Windows® 7 Bible

Jim Boyce

WILEY

Wiley Publishing, Inc.

Windows® 7 Bible

Published by
Wiley Publishing, Inc.
10475 Crosspoint Boulevard
Indianapolis, IN 46256
www.wiley.com

Copyright © 2009 by Jim Boyce

Published by Wiley Publishing, Inc., Indianapolis, Indiana

Published simultaneously in Canada

ISBN: 978-0-470-50909-8

Manufactured in the United States of America

10 9 8 7 6 5 4 3 2

For general information on our other products and services please contact our Customer Care Department within the United States at (877) 762-2974, outside the United States at (317) 572-3993 or fax (317) 572-4002.

Wiley also publishes its books in a variety of electronic formats. Some content that appears in print may not be available in electronic books.

Library of Congress Control Number: 2009933373

About the Author

Jim Boyce has authored and co-authored over 50 books on computers and technology covering operating systems, applications, and programming topics. He has been a frequent contributor to Microsoft.com, techrepublic.com, and other online publications. Jim has written for a number of print publications including Windows IT Pro, WINDOWS Magazine, InfoWorld, and others, and was a Contributing Editor and columnist for WINDOWS Magazine.

Today, Jim is a Sr. Practice Manager for ACS, a premier provider of business process outsourcing and information technology services, where he leads a collaboration team providing collaboration services and development for multiple customers and over 30,000 users.

Credits

Executive Editor
Carol Long

Project Editor
Kenyon Brown

Technical Editor
Todd Meister

Production Editor
Kathleen Wisor

Copy Editors
Susan Christophersen
Kim Cofer

Editorial Director
Robyn B. Siesky

Editorial Manager
Mary Beth Wakefield

Production Manager
Tim Tate

Vice President and Executive Group Publisher
Richard Swadley

Vice President and Executive Publisher
Barry Pruett

Associate Publisher
Jim Minatel

Project Coordinator, Cover
Lynsey Stanford

Proofreaders
Kristy Eldredge, Word One
Scott Klemp, Word One
Jen Larsen, Word One

Indexer
Robert Swanson

Cover Image
Joyce Haughey

Cover Designer
Michael E. Trent

Acknowledgments

A revision of an existing book is much different from a project started from scratch, in large part because the final result builds on the work of the previous author. So, first and foremost, I'd like to express my appreciation to Alan Simpson for all of his efforts in creating the body of work that the Windows 7 Bible is built upon. With such a short project timeline, having a solid foundation was critical.

I'd also like to thank Rob Tidrow, Nathan Kuhn, and Tyler Regas for their help, particularly at the last minute, in pulling together content for the book so we could complete the project on time.

I also want to recognize Carol Long and Carole McClendon for bringing me this opportunity. Finally, I offer my appreciation and thanks to the editorial team for their help in pulling together this project: Kenyon Brown, Todd Meister, Kathleen Wisor, Susan Christophersen, and Kim Cofer. It was a great experience.

Contents at a Glance

Contents at a Glance

Contents

Contents

Contents

Contents

Contents

Contents

Contents

Contents

Contents

Contents

Contents

Contents

Contents

Contents

Contents

Contents

Contents

Contents

Contents

Introduction

Welcome to *Windows 7 Bible*. If you are familiar with Windows, you might know that the Windows operating system has existed for two decades. In that time, OS has transformed in many ways as computer hardware has changed dramatically.

Windows 7 is the latest edition in the Windows family, and builds on the previous edition, Windows Vista. Windows 7 isn't just a new face on Vista, however. Windows 7 not only addresses many of the functional and usability issues that users disliked about Windows Vista, but it also adds new features to improve performance and make Windows easier to use.

While we have tried to cover as many of the features and capabilities as Windows 7 offers, some naturally fall through the cracks because we only have so much space in this book. With a good understanding of the key features, however, you are well on your way to getting the most from your Windows PC.

Who This Book Is For

Not everyone wants to be a computer expert, and few have the time to become one. Most people just want to use a computer to get things done, or even just to have some fun. This should come as no surprise. After all, not everyone who drives a car wants to be a professional mechanic. Not everyone who uses a cell phone wants to be an electrical engineer. So why should everyone who uses a computer want, or need, to be a computer expert? They shouldn't. Some people need to just be computer *users*, people who use the computer without being total nerds about it.

This book is for the computer *users*. The people who just want to use their computers to have some fun and get some things done. It might seem like an awfully big book for such an audience. The only reason it's such a big book is because there are *so many* things you can do with Windows 7.

Most of us prefer to learn by discovery, by exploring and trying things out. It's a lot more fun that way and typically much more effective. However, just a couple of problems are evident with that approach. For one, you can get yourself into a bind from time to time. For another, when you get to a place where you don't know what's going on, sometimes you need to fill in some gaps before you can move on and continue learning by discovery.

A book can help with that by covering all the stuff everyone else assumes you already know. Especially if that book is divided up into sections and chapters that deal with one topic at a time, so you can focus on just the thing you need to know, when you need to know it. Which brings us to . . .

How to Use This Book

A book that supports learning by discovery needs to have some elements of a tutorial and some elements of a reference book. I guess you could say it has to be a reference book divided into multiple mini-tutorials, so you can learn what you need to know about one topic, when you need to know it. To that extent, this book is divided into 10 major parts, each of which covers a large topic.

Each part, in turn, is divided into multiple chapters, each chapter covering a smaller topic. Chapters are divided into sections and subsections, all designed to help you find the information you need, when you need it. The Table of Contents up front covers all the specifics. The index at the back of the book helps you find things based on a keyword or topic. The only thing missing is a high-level view of just the parts. So that's what I'll provide here.

Part I: Getting Started, Getting Secure. How you get started with Windows 7depends on where you're coming from. Part I tries to cover all fronts. If you're an experienced Windows user, then you probably want to know what's new. Chapter 1 covers that turf. If you're relatively new to PCs, you'll likely be interested in learning the most important basic skills for using a computer. Chapter 2 covers that ground. Chapters 3–6 cover important "getting started" topics for everyone. Chapter 6 provides solutions to common problems with getting started.

Part II: Batten Down the Security Hatches. There is no such thing as a 100-percent secure computer. Even with all of its advanced built-in security, there are certain things that you, the user, need to contribute to make sure that your computer is safe and stays up-to-date with ever-changing security threats. The chapters in Part II cover that ground.

Part III: Personalizing Windows 7. We all like to tweak things to suit our personal needs, taste, and style. That's what Part III is all about. But it's not just about changing the look and feel of things. It's about really making the computer a useful tool for whatever your work (or play) requires.

Part IV: Using the Internet. Just about everyone who uses a computer also uses the Internet. And Windows 7 has many tools to make that possible. Chapter 16 covers Microsoft Internet Explorer, the program for using Web sites like eBay, Google, and millions of others. Chapter 17 covers Windows Live Mail, a great new program for e-mail and newsgroups. Other chapters get into lesser-known, but still useful, aspects of the Internet and techniques for troubleshooting common Internet problems.

Part V: Pictures, Music, and Movies. The Internet isn't the only place to have fun with a computer. You can have a lot of fun offline with pictures, music, and movies. The chapters in Part V tell you how.

Part VI: Managing Files and Folders. We all have to make some effort to get our stuff organized and keep it organized. Otherwise, we spend more time looking for stuff than actually doing things. Part VI covers all the necessary housekeeping kinds of chores to help you spend less time looking for things and more time doing things.

Part VII: Printing, Faxing, and Scanning. Sometimes, you just have to get a thing off the screen and onto paper. That's what printing is all about. Sometimes, you need to get a thing off of paper and into the computer. That's what scanning is about. And sometimes you have to use a fax machine rather than e-mail to get a printed page to someone. Such are the topics of VII.

Part VIII: Installing and Removing Programs. Hot topics here include downloading programs, installing programs from CDs and floppies, getting older programs to run, controlling access to programs, getting rid of unwanted programs, and dealing with problem programs and processes. After all, what good is a computer without some programs to run on it?

Part IX: Hardware and Performance Tuning. Hardware is the computer buzzword for physical gadgets you can hold in your hand. As the years roll by hardware just keeps getting smaller, better, faster, cheaper, and, well, cooler. This part covers everything you need to know about adding and removing hardware and troubleshooting hardware problems.

Part X: Networking and Sharing. Whether you have two PCs or 20, eventually you'll want to link them all together into a single private network so they can share a single Internet account and printer, or perhaps several printers. And if you've been wasting time transferring files via floppies, CDs, or some other removable disk, you'll want to replace all that with simple drag-and-drop operations on your screen. Part X tells you how to make all of that happen.

That's a lot of topics and a lot to think about. But there's no hurry. If you're new to Windows, or your experience is limited to things like e-mail and the Web, Chapter 2 is probably your best first stop. Those of you with more extensive Windows experience might want to hop over to Chapter 1 for a quick look at things that are new in Windows 7.

Part I

Getting Started, Getting Secure

Windows users range in experience from people who are just getting started with their first PC to folks with years of Windows experience under their belts. Part I attempts to address both audiences by tackling topics that everyone needs to know in order to get started.

Chapter 1 highlights the new features of Windows 7 and is geared toward people with some experience with a previous version of Windows. The idea there is to point out the main Windows 7 features that make it different from or better than earlier Windows versions.

Of course, if you have little or no Windows experience, you don't really care about what's new versus what's not. All you care about is learning how to work the computer. If you're in that category, you can skip Chapter 1 and go straight to Chapter 2.

Chapter 3 then covers user accounts and the User Account Control (UAC) features of Windows. Chapter 4 moves on to Parental Controls, something that many parents have wanted in their computers for a long time. Beginners and experienced users alike will find much that's useful in those chapters.

Chapter 5 helps you learn where to go in Windows to get help using Windows and your computer. Chapter 6 tackles some common problems you might encounter in getting things to work throughout the first five chapters.

What's New in Windows 7

Welcome to Windows 7! This chapter is for people who have experience with Windows Vista or other versions of Windows and just want to know what's new. If you're new to PCs, this chapter won't help much because *everything* will be new to you. So feel free to skip this chapter and head over to Chapter 2 if you're not a long-time Windows user.

Even though Windows 7 has new features and some new looks (particularly if you are a Windows XP user), that doesn't mean you have to throw away all your existing hard-earned knowledge. In fact, you don't have to throw away any of that, because the old familiar ways of doing things still apply.

If you invest a little time in learning what's new and different, you'll find that you really *can* get things done more quickly and easily in Windows 7. This chapter provides a quick overview of what's new, so you can decide for yourself which of the features are most relevant to how you use your computer.

IN THIS CHAPTER

A new look and feel

Quicker, easier navigation

Built-in security and parental controls

A better Internet experience

And so much more

Taskbar and Full-Screen Improvements

The taskbar at the bottom of the Windows desktop provides, just as it does in previous versions of Windows, quick access to your running programs, the clock, and notification messages. But Windows 7 improves on the taskbar by streamlining it with smaller icons that group your programs together. For example, if you have three different Web pages open in three instances of Internet Explorer, you'll see a single, small Internet Explorer icon on the taskbar that you can use to quickly access one of those windows. The reduced icon size makes more room available on the taskbar for other program group icons, making it easier for you to work with your programs. Figure 1-1 shows an example of the new taskbar.

In addition, Windows 7 now provides preview features to help you move between programs. When you click the mouse on or hover it over a program group icon, Windows displays a preview of each of the program windows in that group, and as you hover the mouse over a preview window, Windows shows you a full-size preview on the desktop of that window's contents. You can then click the preview to open its associated program window (Figure 1-2).

FIGURE 1-1

The new taskbar.

FIGURE 1-2

Window previews from the taskbar.

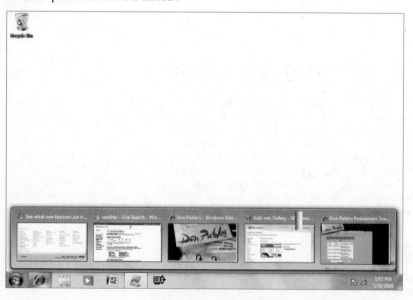

Windows lets you control the taskbar's new behavior. You can direct Windows to always combine like programs into a single group icon, combine them only when the taskbar gets full, or never combine them.

Jump Lists

Jump lists are another new feature in Windows 7. When you right-click a taskbar icon, Windows displays a jump list that contains menu items for commonly-used tasks for the program and quick access to recently-used documents (Figure 1-3).

FIGURE 1-3

A program's jump list.

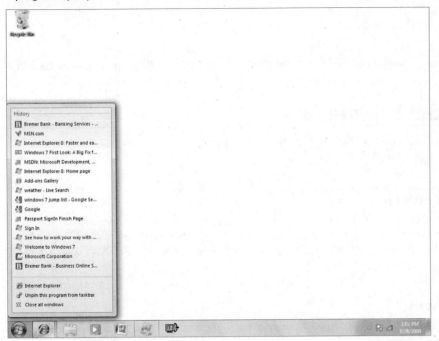

Jump lists are a Windows feature, rather than an application feature, so you'll get a jump list for a program even if it wasn't written specifically to use the jump list. However, program developers can modify the jump list, so programs that are written specifically to do so will likely provide additional options in the jump list menu.

New Ways to Work in Windows

Windows 7 gives you more ways to work with program windows. For example, you have more ways to maximize and arrange windows on the desktop. In addition to the familiar ways of maximizing a window — double-clicking its taskbar or clicking the Maximize button — you can simply drag the window's title bar to the top of the desktop. Windows will then maximize the window. To restore it to a window, just drag the title bar down from the top of the desktop. Is that any faster than using the buttons in the top-right corner of the window? Not really, but on a high-resolution display, those buttons can be kind of small, and dragging the title bar is an easier method.

You can also dock windows to the left or right side of the desktop. Docking the window attaches the edge of the window to the edge of the desktop and sizes the window to fill exactly half of the desktop. You dock the window by dragging the title bar to the left or right edge of the desktop. This is a great feature when you want to copy or move items between two windows.

Finally, remember the Show Desktop icon in previous versions of Windows, which when clicked minimized all running programs to the taskbar temporarily? That feature is now in the bottom-right corner of the taskbar. Just hover the mouse over the small, vertical button at the right edge of the taskbar, and Windows makes all open windows disappear so that you can see the desktop. This is really handy when you want to see your desktop gadgets for a second. To view your program windows again, just move the mouse away from the taskbar.

Tip
To minimize or restore all program windows, click the Show Desktop button at the right edge of the taskbar. ■

Internet Explorer 8

Windows 7 comes with Internet Explorer 8, and IE 8 sports lots of new features. The following sections explore a few of them.

Instant search

In IE 8, as you start typing in the Live Search box, IE offers instant results to match what you are typing. For example, it offers previously visited sites, just as in previous versions of IE. But it also starts searching for that word or phrase within Live Search and within your history. Figure 1-4 shows an example.

Web slices

Web slices in IE 8 let you keep track of content from sites through the IE 8 Favorites Bar. For example, Live Search offers Web slices for weather that you can add to your Favorites Bar, and you can get weather update notifications when they occur. eBay is another example, offering to track an auction and notify you when bid changes occur.

When you visit a page that offers a slice, you see a green icon, which in Figure 1-5 is under the mouse cursor. To subscribe to the slice, click the icon. Internet Explorer opens a dialog box asking whether you want to add the Web slice to your Favorites Bar. Click the Add to Favorites Bar button to add the slice. When the slice is updated, Internet Explorer highlights the item in the Favorites Bar.

Accelerators

Accelerators are another new feature in Internet Explorer 8 that simplify and speed up browsing tasks. For example, if you were using an earlier version of IE and found an address on a Web page for a restaurant you wanted to visit, you'd probably have to copy the address to the Clipboard and then navigate to another site to map that address. With the Map with Live Maps accelerator, all you need to do is highlight the restaurant's address and then click the blue accelerator icon that appears above the text. If you hover the mouse over the Map with Live Search option, IE displays a pop-up window showing the location on a map (Figure 1-6). You can click the menu option to open the map in a new IE tab.

FIGURE 1-4

Live Search at work.

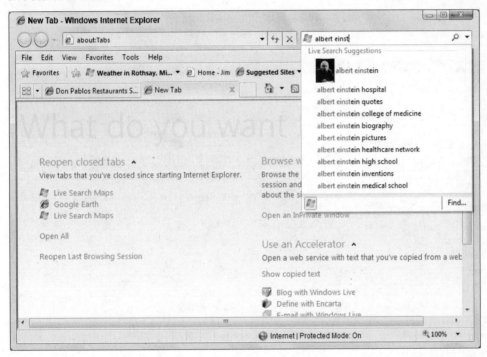

There are lots of accelerators for IE 8 for blogging, research, mapping, music, social networking, and much more. To find more accelerators for your computer, visit `http://ieaddons.com`.

Better navigation

IE 8 adds several improvements to simplify navigation. For example, when you open a new tab from a page, IE 8 places the two tabs next to each other and color codes them so that you can see that they are related. You can right-click a tab and close that tab, close all other tabs and keep that one open, remove the tab from its group, and access a list of recently closed tabs so that you can easily reopen them.

Searching on a page is also improved. The Find on Page toolbar, which you can open by pressing Ctrl+F, performs an instant search as you type. It offers search results as you type each character. It also highlights search results on the page rather than locates them one at a time, as in previous versions of IE (Figure 1-7).

FIGURE 1-5

An icon on a Web page indicates an available Web slice.

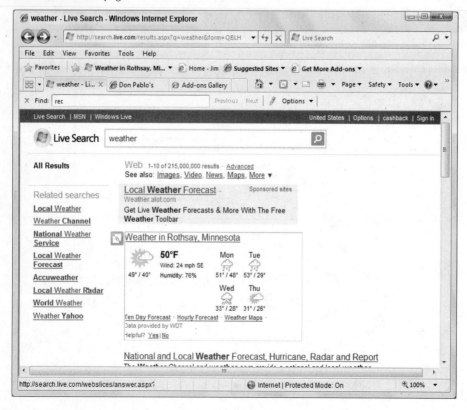

IE 8 offers several other navigation improvements, including a smarter address bar that provides an instant search of your History, Favorites, and RSS feeds; better page zoom; smarter back navigation; and a compatibility view for viewing Web pages that are not fully compatible with IE 8.

InPrivate browsing

InPrivate Browsing in IE 8 helps you minimize your exposure on the Internet. This new feature helps prevent your browser history, temporary Internet files, form data, cookies, and usernames and passwords from being saved by the browser, effectively leaving no evidence of your browsing or search history. InPrivate Browsing also can block content from external sites — sites that the page you are visiting is pulling data from. Blocking these third-party sites can help minimize how and whether your browsing habits are tracked.

FIGURE 1-6

Accelerators speed up browsing tasks.

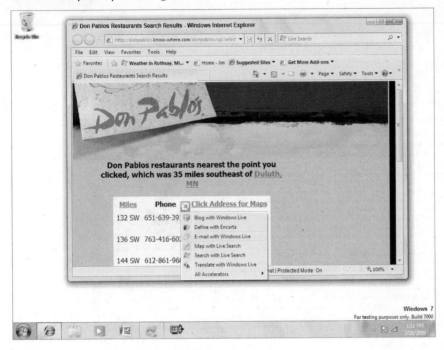

Other new IE features

The new features described in the preceding sections are just some of the new features in IE 8. You'll find better performance, better crash recovery, additional security features for phishing and malware attacks, better favorites management, and more.

Windows Live

If you have been a Windows Vista user, you might be surprised to see that some of the programs you are accustomed to using are no longer included with Windows 7. For example, you won't find Windows Mail included in 7. Instead, these programs have been pulled from Windows and made part of Windows Live, a set of online services and programs from Microsoft. These programs include:

- **Messenger:** Use Messenger to text chat, video chat, or make phone calls to others.
- **Mail:** Formerly Outlook Express, then Windows Mail in Windows Vista, Windows Live Mail lets you send and receive e-mail and work with online newsgroups.
- **Writer:** Use this program to blog and share photos and videos on many blog services.
- **Photo Gallery:** Manage your digital photos, edit them, share them with friends and family, and even stitch together photos to make panoramic shots.

FIGURE 1-7

On-page search in IE 8.

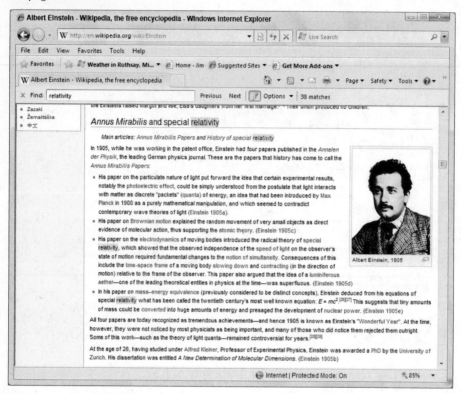

- **Movie Maker:** Create movies and video clips, and add titles, subtitles, music, and special effects.
- **Family Safety:** Control what sites your children can see, view reports about their browsing history, limit searches, and decide with whom they can communicate when they are using Windows Live Messenger.
- **Toolbar:** The Windows Live Toolbar gives you quick access to Windows Live and Live Search in Internet Explorer.

You'll find most of these Windows add-ons covered throughout this book. Visit http://home.live.com to download these Windows Live add-ons.

Better Device Management

Previous versions of Windows provided several different ways to manage hardware such as printers, mice, cameras, scanners, and so on. For example, you managed printers from the Printers object in Control Panel, mice from the Mouse object, keyboard from the Keyboard object, and so on. Windows

7 brings devices together in a new Devices and Printers object that enables you to view and manage devices in one location (Figure 1-8).

Manage devices in one location.

In Devices and Printers, you can manage cell phones, MP3 players, cameras, mice, displays, printers, faxes, keyboards, and other compatible devices. Bringing all these devices under a common management tool simplifies device configuration and troubleshooting.

Homegroup

Windows 7 introduces a new feature called Homegroup to help simplify sharing files and printers in a home network. A homegroup is a collection of computers that are set up to automatically share pictures, music, videos, documents, and printers (or any combination thereof).

In effect, a homegroup lets you share resources on the network using a single password. By default, when you create a homegroup, Windows 7 shares your Pictures, Music, and Videos libraries, along with your printers. You can also share other folders simply by right-clicking the folder, choosing Share With, and then choosing one of the Homegroup options from the menu (Figure 1-9).

Windows 7 includes a Homegroup object to help you access resources that are shared in your homegroup. Click the Windows Explorer icon in the taskbar to open the Libraries window; then click Homegroup in the left pane to open your homegroup. You see the resources there that are shared by others in your homegroup.

Easily share folders in a homegroup.

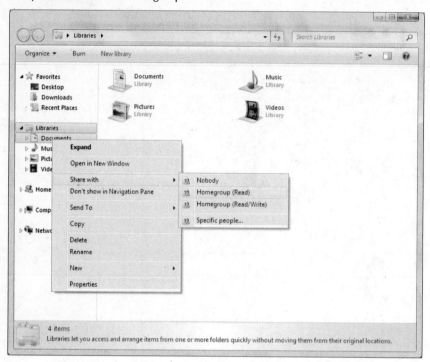

A homegroup is a simplified sharing mechanism, so you have somewhat limited sharing options. For example, you can give those in your homegroup the ability to read or modify files as a group. If you need to enable some people only to view files but others to edit them, a homegroup isn't the right solution for you. Instead, you need to use one of Windows 7 other sharing options to share those files.

Performance and Battery Life

Performance is another area of improvement in Windows 7. If you have worked with previous versions of Windows, you'll find that Windows 7 starts, resumes, and shuts down faster, giving you a snappier experience with your computer. Thanks to some additional power-saving features, Windows 7 should also give you better battery life for your notebook computer.

Look and Feel

Because Windows 7 has its origins in Windows Vista, the look and feel is much the same between the two versions of Windows. As you might expect, however, Windows 7 adds its own features that give this new version its own look and feel.

For example, you find new backgrounds, color schemes, and screensavers bundled with Windows 7. You can also download new themes as they become available. As mentioned earlier in this chapter, changes to the desktop, taskbar, and window preview also give Windows 7 a new look and make it easier to use.

Troubleshooting and Alerts

One of the annoyances in Windows Vista is the frequency of the alerts and pop-up messages that it displays. Windows 7 changes the way it displays alerts; it also gives you more control over those alerts and messages, letting you choose the messages you want to see.

The Action Center consolidates alerts from several Windows features, including the Security Center and Windows Defender. In Windows 7, the Action Center icon appears in the taskbar. Clicking the icon displays messages related to the items that you might need to address, such as the lack of an antivirus program, a problem with a device in the computer, or the need to scan the computer for threats (Figure 1-10).

FIGURE 1-10

Action Center consolidates notifications.

Windows 7 also gives you control over the types of messages you see. For example, if you don't want to see messages about Windows Update, you can turn off those messages by deselecting a check box in the Action Center settings. In addition, you can control how Windows 7 notifies you when changes are being made to your computer. Instead of Windows notifying you and asking you to allow a change that you initiate in Windows, for example, you can have Windows notify you only when programs try to make changes.

Other changes are geared toward troubleshooting. The Devices and Printers folder, for example, gives you a single place to manage and troubleshoot a wide variety of devices connected to your computer. In addition, the Troubleshooting item in the Control Panel consolidates troubleshooting tools in one place (Figure 1-11).

FIGURE 1-11

The Troubleshooting item in Control Panel.

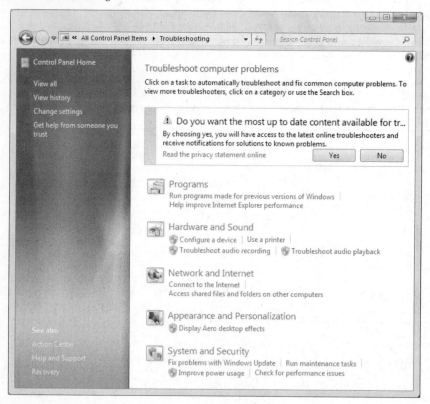

Music and Video Sharing

Windows 7 gives you new ways to enjoy and share your music and videos. With the new homegroup networking feature, you can easily share your music, pictures, and videos with others on your home network. For example, you might consolidate all your photos into one location, where you can easily back them up and share them across the network.

Even more significant is the capability in Windows Media Player 12, which is included with Windows 7 to stream media to other computers, even across the Internet. This means that others on your homegroup can access a central media library — for example streaming music from a home server tucked in your basement that streams to a media center in your living room. Even cooler than that, you can stream music from your home computer to your computer at work — and potentially stream music to mobile devices such as a Windows Mobile smartphone or media player.

To further extend sharing capabilities, Windows Media Player 12 can browse media libraries on other computers, enabling you to browse to and play music stored on other computers on your network. This capability isn't limited to Windows Media Player libraries, either. Media Player 12 can also browse and play from iTunes libraries.

. . . and More

The new Windows 7 features I describe in this chapter are just some of the major new features and capabilities offered by this latest version of Windows. You also find expanded hardware support and other usability features. For example, Windows 7 improves on its touch-screen features to make navigating on touch-screen devices easier. Windows 7 also improves on handwriting-recognition features to improve your experience with tablet PCs and similar devices.

So, don't think of Windows 7 as Windows with just a new look and feel. As you get more familiar with it, you realize that it offers a wealth of new features and capabilities that will make your computer experience more enjoyable and useful.

Wrap-Up

Long gone are the days when people managed a few files and folders on external disks without an Internet connection. In today's connected world, we deal with massive amounts of digital information in many forms, and from many sources. Windows 7 gives you new ways to interact with that information.

This chapter has been a sort of view from 30,000 feet of what's new in Windows 7. Here I've focused on the main things that most users will want to explore. But there's much more than I cover in a single chapter. Here's a quick recap of what's hot:

- The new taskbar makes it easier to work with multiple programs simultaneously.
- Jump lists give you quick access to documents and program functions right from the taskbar.
- New desktop features let you navigate the desktop more easily, quickly move and view program windows, and control the desktop much better than in past versions.
- Internet Explorer brings a big toolbox of new features that make Internet browsing easier and more useful.
- Windows Live makes several Windows features available as optional downloads to streamline Windows, but also makes more features available when you need or want them.
- Consolidated device management makes managing the devices connected to your PC easier.
- Homegroup networking simplifies sharing documents and media across your home network.
- Windows Media Player 12 extends media sharing across the Internet.

Getting Around

In today's busy world, few people have the time to sit down and really learn to use a computer. Many books and online tutorials don't really help because they assume you already know all the basic concepts and terminology. That's a big assumption because the truth is that most people don't already know those things. Most people don't know a file from a folder from a megabyte from a golf ball. These just aren't the kinds of things we learned about in school or from our day-to-day experiences.

This chapter is mostly about the kinds of things everyone else assumes you already know. It's for the kind of people who bought their first computer and discovered it has this thing called Windows 7 on it. Or the kind of people who were getting by with an older computer but now have a new Windows 7 computer and really want to know more about how to use it.

I often refer to the skills in this chapter as "everyday skills" because they're the kinds of things you'll likely do every time you sit down at the computer. I point out the name and purpose of many things you'll see on your screen. All these things combine into a kind of basic knowledge about how you use a computer, in general, to get things done. And it all starts with logging in.

IN THIS CHAPTER

Logging in

Using the Windows desktop

Using the Start menu

Using programs

Shutting down the computer

Terminology for Things You Do

If you're new to computers, the first step is to learn a little terminology about things you do to operate the computer. I assume you know what the *mouse* is. When you move the mouse, the *mouse pointer* on the screen moves in whatever direction you move the mouse. Most mice have two buttons. The one on the left is called the *primary* or *left* mouse button. It's called the primary button because clicking it always makes an action occur directly.

When you rest your hand comfortably on the mouse, the left mouse button should be under your index finger. You don't want to hold the button down, though. Just rest your index finger on it lightly. If you are left-handed, you can switch the orientation of the buttons using the Mouse applet in the Control Panel.

The button on the right is called the *secondary* or *right* mouse button. In contrast to the primary mouse button, clicking the secondary mouse button usually doesn't make an action take place directly; instead, it shows you various actions you take.

Mouse terminology

Everyone uses some specific terms to refer to actions you perform with the mouse. These terms include *point*, *click*, *double-click*, *right-click*, and *drag*.

Point

The term *point*, when used as a verb, means to touch the mouse pointer to an item. For example, "point to the Start button" means to move the mouse pointer so that it's positioned on the Start button (the large, round button at the lower-left corner of your screen that shows the Windows logo). If the item you want to point to is smaller than the mouse pointer, make sure you get the tip of the mouse pointer arrow on the item. Whatever the tip of the mouse pointer is on is the item to which you're pointing.

The term *hover* means the same thing as *point*. For example, the phrase "hover the mouse pointer over the Start button" means the same as "point to the Start button."

When you point to an item, the item's name typically appears in a *tooltip*. For example, if you point to the Start button, the word *Start* appears in a tooltip near the mouse pointer. The tooltip tells you that the item you're pointing to is named Start. Figure 2-1 shows an example of pointing to the Start button with the tooltip showing.

Tip
You can learn the name and purpose of many items on your screen just by pointing to the item and reading the tooltip that appears near the mouse pointer. ∎

Click

The term *click* means to point to an item and then tap the left mouse button. Don't hold down the left mouse button. Just tap (press and release) it. It makes a slight clicking sound when you do. For example, the phrase "click the Start button" means "put the mouse pointer on the Start button and tap the left mouse button." When you do, the Start menu appears. Click the Start button a second time, and the Start menu goes away.

Double-click

The term *double-click* means to point to an item and then tap the left mouse button twice, quickly. Don't hold down the button and don't pause between clicks. Just tap the left mouse button twice. You use double-clicking to *open* items that icons on your screen represent.

Right-click

The term *right-click* means to point to an item and then tap the right mouse button. Again, don't hold down the mouse button, and don't use the left mouse button. Whereas clicking an item usually takes an immediate action, right-clicking presents a shortcut menu of things you can do with the item. You'll see many examples throughout this book.

FIGURE 2-1

Pointing to the Start button.

Drag

The term *drag* means to point to an item and hold down the left mouse button while you're moving the mouse. You typically use dragging to move and size things on the screen. You can see examples a little later in this chapter.

Tip

As you discover in Chapter 29, you can also use dragging to move and copy files from one location to another. ■

Keyboard terminology

The keyboard is the thing that looks like a typewriter keyboard. The keys labeled F1, F2, and so forth across the top are called *function keys*. The keys that show arrows and names such as Home, End, PgUp (Page Up), and PgDn (Page Down) are *navigation keys*.

Tab, Enter, and Spacebar

The Tab key shows two opposing arrows pointing left and right. That key is usually to the left of the letter Q. The Enter key (also called the Carriage Return or Return key) is located where the carriage return key is on a standard typewriter. It may be labeled Enter or Return, or it may just show a bent, left-pointing arrow. The Spacebar is the wide key centered at the bottom of the keyboard. When you're typing text, it types a blank space.

If in doubt, Escape key out

The Esc or Escape key is the one labeled Esc or Escape (or maybe even Cancel). It's usually at the upper-left corner of the keyboard. It's a good one to know because it often allows you to escape from unfamiliar territory.

The Help key (F1)

The Help key is the F1 function key. That's a good one to know because it's the key you press for help. Not the kind of help where someone appears and helps you along. Unfortunately, it's not possible to get that kind of help from a computer. Instead, pressing Help opens a help window. You learn more about getting help in Chapter 5.

The ⊞ Key

If you have a Windows keyboard, you also have a *Windows key*, which shows the Windows logo. In text, that's often referred to as ⊞. That one is usually near the lower-left corner of the keyboard. That key might also show the word Start, because you can tap it to show and hide the Start menu.

Shift, Ctrl, and Alt

The keys labeled Shift, Ctrl (Control), and Alt (Alternate) are *modifier* keys. There are usually two of each of those keys on a keyboard, near the lower left and lower right of the main typing keys. The Shift key may just show as a large, up-pointing arrow. One is to the left of the Z key, the other to the right of the question mark (?) key. They're called modifier keys because they usually don't do anything by themselves. Instead, you hold down a modifier key while pressing some other key. For example, when you hold down the Shift key and press the A key, you get an uppercase *A* rather than a lowercase *a*.

Shortcut keys

The term *press* always refers to a key on the keyboard rather than something you do with the mouse. For example, the term *press Enter* means to press the Enter key. When you see an instruction to press two keys with a + in between (*key+key*), that means "hold down the first key, tap the second key, release the first key." For example, an instruction to

```
Press Ctrl+Esc
```

means "hold down the Ctrl key, tap the Esc key, release the Ctrl key."

You'll often see the term *shortcut key* used to refer to *key+key* combinations. The "shortcut" part comes from the fact that the keystroke is an alternative way of doing something with the mouse. (It may not seem like much of a "shortcut," though, if you can't type worth beans!)

Much as we all hate to learn terminology, knowing the terms and keyboard keys I just described is critical to learning how to use a computer. All written and spoken instructions assume that you know what those terms mean. If you don't, the instructions won't do you any good.

Okay, let's move on to using the computer and to the names of things you'll do, see, and use often.

Logging In

Obviously, the first step to using a computer is to turn it on. Shortly after you first start your computer, the Windows 7 Login screen appears. Exactly how that screen looks depends on what user accounts exist on your computer. By default, Windows 7 comes with a built-in user account named Administrator. But it's unlikely that you'll ever see that user account because it's not for day-to-day computer use. If you've never used your computer or Windows 7 before, you'll likely be taken through a process where it asks you to create a user account. Just follow the on-screen instructions if faced with that question.

If your computer already has user accounts, you'll likely see a *login page* that displays icons (little pictures) and names for one or more *user accounts*. You learn about user accounts in Chapter 3. But for now, all you need to know is that if you see user account icons shortly after you first start your computer, you have to click one in order to use the computer.

Tip
The blue circle near the lower-left corner of the screen provides Ease of Access options for the visually impaired. The red button at the lower-right corner lets you turn off the computer rather than log in. ■

FIGURE 2-2

Typing a password.

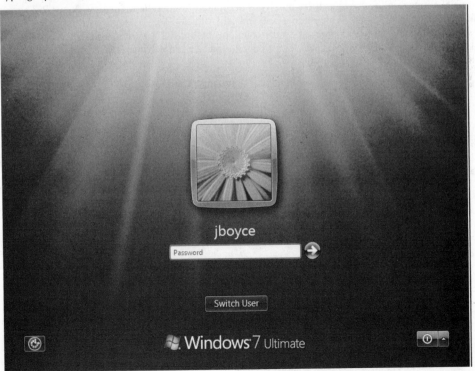

If the user account isn't password-protected, the Windows desktop appears automatically. If the user account you clicked is password-protected, a rectangular box appears instead. You have to type the correct password for the account to get to the Windows desktop. The letters you type won't show in the box. Instead, you'll see a dot for each letter you type, as in the example shown in Figure 2-2. This is to prevent people from learning your password by looking over your shoulder as you type it on the screen. After you type the password, press Enter or click the arrow to the right of the password box.

After you've successfully logged in, the Windows desktop appears.

What's on the Desktop

The interface that Windows 7 provides is called the *Windows desktop*. The name "desktop" comes from the fact that it plays the same role as a real work desktop. You work with programs on the Windows desktop in much the same way as you work with paper on an office desktop.

The desktop is on the screen from the moment you log in to the moment you log off. The desktop may get covered by program windows and other items, but the desktop is still under there no matter how much you clutter the screen. It's the same as a real desk in that sense. Although your real desktop may be completely covered by random junk (as mine is right now), your desktop is still under there somewhere. You just have to dig through the mess to get to it.

The two main components of the Windows desktop are the desktop itself and the taskbar. The desktop is where everything that you open piles up. The taskbar's main role is to make it easy to switch from one open item to another. Everything you'll ever see on your screen has a name and a purpose. Virtually nothing on the screen is there purely for decoration (except the wallpaper). Figure 2-3 shows the main components of the Windows desktop and other items. Your desktop might not look exactly like the picture and might not show all of the components. But don't worry about that. Right now, you want to focus on learning the names of things so that you know what people are talking about when they refer to these things.

Here's a quick overview of what each component represents. The sections that follow the list describe each component in detail.

Tip

You learn to personalize your desktop in Chapter 10. But here's a quick hint: Virtually everything you'll ever see on your screen, including the desktop, is an *object* that has *properties*. To customize any object, right-click that object and choose Properties. ■

- **Desktop:** The desktop itself is everything above the taskbar. Most programs you open appear in a window on the desktop.

- **Desktop icons:** Icons on the desktop provide quick access to frequently used programs, folders, and documents. You can add and remove desktop icons as you see fit.

- **Gadgets:** These are optional components for showing data in a small window. Examples are a clock, weather information, or stock ticker.

- **Start button:** Click the Start button to display the Start menu. The Start menu provides access to programs installed on your computer, as well as commonly used folders such as Documents, Pictures, and Music.

- **Taskbar:** A task is an open program. The taskbar makes switching among all your open programs easy. Right-clicking the clock in the taskbar provides easy access to options for customizing the taskbar and organizing open program windows.

FIGURE 2-3

The desktop, taskbar, and other items.

- **Notification area:** Displays icons for programs running in the background, often referred to as *processes* and *services*. Messages coming from those programs appear in speech balloons just above the Notification area.

- **Clock:** Shows the current time and date.

That's the quick tour of items on and around the Windows 7 desktop. The sections that follow look at each major item. But first, I should point out that your desktop might be partially covered by the Getting Started item. If so, and it gets in your way while you're trying things out in this chapter, you can close the Welcome Center so that it's out of your way. See "The Getting Started Item" near the end of this chapter for more information.

Using the Start Menu

Clicking the Start button displays the Start menu. The left side of the Start menu shows icons for some (but not all) of the programs on your computer. The right side of the menu offers links to commonly used folders and other features. Figure 2-4 shows an example.

The icons on your Start menu won't necessarily match those shown in the figure, so don't worry if yours looks different. The figure is just an example. You will notice, however, that some of the program names on the left side of the Start menu are boldface and some are not. There's a horizontal line separating the two types of names.

FIGURE 2-4

Start menu.

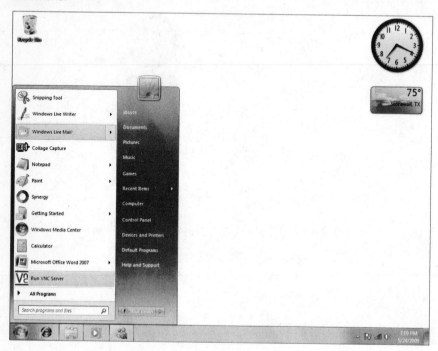

Items above the horizontal line are *pinned* to the Start menu and never change. Items below the horizontal line are *dynamic*, meaning they change automatically based on the programs you use most frequently. As the weeks and months roll by, the left side of your Start menu will eventually list just the programs you use most often.

To see all the programs available on your system, click All Programs near the bottom of the Start menu. In the All Programs menu, some icons look like folders, others like logos. Any icon that looks like a logo represents a program. To start (open) a program, you click its name or logo.

Icons that look like folders represent program groups. To see the names of programs in a group, click the folder icon or name. For example, in Figure 2-5 I clicked the Accessories folder. So now the left side of the Start menu includes programs and program groups from the Windows 7 Accessories program group.

You can choose from many more programs than can fit on the left side of the Start menu. Use the vertical scroll bar just to the right of the program name to scroll up and down through the complete list. If you want to leave the All Programs menu and return to the dynamic menu, click the <Back at the bottom of the list.

The right side of the Start menu

The right side of the Start menu shows menu items for frequently used folders and features. The name at the top of the list (jboyce in the previous examples) is the name of the user account into which you're currently logged. Clicking the user name opens a folder containing icons for other folders that represent things like documents, pictures, music, and other information saved and stored by this user.

FIGURE 2-5

The All Programs menu showing the Accessories group.

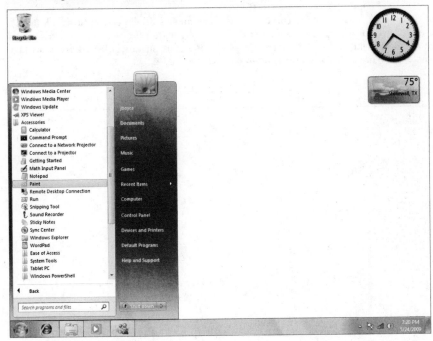

Items labeled Documents, Pictures, and Music open folders in which you can store documents, photographs, songs, respectively. The Games link opens a folder of games you can play on your computer.

Tip

A folder in Windows 7 is like a manila file folder in a filing cabinet. It's a container in which you can store documents. You use folders in Windows to organize things, just as you use folders to organize things in a filing cabinet. ■

The Computer link opens a folder that shows icons representing disk drives, memory card slots, and other connected hardware devices such as DVD drives, cameras, and scanners. Chapter 29 tells the whole story on that folder.

Tip

As with everything else in Windows 7, you can customize many aspects of the Start menu. For instance, you can choose which options you do/don't want to appear on the right side of the Start menu. Right-click the Start button and choose Properties to get to its Properties dialog box. See Chapter 10 for a description of its options. ■

You have plenty of time to get into the various folders and document types described previously. For now, I keep you focused on the Start menu.

The Start menu Search box

Tip

Near the bottom of the Start menu, you see a Search box. As its name implies, it allows you to search for items based on a word or phrase. For example, say that you click the Start button (or press ![Windows logo] or Ctrl+Esc on your keyboard) to open the Start menu and then type the letters *cal*. The Start menu will list all programs that contain "cal." For example, in Figure 2-6, Calculator is listed under Programs. ∎

FIGURE 2-6

Start menu search for "cal."

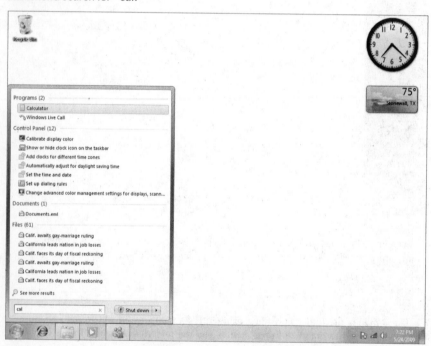

Below the list of programs that contain the search letters, you may see Control Panel items, files, contacts, and e-mail messages that also contain those letters. As you type more letters, the list shrinks to show only the items that contain all the letters you've typed so far. When you see the item you want to open, just click its name in the Start menu.

To cancel a search without making a selection, press Escape (Esc).

Tip

For experienced users, the instant searches from the Start menu are one of Windows 7's best features. It can save you a lot of time you'd otherwise spend opening programs and folders to find something. ∎

The Power button

The Power button at the lower-right side of the Start menu plays several roles and can take one of two appearances. If the Power button has no icon beside it, and reads Shut Down, clicking the button powers down your computer. If you see a shield icon on the button in addition to the words Shut Down, Windows will install downloaded updates and then shut down.

Clicking the arrow on the Power button displays several options, as shown in Figure 2-7 and summarized in the following list (you might not see all of them depending on your computer's configuration).

FIGURE 2-7

The Power button and options.

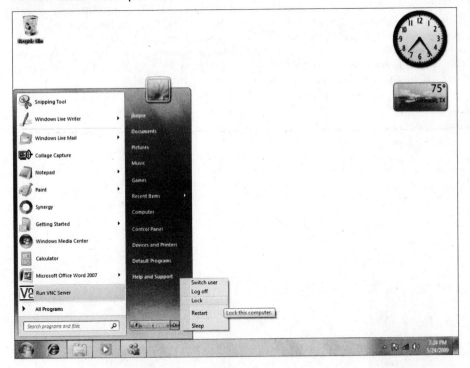

- **Switch User:** Switches to another user account without logging out of the current account.
- **Log Off:** Closes all open items, logs out of the current user account, and returns to the login screen.
- **Lock:** Hides the desktop behind a login screen. Regaining access requires entering the user account password.
- **Shut Down:** Closes all open items and shuts down the computer.
- **Restart:** Closes all open items and restarts the computer (also called a *reboot* or *warm boot*).
- **Sleep:** Puts the computer in a state in which it consumes little power without losing your place on the screen.

- **Hibernate:** Saves what's on your desktop and then shuts down the computer all the way so that it's consuming no power at all. When you restart the computer and log in, your desktop is returned to wherever you left things.

Different types of computers offer different options for sleeping, hibernating, and shutting down. How you restart the computer also varies. For example, when you put the computer to sleep, you can often wake it up just by tapping a key on the keyboard or by moving the mouse. Or, on a notebook computer, simply opening the lid to view the screen may wake up the computer.

When you hibernate or shut down the computer, you have to use the main On/Off switch to turn the computer back on. But because these vary from one computer to the next, I can't say exactly which options your computer offers or how they work. If you have any trouble with those options, refer to the instruction manual that came with your computer for specifics.

At times, the button for powering down the computer might show a shield and exclamation point, as shown in Figure 2-8. When you point to that button, the tooltip shows information like that shown in the figure. The button and tooltip are telling you that your computer has automatically received an update that requires you to click that button. Go ahead and do so. Don't worry: It's not a security risk. Nothing bad will happen, it won't cost you any money, and everything will work the way it did before. The update is just a security patch or minor fix. Go ahead and click the exclamation point button and wait for the computer to shut down on its own.

FIGURE 2-8

Shut Down button and tooltip.

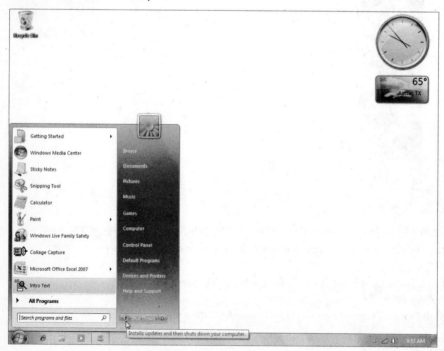

Note
Chapter 9 talks about automatic updates in depth. ∎

Using Jump Lists

Jump lists are a new feature of Windows 7 that enhance the usefulness of the icons on the taskbar. Jump lists add the most recently used objects from the application to a pop-up menu. Just right-click the icon to view the Jump list (Figure 2-9).

FIGURE 2-9

A Jump list for Microsoft Office Word.

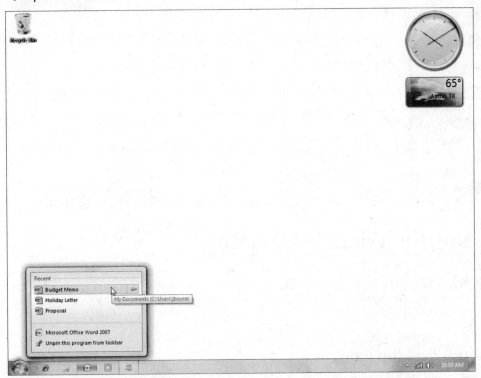

Other applications written for Windows 7 offer additional capabilities in the Jump menu. For example, Internet Explorer 8 offers your browsing history (Figure 2-10).

You don't need to do anything to set up Jump lists — they happen automatically. Whenever you want to use a Jump list, just right-click a taskbar icon and choose from the list the item you want to open.

FIGURE 2-10

Browsing history in the IE jump menu.

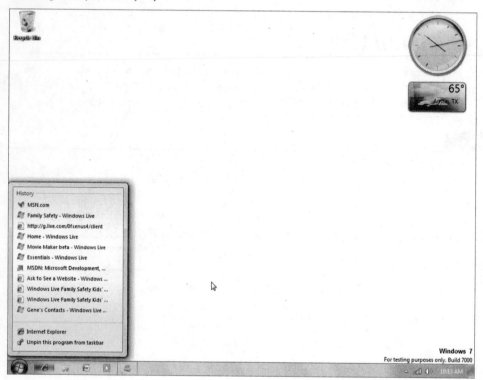

Using the Windows Desktop

As mentioned, the Windows desktop is the electronic equivalent of a real desktop. It's the place where you keep stuff you're working on right now. Every program that's currently open is usually contained within some program window. When no programs are open, the desktop and all your desktop icons are plainly visible on the screen.

About desktop icons

Desktop icons are just like the icons on the Start menu. Each icon represents a *closed* object that you can *open* by double-clicking the icon. Most desktop icons are shortcuts to files and folders. They're shortcuts in the sense that they duplicate icons available elsewhere. They just save you the extra clicks required to get to the same icon through the Start menu or All Programs menu.

Rules always have exceptions. When it comes to desktop icons, the Recycle Bin is the exception. The Recycle Bin icon exists only on the desktop, and you won't find it anywhere else. The role of the Recycle Bin is that of a safety net. Whenever you delete a file or folder from your hard drive, the item is actually just moved to the Recycle Bin. You can restore an accidentally deleted item from the Recycle Bin back to its original location.

In addition to the Recycle Bin, you have other built-in desktop icons from which to choose. If you want to take a shot at adding icons, you have to get to the Personalization page and make some selections. You can use either of the following techniques to get to the Personalization page:

- Click the Start button, type **pers**, and click Personalization.
- Right-click the desktop and choose Personalize.

Note

If you don't see Personalize when you right-click the desktop, that means you didn't right-click the desktop. You right-clicked something that's covering the desktop. You learn to close and hide things that are covering the desktop a little later in this chapter. ■

The Personalization Control Panel applet opens. In its left column, click Change Desktop Icons. You see a *dialog box* like the one in Figure 2-11. It's called a dialog box because you carry on a sort of dialog with it. It shows you options from which you can pick and choose. You make your choices and click OK. You'll see menu dialog boxes throughout this book.

FIGURE 2-11

The Desktop Icon Settings dialog box.

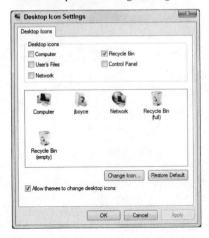

To make an icon visible on your desktop, select (click to put a checkmark in) the check box next to the icon's name. To prevent an icon from appearing on the desktop, click the check box to the left of its name to deselect it (remove the checkmark). In the figure, I've opted to see all icons except the Network and Control Panel icons.

You can choose a different picture for any icon you've opted to show on the desktop. Click the icon's picture in the middle of the dialog box. Then click the Change Icon button. Click the icon you want to show and then click OK. If you change your mind after the fact, click Restore Default.

Click OK after making your selections. The dialog box closes and the icons you choose appear on the desktop. However, you might not see them if that part of the desktop is covered by something that's open. Don't worry about that. You learn about how you open, close, move, and size things on the desktop a little later in this chapter.

If nothing is covering the desktop, but you still don't see any desktop icons, they might just be switched off. I cover this topic in the next section.

Arranging desktop icons

As you discover in Chapter 10, you have many ways to customize the Windows 7 desktop. But if you just want to make some quick, minor changes to your desktop icons, right-click the desktop to view its shortcut menu. Items on the menu that have a little arrow to the right show submenus. For example, if you right-click the desktop and point to View on the menu, you see the View menu, as shown in Figure 2-12.

FIGURE 2-12

Right-click the desktop.

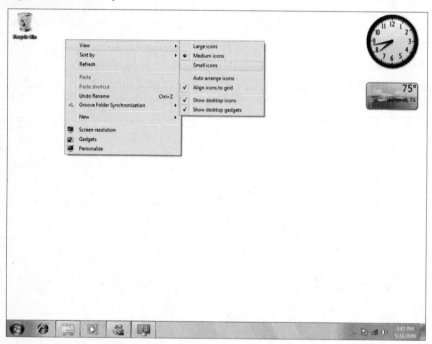

The final item on the View menu, Show Desktop Items, needs to be selected (checked) for the icons to show at all. If no checkmark appears next to that item, click that item. The menu closes and the icons appear on the desktop. When you need to see the menu again, just right-click the desktop again.

The top three items on the menu, Large Icons, Medium Icons, and Small Icons, control the size of the icons. Click any option to see its effect. If you don't like the result, right-click the desktop again, choose View, and choose a different size.

Tip

If your mouse has a wheel, you can also size icons by holding down the Ctrl key as you spin the mouse wheel. This gives you an almost endless range of icon sizes from which to choose. Use one of the three items in the View menu to get them back to one of the three default sizes. ■

The Sort By option on the desktop shortcut menu lets you arrange desktop icons alphabetically by Name, by Size, by Type, or by Date Modified. However, no matter how you choose to sort icons, the built-in icons are sorted separately from those you create. Custom shortcut icons you create yourself are listed after the built-in icons. So if you sort by name, the built-in icons are listed alphabetically first. Then any shortcut icons you created are alphabetized after those. If you sort in reverse order, however (choose Sort, by Name twice), the custom items display first, followed by the built-in icons.

Tip

To create a custom desktop shortcut icon to a favorite program, right-click the program's icon on the All Programs menu and choose Send To ⇨ Desktop (create shortcut). ■

You learn more about personalizing your desktop in Chapter 11. For now, you should stay focused on basic skills such as clicking and right-clicking, as well as on the names of items you see on your screen.

Running Programs

You can start any program that's installed on your computer by finding the program's icon on the All Programs menu and then clicking that icon. You have other ways to start programs as well. For example, if an icon appears on the left side of the Start menu to start the program, just click that instead. If you see an icon for the program in the Quick Launch toolbar, you can click that. If you see a shortcut icon to the program on the desktop, you can click (or double-click) that icon to start the program.

Note

Whether you need to single-click or double-click a desktop icon to open it depends on how you have configured Windows 7. See "To Click or Double-Click" in Chapter 29 for details. ■

Every time you start a program, an *instance* of that program opens in a program window. No rule exists that says you can have only one program open at a time. Nor are you limited to having only one copy of any given program open at a time. You can have as many programs open simultaneously as you can cram into your available memory (RAM). Most programs allow you to run multiple instances. The more memory your system has, the more stuff you can have open without much slowdown in performance.

Note

When it comes to using programs, the terms *start*, *run*, *launch*, and *open* all mean the same thing — to load a copy of the program into memory (RAM) so that it's visible on your screen. You can't use a program until it's running. ■

Any item you open on the desktop usually shows its own name somewhere near the top of the program window. Figure 2-13 shows an example in which I have Getting Started open on the desktop. You see its name in the address bar near the top of the window, appearing either by itself or as part of a string of items.

Most items that you open also have a taskbar button. The name in the taskbar button matches the name of the item. For example, the taskbar button for the open Getting Started also shows the words Getting Started when you hover the pointer over the icon. You can click the Getting Started taskbar button to make the open window appear and disappear. That's a good thing to know, because sometimes you want to get something off the screen temporarily so that you can see something else on the screen.

FIGURE 2-13

Sample title bar and taskbar button.

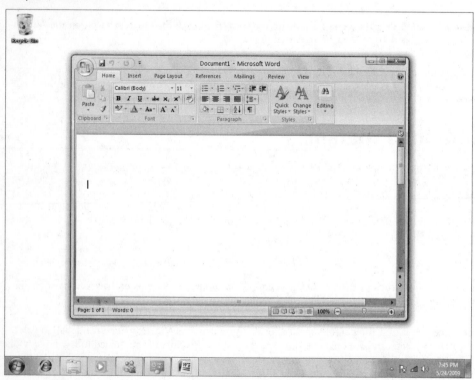

When you have multiple program windows open, they stack up on the desktop the way multiple sheets of paper on your real desktop stack up. When you have multiple sheets of paper in a pile, you can't see what's on every page. You can see only what's on the top page, because all the other pages are covered by that page.

It works the same way with program windows. When you have multiple program windows open, you can see only the one that's on the top of the stack. We call the program that's on the top of the stack the *active window*.

Note
Some programs have an option called "Always on Top" that makes them display on top of the stack even when they are not active. So, a program could be active but not necessarily on top of the stack. For the purposes of this chapter, however, assume that the active window is always the one on top of the stack. ■

The active window

When two or more program windows are open on the desktop window, only one of them can be the active window. The active window has some unique characteristics:

- The active window is usually on the top of the stack. Any other open windows will be under the active window so that they don't cover any of its content. The exception is a window configured for Always on Top, as described previously.
- The taskbar button for the active window is highlighted with a brighter foreground color.
- Anything you do at the keyboard applies to the active window only. You cannot type in an inactive window.

Switching among open programs

Whenever you have two or more programs open at the same time, you want to be able to easily switch among them. You have several ways to switch among open programs, as discussed in the sections to follow.

Caution

The taskbar shows a miniature version of the window by default. Pointing to a taskbar button shows a tooltip with the name of the window or program. You can set the size of the icons used by the taskbar through the properties for the taskbar. ■

Switching with taskbar buttons

As mentioned, almost every open program has a button on the taskbar. When you have multiple open programs, you have multiple taskbar buttons. To make any one particular program active, click its taskbar button. If you're not sure which button is which, point to each button. You see the name and a miniature copy of the program that the button represents, as in Figure 2-14. You also see a full-size preview of the window, a new feature in Windows 7.

Tip

If any portion of the window you want to bring to the top of the stack is visible on the screen, you can just click that visible portion of the window to bring it to the top of the stack. ■

Switching with the keyboard

If you prefer the keyboard to the mouse, you can use Alt+Tab to switch among open windows. Hold down the Alt key and then press the Tab key. You see a thumbnail image for each open program window, as in the example shown in Figure 2-15. Keep the Alt key pressed down and keep pressing Tab until the name of the program you want to switch to appears above the icons. Then release the Alt key.

Tip

The Tab key shows two arrows pointing in opposite directions and is usually just to the left of the letter Q on the keyboard. ■

The last (rightmost) item in the Alt+Tab window represents the desktop rather than an open program. If you release the Alt key with that selected, all windows are minimized to the tasbkar. But you can still bring up any open program by clicking its taskbar button.

FIGURE 2-14

Pointing to a taskbar button.

Switching with Flip 3D

If you're using the Aero Glass interface in Windows 7, you can use Flip 3D to switch among windows. Hold down the ⊞ key and press Tab. The desktop darkens, and any program windows you have open appear in the three-dimensional view, as shown in Figure 2-16.

Note
Flip 3D works only if you use the Aero Glass interface. ■

When you see the three-dimensional stack, you can click any window to bring that window to the top of the stack on your desktop. If your mouse has a wheel, you can cycle through windows by spinning the mouse wheel. If you use the keyboard, keep the ⊞ key held down and press the Tab key until the window you want is at the front of the stack. When you release ⊞ , that same window will be on the top of the stack on the desktop.

In Windows Vista, Flip 3D was accessible from the Quick Launch taskbar. That taskbar isn't included in the Windows 7 interface, but you can create a shortcut for Flip 3D and pin it to the taskbar. Here's how:

1. Right-click the desktop and choose New ⇨ Shortcut.

2. In the Type the Location of the Item text box, type **c:\windows\system32\rundll32.exe DwmApi #105** and then click Next.

FIGURE 2-15

Alt+Tab window.

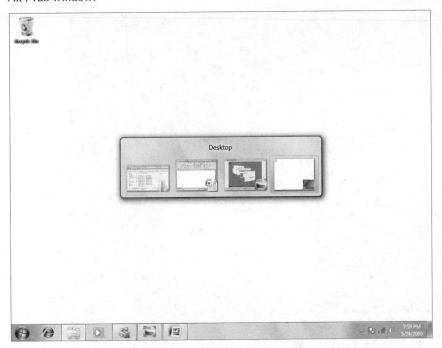

3. Name the shortcut Flip 3D and click Finish.

4. Right-click the shortcut and choose Properties.

5. Click the Shortcut tab of the item's Properties dialog box and then click Change Icon.

6. Click Browse, and in the Windows\System32 folder, locate and select the file imageres.dll; then click Open.

7. Select the Flip 3D icon (or another icon of your choice) and click OK.

8. Click OK to close the Properties dialog box for the shortcut.

9. Drag the shortcut to the taskbar to pin it there. You can then delete the original shortcut from the desktop, if you prefer.

Whenever you want to use Flip 3D, just click the shortcut icon in the taskbar to display the open programs on the desktop, and click the window you want to use. You can also scroll with the mouse to cycle through the windows.

Arranging program windows

You can use options on the taskbar shortcut menu to arrange all currently open program windows. To get to that menu, right-click an empty portion of the taskbar, or right-click the clock in the lower-right corner of the screen. Figure 2-17 shows the options on the menu.

FIGURE 2-16

Flip 3D stack of open windows.

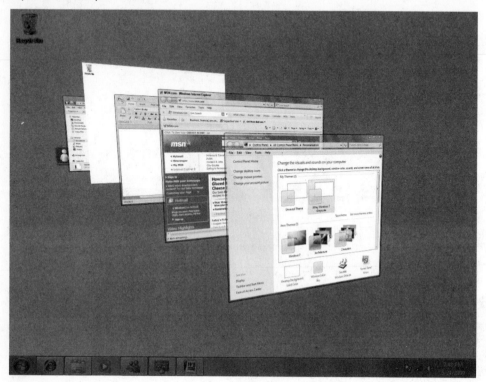

The four options that apply to program windows on the desktop are similar to the options you get when you right-click a taskbar button that represents multiple instances of one program:

- **Cascade Windows:** Stacks all the open windows like sheets of paper, fanned out so that all their title bars are visible, as in Figure 2-18.

- **Show Windows Stacked:** Arranges the windows in rows across the screen, or as equal-sized tiles.

- **Show Windows Side by Side:** Arranges the windows side by side. As with the preceding option, if you have too many open windows to show that way, they'll be displayed in equal-sized tiles.

- **Show the Desktop:** Minimizes all open windows so that only their taskbar buttons are visible. You can see the entire desktop at that point. To bring any window back onto the screen, click its taskbar button. To bring them all back, right-click the clock or taskbar again and choose Show Open Windows.

The only way to truly appreciate these options is to try them out for yourself. Open two or more programs. Then try each of the options described to see their effects on your open program windows.

FIGURE 2-17

Taskbar shortcut menu.

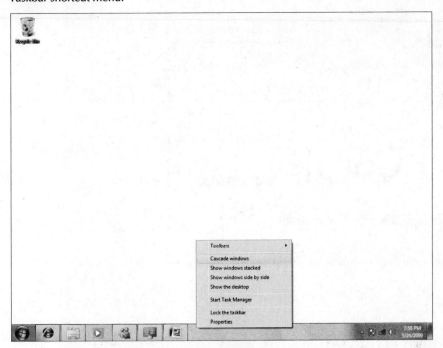

Sizing program windows

As a rule, program windows can be any size you want them to be, but this rule has a few exceptions. For example, the tiny Calculator program can't be sized at all. Some programs, such as Movie Maker, Media Player, and Solitaire, will shrink down only so far. But in general, most open program windows can appear in three categories of sizes:

- Maximized, in which the program fills the entire screen above the taskbar, covering the desktop.
- Minimized, in which only the program's taskbar button is visible, and the program window takes up no space on the desktop.
- Any size in between those two extremes.

Often, you'll want to work with two or more program windows at a time. Knowing how to size program windows is a critical skill for doing so, because working with multiple program windows is difficult if you can't see at least some portion of each one.

Maximize a program window

A maximized program window fills all the space above the taskbar. This makes it easy to see everything inside the program window. If a program window isn't already maximized, you can maximize it in several ways:

- Click the Maximize button in the program's title bar (see Figure 2-19).

39

FIGURE 2-18

Cascaded program windows.

FIGURE 2-19

Maximize button in a title bar.

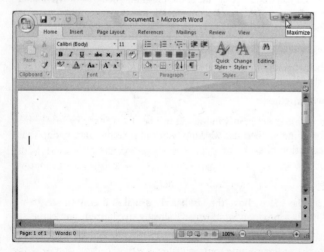

- Double-click the program's title bar.
- Click the upper-left corner of the window you want to maximize and choose Maximize. Optionally, right-click anywhere near the center top of the window and choose Maximize.

Tip

Remember, few buttons on the screen show their name. But you can find out a button's name just by touching the button with the tip of the mouse pointer. ■

Minimize a program window

If you want to get a program window off the screen temporarily without losing your place, minimize the program window. When you minimize the program window, the program remains running. However, it takes up no space on the screen, and therefore can't cover anything else on the screen. When minimized, only the window's taskbar button remains visible. You can minimize a window in several ways:

- Click the Minimize button in the program's title bar (see Figure 2-20).

Minimize button in a title bar.

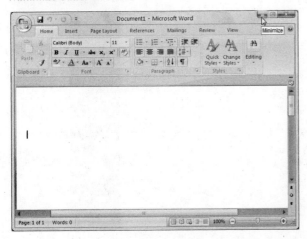

- Click the upper-left corner of the window you want to minimize (or right-click anywhere near the center top of the window) and choose Minimize.
- Click the program's taskbar button once or twice. (If the program isn't in the active window, the first click just makes it the active window. The second click then minimizes the active window.)
- Right-click the program's taskbar button or title bar and choose Minimize.

Size at will

Between the two extremes of maximized (hog up the entire desktop) and minimized (not even visible on the desktop), most program windows can be any size you want them to be. The first step to sizing a program window is to get it to an in-between size so that it's neither maximized nor minimized. To do that:

- If the program window is currently minimized, click its taskbar button to make it visible on the screen.

- If the program window is currently maximized, double-click its title bar or click its Restore Down button to shrink it down a little. Figure 2-21 shows the tooltip that appears when you point to the Restore Down button. Optionally, use the Cascade Windows option described earlier to get all open program windows down to an in-between size.

FIGURE 2-21

The Restore Down button in a maximized program window.

Minimize versus Close

Everything that's "in your computer," so to speak, is actually a file on your hard disk. The stuff on your hard disk is always there, whether the computer is on or off. When you open an item, two things happen. The most obvious is that the item becomes visible on the screen. What's not so obvious is the fact that a copy of the program is also loaded in the computer's memory (RAM).

When you minimize an open window, the program is still in memory. The only way you can tell that is by the fact that the program's taskbar button is still on the taskbar. When you want to view that program window, you just click its taskbar to make it visible on the screen again. It shows up looking exactly as it did before you minimized it.

When you close a program, its window and taskbar button both disappear, and the program is also removed from RAM (making room for other things you might want to work with). The only way to get back to the program is to restart it from its icon. However, this new program window will be an entirely new instance of the program, unrelated to how things looked before you closed the program.

After the program window is visible but not hogging up the entire screen, you can size it to your liking by dragging any edge or corner. You have to get the tip of the mouse pointer right on the border of the window you want to size so that the pointer turns into a two-headed arrow, as in Figure 2-22.

FIGURE 2-22

Mouse pointer positioned for sizing a window.

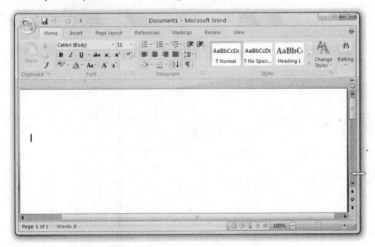

When you see the two-headed arrow, gently hold down the left mouse button without moving the mouse. After the mouse button is down, drag in the direction you want to size the window. Release the mouse button when the window is the size you want.

You can also size a program window using the mouse and the keyboard. Again, the program window has to be at some in-between size to start with. Also, note that you always begin the process from the program window's taskbar button. Here are the steps:

1. Click the program window's control menu button (upper-left corner of the window) and choose Size.

2. Press the navigation keys ($\leftarrow$, $\rightarrow$, $\uparrow$, $\downarrow$) until the window (or the border around the window) is the size you want.

3. Press the Enter key.

Moving a program window

You can easily move a program window about the screen just by dragging its title bar. However, you can't start with a maximized or minimized window. You have to get the program window to an in-between size before you even get started. Then just get the mouse pointer somewhere near the top center of the window you want to move, hold down the left mouse button, and drag the window around. Release the mouse button when the window is where you want it on the desktop.

Dialog boxes work the same way. You can't size or minimize a dialog box, and dialog boxes don't have taskbar buttons. But you can easily drag a dialog box around the screen by its title bar.

Moving and sizing from the keyboard

As you've seen, most of the techniques for moving and sizing program windows rely on the mouse. There are some keyboard alternatives, but they're not available in all program windows. The only way to find out whether these work in the window you're using at the moment is to press Alt+Spacebar and see whether a system menu drops down from the upper-left corner, as in Figure 2-23.

If you see the menu, you just have to press the underlined letter from the menu option you want to select. For example, press the letter x to Maximize or n to Minimize. If you press m to Move or s to Size, you can then use the ←, →, ↑, ↓ keys to move or size the window. Then press Enter when the window is positioned or sized to your liking.

FIGURE 2-23

System menu from a program window.

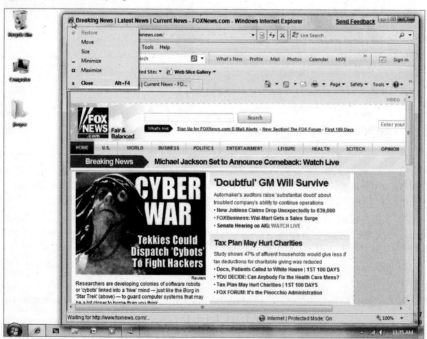

Tip

Sometimes, a window can be outside the viewable area of the desktop. This can happen if you extend your Windows desktop onto another monitor but that monitor isn't connected or turned on. If you can press Alt+Tab and determine that a program is running, but you can't see it on the desktop, press Alt+Tab and select the program (make it active). Then, press Alt+Spacebar, press M, and use the arrow keys on the keyboard to move the window into a viewable area of the desktop. ■

Closing a Program

When you've finished using a program for the time being, that's the time to close it. Every open program and document consumes some resources, mostly in the form of using memory (RAM). When RAM is full, the computer has to start using *virtual memory*, which is basically space on the hard disk configured to look like RAM to the computer.

RAM has no moving parts and, thus, can feed stuff to the processor (where all the work takes place) at amazing speeds. A hard disk has moving parts and is much, much slower. As soon as Windows has to start using virtual memory, everything slows down. So, you really don't want to have a bunch of stuff you're not using anymore open and consuming resources.

You have lots of ways to close a program. Use whichever of the following techniques is most convenient for you, because they all produce the same result — the program is removed from memory, and both its program window and taskbar button are removed from the screen:

- Click the Close (X) button in the program window's upper-right corner.
- Right-click the title bar across the top of the program window and choose Close.
- Choose File ➪ Exit from the program's menu bar.
- Right-click the program's taskbar button and choose Close window.
- If the program is in the active window, press Alt+F4.

If you were working on a document in the program and have made changes to that document since you last saved it, the program will (hopefully) ask whether you want to save those changes in a message box like the example in Figure 2-24.

FIGURE 2-24

Last chance to save a document.

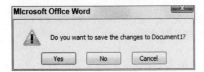

Never take that dialog box lightly, because whichever option you choose is final, and there's no going back and changing your mind. Your options are as follows:

- **Yes:** The document will be saved in its current state; both the document and the program will close.

- **No:** Any and all changes you made to the document since you last saved it will be lost forever. Both the document and the program will close.

- **Cancel:** The program and document will both remain open and on the screen. You can then continue work on the document and save it from the program's menu bar (choose File ➪ Save).

Using the Notification Area

Over on the right side of the taskbar is the Notification area (also called the *system tray* or *tray*). Each icon in the Notification area represents a program or service that's running in the background. For example, antivirus and antispyware programs often show icons in the Notification area so that you know they're running.

To conserve space on the taskbar, Windows 7 gives you the option of hiding inactive icons. When inactive icons are hidden, you see a button with up and down arrows on it at the left side of the Notification area. Click the button to see icons that are currently hidden.

As with any icon or button, you can point to an icon in the Notification area to see the name of that icon. Right-clicking an icon usually provides a context menu of options for using the item. Clicking or double-clicking the icon usually opens a program window that's associated with the running background service.

Note

A *context menu* is a menu that offers commands that are in the context of the selected item. In other words, the commands apply specifically to the selected item, not to other items. To open a context menu, right-click an item (like an icon). ■

For example, the Volume icon provides a simple service: It lets you control the volume of your speakers when sound is playing. To change the volume, you click the icon and then drag the slider (shown in Figure 2-25) up or down. Optionally, you can mute the speakers by choosing the button at the bottom of the slider. Click it again to remove the mute. The Mixer option opens a window in which you can control the volume of different kinds of sounds independently.

The icons in the Notification area don't represent programs that you *can* run. They represent programs that *are* running. The icon simply serves as a notification that the program is running, although in most cases, the icon also provides options for closing the program or changing how it runs. Different computers have different Notification area icons. Some common examples include the following:

- **Network Connections:** You might see an icon that lets you disconnect from the network, view and connect to wireless networks, and open the Network and Sharing Center.

- **Instant Messaging programs:** If you use Windows Live Messenger, Office Communicator, AOL Instant Messenger, or a similar program, the icon will be visible when the program is running.

- **Security programs:** Programs that protect your system from malware (such as viruses and spyware) often display icons in the Notification area.

- **Updates:** An icon notifies you when updates are available for downloading or installing.

- **Safely Remove Hardware:** If you have a USB device connected to your computer, the Safely Remove Hardware icon lets you disable the device before removing it, which you do to make sure that the device doesn't disconnect while it's still in use.

FIGURE 2-25

Volume control slider.

Showing/hiding notification icons

You can choose for yourself which Notification area icons you do and don't want to see at any time. You rarely need to see them all, so you can hide some from yourself just to conserve the taskbar space they would otherwise take up. To make choices about those icons, right-click the clock or blank area of the tray and choose Customize Notification Icons. The Notification Area Icons dialog box, shown in Figure 2-26, opens.

The Notification Area Icons dialog box lists items that are currently active, as well as inactive items that were active in the past. You can choose if and how you want to display an icon by clicking the Behavior icon to the right of the item's name. Your options are:

- **Only Show Notifications:** The icon will be visible only when it's active and serving some purpose.
- **Hide Icon and Notifications:** The item will always be hidden.
- **Show Icon and Notifications:** The item will always be visible in the Notification area.

As always, what you choose to show or hide is entirely up to you. Just make your selections and click OK in each of the open dialog boxes.

FIGURE 2-26

Notification Area Icons dialog box.

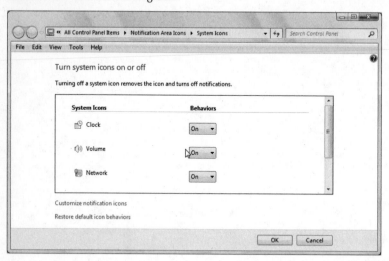

If you always want all Notification area icons to be visible, follow these steps:

1. Right-click the current time in the lower right of the screen and choose Customize Notification Icons.

2. In the Notification Area Icons dialog box that opens, select Always Show All Icons and Notifications on the Taskbar check box.

3. Click OK.

Chapter 10 discusses additional techniques for customizing the desktop, taskbar, and Notification area.

Responding to notification messages

Icons in the Notification area may occasionally display messages in a speech balloon. Many messages just provide some feedback and don't require any response from you, as in the example in Figure 2-27. That kind of message generally fades away on its own after a few seconds. But you can also close the message by clicking the Close (X) button in its upper-right corner.

Icons or messages that show a shield icon, like the one in Figure 2-28, are security related. (The message in Figure 2-28 is a fairly common one.) You can click the balloon or message title to get more information about the items.

Chapters 7 through 9 discuss security in some depth. For now, it's sufficient to note that the message in Figure 2-28 indicates that you *might* not have virus protection. In truth, the message just means that Windows hasn't detected any known virus protection yet. So don't be too alarmed if you see that message and know for a fact that you do have virus protection.

FIGURE 2-27

An informational notification message.

Using scroll bars

Scroll bars appear in program windows whenever the window contains more information than it can fit. You may not see any on your screen right now. But don't worry about that. The trick is to recognize them when you do see them, to know what they mean, and to know how to work them. Figure 2-29 shows an example of a vertical scroll bar and a horizontal scroll bar.

When you see a scroll bar, it means that there's more to see than what's currently visible in the window. The size of the scroll box (the bit inside the scroll bar area that looks like a long button) relative to the size of the scroll bar tells you roughly how much more there is to see. For example, if the scroll bar is about 10 percent the size of the bar, it means you're seeing only about 10 percent of all there is to see.

To see the rest, you use the scroll bar to scroll through the information. You have basically three ways to use scroll bars:

- Click a button at the end of the scroll bar to move a little bit in the direction of the arrow on the button.

- Click an empty space on the scroll bar to move the scroll box along the bar toward the place where you clicked. That moves you farther than clicking the buttons would.

49

FIGURE 2-28

A security warning from the Notification area.

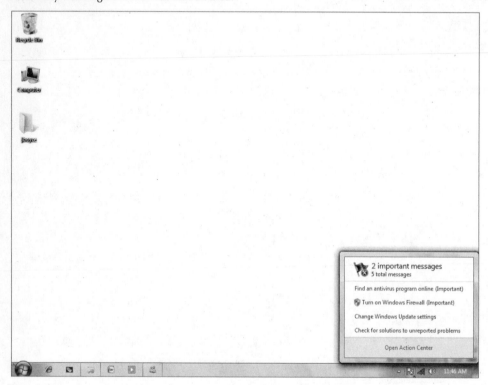

- Drag the scroll box in the direction you want to scroll. To drag, place the mouse pointer on the button and hold down the left mouse button while moving the mouse in the direction you want to scroll.

If your mouse has a wheel, you can use that to scroll as well. If the window shows a vertical scroll bar, spinning the mouse wheel scrolls up and down. If the window shows only a horizontal scroll bar, spinning the mouse wheel scrolls left and right. Some mice have a horizontal scroll button (or wheel) that you can push left or right to scroll horizontally.

You can also use the keyboard to scroll up and down. But understand that they work only in the active window (the window that's on the top of the stack). If necessary, first click the window or press Alt+Tab to bring it to the top of the stack. Then you can use the ↑ and ↓ keys to scroll up and down slightly. Use the Page Up (PgUp) and Page Down (PgDn) keys to scroll up and down in larger increments. Press the Home key to scroll all the way to the top (or all the way to the left). Press the End key to scroll all the way to the end.

Using Back and Forward buttons

Back and Forward buttons help you navigate through multiple pages of items. As with scroll bars, they appear only when useful, so don't expect to see them on your screen right now, or all the time. At times they may be *disabled* (dimmed), as at the top of Figure 2-30. At other times they are *enabled* (not dimmed), as at the bottom half of the same figure. Also, you won't find Back and Forward buttons in every program window.

FIGURE 2-29

Examples of scroll bars.

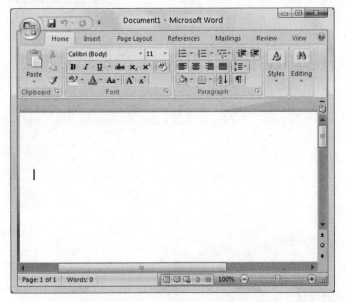

FIGURE 2-30

Back and Forward buttons.

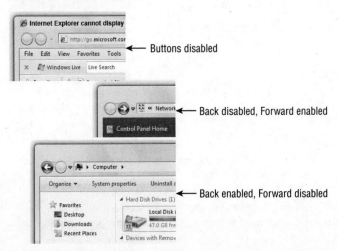

A disabled button isn't broken. When an item is disabled, it's just not appropriate at the moment. For example, when you first open a window, both buttons may be disabled because you have no page to switch to yet. When you click a link that takes you to another page, the Back button is then enabled, because now you *do* have a page to go back to (the page you just left). After you go back to the previous page, the Forward button is enabled because now you have a page to go forward to — the page you just left.

When a button is enabled, you just click it to go back or forward. When a button is disabled, clicking it has no effect.

The Getting Started Item

The Getting Started item is a Control Panel item whose window might or might not appear automatically when you first log in to Windows. It can also appear on the Start menu. It provides some links to a few Windows features and some online resources. Figure 2-31 shows an example. Yours might look a little different.

FIGURE 2-31

The Getting Started item.

When you click an icon in the lower half of the window, the upper half changes to show you more information. An action button with a green arrow and descriptions also appears in the upper half of the window to help you see more information or start a task associated with the described item.

You can maximize, minimize, restore, move, size, and close the Getting Started window as you can any open window. See the sections on sizing, arranging, moving, and closing program windows earlier in this chapter for more information.

Quick Help for Getting Started

Windows Help is a great resource to help you learn about Windows and how to work with your computer. To open Help, click the Start menu and then click Help and Support.

If you're new to computers, the Learn About Windows Basics item in Help provides a quick overview of basic skills and concepts (Figure 2-32).

FIGURE 2-32

Windows Basics help.

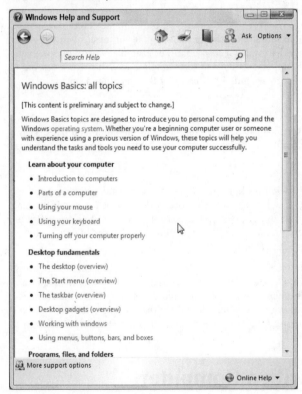

Each short chunk of blue text is a link that takes you to a help topic. Click any link to see that topic. In many of the pages, you need to use the scroll bar to scroll up and down through all the text. You can use the Back and Forward buttons, when enabled, to scroll through pages you've already visited. Using the Help feature in this manner will give you some practice with skills you've learned in this chapter. At the same time, it can help you reinforce what you already know and teach you some things you haven't learned yet.

To leave the Help window, just close it (click the Close (X) button in its upper-right corner). See Chapter 5 for more information on using the Help system.

Tip
You'll often see a little blue button with a white question mark in program windows. That's the Help button. You can click it for information. You can also press the Help key (F1) on your keyboard at any time for help. ∎

Logging Off, Shutting Down

Here's a question a lot of people ask: "Should I shut down my computer if I won't be using it for a while, or should I just leave it on?" Everybody has an opinion about this. So here's mine: It doesn't matter. Personally, about the only time I ever shut down my computers is when I need to, such as when installing certain types of hardware. Aside from that, all my computers are on, and online, 24 hours a day, 7 days a week. With today's green PCs, turning off the computer every day isn't as important as it once was. Perhaps more important, leaving the computer on means you can start working with it almost right away, rather than wait for it to boot. For example, when I'm done with my notebook for the day, I just close the lid and let it go into standby mode. When I need to use it again I open the lid, and within ten or fifteen seconds I can be using the computer again.

Note
Okay, this is more of a gripe than a note. Microsoft, we can send people safely to the moon and back. Why can't we have a computer that has an instant-on feature or at least boots from having the power off to being ready to use in ten seconds? ∎

The Power button on the Start menu is shown back in Figures 2-7 and 2-8. Understand that turning off a PC isn't quite the same as turning off a TV or radio. You usually don't want to just hit the main power switch to shut down while you have things open on the desktop. You want to close everything first. Then click the Start button, click the arrow on the Power button, and choose Shut Down (or just click the Power button if it already says Shut Down).

Don't expect the computer to turn off immediately. It takes a few seconds for Windows to get everything closed up and ready to shut down. On most computers, you don't have to do anything else. The computer will eventually shut itself down completely. Some older computers may show a message stating, "It is now safe to shut down your computer." If you see that message, you need to hold in the main power button on your computer for a few seconds to finish shutting down the system.

Stuff You Can Do with a Computer

There's so much you can do with Windows 7 and your computer, I hardly know where to start. So I'll just throw some ideas out there and point you to the chapter where that topic is discussed. Of course, you can get much more detailed information about the contents of this book from the Table of Contents up front. And you can look things up in the Index at the back of the book. For the folks who are just getting started and don't know quite what to do next, here are some quick suggestions:

- Set up parental controls: Chapter 4
- Get help: Chapter 5
- Personalize the screen to your own style: Chapter 10
- Dictate text: Chapter 11

- Do some basic math with Windows Calculator: Chapter 15
- Type letters and other text with WordPad: Chapter 15
- Surfing the Internet: Chapter 16
- Send and receive e-mail: Chapter 18
- Chat online: Chapter 19
- Organize, fix, and print photos: Chapter 23
- Collect music and make your own CDs: Chapter 24

The terms and skills you've learned in this chapter should be enough to get you started on whichever topic looks most interesting. You will need an Internet connection for e-mail and the Web. But you should be able to do everything else using just Windows 7. You don't need to buy extra programs to do those things.

Wrap-Up

That about wraps it up for the main terminology and basic skills. Much of what you've learned in this chapter is the kind of stuff most people assume you already know. You may have to read the chapter a few times, and practice things, before it all sinks in. Use the Windows Basics help I mentioned for more information and for hands-on practice.

Here's a quick summary of the most important points covered in this chapter:

- The Windows desktop is where you'll do all your work.
- You'll use your mouse and keyboard to operate the computer.
- Most of your work will involve opening and using programs.
- You can start any program that's installed on your computer from the All Programs menu.
- Each open program will appear in its own program window on the desktop. Program windows stack up like sheets of paper.
- Each open program window has a corresponding taskbar button. The taskbar buttons help you switch from one open program window to another.
- You can move and size program windows to see exactly what you need to see, when you need to see it.
- When you've finished using your computer and want to shut it down, don't go straight for the main power switch. Instead, click the Start button and then click the Shut Down button on the Start menu.

That's enough for now about the desktop and programs. These days, with just about everyone using his or her computer to access the Internet, security is a major issue. So I start to address that topic in Chapter 3 with a discussion of user accounts and how they relate to computer security.

Sharing and Securing with User Accounts

Every person who uses your computer is called a *user*, and each user can have his or her own *user account* on the computer. Giving each person a user account is a lot like giving each person his or her own separate PC, but a lot cheaper. Each user can personalize the desktop and other settings to one's liking. Each person can have his or her own separate collection of pictures, music, videos, and other documents. Each user can also set up his or her own separate e-mail account.

User accounts allow parents to create and enforce parental controls in Windows 7. This is a great tool for parents who can't always monitor when and how children use the computer. Parental controls allow you to control and monitor children's computer use 24 hours a day, 365 days a year, even when you're not around to do it yourself.

User accounts also add a level of security to your computer. Many security breaches occur not because of a problem with the computer or Windows, but because the user is in an account that grants malware (bad software) *permission* to do its evil deeds. Of course, people don't realize that they're granting permission, because the program doesn't ask for permission. It gets its permission automatically from the type of user account into which you're currently logged.

Creating and managing user accounts is easy. But before getting into the specifics of all that, let's take a look at how you, as a user, experience user accounts.

Logging In and Out of User Accounts

If you already have multiple user accounts on your computer, you see an icon for each one shortly after you first start your computer. Figure 3-1 shows an example of some icons that represent user accounts.

FIGURE 3-1

Sample user account icons.

To log in to an account, click its picture. If the user account is password-protected, you must also enter the password that protects that account from unauthorized entry.

Where am I now?

To see the name of the user account into which you're currently logged, click the Start button. The name at the top-right side of the Start menu is the name of the user account into which you're currently logged. In Figure 3-2, that user account name is jboyce. But it could be anything on your computer. If Windows 7 came pre-installed on your computer, it might be a generic name like Owner or User.

Logging out of an account

You have a few different ways to switch from the account into which you're currently logged to another account (assuming that you have more than one user account on your computer already). The first step is to click the Start button and then click the arrow next to the Power button, as in Figure 3-3. The first three items have to do with the user account into which you're currently logged:

FIGURE 3-2

Username on the Start menu.

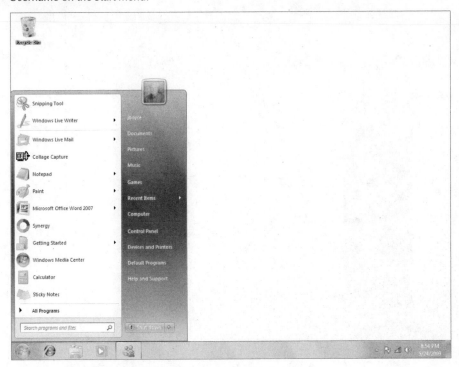

Why Switch User Can Be Bad

When you use Switch User, rather than Log Off, to leave your account, all the programs and documents on your desktop remain open and in memory. This leaves less working memory for other users in their accounts.

If multiple users consistently use Switch User to leave their accounts, you end up with lots of people's stuff in memory all the time. The likely result is that the entire computer will run much slower for everyone.

Ideally, every user should log off from his or her account when finished using the computer. If you find that other users won't stay with that plan, and the computer is often running slower than molasses in Antarctica, you can disable the Switch User option.

- **Switch User:** Lets you go to another user account without losing your place in the current user account. This is fine for temporarily using another account to perform a simple task (such as checking e-mail).

FIGURE 3-3

Logging out options.

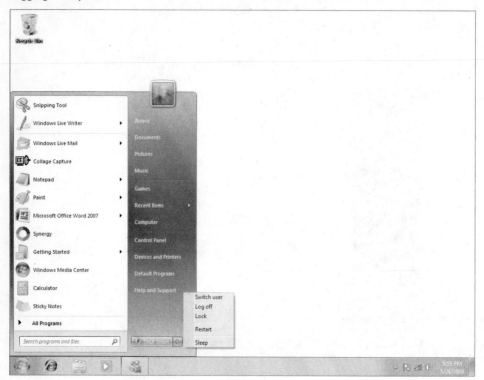

- **Hibernate:** On a notebook computer, this option saves the system state to disk and powers down the computer, but the computer can be restored more quickly than shutting down and starting up.

- **Log Off:** This option closes all open programs and gives you the opportunity to save any unsaved work. Use this option when you plan to be away from the computer for a while.

- **Lock:** If your user account is password-protected, use this option to hide what's on your screen and keep other people from using the computer under your user account. When you log back in, you'll be right back where you left the computer.

If your user account isn't password-protected, other people aren't really locked out of your account. Anyone can come along, click your user account name, and be at your desktop.

Creating Strong Passwords

I talk about techniques for creating, managing, and password-protecting user accounts in a moment. But before I get into the details, I think it might be worthwhile to talk about passwords in general. Not just passwords for user accounts, but for all types of accounts you create, including online accounts.

A password that's easily guessed is a weak password. A strong password is one that's not easily guessed and is immune to *password-guessing attacks*. The two most common forms of password-guessing attacks are the *dictionary attack* and the *brute-force attack*. Both types of attacks rely on special programs that are specifically designed to try to crack people's passwords and gain unauthorized entry to their user accounts.

The dictionary attack tries many thousands of passwords from a dictionary of English terms and commonly used passwords. The brute-force attack tries thousands of combinations of characters until it finds the right combination of characters needed to get into the account.

Admittedly, both types of attacks are rare in a home PC environment. They're also easily frustrated by common techniques such as forcing the user to wait several minutes before trying again after three failed password attempts. Nonetheless, the general guidelines used to protect top-secret data from password-guessing attacks can be applied to any password you create. A strong password is one that meets at least some of the following criteria:

- It is at least eight characters long.
- It does not contain your real name, user account name, pet names, significant date (such as birthday), or any name that's easily guessed by other family members or coworkers.
- It does not contain a word that can be found in a dictionary.
- It contains some combination of uppercase letters, lowercase letters, numeric digits, and symbols (such as !, &, ?, @, or #).

Again, I realize that few of us need Fort Knox security on our personal PCs. You don't want to come up with a password that's difficult to remember and a pain to type. But any steps you take to make the password less susceptible to guessing are well worth some effort. Some Web sites offer password checkers, programs that analyze a password and tell you how strong it is. See `www.microsoft.com/athome/security/privacy/password_checker.mspx` for an example. Or go to any search engine, such as `www.google.com`, and search for *password checker*.

Remembering passwords

The most common problem with passwords is forgetting them after the fact. When you set up a password for a Web site, you can usually find out what it is just by clicking an "I forgot my password" link at the sign-in page. But there is no such link for passwords that protect your Windows user accounts. Therefore, it's extremely important that you *not* forget your Windows passwords!

Before you password-protect a user account, take the time to come up with a password that you (or the user) can remember. Make sure you use exactly the same uppercase and lowercase letters that you'll be typing. All passwords are always case sensitive, which means uppercase and lowercase letters count!

For example, say you jot down your password as `tee4me!0` (where that last digit is a zero). But later you type it in as `Tee4Me!o` (with the last digit being the letter *o*). Still later, you forget the password and dig out the sheet of paper. The `tee4me!0` you wrote down won't work, because the password is actually `Tee4Me!o`.

Caution

On a typewriter, the number 0 is basically the same as an uppercase letter *O*. The number 1 is basically the same as a lowercase letter *l* but that is *not* true of computers. You must use the 1 and 0 keys near the top of the keyboard or on the numeric keypad to type 1 (one) and 0 (zero). ■

Devising a password hint

With Windows passwords, you can also specify a password hint to help you remember a forgotten password. But still, it's tricky. Anyone who uses your computer can see the password hint. So the hint can't be so obvious that it tells a potential intruder what the password is.

By the same token, the hint might trigger your basic memory of the password. But perhaps not the exact uppercase and lowercase letters you used. It's not a good idea to write down your passwords, because it exposes them to others' access. But, if you need to keep track of multiple passwords, consider using a password-protected Excel spreadsheet to store all your passwords. Then, you only need to really remember one — the one for the Excel file. There are also password-keeper applications available that achieve the same result.

Tip

If you decide to store your passwords in an Excel file, make a copy you can open on another computer in case your computer crashes or you forget the password to log on. ■

The bottom line on remembering passwords is simple: You are allowed no margin for error. A password that's "sort of like" the one you specified is not good enough. It must be *exactly* the one you specified. You must treat passwords as though they are valuable diamonds. Keep them safe and keep them secure, but don't keep them so safe that even *you* can't find them!

Okay, that's enough general advice about passwords. Next, you need to find out about types of user accounts.

Tip

As long as your account is an administrator account, or you have a separate administrator account that you can access, you can always reset someone's password on the computer if needed. You don't have to go through a password recovery process; just reset the password. ■

Types of User Accounts

Windows 7 offers four basic types of user accounts: the built-in Administrator account, user accounts with administrative privileges, standard accounts, and a Guest account. They vary in how much privilege they grant to the person using the account.

The built-in Administrator account

A single user account named Administrator is built into Windows 7. This is not the same as an administrative account you create yourself or see on the login screen. This account is hidden from normal view. It doesn't show up on the usual login screen.

The built-in Administrator account has unlimited computer privileges. So while you're logged in to that account, you can do anything and everything you want with the computer. Any programs you run while you are in that account can also do anything they want. That makes the account risky from a security standpoint, and very unwise to use unless absolutely necessary.

In high-security settings, a new computer is usually configured by a certified network or security administrator who logs in to the Administrator account to set up the computer for other users. There the administrator configures accounts on the *principle of least privilege*, where each account is given only as much privilege as necessary to perform a specific job.

When the administrator is finished, he or she typically renames the built-in Administrator account and password-protects it to keep everyone else out. The account is always hidden from view, except from other administrators who know how to find it. All this is standing operating procedure in secure computing environments, though hardly the norm in home computing.

In Windows 7, you really don't need to find, log in to, and use the built-in Administrator account unless you're an advanced user with a specific need, in which case you can get to it through Safe Mode. As a regular home user, you can do everything you need to do from a regular user account that has administrative privileges.

Note

Experienced users who need access to the built-in Administrator account can get to it through Safe Mode. I talk about that in Chapter 13. But if you're not a professional, I suggest you stay away from that and use an administrative account, discussed next. ■

Administrative user accounts

Most of the time when you hear reference to an Administrator account in Windows 7, that reference is to a regular user account that has administrative privileges. This is an account that has virtually all the power and privilege of the built-in Administrator account. But it also has a lot of security built in to help thwart security threats that might otherwise abuse that account's privileges to do harm to your computer.

Ideally, you want to create one user account with administrative privileges on your computer. If you intend to implement parental controls, you'll need to password-protect that account to keep children from disabling or changing parental controls.

Standard accounts

A standard user account is the kind of account everyone should use for day-to-day computer use. It has enough privilege to do day-to-day tasks such as run programs, work with documents, do e-mail, and browse the Web. It doesn't have enough privilege to make changes to the system that would affect other people's user accounts. It doesn't have enough privilege to allow children to override parental controls. And most important, it doesn't have enough privilege to let malware such as viruses and worms make harmful changes to your system.

If you use a standard account all the time, and use a built-in administrative account only when absolutely necessary, you'll go a long way toward keeping your computer safe from Internet security threats.

Guest account

The optional Guest account exists to allow people who don't regularly use your computer to use it temporarily. Basically, it lets them check their e-mail, browse the Web, and maybe play some games. It definitely won't let them make changes to your user account or anyone else's. Its limited privileges also help protect your system from any malicious software they might pick up while online.

Creating and Managing User Accounts

The best way to handle user accounts is for one person to play the role of administrator, even if that person isn't a professional. In a home environment, it would most likely be a parent who needs to define parental controls. It's best to log in to a user account that already has administrative privileges to get started. If you only have one user account, or are taken straight to the desktop at startup, then that account probably has administrative privileges.

As with most configuration tasks, you create and manage user accounts through the Control Panel. There are several pages you can use, and several ways to get to them. As always, there is no right way or wrong way. No good way or bad way. You just use whatever is easiest and most convenient for you at the moment. Here are a couple of ways to get to options for managing the user account you're logged in to at the moment:

- Press ⊞, type **user** in the search box, and click User Accounts.
- Click the Start button, choose Control Panel, click User Accounts and Family Safety, and then click User Accounts.

A Control Panel applet appears that lets you make changes to the account into which you're currently logged, as in the example shown in Figure 3-4. Options marked with shield icons require administrative privileges.

FIGURE 3-4

The User Accounts Control Panel applet.

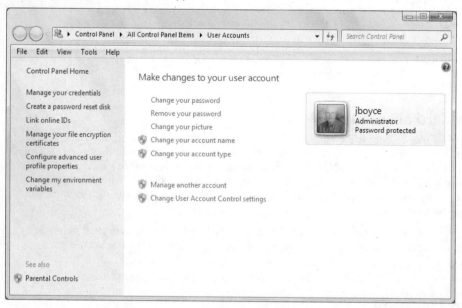

To create a new user account, click Manage Another Account. If you're in a standard account on a computer that already has a password-protected administrative account, you'll have to enter the password for the Administrator account. Or, if the administrative account doesn't have a password, press

Enter to leave the password box empty. You end up in the Manage Accounts page. There you see an icon for every user account on your system. You can also tell the type of each account. Figure 3-5 shows an example with two administrative accounts, jboyce and the built-in Administrator account. The rest are standard user accounts.

Manage Accounts page.

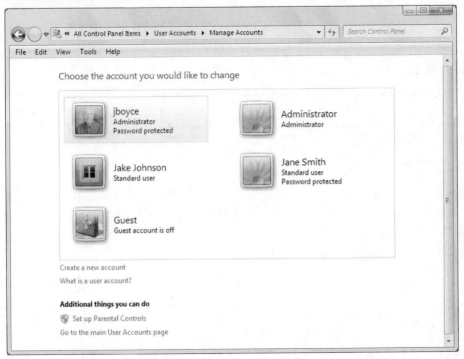

Creating a user account

Creating a new user account is easy. You should have one standard account for your day-to-day computing, plus one standard account for every other person who will use your computer. Ideally, each of these should be password-protected, but this is not a requirement.

Keep in mind that each user account has its own collection of files. If you've been using your administrative account for a while, you may not want to create a new standard account from scratch. Better to create a new administrative account from scratch and then change your current account from an administrative account to a standard account. That way, you won't have to move files from your current account to the new account.

To create a new user account, click Create a New Account to get to the page shown in Figure 3-6.

Type in a name for the user account. If you're creating a new administrative account, consider naming it Admin or something like that. You can't use the name Administrator because that name is already taken by the built-in administrative account. If you're creating a new standard account for yourself or a family member, use the person's first name as the account name.

FIGURE 3-6

Create a new user account.

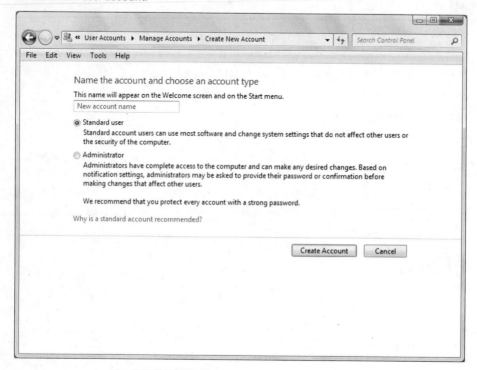

After you've typed the account name, choose Standard User to create a standard user account. Or choose Administrator to create a user account that has administrative privileges. Then click Create Account to create the user account. You're returned to the previous Manage User Accounts page, where you see that the new user account has been added to the system.

You can repeat the process to create as many user accounts as you wish.

Changing user accounts

When you create a user account, you're just giving it a name and choosing a type. After you've created a user account, you can change it to better suit your needs. Use the Manage User Accounts page (refer to Figure 3-5) to make changes to accounts.

Caution

When you delete a user account, you might also delete all the files in that account if you're not careful. Read the section titled "Deleting User Accounts," later in this chapter, before you delete an account so that you don't end up deleting photos or other documents that could be difficult or impossible to recover. ■

Changing a user account type

You can change an Administrator account to a standard account, or vice versa, from the main User Accounts page. For example, if you've been using an administrative account for your day-to-day computing since buying your computer, you might want to change it to a standard account for the added security that a standard account provides. At least one user account must have administrative privileges, so you can make this change only if you have at least one other user account on the system that has administrative privileges.

To change an account's type, click the account's icon or name in the Manage Accounts page. First you're taken to the Change an Account page. As you can see in Figure 3-7, that page lets you change the account in a number of ways, or even delete the account.

FIGURE 3-7

Change an Account page.

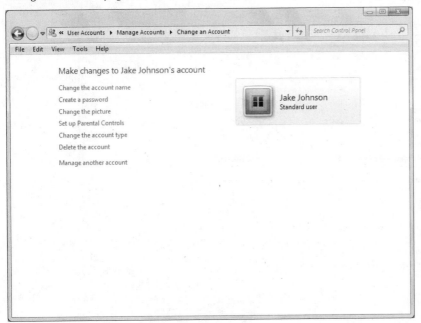

Click Change the Account Type to change the account from an administrative account to a standard account, or vice versa. To change the account type, click Change the Account Type. You're taken to the Change Account Type page. Click the type of account you want this user account to be, and then click Change Account Type.

Password-protecting an account

If you share your computer with other people, chances are you'll want to keep some people out of the Administrator account. Likewise, you'll want to keep some users from having administrative privileges. This is especially important with parental controls. If the administrative account isn't password-protected, it won't take long for the kids to figure out how to bypass any controls you impose.

Password-protecting an account is easy enough. Just remember, you do *not* want to forget the password you set on the administrator account if it is the only one. Otherwise, nobody will have administrative privileges, and that will cause a world of headaches. So think up a good password and password hint, and make sure you enter the password correctly.

To password-protect a user account, go to the main page for the user account. For instance, if you're in the Manage Accounts page, click the user account you want to password-protect. Then click Create a Password. You're taken to a page like the one in Figure 3-8. If you've been using the account for a while without a password, heed the warnings. If it's a brand-new account, you don't have anything to worry about.

FIGURE 3-8

Password-protecting an account.

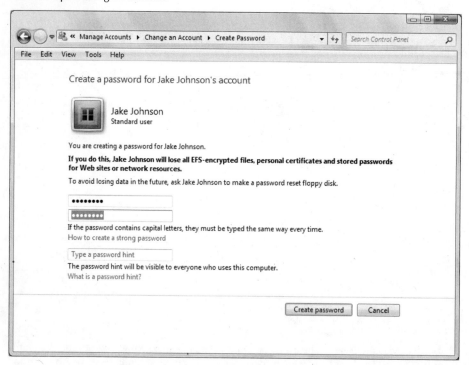

To password-protect the account, type your password in the New Password box. Then press Tab or click the second textbox and type the same password again. You won't see the characters you type, just a placeholder for each character. Typing passwords always works that way to prevent *shoulder surfing*. Shoulder surfing is a simple technique for discovering someone's password just by watching over the person's shoulder as he or she types it on the screen.

Next, type in your password hint. The hint should be something that reminds you of the forgotten password, but not a dead giveaway to someone trying to break into the account. Click Create Password after you've filled in all the blanks.

If you see a message indicating that your passwords don't match, you'll have to retype both passwords. Make sure you type the password exactly the same in both boxes. Then click the Change Password button again. You'll be taken back to the main page for the user account when you've successfully entered the password in both boxes and provided a password hint.

You can repeat the process to password-protect as many accounts as you wish. If you're creating user accounts for people other than yourself, set a default password for the account and then let them manage their own passwords. In my opinion, every account should have a password.

Tip

Why have a password on all accounts? First, it's basic security. Second, if you have more than one child using a shared computer, having a password for each child will help prevent one from using another's account to potentially bypass restrictions. ∎

Changing the account picture

Every user account has an associated picture. The picture is like an icon, giving you a quick visual reference without having to read the name. The picture you choose can be any one of several built-in pictures, or it can be a picture of your own choosing.

If you decide to use your own picture, try to avoid using one that comes straight from a digital camera. The file size on such pictures is really too large for a user account picture. Your best bet would be to crop out a section from a photo, and size it to about 100 x 100 pixels. The picture you choose must be the JPEG, BMP, PNG, GIF, or PNG file type.

Tip

If you don't know enough about pictures to meet all the requirements, you can use built-in pictures. Then, after you've acquired some of the skills covered in Chapter 23, you can create a suitable user account picture and apply it to any user account. ∎

To change the picture for a user account, get to the main page for that user account and click Change the Picture (or Change My Picture, depending on how you got there). Then:

- To use a built-in picture, click the picture you want and click the Change Picture button.
- To use a custom picture, click Browse for More Pictures and navigate to the folder that contains your custom user account pictures, as in the example shown in Figure 3-9. Then click (or double-click) the picture you want to use.

The picture you selected replaces the original picture.

Changing the account name

The account name is the name that appears on the login screen and at the top of the Start menu when you're logged in to an account. If you inadvertently misspelled the name when you first created the account, you may want to change the name to correct that misspelling. Or, if an account has a generic name such as Owner, you might want to change it to a more personal name. But other than that, there wouldn't really be any need to change an account.

To change an account name, just get to the main page for the user account. Click the Change the Account Name link, type the new name, and click the Change Name button.

FIGURE 3-9

Changing a user account picture.

Enabling or disabling the Guest account

The Guest account is for anybody who might need to use your computer on a temporary basis. For example, with a home computer, you might set up a Guest account for any temporary houseguests. Then let those people use the Guest account to check their e-mail, browse the Web, and such. The Guest account has very limited privileges, so you don't have to worry about them messing things up while using your computer.

The Guest account is turned off by default. You can keep it that way until you actually need it. To activate the Guest account, go to the Manage Accounts page and click the Guest account icon. Then choose Turn On. Likewise, should you ever need to disable the Guest account, click its icon on the Manage Accounts page and then click Turn Off the Guest account.

Navigating through user account pages

As you can see, it's pretty easy to create and manage user accounts. It's largely just a matter of choosing options and reading text that's right on the screen. Remember, any blue text you see is a link, meaning you can click it. You can use the Back and Forward buttons to get around from page to page. On most pages, you can click the Manage Another Account link to get to the Manage Accounts page. You can also use the address bar at the top of the window to get around. Click any name in the address bar to jump to that page. Or click the arrow between any two page names, or to the left of the page names (as in Figure 3-10) to get to other pages.

FIGURE 3-10

Use the address bar to get around.

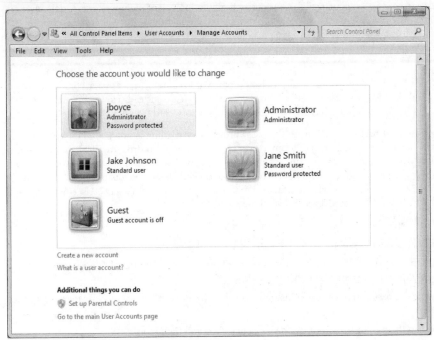

Creating a Password Reset Disk

A password reset disk is an important part of any password-protected PC. It's the only method of password recovery that allows you to retain all data in an account in the event of a forgotten password. Advanced features such as EFS (Encrypting File System) encryption, personal certificates, and stored network passwords can be recovered only by using a password reset disk.

The main trick is to create the password reset disk *before* you forget the password. You can't do it after you've forgotten the password. Keep that disk in a safe place where you can find it when you need it, but where others can't find it to gain unauthorized access to the administrative account.

Jump Drive? Memory Card?

A jump drive (also called a *USB flash drive*) is a small device that plugs into a USB port on your computer and looks and acts like a disk drive. A memory card is a storage device commonly used to store pictures in digital cameras. If your computer has slots for such cards, you can slide a card into the slot and treat the card just as you would a USB flash drive. See Chapter 29 for more information.

continued

continued

To see examples and get an idea of costs, check out some online retailers. Then search the site for *jump drive* or *memory card reader* to view available products. If you're looking at memory card readers, the kind that plugs into a USB will be the easiest to install. Many retail department stores that sell computer or office supplies also carry flash drives.

A floppy disk or jump drive works equally well as a password recovery tool. If your computer doesn't have a floppy disk drive, you can use a jump drive or memory card instead. However, a memory card will work only if your computer has slots for inserting a memory card.

To create a password reset disk, log in to the password-protected administrative account you created. Then insert a blank floppy disk in the floppy drive. Or connect a jump drive to a USB port, or put a spare memory card in a memory card slot. Then get to the main User Accounts page. If you've already closed the user account window, press ▟, type **user**, and click User Accounts on the Start menu. Or go through the Control Panel (click the **Start** button and choose Control Panel ➪ User Accounts and Family Safety ➪ User Accounts). Then follow these steps:

1. In the left column, click Create a Password Reset Disk.
2. Read the first page of the wizard that opens and click Next.
3. Choose the drive into which you inserted the floppy, or the drive letter that represents the jump drive or memory card; then click Next.
4. Type the password for the administrative account into which you're currently logged and click Next.
5. When the progress indicator is finished, click Next and then Finish.

Keep the disk (or drive, or card) in a safe place. If you use a jump drive that you also use for other purposes, make sure you don't erase the userkey.psw file. That's the file needed for password recovery.

Using the password reset disk

If you ever need to use the disk (or drive, or card) to get into the administrative account, first start the computer and click the administrative account for which you created the password reset disk. Take a best guess at the password and press Enter.

If the password is rejected, insert the floppy disk, jump drive, or memory card you created as a password reset disk. Wait a few seconds for Windows to recognize and register the item. Then click Reset Password under the password hint on the login screen.

Follow the instructions presented by the wizard that opens. You won't be required to remember the original password. Instead, you create an entirely new password and hint for the account. Use that new password whenever you log in to the account from that point on.

Cracking into standard user accounts

If a standard user forgets his or her password, you can use an account that has administrative privileges to get the standard user back into his or her account. If you're an administrator and just want to see what a standard user is up to, you can use this same technique to remove the password from the account and have full access to its folders.

Caution

This approach will cause the standard user to lose access to encrypted files and e-mail messages you create in an e-mail program such as Windows Live Mail. If the standard user is advanced enough to use those things, it is better to use a password reset disk to gain access to the account. ■

To remove the password from a standard user account:

1. Log in to a user account that has administrative privileges.
2. Get to the Manage Accounts page (click the Start button and choose Control Panel ⇨ Add or Remove User Accounts).
3. Click the password-protected account for which the user has forgotten the password.
4. Click the Remove the Password button.

The standard user account will no longer be password-protected. Anybody can log in to that account from the login page just by clicking the user's account icon.

Deleting User Accounts

An administrator can easily delete user accounts. If nobody has ever used a user account, then deleting the account is no big deal. But if anybody has used the account, there is much to consider before deleting it because when you delete the user account, you also delete all e-mail messages downloaded to the computer, the e-mail account, and Internet favorites. You could also delete all of that user's saved files if you're not careful. Doing this by accident would be a disaster, because there's no way to undo the deletion. So just to make sure nobody misses this important point, here's a caution:

Caution

Deleting a user account can have very serious consequences. Don't do it unless you fully understand the ramifications. ■

If you want to save the user's e-mail messages and Internet favorites, export them to that user's Documents folder first. How you export depends on the programs you use for e-mail and Web browsing. If those programs are Windows Mail and Internet Explorer, you can use the techniques described in Chapters 19 and 21 to export.

So let's assume you understand the consequences and have no intention of deleting an account just for the heck of it. Only administrators can delete user accounts. So if you're in a standard account, you at least need to know the administrative password to delete a user account. You also need to log in to any account except the one you intend to delete. Then:

1. Click the Start button, choose Control Panel, and click Add or Remove User Accounts.
2. If prompted, enter an administrative password.
3. Click the account you want to delete.
4. Click Delete the Account and read the resulting message. Then click one of the following buttons:
   - Delete files: Click this button only if you intend to delete *everything* associated with the account, including all files that the user has created and saved.

- Keep files: Click this option to save the user's files. You will still lose the user's saved e-mail messages, Internet favorites, and user account.

5. Read the next page to make sure you understand the consequences of your choice. Then click Cancel if you change your mind, or click Delete Account if you're sure you know what you're doing.

If you choose Delete Account, the user's account will no longer exist. If you choose Keep Files, the user's saved files (those from his account's profile) will be in a folder on the desktop. That folder will have the same name as the user account you just deleted. Otherwise, nothing of the user's account, not even his or her saved files, will remain. (If you choose Cancel in step 5, the entire account remains intact and unchanged.)

If you create a new user account with the same name as the one you just deleted, the new account is still an entirely new account. It will not inherit any files or settings from the account you previously deleted.

Note

If the user's Documents folder contains no documents, Windows will not create a copy of the folder on your desktop when you delete the account (because there is nothing to save). ■

Using User Accounts

As mentioned at the start of this chapter, each user account is like its own separate PC. Every user has his or her private Documents, Pictures, Music, and Video folders for storing files. Each user account can have its own e-mail account and Internet favorites. Each user can customize the desktop, Start menu, and other settings to that user's own liking.

When you first start your computer, or log out of your user account, you see a name and icon for each available user account. If you click a user account that isn't password-protected, you're taken straight into the account. But if you click the icon for a password-protected account, a password prompt appears as in Figure 3-11.

To get into the account, you need to enter the appropriate password. Entering the wrong password just displays the password hint and gives you another shot at entering the correct password. You can't get into the user account until you've entered the correct password for the account.

The first time you (or someone else) log in to a new user account, it's just like starting Windows 7 on a brand-new PC. The desktop has the default appearance. All of the document folders in the account are empty. There is no e-mail account, no Internet favorites. To use e-mail, the user (or administrator) needs to set up the account with an e-mail account, preferably an account used only by that user.

The user does have access to all the programs installed on the computer (except for rare cases in which someone installed a program for personal use only). The user will likely have Internet connectivity through the same modem or network as all other user accounts.

If the user account is a standard account, there are some limitations to what the user can do. Basically, the user cannot make any changes to the system that would affect other users. That's where Windows 7's User Account Control (UAC) security comes into play.

FIGURE 3-11

Log in to a password-protected account.

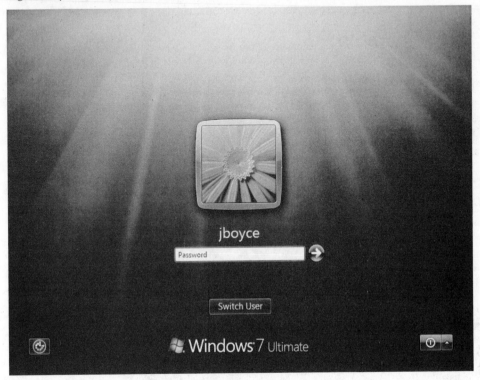

Understanding User Account Control (UAC)

User Account Control (UAC) is the general term for the way administrative and standard user accounts work in Windows 7. As you browse around through various pages in the Control Panel, you'll notice that many links have a shield next to them. For example, if you click the Start button, choose Control Panel, and click User Accounts and Family Safety, you see the options shown in Figure 3-12.

Items that have a shield next to them require administrative approval. Items without a shield don't. For example, any user can change his or her Windows password, with or without administrative approval. You can tell just by the fact that there's no shield next to the Change Your Windows Password link.

Options that do have a shield next to them require administrative approval. But you don't necessarily need to be logged in to an administrative account to use those options. You just have to prove that you have administrative privileges. You do that by entering the password for an administrative account. When you click a shielded option, you see a dialog box similar to the one in Figure 3-13. To prove that you have administrative privileges on this computer, just enter the password for the administrative user account and click Submit (or OK in some dialog boxes).

FIGURE 3-12

User Accounts and Family Safety.

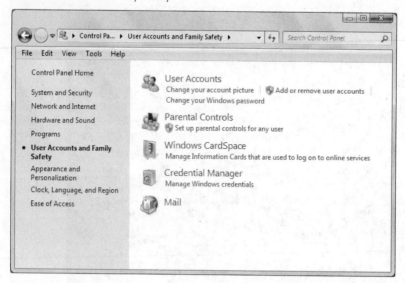

FIGURE 3-13

User Account Control dialog box.

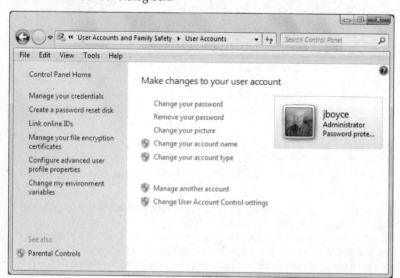

Of course, when someone who doesn't know the administrative account password encounters the User Account Control dialog box, he or she is stuck. Users who don't know the password can't go any further. This prevents the standard user from doing things that might affect the overall system and other people's user accounts. It also prevents children from overriding parental controls. (You learn how to set up parental controls in Chapter 4.)

Privilege escalation in administrative accounts

If you happen to be logged in to an administrative account when you click a shielded option, you don't need to enter an administrative password. After all, if you're in an administrative account, you must already know the password required to get into that account. You don't need to prove that you know that password again. But, you'll still see a prompt telling you that the program you're about to run makes changes to the system, as in the example in Figure 3-14. You have to click Continue to proceed.

FIGURE 3-14

Status-checking prompt.

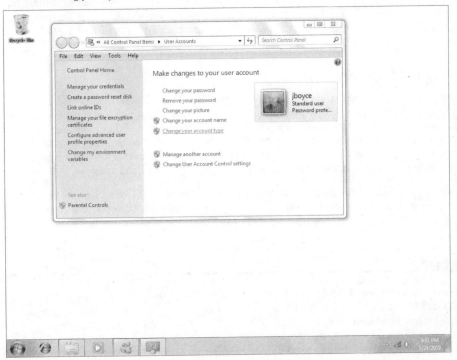

It might seem odd (and irritating) that you still have to click something to get to the item you clicked. But it works that way for a reason. The dialog box lets you know that the program you're about to run is going to make changes to the overall system. You expect to see that dialog box after you click a shielded option. And with time and experience, you'll learn to expect it when you do other things that affect the system as a whole, such as when you install new programs.

Sometimes it occurs when you don't expect to see it. For example, when opening an e-mail attachment, you wouldn't normally expect to see that message. After all, opening an e-mail attachment should just show you the contents of the attachment, not make a change to the system as a whole. Seeing the warning in that context lets you know that something fishy is going on, most likely something bad in the e-mail attachment. You can click Cancel to *not* open the attachment, thereby protecting your system from whatever virus or other bad thing lies hidden within the e-mail attachment.

Note
See Chapter 8 for the full story on protecting your system from viruses and other malicious software. ■

On a more technical note, UAC operates on a principle of least privilege, whereby all users run with a limited set of privileges. When you're in an administrative account, you actually run with the same privileges as a standard user. This is done to protect your system from malware that would otherwise exploit the privileges of your administrative account to make malicious changes to your system.

When you enter a password or click Continue in response to a UAC prompt, you temporarily *elevate* your privileges to allow that one change to be made. After that change is made, you're back to your more secure standard user privileges. This is how things have been done in high-security settings for years, and it is considered a security *best practice*. If at all possible, you should follow suit and keep UAC active on your own computer. But if it proves to be impractical, you can turn off UAC.

Turning UAC on and off

Even though it has been much improved from Windows Visat, User Account Control (UAC) is not always a very popular Windows 7 feature. After all, nobody wants a feature that makes them do more work, even when the extra work is nothing more than an occasional extra mouse click. Furthermore, sometimes UAC is just impractical. For example, if you give your kids standard user accounts, they can't install their own programs. But if you give them administrative accounts, you can't institute parental controls. In such situations, turning off UAC might be your best and safest bet.

Before you turn off UAC, I recommend that you first ensure that all of the other security measures discussed in Part II of this book are installed and working on your PC. UAC is just one component of an overall security strategy. The more components you have on and working, the better.

New Feature

User Account Control is modified in Windows 7 to make it less obtrusive. In contrast to how it functioned in Windows Vista, in which it was an on or off feature, UAC now offers a range of settings to tailor the end user experience.

Changing UAC settings is a simple process. Get to the main User Accounts control panel. From the desktop, press ▧ , type **user**, and click User Accounts. Or click the Start button and choose Control Panel ➪ User Accounts and Family Safety ➪ User Accounts. Click Change User Account Control Settings, and then if prompted to do so, enter an administrative password to get to the page shown in Figure 3-15.

FIGURE 3-15

Turn User Account Control on or off.

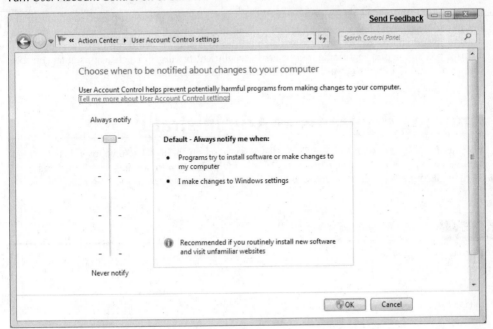

You can choose from the following options:

- **Always Notify:** Windows will notify you if programs try to install software or make changes to the computer, or if you make changes to Windows settings.

- **Default — Notify Me Only When Programs Try to Make Changes to My Computer:** Windows will not notify you when you make changes to your computer, but will notify you, by dimming the desktop and displaying a warning, if programs attempt to make changes.

- **Notify Me Only When Programs Try to Make Changes to My Computer (Do Not Dim My Desktop):** Windows will not notify you when you make changes to your computer, but will notify you when programs attempt to make changes. However, Windows will not dim the desktop, but instead just display a message.

- **Never Notify Me When:** Windows will not notify you of changes (turns off UAC). The only safe time to use this option is when you need to install a program that doesn't work with UAC. Turn off UAC, install the program, and then turn on UAC again.

To turn User Account Control off, drag the slider down to Never Notify. Or, if it was already off and you want better security, drag the slider up to the desired level. Then click OK. If you selected Never Notify to turn off UAC, you'll be prompted to restart the computer. Click the Solve PC Issues button in the tray and then click the message labeled You Must Restart Your Computer to Turn Off User Account Control. You can click Restart Now to activate the change on reboot. Or, click Restart Later if you need to save any work before proceeding.

When the computer restarts, things will still look the same. But when you click a shielded option, you will receive no prompting for credentials or status checking. Things will basically be as they were in Windows XP and other earlier versions of Windows.

You can still institute parental controls, provided that you have one password-protected administrative account and each child has a standard account. (This also assumes that the kids don't know the password to the administrative account.) When a child tries to change or deactivate parental controls, a message box will appear, informing him or her of insufficient privileges. To change parental controls, you need to log in to the password-protected administrative account.

Running Programs as Administrator

Most newer programs work with UAC's privilege escalation on the fly. But sometimes that won't work, especially with older programs. You can run any program with administrative privileges by right-clicking its startup icon and choosing Run as Administrator, as in the example shown in Figure 3-16.

FIGURE 3-16

Run a program as administrator.

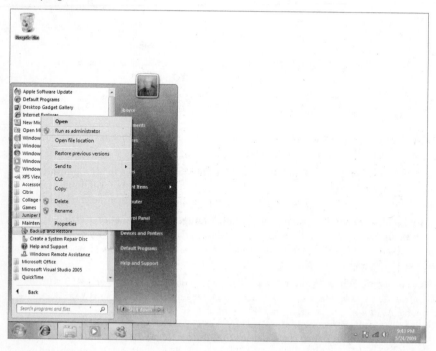

The same method works for programs that you can't launch from the Start menu. Use Windows Explorer to get to the folder that contains the executable file for the program. Then right-click the filename and choose Run as Administrator.

You can make older programs that aren't part of Windows 7 run with elevated privileges automatically by changing program compatibility settings. Right-click the startup icon for the program, or the executable file's icon, and choose Properties. In the Properties dialog box, click the Compatibility tab. Then, under Privilege Level, select Run This Program as an Administrator and click OK.

If the option to run the program as an administrator is disabled, then one of the following is true: the program doesn't require administrative privileges to run; you are not logged in to an administrative account; or the program is blocked from always running elevated.

Add the Built-in Administrator Account to the Login Screen

The built-in Administrator account is intentionally hidden to keep out users who don't have sufficient knowledge to understand the risks involved in using such an account. Typically, the only way to get to it is by starting the computer in Safe Mode. If you're an advanced user and want to be able to get to that account from the login page, you just have to enable the account. Here's how:

1. Log in to an account that has administrative privileges.
2. Click the Start button, right-click Computer, and choose Manage.
3. In the left column of the Computer Management tool that opens, click Local Users and Groups.
4. In the center column, double-click the Users folder.
5. Right-click the Administrator account and choose Properties.
6. Clear the check mark beside Account is Disabled and click OK.
7. Close the Computer Management window.

When you log out of your current account, you'll see the Administrator account on the login page. It will also appear there each time you start the computer.

Stop Entering Password on Lockout

If you leave the computer for a few minutes without logging out, you're taken to a *lockout* screen that shows your user account information. If your user account is password-protected, you need to enter your password to get back to the desktop. This is to prevent other people from using your computer while you're away. But it makes sense only in a work environment. In a home environment, it may be overkill. You can reconfigure 7 so that you don't have to reenter your password to get back to your desktop. Here are the steps:

1. Click the Start button, type **pow**, and click Power Options.
2. In the left column, click Require a Password on Wakeup.
3. If the options under Password Protection on Wakeup are disabled, click Change Settings that Are Currently Unavailable. Then elevate your privileges by clicking Continue or by entering the password for an administrative account.
4. Choose Don't Require a Password.
5. Click Save Changes.

For more information on power options settings, see Chapter 52.

Advanced Security Tools

IT professionals and highly experienced users can continue to use Local Users and Groups and Local Security Policy consoles for more advanced security configuration. Options in those tools are beyond the scope of this book, and not the kinds of things the average user wants to mess with. To get to Local Users and Groups, click the Start button, right-click Computer, and choose Manage. Or press ⊞, type **comp**, and click Computer Management. Then click Local Users and Groups in the left column.

To get to Local Security Policy, press ⊞, type **local**, and click Local Security Policy. To find the new settings related to UAC, expand Local Policies in the left column and then click Security Options. The new UAC settings are at the bottom of the list in the content pane.

Tip
Windows CardSpace lets you set up relationships with online services that require logging in. ∎

About Windows CardSpace

Windows CardSpace lets you store user account information for online services that support the CardSpace feature. It's a means of creating a digital identity that can be used instead of a username and password to log in to online accounts that support the CardSpace feature.

CardSpace adds security to Web relationships by encrypting data in your card before sending the information to a Web site. You can also review cards from Web sites that use them to get more information about a site before signing up for an account.

CardSpace is still relatively new, with a limited number of Web sites supporting it. The idea of CardSpace is fairly simple, however. You can create one or more digital cards, each with whatever information you want to provide to Web sites with which you do business. For example, you might want cards that include only your name and no further identifying information. Other cards might include your street address and phone number.

When you set up an account with an online site that supports CardSpace, you can send your card rather than fill in blanks on that site's user form. After you've established an account, you can submit your card whenever you need to log in to the site.

You can choose from two kinds of cards to use:

- **Personal cards:** These you create yourself and provide to online Web services as you see fit.
- **Managed cards:** These are like membership cards provided to you by organizations and businesses that support the CardSpace identity system.

Use one of the following methods to access Windows CardSpace:

- Click the Start button and choose Control Panel ➪ User Accounts and Family Safety ➪ Windows CardSpace.
- Tap ⊞, type **card** and click Windows CardSpace.

If you're taken to a welcome page, click OK to proceed. To create a personal card, click Add a Card in the right column. Click Personal Card and fill in whatever blanks you're comfortable with. You might want to start by creating a basic card that contains your name, e-mail address, and perhaps a picture or logo. You can create other cards with more information, if necessary, for sites that you trust with that information.

You don't create managed cards yourself. Instead, you set up an account with a service that uses managed cards. When you receive such a card, you'll likely get instructions on its use. But the basic procedure is to go into CardSpace, click Add a Card, click Install a Managed Card, and then import the card that the online service has sent you.

If the CardSpace technology catches on, you'll be able to access your cards right from your Web browser. When you go to log in to a site, you'll see an option to log in the traditional way through a user account and password, or by using CardSpace (or an InfoCard). Click the option to use CardSpace, click the card you want to use, and you're logged in.

Using Credential Manager

Credential Manager (Figure 3-17) enables you to manage your usernames and their associated passwords (collectively called *credentials*) for servers, Web sites, and programs. These credentials are stored in an electronic virtual vault. When you access a server, site, or program that requests a password, Credential Manager can submit the credentials for you so that you don't have to type them yourself. If your password cache has dozens of sets of credentials in it, as mine does, you'll be more than happy to put Credential Manager to work for you.

FIGURE 3-17

Store usernames and passwords in Credential Manager.

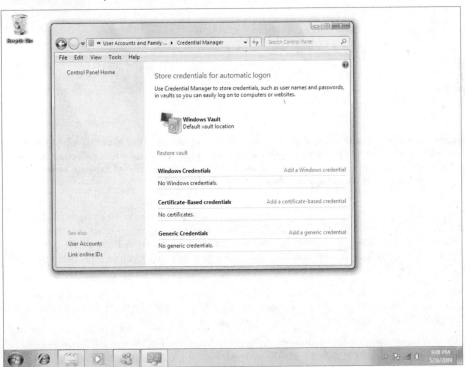

FIGURE 3-18

Windows prompts for credentials.

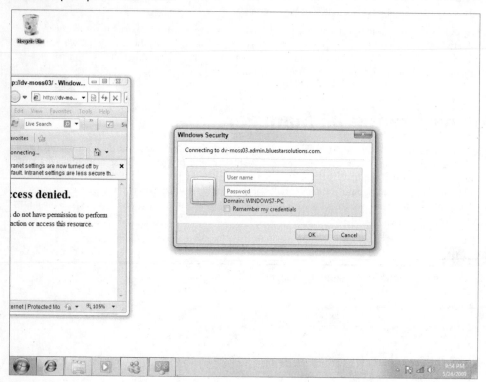

Note

Credential Manager can't interact with every Web site that requests credentials. For example, when you log in to your online banking site, the site probably displays a form in which you enter your credentials. Credential Manager can't store this type of forms-based credentials, but you can have Internet Explorer remember the credentials for you. See Chapter 16 to learn more about Internet Explorer. ■

Although you can add credentials to your vault directly, you don't need to do so in most cases. Instead, you can let Windows do it for you. To do so, navigate to a server or other computer on your network, or to a Web server that prompts you for credentials, as shown in Figure 3-18. Enter the username and password in the Windows Security dialog box, select Remember My Credentials, and click OK. Windows stores the credentials in Credential Manager (Figure 3-19).

You can add credentials to your vault yourself if you want to. For example, if you have lots of credentials you use with multiple servers or sites, you might want to prepopulate your credential vault so that you don't have to enter them the next time you visit that resource.

To add credentials, open the User Accounts and Family Safety item in the Control Panel and then click Credential Manager. Click Add a Windows Credential and in the resulting form, enter the following:

FIGURE 3-19

Credentials are stored in Credential Manager.

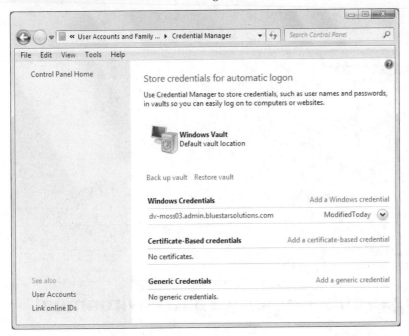

- **Internet or Network Address:** Type the path to the resource. For example, enter **fileserver****Docs** to specify the Docs share on a server on the network named fileserver. Or, enter **portal.mycompany.tld** if your company intranet portal is located at `https://portal.mycompany.tld`.

- **Username:** Enter the username you want to use to log on to the specified service.

- **Password:** Enter the password associated with the username.

You can also add a certificate resource, which associates a network resource with a certificate that is already installed in the Personal certificate store on your computer. In this case, verify that you have already installed the certificate, click Add a Certificate-Based Credential, type the resource URL, and click Select Certificate to select the certificate. You can also choose to use a smart card certificate (a certificate installed on a smart card that you insert in your computer).

The third type of credential you can add is a generic credential, which are credentials used by applications that perform authentication themselves rather than rely on Windows to perform the authentication. As with a Windows credential, you specify the URL, username, and password for a generic credential.

Tip

You can specify a port number in the resource path, if needed. For example, if an application is connecting to a SQL Server at `sql.mydomain.tld` on port 1433, you would specify **sql.mydomain.tld:1433** in the Internet or Network Address field in Credential Manager. ■

FIGURE 3-20

The Environment Variables dialog box.

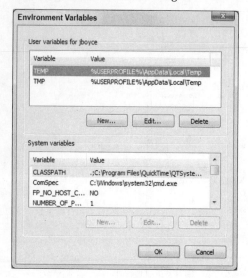

Managing Profile Properties and Environment Variables

From the earliest days of DOS, the PC operating system we old computer geeks used before Windows came along, *environment variables* have been used to store information used by the operating system. For example, the TMP and TEMP variables tell Windows where to store temporary files. The PATH variable tells Windows where to look for programs if it can't find them in the current directory. A number of other system and user variables serve similar purposes.

In most cases, you should not need to change environment variables. But if you do — such as adding a folder to the PATH variable — you can do so through your user account properties. Open the User Accounts object in the Control Panel and click Change My Environment Variables. In the Environment Variables dialog box (Figure 3-20), click the user variable that you want to change, click Edit, modify as needed, and click OK. You can also click New and then add a new user environment variable.

Note

Only the built-in Administrator account can modify the system environment variables. ∎

Linking Online IDs with Windows Accounts

Windows 7 gives you the capability to link online IDs with your Windows account. For example, you might link your Windows Live ID with your Windows account. Linking online IDs enables other people to share files with you on a homegroup using that online ID rather than a Windows account.

The advantage to other people is that they don't have to add an account for you on their computers. Instead, they can use your online ID — such as your e-mail address — to share files with you.

Linking your online IDs with your Windows account is a two-step process. First, you add the online ID provider to Windows, and then you link the ID to your Windows account. For example, you first add the Windows Live ID provider to Windows and then link your Windows ID to your Windows account.

Follow these steps to accomplish both tasks:

1. Log in to Windows using the account you want to link; then open the User Accounts object in the Control Panel.

2. In the left pane, click Link Online IDs.

3. Click the Add an Online ID Provider link near the bottom of the dialog box to navigate to the Windows 7 online ID providers Web site.

4. Click the provider for the service you want to link. As I write this, only Windows Live is supported. However, other providers will potentially be supported by the final release of Windows 7.

5. When you click the provider in the list, you should see a download page that will enable you to download and install the ID provider add-on. Follow the instructions provided by the Web site to accomplish that task.

6. After you have installed the online ID provider, navigate back to the User Accounts object in the Control Panel for your account. You should now see the provider listed (Figure 3-21).

FIGURE 3-21

Online ID provider.

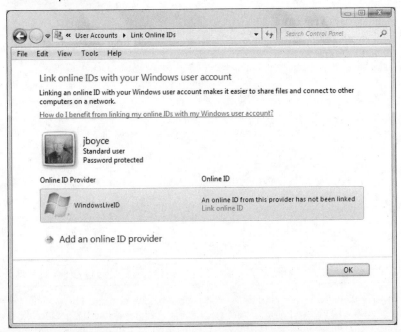

---

7. Click the Add Linked ID link in the Online ID column. What happens at this point depends on the selected provider. For Windows Live, you enter your Windows Live credentials and sign in. The ID is then linked to your Windows account.

To learn how to use a linked ID for sharing, see Chapter 53.

Wrap-Up

When two or more people share a computer, user accounts let each person treat the computer as though it were his or her own. Users can personalize settings to their liking and keep their files separate from other users.

User accounts also work in conjunction with parental controls. A parent can set up a password-protected administrative account and then use that account to set up parental controls. You can create standard accounts for children and allow them to log in to their own accounts only. Parental controls are covered in Chapter 4.

User accounts also add security to your system by making all users run with limited privileges. The general term for security through user accounts is User Account Control (UAC). Some key points to keep in mind:

- At least one person should play the role of administrator for the computer. That person should create a password-protected user account with administrative privileges.

- The administrator should also create a standard account for him- or herself, and one for each person who shares the computer.

- All users (including the administrator) should use their standard accounts for day-to-day computing.

- All accounts should have a password.

- All the tools for creating and managing user accounts are accessible from User Accounts and Family Safety in the Control Panel.

Parental Controls and Family Safety

K eeping kids safe online isn't always easy for parents. Especially for the parent who hasn't exactly been riding the crest of the tech wave in recent years. Parental controls are a great first step to keeping children safe online. Better yet, you don't need to be a computer guru to set parental controls. After you've set up standard user accounts for children (as discussed in Chapter 3), the rest is fairly easy. In this chapter, you see just how easy it is to set up parental controls in Windows 7 and how to extend parental controls with Windows Live.

Before You Get Started

For parental controls to work, your computer must be set up with at least one password-protected administrator user account. If you set up multiple user accounts with administrative privileges, make sure that they're all password-protected. And make sure the kids don't know the password. Otherwise, the kids can easily go in and change any parental controls you import.

Furthermore, each child should have his or her own standard user account. If you have no idea what I'm talking about here, see Chapter 3. There you can learn everything you need to know about setting up user accounts.

Finally, understand that Windows 7 offers a certain set of features for parental control. You can add other features by downloading the Family Safety add-on from Microsoft Windows Live. The first half of this chapter covers the parental controls that are built into Windows 7, and the second half covers the Windows Live add-ons.

Using the Built-In Parental Controls

Windows 7 provides three options for controlling how your children (or even you) can use the computer. These are as follows:

- **Time Limits:** Specify the hours during each day that the child can use the computer.
- **Games:** Specify whether the child can play games on the computer, and set the rating and content types that are allowed.
- **Allow and Block Specific Programs:** Select which programs the child can run.

Getting to the Parental Controls Page

Fortunately, you don't need to be a computer guru to set up parental controls. After you've set up appropriate user accounts, the rest is easy. Here are the steps:

1. Log in to a user account that has administrative privileges.

2. Do whichever of the following is most convenient for you at the moment:

   - Tap 🪟 , type **par** in the search box, and click Parental Controls.
   - Click the Start button, choose Control Panel, and click Set Up Parental Controls for Any User.

3. You come to a page that shows the name and picture for each user account you've created, as in the example in Figure 4-1. Click the user account for which you want to set up parental controls.

Now you're in the parental controls page shown in Figure 4-2. Any options you choose are applied to the account shown in the page. For example, in Figure 4-2, I'm setting up parental controls for a user named Gene.

To activate parental controls for the account, choose On, Enforce Current Settings under the Parental Controls heading. After you turn on parental controls, you can choose which controls to apply for the selected user.

Setting time limits

To specify times when the child is allowed to use the computer, click Time Limits. You see a grid of days and times. Initially, all squares are white, meaning there are no restrictions. You can click any time slot for which the child isn't allowed to use the computer to turn it blue. Or, drag the mouse pointer through a longer stretch of time to block more time.

Optionally, you can place the mouse pointer in the upper-left corner of the grid and drag down to the lower-right corner to block all times. Then drag the mouse pointer through the times that the child is allowed to use the computer. For example, in Figure 4-3, the child is allowed to use the computer from 10:00 am to 7:00 pm on Sunday, 3:00 to 7:00 on Monday, Tuesday, Wednesday, and Thursday, 3:00 to 9:00 on Friday, and 10:00 a.m. to 9:00 p.m. on Saturday.

Click OK after setting allowable times. You can change those settings at any time by clicking Time Limits again when appropriate. For example, if the child needs a "time out" from the computer, you can block out all the times so that the child can't use the computer at all!

Tip

Sometimes you might want to allow your children to use the computer but not use the Internet. For example, they might need to do homework but you don't want them on the Web. You can prevent their access to the Internet by blocking Internet Explorer, but I block Internet traffic at the home firewall instead. With a single click in the firewall interface, I can allow or deny traffic to the kids' computer. Configuring a firewall is outside the scope of this chapter, but I offer this tip to give you another way to control how your children use the computer. ■

FIGURE 4-1

Click a standard account to create parental controls.

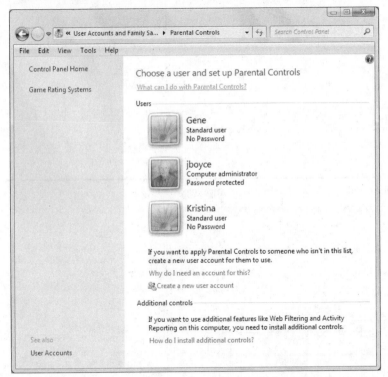

Controlling game play

To control the child's game play, click Games. Doing so opens the page shown in Figure 4-4. If you don't want the child to use the computer for game play at all, choose No. Otherwise, choose Yes.

If you choose Yes, you can block games based on content. Click Set Game Ratings. Your first options will be based on ESRB ratings. ESRB stands for Entertainment Software Rating Board, an independent third party that rates games for age appropriateness and specific content. The ratings are similar to movie ratings (G, PG, R, and so forth), but specific to computer games.

FIGURE 4-2

Setting up controls for a user.

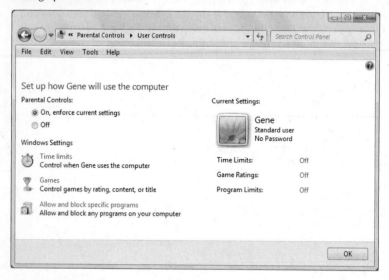

FIGURE 4-3

White squares indicate when your child is allowed to use the computer.

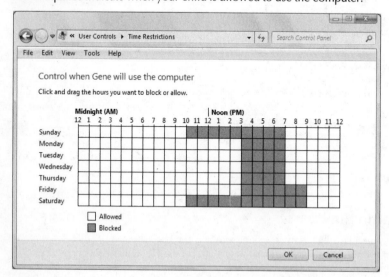

Tip

To use a rating system other than ESRB, click the Back button until you get to the first parental controls page that shows user accounts. Then click Select a Games Rating System in the left column. ∎

FIGURE 4-4

Controlling children's game play.

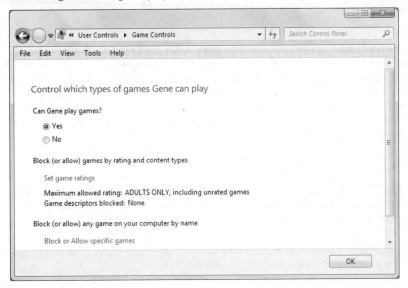

To prevent the child from playing games that have no ESRB rating, choose Block games with no rating. Then read each rating and click whichever rating is the most appropriate for your child. The child will be able to play games up to, and including, the rating you choose.

Then you can scroll down the page and block more games based on content type. To block games based on content, select the type of content you want to block. When you get to the bottom of the list and have blocked all the content that you feel is inappropriate, click OK.

Finally, you can click Block or Allow Specific Games to allow or block games installed on your computer. For each listed game, you can choose User Rating Setting to block based on the ESRB rating. Or you can choose Always Allow to let the child play the game. Or choose Always Block to prevent the child from playing that game. Click OK after making your selections. Then click OK again to return to the main parental controls page for your child.

Blocking and allowing programs

Clicking Allow and Block Specific Programs takes you to a page that lists all the programs installed on your computer. There you can opt to allow the child to use all programs. Or choose <child> Can Only Use the Programs I Allow. If you choose the second option, you need to select the check box next to each program that the child is allowed to use. Click OK after making your selections.

When you've finished setting up parental controls for the child, the account name and picture summarize your settings. You can click OK to return to the list of user accounts. From there, you can click another account to which you want to assign parental controls. Or close the window if you're finished setting up parental controls.

Of course, you can add or change parental controls at any time. Just use any technique described under "Getting to the Parental Controls Page," earlier in this chapter, to get to the main page. Then click the account for which you want to add or change parental controls.

Using Parental Controls from Windows Live

The Windows Live Family Safety add-on adds Web filtering and activity reporting to your toolbox of parental controls. To add these controls to your computer, first make sure you have a Windows Live account. If you don't, you can create one the first time you visit the Web site. Open Internet Explorer, browse to `http://home.live.com`, and log in with your Windows Live ID (or create one). Then, click More and then click Family Safety.

Tip

The preceding links will get you to the download site at Windows Live, which is located at `http://download.live.com`. The Web is a fluid thing, so these links could be different by the time you read this. If all else fails, search at Live.com for downloads and parental controls. ■

Choose your language from the drop-down list and then click the Download button. Follow the displayed download instructions to start and complete the download process.

The Family Safety add-on gives you the following added capabilities:

- **Activity reports:** View reports of the Web activity and other Internet activity for the selected child.

- **Content filtering:** Specify the types of Web sites the child can access.

- **Contact management:** Specify the people the child can communicate with online through Windows Live Messenger, Hotmail, and Spaces on Windows Live. You can also allow the child to manage his or her own contact list.

To access the new Family Safety settings, click Start ➪ All Programs ➪ Windows Live ➪ Windows Live Family Safety to open the Windows Live Family Safety Filter dialog box. Then, click the Go to the Family Safety link to navigate to the Windows Live Family Safety Web site (Figure 4-5).

Through the Family Safety Web site, you can add child and parent accounts, as well as configure settings for each child's account. To configure settings for a child, first add the child's account. Click the Add Child link, and if you have already created the child's Windows Live account, click Sign in with This Child's ID. If not, click Create Child ID.

After the account is created, you see it listed when you browse to the Family Safety Web site. You can click the link under the Web Filtering, Activity Reporting, or Contact Management columns to set the corresponding setting.

Each Windows account by default uses the Windows Live ID that was used to install the Family Safety add-on. Before you allow a child to browse the Web, you need to log in to the computer with his/her account and log in to Family Safety with his/her Windows Live ID. Here's how:

1. Log in to the computer using the child's Windows account.

2. Click Start ➪ All Programs ➪ Windows Live ➪ Windows Live Family Safety.

3. Click Sign Out to switch family members.

FIGURE 4-5

Setting up Family Safety settings.

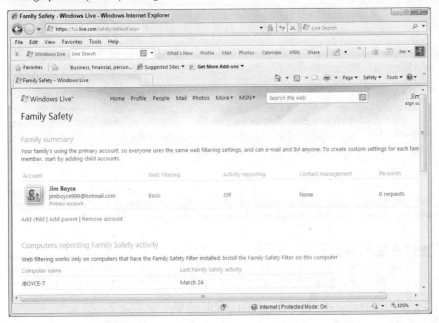

4. In the Sign In to Family Safety dialog box, enter the child's Windows Live credentials. If you don't want the child to have to enter the credentials each time, select the Remember My Password and Sign Me In Automatically options. Then click Sign In.

Tip

You can use a single Windows Live ID for all your children, imposing a common set of restrictions for them all. However, you will not be able to track individual usage. Instead, all usage will be reported against the common ID. For that reason, it's a good idea to create a Windows Live ID for each child. ■

Caution

I need to point out that when you use the Windows Live Family Safety add-on and reporting is enabled, your child's browsing history is maintained on a Microsoft Web site. This can be handy, because you have access to the browsing history from any location, such as at work. However, it could potentially be a privacy risk. If you don't like the idea of your child's Internet usage history being stored on a public server, even if it is secured to prevent others from browsing the history, consider using a third-party Internet control and reporting program that installs on the computer and stores its logs locally on that computer (or e-mails the logs to you). ■

The following sections explain how to manage parental settings.

Defining Web restrictions

The World Wide Web contains millions of Web sites and billions of Web pages. No one person or company has control over what goes on the Web. It's very much a public place where anyone can post any content they wish. Obviously, not all that content is suitable for children. (Much of it isn't particularly appropriate for adults, either.)

To define Web restrictions, navigate to the Family Safety Web site as described previously, and click Add a Child. If the child's account already exists and is listed, just click the child's account. In the resulting Web Filtering page, you can choose between the following three options:

- **Strict:** Block all Web sites except child-friendly sites and sites you've explicitly allowed.
- **Basic:** Block only adult content.
- **Custom:** Choose from multiple types of sites those you will allow the child to access.

In addition to choosing between these three primary options, you can explicitly add sites to the list of allowed or blocked sites. To add a site, click in the text box under Allow or Block a Website, type the site's URL, and choose the desired action from the drop-down list, such as Allow for This Account Only. Then, click Add. When you're satisfied with the settings, click Save.

Tip

For Web filtering to work, the Family Safety Filter must be installed on the computer. If you have more than one computer, make sure the filter is installed on each computer that your children will use. ∎

How Do I Paste a URL?

Every Web site has a unique address called a URL (Uniform Resource Locator). To allow the child to visit a Web site, you either have to type or paste the URL of that site into the box under the Website address heading. To paste rather than type, browse to a Web site (or have the child browse to the site) in Internet Explorer or another Web browser. When you're at the Web site, you know that the URL in the Web browser's address bar is the correct URL for that site.

To paste that URL, you first have to copy it. To do so, select the URL by clicking the icon just to the left of the `http://` in the browser's address bar. If that doesn't work, drag the mouse pointer through the whole URL. When all the letters in the URL are highlighted (that is, they show as white text against a blue background), press Ctrl+C to copy. (You won't see anything happen on the screen.) Then go to the Allow Block Webpages page (by clicking its button in the taskbar). Click in the box under Website address where you would have typed the URL, and press Ctrl+V to paste. Then click the Allow button to add the URL to the list of Allowed sites.

Knowing how to copy and paste is a valuable basic skill because any place you can type text, you can also paste text. So you rarely need to paste text that you can just copy from some other place on the screen. For more information on working with text, including copying and pasting, see Chapter 14.

Get Web sites working

If you've set restrictions on Web sites, you might need to do a little tweaking to get the sites working. Log out of your administrative account (click the Start button, click the arrow next to the lock, and then click Log Off). Then log in to the child's account. Browse to an allowed Web site. If some content from the site is blocked, you'll see a warning in the information bar (Infobar). You can click the Infobar to review portions of the site that are blocked. Typically, allowing the child to see the blocked content is perfectly safe because it's still age-appropriate. But you'll need to choose Always Allow when prompted to make sure the child can visit the site when you're away.

You can also use one of the child's allowed sites as the default home page that appears when the child first opens the Web browser. In Internet Explorer, browse to whatever Web page you want to make the default. Then click the Home button in the toolbar (or press Alt+M) and click Add or Change Home Page. Choose Use this Webpage as Your Only Home Page and click Yes. You might also want to add all the allowed sites to the child's Favorites. For more information on Internet Explorer, Favorites, and default home pages, see Chapter 17.

When you want to get back to performing parental (administrative) tasks, log out of the child's account. Then log back into your administrative account.

Next, you want to specify exactly what the child can and can't do with the computer. Your options are described in the sections that follow.

Viewing User Activity Reports

User activity reports provide a summary of user activity. You can view the report for any user at any time, and you can review a child's computer activity by following these steps:

1. Navigate to the Windows Live Family Safety Web site as described previously.

2. Log in with your Windows Live account and then click the icon beside the user whose reports you want to view.

3. Click the Activity Reporting link (Figure 4-6).

FIGURE 4-6

Viewing an activity report.

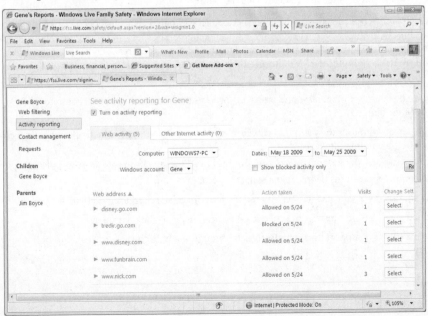

4. In the Web activity tab, choose the range of dates you want to view and click Refresh. By default, the site shows the previous seven days of activity.

5. Click the Other Internet activity tab to view reports for the child's other Internet activity.

Technical approaches to online safety, such as parental controls, are a good thing. But they cannot cover all possible risks. Kids like to get involved with instant messaging and chats in which people aren't always who they claim to be.

Children should be taught some basic ground rules. For example, children should never give out personal information, such as where they live or go to school. If anything makes them feel uncomfortable, they should report it to their parents. They should never agree to meet with anyone.

As a parent, you have many online resources for sharing your concerns with others and getting advice. You don't need to be a technical whiz to take advantage of these sites. Here are some you might want to add to your Favorites:

- **Safe Kids:** www.safekids.com
- **Child Safety:** www.microsoft.com/athome/security/children
- **CyberAngels:** www.cyberangels.org/
- **GetNetWise:** www.getnetwise.org/

Wrap-Up

The Internet is here to stay. Today's children will likely use it as their main source of information and communication throughout their lives. The Internet is also very much a public place, a direct reflection of the world at large. Although most of the people online are perfectly normal, the Internet has its share of wackos and other undesirables, just as the real world does.

Knowledge is a parent's best defense against Internet dangers. A parent who has been out of the loop in terms of technical advances over recent years will feel some helplessness and insecurity about keeping kids safe online. Setting up user accounts and parental controls is a great way to get started in taking control of kids' computer use. Monitoring their activity is another. Here's a quick wrap-up of the main points covered in this chapter:

- A parent should set up at least one password-protected administrative user account to take control of the computer.

- Each person who uses the computer can also have a standard account, which offers greater security than an administrative account.

- The person with the administrative account can use parental controls to set limits on Internet and computer usage for people using standard accounts.

- The administrator can also use activity reports to monitor standard users' activities.

- PC Safeguard lets you restrict the changes a user can make to the computer.

- Parents can find support and stay up-to-date through many Web sites dedicated to online safety.

Help, Support, and Troubleshooting

E ver heard the saying, "If all else fails, read the instructions?" It's sarcastic, of course. But it's also somewhat profound, because it touches on our natural desire for immediate gratification. Believe me, when it comes to wanting and expecting immediate gratification, I'm as guilty as the next person.

Unfortunately, there are no one-size-fits-all instructions for using a computer. If all instructions for all types of computers and programs were gathered into one set, it would be bigger than multiple sets of the *Encyclopedia Britannica* — actually, probably big enough to fill a decent-sized public library. Truth is, you can do so many things with a computer, and such a huge volume of information is available, that no single source of information could possibly exist.

To survive in the digital world these days, you have to be resourceful. And being resourceful means having enough skills to find the information you need, when you need it, wherever that information might be. But being resourceful isn't a skill anyone is born with. You have to *learn* to be resourceful. And that's what this chapter is all about.

IN THIS CHAPTER

Learning about Help and Support

Getting help from people

Troubleshooting

Introducing Help and Support

By far, the most important resource for getting the information you need, when you need it, is the Help and Support built into Windows 7. It doesn't cover everything in great depth. But it does cover all the main features with a focus on the tasks most people want to perform with their computers.

You have a couple of ways to get to Windows 7's Help. When you're in a Windows 7 program such as Photo Gallery, Media Player, or any other, click the Help button (if any) at the upper-right corner of your screen (see Figure 5-1). Or if the program has a menu bar, click Help in that menu bar to see options for getting help. Or press the Help key (F1).

FIGURE 5-1

A sample Help button in a Windows 7 program.

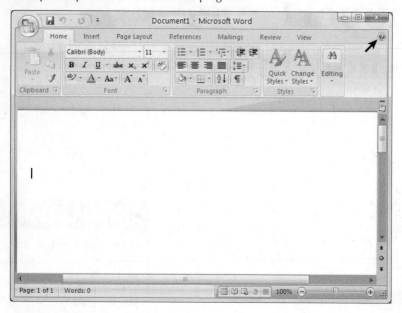

Caution

If your keyboard has a Function Lock (or F Lock) key, the function keys (F1 through F12) work only if that key is on. ■

When you access help from a particular program, you get help that's relevant to the program or component from which you requested the help.

To get more general help with Windows 7, open the Help and Support Center from the Start menu (see Figure 5-2).

If you don't see a Help and Support option on your Start menu, don't panic. Some computer manufacturers replace that with their own Help or Support option. Clicking that option takes you to a help page that's similar to the Windows 7 Help page. It's just rearranged to promote your computer manufacturer.

If you don't see Help and Support on your Start menu, it might also just be turned off. You can probably turn it back on. Right-click the Start button and choose Properties. In the dialog box that opens, click the Customize button. Then scroll down through the list of options and select Help. Click OK in each open dialog box.

Tip

See "Personalizing the Start Menu" in Chapter 10 for the full scoop on Start menu options. ■

The Help and Support Center (see Figure 5-3) provides access to all Help features.

For beginners and casual users, the Learn about Windows Basics topic is the best place to start, especially when you need reminders of key terms and concepts that the rest of Help assumes that you already know. That includes terms such as hardware, software, point, click, double-click, right-click, drag, function keys, navigation keys, keyboard shortcuts, menu, command, desktop, icon, taskbar, Sidebar, program, window, document, minimize, maximize, restore, scroll bar, open, save, close, undo, file, folder, move, copy, delete, and print.

FIGURE 5-2

Help and Support on the Start menu.

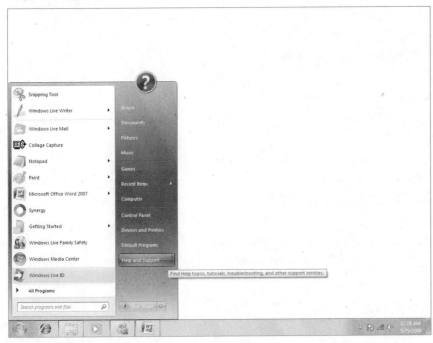

If you already have all those terms and concepts down pat, use the Browse Help topics item to browse through all the Help content. Or, click the Search Help box, type a search keyword or phrase, and click the Search Help button to search for topics.

Navigating Help

Across the top of the Help and Support Center, you see the buttons shown in Figure 5-4. (On your own screen, you can point to any button to see its name.) Here's what each button offers:

- **Back:** Takes you back to the help page you just left (if any). Disabled (dimmed) when there's no page to go back to.

- **Forward:** Returns to the page you just backed out of. Disabled if you didn't just back out of a page.

- **Help and Support Home:** Takes you to the same page that opens when you first open Help and Support.

FIGURE 5-3

The Help and Support Center home page.

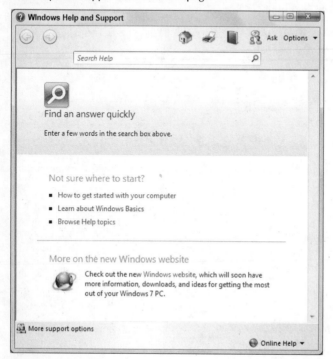

FIGURE 5-4

The Help and Support Center toolbar.

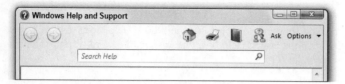

- **Print:** Lets you print whatever help information you're currently viewing.

- **Browse Help:** Takes you to the Table of Contents.

- **Learn about Other Support Options:** Takes you to options for getting online help from humans. (But no one is actually sitting there waiting to answer your questions. It's more complicated than that.)

- **Options:** Provides the following options:

  - **Print:** Same as clicking the Print button.

  - **Browse Help:** Same as clicking the Browse Help button.

- **Text Size:** Changes the size of the text in the Help window. (A lifesaver if the text is too small to read!)
- **Find (on This Page):** Searches the current Help page (only) for a word or phrase you specify.
- **Settings:** Provides options for enabling or disabling online help and participation in Help Experience Improvement program.

Tip

You can point to any button across the top of the Help and Support Center to see its name. ■

Using the Search box

The Search box at the top of the Help and Support Center window is strictly for searching Help. It searches both the Help that's in your computer and the more extensive online Help (if you're online when you use the Search box).

Use the Search box as you would the index at the back of a book. It works best if you know the exact term you're looking for and how to spell that term. But even if you don't know how to spell it exactly, the Search feature works pretty well. For example, a search for *desk top* (wrong spelling) returns roughly the same results as *desktop* (correct spelling).

You can also phrase your search as a question. For example, "What is a user account?" or "How do I create a user account?"

Press Enter or click the magnifying glass button after typing your search term or question. The results will be a series of links to pages in Help that are relevant to your search phrase or question.

Online Help and Offline Help

There are really two types of help in Windows 7. There's *offline Help*, which you can access at any time. There's also *online Help*, which you can access only when you're connected to the Internet. The online Help is more extensive than the offline help.

In the Help window's lower-right corner, you'll see an indicator that tells you which Help you're currently accessing (see Figure 5-5). Click that to choose to use Get Offline Help (only), or Online Help (which includes both offline Help and online Help). To automatically include online Help in your searches, click Options, choose Settings, and then choose Improve My Search Results by Using Online Help (Recommended).

Windows 7's Help Is Only About Windows 7 ⸻

I t's important to understand that the Help and Support in Windows 7 is *only* for Windows 7 and the programs that come with Windows 7. There are at least 100,000 other programs you can purchase separately. Windows 7's Help and Support doesn't cover any of those programs.

continued

continued

When you want help with some program other than Windows 7, you have to look in the Help for *that* program, not Windows 7's Help. Typically, you do so by choosing Help from that program's menu bar or by pressing F1 while that program is open and in the active window.

E-mail Help works the same way. E-mail isn't really a component of Windows 7. E-mail is a service provided by your ISP (Internet service provider) or a third party such as Google for Google Mail or Yahoo! for Yahoo! Mail. Your ISP or mail service provider is your best resource for questions about e-mail. However, the Help content included with your e-mail program (if other than a Web browser, such as Windows Mail or Microsoft Office Outlook), is the best place to learn how to use that program.

FIGURE 5-5

Online/Offline options.

Help from People

When we can't figure something out by guessing, usually our next thought is to call someone on the phone. Whether that strategy works depends on whom you call. Many of the larger companies charge for telephone support, and it can be quite expensive, especially if you don't know all the terminology. When you don't know the terminology, it's hard to ask the question and even harder to understand the answer.

FIGURE 5-6

Resources for live help.

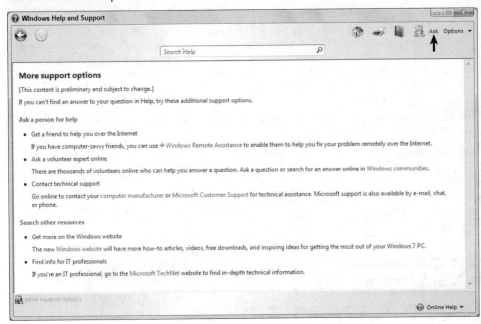

You have some online alternatives to using the phone that enable you to get help from another person without spending a fortune. Clicking the Ask button in the Help and Support Center shows these alternatives (see Figure 5-6). The sections to follow describe what each option is about.

Remote assistance

Remote Assistance is a technology that allows another person to see what's on your computer screen and operate your computer with his or her mouse and keyboard. The idea here is to turn control of your computer over to a trusted expert to resolve your problem.

Unfortunately, you have to provide your own trusted expert. There aren't any companies (that I know of) that have trusted experts willing to hook into your computer and fix things for free. For more information, see "Using Remote Assistance" in Chapter 20.

Windows communities

Windows Communities are *newsgroups* in which other users hang out, ask questions, and answer questions. Nobody gets paid to work on newsgroups. It's all done voluntarily. So there's no charge to access the newsgroups.

Newsgroups aren't an immediate gratification type of help. There isn't anyone there waiting for your questions and standing ready to answer on the spot. It's more like group e-mail: People post messages, and other people reply as convenient. This is another resource you can add to your list of resources for information.

To get to the newsgroups, first make sure that your computer is online. Then click the Ask button in Help and Support and click Windows Communities. Your Web browser opens to the home page for the communities. I can't say exactly how it will look because it's a Web page, and Web pages change all the time. But you should see a Search For box and some basic instructions, as shown in Figure 5-7.

FIGURE 5-7

Home page for online communities.

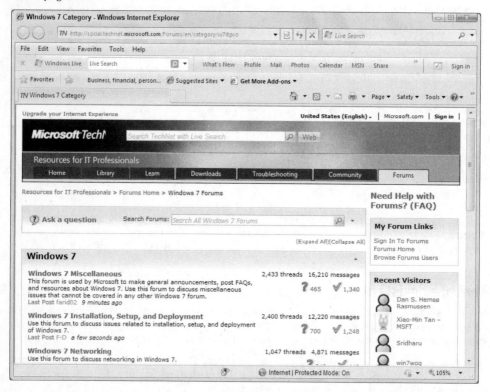

It's important to understand that when you type something in the Search For box, you're not sending your question to an expert to read and answer. There is no live person on the other end to read and respond to your question. Instead, what you get is a list of all the previous newsgroup posts that contain the word or phrase for which you searched, similar to the example in Figure 5-8.

The idea is to scroll through all the messages to see whether one looks as though it might help. Then click its message header (the text in bold) to expand the thread. A *thread* consists of the original message and all the replies to that message. To read any message in the thread, click its header in the left pane. The message text appears in the right pane.

FIGURE 5-8

Results of search for Aero Glass.

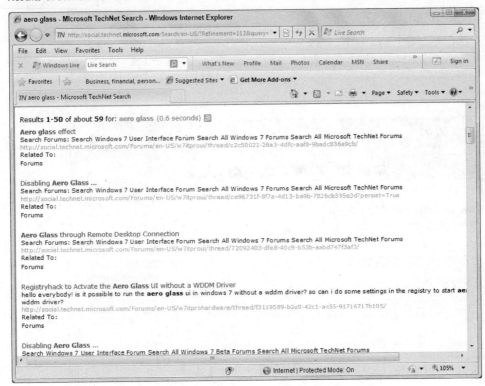

To post your own question to a group, you need to set up an account. Don't worry; you don't have to give up any personal information. Nor will there ever be a charge. You need to set up the account only once, not every time you use the newsgroups.

Posting a question starts with clicking Ask a Question. If you haven't set up an account yet, you'll be given the opportunity to do so on the next page that opens. Otherwise, if you already have set up an account, you can sign in by entering your username and password. After you do so, you'll be able to create a new post, as shown in Figure 5-9.

When you've set up an account, you might find it easier to use a newsgroup client rather than your Web browser to access the newsgroups. You can use Windows Live Mail as that newsgroup client (even if you don't use Windows Live Mail for e-mail). For more information on using newsgroups with Windows Live Mail, see Chapter 20.

Microsoft customer support

Clicking the Microsoft Customer Support link takes you to a Web page that provides still more support options. There, you'll find a ton of links to different kinds of support for different kinds of questions. Take a look at all your options and decide what's best for you.

FIGURE 5-9

Post a question.

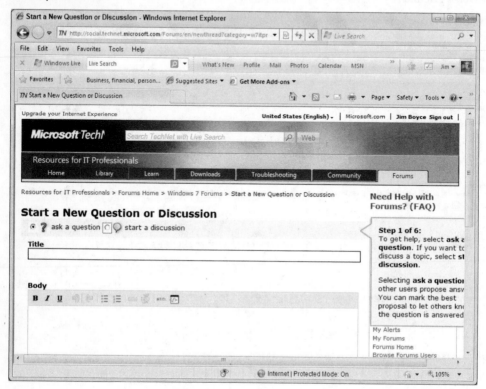

Troubleshooting

Troubleshooting computer problems isn't easy; it involves a host of skills that take a lot of time, education, and experience to build. But you can use some resources to troubleshoot some of the more common problems without being a total computer geek.

First, it's important to understand that troubleshooting comes into play only when you already know how to do something but it's not working as it should. This is not the same as *not* knowing how to do something, or not being able to figure out how to do something by guessing. It's an important distinction to make because if you can't do something because you don't know how, troubleshooting won't help.

As to nongeek troubleshooting, there are many resources for that. The first is Windows 7's automated troubleshooting. Windows 7 can often recognize when something's gone wrong. When it does, Windows 7 may pop up a message asking whether it's okay to send information about the problem to Microsoft. You should always choose Yes. No human will receive the message. Nobody will call or pop up on your screen to solve the problem. Instead, another computer will check to see whether it's a known problem that's already been solved.

If a solution is available, you'll (eventually) see a message in your Notification area offering to solve the problem. Just click that message and follow any additional instructions that appear on the screen. Hopefully, the problem will go away without your having to call in the pricey computer nerds.

You can also use the Troubleshooting link in the Help and Support Center shown back in Figure 5-3. Click that link to find solutions to common problems.

I've also included a troubleshooting chapter at the end of each part of this book. As with the Troubleshooting you get through the Help and Support Center, these chapters cover only some of the more common problems. There isn't a book in the world that's large enough to cover every possibility.

Finally, the communities mentioned in the previous section can be a great resource. Just make sure that you explain exactly what the problem is so that people reading your post can determine what's happening. Chances are, someone who reads your message has already encountered that problem and will offer a solution. Hey, it's free. So it's certainly worth a try.

Wrap-Up

Finding the information you need, when you need it, is a big part of using a computer these days. A single resource, such as a book, a computer course, the built-in Help, communities, the Web, and so on, isn't really enough. The field is much too big now. To survive in the digital world, you need access to many resources. This chapter has touched on the different resources available to you. To summarize:

- Windows Help and Support is one of your best resources for information about Windows 7.

- There are three ways to get to help, which you surely want to memorize: Press the Help key (F1) on your keyboard. Or click a Help button (blue circle with question mark). Or click the Start button and choose Help and Support.

- Most programs that aren't built into Windows 7 have their own help. To get to that help, you typically press the Help key (F1) or choose Help from that program's menu bar.

- If pressing the F1 key has no effect, tap the F Lock (or Function Lock) key on your keyboard and then press the F1 key again.

- Windows Communities are a resource for free help from live human beings.

- You need to invest a little time in learning to use the communities. They're not an instant-gratification thing. But the time you spend will be well worth it.

Troubleshooting Startup Problems

Each major part in this book ends with a troubleshooting chapter like this. The troubleshooting chapters provide quick solutions to common problems. That's about it. You won't catch me yammering on for paragraph after paragraph in these troubleshooting chapters!

The Computer Won't Start

If the computer does absolutely nothing when you first turn it on, your first move is to check all cable connections. Make sure the power plug on every device that plugs into the wall is firmly plugged in. Also, make sure the mouse, keyboard, and all other devices are firmly plugged into their slots.

If it's a desktop computer, look for a 0/1 power switch on the back of the computer and make sure it's on (flipped to the 1 position).

Turn on the computer again and as it's powering up, push the button on the floppy disk drive (if the computer has one) and the CD or DVD drive. If there is a disk in either drive, remove it.

If the computer sounds as though it's starting up but you don't see anything on the screen, make sure all plugs to the monitor are firmly seated. If it's a desktop computer, make sure the monitor's power cable is firmly attached to the monitor and wall socket, and that the cable connecting the computer to the monitor is firmly attached at both ends of the cable. Make sure the monitor is turned on. Then restart the computer.

Non-System Disk or Disk Error message

This message appears when the computer attempts to boot from a disk on which Windows is not installed. If a floppy disk is in the floppy drive, remove it. Likewise for any disk in the CD drive or DVD drive, or any drive that's connected to the computer through a USB port. Press any key to continue startup. If that doesn't work, press Ctrl+Alt+Del or restart the computer with the main on/off switch.

Computer starts but mouse and keyboard don't work

If the computer starts, but doesn't respond to the mouse and keyboard, turn off the computer. Unplug both the mouse and keyboard from the computer. If the mouse connects to a round PS/2 port, make sure you plug it in firmly. If the plug is round, make sure you plug it into the PS/2 port for the mouse (usually colored green). Make sure nothing is resting on the keyboard and holding down a key. Then firmly plug in the keyboard. If the plug is round, plug it into the PS/2 port for the keyboard (usually purple in color). Check *all* cable connections to the computer one more time. Then restart the computer.

Computer keeps trying to start but never gets there

Get to Safe Mode and choose the option to disable automatic restart. If that doesn't help, get to the Safe Mode options again and try the Last Known Good Configuration option. See "Troubleshooting Startup" in Chapter 13.

Screen turns blue during startup and then stops

This is commonly referred to as the Blue Screen of Death (BSOD). It doesn't mean your computer is permanently broken. A frequent cause of this problem is a device driver that doesn't work with Windows 7.

If you recently connected or installed a new hardware device, disconnect or uninstall it. Then start the computer again. That's your best bet.

If you still get the Blue Screen of Death, you'll likely have to boot to Safe Mode and disable the device through Device Manager. This is not the sort of thing the average user normally does. This is more the kind of thing that a professional would handle. But if you want to take a shot at fixing it yourself, see "Troubleshooting Startup" in Chapter 13 and "Dealing with Devices that Prevent Windows 7 from Starting" in Chapter 50.

If the error persists, look for an error number on the Blue Screen of Death page. It will most likely start with the characters 0x. Jot that number down on a sheet of paper. Then, if you can get online through another computer, go to Microsoft's sites (`http://search.microsoft.com` or `http://search.microsoft.com`) or your favorite online search site (such as Google) and search for that number. You might find a page that offers an exact solution to that problem.

If you can get online through another computer, you might also consider posting a question at the Windows Communities site. Be sure to include the error number in your post. You might find someone who has already experienced and solved that very problem.

Computer Takes Too Long to Start

When the computer takes much longer to start than it used to, the problem is usually caused by too many programs trying to auto-start. Consider uninstalling any programs you don't really use, as discussed in Chapter 44. For the remaining programs, use Windows Defender to prevent unnecessary programs from starting automatically. See "Conquering Spyware with Windows Defender," in Chapter 8, for more information. See Chapter 13 for additional information on controlling auto-start programs.

Many things that prevent a computer from starting have nothing to do with Windows 7. It often takes even seasoned pros many hours to diagnose and repair startup problems. But before you resort to the repair shop, here are some other things you can try.

Restore system files to an earlier time

If you can get the computer to start in Safe Mode, try restoring your files to an earlier time. In Safe Mode, click the Start button, type Restore, and then click System Restore on the Start menu. Follow the on-screen instructions to restore system files from a date prior to when the problem began. Choose the most recent date. For example, if the problem started today, restore files from yesterday or the day before.

Repair Install Windows 7

If you have a CD or DVD with Windows 7 on it, you can boot from that disc and do a repair installation. Put that disc in the CD or DVD drive and start the computer. Watch the screen for a message that shows "Press any key to boot from CD or DVD" (or a similar message); then, press Enter or the spacebar.

If the option to boot from the CD or DVD never appears, and the computer won't boot from that disc, you need to change your BIOS options to start from the CD drive. How you do that varies from one computer to the next. Typically, start the computer and then immediately start pressing the F1, F2, or Del key (perhaps all three, if you don't know which is required) repeatedly as the computer is starting. This should take you to the BIOS Setup options. There you can configure the computer to try starting from the CD before it tries starting from the hard drive. Close and save the new settings. The computer will restart, and this time you should be able to boot from the CD or DVD.

If you're able to boot from the CD, the first screen you see will likely ask about your language and locale. Make any necessary changes and click Next. On the next page, click Repair Your Computer (not the Install Now option). Then just follow the on-screen instructions to do a repair install of Windows 7.

The instruction manual that came with your computer

Most computer manufacturers provide some means of helping you troubleshoot and repair startup problems. Be sure to look through whatever documentation you have for your computer manufacturer's recommendations. That could be your best bet, because all computers are unique in some ways. The manual that came with your computer provides information that's specific to your exact make and model of computer.

Resources in this book

I've thrown a lot of technical terms and concepts at you in this chapter. But when it comes to solving startup problems, there's no way around that. Here are some additional resources within this book that might help you solve a startup problem:

- **Using Safe Mode:** The "Troubleshooting Startup" section in Chapter 13 provides information on starting your computer from Safe Mode. If you can get to Safe Mode, techniques described in the chapters referenced in this list might help you solve the problems.

- **Restore from a CompletePC image:** If you've backed up your entire hard disk using Backup and Restore, see "Using the Backup and Restore Center" in Chapter 33 for information on restoring from that backup.

- **Restore to an earlier time:** For information on restoring your computer to an earlier time, see "Using System Protection" in Chapter 33.

- **Removing programs:** If you think a faulty program might be preventing your computer from starting, you can uninstall the program using techniques described in Chapter 42 (assuming that you can get to Safe Mode so that you have access to that program).
- **Removing hardware:** When faulty hardware or drivers are preventing Windows 7 from starting, techniques described under "Removing Hardware" in Chapter 46 might help.
- **Troubleshooting hardware:** Startup problems are often hardware problems. See Chapter 50 for more information on troubleshooting hardware.

Resources in Windows Help

If you can start the computer in Safe Mode, you can get to Windows Help, too. In fact, the Help window should open automatically as soon as you enter Safe Mode. If it doesn't, click the Start button and choose Help and Support. Then search using the keywords *Safe Mode* for additional information on using Safe Mode to troubleshoot startup options.

Online resources

If you can start in Safe Mode with Networking, you can access online resources. You might try searching Windows Communities (which you can get to from Windows Help) for words related to the startup problem you're having. Or post a question describing the problem in as much detail as possible.

You can also search Microsoft's Web site for words that describe the problem you're having. Be sure to include the number 7 in your search. Otherwise, the search result will likely include other irrelevant Microsoft products. Starting your search from http://search.microsoft.com or http://support.microsoft.com will help limit the search to Microsoft, rather than include the entire Web. If that doesn't help, you can try searching the entire Web from www.live.com, www.google.com, or whatever search engine you prefer.

If you're not a technical person, don't expect it to be easy. As I said, startup problems can be difficult to troubleshoot, even for the pros. If all else fails, you may have to take the system to a repair shop to get the problem resolved. Or call a mobile service that will send a computer geek to your home or office.

Programs Won't Start

If a favorite old program won't start, it's most likely an incompatibility issue. Try right-clicking the startup icon for the program and choosing Run as Administrator. If that doesn't help, try the program compatibility features. See Chapter 41 for more information on getting older programs to run with Windows 7.

Part II

Batten Down the Security Hatches

I n the very early years of personal computers, nobody gave much thought to computer security. After all, why would someone need high security on a computer that they alone use? The Internet changed all that. Suddenly, personal computers were connected to an enormous public network fraught with all forms of malicious software. People have suffered many security breaches ever since, ranging from minor annoyances to true data disasters.

Windows Vista was designed, built, and tested from the ground up to be the most secure Windows ever created, and Windows 7 builds on that design. But ask any security professional whether there is such a thing as a 100-percent secure computer, and you'll surely get "No" as your answer. You simply cannot create a machine that's totally programmable and also 100-percent secure. The best you can do is to minimize the likelihood of security breaches.

Virtually everyone today uses his or her computer to access the Internet. You want to make your computer as secure as possible as soon as possible. Part II takes you through the "big three" elements of doing that. Chapter 7 covers the built-in Windows Firewall. Chapter 8 covers tools and techniques for warding off malicious software, including Windows Defender, which comes free with Windows 7. Chapter 9 covers automatic updates, an important component for keeping your computer secure against the latest security threats.

Blocking Hackers with Windows Firewall

If you use the Internet, a firewall is a must-have security tool. It's not the only tool you need, but it's an important one. It protects your computer from hackers and worms. Hackers are people and programs that would attempt to access your computer through the Internet without your knowing it. Worms are bad programs, such as viruses, that are usually written to do intentional harm.

Windows 7 comes with its own built-in firewall. If you didn't know about it before going online, relax. It's enabled by default. So most likely it's been protecting you since the very first moment you went online. In this chapter, you learn how the firewall works and how to configure it for maximum protection.

How Firewalls Work

To understand what a firewall is, you need to first understand what a network connection is. Even though you have only one skinny set of wires connecting your computer to the Internet (through a phone line or cable outlet), that connection actually consists of 65,535 *ports*. Each port can simultaneously carry on its own conversation with the outside world. So, theoretically, you could have 65,535 things going on at a time. Of course, nobody ever has that much going on all at one time. A handful of ports is more like it.

The ports are divided into two categories: TCP (Transmission Control Protocol) and UDP (User Datagram Protocol). TCP is generally used to send text and pictures (Web pages and e-mail), and includes some error checking to make sure all the information that's received by a computer matches what the sending computer sent. UDP works more like broadcast TV or radio, where the information is just sent out and there is no error checking. UDP is generally used for real-time communications, such as voice conversations and radio broadcasts sent over the Internet.

Each port has two directions: incoming (or *ingress*) and outgoing (or *egress*). The direction is in relation to stuff coming into your computer from the outside: namely the Internet. It's the stuff coming into your computer that you have to watch out for. But you can't close all ports to all incoming traffic. If you did, there'd be no way to get the good stuff in. But you don't want to let everything in, either. You need a way to separate the wheat from the chaff, so to speak — a way to let in the good stuff while keeping out the bad stuff.

Antispyware and antivirus software are good tools for keeping out viruses and other bad things that are attached to files coming into your computer. But hackers can actually sneak worms and other bad things in through unprotected ports without involving a file in the process. That's where the firewall comes into play. A *stateful* firewall, such as the one that comes with Windows 7, keeps track of everything you request. When traffic from the Internet wants to come in through a port, the firewall checks to make sure the traffic is something you requested. If it isn't, the firewall assumes this is a hacker trying to sneak something in without your knowing it, and therefore prevents the traffic from entering your computer. Figure 7-1 illustrates how it works.

FIGURE 7-1

How a stateful firewall works.

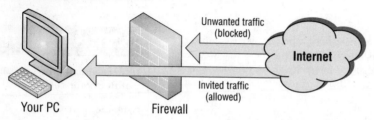

So, there's really more to it than just having a port open or closed. It's also about *filtering*. About making sure that data coming into an open port is something you requested and not some rogue uninvited traffic sent by some hacker. Many of the worms that infected so many computers in the 1990s did so by sneaking in undetected through unfiltered ports. These days, you really want to make sure you have a firewall up whenever you go online to prevent such things.

What a firewall doesn't protect against

It's important to understand that a firewall alone is not sufficient protection against all Internet threats. A firewall is just one component in a larger defense system. Specifically:

- Windows firewall *doesn't* protect you from spyware and viruses. See Chapter 8 for more information on that protection.

- Windows firewall *doesn't* protect you from attacks based on exploits. Automatic updates (Chapter 9) provide that protection.

- A firewall *doesn't* protect you from pop-up ads. See Chapter 16 for information on pop-up blocking with Internet Explorer.

- A firewall *doesn't* protect you from phishing scams. See Chapters 16 and 18 for that protection.

- Windows firewall *doesn't* protect you from spam (junk e-mail). See Chapter 18 for tools and techniques on managing spam with Windows Mail.

So, a firewall isn't a complete solution. Rather, it's an important component of a larger security strategy.

Note

Note that in the preceding list, I indicated that Windows Firewall doesn't provide certain types of protection, such as spam or virus blocking. Many hardware firewalls *do* provide this type of protection. This is sometimes call *perimeter protection*, because it protects your network from threats at the perimeter of your network. These types of firewalls can cost from several hundred to several thousands of dollars, so they aren't always the best bet for a home network. They can be extremely valuable, however, for business networks. ■

Introducing Action Center

Before you get into Windows Firewall, take a look at the Action Center. This is a single point of notification for most of your PC's security. You can open the Action Center in several ways. Use whichever is most convenient for you:

- Right-click the flag icon in the Notification area and choose Action Center.
- Press ▓ , type **act**, and click Action Center.
- Click the Start button, choose Control Panel, click System and Security, and then click Action Center.

Whichever method you use, the Action Center opens. Figure 7-2 shows an example. I clicked the arrow button to the right of each heading so that you can see the descriptive text under each heading. You can click that button to show or hide the same descriptive text.

By default, Windows Firewall is turned on and working at all times, so your Action Center should show "On" beside the Firewall item, as in Figure 7-2 (and you will see only the Network Firewall item in Action Center if you click the arrow beside the Security heading). If yours shows Off or Not Monitored, it might be because you have a third-party firewall program running in place of Windows Firewall. There are many such programs available, such as McAfee, Symantec (Norton), Gibson Research, and other companies. If your firewall is turned off and you don't know why, it would be good to find out — perhaps from your computer manufacturer or someone who knows. If you don't have any firewall up, you should definitely turn on Windows Firewall.

Note

There is no advantage to having two or more firewalls running simultaneously. In fact, more than one firewall is likely to cause unnecessary problems. ■

Turning Windows Firewall on or off

To turn Windows Firewall on or off, you must have administrative privileges. In the System and Security Control Panel window, click Windows Firewall. You should see the current firewall status in the right pane, and options for controlling the firewall in the left pane. Click Change Notification Settings or Turn Windows Firewall On or Off in the left pane to see the options shown in the foreground of Figure 7-3.

Tip

Use the Block All Incoming Connections check box only to temporarily disable exceptions when connecting to public Wi-Fi networks. You can find more on that topic in the sections to follow. ■

FIGURE 7-2

Action Center.

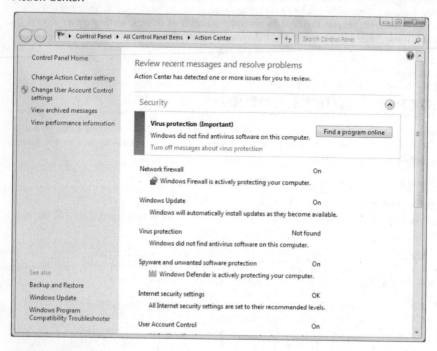

FIGURE 7-3

Settings for Windows Firewall.

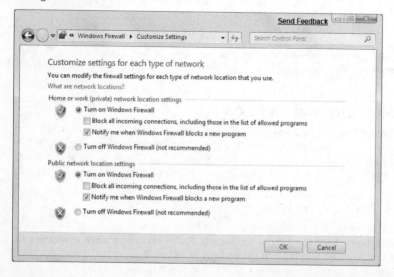

If you have a third-party firewall that you feel is more secure than the Windows Firewall, you can choose the Off option to turn off Windows Firewall. Just make sure you have a firewall up when you go online. Otherwise, you won't have anything to stop uninvited traffic on your network connection.

Tip

If you have a firewall at home, such as a wireless access point (WAP) or a cable or DSL modem that provides firewall features, and those features are turned on, you can safely turn off Windows Firewall. However, there usually is no downside to leaving Windows Firewall turned on even when an upstream firewall is in place. The exception is when you are trying to play multiplayer games or accomplish networking with other computers on the network and can't get the ports right in Windows Firewall to make it work. In these situations, just turn off Windows Firewall on the computers (but make sure your upstream firewall is working)! ■

Making Exceptions to Firewall Protection

When Windows Firewall is turned on and running, you don't really have to do anything special to use it. It will be on constant vigil, automatically protecting your computer from hackers and worms trying to sneak in through unprotected ports. Ports for common Internet tasks such as e-mail and the Web will be open and monitored so that you can easily use those programs safely.

Internet programs that don't use standard e-mail and Web ports may require that you create an *exception* to the default firewall rules for incoming traffic. Examples include instant messaging programs and some online games. When you try to use such a program, Windows Firewall displays a security alert like the one in Figure 7-4.

The message doesn't mean that the program is "bad." It just means that to use the program, the Firewall has to open a port. If you don't recognize the program name and publisher shown, click Cancel. If you want to use the program, first decide for which networks the exception will be allowed. For example, if the traffic is coming from another computer on your local network, select the Private Networks option. For traffic coming from the Internet, select Public Networks (you can select either or both, as needed). Then, click Allow Access. Allowing access for a program doesn't leave the associated port wide open. It just creates a new rule that allows that one program to use the port. You're still protected because the port is closed when you're not using that specific program. The port is also closed to programs other than the one for which you unblocked the port. Should you change your mind in the future, you can always reblock the port as described in the next section.

Manually configuring firewall exceptions (allowed programs)

Normally, when you try to use a program that needs to work through the firewall, you get a message like the example shown in Figure 7-4. Occasionally, you might need, or want, to manually allow or block a program through the firewall. If you have administrative privileges, you can do that via the Allowed Programs page shown in Figure 7-5. To open that page, click Allow a Program Through Windows Firewall in System and Security (by the Windows Firewall item in Control Panel).

Items on the list with a check mark beside them represent programs and features that work through the firewall. You'll also see any exceptions you created in response to a security alert. For example, Trillian isn't a Windows 7 feature, so you might not see that one. It shows in Figure 7-5 because I chose to allow access for it in response to the security alert shown back in Figure 7-4.

You probably aren't familiar with most of the programs listed in the Allowed Programs and Features list, so you should not select or deselect a box just by guessing. But you don't need to guess, either. If you just leave things as they are, everything will be fine. If you later decide to use one of the listed features, you'll be prompted at that point to allow access for the program if it's necessary to do so.

FIGURE 7-4

Windows Firewall security alert.

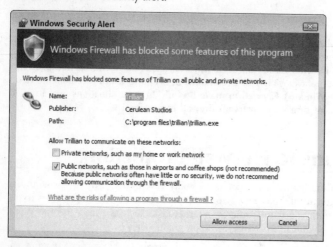

FIGURE 7-5

Windows Firewall Allowed programs and features.

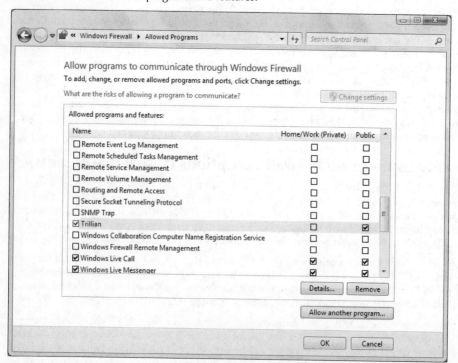

Adding a program exception

You can unblock ports for programs that aren't listed under Allowed Programs and Features. You would do this only if specifically instructed to do so by a program manufacturer you know and trust.

If the program for which you want to create an exception isn't listed under Allowed Programs and Features, first click Change Settings and then click the Allow Another Program button. When you click Allow Another Program, you see a list of installed programs that might require Internet access, as in Figure 7-6. Click the program that you want to add to the list. Optionally, if the program isn't listed, but you know where it's installed, you can use the Browse button to get to the main executable for that program (typically the .exe file).

FIGURE 7-6

Add a Program dialog box.

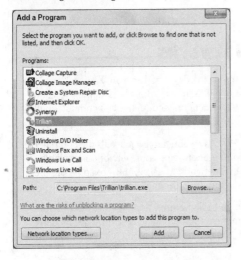

Clicking the Network Location Types button lets you define the addresses from which any unsolicited traffic is expected to originate. For example, if you're using a program that provides communications among programs within your local network only, you wouldn't want to accept unsolicited traffic coming to that port from the Internet. You'd want to accept unsolicited traffic coming only from computers within your own network. When you click Network Location Types, you see the options shown in Figure 7-7. Your options are as follows:

- **Private Networks, Such as Those at Home or at a Workplace:** If the program in question has nothing to do with the Internet, and is for your home or business network only, choose this option to block Internet access but allow programs within your own network to communicate with each other through the program.

- **Public Networks, Such as Those in an Airport or Coffee Shop:** If you want the program to be able to connect to the Internet, choose this option.

Tip

You can choose the scope for the program within the Allowed programs and features list just by placing a check in the Home/Work (Private) or Public columns for the program. ■

FIGURE 7-7

The Choose Network Location Types dialog box.

IP Addresses on Home/Office Networks

When you set up a network using the Network Setup Wizard described in Part X of this book, each computer is automatically assigned a 192.168.0.*x* IP address, where *x* is unique to each computer. For example, if the computers are sharing a single Internet connection, the first computer will be 192.168.0.1, and the subsequent computers will also have addresses in that same address space.

All computers will have the same subnet mask of 255.255.255.0. The subnet mask just tells the computer that the first three numbers are part of the *network address* (the address of your network as a whole), and the last number refers to a specific *host* (computer) on that network. The 192.168 . . . addresses are called *private addresses* because they cannot be accessed directly from the Internet.

To see the IP address of a computer on your local network, go to that computer, click the Start button, and choose All Programs ➪ Accessories ➪ Command Prompt. At the command prompt, type **ipconfig /all** and press Enter. You see the computer's IP address and subnet mask listed along with other Internet Protocol data.

Disabling, changing, and deleting exceptions

The check boxes in the Allowed Programs and Features list indicate whether the exception is enabled or disabled. When you clear a check box, the exception is disabled and traffic for that program is rejected. This makes it relatively easy to enable and disable a rule for a program on an as-needed basis, because the program name always remains in the list of exceptions.

To change the scope of an exception in your exceptions list, click the check box in the Private or Public column, as needed. To remove a program from the exceptions list, and stop accepting unsolicited traffic through its port, click the program name and then click the Remove button.

Tip
You can remove the default programs from the list — only those you have added. ■

Advanced Firewall Configuration

The rest of this chapter goes way beyond anything that would concern the average home computer user. It's for more advanced users and network and security administrators who might need to configure Windows Firewall to comply with an organization's security policy. All these options require administrative privileges. I don't go into great detail on what the various options mean because I assume you are working to comply with an existing policy.

Caution

If you're not a professional administrator, it's best to stay out of this area altogether. You certainly don't want to guess and hack your way through things just to see what happens. Doing so could lead to a real can of worms that makes it impossible or extremely difficult to access the Internet. ∎

Open the Windows Firewall with Advanced Security icon

To get to the advanced configuration options for Windows Firewall, first open Windows Firewall from the System and Security item in the Control Panel. Then click the Advanced Settings link in the left pane. Or press ▝, type **fire**, and click Windows Firewall with Advanced Security. The Firewall console, shown in Figure 7-8, opens.

FIGURE 7-8

Windows Firewall with Advanced Security console.

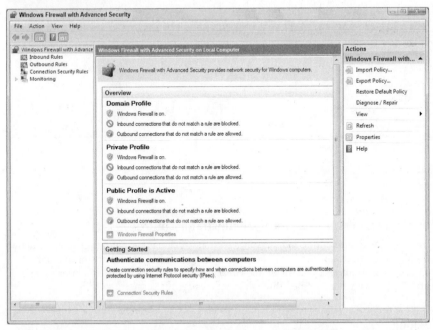

As you can see in the figure, you have three independently configurable profiles to work with. The Domain Profile is active when the computer is logged in to a domain. The Private Profile applies to computers within a local, private network. The Public Profile protects your computer from the public Internet.

Changing Firewall Profile Properties

Clicking the Windows Firewall Properties link near the bottom of the console (or the Properties item in the Actions pane) takes you to the dialog box shown in Figure 7-9. Notice that you can use tabs at the top of the dialog box to configure the Domain, Private, and Public settings. The fourth option applies to IPsec (IP Security), commonly used with VPNs (Virtual Private Networks), described a little later in this section. By default, Inbound connections are set to Block and Outbound ports are set to Allow. You can change either setting by clicking the appropriate button.

FIGURE 7-9

Windows Firewall advanced properties.

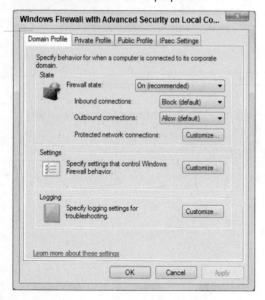

Firewall alerts, unicast responses, local administrator control

Each profile tab has a Customize button in its Settings section. Clicking that button provides an option to turn off firewall notifications for that profile. Administrators can also use options on that tab to allow or prevent unicast responses to multicast and broadcast traffic. There's also an option to merge local administrator rules with rules defined through group policy.

Security Logging

Each profile tab also offers a Logging section with a Customize button. Click the Customize button to set a name and location for the log file, a maximum size, and to choose whether you want to log dropped packets, successful connections, or both. You can use that log file to review firewall activity and to troubleshoot connection problems caused by the firewall configuration.

Customizing IPsec settings

Why Outbound Connections Are Set to Allow

Contrary to some common marketing hype and urban myths, having outbound connections set to Allow by default does not make your computer more susceptible to security threats. Firewalls are really about controlling traffic between trusted and untrusted networks. The Internet is always considered untrusted because it's open to the public and anything goes. It's necessary to block inbound connections by default so that you can control exactly what does, and doesn't, come in from the Internet.

Things that are already inside your computer (or local network) are generally considered "trusted." That's because, unlike the Internet, you do have control over what's inside your own PC or network. Your firewall and antimalware programs also help to keep bad stuff out. Therefore, you shouldn't need to block outbound connections by default.

There are exceptions, of course. In a secure setting in which highly sensitive data is confined to secure workstations in a subnet, it certainly makes sense to block outgoing connections by default. That way, you can limit outbound connections to specific hosts, programs, security groups, and so forth. You can also enforce encryption on outbound connections.

The IPsec Settings tab in the firewall properties provides a way to configure IPsec (IP Security). Clicking the Customize button under IPsec Defaults reveals the options shown in Figure 7-10. The Default settings in each case cause settings to be inherited from a higher-level GPO (Group Policy Object). To override the GPO, choose whichever options you want to apply to the current Windows Firewall instance. When you override the default, you can choose key exchange and data integrity algorithms. You can also fine-tune Kerberos V5 authentication through those settings.

FIGURE 7-10

IPsec Settings dialog box.

Clicking OK or Cancel in the Customize IPsec Settings dialog box takes you back to the IPsec Settings tab. There you can use the IPsec Exemptions section to exempt ICMP from IPsec, which may help with connection problems caused by ICMP rules.

Note

IPsec is a set of cryptographic protocols for securing communications across untrusted networks. It is commonly associated with tunneling and virtual private networks (VPNs). ■

That covers the main firewall properties. You can configure plenty more outside the Properties dialog box. Again, most of these go far beyond anything the average home user needs to be concerned with, so I'm being brief here. Advanced users needing more information can find plenty of information in the Help section for the firewall.

Inbound and Outbound Rules

In the left column of the main Windows Firewall with Advanced Security window shown back in Figure 7-7, you see Inbound Rules and Outbound Rules links. These provide very granular control over Windows Firewall rules for incoming and outgoing connections. Figure 7-11 shows a small portion of the possibilities there. Use scroll bars to see them all.

FIGURE 7-11

Advanced outbound exceptions control.

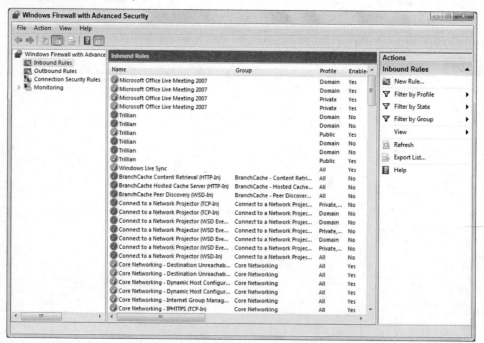

Here we're getting into security matters that go beyond the scope of this book. But I think it will be easy for any professional administrator to figure out what's going on there. Options (and the Help link) in the Actions column on the right tell all. You can also change any exception in the center column by right-clicking and choosing Properties.

Wrap-Up

A firewall is an important component of a larger overall security strategy. Windows 7 comes with a built-in firewall that's turned on and working from the moment you first start your computer. The firewall is automatically configured to prevent unsolicited Internet traffic from getting into your computer, thereby protecting you from worms and other hack attempts. The 7 firewall also provides advanced options for professional network and security administrators who need more granular control over its behavior. In summary:

- A firewall protects your computer from unsolicited network traffic, which is a major cause of worms and other hack attempts.

- A firewall will not protect your computer from viruses, pop-up ads, or junk e-mail.

- You don't need to configure the firewall to use standard Internet services such as the Web and e-mail. Those will work through the firewall automatically.

- When you start an Internet program that needs access to the Internet through a closed port, you'll be given a security alert with options to Unblock, or Keep Blocking, the port. You must choose Unblock to use that program.

- Windows Firewall is one of the programs in the Security Center. To open Security Center, click the Start button and choose Control Panel ⇨ Security ⇨ Security Center.

- From the Start menu, you can search on the keyword *fire* to get to Windows Firewall configuration options.

- Exceptions in Windows Firewall are programs that are allowed to work through the firewall.

- Professional network and security administrators can configure Windows Firewall through the Windows Firewall with Advanced Security console in Administrative Tools.

Conquering Malicious Software

Malicious software (also called *malware*) is any software program that's intentionally designed to cause your computer harm or invade your privacy. These are not programs you purchase, or programs from reputable software manufacturers such as Microsoft, Adobe, Corel, and others. They generally don't have icons, and you don't have to run them yourself. Rather, they're tiny programs that are hidden inside your system and do their dirty work without your knowing it.

As you learn in this chapter, several forms of malware exist including viruses, worms, spyware, and adware. As you also discover in this chapter, you can take actions to prevent your computer from getting malware. And when it's too late for that, you can take steps to get rid of malware. This chapter starts with a discussion of the most prevalent form of malware today, spyware.

IN THIS CHAPTER

Understanding malware

Beating spyware with Windows Defender

Killing and preventing viruses

De-worming with the Malicious Software Removal Tool

Types of Malware

Malicious software comes in many forms. All forms have certain things in common, though. For one, they're invisible — you don't even know they're there. For another, they all do something bad, something you don't really want happening on your computer. Third, they're all written by human programmers to intentionally do these bad things. The differences have to do with how they spread and what they do after they're on your computer. I tell you about the differences in the sections to follow.

Viruses and worms

Viruses and worms are self-replicating programs that spread from one computer to the next, usually via the Internet. A virus needs a *host file* to spread from one computer to the next. The host file can be anything, though viruses are typically hidden in e-mail attachments and programs you download.

A worm is similar to a virus in that it can replicate itself and spread. However, unlike a virus, a worm doesn't need a host file to travel around. It can go from one computer to the next right though your Internet connection. That's one reason it's important to always have a firewall up when you're online — to keep out worms that travel through Internet connections.

The harm caused by viruses and worms ranges from minor pranks to serious damage. A minor prank might be something like a small message that appears somewhere on your screen where you don't want it. A more serious virus might erase important files, or even try to erase all your files, rendering your computer useless.

Spyware and adware

Spyware and adware is malware that's not designed to specifically harm your computer. Rather, it's designed to help people sell you stuff. A common spyware tactic is to send information about the Web sites you visit to computers that send out advertisements on the Internet. That computer analyzes the Web sites you visit to figure out what types of products you're most likely to buy. That computer then sends ads about such products to your computer.

Adware is the mechanism that allows ads to appear on your computer screen. When you get advertisements on your screen, seemingly out of the clear blue sky, there's usually some form of adware behind it. Spyware and adware often work in conjunction with one another. The adware provides the means to display ads. The spyware helps the ad server (the computer sending the ads) choose ads for products you're most likely to buy.

Trojan horses and rootkits

You may have heard the term *Trojan horse* in relation to early mythology. The story goes like this. After 10 years of war with the city of Troy, the Greeks decided to call it quits. As a peace offering, they gave to the people of Troy a huge horse statue named the Trojan horse.

While the people of Troy were busy celebrating the end of the war, Greek soldiers hidden inside the horse snuck out and opened the gates to the city from inside. This allowed other Greek soldiers, lying in wait hidden outside the city, to storm into the town and conquer it. (This is definitely a case in which it would have been wise to look a gift horse in the mouth.)

A Trojan horse is a program that works in a similar manner. In contrast to other forms of malware, a Trojan horse is a program you can actually see on your screen and use. On the surface, it does do something useful. However, hidden inside the program is some smaller program that does bad things, usually without your knowledge.

A Trojan horse can also be a program that hides nothing but could be used in bad ways. Take, for example, a program that can recover lost passwords. On the one hand, it can be a good thing if you use it to recover forgotten passwords from files you created yourself. But it can be a bad thing when used to break into other people's password-protected files.

A *rootkit* is a program that is capable of hiding itself, and the malicious intent of other programs, from the user and even from the system. As with Trojan horses, not all rootkits are inherently malicious. However, they can certainly be used in malicious ways. Windows 7 protects your system from rootkits on many fronts, including Windows Defender.

Conquering Spyware with Windows Defender

Note
Windows Defender was a popular download for Windows XP. It came free with Windows Vista, and is also included for free in Windows 7, so there's nothing to download. ∎

Spyware (and its close cousin adware) isn't specifically designed to cause your computer harm. But even without the direct intent to do harm, spyware can have serious consequences. Too much spyware can bog your system down, causing everything to run slower than it should. Spyware can make unwanted changes to your Internet settings, causing your Web browser to act in unexpected ways. Spyware can lead to many annoying pop-up ads. In the worst cases, it can send personally identifiable information about you to identity thieves.

Most spyware comes from software that you can download for free, such as screen savers, custom toolbars, and file-sharing programs. However, it can also be installed automatically from scripts and programs embedded in Web pages.

There are many programs on the market that are designed to prevent and eliminate spyware (and adware). But you don't have to spend any money or download any third-party programs to protect your system from these threats. You can use Windows Defender, which comes with Windows 7 for free. Despite its focus on spyware, Defender actually protects your computer from any potentially unwanted programs. That includes many types of adware, Trojan horses, and rootkits.

Opening Windows Defender

Windows Defender doesn't need to be open to protect your computer. But you can do other things with Defender that do require opening the program. As with most programs, you have many ways to open Defender. Use whichever is most convenient for you at the moment:

- Open the Control Panel and click the All Control Panel Items link in the left pane; then, open Windows Defender.
- Press ▟ , type **def** in the Search box, and click Windows Defender.

When Windows Defender opens, it looks something like Figure 8-1.

Removing spyware from your computer

Windows Defender offers many tools for fighting spyware. One of them is the ability to scan your system for any spyware that you might have already acquired. You can do a Full Scan, which takes a while but gives you the peace of mind of knowing that your system is free of malicious spyware. Or you can do a Quick Scan. As its name implies, the Quick Scan takes less time because it focuses on areas where spyware is most likely hiding. You can also opt for a Custom Scan, which lets you choose which drives you want to scan. To perform a scan, click the arrow next to the Scan button, as shown in Figure 8-2, and then select the desired scan option.

Note
If you're unable to scan for spyware from a standard account, an administrator may need to enable scanning for you. See "Advanced and administrator configuration options," later in this chapter. ■

A full scan takes several minutes, so you need to be patient. When the scan is complete, you should see a clean bill of health. If not, suspicious items will be *quarantined* (disabled). You should be taken to the quarantined list automatically, though you can get there any time by choosing Tools ⇨ Quarantined Items.

FIGURE 8-1

Windows Defender.

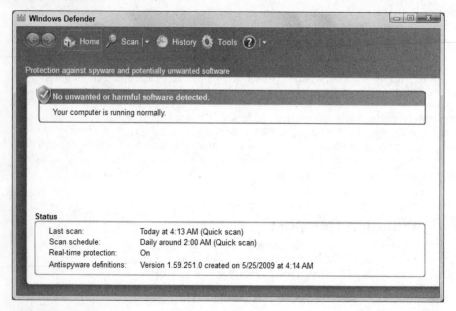

FIGURE 8-2

Scan for spyware.

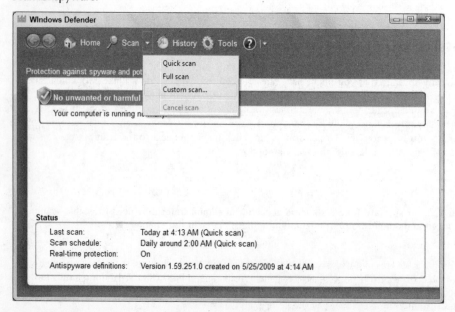

Each item in the quarantined list has an alert level associated with it. Here's what each alert level means:

- **Severe:** This item is known to compromise the security of your computer. It should be removed immediately.

- **High:** This item may be too new to be well known. But all indications point to malicious intent, so the item should be removed immediately.

- **Medium:** This item appears to collect personal information or change Internet settings. Review the item details. If you do not recognize or trust the publisher, block or remove the item.

- **Low:** This is a potentially unwanted item that should be removed if you did not intentionally install it yourself.

- **Not Yet Classified:** This item is unrecognized but is potentially something you don't want on your computer. You may want to check with the Windows Defender newsgroups described later in this chapter for further advice.

To remove an item, click its name and click Remove. You can usually click Remove All, because valid, useful programs are rarely detected as spyware or other potentially unwanted items. If in doubt, you can leave the item quarantined for a while. Use your computer normally to see whether some useful program no longer works. After you've determined that everything is okay, you can go back into Quarantined Items and remove anything you left behind.

Should you ever encounter a false positive (where an innocent program is quarantined), don't remove it. Instead, click its name and then click Restore.

Doing a quick scan

A full scan takes some time because it scans every file on your hard disk. You can save some time by doing a quick scan. A quick scan checks only new files and the kinds of files commonly used by spyware. After you've done a single full scan, quick scans are sufficient.

Doing a custom scan

A custom scan lets you scan a specific drive or folder. For example, if someone sends you a CD or DVD, you might want to check that disk before copying or opening any files from it.

For downloads, you might consider creating a subfolder within your Documents folder, perhaps named Unscanned or something similar. Whenever you download a file or save an e-mail attachment that you don't trust 100 percent, save it to that Unscanned folder. Then scan just the folder to make sure all is well. If the files check out okay, you can then move them to any folder you like. Or, in the case of a downloaded program, click the icon to start the program installation.

To do a custom scan, click Scan in Windows Defender and choose Custom Scan. Then click the Select button and click to select the drive you want to scan. Or, expand any drive icon and select the specific folder you want to scan. Then click OK to start the scan.

Automatic scanning

You can also set up Defender to automatically scan your system daily, weekly, or however often you wish. You must be logged in to an account with administrative privileges to set up automatic scanning. From the Administrator account, start Windows Defender normally. Then click Tools and Options. Automatic scanning options appear as shown in Figure 8-3.

FIGURE 8-3

Automatic scanning options.

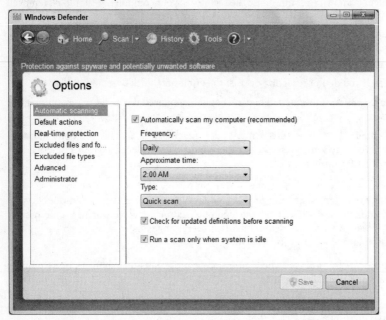

To enable automatic scanning, make sure the Automatically Scan My Computer (Recommended) check box is selected (checked). Then you can set a schedule for scanning. For example, if you use a desktop computer that you leave on 24 hours a day, choose Daily and a time during which you're unlikely to be using the computer. If the computer isn't turned on when the scheduled time arrives, the scan will take place the next time you start the computer. Choose the type of scan you want to perform on the schedule.

If your computer is on and online 24 hours a day, you can also choose Check for Updated Definitions before Scanning. Doing so ensures that Defender is up-to-date with all known spyware when it scans.

Under the Default Actions heading, you can choose how you want an automatic scan to treat Severe, High, Medium, and Low alert items, as follows:

- **Recommended Action Based on Definitions:** Choose this option to take the action that's recommended in the item's definition.

- **Remove:** Choose this option if you want the item removed automatically when found.

- **Quarantine:** Choose this option to have Windows Defender place the item in quarantine and prevent it from running until you review it and choose to either restore it or delete it.

- **Allow:** Have Defender add the software to the allowed list and allow it to run on the computer. This option is available only for the Medium and Low alert items.

If in doubt about what to choose, your best bet is to choose the Recommend Action Based on Definitions option. Each malware item that Defender identifies has a *definition* that specifies its intent, severity, and recommended actions. The definitions are created by human experts who have previously found and analyzed the item. Unless you're an expert yourself, your best bet is to allow those expert definitions to choose a course of action.

Preventing spyware

You've probably heard the saying "An ounce of prevention is worth a pound of cure." That's certainly true of spyware. Getting rid of spyware that has already infected your computer is a good thing. But preventing it from getting there in the first place is even better. That's where *real-time protection* comes into play. The term "real time" means "as it's happening."

The Windows Defender real-time protection analyzes files as they approach your computer from the Internet. Any spyware or suspicious-looking files are blocked to keep your computer from being infected.

Real-time protection is turned on by default. You can control whether it's on or off, and optionally tweak what it monitors by clicking Tools in Defender and choosing Options. Click Real-Time Protection to see the real-time options shown in Figure 8-4.

Following is a description of the options available for real-time protection:

- **Use Real-Time Protection (Recommended):** Turn on real-time protection.
- **Scan Downloaded Files and Attachments:** Monitor ActiveX controls and software installation programs that are downloaded, installed, or run from your Web browser.

FIGURE 8-4

Defender real-time protection options.

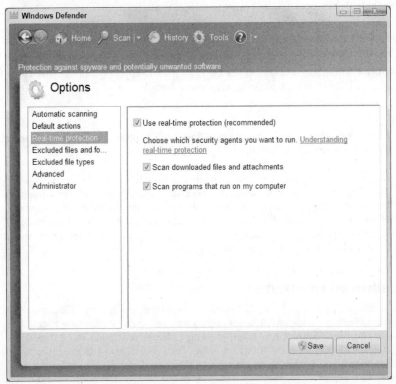

- **Scan Programs That Run on My Computer:** Monitor other programs installed on your computer to search for suspicious activity.

Excluding files and folders

In some situations, you might want to exclude certain files or folders from being scanned by Windows Defender. For example, if there are folders or files that you know are safe but could take a long time for Windows Defender to scan or could cause problems when scanned, you can exclude them. You can also exclude files based on their file type.

To set folder or file exclusions, click the Excluded Files and Folders link in the Windows Defender Options page. Click Add, select a folder or file, and click OK. Repeat the process for any other folders or files you want excluded.

To exclude files by type, click the Excluded File Types link. Click in the text box, type the file extension of the files you want to exclude from scanning, and click Add. Then, click Save to save your changes.

Advanced and Administrator configuration options

If you click Advanced in the Defender Options window, you see the Advanced options shown in Figure 8-5. These options include:

- **Scan Archive Files:** Scan inside archive files such as zip and CAB files for malware.
- **Scan E-Mail:** Scan the contents and attachments of e-mail for malware.
- **Scan Removable Drives:** Scan USB and other removable media for malware.
- **Use Heuristics:** When scanning, detect malware by matching partial malware signatures. This option can enable Defender to identify threats that have been modified (derivative threats) since the signature was released.
- **Create Restore Point:** Create a Windows Restore Point prior to applying actions to detected items to enable you to roll back Windows to its previous state.

Tip
Use the technique described under "Returning to a Previous Restore Point" in Chapter 33 to restore everything to its previous state. ∎

Clicking Administrator in the Options page lets you configure two additional options for Windows Defender. The Use This Program option, when selected, enables Defender. Deselecting this option turns off Defender. Unless Defender is causing a problem with your computer or a specific program, you should leave this option selected to enable Defender to protect your system. The second option, Display Items from All Users of This Computer, enables you to see the History, Allowed items, and Quarantined items for all users. These items are normally hidden.

Disallowing allowed programs

There may be times when you allow a program that you know and trust to run without any warnings from Windows Defender. These get added to the allowed programs list when Windows Defender alerts you about an item and you click Always Allow. Later, you might change your mind about that. If you do, you can click Tools in Defender to open its Options page. Then click Allowed Items. From there you can click any item and choose Remove from List to have Windows Defender start monitoring the program again.

FIGURE 8-5

Advanced Defender configuration options.

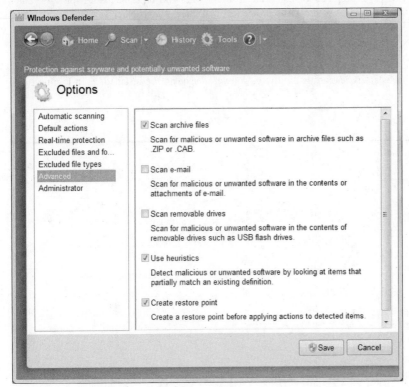

Joining the SpyNet community

The SpyNet community is a huge group of Windows Defender users who keep a watchful eye on potential spyware. Joining the community allows you to see how others are treating suspicious software that hasn't yet been classified by experts. Seeing how others deal with a suspicious file can help you make decisions about suspicious files on your computer. When Defender finds a suspicious file, the community's rating appears as a graph indicating the number of members who have allowed the item.

To join the Microsoft SpyNet community, open Windows Defender, click Tools, and choose Microsoft SpyNet. Then choose the Basic Membership, Advanced Membership, or No Membership option as described on the page that opens.

Windows Defender Web site

The Windows Defender Web site is a great resource for staying up-to-date with spyware threats and tools. The Community link on that page offers further resources for live interaction with others grappling with spyware decisions and experts to help you make those decisions. You can get to the Web site by clicking the Windows Defender Web site link on Defender's Tools page.

Using Antivirus Software

Windows Defender helps to protect your computer from spyware and other malicious software. But it doesn't protect against all viruses. For virus protection, you need a *third-party program* (a program that doesn't come free with Windows 7). The Windows Action Center can detect some (but not all) antivirus programs.

If you don't have antivirus software, or Windows can't recognize the product you're using, you see a security warning that is an indication that antivirus software *might* not be installed, as in Figure 8-6.

FIGURE 8-6

Antivirus software might not be installed.

Note
You might see a warning message briefly even if you do have virus protection, only because the message sometimes appears before your antivirus solution is fully loaded. If your malware protection is On in Security Center, you can ignore the alert. ■

Your ISP (Internet service provider) might provide virus protection. Or your computer manufacturer might have pre-installed antivirus on your system. If you don't know what your situation is, it might be wise to check with your ISP and computer manufacturer before you go out and purchase another product.

Virus protection

There are basically two ways to deal with viruses. The best is to *prevent* them before they infect your system. The other is to detect and remove them after your computer has already been infected. As described earlier in this chapter, you can scan for viruses at your computer or at the perimeter of your network.

Your ISP might provide perimeter protection for viruses, which means viruses are detected and removed by your ISP before they ever get to your computer, as illustrated in Figure 8-7. There is no extra charge for that. You pay for it when you pay the monthly bill for your Internet connection. Furthermore, you don't really have to do anything to keep your virus protection up-to-date. Your ISP takes care of that, too. The same is true if your business provides perimeter protection — a device on your network actively scans all incoming and outgoing traffic looking for and eliminating viruses. However, perimeter protection cannot protect your computer against viruses on a flash drive or other removable media.

FIGURE 8-7

Perimeter protection blocks viruses before they get to your PC.

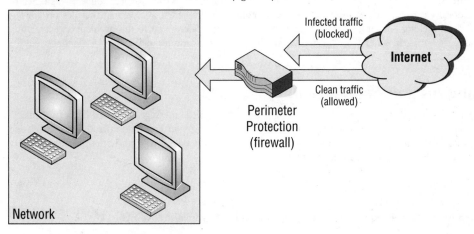

A second approach to virus protection is to have the antivirus program right on your own computer. Some popular brands include Norton Antivirus, McAfee VirusScan, and Trend PC-cillin. Some ISPs actually pay for such a service on your computer. But you still have to take some steps to install the program and keep it up-to-date.

Viruses Mutate

Computer security is always a moving target. The good guys come up with ways to thwart existing malware (including viruses). The bad guys keep inventing new ways to create viruses and other bad programs. To keep up-to-date with current threats, most antivirus programs need to download current *signatures* on a regular basis. Each signature basically tells the antivirus program what to block in order to keep your computer free of viruses.

If neither your ISP nor the computer manufacturer has provided an antivirus program, you should purchase and install one yourself. Although you could try to get by without one, sooner or later your computer is going to get infected, regardless of how careful you are about not downloading programs or opening e-mail attachments.

Even if your ISP or business provides perimeter antivirus protection, you should install and use an antivirus solution on your computer itself. Relying on perimeter protection is better than having no protection at all, and can be quite effective at preventing virus outbreaks, but it isn't the entire solution. Perimeter protection can do nothing to prevent infection from removable media (such as USB flash drives) that you connect to your computer. My preferred solution is to deploy perimeter protection from one vendor and desktop protection from another vendor, giving you two different detection engines for a "more is better" approach to antivirus protection.

You can click the Find an Antivirus program (Figure 8-8 later in this chapter) to browse for available products.

Finally, you might also consider looking into Windows Live OneCare, which combines virus protection with a host of other useful services. See `OneCare.Live.com` for more information.

Whether or not you're a pro, you should scan your computer for viruses at least once a week. Scanning doesn't prevent viruses from infecting your computer. Rather, it analyzes all the files on your hard disk, seeking out viruses hiding there. If it finds any, it alerts you to the problem and lets you remove the virus. In other words, it works just like spyware scanning in Windows Defender.

Antivirus and Action Center

Let's get back to that "Antivirus software might not be installed" message discussed earlier in this chapter. If you have antivirus software installed and protecting your computer already, you won't see that message. That message appears only if (1) Windows can't detect your antivirus program, or (2) you really don't have an antivirus program.

Note
Some options in Action Center require that you use an account with administrative rights. ∎

If you know for a fact that you do have an antivirus program in place, you can make that message stop appearing. You just have to change the notification setting for virus protection.

In Action Center, the Security group of items informs you of virus protection. If the Virus protection item shows "On," you know you have virus protection. All is well and you probably don't need to do anything else, unless you see a message saying you should update your virus definitions or signatures. In that case, you should do as the message instructs.

If the Security section shows the Find a Program Online button (Figure 8-8), you have a decision to make. If you know for a fact that you have an antivirus program installed, click Turn off Messages about Virus Protection. You will still be able to see antivirus status in the Action Center, but the larger box goes away and you see only an indication that virus protection is not monitored.

If you're sure you don't have any virus protection and would like to explore your options, click the Find an Antivirus Program Online link.

FIGURE 8-8

Virus protection is not found in this example.

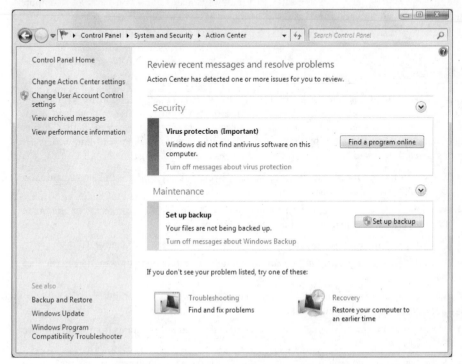

User Account Control and Malware

User Account Control (UAC) is yet another form of malware protection. In contrast to the antimalware programs described in this chapter, which are designed to keep malware out of your PC, UAC prevents malicious programs that have already infiltrated your system from doing their evil deeds. Although Windows 7 significantly reduces the number of alerts it displays, it still might be tempting to turn off UAC, to get rid of that occasional extra mouse click for the approval it requires. But do keep in mind that in doing so, you're lowering your computer's resistance to malware. For more information on User Account Control, see Chapter 3.

The Malicious Software Removal Tool

There is one last malware protection tool you'll want to know about before I put this topic to rest. It's called the Malicious Software Removal Tool (MSRT), a tool that you can download and install on your computer. Its primary focus is on worm and rootkit removal. The page has been at this address for a while:

www.microsoft.com/security/malwareremove/

If you can't find the tool for some reason, perform a search at Microsoft.com for the keywords *Malicious Software Removal Tool* and you should find it.

Also note that the MSRT is also available through Windows Update, and if you have your computer configured to download updates, the MSRT will be included automatically.

Wrap-Up

Malicious software (called malware for short) is computer software that's intentionally written to invade your privacy or cause harm. This is not the kind of thing you purchase or download from legitimate software vendors. Nor does it announce its presence to you on the screen. Rather, it sneaks into your computer through tainted programs and e-mail attachments without your knowledge. This chapter has covered the main types of malware and defenses to take against them:

- Spyware is a form of malware designed to invade your privacy, and it is the largest and most common Internet threat today.

- Windows Defender is a program that comes free with Windows 7 to protect your computer from spyware and similar forms of malicious software.

- Windows Defender can scan your system for unwanted software and remove it.

- Defender's real-time protection prevents spyware from getting on your computer in the first place.

- Viruses and worms are harmful programs that can spread from one computer to the next via the Internet or other network connection.

- Most viruses are spread through e-mail attachments or tainted programs from nonlegitimate Web sites.

- Windows 7 offers no built-in virus protection. Typically, you acquire this from your ISP, your computer manufacturer, or by purchasing it yourself.

- The Windows Action Center alerts you if it cannot find antivirus software on your computer.

- The Malicious Software Removal Tool (MSRT) is an online tool specializing in worm removal. Run it once a month or so to ensure that your computer is free of worms.

Automatic Updates as Security

I nternet security is a never-ending cat-and-mouse game between the security experts and the hackers who seem to have endless amounts of time to search for new ways to exploit the basic programmability of PCs. It seems that every time the good guys find a way to patch some security hole the bad guys have learned to exploit, the bad guys find two more holes to exploit.

Windows 7 is certainly the most secure Windows ever, by a long shot. But there is no such thing as a 100-percent secure computer, because people can always find a way to take something good and turn it into something bad. So in addition to the security features discussed in the preceding chapters, you need to keep your computer up-to-date with security patches as they become available. That's what Windows Update and this chapter are all about.

Understanding Automatic Updates

Many people are afraid of Windows Update. They're afraid that the changes to their system that the updates make will break something that they can't fix. It's certainly true that any change to your system could create a problem. But it's unlikely that keeping up with updates will cause any significant problems — certainly nowhere near as many problems as you expose yourself to by *not* keeping up with updates. In addition, Windows Update creates restore points before installing many updates (but not for all updates), so you have the added security of being able to restore the system to a point prior to the update.

Others fear that Microsoft will somehow exploit them through automatic updates. That's not the way it works. Microsoft has tens of millions of customers and tens of billions of dollars. It doesn't need to exploit anybody to be successful. Desperate people (and companies) do desperate, exploitive things. Microsoft is as far from desperate as you can get.

Microsoft is also a publicly held company on the stock exchange, which means it is subject to constant scrutiny. Such companies are not the ones that distribute malware. Most malware comes from e-mail attachments and free programs from unknown sources. When it comes to knowing who to trust and not to trust, large publicly held companies are by far the most trustworthy, if for no other reason than that they can't afford to be untrustworthy. A third common fear of automatic updates centers around the question "What's this going to cost me?" The answer to that is simple: Absolutely nothing. This brings us to the difference between *updates* and *upgrades*.

Some Hacking Lingo

The hacking world is replete with its own terminology. A *zero day exploit* is one that becomes available before a software product is even released to the public. A *blackhat* is a bad guy who has sufficient technical knowledge to find and publish exploits. A *script kiddie* is an inexperienced programmer who doesn't have enough skill to create or discover his own exploits, but does have enough expertise to create malware based on known exploits. A *whitehat* is one of the good guys — the security experts who find ways to thwart the efforts of blackhats and script kiddies.

Updates versus upgrades

People often assume that the terms *update* and *upgrade* are synonymous. We certainly use the terms interchangeably in common parlance. But in the computer world, there is a big difference. Upgrades usually cost money and involve a fair amount of work. For example, upgrading from Windows Vista to Windows 7 will cost you some money and take some time. You might even need to hire someone to verify that the upgrade will work, and do the upgrade for you.

Updates are much different. Updates are small, simple, and free of charge. Some people turn off automatic updates because they're afraid they'll get some mysterious bill for something they downloaded automatically without realizing it. That will never happen. Turning on and using automatic updates will never cost you a penny.

Why updates are important

Automatic updates are an important part of your overall security. Many forms of malware, especially viruses and worms, operate by exploiting previously unnoticed flaws in programs. The term *exploit*, when used as a noun in computer science, refers to any piece of software that can take advantage of some vulnerability in a program in order to gain unauthorized access to a computer.

Some hackers actually publish, on the Internet, exploits they discover, which is both a good thing and a bad thing. The bad thing is that other hackers can use the exploit to conjure up their own malware, causing a whole slew of new security threats. The good thing is that the good guys can quickly create security patches to prevent the exploits from doing their nefarious deeds. Automatic updates keep your system current with *security patches* that fix the flaws that malware programs attempt to exploit.

Enabling Automatic Updates

Automatic updates are the best way to keep up with security patches. In fact, chances are they are already enabled on your system. To find out, open Windows Update. In case you skipped the preceding chapters, or forgot how, you can use any technique that follows to open Windows Update:

- Click the Start button and choose Control Panel ➪ System and Security ➪ Windows Update.
- Press ⊞, type **upd**, and click Windows Update under Programs.

Figure 9-1 shows the Windows Update applet. To determine Windows Update's status, click the Change Settings link in the left pane. The Important Updates drop-down list shows the current setting.

Windows Update

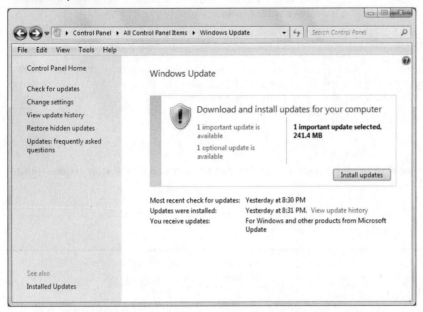

If automatic updates are turned off, seriously consider turning them on. To do so, click the Change Settings link in the Windows Update applet, then choose from one of the three options that enable Windows Update.

Managing Updates

Automatic updates related to security require little or no effort on your part. But sometimes you may be faced with optional updates. These updates aren't security related. Rather, they're new versions of drivers, fixes for minor bugs, or some other type of update. They're optional because your computer is secure whether you install the update or not.

Managing optional updates

To manage optional updates and tweak some settings, use the Windows Update applet in Control Panel. To get to that applet, do one of the following:

- Click the Start button and choose Control Panel; then, click System and Security ➪ Windows Update.
- Press ![windows key], type **upd**, and choose Windows Update.

Figure 9-1 shows the Windows Update applet. If there are any optional updates, click the Optional Updates link to see what they are. The name of each will be listed next to an empty check box (Figure 9-2). You have three options for dealing with each one:

- If you want to download and install the update, select (click to place a checkmark in) its check box.

- If you want to hide the item so that it doesn't show up in the future, right-click it and choose Hide update. (It won't go into hiding until you leave the current window.) Right-click and choose Restore Update to restore a hidden update.

- If you want to get more information about the item before you decide, click its name and view details in for the update in the right pane.

If you selected optional updates to install, you see an Install Update buttons when you click OK to return to the Windows Update window. Click the Install Updates button and follow the on-screen instructions to proceed. If you don't want to install any optional updates, simply close Windows Update.

Tip
To restore updates that have been previously hidden, open Windows Update and click Restore Hidden Updates in the right pane. ■

FIGURE 9-2

Optional updates.

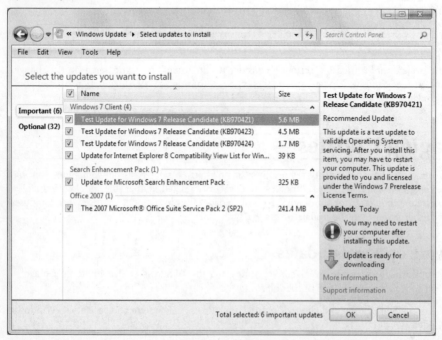

148

Change how updates work

In the left column of the Windows Update page, you can click Change Settings to change how automatic updating works. You come to the options shown in Figure 9-3. The preferred (and most secure) setting is the one shown, which has Windows checking for critical updates daily at 3:00 a.m.

Change update settings.

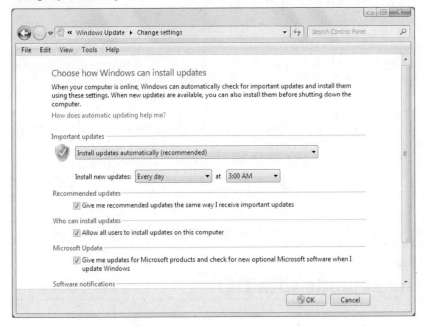

What if your computer isn't turned on and online at 3:00 in the morning? Will you miss out on something important? Not at all. For one thing, there is no time limit on updates. After an update is posted, it stays posted forever. So you can download and install it at any time.

If your computer isn't on and online at 3:00 a.m., it will check for updates and download them in the background as soon as you do go online. ("In the background" means "without interfering with whatever you want to do yourself.") Also, if you shut down the computer before the scheduled time, Windows will offer to check for updates before you shut down. So, you don't have to worry about missing out on anything important.

Of course, you're free to choose a different schedule if you prefer, such as weekly at noon. But daily at 3:00 a.m. is fine.

As an alternative to fully automatic updates, you can choose one of the other options shown on the page. For example, you can have Windows download the updates but ask your permission before actually installing them. Or, you can just be alerted to available updates and then choose whether you want to download or install them.

Finally, you can choose to turn off automatic updating altogether. If you choose that option, the only way to get updates is to click Check for Updates at the left side of the Windows Update page.

By default, only critical updates are downloaded and installed. A critical update is one that's needed to protect your computer against current Internet threats. Choosing Give Me Recommended Updates the Same Way I Receive Important Updates extends that to less-critical updates that aren't directly related to security. Recommended updates are usually things like minor bug fixes or improvements to Windows and other Microsoft products.

Click OK after making any changes to your settings, or click Cancel to leave all settings in their original state.

Reviewing and removing updates

The fact that well over 200,000 hardware and software products are available for Windows means that once in a while an update could cause problems with a particular device or program. Typically, you fix that problem by going to the product manufacturer's Web site and finding out what it recommends. If the manufacturer hasn't fixed the problem yet, and you need immediate access to the device or program, you might want to temporarily remove the conflicting update, especially if it isn't a critical security update.

To review your history of installed updates, click View Update History in the left column of the Windows Update window. If you need to remove any installed updates, you can do so through the Uninstall a Program item in the Control Panel.

Open the Control Panel and click Uninstall a Program. Click View Installed Updates. Right-click the update you want to remove and then click Uninstall. If necessary, you can reinstall the update later by clicking Check for Updates in the left column of the Windows Update page.

Tip
For more information and general troubleshooting, click the Updates: Frequently Asked Questions link at the left side of the Windows Updates page. ■

Thwarting Exploits with DEP

Thwarting malware attacks that exploit software vulnerabilities is the most important element of automatic updates. But Windows 7 offers a second way of thwarting such attacks. It's called Data Execution Prevention (DEP). You don't want to use DEP as an alternative to other techniques described in this part of the book. Rather, you want to use it in addition to other techniques.

To give you a little background, many malware attacks use a technique called *buffer overflow* (or *buffer overrun*) to sneak code (program instructions) into areas of memory that only the operating system (Windows) should be using. Those areas of memory have direct access to everything on your computer. So any bad code that sneaks into that area can do great damage.

More Security Tricks up Its Sleeve

Some malware techniques rely on well-known memory locations to exploit system vulnerabilities. Windows 7 has a surprise for those programs, too. It does not load essential programs to well-known, predictable locations. Instead, it uses Address Space Layout Randomization (ASLR) to load things in a random location each time you start your computer. So malware writers can't really know in advance where a particular exploit resides in memory, making it much more difficult to exploit those memory addresses.

Data Execution Prevention is a security antidote to such attacks. It monitors programs to make sure they use only safe and appropriate memory locations. If DEP notices a program trying to do anything sneaky, it shuts that program down before it can do any harm.

By default, DEP is enabled for essential Windows programs and services only. When coupled with antivirus protection, that setting is usually adequate. You can crank it up to monitor all programs and services. But if you do, you might also have to individually choose programs that are allowed to bypass DEP. Knowing when that's okay may require technical expertise that goes beyond the scope of this book.

To get to options for DEP, first open the System window using whichever technique is most convenient:

- Click the Start button, right-click Computer, and choose Properties.
- Press ![ ], type **sys**, and click System under the Programs heading.

Regardless of the method used, you end up in the System window. In the left column, click Advanced System Settings. That takes you to the System Properties dialog box. In System Properties, click the Advanced tab, click the Settings button on the Performance heading, and then click the Data Execution Prevention tab. At last, you see the options shown in Figure 9-4.

FIGURE 9-4

Data Execution Prevention options.

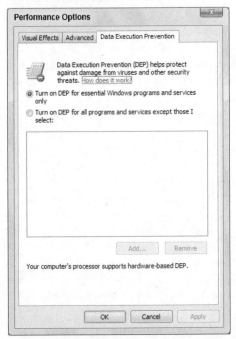

By default, the option to apply DEP to essential Windows programs and services only is selected. For stronger protection, you can turn on DEP for all programs and services. If you choose that option, DEP may sometimes shut down a program to prevent it from running.

Note

Many modern processors offer *NX technologies,* which prevent buffer overflows at the hardware level. When that's the case, Windows supports that hardware-based DEP. For processors that don't have hardware DEP, Windows uses DEP software to achieve the same result. ■

If DEP does shut down a program you need, you have a couple of choices. One is to contact the program manufacturer to find out whether there's a version of the program that runs under DEP. Otherwise, if you trust the program, you can add it to the list of programs that are allowed to bypass DEP. To accomplish that, you need to click the Add button and then navigate to and double-click the executable file (typically, such a file has the extension .exe) that DEP is shutting down.

Wrap-Up

When it comes to general computer security, the "big three" items are (1) a firewall, (2) malware protection, and (3) automatic updates. Chapters 7, 8, and 9 cover those topics. But don't forget that running under a standard user account (Chapter 3) counts, too. Furthermore, you have less technical, "social" threats to consider, such as phishing scams and pop-up ads. Those are covered in Chapters 16 and 18.

As far as this chapter goes, the main points are as follows:

- Automatic updates provide a quick and simple way to protect your computer against current software exploitation malware.

- Unless you have some compelling reason to do otherwise, you should allow Windows 7 to automatically download and install updates daily.

- Data Execution Prevention (DEP) offers yet another layer of protection against threats that work by sneaking errant code into sensitive parts of system memory.

Part III

Personalizing Windows 7

Everybody likes to have a choice. Most of the chapters in this section are about tweaking Windows 7 to look and act the way you want it to. Chapter 10 starts off with the main *look-and-feel* features and how you can customize them to your liking. Chapter 11 moves on to things you can do to adapt Windows 7 to a user's specific sensory and motor challenges, as well as spoken and written languages. You'll also discover the improved Speech Recognition in Windows 7 in Chapter 11.

Chapter 12 moves on to the topic of getting files from an old computer onto a new Windows 7 computer. Chapter 13 covers customization from the standpoint of how Windows 7, as well as other programs, start when you first fire up your computer.

Chapter 14 covers the handy accessory programs that come free with Windows 7. Chapter 15 looks at common customization problems and their solutions.

Personalizing Your Work Environment

T he Windows desktop is your main workplace. Or maybe *play place*, depending on how you use your computer. But the point is, your Windows desktop is similar to a real, wooden desktop. It's where you keep all the stuff you're using right now — the stuff that's *open*. Your hard disk and its folders, by comparison, are more like your filing cabinet, where you keep stuff you might need in the future.

We all like to set up our own desktop and work environment in unique ways. What works best for one person isn't necessarily great for someone else. Fortunately, the way things look and work on your Windows 7 desktop aren't set in stone. You can personalize your desktop and features in a variety of ways to make them look and work the way you like. That's what this chapter is all about — having your Windows environment set up your way.

Most of the options described in this chapter apply only to the user account you're currently logged in to, so any changes you make to your own desktop apply only to you (assuming that you're logged in to your own user account). This means that all users of a computer can have their settings just the way they want them without stepping on each others' toes.

IN THIS CHAPTER

Personalizing your screen, mouse, and keyboard

Customizing your Start menu

Personalizing your taskbar

Using Windows Sidebar and gadgets

Using the Personalization Page

Many options for personalizing the look and feel of Windows 7 are on the Personalization page shown in Figure 10-1. As with most aspects of Windows 7, you have many ways to get to the Personalization page. Use whichever is most convenient for you at the moment.

- Right-click the desktop and choose Personalize.
- Press ⊞ , type **pers**, and click Personalization.
- In Welcome Center, double-click Personalize Windows.
- Click the Start button and click Control Panel ➪ Appearance and Personalization ➪ Personalization.

FIGURE 10-1

Personalization page.

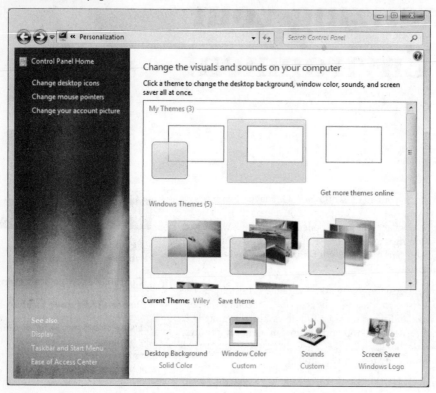

The sections to follow look at how you can use the various options on the page to fine-tune the look and feel of Windows 7 on your screen.

Choosing a theme

A theme is a collection of appearance settings that determine how things look on your screen. For example, Figure 10-2 shows how Windows 7 looks with the Windows 7 theme selected. Figure 10-3 shows how it looks with the Windows Classic theme selected to make the screen look more like Windows 98 or XP.

To choose a theme, open the Personalization window from the Control Panel. You see a selection of themes from which to choose. A good way to personalize your screen is to choose a theme that looks most like how you'd like your screen to look. You can certainly modify it to your preferences or even create your own custom themes. Starting with a predefined theme that has many of the characteristics you like, however, is a good way to get started.

FIGURE 10-2

Windows 7 theme.

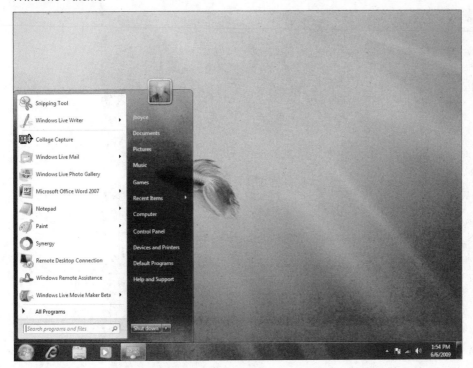

Transparency and Computer Performance

When choosing a color scheme, you might see a warning about transparency affecting your computer's performance. Applying transparency on a computer screen takes a significant number of mathematical calculations. If your computer doesn't have the hardware horsepower to do the task instantly, you might experience a general slowdown in computer performance when you enable transparency. It shouldn't be an issue with newer computers that are specifically designed to run Windows 7.

To try a theme, just click the theme in the Personalization page. The theme is applied to your desktop. If you don't like the results, just click another theme or your previous theme.

Tip
Themes that use Aero Glass have a transparent square at the bottom-left corner of the theme sample. ∎

FIGURE 10-3

Windows Classic theme.

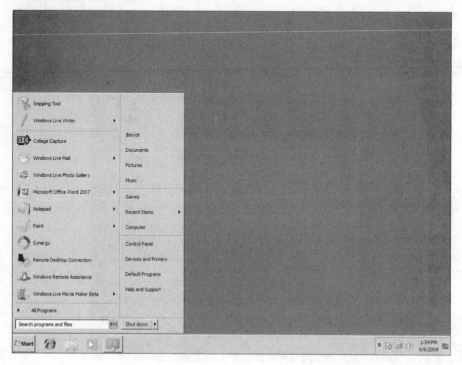

Feel free to try out as many themes as you like. If you plan to further customize things, click Save As. Then enter a name for the theme and click Save.

Tip

You can create as many custom themes as you like. Just remember to give each one a unique name when you save it. ■

Aero Glass Requirements in Depth

To use Aero Glass (which provides window transparency and other cool graphics features), you need a Direct X 9 or higher class graphics processor that supports WDDM, 32 bits per pixel, and Pixel Shader 2.0 in hardware. The graphics card needs at least 64MB of graphics memory, but 256MB of graphics memory (or better) is preferred, especially for higher-resolution displays.

Many newer graphics cards meet all those requirements. But onboard graphics chips rarely do. If you're thinking of adding a graphics card to your system to get all the visual bells and whistles, look for a card that's Windows 7 compatible. You'll also need to get a card that fits in an available slot on your motherboard. If you don't know what slots are available on your motherboard or aren't comfortable installing hardware, your best bet is to take the system to a professional. Tell him or her that you're looking to upgrade your graphics display to full Windows 7 graphics capabilities. A professional can advise you about cards you can purchase and estimates for installation.

Personalizing your desktop background

You can *wallpaper* your desktop with any picture or color you like. In the Personalization window, click Desktop Background to open the Desktop Background page, shown in Figure 10-4.

FIGURE 10-4

The Desktop Background page.

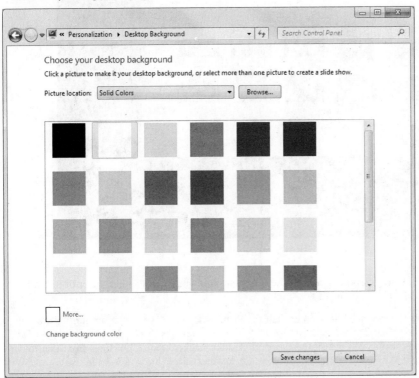

Click the drop-down button and choose Solid Colors to choose a solid-color background for the desktop. Or choose Pictures Library to view pictures from your own Pictures folder and from the shared

Public Pictures folder (Figure 10-5). Of course, if these folders are empty or don't contain any compatible picture types, you won't see any pictures after making your selection. After you choose a category, point to or click any picture to see it applied as your desktop background.

FIGURE 10-5

Choose a desktop background.

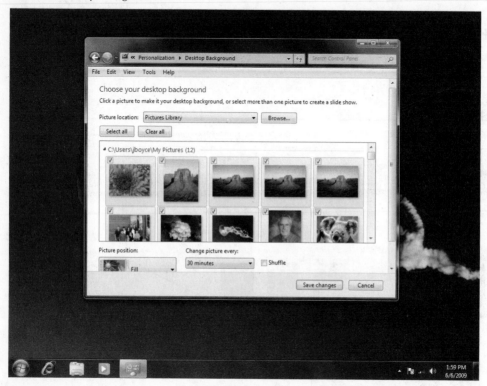

The Top Rated Photos option lets you choose from photos in your own Pictures folder or in the Public Pictures folder that have a rating of 4 or higher.

If you have pictures in some folder other than the Pictures folder for your user account or the Public Pictures folder, click Browse. Navigate to the folder that contains those pictures. Then click (or double-click) the picture you want to use as your desktop background. All pictures from that folder will appear in the Desktop Background window. Click whatever picture you want to use.

If the desktop is covered, hover the mouse over the Show Desktop button at the lower-right corner of the screen to make all windows invisible and show the desktop. Try out different pictures until you find one you like.

You might have noticed that you can choose more than one picture for your desktop. The option Change Picture Every lets you choose how often Windows displays a new desktop picture. Enable the Shuffle option if you want the photos to be shown randomly from the selected group.

Try the options under Picture Position to view it in different ways. The options will have little or no effect on large pictures. But if you choose a small picture of your own, the Tile option will show it repeatedly, like tiles. The Center option will show it centered on the screen. If you choose the Center option, you can click Change Background Color to color the desktop surrounding the picture.

If you don't want a picture on your desktop, choose Solid Colors from the drop-down list. Then click whatever color you like. Or click More for a wider selection of colors. When you've found and chosen a picture or color you like, click Save Changes.

Personalizing your color scheme

To choose a basic color scheme for your screen and selected theme, click Window Color in the Personalization window. If you're using Aero Glass and a theme that uses it, you'll see the options shown in Figure 10-6.

FIGURE 10-6

Change your color scheme.

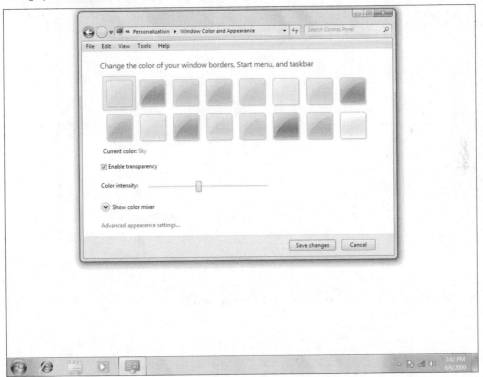

Most of the options are self-explanatory. Click any color sample to apply that color to your windows. Select the Enable Transparency check box to enable or disable the transparency effect on window borders. Use the Color Intensity slider to adjust the amount of color used.

Transparency and Computer Performance

When choosing a color scheme, you might see a warning about transparency affecting your computer's performance. Applying transparency on a computer screen takes a significant number of mathematical calculations. If your computer doesn't have the hardware horsepower to do the task instantly, you might experience a general slowdown in computer performance when you enable transparency. This shouldn't be an issue, however, with newer computers that are specifically designed to run Windows 7.

If you want to create your own colors, click Show Color Mixer to see the additional sliders shown in Figure 10-7. You can use those to create your own color.

FIGURE 10-7

Color mixer sliders.

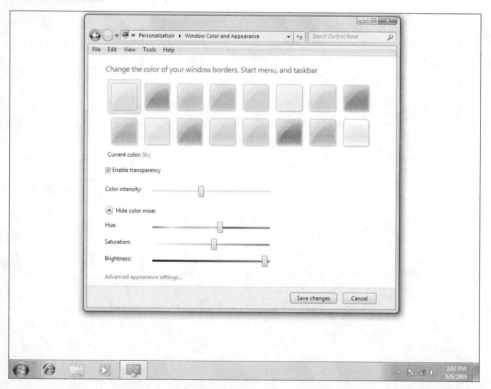

Before you start creating a color, you might find it useful to drag the Intensity slider to the middle or far right end of the bar and deselect the Enable Transparency check box. Also, drag the Saturation and Brightness sliders to the middle. Doing so will make it easier to see your color selection on the window's border.

Drag the Hue slider along the rainbow bar until you find a color you like. Move the Saturation slider to adjust, deepen, or fade your selected color. Use the Brightness slider to brighten or darken the color. You can also enable transparency and adjust the intensity as you go. Just keep playing around with things until you get a color you like.

Making text sharper with ClearType

ClearType is a technology that makes fonts look clearer and smoother on a display. ClearType is particularly effective for LCD displays but can have some effect on CRT displays as well. Windows 7 supports ClearType.

To adjust ClearType on your Windows 7 computer, first open the Control Panel. Then, click Display and click Adjust ClearType Text. You can also press ![win], type **clear**, and click Adjust ClearType Text. The ClearType Text Tuner appears (Figure 10-8).

FIGURE 10-8

ClearType Text Tuner.

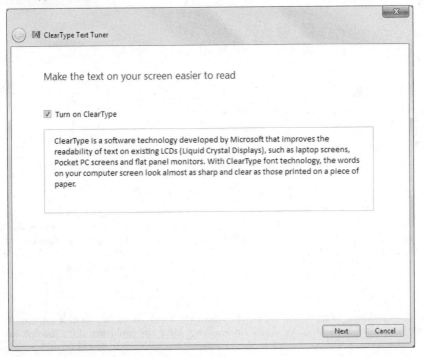

The ClearType Text Tuner is a wizard that steps you through a couple of settings to fine-tune font display on your computer. Select the Turn on ClearType check box and then click Next. Windows 7 checks your computer's display resolution and offers to change resolution to the display native resolution or keep the current resolution. Choose the desired option and click Next. Windows 7 then displays four pages with different text samples, prompting you to choose the ones that look the best to you. Click Finish when you're satisfied with your selections.

Changing individual screen elements

Clicking the Advanced Appearance Settings button in the Window Color and Appearance page takes you to the Window Color and Appearance dialog box, shown in Figure 10-9. You should take care when changing settings in this dialog box. People have been known to do crazy things in this dialog box, such as set everything to the same color and then wonder why they can't see anything on their screen. (They can't see anything because when everything is exactly the same color, the screen is basically one big blob of whatever color they choose.)

FIGURE 10-9

Windows Color and Appearance dialog box.

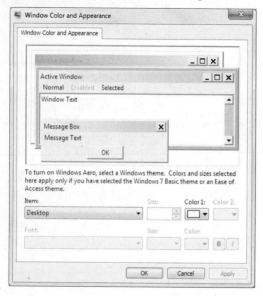

In case you feel savvy or daring enough to tackle these Advanced Appearance options, here's how they work. First, you choose an item from the Item drop-down button. Controls that apply to that item are instantly enabled. Controls that don't apply are disabled. From the enabled options, you can choose colors and fonts, as applicable. Your choices are reflected in the preview above the buttons.

Caution

You definitely don't want to experiment or try things out for the heck of it in Advanced Appearance options. If you plan to use these options to solve some problem, don't. They will not solve any problems. If it's too late for that and you've already made a mess of things, go back to the Theme Settings dialog box described earlier and choose a different theme. ■

Personalizing sound effects

You might have noticed some little beeps and whistles as you do things in Windows 7. Those are called *sound effects,* and you can customize those from the Personalization window. Just click Sounds to open the Windows Sounds dialog box, shown in Figure 10-10.

FIGURE 10-10

Windows Sounds dialog box.

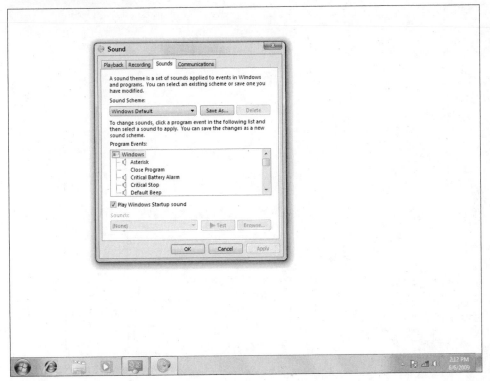

If you don't want to assign sound effects one at a time, you can choose a predefined sound effects scheme from the Sound Scheme drop-down list. Or choose No Sounds if you don't want any sound effects.

The Program Events list shows different events to which you can assign sounds. Items that have a speaker icon to the left already have a sound effect associated with them. To hear one, click any program event that shows a speaker icon. The Sounds drop-down menu below the list shows the filename in which the sound effect is stored. Click the Play button to the right of the sound effect name to hear that sound effect.

Sound effects play only when your computer has a sound card with speakers plugged into the correct jack. If the speakers have their own power switch, they must be turned on. Likewise, if the speakers have their own volume control, the volume must be turned up high enough. And if the speakers have a Mute button, it must be turned off. Likewise, the volume control in the Notification area must have its volume set to a level you can hear and must not be muted, as in Figure 10-11.

Getting back to the Windows Sounds dialog box, you can assign any sound effect you like to any program event. First, click the program event to which you would like to assign or change a sound effect. Then click the drop-down button under Sounds to see a list of built-in sound effects. Click the sound effect you'd like to assign. Then click the Play button to hear that sound effect.

FIGURE 10-11

Windows volume control.

If you have your own sound effect to assign to a program event, click the Browse button and navigate to the folder that contains your sound effects. Then double-click the sound effect you want to assign to the program event.

Tip

Some good Web sites for downloading sound effects include www.ilovewavs.com, www.frogstar.com/wav/effects.asp, and www.partnersinrhyme.com/pir/PIRsfx.shtml. ■

If you change the sound effects associated with program events, you'll want to save all that work as your own sound scheme. Click the Save As button and give the scheme a name.

Personalizing your screen saver

A screen saver is a moving picture or pattern that fills the screen after a period of inactivity. The name screen saver harkens back to the olden days when leaving a fixed image on the screen for too long a time could cause permanent damage to the screen. This type of burn-in can still be a problem with CRT displays, but isn't a problem with LCD displays. So, a screen saver is typically optional nowadays. Still, it's a nice way to have your screen do something entertaining when the computer is on but nobody is using it. Plus, it can be a way to protect your computer from prying eyes when you walk away from it. Better still, lock your workstation before you leave.

In the Personalization window, click Screen Saver. The Screen Saver Settings dialog box shown in Figure 10-12 opens. Click the drop-down button to see a list of screen savers from which you can choose. Click any name in that list to get a sneak peek at how it will look if you apply it.

FIGURE 10-12

Screen Saver Settings dialog box.

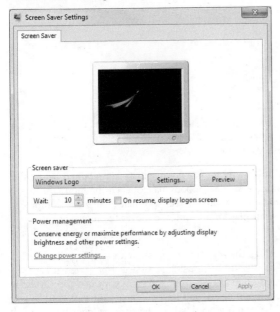

Some screen savers are customizable. Click the Settings button to see whether the screen saver you selected has optional settings you can change. If it does, you'll see those options in a dialog box. Choose whatever options look interesting.

If you have pictures in Photo Gallery, choose Photos from the drop-down button. The screen saver will be a slide show of pictures from your gallery. If you choose Photos from the drop-down list, you can also click the Settings button to see the options shown in Figure 10-13.

Tip

For the goods on photos and Photo Gallery, drop by Chapter 23. ■

As you can see in Figure 10-13, the default setting is for the screen saver to show all pictures and videos from your Pictures library, which includes your own Pictures folder and the Public Pictures folder. You can click Browse to choose a different location, if desired.

Use the Slide Show Speed drop-down button to choose the slide show speed, and choose the Shuffle Pictures option to have Windows randomize the photo selection. Click Save after making your choices.

FIGURE 10-13

Photo slide show options.

Regardless of which screen saver and settings you choose, the small preview window in the dialog box shows you how it will look. For a larger view, click the Preview button. Your selected screen saver will play full screen. To make it stop, just move your mouse.

After you've chosen your screen saver, specify how many minutes of inactivity are required before the screen saver starts playing. A period of inactivity means that nobody has touched the mouse or keyboard. So if you set the Wait option to five minutes, the screen saver will kick in after the computer has been unused for five minutes. The screen saver plays until someone moves the mouse or presses a key on the keyboard.

Choosing On Resume, Display Logon Screen causes the screen saver to show the login page rather than your desktop when someone moves the mouse. If you're using a password-protected user account, showing the login page will prevent that other person from accessing your desktop. It also means that when *you* want to start using the computer again, you have to enter your password to get back to your desktop. Your programs will still be running, so this isn't the same as logging out and logging back in again.

The screen saver won't kick in at all if your power options are set to turn off the monitor before the screen saver kicks in. The Change Power Settings link in the dialog box lets you check, and optionally change, when the monitor goes off.

For example, the Power Save plan turns off the monitor after 20 minutes. If you set the screen saver to kick in after 21 or more minutes, you'll never see the screen saver, because the monitor will be off. If you prefer the screen saver to an empty screen, make sure to set the screen saver timeout to a shorter time period than your screen power-off setting.

Tip

See "The Power Settings" in Chapter 49 for more information on using Power Options. ∎

When you're happy with your screen saver selections, click OK. Remember, the screen saver won't actually play until you've left the computer alone and untouched for the number of minutes you specified in the Wait box on the Screen Saver Settings dialog box.

Personalizing desktop icons

In the left column of the Personalization window, you see a link titled Change Desktop Icons. Click that link to see the dialog box shown in Figure 10-14. Select the check boxes for any icons you want to see on your desktop. Deselect the check box for any icon you don't want to see. As always, choosing icons is purely a matter of personal taste. Also, you can change the icons you see on your desktop at any time. Click OK after choosing the icons you want to see.

Desktop icon settings.

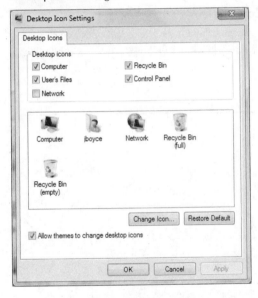

Creating your own desktop icons

The Desktop Icons Settings dialog box shows only the few desktop icons built into Windows 7. Many programs you install create other desktop icons. You're also free to create your own desktop icons. Most desktop icons are actually just *shortcuts* to other places or programs.

Shortcut icons are unique in a couple of ways. For one, they show a little curved arrow like the example in Figure 10-15. For another, deleting a shortcut icon has no effect on the item that the shortcut opens. Instead, deleting a shortcut icon deletes only the icon. The program or folder to which the icon referred still exists. You can still open that item through a non-shortcut method.

If you often go through a series of clicks or steps to open some item, creating a desktop shortcut will make opening that item quicker and easier. Get to the icon you normally click (or double-click) to open a program, folder, or document. Then right-click that icon and choose Send To ⇨ Desktop (Create Shortcut).

Tip
To copy a desktop shortcut icon to the Start menu, drag and drop it onto the Start button. ∎

FIGURE 10-15

FIGURE 10-15

Sample shortcut icon.

Sizing, arranging, showing, and hiding desktop icons

You can size and arrange desktop icons as you see fit. First, minimize or close all open program windows so that you can see the entire desktop. Then right-click any empty area on the desktop and hover the mouse over the View menu.

FIGURE 10-16

View submenu.

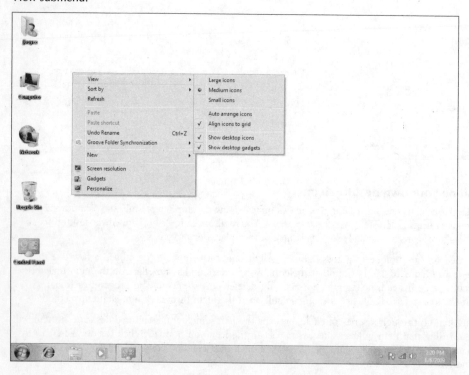

The View submenu, shown in Figure 10-16, contains several options for arranging icons. An item on that menu that has a checkmark is currently selected and active. An item without a checkmark is deselected and inactive. Clicking an item selects it if it's not already selected, or deselects it if it is selected. Here's what each option does:

- **Large Icons:** Shows desktop icons at a large size.
- **Medium Icons:** Shows desktop icons at a medium size.
- **Small Icons:** Shows desktop icons at a smaller size, similar to earlier Windows versions.

Tip

If your mouse has a wheel, you can make desktop icons almost any size by holding down the Ctrl key as you spin the mouse wheel. ■

- **Auto Arrange Icons:** Choosing this option keeps icons neatly arranged near the left side of the desktop. If you clear this option, you can put desktop icons wherever you like. Just drag any icon to wherever you want to put it on the desktop.
- **Align Icons to Grid:** Choosing this option keeps icons aligned to an invisible grid, to make the spacing between them equal.
- **Show Desktop Items:** If this option is selected (checked), desktop icons are visible. Clearing this option makes the desktop icons invisible. It doesn't delete them, however. They'll come back into view when you choose this option again.

The Sort By option on the desktop shortcut menu lets you quickly sort icons by name, size, file extension, or date modified. Regardless of which option you choose, built-in icons are always listed first, followed by your own custom icons in whatever order you specified.

The remaining options are similar to their counterparts in folders. The Refresh option ensures that icons on the desktop are up-to-date with changes you may have made elsewhere in the system. If you accidentally delete a shortcut icon, you can choose Undo Delete (or press Ctrl+Z) to bring it back. The New option lets you create a new folder or document on the desktop. Personalize opens the Personalization page (refer to Figure 10-1).

Customizing icons

To change a built-in icon, open the Desktop Icon Settings dialog box, shown previously in Figure 10-14. Then click the icon you want to customize and click Change Icon. To change the appearance of a shortcut icon, right-click it and choose Properties ➪ Change Icon. The Change Icon dialog box opens, displaying possible alternative icons. Figure 10-17 shows a general example.

Note

Not all programs offer optional icons. If the Change Icon button is disabled, that means you can't change that particular icon. ■

If you have your own .ico files and would prefer to use one of those, click the Browse button in the Change Icon dialog box. Navigate to the folder that contains the .ico file and choose the icon you want to use. Note that many .dll and .exe files also contain icons you can use.

Tip

To explore programs that let you create your own icon pictures, search the Web for icon maker. To find pre-made icons that you can download, search the Web using the keywords download Windows icons. ■

FIGURE 10-17

Change Icon dialog box.

Choosing a screen resolution

One of the changes you might want to make in Windows is to adjust is your screen resolution, because your screen resolution determines how much stuff can fit on your screen. Resolution is measured in *pixels*, with each pixel representing a tiny, lighted dot on the screen. The pixels are too small to see individually. But suffice it to say that the higher the resolution, the smaller everything looks, and the more stuff you can get on the screen. To choose a resolution, right-click the desktop and choose Screen Resolution. Doing so opens the Screen Resolution page shown in Figure 10-18.

There is no right or wrong setting for the screen resolution. A high resolution is good because you can see more stuff on your screen. But a high resolution isn't good if things are so small on your screen that you can't see them. On the Screen Resolutions page, click the Resolution button and then move the slider from one resolution to the next. As you move the slider, you can see a sample of the *aspect ratio* of the current selection. You can't really judge how small things will look on your screen as you move the slider, so it may take a little trial and error to get things just right. But let's stop a second to talk about that *aspect ratio* term here.

Understanding aspect ratio

There was a time when all computer monitors had a 4:3 aspect ratio, which meant that for every 4 pixels of width, you got 3 pixels of height. These days, you'll come across other aspect ratios including 5:4 and the 16:9 ratio found on widescreen TVs. There are some others, too. You can check the manual that came with your monitor or notebook computer for your screen's exact aspect ratio. Or, just choose a resolution that looks good on your screen. Table 10-1 lists some common aspect ratios and resolutions that fit them.

FIGURE 10-18

Screen Resolution page.

TABLE 10-1

Common Aspect Ratios and Resolutions

Aspect Ratio	Shape	Resolutions that Fit
4:3		800 x 600, 1024 x 768, 1152 x 864, 1600 x 1200
5:4		1280 x 1024, 1600 x 1280
16:9		1088 x 612, 1280 x 720, 1600 x 900

Other Ways to Size On-Screen Elements

The resolution you choose sets only a basic default size for items on the screen. There are countless other ways to adjust the size of text, icons, and pictures on your screen, and they work no matter what resolution you choose. For example, holding down the Ctrl button while spinning your mouse wheel affects icon size. In Internet Explorer, you can click the Page button and choose Zoom or Text size to change the size of pictures and text on your screen.

Many programs have a View option in their menus that lets you zoom in and out of things to make them larger or smaller. DPI scaling and the Accessibility Settings described later in this chapter offer many options for making items larger and easier to see on-screen.

So, the trick here is to move the slider to a resolution (for example, 1024 x 768) and then click the Apply button. The new resolution is applied to your screen. If the screen goes blank, don't panic: You just chose a setting that won't work. The setting will be undone automatically in about 15 seconds and everything will be okay again. To try a different resolution, move the slider to another setting and click Apply again. If you find a setting you like, you can click OK and be done with it.

Using multiple monitors

Windows 7 supports the use of multiple monitors in a variety of configurations. In many cases, adding a second monitor is a simple matter of connecting to the external monitor and turning it on. If the device supports Extended Display Identification Data (EDID), Windows will detect the device and adjust the resolution automatically.

If the external monitor is a television set, you may need to connect, turn on the TV, and then use the Input Select or TV/Video button on the TV or remote control to select the external input (often shown as AV1 or Component on the TV screen). You can also add multiple video cards to the PC and connect a monitor to each one.

After you connect to an external monitor and configure it to show input from the plug to which you connected the computer (if necessary), you can configure settings in Windows for the displays. Right-click the desktop and choose Screen Resolution to display the Screen Resolution page shown in Figure 10-19.

The Screen Resolution page will show two displays after you connect the other display to the computer. The displays are identified by the numbers 1 and 2. The graphics on the displays indicate which is the primary (that is, where the Start menu will appear) and which is the secondary. Click the Identify button to have Windows display a large number on the display to help you identify which is which.

The following list explains the controls on the Screen Resolution page:

- **Display:** Use this drop-down button to choose a display to configure.
- **Resolution:** Select the display resolution from this slider button.
- **Orientation:** Choose between Landscape and Portrait modes, as well as Landscape (Flipped) and Portrait (Flipped) modes (which rotate the display).
- **Multiple Displays:** Choose Duplicate These Displays to display the same information on both displays. Choose Extend These Displays to extend the desktop across both displays. The other two options show the desktop only on display 1 or 2, depending on which you select.

FIGURE 10-19

Display settings with two monitors working.

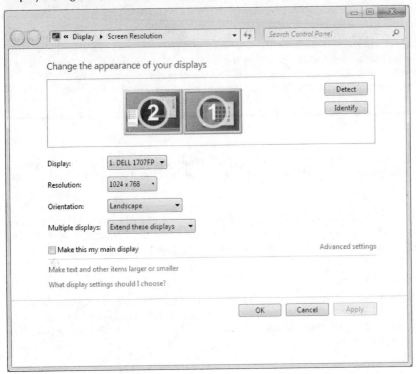

- **Make This My Main Display:** Select this option to make the display number selected in the Display button the main display where the Start menu will appear.

- **Detect:** Click this button to have Windows detect the new display.

- **Identify:** Click this button to display an identifying number on the displays so that you can tell which is which.

- **Make Text and Other Items Larger or Smaller:** Click this link to open a Display page, where you can choose the font size to use on the displays.

Tip

Extending Microsoft Excel across two monitors lets you see twice as many columns! ∎

You can also display content on the second monitor only, leaving the first monitor black. If you're using a mobile computer on batteries, this option conserves battery power.

Regardless of how you set things in the New Display Detected window (or even if it doesn't appear at all), you can use the Display Settings dialog box to configure the second monitor. Open Display Settings as described at the top of this section. Then click the second monitor's box (with the number 2 in it). If that second monitor is grayed out, choose Extend My Desktop Onto This Monitor. If the second monitor still doesn't light up, click Apply.

More Stuff You Can Do with Monitors

Your monitor attaches to a graphics card or graphics chip inside your computer. That card or chip defines the full range of your visual display. Windows 7 might not give you access to the full range of settings available to you, even after you click the Advanced Settings button.

To take full advantage of your graphics card's (or chip's) capabilities, you may want to use the configuration program that came with that device. There are hundreds of such devices on the market, and no rule that applies to them all. To fully understand the capabilities of your graphics card and the programs for using it, refer to the manual that came with the card or your computer.

Note

If you can't get the second monitor to work, make sure it's properly connected and turned on. If the second monitor is a TV, make sure you choose the right input setting using Input Select or TV/Video on the TV or its remote control. ■

You can arrange the squares in the dialog box to match the arrangement of the monitors. For example, if monitor 2 is to the left of monitor 1, drag the 2 square to the left of the 1 square. If the monitors are stacked with 1 on top of 2, drag the 1 square so that it's above the 2 square.

Reducing monitor flicker

If a monitor seems to flicker, adjusting its refresh rate can help. You shouldn't change the refresh rate just for the heck of it, though. Do so only to reduce flicker. First, click the Advanced Settings link. Then click the Monitor tab in the dialog box that opens. Use the drop-down under Screen Refresh Rate to try a higher setting.

Caution

Don't deselect the Hide Modes That This Monitor Cannot Display check box. Doing so will allow you to choose settings that could damage the monitor! ■

After you choose a new refresh rate, click Apply. The monitor might go blank for a few seconds. When it comes back on, see whether the situation has improved. If not, you can try another refresh rate (followed by a click on the Apply button) until you find an optimal setting. When you find the best setting, click OK to close the Advanced Settings dialog box.

Don't forget to click OK after adjusting settings in the Display Settings dialog box. Remember: The settings you choose aren't set in concrete. You can re-open that dialog box and change things any time you like.

Adjusting the font size (DPI)

Windows 7 lets you change the size of text and other items on the display, which can be particularly useful for high-resolution displays, making the screen more readable (which becomes more important the older I get!). To change text size, open the Display item from the Control Panel. Or, right-click the desktop, choose Screen Resolution, and then click Make Text and Other Items Larger or Smaller. Figure 10-20 shows the resulting page, where you can choose among the sizes 100%, 125%, and 150%.

FIGURE 10-20

The Display page.

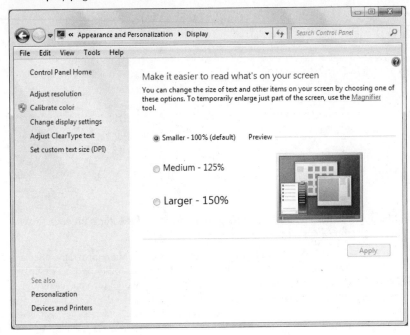

When you change the text size using the Display page, you have to log out and log back in for the change to take effect. (You don't need to restart the computer.)

In addition to setting text size as described previously, you can also choose a custom DPI setting. Here's how:

1. Close all open programs and log in to a user account that has administrative privileges.

2. Open the Display item from the Control Panel, or open the Personalization window (right-click the desktop and choose Personalize); then click Display in the left pane.

3. Click Set Custom Text Size (DPI) to open the Custom DPI Setting dialog box, shown in Figure 10-21.

4. To make text a different size, choose a setting (for example, 125%) from the drop-down list. Or you can also click and drag left or right in the ruler to change the size up to 500 percent.

5. Click OK.

Note

Be careful to increase the current percentage value only slightly. Otherwise, you might make things so huge that hardly anything fits on the screen. ■

6. Click Apply and then click Log Off Now or Log Off Later, depending on whether you want to apply the change now or wait until the next time you log in.

FIGURE 10-21

DPI Scaling dialog box.

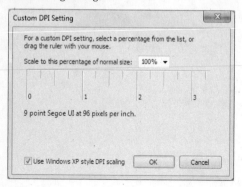

The new setting will be applied after you log out and log back in again. If the items on your screen are too large, repeat the preceding steps, choosing a smaller size in Step 4.

Adjusting the font size DPI isn't the only way to enlarge text on the screen. Many programs offer a Zoom option on their View menus that enables you to resize text. The Accessibility options described later in this chapter also offer some alternatives. But if nothing else really works for you, using the Adjust Font Size (DPI) setting might be your best bet.

Personalizing your mouse

If you grow tired of the same old mouse pointer, or need to make your mouse pointer easier to see, click the Change Mouse Pointers link in the Personalization window. You see the Mouse Properties dialog box with the Pointers tab selected, as shown in Figure 10-22.

To change your mouse pointers, choose a Scheme from the drop-down menu. The list under the Customize heading shows you how the pointers in that scheme look. You can keep all the mouse pointers in the scheme by clicking OK. Or you can assign a mouse pointer of your own choosing to any item. Double-click the pointer you want to change, or click it and click the Browse button. Clicking Browse takes you to a folder named Cursors, which contains all the built-in Windows 7 mouse pointers.

Tip

After you click Browse, you can enlarge the mouse pointer icons in the Browse dialog box for a better look. Hold down the Ctrl key and spin your mouse wheel. Or click the Views button and choose Medium icons or a larger size. ■

If you do assign mouse pointers on a case-by-case basis, click the Save As button to save your selections as a theme with any name you like.

Tip

Don't forget that most dialog box options aren't actually applied until you click the Apply or OK button. ■

FIGURE 10-22

Pointers tab in Mouse Properties.

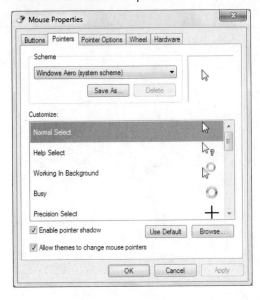

Mice for lefties

If you're left-handed and you want the main mouse button to be below your left index finger, you need to reverse the normal functioning of the buttons. Generally, the left mouse button is the primary button, and the right mouse button is the secondary button. To reverse that setup, first click the Buttons tab in the Mouse Properties dialog box so that you see the options shown in Figure 10-23. Then select the Switch Primary and Secondary Buttons check box.

If you do reverse your mouse buttons, you have to adjust all the standard mouse terminology accordingly. Table 10-2 shows how the various mouse terms apply to right-handed and left-handed settings.

Adjusting the double-click speed

To double-click an icon, you have to tap the primary mouse button twice very quickly. Otherwise, it counts as two single clicks. If it's difficult to tap the button quickly enough, or if you're so fast that two single clicks are being interpreted as a double-click, adjust the Double-click speed slider on the Buttons tab of the Mouse Properties dialog box.

Tip
To do away with the need to double-click anything, switch to single-clicking in the Folder Options dialog box. Tap ▦ , type **fol**, and choose Folder Options for that dialog box. Or see "To click or double-click" in Chapter 28 for details. ∎

To test your current setting, double-click the folder icon. If the closed folder doesn't change to an open one (or vice versa), you didn't double-click fast enough. Move the slider box toward the Slow end of the scale and try again. When the slider is at a place where it's easy to open/close the little folder next to the slider, that's a good setting for you.

FIGURE 10-23

Buttons tab in Mouse Properties.

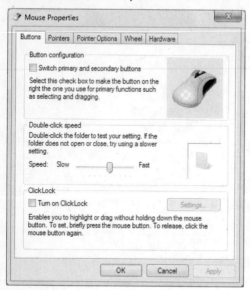

TABLE 10-2

Mouse Terminology for Righties and Lefties

Standard Terminology	Righties	Lefties
Primary button	Left	Right
Secondary button	Right	Left
Click	Left button	Right button
Double-click	Left button	Right button
Drag	Left button	Right button
Right-click	Right button	Left button
Right-drag	Right button	Left button

Using ClickLock

If you find it difficult to select multiple items by dragging the mouse pointer through them, you may want to try activating the ClickLock feature. Enabling that feature lets you select multiple items without holding down the mouse button. First you need to choose Turn On ClickLock on the Buttons tab of the Mouse Properties dialog box. Then, use the Settings button to specify how long you need to hold down the primary mouse button before the key is "locked."

For example, say that you turn on ClickLock and set the required delay to about one second. To drag the mouse pointer through some items, you position the mouse pointer to where you plan to start selecting and hold down the mouse pointer for one second. Then, you can release the mouse button and move the mouse pointer through the items you want to select. Those items will be selected as though you were actually holding down the left mouse button.

When you've finished selecting, just click some area outside the selection. The mouse pointer returns to its normal function, and the items you selected remain selected.

Speed up or slow down the mouse pointer

Clicking the Pointer Options tab in the Mouse Properties dialog box reveals the options shown in Figure 10-24. The first option, Select a Pointer Speed, controls how far the mouse pointer on the screen moves relative to how far you move the mouse with your hand. If you find it difficult to zero in on small things on your screen, drag the slider to the Slow end of the scale. If you feel you have to move the mouse too much to get from one place to another on the screen, move the slider toward the Fast end of the scale.

FIGURE 10-24

Pointer Options tab in Mouse Properties.

Selecting Enhance Pointer Precision makes it easier to move the mouse pointer short distances. It's especially useful if you move the pointer speed slider to the Fast side of the scale.

Tip
The Accessibility options described in Chapter 11 also let you control the behavior of your mouse. ■

Making the mouse pointer more visible

If you keep losing sight of the mouse pointer on your screen, the remaining pointer options can make it easier to find, as follows:

- **Snap To:** If selected, this causes the mouse pointer to jump to the default button (typically the OK button) automatically as soon as the dialog box opens.

- **Display Pointer Trails:** If selected, this causes the mouse pointer to leave a brief trail when you move it, making it easier to see the pointer.

- **Show Location of Pointer When I Press the CTRL Key:** If you select this option, you can easily locate the mouse pointer on your screen by holding down the Ctrl key.

Tip

When you use a projector to give a demonstration on-screen, turn on the pointer trails to make following the mouse across the screen easier for your audience. ■

Yet another way to make your mouse pointer more visible is to use a large or animated mouse pointer.

Changing mouse wheel behavior

The Wheel tab in the Mouse Properties dialog box lets you control how far you scroll when spinning the mouse wheel. The default is usually three lines per notch. But you can change that to any value from one to 100 lines. Optionally, you can configure the wheel to move an entire page with each notch.

Note

The Hardware tab in Mouse Properties shows information about your mouse and provides a means to manually update the mouse driver should the need ever arise. ■

Don't forget to click OK after making your selection in the Mouse Properties dialog box.

That wraps it up for options in the Control Panel's Personalization page. But as you'll see in the sections to follow, there are many more things you can do to tweak Windows 7 to better suit your needs and tastes.

Personalizing the Keyboard

There are a few things you can do to change how the keyboard works. Some are in the Keyboard Properties dialog box, which I cover here. Others come under the heading of accessibility, a topic I address in Chapter 12. To get to the Keyboard Properties dialog box, use whichever of the following methods is easiest for you:

- Press ⊞ , type **key**, and click Keyboard under Programs.

- Click the Start button and choose Control Panel, the arrow to the right of Control Panel in the breadcrumb, and choose All Control Panel Items. Then, click Keyboard.

The Keyboard Properties dialog box, shown in Figure 10-25, opens.

The options in Keyboard Properties are as follows. As always, there is no right or wrong setting. It's all a matter of choosing settings that suit your typing style:

- **Repeat Delay:** Determines how long you have to hold down a key before it starts autotyping (repeating itself automatically).

FIGURE 10-25

Keyboard Properties dialog box.

- **Repeat Rate:** Determines how fast the key types automatically while you're holding it down.
- **Cursor Blink Rate:** Determines how rapidly the cursor blinks in a document.

If your keyboard offers programmable buttons, you may not see any options in the Keyboard Properties dialog box for defining those keys. More likely, you'll need to install and use the program that came with the keyboard to define the keys. There is no "one rule fits all" for that sort of thing. The only places to get the information you need are from the instructions that came with the keyboard and the keyboard manufacturer's Web site.

Note
See "Creating Custom Shortcut Keys," later in this chapter, for tips on launching favorite programs from your keyboard. ∎

Personalizing the Start Menu

The Start button is the gateway to every program currently installed on your computer. The Start menu also provides easy access to commonly used folders such as Documents, Computer, Control Panel, and any others you care to add. As a rule, you want the Start menu to contain items you use frequently so that you can get to those items without navigating through too many submenus.

The Windows 7 menu is split into two columns with icons for programs on the left and icons for folders and other places on the right. The left side of the menu is split into two groups. Icons above the horizontal line are *pinned* to the menu, meaning that they never change unless you change them. Beneath the horizontal line are icons that represent programs you use frequently. Those latter icons change frequently to reflect programs you use frequently. Figure 10-26 shows a sample Start menu.

FIGURE 10-26

Windows 7 Start menu.

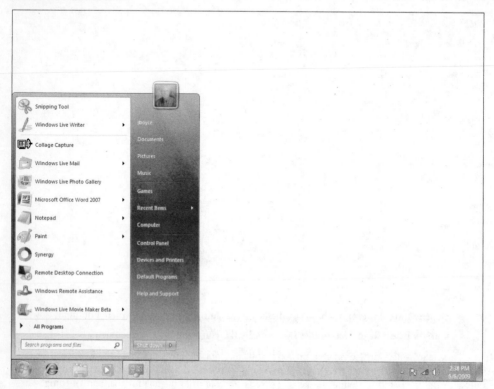

Opening taskbar and Start Menu properties

Use the Start Menu tab of the Taskbar and Start Menu Properties dialog box to personalize the appearance of your Start menu and some of the options it displays. As always, you have a few ways to open that dialog box. Use whichever is most convenient for you:

- Right-click the Start button and choose Properties.
- Click the Start menu, type **sta**, and click Taskbar and Start Menu.
- Click the Start button and choose Control Panel ➪ Appearance and Personalization ➪ Customize the Start menu.

When the dialog box opens, click the Start Menu tab to see the options shown in Figure 10-27.

The Power button action drop-down list lets you specify what action the Power button (at the bottom right of the Start menu) shows. By default, the Power button shows Shut Down, but if you usually only log out of your computer rather than shut it down, you might want to instead choose Log Off or Lock.

Under the Privacy heading, you can choose or clear the following items. But note that if your user account is password-protected, privacy isn't really an issue because no other users (other than administrators) can see your Start menu.

FIGURE 10-27

Start Menu tab in Taskbar and Start Menu Properties dialog box.

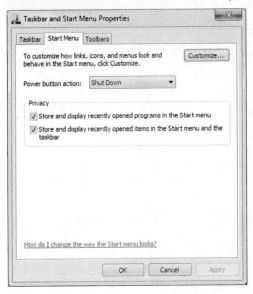

- **Store and Display Recently Opened Programs in the Start Menu:** If you deselect this option, the left side of the Start menu will not show icons for recently used programs.

- **Store and Display Recently Opened Items in the Start menu and the Taskbar:** If selected, this option displays a submenu beside programs on the Start menu with which you have recently opened documents. Clicking that submenu lists recently opened files for that program. That makes it really easy to re-open a file you've worked with recently.

Personalize the right side of the Start Menu

To choose other options for your Start menu, open the Start Menu properties tab as explained in the previous section and then click Customize. Figure 10-28 shows the Customize Start Menu dialog box. Items in the Customize Start Menu dialog box let you choose what appears on the right side of the menu.

Start menu folders

The list box contains options that control the appearance and behavior of your Start menu. Items on the menu that open folders give you these three options:

- **Display As a Link:** Choosing this option tells Windows to open the corresponding folder when you click the menu option. This is the most natural method after you're familiar with working in folders.

- **Display As a Menu:** Choosing this option tells Windows to show items within the folder as options on a menu, without opening the folder. This option is a reasonable alternative for folders that contain few icons but is unwieldy for folders that contain many icons.

FIGURE 10-28

Customize Start Menu dialog box.

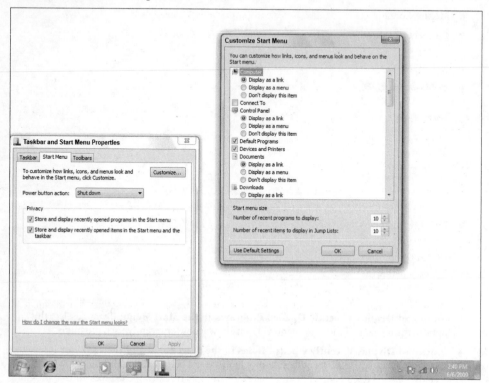

- **Don't Display This Item:** As it says, choosing this option prevents the option from being displayed at all on the right side of the Start menu.

Folders you can open directly from the Start menu are summarized in the following list. If you're new to all this and don't know what might be useful, set them all to Display As a Link. If you later discover that you don't need one, set it to Don't Display This Item.

- **Computer:** Contains icons for all your computer's disk drives. Useful for copying files to and from external disks and memory cards.
- **Control Panel:** Contains all the pages and dialog boxes for personalizing your system and for managing hardware and software.
- **Documents:** Stores all your private documents excluding digital media (pictures, music, video).
- **Downloads:** Stores your downloaded files.
- **Favorites:** Your Internet Explorer favorites.
- **Games:** A folder of saved games and scores. If you don't play computer games, set this one to Don't Display This Item.

- **Personal Folder:** Shows at the top right of the Start menu as your user name. Opening it reveals icons for all your private folders including your Favorites, Documents, Pictures, Music, Videos, Homegroup, Computer, and Network.

- **Music:** Contains songs in your Windows Media Player media library.

- **Pictures:** Contains photos and video clips from your digital camera, Photo Gallery, and any other resources you choose.

- **Recorded TV:** Contains TV programs you have recorded.

- **Videos:** Contains items from your Videos library.

Start menu places

Some check box items in the list box let you access other resources. Of course, all of them are optional. You should choose only those options you'll actually use. Here's a brief description of each and some suggestions:

- **Connect to:** Select this option only if you need to manually connect to a wireless, dial-up, or other connection often.

- **Default Programs:** It's unlikely you'd need to get to this often enough to warrant putting it in the Start menu. You can get to Default Programs through Control Panel or by clicking Start and typing **def**.

- **Favorites Menu:** Choose this option only if you keep track of favorites in Internet Explorer and your Links folder. If you don't use Favorites, this option won't get you much.

- **Help:** If selected, displays a Help and Support option on the right side of the Start menu. Because this is an important resource for information that everyone should learn to use, and use often, it's a good idea to select this option.

- **Network:** Choose this option if your computer is connected to a local network and you need access to shared resources often.

- **Recent Items:** Shows recently accessed items on the Start menu.

- **Run command:** Shows a Run option for more advanced users who run programs that don't have icons. If you don't choose this option, you can type the program name in the Search box and then click its name on the Start menu. Or type **run** in the Search box and click Run on the menu.

- **System Administrative Tools:** If selected, provides quick access to advanced tools often used by system and network administrators. You can choose to display this item on the All Programs menu only or on both the Start menu and All Programs menu. If you choose Don't Display This Item, you can still open Administrative Tools from Control Panel or by clicking the Start button and typing **adm**.

All Start Menu Items Are Shortcuts

Start menu icons are shortcuts, even though they don't show a shortcut arrow. That means when you remove or unpin a Start menu item, you don't lose the program, folder, or file that the item opens. In other words, deleting an icon from the Start menu doesn't delete the program, folder, or file that the item opens.

continued

continued

Therefore, you don't need to be shy about sticking things on the menu as convenient, and removing them as convenient. You can even change the name of an item on the Start menu without changing the actual item's name. Just right-click the item, choose Rename, and give it any name you like. The program, folder, or file that the item opens will retain its original name.

Start menu searching

Tip

Searches in Windows 7 are a huge improvement over searches in earlier versions of Windows. But you need to understand how searching works to take full advantage. See Chapters 30 and 31 for the whole story. ■

A few options in the Customize Start Menu dialog box center around searching. They're all selected by default. Here's what each one means:

- **Search Other Files and Libraries:** If you choose Don't Search, searches launched from the Search box won't include document files in the results. Choose Search with Public Folders to include the shared Public folders in the search, or choose Search Without Public Folders to exclude the shared Public folders from the search.

- **Search Programs and Control Panel:** If selected, searches launched from the Search box include programs and Control Panel items.

Start menu behavior

Some items in the Customize Start Menu list are concerned with how the menu behaves rather than what you see on the menu. Those options are as follows:

- **Enable Context Menus and Dragging and Dropping:** If selected, this allows you to rearrange icons on the All Programs menu by dragging them with the right mouse button, and open context menus for Start menu items.

- **Highlight Newly Installed Programs:** Choose this option to have Windows highlight the Start menu programs that have recently been installed. This helps you locate new programs more easily.

- **Sort All Programs Menu by Name:** Choosing this option keeps items on the Start menu in alphabetical order. Programs are listed first, followed by program groups (folders). If you don't choose this option, you can alphabetize those items by right-clicking any item on All Programs and choosing Sort By Name.

- **Use Large Icons:** Choosing this option displays the large icons on the Start menu. Clearing this option displays smaller icons, which makes room for more items on the menu.

The Number of Recent Programs To Display option dictates how many program icons can appear at the left side of the Start menu. If you set this number too high for your current screen resolution and icon size, you might see the "Some items cannot be shown" message when you click the Start button. The Number Of Recent Items To Display In Jump List option dictates how many recent items are shown in jump lists.

Clicking the Use Default Settings button resets the Start menu options and Number of Recent Programs To Display option back to their original settings.

Customizing the left side of the Start menu

Recall that items above the horizontal line are pinned to the menu and never change. Items below that line reflect programs you use often. So those items are likely to change over time.

Of course, you're never stuck with whatever happens to be on the left side of the Start menu. You can right-click any item, as in the example shown in Figure 10-29. Choose Remove From This List to remove an item. If an item isn't already pinned to the Start button, choose Pin To Start Menu to pin it.

FIGURE 10-29

Right-click a Start menu item.

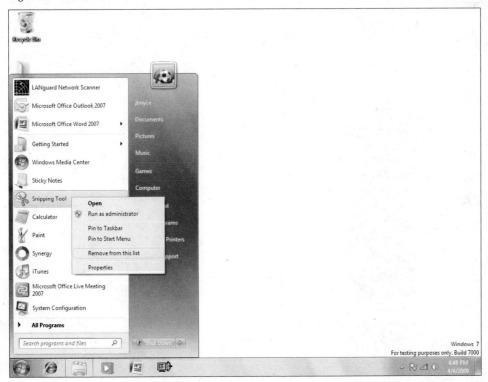

On the All Programs menu, you can right-click any program's icon and choose Pin To Start Menu. That's a quick and easy way to put the icon for a program you use often near the top of the Start menu.

If you use a folder often, you can pin its icon to the Start menu, too. For that matter, if you use a single document often, you can pin its icon to the Start menu as well. Just drag the file or folder icon and drop it right on the Start button. Similarly, you can pin a copy of any desktop shortcut icon to your Start menu. Again, just drag the desktop icon and drop it right on the Start button. To unpin an item from the top-left side of the Start menu, right-click its icon and choose Unpin From Start Menu.

Reorganizing the All Programs menu

The All Programs menu provides access to virtually all application programs installed on your system. Items at the top of the All Programs menu represent individual programs. Items marked with folder icons represent groups of programs. When you click a folder icon, it expands to show programs within that group.

Any program group can contain still more groups, with each group identified by a folder icon. Figure 10-30 shows an example in which I've opened a program group named Microsoft Office.

FIGURE 10-30

Microsoft Office and Tools program groups.

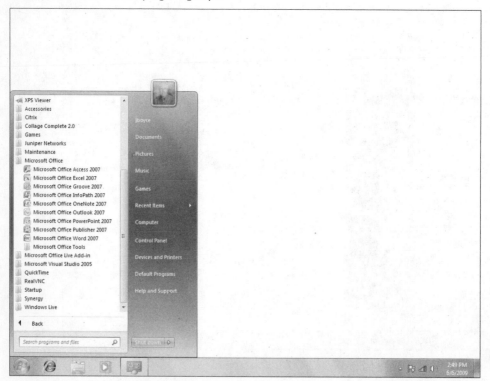

Note

Microsoft Office doesn't come free with Windows 7. It's a program you have to purchase separately. So don't be alarmed if you have no Microsoft Office group on your All Programs menu. I'm just using that as a general example. ■

You can move things around on the All Programs menu using the right mouse button, but doing so can be awkward. As an alternative, you can work in a more typical folder window. Right-click All Programs and choose one of the following options, depending on what you want to accomplish:

- **Open:** Opens a folder containing icons from the current user's Start menu.
- **Open All Users:** Opens a folder containing icons that appear on all users' Start menus.

Note
As always, you need administrative privileges to make any changes that affect all user accounts. ■

A folder named Start Menu opens. Its icons represent items that are on the Start menu. Within that Start Menu folder is a folder named Programs. When you open the Programs folder, you see icons that represent items on the All Programs menu. Any changes you make in that Programs folder are reflected in the All Programs menu.

For example, suppose you have half a dozen game programs on your All Programs menu. You'd like to group them into a single program group, perhaps named Other Games, on the All Programs menu. In the Programs folder, click the Organize button and choose New Folder. Name the folder Other Games. Then move the icons for the game programs into that folder.

Suppose you want to go the other way. Take all or some of the programs from the Microsoft Office group and copy them right onto the All Programs menu. Open the Microsoft Office folder in Programs and select the icons you want to move. Then press Ctrl+C to copy them. Click Programs in the breadcrumb menu to go back up to the Programs folder and press Ctrl+V to paste them. The pasted programs will be on the All Programs menu in addition to appearing in the Microsoft Office group.

Tip
If you prefer, you can press Ctrl+X to cut the items from a folder rather than copy them. ■

When you've finished making changes, close the Programs or Start Menu folder (whichever is open). Then click the Start button and choose All Programs. Any organizational changes you made in the Programs folder show up in the All Programs menu.

Creating Custom Shortcut Keys

Windows 7 offers many shortcut keys that you can use as an alternative to the mouse. They're summarized in Appendix C at the back of this book. Most programs also offer shortcut keys. Those you can discover by looking at pull-down menus or by searching that program's Help using the keywords "shortcut keys."

You can create your own custom shortcut keys for launching favorite programs or opening folders. By default, these custom keys will be a Ctrl+Alt+*key* combination to avoid conflicts with built-in shortcut keys. Also, they'll work only when you're on the desktop. That's because keystrokes apply only to the active window. So if any program window is open on the desktop, your keystrokes apply only to that window.

Tip

You can minimize all open windows to get to the desktop without losing your place in open program windows. Right-click an empty area of the taskbar or the clock and choose Show the Desktop. Or click the Show Desktop button at the far right edge of the taskbar. You can also press ⊞ +M to show the desktop. ■

Before you create a custom shortcut key, make sure it's not already assigned to something else. Get to the desktop and press the Ctrl+Alt+*key* combination you intend to use. If nothing opens, you know the shortcut is available. If something does open, you need to come up with a different shortcut key, or remove the shortcut key from the item to which it's currently assigned.

Tip

You can right-click programs in the Start menu and choose Properties to assign a shortcut key to the item. ■

You can assign a shortcut key to any item that offers a Shortcut Key option in its Properties dialog box. The easiest way, however, is to first create a desktop shortcut to the item. Then define the key in the desktop shortcut icon. So the first step is to get to the icon that opens the program or folder of interest. Then right-click that icon and choose Send To ➪ Desktop (Create Shortcut).

Note

If all your desktop icons are hidden, right-click an empty portion of the desktop and choose View ➪ Show Desktop Items. ■

Next, get to the desktop and locate the shortcut icon you just created. Right-click that icon and choose Properties. Click the Shortcut tab in the Properties sheet. Then click in the Shortcut Key box and type the letter you want to use as the shortcut. For example, Figure 10-31 shows that I typed the letter **C** in the Shortcut Key box for the Calculator shortcut's properties. Windows automatically added the Ctrl+Alt+ in front of that letter **C** I typed.

Click OK to close the dialog box. To test the shortcut, make sure you're at the desktop and then press the shortcut key combination. For example, pressing Ctrl+Alt+C after assigning the key combination just described opens Calculator.

There is one slight disadvantage to assigning the shortcut key in a shortcut icon. If you delete the shortcut icon from your desktop, you also delete the shortcut key. If that's a problem, you can hide, rather than delete, the desktop icon. Just right-click that icon and choose Properties. Click the General tab in the Properties dialog box and select the Hidden check box. Then click OK. The icon will disappear (or go dim) but the shortcut key will still work.

Whether hidden icons are dim or invisible depends on a setting in Folder Options. To get to that dialog box, click the Start button, type **fol**, and click Folder Options on the Start menu. Click the View tab in the dialog box. To make hidden icons invisible, choose Do Not Show Hidden Files and Folders. To make them visible but dim, choose Show Hidden Files and Folders. Click OK after making your selection.

Tip

You can open the Folder Options dialog box by clicking Organize ➪ Folder and Search Options with a folder window open. ■

FIGURE 10-31

Ctrl+Alt+C shortcut assigned to Calculator.

Customizing the Taskbar

The taskbar, which by default is at the bottom of your screen, is one of the most useful tools in Windows. It contains the Start button, a button for each open program window, and the Notification area. It can also contain some toolbars, such as the Address toolbar, which provides an easy way to open Web sites, drives, folders, or other items by their path or URL. You can customize the taskbar in many ways, so don't worry about what you see on yours right at this moment.

Some options for customizing the taskbar are in the Taskbar and Start Menu Properties dialog box. To open that dialog box, use whichever of the following techniques is easiest for you:

- Right-click the Start button, current time, or any empty spot on the taskbar and choose Properties.

- Tap 🗔 , type **task**, and click Taskbar and Start Menu.

- Click Start and choose Control Panel ➪ Appearance and Personalization ➪ Taskbar and Start Menu.

In the dialog box, click the Taskbar tab to see the options shown in Figure 10-32. The options on that tab are as follows:

- **Lock the Taskbar:** If you select this option, you lock the taskbar, which prevents you from accidentally moving or resizing it. If you want to move or resize the taskbar, you first need to deselect this option to unlock the taskbar.

193

FIGURE 10-32

Taskbar tab in the Taskbar and Start Menu Properties dialog box.

- **Auto-Hide the Taskbar:** If you select this icon, the taskbar automatically slides out of view when you're not using it, thereby freeing the little bit of screen space it takes up. After the taskbar hides itself, you can rest the tip of the mouse button on the thin line at the bottom of the screen to bring the taskbar out of hiding.

- **Use Small Icons:** Show small icons rather than the larger, default size icons for taskbar items.

- **Taskbar Location On Screen:** Choose on which edge of the display the taskbar will appear.

- **Taskbar Buttons:** Choose whether Windows combines similar items on the taskbar (such as documents for the same program), and whether it combines icons all the time or only when the taskbar is full.

- **Customize:** Click this button to specify which items appear in the Notification area of the taskbar (tray).

- **Use Aero Peek to Preview the Desktop:** Choose this option to make mini-versions of open program windows available from taskbar buttons. To see the preview of any open program window, point to its taskbar button, as in the example shown in Figure 10-33.

Click OK after making your selections from the dialog box. There are some other things you can do to customize the taskbar, outside that dialog box, as described next.

Locking and unlocking the taskbar

The taskbar doesn't have to be at the bottom of the screen. And it doesn't need to be a specific height, either. When the taskbar is unlocked, you can move and size it at will. If the taskbar is unlocked, putting the tip of the mouse pointer at the top of the taskbar changes the pointer to a two-headed arrow. Also, if you have any toolbars on the taskbar, you'll see a *dragging handle* (columns of dots) next to each toolbar. When you right-click an empty area of the taskbar or the current time, the Lock the Taskbar option on the menu is deselected (see Figure 10-34).

Preview window when pointing to a taskbar button.

If the taskbar is locked, just right-click an empty portion of the taskbar or the current time and click Lock the Taskbar to unlock. The option is a toggle, so you can use the same procedure to lock the taskbar when it's unlocked.

Moving and sizing the taskbar

When the taskbar is unlocked, you can dock it to any edge of the screen as follows:

1. Place the tip of the mouse pointer on an empty portion of the taskbar (not in a toolbar or on a button).

2. Hold down the left mouse button, drag the taskbar to any screen edge, and release the mouse button.

FIGURE 10-34

Unlocked taskbar.

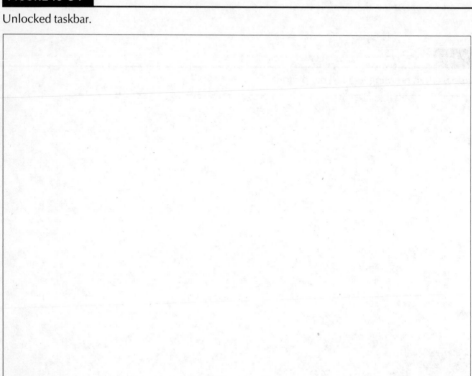

To change the height of the taskbar, put the tip of the mouse pointer on the top of the taskbar so that it changes to a two-headed arrow. Then hold down the left mouse button and drag up or down until the bar is at a height you like. The minimum height is one row tall. The maximum is about a third of the screen.

Tip

If you have any problem getting the taskbar back to the original one-row tall size, close all open toolbars. Then size the taskbar to the height you want and choose which toolbars you want to view. ■

If you want to hide the taskbar altogether, select the Auto-Hide the Taskbar option in the Taskbar and Start Menu Properties dialog box, described earlier in this chapter. The taskbar stays hidden until you move the mouse pointer to the edge of the screen where you placed the taskbar.

Showing toolbars on the taskbar

Windows 7 comes with some optional toolbars you can add to the taskbar or allow to float freely on the desktop. To show or hide a toolbar, right-click the clock in the lower-right corner of your screen or an empty part of the taskbar and choose Toolbars. You see the names of toolbars shown in Figure 10-35 and summarized here.

FIGURE 10-35

Show or hide optional toolbars.

- **Address:** Displays an Address bar like the one in your Web browser. Typing a URL into the bar will open your Web browser and the page at the URL.

- **Links:** Displays the contents of Internet Explorer's Links folder as a toolbar. See "Using the Links toolbar (Favorites Bar)," later in this chapter, for more information.

- **Tablet PC Input Panel:** Displays the handwriting recognition window used with tablet PCs. This one will likely appear jutting out from the side of your screen rather than in the taskbar.

- **Desktop:** Shows all the icons from your desktop in a condensed toolbar format.

Note
You might also see a Language Bar toolbar option. That one applies to multilanguage keyboards as discussed in the "Working with multiple languages" section in Chapter 11. ■

- **New Toolbar:** Create a custom toolbar containing icons from any folder you wish. For example, after choosing this option, click your User Account name in the New Toolbar dialog box and click OK. The new toolbar that appears will provide quick access to all your folders.

On the Toolbars menu, any toolbar that has a checkmark next to its name is "on" and visible in the taskbar. Any toolbar whose name isn't selected is hidden. Click a name to hide, or show, the toolbar.

When you first choose a custom toolbar, there may not be room for it on the taskbar, especially if the taskbar is already loaded up with buttons or other toolbars. The next section explains ways to deal with that.

Sizing and positioning taskbar toolbars

There isn't a lot of room on the taskbar, so it will get crowded if you add too many items to it. If you want a lot of optional toolbars to your taskbar, consider making it taller so that it can show more items. Try moving it to the side of the screen to see whether that helps.

Note

If you want to stretch the taskbar across more than one display, check out UltraMon at www.ultramon.com. This very cool utility adds lots of features for multiple displays. ■

When you have more items on a toolbar than it can show, you see a >> symbol at the right side of the toolbar. Clicking that shows the items that don't fit on-screen on the toolbar. If you have more open program windows than space for taskbar buttons, use the up and down arrows to the right of the visible taskbar buttons to see additional buttons.

Tip

You can also switch from one open program window to the next by pressing Alt+Tab or ▨ +Tab. ■

When the taskbar is unlocked, you see a dragging handle at the left side of each toolbar. You can drag those handles left and right to move and size toolbars. You can also show or hide the toolbar titles and text. Figure 10-36 shows an example of the text, titles, a handle, and taskbar button scrolling arrows.

To show or hide the title or text, right-click the toolbar's title or dragging handle. Then choose Show Title to show or hide the toolbar's title. Click Show Text to show or hide text for icons on the toolbar.

Note

Text always appears next to icons when you click >> on a toolbar. The Show Text option has no effect on that. To change the text that appears next to an icon, right-click that text, choose Rename, type the new name (or edit the existing name), and press Enter. ■

Using the Links toolbar (Favorites Bar)

The Links toolbar offers easy, one-click access to favorite Web sites. In fact, the Links toolbar shows the contents of your Internet Explorer Favorites Bar. So, just understand that Links on the taskbar is actually your Internet Explorer Favorites Bar.

You can make the Favorites Bar visible in Internet Explorer, the taskbar, or both. It's easiest to add links to the toolbar from Internet Explorer. So if you don't see that toolbar in Internet Explorer, click its Tools button and choose Toolbars ➪ Favorites Bar. Normally, it shows up under the Menu bar, as in Figure 10-37. The rest is easy:

FIGURE 10-36

Taskbar and toolbar handles, titles, text, and buttons.

- To create an icon for the page you're currently viewing, drag the icon to the left of the URL in the Address bar to the far-right edge of the Links toolbar (so that the mouse pointer turns to an I-beam). Then release the mouse button.

Tip
As with any toolbar, when there are more links than space, you see >> at the end of the toolbar. Click that symbol to see hidden links. ■

- To create an icon for a link on the current page, drag the link from the page onto the Favorites Bar.
- To remove an icon from the Favorites Bar, right-click the item and choose Delete.
- To rearrange items on the Favorites Bar, drag the item's icon to a new location on the toolbar.

Any changes that you make to the Favorites Bar in Internet Explorer are automatically reflected in the Links toolbar on the taskbar.

FIGURE 10-37

Favorites Bar in Internet Explorer.

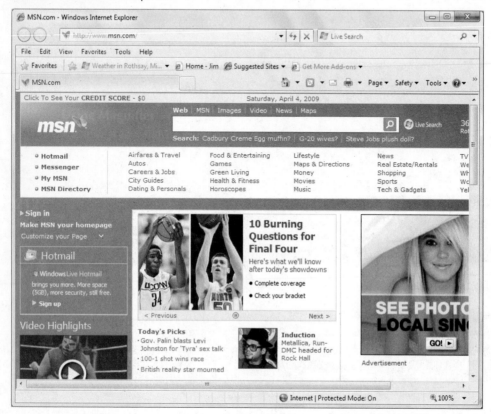

Customizing the Notification Area

The Notification area (also called the system tray) appears at the right side of the taskbar. It contains icons for programs and services that are running in the *background*, which means it's a program that typically doesn't have a specific program window or taskbar button associated with it. Icons in the Notification area represent features such as your antivirus software, volume control, network connection, and Windows Sidebar. Pointing to an item displays its name or other information.

To conserve space on the taskbar, nonessential or inactive icons can be hidden. When you have hidden items, you see a small up-facing arrow at the left side of the Notification area, as shown in Figure 10-38. Click the arrow button (labeled Show Hidden Icons) to see the hidden items.

You can use a couple of different dialog boxes to customize the Notification area. The first is Taskbar and Start Menu Properties, which you've seen in previous sections. To open that, right-click the Start button and choose Properties. Then click Customize in the Notification area group and click the Turn System Icons On or Off link near the bottom of the window to see the options shown in Figure 10-39.

FIGURE 10-38

Notification area.

Use the drop-down buttons to show or hide the Clock, Volume Control, Network, Power, and Action Center icons. Any items that are disabled (dimmed) aren't relevant to your system, so don't worry about those.

Note

As always, the items you turn on or off will have no effect until you click Apply or OK. ■

For more detailed control over the Notification area, click the Show Hidden Icons button and click Customize. Or right-click the current time in the lower-right corner of the screen and choose Customize Notification Icons. Either way, the Notification Area Icons window opens. Chapter 2 explains how to configure these settings.

Getting rid of Notification Area icons

You cannot delete a Notification area icon by right-clicking and choosing Delete. That's because in contrast to toolbars, its icons are not shortcuts for opening programs. Icons in the Notification area represent programs that are already running — albeit in the background, with nothing showing on the screen.

FIGURE 10-39

Notification Area Icons window.

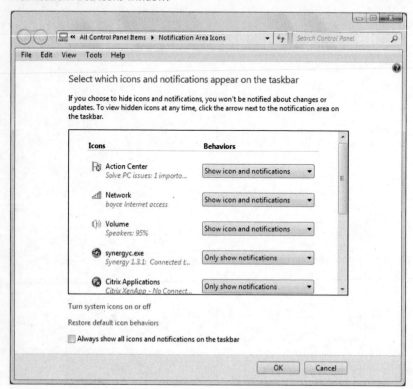

There is no single, simple step you can perform to get rid of a Notification area icon. There are hundreds of programs on the market that can run in the background. To keep such a program from showing up in your Notification area, you might need to prevent that program from auto-starting with your computer. Or you might need to remove the program from your system altogether. Then again, you might need only to get to the program's Options dialog box and deselect the check box that makes it show a Notification area icon.

One thing's for sure: You don't want to delete anything from the Notification area unless you know exactly what you're deleting and why. For example, an icon could represent your virus or spyware protection. You wouldn't necessarily want to delete such programs, or prevent them from auto-starting, because they need to be running in the background to keep your computer secure.

To see what options are available for a Notification area icon, right-click the icon. Some programs that run as icons in the Notification area can show up on the screen in a program window. Double-clicking its Notification area icon will usually open that program window. From there, you can learn more about the program that the icon represents. If it has a menu bar, choosing Tools ➪ Options might take you to a dialog box where you can prevent the program from auto-starting, or prevent it from showing up in the Notification area.

If the Notification area icon represents a program you don't want on your system at all, you can remove the program through Control Panel. Just make sure you don't remove a program you actually need and cannot replace. See Chapter 42 for the goods on removing programs.

If you want to keep a program but also want to prevent it from auto-starting and can't find a way to do that from within the program, there are still a couple of other ways to do that. If the program has an icon in your Startup folder, you can just remove that icon from that folder. Or you can use the System Configuration tool in the Administrative Tools folder to disable auto-starting of specific programs.

Tweaking the clock

The clock in the lower-right corner of the screen doesn't look like much, but you can do quite a few things with it. If you point to it, you see the current date. If you click it, you see the current date marked on a calendar and the time on a clock. If you right-click the time and choose Adjust Date/Time, you come to the dialog box shown in Figure 10-40. There you can do several things with the clock.

FIGURE 10-40

Date and time properties.

Note
You need administrative privileges to change some aspects of the date and time. That might sound silly, but in a home environment, it keeps the kids from getting around parental controls that limit when they can use the computer. ■

First, you want to make sure your clock is set to the time zone you're in. Click Change Time Zone and choose your time zone. If you're in an area that honors daylight savings time, check the option that allows that change to be handled automatically.

If the date or time is wrong on your clock, you can click Change Date and Time to manually enter the correct information. Or click the Internet Time tab and click Change Settings. Then click Update Now to synchronize your calendar and clock with the "official time" on the Internet.

Note

You might see a message that the Windows Time service is not running when you open the Internet Time tab. You can still click Change Settings and click Update Now to set the time. Windows will start the Time service for you. ■

You can also make the clock show the current time for up to three time zones. Click Additional Clocks. Then just follow the on-screen instructions to add one or two more times to your clock. Click OK after adjusting all your time settings.

Back on the desktop, the current time in the Notification area will be accurate. Likewise when you point to the time to see more information. If you set up multiple time zones, you'll see them all when you point to the current time. Clicking the time shows times for all time zones in the form of clocks, as in Figure 10-41.

FIGURE 10-41

Clocks for multiple time zones.

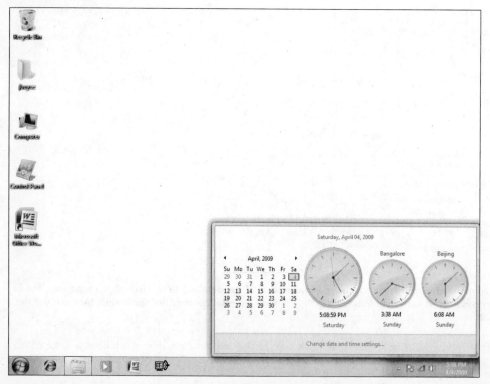

Using Gadgets

New Feature

Gadgets are a handy way to keep things you need often visible on your desktop at all times. Gadgets no longer are locked into the sidebar as they are in Windows Vista, but instead can float anywhere on the desktop.

Gadgets are optional desktop items. Figure 10-42 shows a selection of gadgets on the desktop, with two at the right edge, one at the top, and one at the bottom left. There are many gadgets from which to choose. Some are in the Gadget Gallery (also shown in Figure 10-42). Others you can download from the Internet. If you don't see the sidebar at all, don't worry.

FIGURE 10-42

Four gadgets on the desktop.

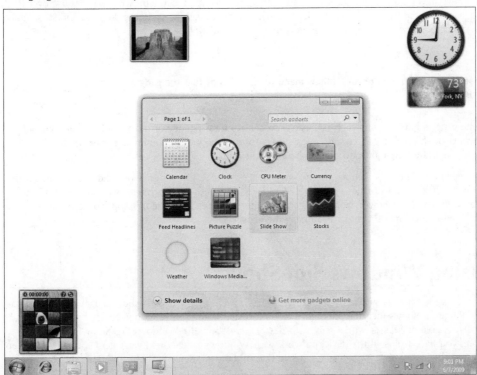

Adding and removing gadgets

There are no required gadgets. Nor are there right, wrong, good, or bad gadgets. The idea is to simply look around through available gadgets and pick ones you like. To add gadgets to the desktop, right-click the desktop and choose Gadgets to open the dialog box shown previously in Figure 10-42.

When the gallery first opens, you see a few sample gadgets. There can be more than one page of gadgets, and the Page control in the upper left of the page lets you scroll through the pages.

After you've checked out gadgets you already have, click Get More Gadgets Online to see more. You're taken to a Web page where you can scroll through many more available gadgets. Just read and follow the instructions on that page to shop around and download any gadgets that look interesting. Downloaded gadgets are placed in your gallery, which makes them easy to get to and put on your sidebar.

To add a gadget to the desktop, just double-click it. You can also right-click it and choose Add or just drag it from the gallery onto the sidebar.

To remove a gadget from your desktop, right-click it and choose Close Gadget. Or point to the gadget and click the Close (X) button at its upper-right corner. A copy of the gadget remains in your gallery in case you want to add it back on later. To remove a gadget from the gallery and your computer, right-click the gadget in the gallery and choose Uninstall.

Using and manipulating gadgets

Different gadgets do different things and work in different ways. But most are easy to figure out. If the gadget has options or settings you can change, you see a wrench icon when you mouse over the gadget. Click that icon to see what it has to offer. Or right-click the gadget and choose Options. When the dialog box opens, the options should generally be self-explanatory.

Note
If you don't see the wrench icon or an Options menu item, it means that the gadget doesn't have any configurable options. ■

Some gadgets have options such as Opacity to control transparency or other options that control how it works. Right-click a gadget and choose Move to turn the mouse pointer to a four-headed "move" arrow; then drag the mouse to put it wherever you want.

Gadgets are meant to be simple, useful, and fun. So feel free to try things out and play around with them. Because no set of rules applies to all gadgets, you need to experiment with any gadget you choose to figure out how it works. Remember, after a gadget is on the desktop, you can right-click it to see options for using and customizing the gadget.

Using Windows SideShow

Windows SideShow is similar to Windows gadgets, except that it doesn't show gadgets on your desktop. Rather, it shows them on alternative display devices found on some notebooks, cell phones, and other portable devices. It works only with devices that sport the Windows SideShow logo. Furthermore, you have to install the device to work with Windows SideShow. I can't help you with that step because there are many such devices and no one rule fits all. Refer to the instructions that came with the device for specifics.

On the computer side of things, you use the SideShow control panel to tweak settings on the alternative screen and to choose gadgets. Use either of the following methods to get to that control panel:

- Press ▊, type **side**, and click Windows SideShow.
- Choose Windows SideShow from the Control Panel.

What you see in the SideShow control panel depends on the device you've installed. But the options should be self-explanatory enough that you can figure it out on your own. Basically, you choose the gadgets you want to display from the list of available gadgets. Click the Get More Gadgets Online link to find other SideShow gadgets. Use the Help links in the control panel for more information about SideShow and configuring it to best work with your hardware.

Wrap-Up

This chapter has been all about the many ways you can customize the Windows desktop, Start menu, and taskbar to set up your screen in a way that works for you. You have many options. The important thing to keep in mind is that they *are* options, and there is no right or wrong way to do things. It's all about making choices that work for you. Here's a quick recap of the essentials:

- The Windows desktop is basically your entire screen — the place where you do all your work.
- Most tools for personalizing your system are in the Personalization page of the Control Panel. To get there quickly, right-click the desktop and choose Personalize.
- To personalize your Start menu, taskbar, or Notification area, right-click the Start button and choose Properties.
- To create a custom shortcut key for launching a program, right-click the program's icon and choose Properties. Then click the Shortcut tab and fill in the Keyboard Shortcut box.
- To add or remove taskbar toolbars, right-click the clock and choose Toolbars.
- To show or hide Notification area icons, right-click the clock or an empty taskbar area and choose Customize Notification Icons.
- Windows SideShow is like a sidebar for alternative display devices. It works only with devices that sport the Windows SideShow logo.

Ease of Access, Speech, and Language

This chapter is all about Windows 7's Ease of Access, Speech Recognition, Text-to-Speech, Handwriting Recognition, and Language options. These features offer alternatives to standard read, type, and click interaction with the computer.

Some features are designed for people with specific sensory, motor, cognitive, or seizure-related disabilities. Others aren't for any specific disability, but rather just offer an alternative way of doing things.

For example, if you just can't type worth beans, speech recognition lets you work your computer by talking. The Text-to-Speech option reads text aloud from the screen, which is good for any preschooler or any over-40 adult whose eyesight isn't what it used to be. In short, this isn't just a chapter for people with physical challenges. There's something for just about everyone here.

If several people share your computer, and different people have different needs, you should set up a user account for each person before you set the options described in this chapter. That way, you can tailor settings for each user. If you haven't gotten around to setting up user accounts yet, take a look at Chapter 3.

Introducing Ease of Access Center

Accessibility features for sensory and motor impairments are in the Ease of Access Center. If you have multiple user accounts, you can get to its options right from the login page after you start your computer or log out of your account. Just click the blue-and-white Ease of Access button in the lower-left corner of the screen (see Figure 11-1).

When the dialog box opens, a voice reads each option aloud and makes the currently selected option larger. To activate an accessibility feature, press the spacebar to select that feature's check box. After you've selected the features you need, a dialog box appears in which you can tweak settings for that feature. I get into the specifics of these settings when I cover each feature in more detail. But I think most are self-explanatory, so feel free to adjust whatever you want, or just click OK to accept the default settings.

FIGURE 11-1

Ease of Access from login page.

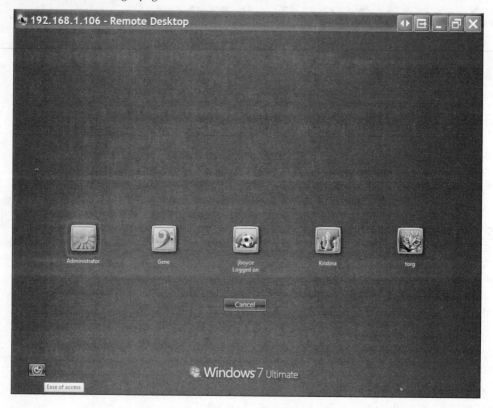

When you've finished choosing Ease of Access options, click the name or picture of your user account. Don't worry if you miss the opportunity to choose Ease of Access options at the login page. You can choose and configure things right from you user account, as described next.

After you've logged in to a user account, you can use the Ease of Access Center to enable, disable, or tweak accessibility options. Use whichever of the following techniques is easiest for you to get to the Ease of Access Center:

- Press ▓▓ , type **ea**, and click Ease of Access.

- Hold down ▓▓ and press U.

- Click the Start button and choose Control Panel ⇨ Ease of Access ⇨ Ease of Access Center.

- Right-click the desktop and choose Personalize; then click Ease of Access Center in the lower-left corner of the Personalization page.

- Click the Start button and choose All Programs ⇨ Accessories ⇨ Ease of Access ⇨ Ease of Access Center.

Regardless of how you get there, the Ease of Access Center, shown in Figure 11-2, opens.

FIGURE 11-2

Ease of Access Center.

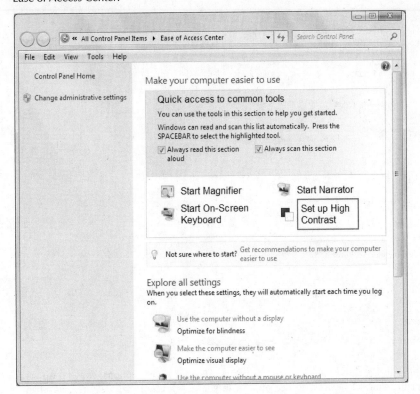

If the Always Read This Section Aloud and Always Scan This Section check boxes are selected, each option will be read aloud and magnified to help with visual impairments. After an option is read aloud, you have a few seconds to press the spacebar and select that feature. If you don't want to turn on a feature, don't press the spacebar. To disable the spoken instructions, deselect those check boxes.

If the preceding approach doesn't work for you, click Get Recommendations To Make Your Computer Easier To Use. Just follow the instructions on each page, selecting (clicking to place a checkmark in) only items that apply to you personally and click Next. Continue on that way until you get to the last page and answer its questions. Then click Done.

After answering questions on the last page, you see a list of recommended settings. None is selected. You need to select all the options yourself, or at least the options that seem most likely to apply to your impairments. Click Save to save the suggested settings and close the window.

Yet a third approach to choosing Ease of Access options is to click an option in the lower half of the Ease of Access Center (see Figure 11-3). Use the scroll bar at the right side of the Ease of Access Center program window to reach the additional options. Again, this is just another way of approaching accessibility options. As are the other approaches, these are self-explanatory. Just click any blue text that applies to you under the Explore All Settings heading. The next page to open provides options, instructions, and information.

FIGURE 11-3

More Ease of Access Center options.

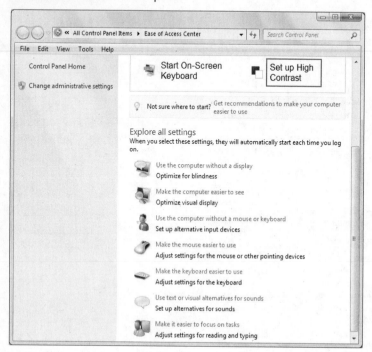

Regardless of which approach you use to choose your basic Ease of Access options, you end up with one or more specific Windows features turned on to help you out. Each of those features has a name, such as Magnifier, Narrator, On-Screen Keyboard, and others. Some have additional settings you can tweak to better suit your own needs. The rest of this chapter is about using those individual tools to improve accessibility.

Help for visual impairments

Visual impairments range from poor eyesight to near or total blindness. The Ease of Access Center provides some helpers for visual impairments. However, total blindness usually requires alternative input devices that go beyond the kinds of things you can do by changing settings in Windows. For more information on such devices, see the assistive technologies Web page at www.microsoft.com/enable.

For visual impairments that don't require special hardware devices, Windows 7 offers the built-in tools described in this section.

Using Magnifier

Magnifier is an assistive tool for those with visual impairments who require magnification of items on the screen. Magnifier offers two ways to magnify the screen to make it easier to see. In the default mode, Magnifier magnifies the screen to 200% of normal size. As you move the mouse, the display pans to show more of the desktop.

FIGURE 11-4

Microsoft Magnifier.

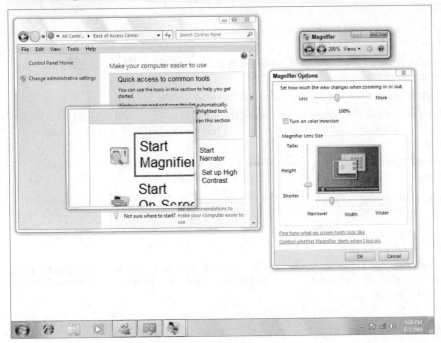

You can also use a window view to magnify a portion of the screen around the mouse pointer (called Lens view). Figure 11-4 shows a portion of the screen magnified. As you move the cursor around on the main screen, the magnifier follows, showing an enlarged version of whatever you're pointing to with the mouse pointer.

If you didn't turn on Magnifier from the Ease of Access Center, you can do so from the Start menu. Click the Start button and choose All Programs ⇨ Accessories ⇨ Ease of Access ⇨ Magnifier. Or press 🪟 , type **mag**, and click Magnifier.

When you start Magnifier, a small control window opens on the desktop, as shown near the top of Figure 11-4, that lets you choose between Full Screen, Lens, and Docked views. This control window changes to a partially transparent magnifying glass after a few seconds. You can click the magnifying glass to open the control window so that you can set options, change views, or close Magnifier. (To close it, just click the Close icon in the window.)

The dialog box shown in Figure 11-4 provides options for tweaking Magnifier settings. To open these options, click the Options gear icon on the control window. The Magnifier Options dialog box shows only some of its options if you are using full screen view. Switch to lens view to view all options.

The options in the dialog box let you tweak things as follows:

- **Set How Much the View Changes When Zooming In or Out:** Specify the percentage by which you want the view to zoom in or out when you click the Zoom In or Zoom Out button on the control window.

213

- **Turn on Color Inversion:** Makes the content inside the magnifier look like a negative of the original.

- **Follow the Mouse Pointer:** If selected, tells the magnification window to always reflect content near the mouse pointer.

- **Follow the Keyboard Focus:** If selected, ensures that any text you type is visible in the magnifier as you're typing.

- **Have Magnifier Follow the Text Insertion Point:** Similar to above but ensures that any text you're editing is magnified.

- **Magnifier Lens Size:** Use the two sliders in this area to set the size of the Magnifier lens.

- **Fine Tune What My Screen Fonts Look Like:** Click this link to start the ClearType Text Tuner, which can help improve the look of text on the display. See Chapter 10 to learn more.

- **Control Whether Magnifier Starts When I Log On:** Click this link to specify whether Magnifier starts automatically when you log on to Windows 7.

To close the control window without closing the magnification window, click the Minimize button in the window or right-click its taskbar button or title bar and choose Minimize.

Tip

To create shortcuts to some Ease of Access tools, click the Start button and choose All Programs ⇨ Accessories ⇨ Ease of Access. Then right-click any item that displays and choose Send To ⇨ Desktop (Create Shortcut), Pin to Taskbar, or Pin to Start Menu. ■

Using Microsoft Narrator

Microsoft Narrator is an assistive technology that reads aloud text on the screen for users with visual impairments. It announces events and things that happen on the screen. If you didn't enable Narrator in the Ease of Access Center, you can start it at any time. Click the Start button and choose All Programs ⇨ Accessories ⇨ Ease of Access ⇨ Narrator. (Or press ⊞ , type **nar**, and click Narrator.)

When Narrator opens, you see the dialog box shown in Figure 11-5. You'll hear the talking voice immediately, or as soon as you start doing things. The dialog box helps you tweak Narrator settings as follows:

- **Echo User's Keystrokes:** If selected, the narrator speaks every key you press at the keyboard.

- **Announce System Messages:** If selected, Narrator reads aloud any system message that appears on the screen.

- **Announce Scroll Notifications:** If selected, keeps you informed of how far down you've scrolled in a window.

- **Start Narrator Minimized:** If selected, starts Narrator with its dialog box minimized rather than open. Clicking the Microsoft Narrator taskbar button opens the dialog box.

- **Quick Help:** Starts spoken help for Narrator.

- **Voice Settings:** Lets you change the voice, speed, volume, and pitch of the speaking voice.

- **Exit:** Closes Narrator and its dialog box. You won't hear any more spoken narration until you restart Narrator. If you want to keep the narration but lose the dialog box, minimize (rather than close) the dialog box.

FIGURE 11-5

Microsoft Narrator options.

Note

Microsoft Narrator is weak compared to more sophisticated assistive technologies for the blind. To explore better Windows 7–compatible devices, browse to www.microsoft.com/enable. ■

Narrator is specifically designed to aid with visual impairments. As such, it reads everything on the screen. If you're looking for a more casual program to have e-books read aloud, consider Adobe Reader and Microsoft Reader. You can download both free from www.adobe.com/reader and www.microsoft.com/reader.

TextAloud is a popular text-to-speech tool designed to read e-mail, Web pages, and similar documents aloud. It's not free, but it's not expensive, either. You can learn more and download a free trial version from www.nextup.com.

Using High Contrast

High Contrast is a Windows feature that shows items in highly contrasting colors to help with visual impairments that make things on the screen look blurry. Click Set Up High Contrast in the Ease of Access Center to get to options for controlling high contrast.

If you don't like the default high-contrast color scheme, open the Personalization item from the Control Panel and choose one of the Basic and High Contrast themes listed there. Try each of the available schemes until you find the one that works best for you.

By default, you can turn High Contrast on and off by pressing Alt+Left Shift+Print Screen (hold down the Alt key, hold down the Shift key next to the letter Z, press the Print Screen [PrtScrn] key, and then release all keys).

Note

If your keyboard has a Function Lock or F Lock key, you might need to turn that off for Alt+Left Shift+Print Screen to work. ■

Using the computer without a display

Down in the "Explore all settings" section of the Ease of Access Center, you see a Use the Computer Without a Display link. Clicking that link presents the options shown in Figure 11-6.

FIGURE 11-6

Use the Computer Without a Display.

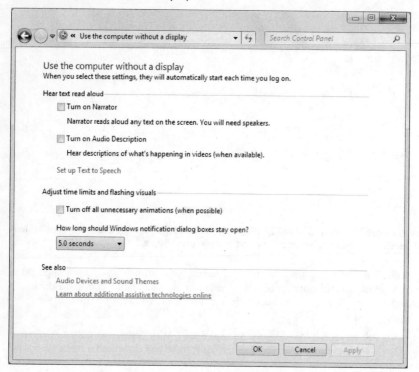

The first option turns on Microsoft Narrator, described in the preceding section. Turn on Audio Description, if selected, uses speech to describe what's happening in videos. Not all videos support that capability. So even if you choose that option, you don't get voice descriptions with every video that plays. Videos that do support audio description use your current text-to-speech settings, described later in this chapter, for voice. The Set Up Text to Speech link takes you to the dialog box for configuring text-to-speech.

Choosing Turn Off All Unnecessary Animations (When Possible) turns off special animation effects that aren't relevant to alternative display devices; it also allows them to work faster. You can also control how long Notification area messages stay on the screen. If they tend to disappear before you get a chance to hear Narrator read them, adjust the slider to make them stay on the screen longer.

If you made any changes in the window, click Apply to apply them without closing the window. Or click OK to apply them and close the window. To return to Ease of Access without saving changes, click Cancel or the Back button.

Optimize visual display

Ease of Access also provides a Make the Computer Easier to See link for visual impairments. Click that link for options related to your visual display. The first few options control High Contrast,

Narrator, Audio Description, and Magnifier, as described earlier. Scroll down to the options shown in Figure 11-7 for some other options, described next.

FIGURE 11-7

Make the Computer Easier to See.

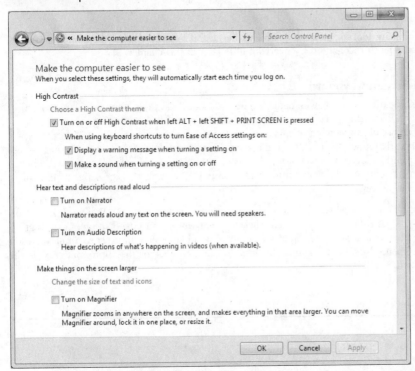

- **Make the Focus Rectangle Thicker:** As you press the Tab key to move from one option to the next in a dialog box, a focus rectangle appears around the currently selected option. Choose this option to make that rectangle easier to see.

- **Set the Thickness of the Blinking Cursor:** When you're typing text, a blinking vertical cursor appears at the place where the next character to type will appear. If it's difficult to see that cursor, use the drop-down button to increase its thickness. The line to the right of the Preview setting shows how wide that cursor will be.

- **Turn Off All Unnecessary Animations (When Possible):** Some animation effects on the screen serve no practical purpose. They're just there for amusement. They might be an unnecessary distraction or annoyance for some visual impairments. Choose this option to get rid of them.

- **Remove Background Images (Where Available):** Background pictures on the desktop, in folders, and in other locations can make it difficult to see text and other content on a page. Choose this option to get rid of those images.

As always, your choices won't be activated until you click OK or Apply. (The only difference is that OK closes the window and Apply leaves it open.)

Help for motor impairments

The Ease of Access Center offers several options for helping with motor impairments that make it difficult to use the mouse and keyboard. These include the On-Screen Keyboard, Sticky Keys, Filter Keys, and others. You can get to these options through the Ease of Access Center and other methods described in the sections that follow.

Tip

Speech recognition is the ultimate tool for motor impairments because it lets you control the computer and dictate text with your voice. Speech recognition is covered a little later in this chapter. ■

Using the On-Screen Keyboard

The On-Screen Keyboard is just what its name implies: It's a keyboard that appears on the screen so that you can type by clicking keys with the mouse pointer rather than by typing. This is useful for those with a variety of motor impairments, but not too bad for one-fingered hunt-and-peck typists, either. You find the option for enabling On-Screen Keyboard in the Ease of Access Center — just click Start On-Screen Keyboard. You can also get to it from the desktop (press ⊞, type **on**, and click On-Screen Keyboard). Or click the Start button and choose All Programs ➪ Accessories ➪ Ease of Access ➪ On-Screen Keyboard.

The keyboard appears in a free-floating window on the screen (see Figure 11-8). You work it as you would a normal keyboard. First, on the screen, click the spot where you intend to type text. That space can be any place that accepts text, from the Address bar in your Web browser to a full Microsoft Word document. Then, just start typing one character at a time by clicking the appropriate key on the On-Screen Keyboard.

FIGURE 11-8

The On-Screen Keyboard.

Use the Backspace (Bksp) and Delete (Del) keys to delete text. To type an uppercase letter, click the Shift key and then type the letter you want to type in uppercase. To press a *key+key* combination, such as Ctrl+Esc, click the first key and then the second key.

When you've finished with the On-Screen Keyboard, click the Close (X) button in its upper-right corner. To see a more complete set of keyboard helpers, use whichever method is easiest and works best for you:

- In the Ease of Access Center, click Make the Keyboard Easier To Use.
- From the desktop, click the Start button and choose Control Panel ➪ Ease of Access ➪ Change How Your Keyboard Works.

FIGURE 11-9

Make the Keyboard Easier To Use.

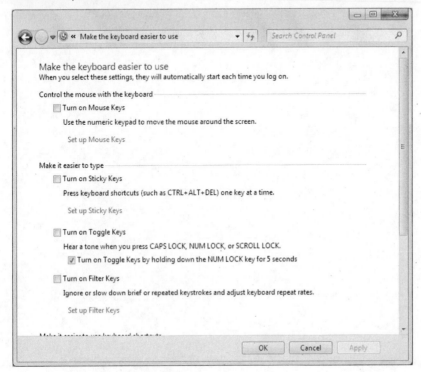

You're taken to the options that are shown in Figure 11-9. Each option is discussed in the sections that follow.

Some of the options show Notification area icons when they're turned on, as in Figure 11-10. That makes it easy to see, at a glance, which features are currently running. When Filter Keys and Sticky Keys are showing their icons, you can double-click either one to change its settings.

Using Mouse Keys

Mouse Keys lets you use your keyboard to move the mouse pointer around on the screen using arrow keys on the numeric keypad instead of the mouse. To use Mouse Keys, first make sure that option is selected in the Make the Keyboard Easier To Use window (refer to Figure 11-9). To configure Mouse Keys, click Set Up Mouse Keys. You see the options shown in Figure 11-11.

Each option is briefly explained within the window and in the following list:

- **Turn On Mouse Keys:** Select this check box to enable Mouse Keys; deselect this check box to disable Mouse Keys.
- **Turn On Mouse Keys with Alt+Left Shift + Num Lock:** Choose this option if you want to be able to turn Mouse Keys on and off using the shortcut key. (To do so, hold down the Alt key, hold down the Shift key to the left of the letter Z, and then press the Num Lock key.)

FIGURE 11-10

Notification area icons for keyboard helpers.

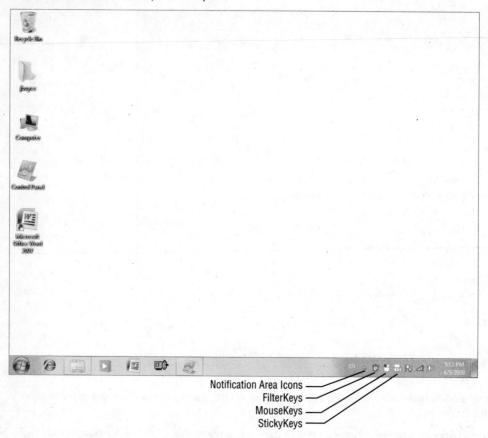

Notification Area Icons ————
FilterKeys ————
MouseKeys ————
StickyKeys ————

- **Display a Warning Message when Turning a Setting On:** Choose this option if you want some visual feedback on the screen so that you know when you've turned on Mouse Keys.

- **Make a Sound When Turning a Setting On or Off:** Choose this option if you want to hear some auditory feedback when turning a feature off.

- **Top Speed:** Use this slider to determine how fast the mouse pointer can go when you hold down an arrow key.

- **Acceleration:** The longer you hold down an arrow key, the faster the mouse pointer moves. Use this slider to determine how quickly that acceleration occurs.

- **Hold Down Ctrl To Speed Up and Shift To Slow Down:** Choose this option if you want to control mouse pointer speed by holding down Ctrl or Shift while moving the mouse pointer with the arrow keys.

- **Use Mouse Keys When Num Lock Is:** Choose when Mouse Keys is operable, either when the Num Lock key is on or when it is off.

FIGURE 11-11

Set Up Mouse Keys.

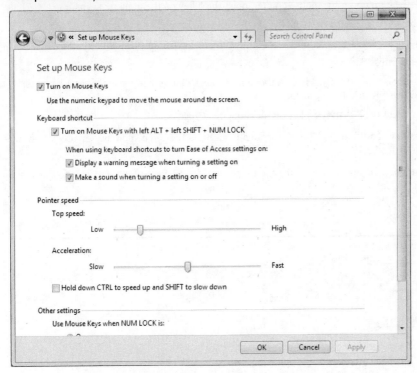

- **Display the Mouse Keys Icon On the Taskbar:** Deselecting this option prevents Mouse Keys from displaying a Notification area icon.

For Mouse Keys to work, several things have to happen. First, you should see the Mouse Keys icon in the Notification area. If you don't, press left Alt+Left Shift+Num Lock or turn it on. Click Yes in the dialog box that opens. Optionally, you can click Make the Keyboard Easier To Use in the Ease of Access Center. Then select the Turn On Mouse Keys check box and click Apply.

If you see a red No symbol on the Mouse Keys Notification area icon, that means the Num Lock key isn't set for moving the mouse pointer. Press the Num Lock key once to make the No symbol go away. Now you can move the mouse pointer using navigation keys on the numeric keypad, as summarized next.

Caution

Navigation keys that aren't on the numeric keypad probably won't move the mouse pointer at all, whether Num Lock is on or off. So make sure you use the navigation keys on the numeric keypad. ∎

To move the mouse pointer while Mouse Keys is active:

- Use the ↑ and ↓ keys on the numeric keypad to move the mouse pointer vertically.

221

- Use the ← and → keys to move the mouse pointer horizontally.
- Use the Home, PgDn, PgUp, and End keys to move the mouse pointer diagonally.
- To click the item under the mouse pointer, press the 5 key on the numeric keypad.
- To double-click, press the + (plus) key on the numeric keypad.
- To right-click, press the – (minus) key on the numeric keypad or press Shift+F10.
- To rename, press F2.
- To drag, press the Insert (Ins) key on the numeric keypad and then move the mouse pointer with the keys previously described.
- To drop, press the Delete (Del) key on the numeric keypad.

To disable Mouse Keys and hide its Notification area icon, press the same shortcut key used to show it: Alt+Left Shift+Num Lock.

You can also customize the appearance of the mouse pointer. In the Ease of Access Center, click Make the Mouse Easier To Use to get to the options shown in Figure 11-12.

FIGURE 11-12

More mouse options.

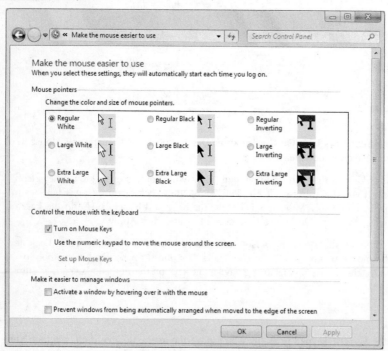

From the top of the dialog box, choose a size and color scheme for the mouse from the nine options provided. If you want to be able to bring a partially covered program window to the top of the stack just by pointing to it, choose Activate a Window By Hovering Over It With the Mouse.

Clicking Mouse Settings takes you to the general mouse personalization dialog box described in the "Personalizing your mouse" section in Chapter 10.

Using Sticky Keys

Sticky Keys eliminates the need to hold down two keys simultaneously to press shortcut keys, such as Ctrl+Esc. When Sticky Keys is active, you need only press the *modifier key* (the first key in the *key + key* sequence) once and then press the second key separately. For example, to press Ctrl+Esc with Sticky Keys active, press the Ctrl key and then press the Esc key.

When Sticky Keys is active, you see its icon in the Notification area (refer to Figure 11-10). If it's not on, you may be able to activate it by pressing the Shift key five times and clicking Yes. If that method doesn't work, click Make the Keyboard Easier to Use in the Ease of Access Center and then select the Turn On Sticky Keys check box in the Ease of Access Center.

Each modifier key that you can make stick is indicated by a little square in the Notification area icon. The square turns blank when the key is in the "on" position. To try it, just pick a key (Ctrl, Alt, Shift, or the Windows Logo key) and press it a few times. You see the little square turn black when the key is locked down. You see that same square turn white when the key is unlocked.

You can tweak Sticky Keys behavior to work best for you. To get to its settings, double-click the Sticky Keys Notification area icon and click Set Up Sticky Keys. Or click Make the Keyboard Easier To Use in Ease of Access Center and then click Set up Sticky Keys. The options shown in Figure 11-13 appear.

FIGURE 11-13

Configure Sticky Keys:

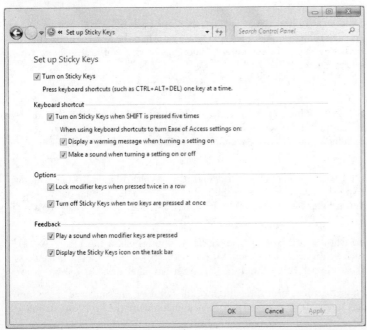

223

Most of the options in the dialog box are self-explanatory, so I don't belabor them here. The first one lets you turn Sticky Keys on or off. The second option controls the Sticky Keys shortcut key behavior. But the following two options deserve some mention:

- **Lock Modifier Keys When Pressed Twice in a Row:** Choose this option if you want to have the ability to lock down a modifier key for more than one subsequent use. For example, if you choose the option, you can press the Shift key twice to keep that key locked down. Each single key you press after that will be typed as though you were holding down the Shift key. The key stays in that locked down position until you tap it a third time.

- **Turn Off Sticky Keys If Two Keys Are Pressed at Once:** Selecting this option lets you disable Sticky Keys by pressing any two keys simultaneously. (If you clear this option, you can turn off Sticky Keys by pressing the Shift key five times.)

The Notifications options control audio and Notification area icons. Make your selections and then click OK or Apply, as always, to activate your selections.

Using Toggle Keys

Toggle Keys is a simple keyboard helper that emits a sound whenever you press a toggle key (Caps Lock, Num Lock, or Scroll Lock). To activate Toggle Keys, select its check box near the center of the keyboard helpers shown back in Figure 11-9. As long as you don't disable its shortcut key, you can turn Toggle Keys on or off by holding down the Num Lock key for five seconds.

Tip

They're called *toggle keys* because each has two possible settings, "on" and "off." When you tap the key, you go to the opposite setting. Many keyboards have little light indicators that go on when the key is in the "on" position. ■

If you turn Toggle Keys on and want to hear the sound, tap the Caps Lock key a few times. You hear a high-pitched tone when the key comes on and a low-pitched tone when the key goes off. There is no Notification area icon for Toggle Keys. The only way to know it's on is if you hear a sound when you tap one of those toggle keys, such as Caps Lock.

Using Filter Keys

The Filter Keys option disables autotyping (repeated typing of the character) when a key is held down long enough or when multiple rapid keystrokes occur. This helps to avoid unwanted keystrokes caused by shakiness and involuntary muscle movements associated with Parkinson's and similar motor impairments.

To activate Filter Keys, select Turn On Filter Keys in the Make the Keyboard Easier To Use window. When Filter Keys is active, you should see its icon in the Notification area, as pointed out back in Figure 11-10. You can also turn Filter Keys on or off by holding down the right Shift key for eight seconds and clicking Yes.

To personalize Filter Keys so that it works best for you, get to its settings (shown in Figure 11-14). You can do so by double-clicking the Filter Keys Notification area icon. Or open the Ease of Access Center, click Make the Keyboard Easier To Use, and then click Set Up Filter Keys.

The first two sections, and Other Settings near the bottom of the window, are similar to those for other keyboard helpers: You can enable or disable Filter Keys and configure the keyboard shortcut. The rest are unique:

FIGURE 11-14

Set Up Filter Keys.

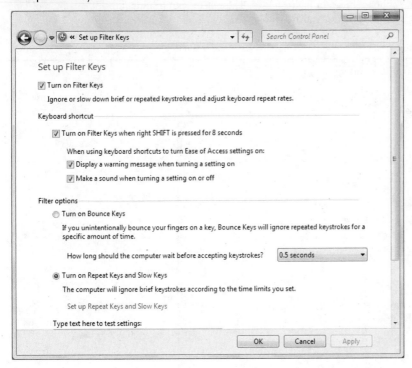

- **Turn On Bounce Keys:** If your fingers unintentionally press a key repeatedly when you mean to press it once, choose this option to ignore repeated keystrokes. Then specify how long you want Windows to wait before considering the next keypress an intentional one.

- **Turn On Repeat Keys and Slow Keys:** Choose this option if you inadvertently hold down a key too long, causing it to repeat, or if you inadvertently brush keys because of involuntary muscle movements. Then click Set Up Repeat Keys and Slow Keys to turn off, or tone down, repeat keys, and to put a minimum duration on how long you have to press a key before it counts as a valid keystroke.

You can test your current settings in the textboxes provided in the window. The last two options allow you to assign audible feedback to accepted keystrokes and show the Filter Keys icon in the Notification area. As always, click OK or Apply to activate your selections.

Don't expect to get all the settings for keyboard helpers right on your first attempt. The best you can do, for starters, is guess what might work. Then use the settings until you get the hang of the feature. After you get a feel for how the keyboard helper works, it will be easier to go back and fine-tune your settings until you find what works best for you.

Note
See "Personalizing your mouse" and "Personalizing the keyboard" in Chapter 10 for other options on configuring your mouse and keyboard. ∎

Help for hearing impairments

Clicking the Use Text or Visual Alternatives for Sounds link near the bottom of the Ease of Access Center presents the options shown in Figure 11-15. These help with hearing impairments by replacing little sound effects and other auditory alerts with visual ones.

FIGURE 11-15

Use Text or Visual Alternatives for Sounds.

Your options in Sounds are as follows:

- **Turn On Visual Notifications for Sounds (Sound Sentry):** Choosing this option replaces the little beeps and other sounds that alert hearing people to events with visual alerts.
- **Choose Visual Warning:** Lets you choose how large you want the warning to be, ranging from none at all to flashing the entire desktop.
- **Turn on Text Captions for Spoken Dialog (When Available):** Choosing this option is similar to turning on closed captions on a TV. Spoken text is displayed on-screen as written text whenever possible.

As always, you need to click OK or Apply to activate any options you've selected or deselected.

Make it easier to focus on tasks

Down at the bottom of the Ease of Access Center is a link titled Make It Easier To Focus On Tasks. Clicking that takes you to the options shown in Figure 11-16. All the options turn on (or off) features described earlier in this chapter.

FIGURE 11-16

Options to make it easier to focus on tasks.

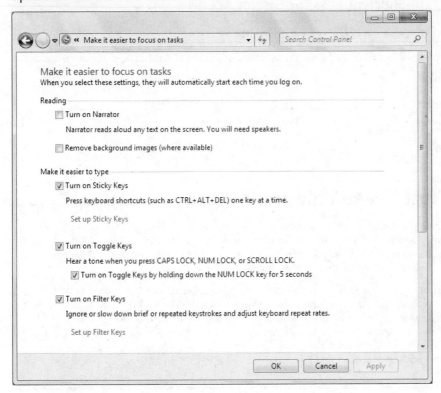

As always, if you do select or clear any options, you need to click OK or Apply to activate those selections.

Ease of Access administrative settings

The Change Administrative Settings option at the left side of the Ease of Access Center allows an administrator to apply the selected Ease of Access options to the login page that all users see when first starting the computer. You need administrative privileges to set that one because it's the only setting that affects all users. You can also set a Restore point from that page as a backup to all the Ease of Access settings in play.

Accessibility keyboard shortcuts

For future reference, Table 11-1 lists shortcut keys used to turn Ease of Access features on or off from the keyboard. Keep in mind, however, that these work only if you didn't disable shortcut access while configuring the feature.

TABLE 11-1

Shortcut Keys for Ease of Access

Open Ease of Access Center	Windows logo key +U
Turn High Contrast on/off	Press left Alt+Left Shift+Print Screen (PrtScrn)
Turn Filter Keys on/off	Hold down Right Shift for eight seconds
Turn Mouse Keys on/off	Press Left Alt+Left Shift+Num Lock
Turn Sticky Keys on/off	Press Shift five times
Turn Toggle Keys on/off	Hold down Num Lock for five seconds

How Do I Turn These Things Off?

Ease of Access options are no different from options you choose in dialog boxes. When you activate a feature, Windows 7 assumes you mean it. Any features you activate will remain activated through the current session and into all future sessions. There isn't a "just experimenting" or "just kidding" mode where they turn themselves off automatically after a while.

To further complicate things, lots of ways to turn these things on or off are available. Also, if you don't remember where or how you turned a feature on, turning it off could be tricky. If you have trouble turning off some features, first clear all the checkmarks at the top of the Ease of Access Center. Then open the first item under Explore All Settings. Deselect the check boxes for features you don't want and then click Save. Then do the same for all the remaining links under the Explore All Settings section until you've turned off everything you don't need.

Using Speech Recognition

Speech recognition is a Windows 7 feature that lets you perform many tasks by talking rather than typing or clicking. It's a great solution to problems caused by motor impairments that make it difficult to use the mouse and keyboard. It can also be useful if you just can't type worth beans. You can use speech recognition to open programs, folders, and files, make selections in dialog boxes, dictate text that you'd normally type by hand, and more.

To use speech recognition, you need a microphone. A USB headset microphone with *noise cancellation* to filter out background sound is best. If you don't have one, you can purchase one at any place that sells computer accessories. To see examples or purchase online, go to an online retailer (www.cdw.com, www.newegg.com, www.tigerdirect.com, www.walmart.com, www.amazon.com, or whichever you like) and search for "USB headset microphone."

After you have a microphone, learn enough about it to plug it into the computer, make sure it's not muted, and control its volume (if it has Mute and Volume controls). Plug it into the computer and wait a few seconds for Windows 7 to recognize it and show you a notification that it's ready to use. Then try to set aside about an hour when you can have some peace and quiet without interruptions so that you can learn how to use speech recognition. If you provide the microphone and time, Windows 7 will provide the training, as discussed in the next section.

Getting started with speech recognition

The first step to using speech recognition is to connect your microphone to the computer according to the manufacturer's instructions. The second step is to open the Speech Recognition control panel using whichever technique is easiest for you.

Note
If the Speech Recognition control panel is already open and running, right-click its microphone or Notification area icon and choose Configuration ⇨ Open Speech Recognition Control Panel. ■

- Click the Start button and choose Control Panel ⇨ Ease of Access ⇨ Speech Recognition.
- Press 🟦, type **spe**, and click Speech Recognition.
- If you're already in the Ease of Access Center, click the arrow next to Ease of Access in the breadcrumb trail and choose Speech Recognition.

The Speech Recognition options, shown in Figure 11-17, appear.

FIGURE 11-17

Speech Recognition control panel.

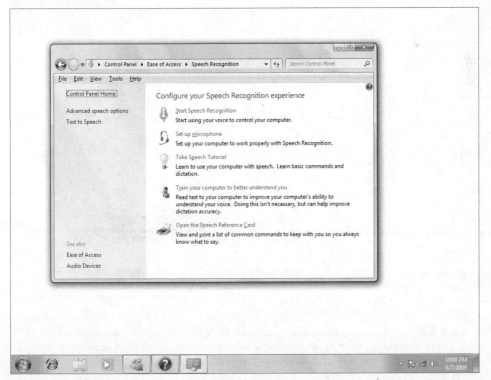

Your first hour of learning to use speech recognition begins when you click Start Speech Recognition. You are taken through the entire process of setting things up and learning how to use this feature (assuming you haven't already been through that process). I don't repeat everything in the tutorial here because you're better off just doing what the on-screen tutorial tells you to do. If you pay attention and try what it tells you to, you'll quickly be up to speed on the basics of using speech recognition.

If you can't make it through the whole tutorial, click Set-Up Microphone or Take Speech Tutorial when you can resume. As in all aspects of using a computer, the hour you invest in learning will save you hours of hair-pulling frustration later.

When you've finished setting things up and taking the tutorial, you should see a round Notification area icon whose tooltip shows the words Speech Recognition when you point to it. Clicking that icon opens the menu shown in Figure 11-18. Double-clicking that icon displays the Speech Recognition microphone shown near the bottom right of that same figure.

FIGURE 11-18

Speech Recognition microphone and Notification area icon.

The rest of this section assumes that you've completed the Speech Recognition tutorial and learned the basics. You should be able to open the menu and Speech Recognition microphone at the bottom of Figure 11-18 on your own. Most of what follows gives you reminders of specific things you can say.

Control speech recognition by voice

When the Speech Recognition Notification area icon is visible, you can speak any phrase at the left side of Table 11-2 to perform the action shown in the right column. (Don't forget to don your headset or activate your microphone first.)

TABLE 11-2

Controlling Speech Recognition by Voice

To do this	Say this
Wake up sleeping speech recognition	Start listening
Move the Speech Recognition icon to top or bottom of screen	Move speech recognition
Hide Speech Recognition microphone	Minimize speech recognition
Show Speech Recognition microphone	Open speech recognition
See special words you can say	What can I say?
Put speech recognition to sleep	Stop listening

Commanding Windows by voice

Table 11-3 lists things you can do by voice to control Windows at that desktop, as well as program windows that are already open. Speak only the text shown in monospace font. Other text is for clarification. Replace italicized text with an actual name. For example, in Open *program name*, say the name of the program in place of *program name*. So to open WordPad, for example, you'd say Open WordPad.

But be aware that if the cursor is in a word processing or text-editing program (WordPad or Word, for example), your speech might be taken as dictation and typed into your document. You can say minimize Word or minimize WordPad to minimize either program to prevent that.

Tip

If you have Folder Options set to single-clicking, it may be difficult to select icons by voice. Consider switching to double-clicking so that you can say Click and Shift Click to select icons. ■

Work anywhere by voice

When it's difficult to refer to things by name, you can use numbers or a mousegrid to click areas by number. Say show numbers to show numbers; say mousegrid to see the mousegrid. Then look to the Speech Recognition microphone for guidance on other things you can say. Table 11-4 shows words you can say while in Click Anywhere mode. If you get stuck in either display and just want to bail out, say hide numbers to get rid of numbers, or cancel to end the mousegrid.

TABLE 11-3

Spoken Words for Windows and Program Windows

To do this	Say this
Open the Start menu	Click Start
Choose Start menu items	*Option name*
Click an item	Click *item name*
Double-click an item	Double click *item name*
Right-click an item	Right click *item name*
Shift+Click an item	Shift click *item name*
Open a program	Open *program name*
Choose menu commands	*Command name* (for example File Open)
Go to a field or control	Go to *field name* or *control name*
Go to next field or control	Tab or Press tab
Undo last action	Undo that or scratch that
Redo last action	Redo
Scroll one line	Scroll up or Scroll down
Scroll multiple lines	Scroll *direction* lines
Scroll by page	Scroll *direction number* pages
Switch to an open program	Switch to *program name*
Maximize open window	Maximize that (for active window) or Maximize *program name*
Restore maximized window	Restore that or Restore *program name*
Minimize open window	Minimize that (for active window) or Minimize *program name*
Minimize all windows	Show Desktop
Close a program	Close that (for active window) or Close *program name*
Show numbers for items	Show numbers
Click numbered item	Click *number*
Double-click numbered item	Double Click *number*
Right-click numbered item	Right Click *number*

To do this	Say this
Hide numbers	Hide numbers
Cut	Cut that or Cut
Copy	Copy that or Copy
Paste	Paste
Delete	Delete that or Delete
Undo	Undo that or Scratch that or Undo

TABLE 11-4

Spoken Words for Clicking Anywhere

To do this	Say this
Number *clickable* items	Show numbers
Click a numbered item	Click *number*
Show the mousegrid	Mousegrid
Zoom in a grid	*Number*
Move the mouse pointer to mousegrid square	*Number* or *numbers*
Click any mousegrid square	Click *number* or Click *numbers*
Select an item to drag with the mousegrid	*Number* mark or *numbers* mark
Drag selected item in mousegrid square	*Number* or *numbers* click
Hide the mousegrid	Cancel

Tip

In Microsoft Internet Explorer, you can say Press tab and Tab to move from one link to the next on a page. When the link you want to click has the focus, say Click that or Click to click that link. Say Click back to return to the previous page. ■

Dictating text

You can dictate text just about anywhere you can type text. Speak one sentence at a time and follow each by saying period (or exclamation point or question mark). To start a new paragraph, say new paragraph. Use the words shown in the right column of Table 11-5 to insert other punctuation marks.

TABLE 11-5

Spoken Words for Punctuation

To type this	Say this
,	Comma
;	Semicolon
.	Period or Dot or Full stop
:	Colon
"	Double quote
'	Single quote or apostrophe
>	Greater than
<	Less than
/	Forward slash
\	Backslash
~	Tilde
@	At sign
&	Ampersand
!	Exclamation mark or Exclamation point
?	Question mark
...	Ellipsis
#	Number sign
$	Dollar sign
%	Percent or Percent sign
^	Caret or Caret sign
(	Open parenthesis
)	Close parenthesis
_	Underscore
-	Hyphen or Minus sign or Dash
=	Equal sign
+	Plus sign
{	Open brace
}	Close brace

To type this	Say this
[	Left bracket or Open bracket
]	Right bracket or Close bracket
|	Pipe sign
:-)	Smiley face or Happy face
:-(	Frown face or Unhappy face
;-)	Wink face
(tm)	Trademark sign
¾	Three-quarter
¼	One-quarter
½	One-half

Table 11-6 shows spoken commands for formatting and editing text. Don't forget that you can also choose menu commands just by saying the names of things on the menu bar and drop-down menus. You can also press special keys such as Home, End, Page Up, Page Down, Backspace, Spacebar, and Tab just by saying their names. You can press any key by saying the word press followed by the letter, number, or name. For example, Press Up, Press Down, Press Left, Press Right, Press Tab, Press Escape. Any time you goof and make matters worse, say Undo that.

Making dictation better

Voice dictation isn't always easy. It's certainly not like *Star Trek,* in which they just say whatever they want and the computer "understands." Real computers don't "understand" anything to say or type. They're just mindless, brainless machines. When you use speech recognition and dictation, you're not really "talking to" or "conversing with" the computer as you would another person. You're trying to control a dumb machine with your voice. Because yours is the only brain in the "conversation," the onus of getting it to work falls on you.

Speech recognition often fails when there are homonyms involved — words that sound alike such as wood/would, to/too/two, and I am/IM (try saying I'm instead on that last one). Names and slang terms that aren't in the dictionary are often mistaken for similar-sounding words from the dictionary. There are things you can do to improve matters, as discussed in the next three sections.

Correct that

When speech recognition gets a spoken word wrong, correcting it by voice helps it to learn your unique speaking style. To correct a wrong word, say Correct *word* (where *word* is the word you want to correct). If that word appears in several places, each will show a number. Say the number of the word you want to correct and then say OK. The Alternatives Panel opens. As instructed in the panel, say the number of the corrected word and then say OK. Or say I'll spell it myself and follow the on-screen instructions.

235

TABLE 11-6

Spoken Words for Formatting and Editing

To do this	Say this
Start a new line	New line
Start a new paragraph	New paragraph
Put cursor before a specific word	Go to *word*
Put cursor after a specific word	Go after *word*
Go to start of current sentence	Go to start of sentence
Go to start of current paragraph	Go to start of paragraph
Go to start of document	Go to start of document
Go to end of current sentence	Go to end of sentence
Go to end of current paragraph	Go to end of paragraph
Go to end of document	Go to end of document
Select a word	Select *word*
Select all text from one word to another word	Select *word* through *word*
Select all text in document	Select all
Select previous *x* words (up to 20)	Select previous **number** words
Select next *x* words (up to 20)	Select next *number* words
Select the last text you dictated	Select that
Boldface selected text	Bold
Italicize selected text	Italic
Delete selected text	Delete that
Undo last change	Undo that **or** Undo
Redo last undo	Redo that **or** Redo
Deselect selected text	Clear selection
Center text	Center
Change next *x* words to uppercase	Change next *number* to uppercase
Change next *x* words to lowercase	Change next *number* to lowercase
Delete previous sentence	Delete previous sentence
Delete next sentence	Delete next sentence
Delete previous paragraph	Delete previous paragraph
Delete next paragraph	Delete next paragraph

Improve voice recognition

Speech recognition offers little five-minute training sessions to help it better recognize your voice. To ensure that it doesn't think you're dictating, close or minimize any open windows (say show desktop or right-click the clock and choose Show the Desktop). Then say stop listening. Right-click the Speech Recognition microphone or Notification area icon and choose Configuration ⇨ Improve Voice Recognition. Then follow the on-screen instructions in the Voice Recognition Wizard that opens.

Tip

You can say Next, **rather than click Next, after reading each line in the Voice Training Wizard.** ∎

There are several different training sessions available from that same set of commands, so don't feel that you can choose Configuration ⇨ Improve Voice Recognition only once. You can choose it whenever you have a spare five minutes to improve speech recognition.

Add words to the speech dictionary

Speech recognition operates by comparing sound waves of words you say to words in its dictionary. You can add your own words to the dictionary, remove words, or change words. Adding words is especially useful for things like people's names, domain names, e-mail addresses, and slang terms.

To open the speech dictionary, right-click the Speech Recognition microphone or Notification area icon and choose Open the Speech Dictionary. You see the options shown in Figure 11-19. Just click whichever action you want to do and follow the on-screen instructions.

FIGURE 11-19

Speech Dictionary.

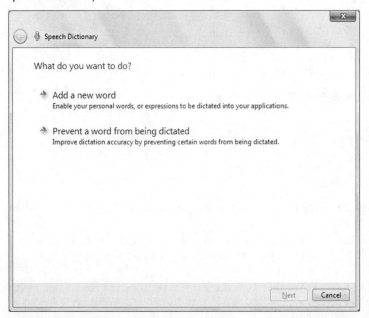

237

Advanced speech recognition configuration

Advanced Speech Recognition options let you choose a speech recognition engine (language), control automatic startup, and more. To get to those options, open the Speech Recognition Control Panel. Right-click the Speech Recognition microphone or Notification area icon (if available) and choose Configuration ➪ Open Speech Recognition Control Panel. Otherwise, use any method described in the "Getting started with speech recognition" section, earlier in this chapter. Then click Advanced Speech Options to see the Speech Properties dialog box shown in Figure 11-20.

FIGURE 11-20

Speech Properties dialog box.

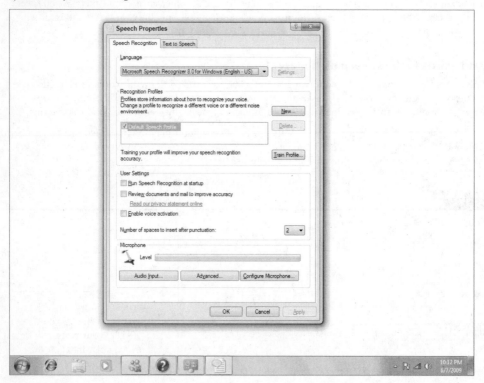

The advanced options are as follows:

- **Language:** Choose the speech recognition option that matches the language in which you'll be speaking.

- **Recognition Profiles:** Use this option to allow multiple users to define their own unique speech profiles. Each user can then train speech recognition independently for the best accuracy.

- **Run Speech Recognition at Startup:** If you deselect this check box, you can still start speech recognition manually by clicking Start and choosing All Programs ➪ Accessories ➪ Ease of Access ➪ Speech Recognition.

Tip

As with any program, you can create desktop shortcuts to speech recognition. ■

- **Review Documents and Mail to Improve Accuracy:** Clear this option only if you think the review is slowing down your computer.

- **Enable Voice Activation:** This option enables speech recognition to be activated vocally.

- **Number of Spaces to Insert after Punctuation:** Sets the number of spaces to type after end-of-sentence punctuation. The standard has traditionally been 2 in English, but is now more commonly 1.

- **Microphone:** Use this option to make sure your microphone hears you or to adjust its settings.

- **Audio Input:** Click this button to open the Sound properties dialog box to configure speakers, microphone, and other sound properties.

- **Advanced:** Click this button to specify audio input settings (choose a specific microphone, for example) and configure related settings.

- **Configure Microphone:** Click this button to start the Microphone Setup Wizard, which you use to configure your microphone settings.

As always, click OK or Apply after changing anything in the dialog box to implement your changes.

More speech recognition help

To get the most from speech recognition, you want to have easy access to all your resources. You'll find lots of information in Windows Help and Support. Click the Start button, choose Help and Support, type **Speech Recognition**, and press Enter. Or say the following (but don't say anything where you see a hyphen; the hyphen means to just pause briefly until the computer responds to what you just said): `Click Start - Help and Support - Search - 1 - OK - Speech Recognition - Press Enter`.

Regional and Language Settings

Different regions and languages show numbers, dollar amounts, dates, and times in different ways. For example, in the United States, dollar amounts are shown in $1,234.56 format. The United Kingdom uses a £1,234.56 format. French Canada would show that as 1 234,56 $. If your computer isn't showing numbers, dollar amounts, times, or dates correctly for your region, you can fix that. First, you need to open the Regional and Language Settings dialog box using whichever method is easiest for you:

- Press ⊞ , type **lang**, and click Regional and Language.
- Click the Start button and choose Control Panel ➪ Clock, Language, and Region ➪ Regional and Language.

The dialog box opens, looking something like Figure 11-21. Click the Formats tab (shown in the figure) to change your regional settings.

Change how numbers, dates, and times look

The Formats tab of Regional and Language Options shows how numbers, currency values, dates, and times are displayed on your screen. You're not stuck with those formats, however. To change them, click the drop-down button under the Format heading and choose whichever option best describes your region. The formats beneath your selection will change to reflect how things are shown in that region.

FIGURE 11-21

Formats tab of Regional and Language Options.

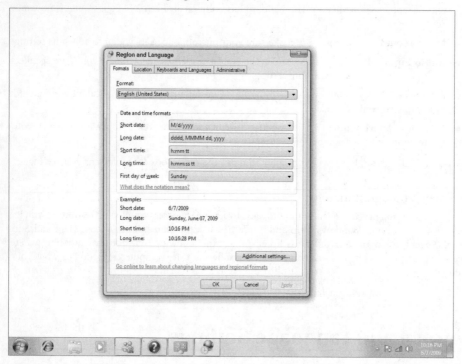

If you need to change one or more of the formats shown under your selected language, click Additional Settings. In the dialog box that opens, specify exactly how you want Windows 7 to show Number, Currency, Time, and Date formats on your screen. When you're happy with the examples shown in your Formats tab, click Apply. You might want to take a look at the next section before you close the dialog box.

Let them know your correct location

Some programs and online services tailor their content to match the location in which your computer is located. If that information seems incorrect, click the Location tab in the Regional and Language dialog box. Choose your actual location from the drop-down button and then click Apply.

Working with multiple languages

For people who work in multiple languages, Windows 7 offers some handy options for adjusting your keyboard to work in a specific language. These features are especially useful for translators who need to switch from one language to another. You can work with two different types of languages:

- **Input Language:** The language you use to type, edit, and read documents is called the input language. Input languages come pre-installed. You don't need to download or buy anything. When you install an input language for reading and typing, you can also choose to use that language for speech recognition.

- **User Interface Language:** The user interface language determines the language displayed on menus, in dialog boxes and wizards, and elsewhere on the screen. A few of these are installed by default; others have to be installed separately. There are two different types of user interface languages you can install:

  - **Language interface packs (LIPs):** These user interface languages translate about 80 percent of the user interface. These are preferred if your goal is to change the language that's on your screen for everyone who uses the computer. These work with all versions of Windows, are free, and are easy to install.

  - **Multilingual user interface (MUI) packs:** These user interface languages translate the entire user interface. They can be applied to individual user accounts. So if some users need an English version of Windows, whereas others need a Spanish version, these are the way to go. But MUI packs work only with Windows 7 Ultimate edition. They can be installed from your original Microsoft Windows DVD or downloaded from Microsoft's Web site.

Tools for adding input languages and user interface languages are on the Keyboard and Languages tab of the Regional and Language dialog box. As you can see in Figure 11-22, the top box is strictly for input languages (how you type, read, and edit documents). The bottom half is for user interface languages (text that appears in menus, dialog boxes, and wizards).

I explain techniques for working with all the different types of languages and files in the sections to follow.

Tip

You don't need anything described in this chapter to type special characters. Those you can insert with Character Map. See "Typing Special Characters with Character Map" in Chapter 14. ∎

Using input languages

If you're a translator or need to type, edit, and read documents in multiple languages, input languages, described here, are for you. To install an input language, click the Change Keyboards button. The Text Services and Input Languages dialog box, shown in Figure 11-23, opens.

To install an input language, click the Add button. A dialog box containing a long list of languages appears. Scroll through that list until you find the language you need. Then click the + (plus) sign next to that language. You can choose which keyboard style you want to use with that language. Click the Preview button to see the layout of whichever keyboard you choose.

FIGURE 11-22

Keyboards and Languages tab.

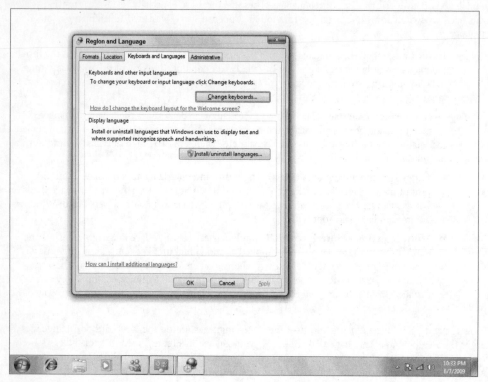

Tip

You can translate text electronically without using input languages. Copy and paste text from any language to a translator such as that found at `http://babelfish.altavista.com/`. **Then copy and paste the translated text to any document.** ∎

For languages that use complex characters, you can also choose an Input Method Editor (IME). This type of editor allows you to use alternatives to the keyboard, such as a pad, for typing.

You can select the Speech check box for most languages. However, speech recognition engines are available for a limited number of languages. To see which speech recognition engines are currently available, go to the Windows Web site (`www.microsoft.com/windows`) and search for "speech recognition engines." Click OK after making your selection.

You can install as many languages and keyboards as you wish. You don't have to do them all in one fell swoop, either. You can add them on an as-needed basis. Each language you add appears in the Installed Services list. Figure 11-24 shows an example in which I've added Chinese and Spanish.

Note the two-letter acronym next to each language in Figure 11-24. That's important because that's how you'll know, later, which language is currently selected. As always, you can click OK after adding input languages.

FIGURE 11-23

Text Services and Input Languages dialog box.

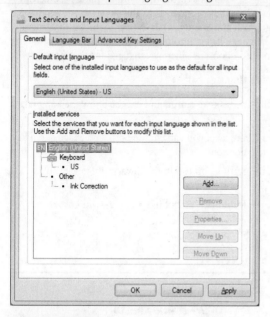

FIGURE 11-24

Chinese and Spanish added as input languages.

Switching languages and keyboards

When you have two or more input languages installed, only one is active at any given time. You need to be in a program that can use alternative languages, such as WordPad, Word, or the On-Screen Keyboard, for the language bar to be relevant at all. When that program is in the active window, you see which language is currently in use for that program. If the language bar is open, you see the language in the bar as at the top of Figure 11-25. If the language bar is minimized, you see the two-letter language abbreviation in the taskbar. Click either one to choose a different language for that program.

Here are some basic, good-to-know facts about the language bar:

- When the language bar is minimized, click its taskbar button and choose Show the Language bar to make it visible.

- If you've selected multiple keyboards for a language, you can choose both a language and a keyboard for whatever program is in the active window.

- When the language bar is visible, click the Settings button in the lower-right corner to set default behavior and appearance options.

- When the language bar is visible, click the Minimize symbol in its upper-right corner to minimize it.

FIGURE 11-25

Language bar and taskbar icon.

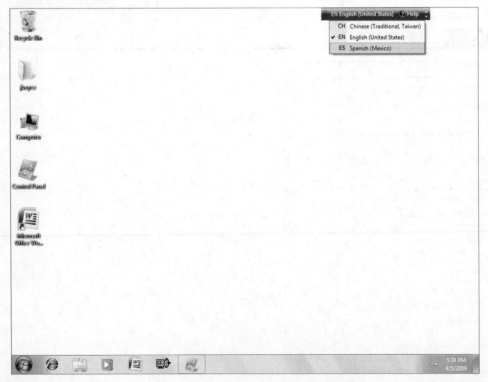

FIGURE 11-26

On-screen Spanish keyboard.

Keep in mind that you can choose different languages and keyboards for different programs. If you have multiple programs open, make sure you first click the title bar of the one you want to configure so that you can see the language and keyboard currently assigned to that program.

When you choose a different language and keyboard from the language bar, the symbols on your keyboard's keys don't change to show the keyboard you've selected. Ideally, you would want to plug in a keyboard that already has the keys in the right layout, or at least use some kind of template that shows how keys are laid out. In a pinch, you can use the On-Screen Keyboard or an on-screen layout to see the keyboard layout. You can find small layouts for the screen by browsing to www.microsoft.com with Internet Explorer and searching for "windows keyboard layouts."

Figure 11-26 shows an example in which I selected the On-Screen Keyboard and then chose Spanish as the keyboard. The keyboard looks almost the same as the English keyboard, but there are some differences. For example, there is an upside-down question mark to the left of the Backspace (Bksp) key that doesn't exist on English keyboards. Pressing the Shift key turns that to an upside-down exclamation point.

Languages that don't use standard keyboard layouts will offer an IME as an alternative. For example, in Figure 11-27 I've chosen Chinese as the language and IME Pad from the language bar. The IME pad lets you compose Chinese characters on the screen.

FIGURE 11-27

Chinese language bar and IME pad.

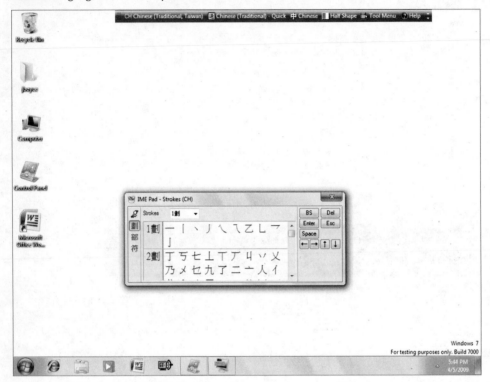

Removing input languages

Removing an input language follows much the same process as adding one. Get back to the Keyboards and Languages tab or Regional and Language and click the Settings button. Click the language or keyboard you want to remove and then click the Remove button. Then click OK.

Installing user interface languages

In contrast to input languages, user interface languages change the language used in menus, dialog boxes, and wizards. You need administrative privileges to install these languages because they affect all user accounts. To download, go to http://download.microsoft.com and search for "Windows 7 Language Interface Pack." Download according to instructions at the site. After you have the file, just double-click its icon and follow the on-screen instructions to install.

Multilingual user interface language packs work only in Ultimate edition of Windows 7. These come with the product on the DVD. Or you can search http://download.microsoft.com for "multilingual user interface" to see what's available online.

After you have an MUI file and know its location on your system, follow these steps to install:

1. Open the Regional and Language dialog box, as described earlier in this section.

2. Click the Keyboards and Languages tab and then click Install/Uninstall Languages (available only in the editions that support MUI).

3. Follow the on-screen instructions to install the MUI of your choice.

After you change the user interface language, verify settings on the Formats tab of Regional and Language Options. If necessary, you can choose a different format as described in the "Change how numbers, dates, and times look" section, which appears previously in this chapter.

Wrap-Up

Windows 7's Ease of Access options provide many alternatives to traditional mouse-and-keyboard computer interaction. Speech Recognition lets you control your computer and dictate text by voice. Regional and Language options provide a means of internationalizing your copy of Windows 7. Here is a quick rundown of the most important things to know:

- To open Ease of Access from the login screen, click the blue Ease of Access button near the lower-left corner.

- To open the Ease of Access Center from the desktop, hold down the Windows logo key and press U. Or click the Start button and choose Control Panel ➪ Ease of Access ➪ Ease of Access Center.

- Microsoft Magnifier, Narrator, and High Contrast help with visual impairments.

- The On-Screen Keyboard, Mouse Keys, Sticky Keys, Toggle Keys, Filter Keys, and Speech Recognition can help with motor impairments.

- Speech recognition takes some time and practice on your part but can be used both to control Windows and to dictate text.

- Regional and Language input languages let you choose languages and keyboards for reading and editing text.

- User interface languages control the language of text displayed in menus, dialog boxes, and wizards.

Transferring Files from Another Computer

I f you bought a new computer with Windows 7pre-installed, you may want to bring some files from an older computer into the new one. If both computers are on the same network, this is a simple matter of using drag-and-drop across folders. But if the two computers are not on the same network, it's a little trickier.

You could copy files from the old computer to a jump drive or other external drive. Then copy files from that drive into corresponding folders on the new computer. But that could take some time, especially if you have hundreds or thousands of files to copy.

Windows Easy Transfer provides a better way to get files from an old computer to a new one. You connect the two computers using a special cable. Then you run the program, tell it what you want to copy, and go to lunch. (Or possibly to bed, because the copying could take several hours.) This chapter explores all the possibilities. But first, let's talk about what you can and can't transfer so that you come into the whole thing with realistic expectations.

What You Can Transfer

You can't transfer everything from your old computer to the new one. But you can transfer just about everything you created or downloaded yourself. Specifically, you can transfer the following:

- **Files and folders:** Everything within the My Documents and Shared Documents folders and their subfolders to corresponding folders on the new computer.

- **Media Files:** Music, playlists, album art, pictures, and videos — most of which are likely stored in your My Music, My Pictures, My Videos (or their Shared) folder equivalents.

- **E-mail settings and messages:** The settings you need to access your e-mail. You can also transfer all saved e-mail messages.

- **Contacts:** If you stored names and address in Windows Address Book (WAB) or Microsoft Outlook on your old computer, you can transfer those to the new computer.

- **Internet settings and favorites:** Settings required for your Internet connection to work, as well as Favorites you've collected. You can also transfer cookies, which retain information that allows you to gain access to certain Web sites that might otherwise require logging in.

- **Personal settings:** Windows personalization settings such as desktop backgrounds, screen savers, Start menu and taskbar options, fonts, network connections, color schemes, accessibility options, and so forth. However, don't expect everything to look and work exactly as it did on your old computer, because there are some changes in Windows 7.

- **User accounts:** If you have multiple user accounts on your old computer, you can transfer those as well. Each user account will retain its documents and settings.

- **Program settings:** Settings you chose within programs to personalize things can be transferred. However, it's important to keep in mind that the programs themselves are not transferred.

What you can't transfer

About the only things you can't transfer are the old version of Windows and programs on the old computer. That's because all programs (including Windows) need to be *installed* on the computer on which they'll run. Copying an installed program from one computer to another just flat-out won't work in almost all cases. The exceptions are too few to consider it a possibility.

Getting programs onto the new computer

Even though you can't transfer installed programs from one computer to another, you can install those same programs on the new computer. For programs you purchased on CD, just insert the CD into the new computer's CD drive and install as you normally would.

Caution

Do not install old utility programs (virus scanners, file managers, firewalls, and such) on your Windows 7 computer. (See "What not to install," later in this chapter, for more information.) Stick with *application* programs such as word processors, spreadsheets, graphics programs, and such — the types of programs used to create and edit documents. ∎

For programs you downloaded, the rules are a little different. If you chose the Save option when downloading and kept that file, you can transfer the saved file to the new computer. Then open that file to start the installation process again. Otherwise, you have to go back to the Web site from which you originally downloaded the program and download again. That's not necessarily a bad thing, because the company might have released an updated version designed for Windows 7 or which has other useful improvements.

As far as Windows goes, you first have to understand that a computer can run only one operating system at a time without a virtualization tool such as VMware or Virtual PC. It makes no sense to try to "transfer" Windows Vista, Windows XP, or Windows 2000 to the new Windows 7 computer.

One Computer, Multiple Operating Systems

You can install and use multiple operating systems on a single PC in a couple of ways. One method, called *dual booting*, involves installing each operating system on its own hard drive *partition*. You can use the Disk Management tool described in Chapter 46, or a third-party program such as Partition Magic to create the partitions. Either way, you risk losing everything on your hard drive, so you must make backups first. If you're not a drive disk or computer expert, you might seriously consider having multiple operating systems installed professionally rather than try to do it yourself.

Virtual machine software provides another approach to using multiple operating systems on a single computer. You can download and use Microsoft Virtual PC for free from www.microsoft.com/windows/virtualPC. Or browse to search.microsoft.com and search for "Windows 7 Virtual PC" for more specific information. You can also use a third-party product such as VMware described at www.vmware.com/products/.

What not to install

Utility programs are specifically designed for security or to enhance features of the operating system. Each is generally designed to work with a specific operating system or family of operating systems. You should never install a utility program that wasn't specifically designed for Windows 7 on your Windows 7 computer. If in doubt, you should contact the program manufacturer to find out whether installing it is okay.

Also, before you even bother installing such programs, learn what's available in Windows 7 and how to use it. Chances are, you won't even need those old utility programs. For example, Windows 7 has extensive security built right into the very core of the operating system, plus lots of extras to protect your computer from many kinds of security threats. You can learn what those are and how to use them in Part II of this book.

Choosing a Transfer Method

To make transferring files as safe and painless as possible, Windows 7 comes with a program named Windows Easy Transfer. The program takes you step-by-step through the process of getting usable files and settings from your old computer to your new Windows 7 computer. Windows Easy Transfer works only with Windows XP, Windows 2000, and Windows Vista. If the computer from which you're transferring files is not running one of those operating systems, you'll have to use an alternative method described later in this chapter.

Easy Transfer provides several methods of transferring files. You need to choose a method that both of your computers can support. The sections to follow describe the three methods: Easy Transfer cable, home network, and external drives or discs.

Note
If you upgraded your operating system from Windows Vista, there's no need to transfer files. Your old files are still on your computer and should be available in Windows 7 automatically. ■

Using a USB Easy Transfer cable

If at all possible, you should use the USB Easy Transfer cable method to transfer files from your old computer to your new computer. You'll need a USB Easy Transfer cable. If your new computer came with Windows 7 pre-installed, it might also have come with a USB Easy Transfer cable. Check the documentation that came with your computer if you're not sure, or contact your computer manufacturer.

If you don't have a USB Easy Transfer cable, you can purchase one online or at any retailer that sells computers or electronics equipment. Online, go to any computer retailer's site (www.cdw.com, www.newegg.com, www.tigerdirect.com, www.amazon.com) and search specifically for "USB Easy Transfer Cable." Or ask for it by name at your local retailer. It should come with a CD that includes the programs you need to make it work. Insert that CD in the old computer's CD drive and follow the on-screen instructions to install the drives and connect the cable.

Caution

Don't use the Easy Transfer CD in your new Windows 7 computer. That computer already has everything you need. ∎

If the transfer cable isn't long enough to connect the two computers, and there's no way to resituate one computer, you might consider using a USB extension cable with the Easy Transfer cable. You can find these at many electronics stores. Or search the Web or an online retailer for "USB extension cable."

Using a home network

If you already have a home network and your new Windows 7 computer is on that network, you can run Windows Easy Transfer on the new 7 computer without connecting any more cables. However, this works only if the Windows 7 computer is already part of your home network. See Part X for more information on creating and using a home network.

Using external drives or discs

If you have no way to connect the new 7 computer to the old computer, you can use external drives or discs. First you need to choose which type of disk you can use. The following sections describe these types.

Using a flash drive or external hard drive

You can use a *flash drive* (also called a jump drive) or an external hard drive that connects via USB. An external hard drive would be the quickest and easiest. If you use a flash drive, you need one with enough storage capacity for the largest file. It doesn't need capacity for *all* the files because you can make the transfer in several steps. If the flash drive contains backups of many important files, consider moving those to another location temporarily during the transfer. The more room you have on the flash drive, the better.

Using CDs or DVDs

You can use CD-RW, DVD-RW, or DVD+RW discs to transfer files. Both computers must have a drive that can read and write to the type of disc you choose. For example, if one computer can read and write CD-RW discs only, then you have to use CD-RW discs.

What about Floppy Disks?

By the way, you may have noticed that I didn't mention floppy disks. That's because you can't use floppies with Windows Easy Transfer. The floppy disk's extremely small capacity (1.4MB) makes it an unrealistic medium for this sort of thing. In fact, most people would call it an unrealistic medium for much of anything, which is why many computer manufacturers don't even bother to put floppy drives in many systems they sell. Floppies are basically in the "obsolete" category of computer media — except for making backups of small files such as digital licenses and certificates.

How Long Does It Take?

How long it takes to transfer files from your old computer to the new one depends on how much stuff you're transferring and the method you use. But it could be several hours, so you should definitely start the process when you can concentrate on it for a while without interruptions.

If you have a lot of old junk on your old computer that you've been ignoring, a little spring cleaning may be in order. Delete anything you know for sure you will never need again for the rest of your life. No sense transferring trash. If you do, you'll eventually have to clean it off of both computers!

Make sure that you have at least one empty CD-RW or DVD-RW disc on hand before you begin the transfer. Put it in the appropriate drive on the new Windows 7 computer. If AutoPlay or a program opens after you insert the disc, just close that item by clicking the Close (X) button in its upper-right corner.

Note
A DVD holds much more information than a CD. So if you can use DVDs, you'll use fewer discs. You can use dual-layer (8.5GB) DVDs only if the DVD drives in both computers support that format. ∎

Doing the Transfer

After you've decided on a transfer method, Windows Easy Transfer takes you through the steps required to complete your transfer. To get started, sit at your new Windows 7 PC and use whichever of the following techniques works and is easiest for you:

- Press ⊞, type **trans**, and click Windows Easy Transfer on the Start menu.
- Click the Start button and choose All Programs ➪ Accessories ➪ System Tools ➪ Windows Easy Transfer.

Windows Easy Transfer opens, looking like Figure 12-1.

Tip
The Windows Easy Transfer on Windows 7 asks you whether you have installed the Windows Easy Transfer software on your old PC and prompts you to select an external hard drive, shared network folder, or USB flash drive. It will then copy the software to the specified location, and you can use that software to install on your old PC. Run MgSetup.exe from the target location to install the software. ∎

FIGURE 12-1

First page of Windows Easy Transfer.

The program will take you step-by-step through the rest of the process. Make sure you read all the text on a page and accurately answer any questions before you click Next (or any other button) at the bottom of a page. A couple of things you might notice along the way:

- If you left any other programs open before you started Easy Transfer, you'll be prompted to close them. Click Close All and, if prompted, save any unsaved work you left behind.

- If asked for permission to work through your firewall, click Yes or OK. Don't worry, you're not making your computer vulnerable to hackers or malware. You're just giving Easy Transfer the right to do what it needs to do and nothing more.

- If you'll be using discs to make the transfer, you need to follow instructions to copy Easy Transfer to a disc. Then you need to insert that disc in the other computer, choose the option to run Easy Install on that computer, and continue the transfer from that computer.

Regardless of which method you use, you'll eventually come to a page like the one in Figure 12-2. You can choose which user account files and shared items to transfer. To choose only certain items under each account or under the Shared Items, click the Customize link under the item to open the pop-up menu shown in Figure 12-2. You can simply check / uncheck items to specify whether they are included, and also click the Advanced link at the bottom of the pop-up window to open a Windows Explorer-like dialog box in which you can choose or exclude individual folders and files.

After you've made your selection, you're back to just reading and following instructions on the screen. Those instructions will be tailored to the method you're using and the files you're transferring. If you are transferring using the network, Windows Easy Transfer will issue you a key. You enter this key in Windows Easy Transfer on the new computer to enable it to connect to your old one and begin the transfer.

FIGURE 12-2

Decide what to transfer.

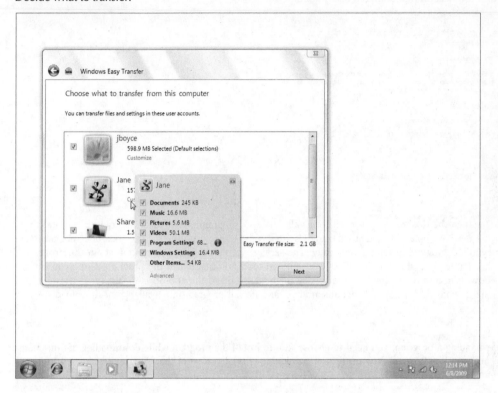

When the Transfer Is Finished

When Easy Transfer has completed its task, your new computer will contain whatever you opted to transfer. Keep in mind that some folder names are different in Windows 7. The "Shared" folders are now "Public" folders (Public Documents, Public Pictures, and so forth).

Note
The `Documents and Settings` folder from Windows XP is named `Users` in Windows 7. The `All Users` subfolder is named `Public` in Windows 7. ■

Remember, programs from your old computer are typically not transferred unless they are standalone executables that do not require installation or setup. All programs must be installed to the computer on which they'll run. You need to start that installation from the original program CD or a download.

Documents for which there is no program on the new computer will not open on the new computer. When you attempt to open such a document, you'll see an error message like the one in Figure 12-3.

FIGURE 12-3

No program on this computer can open this document.

To open the document, you need to install whatever program you used on the older computer to the new computer. Note that choosing Use the Web Service from the message box does not make the required program install automatically. The service simply provides information about the program needed to open that type of file; it also links to more information. If the program is one you can download and install for free, the service might take you to the appropriate page for performing the download. But not all programs are free, and not all programs are available for download.

Note
When downloading a program, you need to choose Run to install the program while downloading. If you choose Save, the program won't install. You need to open (double-click) the icon of the file you downloaded to install the program. ■

Transferring without Windows Easy Transfer

In some situations you might want to use a manual method to copy files and other items from your old computer to your new Windows 7 computer. For example, perhaps you can't use Windows Easy Transfer because of limitations of the PC or your working environment, or maybe you just want some manual alternatives.

One choice is to copy any files you need on the new computer to some external medium. A flash drive or external hard drive would be best. You can use CDs or DVDs if both computers have appropriate drives. After you've copied all the necessary files to that external medium, connect it to or insert it into your Windows 7 computer and copy files from it to appropriate folders on your hard drive (for example, Documents, Pictures, Music, Videos).

Copying files won't help with Internet favorites, e-mail messages, contacts, and such. But you can usually *export* those items to files. Copy those files to your external medium and then *import* those files to corresponding programs on your Windows 7 computer. Options to import and export are usually on a program's File menu. If in doubt, you can search that program's Help for "Export" or "Import," depending on which you need to do.

The sections that follow offer a few handy tips and techniques. First, however, I offer a couple of cautions for people who skipped or didn't understand the preceding sections of this chapter.

Caution

The techniques assume that you know how to navigate folders, use your My Computer folder (or Computer folder in Windows Vista and Windows 7), and copy files. Most of the concepts and skills presented in Part VI of this book apply to all versions of Windows. ■

Manually transfer Internet Explorer Favorites

To export Internet Export Favorites on the old computer, choose File ➪ Import and Export ➪ Export Favorites. Put that file on your external drive or disc. Or put it in your Documents folder (or someplace else that's easy to get to) and copy it to the external drive or disc. The Favorites are stored in a file named bookmark.htm.

Tip

It's really not necessary to export cookies to your new computer. Those files are created and deleted on the fly by Web sites you visit and are rarely "necessary" for accessing a Web site. But if you really want to do so, you can choose to export and import cookies. Note that if you don't copy over cookies, you'll have to reauthenticate on any sites that use cookies to store authentication information. ■

On the Windows 7 computer, open Internet Explorer. Press the Alt key to see the classic menus. Choose File ➪ Import and Export, and in the wizard, choose Import Favorites. Browse to your external drive or disc and double-click the bookmark.htm file. Continue on through the wizard, clicking Next, Import, OK, and Finish where appropriate. When you're done, click the Favorites Center star at the left side of the toolbar. You should see all your imported favorites.

Manually transfer contacts

If you use Outlook Express or Microsoft Outlook on the old computer to manage contacts, you can export them to a .csv file on an external drive or disc. Then connect that drive or insert the disc in the Windows 7 computer and import your contacts to your Contacts folder.

To export Windows Address Book contacts from Outlook Express, open Outlook Express and click Address Book. Or open Windows Address Book from the Start menu. When you're in Windows Address Book, choose File ➪ Export ➪ Other Address Book ➪ Text File (Comma Separated Values). Then browse to your external drive and enter a filename. When you get to the Select Fields page, you can select every check box and then click Finish.

To export Contacts from Microsoft Outlook, open Outlook and click Contacts so that you're viewing your contacts. Choose File ➪ Import and Export from the menu. In the wizard that opens, choose Export to a File, Comma Separated Values (Windows), and Contacts. Use the Browse button to navigate to your external drive, give the file a name, and click Next and Finish until the copy is complete.

In Windows 7, you'll use your Contacts folder to manage names and address. Chapter 21 provides all the details. In terms of importing contacts from that .csv file, the process goes like this: First, insert the disc or connect the drive that contains the exported contacts. Then open your Contacts folder: Log in to your user account, click the Start button, click your user name, and open the Contacts icon.

In your open Contacts folder, click Import in the toolbar. If you don't see Import in the toolbar, click >> at the end of that toolbar and then click Import. Click CSV (Comma Separated Values) and click Import. On the next page, click the Browse button and navigate to the disc or drive that contains those contacts you exported. Click the filename that contains the contacts and click Open. Then click Next and Finish. Each imported contact is represented by an icon in your Contacts folder.

Manually transfer Outlook Express e-mail messages

Windows Live Mail, covered in Chapter 18, includes a capability to import messages from Outlook Express 6. Here's how to accomplish that task:

1. Open Outlook Express on your old computer and click Tools ➪ Options.

2. Click the Maintenance tab and click Store Folder to view the location of your current mail store.

3. Copy all of the contents of the Outlook Express mail store folder identified in step 2 to a flash drive or other removable media.

4. On your Windows 7 computer where Windows Live Mail is installed, open Windows Live Main and click File ➪ Import ➪ Messages.

5. In the Windows Live Mail Import wizard, choose Microsoft Outlook Express 6 from the list of e-mail sources and click Next.

6. Browse to the location where the files you copied in step 3 are located, and then click Next. Follow the remaining wizard prompts to complete the import.

There isn't really any sure-fire simple way of transferring e-mail messages from all older versions of Outlook Express to Windows 7. But the method described in this section seems to work with many versions. The idea is to open Outlook Express normally. Drag the message headers of any messages you want to transfer to a folder window for your external drive or disc. You can select multiple headers using the standard Ctrl+Click and Shift+Click methods and then drag any one of them. Each e-mail message then becomes an .eml file on the external drive.

Now comes the strange-but-true part of the transfer. Connect the drive or insert the disc that contains the .eml files in the Windows 7 computer. Open Windows Live Mail and click your Inbox (or any folder under your Inbox). Or maybe better still, create a folder under your Inbox and name it something like Imported (in case this manual transfer method doesn't work with *all* versions of Outlook Express). Select all the icons for the .eml files on the external drive or disc and drag them to the main pane in Windows Live Mail where you normally see message headers. They should just fall right into place, no problem (although they'll be at the bottom of the list of message headers that are already in that folder).

As an alternative to transferring by drive or disc, you can forward any saved messages to yourself so that they end up back on your ISP's mail sever. Just make sure you don't download the messages to your old computer again. When you check your e-mail on the your new Windows 7 computer, the forwarded messages will download to your Inbox there.

Note

E-mail is an Internet service provided by your ISP. Not all ISPs provide the same service. If you have questions about, or problems with, your e-mail, contact your ISP. Its staff members are the only people who can help you with the service that ISP provides. ■

Transferring fonts

If you purchased or downloaded any TrueType or OpenType fonts and want to copy them over, open the Fonts folder on the old computer. This is typically C:\Windows\Fonts. Open that folder and copy any fonts you want to transfer to your external drive or disc. Stick with TrueType and OpenType fonts (with .ttf extensions) that you acquired on your own. Don't try to copy all fonts. Windows 7 already has many fonts built into it, and you don't want to replace those fonts with older versions of similar fonts.

After you've copied fonts to an external drive or disc, connect that drive or insert that disc into the Windows 7 computer. Log in to an administrative user account. Then, simply right-click the font file you want to add and click Install.

Wrap-Up

Transferring files and settings from an old Windows 2000 or Windows XP computer is fairly easy. Use the USB Easy Transfer cable that came with your new computer. Or purchase one from any computer retailer. If the old computer isn't running Windows 2000 or XP, you can't use the Easy Transfer program and cable. But there are still ways to get files to the new computer, provided that you have sufficient basic skills to locate and copy files. To summarize:

- Windows Easy Transfer is the quickest and easiest way to transfer user accounts, folders, files, and settings from an old Windows 2000 or XP computer to your new 7 computer.

- You cannot transfer programs from an old computer to a new one through any means unless the programs are standalone executables. That's because most programs must be *installed* — not transferred or copied to the computer.

- Do not install older utility programs (virus scanners, firewalls, file managers, and such) on Windows 7. Such programs are designed to work with a specific version or family of Windows, and may cause problems if installed on Windows 7.

- Windows Easy Transfer, which comes free with Windows 7, provides the quickest and easiest method of transferring user accounts, files, and settings from a Windows 2000, XP, or Vista computer to a new Windows 7 computer.

- To start Windows Easy Transfer, click the Start button, type **trans**, and click Windows Easy Transfer. To transfer files, just read the Windows Easy Transfer instructions and choose options that make sense for your equipment.

- To transfer files from earlier versions of Windows, copy those files to an external drive or disc. Then copy from that same drive or disc onto the Windows 7 computer.

- To transfer contacts from an older computer, export them to a CSV file on an external drive or disc. Then import them from that drive or disc into your Contacts folder on the Windows 7 computer.

Customizing Startup Options

A computer is basically a machine that's designed to do one thing: run programs. There are more than 100,000 different programs that can run on your computer. Nobody owns them all or needs them all. But there are certainly many to choose from.

Your computer already has many programs installed on it. Many are programs that you can start at will from icons on the Start menu and All Programs menu. Some programs start automatically when you log in. Often, these programs run in a window, as an icon on the taskbar, or both.

Another type of program starts automatically as soon as you start your computer. These are referred to as *services*, and services are most often part of the Windows operating system itself or programs that control hardware or other underlying functions. Services generally don't have program windows on your desktop or taskbar buttons. In fact, you would likely never know that services existed unless you went looking for them.

This chapter is about controlling exactly which programs and services do, and don't, start automatically when you first start your computer and Windows. By controlling these programs, you can streamline the Windows startup and fix problems with performance or function.

First Things First

First, I need to make a distinction between application programs and services. For this chapter's purpose, I refer to such a program as an application program (or *application*, or *app* for short). These are programs that, when open, usually have a program window on your desktop and a rectangular button in the taskbar. Typically, you open and use such a program to perform some specific task, such as to check your e-mail or browse the Web. Then you close the program when you've finished that task. To close such a program, you can typically click the Close (X) button in the program's upper-right corner or right-click the program's taskbar button and choose Close. You can reopen the program at any time by clicking its icon on the Start or All Programs menu.

Even though most application programs run in a window and live on the taskbar, not all do. Many utility applications run as icons on the Notification area (tray). The Ultramon program, which I discussed in a previous chapter, for example, runs as an icon on the tray and provides special features for using multiple displays. Typically, when you rest the mouse pointer on a tray icon such as Ultramon's, a tooltip appears, showing the name of the program that the icon represents. Clicking or double-clicking such an icon often opens a dialog box or similar window. Right-clicking such an icon often displays a list of things you can do with the program. Figure 13-1 illustrates this distinction between applications and services.

FIGURE 13-1

Examples of application programs and tray icons.

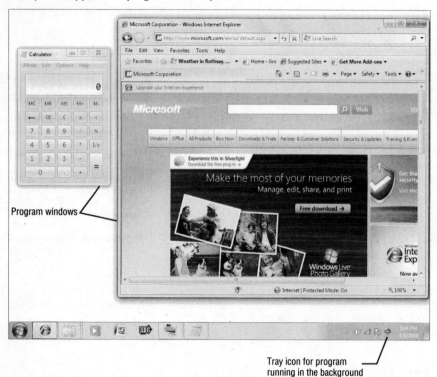

Program windows

Tray icon for program
running in the background

Tip

In many cases, you can control whether a program's icon appears in the tray. You can also control which of the Windows 7 tray icons appear in the tray. See Chapter 10 to learn how to customize the taskbar and tray. ■

Services are also application programs, but services generally do not provide any means for the user to interact with them. Many services are actually included as part of the operating system. For example, the Windows Time service provides time synchronization functions for Windows, enabling it, for example, to set the computer's time from a remote time server. The DHCP Client service is another example. It is responsible for obtaining an IP address for your computer when the computer starts up, enabling your computer to participate on the network.

Neither of the services described above provides any means for you to interact with them; they do their thing in the background with no input from you. By contrast, the Windows Firewall service does provide a means for you to interact with it. Even so, Windows Firewall is still a service, and most of the time, you don't interact with it. Services such as this that provide a means for user interaction are by far the exception rather than the rule.

Why am I telling you about services and how they differ from other programs? In most cases, you won't need to manage services or control their startup, but in some situations, doing so is necessary. Most of the time, you'll be more concerned with which application programs start automatically. But it's important for you to understand the difference so that you can make an educated decision as to how to handle them. One of the main focuses of this chapter is to help you understand how to make programs start automatically that normally don't do so, how to stop certain programs from starting automatically, and why you would want to do either. So, let's start with how you make programs start automatically.

Starting Application Programs Automatically

If you always use a certain application program when you start your computer, you can configure Windows to start that program automatically. For example, maybe you use Microsoft Office Outlook all the time for your e-mail and want it to open as soon as you log in to the computer so that you don't have to start it yourself.

You can also make folders open automatically. For example, you can have Windows automatically open the main folder for your user account at startup so that you can quickly get to other folders, such as Documents, Pictures, or Music.

You have a couple of ways to make programs start automatically when you log in. The first is to add a shortcut for the program to one of the two Startup folders provided by Windows. One Startup folder is for your user account; the other is for all users of the computer. Your Startup folder is located in the folder `\Users\<user>\AppData\Roaming\Microsoft\Windows\Start Menu\Programs`, where `<user>` is your username (such as *jim*). The Startup folder for everyone who uses the computer is located in the hidden folder `\ProgramData\Microsoft\Windows\Start Menu\Programs`.

If you want a program to start automatically for you, put a shortcut for the program in your Startup folder. If you want a program to start automatically for everyone, you can instead put it in the Startup folder for all users.

Assuming that you're already logged in to your user account, the steps to open your own Startup folder are easy:

1. Click the Start button and choose All Programs.

2. If necessary, scroll down until you see the Startup folder icon on the menu.

3. Right-click that Startup icon and choose Open. It opens as a folder on the desktop.

Optionally, to give yourself some elbow room, size and position the window as shown in Figure 13-2. You don't need the Navigation pane here, so you can close that if it's open (click the Organize button and choose Organize ➪ Layout ➪ Navigation Pane).

To make an application program auto-start, right-drag (drag with the right mouse button) its icon from the All Programs menu into the main pane of the Startup folder and drop it there; then choose Create Shortcuts Here. Keep in mind that the more programs you add to the folder, the longer it will take for your computer to start. So don't get carried away and put all your favorite programs in there. One or two should be sufficient.

FIGURE 13-2

Startup folder.

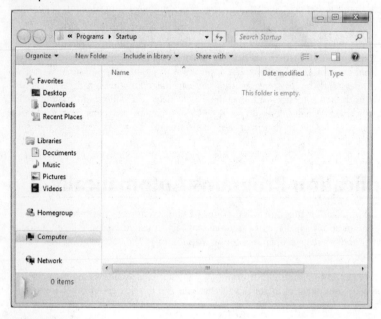

Caution

If you accidentally moved a shortcut from the Start menu instead of copying it, right-click some empty space in the Startup folder and choose Undo Move. Or just drag it back to its old location on the Start menu. ■

When you've finished, close the Startup folder. Windows Defender may show a message alerting you to the fact that your startup options have changed. No cause for alarm. In this case the message is superfluous because you intentionally changed your startup programs. Defender doesn't know that, however. It's just doing one of its many jobs, which in this situation is to keep you informed of changes to your Startup options.

Tip

To add a program's shortcut to the Startup folder for all users so that it starts for everyone, use the same process as described previously except drag the icon to the all users Startup folder rather than your personal Startup folder. ■

Bypassing all Startup folder programs

Windows gives you a quick and easy way to bypass all programs that start automatically from either of the Startup folders. For example, if you are having problems with a particular program causing startup problems, or you have lots of programs and just want to get to your desktop quickly, you can bypass all Startup programs so that none of them start. To do so, click your user account in the login screen, type your password, and press Enter. Immediately press and hold the left Shift key. Keep pressing the Shift key until the Start menu, desktop icons, and taskbar all appear. If programs from the Startup folders still start automatically, you're not holding the Shift key long enough.

Stopping auto-start applications

Should you ever change your mind about auto-start applications, you just need to reopen that Startup folder for your user account. Then delete the shortcut icon for any program you don't want to auto-start. Or, if you moved it from another location, move it back (out of the Startup folder.) However, not all programs that auto-start will be in the Startup folder for your user account. Some may be in the Startup folder for all users. (Still others will be in other locations. I get to those in the section on Windows Defender later in this chapter.)

To view, and optionally remove, programs that start automatically in all user accounts, you need to get to the all users Startup folder. You may need administrative privileges to make changes to that folder, so be prepared to enter an administrative password if you're working from a standard account. The basic procedure is easy: Click the Start button and choose All Programs. Right-click the Startup folder again, but this time choose Open All Users (see Figure 13-3).

FIGURE 13-3

Open the Startup folder for all user accounts.

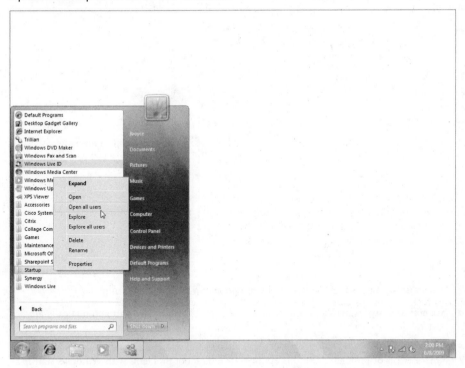

The All Users Startup folder works just like the Startup folder for a single user account. If you want a program to auto-start in all user accounts, drag that program's icon into the folder. If you want to stop a program from auto-starting in all user accounts, delete its icon from that Startup folder. But again, stick with programs you know. Removing programs from the All Users Startup folder at random could have unpleasant consequences that you weren't expecting.

Note

Windows Defender in Windows Vista includes a Software Explorer component that enables you to control startup programs, but Software Explorer has been removed from Windows Defender in Windows 7. Instead, you can use the System Configuration tool described in the next section to control program startup. ■

Using the System Configuration Tool to Control Startup

One tool that has existed in multiple versions of Windows that lets you control program startup is the System Configuration program. That program is also available in Windows 7. To open System Configuration, open the Control Panel, click All Control Panel Items, and click Administrative Tools. Figure 13-4 shows the System Configuration program window.

FIGURE 13-4

System Configuration program.

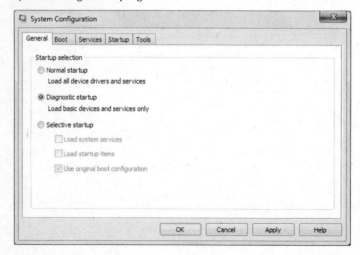

The General tab, shown in Figure 13-4, offers three options for controlling startup:

- **Normal Startup**. Start Windows normally. All items that normally start automatically are started.

- **Diagnostic Startup**. Load only basic device drivers and operating system services but not other services or programs. Use this option to troubleshoot problems with Windows startup that might be caused by a third-party service, device driver, or program.

- **Selective Startup**. Choose which types of items will start automatically. Start Windows with basic devices and services, and optionally other system services and startup programs.

The Boot tab, shown in Figure 13-5, lets you control how Windows boots. The large text box lists all the operating system boot selections. If Windows 7 is the only operating system on the computer, it will be the only one listed in the text box. If you have a dual-boot system (for example, with Windows

XP and Windows 7 on the same computer in different partitions), those additional operating system instances will also be listed. Click an instance and then click Set As Default to make that operating system boot by default when the computer starts.

FIGURE 13-5

The Boot tab.

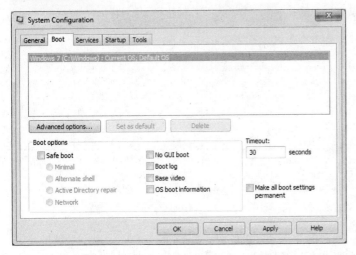

The other options under the Boot Options group let you configure options for a safe boot so that the next time you start Windows, it will boot with the specified safe boot option. You can also set other boot options. Because you likely will use these options rarely, if ever, I point you to the Help content rather than cover them here. Just click the Help button on the Boot tab to view an explanation of these options.

Note
Use the option Make All Boot Settings Permanent to have the settings apply every time you boot the computer. ∎

The Services tab gives you a means to disable services so that they do not start when Windows boots. This tab also shows the current state of the services on the computer. Selecting the check box beside a service indicates that the service is enabled. You can disable a service by deselecting its check box. If you want to view only third-party services, select the Hide All Microsoft Services check box. This helps you identify services that are not part of the Windows 7 operating system.

In general, you should avoid disabling services unless you know exactly what the service does and what the consequences of disabling it will be. Usually, you want to disable a service only if a tech support engineer or some troubleshooting documentation has directed you to do so.

The Startup tab (Figure 13-6) shows programs that start through an entry in the Windows registry. Typically, these programs are listed in the registry key HKEY_LOCAL_MACHINE\ SOFTWARE\Microsoft\Windows\CurrentVersion\Run. You can disable a program from starting from its registry entry by deselecting the check box.

FIGURE 13-6

The Startup tab.

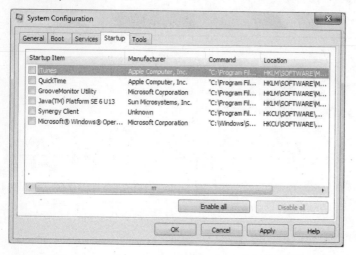

Caution

The Windows registry is a group of files that store configuration information for Windows and applications. The Registry Editor program offers another means for viewing and changing the contents of the registry. However, you should never change registry settings unless you know exactly what you're doing, because an incorrect change could potentially prevent Windows from booting or working properly. ■

Often, program developers will design their programs to start from the registry instead of the Startup folder when they don't want the user to be able to turn off the program without uninstalling it. This is typical for antivirus programs and other utility programs. If you are trying to turn off a program and you don't find it in one of the Startup folders, there is probably an entry for the program in the registry that causes it to start automatically.

The Tools tab gathers a selection of useful tools for troubleshooting problems with your computer and getting more information about programs. Just click a tool and click Launch to open the tool.

After you make changes to configuration settings in the System Configuration tool, you need to click OK and then restart the computer to make the changes take effect.

Controlling Services with the Services Snap-In

Windows 7 includes a system management framework tool called the Microsoft Management Console (MMC). The MMC provides access to various *snap-ins*, with each snap-in providing options for different types of configuration options or an interface to manage items such as policies, accounts, and so on. One of these snap-ins is named Services.msc. It's not a user-friendly program but is rather designed for professionals. Beginners and casual users are better off sticking with the Startup folders as a means of working with auto-start programs. Even so, beginners can start to understand how some of the underlying pieces of Windows work by looking through the Services console and checking out what some of the services do.

Note

If you want to make any changes in the Services snap-in, log out of any standard accounts and in to an account that has administrative privileges. Or, right-click Services and choose **Run As Administrator.** ■

To start the Services snap-in, click the Start button, type **serv**, and click Services under the Program heading on the Start menu. When the Services snap-in is open, use the View menu options to choose how you want to view icons. Figure 13-7 shows how things are displayed in the Details view. The toolbar contains a couple of buttons for showing and hiding optional Console Tree and Action panes. (Both are hidden in Figure 13-7.) Extended and Standard tabs are near the bottom of the window. The figure shows how things look in the Extended tab.

Services snap-in.

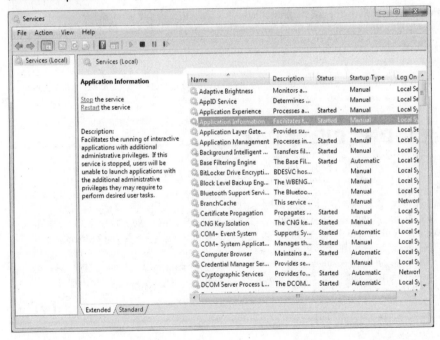

Tip

You can also start the Services console by running Services.msc, by opening it in the Administrative Tools folder, or by right-clicking Computer, choosing Manage, and clicking the Services node in the left pane of the Computer Management console (expand Services and Applications in the left pane if needed to access the Services console). ■

Clicking the Extended tab opens a new pane at the left side of the program window that shows detailed information about any service name you click. It also provides options to start a service that's not running, or to stop or restart the service if it's not running.

Note

Because of enhanced security in Windows 7, you do not have as much leeway in starting and stopping services as you did in earlier Windows versions. Some services cannot be stopped at all! ■

If you scroll through the list of services, you'll probably see quite a few. Exactly which services are listed will vary from one computer to the next. Few, if any, of the services will have any meaning to the average computer user. These things are really only of use to professional programmers, network administrators, support technicians, or other experienced professionals. What follows is mainly for those folks. I don't bother to summarize what each service does because doing so would eat up several pages and only repeat the information that's already in the Description column.

The Status column shows Started for those services that are currently running. It shows nothing for services that aren't running. The Startup Type column shows whether the service is configured to run automatically, if at all. Common settings are:

- **Automatic:** The service starts automatically when the computer starts or when a user logs in.

- **Manual:** The service doesn't start automatically. You can start the service, however, by right-clicking the service name and choosing Start or by choosing Start from the Action menu.

- **Disabled:** The service is disabled and must be enabled from the Properties dialog box before it can be started.

To get more information about a service or change its Startup type, right-click the service name and choose Properties. You see a dialog box like the one in Figure 13-8.

What Does the DNS Client Do?

IP addresses are what routers (networking hardware that moves data around) use to locate devices such as servers on the Internet and send traffic back and forth between devices. The DNS client service is called a *DNS resolver* and is critical for networking because it resolves hostnames like www.wiley.com to IP addresses such as 208.215.179.146. When you type a URL into your Web browser and press Enter, the DNS service contacts a DNS name server and gives it the hostname (in this example, www.wiley.com), and the name server responds with the IP address that corresponds to the hostname. Then, the traffic (in this case, the request for the specified Web site) gets routed on the Internet to the server based on its IP address. Of course, you can browse the Web for the rest of your life without knowing anything about DNS or IP addresses. You couldn't browse the Web without a DNS resolver service running, however.

The options you see in Figure 13-8 are typical of the items listed in the Services snap-in. The Description textbox provides a description of the services and tells what will happen if you disable or stop the service. The Path To Executable textbox shows the location and name of the program that provides the service. The Startup type option provides the Automatic, Manual, and Disabled options.

The buttons let you stop, pause, resume, or start the service. Some programs accept parameters, which you can add to the Start Parameters textbox.

The Log On tab provides options for granting rights to services that need permissions to run. The Recovery tab provides options for dealing with problems when a service fails to start.

FIGURE 13-8

FIGURE 13-8

Properties for the DNS client service.

The Dependencies tab is one of the most important of the bunch because it specifies which services the current service depends on (if any) and which services depend on the current service. For example, DNS is a TCP/IP thing (which is the protocol used by the Internet and most modern local networks). If a service isn't starting and you can't figure out why, seeing what services the current one depends on might provide a clue. If that service isn't running, the one you're looking at can't start, so you need to go to that service and make sure it's starting.

If you're interested in learning more about TCP/IP and how the Internet works, a Windows book isn't the best place to look. Any book on TCP/IP, however, or any book or course that prepares you for MCSA (Microsoft Certified Systems Administrator) or MCSE (Microsoft Certified Systems Engineer) certification would explain all that in depth. For broader technical coverage of services, consult a technical reference such as *Microsoft Windows 7 Resource Kit*.

Note

For more information on Microsoft certifications, see www.microsoft.com/learning/mcp. ∎

Bypassing the Login Page

This is one of those little Windows 7 secrets everyone likes to know about but should be cautious about using. It lets you bypass the login screen and start up Windows 7 in a specific user account automatically. Though it does save you one click at startup, it means anyone who sits at your computer can just turn on the power switch and have full access to everything in your user account. So don't do this if you want to keep other people out of your user account.

Doing this trick requires administrative privileges. So know the password or log in to an administrative account first. Here are the steps:

1. Click the Start button, type **netplwiz**, and then click netplwiz in the Start menu.

2. Grant permission or enter an administrative password if prompted.

3. Deselect the Users Must Enter a Username and Password to Use This Computer check box.

4. Click Apply.

5. In the dialog box that opens, type the name of the user account to which you want to log in automatically.

6. If that user account requires a password, type the password once in the Password box and then again in the second box for confirmation. If the user account isn't password-protected, leave both boxes empty.

7. Click OK in each open dialog box.

That's it. The next time you restart your computer, there will be no login page. You'll be taken straight into your user account. If there are other user accounts on the computer, and you want to let another user log in, log out of your account (click the Start button, the arrow next to the lock symbol, and choose Log Off). You're taken to the login page, which works normally. For example, if you want to get into a password-protected administrative account, you'll still click that account's icon and will have to enter the correct password.

If you ever change your mind about doing this, just repeat Steps 1 and 2 in the preceding list. This time, though, select the Users Must Enter a Username and Password to Use This Computer check box and click OK.

Troubleshooting Startup

Many things can prevent Windows from starting properly. There is no simple solution to the problem because too many things might be wrong. Typically, you need a professional to fix such problems. But I can tell you a few things that even the average user might try to get things going again.

Get rid of disabled devices

If your computer contains a hardware device that Windows 7 can't use, you should still be able to get to the desktop. But each time you do, you'll see a notification message about a device being disabled. That can get tiresome. If you manually disable the device through Device Manager, you won't see that message anymore. Also, it should take a little less time for Windows 7 to start.

Caution

Don't take wild guesses here. If you disable a hardware device you really need, you might not be able to start Windows 7 at all! If in doubt, it's better to take the computer into a repair shop and let the pros figure it out. ■

To disable a device, you need to first log in to a user account that has administrative privileges. Then press ⊞, type dev, and click Device Manager on the Start menu. Or right-click Computer in the Start menu, choose Manage, and click the Device Manager node in the left pane. Expand the category to which the device belongs. If you're not sure which category to look in, try the Other Devices category.

You'll be looking for a device whose icon shows an exclamation point in a tiny yellow circle. After you find the device, right-click its name and choose Disable.

When you've disabled the device, the yellow icon changes to a white downward-pointing arrow. That means the device is disabled and Windows 7 won't try to reinstall it on future bootups, which should mean a slightly quicker boot-up time and no irritating message about the disabled device.

When Windows won't start at all

If Windows won't start at all, try to start Windows 7 in Safe Mode. This is a special mode in which Windows 7 loads only the minimum services, drivers, and programs it needs to get going. Getting to Safe Mode isn't always easy. You have to restart the computer and then press the F8 key after the POST (Power on Self Test) but before Windows starts to load. If your keyboard has a Function Lock (F Lock) key, you have to make sure that it's on before you press F8. In a pinch, you can restart the computer and then press F8 repeatedly for the first few seconds. But again, keep an eye on the Function Lock key because it might go off once or twice during the restart.

When you've pressed the F8 key at just the right time, you'll see a screen that shows several options for starting Windows, as summarized here:

- **Safe Mode:** Starts Windows with a minimal set of drivers and services so that you can use other tools such as System Restore, Device Manager, Installed Programs, and others to try to fix the problems. For example, you could uninstall known faulty programs and devices and then return to an earlier restore point.

- **Safe Mode with Networking:** Same as previous, but provides access to the Internet and a private network.

- **Safe Mode with Command Prompt:** Starts windows without the GUI (graphical user interface).

- **Enable Boot Logging:** Creates a log file named ntbtlog.txt that lists all drivers that were loaded during startup.

- **Enable Low-Resolution Video (640x480):** Starts with low resolution and refresh rates to reset display settings.

- **Last Known Good Configuration:** Starts Windows with the last successful configuration (an easy fix for many problems!).

- **Directory Services Restore Mode:** Starts a domain control running Active Directory so that directory services can be restored.

- **Debugging Mode:** Starts in an advanced troubleshooting mode for professionals.

- **Disable Automatic Restart on System Failure:** Prevents Windows from automatically restarting during a failed startup. This gets you out of the endless loop of crashing and restarting.

- **Start Windows Normally:** Starts normally with all drivers and services.

- **Disable Driver Signature Enforcement:** Allows improperly signed drivers to be loaded at startup.

- **Repair Your Computer:** Use this option to repair your installation of Windows 7.

Often, choosing the Last Known Good Configuration option will get you back to the desktop. Or you can go into Safe Mode to get to a minimal desktop. Either way, when you're at the desktop, you may be able to fix the problem. For example, if the problem started right after you installed new hardware, use Device Manager to uninstall the device driver. Then shut down the computer, physically remove the device, and restart. See Chapter 46 for more information.

If a program is causing the problem, uninstall that program through Control Panel. See Chapter 42 for the details on uninstalling programs.

You can also use System Restore to restore to a previous restore point. For more information, see "Using System Protection" in Chapter 33.

If you're not sure what's causing the problem, you can use System Configuration, described earlier in this chapter, as a diagnostic tool for finding out.

You can start by choosing Diagnostic Startup and closing System Configuration. Then restart the computer but don't go into Safe Mode. The computer will start with a minimal set of drivers and programs, and System Configuration will open. Then you can use options on the Boot, Services, Startup, and Tools tabs to choose other options. For example, you might want to try enabling a few services or programs on the Services and Startup tabs and then restart the computer again to see whether it will boot. Repeat the process until you find the specific program or service that won't allow normal startup. When you've diagnosed the problem that way, you can prevent the service or program from auto-starting. Or uninstall the problem program.

When everything is back in shape, you should be able to choose Normal Startup from System Configuration and have the computer start normally.

Of course, the tools I've described here are really for pros. This is a book for users, and there really isn't room to go into great depth on these more technical topics. But you can find plenty more information in Help and online. For example, you can click Start and choose Help and Support to use Windows Help. Then search for terms like "safe mode," "system configuration," or "startup repair" for more information. Or go to Windows Live Search or `http://search.microsoft.com` and search for any of those terms preceded by Windows 7. For example, search for "Windows 7 safe mode" or "Windows 7 system configuration."

Wrap-Up

This chapter has covered all the different ways you can control which programs do, and don't, automatically start when Windows first starts up or when you first log in to your Windows user account.

- Some programs have their own built-in options for choosing whether the program starts automatically and appears in the Notification area.

- You can start any application program automatically, or even open a folder automatically, by adding a shortcut for the program to the Startup folder.

- The full set of services that can be started and stopped automatically are listed in the Services.msc snap-in.

- The Services.msc snap-in is an advanced tool designed for professional programmers and network engineers. As such, it contains very little information that would be useful to the average computer user.

- You can use netplwiz to bypass the login page and go straight to any user account you wish.

- Safe Mode provides a means of starting Windows 7 with the fewest drivers and services. It helps you get the system started so that you can diagnose and repair whatever is preventing normal startup.

Using Windows 7 Programs and Accessories

Windows 7 is your computer's operating system (often abbreviated OS). As such, it's mainly responsible for getting your computer started and making sure that all the programs in, and devices attached to, your system work together. It's also responsible for defining how you operate the computer. In that regard, it's by far the most important program on your system. Without an operating system, a computer won't even start. It's little more than a very expensive boat anchor.

Windows 7 also comes with many application programs that aren't really part of the system. Rather, they're extra goodies you can use to view and create things. Many of those programs are so large and sophisticated that they get entire chapters of their own in this book. Internet Explorer (Chapter 16), Writer (Chapter 17), Windows Live Mail (Chapters 18 and 20) Messenger (19), Windows Contacts (Chapter 21), and Windows Media Player (Chapter 24) are just a few examples of such programs.

This chapter looks at some of the smaller, easier programs that come with Windows 7. Many of these are referred to as *accessories*. In fact, you'll find many of them in the Accessories program group on your Start menu. Before we get started with specific programs, let's take a look at some general topics that apply to virtually every program you'll ever use.

Important Stuff About Programs

There are more than 100,000 different programs that you can run on your computer. Nobody owns them all or needs them all. But everyone has some programs on his or her computer already. For example, you have Windows 7 and all the programs that came with Windows 7. If you bought your computer with Windows 7 pre-installed, your computer manufacturer may have pre-installed some other programs as well.

Most of the programs at your disposal have icons on the All Programs menu (or in one of the folders on the All Programs menu). To start a program, you click its icon on that menu. When you start a program, it opens in a program window on your desktop. You can move and size that window, switch among multiple open program windows, and close a program (and its window) when you've finished using it.

Note

See Chapter 2 for more information on the Start menu and working with program windows. ∎

Of all the general things to know about programs, the most important is this: Every program has its own built-in Help. You don't need to try to "figure out" a program by guessing. After you understand that every program has its own built-in help, you can find out how to use that program or one of its features without all the hair-pulling frustration and ensuing problems of trial-and-error guesswork.

Many people make the mistake of looking in the wrong place for help with a program. For example, the Help described in Chapter 5 of this book is help for Windows 7. That's not the place to look for help with any other programs. Many people search the Web for help. But there you're searching through billions of pages of text, most having nothing to do with the program you're seeking help on. When you need help with a specific program, the first place to look is the Help for that program. It's as simple as that.

You have two ways to get to a program's Help. First, the program must be open. Then, do the following:

- Choose Help from that program's menu bar and click the first option on the Help menu. Figure 14-1 shows an example.

FIGURE 14-1

Sample Help menu in a program.

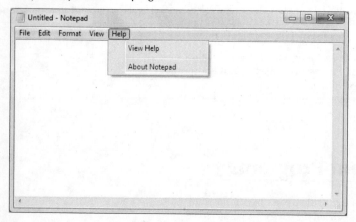

- If you see a Help button, click it. Often, the button shows just a question mark, as in the example shown in Figure 14-2.
- Make sure that the program is in the active window and press the Help key (F1) on your keyboard.

After the Help opens, you should easily find your way around. It's largely a matter of reading what you see and clicking the topic you need help with.

Sample Help button near the mouse pointer.

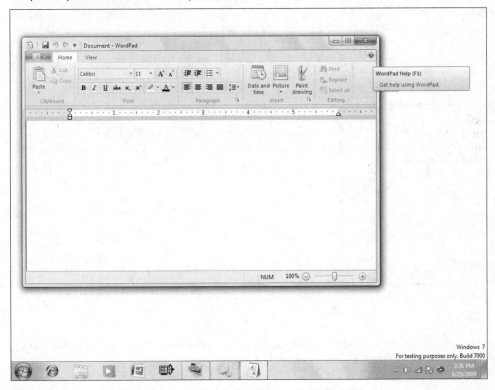

The rest of this chapter looks at most of the programs and accessories that come with Windows 7. This book doesn't have enough room to cover each one in great depth. So if you find a program that's useful for you, keep in mind that you can use its Help (not Windows Help) for more information about that program.

Using Windows Calculator

The easiest (and sometimes the handiest) little program in 7 is Calculator. It looks and acts just like a pocket calculator. To open it, click the Start button and choose All Programs ➪ Accessories ➪ Calculator. Or press ⊞ , type **cal**, and choose Calculator. When it's open on the screen, you can use the standard view shown at the top of Figure 14-3. Or you can use the more advanced views shown in the same figure. They are, clockwise, Scientific, Statistics, and Programmer.

FIGURE 14-3

Four ways to view Windows Calculator.

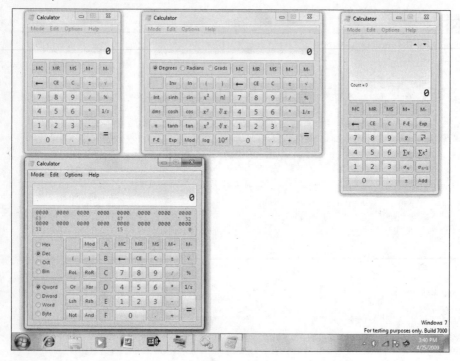

Note
You can move Calculator around by dragging its title bar. You also can minimize it to a taskbar button. But you can't maximize it or size it by dragging a corner or edge. ■

If you know how to work a pocket calculator, you know how to work the calculator on your screen. The only difference is that you click the buttons with your mouse rather than press them with your finger. For example, to multiply 123.45 by 678.9, you click the following buttons:

```
123.45*678.9=
```

To clear the current entry and start a new calculation, click the button with the large red C. For help with Calculator, choose Help ➪ View Help from its menu. Or press F1 when Calculator is in the active program window.

Typing with WordPad

As most readers probably know, *word processing* is all about using a computer as sort of a high-tech typewriter. Windows 7 comes with its own built-in word processor named WordPad. It's not as fancy as Microsoft Word or WordPerfect. But it is free, and it's sufficient for typing basic letters and reports.

To open WordPad, click the Start button and choose All Programs ⇨ Accessories ⇨ WordPad. Or press ▨ , type **wor**, and choose WordPad from the Start menu.

Note

If you can't find WordPad on your Accessories menu, your computer manufacturer may have left it off because you already have a better word processor, such as Microsoft Word or WordPerfect. If you have one of those, you're better off using it than WordPad. ■

WordPad, Word, WordPerfect – What's the Diff?

Just as there are many brands of toothpaste, shampoo, and cars, so are there many brands of word processing programs. WordPad, Microsoft Word, and WordPerfect are basically different "brands" of word processing programs. WordPad is a simple word processor that comes free with every copy of Windows 7. You don't have to buy or install anything to use it. It's just there.

Microsoft Word is Microsoft's professional-grade word processing program. WordPerfect is Corel's professional-grade word processing program. Neither Word nor WordPerfect comes free with Windows 7. If you have one or the other but don't know why, it's because your computer manufacturer bundled it with your system.

When WordPad opens, you see a menu ribbon that gives you access to WordPad's functions (such as formatting). At the left of the ribbon is the WordPad button, which gives you access to other functions, such as printing. The large document area beneath that is basically a blank sheet of paper on which you type your document. Typing on a computer screen is different from typing on paper. So for those of you who are new to all this, the following sections explain some things you really need to know about typing with computers in general.

Typing and navigating text

Typing in a document, e-mail message, or anywhere else on a computer screen is similar to typing with a typewriter. The main difference is that when you type on a computer screen, you don't press Enter at the end of each line. You press Enter only after typing the entire paragraph. Pressing Enter a second time adds a blank line above the next paragraph you type.

Figure 14-4 shows an example in which a bent arrow ◀┘ shows where I pressed the Enter key to end a line or paragraph or to insert a blank line. (When typing your own document, you won't see any bent arrows. They're just for illustration in the figure.)

When typing your own document, don't worry about making, or leaving, space for margins. The program takes care of that for you.

As long as your WordPad window is enlarged to be wide enough to show both margins, what you see on the screen is pretty much how the document will look when printed. To see how your document will look for sure when you print it, click the WordPad button and then choose Print ⇨ Print Preview from the WordPad menu bar. To return to your document for more editing, click the Close Print Preview button at the top of the Print Preview window.

FIGURE 14-4

The bent arrows show where I pressed the Enter key.

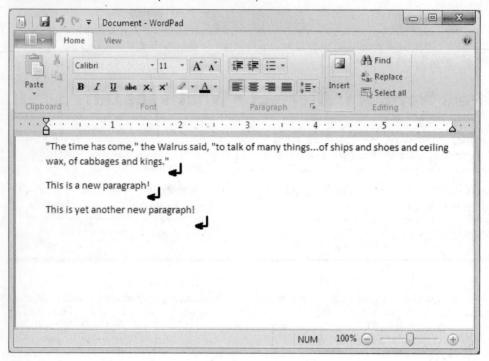

Tip

Most programs have a Print Preview option. You can use it to get a sneak peek at how your document will look before you print it. ■

If you make a mistake while typing, use the Backspace key to back up and erase what you just typed. If it's too late for that because you've typed a whole lot of text since the mistake, use the basic editing techniques described in the next section to make corrections.

Basic text editing

To insert or delete text, first get the *cursor* to where you want to make the change. Note that the cursor is not the same as the mouse pointer. The cursor is usually a blinking vertical bar that shows where the next character you type will appear. One way to get the cursor where you want it is to get the tip of the mouse pointer right where you want to put the cursor and then click the left mouse button.

You can also move the cursor around using the keys listed in Table 14-1. I titled that table "*Almost Universal*" because you never know where there will be some exception to the rule. Note, however, that you cannot use those keys to move the cursor *outside* text. If the cursor is at the bottom of your document and you need to move down, press the Enter key to insert blank lines. If you need to move the cursor to the right in an empty line, press the Tab key or spacebar.

TABLE 14-1

(Almost) Universal Keys for Moving the Cursor Through Text

Key	Where it moves the cursor
→	One character to the right
←	One character to the left
↑	Up one line
↓	Down one line
Home	Beginning of the line
End	End of line
Ctrl+Home	Top of document
Ctrl+End	End of document
Page Up (PgUp)	Up a page (or screenful)
Page Down (PgDn)	Down a page (or screenful)
Ctrl+←	One word to the left
Ctrl+→	One word to the right
Ctrl+↑	Up one paragraph
Ctrl+↓	Down one paragraph
Ctrl+Page Up (PgUp)	To top of previous page
Ctrl+Page Down (PgDn)	To top of next page

To delete text near the cursor, do one of the following:

- Press Backspace to delete the character to the left of the cursor.
- Press Delete (Del) to delete the character to the right of the cursor.

To insert text at the cursor position, just start typing. If you're in Insert mode, the new text will be inserted without replacing any existing text. If you're in Overwrite mode, the new text will replace (overwrite) existing text. To switch from Insert to Overwrite mode, or vice versa, press the Insert (Ins) key once.

Note

If pressing the Insert key doesn't switch from Insert to Overwrite mode and your keyboard has a Function Lock (or F Lock) key, press that key first. Then try the Insert key again. ■

Selecting text

If you want to work with larger chunks of text (as opposed to working with one character at a time), you first need to *select* the text with which you want to work. Selected text is highlighted.

For example, in Figure 14-5, I selected the highlighted paragraph by dragging the mouse pointer through it.

FIGURE 14-5

One paragraph of text selected.

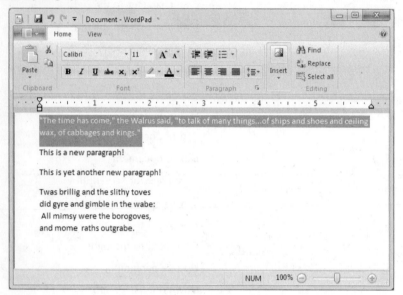

Tip
To drag, hold down the left mouse button while moving the mouse. ■

You can select text using either the mouse or the keyboard. With the mouse, you can just drag the mouse pointer through any chunk of text you select. There are some optional mouse *shortcuts* you can use in most programs for selecting specific chunks of text, as follows:

- **Select one word:** Double-click the word.
- **Select one line:** Move the cursor into the whitespace to the left of the line and then click.
- **Select one paragraph:** Triple-click the paragraph (works in WordPad, Word, Internet Explorer, and some other programs). If triple-clicking doesn't work, drag the mouse pointer through the paragraph.
- **Select multiple paragraphs:** Drag through all of them, or click where you want to start the selection. Then hold down the Shift key and click the location you want to extend the selection to.
- **Select all text in the document:** Click Select All in the Editing group on the ribbon or press Ctrl+A.

If one of the preceding methods doesn't work in the program you're using, dragging the mouse pointer through the text you want to select should work.

If you make a mistake while selecting and want to start over, just deselect the text. Clicking just outside the selected text will usually do the trick. Or press the ↑, ↓, ←, or → key by itself (without holding down the Shift key).

To select text using the keyboard rather than the mouse, just hold down the Shift key as you press any of the navigation keys that are listed in Table 14-1.

Formatting text

Many forms of text formatting are based on a *select, then do* principle. First you select the text to which you want to apply formatting (using any selection technique previously mentioned). Then you *do* the necessary command, either by making selections from the program's menu bar or ribbon or by clicking buttons in its toolbar. For example, in WordPad you can apply a font (print style) to any text you've typed.

As an example, Figure 14-6 shows where I've selected a small portion of text I typed into a WordPad document.

FIGURE 14-6

Some text selected for formatting.

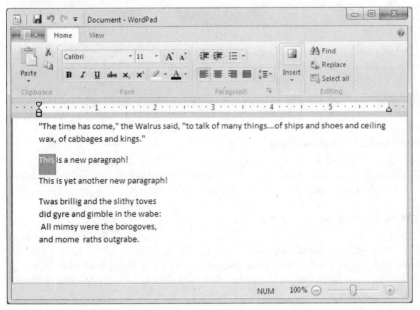

Next, click the Home tab on the ribbon and choose the font, size, and color you want from the controls in the Font group, as in the example shown in Figure 14-7.

Your selections are applied to the selected text, as in the example shown in Figure 14-8.

The *select, then do* approach also works for deleting, replacing, copying, and moving text.

FIGURE 14-7

Choose a font, size, and color.

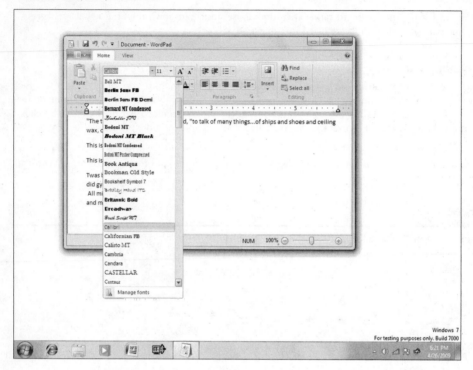

Deleting and replacing chunks of text

To delete a large chunk of text, select the text you want to delete and then press the Delete key. Optionally, you can select the text and then just start typing new text. The selected text will disappear the moment you start typing, and only the new text you type will remain.

Using copy and paste and cut and paste

Anywhere you can select text, you can copy text. Anywhere you can type text, you can paste text. So you never need to retype text you already see on your screen. You can just copy and paste it instead. For example, if you have some text in a Web page that you want to add to a WordPad or other document you're creating, you don't need to retype the text that's already in that page. Just copy and paste it.

For this to work, you need to know how to have multiple program windows on the screen and how to switch between them. These kinds of basic skills are described under "Running Programs" in Chapter 2. After you've mastered those basic skills, copying and pasting should be fairly easy for you. First, understand that two documents are involved:

- **Source:** The document or page that already has the text you want to copy. In other words, the place you're copying *from*.

- **Destination:** The place where you would have typed the text yourself if you had to. In other words, the place you're copying *to*.

FIGURE 14-8

Font selections applied to the (previously) selected text.

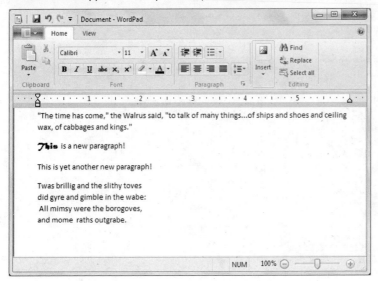

So assuming that you can see the text you want to copy and can get to the place where you want to paste it, here are the steps:

1. At the source, select the text you want to copy using any method cited earlier.

2. Copy the selected text using whichever of the following methods is most convenient at the moment:

   ● Press Ctrl+C.

   ● Right-click the selected text and choose Copy.

   ● Click the Copy button in that program's toolbar or ribbon.

   ● Choose Edit ⇨ Copy from that program's menu bar.

   Figure 14-9 shows an example in which I've selected a chunk of text in a Web page, right-clicked that text, and am about to click Copy.

3. Get to the destination and click where you want to paste the text. The cursor should be where it would be if you intended to type that text yourself.

4. Use whichever method is most convenient to paste the text you copied:

   ● Press Ctrl+V.

   ● Right-click near the cursor and choose Paste.

   ● Click the Paste button in the destination program's toolbar or ribbon.

   ● Choose Edit ⇨ Paste from the destination program's menu bar.

The text you copied is placed right where you pasted it.

FIGURE 14-9

Text selected in a Web page.

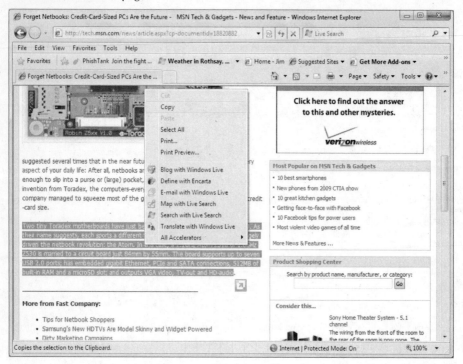

Moving text within a document

If you want to move a chunk of text within a document, the technique is similar to copying and pasting except you cut and paste. As the word implies, when you *cut* text, you remove it from its present location. This method works only in documents that you *can* edit. For example, you can't cut and paste from a Web page because you don't own the Web page and aren't allowed to change it. You can only copy from a Web page.

But when you create a document yourself, you can do anything you want to it, including cut and paste. The steps are the same; it's just a matter of cutting rather than copying:

1. Select the text you want to move using any selection technique you like.

2. Cut the text using whichever method here is most convenient at the moment:

   - Press Ctrl+X.
   - Press Shift+Delete
   - Right-click the selected text and choose Cut.
   - Click the Cut button in the program's toolbar or ribbon.
   - Choose Edit ⇨ Cut from that program's menu bar.

3. Move the cursor to wherever you want to put the cut text.

4. Paste the text (press Ctrl+V, press Shift+Insert, or right-click and choose Paste, or click the Paste toolbar or ribbon button, or choose Edit ⇨ Paste from the program's menu bar).

The methods given here work the same in small textboxes, not just word processing documents. You can, for example, copy a URL (Web site address) from any page and then paste it into the Address bar of your Web browser to get to that page.

Copy and paste a picture

You can copy and paste a picture from an open document into a WordPad document. The picture needs to be open for this method to work. By "open," I mean already visible in some other open document (such as a Web page) or in a graphics program. Right-click the picture and choose Copy. Then click at about where you want to put the picture in your WordPad document and paste (press Ctrl+V or right-click near the cursor and choose Paste).

When the picture is in your document, clicking the picture will display sizing handles (little black squares around the border of the picture). You can drag any one of those handles to make the picture larger or smaller.

Note

WordPad isn't a great program for creating complex documents with pictures. You can do some basic things with pictures in a WordPad document. If you're serious about creating complex documents with many pictures, however, you need a serious word processor such as Microsoft Word or WordPerfect. ∎

Saving a WordPad document

Any typed document you create with WordPad (or Microsoft Word, or WordPerfect, or any other program) exists on your screen (so that you can see it) and in your computer's *memory* (RAM). There is nothing permanent about it. If you shut off your computer without saving the document, that document simply ceases to exist. There is no way to "get it back" because it is gone forever and no record of it exists anywhere in the known universe.

About the Windows Clipboard

When you cut or copy text using any of the preceding techniques, whatever you cut or copied is placed in an area of your computer's memory called the Windows Clipboard. The formal name often confuses people because they figure they should be able to see something named Clipboard on the screen, in their menus, or someplace. But there is no such thing to be concerned about.

The Clipboard is nothing more than a place in your computer's memory where Windows temporarily stores the latest item you copied or cut. When you shut off the computer, the Clipboard is emptied. So you should make no attempt to use the Clipboard for any form of long-term storage. The Clipboard is not for documents and files or for long-term storage.

Every time you copy and paste or cut and paste you should do so in one smooth motion. Select the text you want, copy or cut it, and paste it where you want to put it.

When you do save something, you have to think about where plan to put it and what you want to name it. Otherwise, if you just save it "someplace," you may not be able to find it again when you need it. This topic is covered under "Saving Things in Folders" in Chapter 29. Here I just tell you about saving documents you create in WordPad or similar programs such as Microsoft Word and WordPerfect. Here's how saving works:

1. Choose File ➪ Save from the menu bar, or if the program has a ribbon like that in WordPad or Word 2007, click the Save button in the program's title bar above the ribbon at the upper left. The first time you save a new document, the Save As dialog box opens.

2. Tell Windows *where* you want to put the document by navigating to that folder.

   If you don't know and don't have a preference, use your Documents folder. Most likely it will already be selected for you (you see the name Documents at the right side of the breadcrumb trail). If you see some other name there, click the arrow next to your user name and choose Documents. Or click Documents in the navigation pane at the left.

3. In the File Name box, enter a brief filename that will make it easy to identify the file later (when all you can see is the name).

   Figure 14-10 shows an example in which I've opted to put the new document in the Documents folder for my user account (jboyce). I've named the document Lewis Carrol.rtf.

FIGURE 14-10

Ready to save a document in my Documents folder.

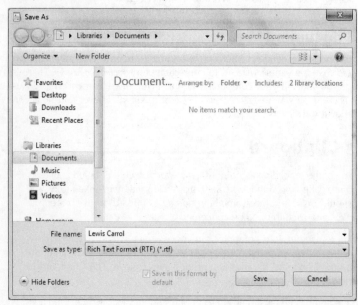

4. Near the lower-right corner of the dialog box, click the Save button.

Everything that's currently in the document is now saved in a file in the folder you specified. Note, however, that any additional changes you make are *not* saved unless your program is capable of and configured to save changes automatically. If you make more changes and want to save those, do any of the following to save:

- Press Ctrl+S.
- Click the Save button on the toolbar or above the ribbon.
- Choose File ➪ Save from the menu.

You won't get any feedback on the screen. Nor will Windows ask you where to put the file or what to name it. You already gave Windows that information. Subsequent saves just ensure that all changes you've made since that last save are added to that file.

Caution

Never turn off your computer without first closing all open programs and saving all unsaved work! Always shut down properly by clicking the Start button, clicking the arrow next to the lock symbol, and choosing Shut Down. ■

To print your document, click the WordPad button and choose Print ➪ Print from WordPad's menu. Then click the Print button in the Print dialog box that opens. For the complete lowdown on printing, see Chapter 36.

When you've finished using WordPad and working on your document, close them both. (Actually, you just need to close WordPad because in doing so you'll also close the document.) To close WordPad, click the Close (X) button in its upper-right corner. Or click the WordPad button and choose Exit from its menu. If you've left any unsaved work behind in your document, you'll see a message like the one in Figure 14-11.

FIGURE 14-11

Warning and last chance to save unsaved work.

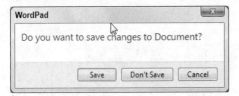

This is your last chance to save your work and any changes you've made since the last time you saved. If you choose No, you lose everything you accomplished since your last save. So you should choose Yes unless you're certain you don't want to save that work.

Both WordPad and your document close (meaning they are no longer visible on your screen).

Opening a WordPad document

Anytime you want to start WordPad again in the future, just click the Start button and choose All Programs ➪ Accessories ➪ WordPad again. But don't expect that last document you worked on to appear automatically. Documents are separate from programs. You can create all the documents you want in any program. Most programs don't automatically reopen the last document you worked on. They presume that you want to create a new document, so they open with a new, blank screen.

You can, of course, open any document you created and saved in WordPad. If it's a document you created recently, and WordPad is pinned to the Start menu, just click the WordPad button and then click the document's name in the right side of the menu in the Recent list, as in Figure 14-12.

FIGURE 14-12

Opening a recently saved document.

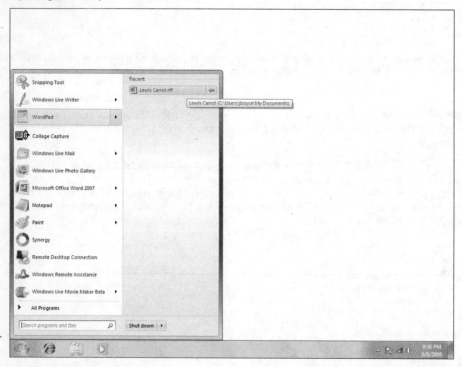

If the document is one you haven't worked on recently, its name might not be in the Recent list. In that case, open WordPad, click the WordPad button and click Open from the menu. That brings up an Open dialog box, where you can navigate to the folder in which you placed the document and then double-click its icon. When the document opens, it will appear in WordPad looking exactly as it did the last time you saved it.

Tip

In programs that have a traditional Windows menu bar and not a ribbon, choose File ⇨ Open to open the Open dialog box and select a file to open. ■

It's not necessary to open the program first. The Recent Items option on the right side of the Start menu lists documents you've worked with recently. Often you just have to click the Start button, click Recent Items, and then click the name of the document you want to open. No need to open the program first.

Similarly, you can navigate to any folder and double-click the icon of the document you want to open. You don't need to open the program first. When you double-click the document's icon, the default program for that file type opens to display the document. See Chapter 29 for the full story on folders and files.

Note

If you double-click the icon for a saved WordPad document, Microsoft Word (if installed on your system) will open the document. That's because after being installed, Microsoft Word becomes the default program for many kinds of text documents. If you have Microsoft Word, you have no compelling reason to use WordPad. ■

Typing Special Characters with Character Map

There are many characters you can type right from your keyboard. There are many you can't, such as ®, ©, ™, ∑, ≠, and ÷, to name a few. Any character you can't type, you can insert from Windows Character Map. First, place the cursor where you want to type the character. Then click the Start button and choose All Programs ⇨ Accessories ⇨ System Tools ⇨ Character Map. Or press 🪟, type **char**, and click Character Map. The Character Map opens, as shown in Figure 14-13.

Character Map.

You have thousands of characters to choose from in Character Map. Finding just the one you want isn't always easy. But a good starting place is the Symbols font, which you can view by choosing Symbol from the Font drop-down list. Then use the scroll bar at the right side of the map to look through all the available symbols. To see a larger version of any character, click it.

When you find the character you want to insert, click it and then click the Select button. You can select a bunch of characters if you want. They line up in the Characters to Copy box. When all the characters you want are in the box, click the Copy button. Then switch back to the document you're typing and paste (press Ctrl+V). The characters are pasted at the cursor position.

If you don't find the character you want in the Symbol set, try a different font. The Wingdings and Webdings fonts contain many special characters. If you're looking for non-English characters, such as ñ, é, ¿, and ¡¡, select the same font in which you're typing (Arial or Times New Roman) from the Font drop-down list. Then scroll through the list of available characters.

To search for a character by name, choose the Advanced View check box. Type the name of the character you want and click Search. For more information on using Character Map, click its Help button.

Working with Fonts

Windows 7 comes with a large selection of fonts. You'll see just how many when you apply a font to selected text. Each font that you can apply to text is stored as a file in your Fonts folders. You can use either of the following techniques to open that folder:

- Press ![start], type **font**, and click the Fonts folder icon under Programs on the Start menu.
- Click the Start button and choose Control Panel ➪ Appearance and Personalization ➪ Fonts.

Figure 14-14 shows an example of how things might look in that folder. Because it's a folder, you can use the Views button to control the size of icons.

FIGURE 14-14

The Fonts folder.

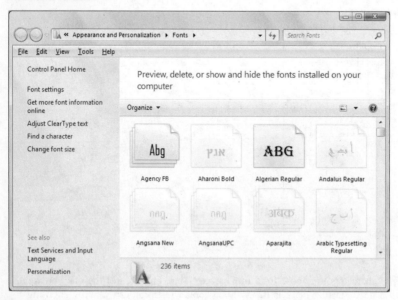

Note

The Fonts folder has nothing to do with *applying* fonts to text. You apply fonts in programs in which you can type and format text, such as WordPad. The Fonts folder is just a repository where all your available fonts are stored. ■

To see what a font looks like, double-click its icon. A window opens showing a sample. Close that window after viewing the font.

Using Notepad

Notepad is similar to WordPad in that it's mainly about typing text. The basic typing and editing skills, and techniques for saving and opening files, apply as well. The main difference is that Notepad is about creating *plain text documents*. These are files that contain only unformatted text with no pictures or other nontext items.

If you have Microsoft Word or WordPerfect, use that for typing text documents. Each has its own Help so that you can learn more. There are also entire books about those products. If you don't have Word or WordPerfect, you can get by with WordPad. You just won't have some of the more advanced features, such as spell checking.

Don't use Notepad at all unless you specifically need to create a text file that contains only plain text. If you do want to use Notepad, you can start it in the usual manner. Press ⊞ , type **note**, and choose Notepad. Or click the Start button and choose All Programs ➪ Accessories ➪ Notepad.

Zipping and Unzipping Files

Zipping is a way of combing multiple files and folders into a single *compressed folder*. This is often done to make e-mailing a large number of files as a single attachment easier. For example, when I write a book, each chapter contains many files — one file containing all the text and a separate file for each picture. Before I submit a chapter to the publisher, I combine all the files into a single compressed file named Chapter *x* (where *x* is the chapter number). Then I transmit that file via e-mail.

When the editor receives the file, it's easy for him or her to pass on a copy to each editor who needs to see it. Well, certainly a lot easier than if I'd sent 20 or 30 separate little files for that one chapter.

In Windows 7, the terms *compressed folder* and *Zip file* mean the same thing — a single file with a .zip extension that contains still more files and/or folders. The icon for a Zip file looks like a manila file folder with a zipper on it. If filename extensions aren't hidden, the extension is .zip, as in the example shown in Figure 14-15.

A side benefit to using compressed folders is that Windows will attempt to make the files smaller by compressing them. This means that the compressed folder will consume less disk space, and transfer more quickly than the individual uncompressed files will. Exactly how much compression you get, though, depends on what kinds of files you put into the Zip file. Many file formats, such as JPEG, PNG, WMV, MPEG, WMA, and MP3, are already compressed, so they don't shrink much (if at all) when you zip them. But many other kinds of files will shrink when placed in a Zip file.

Note
The compression affects only the amount of disk space the files consume. It doesn't make the files visually smaller on the screen or remove any content from the files. ■

FIGURE 14-15

Sample compressed folder (Zip file).

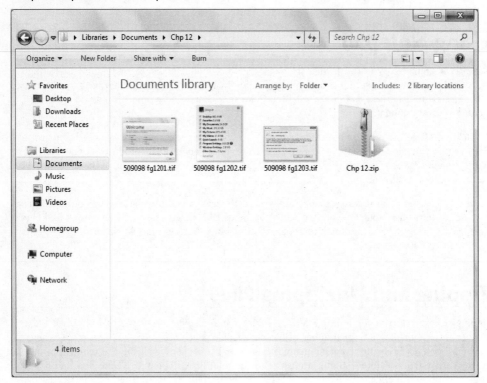

Zipping files

To place two or more files into a Zip file, you first need to select their icons. If you don't know how to do that yet, see Chapter 29. Then, right-click any selected icon and choose Send To ➪ Compressed (zipped) Folder, as shown in Figure 14-16.

You get some brief feedback and then see the compressed folder icon. The original files remain intact and unaffected. This means that you can send the Zip file to someone by e-mail, transfer it across the network to another computer, or perhaps put it on a removable drive.

Tip

To add more files to a Zip file, drag icons for those files to the Zip file's icon and drop them right on that icon. ■

Assuming that you do want to e-mail the Zip file to someone, and you're using Windows Live Mail or some other compatible POP3 or MAPI e-mail client, you can right-click the Zip file's icon, choose Send To ➪ Mail Recipient, and you're on your way. If that approach doesn't work for you because you use some incompatible e-mail system, you can still attach the file to an e-mail message using the standard method for your e-mail account.

Note

See Chapter 18 for more information on Windows Live Mail. If you don't use Windows Live Mail and don't know how to attach files or save attachments, check the Help page for your e-mail service or contact your ISP. ■

FIGURE 14-16

About to zip selected files.

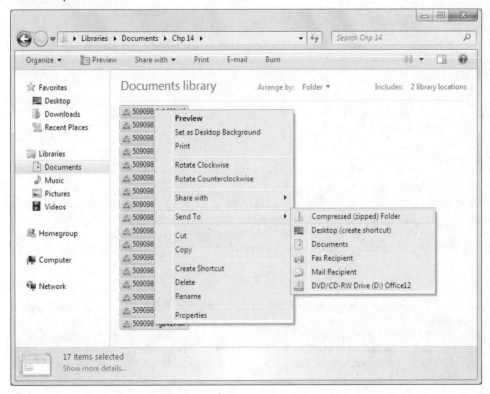

Unzipping files

If someone sends you a Zip file, the first thing you need to do is save the attachment as a file. In Windows Live Mail, this is a simple matter of clicking the message header, clicking the paper clip icon in the preview area as shown in Figure 14-17, and then clicking Save Attachments. In many e-mail clients, it's a matter of right-clicking the attachment icon and choosing Save As.

Regardless of how you save the attachment, it's important to know where you saved it because you need to get to the saved file to extract its contents. If in doubt, save the file to your Documents folder.

Next, you need to navigate to the folder in which you saved the Zip file. Then right-click its icon and choose Extract All, as shown in Figure 14-18.

FIGURE 14-17

Saving an e-mail attachment with Windows Live Mail.

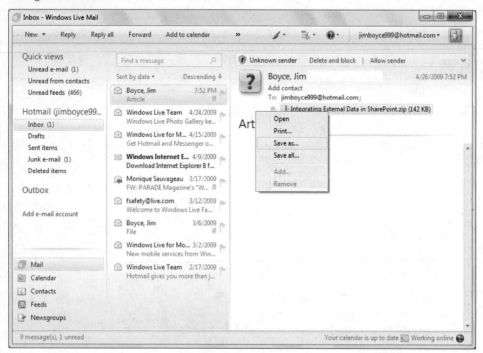

The Extract Compressed (Zipped) Folders Wizard opens. You can specify where you want to put the extracted files, if you like. Or do the easy thing and just accept the suggested location and click Extract. If you use that method, you end up with a new, regular folder with the same name as the compressed folder, as in the example in Figure 14-19. You can delete the Zip file because you really don't need it anymore. Use the files in the uncompressed folder for whatever you intend to do with them.

Zipping and unzipping are built into Windows. There is no program window or menu bar from which to get Help. But there is information in Windows general help. Click the Start button, choose Help and Support, and search for "compressed folder" or "Zip file."

Tip

Check out www.winzip.com for a program that gives you many more features for creating and working with Zip files. ■

FIGURE 14-18

About to extract files from a compressed folder (Zip file).

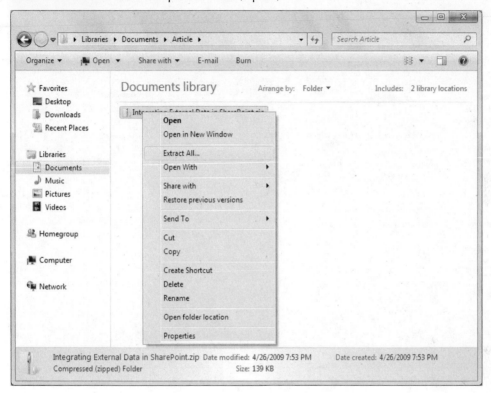

Annotating Screenshots with Snipping Tool

Snipping Tool is a program that makes taking a snapshot of part of the screen easy. You can annotate that picture with text and highlights. Here's how it works. First, set up the screen so that you can see what you want to capture to a picture. Then use either of the following techniques to open the Snipping Tool:

- Click the Start button and choose All Programs ➪ Accessories ➪ Snipping Tool.
- Press ▮ , type **snip**, and choose Snipping Tool.

A small window with some instructional text appears, as shown in Figure 14-20. Everything behind that window may be dimmed.

FIGURE 14-19

Regular folder extracted from compressed folder.

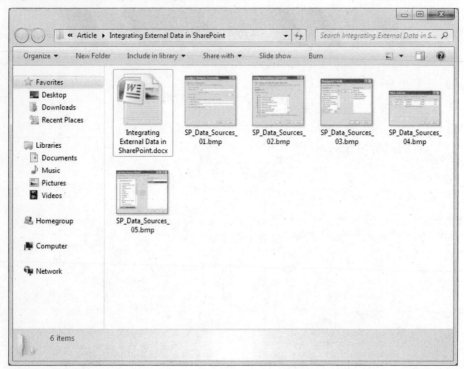

FIGURE 14-20

Snipping Tool with no picture.

When the Snipping Tool is open, follow these steps to capture a screenshot:

1. Click the arrow on the New button and choose how you want to take your screenshot:

   - **Free Form Snip:** Take a snapshot of any area you like in any shape you like.
   - **Rectangular Snip:** Take a snapshot of any rectangular portion of the screen.
   - **Window Snip:** Take a snapshot of any open program window.
   - **Full-screen Snip:** Take a snapshot of the entire screen.

2. Specify what area of the screen you want to snip, as follows:

- If you chose the Free Form or Rectangular Snip, drag a circle or rectangle around the area you want to snip.

- If you chose Window Snip, click anywhere within the window you want to snip.

- If you chose Full-Screen Snip, do nothing. The entire screen is snipped automatically.

A larger version of the Snipping Tool opens showing whatever you snipped. For example, in Figure 14-21, I snipped Windows Media Player as it was playing a song.

FIGURE 14-21

Snipping Tool with snapshot of Media Player.

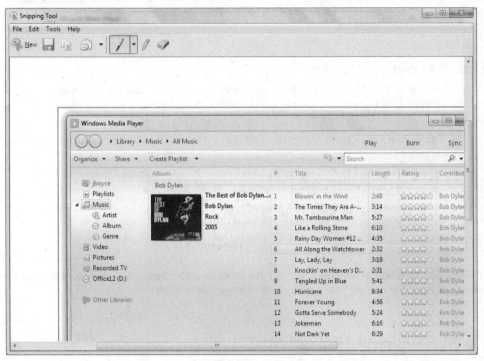

With the snapshot in place, you can use the Pen to draw on the picture. Choose Tools ⇨ Pen and a pen color, or choose a pen from the toolbar. Or choose Tools ⇨ Pen ⇨ Customize to define your own pen color, thickness, and tip. Choose Tools ⇨ Pen ⇨ Custom Pen to use your custom pen. Then just draw on your screenshot by dragging. If you make a mess of things, click the Eraser and click the thing you messed up.

To highlight an area in yellow, click the Highlighter tool and drag the mouse pointer through the item you wish to highlight. Again, if you mess up, click the Erase tool and click the bad highlight.

Saving a snip

To save the screenshot, click the Save Snip button or choose File ➪ Save As from the menu. Navigate to the folder in which you want to place the saved picture. Name the snapshot as you would any other file. From the Save As type drop-down list, choose a picture format (JPEG, PNG, or GIF). If you don't have a preference, JPEG is likely your best bet because it conserves all colors and is compatible with most graphics programs.

Optionally, you can save the snip as an HTML file with an .mht extension. However, it won't be a standard graphics image if you choose that option. You'll be limited to opening the picture in Internet Explorer and Microsoft Word. And you won't be able to do further editing in a graphics program.

Copy and paste a snip

To copy and paste the snip into an open document, click the Copy toolbar button or choose Edit ➪ Copy. Then navigate to where you want to insert the picture and paste as usual (press Ctrl+V or right-click and choose Paste).

E-mail a snip

If you use Windows Live Mail or a similar compatible e-mail client, you can e-mail the snip to someone directly from the program. Click the arrow on the Send Snip button or choose File ➪ Send To. Then choose one of the following options:

- **E-mail Recipient:** Opens a new e-mail message with the snip embedded in the body of the message.
- **E-mail Recipient (As Attachment):** Allows you to specify a size for the picture and then attaches to a new, empty e-mail message as a JPEG image.

When the e-mail message opens, fill in the recipient address (or addresses) and Subject line as usual. You can also type in the body of the message as usual. Then click Send.

Tip

If you can't e-mail directly from the Snipping Tool, save the image as a file. Then attach that saved file to an e-mail message using whatever method your e-mail client or service provides. ■

Change Snipping Tool options

To change how the Snipping Tool works, choose Tools ➪ Options from the menu. Make your selections as summarized here:

- **Hide Instruction Text:** Choose this to hide the small instructions that appear at the bottom of the empty Snipping Tool.
- **Always Copy Snips to the Clipboard:** Choosing this option copies every snip straight to the Clipboard, which means that you can paste the snip into an open document without first clicking the Copy toolbar button.
- **Include URL below Snips (HTML Only):** If you use the Snipping Tool to capture screenshots of Web pages, choose this option to automatically annotate each snip with a link to the page from which it was taken. When saving the snip, you must choose HTML as the Save As Type.

- **Prompt to Save Snips before Exiting:** If you deselect this option, you won't be asked whether you want to save the latest unsaved snip when you close the Snipping Tool.

- **Show Screen Overlay when Snipping Tool Is Active:** If you deselect this option, the screen won't go dim when waiting for you to take your snapshot.

- **Ink Color:** Specify a color for the border that surrounds each snipped image.

- **Show Selection Ink after Snips are Captured:** If you deselect this option, the border that normally surrounds each snip won't appear inside the Snipping Tool.

To activate your selections, click OK in the Options dialog box. Some changes might also require you to exit the Snipping Tool and reopen it.

Screenshots the old-fashioned way

The old method of capturing screens with the Print Screen key still works. It may be a better choice when you need to hold down the mouse button to show something, because the Snipping Tool doesn't provide a means for doing that. For more information on taking screenshots with the Print Screen key, see "Taking Screenshots" in Chapter 23.

Using Paint

Paint is a simple drawing and graphics editing tool that comes free with Windows 7. Just about any graphics editing program on the market can do everything Paint can do and much more, but Paint can still be a very useful program.

Tip

If you want to crop or edit photos, use the Fix feature in Windows Live Photo Gallery (Chapter 23). ∎

One thing that Paint is still good for is resizing large photos. For example, your digital camera might shoot enormous 5-megapixel pictures that look great on the screen and in print. But those huge dimensions and potentially large file size can be a pain when trying to e-mail photos or post them on a Web site.

If you use Windows Live Mail to e-mail photos, solving that problem is simple. When you send the pictures, you'll see a prompt asking what size you want them to be. Just choose 640 × 480 (or whatever). The e-mailed copies of the pictures will be reduced in size without compromising the size or quality of the originals.

If you don't use an e-mail client that automatically reduces picture sizes, or if you need to shrink some pictures for Web publication, you can use Paint to reduce their sizes. Unfortunately, it doesn't let you reduce to specific dimensions. So you're better off using a "real" graphics program if you can. But in a pinch, you can pull it off with Paint.

First you need to know the dimensions of the original picture. One way to do that is to open the folder in which the picture is contained. Use the Details view. If you see no Dimensions column, right-click a column heading and add a Dimensions column. In Figure 14-22, I added the column and dragged it over so that it's next to the Name column.

If you just want to see the dimensions of a single picture, you don't need to use the Details view. Instead, you can right-click the picture's icon and choose Properties. Then click the Details tab in the

Properties sheet. Scroll through all the details, if necessary, to see whether you can find the picture's dimensions.

FIGURE 14-22

Viewing picture icons in Details view.

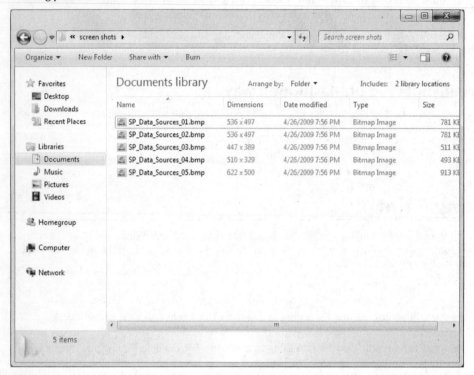

Note

Not all file types store or can display picture dimensions. I use JPEGs in this example, which does contain dimension information. ■

Now you need to do a little math to figure out how much you need to reduce the picture to get it to the size you want. In this case, I'd probably just shrink a picture to about 25 percent of its current size, which gets it down to about the 640 x 480 range (give or take a few pixels).

The next step is to make a copy of the picture. You never want to shrink or reduce the quality of your original picture. You always want to keep that one because it's the best one for printing and editing. A simple way to copy it is to right-click the picture's icon and choose Copy. Then press Ctrl+V to paste. The copy has the same name as the original picture followed by - Copy. You can rename that to something more meaningful. For example, change - Copy to (Small).

Next, right-click the copied picture's icon and choose Open With ➪ Paint. (This method works only if Paint is installed and the picture you're working with is compatible with Paint.) When Paint is open, click the Resize and Skew button in the Image group on the ribbon. Then set the Horizontal and Vertical Size options to the percent value you want. For example, in Figure 14-23 I set those each to 25 percent.

FIGURE 14-23

Reducing a picture to 25 percent of its current size.

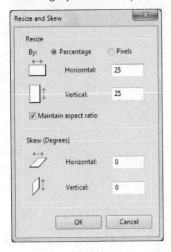

Click OK in the Resize and Skew dialog box, close Paint, and choose Yes when asked about saving your changes. You're done.

Using Sound Recorder

Sound Recorder is a simple program for recording sounds from a connected microphone. To use it, first make sure that your microphone is properly connected to your sound card or computer. To avoid potential problems, you might want to make sure that the microphone you're using is properly configured.

Tip
Use Windows Media Player to copy songs from CDs (Chapter 24). To dictate text, use Speech Recognition (Chapter 11). ■

To check and configure your microphone, right-click the speaker icon in the Notification area and choose Recording devices. If you see no such icon, click the Start button, type **audio**, and click Manage Audio Devices. In the dialog box that opens, click the Recording tab to view all your recording devices, as shown in Figure 14-24.

First, make sure that the microphone you intend to use is set as the default (shows a checkmark in a green circle). If it's not, right-click the icon for that microphone and choose Set As Default Device.

FIGURE 14-24

Audio Devices.

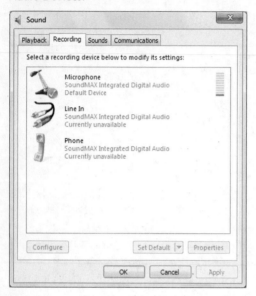

Next, speak into the microphone to make sure that it detects your voice. You should see some activity on the meter that's on the icon. If you see little or no activity:

- Make sure that the microphone is plugged into the correct port on your computer.
- If the microphone has any switches or controls, make sure it's on, not muted, and doesn't have its volume turned down too low.
- Right-click the microphone's icon and choose Properties. Click the Levels tab in the dialog box that opens and drag the slider to the right. Then click OK.

When you can see activity on the default microphone's icon, you know you're ready to go. Click OK in the Audio Devices window.

To start Sound Recorder, do either of the following:

- Press ![start], type **sou**, and click Sound Recorder.
- Click the Start button and choose All Programs ➪ Accessories ➪ Sound Recorder.

Sound Recorder, shown in Figure 14-25, opens.

When you speak into your microphone, you should see a green indicator moving with your voice. This lets you know that Sound Recorder is hearing you. To start recording, click the Start Recording button and say whatever you want to record.

When you've finished recording, click Stop Recording. A Save As dialog box opens so that you can save what you recorded. Navigate to the folder in which you want to save the recording, name the file, and click OK. (Or if you don't want to save the recording, click Cancel.)

FIGURE 14-25

Sound Recorder.

For help with Sound Recorder, click its Help button (the blue one with the question mark).

When you've finished recording, you can close Sound Recorder. To play the file you recorded, navigate to the folder in which you saved the recording and double-click its icon.

Wrap-Up

This chapter has covered some of the relatively small and simple accessory programs of Windows 7. I devote entire chapters to the bigger programs elsewhere in the book. Here's a quick review of what I covered in this chapter:

- Most programs have their own built-in help. You should always refer to the Help for information that's specific to that program.
- Use Calculator as you would a simple pocket calculator or a more advanced scientific calculator.
- WordPad is a limited-feature word processor that comes free with Windows 7. You can use it to type letters and other relatively simple documents.
- The basic skills for typing and editing text in WordPad apply to virtually all programs that allow you to work with text. Most of these basic skills even work in small textboxes found on forms.
- Copying and pasting, which work in WordPad, are universal Windows 7 basic skills that every computer user needs to learn.
- To type special characters into a document, use Character Map.
- To add new fonts to your system, use the Fonts folder.
- To combine multiple files and folders into a single compressed folder (Zip file), select their icons. Then right-click any selected icon and choose Send To ⇨ Compressed (zipped) Folder.
- To extract files and folders from a Zip file, right-click its icon and choose Extract All.
- To take and annotate screenshots, use the Snipping Tool.
- To resize pictures, use Paint (unless you have a better graphics program installed).
- To record your spoken voice, use Sound Recorder.

Troubleshooting Customization Problems

Desktop Problems

T he desktop is where you'll spend most of your time. To keep it looking the way you want, here are some tips for solving common problems you might run into while configuring your desktop.

My screen is too large/small; my screen colors look awful

For the best view of your desktop, your screen resolution should be set to at least 800 × 600 and color depth to at least 16 bits. To change your settings, follow these steps:

1. Right-click the Windows 7 desktop and choose Screen Resolution.

2. Set the Resolution option to 800 × 600 or greater, as shown in Figure 15-1 (in which it's set at 1024 × 768), and click Apply.

3. Click Advanced Settings, click Monitor, and set the Colors setting to at least 16 bit.

4. Click OK.

If you're not happy with the results, you can repeat the steps to try other resolutions and color depths. If the desktop doesn't fit right on the screen after you change the resolution, see the next troubleshooting section.

If you can't get your screen to show anything better than the absolute minimum, the driver for your card probably isn't compatible with Windows 7. See "Updating your Display Driver," later in this chapter.

IN THIS CHAPTER

Troubleshooting desktop problems

Handling Start Menu issues

Dealing with the taskbar

Fixing accessibility and language glitches

FIGURE 15-1

Screen Resolution settings.

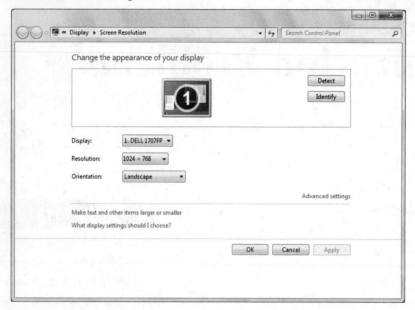

When I right-click the desktop, I don't get a Personalize option

If you can't see the Personalize option, you're most likely right-clicking something that's covering the desktop, such as an icon or program window. Click the Show Desktop button to the right of the clock in the system tray. Then you'll see, and can right-click, the actual Windows 7 desktop.

As an alternative, click the Start button, type **pers**, and click Personalization to get to the Personalization options.

Parts of my screen are cut off or blank

When the desktop doesn't fill the screen correctly, you need to adjust settings on the monitor. You use knobs or buttons on the monitor to do that, not your mouse or keyboard. Exactly how you do it varies from one monitor to the next, but the typical scenario is to use the monitor's OSD (on-screen display) options. In particular, you need to adjust the Height, Vertical Centering, Width, and Horizontal Centering settings.

If you can't figure out how to use the monitor buttons, your only other recourse is to check the documentation that came with the monitor or notebook computer. Or search the manufacturer's Web site for information on that specific model of monitor or notebook computer.

My desktop picture doesn't fit right

You can use any picture that's on your computer as the background (also called a *wallpaper*) for your desktop. Any picture that's as large as, or larger than, your screen (as defined by the Resolution setting in Display Settings) will automatically fill the screen. Smaller pictures can be centered, tiled, or stretched to fill the screen. To choose a picture and how you want it displayed, follow these steps:

1. Right-click the Windows desktop and choose Personalize.

2. In the Personalization window that opens, click the Desktop Background link.

3. Clicking the drop-down box lists different categories of backgrounds. Selecting one of the options in the drop-down list will display all the available backgrounds for that category. After you've selected a category, you can select the background or click the Browse button to find a different picture.

4. If the picture does not fit the desktop, choose one of the following options from the Picture Position button, as shown in Figure 15-2:

FIGURE 15-2

Available options for setting the appearance of the desktop background.

- **Fill:** Enlarge the picture to completely fill the screen.
- **Fit:** Match the image's width to the width of the screen.
- **Stretch:** Stretch the picture's horizontal and vertical dimensions to match the screen's dimensions. The image could be distorted.
- **Tile:** The picture is shown at actual size but tiled to fill the screen.
- **Center:** The picture is shown at actual size, centered on the screen.

5. Click Save Changes.

If you choose the Tile option but the picture doesn't repeat, it's because the picture is as large, or larger, than the desktop. The Tile option works only with pictures that are smaller than the desktop.

Everything is huge; I can't see all of dialog boxes

If you get carried away with setting a larger DPI (dots per inch), you could end up in a situation in which everything is so large, you can't even get to the buttons needed to change things back to the way they were. Follow the steps under the heading "Adjusting the font size (DPI)" in Chapter 10.

Icon names are too big or too small

In Chapter 10, you learn how to get your screen looking just the way you want. For now, if you just want to increase the size of the text on your screen, follow these steps:

1. Right-click the desktop and choose Personalize.

2. Click Window Color.

3. Click the Advanced Appearance Settings link.

4. From the Size drop-down list associated with the font, choose the size of the font desired, as shown in Figure 15-3. Optionally, you can choose a different size and color, and set the Bold and Italics settings for your Icon font.

5. Click OK then Save Changes to return to the Personalization screen.

FIGURE 15-3

Adjust the icon desktop font.

That should make the text large enough to read.

Tip

To make the icons larger or smaller, click any empty area on the desktop. Then hold down the Ctrl key as you spin your mouse wheel. ■

I don't have any desktop icons (or don't like their size)

If you don't have any desktop icons, they're probably turned off. Right-click the desktop and choose View ➪ Show Desktop Icons. To change their size, right-click the desktop and choose View. Then click one of the icon sizes to the right (Large Icons, Medium Icons, Small Icons). If your mouse has a wheel, hold down the Ctrl key while spinning the wheel for other sizes.

I can't put my desktop icons where I want them

If you drag an icon to a new location on the desktop and it moves right back to where it was, right-click the desktop and choose View ➪ Auto Arrange Icons to turn off that feature.

To sort desktop icons, right-click the desktop, choose Sort By, and try different options on the submenu to see different sort orders.

My screen saver never kicks in

If your monitor is set to power down before your screen saver starts, you'll never see the screen saver. You either have to make your screen saver start sooner or make your monitor turn off later. To make the monitor turn off later, press 🪟 or click the Start button, type **pow**, and click Power Options. In the left column, click Choose When to Turn Off the Display and set a time limit that's longer than the screen saver delay. Similarly, if the computer goes to sleep before the screen saver kicks in, you'll never see the screen saver.

See Chapter 49 for more information on power options.

Missing Aero Flip 3D, or Switch between Windows button

Aero Glass is an optional interface that's available only with certain kinds of video cards. To use Aero Glass, you must have a compatible video card and choose an Aero theme. To ensure that you're using an Aero theme, follow these steps:

1. Click the Start button, type **pers**, and click Personalize. Or right-click the desktop and choose Personalize.

2. In the Personalization window, select one of the themes in the Aero Themes group.

If your video card supports Aero, you should see the transparency effect. If you hold down 🪟 and press Tab, you should see the Flip 3D effect.

If your video card is supposed to support Aero Glass but doesn't, you might need to update its driver. See "Updating your Display Driver," near the end of this chapter.

Start Menu Problems

Most applications will install an icon on the Start menu. When your Start menu stops looking the way it should, it can really slow you down. Here are some tips to keep your Start menu looking the way you want.

Some Start items can't be displayed

If clicking the Start button displays Some Start items can't be displayed, you need to reduce the number of items on the Start menu or use small icons. Try reducing the number of items first by following these steps:

1. Right-click the Start button and choose Properties.

2. Click the Customize button on the Start Menu tab.

3. In the Customize Start Menu window, scroll to the bottom and then:

   - If you want to use smaller icons, scroll down the list of options and deselect the Use Large Icons option.

   - If you want to keep using large icons, reduce one or both of the numbers in the Start Menu Size group.

4. Click OK in each open dialog box.

Eventually, you'll get a sense of how many icons can fit in the lower-left side of the menu. If you set the Start Menu Size number to the number of icons that can fit in that space, you'll get just the right amount of icons in that space without seeing the Some Start menu items can't be displayed message.

The right side of my Start menu is missing some options

Chapter 11 explains how to customize your Start menu. If you're just looking for a quick fix right now, follow these steps:

1. Right-click the Start button and choose Properties.

2. Click the Customize button on the Start Menu tab.

3. In the list box that appears on the Customize Start Menu window, select any items you want on the menu and deselect any items you don't want.

4. Click OK in each of the open dialog boxes.

Taskbar Problems

The taskbar provides quick access to all your open applications, assuming that it's working correctly. The taskbar includes the Quick Launch toolbar, which enables you to run applications that have shortcuts created in this area. Here are some tips for managing your taskbar problems.

My taskbar is missing

It's probably just hidden. Touch the mouse pointer to the very bottom of the screen and it should scroll up into view. To make it stop going into hiding:

1. Right-click the Start button and choose Properties

2. Click the Taskbar tab and deselect Auto-Hide the Taskbar check box.

3. Click OK.

My taskbar is too tall (or messed up)

First, make sure the taskbar is unlocked and close all optional toolbars so that you can better see what's going on. Here's how:

1. Right-click the Start button and choose Properties.

2. Click the Taskbar tab and click the Lock the Taskbar check box to deselect it.

3. Click the Toolbars tab and deselect all check boxes.

4. Click OK or press Enter.

5. Put the tip of the mouse pointer on the top of the taskbar until the mouse pointer turns into a two-headed arrow; then hold down the left mouse button while moving the mouse toward you to shrink the taskbar to one row tall.

6. Right-click the current time in the lower-right corner of the screen and choose Lock the Taskbar to lock the taskbar to that height.

See "Customizing the Taskbar" in Chapter 10 for more information.

I don't have a Quick Launch toolbar

If you have previously used Windows Vista and now don't see the Quick Launch toolbar in Windows 7, don't be surprised. It's no longer included on the taskbar. The new features of the Windows 7 taskbar essentially make the Quick Launch toolbar unnecessary.

Updating Your Display Driver

Problems that prevent you from setting a reasonable desktop size and color depth are often caused by the device driver for the video card. Similarly, if a video card meets all the requirements for Aero Glass, and you still can't get Aero Glass to work, you might need to update your display driver. To do so, follow these steps:

1. If you're in a standard user account, log in to an account that has administrative privileges.

2. Connect to the Internet so that Windows can look for a new driver online.

3. Open Device Manager (press ⊞ or click the Start button, type **dev**, and click Device Manager).

4. Click the arrow (if any) next to Display Adapters.

5. Right-click the icon that represents your video card and choose Update Driver Software. Figure 15-4 shows an example.

FIGURE 15-4

Updating the device driver for a video card.

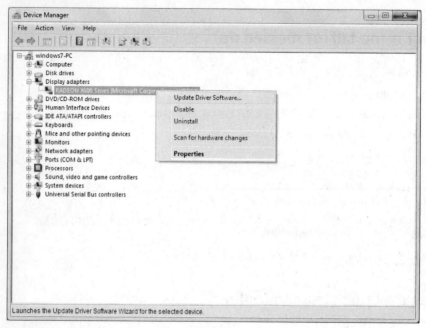

Note
The name that shows under Display Adapters will likely be different on your computer. Also, only one name will likely be listed. ■

6. Follow the on-screen instructions.

If the search doesn't find an updated driver, you might already have the latest driver for your video card. The only way to know for sure is to visit the card manufacturer's Web site and look up the latest driver for your specific video card.

Part IV

Using the Internet

The Internet has become so interwoven into our daily lives that getting things done without it is nearly impossible. Without a doubt, most people use their PCs to access the Internet more than anything else. This part of the book is all about the tools that come with Windows 7 to do just that — use the Internet.

Chapter 16 starts with an in-depth look at Microsoft Internet Explorer, the Web browser that comes free with Windows 7. You need a Web browser to access Web sites such as eBay, Google, Windows Live, and others.

Chapter 17 covers the new Windows Live Writer program that enables you to blog with services such as Windows Live Spaces, Blogger, WordPress, TypePad, and others.

Chapter 18 covers Windows Live Mail, the built-in program for doing e-mail and accessing newsgroups such as the Windows Communities. Windows Live Mail is a big improvement over its predecessors Outlook Express and Windows Mail and is well worth a look. It ties in with Windows 7's new search features, which makes it easy to find e-mail messages right from the Start menu, without opening the program first and digging around through folders.

Chapter 19 explores Windows Live Messenger, another downloadable add-on from Windows Live. You can use Messenger to chat online, hold video calls, and even text someone's cell phone.

Chapter 20 moves on to other Internet-related topics such as newsgroups, FTP, and Remote Assistance. Chapter 21 covers

Windows Contacts, a handy feature for managing names and
addresses and a big improvement over the Windows Address
Book (WAB) of yesteryear. Chapter 22, the final chapter
in this part, covers some solutions to common Internet
problems.

Using Internet Explorer

Next to e-mail, having access to the World Wide Web is one of biggest reasons people own computers. The Web consists of billions of pages of information as well as pictures, music, and video. The Web is also home to Windows Live, which brings Web content to your computer in fun and novel ways.

To use the Web, you need an Internet connection and a *Web browser*. A Web browser is a program that lets you browse (explore) the Web and find whatever you're looking for. The Web browser that comes with Windows 7 is named Internet Explorer 8, and that's what this chapter is mainly about. It starts with a brief look at how the Web works.

Understanding How the Web Works

The Internet consists of tens of millions of computers throughout the world connected by cables. A few million of those computers are *Web servers*, computers that store, and dish out, copies of Web pages to anyone who asks for them. The program you use to access and view Web pages is called a *Web browser*. Many brands of Web browsers are on the market, including Firefox, Safari, Google Chrome, and Windows Internet Explorer. This chapter covers Windows Internet Explorer Version 8, the Web browser that comes free with Windows 7.

Most Web sites use the HyperText Transfer Protocol (HTTP). For that reason, the URL (Uniform Resource Locator) for every Web page starts with `http://`. After the `http://` comes the host name, which in the early days of the Internet typically indicated the name of the Web server to which you were connecting. Today, however, many Web servers host more than one Web site, and therefore the host name often identifies the Web application (web app) on the server that is serving up that particular site, rather than the server name itself.

Tip
The Secure Sockets Layer (SSL) protocol is used by secure Web sites to encrypt traffic between the client (your computer) and the server. These secure sites use `https://` rather than `http://` at the beginning of the URL. ■

A Web site can consist of any number of pages. The first or main page for a Web site is often called its *home page*. In almost every case, you don't have to add the name of the site's home page in the URL, but instead just enter the protocol, host name, and domain name. For example, you can get to Microsoft's home page at `http://www.microsoft.com`. Google's home page is at `http://www.google.com`. eBay's home page is at `http://www.ebay.com`.

Tip

The reason you usually don't have to include the home page name in the URL to get to the site home page is that the server sets a default name and serves up that page for all requests that don't specify any other page. Often, the home page is named `default.htm`, `index.htm`, **or some variation of that, such as** `index.aspx`. ■

Notice how some URLs end in `.com`. That last part of the URL is called the top-level domain (TLD). Web sites that end in `.com` are *commercial* (business) Web sites. There are other types of sites as well; the most common top-level domains, their meaning, and examples are shown in Table 16-1.

TABLE 16-1

Examples of Top-Level Domains and URLs of Web Sites

Top-Level Domain (TLD)	Type	Example URL
.com	Commercial	www.amazon.com
.edu	Education	www.ucla.edu
.gov	Government	www.fbi.gov
.org	Nonprofit organization	www.redcross.org
.net	Network	www.comcast.net
.mil	Military	www.army.mil

Notice that I don't have the `http://` in front of the example URLs in Table 16-1. You rarely see the `http://` used at the front of a URL. Typically, you just see them expressed as `www.microsoft.com` or `www.ebay.com`. That's because virtually all public, nonsecured Web pages use `http://` as the protocol. In fact, when you type a URL into your Web browser's address bar and leave off the `http://` part, the browser just fills it in for you and makes the connection.

All Web browsers work the same way. You type a URL into the address bar and press Enter or click Go. That sends a packet of information off to your ISP (Internet service provider), which in turn routes it to the Internet. After traversing the Internet, the packet arrives at the Web server as a request that means "Hey, send me your Web page." The Web browser dutifully responds by sending out the requested page, which makes its way back to your ISP and then to your PC. You see the results as a Web page in your Web browser. Figure 16-1 illustrates the basic idea.

FIGURE 16-1

Requesting and viewing a Web page.

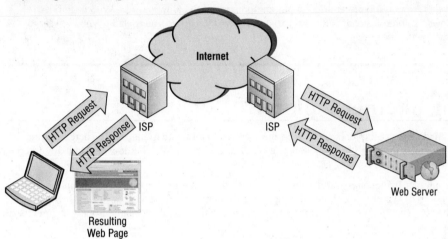

Remember, the Web contains billions of pages. You can access any one of them with any Web browser and any type of Internet connection. It doesn't matter who your ISP is or what Web browser you're using.

The time it takes from when you first make the request for a page and when you actually see the page depends on the speed of your Internet connection. It's usually only a matter of seconds. With really fast Internet connections, it might seem like no time at all.

Windows Explorer Versus Internet Explorer

People often confuse Windows Explorer and Internet Explorer because of their similar names, but there is a big difference between them. Windows Explorer (often called Explorer for short) is a program for exploring things *inside* your computer — things like disk drives, folders, and files that you can use without being online. Its program file is named Explore.exe. If your computer is part of a local network, you use Windows Explorer to access shared resources on those nearby computers as well.

Internet Explorer is typically for exploring stuff *outside* your computer, mainly World Wide Web pages on the Internet. Its program file name is Iexplore.exe. You have to be online (connected to the Internet) to explore those outside resources. The items outside your computer are mostly Web pages, rather than drives, folders, and files. Web pages have longer names, usually in the form of www.something.com, rather than short, simple names such as Computer, Documents, Pictures, and such.

continued

continued

Finally, note that you can open a Web page from a Windows Explorer window by typing the Web page's URL in the Windows Explorer address bar and pressing Enter. However, the Web page doesn't open in Windows Explorer. Instead, Windows Explorer passes the URL to your default Web browser to open the page; it then closes itself.

Using Internet Explorer

As mentioned, Internet Explorer is the Web browser that comes with Windows 7. There's no rule that says you must use that Web browser. But you certainly can, because it should work with any Internet account with any ISP.

You start Internet Explorer as you do any other program. If Internet Explorer is configured as your *default* (preferred) Web browser, click the Internet Explorer icon on the taskbar just to the right of the Start menu. Or, click Start ➪ All Programs ➪ Internet Explorer. Both are pointed out in Figure 16-2.

FIGURE 16-2

Starting Internet Explorer.

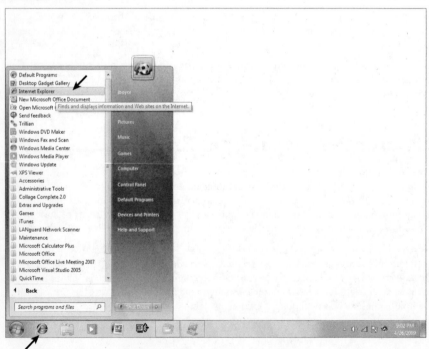

When Internet Explorer opens, you're taken to your *default home page*. That's just the fancy name for the first Web page you see when you open your Web browser. As discussed later in this chapter, you can choose any page you like as your default home page.

Tip

You can minimize, maximize, move, and size Internet Explorer's program window using the basic skills described under "Arranging program windows" in Chapter 2. ■

Browsing to a Web site

To browse to a Web site for the first time, click inside Internet Explorer's address bar and type the URL. You don't need to type the `http://` part. But you do need to type everything that comes after that part. Don't type any blank spaces, and be sure to use forward slashes (/), not backslashes (\). After you've typed the URL, press Enter or click the Go button to the right. Figure 16-3 shows an example of the URL for the Google search site typed into Internet Explorer's address bar.

FIGURE 16-3

Typing a URL.

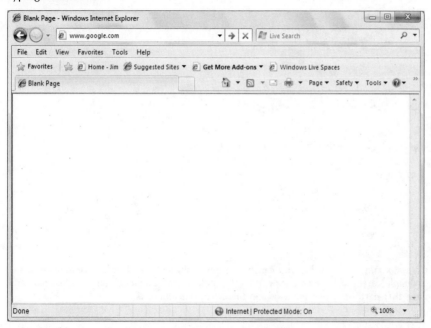

After you press Enter or click Go, Internet Explorer adds the leading `http://` part for you. The page at that URL shows up on your screen shortly thereafter. If it seems to be taking forever for the page to appear and you don't want to wait any longer, click the Stop button. Then click the Back button, if necessary, to return to the previous page.

Tip

URLs aren't case sensitive, so it's okay to type them in all lowercase letters. ■

It's not entirely necessary to type the entire URL. If the URL that's currently in the address bar is similar to the one you're about to type, you can select just the part you want to change. Then type in the new part. For example, Figure 16-4 shows the google portion of a URL selected by dragging the mouse pointer in it. Type another name, such as ebay, at that point, replacing google with ebay so the URL becomes www.ebay.com. Press Enter or click Go to browse.

FIGURE 16-4

Editing an URL.

Tip

To highlight just part of the domain name so that you can type a new one, just double-click the domain name in the address bar. For example, if you are viewing www.google.com, just double-click the google part and then start typing to replace that part and leave the www and the com parts alone. ■

Using AutoComplete

Internet Explorer remembers URLs you've typed in the past. When the URL you're typing matches ones you've typed in the past, a *history menu* will drop down, showing those previous URLs. For example, you can select (drag the mouse pointer through) all the text after the http://www. to select it. Start typing the replacement text, and the drop-down menu will show previously visited pages that start with the same letters.

For example, the top of Figure 16-5 shows all the text to the right of the www. selected and deleted after browsing to Google. Typing the letter g then shows all previously visited URLs that start with http://www.g, as shown in the bottom of that figure. Rather than continue typing the URL, just click the full URL in the drop-down list.

FIGURE 16-5

Drop-down menu of previous URLs.

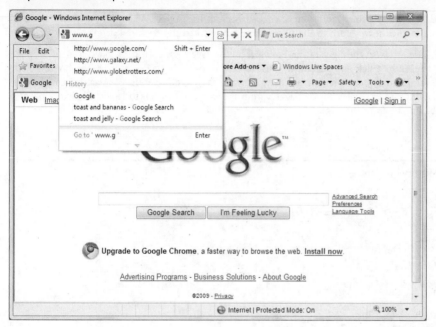

Tip

The drop-down list in IE8 includes your browsing history and favorites, so you can get to these sites quickly and easily. To clear out or disable the drop-down list, see "Deleting the Browser History," later in this chapter. ■

Using hyperlinks

When you're at a Web site, you may not have to do much more typing of URLs. After you're at a page, you can click any *hyperlink* (also called a *link*) to go to whatever page the link represents. A hyperlink can be text, a picture, or a button. A text hyperlink is usually blue, underlined text. However, if you've already visited the page that a text hyperlink points to, the hyperlink is purple.

A picture hyperlink might not look like anything special. But you can tell whether a picture is a hyperlink by putting the mouse pointer on it. If the mouse pointer changes to a small, pointing hand, you can click the picture to go to the page or item that's linked to the picture.

Using Back, Forward, and History buttons

The Back and Forward buttons maintain a history of your current Web-browsing session. A session starts when you first open your Web browser. The session ends when you close your Web browser. For this reason, the Back button is always disabled (dimmed) when you first open your browser. That's because there's no page to go back to when you first open your browser. But as soon as you go to another page, the Back button is enabled so that you can click it to return to the previous page.

Tip

You can also press the Backspace key to go back to the previous page. ■

The Forward button is disabled until you've clicked Back at least once. When the Forward button is enabled, you can click it to return to the page where you clicked the Back button.

Clicking the little arrow to the right of the Forward button (see Figure 16-6) displays a menu of pages you've visited recently. Click any page in that list to return to it. Or click History at the bottom of the menu to see the History pane. The History pane shows a more extensive list of recently visited Web sites. Click any one to expand it to see pages within the site you've been to lately. Click any page under the heading to go to the page.

FIGURE 16-6

Back, Forward, and History buttons.

To delete a link from the History pane, right-click it and choose Delete. To close the History pane so that it's out of your way, click the X button near its upper-right corner.

Magnifying a page

If it's difficult to read the small text on a Web page, you can zoom in for a closer look. There are actually two ways to do this. You can enlarge only the text and keep pictures at their current size. Or you can zoom in on pictures and text.

FIGURE 16-7

Page button and menu.

- To change the text size only, click the Page button (see Figure 16-7), click Text Size, and then click a text size.

- To change the size of text and pictures, click the Page button, click Zoom, and choose a magnification.

Tip

For quick zooming from the keyboard, hold down the Ctrl key and tap the + key repeatedly to zoom in. Hold down the Ctrl key and press the − (hyphen) key to zoom out. If your mouse has a scroll wheel, hold down the Ctrl button and scroll up or down to resize the page. Or, use the Zoom button at the bottom right of the window. ■

Panes and toolbars

In common with many programs, Internet Explorer has optional panes and toolbars. These are all accessible from the View menu on the menu bar. If you don't see the menu bar, press the Alt key or click Tools and choose Menu bar.

- To show or hide an optional pane, choose View ➪ Explorer Bars and click a pane name.

325

- To show or hide a toolbar, choose View ➪ Toolbars from the menu bar.

- You can widen or narrow a pane by dragging its inner border left or right.

- To customize the Command Bar (the one with the Page and Tools buttons), right-click an empty area at the right side of the menu bar or links bar and choose Customize. You'll see a handful of options that control text and icons, as well as add or remove toolbar buttons.

Full-screen viewing

When you're viewing a large Web page that's partially cut off, you can switch to full-screen view. That will get Internet Explorer's program window out of the way temporarily so that you can see more of the page. To go to full-screen view, choose View ➪ Full Screen from the menu, or press F11.

While you're in full-screen view, you can bring down just the address bar and toolbar so that you can go to another page, print the current page, or whatever. Just move the mouse pointer to the top of the screen, and those items will drop down into view. They'll slide out of view again when you move the mouse pointer back to the page.

To leave full-screen view and get back to the regular program window, press F11. Or move the mouse to the top of the display, and after the menu drops down again, choose View ➪ Full Screen.

Change your default home page

The page that first appears when you open your Web browser is called your *default home page*. Initially, it's whatever Microsoft or your computer manufacturer wanted it to be. But you can change that at any time. It's a simple process:

1. Browse to the page that you want to make your new default home page.

2. Click the arrow on the Home button, called out in Figure 16-8, and choose Add or Change Home Page.

3. If you haven't yet used multiple tabs (discussed next), choose Use This Webpage As Your Only Home Page and click Yes.

No matter where you are on the Internet, you can always get back to your default home page just by clicking the Home button in Internet Explorer.

If you have two or more Web sites you visit regularly, you can set up multiple home pages using tabs.

Using Tabs

Tabbed browsing lets you view multiple Web pages at one time within a single Internet Explorer window. Tabs appear under the menu bar. When you use multiple tabs, each tab shows the title of the page that's currently open in that tab. To open a new tab and display a page in it, click the empty tab to the right of the open tabs, or press Ctrl+T. Then enter the URL of the page you want to visit in the address bar.

Note
If tabs aren't available in your Internet Explorer, see "Personalizing tabbed browsing," later in this section. ■

FIGURE 16-8

Home button.

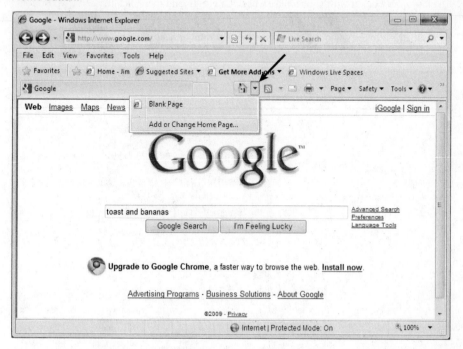

You can switch from one tabbed page to the next just by clicking any tab. To switch from tab to tab using the keyboard, press Ctrl+Tab to go to the next tab. Press Shift+Ctrl+Tab to go to the previous tab.

You can also open tabs in the background. When you do, the new tab opens to display a page. But you're not taken directly to that page. You stay where you are so that you can open additional tabs from the current page. To open a tab in the background, do any of the following:

- Hold down the Ctrl key while you click any hyperlink.
- Right-click any hyperlink and choose Open in New Tab.
- If your mouse has a wheel, click the hyperlink with the mouse wheel.

The new page opens in a separate tab, but you'll see only the tab, not the page. When you're ready to view the page, just click its tab.

When you close Internet Explorer with multiple tabs open, you'll see a prompt asking whether you want to close all tabs. Click Close Current Tab if your intent was to close only one tab. Otherwise, click Close Alls Tabs to close all open tabs and Internet Explorer. To stop seeing that message, select the Always Close All Tabs check box.

Here are some other good things to know about tabs:

- To open a page in a new tab and bring it to the foreground, hold down the Ctrl and Shift keys when you click a hyperlink.

- To open a new page in the foreground from the address bar, type the URL in the address bar and press Alt+Enter.

- To close a tab, click it with your mouse wheel. Or click it and then click the Close (X) button on that tab or press Ctrl+W.

- To close all tabs except one, right-click the tab you want to keep and choose Close Other Tabs. (See Figure 16-9.)

FIGURE 16-9

Right-click a tab.

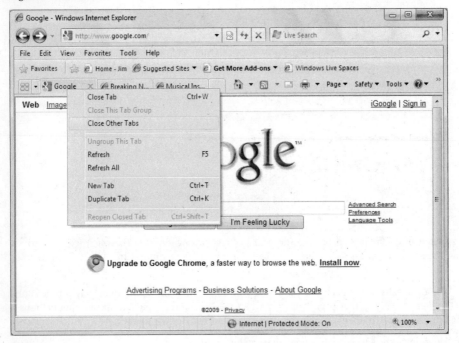

Tip

You can also save tab groups as favorites. See "Managing Favorite Sites," later in this chapter. ■

Using Quick Tabs

You can click the Quick Tabs button, or choose View ⇨ Quick Tabs, or press Ctrl+Q to see a miniature version of each open page. Click any miniature page to open and view its tab. Click any miniature page to bring the full page to the foreground.

A better alternative is to simply hover the mouse over the Internet Explorer icon in the taskbar. Windows displays a preview of the pages on the desktop, and you can simply click the one you want to open it. (See Figure 16-10.)

FIGURE 16-10

Preview Internet Explorer windows.

Creating multiple home page tabs

You can create multiple default home pages that all open automatically as soon as you start your Web browser. They're called *home page tabs* and are easy to set up. First click the empty tab. You see a blank page. Use the address bar to browse to the page that you want to use as the default home page for that tab. Then click the Home button and choose Add or Change Home Page ➪ Add This Web-page to your home page tabs ➪ Yes.

You can have as many home page tabs as you wish. But keep in mind that the more you have, the longer it will take for Internet Explorer to start. You don't want to use home page tabs as a substitute for Favorites. Limit them to perhaps the three or four Web sites you visit most often. If you get carried away, you can always remove a home page tab. Click the Home button, choose Remove, click the page you want to remove, and click Yes.

When you have all the default home pages you want open, each in its own tab, click the Home button, choose Add or Change Home Page, click Use the Current Tab Set As Your Home Page, and click Yes.

329

Tip

If you are a fast typist, choose Tools ➪ Internet Options, and on the General tab, click in the Home Page text box and type the addresses of the pages you want to add as your default page tabs, one to a line. Then click OK. ■

To test your multiple home pages, close Internet Explorer. Then reopen it. All the home pages should open, each in its own tab. No matter where you happen to be in Internet Explorer, you can always get back to any one of your default home pages. Just click the arrow on the Page button and click the page you want to jump to.

Tip

To browse without changing the contents of any tab, click the new, empty tab before entering an address. Or right-click a link in an existing tabbed page and choose Open in New Tab. ■

Rearranging and removing home page tabs

When you open Internet Explorer with multiple home page tabs, only the page in the first tab is visible. You may decide that you want to rearrange those pages after you've been using them for a while. To rearrange home page tabs:

1. Click the Tools button and choose Internet Options or choose Tools ➪ Internet Options from Internet Explorer's menu bar. The dialog box shown in Figure 16-11 will open.
2. On the General tab, select the URL you want to move.
3. Press Ctrl+X to cut the line.
4. Press Delete (Del) to delete the blank line.
5. Move the cursor to the start of the line where you want to place the URL.
6. Press Ctrl+V to paste; then press Enter.
7. Make sure that each URL appears on its own line and click OK.

To test the new arrangement, close and reopen Internet Explorer.

To remove a page from your home page tabs, remove its URL from the list on the General tab. To do that, select the line and press Delete (Del) twice, once to remove the text and a second time to delete the blank line left behind. Then click OK.

Personalizing tabbed browsing

You can enable or disable tabbed browsing, or tweak how tabs work. Click Tools and choose Internet Options or choose Tools ➪ Internet Options from Internet Explorer's menu. Then click the Settings button under the Tabs group. You'll see the options shown in Figure 16-12.

Here's what each option offers:

- **Enable Tabbed Browsing:** If you deselect this check box, tabbed browsing is disabled and all options that apply to tabbed browsing are disabled. Select this option to allow tabbed browsing. If you change this setting, you need to click OK. Then close and reopen Internet Explorer.
- **Warn Me When Closing Multiple Tabs:** Deselect this option to get rid of the warning that appears when closing Internet Explorer. Select this check box to bring the warning back.

FIGURE 16-11

Home pages in Internet Options.

- **Always Switch to New Tabs When They Are Created:** Choose this option to have new tabs open in the foreground automatically. For example, if this option is enabled and you right-click a link and choose Open in New Tab, the link opens in the new tab and that new tab appears in the foreground.

- **Show Previews for Individual Tabs in the Taskbar:** Select this option to have Windows display a preview for each tab when you hover over the Internet Explorer icon in the taskbar.

- **Enable Quick Tabs:** Deselecting this option removes the Quick Tabs button. The Quick Tabs button won't be visible to the left of the tabs. The Quick Tabs option on the View menu is disabled, and pressing Ctrl+Q has no effect. Select this option to enable Quick Tabs. After you change this option, click OK, close Internet Explorer, and then reopen Internet Explorer.

- **Enable Tab Groups:** When this option is enabled, Internet Explorer places new tabs that are opened from an existing page next to the original page, and color-codes the tabs the same, providing a logical and visual grouping for the related tabs.

- **Open Only the First Home Page When Internet Explorer Starts:** Select this option to allow for quicker startup. Only the first tabbed home page opens when you open Internet Explorer. To bring up other home pages, use the Home drop-down button on the toolbar.

- **When a New Tab Is Opened, Open:** Choose what you want Internet Explorer to display when you open a new tab.

- **When a Pop-Up Is Encountered:** A pop-up is any Web page that tries to open in a new Web browser. You learn more about pop-ups later in this chapter. But in the Tabbed Browsing Settings dialog box, your options are as follows:

FIGURE 16-12

Tabbed browsing settings.

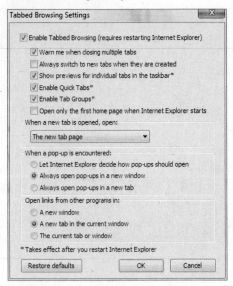

- **Let Internet Explorer Decide How Pop-Ups Should Open:** Choose this option to let Internet Explorer decide how to open pop-ups based on your pop-up blocker settings and the URL of the pop-up.

- **Always Open Pop-Ups in a New Window:** Choose this option to have acceptable pop-ups open in a new, separate instance of Internet Explorer.

- **Always Open Pop-Ups in a New Tab:** Choose this option to have acceptable pop-ups open in a new tab rather than in a new instance of Internet Explorer.

- **Open Links from Other Programs In:** These settings apply to other programs that can open Web pages, such as Windows Live Mail. They apply only if Internet Explorer is already open when you click a link in that other program:

  - **A New Window:** Pages you open from outside Internet Explorer open in a separate program window.

  - **A New Tab in the Current Window:** Keeps current tabs intact by opening the new page in a new, separate tab.

  - **The current tab or window:** The new page opens in the current Internet Explorer window, replacing what was showing before. Clicking Internet Explorer's Back button takes you back to the page that was showing before.

- **Restore Defaults:** Click this button to restore all Tabbed Browsing Settings.

Don't forget to click OK after making your choices. If you chose an option that requires restart, close Internet Explorer and restart it.

Shortcut keys for tabs

I mention several shortcut keys for using tabs in the preceding sections. For easy reference, Table 16-2 lists them all.

TABLE 16-2

Shortcut Keys for Tabs

Action	Shortcut
Open linked page in background tab	Ctrl+click the link or click with mouse wheel
Open linked page in foreground tab	Shift+Ctrl+Click the link
Open new tab in foreground from the address bar	Type the URL and press Alt+Enter
Open a new, empty tab in the foreground	Ctrl+T
Open Quick Tabs	Ctrl+Q
Switch from tab to tab	Ctrl+Tab, Shift+Ctrl+Tab
Go to a specific tab	Ctrl+n, where n is a number from 1 to 8
Go to the last tab	Ctrl+9
Close the current tab	Ctrl+W or click with mouse wheel
Close all tabs except the one in the foreground	Ctrl+Alt+F4

New Feature

Web slices let you view snippets of content from multiple Web pages.

Using Web Slices

Web slices in IE 8 let you keep track of content from sites through the IE 8 Favorites Bar. For example, Live Search offers Web slices for weather that you can add to your Favorites Bar, and get weather update notifications when they occur. eBay is another example, offering to track an auction and notify you when bid changes occur.

When you visit a page that offers a slice, you see a green icon on the page where the slice is offered, and the Feeds button on the command bar also looks green. To subscribe to the slice, click the icon. Internet Explorer opens a dialog box asking whether you want to add the Web slice to your Favorites Bar. Click the Add to Favorites Bar button to add the slice. When there is an update to the slice, Internet Explorer highlights the item in the Favorites Bar.

Tip
Click the down arrow next to the Feeds button to view multiple slices from the page as well as RSS feeds, if any, that are published to the page. ■

New Feature

A ccelerators speed up common browsing tasks such as mapping an address.

Using Accelerators

Accelerators are another new feature in Internet Explorer 8 that simplify and speed up browsing tasks. For example, if you were using an earlier version of IE and found an address on a Web page for a restaurant you wanted to visit, you'd probably have to copy the address to the Clipboard and then navigate to another site to map that address. With the Map with Live Maps accelerator, all you need to do is highlight the restaurant's address and then click the blue accelerator icon that appears above the text. If you hover the mouse over the Map with Live Search option, IE displays a pop-up window showing the location on a map. You can click the menu option to open the map in a new IE tab.

IE 8 has lots of accelerators for blogging, research, mapping, music, social networking, and much more. To find more accelerators for your computer, visit `http://ieaddons.com`.

New Feature

V isual search adds images to search results.

Using Visual Search

Visual Search is another new IE 8 feature that enhances searching. Visual Search presents images along with search results when those results offer images. For example, click in the Search text box and begin typing **Albert Einstein.** You should see at least one result with an image of Albert Einstein beside it.

Using RSS Feeds

Tip
You don't have to browse all your sites to see what's new. Use RSS feeds to have your favorite Web content delivered straight to your door. ■

RSS stands for Really Simple Syndication, and RSS provides a means for syndicating Web content. To put it simply, an RSS feed is Web content that is delivered to you using one of a handful of possible methods.

The main difference between an RSS feed and a Web page is that RSS feeds are delivered to you automatically; you don't have to browse to the feed's content to see what's new. When you subscribe to a feed, new content comes to you automatically as soon as it is published. For example, depending on how you subscribe to the feed, you might receive an e-mail notification with some of the content and a link to click so that you can view the entire content. Or, if you visit a Web page that hosts an RSS feed Web part, the RSS feeds are displayed on that Web page, and you can click the links to view the content. RSS feeds are often used for publishing news, so you're likely to find feeds at news sites, such as your local newspaper or TV station's Web sites. But any site can host RSS feeds. Press releases are often published as RSS feeds, as are blogs.

Note
See Chapter 17 to learn more about blogs. ■

When you browse to a Web page, take a look at the Feeds button in the Command Bar. (See Figure 16-13.) When it displays as orange and enabled, one or more are feeds available from that page. Click the Feeds button to learn more about the available feeds. You might see several feeds when you click the Feeds button.

FIGURE 16-13

Feeds button.

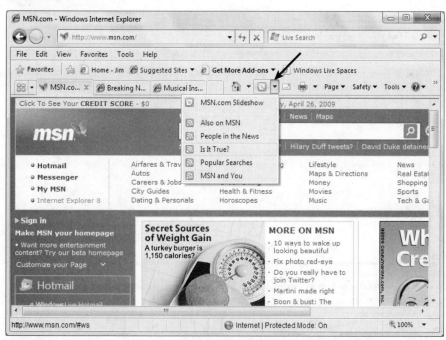

Tip
If the Feeds button is green, Web slices are available on the page. See "Using Web Slices," earlier in this chapter, for more information. Click the down arrow beside the button to view any RSS feeds available on the page. ■

If you see a feed that looks interesting, click it in the drop-down menu under the Feeds button. You come to a new page that shows information about the feed. If it looks interesting, you can subscribe to the feed. Most subscriptions are free. You can unsubscribe at any time, so you're not making any big commitment when you subscribe to a feed. To subscribe, click + Subscribe To This Feed on the feed page (Figure 16-14). In the resulting dialog box, just click the Subscribe button to subscribe to the feed.

You can subscribe to as many feeds as you like. Internet Explorer automatically checks all feeds in the background for fresh content. To view feeds, click the Favorites Center button and then click Feeds. (See Figure 16-15.) You see a link to each subscribed feed. Click any feed's link to see current content.

FIGURE 16-14

Subscribe to a feed.

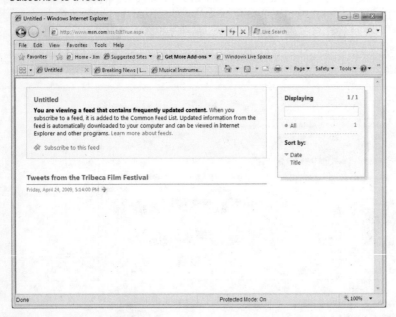

Finding Feeds

Yoou'll discover many on your own in your day-to-day Web browsing. As you browse from page to page, just glance up at the Feeds button to see whether it's enabled. Here are some sites you might want to check out to get started:

- www.mtv.com/rss

- www.microsoft.com/windows

- feeds.foxnews.com/foxnews/latest

- news.google.com

- www.si.com
- www.microsoft.com/ie
- abclocal.go.com
- www.ieaddons.com
- online.wsj.com
- weather.msn.com
- www.reuters.com
- www.nytimes.com

FIGURE 16-15

Feeds in the Favorites Center.

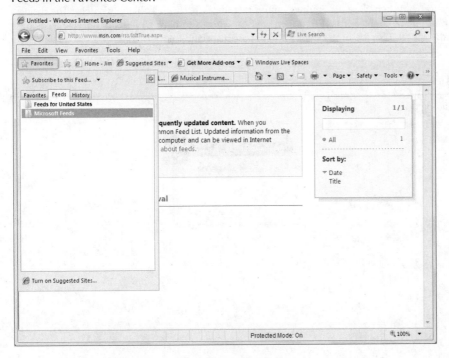

Optional settings for RSS feeds

You can tweak a couple of settings to change how RSS feeds behave. To get to them:

1. Click Tools on the Command Bar and choose Internet Options or choose Tools ⇨ Internet Options from Internet Explorer's menu.

2. Click the Content tab in the dialog box that opens.

3. Under the Feeds and Web Slices group, click the Settings button.

The options in the dialog box that opens are largely self-explanatory. You can control if, and how often, feeds and Web Slices update automatically. The Automatically Mark Feed As Read When Reading a Feed option automatically colors feeds you've read differently from unread feeds to help you keep track. That option is available only if you also choose Turn on Feed Reading view. If you disable the Feed Reading view, your feeds will be difficult to read because they're displayed in the native XML format. Choosing Play a Sound When a Feed or Web Slice Is Found for a Webpage is a good way to get a heads-up beep when you land on a page that offers feeds. Choosing Turn On in Page Web Slice Discovery enables IE 8 to identify and display available Web Slices on the page. Use Play a Sound When a Monitored Feed or Web Slice is Updated to receive an audible notification when feeds and slices are updated.

As always, click OK in all open dialog boxes after making your selections.

Using the RSS Feed Headlines gadget

You can use the RSS Feed Headlines gadget to keep an eye on feeds. Right-click the desktop and choose Gadgets, and then drag the Feed Headlines gadget onto the desktop. Hover the mouse pointer over the gadget and then click the Settings button that appears. (It looks like a wrench.) The dialog box shown in Figure 16-16 opens. From there you can choose to have all feeds or specific feeds displayed in the gadget. Use the drop-down list to choose a specific feed.

FIGURE 16-16

RSS Feeds gadget dialog box.

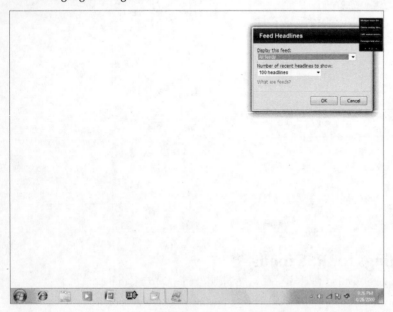

Note
For the full lowdown on gadgets, see "Using Gadgets" in Chapter 10. ■

You can have multiple Feed Headlines gadgets on the desktop. For instance, you might use one gadget to show content from a favorite feed and use a second gadget to show content from all feeds.

Managing Favorite Sites

Getting back to favorite Web sites by retyping the URL each time gets tiresome. Fortunately, it's also unnecessary because you can get to any favorite site with a simple mouse click. You just have to remember to add the site to your Favorites while you're there. That's easy to do:

1. If you're not already at a favorite Web site or page, browse to one.
2. Do any of the following to add the page to your Favorites:
    - Click the Favorites button and choose Add to Favorites.
    - Right-click some empty white space on the page and choose Add to Favorites.
    - Choose Favorites ➪ Add to Favorites from Internet Explorer's menu.

Tip

You can create folders, rename folders, change page titles, and organize favorites into folders at any time. So feel free to skip all the optional steps that follow. ■

3. Optionally, if you want to type your own descriptive title for the page, replace the text shown in the Name box with your own name.
4. Optionally, if you've already set up custom Favorites folders, click the Create In button and choose the folder in which you want to place the favorite.
5. Optionally, to create a new Favorites folder, click New Folder, type the new folder name, and click Create.
6. Click Add.

The Web site's title is added to your Favorites menu and the Favorites Center. To return to the site at any time in the future, choose Favorites from the menu and click the Web site's title. Or click the Favorites Center button (star) and click the site's title there.

Tip

To create a desktop shortcut to the page you're currently viewing, choose File ➪ Send ➪ Shortcut to Desktop from Internet Explorer's menu. To e-mail a link or Web Page to someone, click File ➪ Send and then choose Page by E-mail (to send the page itself) or Link by E-mail (to send a link to the page). ■

Adding tab groups to Favorites

You can add a whole group of pages organized into tabs to your Favorites. For example, you might open several favorite shopping sites, music sites, sports sites, or whatever, each in its own tab. To save the whole tab group to your Favorites:

1. Choose Favorites ➪ Add Current Tabs to Favorites from the menu.
2. Type in a folder name that describes the pages in the tab group (for example, **Shopping Sites**) and click Add.

The tab group is added to the Favorites Center and Favorites menu. To reopen the tab group and all its pages in the future, click the Favorites Center button (the one with the star in Figure 16-17). Then point to the name of the tab group and click the blue arrow that appears to the right. Or right-click the tab group name and choose Open in Tab Group.

FIGURE 16-17

Tab group in Favorites Center.

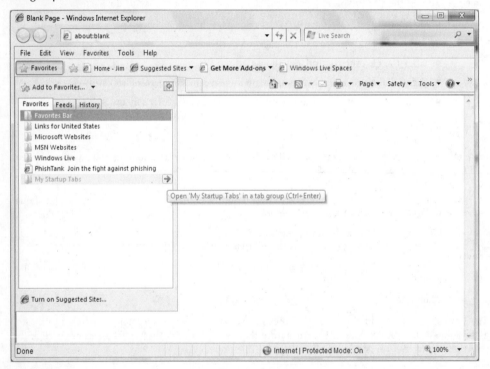

Starting Your Favorites Collection

If you're new to the Web and want to visit some useful Web sites that you might want to add to your Favorites, here are a few to help you get started. Not everyone will want to add all these to his or her Favorites, of course. But you're likely to find some sites you'll want to revisit:

- www.dictionary.com: Look up a word in a dictionary or thesaurus, or translate text from one language to another.

- www.wikipedia.org: Research a multitude of topics in many languages through this online encyclopedia. Anyone can contribute to Wikipedia, however, so consider it a good source of information but not necessarily a source of *completely accurate* information.

- `www.ebay.com`: Find myriad goods at this ever-popular buy-and-sell-anything-and-everything site.

- `www.fandango.com`: Find out what movies are playing in your local theaters, their start times, and so forth.

- `www.google.com`: Search the World Wide Web on this popular site.

- `www.mapquest.com`: Use this as a great resource for maps and driving directions.

- `search.microsoft.com`: Search Microsoft's Web site for technical support. Other useful Microsoft pages include `www.microsoft.com/windows`, `download.microsoft.com`, and `www.windowsmarketplace.com`.

- `www.tucows.com`: Locate hard-to-find programs that you can download and try for free.

Organizing Favorites

As your collection of favorite Web sites and RSS feeds grows, you might find it useful to organize them into folders. That way, you won't be faced with a huge list of favorites each time you open your Favorites bar. To organize your favorites, choose Favorites ➪ Organize Favorites from Internet Explorer's menu bar. You see the Organize Favorites window shown in Figure 16-18.

FIGURE 16-18

Organize Favorites.

To create a new folder, click the New Folder button, type a folder name, and press Enter. To create a subfolder within an existing folder, first open the parent folder. Then click New Folder and enter the subfolder name.

To move a page or tab group into a folder, choose the item you want to move and then click Move. Click the folder into which you want to move the item and click OK. Or, just drag the item onto the folder into which you want to move it.

To rename a link or folder, choose the item you want to rename, click Rename, type the new name, and press Enter.

Caution

Deleting a folder deletes all items in that folder. If the folder contains any items you want to keep, move them to another folder before you delete. ■

To delete an item or folder, choose the item you want to delete, click Delete, and click OK.

To put items into alphabetical order, right-click a folder name or some empty space and choose Sort by Name.

Click Close when you've finished organizing your Favorites. To view your reorganized favorites, click the Favorites Center button.

Importing and exporting Favorites

If you've been using another Web browser for a while and want to start using Internet Explorer, you can import your Favorites and other items from your other browser. That way, Internet Explorer will have all the favorite Web sites you're accustomed to from your previous browser.

Similarly, if you want to use some browser other than Internet Explorer, you can export Favorites and other items from Internet Explorer to your other browser. Either way, the steps are as follows:

1. Choose File ➪ Import and Export from Internet Explorer's menu.
2. On the next wizard page, choose whichever option describes what you want to do and click Next.
   - To import from another browser installed on your computer, choose Import From Another Browser.
   - To import from a file that you exported from some other program, choose Import From A File and click Next.
   - To export directly to a file, choose Export To A File and click Next.
3. Choose the items to import or export (Favorites, Feeds, and Cookies) and click Next.
4. Follow additional instructions for selecting files if required, and click Import if importing data, or click Export if exporting data.

Why Would I Import/Export a File?

If the program you want to import from or export to isn't on the same computer, you can use a file as a go-between. Let's say you have two computers, which we'll call OldComputer and NewComputer. To get Favorites from OldComputer to NewComputer, you would log in to OldComputer and there you would export Favorites to a file named `bookmark.htm` on a jump drive. Then log in to NewComputer and import them from `bookmark.htm` on the jump drive.

Blocking Pop-Ups

A pop-up is any Web page that opens in its own separate browser window. Some pop-ups are OK. For example, a pop-up might open to display a larger copy of a small picture. Or it might open so that you can still see the page that contains the link that opened the page. Other pop-ups, such as advertisements, aren't so great. These are often referred to as automatic pop-ups because they appear on their own, without your clicking a link.

Microsoft Internet Explorer has a built-in pop-up blocker to help you deal with pop-ups. To activate or deactivate the pop-up blocker:

1. Click Tools and choose Internet Options or choose Tools ⇨ Internet Options from Internet Explorer's menu.

2. Click the Privacy tab.

3. To block pop-ups, select (check) Turn on Pop-up Blocker. To allow all pop-ups through, deselect that check box.

If you opt to use the pop-up blocker, you can click the Settings button to configure it to your own tastes. When you click the Settings button, the dialog box shown in Figure 16-19 opens.

First you can choose how aggressively you want to block pop-ups (remember, they're not all ads). Use the Blocking Level drop-down list at the bottom of the dialog box to choose one of the following blocking levels:

- **High:** Blocks all pop-ups, even when you click a link to open the pop-up. If you choose this setting, you have to hold down the Ctrl and Alt keys while clicking a link to allow a legitimate pop-up page to open.
- **Medium:** Blocks most automatic pop-ups, but not pop-ups that open when you click a link.
- **Low:** Blocks relatively few pop-ups. Always allows pop-ups from secure and trusted Web sites.

The Notification options let you hear a sound and display the Information bar when a pop-up is blocked. It's a good idea to select both those options so that you know when a page has been blocked. That way, you can decide whether you want to allow a Web site to show pop-ups. (Remember, not all pop-ups are bad.)

If you already know that you want to allow pop-ups from a specific site, you can type the site's URL under Address of Website to Allow and then click the Add button. Doing so is not really necessary, however; if you choose the Show Information Bar when a pop-up is blocked option, you can allow sites as you go. Click the Close button at the bottom of the Pop-up Settings dialog box after making your selections. Then click OK to close the Internet Options dialog box.

FIGURE 16-19

Pop-up blocker settings.

Using the Information bar

The Internet Explorer Information bar appears whenever the pop-up blocker prevents a page from opening. It also appears when you're about to download certain kinds of programs, such as ActiveX controls. Typically, you hear a beep when the Information bar opens. You also may see the message shown in Figure 16-20.

The Information bar is the one below the tabs. To use it, you need to click the Close button in the information box. When you get accustomed to recognizing the Information bar, you can choose Don't Show This Message Again to keep the message box from alerting you to the Information bar. After closing the message, click the Information bar and choose what you want to do:

- **Temporarily Allow Pop-Ups:** Choose this option to take a look at the pop-up to see if it's something useful. If it is okay, you can close the pop-up window, click the Information bar again, and choose the option described next.

- **Always Allow Pop-Ups from This Site:** Choose this option if you trust the current Web site enough to always allow pop-ups. Choose Yes when asked for confirmation.

- **Settings:** Use this menu to access settings that control how the pop-up blocker works.

If you later regret choosing to always allow pop-ups, go back to the Pop-up Blocker Settings dialog box shown in Figure 16-19. Click the Web site's URL and click Remove.

FIGURE 16-20

Information bar.

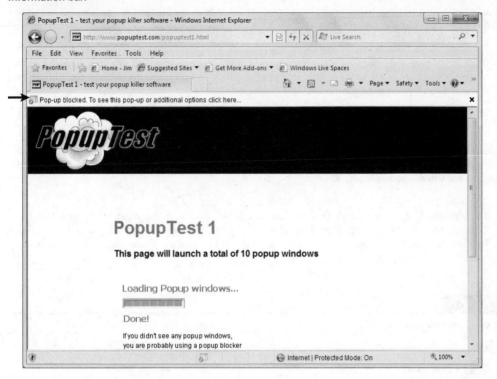

When pop-ups still get through

If you've enabled Internet Explorer's pop-up blocker but still get pop-up ads when you use it, your computer may be infected with spyware or adware. Consider using Windows Defender, discussed in Chapter 8, to scan your entire system for spyware. Remove any spyware it finds.

Internet Explorer never blocks pop-ups from Web sites in your Local Intranet zone. See "Using Internet Security Zones," later in this chapter, for more information.

Using the SmartScreen Filter

Phishing is a technique used by thieves to get passwords and PINs (Personal Identification Numbers). It usually works something like this: You get an e-mail message that appears to be from a legitimate bank, business, or your IT department. PayPal, eBay, and banks are favorite targets because people have accounts and deal in money at those sites. The message tells you that you need to respond to some message or check your account.

When you click a link in the e-mail message, your browser opens and appears to take you to the normal sign-in page for your account. However, it only *looks* like the real sign-in page. It's really a page at some other Web site. You type in your user name and password and then the phishers send you to the real site. In the meantime, the thieves have stored your user name and password in their own database and can now get into your account and get all the personal information in that account, which can be used for identity theft. Depending on the type of site, they may even be able to transfer money out of your account and into their own.

The scam works because everything looks legitimate, both in the e-mail message and on the sign-in page. In the past, the only way you would know it was a scam would be if you took a close look at where the links are really sending you, or if you happened to notice that the URL in the address bar at the account sign-in page wasn't really the business's URL.

Tip

In Windows Mail, point to any link in any e-mail message. The status bar at the bottom of the program window shows where the link really takes you. In Internet Explorer, you just have to look at the address bar at the sign-in page to see where you really are. ■

The phishing filters in Windows Mail and Internet Explorer keep an eye out for you. In Internet Explorer, the address bar turns a reddish color and shows a red shield with a white X. You see a large warning page with a red background if the site has been reported as unsafe. Figure 16-21 shows an example.

FIGURE 16-21

Phishing Web site blocked.

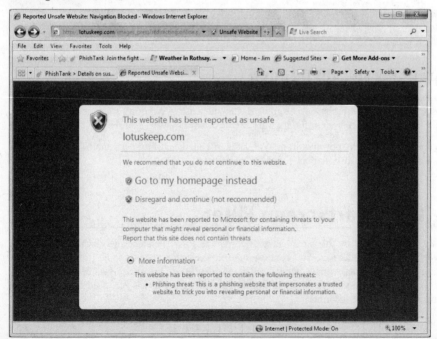

Another dead giveaway is when the address bar shows an IP address in front of a legitimate site name. For example, `http://206.83.210.40/chase-online.com` looks as though it has something to do with Chase bank. However, the IP address (`206.83.210.40`) is the actual Web server address. The part after the IP address, `chase-online.com`, is just a folder on that server and can be any name the crooks want it to be. It's unlikely that a legitimate business would show an IP address instead of its registered domain name.

In addition to checking for phishing sites, the SmartScreen Filter also checks for sites that offer malicious downloads. This means that the SmartScreen Filter can help protect your computer against infection by malware.

How the SmartScreen Filter works

Internet Explorer's SmartScreen Filter takes a three-pronged approach to detecting phishing scams. First, SmartScreen analyzes sites you visit for tactics commonly used by phishing sites. If it finds suspicious content, SmartScreen displays a warning message and gives you the opportunity to provide feedback.

Second, SmartScreen sends URLs of sites you visit to a Microsoft database of reported phishing sites to catch them before you get there. If you are trying to visit a site that is listed in the database, SmartScreen blocks the site and shows the red warning page described previously. This page offers you the option of ignoring the warning and visiting the page, but that's generally a bad idea.

Third, SmartScreen checks downloaded files against the same dynamic database, and if SmartScreen finds a match, it blocks the download and displays a warning message.

Most of the time when SmartScreen reports a suspicious Web site, it's correct. Occasionally, you might see a *false positive*, meaning that a legitimate site is marked as suspicious. The SmartScreen page offers a link that will open a page on one of Microsoft's Web sites that you can use to report that you believe the site is safe.

Getting the most from the SmartScreen Filter

By default, SmartScreen Filter is enabled and checks visited sites against the Microsoft database. If desired, you can turn off SmartScreen Filter by clicking the Safety button on the toolbar and choosing SmartScreen Filter ➪ Turn Off SmartScreen Filter. In the resulting Microsoft SmartScreen Filter dialog box, click Turn off SmartScreen Filter and click OK.

If you turn off SmartScreen Filter, you can manually check the page you're currently viewing by clicking Safety ➪ SmartScreen Filter ➪ Check this Website.

Caution
Some fraudulent Web sites will tell you to ignore phishing filters. Don't believe it. Why would a valid Web site tell you to ignore a safety feature like that? It's like someone telling you it's OK to run a stop sign. ∎

If you have turned off SmartScreen Filter, you can easily turn it back on. Click Safety ➪ SmartScreen Filter ➪ Turn On SmartScreen Filter. What if I've already been tricked?

If you think you may have given away your password to a phishing scam already, change your password or PIN as soon as possible. Log in to your account through your Web browser, not from a link in any e-mail message. Then use whatever means that Web site provides to change your password.

How do I protect myself in the future?

When you get an e-mail concerning any online account you have, don't click links in the e-mail message. Go to the Web site directly with your browser, using the same URL you always do. Also, never give out a password or PIN in an instant message, e-mail message, or over the phone.

Remember, when it comes to protecting your online assets, knowledge is power. Ignorance is vulnerability. To keep abreast of current scams and ways to stay safe online, visit www.microsoft.com/athome/security. Also, consider subscribing to the Security At Home RSS Feed at www.microsoft.com/athome/security/rss/rssfeed.aspx.

Tip
Parental controls, discussed in Chapter 4, provide tools and techniques for keeping children safe online. ■

Deleting the Browser History

The term *browser history* covers the many different things that Internet Explorer tracks automatically. This includes Web site addresses, things you type into forms, cookies, and even entire pages. Here I look at ways you can clear those things and disable them entirely where appropriate.

Clearing AutoComplete entries

AutoComplete is a feature of Internet Explorer that remembers passwords and other data you've entered in the past. When you go to a Web site with a remembered password, it types in the password for you automatically. When you start filling in the Name, Address, or a similar item on a form, it displays text that matches what you've typed into similar form fields in the past.

AutoComplete also keeps track of URLs you've typed in the past. Whenever you type a new address into your Web browser's address bar, it displays past URLs that match what you've typed so far.

Tip
To remove a single item rather than all items from a drop-down menu, point to the item you want to delete and press Delete. It doesn't work on all drop-down menus, but it works on many of them. ■

If you're using a public computer, you certainly don't want to leave that behind. Even on your own personal computer, you might want to delete those things if you've made a lot of mistakes in the past. Or if you share your user account with many people, you may want to clear those items for your own basic privacy. Whatever the reason, it's easy to empty those things out and start with a clean slate. For precise control of what gets deleted, follow these steps:

1. Click the Tools button and choose Internet Options, or choose Tools ➪ Internet Options from the menu bar.

2. On the General tab, in the Browsing history group, click Delete to see the Delete Browsing History dialog box, shown in Figure 16-22.

3. Select the items you want Internet Explorer to delete, click Delete, and click OK.

FIGURE 16-22

Delete Browsing History dialog box.

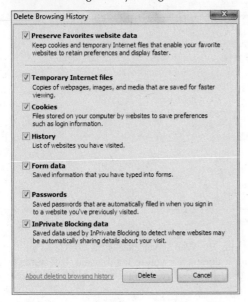

Configuring AutoComplete

If you don't want AutoComplete to keep track of things you type, you can turn it off. Here's how:

1. Click Tools and choose Internet Options or choose Tools ➪ Internet Options from the menu bar.

2. Click the Content tab.

3. Under the AutoComplete group, click Settings. You see the options shown in Figure 16-23.

4. Deselect any type of AutoComplete options you don't want to use.

5. Click OK.

The Delete Browsing History dialog box, shown earlier, lets you delete your temporary Internet files and cookies. It seems that almost everyone who browses the Web has heard of those things but there's a lot of confusion about what they are. So in the sections that follow, I take a crack at explaining them without boring you to tears in the process, I hope.

Understanding cookies

A cookie is a tiny file placed on your computer at the request of a Web site. The vast majority of cookies are perfectly harmless and are necessary for using certain types of sites. Most often, cookies are used to keep you signed into a Web site that requires logging in. When you log in, a cookie is created that contains information about your current session. Typically, this is just some randomly assigned number that contains no information about you or your computer.

FIGURE 16-23

AutoComplete settings.

As you browse from one page to the next within the site, the Web server checks the cookie to see whether you're already logged in. If you are logged in, it doesn't ask you to log in again. If it weren't for cookies, you'd have to log in every time you switched from one page to the next within the Web site. That would be a major pain.

Deleting cookies

You can easily wipe your computer clean of all cookies at any time. There's no such thing as a "required" cookie, so you usually don't have to worry about eliminating some important, necessary cookie. The worst that can happen is that you have to log into a secure Web site that might otherwise be able to log you in automatically. Or, you could lose the contents of a online shopping cart if you haven't checked out yet.

If you're not concerned about losing any data, however, you can delete the cookies. To wipe your computer clean of all cookies:

1. Click Tools and choose Internet Options or choose Tools ⇨ Internet Options from Internet Explorer's menu.

2. Under the Browsing History heading, click Delete.

3. Select Cookies and click Delete.

4. Click OK.

Adjusting cookie privacy settings

You can easily protect your computer from unacceptable cookies by setting a security level for privacy. If your Internet Options dialog box isn't already open, choose Tools ⇨ Internet Options from Internet Explorer's menu. Then click the Privacy tab. You see the slider shown in Figure 16-24.

Drag the slider to Medium (if it isn't already there). You can set it higher for even better protection. You might, however, find using some legitimate Web sites difficult if you do.

FIGURE 16-24

Privacy settings for cookies.

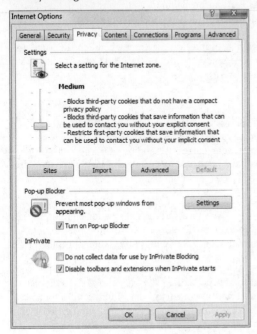

Looking at cookies and privacy policies

The main threat posed by cookies is invasion of privacy. As mentioned, unacceptable cookies might contain personal information that could be exploited.

Many Web sites that use cookies these days will back them up with a compact privacy policy. The privacy policy specifies how the site will protect your privacy. You can check to see what cookies, if any, a Web page has put on your system:

1. If you're not already at the Web page in question, browse to it normally.

2. Choose View ➪ Web page privacy policy from Internet Explorer's menu.

A list of files downloaded from that page appears in a dialog box. If the page loaded a cookie, you see Accepted or Blocked in the Cookies column. To see whether the cookie has a compact privacy policy, click the address to the left of Accepted or Blocked and then click Summary.

If your current privacy settings blocked a cookie that you need for the page, you can choose Always Allow This Site to Use Cookies to loosen the restrictions on that site. Similarly, if a cookie was accepted, you can choose to block future cookies from that site. If trying to manage cookies on a case-by-case basis gets to be too much trouble, click the Settings button to get to the Privacy slider. Then drag the slider down a notch or two to loosen your restrictions.

Note
Third-party cookies, which come from a site other than the one you're visiting, are the greatest offenders. That's why most of the privacy settings focus on third-party cookie handling. ■

Understanding temporary Internet files

To understand temporary Internet files, you have to understand a little about how the Web works. When you type a URL into your browser's address bar and press Enter, your computer sends a little *packet* of information to the Web server at that address. You don't actually "connect" to the server, you just send a message that says, "Hey, server, send your page to me at *my IP address*." The *my IP address* part is a number that uniquely identifies your computer on the Internet, much the same as your phone number uniquely identifies your telephone among all the phones in the world.

Tip

If you have a standard home Internet connection, your IP address could change periodically. If you want to see what it is right now, go to a search engine such as www.google.com. Search for "what is my IP address?" You receive a list of Web sites that display your current IP address. Or you can visit "http://whatismyip.com" to view your address on the page or www.boyce.us and view your IP address under the date in the navigation bar. ∎

When the Web server gets the packet, it sends out the Web page, addressed to your computer. The page isn't sent as one big file, per se. It's sent as hundreds or thousands of tiny little packets. These packets don't even take the same path to your computer. They travel more like water dripping down a net, each following its own path but eventually ending up in the same place.

The packets don't even arrive at your computer in the proper order. They have to be reassembled into the proper order. The reassembled packets are stored in your temporary Internet files folder as a single file. (Well, actually, it might be several files: One for the text of the page, another for each picture on the page, and perhaps even others. But that's not important here.)

As all the pieces come together in your temporary Internet files folder, your Web browser displays the page. With a fast Internet connection, this all happens so quickly that you would never guess it is being built from these little bits and pieces.

Anyway, the bottom line is that when you're looking at a Web page in your Web browser, you're not really looking at some faraway document on another computer. You're actually looking at a copy of that document that's on your own computer, in your temporary Internet files folder.

When you've finished viewing the page and you move on to the next page, Internet Explorer doesn't erase the copied page. It keeps it. That way, if you click Back to go back to that page, it doesn't have to go through the whole process of getting the page from the Web server again. It just shows the copy of the page that's already in your temporary Internet files folder.

So what's to keep these temporary Internet files from filling up your entire hard disk? Easy. There's a limit to how much stuff that temporary Internet files folder can hold. When it starts to get full, old pages you haven't viewed in a long time are automatically deleted to make room for new pages you're viewing. Hence the name *temporary* Internet files. They don't last forever.

Why It's So Fast

The reason it's all so fast is that the electrons carrying the packets of information are moving at nearly the speed of light, 186,000 miles per second. That's fast enough to circle the earth at the equator seven times a second. The distances the electrons have to travel across the Web and inside your computer are so tiny that it takes virtually no time at all.

The only reason a dial-up connection seems slow is that the telephone lines put a stranglehold on the information, similarly to how water runs through a very skinny tube rather than a big fat drainage pipe. It takes longer to drain a pool with a tiny tube than with a wide drainage pipe. Likewise, it takes longer to get Internet data from your ISP to your computer with a "skinny" dial-up connection than it does with a "wide" broadband connection.

DSL uses telephone lines, too, just as dial-up connections do. But DSL is faster because the information is transmitted over the telephone line digitally. With a dial-up connection, the information is transmitted in analog format. It's really the combination of telephone lines and analog format that makes dial-up connections so slow.

Clearing temporary Internet files

You can clean out those temporary Internet files any time you want. It's never necessary to do so, though doing it just before performing some task that operates on all files in your system, such as a virus scan or disk defragmentation, is useful. Also, there's no such thing as a "necessary" or "required" temporary Internet file. So you can never do any harm by wiping them off of your computer.

Deleting temporary Internet files is much like deleting cookies. The steps are as follows:

1. Click Tools and choose Internet Options or choose Tools ⇨ Internet Options from Internet Explorer's menu bar.

2. Under the Browsing History group, click Delete.

3. Select Temporary Internet Files and then click Delete.

4. Click OK.

If you have a slow Internet connection, viewing pages you've viewed in the past might seem to take a little longer. That's because Internet Explorer has to download everything from scratch again. No temporary Internet files are left that Internet Explorer can use as an alternative. If you have a fast Internet connection, you might not notice any difference at all.

Temporary Internet files settings

You can change some settings that apply to temporary Internet files. Once again, click Tools and choose Internet Options or choose Tools ⇨ Internet Options from Internet Explorer's menu bar. This time, though, click the Settings button under Browser History. The Temporary Internet Files and History Settings dialog box, shown in Figure 16-25, opens.

The first set of options determines how and when Internet Explorer checks for new versions of files that are in your temporary Internet files folder. Automatic is the preferred setting. This allows Internet Explorer to use its own built-in programming logic to make a best guess about whether it's worth taking the time to check for newer versions of files. The guess is usually right. But you can always click the Refresh button or choose View ⇨ Refresh to download the page to be sure.

The first two options force Internet Explorer to check every time you visit the page or every time you start Internet Explorer. Theoretically, either of these options would ensure that you always have the most up-to-date content. Both, however, will also likely force Internet Explorer to check more than is necessary, and perhaps slow down your whole Web-browsing experience, especially if you have a slow Internet connection.

Temporary Internet Files and History Settings dialog box.

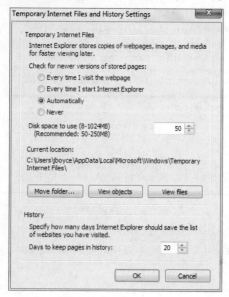

The Never option is risky because you really have no way of knowing whether the page you're viewing in your browser is in sync with what's currently on the Web server. You would have to use the Refresh button every time you visit a page to make sure you have the most current content.

The Disk Space to Use option lets you decide how much hard drive space you're willing to sacrifice for storing temporary Internet files. Keep in mind that hard drive space is measured in gigabytes (GB), and the setting is measured in megabytes (MB). A gigabyte is 1,024MB, so even the largest setting is still relatively small.

The Current location shows where your Temporary Internet Files folder is located on your hard disk. If your drive C is running low on space and you have a second hard drive in the computer, you can click the Move Folder button to place the temporary files on that other drive.

Note

The Temporary Internet Files folder is hidden and protected. If you try to get to it with Windows Explorer, you may not have any luck. You have to choose Show Hidden Files and Folders and deselect the Hide Protected Operating System Files check box in the Folder Options dialog box to see the folder. ■

The View objects button shows icons for Web objects in the Temporary Internet Files folder. Objects are different from pages and pictures. They're small programs that allow you to use more advanced

Web features. For example, you'd likely find things such as the Adobe Flash Player and Windows Genuine Advantage tool in there, if you've downloaded those items.

Objects aren't deleted when you clear out your Temporary Internet Files folder. If they were, you would have to manually download and install them again. But if you ever needed to delete some object, on the advice of a professional, you could do so in that folder.

The View Files button shows the files that are currently stored in the Temporary Internet Files folder. Some of these may be retained when you clear your temporary Internet files, because the convenience of keeping them outweighs the benefits of clearing them. But if there was some problem with the site and the Webmaster recommended eliminating the file, you could do so from the folder.

The Days to Keep Pages in History setting relates to the History pane at the left side of Internet Explorer's program window. To see that pane, press Ctrl+H or click the Favorites Center button and then click History. Or choose View ➪ History. The number you enter specifies how bar back your History keeps track of visited Web sites. For example, if you set it to 7, your History list will never show addresses of sites you visited more than a week ago.

A note on certificates

As you go through all the optional settings in the Internet Options dialog box, you eventually notice the Certificates section on the Content tab. First, let me just say there's really nothing you need to do, or should do, with those options unless you're specifically instructed to do so by a trusted Web site or certificate authority. Otherwise, it's all handled automatically without any intervention on your part.

But because I'm getting into some of the more obscure aspects of secure Web browsing here, it might be worth learning what certificates are about and how they provide secure Web browsing. After all, when it comes to Internet security, knowledge is your best defense.

Here's the basic problem. Virtually all Web traffic takes place in *plain text*, meaning that no effort is made to disguise or hide the content being transmitted between a Web server and a Web browser. There's no need to disguise it. Most information on the Web is there for public consumption. And there's no need to disguise information that anybody and everybody can access from their own computer.

It's a different story when you make an online purchase and need to send your credit card information to the online store. That kind of information is most definitely not for public consumption. To make sure that it doesn't fall into the wrong hands, credit card information (and some other types of personal information) is encrypted before it's put on the Internet.

Encryption means that the information is encoded in such a way that if someone did manage to intercept it, it would do that person no good because opening the intercepted file would display nothing but meaningless gobbledygook. It can't be deciphered without the appropriate "secret decoder ring." Or, in correct terminology, the interceptor doesn't have the appropriate *private key* to decode the message. Only the company to which you're sending the sensitive information has that private key.

A certificate is a means of making sure that the whole encryption process stays legitimate and safe. A site that wants to offer secure Web browsing to its customers applies to a company called a Certificate Authority (CA) for a certificate. The company has to prove its legitimacy as a business, have a stable place of business, and have people who will be held criminally responsible for any shenanigans.

When the company gets the certificate, it also gets a *public key* for encrypting files and a *private key* for decrypting files. (It's not a physical key; it's a computer file.) The company then sets up a secure Web server that has an https:// address. The *s* stands for *secure*.

When you browse to a secure Web site (one that starts with `https://`), some things happen behind the scenes to protect you. First, the server has to prove it's the actual Web site to your computer by sending its certificate. Your computer then checks the certificate holder's status with the CA to verify that the server is not an imposter and that the business hasn't had its certificate revoked for doing bad things with it.

Note

If a certificate holder uses the certificate to commit a crime (such as ripping off customers), the certificate is revoked. You see a warning message not to do business with the site. ∎

The certificate the server sends you also contains the site's public encryption key. So let's say you fill in your credit card information on a form on your screen. Then you click Submit to send it. Before that information leaves your computer, it's encrypted with the site's public key. It remains encrypted until it gets to the already-proven-safe Web server.

When it gets to that safe server, it can be decrypted with the company's private key to complete the transaction. Overall, the whole process is probably much safer than handing your credit card over to an unknown waiter, waitress, gas station attendant, or store clerk.

The trick is knowing when you're on a secure site. The easy way to tell is by looking at the address bar when you're on the page where you conduct the transaction. If its address starts with `https://`, it's okay. You might also see the message shown in Figure 16-26 when you first enter the page. (If you previously chose the option not to see that message anymore, you won't see that message.)

FIGURE 16-26

Message about entering a secure site.

Assuming that you haven't already turned off that message, you also see a message when you leave the secure connection, as in Figure 16-27. Also, the address of the page you go to will start with `http://` rather than `https://`.

Both of the preceding messages are just there to keep you informed of when it is, and isn't, safe to send sensitive data across the Internet. If you did turn off those messages and want to see them again in the future, follow these steps:

1. Click Tools and choose Internet Options or choose Tools ➪ Internet Options from Internet Explorer's menu bar.

2. In the Internet Options dialog box, click the Advanced tab.

3. Scroll to the bottom of the list.

4. Select the Warn If Changing Between Secure and Not Secure Mode and click OK.

FIGURE 16-27

Message about leaving a secure site.

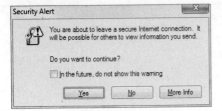

Using Internet Security Zones

Internet Security Zones offer a means of separating Web sites you do trust from those you don't. You have four different security zones to choose from:

- **Internet:** Every Internet Web site you visit automatically falls into the Internet security zone unless you move it to another zone.

- **Local Intranet:** In large networks that have their own non-Internet Web sites, every Web site within that network automatically falls into the Intranet zone.

- **Trusted Sites:** Initially, no sites fall into this category. But you can move any trusted site into this category so that you don't get a security warning every time you visit.

- **Untrusted Sites:** Initially, no sites fall into this category, either. But you can move any Web site that you use but don't fully trust into this zone to enforce maximum security.

To get to the Security Zones dialog box, choose Tools ➪ Internet Options from Internet Explorer's menu. Then click the Security tab. You see the options in Figure 16-28.

Each zone has its own security settings. Click one of the security zone icons near the top of the dialog box. The slider under Security Level for This Zone changes to show that zone's security level. For example, the security level for the Internet zone is Medium-High. This is the default setting and is appropriate for the vast majority of Web sites you're likely to visit. Characteristics of the security level include:

- **Internet Explorer Protected Mode Enabled:** In Protected Mode, Internet Explorer protects your computer from malware (malicious software) that could harm your computer. It also allows you to install safe downloaded software from a standard user account.

- **Prompts before Downloading Potentially Unsafe Content:** Displays a warning whenever you're about to download *potentially* unsafe software. If you trust the software you're about to download, it won't prevent you from doing so. But it will prevent bad Web sites from sneaking malware onto your computer without your knowledge.

- **Unsigned ActiveX Controls Will Not Be Downloaded:** An ActiveX control is like a tiny program that can make your computer do things. (Web pages and pictures can't make your computer do things.) A signed ActiveX control is one in which the author of the control can be identified and held accountable for any harm it causes.

There probably is no reason to change the Security level for the Internet zone. If you have an account at a trusted Web site that won't work properly with these settings, it's really not necessary to lower the security level for all sites just to accommodate that one site. Instead, you can put that site in your Trusted Sites zone and lower the security settings there. (More on the Trusted Sites zone in a moment.)

FIGURE 16-28

Security Zones in Internet Options.

Rather than settle for one of the security levels along the slider, you can click Custom Level and define your own security restrictions for the zone. However, many of the options provided require advanced professional knowledge that goes beyond the scope of this book.

The Trusted Sites zone is where you can put Web sites you trust that don't work properly in the Internet zone. To put a site in that zone, click the Trusted Sites icon and click Sites. Type the site's URL (if it isn't already in the box) and click Add. By default, you're limited to adding secure sites to that zone. A secure site is one whose address starts with `https://` rather than `http://`. But you can eliminate that restriction by deselecting the Require Server (https://) for All Sites in This Zone" check box. The security level for Trusted sites is Medium. You can reduce that to Medium-Low or Low.

How Does a Beginner Know Whom to Trust?

It's hard to know whom to trust when you're just getting started with computers. But a key issue is whether you can find and hold responsible the party that owns the site. Large businesses that have physical stores and shopping malls and such are generally trustworthy. After all, their online business wouldn't last too long if word got out that they were downloading bad software to their customers.

The same is true with software companies. Software giants such as Microsoft simply cannot afford to allow anything bad to leave their Web servers and harm customers' computers. So you can trust them.

Any site that has a large customer base can also be considered trustworthy. After all, if they were doing something dishonest, word would get out and they wouldn't have many customers.

Sites that publish unsavory content, make promises that seem too good to be true, and have no real presence off the Internet are the most dubious. If you know an Internet-savvy computer geek, you can ask them what they think.

Keep in mind that the Medium-High security level applied to all Web sites will make it tough for a malicious site to sneak anything past you. The security measures discussed in Part II make it all the more difficult for the bad guys to do any harm. So you're never really flying blind with no security at all.

Use the Restricted Sites zone for sites you visit regularly but don't really trust. The security level for Restricted sites is High, which will make it extremely difficult for the Web site to sneak anything past you.

Printing Web Pages

Printing a Web page is basically the same as printing any other document. If you haven't fully mastered the art of printing, you might want to read Chapter 36 to discover all the possibilities. Here I focus on tools and techniques that are unique to printing Web pages. Some things to consider before you print are listed here, as follows:

- Look around the page for a *printer-friendly* or *printable page* link. If you find such a link, click it for a version of the page that's likely to work better with your printer.

- If the Web site consists of multiple individually scrollable frames and you want to print only one frame, click some plain text or white space in the frame you want to print.

- If you want to print only a portion of the Web page, select the content you want to print.

- Consider using Print Preview, discussed next, to see how the printed document will look before you actually print. That way, you won't waste paper on disappointing results.

To print the page, click the drop-down arrow beside the Print button and choose Print (see Figure 16-29). Or choose File ➪ Print from the menu, or press Ctrl+P.

The Print dialog box, shown in Figure 16-30, opens. First, click the printer you want to use. If you want to create an XPS document rather than go straight to paper, choose Microsoft XPS.

Before you click the Print button, consider the following:

- If the page has multiple frames and you want to print only the one you previously clicked, click the Options tab, choose Only the Selected Frame, and click the General tab again.

- If you want to print only the content that you previously selected, choose Selection.

- If you want to print only a portion of a multipage document, choose any option other than All. For example, click Current Page to print only the page you're viewing. Or choose Pages and enter a page range.

- To conserve color ink, consider clicking Preferences ➪ Paper/Quality ➪ Black and White ➪ OK. (Not available on all printers.)

- To preview how things will look before you print, click Apply and then click Cancel. Then use Print Preview as described next to take a close look. Otherwise, click Print to start printing.

FIGURE 16-29

Print button and menu.

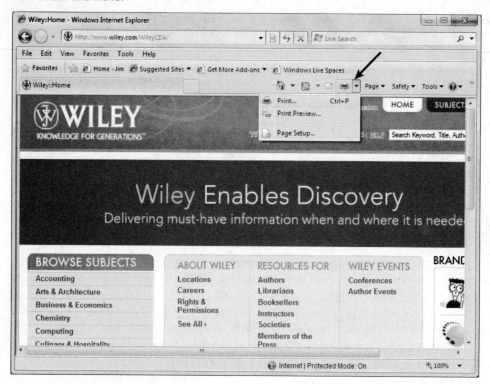

Using Print Preview

Print Preview is a great way to get a quick peek at how your printed pages will look. As when printing directly to paper, you start by clicking the frame you want to print (if the page has multiple frames). If you want to print a portion of the page, select the content that you want to print. Then click the Print button and choose Print Preview. Or press Alt+F+V or choose File ⇨ Print Preview from the menu. The page opens in Print Preview. Figure 16-31 shows an example of a page in Print Preview.

Across the top of the Print Preview window are several buttons and other controls. As always, you can point to any one of them to see its name. If the page has multiple frames and you want to print only the frame in which you clicked, press Alt+F or choose Only the Selected Frame from the Select Content drop-down menu. If you selected specific content to print first, choose As Selected On Screen to see only that content.

To get a close-up view of how the printed page will look, click the View Full Width button or press Alt+W. If it looks as though you're likely to have problems with text being cut off at the right margin, choose Shrink to Fit from the Choose Print Size drop-down list.

To adjust margins, first click the View Full Page button or press Alt+1. You see little lines and arrows around the corners of the page. Drag those in the directions indicated by the arrows to adjust the margins. Or click the Page Setup button and set the Left, Top, Right, and Bottom margins in inches. Then click OK.

FIGURE 16-30

Print dialog box.

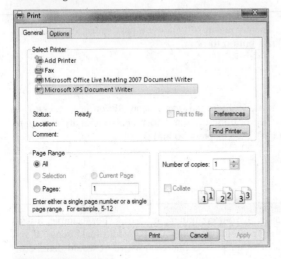

FIGURE 16-31

Sample page in Print Preview.

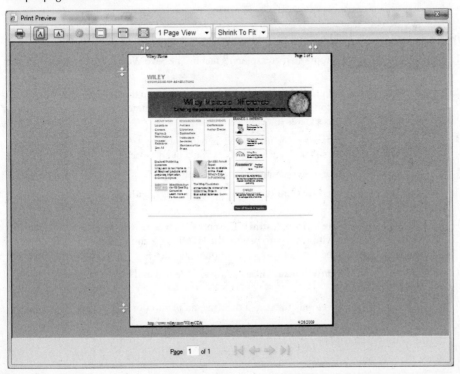

At the bottom left of the Print Preview window, use the arrows to scroll through pages. Depending on how many pages there are, use the Show Multiple Pages button to zoom out and see how multiple pages will look when printed.

When you're happy with the way things look in Print Preview, click the Print button near the upper-left corner. The Print dialog box opens. There you can still choose a page range, Paper/Quality, or other printing features before clicking the Print button to print.

Important printing tip

Don't expect the printer to start printing immediately. There's always a delay. If you keep clicking the Print button to hurry things along, you end up printing the same document repeatedly. For more information on printing (and stopping the printer), see Chapters 36 and 37.

Saving Web Pages

Occasionally, you might want to save a Web page on your computer's hard disk. For example, if it's a lengthy document that you want to be able to refer to offline, saving a copy would make sense. If you want to be able to work with the material in a program such as Microsoft Word, it would definitely make sense to save a copy of the page to your own computer first. Or perhaps you want to save a copy of an online receipt or airline boarding pass. To save a copy of the Web page you're currently viewing:

Tip

A good alternative for saving receipts and boarding passes is to print them to a PDF or XPS file. ■

1. Choose File ➪ Save As from Internet Explorer's menu. The Save Webpage dialog box opens, as shown in Figure 16-32.

2. Use the Favorite Links, Folders List, or address bar to navigate to the folder in which you want to save the page. If you don't have a preference, just choose Documents from the Favorite Links pane to put it in your Documents folder.

3. Optionally, change the page's name using the File name option. To improve searching later, consider naming the file so that it contains words you'd likely search for.

4. Optionally, choose a Save As type from one of these options:

   - **Web Archive, Single File (*.mht):** Stores the entire page, with pictures, in a single file with a single icon.

   - **Web Page, Complete (*.htm,*.html):** The entire Web page with all pictures is down-loaded. You end up with two icons, one for the HTML page and the other for a folder containing pictures and perhaps other miscellaneous code files.

   - **Web Page, HTML Only (*htm,*.html):** Saves all the text and HTML of the page, but no pictures.

   - **Text File (*.txt):** Saves only the text of the page, no pictures or HTML tags.

5. Optionally, change the Encoding option, but only if you have a good reason, such as when saving non-English pages.

6. Click the Save button.

FIGURE 16-32

Save Webpage dialog box.

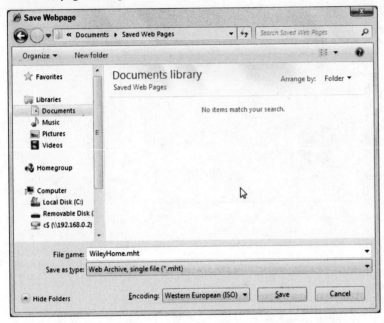

The page is saved to whatever folder you specified in Step 2. When you open that folder, you see one or two documents for the page. If you chose the Web Page, Complete option, you see two icons. One will be a document icon with whatever filename you entered in Step 3. The other icon will be a folder that has the same filename followed by _files. Figure 16-33 shows an example with the icons shown in Tiles view.

Note

For more information on folders, the Tiles view, and related topics, see Chapter 29. ■

To view the saved page offline, double-click the document icon (the one on the left). Or if you have multiple programs that are capable of opening HTML documents, right-click the document icon, choose Open With, and click the name of the program you want to use.

The _files folder contains pictures and other non-HTML page elements. Those extra items are required because the document file doesn't actually contain pictures or other elements. They only appear to be in the page when you open the page with your Web browser.

Note

To see what's *really* in the Web page, right-click the document icon and choose Open With ➪ Notepad. If you're not familiar with HTML, it will look like a bunch of nonsense. But you will notice that there no pictures when you view the document in Notepad. ■

FIGURE 16-33

Web page saved using the Webpage, Complete option.

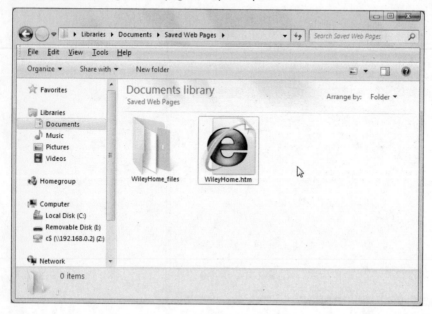

In a sense, the document file and folder are joined at the hip. If you delete one, you automatically delete the other. But the reverse isn't true. If you decide to fish them out of the Recycle Bin, you need to restore each one individually.

If you chose the Web Page, HTML Only option, you get a document icon similar to the one on the right in Figure 16-34. But you don't get the folder icon. When you open that document, you see all the formatted text, but no pictures.

If you chose the Web Archive, Single File option, the icon looks more like the top example in Figure 16-34. That one contains text and pictures. You can double-click it to open it in your Web browser. Or right-click it, choose Open With, and then choose the program you want to use.

If you saved the page as a text document, it will show a blank page icon rather than an Internet Explorer page icon. Because that's a plain text document, it contains only unformatted text, no pictures. When double-clicked, it will likely open in a simple text editor such as Notepad. Optionally, you could right-click its icon, choose Open With, and then choose a word processing program such as Microsoft Word. Then format the document using the features and capabilities of that word processing program.

Copying content from Web pages

As an alternative to saving a whole Web page as a file, you can copy and paste it (or any portion of it) to a word processing document. While you're viewing the Web page, press Ctrl+A to select everything in the document. Or hold down the left mouse button and drag the mouse pointer through the content you want to copy. Then press Ctrl+C to copy the selection to the Clipboard.

FIGURE 16-34

Web page saved as archive and text.

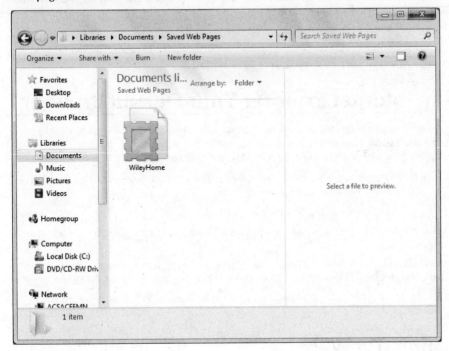

Next, open the document into which you want to paste the content. Then click where you want to put the copied content. Or open Microsoft Word or WordPad so that you start with a new, empty document. Then press Ctrl+V or right-click at about where you want to paste; next, choose Paste.

To copy just a single picture from a Web page, right-click the picture and choose Copy. Then open a graphics program and press Ctrl+V to paste. Or open a word processing document that can accept pictures and then click where you want to put the picture to position the cursor. Then press Ctrl+V or right-click that same spot and choose Paste.

Downloading pictures and videos

You can often (though not always) download multimedia items from Web pages as independent files on your own computer:

- To copy a picture you see on a Web page, right-click the picture and choose Save Picture As.
- To download a video or sound, you first need to get to the link that leads to that object. Right-click that link and choose Save Target As.

The Save As dialog box opens as usual, and you can choose a folder and specify a filename for the item you're copying. If you don't have a preference, put pictures in your Pictures folder and videos in your Videos folder.

Tip

If you're unable to copy a picture by right-clicking and choosing Copy, you can also take a picture of the entire screen with the picture visible. Then, paste the screenshot into a graphics program and crop out whatever you don't want. See "Taking screenshots" in Chapter 23. ■

Tip

Streaming audio and video generally can't be saved to your local system. ■

Making Internet Explorer Your Default Browser

Your default Web browser is the one that opens automatically when you double-click (or click) an HTML file. It's also the one that usually appears at the top of the Start menu. If Internet Explorer isn't your default Web browser but you'd like it to be, follow these steps:

1. Open Internet Explorer. Then click the Tools button and choose Internet Options, or choose Tools ➪ Internet Options from its menu.

2. In the Internet Options dialog box, click the Programs tab.

3. Click the Make Default button if it's enabled. If it's dimmed, Internet Explorer already is your default browser.

4. Optionally, to have Internet Explorer prompt you to be your default browser, in case it loses that status to another browser, select the Tell Me If Internet Explorer Is Not the Default Browser option.

5. Click OK.

Searching the Web

The World Wide Web contains billions of pages of information. You can find anything on the Web; you just need to know where to look and how to look for it. You can use the standard method of browsing to a search engine such as www.google.com, www.yahoo.com, or whatever. Or you can configure Internet Explorer to make it all a bit more automatic. First, click the arrow next to the Search box, as shown in Figure 16-35, to get your bearings. That's where you'll do most tasks related to searching.

Choosing search providers

If you already have a favorite search engine, you can use it as your default search provider. If you have several favorites, you can add them all and make any one the default provider. In case you're new to all this, I give you some advice on search providers to try. Here are the steps to follow to choose search providers:

1. Click the arrow on the Search box and choose Find More Providers. A Web page opens showing names of several search engines and searchable Web sites.

2. Click a provider name (such as Google) and click Add to Internet Explorer.

3. Repeat Step 2 for each provider you want to use. If you don't have any preferences, here are some examples:

   - AOL, Ask.com, Google, Lycos.com, MSN, and Yahoo! are all general-purposes sites that cover most of the World Wide Web.

FIGURE 16-35

Search box drop-down menu.

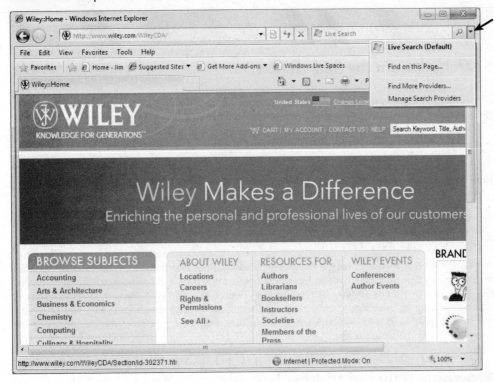

- About.com, www.cnet.com, and Microsoft.com are good resources for computer information.

- Wikipedia.org is a great online encyclopedia for information about virtually any topic, although accuracy isn't guaranteed because anyone can edit an entry.

- Amazon, BestBuy.com, eBay, Overstock.com, Shopzilla, Target, and Wal-Mart are all shopping-related sites.

- Monster is for job searching, ESPN for sports, USA Today for news.

When you've finished making selections, click the arrow on the Search box again. This time, all the search providers you've chosen appear.

Choosing a default provider

Searching all your providers would probably be a bit extreme. You could end up with links to more Web pages than you could explore in a lifetime. So you need to pick one to be the default provider. The default provider is just the one that's used unless you specify otherwise. To choose a default provider:

1. Click the down arrow button on the Search box again and click Manage Search Providers.

2. Click the provider you want to use as your default and click Set As Default.

3. Optionally, you can remove any provider by clicking its name and clicking Remove.

4. Click Close.

The text inside the Search box changes to reflect your default provider.

Searching from the Search box

Click the Search box and type the word or phrase you want to hunt for. This need not be in the form of a question. In fact, words such as how, do, I, what, is, why, the, a, an, and other words that appear in virtually all pages are largely ignored. You're not asking a person (or the Internet) a question here. You're asking it to show you pages that contain a particular word or phrase. The more specific you make that word or phrase, the better the results will be.

After you type the word or phrase, press Enter or click the magnifying glass. The search results from your default search provider appear in the main document area where all Web pages appear.

To try the same search on a different search provider, click the arrow next to the Search box and choose the search provider you want to try. It's simple. Try your search on a few search providers. Try several searches. You'll get the hang of it in no time.

Just remember that if you get far too many search results, your best bet is to try to be more specific in your search. For example, if you're looking for parts for a 1966 Ford Mustang convertible, don't search for *cars* or *Ford* or *Mustang* or *Mustang parts*. Search for *1966 Ford Mustang convertible parts*. If you're looking for Swarovski Crystal rhinestone wholesalers, don't search for one or two of those words. Search for *Swarovski Crystal rhinestone wholesalers*. Remember, the more specific the search, the fewer and better the search results.

Searching from the address bar

Normally you use the address bar to type the URL (address) of the page you want to visit. If you type regular text in the address bar, it's treated like text you enter in the Search box. A page from your default provider opens showing links to pages that contain the word or phrase you typed.

You can control a couple of options for searching from the address bar. Click Tools, choose Internet Options, and click the Advanced tab. Scroll through the list and find the options under Search from the address bar.

Searching the Current Page

Some Web pages are large. There may be times where you just want to search the page you're currently viewing for a word or phrase. To do that, click the arrow on the Search box and choose Find on This Page. A Find box opens. Type the word or phrase you're looking for and click Next. The first occurrence of that word is highlighted. From there, you can use the Next and Previous buttons to search down, and up, the page for your word. When you've found what you're looking for, close the Find box by clicking the X at the left edge of the Find box.

Getting More with Add-ons

Add-ons are programs used to extend the functionality of Internet Explorer. Some examples with which many readers will be familiar include Apple's QuickTime, Adobe Acrobat Reader, and Macromedia Flash Player. QuickTime and Adobe Reader are full stand-alone programs. But each also has an Internet Explorer add-on component that installed automatically with the application.

Shopping for add-ons

There are many add-ons for Internet Explorer, beyond the free and popular examples mentioned. They range in price from free to hundreds of dollars. They are entirely optional, so you're never required to download such add-ons.

You should wait until you've fully mastered all the capabilities of Internet Explorer before you consider using add-ons. Many older add-ons duplicate capabilities already available in Internet Explorer and Windows 7. (Parental controls and pop-up blockers are good examples.) You're much better off using what you already have, if possible, than using an old program designed for older systems.

FIGURE 16-36

Manage add-ons.

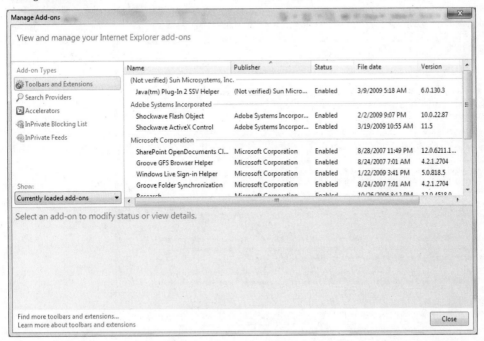

Note

See Chapter 4 for more information on using Windows 7 parental controls. ∎

You should use only add-ons that are specifically designed for Internet Explorer Version 8 and Windows 7. Using add-ons designed for older versions of Windows or Internet Explorer can cause Internet Explorer to freeze up or crash often.

All those caveats aside, to see what add-ons are currently available, click the Tools button and choose Manage Add-ons. Then click the Find More Toolbars and Extensions link. You're taken to the Internet Explorer Add-ons page (www.ieaddons.com), where you can shop around at your leisure.

Managing add-ons

To view add-ons already in Internet Explorer, choose Tools ➪ Manage Add-Ons. The Manage Add-Ons dialog box opens (see Figure 16-36). Use the Show drop-down button to view add-ons as follows:

- **All Add-Ons:** Shows all add-ons in your computer.

FIGURE 16-37

Internet Explorer Help and Support.

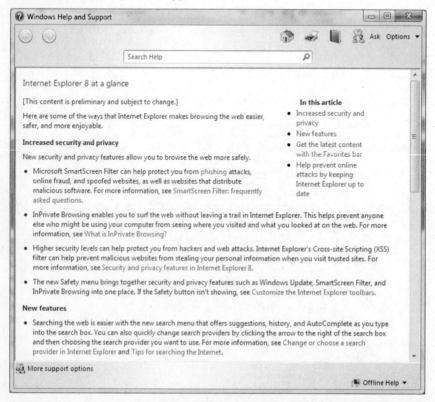

- **Currently Loaded Add-Ons:** Lists add-ons that were needed or used by the current Web page or recently visited pages.
- **Run without Permission:** Shows add-ons that were preapproved as safe by your ISP, computer manufacturer, or Microsoft.
- **Downloaded Controls:** Lists installed ActiveX controls.

If you think an add-on is causing problems, disable it. Just click its name and then click the Disable button. If that doesn't resolve the problem, or causes new problems with another site, reenable the add-on. As before, click its name and click Enable.

To disable an ActiveX control add-on, click its name and then click the Disable button. If you're confident that one is causing a problem, remove the larger application program through Add or Remove Programs in Control Panel.

Internet Explorer Help and Troubleshooting

As do most programs, Internet Explorer has its own built-in help. To get to it, click the Help button on the Command Bar. Or, click >> at the end of the bar and choose Help. Or choose Help from its menu bar.

If you're having difficulty getting online, try choosing Tools ⇨ Diagnose connection problems from Internet Explorer's menu. If that doesn't help, contact your ISP's tech support by phone. Be sure to tell them you're having difficulties connecting with Internet Explorer 8 in Windows 7.

Wrap-Up

In this chapter, you've learned about the World Wide Web and Internet Explorer. The Web is the most comprehensive and widely used resource ever. The program you use to access the Web is called a Web browser. Internet Explorer is the Web browser that comes with Windows 7. Here's a quick summary of the key points made in this chapter about Internet Explorer 8:

- Internet Explorer tabs let you browse with multiple pages open simultaneously.
- RSS feeds are Web content that's delivered to you automatically.
- Favorites let you organize links to favorite Web sites for easy one-click return visits.
- Internet Explorer's pop-up blocker helps to keep annoying pop-up ads to a minimum.
- Internet Explorer's SmartScreen Filter alerts you to potentially fraudulent Web sites designed to steal your password, and possibly your identity.
- The Search box lets you search any number of search engines and Web sites for any word or phrase.

Blogging with Writer

Y ou might have heard of the term *Web 2.0*, which loosely refers to the transition from relatively static HTML pages to more dynamic Web content that is geared toward collaboration and *social networking*. Social networking refers to ways in which people can connect and share information online.

Some of the social networking tools in the Web 2.0 world include wikis and blogs. This chapter explores blogging and the Windows Live Writer application, which you can use to create your own blog posts. But first, I offer a better explanation of blogging.

What Is Blogging?

The word *blog* comes from the term Web log. A blog is essentially a personal online journal. People use blogs for lots of purposes, but a typical one is to publish information about themselves, their interests, and the things they are working on or thinking about. Other people use their blogs to publish political or social opinions, or to write about a host of topics. Several blog sites are considered by many to be more reliable than the "mainstream" media, which illustrates the power that blogging and the Internet in general have amassed.

Figure 17-1 shows my blog space on live.com. You can view my blog posts there, comment on an entry, send messages, subscribe to the blog (so that you receive new items by RSS), and more. Keep in mind that this is how the live.com blogs look; other blog sites look different, naturally, because they are hosted at different Web sites.

There are several places on the Internet where you can set up your own blog. In this chapter, I focus on live.com, but keep in mind that you can use Writer to blog at many different blog sites. In fact, you can set up multiple blog accounts in Writer and use it to create and publish blog posts to all of them.

IN THIS CHAPTER

Understanding blogs and blogging

Setting up your own blog space

Using Windows Live Writer to create blog posts

Adding video and photos to a blog

Using plug-ins with Writer

FIGURE 17-1

A blog site at live.com.

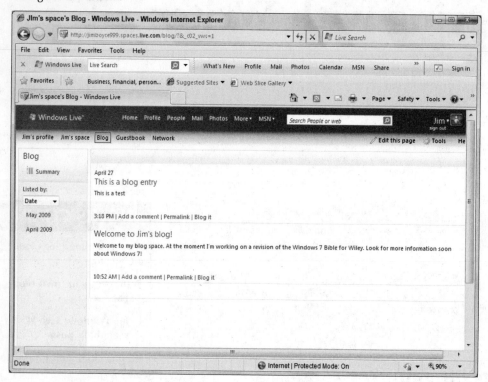

Adding Windows Live Writer to Windows

If you don't already have Windows Writer installed on your computer, you need to add it. First, however, click Start ➪ All Programs ➪ Windows Live and make sure you don't see Windows Live Writer in the menu. If you do see it, Writer is already installed and you can skip to the next section to start learning how to use it.

To add Writer, open Internet Explorer and browse to home.live.com. Log in with your Windows Live account. (If you don't already have one, you can easily sign up for one right from the login page.) Then, in the Windows Live Web site, click More ➪ Downloads. In the Blogging section, click Writer to open the download page (Figure 17-2).

Click the Download button, and when the File Download dialog box appears, click Run. If User Account Control displays a security warning, click Yes to allow the Windows Live Setup program to run. In the Windows Live installer (Figure 17-3), click the button beside Writer. You can also choose to download other Windows Live add-ons at this time, or run the installer again later to add other add-ons. If the installer shows that Writer is already installed, as shown in Figure 17-3, you don't need to install it again. You can certainly add any other Windows Live programs that are not yet installed, however.

FIGURE 17-2

Download Windows Live Writer.

FIGURE 17-3

The Windows Live installer.

Setting Up Your Blog Account

After you have installed Writer or ascertained that you already have it, you need to configure at least one blog account. The following section explains how.

Adding a blog account

Writer automatically should run a configuration wizard the first time you start the program. If you need to start the wizard yourself, choose Blogs ➪ Add Blog Account to start the Windows Live Writer Wizard, shown in Figure 17-4.

If you already have a blog, in the first page of the wizard choose the type of service where it is hosted:

- **Windows Live Spaces:** Choose this option if your blog is already set up on Windows Live.
- **SharePoint blog:** Choose this option if your blog is set up on a Microsoft Office SharePoint Server (MOSS) site.
- **Other blog service:** Choose this option if your blog is hosted by a different site.

If you don't have a blog already, you can use the wizard to set up one at Windows Live. That's the option I focus on in this section. If you already have a blog site, all you need to do is enter the blog site URL in the wizard and provide login credentials when prompted.

FIGURE 17-4

The Windows Live Writer Wizard.

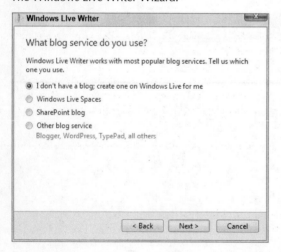

To create a Windows Live blog site through the wizard, choose the option I Don't Have a Blog; Create One on Windows Live for Me. Then click Next. The wizard then prompts you for your Windows

Live ID (Figure 17-5). Enter your Windows Live ID and password in the textboxes provided for that purpose in the wizard and click Next.

Enter your Windows Live ID.

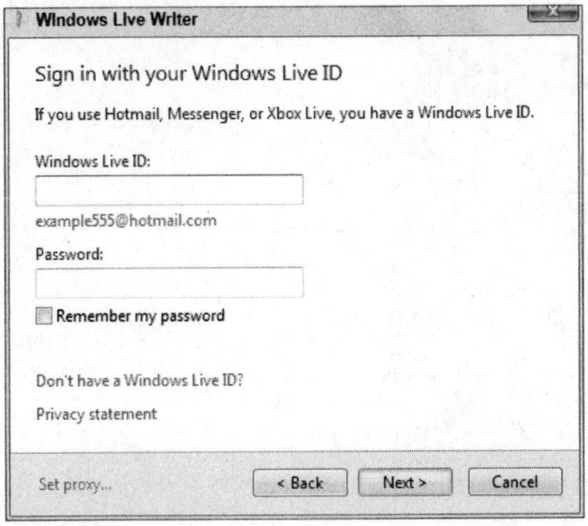

Tip

If you don't already have a Windows Live ID, click the Don't Have a Windows Live ID link, which opens the Windows Live Web site. Then follow the prompts to create one. ■

After you click Next, the wizard creates a blog for you on Windows Live, copies some files to your computer, and then prompts you for a nickname for the blog. This is the account name in Writer for your blog, as well as the name that gets added to your blog site. In Figure 17-1, for example, "Jim's blog" is the nickname in Writer and the blog name at the blog site.

You can create multiple blog accounts in Writer. Just run the wizard once for each blog account that you have.

Setting your URL

When you first create a blog site at live.com, the URL for the site will be mostly gibberish. For example, when I set up my site, the URL was `http://cid-3ad7f7dae4757a35.spaces.live.com`. More than likely, you'll want to change your URL to something more memorable. As Figure 17-6 illustrates, one of the tasks you can perform for your blog site is to choose a Web address for your site, essentially renaming the site. To do so, open Windows Live Writer and click the Edit Your Space link. In the resulting Web page, click the Choose Web Address link to open the page shown in Figure 17-7.

FIGURE 17-6

Options for editing your site.

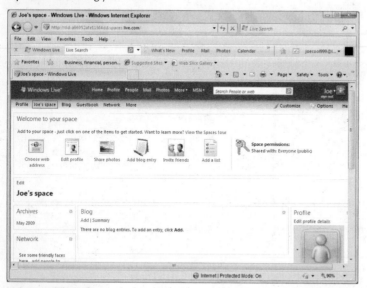

FIGURE 17-7

Choose a Web address.

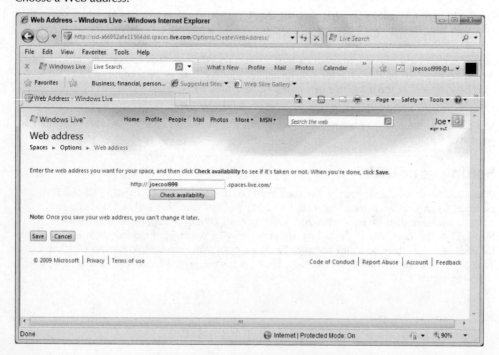

In the URL textbox, type the Web address you would like to use for your site. For example, you might use your name, the first part of your e-mail address, or other address that is easy for your blog visitors to remember. Then, click Check Availability to see whether that address is available. If so, click Save to apply the change to your blog URL.

Caution

You can't change your URL again after you save it, so make sure it is truly what you want before you click Save. ∎

Editing your profile

Part of your online presence includes your profile, which includes details such as your contact information, where you went to school, your occupation, marital status, and other information. You can leave all this blank if you want, share some items but not others, or share everything (probably not the best idea).

To edit your profile from Writer, click the Edit Your Space link, and in the resulting Web page, log in to Windows Live. Then, click Edit Profile to open the page shown in Figure 17-8. The page contains several categories of information. Click the Edit link in a category to open a form and enter the information.

FIGURE 17-8

Edit your profile.

The profile categories each include a link that lets you specify who can view the information you enter for that particular category. Just click Edit under a category to edit that item, then on the resulting page, click the link beside Shared With. As you can see in Figure 17-9, you can share the information with everyone or any combination of your network (people in your Messenger contacts), coworkers, family, friends, or specific individuals.

FIGURE 17-9

Specify who can see your profile categories.

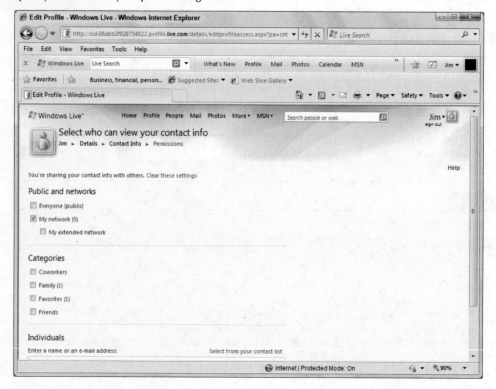

I don't go into detail about editing your profile because the tasks are self-explanatory. I just offer the advice that you consider what information you want to be visible to only your friends and family versus what you want to be publicly available. Set permissions on each category accordingly. If you are allowing your children to create an Internet presence, you should definitely take the time to review what their spaces contain and what is visible to the public.

Creating and Publishing Blog Posts

Writer makes creating and posting blog posts easy because it works similarly to word processors such as Microsoft Office Word and WordPad. For that reason, I don't cover every little feature in Writer. With a half an hour or so of experimentation, you should be a pro at using Writer's features. Instead, I focus on some basics to get you started, followed by some of the less intuitive tasks.

Creating a blog post

Start by opening the Windows Live Writer program. After you open the program, click in the Enter a Post Title text box (Figure 17-10) and type the name for your new post.

Next, click below the title and start typing your blog post. The controls in the program's toolbar let you format paragraphs and text as well as insert a variety of objects, including hyperlinks, pictures, photo albums, tables, maps, tags, and video. You can also use the tools in the right pane to insert items into the blog post.

FIGURE 17-10

Title for a new post.

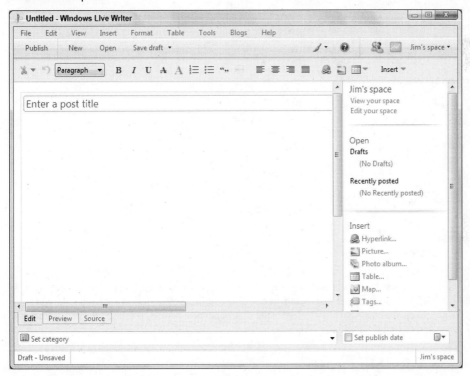

Saving a draft

Your blog post isn't visible to others until you publish it. Before you do that, however, you need to save it as a draft. You can either save your blog post locally on your computer or on your blog site. In either case, to save your blog post as a draft, click the Save Draft button on the Writer toolbar. Doing so saves the draft to your local computer. To post a draft to your blog site, click the down arrow beside the Save Draft button and choose Post Draft to Blog. If you are not logged in to the blog site, Writer will prompt you to enter your credentials before publishing the draft to the site.

Tip

Saving your blog posts locally enables you to work on them when your computer is offline. ■

Opening an existing blog post

Just as you can with most other types of documents, you can open an existing blog post, whether draft or published, to edit it. To open a blog post, in Writer choose File ➪ Open to display the Open dialog box (Figure 17-11). Here you can choose the location where the blog is stored, whether in the Drafts folder or on your blog site(s). Writer also keeps track of recently posted blogs, so you can quickly locate blog posts you've worked on lately.

FIGURE 17-11

Open an existing blog post.

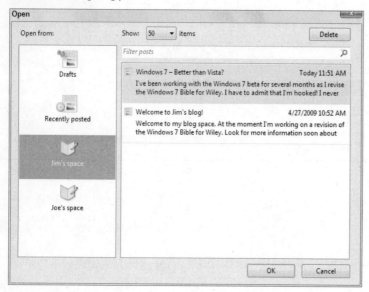

If you have many entries in the selected location, use the Show drop-down button to choose whether to show all of them or a limited number. You can also use the Delete button to delete any you no longer want. Keep in mind that if you delete one that is already posted, it will be deleted from your local computer as well as from your blog site.

Preview your blog post

As you are working on a new blog post, you'll probably want to see what it will look like when you publish it. This is particularly true if you have graphics, hyperlinks, or even custom HTML code in it. Writer does a great job of showing you what the blog will look like right in the Edit window, but you might want to see it in the context of your site.

To see how it looks on your site, save the blog post as a draft to your blog site. Then click the Preview button near the bottom left of the Writer window (Figure 17-12).

Viewing and editing source code

As does most other Web content, a blog post consists of HTML code. HTML is an acronym for Hyper-Text Markup Language, the most common language generally used to create Web content.

FIGURE 17-12

The Preview window.

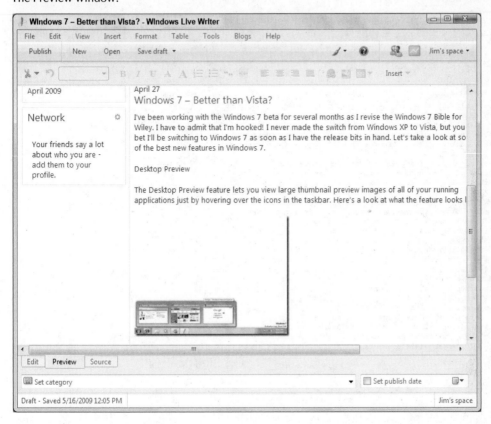

The beauty of an editor such as Writer is that it gives you a WYSIWYG view of your document. That's an acronym for What You See Is What You Get — what you see in the program as you are editing the document is pretty close (or exactly) what you'll see in the finished document. In the case of Writer, the Edit window displays a pretty good idea of what the blog post will look like when published.

But what you see in the Edit window, the Preview window, and when the blog post is published is a *rendering* of the content. The actual content is all text, as shown in Figure 17-13, which shows Writer's Source window.

If the Edit window does such a good job of showing you what the blog post will look like, why do you need the Source window? Although Writer gives you lots of capability to add content, it doesn't cover every possible thing you can do with content on a Web site. So, you can use the Source window to view and edit the source code. For example, you might want to fine-tune some text formatting, or perhaps you are an HTML expert and just prefer working right in the code. Whatever the case, the Source window lets you edit the source code to your heart's content.

FIGURE 17-13

The Source window.

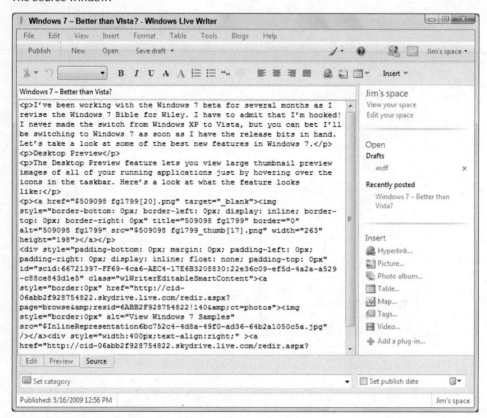

Publishing your blog post

When you are ready to make the blog post visible to others, you need to publish it. Publishing is a simple process — just click the Publish button in Writer's toolbar, and Writer publishes the blog to your blog site.

Tip

Writer doesn't give you the capability to cancel the publish process after it's started. This usually isn't a problem unless you are publishing a blog with lots of photos or a photo album. Uploading many photos can take a lot of time, so if you need to stop in the middle of uploading, all you can do is terminate the Writer program itself. ■

In addition to publishing a blog post explicitly, you can also set the publication date and let it essentially auto publish. For example, perhaps you want to post a blog post but not make it visible for a week. You set the publish date and post the entry, and it becomes visible on the specified date. To set the publish date, click the small calendar icon in the bottom-right corner of the Writer window. In the resulting pop-up calendar, click the date on which you want the item to be visible.

Note

Not all blog sites support saving entries for future publishing. If that is the case with your service, Writer notifies you of that fact when you publish the item and gives you the option to cancel or publish the item immediately. ■

Working with Photos

Sooner or later, you'll probably want to add some photos to your blog. With Writer, you can easily add individual photos or add a photo album with multiple photos.

Adding a photo

To add a single photo, open the blog post in Writer, position the cursor where you want the photo to be inserted, and click Picture in the Insert group on the Taskpane. Writer opens an Insert Picture dialog box. Browse to and select the file; then click Open to insert it at the selected location.

Tip

If the Taskpane isn't visible, choose View ⇨ Taskpane in Writer's menu bar. ■

After the photo is added, you have several options to control the way it looks. Click the photo in the Edit window and note the options that appear in the Taskpane (Figure 17-14). The Picture tab lets you specify the following properties:

- **Text wrapping:** Specify how text wraps around the image.
- **Margins:** Add margins around the photo to control the space between the photo and the surrounding text (or other photos).
- **Borders:** Use the Borders drop-down list to choose the type of border, if any, to add around the photo.
- **Link To:** Use this drop-down list to add a hyperlink to the image. The default is Source Picture, which causes the image to be opened in the user's browser when he or she clicks the photo. If you want to have a Web page open instead, choose the URL option. Writer opens an Edit Hyperlink dialog box that you use to specify the URL, text, title, tags, and other properties.
- **Options:** Click this button to change the options for the selected Link To property. For example, if you are linking to a URL, clicking Options opens the Edit Hyperlink dialog box. If you are linking to the source picture, clicking Options opens the Source Picture Options dialog box (Figure 17-15), which you use to set the image size and how it appears in the browser.

The Advanced tab of the Picture Taskpane lets you control the size of the image as well as perform a handful of actions on the image:

- **Rotate:** Click to rotate the image clockwise 90 degrees with each click.
- **Contrast:** Open a simple Contrast dialog box to set the Brightness and Contrast properties for the image.
- **Crop:** Open a Crop window (Figure 17-16) that you can use to crop the image. Choose a size from the Proportion drop-down list or choose Custom and then click and drag the cropping frame to size it. Click OK to apply the crop.

FIGURE 17-14

Photo options in the Taskpane.

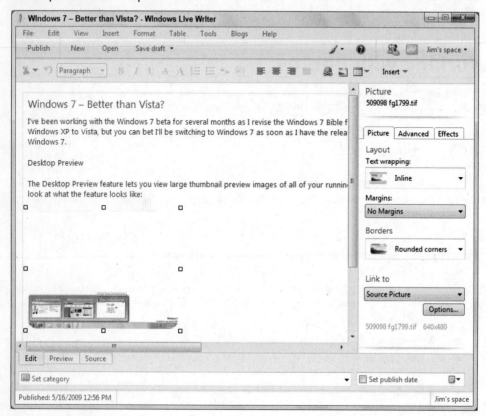

FIGURE 17-15

Source Picture Options dialog box.

FIGURE 17-16

Crop a photo.

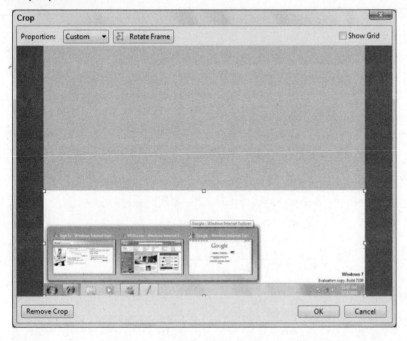

Tip

Click Remove Crop to restore the photo to its original content. Use the Rotate Frame button to rotate the cropping frame 90 degrees. Use the Show Grid option to show a grid on the frame. ∎

- **Tilt:** Click to open the Tilt dialog box, where you specify the angle of tilt for the photo.

- **Watermark:** Click to open the Watermark dialog box shown in Figure 17-17, which you can use to add a watermark to the photo. You specify the watermark text, the font to use, and the position of the watermark on the photo.

- **Alternate Text:** Use this text box to specify the text that the browser will display if it can't show the photo.

The Effects tab of the Picture Taskpane lets you apply a handful of special effects to the selected photo, including making it a black-and-white image, applying a sepia tone, adjusting color, and other effects.

Adding a photo album

Writer makes it easy to add a group of photos to your blog site as a photo album. The photo album shows as thumbnails (small images) on the page. Clicking the album opens a page where you can view thumbnails for all the photos and open individual photos (Figure 17-18).

FIGURE 17-17

A watermark on a photo.

FIGURE 17-18

A photo album.

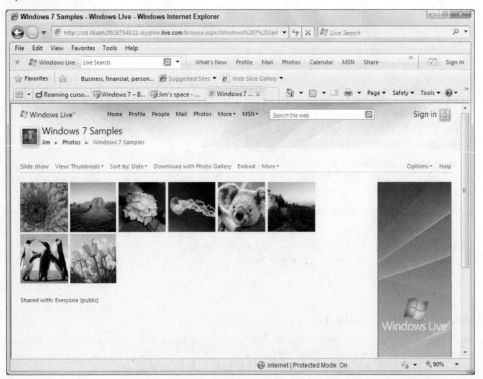

FIGURE 17-19

The Insert Photo Album dialog box.

To add a photo album, click in the blog where you want the album to be inserted and then click Photo Album in the Taskpane. Writer opens the Insert Photo Album dialog box (Figure 17-19), where you specify a name for the album and add the desired photos to the album. You can simply drag photos from your Pictures folder or any other location into the dialog box to add them.

Tip

Click the From Existing Album tab to add photos from an existing photo album you have already published to your blog site. ■

After you insert the album and photos, you can modify the album's properties. When you click the photo album in Writer, the Taskpane options change to offer properties for the album (Figure 17-20).

The Album Style drop-down options let you choose how the album appears within the blog post, arranging the thumbnails in different ways. You can also click the Change Cover Pictures link to change the order of the photos. Use the Text Wrapping drop-down list to specify how the photo album wraps within the text on the blog, and the Margins drop-down list to specify margins between the album and the surrounding text.

Uploading Pictures with FTP

Many blog sites give you the capability to upload your photos through a Web browser or directly from Writer. Others use File Transfer Protocol (FTP) for photo upload. If your blog account requires

FTP, you can configure Writer to use FTP to upload your photos. To do so, choose Blogs ➪ Edit Blog Settings to open the Edit Blog Settings dialog box. Click Pictures in the left pane and then click the Upload Pictures to an FTP Server option. Click Configure FTP to open the FTP Server Configuration dialog box, where you enter the FTP hostname, account information, target folder, and URL of the FTP publishing folder. Then click OK to close the dialog box.

FIGURE 17-20

Photo album options in the Taskpane.

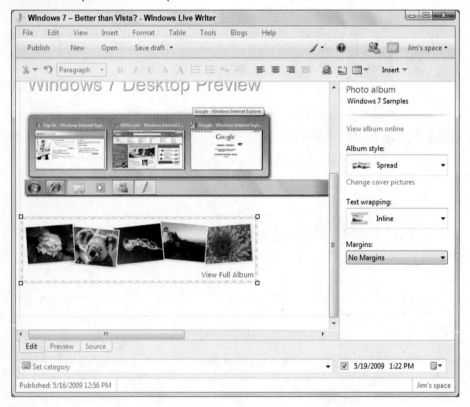

Working with Videos

Writer makes it easy to add videos to your blog. You can add videos from a Web URL, from a file, or from a video service such as Soapbox or YouTube. To add a video, click in the blog post where you want the video to be inserted; then click Video in the Taskpane to open the Insert Video dialog box (Figure 17-21).

The From Web tab lets you specify the video's URL or embed code from a video already hosted on another Web site. Enter the URL to the video or the embed code in the textbox. Then, click Preview to preview the video in the Insert Video dialog box.

FIGURE 17-21

Insert Video dialog box.

Note

Note that not all Web sites will offer to embed code for videos. ∎

The From File tab, shown previously in Figure 17-21, lets you accomplish two tasks at one time: add the video to your blog and upload the video to either Soapbox or YouTube. In the Video File textbox, specify the location of the video file on your computer. Then, add a title and description in the Title and Description fields, add tags in the Tags field, and choose a category from the Categories drop-down list. You can also choose permissions for the video from the Permissions drop-down list. Finally, click the Terms of Use check box for the selected service and then click Insert.

The From Video Service tab in the Taskpane lets you insert an existing video from your Soapbox or YouTube account. In the left pane of the dialog box, click either Soapbox or YouTube. If you are not yet signed in to the service, you'll see username and password fields in the dialog box. Log in to select the video you want to insert.

Using Tables

Tables are particularly useful when you want to align or arrange objects in your blog post. After you insert a table, you can insert text or other items (such as photos and links) in the table's fields. To add a table, click in the blog post where you want the table to be inserted. Then, in the

Taskpane, click the Table link under the Insert group. Writer displays the Insert Table dialog box, shown in Figure 17-22. Specify the number of rows and columns for the table, the width of the table in pixels, border width, cell padding, and cell spacing. Then click Insert.

FIGURE 17-22

Insert Table dialog box.

FIGURE 17-23

Change table properties.

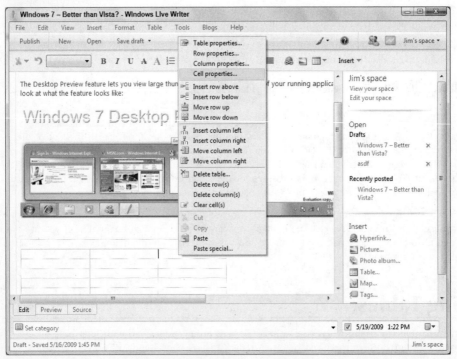

Tip

The cell padding is the margin inside each cell. The cell spacing is the distance between cells, in pixels. ■

After you insert the table into the blog post, you can add or remove columns or rows, change column width, and set other properties. To change column width, simply click and drag a column's border. To change other properties, right-click the table to view the menu shown in Figure 17-23. Then choose the appropriate option from the menu. I don't cover each table, column, row, or cell property because they are generally self-explanatory.

To insert something in a cell within a table, just click inside the cell and then type text or use the links in the Insert group on the Taskpane.

Using Tags

In the context of blogs, tags are categories or keywords that you can add to your blog post. Tags make it easier for people to find your blog posts. For example, if I'm writing a blog post on Windows 7, I add a tag of Windows 7 to the blog post. People searching for blog posts about Windows 7 can then more easily find my blog.

Tags comprise a relatively complex subject that would take a chapter of its own to describe in detail, particularly when considering the number of tag providers on the Internet. Instead, I assume that you've done your homework and understand how tags work, and just need to know how to add them in Writer. That's the easy part!

To add a tag, click in the blog post where you want the tag inserted. Then click the Tags link in the Insert group on the Taskpane. In the resulting Insert Tags dialog box (Figure 17-24), select a tag provider from the drop-down list and then type the tags, separating them by commas. When you're done, click Insert.

FIGURE 17-24

The Insert Tags dialog box.

If the tag provider you need to use isn't listed by default in Writer, click the Tag Provider drop-down list in the Insert Tags dialog box and choose Customize Providers to open the Tag Options dialog box. Click the Add button to display the Create New Tag Provider dialog box (Figure 17-25), enter the configuration information in the provided fields, and click OK. If you're not sure what to enter in the textboxes, check the Support area on the tag provider's Web site for help.

FIGURE 17-25

The Create New Tag Provider dialog box.

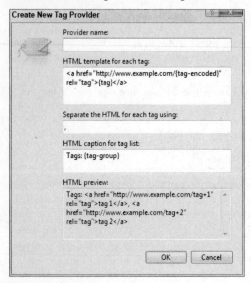

FIGURE 17-26

The Insert Map dialog box.

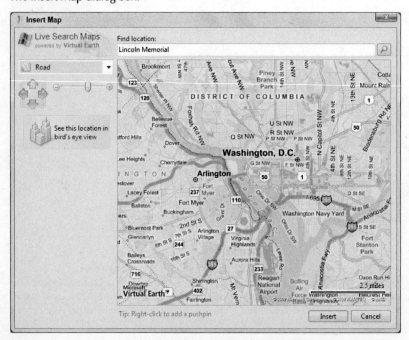

Inserting Maps

You can insert a map in your blog post from Microsoft's Live Search Maps. For example, maybe you're blogging about an event that you are hosting or attending and want everyone who reads your blog to be able to find that event.

To insert a map, click in the blog post where you want the map inserted and then click the Map link in the Insert group on the Taskpane. In the resulting Insert Map dialog box (Figure 17-26), in the Find Location text box, type the place or address you want to find and then click the Search button. Figure 17-26 shows the results of a search for the Lincoln Memorial.

You can choose from three different display types using the drop-down list in the left pane of the Insert Map dialog box. The Road view shows a road map like the one in Figure 17-26. Aerial view shows a straight-down satellite image of the specified location. The bird's eye view shows the location in perspective from above (also a satellite view). Figure 17-27 shows the Lincoln Memorial in bird's eye view. Use the large and small icons in the left pane to zoom the image in or out. Use the direction buttons to pick from which direction you want to view the location.

Tip

Use the slider for Road and Aerial views to zoom in or out. Use the Show Labels option with Aerial view to add street names and other place labels to the image. ■

FIGURE 17-27

Bird's eye view of the Lincoln Memorial.

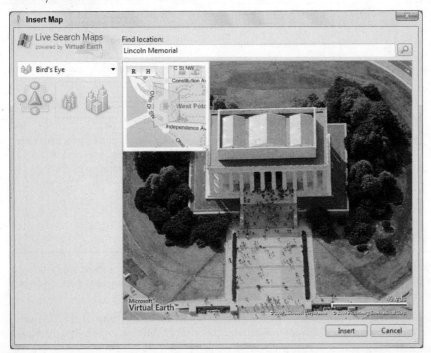

FIGURE 17-28

A map added to a blog post.

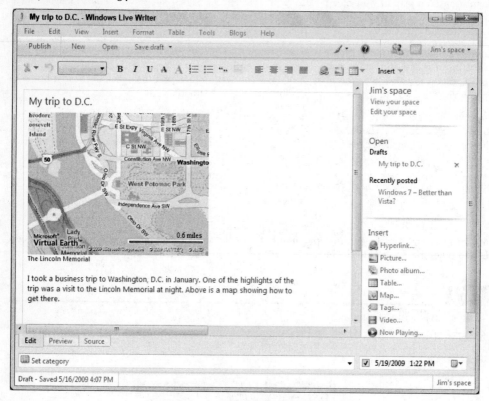

When you're satisfied with the results, click the Insert button to add the map to your blog post. Figure 17-28 shows the results in Writer.

As with other types of items you insert in a blog post, you can modify the properties of a map after inserting it. Just click the map to show its properties in the Taskpane. There you can click a link to change the map view, specify a caption to go beneath the map, and set text wrapping and margins for the map.

Using Plug-Ins

Writer gives you several tools for adding items to your blog posts, and although those are certainly useful, you might want to add plenty more to your blog. Fortunately, Writer supports plug-ins, which enable developers to add functionality to Writer.

To add a plug-in, open Writer and click the Add a Plug-In link in the Insert group on the Taskpane. Writer opens a Web browser and displays the Windows Live Gallery Web site, which lists the available plug-ins. Locate the plug-in you want and click Download. After the plug-in is downloaded to your computer, run the downloaded installer file to add the plug-in. Then close and restart Writer to use the new plug-in.

To modify plug-in settings, in Writer choose Tools ⇨ Options to open the Options dialog box; then click Plug-Ins in the left pane. You'll see a list of all installed plug-ins and can configure options for them, enable or disable a plug-in, and even add a new plug-in (Figure 17-29)

FIGURE 17-29

Manage plug-ins in the Options dialog box.

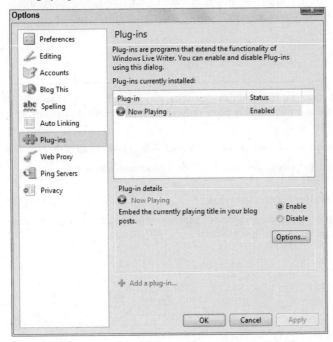

Setting Writer Options

Writer provides several pages of options you can use to change the way the program looks and works. To access these options, choose Tools ⇨ Options to open the Options dialog box (shown previously in Figure 17-29). This dialog box offers several pages, as follows:

- **Preferences:** Use the page to view general options that control how the Writer window looks and how posts are published.

- **Editing:** Set options for entering text, viewing word count, and determining how often Writer automatically saves drafts (if at all).

- **Accounts:** View, add, and configure blog accounts.

- **Blog This:** Specify settings that Writer will use when it is launched by other applications.

397

- **Spelling:** Set options for checking spelling in your blog posts.
- **Auto Linking:** Configure settings for automatic linking, which enables Writer to automatically create links for terms in your blog post.
- **Plug-Ins:** View, manage, and add plug-ins.
- **Web Proxy:** Specify the custom proxy server settings you want to use for Writer if your network requires that you use a proxy server. A proxy server acts as a gateway to the Internet for outgoing Web requests.
- **Ping Servers:** Specify the servers that you want to notify each time you publish new blog posts.
- **Privacy:** Choose whether to allow Microsoft to automatically collect information about your computer and how you use Microsoft's software.

Wrap-Up

Windows Live Writer is an add-on program that you can download and install from the Microsoft Live Web site. Writer lets you create and publish blog posts on your blog sites. Some key points to remember about Writer are the following:

- You can create multiple blog accounts and use Writer to publish blog posts to all of them.
- You can add hyperlinks, photos, photo albums, tables, maps, and much more to your blog posts.
- You can use plug-ins to add other features to Writer.
- See "Windows Live Essentials," from Wiley, for more information on the add-on programs that are part of the Windows Live family, including Writer.

Using Windows Live Mail

It seems that just about everyone knows what e-mail is. (The *e* stands for *electronic*.) With e-mail, you type a letter or message on your computer and send it to the recipient's e-mail address, and it ends up in the recipient's e-mail Inbox, sometimes as quickly as a few seconds later. You can attach things such as pictures and other files to the message so that the recipient gets those, too.

To use e-mail, you need an Internet connection, an e-mail address, and an e-mail client (or a Web browser for web-based e-mail). All e-mail addresses follow the format *someone@somewhere.tld*, where *someone* is your user name and *somewhere.tld* is your mail provider's domain name. The e-mail client is the program you use to send and receive e-mail. This chapter is about Windows Live Mail, the optional e-mail client that is available as a download from Microsoft's Windows Live Web site.

How E-Mail Works

When you send an e-mail message to someone, it goes from your computer to an outgoing mail server (a computer) on your office network, at your ISP, or another mail provider (such as Hotmail). That server looks up where the message needs to go based on the delivery addresses and then sends the message to an incoming mail server at the other end. That incoming mail server delivers the message to the recipient's inbox.

Figure 18-1 shows the basic idea.

New Feature

Windows Live Mail, a downloadable add-on program, replaces the Windows Mail program included with Windows Vista. Windows 7 does not include its own e-mail client.

FIGURE 18-1

E-mail delivery across the Internet.

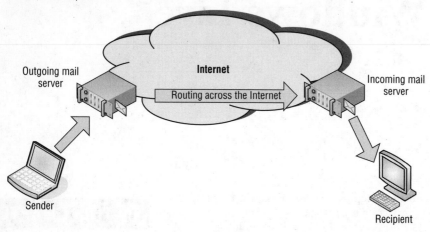

Introducing Windows Live Mail

Although Windows 7 doesn't come with an e-mail client, you can download and use the Windows Live Mail program for the Windows Live Web site. If Windows Live Mail is your default e-mail client (the main program you use for sending and receiving e-mail), you can start Windows Live Mail by clicking the Start button and choosing Windows Live Mail. Figure 18-2 shows its icon (at the mouse pointer).

The first time you open Windows Live Mail, you might be taken to a wizard for setting up your e-mail account. If you have all the factual information you need about your account, you can proceed through the wizard to set up the account. Otherwise, you can click the Cancel button, open Windows Live Mail, and set up your account later. Figure 18-3 shows how the Windows Live Mail program looks, and points out some of its main components. Don't be alarmed if you're missing some components. Many are optional and easily turned on and off with a mouse click or two.

If Windows Live Mail isn't an option on your Start menu, you can still open it. Click the Start button and then click All Programs ➪ Windows Live ➪ Windows Live Mail. Whether you can *use* Windows Live Mail is an altogether different matter, which I tackle in a moment. The title bar and toolbar appear near the top of the program window and work the same as in other programs. The other components are as follows:

- **Folder pane:** Shows folders into which you can organize e-mail messages, as well as selected search folders that are virtual folders used to display specific types of messages, such as all unread e-mail.

- **Folder Shortcuts:** These icons give you quick access to your primary folders, including Mail, Calendar, Contacts, Feeds, and Newsgroups.

- **Message list:** Every e-mail message displays a header showing who sent the message, the Subject of the message, and the date you received it.

FIGURE 18-2

Windows Live Mail icon on the Start menu.

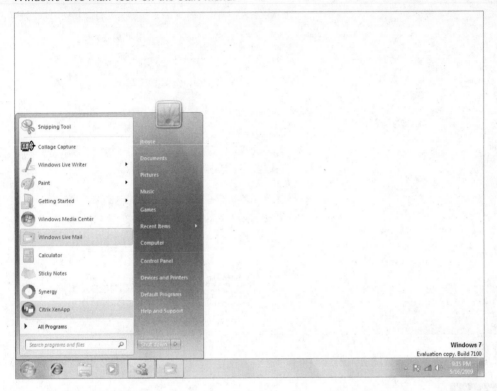

- **Preview pane header:** Shows the message header information in a large and more detailed format.

- **Preview pane:** Shows a portion of the e-mail message whose message header is selected in the message list.

- **Status bar:** Tells you the status of various program facts and operations.

As with most programs, you can customize the appearance of Windows Live Mail to your liking. Choose View ➪ Layout from its menu bar to display the dialog box shown in Figure 18-4. Or, click the Menus button on the toolbar and choose Layout. Items that have checkmarks are currently "on" and visible in the program window. Items without checkmarks are "off."

The Layout dialog box contains four groups of settings:

- **Reading pane (Mail):** Turn on or off the reading pane and, if on, specify whether it is at the bottom or to the right of the message list.

- **Message list:** Specify whether the message list shows one line or two lines, or decides on this number based on the width of the message list.

FIGURE 18-3

Windows Live Mail program window.

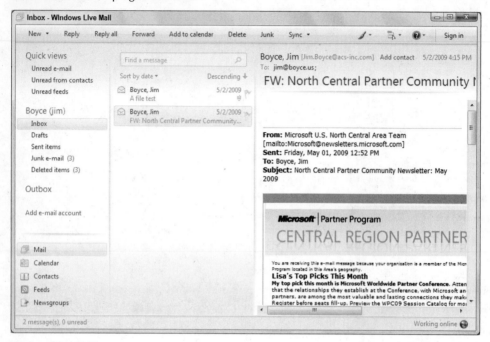

FIGURE 18-4

Layout dialog box.

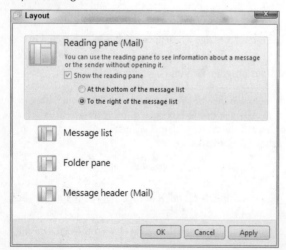

- **Folder pane:** Specify how the various folders appear in the folder pane. Options include:

  - **Use Compact View For Folder Pane:** Uses small icons instead of words to represent the folders and other items in the folder pane.

  - **Use Compact Shortcuts:** Displays only small icons for the folder shortcuts, rather than icon and name.

  - **Show Storage Folders:** Shows Drafts, Sent Items, and Deleted Items folders in the folder pane.

  - **Show Quick views:** Displays the quick view search folders Unread E-Mail, Unread from Contacts, and Unread Feeds.

- **Message header (Mail):** Shows in the reading pane the message header of the selected message.

To change an option, select check boxes as appropriate and then click Apply. If you don't like the results, click that same check box again and click Apply again. When you're happy with how things look, click OK to save your current settings and close the dialog box.

Before you can use Windows Live Mail to send and receive e-mail, you have to configure it to work with your e-mail account. Your company, ISP (Internet service provider), or e-mail provider (such as Hotmail) supplies your e-mail account. Windows Live Mail is just the e-mail client (program) that lets you send and receive messages through that e-mail account.

What you need to know to get started

Before you attempt to use Windows Live Mail as your e-mail client, you need to acquire some basic facts about your e-mail account. Only your e-mail provider can give you that information. Here's a quick overview of the information you need:

- **Compatibility:** You need to find out whether you can use Windows Live Mail with your e-mail account.

- **E-mail address:** You must know your own e-mail address, the one that people use to send you e-mail messages. You get your e-mail address from your e-mail provider.

- **Account type:** Typically, this would be either POP3 or HTTP (Hypertext Transfer Protocol). Windows Live Mail supports POP3, IMAP, and HTTP.

- **User account name, a.k.a. username:** The name you use to sign into your e-mail service.

- **E-mail password:** You should be able to define your own password. But if your mail provider has set up a temporary password, you need to know what that is to set up your account.

- **Outgoing (SMTP) mail server:** You need to know the fully qualified domain name (FQDN) of your outgoing mail server. The FQDN typically takes the form `server.domain.extension`, such as `smtp.somedomain.com`.

- **Incoming (POP3) mail server:** You need to know the exact name of your incoming mail server.

Feel free to use Table 18-1 to jot down the facts about your account. If you're tempted to fill in your own information by guessing, don't. Windows Live Mail won't work until you get exactly the right information in place.

Keep in mind that if you're dealing with multiple e-mail addresses and accounts, you need to fill in the blanks in Table 18-1 for each e-mail account. You need to set up a separate Windows Live Mail account for each e-mail address.

TABLE 18-1

Information You Need to Set Up Windows Live Mail

Line	Information Needed	Example	Write Your Information Here
1	Provider allows Windows Live Mail as e-mail client?	Yes or No	
2	Your e-mail address	somebody@ somewhere.com	
3	E-mail account type	POP3, IMAP, HTTP, Web mail, or some other protocol	
4	Incoming (POP3) mail server	Mail.somewhere.com	
5	Outgoing (SMTP) mail server	Smtp.somewhere.com	
6	Server requires authentication	Yes or No	
7	Your e-mail user name	Somebody	
8	Your e-mail password	********	

After you've filled in the Table 18-1 blanks for an e-mail account, you're ready to configure Windows Live Mail to use that account. Remember, Windows Live Mail doesn't work with all e-mail systems. So ...

- If your answer to Line 1 is No, ignore this entire chapter. Use whatever e-mail client and methods your mail provider supports. This might be Microsoft Office Outlook (for Exchange Server accounts) or simply a Web browser.

- If your information for Line 3 is *not* POP3, or IMAP, check with your ISP for specific instructions on setting up Windows Live Mail as your e-mail client.

Assuming you know that Windows Live Mail will work with your e-mail account and you've accurately filled in the blanks in Table 18-1, you're ready to configure your e-mail account.

Setting up your e-mail account

If several people share a single computer, each user should have his or her own user account and e-mail address. (See Chapter 3 if you need to set up user accounts.) Before you configure Windows Live Mail, make sure you log in to the user account for the e-mail address you're about to configure. Then configure Windows Live Mail for that user's e-mail address only. Start Windows Live Mail as described earlier in this chapter and follow these steps (use your account checklist as a guide):

1. From the Windows Live Mail menu bar, press Alt and choose Tools ⇨ Accounts and click Add. Or click the Add E-Mail Account link in the folder pane.

2. In the Add an Account dialog box that opens, click E-mail Account and click Next.

Caution

When typing information in the remaining steps, be aware that even the tiniest typographical error, misspelling, or a blank space will prevent your account from working. ■

3. Type your e-mail address exactly as provided by your mail provider and then enter your password in the Password field. Type your name as you want it to appear in the From line when people receive messages from you.

4. At this point, you can simply click Next and let Windows Live Mail attempt to configure your account settings automatically. Assuming that the program can't configure your settings automatically and you need to configure them yourself, select the check box labeled Manually Configure Server Settings for E-Mail Account and then click Next.

Tip

If you don't want to enter your password every time you check your e-mail, select Remember Password. However, don't choose that option on a public computer, because it will allow anyone to use your e-mail account. ■

5. When prompted for incoming and outgoing e-mail servers (see Figure 18-5), choose options and fill in the blanks according to what you entered for your mail servers in your account checklist. See the following list of options as a guide. When finished, click Next.

FIGURE 18-5

Settings for e-mail servers.

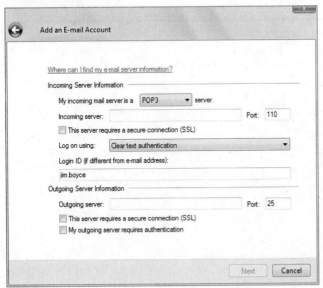

- **My Incoming Mail Server Is A:** Choose from POP3, IMAP, or HTTP.
- **Incoming Server:** Specify the FQDN of the server from which you will be retrieving your e-mail.
- **Port:** Specify the port on which Windows Live Mail needs to communicate with the incoming mail server. The default for POP3 is port 110; for IMAP it's 143.

- **This Server Requires a Secure Connection (SSL):** Choose this option if the incoming mail server requires that traffic be encrypted between Windows Live Mail and the server.

- **Log On Using:** Choose between Clear Text Authentication (no encryption for the user credentials), Authenticated POP (APOP), and Secure Password Authentication.

- **Login ID (If Different from E-Mail Address):** Specify the account to use to log in to the server. Sometimes this item takes the form of just a username and sometimes it is the e-mail address for the account. However, the account name must match exactly the account name on the incoming mail server.

- **Outgoing Server:** Specify the FQDN of the server to which Windows Live Mail will send outgoing e-mail.

- **Port:** Specify the port on which Windows Live Mail must communicate with the outgoing mail server. The default is port 25.

- **This Server Requires a Secure Connection (SSL):** Choose this option if the outgoing mail server requires that traffic be encrypted between Windows Live Main and the server.

- **My Outgoing Server Requires Authentication:** If the outgoing mail server requires that you log in when sending e-mail, select this option.

6. On the final page, click the Finish button.

The new account will be added to the Accounts dialog box under the Mail heading. The sample account shown in Figure 18-6 is just an example. Yours will be different.

FIGURE 18-6

Sample e-mail account.

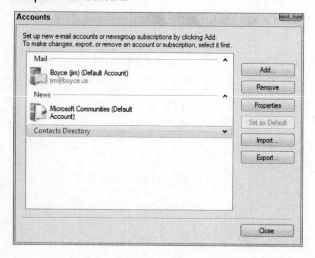

To test your account, click the Sync button. If you get an error message, you made a mistake or entered wrong information somewhere in the previous steps. To review, and optionally change, any information you entered, press Alt, and choose Tools ➪ Accounts from the menu bar. Then click the name of the account you just created and choose Properties. In the Properties dialog box that opens, review what you entered and make any necessary corrections. Remember, only your e-mail account provider or the company's technical support desk can help you troubleshoot any problems you might have.

Tip

To give the account a more meaningful name of your own choosing, click its name in the Accounts dialog box (choose Tools ➪ Accounts) and click Properties. In the first text box on the General tab, replace the current name with a name of your own choosing. Then click OK. Click Close to close the Accounts dialog box. ■

Writing E-Mail with Windows Live Mail

After your e-mail account is properly configured, you're ready to send and receive e-mail. You can send an e-mail message to anyone who has an e-mail address. You can even send messages to yourself. That might be worthwhile if you're new to all this and just want to test things for starters. To write an e-mail message:

1. With the Mail folders selected, click New in the toolbar. You can also press Ctrl+N, choose File ➪ New ➪ E-mail Message from the menu bar, or click the down arrow beside the New button on the toolbar and choose E-Mail Message. An empty message window titled New Message opens.

Tip

To add a background to your message, click the Stationery button on the message window's toolbar and then click a stationery name. Or click More stationery to choose from several other predefined designs or create your own. ■

2. Type the recipient's e-mail address in the To field. If you want to send the message to several people, you can type several addresses separated by semicolons (;).

   ● Optionally, to send carbon copies of the message to other recipients, put their e-mail addresses in the Cc field. Again, you can separate multiple e-mail addresses with semicolons. Choose View ➪ Cc and Bcc from the menu bar to show the Cc and Bcc fields.

   ● Optionally, to send blind carbon copies of the message to other recipients, type their e-mail addresses into the Bcc field, again separating multiple addresses with semicolons.

Tip

A blind carbon copy sends the e-mail message to the Bcc recipients with their names hidden from recipients in the To and Cc fields (and yours is hidden from the other Bcc recipients). This protects the privacy of the Bcc recipients. If you want to send a message to a group of people and have none of them see who is receiving the e-mail other than themselves, put all the address in the Bcc field. If you don't see Cc and Bcc fields, click the Show Cc & Bcc link beside the Subject field. If you have multiple e-mail accounts and want to change the account from which you're sending, use the From: drop-down menu to choose the account. ■

3. In the Subject: box, type a brief description of the subject of the message. This part of the message appears in the recipient's Inbox and is visible prior to the recipient's opening the message.

4. Type your message in the large editing window below the address portion of the e-mail. Figure 18-7 shows an example of a simple test message typed in the New Message window.

   ● Optionally, use the basic editing techniques and spell checker described later to clean up your message before sending.

- Optionally, set the message priority or request a read receipt using techniques described in the sections to follow.

5. Click the Send button in the toolbar.

FIGURE 18-7

A simple test message.

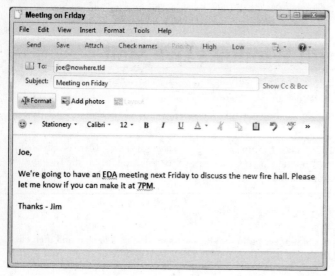

Windows Live Mail puts the message in your Outbox. Depending on how Windows Live Mail is configured, the message will either wait in the Outbox until the next time you synchronize folders or be sent immediately. While messages are sitting in your Outbox, you see a number next to that folder name indicating the number of messages awaiting delivery (see Figure 18-8). To send the message, click Sync in the toolbar.

If you sent the message to yourself, it might not appear right away. You have to wait a few seconds — maybe longer — as the message makes the trip from your computer to the outgoing mail server and then to the incoming mail server. Then click Sync to retrieve your messages from your mail provider's incoming mail server.

Typing and editing tips

Here are some basic things to keep in mind when typing an e-mail message (or just about anything else on a computer screen):

- When typing a paragraph, don't press Enter at the end of each line. Press Enter only at the end of the paragraph.

- To insert a blank line, press Enter (for example, press Enter twice at the end of a paragraph).

- To start a new line without starting a new paragraph, press Shift+Enter.

- The blinking cursor on the screen shows where the text you type next will appear. To change text, click where you want to make your change to get the blinking cursor to that spot. Then type your new text.

- To delete a few characters, click where you want to delete. Press Delete (Del) to delete characters to the right of the cursor or a blank line. Press Backspace to delete characters to the left of the cursor.

- To delete a larger chunk of text, select the text you want to delete. Then press Delete (Del).

- To undo a recent change to your text, press Ctrl+Z or click the Undo button in the toolbar, or choose Edit ➪ Undo from the menu bar.

- Use standard copy-and-paste techniques to paste text into an e-mail message and to move or copy text out of a message. See "Using copy and paste and cut and paste" in Chapter 14.

FIGURE 18-8

Message waiting in the Outbox.

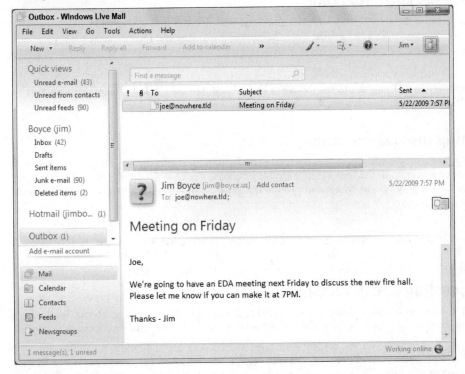

Tip

You rarely need to retype text you can already see on your screen. Just copy and paste the text instead. Any place you can type text, you can also paste text. ■

Check your spelling

To check your spelling in an e-mail message, press F7 or click the Check Spelling (abc) toolbar button. The spell checker will compare each word in your message to an internal dictionary. When it finds a word that doesn't exist in its dictionary, the Spelling dialog box opens. From there you can do any of the following:

- If the Spelling box offers suggested words, click the word that's spelled correctly then click Change.

- If the word is already spelled correctly (because it's a person's name or some other word not normally found in the dictionary), click Ignore.

Tip

If you already know how to use a word processing program such as Microsoft Word or WordPerfect, you can type, edit, and spell-check your message in that program. Press Ctrl+A and then Ctrl+C in the word processing program to select and copy all text. Then click in the body of your e-mail message and press Ctrl+V to paste that copied text into the e-mail message. ■

Add a background color

When you're in the New Message window writing your e-mail message, you can add a background color. To do so, click the Background Color button on the toolbar and then click the color you want to use from the color palette.

Tip

You can use stationery to add graphics to the message's background. See the section "Composing Rich-Text Messages with HTML," later in this chapter. ■

Setting message priority

Every e-mail message you type will automatically be set to normal priority. To change that, click the High or Low buttons in the New Message toolbar or choose Tools → Set Priority from the menu bar. Then choose a priority. The appropriate symbol will show up in the Priority column of the recipient's Inbox.

Tip

To see how priorities and read receipts work, apply those features to some test messages sent to your own e-mail address. ■

Requesting a read receipt

If you want to verify that a recipient has received and read your e-mail message, choose Tools → Request Read Receipt from the New Message window's menu bar. Then send your message normally.

When the recipient receives and reads the message, she will see a box indicating that you've requested a read receipt. If she chooses Yes to send a read receipt, you will receive an e-mail message with the word Read in the Subject line. That message tells you the date and time that the recipient read the message.

Note

There's no guarantee that you'll always get a read receipt, because the recipient can opt not to send you one. Likewise, you can receive read receipts even if the recipient does nothing, if his mail program is configured to send read receipts automatically. Also, understand that delivery receipts and read receipts are two different things. A delivery receipt indicates that a message has been delivered, whereas a read receipt indicates that a message has been opened (read) on the recipient's computer. Windows Live Mail does not support delivery receipts, although some other e-mail programs, such as Microsoft Office Outlook, do support them. ■

Getting Your E-Mail

To get e-mail messages addressed to you, you have to download them from your mail provider's incoming mail server. Depending on how Windows Live Mail is configured, that might happen automatically as soon as you open the program. It might even happen automatically every few seconds or minutes. It all depends on how you configure Windows Live Mail. But regardless of how the program is configured at the moment, you can always download waiting messages by clicking Sync in the toolbar.

New messages you receive might go straight to your Junk Mail folder or your Inbox. It all depends on (you guessed it) how you've configured Windows Live Mail. (I talk about junk mail a little later in the chapter.) Every folder shows a little number indicating how may unread messages it contains. To see unread messages, click the folder in the Folder list (either Inbox or Junk Mail). The contents pane shows message headers for every message currently in the folder. Headers for unread messages are in boldface.

To preview what's in the message, click its message header. The reading pane shows the message (or at least, part of it). In Figure 18-9, I clicked the Inbox folder, and then clicked a message header. The body of that message appears in the reading pane.

An unread message turns to a read message within a few seconds of clicking its message header in the Message list. So its message header won't stay boldfaced for long. The number next to the folder name also goes away after you've read all the messages in that folder.

The reading pane might not be tall enough to show the entire message, but you have several ways to address that issue. You can use the scroll bar at the right side of the message to scroll up and down, or you can adjust the height of the preview pane by dragging its upper border up or down. Or you can double-click the message header to *open* the message. An open message appears in its own window. You can position and size that window to your liking using the techniques described in Chapter 2.

Replying to a message

If you want to reply to the e-mail message you're currently reading, click one of the following:

- **Reply:** Click this button to reply to the original sender only.
- **Reply All:** Click this button to reply to the original sender plus everyone else to whom that sender sent the same message.

The message opens in a new window with some empty space at the top for you to type your reply. You don't need to delete the original message below that space. In fact, it's better to leave it there because that way, the person to whom you're replying can review, if necessary, the original message to which you're responding. When you've finished typing your reply, click the Send button in the toolbar.

Forwarding a message

To pass the message you're reading on to someone else, click the Forward button. Add recipient addresses as described previously and then click Send. The message awaits you in the Outbox until the next time the folder is synchronized.

FIGURE 18-9

Viewing a received message.

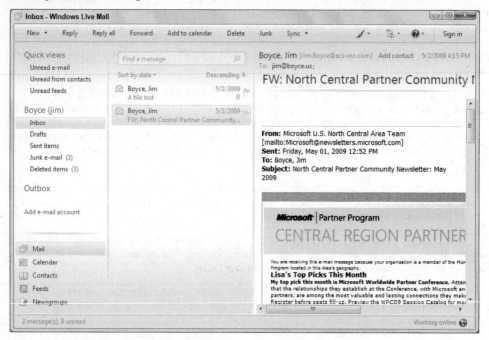

Other things you can do with a message

To see other things you can do with a message, right-click the message header in the Message list. You see a menu like the one in Figure 18-10. The first few options let you do things I've already told you about (open, print, reply, forward). The rest are summarized in the following list.

In a nutshell, here is what the rest of the options offer. Some options are covered in more detail later in this chapter:

- **Open:** Opens the e-mail message in a separate window. You can move, size, and position that window to your liking using the techniques described in Chapter 2.

- **Print:** Prints a copy of the message. See Chapter 36 if you need help with printing.

- **Reply to Sender**, **Reply to All**, **Forward:** See the "Replying to a message" and "Forwarding a message" sections, previously in this chapter.

- **Forward As Attachment:** Forwards the message to senders of your choosing as an attached file rather than as a message. See "Using E-Mail Attachments," later in this chapter, for more information on attachments.

- **Mark as Read:** Removes the boldface from the message header in the Message list.

- **Mark as Unread:** Makes the message header boldfaced in the Message list.

- **Move to Folder:** Moves the message to any folder in the Folder list. (Optionally, you can drag any message header to any folder in the list.)

FIGURE 18-10

Right-click a message header.

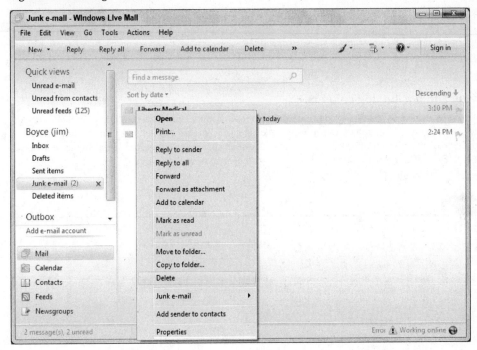

- **Copy to Folder:** Puts a copy of the message in a folder you specify without removing it from its current folder.

- **Delete:** Sends the message to the Deleted Items folder.

- **Junk E-mail:** Offers numerous options for deciding how to treat future messages from the message sender.

- **Add Sender to Contacts:** Adds the message sender to your Contacts folder (which is similar to a personal address book).

- **Properties:** Shows some detailed information about the message.

Magnifying e-mail text

To change the text size of an e-mail message, choose View ➪ Text Size from the menu bar and then click a text size. To return to the normal text size at any time, choose View ➪ Text Size ➪ Medium. Note that changing text size in this way doesn't necessarily change the appearance of all of the text in the message.

Sorting messages by message headers

As in any columnar display of data, you can sort messages using message headers however you see fit. Just click the column heading by which you want to sort. For example, to sort messages by Date

Received, with the most recent messages at the top of the list, click the Received column until the little triangle in that heading points down. Or to find a message by subject, click the Subject column header to sort by subject.

When the Message list is displaying its two-line view, a button appears at the upper left of the Message list. By default, messages are sorted by date, so this button's caption reads Sort by Date. To sort by other fields, click the button and choose from the resulting drop-down menu. The button's caption then changes to indicate the new sort field.

Sizing and positioning columns

As in most columnar displays of data, you can choose, arrange, and size columns in the Message list. To widen or narrow a column, position the tip of the mouse pointer right on the line at the right side of the column title so that the mouse pointer changes to a two-headed arrow as shown in Figure 18-11. Then slowly drag left or right to widen or narrow the column.

FIGURE 18-11

Size a column.

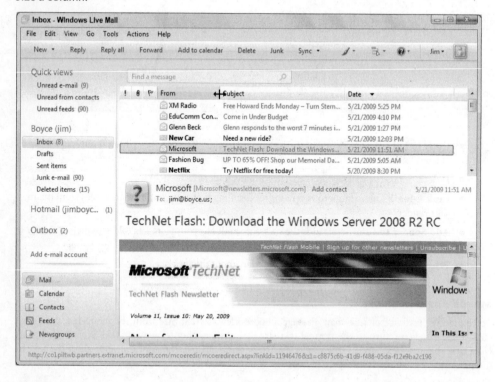

Tip

To view the Message list in single-line mode, choose View ➪ Layout, click Message List, and choose One-Line View, then click OK. ∎

To move a column left or right, position the tip of the mouse pointer right on the column name. Then drag the column name left or right.

Note
To deal with blocked content and warning messages, see "E-Mail security options," later in this chapter. ■

Sizing the reading pane

The reading pane shows the contents of whatever message header you click. You can size it as you would most other panes: When the reading pane is below the Message list, position the tip of the mouse pointer on the upper border of the preview pane so that the mouse pointer changes to a two-headed arrow. Then slowly drag up or down until the pane is the size you like. When the reading pane is to the left of the Message list, drag the left edge of the reading pane left or right to resize it.

Don't forget that the reading pane is just a sneak peek at what's in an e-mail message. You can double-click any message header to open the full message in its own window. You can size, position, and close that window using the standard methods described in Chapter 2.

Using E-Mail Attachments

Attachments provide a means of sending documents and other files through e-mail. For example, to send a picture, song, video, spreadsheet, or Microsoft Word or other document from a folder to someone, you *attach* that document to an e-mail message.

Every mail provider puts a limit on how large a file you can attach. The number varies from one provider to the next. The limits typically range between 1 and 10MB. To find out what your attachment size limit is, browse around your provider's help documentation for e-mail or contact it by phone.

You can attach multiple files to an e-mail message, but their combined sizes must be within the limit imposed by your mail provider. Optionally, you can combine multiple files into a single compressed file first. That allows both you and the recipient to handle multiple files as one; it can also reduce the overall file size. See "Zipping and Unzipping Files" in Chapter 14 for more information on using Zip files.

You can attach files to e-mail messages in Windows Live Mail in several ways. There isn't a right way or wrong way. The end result is the same no matter which method you use: The e-mail recipient gets your e-mail message with the files you attached. So choosing one method or another is just a matter of deciding what's easiest for you based on what you're sending and how much you know about files and folders. In the following section, I start with the basic method of writing an e-mail message and then attaching one or more files.

Attaching a file to a message

You can write an e-mail message in Windows Live Mail first and then attach one or more files to it. The file(s) can be anything: word processing documents, spreadsheets, pictures, music, video — whatever. You just need to know what folder the file(s) are in and how to navigate to that folder. Here are the steps:

1. In Windows Live Mail, click New to start a new message, fill in the To and Subject lines, and type the body of the message as you would with any other e-mail message. Don't send the message yet.

2. Click Attach in the toolbar or from the menu bar above the new message and choose Insert ⇨ File As Attachment. An Open dialog box opens, as shown in Figure 18-12.

FIGURE 18-12

Insert Attachment dialog box.

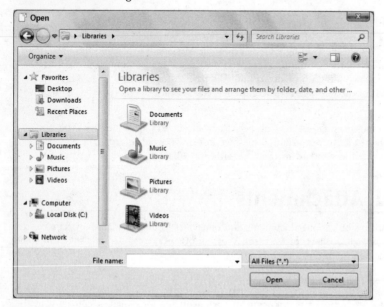

Tip

To get to the main folders for your user account as in the example shown in the figure, click your user account name in the address bar. To size icons in the center pane, right-click an empty space within that main pane and choose View; then choose an icon size or view type. ■

3. Navigate to the folder that contains the files you want to attach to your message.

4. Click the icon for the file you want to attach or select icons for all the files you want to attach. Then click Open. The file(s) you selected appears in the Attachment list under the Subject field. Figure 18-13 shows an example in which I've attached two files to a message.

5. Optionally, to attach additional files from other folders, repeat Steps 2–4.

6. Click Send in the New Message window toolbar.

E-mailing documents from folders

The preceding steps assume that you want to create your e-mail message first and then attach files to it. But you can do it another way. If you happen to be in the folder that contains the file(s) you want to e-mail, there's no reason to open Windows Live Mail first. Instead, you can follow these steps:

1. If you haven't already done so, open the folder that contains the file(s) you want to send.

2. Optionally, to send multiple files from the same folder, select their icons.

FIGURE 18-13

Icons for attached files.

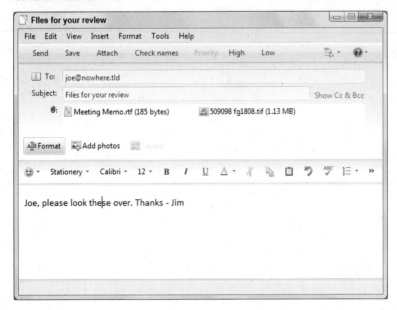

Tip

See "How to Select Icons" in Chapter 30 if you haven't yet learned how to select multiple icons. ■

3. Right-click the icon (or any selected icon) of the file that you want to e-mail and choose Send To ➪ Mail Recipient. (See Figure 18-14.)

4. If you're sending pictures, the Attach Files dialog box opens. Choose whatever size you want the pictures to be. Just make sure that the resulting Total Estimated Size is within the attachment size limit imposed by your mail provider. Then click Attach. Try a smaller picture size if you go over the limit.

Tip

If you using a Windows Live account and are attaching a photo, Windows Live Mail asks whether you want to upload the image to the Web and send a link instead. For now, I assume that you click No. The picture is then added to the new message as a file attachment. ■

5. A new e-mail message opens in the New Message window with the files already attached. Fill in the To and Subject lines as you would with any other e-mail message.

6. Optionally, change the text of the message to whatever you want to write in your e-mail message.

7. Click the Send button in the New Message toolbar.

FIGURE 18-14

E-mailing from a folder.

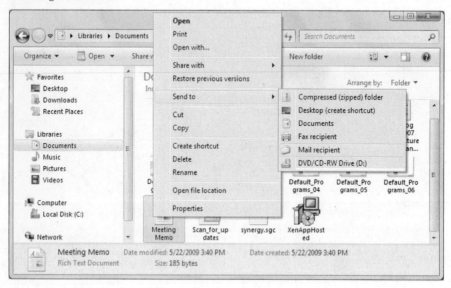

E-mailing pictures from Windows Live Photo Gallery

If you've already learned how to use Windows Live Photo Gallery (Chapter 23), you can e-mail photos and video clips straight from the gallery. Here are the steps:

1. Open Windows Live Photo Gallery.

2. Choose options in the navigation pane so that you can see the photos and video clip icons of the items you want to send.

3. Select the icons of the items you want to send using the standard selection methods for Windows Live Photo Gallery (see "Selecting thumbnails in the gallery" in Chapter 23 to learn how).

4. Click E-mail in the toolbar. The image thumbnail appears in the New Message window (Figure 18-15).

5. Use the options on the Photos toolbar in the New Message window to add a frame, special effects, and more photos, as well as to specify other settings. Use the options on the Layout toolbar to organize the photos in the message.

6. Fill in the To and Subject lines as you would with any e-mail message.

7. Optionally, change the text in the body of the e-mail message to whatever message you want to write.

8. Click the Send button in the New Message window.

You can use the same technique to send pictures from your Pictures folder or any folder that contains pictures. Open the folder, select the pictures you want to send, right-click any selected icon, and choose Send To ➪ Mail Recipient.

FIGURE 18-15

Photo in a new message.

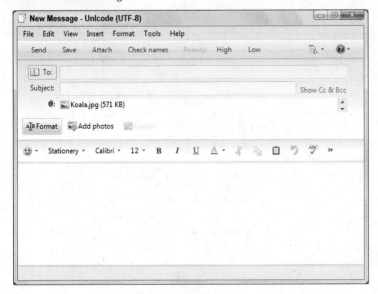

Opening received attachments

When somebody sends you an e-mail message with files attached, the header for that message shows a paper clip icon. For example, the first message in Figure 18-16 has an attachment. When you click the message header of such a message, the reading pane also shows a paper clip. Right-click an attachment in the reading pane to access commands for opening, printing, and saving attachments.

Caution

Most malware (viruses and such) can spread by e-mail attachments. Never open any e-mail attachment unless you know whom it's from and what it contains. Do not trust e-mail messages that claim to be returning failed messages from your account. Most of the time they're fake. Their attached files contain viruses and other malware! ■

The name of each attached file appears in the header as shown in Figure 18-16. To view the contents of an attachment, double-click its icon. You will probably get a security warning. If you're confident that the attachment is safe, click Open to open it.

Note

Disabled (dimmed) items on the paper clip menu can't be opened or saved because of your current security settings. See "E-mail security options," later in this chapter, for more information. ■

The attachment will open in whatever program is currently configured for that file type on your system (assuming that there *is* a program for that file type on your system). If it opens, you can view it, save it to a regular file, print it, or do whatever you like with it in that program (assuming that you know how to use that program to do all those things). Close that program when you're done viewing the attachment.

FIGURE 18-16

E-mail message attachments.

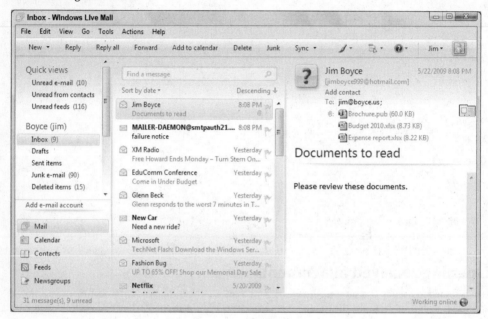

You can open files (attachments) for a file type only if you have a program that *can* open that file type. If you don't have an appropriate program installed on your system, you see a message, perhaps like the one in Figure 18-17, when you try to open an attachment.

As an example, suppose someone sends you a Microsoft PowerPoint file with a .ppt or .pptx extension. If you don't have the PowerPoint program (or a PowerPoint viewer), you can't open that attachment until you get the PowerPoint viewer or install PowerPoint on your computer.

Table 18-2 lists some common file types, the name of the viewer you need to open that type of file, the Web site from which you can download the viewer, and the word(s) to search for (if needed) when you get to the suggested page in order to find the download.

If you can't find a viewer for an attachment but you know the sender, you may be able to get the sender to resend the file in a format you can open. For example, a WordPerfect user might be able to save a document in Rich Text Format (.rtf) or as a Word document (.doc) and then send you that copy of the file as an e-mail attachment.

Note
Digitally licensed files, such as music you purchase online, will play only on the computer to which you downloaded the file. That's true even if you already have the correct player for the file. ■

Message for attachment.

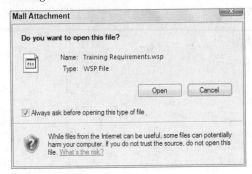

Some Common File Types and Available Viewers

Extension	Program Needed	Web Site	Search for
.doc/.docx	Microsoft Word	http://download.microsoft.com	Word Viewer
.kmz	Google Earth	http://earth.google.com/download-earth.html	
.mov	QuickTime	www.apple.com/quicktime	
.pdf	Adobe Reader	www.adobe.com/products/reader acrobat/readermain.html	
.ppt/.pptx	Microsoft PowerPoint	http://download.microsoft.com	PowerPoint Viewer
.snp	Snapshot Viewer	http://download.microsoft.com	Snapshot Viewer
.vsd	Microsoft Visio	http://download.microsoft.com	Visio Viewer
.xls/.xlsx	Microsoft Excel	http://download.microsoft.com	Excel Viewer

Saving attachments as files

Files attached to e-mail messages don't automatically go to a regular document folder such as the Documents, Pictures, and Music folders in your user account. Instead, they remain in your mailbox until you save them to your hard drive or another medium. Here's how:

1. In the Reading pane, right-click attachment that you want to save as a file.
2. Click Save As in the context menu (see Figure 18-18).

FIGURE 18-18

Context menu for an attachment.

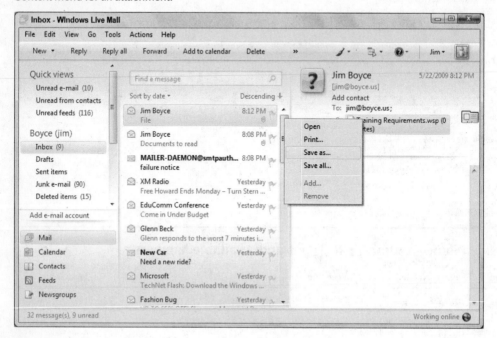

Note

If the message is from an unknown sender, Windows Live Mail displays a warning above the header in the reading pane. You can click Delete and block to delete the message and add the sender to the Blocked Senders list. Or click Allow to add the sender to the Allowed Senders list. ■

3. The Save Attachment As dialog box opens. Initially, all the filenames will be selected, as in Figure 18-19. You can hold down the Ctrl key and click the names of any files you do or don't want to save. Only selected files are saved.

4. Navigate to the folder in which you want to put the saved files. For example, if you're saving a picture, choose your Pictures folder. For a text document or worksheet, choose your Documents folder.

5. Click Save.

The Save Attachment As dialog box closes and you're returned to Windows Live Mail. The original files will still be attached to the message. You can also find copies of those same attached files in whatever folder you specified in the preceding Step 4. Use those saved copies of the attachments for day-to-day editing of files, printing, and so forth.

After you've verified that the files are in the folder to which you saved them, feel free to delete the e-mail message. You don't need the message or the files attached to it anymore. Or you can keep the message and its attached files as a backup to the files in your document folder or so that you remember who sent them to you.

FIGURE 18-19

Save Attachment As dialog box.

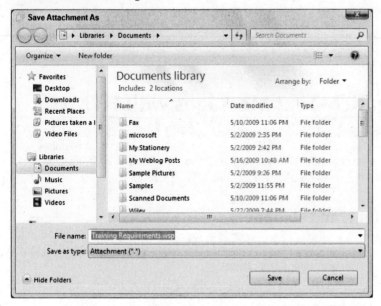

Saving embedded pictures as files

If you get an e-mail message that contains an embedded picture, you might want to keep a copy of the picture as a regular file in Windows Live Photo Gallery. That way, the picture is just like any picture you get from a camera or other source and not hidden away in an old e-mail message.

Saving a picture that's embedded in an e-mail message is the same as copying a picture from a Web page in Internet Explorer. Right-click the picture and choose Save Picture As. Choose a folder — your Pictures folder if you don't have a preference — and give the picture a filename of your own choosing. Then click Save.

The saved picture will be graphics ⇨ file in whatever folder you specified. If you chose a folder that Windows Live Photo Gallery monitors, the picture shows up in your gallery as well, most likely as an untagged picture. But you can tag it, open it, edit it, fix it, print it, and do anything else you can do with other pictures in your gallery.

Converting e-mail messages to files

Each e-mail message you receive is a file with an .eml filename extension stored in the Windows Live Mail folder for your user account. But you can save a copy of any message to a regular folder, such as the Documents folder for your user account. Click the header of the message you want to save. Then choose File ⇨ Save As from the Windows Live Mail menu bar. Specify a document folder in which to store the message. Optionally, give the file a name of your own choosing and click Save. The message is saved as a file with the .eml filename extension. Although you can open a message file in Notepad or other text editor, in almost all cases you want to open the message in Windows Live Mail. To do so, just double-click the .eml file, and it will open in a Windows Live Mail message window.

If you have a word processing program such as Microsoft Word or WordPerfect, you can copy and paste any e-mail message to a document in that program. Open the e-mail message by double-clicking its message header. Then press Ctrl+A (Select All) and Ctrl+C (Copy) to copy the message content to the Clipboard. Then open your word processor, click inside a document, and press Ctrl+V to paste in the message. Save the document in your Documents folder or some other Windows folder that makes sense for you. That copy of the message will be a normal, editable document. You can then delete the original e-mail message or perhaps keep it as a backup.

Composing Rich-Text Messages with HTML

HTML (Hypertext Markup Language) is the formatting language used to create most static content in Web pages. You can also use it to compose e-mail messages. When you use HTML to compose messages, your message can contain much more than plain text. You can use fonts, hyperlinks, pictures, and other formatting features in your messages.

HTML, default font, and stationery

The first step to creating rich-text messages with HTML is to configure Windows Live Mail to use that setting automatically. HTML is the default, but you can change it back to HTML if for some reason the default has been set to plain text. Here are the steps:

1. In Windows Live Mail, choose Tools ➪ Options from the menu bar.

2. In the Options dialog box that opens, click the Send tab.

3. Under Mail Sending Format, choose HTML, as in Figure 18-20.

4. If you want to also set a default font and stationery, continue with the following steps. Otherwise, you can click OK now and skip the remaining steps.

5. Click the Compose tab.

6. To set a default font, click Font Settings next to Mail. Choose your font name, size, and color; then click OK.

7. Optionally, to choose a stationery (typically a background picture, but it can be other HTML content), select the Mail check box under the Stationery heading, and then click the Select button at the right.

8. In the Select Stationery dialog box that opens, point to each icon to see what it looks like in the preview pane to the right. (Make sure that Show Preview is selected if you don't see previews.) Take a look at each one. If you find one you like, click it and then click OK.

Tip
If you want to try your hand at creating your own custom stationery, click Create New in the Select Stationery dialog box. ■

9. Click OK to save your settings and return to Windows Live Mail.

To compose a new e-mail message, click the New button. If you chose stationery in the preceding steps, the new message has that stationery automatically. Fill in the To and Subject lines as you normally do and then type your message. If you chose a default font, text you type in the body of the message is in that font.

FIGURE 18-20

Send messages as HTML.

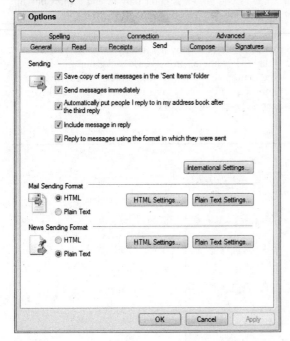

Tip

To choose or change the stationery for an e-mail message that you're currently typing, click the Stationery button in the toolbar or choose Format ⇨ Apply Stationery from the New Message window's menu bar. ∎

You don't have to worry about applying any formatting while typing your message. You might find just typing the text of your message easiest. Then go back and apply formatting using the *select, then do* method. That is, you *select* (drag the mouse pointer through) the text you want to format and then *do* by clicking a button in the formatting toolbar just above the text. You can see examples as you continue reading here.

Tip

The *select, then do* approach described here works in virtually all word processors and Web page editors. When you learn to do it in one program, you know how to do it in all programs. Also, pressing Undo (Ctrl+Z) to undo your last formatting change applies to virtually all formatting in all programs. ∎

Using fonts, sizes, boldface, underline, italics, colors

The first few buttons in the New Message formatting toolbar let you apply a font, size, paragraph style, boldface, italics, underline, and a color to selected text. To apply formatting to a chunk of text, first *select* the text by dragging the mouse pointer through it. The selected text is highlighted. If you select too much or too little, just click any text and try again.

Tip

When typing a paragraph, don't press Enter at the end of each line. Just keep typing as though right off the edge. The text will automatically wrap down to the next line as you go. Press Enter only to end a short line of text or an entire paragraph. Press Enter again to insert a blank line. ■

For example, in Figure 18-21 I selected the first sentence of text by dragging the mouse pointer through it. Notice how the selected text is highlighted (white against a dark background). After you've selected a chunk of text, you can click any button in the Formatting toolbar. The formatting is applied only to the selected text. If you're not sure what a button is for, just point to it (rest the tip of the mouse pointer on it). The name of the button appears in a tooltip at the mouse pointer.

FIGURE 18-21

Selected text and the Formatting toolbar.

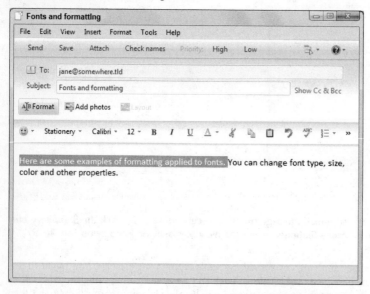

Figure 18-22 shows some text with different formats applied. The best way to get the hang of all this is to just experiment and practice with a fake e-mail that you don't intend to send anyone. Type a bunch of text. Then select any chunk of text and choose an option from the Font, Font Size, Paragraph Style, or Font Color button in the Formatting toolbar. Or just click the Bold, Italic, or Underline button. If you don't like what you see, press Ctrl+Z to undo that change.

Try combining types of formatting, too. For example, you might want to apply a font, size, bold face, italic, and a font color to a chunk of text. You can't do any harm by experimenting, especially if you practice in a message you don't intend to send.

Typing a list

Numbered and bulleted lists are useful ways of organizing text. For example, you might want to show some numbered steps or a list of points or options in your text. To do so, type each item in the list, pressing Enter once at the end of each line. Do not type a number or symbol at the start of each line. Those are added when you apply formatting later.

FIGURE 18-22

Examples of formatted text.

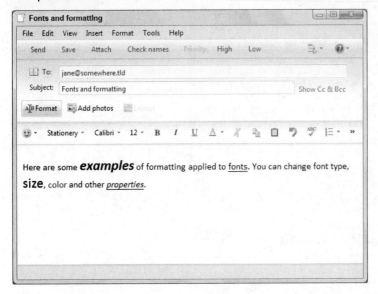

Next, select all the items in the list by dragging the mouse pointer through them. Figure 18-23 shows an example in which I've selected multiple lines in a list. Next, click the Format As List button in the Formatting toolbar (also shown in Figure 18-23) and choose Numbered List or Bulleted List.

Indenting and aligning text

Use the Format Paragraph button in the toolbar (see Figure 18-24) to align or indent text. As always, you can start by typing a line or paragraph of text. Then select the text you want to align or indent and click the Format Paragraph button, followed by the appropriate formatting command to apply formatting. That same figure shows examples of text to which indentation and alignment have been applied.

Inserting inline pictures

You can insert a small photo or picture into the body of your e-mail message. In contrast to attaching a picture, in this case your picture appears right in the body of your e-mail message; this is called an inline picture. If the picture is small enough, you can even wrap text around the picture.

Note

Windows Live Mail enables you to create a photo e-mail that uploads your images to a Windows Live space and sends only a thumbnail of the images with a link to the image online. That type of e-mail is covered later, in the section, "Creating Photo E-Mails." ■

FIGURE 18-23

Example of selected list.

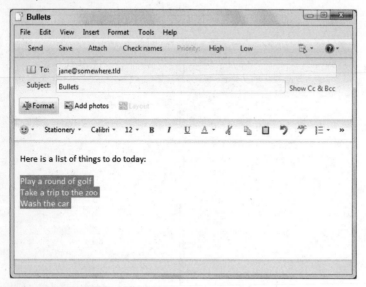

FIGURE 18-24

Alignment and indentation examples.

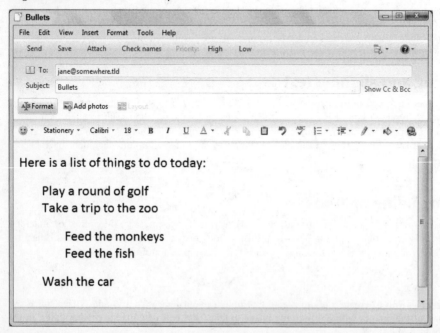

There is one catch to inserting pictures in e-mail messages. You can insert only BMP, DIB, JPEG, JPG, JPE, JFIF, and PNG file types. If the picture you want to insert isn't one of those types, you can still attach it to an e-mail message as described under "Attaching a file to a message," earlier in this chapter. Or you can open the picture in a graphics program and then use that program to save a separate copy of the picture as one of the supported file types.

Tip

For more information on pictures and picture types, see Chapter 23. The more you know about pictures in general, the easier it will be to use them with e-mail messages. ■

Inserting an inline (embedded) image is easy. Use the New button to create a new e-mail message. Fill in the To and Subject lines, and type your message in the large pane — just as you do when sending any other e-mail message. Then follow these steps:

1. In your message, click where you want to put the upper-left corner of the picture.

2. Choose Insert ➪ Image ➪ Inline from the menu bar.

3. Navigate to the folder that contains the picture, click the picture's icon, and then click Open. The image appears in the message. When the picture is in the message, you can make adjustments to its size. Click the picture so that it shows sizing handles (little squares around its border). Then drag any handle to increase or decrease the height or width of the picture. To move the picture, just drag it to some new location within the message. To rotate the picture, click and drag the handle on top of the picture. When the mouse is on the tip of the rotation handle, the mouse pointer changes to a partial circle. Figure 18-25 shows a couple of photos rotated in an e-mail message.

Windows Live Mail doesn't offer a lot of editing capabilities for placing inline images in a message. For example, you can format the paragraph in which the image is inserted to align the photo to the left, center, or right. You can't, however, simply drag a photo to any point in the body of the message. Instead, the image is still constrained by the properties of the paragraph in which it is embedded. You can drag it to a different paragraph in the message, but you can't format the picture to wrap the text around it.

Inserting a line

If you want to insert a line in an e-mail message, first click where you want the line to appear. Then choose Insert ➪ Horizontal Line from the menu bar.

Adding hyperlinks to e-mail messages

A hyperlink is text you can click in a message to browse to a Web page or create a new e-mail message. You can add hyperlinks to e-mail messages in several ways. Here, I assume that you're already in the New Message window and have started typing your message.

Type a link

One way to insert a link into a Web page is to simply type the page's URL (address). For example, you can type a URL such as www.google.com right into an e-mail message. As you move on to continue typing, that text automatically turns to a clickable hyperlink (it turns blue and gains an underline).

FIGURE 18-25

Rotated photos in an e-mail message.

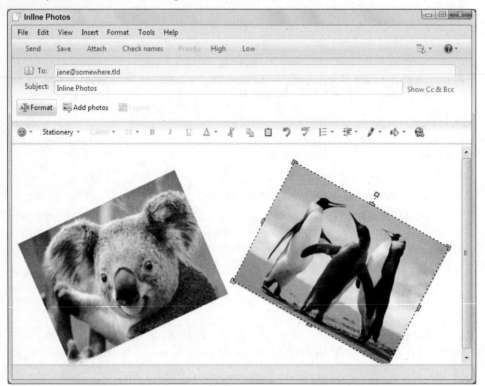

Copy and paste a link

If you want to send the address of a page you're currently viewing to someone, you can copy and paste that page's URL rather than retype it. For example, say that you're viewing the page in Internet Explorer. Click just to the right of the page's URL in the address bar. Or drag the mouse pointer through the URL in the address bar to select it. You know the address is selected when the text turns white against a blue background. Then press Ctrl+C to copy that selected URL.

Next, click in your e-mail message where you want the address to appear. Then press Ctrl+V to paste in the URL. If necessary, you can press the spacebar to insert a blank space or Enter to start a new line. The URL will automatically become a hyperlink, as indicated by its color and underlining.

Custom links

The links you put in an e-mail message don't have to exactly match the link. For example, you can use the words Click here as the visible part of the link. There's a big drawback to this approach, though. The recipient's e-mail client might flag your message as a potential phishing scam, because those scams use the same technique to hide actual URLs. You don't want people thinking your e-mail message is a scam. So I suggest you avoid using this technique in e-mail messages.

Nonetheless, Windows Live Mail lets you create such links. So if you want to give it a try, here are the steps:

1. Type the text you plan to use as a URL (for example, the words Click here).

2. Select the text that will act as a hyperlink.

3. Click the Insert a Link button in the New Message toolbar, or choose Insert ➪ Hyperlink from the New Message menu bar.

4. In the Insert Hyperlink dialog box that opens, type in the Text to Display box the words you want to appear in the message body. Then type (or paste) the URL of the Web site into the Address text box.

5. Click OK in the Insert Hyperlink dialog box.

The text you selected in Step 1 will be colored and underlined as a hyperlink. The recipient of your e-mail message only needs to click that link to visit the site.

Tip

If you highlight some existing text in the message before you open the Hyperlink dialog box, Windows Live Mail uses that text as the Text to Display text. ■

Adding a signature automatically

You can automatically add a signature to the bottom of every e-mail message you send. The signature can be as simple as your name. Or it can be your name, e-mail address, and any other text you want. For example, if you have your own Web site, you can include its URL in your signature. Creating a signature is easy:

1. From the menu bar in Windows Live Mail, choose Tools ➪ Options.

2. In the Options dialog box, click the Signatures tab.

3. Click the New button.

4. Click Text under Edit Signature.

5. To the right of the Text option, type the text of your signature. You can type as many lines as you wish.

6. Choose Add Signatures to All Outgoing Messages.

7. Optionally, select or deselect Don't Add Signatures to Replies and Forwards depending on whether you want to sign replies and forwards. Figure 18-26 shows an example.

8. Click OK.

To test it, click the New Message button. A new empty e-mail message opens with your signature already added to the bottom. As you type text above the signature in your message, the signature moves down so that it stays at the bottom of the message.

If you manage multiple accounts with Windows Live Mail, you can create different signatures for different accounts. Follow the basic steps described earlier to create each signature. To assign a signature to an account, click its name under Signatures. Then click the Advanced button. Select the accounts for which you want to use that signature; then click OK.

Tip

Advanced users who know HTML can create a fancier signature in Notepad or an HTML editor leave out the <head>, <body>, and <meta> tags used in Web pages. ■

FIGURE 18-26

Sample signature.

Creating Photo E-Mails

Earlier in this chapter, you learned how to embed inline images in an e-mail message. Windows Live Mail provides another capability for sending photos, which is called a *photo e-mail*. With a photo e-mail, you embed thumbnails of the pictures in the e-mail message, but the photos themselves are actually uploaded to Windows Live servers. The e-mail contains a link for each image, and when someone receives your message and clicks a photo thumbnail, the image is downloaded from the server. This method helps reduce the amount of data in the recipients' mailboxes and can be a great help in bypassing e-mail attachment limits. Plus, a photo e-mail gives you additional options for formatting the images in the e-mail than when using an inline image.

To create a photo e-mail, click the down arrow beside the New button and choose Photo E-Mail. Or simply click New to start a new message and then click the Add Photos button. Either way, Windows Live Mail opens the Add Photos dialog box, shown in Figure 18-27.

Select one or more photos and click Add. When you are finished adding photos, click Done to close the Add Photos dialog box. The image thumbnails then appear in the body of the message (Figure 18-28).

As you can tell from the toolbar shown in Figure 18-28, you can add a different type of frame around each photo, rotate photos, use autocorrect to fine-tune image colors, set photos to black and white, and specify the quality of the images that will be uploaded to the server. The editing tools are fairly straightforward, so I focus on the upload options.

FIGURE 18-27

The Add Photos dialog box.

The three options — Low, Medium, and High — determine the quality of the images that are uploaded to the Windows Live servers. Depending on your selection, Windows Live Mail changes the quality of the photos before uploading. Pick a value based on how much data you want to place on the servers, the upload time, and how good you really need the photos to look when they are downloaded by the e-mail recipients.

Note
You must have a Windows Live account to upload photos. You are limited to 500 images per month and 500MB worth of images in each photo e-mail. ■

If you click the Layout button, Windows Live Mail offers multiple options for arranging the photos in the e-mail. Although you can use very large thumbnails, doing so partly defeats the purpose of using thumbnails instead of inline images. But whatever layout you choose (except Small Thumbnails), you can add text to each image.

To change an image, double-click the image to display the Open dialog box. You can also click the Add More Photos button to add other photos to the e-mail.

When you're satisfied with the layout of the photos and have added text and other content to the e-mail, click Send. Windows Live Mail places the message in your Outbox and takes care of uploading the images to the Windows Live servers.

When the photo e-mail arrives at its destination, the e-mail looks just as it did when you sent it. When you click one of the thumbnails, however, the image is downloaded from the server and displayed on the recipient's screen.

FIGURE 18-28

Thumbnails in a photo e-mail.

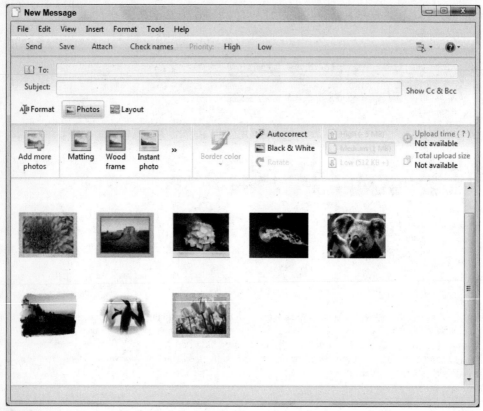

Note

Junk Mail filtering in Windows Live Mail provides a simple yet effective means for filtering out the junk without all the effort of defining countless rules. ■

Dealing with Spam (Junk E-Mail)

Spam, the electronic equivalent of junk paper mail, is an unpleasant fact of life. Windows Live Mail offers some tools and strategies for dealing with it. But before I get into the specifics, it's important to understand that Windows Live Mail can't really tell a junk e-mail from a valid e-mail with absolute certainty. No computer program can do that. That's because junk mail messages don't carry any special information that explicitly identifies them as junk.

Nonetheless, you have many ways to configure Windows Live Mail to minimize your exposure to junk mail. To see them, choose Tools ➪ Safety Options from the Windows Live Mail menu bar. The dialog box shown in Figure 18-29 opens. Your first step is to choose the level of junk e-mail protection from the options given.

FIGURE 18-29

Safety Options dialog box.

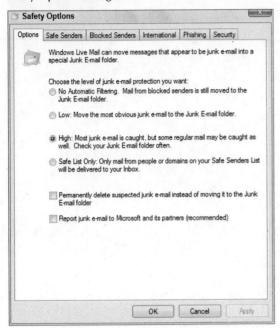

The most effective way to deal with junk e-mail is to choose the Safe List Only option, but it is also the most restrictive. This option lets you accept e-mail from specific people and domains only. If you accidentally forget to include someone as a safe sender, you can easily make him or her one later. But you can read all the options and choose whichever one best describes the strategy you want to try or use.

Caution

Don't choose the Permanently Delete Suspected Junk E-Mail option until you're confident that your strategy will never accidentally identify a valid e-mail message as junk. ■

Identifying safe senders

A safe sender is any person or domain from which you're willing to accept e-mail. To specify safe senders, click the Safe Senders tab. Use the Add button to add safe senders to your list. To accept e-mail from anyone with an e-mail account in a specific domain, you can enter just the domain name of the safe sender (the part of the e-mail address that comes after the @ symbol). For example, to receive e-mail from any e-mail account at Microsoft, you enter **Microsoft.com**.

In Figure 18-30, I've listed the domain names of several domains. Listing only the domain name ensures that I get e-mail sent by anyone who works for the company or who has an e-mail account in that domain. In other words, it means I trust e-mail sent by anyone within that e-mail domain.

FIGURE 18-30

Safe Senders tab.

You wouldn't want to list large domains such as Aol.com, Hotmail.com, Comcast.net, or Yahoo.com as safe senders. That's not because those companies are bad. Rather, they have millions of customers, most of whom you don't even know. But you might want to receive e-mail from people you *do* know from those domains. In that case, you enter the exact e-mail address of the person from whom you're willing to accept e-mail.

You can choose Always Trust E-Mail from My Contacts to always trust e-mail from people who you know well enough to put in your Contacts folder. Likewise, you can choose Automatically Add People I E-Mail to the Safe Senders list. When you do so, you're assuming that if you know or trust someone enough to send him or her an e-mail, you're also willing to accept e-mail from that person.

As in all dialog boxes, you're not making any lifelong commitments in the Safe Senders list. You can add more safe senders at any time. Remove one at any time by clicking it and then clicking Remove.

Blocking specific senders

The Blocked Senders tab is the opposite of Safe Senders. There you can list specific domains or addresses that should be blocked. Of course, there are millions of addresses from which you don't want to accept e-mail, and it wouldn't make sense to try to list them all. Furthermore, if you chose Safe Senders Only on the first page of the dialog box, you don't need to list any domains or addresses in Blocked Senders because everyone except your safe senders will be blocked automatically.

Blocking by country and language

Most of us get junk e-mail messages written in other languages or from other countries. The International tab in Junk E-Mail Options lets you block messages from entire countries based on the top-level domain for that country. For example, you can click the Blocked Top Level Domain List button to see a list of all countries that have a specific abbreviation in their international domain (US for United States, AU for Australia, and so forth).

You can really minimize your foreign junk mail by clicking the Blocked Top Level Domain List. When the list opens, click Select All. Then scroll down through the list and clear the checkmark next to any country from which you are willing to accept e-mail.

Tip

Blocking a specific country doesn't prevent e-mail coming to you from that country. It only blocks e-mail with addresses that use the country's top-level domain. For example, if you block the US domain, my address of jim@boyce.us would never make it to your Inbox. However, my address of jimboyce999@hotmail.com *would* make it to you, even though it probably comes from a server in the United States. Understand that Windows Live Mail has no way of knowing exactly where a message originated; it can tell only what the e-mail address is. ∎

Different languages require different encoding (characters). The Blocked Encoding List lets you block and accept messages based on that encoding. So again, you can click that option. Then select encodings that support languages you can't read. Be careful, however. Just because you don't know what an encoding means doesn't mean you can't read text written in that language. You should block an encoding only if you're sure it's for a language you can't read.

Blocking phishing scams

Phishing is perhaps the most prevalent threat on the Internet today. *Phishing* is when people send out e-mail messages that appear to be from legitimate banks and businesses where people have accounts. They tell people that there's a problem with their account or offer a special promotion and instruct them to log in to their accounts. Unaware, users dutifully follow the instructions, not realizing that the place where they're signing in and divulging their user name, password, and other personal information is *not* the company the message and Web page purport to be. It's an imposter posing as a legitimate business to steal information.

Phishing scams such as that are prevalent because they work. People see a name and logo they recognize, so they assume that the e-mail and page are legitimate. Unfortunately, names and logos mean nothing in e-mail messages and Web pages. Anyone with even rudimentary computer skills can copy them from legitimate Web sites and paste them into their own fraudulent e-mails, and they do it all the time. This is how they lure innocent folk into divulging information that leads to identity theft and unauthorized withdrawals from bank accounts.

On the Phishing tab of the Junk E-Mail Options dialog box, I *strongly* advise choosing both options, Protect My Inbox from Messages with Potential Phishing Links and Move Phishing E-mail to the Junk Mail Folder, as shown in Figure 18-31.

Click OK after choosing your Junk E-mail Options. Next, I show you ways of dealing with junk e-mail.

FIGURE 18-31

Protection from phishing scams.

Managing junk mail and good mail

Whatever settings you chose in the Junk E-mail Options dialog box will be active from that point forward. So when you click Sync to check your mail, some messages will go straight to your Junk Mail folder, others to your Inbox. For example, if you chose the Safe List Only option, only e-mail messages for senders on your safe list land in your Inbox. Everything else goes to the Junk Mail folder.

Regardless of how you set up your Junk Mail Options, you should occasionally click Junk E-Mail in the Folders list and take a quick look through your junk mail. Remember, Windows Live Mail doesn't really know whether a message is junk. It's just acting in accordance with options you chose in the dialog box, which are based on different levels of analysis by Windows Live Mail. So some perfectly legitimate e-mail messages might occasionally land in your Junk Mail folder.

If you find a valid e-mail message in your Junk Mail folder, right-click its message header and choose Junk E-mail. You see the options shown in Figure 18-32. Choose whichever option best describes what you want to do. For example, you can choose Add Sender to Safe Senders List so that no future messages from that sender end up in your Junk Mail folder.

Tip

Phishing scams are a favorite form of identity theft, largely because they work. The Phishing Filter alerts you to potentially fraudulent messages. ■

FIGURE 18-32

Junk E-mail Options for a message.

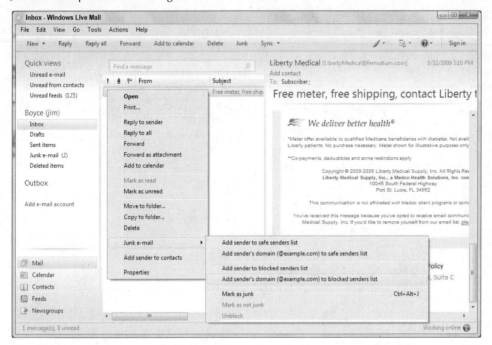

Phishing scam e-mails

If you've enabled phishing scam protection, e-mail messages that could be phishing scams are marked by a red shield with the message header shown in red. Windows Live Mail also displays a warning dialog box like the one shown in Figure 18-33. When you click the message header in the Message list, you see Delete and Unblock options in the header in the reading pane, as shown in Figure 18-34. There's no way for Windows Live Mail to know for sure whether an e-mail is really a phishing scam. It's just looking for indicators in the message.

FIGURE 18-33

Phishing attempt warning dialog box.

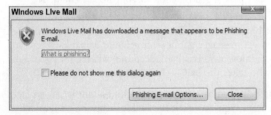

FIGURE 18-34

Phishing attempt warning in reading pane.

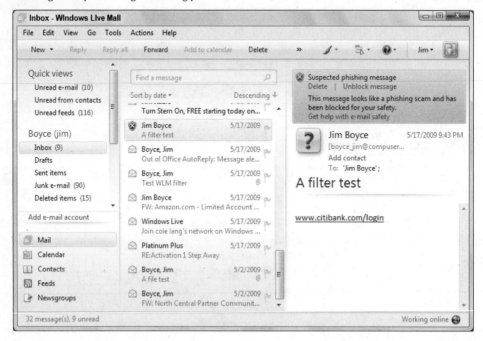

For example, the bogus message I created and show in Figure 18-35 has been marked as a potential phishing scam because of the Click Here to Active Your Account link. An obvious grammatical error like this is usually a pretty good indication of a scam in itself. Legitimate companies tend to be more careful about such things. But that's not the reason that Windows Live Mail marked it as a phishing scam.

The real reason shows in the status bar at the bottom of the window. The message is supposedly from a bank. But when I point to the link, the status bar shows that the link target isn't the bank's Web site. Rather, it's a link to a server's IP address. That's the main reason that this message is marked as a potential phishing scam. The message appears to be from a legitimate bank, but a link in the message actually sends you to some other Web site that doesn't match the URL's text.

Tip

You can point to any hyperlink in any e-mail message to see the link target in the status bar. You can use this simple technique to bust any phishing scam, with or without phishing protection in your e-mail client. ■

PayPal and eBay accounts are favorite targets of phishing scams. Banks are also favorite targets because that's where the money is. That's why you often get messages about your account at banks where you don't even have an account. The scammers don't know who has bank accounts where. They just send the scam message to virtually everyone to see who takes the bait — hence the name "phishing."

Once in a while, you get an e-mail message that's flagged as a potential phishing scam when, in fact, it's not. If you're certain that a message isn't a scam, you can click the Unblock button to unblock

FIGURE 18-35

Status bar shows true destination of a link.

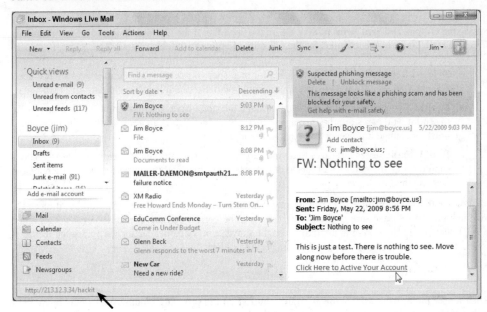

the message. If the message is in your Junk Mail folder, it will disappear into your Inbox, where you can treat it as any other normal e-mail message. But if you're not absolutely sure, your best bet would be to delete the message. Or forward it to the company that the scammers are impersonating.

Tip

The Microsoft Safety home page at `www.microsoft.com/mscorp/safety/` is a good resource for keeping abreast of trends in online safety. ■

Managing Mail Folders and Messages

All your e-mail messages are organized into *mail folders*. Those mail folders are different from the document folders discussed in Chapter 28 because you get to them through the Windows Live Mail program, not from Explorer. Windows Live Mail comes with several predefined folders for storing messages. Those folders are listed in the Folders list at the left side of the Windows Live Mail program. They include

- **Inbox:** If you don't use junk mail filtering, every e-mail message you receive is stored in this folder. With junk mail filtering, only messages that get through the filter are stored in this folder.

- **Outbox:** Messages you send are stored in this folder until you click the Sync button or Windows Live Mail automatically performs a synchronization.

- **Sent Items:** Stores a copy of every e-mail message you send, provided that Windows Live Mail is configured to store copies of sent messages.

Note

Options for using the Outbox and Sent Items folders are on the Send tab of the Options dialog box. See "Personalizing Windows Live Mail," later in this chapter, for the full suite of options available to you. ■

- **Deleted Items:** Acts like a wastebasket for messages you delete. Deleted messages are not permanently removed from your computer until you delete them from this folder.

- **Drafts:** If you start writing an e-mail message but don't have time to complete it or aren't ready to send it, you can store the message in this folder. Later, you can come back to the message, finish or change it however you like, and send it.

- **Junk E-mail:** Stores messages that your junk mail filter settings have deemed junk mail. You should check the contents of this folder to make sure that nothing important got in there before deleting them.

Mail folders that contain unread e-mail messages have a number to the right. The number indicates how may unread messages are in that folder. To view the contents of any e-mail folder, click its name in the folder pane. The contents pane to the right shows a message header for each message in the folder. The message headers for unread messages are boldfaced.

Tip

When you click a mail folder name, the status bar at the bottom of the program window shows how many messages are in that folder and how many of them are unread. ■

Choosing columns for the Message list

The Message list shows a message header for each message in a mail folder. You can customize that list to show information that's relevant to how you use Windows Live Mail. For starters, when the Message list is displaying single-line view, you can choose columns for display in that list. If the Message list is showing two-line view, first switch to one-line view (choose View ➪ Layout, click Message List, select Two-Line View, and click OK). Then, follow these steps to add columns:

1. Choose View ➪ Columns from the Windows Live Mail menu bar. Or right-click a column and choose Columns. The Columns dialog box shown in Figure 18-36 opens.

2. Select the columns you want to see. Deselect columns you don't want to see. Your choices are:

   - **Priority:** This column shows an exclamation point for messages marked high-priority by the sender; it shows a blue down-arrow for messages marked low priority; and it shows nothing for normal priority messages.

   - **Attachment:** Shows a paper clip for messages that have attached files.

   - **Flag:** Provides an easy way for you to mark messages that require more attention later.

   - **From:** Shows the sender's name.

   - **Subject:** Shows the subject of the message.

   - **Date:** Shows the date and time received.

   - **To:** Shows to whom each message is addressed. This is especially handy if you use Windows Live Mail to manage multiple e-mail accounts.

FIGURE 18-36

The Columns dialog box.

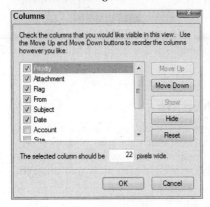

- **Account:** Shows the name of the e-mail account from which each message was downloaded. This is handy if you use Windows Live Mail to manage multiple accounts.

- **Size:** Shows the file size of the message and its attachments (if any).

- **Sent:** Shows the date and time that each message was sent.

- **Watched Items:** Used mainly with newsgroups (see Chapter 20) to color-code ongoing conversations you're watching.

3. Optionally, click any selected column name and use the Move Up or Move Down button to change its position in the list. (You can also rearrange columns after you exit the Columns dialog box.)

4. Optionally, click any selected column name and set its width in pixels.

Tip

You may find moving and sizing columns easier after you exit the Columns dialog box. See "Sizing and positioning columns," earlier in this chapter. ■

5. Optionally, click the Reset button if all you want to do is get back to the columns that Windows Live Mail displays by default.

6. Click OK.

Tip

Clicking the Show and Hide buttons has the same effect as selecting and clearing check boxes. ■

The column names appear across the top of the contents pane. If there are more than will fit in the available space, use the horizontal scroll bar below the message headers to scroll left and right. You can also rearrange columns and change their widths using techniques described in "Sizing and positioning columns," earlier in this chapter.

You can sort message headers based on information in any column. Just click the column heading on which you want to base the sort.

- An up-pointing arrow in the column heading means that the headers are in ascending order (A to Z, or newest to oldest, or smallest to largest).

- A down-pointing arrow indicates descending order (Z to A, or largest to smallest, or oldest to newest).

Click the heading to switch between ascending and descending order. For example, to put the newest messages at the top of the list, click the Received column heading until that column heading shows a down-pointing triangle.

Flagging messages that need more attention

The Flag column is wonderfully simple to use and worth its weight in gold. Say that you read a mail message and know it needs more attention but you can't give it the time right now. Click the Flag column for that message header. A little red flag appears, which acts as a perfect visual reminder. Of course, you can click the Flag column heading (once or twice) to quickly move all flagged messages to the top of the list.

When you've finally given the message the attention it needs, click the little flag next to its header. The flag disappears.

Grouping conversation messages

Sometimes you get into an e-mail situation in which someone writes you a message and you send a reply. That person replies to your reply. Then you in turn reply. This kind of back-and-forth communication is often referred to as a *conversation* because it is like a spoken conversation. It is also referred to as a *message thread*.

The message headers for these conversations don't usually look special in Windows Live Mail, other than the fact that messages to which you've already replied have a reply arrow in their icon.

You can get better organized and save some space by grouping those conversational messages together. Just choose View ➪ View by Conversation from the menu bar.

When the messages are grouped, you have two ways to view them. In the *collapsed* view, only one of the message headers is visible. Reducing all the messages in the conversation to a single header like that can save a lot of space, as well as make it easier to treat the whole conversation as a unit.

When you need to see messages within the conversation, just click the plus (+) sign. The conversation expands to show all the original message headers. In that view, you can click any message header to review its contents. When you're done with that, just click the minus (−) sign next to the first header to collapse all the messages into a single unit again.

Of course, these are all just different ways you can organize and view messages in a conversation. If you decide you want to go back to the old way, just choose View ➪ View by Conversation from the menu again to turn that option off.

Filtering messages

Normally, Windows Live Mail makes all messages in a folder visible. Often, that's more messages than you really want or need to see. You have many ways to put some messages into hiding temporarily so that you don't have to go digging through them to find what you need. In this section I tell you about different ways you can put some messages into hiding temporarily to get them out of your way.

FIGURE 18-37

Views in the View menu.

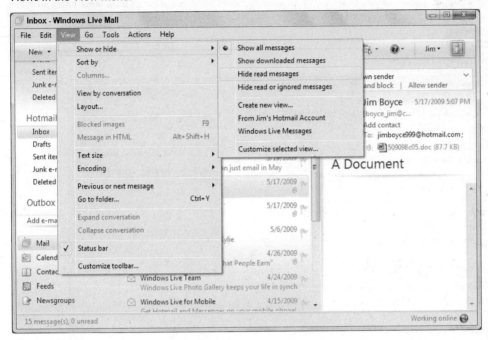

Choose View ➪ Show or Hide to display the menu shown in Figure 18-37. By default, this menu shows three views from which you can select to determine which messages appear in the Message list.

Note

Ignored messages are more relevant to newsgroups than e-mail. Therefore, I cover them in Chapter 20. ■

Each of those options on the cascading menu in Figure 18-38 is called a *view*. You can define your own custom views to gain more control over exactly which messages you want to put into hiding. To create a view, choose Views ➪ Show or Hide ➪ Create New View. The Define Views dialog box opens. It lists all your current views. Click the New button to open the New View dialog box and define a new view.

The first list in the New View dialog box contains options that let you specify conditions for your view. Scroll through the list in Box 1 to see all the different ways you can specify a condition for your view. Select the check box of whichever one helps you define a condition; then click the blue underlined text in Box 2 and type what you're looking for. For example, choose Where the From Line Contains People. In Box 2, click the Contains People link and type something from the sender's e-mail address that will identify his or her messages. Then click Add and OK.

You can repeat the process to define multiple conditions. Then at the bottom of Box 2, click the Show/Hide prompt and choose whether you want to show or hide messages that meet the conditions. When you're done, give the view a meaningful name of your own choosing. Then click OK. With the new view listed in the Define Views dialog box, click the view and then click Apply View. Choose whether to apply the view to the currently selected folder only or to all folders. Next, click OK to apply the view.

For example, Figure 18-38 shows a custom view named This Week. That custom view hides all messages received more than seven days ago.

Sample view named This Week.

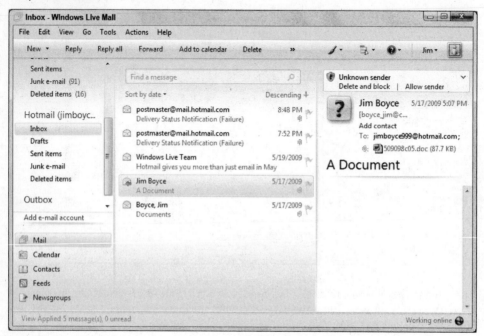

As your collection of e-mail messages grows, you'll probably come up with ideas for new views. That's not a problem because you can create a new view at any time. You can have as many views as you like. You can change or delete any view at any time. Just choose View ➪ Show or Hide ➪ Create New View from the Windows Live Mail menu bar and the rest is easy.

Once a custom view has been applied to a folder, it is listed on the View button. For example, you can see my new This Week view on the cascading menu in Figure 18-39. To apply a view, just click that view's name. To remove the view (un-apply, not delete), choose the Show All Messages view.

Filtering is a great way to quickly narrow down visible messages to those you wish to see. Still, you may not want to keep all your e-mail messages in your Inbox, especially when you have hundreds or thousands of them. You might want to organize your e-mail messages into folders and subfolders, as you do with documents. No problem, because you can always . . .

Create your own mail folders

If you keep many of the e-mail messages that you receive, you might find it easiest to organize them into folders you've created yourself. That way, you don't have to go digging through every message in your Inbox each time you want to find a specific message.

FIGURE 18-39

Custom views on the drop-down menu.

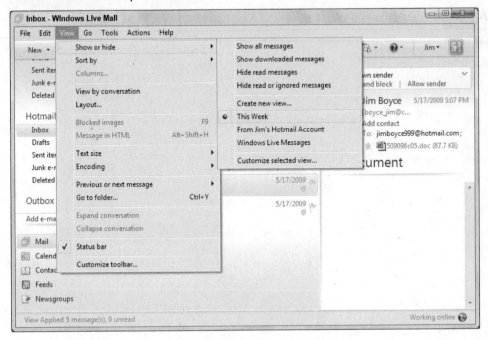

As you'll discover later in this chapter, any searches you conduct will look at your Inbox and its sub-folders by default. So to keep life simple, you should make any new folders as subfolders of the Inbox, or subfolders of some other folder you already put under Inbox. Either way, here's how you create a new folder:

1. Right-click the Inbox folder, or a custom folder that will act as parent to the new folder, and choose New Folder to open the Create Folder dialog box.

2. Type a name of your own choosing for your new folder.

3. If you didn't right-click the appropriate parent folder in Step 1, you can do so at the bottom of the Create Folder dialog box.

4. Click OK.

You can create as many folders as you wish. Figure 18-40 shows an example in which I've created folders for messages for various projects, companies, and categories. There is no right or wrong way to organize folders. Whatever makes sense to you is right for you.

Moving, renaming, and deleting mail folders

If you goof or change your mind after creating folders, it's no big deal. Use the following techniques to change things:

- To change the name of a folder, right-click its name and choose Rename. Edit the existing name or type the new name and then click OK.

- To move a folder (so that some other folder becomes its parent), drag the folder to the parent folder's name.

FIGURE 18-40

Custom mail folders.

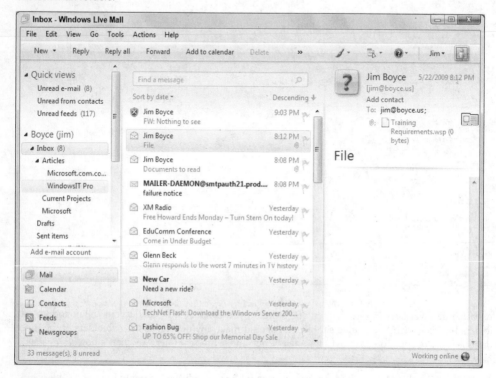

Caution

Deleting a folder also deletes all the messages in that folder. If the folder already contains messages you want to keep, make sure you move those messages to a different folder before you delete the folder. ■

- To delete a folder, right-click its name and choose Delete. Click Yes (if you're sure) when asked for confirmation.

Tip

To undelete a deleted folder, click the triangle next to the Deleted Items folder. If the deleted folder's name appears, drag it to some other folder to get it out of Deleted Items. ■

Showing/hiding mail folders

Mail folders form a collapsible tree, meaning you can show and hide things at will. If a folder contains subfolders, it will have either a black triangle or a white triangle to its left. A white triangle indicates that subfolders are hidden. Click that triangle to bring subfolders out of hiding. A black triangle means that subfolders are visible. Click that black triangle to put subfolders into hiding.

Tip

Don't forget that you can widen or narrow the Folder pane by dragging its inner border left or right. ∎

Managing messages

When you have some custom folders in place, you can start organizing your existing messages into those folders. If you already have many messages to deal with, you may not want to work with one message at a time. If you want to move (or delete) multiple messages, you first have to select their message headers.

Selecting multiple e-mail messages

You can select multiple messages and then move (or delete) them all in one fell swoop. Selected message headers are highlighted to look different from unselected headers. Figure 18-41 shows an example.

FIGURE 18-41

Selected message headers.

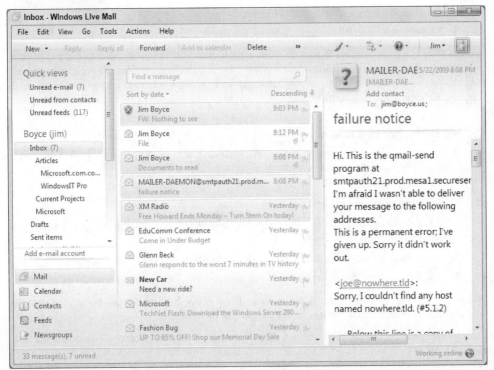

Before you select multiple headers, you might find it easiest to sort the messages in some order that clumps together the ones you want to select. Or if you've already created a view that isolates messages, choose that view name from the View menu to filter out messages you don't want to select. It's not necessary to sort or filter first — just an option worth considering.

You can use any of the following techniques to select multiple message headers. You know which headers are selected because they're highlighted:

- To select one message header, click anywhere on that header.

- To select message headers above that one, hold down the Shift key while pressing the up arrow (↑) or Page Up. Or to select messages below that one, hold down the Shift key while pressing the down arrow (↓) or Page Down.

- Press Shift+End to select all messages to the end of the list. Or press Shift+Home to select to the top of the list.

- To extend the selection range to another message header, Shift+click the header to which you want to extend the selection.

- To select (or deselect) a single message without deselecting all selected messages, Ctrl+Click the message header you want to select or deselect.

Tip

Shift+click means "hold down the Shift key on the keyboard while you click." Ctrl+click means "hold down the Ctrl key on the keyboard while you click." ■

- To select all message headers, press Ctrl+A.

- To deselect all selected headers, click any message header.

You can right-click any selected header to open, print, forward, or delete all the selected messages or to mark them all as read or unread. If you use the Flag column, you can click Actions and choose Flag Message to flag them all. You can also click any active toolbar button to perform a task on all the selected messages. You can also move all the selected messages to another folder, as described next.

Moving messages to a folder

The simple way to move a message to a folder is to just drag it from the contents pane to whatever folder you want to put it in. To move a bunch of messages, select their headers first. Then drag any selected header to the target folder.

Alternatively, if you don't like dragging, you can use this method:

1. Click the message header of the message you want to move or select the message headers you want to move.

2. Right-click the message header (or any selected header) and choose Move to Folder.

3. Click the name of the folder to which you want to move the message(s) and click OK.

Whichever method you use, the result is the same. The message headers disappear from the contents pane. To see them again, click whichever folder you put them in.

You can use Steps 1–3 to copy, rather than move, messages to a folder. You just have to choose Copy to Folder rather than Move to Folder in Step 2. Of course, with that approach, you end up with two copies of each message, one still in the original folder and another in the folder to which you copied.

Deleting messages

Deleting messages is easy to do. Click the message header for the message you want to delete or select headers of multiple messages to delete. Then do one of the following:

- Right-click the header (or any selected header) and choose Delete.
- Press the Delete key (Del).
- Drag the header or any selected header to the Deleted Items folder.

Regardless of which method you use, the messages are moved into your Deleted Items folder. They remain there until you clear out the Deleted Items folder or move the messages to a different folder. Just click the Deleted Items folder and drag any message you intended to keep to some other folder.

Permanently deleting messages

The messages aren't really deleted until you empty the Deleted Items folder. In that regard, they're still taking up space on your hard drive. To really get rid of the unwanted messages, you need to *empty* the Deleted Items folder. Emptying the Deleted Items folder permanently deletes the messages. There's no changing your mind and getting messages back after that point. So before you empty your Deleted Items folder, you may want to review the messages that are in there and move out any that you intended to keep.

To empty your Deleted Items folder, right-click its name in the folder pane and choose Empty Deleted Items folder (see Figure 18-42). Or choose Edit ⇨ Empty 'Deleted Items' Folder from the menu bar.

You see a message warning that the messages will be permanently deleted. You should have already verified that your Deleted Items folder doesn't contain anything you intended to keep before you go this far. If you didn't, you should choose No because that's your last chance to change your mind. But if you're certain that your Deleted Items folder contains nothing worth keeping, click Yes. The folder is emptied and the space they occupied on your hard drive is now available.

Auto-organizing messages through rules

If you're looking for the ultimate in organization, consider have Windows Live Mail organize your messages into your custom folders for you, as soon as they arrive. That'll save you from having to move them after the fact. To organize your messages automatically, you have to define some *message rules* that apply actions to messages based on certain conditions. The conditions can be just about anything: the sender's e-mail address or domain, a word or phrase in the Subject line, or a word or phrase in the body of the message.

You have a couple of ways to create a message rule. You can start from scratch or you can use an existing message as sort of a template for defining message rules. You can do either of the following to get started:

- To start from scratch, choose Tools ⇨ Messages Rules ⇨ Mail.
- To use an existing message as a template, click that message's header and choose Actions ⇨ Create Rule from Message.

Either way, the New Message Rule dialog box opens. In the first box, you define your conditions. You can define one condition or several. First, select the check box that best describes what part of the message contains the condition. For example, choose Where the Subject Line Contains Specific Words if you want the rule to be based on text in the Subject of the message.

FIGURE 18-42

Empty the Deleted Items folder.

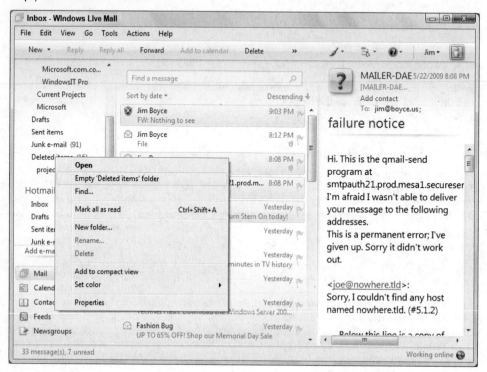

Then, in the box labeled To Edit This Description Click the Underline Words, click the link and type exactly what you're looking for. A new dialog box opens so that you can specify what you're looking for. Type in the word, phrase, or address you're looking for. Click the Add button. You can specify multiple terms, clicking Add after each one. Then click the Options button to specify the logic of the condition, such as the item does or does not contain the specified word, phrase, or address. Click OK.

Then go to the box labeled Select One or More Actions and specify what you want to do with messages that meet your condition. For example, choose Move It to the Specified Folder and then navigate to the folder in which you want the message placed. Next, in the Enter a Name For box, give your rule a name that will help you recognize it. Finally, click Save Rule.

Figure 18-43 shows an example. I've created a message rule that says "When you get a message that has 'Your order with Amazon.com,' put it into my 'Pending' folder" (which is a subfolder under my Online Purchases folder). I named that rule New Amazon Purchases.

To view existing rules or create new rules, choose Tools ➪ Message Rules ➪ Mail to open the Rules dialog box, which is where Windows Live Mail keeps all your rules. You can create as many rules as you like to move different kinds of messages to different folders, automatically delete certain messages, automatically forward certain messages, and even automatically reply to certain types of messages with a canned response. (More on that in a moment.)

FIGURE 18-43

A sample mail rule.

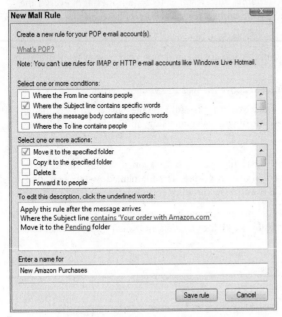

Of course, you don't have to define all your rules in one sitting. You can create, change, and delete message rules at any time. Most people create rules slowly over time. The trick is mainly to remember that you *can* create message rules. When you find yourself doing the same thing every time you get a certain type of message, think to yourself, "Hey, I could create a message rule to do this automatically." Then go in and create your new rule. Likewise, if you find that an existing rule isn't quite working out as planned, you can change the rule. Or you can delete it and come up with a better rule.

Tip

On the General tab of the Options dialog box, you should enable the Automatically Display Folders with Unread Messages option to ensure that you always see folders that contain new, unread messages in the folder pane. See "Personalizing Windows Live Mail," later in this chapter, if you need help with that. ∎

Auto-responding to messages

You can create a message rule that automatically responds to certain incoming messages (or all incoming messages). But before you go to the trouble, think about this: If the idea is to send an auto-response while you're away on vacation, the auto-responder works only if you leave your computer on and online the whole time you're away, and you configure Windows Live Mail to automatically check your messages occasionally.

If that's not realistic, you have to set up your auto-responder at the e-mail server, not in Windows Live Mail. Whether you can do that, and how, depends entirely on your mail service provider. You need to search its Web site or contact the company to find out whether an auto-responder is even an option, and if so, how to set one up.

Getting back to Windows Live Mail, you can certainly auto-respond to certain messages every time you check your mail. The first step is to define your canned response. Here's how:

1. Open Windows Live Mail and click the Create Mail button.

2. Leave the To and Cc lines empty. Fill in the Subject line and type your canned response in the body of the message.

3. Choose File ⇨ Save As from the menu bar above the message you just typed.

4. Navigate to the document folder in which you want to store the message (your Documents folder will do just fine), type in a filename of your own choosing, and click Save.

5. Close the window in which you wrote the message.

Now you have a canned response stored as an .eml file. To verify that, open the document folder in which you placed the message. Its icon looks like an envelope. The file named Auto-Rep.eml in Figure 18-44 shows an example. I use it as the example in the steps to follow.

Next, you need to set up a message rule that defines which messages get an auto-response. In Windows Live Mail, choose Tools ⇨ Message Rules ⇨ Mail to create a new mail message rule. Specify

Icon for a saved e-mail message (.eml file).

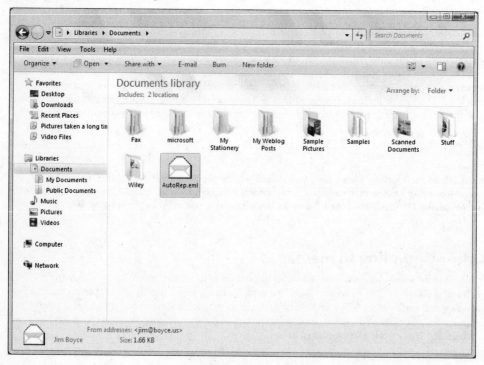

FIGURE 18-45

A sample message rule to auto-respond to some messages.

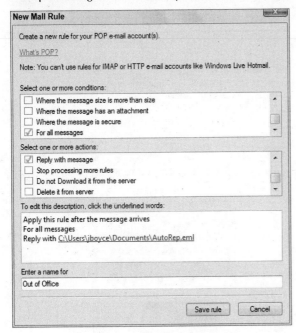

conditions that define messages that will get an auto-response. Use For All Messages to have the auto-response execute for all messages, or specify a more restrictive set of conditions.

For the rule action, choose Reply with Message. Then click the message link in the box below, navigate to the folder that contains your auto-response message, and double-click its icon. Figure 18-45 shows the basic design of my sample rule.

Unfortunately, you can't test the auto-responder by sending an e-mail message from your own account. If you try, you see a message indicating that no reply was sent because the incoming message was from your own account. But if you have access to some other account with a different e-mail address, you can test it from there.

Searching for Messages

As your collection of e-mail messages grows, it will become increasingly difficult to find specific messages, especially old messages you haven't looked at in months. Fortunately, Windows Live Mail has many of its own Search tools to help you find things.

To do a quick search for a word or phrase in a message header, use the Search box above the Message list. In Figure 18-46, it contains the phrase *Find a message*. As you type a word or phrase to search for, message headers that don't contain that word or phrase disappear. If no message headers contain the word or phrase, all the headers disappear. Press Esc or click the X at the right of the Search box to cancel that search and bring back all the message headers.

FIGURE 18-46

Search box and Find button.

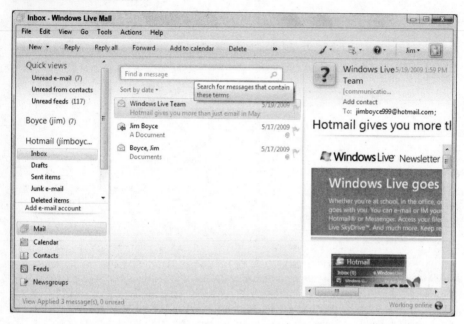

When you type a search phrase, a search scope drop-down list appears beside the Search box. By default, the drop-down list shows the name of the current folder. You can click All E-Mail to search all your mail folders.

Advanced Search

The Search box is great for quickly finding messages based on a word or phrase. In some situations, however, you might want to use more complex search criteria. For example, perhaps you want to search based on date received, or whether the message has an attachment or text in the subject, or some other basis.

To start an advanced search, choose Edit ➪ Find ➪ Message. Then just fill in the blanks to describe what you're searching for. You can fill in any number of boxes. For example, to search for messages that have a specific word or phrase in the subject line, type that word or phrase in the Subject box. To look for messages that have a certain word or phrase in the body of the message, type that word or phrase in the Message box.

You can also limit the search to messages sent before or after some date, to flagged messages, or to messages that have attachments. When you've finished filling in the blanks, click the Find Now button. Headers for messages that match your search criteria (if any) appear at the bottom of the Find Message window. If necessary, use the scroll bar to the right of the message headers to scroll through them. Optionally, you can enlarge the window to see more message headers.

If no messages match your search criteria, maybe you spelled a word wrong or used too many criteria. Click the New Search button and try again.

To open a found message, double-click its header in the lower pane. Optionally, you can right-click any message header to perform some task on that message. Or use commands from the menu bar at the top of the Find Message dialog box to do things with the message. As in the main Windows Live Mail program, you can select multiple found messages to perform some task on all of them in one fell swoop.

When you've finished with the Find Message dialog box, click its Close (X) button. Or choose File ➪ Close from its menu bar.

Tip
You don't really need to open Windows Live Mail to search for messages. You can launch your search right from the Start menu or the Search window. ∎

Searching from the Start menu

One of the beauties of Windows Live Mail is that all your messages are included in the search index of Windows 7. This means that you can search for any word or phrase in the body of any mail message right from the Start menu. For example, you can press ⊞, type a word, and see all files (including e-mail messages) that contain that word.

When typing in the Search box, you can also use To or From to limit the search to messages that are to or from a specific person or domain. For example, a search for from:susan finds only messages that have Susan in the From address. A search for to:susan finds only messages you sent to Susan. Use the keyword about: to search contents. For example, a search for body:deadline finds all messages that contain the word *deadline*. To limit the search to the message subject line, use the subject: keyword. For example, a search for subject:7 finds only messages that have "7" in the Subject line.

You can use AND and OR (uppercase letters) to specify multiple criteria. For example, a search for

from:alan AND body:excel

displays only messages from Alan that have the word *Excel* in the message body. A search for

to:susan OR from:susan

finds all messages that you sent to, or received from, Susan.

Tip
If you have lots of files and messages to deal with, the search index in Windows 7 is worth its weight in diamonds. But it takes a little time and knowledge to take advantage of all that it has to offer. See Chapters 30 and 31 for the whole story. ∎

Personalizing Windows Live Mail

You have many options for personalizing Windows Live Mail. Most are in its Options dialog box. You can open that dialog box at any time, and change any settings you like, by choosing Tools ➪ Options from the Windows Live Mail menu bar. The sections to follow look at settings on each tab of the Options dialog box. Some are more relevant to newsgroups than to e-mail. Newsgroups are covered in Chapter 20.

FIGURE 18-47

General tab.

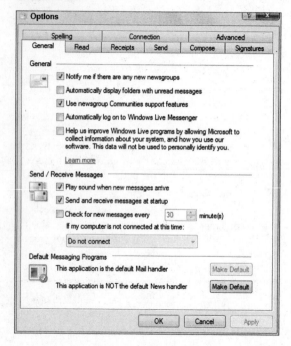

General options

The General tab displays the options shown in Figure 18-47. Here's a rundown of what they offer:

- **Notify Me If There Are Any New Newsgroups:** If you use Windows Live Mail to participate in newsgroups, choosing this option will ensure that you'll be notified when new newsgroups become available.

- **Automatically Display Folders with Unread Messages:** If you use message rules to automatically route messages to folders, you should choose this option. Otherwise, if a message gets routed to a subfolder that's currently hidden in the Folders list, you might not be aware of the new message.

- **Use Newsgroups Communities Support Features:** Choose this option to participate in newsgroups that offer technical support for Windows and other products.

- **Automatically Log On to Windows Live Messenger:** Choose this option to log in to Windows Live Messenger when you start Windows Live Mail.

Under the Send/Receive Messages heading, you find the following optional settings:

- **Play Sound When New Messages Arrive:** Choose this option to get a sound alert when new e-mail messages are downloaded to your Inbox.

- **Send and Receive Messages at Startup:** Choose this option if you want Windows Live Mail to automatically send and receive messages as soon as you open Windows Live Mail. If you don't choose this option, you must manually send and receive messages. Choose Tools ➪ Send/Receive from the menu bar, or click the Send/Receive button in the toolbar to manually send and/or receive messages.

- **Check for new messages every _x_ minutes:** Choose this option if you want Windows Live Mail to automatically check for new e-mail messages. If you choose this option, you can also set the number of minutes between checks.

- **If My Computer Is Not Connected at This Time:** If you've opted to let Windows Live Mail automatically check for new messages, use the drop-down button to choose whether you also want Windows Live Mail to connect automatically if it's offline. You can also specify whether this option overrides the Work Offline option, described in the following sidebar.

Under the Default Messaging Programs, you find options for making Windows Live Mail your default mail handler. If you use multiple e-mail clients and messaging programs, only one can be the default. The _default_ program is the one that appears when you perform a messaging-related task from outside your messaging program (such as double-clicking an e-mail message stored on disk).

If either Make Default button is dimmed, that just means that Windows Live Mail is already the default messaging program, so you don't need to do anything else there. But if some other program becomes the default messaging program, and you want to switch back to Windows Live Mail, the Make Default button(s) will be enabled so that you can go back to using Windows Live Mail as your default program.

Working Offline

Working offline is a means of using Windows Live Mail to manage messages without being online. This allows you to read and reply to e-mail messages without being online. You might want to use this feature to minimize your connection time if you use your regular voice telephone line to connect to the Internet, or if your ISP charges by the hour.

To work offline, choose File ➪ Work Offline from the Windows Live Mail menu bar. You see a Working Offline indicator in the status bar. You can read and reply to e-mail messages, but your replies will be stored in your Outbox. To get back online and send your replies, choose File ➪ Work Offline to deselect that option and go back online. Then click Sync to send out your pending messages.

Read options

The Read tab in the Options dialog box, shown in Figure 18-48, offers options for personalizing how Windows Live Mail displays and handles messages you receive. Most options are fairly simple and don't have any big effect on how you handle messages. The sections to follow relate to options on that tab.

FIGURE 18-48

Read tab.

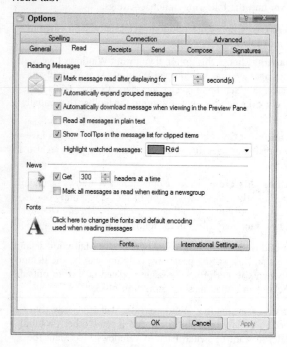

Mark message read after displaying for x seconds

When you first get a new batch of messages, their message headers are boldfaced and their icons show a closed envelope to distinguish them from older messages. The boldface signifies an unread message. When you click an unread message header to read the message, the header stays boldfaced for a few seconds. Exactly how many seconds depends on the number you specify for this setting. So if you feel that your messages are being switched from Unread to Read too quickly, you can change the default of 5 seconds to 10 or 15 seconds.

Then again, you can disable this setting altogether. If you do, unread messages will never be changed to read messages automatically. Every message will remain boldfaced until you right-click the message header and choose Mark As Unread.

Automatically expand grouped messages

If you use the Group Messages by Conversation feature, choosing this option causes messages to appear in the expanded rather than collapsed view. In newsgroups, it means that you see every message header rather than just the initial post for a thread. You can still expand or collapse any conversation by clicking the plus (+) or minus (−) sign in the message header.

Automatically download message when viewing in the Preview Pane

The option that sports this section's title is a newsgroup thing. Some newsgroup messages are quite large, and you don't necessarily want to download and install copies of them on your own computer.

Normally, it's not even necessary to download newsgroup messages because you can always view them on the newsgroup server.

But if you want to access the newsgroup messages offline, you can choose the Automatically Download Message When Viewing in the Preview Pane option so that each newsgroup message is downloaded as soon as you display it in your Preview pane.

Read all messages in plain text

Choosing this option removes HTML and graphics from e-mail messages you receive so that every message contains plain text. There's no technical advantage to this. Some people just prefer plain text to fancy formatting.

Show ToolTips in the message list for clipped items

Here's another simple option for message headers. If selected, this option lets you see information that's clipped off in a column. For example, say that the Subject line for a message is too wide for the Subject column in the contents pane. When this feature is selected, you just have to touch the tip of the mouse pointer to that subject line. The entire line will appear in a tooltip near the mouse pointer.

Highlight watched messages

This setting relates to the optional Watch/Ignore column in the contents pane. When you click in that pane to watch a conversation, the text of that header usually turns red. Use this option to make the message turn to some color other than red.

News settings

Options under the News heading control how many message headers get downloaded each time you connect to the group, and whether they're marked as Read. These settings apply only to newsgroups. I talk about these options in Chapter 20, where they're more relevant.

Fonts settings

The Fonts settings on the Read tab set default fonts and encodings for reading (not writing) e-mail messages. The default encoding should be Western European for English and similar languages. Use other encodings for Chinese, Arabic, and other languages that require special characters. But the fonts you choose and their size are entirely up to you.

Receipt options

The Receipts tab of the Options dialog box lets you configure both sending and receiving read receipts. A read receipt is a message that is sent to the sender of a message when that message that has been read. Depending on how Windows Live Mail is configured, it will either send the read receipt automatically or prompt you to let it send the receipt. In the latter case, if you click Yes, the sender gets an e-mail message verifying that you read the message. Options on the Receipts tab are mostly self-explanatory.

If you choose the Request a Read Receipt for All Sent Messages option, every e-mail message you send will automatically request a read receipt. If you don't choose this option, you can still request a read receipt for any message you write. Just choose Tools ➪ Request Read Receipt before you click the Send button in the New Message window.

The options under Returning Read Receipts apply to how you respond when someone sends you a read receipt. They are self-explanatory.

Caution

For security reasons, choosing Always Send a Read Receipt is a bad idea. Spammers and identity thieves can use read receipts to verify e-mail addresses. ■

Clicking the Secure Receipts button displays the options shown in Figure 18-49.

Secure Receipt Options dialog box.

Those options apply only if you already have a digital signature. (I talk about digital signatures earlier in this chapter.) The options are the same as for regular receipts but apply only to e-mail messages that you digitally sign.

Send options

The Send tab (see Figure 18-50) offers options that control how and when the messages that you write are sent. Here's what each option means:

- **Save Copy of Sent Messages in the 'Sent Items' Folder:** Select this option to keep a record of all sent e-mail messages in your Sent Items folder. It's a great way to keep track of what you've sent.

- **Send Messages Immediately:** If you choose this option, every message you write is sent as soon as you click the Send button. Otherwise, each sent message goes to your Outbox and isn't actually sent until you click Send/Receive.

- **Automatically Put People I Reply To in My Address Book after the Third Reply:** Choose this to automatically add people to your Contacts list after you have replied to e-mails from them for a third time. You can add, change, or remove contacts at any time.

- **Include Message in Reply:** Choosing this option just ensures that when you reply to an e-mail message, a copy of the message to which you're replying appears below your reply. This is a good thing because it allows the original sender to review the message to which you're responding.

FIGURE 18-50

The Send tab of the Options dialog box.

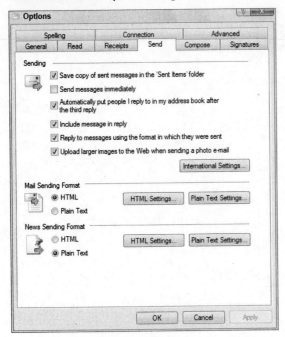

- **Reply to Messages Using the Format in Which They Were Sent:** Choosing this option keeps your replies in sync with messages received. For example, if someone sends you a plain-text message, your reply is also in plain text, even if you chose HTML as your Mail Sending Format.

- **Upload Larger Images to the Web when Sending a Photo E-Mail:** For a Windows Live Mail e-mail account, when this option is enabled Windows Live Mail uploads photos to your Windows Live Mail account when you send a photo e-mail.

- **Mail Sending Format:** Choose HTML or Plain Text as the default for new messages you compose. See "Composing Rich-Text Messages with HTML," earlier in this chapter, for more information.

- **News Sending Format:** Same idea as above but applies only to newsgroup messages. See Chapter 20 for more information on newsgroups.

Compose options

The Compose tab in the Windows Live Mail Options dialog box, shown in Figure 18-51, lets you define default settings for the e-mail messages you write.

Compose font

Use the Font Settings button next to the Mail heading to choose a default font for the e-mail messages you type. You can choose a different default font for newsgroup messages.

FIGURE 18-51

The Compose tab of the Windows Live Mail Options dialog box.

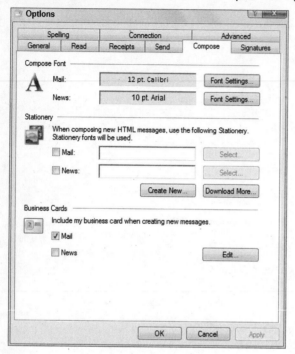

Stationery

A stationery is a background color, picture, or pattern for electronic messages. If you want to use stationery on all (or most) of the e-mail messages you send, select the Mail check box. Then click Select and pick whichever stationery you like best. You can do the same for newsgroups. But you might not want to do so because newsgroup folk tend to prefer to keep things plain and simple.

If you define a default stationery, it appears as the background every time you click Create Mail to create a new e-mail message. If, for whatever reason, you don't want to use the stationery in the message you're about to write, choose Format ⇨ Apply Stationery ⇨ No Stationery to remove the stationery from that one message.

Tip

Click Create New in the Select Stationery dialog box to create your own custom stationery. ■

Business cards

In the online world, the goal is generally to *never* expose personally identifiable information such as your home address and phone number unless you're setting up an account through a secure Web site with a business you know and trust. People who expose personally identifiable information online expose themselves to identity theft and other risks.

FIGURE 18-52

The Edit Contact dialog box.

However, if you have a Web site, an eBay store, or your own business, chances are you do want to promote it online. One way to do that is by creating a signature that shows relevant information at the bottom of e-mail messages you send. Another way is to attach a virtual business card to your e-mail messages. A virtual business card is like a real business card, except that no paper is involved. A virtual business card makes it easy for people to add your business or site to their Windows Contacts or Windows Live Mail Contacts.

The first step to adding a virtual business card is to edit your business card information. To do so, choose Tools ➪ Options, click the Compose tab, and click Edit. In the Edit Contact dialog box (Figure 18-52), enter your information. Include only the information you would put on a real business card. That is, don't include your home address or phone number but rather the business URL, e-mail address, or whatever else seems appropriate. Click Save to save the changes.

Tip

See Chapter 21 for more information on creating and using Windows Contacts. ■

To add the business card to your e-mail messages, get back to the Compose tab of the Windows Live Mail Options dialog box and select Mail under Include My Business Card When Creating New

Messages. Select the Mail check box. Optionally, click the Edit button to review or edit the contact information.

After you've activated the card and clicked OK to leave the Options dialog box, every message you send includes your business card. When a recipient receives your message, the card appears as an icon in the preview pane header, as shown in Figure 18-53. The recipient can click the card icon to open and view the card, and then click Add to Contacts to add the card to his or her Windows Contacts.

FIGURE 18-53

Business card icon.

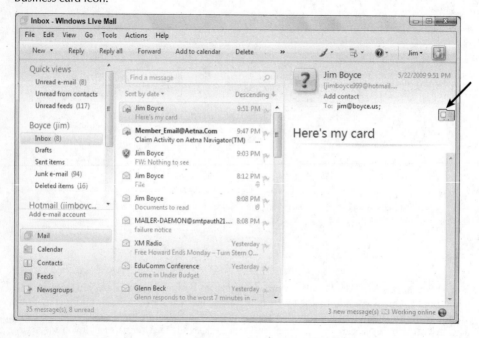

Signature options

The Signature tab of the Options dialog box allows you to create one or more signatures for your e-mail messages. The signature appears at the bottom of every e-mail message you compose. For more information on signatures, see "Adding a signature automatically," earlier in this chapter.

Spelling options

The Spelling tab in the Options dialog box lets you configure spell-checking in e-mail messages. Most options are self-explanatory. The main option to consider is the one named Always Check Spelling before Sending. Selecting that option causes the spell checker to check your spelling as soon as you click Send after writing a message.

If you don't select the Always Check Spelling before Sending option, spell-checking never kicks in automatically. You have to click the Spelling button, or press F7, or choose Tools ➪ Spelling from the New Message menu bar to start the spell-checker manually.

Connection options

The Connection tab of the Windows Live Mail Options dialog box lets you configure Windows Live Mail for a dial-up Internet connection. The first option, Ask before Switching Dial-Up Connections, just displays a prompt if Windows Live Mail has to switch to a separate dial-up account to access e-mail.

The second option, Hang Up after Sending and Receiving, is self-explanatory. It's designed to minimize connection time.

By default, Windows Live Mail uses the same dial-up connection that Internet Explorer uses to access the Web. If you need to use a different account for Web mail, click the Change button and specify the account you want to use for e-mail.

Advanced options

The Advanced tab in the Windows Live Mail Options dialog box, shown in Figure 18-54, offers a mish-mash of options, mostly of interest to more advanced users. Options in the Settings list are described in the following sections.

FIGURE 18-54

Advanced tab in Windows Live Mail Options.

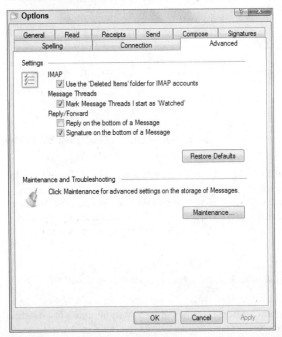

IMAP

IMAP stands for Internet Message Access Protocol. Most ISPs use POP3 (Post Office Protocol, Version 3) for e-mail. But if you happen to be configuring an IMAP account, know that when you delete a message from an IMAP folder, Windows Live Mail marks the message as deleted but leaves the message in your message list until that message has been deleted from the IMAP server.

If you want to remove messages from the IMAP message list when you delete them in Windows Live Mail, select the Use the Deleted Items Folder for IMAP Accounts check box. That way, when you delete an IMAP message in Windows Live Mail, you also delete it from the Message list.

Message threads

A message thread is an e-mail or newsgroup conversation. In Windows Live Mail, you can mark conversations as Watch or Ignore by clicking in the Watch/Ignore column. Message headers in watched conversations are colored to draw attention. If you choose the Mark Message Threads I Start As 'Watched' option, any new conversation you start is automatically marked as watched.

Reply/forward

The Reply/Forward options on the Advanced tab control where things appear in messages you reply to and forward. Normally, any text you type in a reply or forward appears above the original message. Similarly, if you use a custom signature, that signature appears above the original message (below the text you type in your message). The options under Reply/Forward change that positioning as follows:

- **Signature on the Bottom of a Message:** Choosing this option causes signatures to appear at the very bottom of a message to which you reply.

- **Reply on the Bottom of a Message:** Choosing this option causes any text you type in a reply to appear below, rather than above, the original message to which you're replying.

Outside the Settings list are a couple of buttons, described next.

Restore defaults

Clicking the Restore Defaults button changes the options listed under Settings back to their original default settings.

Maintenance and troubleshooting

Clicking the Maintenance button on the Advanced tab opens the Maintenance dialog box for Windows Live Mail, shown in Figure 18-55.

The Maintenance dialog box in the Windows Live Mail Options dialog box provides a few options for automatically managing e-mail messages. The first option, Empty Messages from the 'Deleted Items' Folder on Exit, permanently deletes all messages in the Deleted Items folder when you close Windows Live Mail. The advantage is that you free that disk space immediately. The disadvantage is that you lose the safety net of being able to restore accidentally deleted items before you permanently delete them.

The second option, Purge Deleted Messages When Leaving IMAP Folders, applies only to IMAP e-mail accounts. If selected, this option permanently deletes any messages you marked for deletion as soon as you leave the folder.

The Purge newsgroup message in the background option is for newsgroups only. Purging has no effect on e-mail. The Delete Read Message Bodies in Newsgroups option deletes the body of any newsgroup message after you've read the message. The Delete New Messages *X* Days after Being Downloaded automatically deletes messages after *x* number of days.

FIGURE 18-55

Windows Live Mail Maintenance options dialog box.

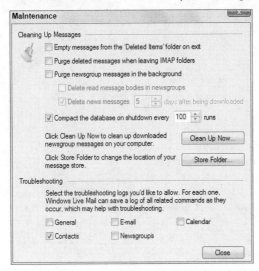

All Windows Live Mail messages are stored as files on your computer's hard drive. Although that's not a true database, Microsoft refers to it as such. As your collection of messages grows, so does that database. Compacting the database helps keep it to a reasonable size. Windows Live Mail doesn't compact the database in the sense of compressing it as you would a Zip folder. Instead, it deletes certain items to take up less space on disk.

The Compact the Database on Shutdown Every *X* Runs option, if selected, automatically displays a little message that reminds you to compact that database occasionally. The default is to display it after every 100 runs, which is fine. But you could change that number to compact more or less frequently. If you deselect the check box, Windows Live Mail will never remind you to compact the database.

The Clean Up Now button lets you delete message bodies, or headers and bodies, from subscribed newsgroups. It has no effect on e-mail messages. Optionally, you can reset all the newsgroup folders so that newsgroup headers are downloaded the next time you connect.

The Store Folder button shows you where messages are stored. By default, this is `C:\Users\ UserAcct\AppData\Local\Microsoft\Windows Live Mail`, where *UserAcct* is the username for the user account into which you're currently logged.

You can change the message store folder to some other location. That might be handy if you need to store your mail on a drive with more space than the default location.

The Troubleshooting options create log files of activity for advanced troubleshooting. The log files are stored in the message store folder. The log files contain copies of commands sent to and from servers. There is no "user friendly" information in the log files. These log files are strictly for advanced network and system administrators who are familiar with the commands sent to and from servers.

FIGURE 18-56

Security tab of the Safety Options dialog box.

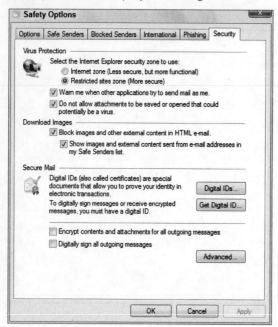

E-mail security options

To access the security-related settings for Windows Live Mail, choose Tools ➪ Safety Options and then click the Security tab. The Security tab in the Safety Options dialog box (see Figure 18-56) provides some options for protecting yourself from e-mail security threats. These are no substitute for the full set of security tools discussed in Part II of this book. Rather, they're extra touches provided by Windows Live Mail for making e-mail safer. The options on the tab are divided into three categories, as described next.

Virus protection

In the Virus Protection section, your first option is to choose between Internet Zone and Restricted Sites Zone. The Internet Zone uses settings defined in Internet Explorer. This setting allows certain scripts and add-ons to work in Windows Live Mail. However, this setting is best used only by professionals who need scripts and add-ons and can distinguish between those that are safe and those that aren't.

For everyone else, the Restricted Sites Zone is the preferred choice. Although slightly more restrictive, it's also a lot safer. Most likely, the things the Restricted Sites Zone prevents you from using are things you don't want on your computer in the first place.

Most viruses spread through e-mail attachments. After your computer is infected, the virus sends copies of itself to people in your Contacts list. You won't be aware this is happening unless you choose Warn Me When Other Applications Try to Send Mail As Me. With that option selected, you see a warning message when the virus attempts to spread itself to one of your e-mail contacts. At that point, you know you picked up a virus and your first task should be to get rid of that virus.

The Do Not Allow Attachments to Be Saved or Opened That Could Potentially Be a Virus option blocks e-mail attachments that could be a virus. It does not detect actual viruses. Unfortunately, there are many file types that *could* contain a virus. So choosing this option will prevent you from opening or saving many attachments that are virus-free and perfectly safe. If you have virus protection through your ISP or on your system that's blocking infected attachments, it's okay to deselect this option. You don' need to worry about files that could contain a virus if your antivirus software is already preventing such attachments from reaching your Inbox.

Download images

The Block images and other external content in HTML e-mail option is designed to protect you from certain types of spyware attacks associated with pictures and other external content in e-mail messages. Choosing this option also has the fringe benefit of speeding up your message downloads, especially if you're using a dial-up connection.

Blocked images in e-mail messages appear as a box with a red X and some text in place of the picture. Above such messages, you see a bar telling you that pictures have been blocked along with an instruction to click that bar to download the images, as in Figure 18-57.

FIGURE 18-57

Blocked images example.

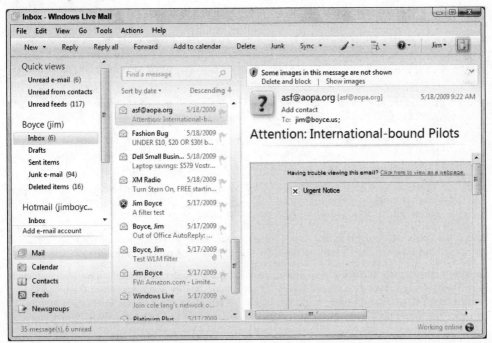

What you do from here depends on whom the e-mail message is from:

- If the message is from someone you know and trust, and you want to see the images, just click the bar as instructed. The images are downloaded and placed right where they belong.

- If the message is not from someone you know and trust, your safest bet is to *not* download the images. Just move on to the next message. Or take a look at the text of the message without the images in place and then decide whether you really want to see the missing pictures.

Secure mail

The Secure Mail options all concern the use of digital IDs. These options are relevant only if you already have a digital ID or you acquire one by clicking Get Digital ID. Digital IDs are a fairly large topic that I address later in this chapter, in "Securing E-mail with Digital IDs."

New Feature

Windows Live Mail adds its own Contacts folder, which you can use to store e-mail addresses, phone numbers, and other contact information.

Working with Contacts

Windows Live Mail includes a Contacts folder that you use to store contact information for people with whom you regularly communicate, whether by e-mail or other method. If you are familiar with the Windows Contacts folder discussed in Chapter 21, you should have no problems working with Contacts in Windows Live Mail. Understand, however, that the two are not the same thing. The contacts stored in Windows Live Mail are separate from the contacts stored in your Windows Contacts folder.

To open the Contacts folder, just click the Contacts shortcut icon in the folder pane. Figure 18-58 shows the Contacts folder with a couple of sample contacts.

What the Contacts folder displays depends on the type of e-mail account you are using. If you have a Windows Live account, the Contacts folder shows the contacts from that account. If you have a POP3 account with another mail provider, the contacts for that account appear in the folder.

By default, Windows Live Mail creates a contact for you using the name and e-mail address you specified when you set up the account (unless you are using a Windows Live account). To view or modify a contact, simply double-click the contact to open it (Figure 18-59).

Editing the contact is straightforward. Just click a category link on the left side of the Edit Contact dialog box and then use the controls in the right side to edit your contact information.

Creating a new contact is equally easy. Just open the Contacts folder in Windows Live Mail and click New. Windows Live Mail displays an Add a Contact dialog box in which you enter the contact's information. The Quick Add page, shown in Figure 18-60, gives you a means for quickly adding a contact when you need only the name, e-mail address, phone, and company fields. When you're satisfied with the contact's content, click Add Contact to save the contact and close the Add a Contact dialog box.

FIGURE 18-58

The Contacts folder.

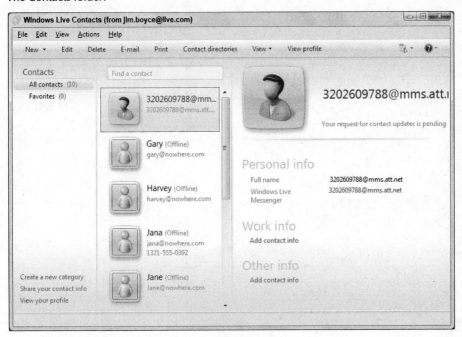

Sending e-mail to contacts

You almost surely want to use the Contacts folder to address e-mail, and Windows Live Mail gives you a couple of ways to do just that. First, you can click the To, Cc, or Bcc button in the message form to open the Send an E-mail dialog box, which lists the contacts in your Contacts folder. Just click a contact in the list and click To, Cc, or Bcc to add the contact to the message.

You can also start an e-mail from the Contacts folder. With the Contacts folder open, select one or more contacts and then click E-mail in the toolbar. Windows Live Mail starts a new e-mail message with the selected contacts as the recipients. You can also select contacts and then right-click one of the selected contacts and choose Send E-mail from the context menu to start a new message to those recipients.

Tip

If you select a single contact that has more than one e-mail address, when you right-click the contact and choose Send E-mail, Windows Live Mail displays a cascading menu from which you can choose the e-mail address to use. ■

FIGURE 18-59

A contact in Windows Live Mail.

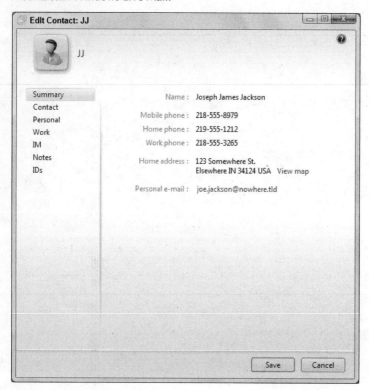

Printing contacts

As you might expect, Windows Live Mail gives you the capability to print the contacts stored in your Contacts folder. You have two formats from which to choose: memo or phone list. The memo format prints each contact with extended information, whereas the phone list prints only the name and phone numbers for the contacts, sorted alphabetically.

To print contacts, select one or more contacts in the Contacts folder and click Print in the toolbar. In the resulting Print dialog box, choose the printer, print type (Memo or Phone List), and whether to print all contacts or just the selected contacts. Set other print options as needed and then click Print.

Note

For more detailed information on working with the Windows Live Mail Contacts folder, see "Windows Live Essentials," from Wiley. ■

FIGURE 18-60

The Quick Add page.

New Feature

Windows Live Mail adds a Calendar folder, which you can use to keep track of appointments and events.

Using the Calendar

Windows Live Mail includes a Calendar folder that you can use to keep track of appointments and events. Figure 18-61 shows the Month view, but Calendar also offers Day and Week views.

On the left side of the Calendar window, the Navigation pane provides a date picker (small calendar for choosing dates) and access to the Calendar folder and Windows Live Mail folder shortcuts. The toolbar offers a small selection of commands for creating new events, choosing the view option, and printing calendar items. You can also choose a color for the calendar, access options, and view Help content.

FIGURE 18-61

The Calendar Month view.

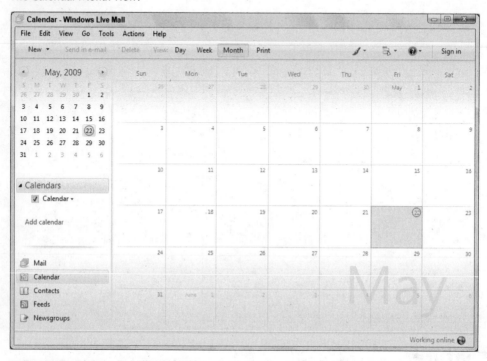

Adding an event

To add an event to the Calendar, open Windows Live Mail, open the Calendar folder, and click New in the toolbar. Windows Live Mail displays the New Event dialog box, shown in Figure 18-62.

Most of the fields on the New Event form are self-explanatory. If you have multiple calendars, you can choose on which calendar to add the item by selecting the calendar from the drop-down list. You can also choose how your availability will be seen by others, whether free, busy, tentative, or away.

If you upgraded to Windows 7 from Windows Vista and you had calendar items created in Windows Calendar, Windows Live Mail Setup imports those items when you install Windows Live Mail. In addition, if you have a Windows Live ID, Windows Live Mail can send you reminders before each event starts. So, if you have a Windows Live ID, you see an additional drop-down button in the New Event dialog box that lets you choose how far ahead of the event the reminder will be sent.

Creating a new calendar

As mentioned in the previous section, you can use multiple calendars in Windows Live Mail. For example, perhaps you want to maintain a personal calendar and a work calendar. Or, if you have a

Windows Live account, you can view your online calendar. That second option is covered in the next section. For now, I assume that you want to create a new calendar in Windows Live Mail.

FIGURE 18-62

The New Event dialog box.

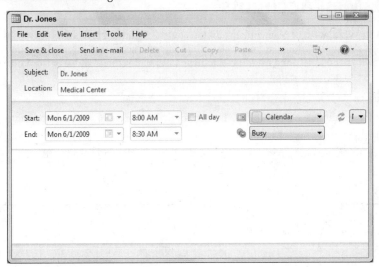

To create a new calendar, open the Calendar folder and click the down arrow beside the New button; then choose Calendar. In the Add a Calendar dialog box, type a name for your calendar, choose a background color, and add an option description. If this is to be your main calendar, select the Make This My Primary Calendar check box. Then click Save to create the new calendar.

After the new calendar is created, you can overlay it with your other calendar(s). In the folder pane, just select each of the calendars you want to view. Windows Live Mail automatically displays a merged view of all the selected calendars.

Working with your Windows Live Calendar

As discussed earlier, Windows Live Mail provides great integration with your Windows Live Calendar. You can manage your calendar on the Web at Home.live.com, or you can manage it within Windows Live Mail. If you make a change at either location, that change appears in both places. So, when you add an event in Windows Live Mail, it becomes visible from the Windows Live Web site.

Adding your Windows Live Calendar in Windows Live Mail is easy. Just log in to Windows Live and then open Windows Live Mail (or log in when you open Windows Live Mail). The calendar then shows up in the folder pane under Hotmail. You can view it along with any other calendars that you have created.

In the earlier section, "Adding an event," I explain that you can specify on which calendar to add a new event when you create the event. When you are working with a Windows Live Calendar, this is particularly important. You want to make sure you add the event to the right calendar because your Windows Live Calendar might be shared. You don't want to accidentally add a personal event or appointment to your shared calendar.

For more detailed information on using the Calendar in Windows Live Mail, see "Windows Live Essentials," from Wiley.

Managing E-Mail Accounts

The Options dialog box in Windows Live Mail contains options for the Windows Live Mail program as a whole. You can manage as many accounts as you wish within any user account. Each mail account that you create has its own settings, separate from the Windows Live Mail settings and separate from other mail accounts. To get to account settings:

1. From the menu bar in Windows Live Mail, choose Tools ➪ Accounts.

2. Under Mail in the Accounts dialog box, click the icon for the mail account you want to change and click Properties.

The Properties dialog box to the account opens, as shown in the example shown in Figure 18-63.

FIGURE 18-63

Properties for an e-mail account.

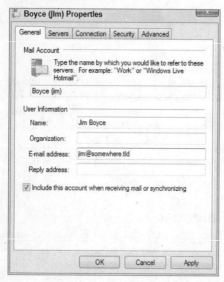

General

The settings on the General tab include:

- **Mail Account:** The name of the account. This can be any name you like.

- **Name:** Your name, a business name, or a nickname of your choosing. The name you type appears in the From column of recipient message headers.

- **Organization:** Can be any name you like. Does not appear in Windows Live Mail message headers.

- **E-Mail Address:** Your e-mail address. This address appears next to From when someone opens an e-mail message you sent.

- **Reply Address:** When a user replies to your message, this e-mail address is placed in the To line and the reply is sent to that address. It can be any e-mail address and need not be the same as the mail account you're configuring.

- **Include This Account When Receiving Mail or Synchronizing:** Clearing this option prevents the Send/Receive button from downloading messages from this account.

Servers

The Servers tab contains information about the incoming and outgoing mail servers, as well as authentication options. Change this information only if the account isn't working. Do not attempt to fix a broken account by guessing. The information you put on this tab must be exactly as required by your mail provider.

Connection

The Connection tab allows you to configure a specific network connection for the account. You don't need to change anything there if you have only a single Internet account.

Security

Use the Security tab to specify a certificate that will be used when you digitally sign outgoing e-mail messages, as well as for encrypting outgoing messages. Digitally signing a message provides digital proof that the message came from you, and was not spoofed (faked) by someone else. Encrypting a message prevents it from being read in transit. The certificates must already be installed on your computer before you set it in the Security tab. Last, you can specify the encryption algorithm from the drop-down list on the Security tab.

Note
I assume that if you need to use digital signing or encryption, you are using Windows Live Mail for work. That implies that you also probably have a technical support group that can help you with obtaining the needed certificates from a certification authority (CA). If not, visit www.verisign.com or www.thawte.com, or search the Web for a CA that provides certificates for digital signing and message encryption. ■

Advanced

The Advanced tab (Figure 18-64) lets you configure the ports used by the outgoing and incoming mail servers and determine whether those servers use SSL (covered previously). In addition, you can set the server timeout value that specifies how long Windows Live Mail waits for a response from the mail servers before timing out the connection.

The Break Apart Messages Larger Than nn KB option on the Advanced tab, if enabled, causes Windows Live Mail to divide messages larger than the specified size into multiple messages. I recommend that rather than use this option, you simply compress the file you are sending using WinZIP, Windows 7's Zip compression or other file compression tool.

FIGURE 18-64

Advanced tab of e-mail account properties.

The Delivery options on the Advanced tab include:

- **Leave a Copy of Messages on Server:** Windows Live Mail downloads a copy of the messages from the incoming mail server and leave the message on the server so that it can be retrieved again if needed. This is useful if you work from multiple computers and need to be able to check your mail from both of them.

- **Remove from Server after *nn* Day(s):** If you enable this option, Windows Live Mail removes messages from the server when they have been on the server longer than the time specified. Use this option to keep only a specified range of messages, such as from the last 30 days, on the server.

- **Remove from Server When Deleted from 'Deleted Items':** Remove items on the server when you delete them from your local Deleted Items folder.

Customizing the Toolbar

As do most programs, Windows Live Mail has a toolbar that provides one-click access to commonly used menu commands. Its buttons aren't set in stone, however. You can add and remove buttons at any time. To get started, right-click the Windows Live Mail toolbar and choose Customize Toolbar. The Customize Toolbar dialog box, shown in Figure 18-65, opens.

The rest is pretty easy. To add a button to the toolbar, click its name in the left column and click Add ►. To remove a button from the toolbar, click its name in the right column and choose ◄ Remove.

The top-to-bottom order of items in the right column reflects their left-to-right order on the toolbar. You can arrange buttons by dragging them up and down that right column. Or click any button name and use the Move Up and Move Down buttons to position the button.

FIGURE 18-65

Customize the Windows Live Mail toolbar.

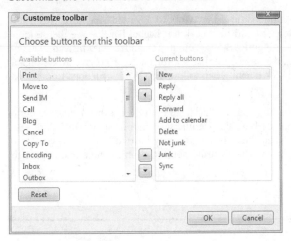

You can also customize the toolbar in the New Message window. Click Create Mail to open that window. Then right-click its toolbar and choose Customize Toolbar. In fact, you can customize the toolbar in most programs and windows that way. If in doubt, right-click the toolbar to find out.

Securing E-Mail with Digital IDs

Digital IDs are a form of security that brings confidentiality, integrity, and authentication to e-mail. The authentication part refers to the fact that when people get a digitally signed message from you, they know for a fact that it's from you and not some imposter posing as you. This is accomplished by digitally signing your e-mail message with your digital ID. You can digitally sign any and all messages, if you like.

The confidentiality and integrity parts mean that both you and the sender are assured that nobody has seen or tampered with the message in transit. This is accomplished through encryption. When you send the message, it gets encrypted into a secret code before it leaves your computer. If someone manages to grab hold of the message before it reaches the intended recipient, it doesn't do them any good. The message looks like meaningless gobbledygook and is impossible to decrypt.

When the intended recipient gets the message, however, it's automatically decrypted, and that person sees what you sent in its original form. To use encryption, both sender and recipient must have digital IDs.

Getting a digital ID

If you work for an organization that requires secure e-mail, your security administrator will likely acquire and install a digital ID for you. So you can skip this section if someone has already taken care of that for you. Otherwise, you have to get your own digital ID. The steps involved depend on the type of ID you get and who you get it from, so I can't really help you there. I should warn you, however, that this requires some technical expertise beyond the basic day-to-day stuff and beyond the scope of this book. You may need some help from a person who has a background in computer security.

The first step is to choose Tools ➪ Safety Options from the Windows Live Mail menu bar. Click the Security tab in the Safety Options dialog box and then click Get Digital ID. You see the options described previously in this chapter (refer to Figure 18-56). You aren't handed one. Instead, you're presented with links to various *certificate authorities* (CAs) that sell (or maybe even give away) digital IDs. You need to find one that's specifically for e-mail. Then follow the CA's instructions to download and install the ID.

When you've completed all the steps required by your certificate authority, click the Digital IDs button on the Security tab of the Safety Options dialog box. The Certificates window, shown in Figure 18-66, opens. You should see your certificate listed there. If not, you may have to Import it. Again, it all depends on whom you get your certificate from. There's really nothing I can say here that applies to all certificate authorities.

FIGURE 18-66

Security tab.

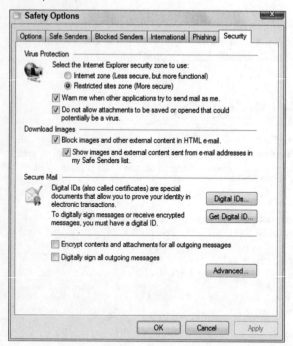

In the Certificates window, click your certificate and then click the Advanced button. Scroll through the list of certificate purposes. If Secure E-mail is listed but not selected, make sure you select that option. Click OK and Close, as necessary, to get back to the Windows Mail Options dialog box. If you have any problems, you need to consult your certificate authority for help.

At the bottom of the Security tab, you see two options related to digital IDs:

- **Encrypt Contents and Attachments for All Outgoing Messages:** Do *not* select this option unless you send e-mail only to people who can decrypt your messages. Better to leave this option deselected and encrypt messages on a case-by-case basis, as described later in this chapter.

- **Digitally Sign All Outgoing Messages:** You can choose this option to digitally sign all messages. Recipients don't need anything special to read digitally signed messages. Optionally, you can leave this option deselected and sign messages on a case-by-case basis.

Click OK to leave the Safety Options dialog box. You use your digital ID when composing messages to send to people.

Using your digital ID

To secure an e-mail message with your digital ID, compose your e-mail message as you normally do. Before you click Send, however, decide whether you want to digitally sign or encrypt the message, or both. You can also opt to request a digital receipt. (Only people who have their own digital ID can send a secure receipt.) Use the Digitally Sign Message and Encrypt toolbar buttons to sign and encrypt the message. Or choose Tools from the menu bar and choose whichever options you want.

Remember, you can send encrypted messages only to other people who have digital IDs. Furthermore, you must have a copy of that person's public encryption key. If you have trouble encrypting a message to such a person, have him or her send you a digitally signed e-message. When you get the message, open it. If you haven't already done so, add that person to your Contacts, (Right-click the message header and choose Add to Contacts.) The sender's public encryption key is added to Windows Live Mail so that you can send encrypted messages to that person from that point on.

If you're still unable to send an encrypted message to the person, open the digitally signed message he or she sent you by double-clicking its message header. In the open message, choose File ➪ Properties from the menu bar. Click the Security tab, click View Certificates, and then click Add to Contacts. Click OK in all open dialog boxes, close the message, and try again.

Note

A public encryption key is a file that allows you to send encrypted messages to a digital ID holder. When the recipient gets the message, that recipient's private key decrypts it. That's what keeps the messages confidential and tamper-proof. The holder of the digital ID is the only person who has the private key required to decrypt the message. ■

Figure 18-67 shows an example in which I've opted to digitally sign and encrypt a message to myself (for testing purposes). I've also requested a secure receipt. Checkmarks on the Tools menu show which options I've selected. The icons selected in the figure also show that the message is digitally signed and encrypted.

Tip

Use the Receipts tab of the Windows Live Mail Options dialog box to configure secure receipt defaults. ■

When you receive digitally signed messages, the only difference you notice is a small ribbon symbol to the left of the Subject in the message headers. When you click the message header, the preview pane header shows a similar ribbon. That symbol is your guarantee that the message is from the person who digitally signed the message and not from an imposter.

FIGURE 18-67

Tools menu in the New Message window.

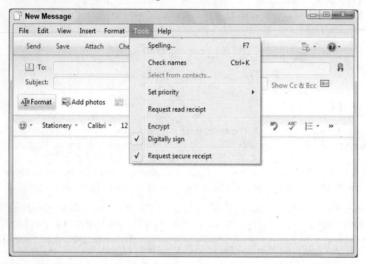

If the message was digitally encrypted, you see a lock symbol in the preview pane header. The message will be perfectly readable on your screen because Windows Live Mail will have already decrypted the message. The lock symbol is your guarantee that the message was encrypted during transit. Thus, nobody else has seen or tampered with the message since it left the sender's computer.

Importing Messages from Other Programs

If you were already using some other e-mail program prior to using Windows Live Mail, you may want to bring its messages into Windows Live Mail. This is called *importing messages*. You can also import account information if you haven't already set up Windows Live Mail to use an account.

There are limits to the types of message you can import. For example, it may not be possible to import messages from Web mail accounts that you manage through your Web browser. But it all depends on your ISP and e-mail client. So I can't tell you how to do this in a step-by-step manner. You may need to contact your ISP or e-mail service provider for help. All I can really show you is how to get the ball rolling:

1. Open Windows Live Mail (if you haven't done so already) and choose File ➪ Import ➪ Messages.

2. A wizard opens. Follow the instructions presented by the wizard to import messages.

How you proceed through the wizard depends on what you're importing. As with any wizard, it's simply a matter of reading and responding to whatever appears on the wizard page and clicking Next. Do so until you get to the last page and click Finish.

Exporting Messages to Other Programs

To copy messages from Windows Live Mail to another program, you *export* them. There's a limit to which programs you can export to, and no single set of rules applies to all. I can't take you step-by-step through the process for every e-mail client on the planet. There are just too many of them and not enough pages in this book to cover all the possibilities. If you have any problems with this, you might need to get some support from the manufacturer or Web site of the program to which you're exporting. But the basic idea is as follows:

1. Open Windows Live Mail (if it isn't already open).

2. Choose File ⇨ Export ⇨ Messages.

3. Follow the instructions in the wizard that opens.

Where and How Messages Are Stored

By default, all the Windows Live Mail e-mail messages for a user account are usually in the folder C:\Users*username*\AppData\Local\Microsoft\Windows Live Mail (where username matches the account name). You can find the exact location by clicking the Store Folder button in the Maintenance dialog box, shown back in Figure 18-55.

Caution

This section is for experienced users with in-depth understanding of drives, folders, files, user accounts, and file types who need to move or copy messages from one message store to another. Nothing in this section is required for normal sending and receiving of e-mail. ■

When you know the location, you can navigate to that folder through Explorer. (Or just copy the path from the Store Location dialog box and paste it into the breadcrumb trail in any Explorer window and press Enter.) E-mail folders and messages are in the Local Folders folder. When you open that folder, you see folders that correspond to folders in the navigation pane (Deleted Items, Drafts, Inbox, and so forth).

Within any folder, subfolders and e-mail messages are represented by icons. Subfolders are usually listed first and indicated by the standard manila file folder icon. Each message is a file with a numeric name and an .eml filename extension. Figure 18-68 shows an example in which I've opened the Inbox folder for a mail account. The folders you see there are custom subfolders within the Inbox. The files with numeric names are e-mail messages within the current folder.

In Explorer, you can treat the mail folders and files as you do document folders and files. For example, if you want to copy the entire Inbox to an external disk or a separate folder, choose Select All from the Organize button, or press Ctrl+A to select everything in the folder. Then click Copy to CD to copy them to a CD. Or just right-drag them to some other folder or drive and choose Copy Here after you release the mouse button.

Caution

You *don't* want to move the files to another location. Otherwise, they won't exist in Windows Live Mail anymore. At least, not until you move or copy them back! ■

To copy the messages and subfolders to another user account, you first need to set up Windows Live Mail in that user account. Then navigate to its data store and copy messages and subfolders to the corresponding folder in the new user's message store.

FIGURE 18-68

Windows Live Mail Inbox when viewed through Explorer.

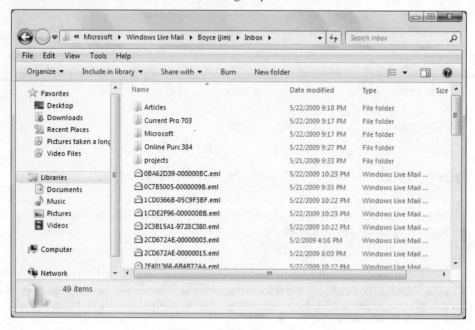

More on Windows Live Mail

I've covered a lot of ground here in this chapter. But e-mail is one of those infinitely long topics for which covering every nook and cranny is impossible. When it comes to e-mail, Windows 7 and even Windows Live Mail are relatively minor players. The real meat of how your e-mail works depends on your mail provider.

Any time you have problems with e-mail, the first place to go is your mail provider's tech support site. They're the ones who provide the service. They're the ones who know their service. Keep in mind that Windows Live Mail has its own built-in help, just as any other program does. Just choose Help ➪ Get Help with Mail from its menu bar, or press F1 while Windows Live Mail is in the active window.

Microsoft Communities is another great resource for help. There are too many different e-mail services out there for any one person to know them all. But when you ask a question through the communities, there's a pretty good chance you'll find someone who is familiar with that service. You learn to use Microsoft Communities in Chapter 20.

Wrap-Up

E-mail is a major application these days. In fact, many people use their computers strictly for e-mail and the Web, so I've given Windows Live Mail some substantial coverage in this chapter. Too much coverage for some readers, and not enough for others, I'm sure. Here's a quick recap of the main points:

- Windows Live Mail is an optional e-mail client for POP3, IMAP, and HTTP e-mail accounts.
- Before you can use Windows Live Mail, you must configure it to work with your e-mail account.
- To write an e-mail message in Windows Live Mail, click the New button in its toolbar.
- To add an attachment to a message, click Attach on the New Message toolbar.
- To download messages from your mail server, click Sync.
- To save received attachments as regular document files, right-click the attachment and choose Save As.
- To control junk mail, choose Tools ⇨ Safety Options.
- To call attention to potential phishing scams, choose Tools ⇨ Safety Options and choose settings on the Phishing tab.
- To block or unblock risky pictures and attachments, choose Tools ⇨ Safety Options from the menu bar and click the Security tab.
- To manage one or more e-mail accounts, choose Tools ⇨ Accounts from the menu bar.

Chatting and Texting with Windows Live Messenger

I n the earliest days of personal computing, people communicated with others mostly by e-mail. Today, people have many different ways to communicate online in addition to e-mail. Online chat is one of those ways. With a chat program, people can communicate in real time by sending text messages back and forth to one another. All it takes is a chat program and an account with an online chat provider.

Windows Live Messenger is an add-on program from Microsoft and part of the Windows Live family of applications, which you can add to your computer and use to communicate with others online in a variety of ways. For example, you can chat online, send text messages, share photos, and even hold a video or audio conference. This chapter offers a brief overview of Windows Live Messenger to get you started. I start with a quick overview of the technology and then explain how you can download and install Windows Live Messenger on your computer. Then, I show you how to use Messenger to chat, text, and share photos. Although this chapter doesn't offer a complete look at all of Messenger's features, you'll find enough information here to help you understand what Messenger can do, as well as where to go for more information.

Tip

For detailed coverage of Messenger, see "Windows Live Essentials," from Wiley. ■

Overview

Online chat, also called *instant messaging* (IM for short), is a very simple concept. You open a chat program, choose a person you want to communicate with, and then type a text message. That message goes across the Internet to a chat server and from there to the other person's computer, where it appears on his screen in his chat program. Then, he types a response and sends it back to you to respond to if you choose. A chat conversation could comprise a few messages or it could go on for hours, the same as any conversation.

Note

The terms *chat* and *IM* are used synonymously in this chapter. ∎

Why IM? I admit that for a long time I really didn't see the usefulness of it, and it was often an annoyance more than anything else. For one, I type about 80 words a minute, and many of the other people I chatted with type much more slowly. So, I spent a lot of time waiting for responses to what I typed. What's more, I usually focused on the chat session to the exclusion of whatever else I was doing at the time, which added to my frustration — it was much easier to me to pick up the phone, have a short conversation, and be done.

I have a much better appreciation for online chat now because I use it extensively in my day job. As an IT manager, I spend at least four or five hours each day on the phone in conference calls. If the phone were my only source of communication, I'd get very little done. Throw e-mail and chat into the mix, however, and I can get a lot done. So, when I'm on a call, I'm also writing and receiving e-mail, chatting online with others, and, occasionally, talking on yet another phone call. In fact, quite often I'm chatting with other people who are on the same conference call while someone else is speaking. This behind-the-scenes communication is particularly useful when customers are on the call and you need to share some internal-only information.

Following are the benefits that IM brings to a typical work environment:

- **Easy access to others:** A chat conversation is just a couple of clicks away, and I can tell from the chat program (in this case, Messenger) that the other person is online.

- **Quick conversations:** If I just have a quick question, I can ask it in a chat session and get a response back usually fairly quickly.

- **Multitasking:** Usually, a one-on-one phone call consumes the majority of your attention. With a chat session, you can send a message and then focus on other tasks while you wait for a response.

- **Instant notes:** I routinely use IM to send or receive information about servers, applications, and the like. I can copy that information right from the IM program and use it in other programs. The phrase "IM that to me" is pretty common these days.

IM is much the same for a home user, except that the conversations are generally personal in nature, such as you might have over the phone. The difference is that, unlike with a phone, you might be carrying on several IM conversations at the same time.

Programs such as Windows Live Messenger enable you to communicate with people in real time, whether they are in the next room or on the other side of the planet. In general, IM is free, other than the cost of having your Internet connection. To use IM, you need only an IM program (such as Messenger) and an online account, which are generally free.

In this chapter, I assume that you have a Windows Live account (which includes Hotmail accounts). You need one of those to use Messenger. Also, you need a microphone if you want to take advantage of Messenger's voice chat capabilities, and a webcam (a camera either built in to your computer or attachable to it) to do video chat.

Adding Messenger to Windows

As mentioned earlier, Windows Live Messenger is not included with Windows 7. Instead, it is available as a download from the Microsoft Live Web site. Before you download it, first check to see whether it is already on your computer. Click Start ➪ All Programs and look for a Windows Live folder. If you find one, click it and look for Windows Live Messenger. If Messenger doesn't show up, you need to add it. Doing so is easy:

1. Open your Web browser and navigate to `http://home.live.com`.

2. If you don't have a Windows Live account, sign up for one at the Windows Live login page. If you already have one, sign in with it.

3. When the Windows Live home page appears, click More ⇨ Downloads.

4. Click the Download button to download the Windows Live Installer.

5. Click Run when prompted to either run or save the file.

At this point, completing the installation is a simple matter of specifying which Windows Live programs you want to install. Make sure to select the box next to Windows Live Messenger and then follow the remaining instructions to complete the installation. Setup will download the programs you specify, and depending on the speed of your Internet connection, downloading and installing the programs you choose can take several minutes.

Setting Up Your Account

Setting up an account in Messenger is even easier than installing the program. First, you need to open the program, so click Start ⇨ All Programs ⇨ Windows Live ⇨ Windows Live Messenger. Figure 19-1 shows the Messenger window.

FIGURE 19-1

Windows Live Messenger.

To set up your account, simply type your Hotmail or Windows Live e-mail address in the account text box and type the password for that account in the password text box. You can use the following options to control sign-in:

- **Remember Me:** Messenger will remember your e-mail address so that you don't have to type it each time you sign in.

- **Remember My Password:** Messenger will remember your password so that you don't have to type it each time you sign in.

- **Sign Me In Automatically:** If you directed Messenger to remember your account and your password, you can use this option to have Messenger sign you in automatically when the program opens.

- **Sign In As:** From this drop-down list, choose the online status that you want others to see. You can choose between Available, Busy, Away, or Appear Offline.

The options for Sign In As determine how others see your online status. In each case, others can still send you messages. However, the option you choose can set their expectation of a reply. If you sign in as Busy, others will likely not expect an immediate answer from you if they send you a message.

FIGURE 19-2

Messenger window with no contacts.

After you specify your sign-in options, click Sign In. The Messenger window changes as shown in Figure 19-2. If you have no contacts, Messenger displays a Welcome message and gives you a link to click to add contacts. If you already have contacts added, Messenger displays their status and also opens the Today window, which gives you quick access to news, e-mail, and other online resources (Figure 19-3).

Contacts and their status.

Adding contacts

Before you can communicate with someone using Messenger, you need to add her as a contact. To add a new contact, click the Add a Contact or Group button in Messenger's toolbar (the one with the green plus sign on it) and click Add a Contact. Messenger displays the dialog box shown in Figure 19-4, where you can enter an IM address, mobile device number, or both. Click Next when you're finished.

Windows Live Messenger also gives you a means to add contacts from other services such as Facebook, MySpace, LinkedIn, hi5, and Tagged. To add these contacts, click the Add a Contact or Group button and choose Add People from Other Services. Messengers opens a Web browser at the Windows Live site, and on the resulting Web page, you can select the service provider you want to use (such as Facebook). Make you selection and click the Next button. You are redirected to the service provider's Web site, where you can sign in and select users to add. Follow the prompts at the site to complete the process.

FIGURE 19-4

Add a contact.

FIGURE 19-5

Creating a group.

Adding and using groups

Groups in Messenger enable you to hold a group chat with more than one person (who also use Messenger). To create a group, click Add a Contact or ⇨ Create a Group. Click OK to dismiss the informational dialog box, type a name for your group, and click Next. In the resulting dialog box (see Figure 19-5), type the e-mail addresses of the people you want to add, separated by semicolons. Optionally, include a message in the message text box and then click Next. An e-mail will be sent to each person in the group asking them to accept the invitation. After they have accepted, you can begin a group chat. To do so, just right-click the group in Messenger and choose Send Instant Message to Group.

Tip

Use Categories such as Family, Friends, Co-workers, and so on group together contacts. To create a category, click Add a Contact or Group ⇨ Create a Category and follow the prompts to name the category and add existing contacts to it. ■

Chatting Online

After you have added some contacts, you can start chatting with them in Messenger. To start a conversation with a single contact, just double-click the contact's name. Messenger opens a window similar to the one shown in Figure 19-6. Type your message and press Enter. If you want to add a smiley (such as a happy face) or a wink, select it from one of the buttons on the toolbar under the chat text box. You can also click the Nudge button to nudge everyone in the conversation (which shakes the Messenger window on their desktops).

FIGURE 19-6

A new chat window.

To chat with a group of people, double-click the group name to open the chat window. Now when you type, the message goes to everyone in the group who is online. All of them can reply back to you, and those replies show up in your chat window, just as they do for a chat session with one contact.

Changing the font

Messenger uses a default font, but you change the font if you prefer a different one. Everything you type then shows up in that font in the text box as you type. Your text shows up on the other contacts' chat windows with the new font as well.

To change the font, click the Change Your Font or Text Color button below the text box in the chat window. Messenger displays a Change Font dialog box in which you can choose a font, style size, color and other font properties. Click OK when done and then start typing to use the new font.

Using ink

Messenger also lets you draw and send those drawings to the others in your chat session, although drawing with a mouse isn't easy. If you have a digitizing tablet, you can get better results. Figure 19-7 shows an example of ink used in a message.

FIGURE 19-7

Ink in a message.

Note

If not all of the recipients in the chat session can receive ink, you'll see a message indicating that the message will be sent as text. ∎

To use ink (draw) in Messenger, click the button labeled Write and Send Messages in Your Handwriting (which looks like a pen). The toolbar changes to display drawing tools that let you choose a point size, erase, redo and undo ink changes, choose a color, and set a grid size. After you choose a point size and color, just click and drag in the drawing area within the Messenger window. Click Send to send the drawing to the other chat session participants. Click the Enter and Send Messages as Text button to switch back to using text.

Tip

Maximize the Messenger window to make more room available horizontally for drawing. Drag the top edge of the drawing area up and down to change the size vertically. ■

Sending Text Messages

You can send text messages to your contacts' cell phones or other mobile devices that are capable of receiving text messages. Mobile devices with a phone number show up in Messenger with a cell phone icon, as shown in Figure 19-8.

FIGURE 19-8

Texting a mobile device.

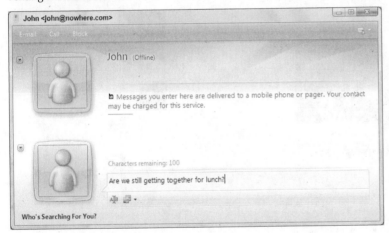

To send a text, double-click the contact's mobile number. Messenger opens a chat window similar to the one shown in Figure 19-8. Type your message in the text box and press Enter. If the person replies, the reply shows up in your chat window.

Sharing Photos

Messenger makes it easy to share photos with others in an IM conversation. The photos show up in the other participants' chat windows, where they can view them and optionally save them to their own computers.

To share a photo, start a chat session with one or more others. Then, click the Photos button in the chat window toolbar. Messenger opens a Select Images to Start Sharing dialog box, which is a standard Open dialog box. Locate the photos you want to share, select them, and click Open. You can also click the Add button in the chat window (Figure 19-9) to open the dialog box and select more photos to share. As soon as you click Open, the photos appear in your chat window as well as on the other participants' windows (after a short delay for upload and download).

Other participants in the conversation can share their pictures, too. They can click Add, select a photo, and click Open, and the photo appears on your computer as well as theirs. To save a photo, mouse over the photo and click the Save Photo button. Type a filename in the resulting dialog box and click Save.

FIGURE 19-9

Sharing photos.

Audio, Video, and More

I've touched on only the very basics of Windows Live Messenger in this chapter. Messenger offers a lot of other features that I don't cover. For example, if you and the other participants have the appropriate recording and playback hardware (typically a microphone and speakers) you can hold an audio conversation. This is a great way to save on long-distance phone charges, particularly if the other person is in another country. If you have the appropriate hardware connected to your computer, you can even call another person's phone and carry on a conversation through Messenger. You can also hold a video chat, assuming that both you and the other person have webcams. If only one of you has a webcam, the other person can still view that webcam.

Messenger's features don't stop there. You can also play games online with your contacts, send files, send an e-mail message, and lots more. To learn more about these other features, spend some time experimenting with Windows Live Messenger and check out "Windows Live Essentials," from Wiley.

Wrap-Up

Windows Live Messenger, a free add-on for Windows computers, provides a great set of tools for communicating with others. These include instant messaging (IM), audio and video conferencing, Internet phone, and photo and file sharing. Following are key points covered in this chapter:

- Windows Live Messenger is a free add-on for Windows, available at `http://home.live.com`.
- You can use Messenger to chat with others online, either singly or in a group.
- With a microphone and speakers, or a compatible phone system, you can hold voice chat sessions with your online contacts across the Internet.
- With a webcam, you can hold a video chat session with your contacts.
- You can share files, share photos, and play online games using Messenger.

Beyond E-Mail and the Web

N ewsgroups are online communities where people exchange information. When you have a question but don't know whom to ask, newsgroups may be your best bet. You post your question so that everyone in the group can read it and then come back a little later and see what kind of answers you've received.

File Transfer Protocol (FTP) is an Internet service used for transferring files from one computer to another across the Internet. In contrast to sending files as e-mail attachments, FTP puts no limitations on file size and doesn't require adding an attachment to an e-mail. You can just drag and drop to move or copy any number of files and folders from one computer to another.

Remote Assistance lets you turn control of your computer over to a trusted expert for advice, troubleshooting, or general support. Remote Desktop allows you to control a remote computer from whatever computer you happen to be using. All these topics are covered in this chapter.

About Newsgroups

Millions of people on the Internet communicate through newsgroups every day. You can find newsgroups that discuss just about any subject imaginable. Following are some terms you're likely to encounter as you engage with newsgroups:

- Each message in a newsgroup is typically called a *post* (short for *posted message*). From the standpoint of Windows Live Mail, each item is a *message*, just as every e-mail you send and receive is a message.

- Posts that you send to multiple newsgroups are called *cross-posted*.

- A series of messages that originate from a single post is called a *conversation* or *thread*. For example, if I post a question and nine people respond, those ten messages constitute a conversation, or thread.

- Many newsgroups are *moderated* by people who screen messages for suitability to the newsgroup. Others are *unmoderated*, and messages pass through to the newsgroup unscreened and uncensored.

- *Lurking* is hanging around a newsgroup to see what's being said without actually contributing anything. When you're new to a newsgroup, lurking for a while is a good idea, just to get an idea of what subject matters the group treats as appropriate.

- *Spamming* is sending blatant advertisements or ads disguised as newsgroup messages to a newsgroup. Spamming is highly unacceptable and sure to get you flamed!

- *Flaming* is sending nasty messages to people in the group. If you post irrelevant messages to a group, you might get flamed!

- *Ranting* is yelling, whining, and complaining about things you don't like. Even if you feel like ranting, never type in all caps. IT COMES ACROSS AS SHOUTING and gets on people's nerves.

- *Netiquette* is observing proper newsgroup etiquette by not sending irrelevant comments and not spamming the group. A good *netizen* (network citizen) follows proper netiquette.

Tip

For information on netiquette (newsgroup etiquette), see www.microsoft.com/protect/computer/ basics/netiquette.mspx. ■

Newsgroups reside on *news servers* (also called *NNTP servers*, where NNTP stands for Network News Transport Protocol). Most news servers have a three-part name, as Web sites do. For example, the Microsoft news server I show here is at msnews.microsoft.com. Each newsgroup has its own name specifying the topic of the group. For example, microsoft.public.windows.7.general is a public newsgroup where people ask general questions about Windows 7.

Tip

You can also access newsgroups and other kinds of support communities from your Web browser. See www.microsoft.com/communities for Microsoft's support options. ■

You participate in newsgroups by posting questions, comments, or replies to the group. Your post is basically an e-mail message sent to anyone in the group who cares to look at it. In fact, newsgroups share so many similarities to e-mail, you can use Windows Live Mail to manage your newsgroup messages along with your e-mail messages.

Note

Windows Live Mail is not included with Windows 7, but rather is available as a downloadable add-on. See home.live.com to learn more about Windows Live and to download a copy of Windows Live Mail. See Chapter 18 to learn about using Windows Live Mail as your e-mail client. ■

Creating a newsgroup account

You don't have to create a newsgroup account in Windows Live Mail to use the Microsoft Communities. That account already exists. That's why you can see its name in the navigation pane at the left side of the Windows Mail program window. As mentioned, that's a great place to get answers to your questions about Windows 7 and other Microsoft products. The only thing you need is a Windows Live ID. The ID is just a username and password that provides access to many of Microsoft's online services. If you don't already have a Live ID, you can pick one up for free at home.live.com. If that address changes, you should be able to pick up an ID just by clicking the appropriate link when prompted for a Live ID.

Note

There is no cost for a Windows Live ID. ■

The first step to getting to any newsgroup is to open Windows Live Mail. Click Start ⇨ All Programs ⇨ Windows Live ⇨ Windows Live Mail to open the program.

If prompted, sign in with your Windows Live ID. Or set up a Live ID by following the prompts on the screen. Then you can skip to the upcoming section "Downloading newsgroup names."

If you're trying to set up an account at another news server, you need to set up the account. First make sure that you know the address of that server. Many ISPs provide NNTP servers as part of their service. Check your ISP's Web site, or give it a call to find out whether it offers this feature. You need to know the name of the server, which will be in the format *name.yourdomain.xxx*, where *name* is the name of the server and *yourdomain.xxx* is your ISP's domain name. Also find out whether the news server requires logging in. After you've gathered that information, follow these steps to set up an account:

Caution

Parents need to be aware that many public newsgroups contain content that's inappropriate for children. I'm not talking about Microsoft Communities here, but rather the public UseNet newsgroups that you might be able to access through your ISP or a third-party service. ■

1. Choose Tools ⇨ Accounts from the Windows Live Mail menu bar. The Accounts dialog box, shown in Figure 20-1, opens.

2. To add a newsgroup other than Microsoft Communities, click the Add button to start the Add an Account wizard.

3. Click Newsgroup Account and click Next.

4. Enter a Display Name. This is the name that others in the group will see and how they'll identify you. The name can be anything you like. Click Next.

FIGURE 20-1

Accounts dialog box.

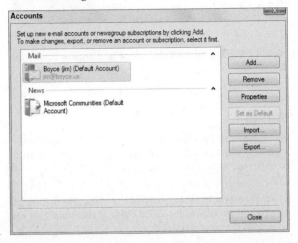

5. Enter your e-mail address and click Next.

6. Enter the name of your news server. If the news server requires that you log in, check the My News Server Requires Me to Log On check box. Then click Next.

7. If your newsgroup requires logging in, fill in your account name and password, as instructed by your ISP or the newsgroup on the next page. Click Next.

8. Click Finish when you get to the last wizard page.

9. At the completion of the wizard, Windows Live Mail displays the dialog box shown in Figure 20-2. You can choose not to download newsgroup names, or choose to download them and optionally turn on Communities if supported by the news server. For details on downloading newsgroups, see the next section.

FIGURE 20-2

Subscribe to newsgroups and turn on Communities.

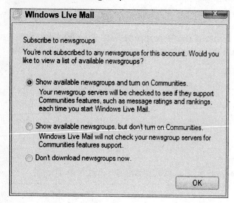

The news server is added to your list of Accounts. For future reference, any time you need to change or delete an account, you do so from that Accounts dialog box. Just click the name of the account you want to change or delete. Then click Properties to change the account, or Delete to remove it.

Tip

To give an account a more user-friendly name, right-click the account in the Folder pane and choose Properties. Change the name in the first text box and click OK. ∎

Downloading newsgroup names

After you've set up an account for a news server, you can *download* newsgroups. The term *download* is a little misleading here because you don't actually download all the newsgroup messages to your computer. Basically, you download just a list of newsgroup names. From there, you can decide which groups you want to subscribe to.

If you just set up a new newsgroup account, you'll be prompted to download newsgroups as soon as you click Close in the Accounts dialog box. If you choose not to download them at that time, you can download newsgroups at any time. You'll see how in the next section.

Subscribing to newsgroups

After you've added a newsgroup server to your Internet accounts, its name appears under e-mail folder names in the left column. If you didn't download newsgroup names right after setting up your account, you can right-click that name in the Folder pane and choose Newsgroups to view a list of newsgroups on that server. Figure 20-3 shows an example using newsgroups from Microsoft Communities.

Most news servers are home to hundreds of newsgroups, which is far more than you'll want to participate in. To narrow the field to newsgroups that cover your topics of interest, type a word in the box under Display Newsgroups That Contain. For example, you might type **Windows 7** to see newsgroups about Windows 7.

After you've narrowed the field, you can subscribe to any newsgroups that look interesting. Subscribing to a newsgroup has no cost, and you can unsubscribe from any newsgroup at any time. You're not making any commitments when you subscribe to a newsgroup. To subscribe to a newsgroup, just click its name and then click the Subscribe button. You can subscribe to as many newsgroups as you like.

Note

At Microsoft Communities, the public newsgroups are available in several languages. Newsgroup names for languages other than English include a two-letter language identifier in the newsgroup name, such as German (.de), Spanish (.es), French (.fr), Italian (.it), and Japanese (.jp). Newsgroups in English don't have a two-letter abbreviation after microsoft.public. ■

The names of any newsgroups to which you've subscribed appear under the newsgroup server name in the left column.

FIGURE 20-3

Newsgroups on a news server.

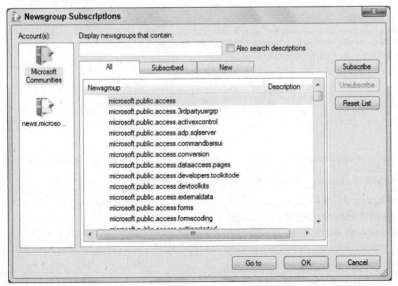

Viewing newsgroup messages

To see what's happening in a newsgroup, just click its name in the Folder pane. Any new messages since your last visit will be downloaded to your computer and displayed in the pane on the right. That may take a couple of minutes, depending on the speed of your connection.

As with e-mail, the top-right pane in Windows Live Mail shows *message headers*. Unread messages are boldfaced. By default, replies to a message are collapsed beneath the message that started the conversation. Click the plus (+) sign next to any collapsed message to see replies. Click any message header to see the content of the message in the Preview pane below the headers, as shown in Figure 20-4.

FIGURE 20-4

Newsgroups in Windows Live Mail.

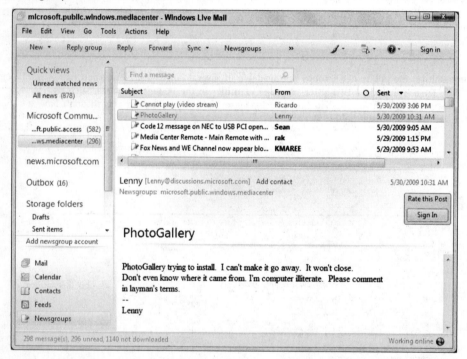

Also as with e-mail, the following visual cues, tools, and techniques apply to newsgroup messages:

- Boldface in the From column indicates an unread message or thread.

- The number in parentheses to the right of a boldface newsgroup name indicates the number of unread messages in that newsgroup.

- A triangle button next to a message header indicates a collapsed conversation. Click the triangle button to expand the conversation. Click it again to collapse a conversation or portion of a conversation.

- To choose columns to display, choose View ➪ Columns from the menu bar.
- To move a column, drag the column heading left or right.
- To size a column, drag the border at the right side of the column heading left or right.
- To mark a conversation of interest as Watched, click the Watched Items column to the left of the message header. The message header turns red and the Watched Items column shows an eyeglass icon. To ignore a conversation, click in the Watched Items column a second time so that the No (circle and slash) symbol appears.

Tip

The Watched Items column has an eyeglass symbol in its column heading. ∎

- Right-click any newsgroup name or message header for quick access to commonly used commands.
- To mark an entire conversation as read, right-click the message header and choose Mark Conversation as Read.
- To mark all the messages in a newsgroup as read, right-click the newsgroup name in the left column and choose Catch Up.

Tip

To automatically mark all newsgroup messages as read when you leave a newsgroup, choose Tools ➪ Options, click the Read tab, select Mark All Messages As Read When Exiting a Newsgroup, and click OK. ∎

- To mark a conversation as Useful or Not Useful, right-click the message header and choose Rate. Or click the Rate button in the Preview pane header. You need to sign in to your Windows Live account.

Tip

Choose View ➪ Show or Hide ➪ Show Only Useful Conversations to filter out messages you haven't marked as Useful. Repeat that menu sequence to bring nonuseful messages back out of hiding. ∎

Tip

If you skipped Chapter 18, you may want to take a quick read through that for a more thorough description of things you can do in the Windows Live Mail program. ∎

Hide Your Real E-Mail Address

When you post or reply to messages in a newsgroup, your e-mail address is posted along with it. Spammers are known to scout newsgroups for valid e-mail addresses. Therefore, it's a good idea not to post your real e-mail address in newsgroups unless you want other users of that news server to be able to contact you.

To hide your real e-mail address, choose Tools ➪ Accounts from the Windows Live Mail menu bar. Click the name of the newsgroup and click the Properties button. Set the Name to whatever name you want to use within the newsgroup. This can be any name you like; it doesn't have to be your real name. Set the E-mail address to something fake, such as noreply@nospam.tld. Leave the Organization and Reply Address fields empty. Click OK and then click Close.

Posting a newsgroup message

To post a question or comment to the newsgroup, create a new message. Before you do, there's an important little setting you might want to change to make your own posts more visible. Here are the steps:

1. Choose Tools ➪ Options from the Windows Live Mail menu bar.

2. Click the Advanced tab.

3. Select Mark Message Threads I Start As "Watched" (if it isn't already selected).

4. Click the Read tab.

5. Next to Highlight Watched Messages, choose a color for displaying watched messages (or keep the default Red).

6. Click OK.

You need do these steps only once, not each time you post a message. Choosing those options will highlight questions that you've posted so that they're easier to find later.

Before you post a message, click the subscribed newsgroup that you think best covers the topic of your question. (Some people get cranky when you post messages that aren't relevant to the newsgroup.) Then click the New button at the left side of the toolbar, or choose File ➪ New ➪ News Message from the menu bar. A New Message window opens, similar to the one shown in Figure 20-5.

FIGURE 20-5

New Message window for newsgroups.

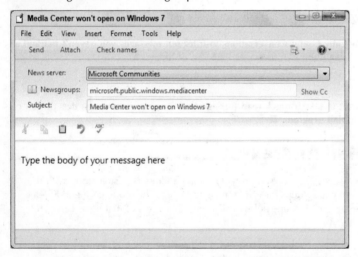

You don't need to change the Newsgroups field of the message. It's already addressed to whatever newsgroup name you clicked in the Folders pane. The exception is when you want to cross-post to multiple newsgroups. In that case, either type the newsgroup names, separating them by semicolons or commas, or simply click the Newsgroups button and choose the other newsgroup(s) you want to add.

When typing your Subject, be as brief and specific as you can be. Many newsgroup members ignore messages with vague subject lines such as "Bug?", "Help!!!!!!!", or "What am I doing wrong?" Under the Subject line, choose Comment, Question, or Suggestion to identify the type of message you're posting.

When typing the body of your message, don't bother trying to do any fancy formatting. Most message boards are plain text, anyway, so all your formatting will likely be for naught. Just try to phrase your comment in a way that's specific and easy for someone to answer. Consider clicking the Spelling toolbar button to clean up any spelling errors before you send.

If you click the Show Cc link to the right of the Newsgroups field, the New Message window expands to show additional fields (Figure 20-6). The additional fields include:

- **Follow-Up To:** Specify the names of newsgroups to which you want replies of your message to be posted. Normally, you leave this field blank so that replies are posted to the same newsgroup where the original post resides.

- **Cc:** Enter one or more e-mail addresses to which you want to send a copy of your post.

- **Reply To:** Specify one or more e-mail addresses to which you want reply posts sent.

- **Distribution:** Specify how widely the post should be propagated.

- **Keywords:** Specify keywords for the post to enable others to search for this message using those keywords.

FIGURE 20-6

Additional message fields.

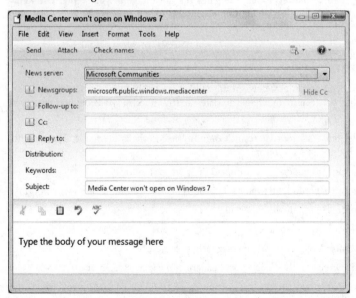

When you've finished typing your message, click Send in the New Message toolbar. The message is added to your Outbox. Click Send/Receive to send the message to the newsgroup, or let Windows Live Mail send it during the next automatic send/receive.

Don't expect new messages to appear immediately (and don't keep sending the same message over and over again!). In a moderated newsgroup, it could take days for your message to be approved and posted. But even in an unmoderated group, it may take a little time for your post to find its way to the group and then back to your downloaded messages.

When you want to view any replies to your post, click the name of the newsgroup to which you posted the message. When your message does show up, any replies may be collapsed beneath it. So if you see a triangle button to the left of your message header, just click it to see replies. Again, be patient. It may take a little time for the right person to find and reply to your message.

Replying to newsgroup messages

If you read a message and decide to post a reply, you can do so in a couple of ways:

- **Reply to Group:** Your message is sent to the news server, and all newsgroup members can see it.

- **Reply:** Your message is sent to the poster's e-mail address, where only he or she will see your response.

To choose a reply option, click the Reply to Group or Reply button on the toolbar. Alternatively, right-click the message header to which you want to reply and choose Reply to Group or Reply to Sender. Then just type your reply and click Send.

Note

In most cases, it's best to reply to the group so that everyone else gains the advantage of your reply. Use Reply to Sender when you don't want the rest of the people viewing the newsgroup to see your reply. ■

Getting the latest messages

Most of the time, the messages you see in any newsgroup will be reasonably up-to-date with what's actually on the news server. But you can manually get updates at any time by synchronizing messages. Here's how:

1. Click a news account name (such as Microsoft Communities) in the Folder pane. The contents pane shows your subscribed newsgroups.

2. Right-click a newsgroup and choose Synchronization Settings (Figure 20-7).

3. By default, each account is configured to not synchronize. Choose from the following options:
   - **Don't Synchronize:** Do not download headers or messages.
   - **All Messages:** Download all messages from the newsgroup.
   - **New Messages Only:** Download only messages that are new.
   - **Headers Only:** Download only the message headers, not the message bodies.

4. Click Sync on the toolbar to synchronize the current newsgroup. Or click the arrow beside the Sync button and choose all newsgroups or all content, including e-mail accounts.

You shouldn't have to repeat these steps often. The way things are set up by default, simply clicking a newsgroup name in the navigation pane downloads all new messages right on the spot.

FIGURE 20-7

Choose a synchronization option.

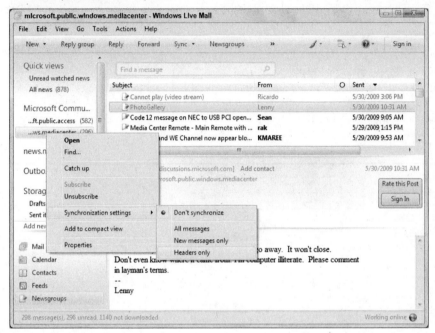

Newsgroup Slang

When you get into a newsgroup, you may come across some unfamiliar acronyms. Here's what they mean:

- AFAIK: As far as I know
- BTW: By the way
- FWIW: For what it's worth
- GMTA: Great minds think alike
- IMHO: In my humble opinion
- IMO: In my opinion
- LOL: Laughing out loud
- NG: Newsgroup
- OIC: Oh, I see
- OTOH: On the other hand
- ROFL: Rolling on the floor laughing
- TIA: Thanks in advance

Searching newsgroup messages

You can quickly search for newsgroup messages that contain a specific word or phrase. Here's how:

1. In the Windows Live Mail Folder pane, click the server or newsgroup you want to search. (For example, click Microsoft Communities to search all your subscribed newsgroups in that news server.)

2. Press Ctrl+Shift+F or choose Edit ➪ Find ➪ Message from the menu bar. The Find Message window opens.

3. Fill in the blanks to define your search. For example, if you want to see all posts about Movie Maker, type that name in the Message box, as shown in Figure 20-8.

4. Click Find Now.

FIGURE 20-8

Find Message dialog box.

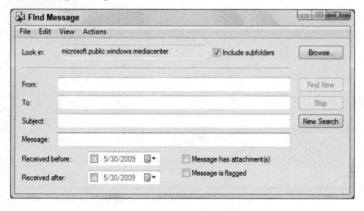

Message headers for posts that match your search criteria appear at the bottom of the Find Message window. Double-click any message header to read the message.

Quick Searches from the Search box

The Search box above the Message list provides a quick way to search just the selected newsgroup. In the navigation pane, click the name of the newsgroup you want to search. (You can't search the whole server or account. It has to be one of the newsgroups under the account name.) Then type a word or phrase into the Search box. As you type, headers for messages that *don't* contain the word or phrase disappear.

To clear the Search box and see all headers again, press Escape (Esc) or click the X beside the Search box.

Searching from the Start menu

Newsgroup messages are included in the Windows 7 search index, which means you can search for messages right from the Start menu. You don't even have to open Windows Live Mail first. Just press or click the Start button. Then, type a word or phrase into the Search box. Newsgroup messages that contain the word or phrase appear on the Start menu.

Hiding irrelevant messages

As with e-mail messages, you can apply a view to any newsgroup to hide irrelevant message headers. Choose View ➪ Show or Hide and then click the name of any view you want to apply.

You can create custom views for newsgroup messages, much as you can for e-mail. Here's how:

1. In the Folder pane, click the name of any subscribed newsgroup.

2. Choose View ➪ Show or Hide ➪ Create New view from the menu.

3. Click New to define a new view.

4. Specify conditions and criteria for the view and give it a name. For example, Figure 20-9 shows settings for a view named This Week, which hides all messages sent more than seven days ago.

5. Click OK in each open dialog box to get back to Windows Mail.

FIGURE 20-9

Custom view to hide messages sent more than seven days ago.

Tip

See "Introducing Windows Live Mail" in Chapter 18 for the basics of using the Windows Live Mail program window. See "Filtering messages" in Chapter 18 for more information on views. ■

Creating newsgroup message rules

As with e-mail messages, you can automate newsgroup message management using rules. From the Windows Live Mail menu bar, choose Tools ➪ Message Rules ➪ News. The New Message Rule window opens.

In the New Message Rule window, choose the Conditions and Actions for your rule and give the rule a name. Figure 20-10 shows an example of a rule named Watch TV, Movie, Video Posts, which automatically highlights any message header that contains *TV*, *video*, or *movie*.

After creating a new rule, click OK to return to the Message Rules dialog box. From there you can create new rules, change existing rules, or delete rules.

FIGURE 20-10

Sample newsgroup message rule.

Rules are applied only to new message headers that you download after you've defined a new rule. But you can apply any rules to messages you already have by following these steps:

1. If you already closed the Message Rules window, choose Tools ➪ Message Rules ➪ News from the Windows Live Mail menu bar.

2. Click Apply Now.

3. Select the name of the rule you want to apply or select all rules to apply all of them.

4. Specify the newsgroup or server to which you want to apply the rule. For example, to apply the rule to all messages from Microsoft Communities, click Browse, click Microsoft Communities, and then click OK.

5. Click Apply Now. Then click OK after the rule is applied.

6. Click the Close and OK buttons to get back to Windows Live Mail.

Messages in whatever newsgroup(s) you specified in Step 4 will be marked according to the rules you specified in Step 3.

Unscrambling messages

Some newsgroups allow members to scramble messages that contain sensitive or offensive text. These are typically identified by the characters ROT13 in the message body. To read such a message, double-click its message header. From the menu bar of the message window that opens, choose Actions ➪ Unscramble (ROT13).

Unsubscribing from a group

If you joined newsgroups that you find you're not using much and want to stop downloading their messages, just unsubscribe from the group. To do so, right-click the newsgroup's name in the Folder pane and choose Unsubscribe.

Personalizing newsgroups

Many of the features described in "Personalizing Windows Live Mail" in Chapter 18 apply to newsgroups. If you skipped that chapter, take a look through that section now for optional settings that apply to newsgroups.

Using FTP

FTP stands for File Transfer Protocol, a standardized method of transferring files from one computer to another on the Internet. FTP is not the same as peer-to-peer (P2P) file sharing, which enables you to download files from any computer that's on the network. Nor is it like transferring files with Windows Live Messenger, through which you can send and receive files with whomever you're having a conversation. Rather, FTP allows you to copy files from, and perhaps to, a computer called an FTP server.

In FTP, the words *upload* and *download* have very specific meanings:

- **Download:** To copy files from the FTP server to your own computer
- **Upload:** To copy files from your computer to the FTP server

Every FTP server has a URL (address) that takes the general form:

ftp://*host.domain.tld*

where *host* is a specific computer's name, *domain* is the name of the company or site that owns the server, and *tld* is one of the common top-level domain names, such as .com or .net.

Anonymous FTP versus FTP accounts

There are two basic ways to do FTP. *Anonymous FTP* allows you to download files from the FTP server without having an account name and password. Often, you can download files using anonymous FTP. However, the ability to upload to an FTP server using anonymous FTP is rare because the owner of the FTP site doesn't want millions of people uploading files randomly.

To upload files to an FTP server, you generally need an account that includes a username and password. As an example, say that your ISP provides some empty space on a Web server on which you're allowed to publish your own Web pages. Or maybe you've rented space on a Web server somewhere to publish your Web pages. Either way, the service provider may give you the URL of the Web server, a user account name, and a password that allows you to upload Web pages from your computer to the Web server. After the pages are on the Web server, anyone with an Internet account and Web browser can view those pages.

To upload and download files with FTP, you may need an *FTP client*. As the name implies, the FTP client is a program that lets you transfer files between your computer and the FTP server to which you have access. However, you can use Microsoft Internet Explorer, and perhaps other Web browsers, to upload and download files.

Using Internet Explorer as an FTP client

You can use Internet Explorer to access FTP sites. In Internet Explorer, type or paste the FTP site's address into the address bar and press Enter. If the FTP site requires you to log in, IE displays a dialog box prompting you for your site user name and password. Fill in the dialog box as follows:

Tip

You can also open an FTP site from Windows Explorer. Open any folder (Documents will do). Then type or paste the FTP site's address (including the ftp://prefix) into the Breadcrumb menu box and press Enter. ■

If you want to log in with a different username than the one currently being used (which could either be anonymous a specific user name), you can do so if you have opened the FTP site in Windows Explorer. Choose File ➪ Log On As from the menu bar to open the Log On As dialog box, shown in Figure 20-11.

FIGURE 20-11

Log On As dialog box.

Tip

If you don't see a menu bar in Internet Explorer, press the Alt key or click the Organize toolbar button and choose Layout ➪ Menu bar. ■

- If the FTP site allows anonymous access, choose Log On Anonymously and then click Log On.
- If you can't use anonymous access, enter your username and password. Optionally, choose Save Password so that you don't have to log in each time. Then click Log On.

Either way, the FTP site opens looking much the same as any folder on your local computer.

To copy files to or from the FTP site, first open a local folder without disturbing the folder that's showing the FTP site. For example, click Start and then click your username. Then navigate to a local folder to which you want to copy files, or to the local folder that contains files you want to copy to the FTP site. Then size and position the two folder windows so that you can see at least a portion of each, such as in the example in Figure 20-12.

FIGURE 20-12

Local folder and FTP site.

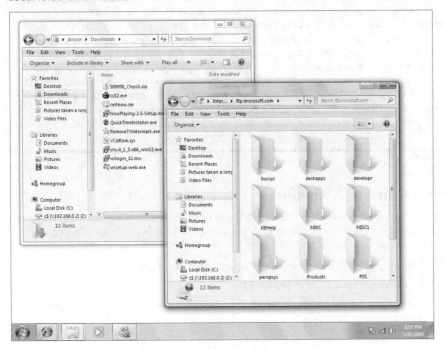

After you have the two windows open like that, you can just drag items from the FTP folder to the local folder to download them. To upload, drag items from the local folder to the FTP folder.

Tip

See "Moving and copying by dragging" in Chapter 29 for info on moving and copying files between folders. ■

Tip

If you prefer, you can include the username and password in the URL when you open the FTP site. Use the format `ftp://user:password@ftpsite.domain.tld`, where `user` is your FTP account name, `password` is the password for the account, and `ftpsite.domain.tld` is the FTP server name. ■

Using Remote Assistance

Remote Assistance is a way to give control of your computer to a trusted expert. A trusted expert is any computer expert you know well enough to trust not to damage your computer or steal any personal information. It might be someone from Desktop Support at your place of business. It may be a friend or relative who just happens to be a computer expert. Whoever it is, you have to find him or her yourself. Remote Assistance provides only the *ability* for a trusted expert to operate your computer from afar. It doesn't provide the trusted expert.

Remote Assistance and Firewalls

If you have any trouble using Remote Assistance, make sure that it's listed as an exception in Windows Firewall. To do so, open Windows Firewall from the Control Panel.Click the Allow A Program Or Feature through Windows Firewall link. Select Remote Assistance and click OK. Note that to send e-mail requests for Remote Assistance, you must enable Windows Remote Assistance for Public connections. In addition, if your computer sits behind a perimeter firewall (DSL router, wireless access point, or other hardware firewall), both your local firewall and the remote firewall must support Universal Plug and Play (UPnP) to support Remote Assistance without any special configuration. Or, if the firewall in front of the system requesting remote assistance doesn't support UPnP, you need to use port forwarding to get the incoming remote assistance traffic to the computer. How you set up port forwarding depends entirely on the type of firewall you have. Essentially, you need to create a rule in the firewall to forward incoming traffic for port 3389 to the computer that needs remote assistance.

Setting up Remote Assistance

Before you try to use Remote Assistance, make sure it's enabled in your user account. This requires administrative privileges. You find options for enabling and disabling it in the System Properties dialog box. Here's a quick and easy way to get to those options:

1. Click the Start button, right-click Computer, and choose Properties.

2. Click the Remote Settings link in the left pane.

3. If prompted, enter an administrative password. The Remote tab of the System Properties dialog box, shown in Figure 20-13, opens.

FIGURE 20-13

System Properties Remote tab.

4. If you want to allow the computer to be used in Remote Assistance sessions, select the first check box. Otherwise, the computer cannot be used for Remote Assistance.

5. Optionally, click the Advanced button. Then, to allow trusted experts to control the computer remotely, select the Allow This Computer to Be Controlled Remotely option.

6. Optionally, set a time limit on how long remote assistance invitations remain open. Also, you can limit remote assistance to other computers running Windows Vista or later versions of Windows.

7. Click OK.

The next section assumes that you've allowed Remote Assistance in the preceding steps.

Requesting Remote Assistance

Before you allow a trusted expert to take over your computer online, you need to agree on a time and a password. For security reasons, it would be best to agree on a password over the phone or in person.

If you know the e-mail address of an expert you can trust to help with your computer, follow these steps to send a remote assistance request:

- Press ![icon], type **remote**, and click Windows Remote Assistance.
- Or click the Start button, choose Help and Support, click Ask in the toolbar, and click Windows Remote Assistance.

Next, click Invite Someone You Trust to Help You. How you proceed from there depends on how you use e-mail. If you use Windows Live Mail or another e-mail client that's compatible with Windows 7, follow these steps:

1. Click Use E-Mail to Send an Invitation.

2. Type the expert's e-mail address in the To box and click Send.

3. If your e-mail client isn't configured to send mail immediately, open that program and perform a Send/Receive.

If you use Web mail, follow these steps instead:

1. Click Save This Invitation As a File.

2. Choose a location in which to save the file and click Save.

3. Compose an e-mail message to the expert and attach the Invitation (or Invitation.msrcincident) file to that message using the standard method for your e-mail service. Then send the message normally.

Tip
If you don't know how to attach files to messages, search your e-mail service's support using "Attach" as the keyword, or ask your trusted expert. ■

The e-mail message is sent to the trusted expert. You see the Windows Remote Assistance window, shown in Figure 20-14.

Windows Remote Assistance window.

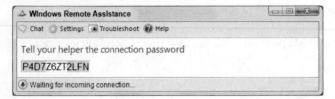

Caution

If you close the Remote Assistance window, your invitation will expire and the expert won't be able to connect. ■

The trusted expert needs to receive your e-mail and open the attached file. You also need to provide the password in the Remote Assistance window to your trusted expert. Remote Assistance doesn't send that in the e-mail, so you need to send that to the other person in a separate e-mail or by phone. Then, he can enter the password in the Remote Assistance window on his end.

After your expert has done all that, you see a new message on the screen asking whether you're willing to allow your helper to connect to your computer. Choose Yes.

When connected, the trusted expert sees your screen and options for chatting, requesting control of the computer, sending a file, and starting a voice conversation. To operate your computer from afar, the expert needs to take control of your computer, which she can do by clicking Request Control at her end.) You see another message asking if you're willing to share control. Again, you have to choose Yes.

You'll be able to see everything the expert is doing. Icons in the Remote Assistance window offer some things you can do while the expert is connected:

- **Disconnect:** Terminates the connection. The expert loses all access to your computer.
- **Stop Sharing:** Keeps the expert connected visually but the expert can't operate your computer.
- **Pause:** Temporarily breaks the expert's connection to your computer. Click Continue to reestablish the connection.
- **Settings:** Takes you to a Settings dialog box, where you can control some optional remote assistance settings. (Click "What do these settings do?" in that dialog box for details.)
- **Help:** Opens Windows Help and Support.
- **Chat:** Opens a chat window so that you and the expert can communicate during the session.
- **Send File:** Lets you send one or more files to the expert.

When you've finished with your Remote Assistance session, click the Disconnect button and close the Remote Assistance window.

Using Remote Desktop

Remote Desktop is a feature that allows you to control a computer from a remote location. It's often used to access computers on a corporate network from a home PC or vice versa. It is also very commonly used by system administrators to remotely manage Windows servers. Remote Desktop is different from Remote Assistance in that with Remote Desktop, you are remotely logging on to a computer and controlling it remotely as a single user. With Remote Assistance, the session includes the local user and the remote expert.

Before you can connect to a remote computer on your office network, a network administrator on the corporate side needs to set up that capability, enabling remote desktop connections inbound to the network (or providing a VPN connection to the remote network for the user). Likewise, if you want to connect to your home computer from the office, you need to configure your home firewall to forward port 3389 to the home computer you want to manage. How you configure the firewall depends on the firewall, so I can't give you specific steps. At this point, I assume that whichever direction you're going, the necessary network and firewall changes are in place to make it possible.

Tip

If you are connecting to another computer on the same network segment as the one your computer is on, no firewall configuration is needed other than having Remote Assistance in Windows Firewall enabled. ■

To connect to the remote computer, you need to know either the hostname of the computer or its IP address. If the computer is on your local network segment, you can use just the computer name. To connect to a computer on a remote network segment, you need to use either the FQDN of the remote computer or its externally facing IP address. This IP address is the public address that is mapped in the firewall to the private address assigned to the computer.

Note

A fully qualified domain name (FQDN) is a name in the common *host.domain.tld* format. ■

When you have the information you need, making the connection should be easy. You have to be online, of course. If the company requires connecting through a modem or VPN (Virtual Private Network), make that connection as specified by your company's network administrator.

Next, open Remote Desktop Connection from the Start menu. As always, you can use the Search box at the bottom of the Start menu to find it. Or click All Programs ➪ Accessories ➪ Remote Desktop Connection. The Remote Desktop Connection window opens. Clicking its Options button expands it to look like Figure 20-15.

Before you connect to a remote computer, you might want to click the Options button and take a look at the options on the various tabs. The only required option is the name or IP address of the computer to which you're connecting. The following sections describe the tabs and options.

Display

Use the Display Configuration settings on the Display tab to specify the screen resolution for the Remote Desktop connection. If you have multiple monitors connected to the local computer, you can select the option Use All My Monitors for the Remote Session to span the remote desktop session across your multiple monitors.

Use the Colors drop-down list to specify the color depth for the remote session. A lower color depth provides faster response for the remote session.

The Display the Connection Bar When I Use the Full Screen option, if enabled, causes Remote Desktop to display a connection bar at the top of the display when the remote session is using full-screen mode. Moving the mouse to the top of the display shows the connection bar, which then enables you to minimize, restore, or close the remote session window.

FIGURE 20-15

Remote Desktop Connection.

Local resources

The settings on the Local Resources tab enable you to configure how Remote Desktop uses local and remote resources. For example, use the Settings button in the Remote Audio group to open a dialog box that lets you specify whether Remote Desktop plays audio from the remote computer at the remote computer, brings it to your local computer, or does not play the sounds. You can also specify similar settings for remote recording.

Use the drop-down list in the Keyboard group to specify how Remote Desktop treats Windows key combinations such as Alt+Tab, sending them to the local computer or remote computer, or sending them to the remote computer only when using full-screen mode.

The Local Devices and Resources group lets you specify how local resources such as your printers, Windows Clipboard, ports, disk drives, and other resources are made available during the remote session. This capability can be extremely useful. For example, by enabling the drives on your local computer for the connection, you make them accessible within My Computer on the remote computer. This means that you can easily drag and drop files between the two systems. By enabling the Clipboard, you can cut and paste between the systems.

Programs

On the Programs tab, you can specify a program to start on the remote computer. Only the program you specify runs on that remote computer. You can exit the session, which closes the program, or you can close the session and leave the remote program running.

Experience

The options on the Experience tab help you control the performance for the remote session. You can choose an option from the drop-down list, which determines which options in the list below the drop-down are enabled. You can also simply select which options you want to use.

Advanced

The Advanced tab offers options that control authentication alerts and Remote Desktop Gateway. The drop-down list on the Advanced tab lets you specify what action Remote Desktop Connection takes when you connect to a remote computer that doesn't satisfy the security requirements as defined by your local system security policy. You can choose to have Remote Desktop Connection drop the connection, warn you so that you can choose the action to take, or connect without warning you.

The Setting button opens the RD Gateway Server Settings dialog box (Figure 20-16), which lets you specify how Remote Desktop Connection works with a Terminal Services Gateway Server, now called Remote Desktop Gateway Server. RD Gateway acts essentially as an intermediary between your computer on the Internet and remote computers behind a firewall, such as at your office. RD Gateway uses SSL (port 443) rather than the usual port 3389 used by Remote Desktop connection. RD Gateway therefore makes connecting to remote computers possible without having a VPN or opening port 3389 in the firewall. What's more, it enables connection to multiple back-end computers, rather than just the one that would otherwise be possible with a hole in the firewall for port 3389.

Remote Desktop Connection can detect the RD Gateway server settings automatically, or you can specify them manually. The first two options on the RD Gateway Server Settings dialog box let you specify which method to use. If you choose to specify the settings yourself, you can enter the server name, login method, and whether to bypass the gateway for computers on your local network. If you enter the settings manually, you also have the option of specifying that Remote Desktop Connection will use your RD Gateway credentials to authenticate on the remote computer to which you are connecting.

FIGURE 20-16

RD Gateway Server Settings.

Tip

In most cases, you can open a remote session in Remote Desktop Connection without changing any options. ■

Allowing remote connections on a home network

You can also use Remote Desktop to control your Windows 7 PC from any other PC within your home network. For example, I have a notebook computer that I use for work and a home computer that I use for personal use. I no longer have a monitor, keyboard, or mouse hooked up to the home computer, but instead simply open a Remote Desktop Connection to it anytime I need to use it. Likewise, I can connect to the other computers in the house when I need to fix something on them.

Note

Remote Desktop is not required for normal home networking tasks such as sharing folders, files, and printers. Nor is it required to access those shared resources. You use Remote Desktop only if you want to operate the remote computer from the screen, keyboard, and mouse on another computer in the network. ■

Because the notebook computer has a wireless connection to my home network, I can use my personal PCs from anywhere in the house, even outside on the deck when the weather is nice.

To set up this type of remote connection, you first need a home network. The computer you want to control remotely needs Windows 7 Ultimate or some other edition that offers Remote Desktop. Finally, you can log in only to password-protected accounts on the Windows 7 computer. It can be a standard account, but it has to be password-protected.

The remote computer also needs to have a version of Windows that supports Remote Desktop. Home versions of Windows, such as Windows XP Home, do not include Remote Desktop capability that would allow you to connect to them remotely, but they include a client that enables them to connect to other computers that do support it.

Assuming that you have all the hardware and software to meet the requirements, the first step is to set up the Windows 7 computer to allow remote connections. Doing so requires administrative privileges and the following steps:

1. On the Windows 7 computer, log in to an account that has administrative privileges.
2. Open System Properties. (Click the Start button, right-click Computer, and choose Properties, or go through Control Panel.)
3. Click Remote Settings in the left pane.
4. On the Remote tab, under the Remote Desktop heading, choose one of the Allow Connections options.

Note

NLA (Network Level Authentication) provides more secure remote desktop connections but isn't available in older Windows versions. For more information, click the Help Me Choose link. ■

5. Click the Select Users button.
6. Use the Add button to add usernames of people who are allowed to connect remotely. The administrator is added to the list automatically. In Figure 20-17, I've added the username jboyce as the second person who can connect remotely.
7. Click OK in each open dialog box.

FIGURE 20-17

Added user jboyce as Remote Desktop user.

Make sure you know the computer name or IP address of the Windows 7 computer. You can see the name to the right of the Computer Name label on the main page of System Properties. For the sake of example, I'm naming the Windows 7 computer Bowser. To find the IP address of the computer, log in to the computer you want to control remotely. Open the Network and Internet object in the Control Panel, and then click View Network Status and Tasks. Click See Full Map and then hover the mouse over your computer to view the IP address in a tooltip window.

Tip

A quicker way to view your IP address is to click the Start button, type **cmd**, and press Enter. Then enter **ipconfig** in the command console window. (The term *command console* is synonymous with *DOS prompt*.) ■

Connecting from a remote home network PC

To connect remotely to the Windows 7 PC from another network in your LAN, open Remote Desktop Connection on your local computer.

In the dialog box that opens, enter the remote computer's IP address or name (Bowser, in my example) and click Connect. If the user account name of the computer at which you're sitting is different from the user account on the Windows 7 computer, click Log On As Another User. Type in the username and password for the user account on the Windows 7 computer and press Enter.

Depending on the display settings you used for the connection, the remote computer's screen will either appear in a window or will fill your local display. If you are running the connection in full-screen mode, move the mouse to the top of the screen to access the Connection Bar, which you can use to minimize, restore, or close the connection. From the local computer, you use the remote computer exactly as you would if you were sitting at that computer. When you've finished with your remote session, log out of the remote user account. That is, click the Start button on the remote computer and choose Log Off.

For more information, check the Remote Desktop Help on both computers that you intend to use in your own local network.

Access multiple computers behind a home firewall

I confess: I'm a computer geek. I have lots of computers at home. I have one, my wife has one, the kids have one, and occasionally there are a couple of others for ongoing projects, such as this book. I generally need to connect to only my own computer at home, but sometimes I do need to connect to the others. This section takes a look at how to set up your firewall for one computer and then extends that concept to multiple computers.

In a typical home network, a DSL modem, cable modem, or other device acts as a perimeter firewall for the home network. Being a computer geek, I have a dedicated hardware firewall connected between my DSL modem and my home network. With such a perimeter firewall in place, setting up a Remote Desktop Connection for a single computer isn't very difficult. You just need to create a static port mapping in the firewall to forward all port 3389 traffic coming in from the Internet to the computer that you want to control remotely.

On the FortiGate firewall that I use, setting up this connection takes two steps:

1. Create a virtual IP object that sets up port forwarding of port 3389 to the internal IP address of the computer (see Figure 20-18). Essentially, this virtual IP object associates port 3389 with that private IP address.

FIGURE 20-18

A virtual IP object for port forwarding.

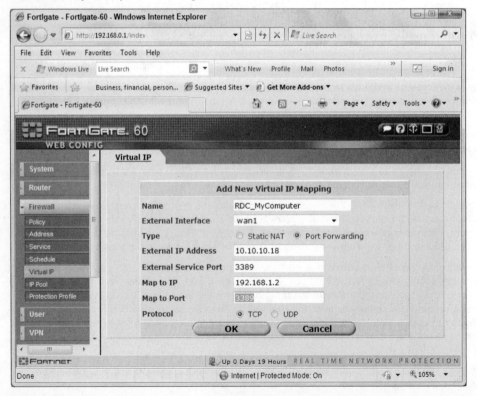

2. Create a rule in the firewall to allow incoming traffic to that virtual IP object. In effect, this allows port 3389 traffic through the firewall, and the virtual IP object causes that traffic to be forwarded to the computer I want to control remotely.

On a more common home network device, such as the D-Link wireless access point I use for wireless devices in the house, the process is a little easier. In this case, you set up a *virtual server* object for the computer you want to control remotely. Figure 20-19 shows an example. In this example, I have configured port 3389 to forward to 192.168.1.2, the IP address of my computer on the home network.

FIGURE 20-19

A virtual server object.

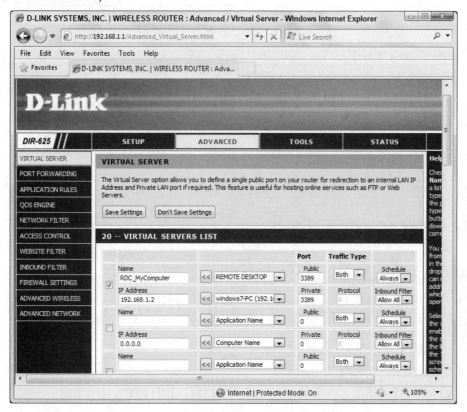

Many networking devices use the virtual server concept to configure port forwarding. The virtual server is just a computer on the network that will accept traffic on the specified port. In this case, that is port 3389 for Remote Desktop Connection.

Too easy, right? Now, extend that concept to enable remote connections to multiple computers. You can specify forwarding for any given port to only one computer on the internal network. So, only one computer can use port 3389 for Remote Desktop Connection. Fortunately, you can configure Remote Destkop Connection on a computer to use a different port, which means that you can assign a different port for each computer on the network. So, one computer might use port 3389, another 3390, another 3391, and so on.

Setting up the firewall for these additional computers is just like setting them up for the first one. Create a port-forwarding object and rule to forward the required port to the appropriate internal IP address. Table 20-1 shows some examples.

TABLE 20-1

Port	Internal IP
3389	192.168.1.2
3390	192.168.1.3
3391	192.168.1.4

In the scenario represented in Table 20-1, you create three different firewall port-forwarding objects so that 3389 goes to 192.168.1.2, 3390 goes to 192.168.1.3, and 3391 goes to 192.168.1.4.

With these firewall changes in place, you need to change the port on which each of the other two computers will listen for Remote Desktop Connection requests. You don't need to change the computer that will use 3389 because it's the default port. Here's how to change the other two computers to use their own ports:

Caution

Also be careful when editing the registry! ■

1. Log in to the computer with an administrative account.

2. Click Start, type **regedit**, and press Enter.

3. In the Registry Editor, locate the following key:

   ```
   HKEY_LOCAL_MACHINE\System\CurrentControlSet\Control\TerminalServer\
   WinStations\RDP-Tcp
   ```

4. Double-click the PortNumber value in the right pane.

5. In the Edit DWORD dialog box, click the Decimal option and then type the port number (in this case, 3390).

6. Click OK and then close the Registry Editor.

7. Repeat the process on the other computer to change its port to a unique number, such as 3391. Repeat again for any other computers you need to control remotely, assigning each a unique port number.

Tip

To check whether a computer is listening on the expected port, open a command console and type netstat -an. This command displays all connections and listening ports. If your computer is configured to use port 3389, for example, you'll see an entry for port 3389 with a status of Listening. ■

Wrap-Up

As are e-mail and the Web, newsgroups and FTP are Internet services that everyone can use. Newsgroups provide a virtual meeting place for people to discuss topics, get and give help, or to just hang out. FTP provides a simple means of transferring files of any size between an FTP server computer and your local computer. Remote Assistance and Remote Desktop Connection both provide a means to view and remotely control other computers. Key points of this chapter are:

- Newsgroups allow people to communicate online by posting and replying to messages.
- You can use Windows Live Mail to subscribe to and participate in newsgroups.
- FTP (File Transfer Protocol) is a technology for transferring files from one computer to another over the Internet.
- One of the easiest ways to transfer files with FTP is with Microsoft Internet Explorer because it allows you to manage files using the same techniques you use on your own computer.
- If you know a trusted computer expert who can help with your computer, use Remote Assistance to get live help online.
- Some corporations allow employees to connect to a corporate network from home using Remote Desktop Connection.
- If you have a home network and suitable versions of Windows, you can use Remote Desktop to control one PC on the network from another PC in the same network, or from the Internet.

Managing Names and Addresses

I n Windows 7, the Contacts folder is your electronic address book. Each
file in that folder is a *contact*, someone with whom you communicate. It
doesn't have to be only people you contact online. You can store anybody's
contact information in your Contacts folder. As with pictures, songs, videos,
and other documents, each user account has its own Contacts folder. So each
person who has a user account can have his or her own collection of names
and addresses.

Note

Keep in mind that the Windows Contacts folder and the contacts in it are separate from the contacts in your e-mail program. For example, if you opt to download and use Windows Live Mail as your e-mail program, it has its own set of
contacts. Although you can import your Windows Contacts into Windows Live
Mail, the contacts are not synchronized. So, if you import your Windows Contacts into Windows Live Mail and then make a change to one of your Windows
Contacts, that change will not show up in Windows Live Mail because there are
actually two separate contacts. ■

Why use Windows Contacts? If you are one of the few people who use a
computer but don't use e-mail, the Windows Contacts folder provides a place
for you to keep your own address book for letters, phone list, and other uses.
Or you might use Windows Contacts to store your personal contacts and your
e-mail program to store your business contacts. Whatever the case, you can use
your Windows Contacts for addressing e-mail, as described later in this chapter.

Opening Contacts

To create or manage contacts, open your Contacts folder using whichever of the
following methods is most convenient for you:

- Click the Start button, click your user name, and then click (or
  double-click) the Contacts folder.

- Press ⊞ , type **cont**, and click Windows Contacts.

- If you're already in a folder, click your user name in the breadcrumb trail, and then click (or double-click) the Contacts folder icon.

If you've never used your Contacts folder before, it will likely be empty except for an entry for your own user account. Figure 21-1 shows a sample Contacts folder with a few contacts already in place.

FIGURE 21-1

Sample Contacts folder.

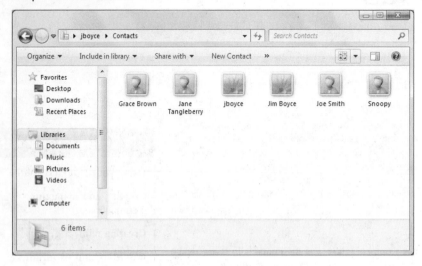

Changing how you view contacts

Because Contacts is a folder, you can control how things look using the standard techniques described in Chapter 29. For example:

- To show or hide the Preview pane, click Organize and choose Layout ⇨ Preview Pane.
- To show or hide the Navigation pane, click Organize and choose Layout ⇨ Navigation Pane.
- To show or hide the menu bar, press the Alt key or click Organize and choose Layout ⇨ Menu Bar.
- To size icons, click the arrow next to the Change Your View button and choose an icon size, or hold down the Ctrl key while spinning your mouse wheel.
- To sort or group contacts in Details view, point to any column heading and click the arrow that appears.

Making shortcuts to contacts

Before I go any further with Contacts, let me point out some easy ways to create shortcuts to your Contacts folder. These make opening the folder in the future easier. You don't have to create any of these shortcuts, of course. They're entirely optional. But if you use your Contacts folder often, you'll probably find them handy.

First, click your username in the breadcrumb menu so that you're in the main folder for your user account. Or, click Start and click your username. Right-click the Contacts icon, as shown in

Figure 21-2, and choose Send To ⇨ Desktop (Create Shortcut). Then, drag the shortcut from the desktop to the Start menu and release it to pin it to the Start menu.

To add a shortcut to the Favorites pane in the navigation bar, click the Start button and then click your username. Then drag the Contacts folder into the Favorites box and drop it there.

FIGURE 21-2

Right-click Contacts.

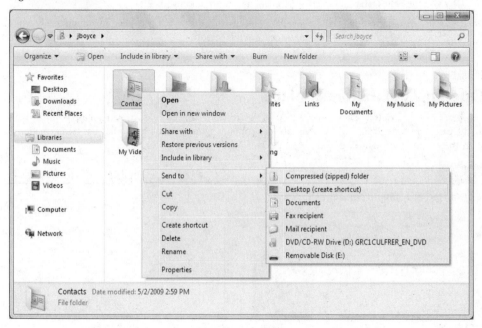

Creating a contact

Creating a contact is simple. First open your Contacts folder if you haven't already. Then click the New Contact toolbar button. Or right-click some empty space in your Contacts folder (not on an icon) and choose New ⇨ Contact.

An empty, fill-in-the-blanks form opens. (The blanks are called *fields*.) It's divided into multiple tabs. You don't have to fill in everything for a contact. Fill in only as much information as you need or want for the contact. Here are some tips for filling in a contact:

- After filling in a field, press the Tab key to move to the next one. Or click the next blank you want to fill.

- After filling in the first and last names, click the Full Name drop-down button to choose how you want the name displayed for alphabetizing.

- To add an e-mail address, type it into the E-mail box and click Add. If the contact has several e-mail addresses, repeat the process to add each one. Then click the e-mail address you use most often for that person and click Set As Default.

- To add a picture, click the picture box and choose Change Picture. Then navigate to the folder that contains the picture you want to add and click (or double-click) the desired picture. The picture becomes the contact's icon in the Contacts folder.

- If this is a personal contact, use the Home tab to fill in the person's home address.

- Use the Work tab to fill in the work address and other information.

- Use the Family tab to fill in personal information such as birthday, anniversary, spouse, children, and so forth.

- Use the Notes tab to fill in any miscellaneous information you desire.

- The IDs tab shouldn't require any intervention on your part. It gets filled in automatically when you receive a digitally signed message from the person.

- When you've finished entering the contact, click OK.

Opening and editing contacts

To open a contact, double-click its icon (unless you're using single-clicks, in which case you just have to click it). You see a Name and E-Mail tab that contains name, e-mail, and other basic information, as in the example in Figure 21-3.

FIGURE 21-3

Name and E-Mail tab of a sample contact.

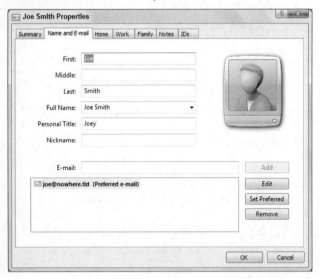

While viewing a contact's information on the Summary tab, you can do any of the following:

- To send the person an e-mail, click the e-mail address.

- To visit that person's Web site (if any), click the URL.

- To add, remove, or change the picture, click the Name and E-mail and then click the picture.

- To see or change any other information, click the appropriate tab.

Tips for Contacts Pictures

For best results, you'll want to create copies of pictures appropriately sized and cropped for contacts. You might want to create a subfolder, perhaps named Contact Pix, in your Pictures folder just for those pictures. That will make them easy to find.

If you want to use a photo you took with a digital camera, start with a copy of the photo so that you don't compromise the original. Try to crop out a perfect square around the person's face. Then size that cropped image to about 250 x 250 pixels. Save it in BMP, JPEG, TIFF, or PNG format. If you're using a logo or icon rather than a photo, you can use the GIF or ICO extension. For picture-editing tools and techniques, see Chapter 23.

Note

Each contact you create in your Contacts file is stored as a `.contact` file. The extension, however, is visible only if you deselect the Hide Extensions for Known File Types check box on the View tab in the Folder Options dialog box. ■

Create a "me" contact

Windows creates a contact for your user account automatically, but you will probably want to fill in more fields, such as your e-mail address. You can e-mail that to folks so that they don't have to type your contact information themselves. After you create a contact for yourself, right-click its icon and choose Set As My Contact.

Tip

Your default user account contact is already set up as your contact. If you right-click your contact, you should see This Is Me in the menu in place of Set As My Contact. You don't have to use the default contact as your own. You can create a new one for yourself, if desired. ■

If you want to e-mail your contact information to others who aren't using Windows 7, attach a `.vcf` file to an e-mail message. To do that, right-click your Contact icon and choose Send Contact. A new message window opens with the card already attached as a `.vcf` file. Fill in the To and Subject lines. Fill in the body of the message informing the recipient that your contact information is attached.

Tip

Contact Groups make sending and forwarding messages to multiple recipients easy. ■

Creating Contact Groups

A contact group is any collection of contacts that have something in common. It could be people who go to the same church as you, members of the same club, work colleagues, or just pals. You might also think of a contact group as a mailing list (or distribution list). The beauty of a contact group is that you can send or forward an e-mail message to everyone in the group in one fell swoop.

Visually, a contact group is just a collection of contact names. For example, Figure 21-4 shows a contact group named Family.

FIGURE 21-4

Sample contact group.

To create a contact group in your Contacts folder:

1. Click the New Contact Group toolbar button.

2. In the Group Name box, enter any name that describes the group.

3. Add members using any of the following methods:

   - To add existing contacts, click Add to Contact Group. Click the first person who should be in the group. Then hold down the Ctrl key as you click everyone else who belongs in the group. Then click Add.

   - To add a new person to the group as well as create a contact for that person, click Create New Contact. Fill in contact information for that person and click OK.

   - To add a person's name and e-mail address without creating a contact icon for that person, fill in the Contact Name and E-mail boxes near the bottom of the window and click Create for Group Only.

4. Optionally, click the Contact Group Details tab and fill in details about the group. For example, if you're all members of the same club or church, you can add address and phone information for the building where you meet.

5. Click OK.

The group window closes and appears as an icon in the Contacts folder. You can use and treat the group in much the same way as you do an individual contact:

   - To send an e-mail to the group, right-click the group icon and choose Action ➪ Send E-mail.

   - To change the group, double-click the group's icon in Contacts.

- To delete the group, right-click its icon and choose Delete. Contacts within the group will remain. Only the group icon and noncontacts are deleted.

Don't forget that you have much leeway in how you view the contents of folders. For example, to view and organize your contacts as a list or table, choose Details from the Views menu. To choose columns to display, right-click any column heading, as shown in Figure 21-5. If the drop-down menu doesn't show a column you want to include, click More for a more complete list.

FIGURE 21-5

Choose columns to display.

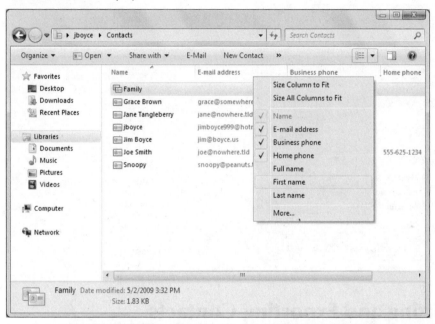

Family   Date modified: 5/2/2009 3:32 PM
Size: 1.83 KB

After you've selected the columns you want to view, you can arrange them however you like. Just drag any column heading left or right to place it where it's easy to see. You can sort, group, and filter contacts as you would files in any folder. For more information on how that works, see Chapters 29–32.

Printing Contacts

Printing contact information is easy. If you want to print only certain contacts, select their icons using any of the standard techniques, such as Ctrl+Click. Then click the Print toolbar button. If that button isn't visible, click >> at the end of the toolbar and then click Print. The Print dialog box opens, looking something like the example in Figure 21-6.

To print all contacts, choose All Contacts under Print range. To print only selected contacts, choose Selected Contacts. Then choose a print format:

- **Memo:** Prints most business and address contact information.
- **Business Card:** Prints business address and phone information.
- **Phone List:** Prints phone numbers.

If you have multiple printers, click the one you want to print with. Then click the Print button.

If none of the available print formats fits what you need, you can export contacts to a file. Then import those contacts into some other program that gives you the flexibility you need to print as you see fit.

Print options for contacts.

Importing and Exporting Contacts

Importing allows you to copy contacts from external programs into your Contacts folder. Exporting lets you copy contacts to another program or a format that's compatible with an outside program. I start this section with importing.

Importing people to your Contacts folder

You can import names and addresses from the following formats into your Windows Contacts folder:

- **CSV (Comma-Separated Values):** This is a generic format to which many programs can export data. You start in the other program by exporting names and addresses to a CSV file. Then you open your Contacts folder and import the CSV file you created from the original program.

- **LDIF (LDAP server):** Use this format to import contacts from a directory server that uses Lightweight Directory Access Protocol (LDAP).

- **vCard (VCF file):** This format is used by many programs to store virtual business card data. In contrast to other options described here, you might use this format to import a single contact whose data is stored in a .vcf file.

- **WAB (Windows Address Book):** This format imports contacts from the `.wab` file used by Windows Address Book and Outlook Express in earlier versions of Windows. Typically, you find that file in the `x:\Documents and Settings\`*`UserName`*`\Application Data\Microsoft\Address Book` folder, where *x* is the disk drive and *UserName* is the name of the user account.

If the data you want to import isn't already in one of these formats, open the program that you normally use to manage those contacts. Then search its Help for "export" to see whether you can export to CSV or another compatible format.

When the data you want to import are in an appropriate format and you know the location of the file, follow these steps to import the data to your Contacts folder:

1. Open Windows Contacts.

Tip

If you plan to import from Application Data or another hidden folder, click the Organize button and choose Folder and Search Options. Click the View tab and then click Show Hidden Files, Folders, and Drives ⇨ OK. Doing so ensures that all folders and files are visible in the steps to follow. ∎

2. Click the Import toolbar button.

3. Click the format in which the data to be imported are stored; then click Import.

4. Navigate to the drive and folder in which the data to be imported are stored; then click (or double-click) the file to import. Click Next.

5. If importing from a CSV file, in the CSV Import dialog box, verify the field mapping to use for the import. To change a field, click the field, click Change Mapping, choose the field you want to map to, and click OK.

6. When you are satisfied with the mapping, click Finish.

You should see an icon for each imported contact.

Exporting contacts to vCards

Many programs store contact information in virtual business cards, where each contact is a file with a `.vcf` extension. Before you get started, you might want to create a folder to store the exported data. That way, all the exported contacts will be together in a single folder.

To export contacts in vCard format:

1. Open Windows Contacts.

2. Click the Export toolbar button.

3. Click vCards (folder of `.vcf` files).

4. Click Export.

5. Navigate to the folder in which you want to place the exported vCards.

6. Click OK.

7. When the export is complete, click OK.

To verify the export, open the folder to which you exported. You should see an icon for each exported contact. The contacts won't show any pictures because the vCard format doesn't support the use of pictures.

Exporting to a CSV file

You can export contacts to a single Comma-Separated Values (CSV) file for later import to another program. For example, after exporting contacts to a CSV file, you can open them in Excel, import them to a Microsoft Access table, or use them for a Microsoft Word mail merge. With Word and Access, you can print form letters, mailing labels, and envelopes from the CSV file.

To export contacts to a CSV file, open Windows Contacts as you normally would. Then:

1. Click the Export toolbar button.
2. Click CSV (Comma-Separated Values) ➪ Export.
3. Type a name for the exported file. Or click the Browse button, navigate to the folder in which you want to store the file, enter a filename, and click Save.
4. Click Next.
5. Select (check) the fields you want to export and click Finish.
6. Click OK when the export is complete.

To verify that export, open the folder to which you exported the file. To view the contents of the file using Notepad, right-click its icon and choose Open With ➪ Notepad. That will show you the file in its raw form. But in actual practice, you'll likely import it into whatever program you want to use.

Searching for Contacts

You don't need to open Windows Contacts to find a person's contact information. Just click the Start button or press ⊞ . Type a few characters from the person's first or last name until you see that name on the Start menu. Then click the person's name on the Start menu. When the contact opens, click the Summary tab and then click the contact's e-mail address to send an e-mail. It's quick and easy.

You can do the same kind of thing using the Search box in the upper-right corner of the Contacts window. Type a few characters from the person's name. The contact list shrinks to contain only the people whose names contain those letters, and highlights the search text in the contact information (such as name or e-mail address). When you see the person you want, double-click the name to open. To unfilter and see all contacts again, click the x at the right side of the Search box.

Sharing Contacts on a Network

If your computer is part of a network, you can share a contact with other Windows 7 computers in that network. The process is the same as that for sharing any other file. Right-click the contact and choose Share With. Choose the people with whom you want to share, and set permission levels. For more information, see Chapters 54 and 55.

Wrap-Up

Names and addresses are easy to manage in Windows 7, thanks to the Contacts folder. Here's a summary of all the things you can do:

- To view contacts, open your Contacts folder. From the desktop, you can click Start and click your username, then double-click the Contacts folder.

- To create shortcuts to your Contacts folder, click the Start button and choose your username. Click the arrow to the left of Libraries in the breadcrumb and choose your username. Then drag the Contacts folder to the Libraries branch in the navigation pane or to the Start button, depending on where you want to place shortcuts.

- To create a new contact, click the New Contact toolbar button in your Contacts folder.

- To open or change a contact's information, open the contact icon.

- To identify a contact as yourself, right-click your own contact icon and choose Set As My Contact.

- To create a mailing list, click New Contact Group in the toolbar.

- To send an e-mail to a contact group, right-click the group icon and choose Action ⇨ Send E-mail. Or from a new message or forwarded message, click To in the address field and choose the group as the recipient.

- To print contacts, click the Print toolbar button.

- Click Import or Export on the toolbar to import contacts from an external source, or copy contacts to an external file.

- To quickly find a contact without opening your Contacts folder, press and type a few characters from the person's first or last name. When you see the name on the Start menu, click it.

Troubleshooting Internet Problems

I nternet problems can be caused by your connection, a problem with the page you're viewing, or a problem with your Web browser.

Troubleshooting Internet Explorer

In this chapter, we focus on problems that are related to Microsoft Internet Explorer.

Clicking a hyperlink has no effect

The link you clicked may open in a new window that is being blocked as a pop-up. Click the Information bar to allow pop-ups, or click the No symbol in the status bar (see Figure 22-1) and choose an option to allow pop-ups. Another possibility is that the window is opening in the background. Look on the taskbar for the new window.

Note
Everything described in Chapter 16 applies to Web pages that open in new browser windows as well. ∎

Can't download program or ActiveX control

Windows 7 adds extra security, preventing downloads from occurring without your permission. When you click a link to start a download, you might see the window shown in Figure 22-2. Click either Run or Save to continue.

Caution
Do not accept unsolicited downloads. Download only programs from sites you know and trust. ∎

FIGURE 22-1

Choose an option to allow pop-ups.

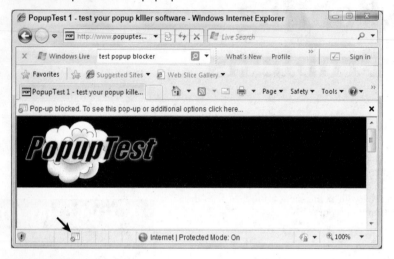

FIGURE 22-2

Specify whether you want to download or run the application.

Security alert about leaving a secure Internet connection

Many sites on the Internet require personal information. Ordering products from Amazon or setting up your account on eBay require that you provide information about yourself. Reputable sites require that you enter this type of information in a secure manner. After entering information and submitting it, you may be prompted with the dialog box shown in Figure 22-3.

This warning is indicating that you were previously at a page that was passing encrypted information to the server and you are now being redirected to a page that does not require encryption. In most cases, this is not a problem because your information has already been sent to the server in a secure manner. Clicking the More Info button will provide additional details; if you are comfortable, you can select the In the Future, Do Not Show This Warning check box.

FIGURE 22-3

Internet Explorer warning that you are leaving a secure site.

Error message: "This page cannot be displayed"

The two most common causes of this problem are trying to browse to a Web page when you're offline and mistyping a URL. If you have a dial-up account, first make sure that you're online. (If you can check your e-mail, you know you're online.)

Keep in mind that you are allowed no margin for typographical errors when typing a URL. Even a minor misspelling, such as www.windowscatalogue.com rather than www.windowscatalog.com, will cause this error. Putting a blank space in a URL will almost always cause the same problem. (The blank space is changed to %20 after you press Enter.)

For additional causes of frequent Page Not Found Errors and solutions, go to support.microsoft.com and search with the keywords "Page Cannot Be Displayed."

Tip

Consider enabling more descriptive error messages in IE. To do so, click Tools ➪ Internet Options ➪ Advanced, and then clear the checkbox beside Show Friendly HTTP Error Messages. ∎

Can't change the default home page

Normally, you can change your default home page (the page that opens automatically when you first open Internet Explorer) at any time. You just browse to whatever Web page you want to make your home page, choose Tools ➪ Internet Options from Internet Explorer's menu bar, and then click Use Current and click OK. You can add several home pages if you like, and each will open in its own tab when you start Internet Explorer.

Note

In a corporate environment, an administrator can also control your home page by using the Internet Explorer Administration Kit. In that case, you can't override the change without the administrator's consent. ∎

If you find that your default home page keeps being reset to something else, look in Add or Remove Programs for programs that know how to do this, such as SecondPower Multimedia Speedbar, GoHip! Browser Enhancement, and Xupiter toolbar, and uninstall those products. Similarly, you can choose Tools ➪ Manage Add-Ons ➪ Enable or Disable Add-Ons and disable any add-ons that include those names.

If the options to change your default home page are disabled (dimmed), your computer has probably been infected with a virus or worm. Use your antivirus software to scan your entire system for viruses, and delete everything that the scan finds. In addition to your antivirus software, you can use Microsoft's Windows Defender, discussed in detail in Chapter 8. Defender is designed to remove unwanted applications.

Tip

You can also try running IE with no add-ons. Click Start ⇨ All Programs ⇨ Accessories ⇨ System Tools ⇨ Internet Explorer (No Add-Ons). ■

Saved pictures stored as bitmaps (.bmp files)

When you right-click a picture on a Web page, it is normally saved as a JPEG or GIF file with whatever filename you provide. If all your images are saved as bitmaps instead, follow these steps:

1. Choose Tools ⇨ Internet Options from Internet Explorer's menu bar.

2. Click the Delete button, select Temporary Internet Files, and then click the Delete button. (Don't worry; you won't lose any programs, documents, or anything else worth keeping.)

3. When the deletion is complete, click the Advanced tab in the Internet Options dialog box.

4. Scroll down to the Security heading in the Advanced Settings list and deselect, if necessary, the Do Not Save Encrypted Pages to Disk option.

5. Click OK to close the dialog box.

6. Click the Refresh button in Internet Explorer's toolbar or press F5.

All other Internet Explorer problems/features

Internet Explorer is a large program that has more to do with the Internet than Windows 7 per se. So, it's not something I can cover in depth in a general Windows book like this. But there's plenty of information available to you. I suggest that you start with the Help that's built into Internet Explorer, as follows:

1. Choose Help ⇨ Internet Explorer Help from Internet Explorer's menu bar. (Press the Alt key if you don't see the menu bar.)

2. In the Help window that opens, click the Browse Help button, which looks like a small book in the toolbar. Then:

   ● Click any item that displays a book icon to see topics within that category.

   ● Click any icon that shows a page with a question mark to open the information for that topic.

At any point, you can type text in the box labeled Search Help. You also can post questions to the online community by clicking the Ask icon in the toolbar and then clicking the Windows Communities link.

For current news, downloads, and more information about Microsoft Internet Explorer, visit the IE home page at www.microsoft.com/ie.

Troubleshooting Windows Live Mail

If you're having problems with e-mail and use Windows Live Mail as your e-mail client, the troubleshooting tips that follow may help solve the problem. Microsoft occasionally adds more security to Windows Live Mail through automatic updates.

Error message: "The host *name* could not be found . . ."

This error message occurs when the host name for your ISP or e-mail server is specified incorrectly for your service. To use Windows Live Mail as an e-mail client, you must (1) make sure that your e-mail provider supports the use of Windows Mail, and (2) use the name, e-mail address, password, incoming mail server name, and outgoing mail server name specified by your ISP. If you have the correct information from your e-mail provider, here's how you can correct the entries for your account:

1. Click Start ➪ All Programs ➪ Windows Live ➪ Windows Live Mail.

2. In the left pane, right-click the account and choose Properties.

3. In the Account Properties dialog box, click the Servers tab to get to the options shown in Figure 22-4.

FIGURE 22-4

The Servers tab of an e-mail account's Properties sheet.

4. Fill in the blanks using exactly the information provided by your ISP or e-mail service provider.

Caution

Attempting to "figure out" appropriate entries on the Servers tab by guessing is like trying to guess a total stranger's phone number — futile. (The sample data shown in the figure is hypothetical and won't work.) ■

5. Follow any other instructions provided by your ISP to fill in information on other tabs.

6. When you've finished entering all your account information, click OK in the Properties dialog box.

Click the Sync button in the Windows Live Mail toolbar to test the new settings.

Some of my mail is not showing up in my Inbox

Windows Live Mail includes a Junk Mail filter. If you receive a notification that you just received mail — either a sound or the small message icon that shows up in Notification bar — but you're unable to locate it, check in your Junk Mail folder. When you receive a message that looks questionable, you might see the dialog box shown in Figure 22-5.

FIGURE 22-5

Windows Live Mail notifying you that there may be something suspect about the message.

You can alter the settings for junk mail by selecting Tools ➪ Safety Options. To learn more about Junk Mail, see the section titled "Dealing with Spam (Junk E-mail)" in Chapter 18.

Tip

Your e-mail provider might also filter your mail before it gets to your Inbox. ■

Pictures are missing from e-mail messages

Windows Live Mail intentionally replaces the pictures in some e-mail messages with a box containing a red X. Doing this protects you from *Web beacon* software, which alerts an online server when you click the picture. It also saves you from having to wait for all the pictures in your junk e-mail to download.

When you get a legitimate e-mail with pictures that you do want to see, just click Show Images in the Information bar (see Figure 22-6) to download and view images for that message only.

Can't open or save e-mail attachment

Windows Live Mail blocks access to potentially unsafe e-mail attachments. When it blocks such an attachment, you should see the following message in the Information bar: *This message contains an attachment whose file type is considered dangerous. The file has been deactivated.* See "Using E-mail Attachments" in Chapter 18 for details.

Caution

Don't trust the extension you see on an e-mail attachment, because there may be another hidden extension behind the one you see. For example, the ILOVEYOU virus was spread in an e-mail attachment named `Love-letter-for-you.txt.vbs`**, and *a lot* of people fell for it. Never open any attachment unless you know exactly what it is and whom it's from.** ■

FIGURE 22-6

Information bar and a blocked image.

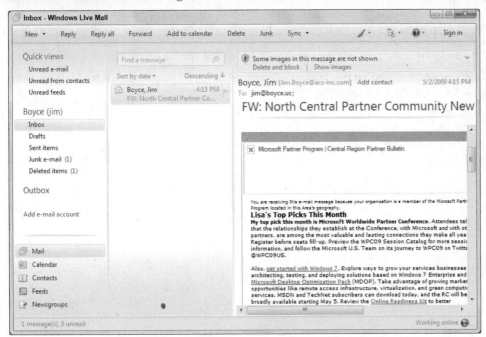

Error Message: "Your current security settings prohibit running ActiveX controls . . ."

This is usually a good thing because an ActiveX control in an e-mail message is likely to be spyware or some other malicious code that you don't want. Click OK and delete the message.

All other Windows Live Mail problems/features

Microsoft provides Windows Live Mail as an optional e-mail and newsgroup client for people who use ISPs that support that program. As such, it's not directly relevant to Windows 7, the operating system, which is the main topic of this book. I don't have room in this book to cover Internet programs in great depth. But you can get plenty of information from the Help in the program.

Keep in mind that when it comes to e-mail, the only people who can really help with your account are the people who have provided you with that account — either your ISP or the e-mail service with which you created the account.

More Internet Troubleshooting

The built-in help that comes with 7 offers many helpful suggestions for troubleshooting Internet connections, Web browsing, Windows Live Mail, FTP, and some other Internet resources. Click the Start button and choose Help and Support. The Help screens are subject to change because computer manufacturers are allowed to customize, and because some help comes from the Internet. If you can't find the topic you're looking for, use the Search Help box to find specific information.

If you can get online and get into Microsoft Communities, you'll find several good resources for asking questions about Internet Explorer and Windows Live Mail.

Part V

Pictures, Music, and Movies

Part V gets into the fun and creative things you can do with pictures, music, and video. Chapter 23 starts off with pictures and all the cool new things you can do with Windows Live Photo Gallery.

Chapter 24 covers Windows Media Player, a great tool for creating and organizing a music collection and creating your own custom music CDs.

Chapter 25 moves on to video files and DVD movies, mostly centering on using Windows Media Player.

If you have the Premium or Ultimate edition of Windows 7, you also have Windows Media Center. Media Center lets you access your entire media collection through a computer or TV screen. If you have the right equipment, you can work it all with a remote control like the one you use to operate your TV.

Despite all the potential fun, multimedia can pose some real technical challenges. Chapter 27 provides solutions to the most common problems faced when working with digital media.

Working with Pictures

I n the computer world, the terms *picture*, *photo*, *image*, *graphic image*, and *digital image* all refer to the same thing — a still picture. Windows 7 offers lots of great tools for organizing, editing, printing, and e-mailing pictures.

Today's hard disks have room to store many thousands of photos. The Windows Live Photo Gallery, an optional add-on for Windows, provides an easy way to organize and find photos based on keywords called *tags*. The Fix pane in Photo Gallery makes common tasks like cropping and red-eye removal a breeze.

Much of this chapter focuses on Windows Live Photo Gallery as the primary tool for managing photos. You can download Windows Live Photo Gallery from home.live.com.

Getting Pictures into Your Computer

You can acquire pictures to use in your computer in several ways. You can store pictures in any folder you like. If you don't have a preference, use the Pictures folder for your user account. You can always move or copy the pictures to another location later, should the need arise.

Getting pictures from a digital camera

Before I tell you how to get pictures from a digital camera, you should understand that I'm talking about the digital cameras that connect through a USB cable and appear as a USB mass storage device. If the method described doesn't work for your camera, see the manual that came with that camera for details. You may have to install and use the software that came with your camera to get pictures from it, but the following steps will work with most modern digital cameras:

1. Use a USB cable to connect your camera to your computer and turn on the camera.

2. Wait a few seconds, then:

   - If you see an AutoPlay dialog box like the one in Figure 23-1, click Import Pictures and Videos. Then skip to step 4.

553

FIGURE 23-1

AutoPlay options for a digital camera.

- If nothing happens within a minute or so of connecting and turning on your camera, open Windows Live Photo Gallery (click the Start button and choose All Programs ⇨ Windows Live ⇨ Windows Live Photo Gallery). Click File in its toolbar and choose Import from Camera or Scanner. Then click the icon for your camera and click Import.

3. In the dialog box shown in Figure 23-2, enter a *tag* (keyword) that will later help you identify pictures. For example, enter the event, location, or subject of the photos.

FIGURE 23-2

Add a tag to pictures.

Tip

Entering a tag is optional, but very useful. Try to think of a single word that describes the pictures you're importing. You can add, change, or delete tags at any time. So don't knock yourself out trying to find a word that applies to every picture. ■

4. Click Import.

5. The next dialog box keeps you apprised of the progress. If you want to delete pictures from the camera after copying, select the Erase after Importing checkbox.

Tip

If you miss the opportunity to erase pictures after importing, you can still erase those using buttons on your camera. Or, open the camera from your Computer folder and delete the pictures using standard techniques described in Chapter 29. ■

6. When copying is finished, turn off and disconnect the camera.

Depending on your camera and the types of pictures (and videos) you imported, Windows Live Photo Gallery might open and display thumbnails of your pictures. However, the pictures aren't actually stored in Photo Gallery, so don't worry if you don't see them there. The pictures are actually in your Pictures folder as described under "Using Your Pictures Folder" later in this chapter.

Getting pictures from a memory card

If you have pictures on a memory card, and your computer has slots for those cards or a card reader attached, you can copy pictures directly from the card. Once you've inserted a memory card into a slot, the card is basically the same as any external disk drive. You can use all the standard techniques discussed in Chapter 29 to move, copy, and delete files as you see fit.

Exactly what happens on your screen after you insert a memory card depends on your AutoPlay settings for cards. See "Change Autoplay Settings" in Chapter 43 for more information on AutoPlay. Regardless of what happens after you first insert a card, you can always get to its contents through your Computer folder. Here's how:

1. Click the Start button and choose Computer.

2. If necessary, scroll down through your removable drives. If you have multiple card slots, look for the one that shows a specific name. For example, in Figure 23-3, drive H is a slot that contains a memory card taken from a Canon camera.

3. Open the card's icon. Then navigate through folders on the card until you find the icons that represent pictures.

4. Select the icons for the pictures you want to copy, or click Organize ➪ Select All (or press Ctrl+A) to select them all.

5. Drag or copy-and-paste the selected icons to your Pictures folder and ignore the following steps. Optionally, use the following steps to copy without dragging or copy-and-paste.

6. If the menu bar isn't visible, tap the Alt key. Choose Edit ➪ Copy from the menu (or Cut if you want to delete the pictures from the memory card).

7. Open the destination folder for the images and press Ctrl+V to paste them into the folder.

The pictures are copied to the destination folder. You can close the folder that's open and remove the memory card. Open the destination folder to see the copied pictures.

No Memory Card Slots?

I f your computer doesn't have slots for memory cards, you can easily add those slots by purchasing and connecting a card reader. Go to any online site that sells computer accessories. Then search for

continued

continued

memory card reader. If you're not interested in installing hardware inside your computer, choose a product that connects through a USB port. Make sure you know what physical size card you need to read and get an appropriate reader. Or, choose a reader that works with all types of memory cards.

FIGURE 23-3

Drive H contains a memory card.

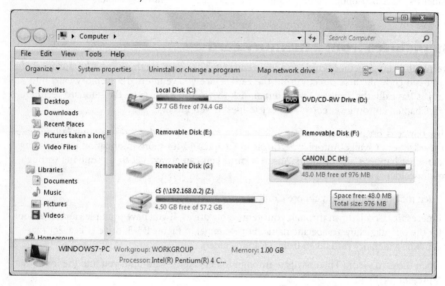

Tip

After (not before) you've verified that pictures have been copied, you can delete them from the memory card. Select all the icons in the card as in step 4. Then press Delete (Del) or right-click any selected icon and choose Delete. ∎

Getting pictures from a CD or DVD

You can store pictures and copy them in many ways on CDs and DVDs. If someone sends you a CD or DVD that contains only pictures, you will likely see a prompt on the screen shortly after you put the disk into your drive. A simple way to import the pictures from that prompt is to click Import Using Windows Picture and Video Import. Then just follow the instructions that appear on the screen. If you're prompted to enter a tag, just type in any word or short phrase that describes the pictures. All the pictures will be copied (imported) to your Pictures folder, where you can access them at any time without using the CD or DVD. But you should keep that disk as a backup.

Tip

You can also copy pictures from a CD using the standard techniques described in Chapter 29. ∎

Some commercial CDs might automatically launch some program when inserted. That might leave you wondering how in the heck you're going to copy pictures from the disk to your computer. The trick is to simply close that program and get to the CD's contents directly. The process goes something like this:

1. Insert the disk into your CD/DVD drive and wait a few seconds. Then:

   - If an AutoPlay dialog box asks what you want to do with the disk, click Open Folder to View Files and go to step 3.

   - If some program opens automatically to show the pictures, close that program and go to step 2.

   - If nothing at all happens within a minute or so of inserting the disk, continue with step 2.

2. Click the Start button and choose Computer. Right-click the icon that represents your CD/DVD drive and choose Open.

3. Now you're viewing the contents of the CD. If necessary, navigate through any folders you find until you find icons for the pictures.

4. Select the icons for the pictures you want to copy. Click Organize ➪ Select All or press Ctrl+A to select them all.

5. Drag or copy-and-paste any selected icon to the Pictures folder in the Navigation pane. Make sure you get the mouse pointer right on that Pictures folder icon so that you see Copy to My Pictures near the mouse pointer. Then release the mouse button.

6. Wait for all of the pictures to copy and then remove the CD from the drive.

You won't need the CD to access those pictures anymore. You'll be able to access them directly from your Pictures folder. But keep the CD as a backup, in case you accidentally delete or destroy any of the copied pictures.

Getting pictures from a scanner

To get photographs on paper into your computer, you use a scanner. Optionally you can use a film scanner or slide scanner to get pictures from film or slides, but those are a bit more expensive than traditional paper scanners.

The first step is, of course, to install the scanner and any required software as per the instructions that came with the scanner. The second step is to read the instructions on how to work your scanner. The steps I'm about to give you work with most, but not all scanners and there may be differences among different products. So if all else fails here, read the instructions that came with *your* scanner to best understand the product you own.

The standard operating procedure for more modern scanners goes like this:

1. Turn on the scanner and put in the picture you want to copy.

2. Click the Start button and choose All Programs ➪ Windows Live ➪ Windows Live Photo Gallery.

3. Click the File toolbar button and choose Import from Scanner or Camera.

4. In the Device Selection window that opens, click the scanner's icon and click Import.

5. Select the scan settings from the options provided as summarized in the following list:

Tip

If you previously saved settings in a scan profile, click Select Profile and then click the profile you want to use. ■

- **Paper Source:** Select the type of scanner you have (flatbed, feeder, or film scanner).
- **Paper Size:** If you're using an automatic document feeder to scan multiple items, select the size of the paper you're scanning. Otherwise, leave this empty.
- **Color Format:** Choose Color, Grayscale, or Black and White.

Note

For a black and white photo, choose Grayscale. The Black and White option provides only black and white with no shades of gray. Black and White, in this context, is best used only for typewritten documents (black ink on white paper). ■

- **File Type:** Choose a file format. Bitmap Image offers the highest quality at the cost of a large file size. Also, bitmap is an older format that doesn't support tagging and metadata as well as newer formats. Better to use JPEG or PNG for a photo. Use Microsoft Document Imaging File only for typewritten documents, not photos.
- **Resolution (DPI):** Select your resolution dots per inch (DPI). The larger the DPI the better the quality of the scanned image, but the larger the file will be. Your best bet for color photos is 300 DPI. Use 75 DPI only for black-and-white text documents. The 150 DPI setting is okay for photos you don't intend to print. You can't change resolution after scanning, but you can rescan the item.
- **Brightness and Contrast:** Use these, if necessary, to enhance the picture's brightness and contrast. You'll need to do a Preview scan to see the effects of any changes you make.

Optionally, if you plan to scan more pictures at the current settings, click Save Profile and give your profile a name.

6. Click Scan.

When the scan is complete, the picture will appear in the Photo Gallery. The actual picture file is in your Pictures folder.

Note

For information on Windows Fax and Scan, see Chapter 38. ■

Using pictures you get by e-mail

Pictures that are embedded in, or attached to, e-mail messages you receive won't show up in Photo Gallery at first. You need to save the picture(s) to your Pictures folder if you want to access and edit them using techniques described in this chapter.

Exactly how you save attachments and embedded pictures depends on your e-mail program. If you use Windows Live Mail, see "Saving attachments as files" and "Saving embedded pictures as files" in Chapter 18.

For most other e-mail clients, it's usually a simple matter of right-clicking the attachment's icon and choosing Save As. In the case of a picture that's visible in the body of the message, right-click the picture and choose Save Picture As. However, do keep in mind that all e-mail clients and systems are different. If you can't figure out how to save attachments or pictures in your e-mail, search your ISP or e-mail provider's e-mail support for attachment, or contact its technical support.

Copying pictures from Web sites

Needless to say, billions of pictures exist on the Internet. You can often find just the picture you're looking for by going to a site like images.google.com and searching for an appropriate word or phrase.

If you find a picture you can use (and you're not infringing on anyone's copyright in the process), you can store a copy of the picture in any folder of your choosing. If the picture you see on the screen is a link to a larger copy of the image, click to get to the larger copy of the picture. Then use whatever options your Web browser provides to save a copy of the picture. Here are the steps for Internet Explorer, the Web browser that comes with Windows 7:

1. In Internet Explorer, right-click anywhere on the picture you want and choose Save Picture As.
2. Click Pictures in the Navigation pane (see Figure 23-4). Of course, you can choose some other folder if you prefer. For example, double-click any subfolder icon in the main pane to store the picture in that subfolder.

   - Optionally, to put the picture in a subfolder of the folder you just opened, double-click that subfolder's icon.

   - Optionally, change the filename of the picture to a filename of your own choosing.

   - Optionally, click to the right of the Save As Type label and choose a format. (JPEG works best if you plan to use Windows Live Photo Gallery.)

3. Click Save.

A copy of the picture is saved in whatever folder you specified in step 2.

FIGURE 23-4

Save Picture.

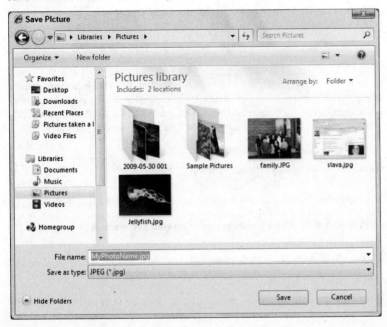

Note

For more information on saving files, see "Saving Things in Folders" in Chapter 28. ∎

Copy-and-paste pictures

You can copy an open picture from just about any document to any document that accepts pictures. For example, you can copy and paste a picture from a Web page to a Microsoft Word document. You just have to make sure the picture is open (not just an icon or thumbnail). To copy-and-paste an open picture:

1. Right-click the picture and choose Copy.
2. Right-click where you want to put the picture and choose Paste.

You can use the same technique to make a copy of a picture within a folder or Windows Live Photo Gallery. Right-click the icon or thumbnail of the picture you want to copy and choose Copy. Then right-click some empty place within the folder (perhaps after the last icon) and choose Paste. The copy will have the same filename as the original followed by -Copy.

Taking screenshots

Caution

The Snipping Tool lets you take a screenshot and also annotate it with your own text. Be sure to check that out under "Annotating Screenshots with Snipping Tool" in Chapter 14. ∎

A screenshot is like a photo of something you see on your screen. Most of the pictures in this book are screenshots. You can create screenshots in Windows 7 in two ways. One is to use the Snipping Tool, described in Chapter 14. The other is to use the Print Screen key.

Using the Print Screen key

The Print Screen key gets its name from the early days of computers where pressing it actually printed whatever was on your screen at the moment to paper. It hasn't worked that way in a long time. Today the Print Screen key takes a snapshot of the screen and puts it in the Windows Clipboard where it just sits until you paste the Clipboard contents. You can use the Print Screen key in two ways:

- **Print Screen:** Takes a snapshot of the entire screen.
- **Alt+Print Screen:** Takes a snapshot of the active window only.

Note

The Print Screen key may be labeled Prnt Scrn, PrtScn, or something similar on your keyboard. ∎

To make a screenshot, get the screen looking the way you want. Then follow these steps:

1. Press Print Screen or Alt+Print Screen.
2. Open your favorite graphics program. If you don't have one, click the Start button and choose All Programs ⇨ Accessories ⇨ Paint to open Paint (which comes with Windows 7).

Note

You can paste the snapshot into a document (like a Microsoft Word document). But if you do, you won't be able to treat it like a normal editable picture that is saved separately on disk. It's a good idea to paste it into Paint or some other graphics program and save it as a JPEG or PNG file. You cannot paste the snapshot into a folder or Windows Live Photo Gallery. ■

3. Choose your program's Paste command (usually located in the Edit menu, or for Paint, in the Home toolbar), or press Ctrl+V. The screenshot is pasted into the program.

4. Exit Paint or your graphics program by clicking its Close (X) button.

5. When you see a message asking if you want to save your changes, click Yes. The Save As dialog box opens.

6. In the Save As dialog box, type a File name of your own choosing.

7. The Save location should already be your Pictures folder (for example, C:\Users\Your User Name\Pictures). If it's not, navigate to your Pictures folder (or the folder in which you want to store screenshots).

8. Set the Save As Type option to PNG or JPEG unless you have a good reason for using a different format.

9. Click the Save button.

My Print Screen Key Doesn't Work

If the Paste option on Paint's Home toolbar is disabled (dimmed), that means there is nothing in the Clipboard. That might happen for a couple reasons. You might have forgotten to press Print Screen or Alt+Print Screen. Or perhaps you copied something else to the Clipboard after pressing Print Screen. And that "something else" isn't a picture.

The second possible problem is that your keyboard works differently. For example, on some keyboards you have to press Shift+Print Screen or Shift+Alt+PrintScreen. On one of my laptop computers, I have to click Fn+Print Screen. On another keyboard, I have to make sure the F Lock key is turned off before pressing the Print Screen key.

If you can't find the right combination of keystrokes for your system, see if you can find the information in the manual that came with your computer, or contact your computer manufacturer and see if they can help.

You won't see anything on your screen. But rest assured, the screenshot is saved as a file in whatever folder you specified in step 7, with whatever filename you specified in step 6. If you chose your Pictures folder in step 7, you'll find the file when you open your Pictures folder, described next.

Using Your Pictures Folder

As its name implies, the Pictures folder is the place to store pictures. Many of the techniques described in the preceding section will put pictures in that folder automatically. To view pictures, just open your Pictures folder using whichever technique is most convenient at the moment:

- Click the Start button and click Pictures (see Figure 23-5).

FIGURE 23-5

Pictures link on the Start menu.

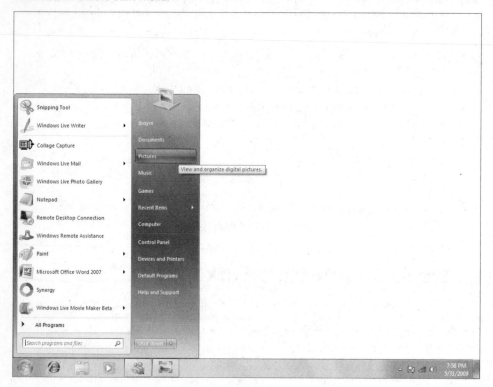

- Click Pictures in Explorer's Navigation pane (see Figure 23-6).

- Click your username in a breadcrumb menu and choose Pictures (see Figure 23-7).

Your Pictures folder opens in Explorer. Your Pictures folder is no different from any other folder. You can use all the tools and techniques described under "Using Windows Explorer" in Chapter 28 to size and arrange icons, hide and show panes, and so forth.

Pictures that you copied from a camera or scanner will likely be stored in subfolders. The name of the subfolder will be the same as the date on which you acquired the pictures, followed by any tag word you added. Figure 23-8 shows an example. The folders whose names start with 2009-0530 001 contain pictures I copied from a digital camera on that date.

When you open a subfolder that contains pictures, you'll see a thumbnail icon for each one. The size of that thumbnail and the amount of textual information shown with each depends on where you place the Views slider in the toolbar. If the Preview pane is open, pointing to a thumbnail displays an enlarged copy of the thumbnail. Figure 23-9 shows an example. To choose which panes you want to show or hide, click the Organize toolbar button and make your selections on the Layout submenu.

FIGURE 23-6

Pictures link in Navigation pane.

FIGURE 23-7

Pictures link from breadcrumb menu.

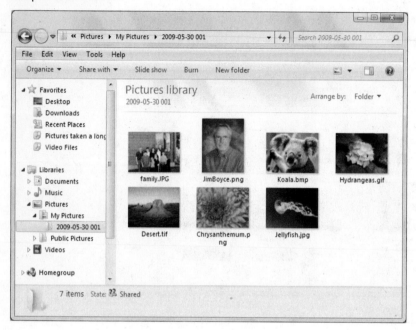

FIGURE 23-8

Sample Pictures folder.

Pictures folder quick tips

Caution

Icons in folders in Windows Vista and Windows 7 are different from the way they were in earlier Windows versions. There is no Filmstrip view in Windows 7, but you can make icons large enough to get a good preview of any picture without opening it. ■

Here are some quick tips that apply to most folders, with a few things that are unique to your Pictures folder:

- If your mouse has a wheel, hold down the Ctrl key while spinning the wheel to size thumbnails and change views.

- Drag the inner border of the Navigation or Preview pane to widen or narrow the pane.

- To open a subfolder, click (or double-click) its icon. To leave a subfolder, click the Back button or press Backspace.

Tip

Whether you need to click or double-click depends on settings in Folder Options. Click the Organize toolbar button and choose Folder and Search Options. Make your selection under Click Items As Follows and click OK. ■

- To rotate a picture, right-click its thumbnail and choose Rotate Clockwise or Rotate Counter-clockwise.

FIGURE 23-9

Folder of pictures.

Note

If the Rotate options are disabled or missing, the picture's file type can't be rotated in Windows, but you can open and rotate it in many graphics programs. ■

- To preview a larger version of a picture, click (or double-click) its thumbnail.

- To view all the pictures in the folder as a slide show, click the Slide Show toolbar button.

- Right-click any thumbnail icon for a shortcut of things you can do with that item.

- Use standard techniques described under "How to Select Icons" in Chapter 29 to select multiple icons that you want to print, copy, burn to CD, and so forth. To select all icons, click Organize ⇨ Select All or press Ctrl+A.

- To e-mail pictures using your default e-mail program, select their thumbnail icons. Then click the E-mail toolbar button.

Note

The E-mail button isn't visible until you select one or more icons in the folder. Also, it doesn't work with all e-mail programs. See Chapter 18 for more information. ■

- Click Burn to copy all pictures in a folder to a writable CD or DVD. To copy only specific items, select their icons and click Burn.

Note

Copying to CD and DVD isn't like copying to other media. Chapter 32 provides the full story. ■

- Right-click any column heading in Details view to choose which columns you want to show or hide.
- Click any column heading to sort thumbnails into ascending or descending order by Name, Date Taken, Rating, or any other heading.
- Click the arrow next to any column heading as in Figure 23-10, or right-click empty space between icons to arrange or filter by Name, Date Taken, Tags, or Rating.

FIGURE 23-10

Grouping options.

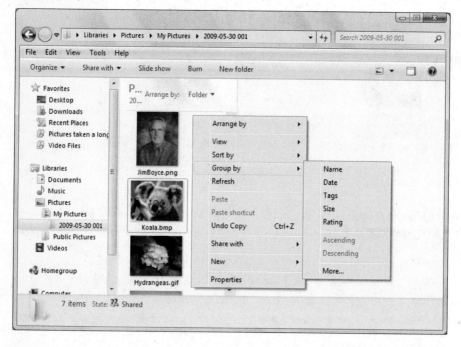

Tip

See "Using Windows Live Photo Gallery" later in this chapter for more information on tags. See "Using Windows Explorer" in Chapter 28 for more info on grouping, stacking, and filtering. ■

- When the Details pane is open, you can use it to add a tag or title to any selected pictures or multiple selected pictures.
- If you have multiple programs that can open a picture type, right-click the thumbnail and choose Open With to open the picture in whatever program you like, or choose a program name from the Preview toolbar button.

FIGURE 23-11

Layout options on Organize menu.

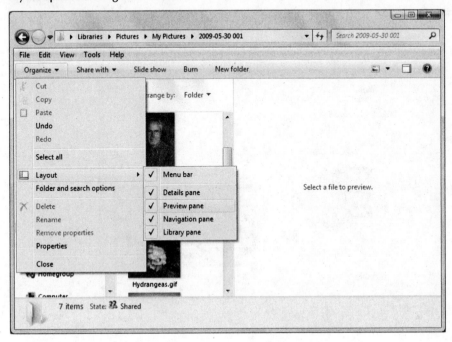

- To show or hide the menu bar, tap the Alt key or click the Organize button and choose Layout ➪ Menu Bar (see Figure 23-11).

- To show or hide filename extensions, click Organize and choose Folder and Search Options. Click the View tab, select or clear the Hide Extensions For Known File Types checkbox, and click OK.

Why some pictures show icons

Not all file types show as pictures in your Pictures folder. Some, such as videos you import from a camera in MP4, MOV, or some other format, show only icons. For example, in Figure 23-12 the icon on the right is a video stored in the Windows Media Video format (a .wmv file). The icon on the left is a video stored in Apple's QuickTime format (.mov format).

If you have an appropriate player for a file type, you can still open it by double-clicking. For example, if you have the QuickTime player (available for free from www.apple.com/quicktime), you can double-click any QuickTime movie's icon to watch it.

Caution
Changing the filename extension using Rename will not work. In fact, if you do that, you may not be able to open the file at all until you rename it back to the original filename extension! ■

FIGURE 23-12

Icon for a QuickTime movie.

If it's important to be able to see the thumbnail of a picture or icon, you have to convert the image or video to a compatible format like JPEG (for a picture) or WMV (for a video). For a single picture, you can often achieve this just by opening the picture in a graphics program. If you don't have a favorite graphics program, you can use Paint (right-click any picture and choose Open With ⇨ Paint). From the menu bar in your graphics program, choose File ⇨ Save As. Use the Save As Type option in the Save dialog box to save the picture as a JPEG or some other compatible format and click Save.

Some graphics programs, like Corel's Paint Shop Pro, will let you convert a whole group of pictures from one format to another without doing them one at a time. You can also go to any online shareware service like www.tucows.com or www.download.com and search for convert picture to find programs that specifically offer batch conversions. Search for convert video for programs that can convert videos.

Tip

If you want to put videos on your mobile devices, such as an iPod, Pocket PC, or other device, check out www.pqdvd.com for a converter. ■

Videos in your Pictures folder

If your digital camera lets you shoot video clips, those will be imported along with your still pictures. If the video is in a compatible format, its thumbnail will show the first frame of the video. It will also show a film-like border and the icon of the default program for playing that type of video.

FIGURE 23-13

Video thumbnail icon selected.

When you select a video thumbnail, the Preview pane turns to a small video screen with controls that work like a VCR or DVD player. Figure 23-13 shows an example where I've selected a video. The video preview pane to the right shows the first frame of the video. To watch the video in that preview, click the Play button under the video.

Once the video starts playing you can click the Full Screen button under the preview window to watch it full-screen. Click anywhere on that full-screen video to return to the desktop and your Pictures folder.

Renaming pictures and videos

Pictures and videos from cameras often have obscure meaningless filenames like 100_9630 or DCM1234. You can change the name of any file by right-clicking its thumbnail and choosing Rename. Or, you can select multiple thumbnails, right-click any one of them, and choose Rename. The current filename is highlighted.

Type the new name. (Never change the extension that comes after the period.) Then press Enter. If you renamed one file, only that file's name will be changed. If you renamed several files, they'll all have the same name followed by a number; for example, Swans (1), Swans (2), Swans (3), and so forth.

If you change your mind after renaming, press Undo (Ctrl+Z). But you have to do it right after pressing Enter. If you move on to other tasks, you may not be able to undo the rename.

There's much more to pictures and videos than looking at them in your Pictures folder. Next you take a look at Windows Live Photo Gallery, a handy tool that comes with Windows 7.

Using Windows Live Photo Gallery

Tip
Windows Live Photo Gallery is a great tool for managing a large photo collection. ■

Windows Live Photo Gallery is a program that helps you bring together pictures and videos from all the subfolders in your Pictures folder. The program is not included with Windows 7, but you can download it from home.live.com.

Photo Gallery isn't a folder where you store files. Rather, it's a way of organizing and accessing files without having to navigate around through multiple folders. For example, you can view all your photos at once, regardless of what folders they're in. Or better yet, you can locate and work with pictures that have certain things in common, such as all the pictures of your child (if you're a parent).

The only disadvantage of Windows Live Photo Gallery is that it doesn't show icons for all pictures and videos. Anything that doesn't show a thumbnail in your Pictures folder doesn't show up at all in Photo Gallery! Photo Gallery shows thumbnails for BMP, JFIF, JPEG, PNG, TIFF, and WDP photos and WMV, AVI, ASF, and MPEG movies.

The easiest way to understand what Windows Live Photo Gallery is all about is to fire it up and take a look for yourself. Use whichever method shown here is easiest for you:

- Click Start and choose All Programs ➪ Windows Live ➪ Windows Live Photo Gallery.
- Tap ⊞, type **gal**, and click Windows Live Photo Gallery.

Figure 23-14 shows an example of how Photo Gallery might look when you first open it. Of course the pictures you see will be your own (if you have any).

Like any program window, you can minimize, maximize, move, and size Photo Gallery to your liking. (Though there is a limit to how small you can make it.) Photo Gallery has its own Help. Click the blue Help button at the right side of its toolbar to open Help (or press F1 if Photo Gallery is the active window).

Choosing what to view and how

The Photo Gallery can show you all the photos and videos on your hard drive (or multiple hard drives), or it can show only certain ones. To get started, you'll want to see everything that's in the Photo Gallery right now. To do that, click All Photos and Videos at the top of the Navigation pane. If you just want to see pictures, click My Pictures under the All Photos and Videos heading. If you just want to see Videos, click My Videos under that same heading.

The gallery to the right of the Navigation pane shows a thumbnail for each photo and video currently in the gallery.

Use the slider at the bottom of the Photo Gallery window to change the size of the thumbnails. The button to the left of the slider lets you choose between Details view and regular thumbnail view. Details view shows the filename, date taken, file size, rating, and other details about each image.

FIGURE 23-14

Windows Photo Gallery.

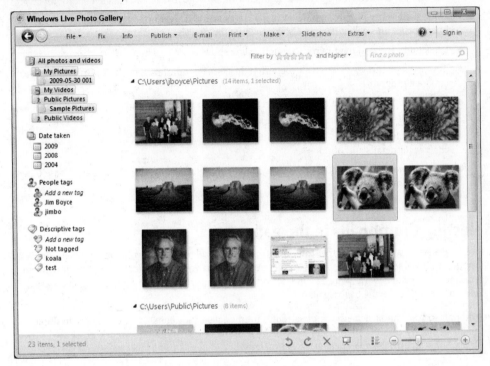

To group or arrange pictures in the gallery, right-click in the right pane and choose View, Sort By, or Group By and whatever option best describes how you want things organized.

Also in the context menu when you right-click is a Table of Contents option. Clicking that opens a Table of Contents pane to the left of the Thumbnails. The Table of Contents works in conjunction with the current Group By option on the Thumbnail View button. For example, if you group by Month, the Table of Contents lets you jump to all pictures taken in a specific month and year. If you group by Image Size, the Table of Contents provides links to large, medium, and small pictures, and so forth.

Go ahead and play around with those buttons and options for a while. You can't do any harm. But some of the grouping and arranging options won't have any real effect until you've built up a sizable collection of pictures. Remember, anything you choose right now you can change at any time in the future. You're not making any long-term commitments here while experimenting with views and arrangements.

Photo Gallery quick tips

Following are some other good things to know. If any item listed doesn't work for you, see "Choosing Photo Gallery options" later in this chapter.

- Rest the mouse pointer on any thumbnail to see a larger view of the picture.

571

- To rotate a picture, right-click it and choose a Rotate option.

- Click Info in the toolbar to open the Info pane, then click any picture to see its information in the Info pane where you can rate it, add, change, or remove tags, or change its caption.

- Double-click any picture to preview it at a larger size and view options for adjusting the photo's image properties. Click Back to Gallery to leave the preview.

- Click Slide Show in the toolbar to watch a slide show.

- To open a picture or video in a program, right-click its thumbnail, click the Open With, and choose a program.

- Click the File button and choose Import from Camera or Scanner to import pictures from a digital camera or scanner.

- To print selected pictures, click the Print toolbar button. (See "Printing Pictures" later in this chapter for details and options.)

- To open the folder in which a picture is contained, right-click its thumbnail and choose Open File Location.

Selecting thumbnails in the gallery

As in folders, you can select multiple thumbnails in Photo Gallery. This can be handy when you want to apply a similar rating, tag, or caption to pictures, or when you want to create a slide show from several pictures, print several pictures, and so forth. You can use the same techniques you use in folders to select thumbnails in the gallery.

In addition to the standard methods of selecting thumbnails (and icons), you can select multiple thumbnails just by clicking their checkboxes. Any thumbnail that has a checkmark is selected. Any thumbnail that doesn't have a checkmark is unselected.

To select all the pictures in the gallery, click any single picture and press Ctrl+A, or right-click some empty space just outside the thumbnails and choose Select All. If you want to select most (but not all) of the pictures, select them all first. Then Ctrl+Click the pictures you want to un-select, or clear their checkboxes.

Dating, rating, tagging, and captioning

Tagging is one of the biggest advantages to having all of your pictures in Windows Live Photo Gallery. A tag is simply some keyword or phrase that you make up to identify pictures; for example, the location where the picture was shot, the subject of the picture, or the names of people in the picture. You can apply as many tags as you want to a picture, and you can add, change, or delete tags at any time.

Rating allows you to rate photos on a scale of 1 to 5 stars based on how much you like the picture. Captions allow you to title pictures with words of your own choosing. Use the Info pane to rate, tag, and caption pictures.

First, click the thumbnail picture that you want to rate. Or, if you want to apply the same rating, tags, or caption to multiple pictures, select all of their icons. Then:

- To rate the selected picture(s), click any star near the top of the Info pane (see Figure 23-15). To give a zero rating, click the first star, then click it again.

FIGURE 23-15

Info pane.

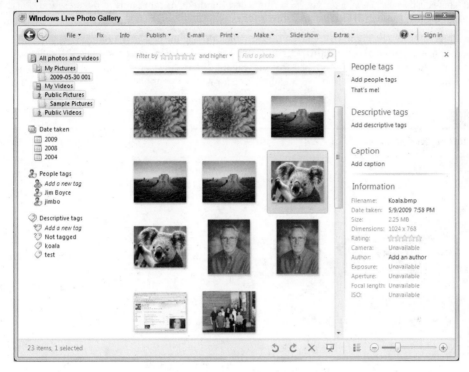

- To tag the selected picture(s), click Add Descriptive Tags. Type one tag (preferably a single word or two) and press Enter. Optionally, type more tags in the same manner, pressing Enter after each tag.

Tip

If the picture contains people you know, consider typing each person's name as a separate tag. That way you can later search for pictures of that person, or pictures that contain several specific people. Don't use commas or semicolons in an attempt to apply multiple tags to a picture. Always press Enter after typing a single tag. ■

- To caption, click Add Caption, type a caption in the Add a Caption box, or replace the text that already appears there with a caption of your own.

- Optionally, if you want to change the date or time that the picture was taken, click the current date and time shown above the Ratings stars.

Tip

In the Details view, you can rate and caption pictures right from the thumbnail without using the Info pane. ■

Filtering pictures

The coolest thing about tagging pictures is that it makes specific pictures very easy to find in the future. This is especially useful after you've accumulated hundreds or thousands of pictures, and don't want to go digging through folders to find specific ones.

To see all pictures to which you've applied a tag, just click the tag in the Navigation pane. If you don't see those tags, click the triangle next to Tags to expand that list. When you click a tag, the gallery shows all pictures to which you've applied that tag. Figure 23-16 shows an example where I clicked the tag koala. The gallery to the right shows all pictures to which I've applied that tag.

FIGURE 23-16

Viewing all pictures tagged koala.

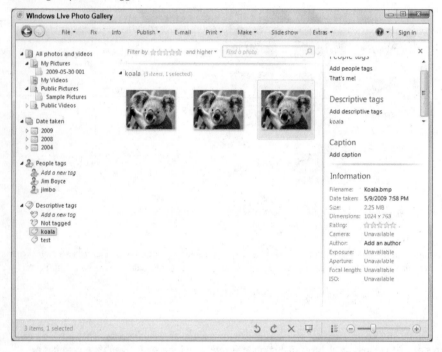

To see pictures that contain multiple tags, use the Search box. For example, suppose you entered each person's name as a separate tag in your photos. First click All Pictures and Videos in the Navigation pane so you're viewing all pictures. Then in the Search box type the names separated by a space. For example, a search for `Ashley Alec` shows only pictures that contain both Ashley and Alec.

To see all pictures to which you haven't yet applied any tags, click Not Tagged near the top of the tag list. From there you can start adding tags to any pictures that appear in the gallery.

In the Navigation pane you'll see the heading Date Taken. Click the triangle next to any heading to expand or collapse its contents. Use them in the same way you use tags. For example, to see all pictures taken in a given year, click a year number. To see all pictures taken on a given day, expand the appropriate year and month, and then click the appropriate date.

To see all the pictures you took in a certain year, month, or day, click the year, month, or date. To see all the pictures to which you've applied a rating (or no rating), click an option under the Ratings heading. To see all the pictures in a particular folder, click the folder name at the bottom of the Navigation pane.

To see all the pictures to which you applied a particular rating, click a rating at the top of the thumbnail pane. To see all the pictures that have zero stars, leave no stars selected and choose Only from the drop-down list. Having all your unrated pictures in the gallery is a good place from which to start rating. To remove the filter, click Clear filter.

Tip

To clear ratings, right-click a thumbnail (or any selected thumbnail) and choose Clear Rating. This sets each selected thumbnail back to Not Rated. ■

To search for pictures or videos by name, tag, or other keyword, first click All Photos and Videos at the top of the Navigation pane. Then type a word in the Search box. You can also narrow the search by first clicking Pictures, Videos, a tag, a year, or whatever to reduce the number of items in the gallery. Your next search will search only within items currently in the gallery.

Changing tags

Tags are flexible. You can add, rename, and change them at will. To change the spelling of a tag, just right-click it in the Navigation pane and choose Rename. Type in the corrected name and press Enter. The spelling will automatically be corrected in every picture that contains that tag.

To delete a tag from a single picture, without removing the tag from any other pictures, first select the picture's thumbnail. Or if you want to delete the tag from a few pictures, select their thumbnails. Then right-click the tag you want to remove and choose Delete. Note that deleting a tag will not delete any pictures. It simply removes the tag from any pictures to which you previously applied the tag.

Use a picture as your desktop background

If you have a favorite photo you'd like to use as a desktop background, right-click its thumbnail and choose Set as Desktop Background.

If you can't see the desktop, click the Show Desktop button at the far right of the taskbar. Then click the Windows Photo Gallery taskbar button to bring Photo Gallery back onto the desktop.

Tip

See "Using the Personalization Page" in Chapter 10 for more ways to personalize your Windows desktop. ■

Adding pictures to Photo Gallery

Photo Gallery doesn't scan your entire hard disk for photos. By default in includes only pictures from the Pictures folder in your user account. If you have pictures in other folders, you can add them to Photo Gallery in several ways. If the pictures are in some arbitrary location where they just happened to end up, consider moving them to your Pictures folder. Use any technique described in Chapter 29 to move and copy files.

If the pictures are in some other folder for good reason, you can add that folder to Windows Live Photo Gallery. This has no effect on the pictures or the folder, so you won't mess up your existing organization. To add a folder to the Photo Gallery:

1. Click the File menu and choose Include a Folder in the Gallery.

2. Navigate to any folder that contains pictures and videos you'd like to include in your gallery and click OK.

Repeat steps 1 and 2 for each folder you want to add. As you add new pictures to those folders in the future, they'll show up automatically in Photo Gallery.

Use your Photo Gallery as a screen saver

To use photos in your Photo Gallery as a screen saver, click the File toolbar button and choose Screen Saver Settings. Set the Screen Saver name to Windows Live Photo Gallery. Then click the Settings button. You can choose to show all photos and videos or narrow the selection to a specific folder. If you like, you can also narrow things down to only pictures that have a certain tag or rating, and exclude files with specific tags. You can also set the general speed of the screen saver slide show. Select Shuffle Contents to randomize the photo and video selection. Click Save after making your selections. Click Preview for a preview of how the screen saver will look. Click OK when you're happy with your selections to return to Photo Gallery.

Fixing photos

Tip
The Fix pane makes it easy to touch up your photos. It's a far cry from a "real" graphics editor like PhotoShop or Paint Shop Pro, but it can fix the most common photo problems. ∎

Windows Live Photo Gallery comes complete with a simple graphics editor specifically designed to work with photos. It's called the Fix pane and you can get to it simply by clicking a thumbnail and then clicking Fix in the toolbar.

The Fix pane replaces the Info pane on the right as in Figure 23-17. Before you try anything, notice the Undo button at the bottom. If you don't like the results of a change, click that to undo the change. If you change your mind after Undo, click Redo to bring the change back. When you point to Undo and Redo after making changes to a picture, you'll see a little arrow on the button that you can click to Undo only one change, or all changes. The buttons are disabled (dimmed) when there's nothing to undo or redo.

The sections that follow describe each tool on the Fix pane.

Why Can't I Fix My Photo?

Sometimes clicking the Fix button won't work. This can happen for several reasons. First, you cannot make changes to a read-only file. Every file on a CD or DVD is read-only. If the picture you're trying to fix is on such a disk, you need to copy it to your Pictures folder first, and then edit the copy that's in your Pictures folder. The picture might also be in some remote location rather than on your own hard disk. You need to get a copy of that picture onto your own hard disk before you can edit it. If the picture is on your hard drive already, it may be marked read-only in its properties sheet. Right-click the picture's icon, choose Properties, clear the Read-only checkbox, and click OK.

The type of file you're editing plays a role as well. Windows Live Photo Gallery supports only modern file formats commonly used for digital photos, such as JPEG and TIFF. You cannot edit .GIF, .BMP, .WMF, and other older or non-photographic file types with Windows Live Photo Gallery. If you try, you'll see the message "Photo Gallery can't edit this picture in its current format." Click the Help link, or see "Changing a picture type or size" later in this chapter for information on how you can change a picture from an incompatible format (like BMP) to a compatible format (like TIFF or JPEG).

FIGURE 23-17

The Fix pane at right.

Auto Adjust

Click Auto Adjust to let Photo Gallery take a shot at cleaning up the brightness, contrast, and such. Don't expect miracles though. Sometimes Auto Adjust might make things worse. If so, just click Undo.

Adjust Exposure

Click this option to adjust the brightness and contrast of the picture. The Brightness slider is especially useful for pictures that are poorly lit. You may need to adjust the contrast as well to bring some depth to the picture. Just move the sliders around until you find a combination you like. If you can't seem to make an improvement, drag the slider boxes back to the middle of each bar, or click Undo until the picture is back to its original form.

Adjust Color

Click Adjust Color to change the Color Temperature, Tint, and Saturation. Adjust each by dragging the slider left or right. Each item has a different effect on the photo as follows:

- **Color Temperature:** The overall tone of your picture. Dragging to the left tends toward cool (bluish tint). Dragging to the right moves toward warm (reddish tint). Best used for pictures taken outdoors.
- **Tint:** Changes the color cast in a picture by adding or removing green from your picture.
- **Saturation:** Drag the slider left and right to change the intensity of all colors. Dragging all the way to the left converts the pictures to grayscale (black and white).

Straighten Photo

This option overlays a grid on the photo and gives you a slider you can use to tilt the photo left or right. If you took a photo with the camera at a slight angle, use this option to straighten the photo.

Crop Photo

Cropping a picture lets you get rid of any unnecessary background. This is useful when the main subject of the photo looks too small or far away. Figure 23-18 shows an example. The photo on the left is the entire original photo. The cropped photo on the right brings attention to a single feature by eliminating much of the background.

Tip

Figure 23-18 is also a good example of why you might want to make a duplicate of the original before cropping. The photo on the left is a great photo, and is worth keeping. The cropped copy on the right is good for showing one of the main subjects of the photo. ■

To crop a photo, first click Crop Photo in the Fix pane. A white box with sizing handles (little squares) appears on the picture. The idea is to get exactly what you want the finished photo to look like inside that box. Anything you want to crop out of the picture should be outside the box.

If you plan on printing the finished photo on pre-sized photographic paper, click the Proportion button and choose your print size. Doing so will keep the proportions of the cropping box at the proper aspect ratio for that goal. Click Rotate Frame to switch between landscape (wide) and portrait (tall) orientations.

Note

The aspect ratio is the ratio of the width of the photo to its height. Different print sizes have slightly different aspect ratios. ■

FIGURE 23-18

Original photo (left) and cropped (right).

If you want to retain the original aspect ratio, click Original. If you're not concerned about printing on pre-sized photo paper, choose Custom. With that setting you can make the cropped picture any shape you like.

Here's how you use the cropping box that's on the picture:

- To make the box larger or smaller, drag any sizing handle (little square) around the box border.
- To re-center the box around the main subject of the photo, put the mouse pointer inside the box and drag it to a better location on the picture.
- To zoom in and out while cropping, spin the mouse wheel or use the Zoom slider.

When the inside of the box looks the way you want your photo to look, click the Apply button. The picture is cropped. (If you change your mind, click Undo.)

Fix Red Eye

Red eye is a common problem caused by the retina at the back of the eye reflecting the flash back to the camera. Fixing it isn't too tough. First, if the eyes are very small in the photo, spin the mouse wheel or use the Zoom button to zoom in on the eyes. You may need to zoom a little, pan a little, zoom a little. The idea is to make the eyes as large as possible in the viewing area. Next, click Fix Red

Eye in the Fix pane and follow the instructions that appear there. Drag a rectangle around the pupil of the eyeball, not the entire eye. Figure 23-19 shows an example where I've dragged a rectangle around a child's eye.

FIGURE 23-19

Fixing red eye.

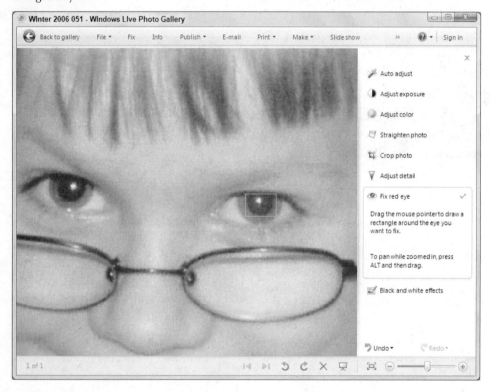

If dragging a rectangle around the eye once doesn't fix the red eye, drag another rectangle around the same eye. Keep doing so until all of the red is gone. Then, pan over to the other eye, if necessary, and drag a square around that eye. If you don't like the results, click Undo. Then try again.

Black and White Effects

You can use the Black and White Effects option to turn your photo into a black and white image with no filter or a choice of orange, yellow, or red filter. Each filter gives a different result. You can also create a sepia tone or cyan tone image.

Saving Fix pane changes

When you've finished touching up your photo in the Fix pane, click Back to Gallery. Your changes are saved automatically.

If you made a mess of things in the Fix pane and were hoping Back to Gallery *wouldn't* save your changes, don't panic. Click the Fix button again to open that same picture with the Fix pane. Then click Revert at the bottom of the Fix pane to undo your previous changes.

Tip

You can recover previous versions of many different kinds of files, not just photos. If you're interested in that sort of thing, see "Using System Protection" in Chapter 33 for the whole story. ■

Using people tags

Window Live Photo Gallery adds a new feature called *people tags* that you can use to identify people in your photos. People tags work in conjunction with Photo Gallery's face detection capability, enabling you to assign a tag to a person's face, rather than just to the photo. So, instead of just adding Edna as a general tag to a photo with 20 people in it, you can assign the people tag to Great Aunt Edna's face, so you can remember who she is in that family reunion photo.

Photo Gallery's face detection capability does not equal *facial recognition*. Photo Gallery won't tag all the photos that contain Aunt Edna automatically. Instead, face detection simply enables Photo Gallery to identify faces in a picture. You can then assign tags to each face.

Assigning a people tag is easy. First, just click a photo. If Photo Gallery is able to detect faces in the photo, you'll see a People Found link in the Info pane. Click Identify, then type the name of the person whose face is highlighted. Repeat the process for other faces in the photo.

If Photo Gallery can't detect faces in the photo, you can add the people tags manually. Double-click the photo to preview it. Then, in the Info pane, click Tag Someone. Click and drag in the photo to draw a frame around the face you want to tag, then select an existing person from the Tag Someone dialog box (Figure 23-20) or type a new name. Repeat the process for any other people in the photo.

As it does with other tags and properties, Photo Gallery shows the people tags in the Navigation pane. You can quickly filter the view to show photos with a specific person in them just by clicking that person's name in the Navigation pane.

Tip

If you log in to your Windows Live account, Photo Gallery downloads your list of Windows Live contacts so you can use those to tag faces in your photos. ■

Other new features

The features I've covered in the previous sections should give you a feel for what Photo Gallery can do. Here's a list of some other key new features in Windows Live Photo Gallery:

- **Gallery Sync:** This feature lets you synchronize photos between two computers, which is a good way to share files with someone else or simply back up your photos on a different computer. You'll need Windows Live Photo Gallery on both computers, as well as a Windows Live account.

- **Publishing:** With Windows Live Photo Gallery you can publish photos and photo albums to photo, event, and group albums on Windows Live. You can also publish videos on Soapbox or publish photos on Flickr.

FIGURE 23-20

Adding a people tag.

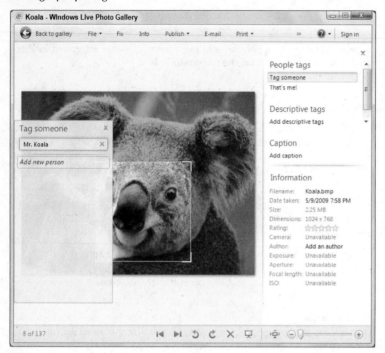

- **Blogging:** If you have Windows Live Writer installed, you can easily create a blog post for a photo. Just select the photo and click Make ➪ Make a Blog Post. Photo Gallery opens Windows Live Writer and inserts a copy of the photo in a new blog entry.

- **More photo tools:** Windows Live Photo Gallery is extensible, which means to you can add other features to it. Examples include Photosynth (cool new way to share photos), Image Composite Editor (enhanced panoramic photo stitcher), and AutoCollage (create a collage from your photos). Click Extras ➪ Download More Photo Tools to see what is available.

- **Panoramic photos:** Photo Gallery enables you to create a panoramic photo from multiple snapshots. Just select the photos and click Make ➪ Create Panoramic Photo. Photo Gallery stitches them together for you automatically.

To learn more about Windows Live Photo Gallery and about the features I've described in this chapter, see "Windows Live Essentials," from Wiley.

Choosing Photo Gallery options

Like most programs, Windows Live Photo Gallery has an Options dialog box that lets you tweak certain program features to your own work style. To open Live Photo Gallery's Options dialog box, click the File toolbar button and choose Options. Figure 23-21 shows the Windows Live Photo Gallery Options dialog box, which contains three tabs: General, Import, and Tags.

FIGURE 23-21

Windows Live Photo Gallery options.

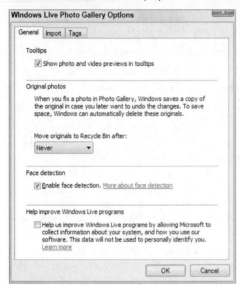

Selecting the first option, Show Photo And Video Previews In Tooltips, ensures that when you point to a thumbnail in Photo Gallery, you see a larger version of the thumbnail or video. Clearing that checkbox prevents the tooltips from showing.

The Original Photos section has to do with the Revert button in Fix. By default, previous versions of photos stay on the hard disk permanently, even though you don't see them. After a few years, or even months, the storage space they require could be significant. Choosing Move Original Files to Recycle Bin After lets you put a time on those saved originals. You can choose from among several time frames ranging from One Day to Never.

Note
The Recycle Bin is much like a wastepaper basket. It holds your trash (deleted files) until you empty it. See "Deleting Files" in Chapter 29 for more information. ■

Keep in mind that you will not be able to revert a modified picture to its original form, or find a previous version of a file after the time limit expires. If you consistently work with duplicates of pictures rather than originals, this isn't a big deal because you always have the original in plain sight in its folder.

The Enable Face Detection option on the General tab turns on or off face detection, described previously.

The Import tab lets you customize how pictures that you import to Photo Gallery are handled. You can import pictures into Photo Gallery by clicking File in its toolbar and choosing Import from Camera or Scanner.

- **Settings For:** Specify the device or medium for which you want to define settings.

- **Import To:** Choose the folder to which pictures and videos will be imported. The default is the My Pictures folder for your user account.

- **Folder Name:** Imported pictures are automatically placed in a folder. Use this option to specify how you want that folder named. You can choose from various combinations of the following:

  - **Date Imported:** Today's date (the date on which you're performing the import).

  - **Name:** Photo or video name.

  - **Date Taken:** The date in the first picture's Date Taken property.

  - **Date Taken Range:** The Date Taken property of the first and last pictures being imported.

- **File Name:** Each imported picture is automatically assigned a filename. To use the original filename as assigned by the camera, choose Original File Name. Some digital cameras organize photos into folders. To preserve both the camera folder and filenames, choose Original File Name (Preserve Folders).

- **Delete Files From Device After Importing:** If selected, pictures and videos will be erased from the camera automatically after importing. If you clear this option, you either have to choose the Erase Pictures During The Import option or manually erase the pictures from the camera after the import.

- **Rotate Photos During Import:** Some digital cameras can sense when you're holding the camera vertically and mark each such picture accordingly. Choosing this option causes those pictures to be rotated to the correct upright position automatically when imported.

- **Open Windows Live Photo Gallery After Importing Files:** When selected ensures that Windows Live Photo Gallery opens automatically as soon as you've finished importing pictures.

- **Restore Defaults:** Sets options back to the original factory settings.

Click OK after making your selections. Your choices on the Import tab will be applied only to pictures you import in the future. They have no effect on pictures you've already imported. Of course, you can rename, rotate, tag, and move pictures at any time, regardless of settings in the Options dialog box.

The Tags tab offers options that determine what metadata is included with photos when you publish them via Windows Live Photo Gallery. You an also delete unused tags from the Tags tab.

Making movies from Photo Gallery

The Make A Movie option in the Make toolbar button in Windows Live Photo Gallery is really just a shortcut to Windows Live Movie Maker. The idea is to get all the pictures and videos you want to put in a movie into the gallery, perhaps by giving all those items a tag, then clicking the tag name in Photo Gallery's Navigation pane. Then you select all those items and click Make ➪ Make a Movie. Movie Maker opens with all the selected items, ready to insert into a new movie.

Printing Pictures

You can print pictures to almost any printer, although photo printers will give you much better results. However, you'll need to refer to the instructions that came with that printer for specifics on connecting the printer. You might also need to install or download a special driver from the printer manufacturer. If in doubt, refer to the manual that came with the photo printer or the manufacturer's Web site.

Most modern inkjet and laser printers let you print on either plain paper or photographic paper. Photographic paper is considerably more expensive, so you might want to stick with plain paper for drafts and informal prints. Use photographic paper for more formal prints of your best photos.

Printing from Windows Live Photo Gallery

If the pictures you want to print are in Windows Live Photo Gallery, you can print from there. Use the Navigation pane to display the pictures you want to print. Then select (check) the picture (or pictures) you want to print. If you want to print all the pictures showing in the gallery, you can click the group heading to select all the icons, or click any one picture in the gallery and press Ctrl+A. If you want to print only some pictures, select their icons. You can do so by pointing to any image and clicking its checkbox. Or you can use the universal techniques for selecting icons discussed in Chapter 29.

After you've selected the pictures you want to print, click the Print toolbar button and choose Print. The Print Pictures window shown in Figure 23-22 opens.

FIGURE 23-22

Print Pictures window.

Note
Don't worry about sideways pictures in the Print Pictures window. You don't need to rotate them. The printed pictures will look fine even if they're sideways in the Print Pictures window. ■

Now you get to make a whole bunch of choices as to how you want to print your picture (or pictures). The choices available to you depend on what kind of printer you're using. If you have multiple printers attached to your computer, the first step is to select the printer you want to use from the Printer drop-down list.

If your printer supports multiple paper sizes, click the Paper Size button and choose the size paper you want to print to. Depending on your printer, you might also be able to click the Quality button and choose the output resolution. The higher the dpi, the better the quality of the print, and the longer it takes to print.

If your selected printer supports multiple paper types, click Paper Type and choose the paper you're using.

If you're printing multiple pictures on large paper, choose a layout from the right column. Use the scroll bar at the right side of the window to view all your options. Typically, you can choose any size from a full page photo down to tiny wallet-sized prints. After you scroll, be sure to click the layout you want to use. The preview area shows you how things will look on each printed page.

Note
If you change your mind about the pictures you selected to print, click Cancel to return to Photo Gallery. ■

To print more than one copy of each picture, specify how many you want to Print Next To Copies Of Each Picture. Choose Fit Picture To Frame to ensure that any small pictures are expanded to fill the page on which they're printed.

With all the choices made, just click Print and wait. Don't expect the printer to start right away. It takes some time for the computer to get everything together before sending it to the printer. Be patient. When your pictures are finished printing, click Finish in the window that appears.

Printing pictures from a folder

If you have pictures that don't show in Windows Live Photo Gallery, you can print them straight from the folder in which they're stored. Open the folder that contains the pictures. Then select the icons of the pictures you want to print. Be careful you don't select any icons for non-picture files, or this technique won't work.

Once you've selected the picture icons, click the Print button in the toolbar. If the Printer button isn't visible, first click >> at the end of the toolbar to see if it's just off the edge. If you still don't see a Print option, chances are one or more of your selected icons isn't a picture. When you do see the Print button, click it. You'll be taken to the Print Pictures window. Choose your settings, as described in the previous section, and click Print.

Using the Slide Show Gadget

Tip
You can use the Slide Show gadget to keep a slide show of all your favorite pictures playing. ■

The Slide Show gadget is a fun way to keep a slide show of all your favorite pictures playing on the desktop. By default, it will display all pictures in your Pictures library, although you can change that to have it show any folder you like.

If you want precise control over the pictures in the slide show, create a subfolder in your Pictures folder. Name it Slide Show Gadget or something similar, then copy into that folder all of the pictures you want the slide show to show.

Note

For details on using gadgets, see "Using Gadgets" in Chapter 10. ■

To add the Slide Show gadget, right-click the desktop and choose Gadgets. In the Gadgets window that opens, find the Slide Show gadget and drag it to the desktop. It will show pictures from your Pictures library in a slide show.

When you point to the Slide Show gadget, you'll see the tools pointed out in Figure 23-23. In addition to the tools shown, you can right-click the gadget to remove it or open its settings.

FIGURE 23-23

Slide Show gadget.

To customize the gadget, click the Options button, or right-click and choose Options. The Slide Show dialog box opens as in Figure 23-24. To have the gadget show pictures from a particular folder, choose an option from the Folder drop-down list. Or, click the ... button, navigate to the folder that contains the pictures, and click OK. Select the Include Subfolders option if you want the Slide Show gadget to show photos from subfolders of the selected folder.

The other two options let you determine the type of transition effect between pictures, how long each picture shows, and whether to randomize (shuffle) the photos.

FIGURE 23-24

Slide Show gadget settings.

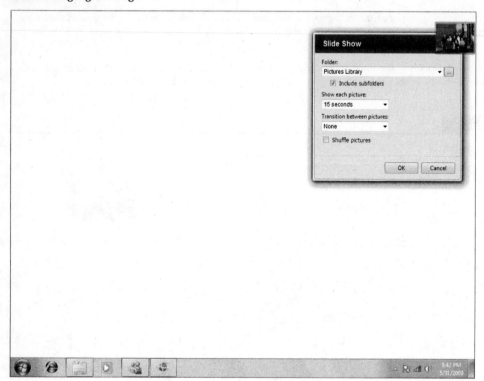

Pixels and Megapixels

Every picture you see on your screen is actually a bunch of little lighted dots on the screen called pixels. You don't see the individual pixels because they're too small, but if you take a small original picture and zoom way in, each pixel reveals itself as a small colored square. Figure 23-25 shows an example. The small inset picture is the original. The larger picture is an extreme zoom in. There you can see how the picture is actually lots of pixels — little colored squares.

When shopping for digital cameras, *megapixels* is a key pricing factor. A megapixel isn't one humongous pixel. It's a million regular-sized pixels. The basic rule of thumb is, the more pixels, the better the quality of the pictures. The term "quality" in this context really means how big you can make it (or print it) without the picture looking *pixilated*. A pixilated picture looks, at best, blotchy. At worst, it looks like a bunch of pixels rather than a coherent picture.

Table 23-1 provides some general guidelines on how the number of megapixels translates to print quality. You can always print any picture at any size, of course, but you start to lose quality if you go above the recommended maximum size shown in the second column. All numbers are approximate, of course, because many other factors come into play in determining overall print quality.

FIGURE 23-25

Zoomed-in to see pixels.

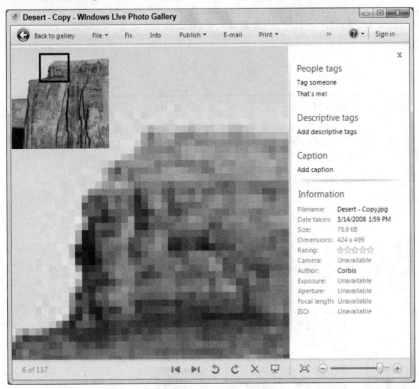

TABLE 23-1

Megapixels and Print Size

Megapixels	Recommended Maximum Print Size
1–2	3 × 5
2–3	5 × 7
3–4	8 × 10
4–5	11 × 14
>5	18 × 24

File extension, size, and dimensions

Every picture has a type, indicated by its filename extension. It also has a size measured in kilobytes (KB) or megabytes (MB). And it has dimensions. You see that information when you point to a picture's thumbnail in a folder (see Figure 23-26). The Details view in a folder can show the Dimension, Size, and Type of every picture in the folder. Right-click any column heading and choose the name of the column you want to see.

FIGURE 23-26

Pointing to a picture in a folder in Windows Explorer.

In Windows Live Photo Gallery, the file extension, size, and dimensions of a photo show when you point to a thumbnail or use the Details view.

A picture's dimensions are its width and height measured in pixels. As a rule, the bigger the dimensions the better, because it means you can print the picture at a very large size with no loss of quality. You can also zoom in quite far, and crop out quite a bit and still end up with a picture that has significant detail.

Recall that the term megapixels refers to the number of pixels in a picture, where one megapixel equals a million pixels. A 5-megapixel camera will create pictures with dimensions of around 2,576 × 1,932. Multiplying those two numbers gives you the total number of pixels in the picture, 4,976,832. That's just abut 5 million pixels, hence the 5-megapixel rating.

The file size is the amount of disk space required to store the picture. Bigger is better in terms of picture quality because a large file size indicates that there's lots of information in the file, which means you can print it at large sizes and zoom in on any portion of the picture without losing much clarity.

The filename extension is the picture's file type. Many types of picture files exist. Table 23-2 lists some examples. Some file types are so old or so rare you may never see one. The most commonly used picture types are TIFF, JPEG, PNG, BMP, and GIF, described next.

TIFF pictures

TIFF (Tagging Information File Format) is the preferred method of storing high-quality photos for printing. In fact, TIFF is widely used by the publishing industry for that very reason. TIFF files tend to be large, because they contain much detailed information and generally use little or no compression to reduce file size.

JPEG pictures

JPEG (Joint Photographic Experts Group) is the most widely used photo format for photos displayed in Web pages. JPEG uses compression to reduce file size while maintaining large dimensions. The compression results in some small loss of picture quality. That loss usually isn't noticeable until you zoom in very tightly on some small area within the picture.

The amount of compression applied to a JPEG can vary. In fact many high-end graphics programs allow you to choose exactly how much compression you want when saving a picture as a JPEG. Many digital cameras save pictures as JPEGs with minimal compression to conserve picture quality while at the same time conserving storage space on memory cards.

GIF pictures

GIF (Graphics Interchange Format) is commonly used in Web pages for illustrations and animations. It's limited to 256 colors, which makes it unsuitable for photos. Photos need millions of colors and tend to look blotchy when saved in GIF format. GIF also allows for transparency and simple animations.

PNG pictures

PNG (Portable Network Graphics) format is a compressed format that's gaining popularity as a format for Web pictures. Like JPEG, it supports millions of colors, and is therefore suitable for photos. Like GIF, it allows for transparency, and is therefore useful for creating images with a transparent background.

BMP pictures

BMP (Windows Bitmap) is an older uncompressed format that conserves picture quality at the cost of a large file size. Though once widely used in Windows, BMP is quickly becoming obsolete in favor of the more widely used TIFF and JPEG formats.

Changing a picture type or size

Sometimes you'll need to change a picture's type, perhaps so you can edit it in Photo Gallery or publish it on a Web site. There may also be times when you want to reduce the file size and/or dimensions of a picture to send it by e-mail or, again, to post it on a Web site.

TABLE 23-2

Examples of File Formats for Pictures

Filename Extension	Format
.art	AOL Art file
.bmp	Windows Bitmap
.cdr	CorelDraw Drawing
.cgm	Computer Graphics Metafile
.clp	Windows Clipboard
.cmx	Corel Clipart
.cut	Dr. Halo
.dcx	Zsoft Multipage Paintbrush
.dib	Windows Device Independent Bitmap
.drw	Micrografx Draw
.dxf	Autodesk Drawing Interchange
.emf	Windows Enhanced Metafile
.tif, .ai, .ps	Encapsulated PostScript
.fpx	FlashPix
.gem	Ventura/GEM Drawing
.gif	CompuServe Graphics Interchange
.hgl	HP Graphics Language
.iff	Amiga
.img	GEM Paint
.jpg, .jif, .jpeg	Joint Photographic Experts Group
.kdc	Kodak Digital Camera
.lbm	Deluxe Paint
.mac	MacPaint
.msp	Microsoft Paint
.pbm	Portable Bitmap
.pcd	Kodak Photo CD
.pct	Macintosh PICT
.pcx	Zsoft Paintbrush

Filename Extension	Format
.pgm	Portable Greymap
.pic	Lotus PIC
.pic	PC Paint
.png	Portable Network Graphics
.ppm	Portable Pixelmap
.psd	Photoshop
.psp	Paint Shop Pro
.ras	Sun RasterImage
.raw	Raw File Format
.rle	Windows or CompuServe RLE
.sct, .ct	SciTex Continuous Tone
.tga	Truevision Targa
.tif, .tiff	Tagged Image File Format
.wdp	Windows Digital Photo
.wmf	Windows Meta File
.wpg	WordPerfect Bitmap or Vector

If you use Windows Live Mail to e-mail photos, you'll automatically be given the option to reduce the dimensions of large pictures. (See "Using E-mail Attachments" in Chapter 18.) Note that only the copies of images sent through e-mail will be reduced in size. Your original photo on your computer's hard disk remains unchanged.

If you don't use Windows Live Mail, you can manually create a smaller image for e-mailing, without losing your original picture. This also works if you want to post a picture on a Web site. Just about any graphics program on the market will allow you to resize a picture and save it in a different format. If you don't have a graphics program, you can use the Paint program that comes with Windows 7.

1. Right-click the icon or thumbnail of the picture you want to reduce and choose Open With ➪ Paint. Don't be alarmed if you see only a small portion of a large picture. Paint doesn't automatically scale the picture to fit in the program window.

2. Choose File ➪ Save As and type a new name for this copy of the picture. For example, use the existing filename followed by TIFF if you're just changing the file type, or the word Small if you're also reducing the picture's dimensions.

3. If the picture isn't already a TIFF, JPEG, or PNG, click the current file type next to Save as type and choose JPEG or PNG.

4. Click Save.

Note

TIFF is best for pictures you intend to print, but don't intend to e-mail or post on a Web site. JPEG and PNG are best for pictures you do intend to e-mail or post on a Web site for editing and printing purposes. ■

5. If your goal is simply to change the picture's type (like from BMP to another format), skip to step 10. Otherwise continue with the following steps.

6. To reduce the picture's size, click the Resize button in the toolbar.

7. Under Resize in the Resize and Skew dialog box, enter a percent value for both Horizontal and Vertical. Make sure to use equal numbers so as not to skew or stretch the pictures. For example, to resize a 2576 × 1932 picture down to near 644 × 483, enter 25% for both Horizontal and Vertical.

8. To see the picture as it will appear on a Web page or to an e-mail recipient, click the Edit tab and then click 100%. (If Paint's program window is small, double-click its title bar to maximize it to full screen.)

9. If the picture it too large or too small, press Ctrl+Z to undo your changes, and repeat steps 6–7 until you find a size you like.

10. Close Paint (click its Close button or choose File ➪ Exit from its menu bar). If asked about saving your changes, choose Yes.

If you started from Photo Gallery, the new copy of the picture may not show up right away. You might have to close Photo Gallery and re-open it. Also, the new picture may not contain the tags that the original picture had, so you might find it in the Not Tagged category in Photo Gallery.

Pictures, Tags, and Virtual Folders

Note

Photos Gallery's tagging capabilities are just the tip of the proverbial iceberg in Windows 7. Tagging applies to many file types, and is a key component in Windows 7's search capabilities. ■

You can use the Search box in Photo Gallery to find pictures based on rating, tags, name, and other properties. Outside of Photo Gallery you can do much more with tags and other photo properties when searching, enabling you to find and organize pictures in ways that transcend tags.

For starters, you can click the Search button or tap ![Windows icon], type in a tag name, and see icons for all pictures that contain that tag. Then, on the Start menu, just click any picture to open it. Or, right-click the picture's icon and choose Open File Location or right-click it and choose Open With, Preview, Send To, or whatever it is you want to do with that item. That's pretty cool. If you prefer, you can open your Pictures folder and use the Search box in its upper-right corner to search for a tag. That will limit the search to pictures in your Pictures folder and its subfolders.

When you search from the Start menu, you can opt to search for all files or just pictures.

If you want to find pictures that contain two tags, separate the tags with a space. For example, a search for

    Ashley Alec

searches for pictures that contain both Ashley and Alec. Use OR to broaden the search to find pictures that contain either Ashley or Alec as here:

`Ashley OR Alec`

If you need to specify your search condition more stringently, use the Search box in the upper-right corner of the Search window. For example, here's a search that finds only TIF files that contain either Ashley or Alec:

`type:tif AND tag:(ashley OR alec)`

Here's a search that finds all JPEG images that have Hawaii as a tag:

`type:jpeg AND tag:Hawaii`

You can still use DOS and Windows wildcard characters to search for filenames. For example, you could type

`haw*`

into the Filename box and click Search, or type

`filename:haw*`

into the Search box to find all pictures whose filenames start with haw.

You can save the results of any search as a virtual folder. When you open that folder, it shows all pictures that currently meet the search condition. For people who have a lot of pictures to deal with, these kinds of searches can be an extremely valuable tool. For more information on searching and virtual folders, see Chapters 30 and 31.

Wrap-Up

You can do lots of things with pictures and photos in Windows 7. You don't get the kind of power and flexibility you would with a dedicated graphics program like Adobe PhotoShop or Corel Paint Shop Pro. But nonetheless, you can perform the most basic operations like cropping, red-eye removal, and some file type conversions with just the built-in Windows 7 tools and programs.

- To get pictures from a digital camera, connect the camera to the computer, turn it on, and choose Import.
- To get pictures from a CD or memory card, insert the card or disk and choose Import. Or open the disk or card and copy files using standard methods.
- To copy-and-paste a picture, right-click the picture and choose Copy. Then right-click at the destination and choose Paste.
- Your Pictures folder is the best place to store pictures.
- Windows Live Photo Gallery lets you organize and find photos as though they were all stored in a single folder.
- Use the Fix button in Photo Gallery to crop and improve pictures.
- Use the Print button in your Pictures folder or Photo Gallery to print pictures.
- Large photos are good for printing and editing. Smaller, compressed photos are best for e-mail and Web publishing.

Making Music with Media Player

U sing your computer to collect, manage, and play music is a lot of fun. You can build up a collection of all your favorite songs, make custom CDs from those songs, or copy them to a portable MP3 player. You can use your computer as a stereo to play any songs you like in any order you like. If your computer is part of a network, you can share songs and play them on any computer that's in the network.

Windows 7 comes with two programs for collecting and playing music. One is Windows Media Player, which we discuss in this chapter. The other is Media Center (not included with all editions of Windows 7). If you prefer to use Media Center, see Chapter 26.

IN THIS CHAPTER

Playing music with Media Player

Copying CDs to your PC

Using your Media Library

Creating your own music CDs

Copying songs to portable players

Controlling Sound Volume

Before we get into Windows Media Player, you need to know a few things up front about music and video. In particular, you want to get your sound working and under control, so you can listen to whatever you like, without blasting your eardrums out!

Before you get started, make sure that you can control the volume of your speakers. At any given time, you're likely to have at least three volume controls available to you. Whichever control is set the lowest wins, in the sense that it puts an upper limit on the other volume controls.

If you have powered speakers, you need to make sure that the speakers are plugged in and turned on and connected to the Speaker output jack on your computer. If the speakers have a Mute button, make sure that it's turned off. If the speakers have a volume control button, that needs to be turned up.

You can control the volume of sound coming from your computer's speakers using the Volume Control icon in the Notification area. It looks like a little speaker with sound waves coming out. Pointing to that icon shows the current volume setting as in the left side of Figure 24-1. Clicking that icon displays a volume control slider and a Mute button, as in the right side of Figure 24-1.

FIGURE 24-1

Volume control icon and slider.

To adjust the volume, just drag the slider handle up or down the bar. To mute the sound, click the Mute button at the bottom of the slider. When the sound is muted, the icon shows a little red international No symbol (circle and slash) and no sound comes from your computer. To get the sound back, click the Mute button a second time.

Tip

If you don't see a speaker icon in your Notification area, chances are it's just hidden. To bring it out of hiding:

1. **Right-click the clock or any blank area in the Notification area and choose Customize Notification Icons.**
2. **Locate Volume in the Icons list, and choose Show Icon and Notifications from the drop-down list.**
3. **Click OK.**

Now you should have a speaker icon in your Notification area. Click it to see the volume control slider and Mute button. To ensure that you can hear any music you play, make sure the sound isn't muted and that the volume isn't turned down too low to hear. ■

With your speakers and volume control slider under control, you're ready to start using Media Player for Music.

Tip

If you have multiple sound cards and can't get any sound, make sure the default sound card is the one that's connected to the speakers. Click the Start button, type sou, and click Sound (or open the Sound applet from the Control Panel). On the Playback tab, click the icon of the sound card you're using and click Set Default. If both sound cards have speakers attached, you can configure each to act as the default for different types of audio using the down arrow next to the Set Default button. ■

Starting Windows Media Player

To start Windows Media Player, use whichever method is easiest for you:

- Click the Start button and choose All Programs ➪ Windows Media Player.
- Press ▟, type **med**, and choose Windows Media Player.
- Open any music file for which Windows Media Player is the default program.

The first time you open Windows Media Player, it will take you through a series of steps asking for your preferences. Don't worry if you don't know how to answer some questions. You can change your answer at any time. So if you see a window titled "Welcome to Windows Media Player" and don't know what to do, just click Recommended Settings and then click Finish. You can change settings at any time, so you're not making any settings permanent by accepting the suggested defaults.

Media Player program window

Like most programs, Windows Media Player opens in its own program window and has a taskbar button. The player can have many different appearances. Exactly how it looks at any time is up to you. You see different ways to display things in a moment. For now, we need to cover the names of things so you know what I'm talking about in the sections that follow.

Figure 24-2 points out the major components of Media Player's Player Library program window.

The features taskbar across the top of the program window represents different areas of Media Player, each of which helps you perform a specific task. In Figure 24-2, the Play tab is selected. Here's a quick summary of the program components and what each tab offers:

- **Navigation pane:** Takes you to your collection of songs and other media files.
- **Details pane:** Shows details for the currently selected library, album, genre, video, and so on.
- **List pane:** Shows information about the current play list and item.
- **Playback controls:** Provides controls for playing the currently selected media, and for switching to Now Playing mode.
- **Play:** Shows the movie or video you're currently watching, or song that is currently playing (if any). You can also rip (copy) CDs to your computer.
- **Burn:** This tab lets you create custom CDs from songs in your media library.
- **Sync:** Use this tab to copy songs and other media files to a portable media player.

FIGURE 24-2

Major Media Player components.

The toolbar

The Media Player toolbar gives you quick access to frequently used commands and options. The buttons in the toolbar change depending on what you have selected at the moment. The following list summarizes the available buttons:

- **Organize:** Manage your media libraries, sort media, customize the Navigation pane, change the Player Library layout, and access Media Player options.

- **Stream:** Enable Internet access to your home media and turn on media streaming, which allows you to send your media to other computers on the local network or the Internet.

- **Create Playlist:** Create a playback list (playlist) of media so you can play the selected items as a group. For example, you might create a playlist called My Top 100 that contains 100 of your favorite songs.

- **Rip CD:** Copy music from a CD to your media library on your computer so you can play it from your computer and optionally share it.

- **Rip Settings:** Specify settings to control the way Media Player rips music from CDs to your computer.

- **View Options:** Choose between Icon, title, and Details views for the List pane.

- **Search:** Search for media in your library.

- **Help:** Open Media Player's Help content.

Tip

Rip CD and Rip Settings only appear in the toolbar if an audio CD is inserted in the drive. ■

Media Player menus

Media Player has lots of menus. They're hidden from view most of the time, but they're also easy to get to. Many of the toolbar buttons have their own menu. You'll see a little down-pointing triangle at the right of the button if it offers commands. Get the tip of the mouse pointer right on that little triangle and click the left mouse button to see the menu for that taskbar button. Figure 24-3 shows an example in which I'm viewing the menu for the Organize button.

To see the main menu, right-click an empty area near the play controls, as at the bottom of Figure 24-4. Optionally, you can right-click an empty spot on the left or right side of the features taskbar to get to the same menu. To make those same options visible in a menu bar, choose Show Menu Bar from the bottom of that main menu.

FIGURE 24-3

Organize button menu.

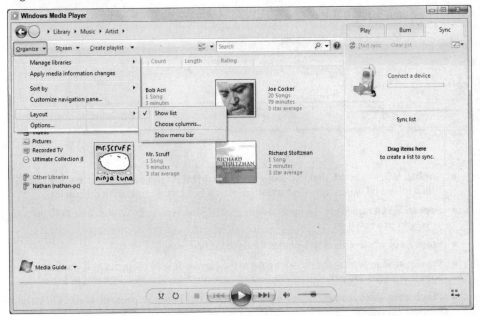

Play controls

The play controls (also called the *playback controls*) are at the bottom of Media Player's program window (see Figure 24-4). They work only when you're playing a song or video or have selected something to play. They work much like the controls on a VCR, stereo, or DVD player. The exact role of each button varies slightly with the type of content you're viewing. Here's what each of the play controls offers:

- **Seek bar:** When content is playing, a green indicator moves along the seek bar. You can click anywhere along the seek bar to jump forward or backward in the playing item. When you point to the end of the green indicator, a button appears. You can drag that button left or right to move back or forward within the item that's playing.

FIGURE 24-4

Media Player play controls.

- **Shuffle:** When selected, multiple songs from the current playlist are played in random order. When turned off, songs from the playlist are played in the same order as in the playlist.

- **Repeat:** When turned on, the same song or playlist plays repeatedly. When turned off, the song or playlist plays only once.

- **Stop:** Stops whatever is playing and rewinds to the beginning.

- **Previous:** Skips back to the previous song in the playlist or DVD chapter. Or, if you point to the button and hold down the left mouse button, plays the current item backwards in fast motion.

- **Play/Pause:** When content is playing, you can click this button to pause playback. Click again to resume playback.

- **Next:** Skips to the next song in the playlist or next chapter on a DVD. Point to this button and hold down the left mouse button to fast forward through the content that's playing.

- **Mute:** Click to mute playback sound. Click a second time to hear the sound again.

- **Volume:** Drag the handle left or right to increase or decrease the volume.

- **Now Playing:** Switches to Now Playing mode, a simplified version of the Media Player window. Also useful when you want to see a video or DVD played at full-screen size. Once in the full-screen mode, right-click anywhere on the screen and choose Exit Full Screen to return to the Player Library window. Or, click Switch to Library to return to the Player Library window.

Other items in the features taskbar are discussed later in this chapter. For now, let's stick with some of the basics of using Media Player's program window.

Closing/minimizing Windows Media Player

You can close Windows Media Player as you would any other program:

- Click the Close (X) button in the upper-right corner of Media Player's program window.
- Choose File ⇨ Exit from Media Player's menu.
- Right-click Media Player's taskbar button and choose Close.
- If Media Player is in the active window, press Alt+F4.

When you close Media Player, it stops playing whatever it was playing.

If you want to continue to listen to music, but want Media Player off the screen, minimize Media Player's program window. Use any of the following techniques to minimize Media Player's program window:

- Click the Minimize button in Media Player's title bar.
- Right-click Media Player's title bar and choose Minimize.
- Right-click Media Player's taskbar button and choose Minimize.

The Media Player icon appears on the Windows taskbar by default, even if the program is not running. Clicking the icon opens Media Player. If Media Player is running, pointing to it on the taskbar displays a preview window as shown in Figure 24-5. You can click the controls at the bottom of the preview to play, stop, or skip forward or back in the playlist. Click the small preview window or the taskbar icon to open Media Player.

FIGURE 24-5

Media Player on the Windows taskbar.

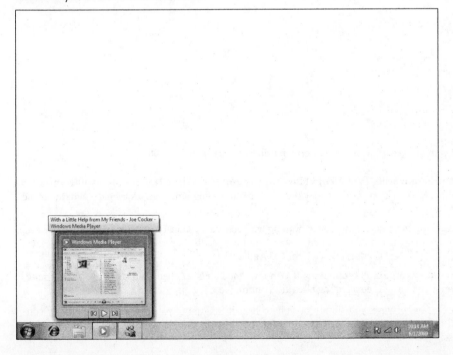

If the Media Player icon doesn't appear on the taskbar, you can easily add it. Click Start ➪ All Programs, right-click Media Player, and choose Pin to Start Menu. If you want to remove Media Player from the Start menu, right-click its taskbar icon and choose Unpin this Program from Taskbar.

That should be enough to get you started using Media Player. Next you look at various ways in which you can use Media Player to listen to music or watch videos.

Listening to a CD

A *music CD* (also called an *audio CD*) is the kind of CD you normally play in a stereo or CD player. Typically you buy these at a music store. As you learn later in this chapter, you can also create your own custom music CDs.

To listen to a music CD, just put it in your CD drive, label side up, and close the drive door. Then wait a few seconds. Windows Media Player might open and start playing the CD automatically. However, other things could happen:

- **A dialog box asks what you want to do:** If you see a dialog box like the example in Figure 24-6, click Play using Windows Media Player, then click OK.

Dialog box asking about a music CD.

Tip

To choose how your computer reacts when you insert a music CD, see Chapter 32. ∎

- **A program other than Media Player opens and plays the CD:** If a program other than Windows Media Player opens to play the CD, close that program. Then, do as indicated under the next item.

- **Nothing happens:** If absolutely nothing happens after you insert an audio CD, or if some other program opened and you closed it, start Windows Media Player. From Windows Media Player's menu, choose Play ➪ DVD, VCD, or CD Audio.

- **Windows Media Player opens:** If Windows Media Player opens and starts playing the song, you don't have to do anything else. Just continue reading on.

After the CD starts playing, you should be able to hear it (assuming your speakers are properly connected and not turned down too far). Use the Volume slider in the play controls to adjust the volume of the music.

Now Playing, Visualizations, and Enhancements

When music is playing, Media Player by default shows the album art, if available, in the Now Playing window. However, you can instead watch a *visualization* of the music. The visualization is a pattern of colors and shapes that change in rhythm to the music. Media Player offers many visualizations from which to choose.

To try a different visualization, first make sure that you're viewing the Now Playing window (press Alt and choose View ➪ Now Playing). Then right-click in the Now Playing window and choose Visualizations, then choose an option from the resulting cascading menu (Figure 24-7).

Choosing a visualization.

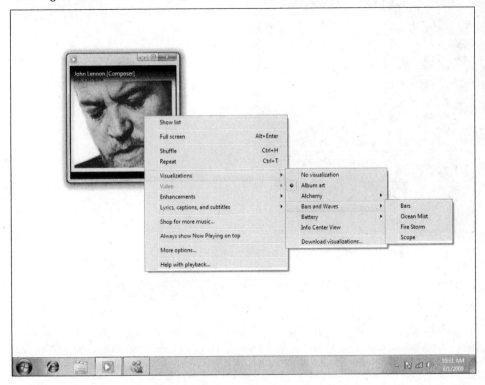

Regardless of which method you use, you'll see a menu of visualization names. Clicking a name displays a submenu of still more visualizations. Just pick any one to see how it looks. Go ahead and try a bunch while a song is playing to find one you like.

Tip

You can download plenty of visualizations for free. Right-click in the Now Playing window and choose Visualizations ➪ Download Visualizations. ■

Using the playlist in Now Playing view

When you're playing a music CD in Now Playing view, the playlist pane to the right of the visualization (see Figure 24-8) shows songs from the CD. That pane is optional. To show or hide that pane, right-click in the Now Playing window and choose Show List.

Playlist pane on right side of window.

In the playlist pane, you might see the song titles, as in Figure 24-8. Or you might just see more generic names like Track1, Track2, and so forth. Many CDs don't have song titles stored on CD, so the song titles have to be downloaded from the Internet. You'll only see song titles if they are available on the CD or have been downloaded from the Internet.

Note

Song titles are a form of media information. I discuss how all of that works under "Options for ripping CDs" later in this chapter. ■

If you want to listen to a specific song on the CD, just double-click its title in the playlist pane. Or, use the Previous and Next buttons in the play controls to highlight the song you want to listen to.

To change the width of the playlist pane, get the tip of the mouse pointer right on the left border of the pane, so the mouse pointer turns to a two-headed arrow. Then drag left or right.

Using Enhancements

While you're listening to music and are in the Now Playing area, you can also use Enhancements to adjust the sound and perform other tasks. The many Enhancements windows are invisible until you open them.

To show or hide Enhancements, right-click in the Now Playing window and choose Enhancements. Or, press Alt to open the menu bar, and then choose View ➪ Enhancements from Media Player's menu. When the Enhancements menu is open, you can choose which type of enhancement you want to see. Your options are summarized here:

- **Crossfading and Auto Volume Leveling:** When Crossfading is turned on, one song gradually fades out while the next song fades in. Auto Volume Leveling keeps songs at roughly equal volumes.

- **Graphic Equalizer:** Adjust the relative strengths of low, middle, and high tones. Optionally, click Default and choose a music type such as Rock or Classical. Click Reset to return to the default settings.

- **Play Speed Settings:** Use this to adjust the play speed of content. This option only works when playing .wma, .wmv, .wm, .mpe, and .asf files. Careful with this one. You don't want all your albums sounding like The Chipmunks!

- **Quiet Mode:** Adjusts the audio dynamic range of music (the difference between the loudest and softest sounds). You'd most likely use this option when listening to headphones or watching a movie in Media Player.

- **SRS WOW Effects:** When activated, SRS WOW effects add depth to your music. This one is definitely worth turning on and trying out if you have good speakers attached to your system.

- **Video Settings:** Adjust the brightness, contrast, hue, saturation, and size of video when viewing a movie or video in Media Player.

- **Dolby Digital Settings:** Choose between three options that adjust the audio range for different listening situations.

The selected Enhancements appear in a separate window, as show previously in Figure 24-8. You can cycle through the various Enhancements options by clicking the Next or Previous buttons in the upper-left corner of the Enhancements window.

Tip
You can drag the Enhancements window and resize it as needed. Click the red X icon to close the window. ■

Stopping a CD

When you've finished listening to a CD, click the Stop button in the play controls. To eject the CD, choose Play ➪ Eject from Media Player's menu, or push the Eject button on your CD drive.

Play CDs automatically with Media Player

If you want to ensure that Media Player opens and plays music CDs automatically, you need to make Media Player the default player for CDs. Here's how:

1. Click the Start button and choose Control Panel.

2. Click Hardware and Sound.

3. Click AutoPlay.

4. Next to Audio CD, choose Play Audio CD using Windows Media Player.

5. If you also want Media Player to play DVDs automatically, next to DVD Movie choose Play DVD Video Using Windows Media Player.

6. Click the Save button.

7. Close Control Panel.

From that point on, whenever you put a music CD in your CD drive, Windows Media Player should open and play the CD automatically.

Tip

Here's a shortcut to the AutoPlay options: Click the Start button or tap ⊞. Type auto and choose AutoPlay from the Start menu. ■

Ripping (Copying) Music CDs

Media Player isn't just about playing CDs. The real idea is to build up a library of digital media on your hard drive, from which you can create custom playlists and music CDs. If you already own some music CDs, ripping a few CDs will be a great way to start creating your personal media library. Though the term "rip" might sound like something bad, it's not. It simply means to "copy," and no harm will come to the CD when you rip songs from it to your media library.

When you rip a CD, you store a copy of each song from the CD on your hard drive. That song is in a format that's more suitable for computers than the song that's on the CD. You can put the original CD back in its case, and leave it there so it doesn't get scratched up. Play the songs straight from your PC, or make your own CDs to play the songs in a stereo. Keep the original CD as a backup in case you accidentally delete some songs you've copied.

Ripping CDs is easy, as you'll see. But you need to make a few decisions up front, like where you want to put the songs, how you want them titled, what format you want them stored in, and so forth. The sections that follow look at all of your options.

Options for ripping CDs

To choose options for how you want to copy CDs to your hard disk, use the Rip Music tab in Media Player's Options dialog box. To get to those options:

1. Open Windows Media Player (if it isn't already open).

2. Insert an audio CD in the drive and click the drive in the Library pane so that the Rip and Rip Settings buttons are available in the toolbar. Then, choose More Options to open the Rip Music tab of Media Player's Options dialog box.

You're taken to the Rip Music tab in Media Player's Options dialog box, shown in Figure 24-9.

The following sections describe what each option offers. Note that you don't need to make selections from the dialog box for every CD you copy. Rather, you choose your options once. All CDs that you copy from that point forward will use whatever settings you chose.

FIGURE 24-9

Rip Music tab in Media Player's Options dialog box.

Choosing where to put songs

By default, all songs you copy from CD will be placed in your Music folder. That's a perfectly fine place to put them, but there's no rule that says you have to put them there. You can store them in any folder you want. For example, you might put them in the Public Music folder if you want everyone who uses the PC to access the songs. Or, if you have multiple hard drives, you can put them in a folder on some drive other than C:.

Note
If you're not very familiar with the concepts of drives and folders, don't worry about it. Just leave the Rip Music to this Location setting alone. Your songs will end up in your personal Music folder. Note that whatever folder you choose is referred to as the *rip music folder* in Media Player options. ■

To choose a drive and folder for storing CDs, click the Change button in the dialog box. Then navigate to the drive and folder in which you want to store the songs. For example, if you want to put the songs in your Public Music folder, expand the Computer, Local Disk (C:), Users, and Public folders, and click Public Music. Then click OK.

The path in the dialog box shows where the songs will be stored. For example, in Figure 24-9, C:\Users\jboyce\Music tells me that the songs will be stored in the personal Music folder for the user account named jboyce. (C: is the hard disk and Users is the name of the folder in which all user accounts are stored.)

Choosing how to name files

Each song you copy from a CD is stored as a file. Like all files, each song will have a filename. Windows Media Player names the files automatically, based on the track number, song title, and other media information.

You're free to choose how you want song files named. How you name the songs is entirely up to you, and won't affect how they play. The default filename is the CD track number followed by the song name. You might prefer to have the song name first. To make your selections, click the File Name button on the Rip Music tab of the dialog box. The File Name Options dialog box shown in Figure 24-10 opens.

FIGURE 24-10

The File Name Options dialog box.

Choose the elements you want to use in each song's filename. At the very least you should choose Song Title, because that is certainly a key piece of information. Use the Separator drop-down list to choose which character will separate each portion of the name.

To change the order of items in the filename, click any selected item and use the Move Up or Move Down button to change its position in the filename. As you choose components and change their order, the generic filename under Preview gives you a sense of how each song title will look with your current settings.

Click OK after deciding how you want your filenames to look.

Choosing a file format and quality

Under Rip Settings on the Rip Music tab, the Format drop-down list lets you choose a format and quality in which to store songs you copy. Basically this all boils down to a trade-off between file size and music quality. File size has to do with how much hard disk space each song consumes. Quality has to do with the depth, clarity, and richness of the music when you listen to it. Music quality is measured in kilobits per second, abbreviated Kbps. The higher the Kbps number, the better the music quality, but the more disk space each song consumes.

Options for choosing are under the Rip Settings heading in the Options dialog box. First, use the Format drop-down list to choose one of the following formats:

- **Windows Media Audio:** Songs are copied to Windows Media Audio (.wma) format files and compressed to conserve disk space. You can choose the amount of compression using the Audio Quality slider in the same dialog box. This is a good general-purpose format that plays on all Windows computers and many portable media devices.

- **Windows Media Audio Pro:** Similar to the preceding format, but includes features that make the music sound better on high-end multi-channel sound systems.

- **Windows Media Audio (Variable Bit Rate):** Same as the preceding format, but the amount of compression varies with the complexity of the information being stored. As a rule, you get better quality with smaller file sizes using a variable bit rate. This format is not compatible with all portable music players.

- **Windows Media Audio Lossless:** Same as the preceding format, but files are not compressed at all. The sound quality is excellent, but the files are huge. Still, if you're a true audiophile, or are interested in creating HighMAT CDs (High-Performance Media Access Technology), this is an excellent choice.

- **MP3:** MP3 is the most widely used format for digital music. It's been around the longest. Unlike the .wma formats, you're not limited to playing the songs on Windows-based computers. You can play MP3 songs on any MP3-compatible player.

- **WAV (Lossless):** Stores each song as a WAV file. These offer high quality, but create enormous files. So you probably want to stay away from this format unless you have some good reason to use it.

If you're new to all of this, and at a complete loss as to what to choose, go with WMA or MP3. Those are common formats that almost any device can play.

If you choose anything but a lossless format, you can then use the Audio Quality slider to choose what quality setting you want. Again, the basic rule of better quality creating larger files applies. Hard disk space is cheap and plentiful, so there's no need to settle for the lowest-quality setting. If in doubt, don't go below 128 Kbps or your music may all end up sounding shallow or kind of "tinny."

As you move the Audio Quality slider to different settings, text beneath the slider tells you roughly how much disk space an entire CD will consume at that setting. To better illustrate how format and audio quality relate to disk space consumption, I ripped a 3-minute song at various sound qualities, and I put their sizes in Table 24-1. The last column, "Songs per GB," gives you a sense of how many songs you can get into a single gigabyte of hard disk space at various quality settings.

Tip

See "Understanding Disks and Drives" in Chapter 28 for more information on disk drives, capacities, and discovering how much space you have. You might want to take a peek at your available space each time you copy a CD, so you can get a sense of how much free space each copied CD consumes. ∎

After you've chosen a format and audio quality, you have a few more options on the Rip Music tab to choose from.

TABLE 24-1

A Three-Minute Song at Formats and Bit Rates

Format/Quality	Bit Rate	Size	Songs per GB
Windows Media Audio	192 Kbps	4.17 MB	246
Windows Media Audio Pro	192 Kbps	4.18 MB	245
WMA Variable Bit Rate	103 Kbps	2.22 MB	461
Window Media Audio Lossless	480 Kbps	14.20 MB	72
MP3	192 Kbps	4.12 MB	249
WAV (Lossless)	320 Kbps	30.30 MB	34

Copy protect music

The Copy Protect Music option on the Rip Music tab lets you decide whether or not you want to put copyright protection on the songs you copy. I think a lot of people choose that option thinking it will somehow protect them from messing up the songs. But that's not how it works. The protection that the option offers is for the copyright holder, not for you.

If you choose the Copy Protect option, the songs you copy will play only on the computer at which you're sitting. You'll also put other restrictions on the songs. For example, you won't be able to import them into Movie Maker or other programs that normally let you edit music. If you want to keep things simple and make sure you can use your copied songs freely, I suggest you leave the Copy Protect Music check box empty.

Rip CD automatically

If selected, this option tells Windows Media Player to copy all the songs from a CD as soon as you insert the audio CD. Choosing this option, along with the Eject CD option described next, makes it easy to rip a whole collection of CDs in assembly-line fashion. For example, if you have a few dozen CDs you want to rip, you can just insert a CD, wait for it to be copied and ejected, and then insert the next CD.

When you've finished ripping your CD collection, you can then clear this option so that you have more flexibility in deciding what you want to do with each CD you insert into your hard drive.

Eject CD after ripping

If selected, this option just tells Media Player to eject the CD from the drive when it's finished copying the CD. As mentioned, choosing this option along with the *Rip CD Automatically* option is a great way to copy multiple CDs in a quick, assembly-line manner.

Still more rip options

Media Player's Options dialog box contains some additional options that affect what happens when you rip CDs. While you still have the Options dialog box open, click the Privacy tab. Then choose your options as summarized next. But remember, not all CDs have media information posted on the Internet. Therefore, even if you do select options as indicated, you may need to manually update media information for a song or album.

- **Display Media Information from the Internet:** Choose (check) this option to have media information, such as song titles, appear automatically when you play or copy a CD.

- **Update Music Files by Retrieving Media Info from the Internet:** Choose this option to have Media Player automatically fill in information from songs you've already copied to your computer.

When you've finished making all of your selections, click OK in the Options dialog box. Now you're ready to start ripping CDs. Remember, you need not change the preceding settings every time you copy a CD. The settings you choose apply to all CDs that you copy.

Copying songs

With all the details of choosing how you want to copy CDs out of the way, you're ready to start copying. Here are the steps:

1. If your Internet account requires logging in, get online so that you're connected to the Internet and Media Player can download media information (song titles).

2. Insert the music CD you want to rip (copy) into your CD drive and close the drive door.

3. If Windows Media Player doesn't open automatically, open it yourself. (If some other program opened when you inserted the CD, close that program, then open Media Player.)

4. If you chose the Rip CD Automatically option described earlier in this chapter, skip down to step 10 now.

5. If the CD starts playing, click the Stop button down in the play controls.

6. Wait for song titles to appear. If song titles don't appear within 30 seconds or so, the CD might not be in the CDDB. In that case, you can go ahead and rip the CD, and then fill in the details later in your media library.

Note
CDDB stands for Compact Disk Database. It's an online database that contains song titles for most (but not all) commercially sold CDs. ■

7. Optionally, clear the checkmark to the left of any songs that you don't want to copy. Media Player will only copy songs that have a checkmark.

8. Click the Rip CD button in the toolbar. Figure 24-11 shows Media Player ripping a Led Zeppelin CD to disk.

9. Wait until the Rip Status column shows *Ripped to Library* for all songs you've opted to copy. If the CD doesn't eject automatically, go ahead and eject it.

10. Put the CD back to wherever you normally keep your CDs. You won't need it any more to play songs from your computer, or to copy files to custom audio CDs or an MP3 player.

That's it for ripping one CD. To rip more CDs, just repeat steps 4 to 10 for each CD. If at any time you want to check your available hard disk space, open your Computer folder. If you don't see any indication of available disk space for your hard disk (typically Local Disk C:), choose Tiles from the Views menu in that folder.

Copying songs from CDs you already own is one way to build up your Media Player music library. Any songs you don't already own, but would like to, you can purchase online and download to your Media Player library. I discuss how that works in the next section.

FIGURE 24-11

Media Player ripping a CD to disk.

Getting Music Online

In addition to ripping CDs you already own, you can download music from online stores. The exact procedure varies from one online store to the next. Some are membership sites. Some let you purchase and download songs without joining or paying a membership fee. New stores and services come online all the time, so there's little that I can tell you specifically that applies to all of the available vendors, other than you should shop around and not necessarily sign up with the first vendor to pop up on your screen. In the bottom left of the Navigation pane, click the arrow beside the Media Guide button and choose Browse All Online Stores to see other options. The button changes to Online Stores. Click the arrow and choose Media Guide if you want to view the Media Guide.

Using the Media Player Library

The whole point of a program like Windows Media Player is to build and manage a library of digital media. That includes music, pictures, video, and recorded TV (even though we're focusing on music in this chapter).

To see and manage your Media Player library, open Media Player in Library mode. If Media Player is currently running in Now Playing mode, click the Switch to Library button.

Navigating the library

There is almost no limit to the ways in which you can view, organize, and change things in the library. You can view media by artist, album, genre, playlist, and other ways. If you want to add other properties to your Navigation pane, click Organize ➪ Customize Navigation Pane to show the Customize Navigation Pane dialog box shown in Figure 24-12.

FIGURE 24-12

Customize Navigation Pane dialog box.

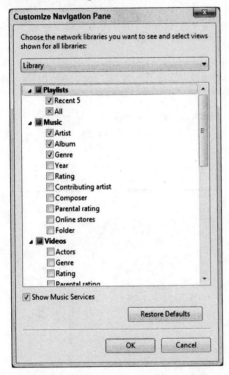

If your Media Player library doesn't show songs, but instead shows pictures or other kinds of media, click an option under Music in the Navigation pane.

In the Navigation pane, you can click the triangle button (if any) next to an item to view different categories such as Artist, Album, Genre, and so on. The following lists views you can add to the Navigation pane for music:

- **Artist:** Shows artist names in alphabetical order.
- **Album:** Shows album titles in alphabetical order.
- **Genre:** Shows names of music genres (such as Classical, Rock, Jazz).
- **Year:** Shows albums organized by publication year.

- **Rating:** Shows songs organized by rating (one to five stars). The songs are separated into those you have rated and those that are rated automatically based on your listening habits. Songs that are unrated appear under the Unrated category.

- **Contributing Artist:** Shows songs organized by contributing artists, if any.

- **Composer:** Shows songs organized by composer.

- **Parental Rating:** Shows songs organized by parental rating.

- **Online Stores:** Shows songs based on the store from which it was obtained.

- **Folder:** Shows songs organized by the folder in which they are stored.

You'll be better able to appreciate the library if you have at least 30 or 40 songs in your library before reading this section. Or better yet, several hundred songs. As you explore your library, keep in mind that you can right-click any icon, stack, category name, or whatever to view, edit, or play items.

Use the View Options button to choose how you want to view things. Depending on where you are at the moment, some View options will be disabled (dimmed) because they're not applicable to the current way of looking at things. But in general, you can choose from the following views:

- **Icon:** Each item is represented by a single icon or stack of icons, as in the example shown in Figure 24-13.

FIGURE 24-13

Sample Icon view.

- **Tile:** Similar to the icon view, but with some additional information about each item or stack to the right. Figure 24-14 shows an example.

Sample Tile view.

- **Expanded Tile:** Shows the album cover and a list of songs on each album. Available in the Recently Added and Songs categories only. Figure 24-15 shows an example.
- **Details:** Shows detailed textual information about each item in a tabular format. Figure 24-16 shows an example.

Of course, there's no right way or wrong way to view icons. Just choose whichever view works best at the moment. Feel free to try things out. You can't do any harm by checking out different ways to view things. And nothing you choose is set in stone. You can change your view at any time.

How you use a view depends on what you're viewing. For example, if you're viewing Genres, you'll see an icon or stack for each genre in your library. Double-clicking an icon or stack shows you all the songs in that genre. Double-clicking an icon that represents a single album displays songs on that album. To play all the items that an icon represents, right-click the icon and choose Play. Again, doing some exploring on your own is your best bet. You're not permanently changing anything as you explore, so there's no need to be worried.

FIGURE 24-15

Sample Expanded Tile view.

FIGURE 24-16

Sample Details view.

Choosing columns for Media Library

In addition to choosing how you want media information to look, you can choose exactly which information you do and don't want to see. The exact options available to you depend on what you're viewing and how you're viewing it at the moment. To see the full set of options, click Music in the Navigation pane, then choose Details from the View Options button. You'll see detailed information about each song organized into rows and columns.

To choose which columns you want to view, right-click a column heading, such as Title or Length, and click Choose Columns on the menu. The Choose Columns dialog box shown in Figure 24-17 opens.

The Choose Columns dialog box.

In the Choose Columns dialog box, select (check) the columns you want to see. Clear (uncheck) columns you don't want to see. You can also control the order of columns, either in the dialog box, or after you exit the dialog box. To control the order of columns while you're in the dialog box, click any selected column name, and then click the Move Up or Move Down button to move it up or down. The higher a column name is in the dialog box, the farther to the left it is in the Details view.

After you've chosen the columns you want to view, click OK. Most likely you won't be able to see all the columns at the same time. But you can use the horizontal scroll bar under the columns to scroll left and right through columns.

Sizing columns

To adjust the width of any column, get the mouse pointer to the right side of the column heading. You'll know the mouse pointer is in the right place when it turns to a two-headed arrow. Then, just drag the column to the width you want.

Moving columns

To move a column left or right, first put the mouse pointer right on the column heading, for example, the word Title, Length, Album, or Album Artist. Then hold down the left mouse button and drag the column left or right. Release the mouse pointer when the column is where you want it to be.

Sorting songs

When you're in a Details view you can also sort items by any column. For example, you can sort them by Title, Length, Album, Album Artist, or any other column heading. The first time you click, items will be sorted into ascending order (alphabetically, or smallest to largest). The second time you click, items will be sorted into descending order (reverse alphabetical, or largest to smallest).

Tip

The techniques for sizing, moving, and sorting by columns apply to most columnar views of data in most programs. This feature is not unique to Media Player. ■

Getting missing media information automatically

Recall that media information refers to things like song titles, artist name, and so forth. That information might be missing from some of your songs for a couple of reasons. One reason might be that the information isn't available from the Internet. In that case, you may have to fill in the missing information manually, using techniques described later in this chapter.

A second reason why you might be missing media information is that you weren't online when you copied some CDs. If that's the case, it's not too late to retrieve that information. It's quicker and easier to retrieve the information automatically. So before you start manually changing media information, use the technique described in this section to see how much of that information you can get automatically.

First you need to check your options for updating media information automatically. Click the Organize button and choose Options. The Library tab in Media Player's Options dialog box appears, shown in Figure 24-18.

Under the Automatic Media Information Updates for Files heading, choose (check) Retrieve Additional Information from the Internet.

- If you've already added some media information manually and don't want the new information to replace that, choose Only Add Missing Information.

- Otherwise, choose Overwrite All Media Information if you want information you've added yourself to be replaced with information from the Internet.

When you've finished making your selection, click OK in the dialog box. Then click the Organize button and choose Apply Media Information Changes.

There's no guarantee that all missing information will be filled in. You may have songs for which there is no online media information. You'll still have to edit those manually. To change the title of a single song, right-click the current title (Track1, Track2, or whatever), choose Edit, and type the correct song title.

Information other than the title is likely to be the same for all the songs on a given album. It's not necessary to change that information one song at a time. You can select multiple songs to which you want to make a change. The change you make is then applied to all the selected songs. We'll get to that in a moment. First let's look at how you can add songs that you have elsewhere on your computer to your Media Player library.

FIGURE 24-18

The Library tab in the Options dialog box.

Choosing what files to include in your library

If you set up multiple user accounts on your computer, each user gets to have his or her own media library. Parents don't have to dig through the kids' songs and vice versa. But you're not stuck with only those songs. Each user also has the option to share songs, and each user has the option to choose or reject songs shared by others. To choose which songs display in your own media library:

1. Click Organize in the taskbar and choose Manage Libraries ⇨ Music to open the Music Library Locations dialog box (Figure 24-19).

2. Click the Add button. The Include Folder in Music dialog box opens.

Note
Even though we're focusing on music here, Media Player can also display pictures, videos, and recorded TV. You can add folders for those types of files using the same process for those libraries. ■

3. To add a new folder to the list of monitored folders, so the songs show up in your library, click the Add button. Then browse to the drive and folder that you want to include and click OK. You can repeat this step to monitor as many folders as you wish.

FIGURE 24-19

The Music Library Locations dialog box.

4. To prevent songs from a folder from being added to your library, click the folder you want to exclude and click the Remove button.

5. Click OK after making your selections to have Media Player search any newly added folders.

Media Player will update your library according to the selections you made.

Sharing (streaming) your media library

New Feature

N ow you can stream your music to another computer across the Internet.

Each user can opt to share all songs or some songs with other user accounts on the same computer. Likewise, if your computer is part of a private network, each user can choose to share songs with other Windows Vista or Windows 7 computers or Windows 7–compatible devices (like the Xbox 360). A great new feature in Windows Media Player 12 is the capability to stream music to the Internet. So, you can enjoy the music library stored on your home computer when you are at work.

The first step in sharing your music is to enable streaming. To do so, click the Stream button in the toolbar and choose Turn On Media Streaming, then click Turn On Media Streaming in the Media Streaming Options dialog box. (If streaming is already enabled, click More Options.) At this point, the options shown in Figure 24-20 appear.

FIGURE 24-20

Media streaming options.

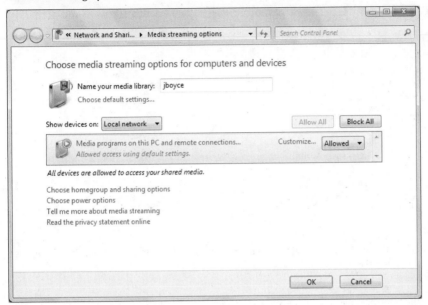

Tip
If you don't see a Turn On Media Streaming command in the Stream menu, streaming is already enabled. ∎

In the Media Streaming Options dialog box you can assign a name to your shared media library, specify streaming settings for specific devices, allow or block access for devices, and access other settings that potentially affect streaming (such as the streaming computer's power settings).

To configure default settings, click the Choose Default Settings link to open the Default Media Streaming Options dialog box shown in Figure 24-21.

In the Default Media Streaming Options dialog box you can specify which media is shared based on star and parental ratings. The default is to share all media. Click OK when you have finished configuring default settings.

Back in the Media Streaming Options dialog box, you can configure settings for specific devices. For example, you might limit access from a specific device (such as your children's computer) based on parental ratings, but allow all ratings from others. The device labeled Media Programs on This PC and Remote Connections defines the settings for programs on your local computer (the one you are setting up to stream) as well as connections from the Internet. Click the Customize link beside a device to configure its streaming settings. The resulting dialog box is identical to the one that's shown in Figure 24-21.

Allowing Internet streaming

As mentioned previously in this chapter, you can use Media Player to stream media to other devices on the Internet. For example, you might listen to your home music library while you are at work. Whatever the case, you must first set up that capability, because it is not enabled by default.

FIGURE 24-21

Default media streaming options.

The first step is to link a Windows Live ID to your account on the computer that will be sharing its library. The Link Online IDs applet in the Control Panel lets you do just that, and you have a couple of ways to get there:

- Open the Control Panel, click User Accounts and Family Safety ⇨ User Accounts and click Link Online IDs in the left pane.

- In Media Player, click Stream ⇨ Allow Internet Access to Home Media ⇨ Link an Online ID.

For help linking your Windows Live ID to your Windows account, see, "Linking Online IDs with Windows Accounts," in Chapter 3.

After you link your Windows Live ID, open Media Player and click Stream ⇨ Allow Internet Access to Home Media. In the resulting Internet Home Media Access dialog box, click Allow Internet Access to Home Media. If prompted for an administrative password, enter it, or if prompted with a User Account Control dialog box, click Yes. Click OK when Windows 7 indicates it has successfully enabled sharing.

Using a remote stream

After you configure streaming on a computer, you can then access that stream from another computer, whether on the local network or on the Internet. To play a stream from another computer, first open Media Player. Then, in the Library view, look under the Other Libraries branch in the Navigation pane. You should see the other computer(s) listed there (Figure 24-22). Click the server from which you want to play, and then play items from the List pane just as you would for a local library.

Tip

If you don't see devices listed in the Other Libraries branch in the Navigation pane, click Organize ⇨ Customize Navigation Pane. Choose Other Libraries from the drop-down list, and then place a check beside each device you want to see listed in the Navigation pane. ■

FIGURE 24-22

Remote libraries in the Navigation pane.

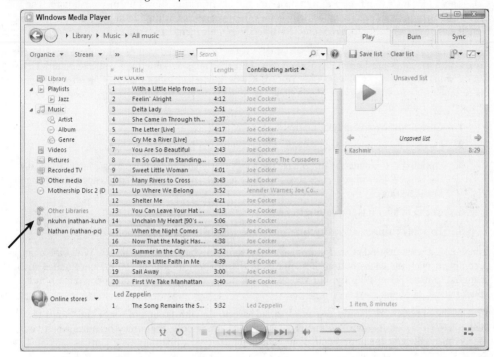

Allow remote control

If you want to let other computers and devices push music, video, and photos to Media Player on your computer, you need to enable remote control of Media Player on your computer. To do so, open Media Player and click Stream ➪ Allow Remote Control of My Player. In the resulting Allow Remote Control dialog box, click Allow Remote Control on this Network.

Pushing media to another computer

If you have a media player at home, such as an Xbox 360, Roku SoundBridge, D-Link MediaLounge, or other device, you can stream music from your computer to that device using Media Player. For example, let's say you have a MediaLounge in your living room hooked up to your entertainment center. Your music collection is on your home PC. No problem, just push the music from your PC to the MediaLounge. Here's how.

Open Media Player, and then create the playlist that you want to stream to the remote device. At the top of the List pane, click the Play To button and choose the device from the list.

Tip

See Part X for more information on private networks and sharing. ■

Automatically renaming songs

Earlier in this chapter you learned how you could control filenames of songs you rip (copy) from CDs. Those filenames don't have a big impact on how information shows up in your library. The media information from each song actually comes from properties in the file rather than the filename. Nonetheless, it never hurts to have some consistency in your filenames.

For example, suppose you ripped a bunch of CDs before you realized you could control how the filenames of those songs are formatted. You change the rip settings to something you like better. That change won't affect songs you've already ripped; it will only affect songs that you rip after changing the setting. You can, however, get Media Player to rename previously named songs according to your new settings. Here's how:

1. Click Organize and choose Options.

2. On the Library tab, choose Rename Music Files using Rip Music Settings.

3. Optionally, if you also want to have the songs rearranged in your rip music folder (typically the Music folder in your user account), choose Rearrange Music in Rip Music Folder Using Rip Music Settings.

4. Click OK after making your selections.

5. To apply changes, click Organize and choose Apply Media Information Changes.

It may take a while to update and rearrange all the songs in your rip music folder. When the change is complete, click the Close button that appears in the progress indicator. You may not notice any changes in Media Player's library, but you likely will notice changes when you open your rip music folder outside of Media Player.

Most of the options and settings discussed so far have to do with groups of songs and things the Media Player does on its own. No matter what settings you choose, there may be times when you need to manually edit (or remove) items in your library.

In some cases, you may need to change a single song title. For example, suppose you have songs named Track1, Track2, Track3, and so forth. You've already tried updating that information through techniques described earlier, but the song titles still don't appear because the song titles aren't available online. When that happens, you'll need to manually change the media information.

When changing a song title, you'll want to work with one song at a time. In other cases, such as when changing a genre or artist name, you may want to make the same change to several songs at once. To make the same change to multiple songs in your library, you first have to select the songs you want to change. So before talking about manually editing songs, let's look at techniques for selecting the songs you want to change.

Selecting in Media Library

Your media library isn't set in stone. You can change the information you see at any time. Typically you just right-click the thing you want to change and choose Edit to change it or Delete to remove it. I'll get to the specifics in a moment. But first let's talk about *selecting* items in the library. Selecting two or more items allows you to make the same change to all those selected items in one fell swoop.

Selecting items in Media Library is much like selecting icons in folders, so if you already know how to do that you're ahead of the game. You can select items in any view, but you might find it easiest to work in the Details view. For example, click Music in the Navigation pane at the left side of the window. Then choose Details from the View Options button. Finally, click whatever column heading arranges the songs in a way that groups them in whatever way is easiest for you to work with at the moment.

One way to select all the items in a group is to click the heading that precedes the group. For example, in Figure 24-23, I clicked the artist name Joe Cocker to select all the songs under that category. The selected songs are highlighted. Any change you make to one of the selected songs is applied to all the selected songs.

FIGURE 24-23

Selected songs under Joe Cocker heading.

Another way to select multiple adjacent songs is to click the first one you want to select. Then hold down the Shift key and click the last one you want to select. The two songs you clicked and all the songs in between are selected.

To select multiple songs that aren't adjacent to one another, click the first one that you want to select. Then hold down the Ctrl key while clicking other songs you want to select. That same technique lets you unselect one selected song without unselecting any other songs.

You can also use the keyboard to select songs, as follows:

- To select every song in the library, click Songs in the Navigation pane, click a song title, and press Ctrl+A.

- To select all the songs from the current song to the bottom of the list, click the first song you want to select and press Shift+End.

- To select all the songs to the top of the list, click the first song and press Shift+Home.

To deselect songs, click a neutral area in the program window, such as the empty space to the left of the play controls.

627

Selecting songs doesn't have any effect on them, other than to highlight them. However, any action you take while the songs are selected is applied to all of the selected songs. The following sections look at things you can do with any one song or any number of selected songs.

Changing a song title

Every song on a CD is likely to have its own unique title, so you generally have to change titles one at a time. To change just one song title, first make sure you don't have multiple songs selected. (Click the song you want to change so that only that song it selected.) Then right-click the title you want to change and choose Edit. Type the new title and press Enter.

Changing genre, artist, and such

You can change the genre, artist, album title, or any other media information for a song by right-clicking in a specific column and choosing Edit. But because all the songs on a CD may have that same artist, or belong to the same genre, you might want to make the change to several songs. First select all the songs to which you want to apply the change. Then click the word or name you want to change in any one of the selected songs and choose Edit. Type in the new name or word and press Enter. The change will occur in all the selected songs.

Changing incorrect media information

Sometimes Media Player will get media information from the Internet, but it's the wrong information. This is especially true when working with multiple CD sets. Rather than manually typing all the information for the CD, you can take a shot at finding the correct information online. To do so, click Album in the Navigation pane. Then scroll to the album that has the incorrect icon, right-click its icon, and choose Update Album Info. Then double-click the album's icon to see whether the situation has improved at all.

If updating the album info didn't help, you can try right-clicking the album title just above its song titles and choosing Find Album Info. Most likely you'll get the same faulty information you got the first time. But you can click the Search button in the lower-left corner of the Album Info window that opens and try searching by the artist's name or album title. You may get lucky and find the exact album you're looking for. The Album Info window acts like a wizard, so you can just follow the instructions on the screen and use the buttons along the bottom of the window to aid in your search.

If you do find the exact album you're looking for, click the Finish button in the Album Info window and Media Player will copy the media information to the album in your media library. If you don't have any such luck, you can still manually enter the correct information for each song on the album using the techniques described in the previous sections.

Rating songs

You've probably noticed the star ratings that Media Player adds to each song. By default, the ratings are all the same (three stars) because the idea is for you to rate each song according to your own likes and dislikes. Give five stars to your favorite songs, one star to songs you don't like, and something in between for all the rest.

To change the rating of a single song, right-click the title of the song you want to rate, choose Rate, and enter the number of stars you want to give it. To rate multiple songs, first decide what rating you want to apply (such as five stars). Then select all the songs to which you want to apply that rating. (You can use the Ctrl+Click method to select multiple non-adjacent songs.) After you've selected all the songs to which you want to apply a rating, right-click any selected song, choose Rate, and choose the desired rating.

Any time you want to view all the songs to which you've applied a rating, click Organize ➪ Sort By ➪ Rating. The contents pane in the center of the program window will show rating categories; one category for ratings you've applied and another for songs you haven't rated yet but were given ratings automatically, like the example in Figure 24-24.

To play all the songs to which you've given a certain rating, right-click the rating icon and choose Play. To see all the songs to which you've applied a given rating, double-click the rating icon.

FIGURE 24-24

Stars representing ratings.

Making Custom Playlists

A playlist is a group of songs. In Media Player's library, every icon, stack, and Navigation pane category is a playlist in its own right, which you can play by right-clicking and choosing Play. So every time you open Windows Media Player and click the Library button in the features taskbar, you have many playlists from which to choose.

A custom playlist is one you create yourself. A custom playlist can contain any songs you like, in any order you like. For example, you can create a Party playlist of songs to play during a party. You can create a Favorites playlist of just your favorite songs. You can also create custom playlists of songs you want to copy to your own custom CDs, DVDs, or portable music player.

To get started on creating a custom playlist, follow these steps:

1. If you haven't already done so, open Windows Media Player.

2. Open the Library view if currently in Now Playing view.

3. If you don't see the Playlist pane at the right side of the program window, do either of the following to make it visible:

   • Click the Play tab.

   • Click the Organize button and choose Layout ⇨ Show List.

To create your own custom playlist, you'll need to start with an empty one, like the example at the right side of Figure 24-25. If your List pane isn't empty, click the Clear List button pointed out in that figure.

FIGURE 24-25

Empty List pane.

To create your custom playlist, drag any song titles you want from the contents pane to the left of the playlist into the playlist. As an alternative to dragging one song title at a time, you can select multiple songs and drag them all at once. As an alternative to dragging, you can right-click any song title and choose Add to Playlist. Or select multiple songs, right-click any selected song, and choose Add to Playlist.

Note

If you skipped the earlier section, "Using the Media Player Library," you'll need to go back and learn some basic library navigation skills before you can find songs to add to your playlist. ■

To add all the songs from an album to the playlist, right-click the album's icon and choose Add to Playlist. Likewise, you can right-click any icon or stack that represents a category of songs — such as a genre, artist name, or rating — and choose Add to Playlist. All the songs within that category are added to the playlist.

Don't worry about adding too much stuff to the playlist. There's almost no limit to how large a playlist can be. And you can also remove any song from the playlist at any time.

Managing songs in a playlist

After you have some songs in a playlist, you can arrange them as you see fit. Use any of the following techniques to do so:

- Drag any song title up or down to change its position in the list.
- Right-click any song title and choose Move Up or Move Down.
- Click the List Options button above the list, and choose whichever option best describes how you want them sorted (see Figure 24-26).

FIGURE 24-26

Sorting songs in a playlist.

- To put the songs in random order, choose Shuffle List from the menu that's shown in Figure 24-27.

Tip

To widen or narrow the List pane, drag its inner border left or right. ■

To remove a song from the playlist, right-click the song title and choose Remove from List. Optionally you can select multiple songs using the Ctrl+Click or Shift+Click method. Then press Delete (Del) or right-click any selected item and choose Remove From This List.

Saving a playlist

To save a playlist, name the list by clicking Untitled Playlist and entering a name. To rename a list, simply click the name and type a new one, then press Enter.

Viewing, playing, and changing playlists

To play all the songs in a playlist, or change a playlist, first click the Play tab. If the Navigation pane isn't open, use the Layout Options button to open it. The playlists appear under the Playlists branch in the Navigation pane. If you click Playlists in the Navigation pane, you'll see all of your saved playlists in the contents pane as icons. Recent playlists will be listed first, followed by all playlists, as in Figure 24-27. In that example I chose Tile from the View Options to show the playlists.

FIGURE 24-27

Playlists.

632

To use a playlist, right-click its icon or name and choose an option, depending on what you want to do:

- **Open:** Shows the contents of the playlist in the contents pane.
- **Play:** Plays all the songs in the playlist.
- **Add To:** Adds the songs from the playlist to whatever playlist is currently in the List pane.
- **Rename:** Lets you change the name of the playlist.
- **Delete:** Deletes the playlist.
- **Open File Location:** Opens the folder in which the playlist is stored.

Using and creating Auto Playlists

An Auto Playlist is one that gets its content automatically. You can also create your own Auto Playlists based on any criteria you like. To create an Auto Playlist, click the arrow beside the Create Playlist button in the toolbar and choose Create Auto Playlist. The New Auto Playlist dialog box opens as shown in Figure 24-28.

FIGURE 24-28

New Auto Playlist dialog box.

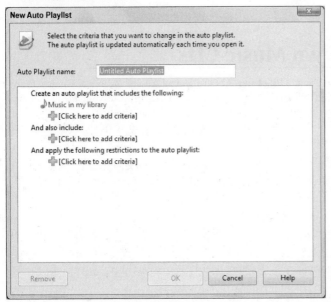

To specify a criterion for the Auto Playlist, click the + sign under Music in My Library and choose an option from the resulting drop-down list. Then specify criteria by clicking options that appear next to the funnel icon. For example, if you wanted to create an Auto Playlist for songs in which Carlos Santana is a contributing artist, choose Contributing Artist from the list, then click the Click to Set link and either choose an artist's name or type the artist's name.

You could create an Auto Playlist, perhaps named "Today's Tunes," by choosing Date Added from the drop-down list, and then choosing a date specification (such as Last 7 Days) from the links that appear beside the new criteria item.

Suppose you have many different types of files in your library and you want to be able to quickly view just the MP3 files. You could create an Auto Playlist named MP3s (or whatever) and use the criteria File Type and MP3.

You can specify multiple criteria if you like. Multiple criteria are always treated as "and" logic, which means each new criterion will narrow, rather than expand, the Auto Playlist's contents. For example, if you specify the criteria Contributing Artist Contains Santana and Date Added to Library Is After Last 30 Days, you'll see all songs added to the library in the last 30 days where the Contributing Artist is Santana.

To include pictures, video, or TV shows in the Auto Playlist, choose an option under the And Also Include heading. Or, to place additional restrictions on the content, choose options under And Apply the Following Restrictions to the Auto Playlist.

When you've finished specifying criteria for your Auto Playlist, click OK. The Auto Playlist will be listed in the Navigation pane along with all others. To play the Auto Playlist, and see its current contents, double-click its name or icon. To change the criteria that define the Auto Playlist's contents, right-click its icon and choose Edit.

Creating Your Own Music CDs

Creating your own custom music CDs is a lot of fun. It's also a great way to protect any new CDs you purchase from getting scratched and ruined. When you buy a new CD, rip it to your Media Library, then put it back in its case for safe-keeping. Burn a copy of the CD (or just your favorite songs from the CD along with some other favorite songs), and use the copy in your home or car stereo. You can also copy songs you purchased online to CDs.

If you buy blank CDs in spindles of 50 or more, they are typically very inexpensive. You won't get the little plastic jewel case, but you can buy paper sleeves or jewel cases separately. Or you can keep all the CDs in a CD binder.

Types of music CDs

Before I get into the specifics of burning CDs, it's important to understand that you can create two different types of music CDs:

- **Audio CD:** This type of CD will play in any home stereo, car stereo, or portable CD player, as well as on computers. You must burn songs to a CD-R disk (preferably an Audio CD-R) to create this type of CD because most non-computer players can't play CD-RW disks or DVD disks.

- **Data CD:** This type of music CD will play in computers, or in any stereo that's capable of playing this type of CD. You can use CD-R or CD-RW disks. However, you must choose a disk type that is compatible with both your computer's CD/DVD burner and the device on which you want to play the disk.

Tip

CDs and DVDs are examples of *optical media*, so-named because they use a laser rather than magnetism to read and write data. All the different types of disks (CD-R, CD-RW, DVD-R, DVD+R, DVD-RW, DVD+RW, and so forth) make things woefully confusing. Chapter 32 untangles the mysteries of the different types of optical media. ■

If you don't know what type of disks your stereo can play, refer to the instructions that came with that device. Optionally, create an RW (Read/Write) disk and try it out. There's no loss if the disk doesn't play, because you can always erase the disk and use it for something else. Once burned, R (Recordable) disks cannot be erased or changed.

Choosing music disk options

The first step to creating a music CD is to specify which type of disk you want to create, and perhaps some other options. In Media Player, click the Burn tab, then click the Burn Options button to see the menu shown in Figure 24-29. Choose options as summarized in the following list.

- **Audio CD:** Choose this option to create the type of CD that all stereos and players can play. For best results use an 80-minute Audio CD-R disk.

FIGURE 24-29

Burn options.

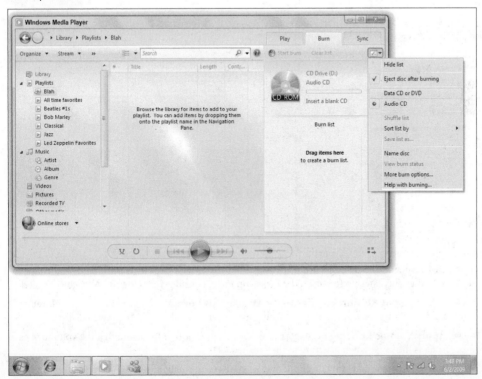

- **Data CD or DVD:** Choose this option if you want to create a music CD or DVD that plays only on computers and devices that are capable of playing non-traditional music CDs.

- **Eject Disc after Burning:** Choose this option to have the CD be ejected automatically when it's ready for use. This is especially useful when burning multiple CDs from a single Burn list.

- **Help with Burning:** Choose this option for help with burning music CDs.

- **Hide list:** Hide the burn list.

- **More Burn Options:** Choose this option to choose additional options described following this list.

- **Name Disc:** Specify a name for the disk.

Choosing More Burn Options takes you to the Burn tab of Media Player's Options dialog box, shown in Figure 24-30. Most of the options duplicate options on the menu. The ones that are unique are summarized in the following list.

Burn tab of the Options dialog box.

- **Burn Speed:** The default setting is Fastest. But if you have problems burning disks, or the sound quality isn't up to par on the disks you burn, consider reducing this to a slower speed.

- **Add a List of All Burned Files to the Disc in this Format:** Choose WPL if your player can read Windows playlists. Choose M3U if your player can only read MP3-style playlists.

- **Apply Volume Leveling across Tracks:** Choose this option to ensure that the volume of each song is the same when listening to the finished CD.

- **Burn CD without Gaps:** Omit the two-second gap normally inserted between audio tracks.

- **Use Media Information to Arrange Files in Folders on the Disc:** If selected, items on the CD will be organized into folders. If you are unsure about whether or not your player can handle folders, clear the check box for this option.

Click OK in the Options dialog box to save any settings you changed. With your options selected and squared away, you're ready to choose which songs you want to copy to your custom CD.

Choosing songs to put on the CD

The skills needed to choose songs to put on a CD are the same as those for creating a custom playlist. You can drag songs individually, or you can drag an entire album or other category. But you have to make sure you're dragging to the Burn list, not just any playlist. Here's the basic process:

- Click the Burn tab to make sure you're viewing the Burn list.

- If your Burn list contains songs from a previously burned CD, and you want to create a new one, click Clear List at the top of the Burn list. Click the Burn Options button and choose Audio CD if you're burning a music CD for stereos. Otherwise you can choose Data CD or DVD if you're creating a music disk for computers and appropriate players.

- Use a felt-tip pen or disk labeler to write the name of your custom CD on a blank CD. Then put that CD in your CD drive.

At this point, your Media Player window should look something like Figure 24-31. The songs that appear in the center contents pane will, of course, be songs you have in your own library. How your icons look depends on what category you're viewing and what option you've selected from the View Options button.

FIGURE 24-31

Ready to copy songs to a Burn list.

At this point, just drag the songs you want to burn to your custom CD to the Burn list, or right-click any song title and choose Add to Burn List. As you add songs, the indicator at the top of the Burn list keeps you informed of how much space will be used on the CD. You can keep adding songs until the disk capacity is exhausted. Any additional songs you add at that point are added to a new disk. Media Player numbers the disk sequentially in the list.

Tip

Clicking the Length column heading sorts songs from longest-to-shortest or vice versa. When you have little time left on a CD, that order can make it easy to find a song that will fit. ■

Options that apply to custom playlists also apply to the Burn list. For example, to remove a song from the Burn list, right-click its title and choose Remove from List. To change the order of songs, click the Burn Options button, choose Sort List By, and choose a sort option. Or, drag any song title up or down within the list.

When you're happy with the songs you've selected and their order, you're ready to burn the CD.

Creating the disk

When the Burn list contains all the songs you want to copy to the CD, click the Start Burn button at the top of the Burn list. Then wait. How long it takes depends on the type of CD you're creating, the speed of your drive, and other factors. The status column in the contents pane and an indicator below the Burn list will keep you apprised of progress.

When the CD is finished, remove it from the CD drive. If you created a standard Audio Disk, you can insert and play it in a stereo as you would any other disk. If you created a Data Disk, you can play it in any device that supports the type of disk you created.

Saving a Burn list

It's a good idea to save each Burn list you create. That way, if you ever want to create another copy of the same CD, you can just open the saved Burn list. To save a Burn list, click the Burn Options button and choose Save List As. Change the name to something that describes the Burn list and click Save. Then to create a new Burn list, click the Clear List Pane button.

Copying Music to Portable Devices

A portable device is an MP3 player or similar device that lets you take your music with you. To put songs (or other media) on your portable device, you *sync* songs from Media Player's library to the device. You can put any songs you wish onto your player. The only limit is the storage capacity of the device.

Windows Media Player works with many MP3 players. However, it does not work with the Apple iPod (you use iTunes to sync to the iPod). Nor does it work with some older devices.

Tip

See "Converting File Types" later in this chapter for tips on using iTunes files with Windows Media Player. ■

If you don't already have a portable device, but are thinking of getting one, visit the www.microsoft.com/mediaplayer and click the Cool Devices link. There you can see the full range of devices that work with Media Player.

Different devices work a little differently. So if you already have a device, the first step is to learn the basics of using it and connecting it to your computer. That information you can get only from the instructions that came with the device. Despite the differences among devices, I can tell you generally how synchronization works with Media Player.

The first step is to open Windows Media Player and click the Sync tab. Then connect your device to the computer and turn it on. If a dialog box opens asking you to name the device, type in a name of your own choosing and click Finish. What happens next depends on the storage capacity of the device:

- If the device capacity is 4 GB or greater, and your media library can fit within that capacity, Media Player automatically copies your entire library to the device. Each time you connect the device in the future, Media Player will copy any new songs you've acquired since the last connection, so that the device stays in sync with your library.

- If the device capacity is less than 4 GB, or your library is too large to fit in the device, nothing is copied automatically. But you can manually copy any songs you like to the device.

You can change what happens when you connect your device. We'll get to that in a moment. First, let's look at how you manually choose songs to put on your device.

Manual syncing

When your device is connected to your computer and you want to choose songs to copy to the device, click the Sync tab. The List pane at the right side of the program window shows the storage capacity of the device, and the amount of space that's currently on the device. Beneath that is an empty playlist, called the Sync list.

To add songs to the device, you need to drag them from the contents pane to the Sync list, just as you would when burning a CD or creating a custom playlist. As always you can select multiple songs and drag them all at once. You can also right-click any song, album, icon, or category name and choose Add To "Sync List."

As you add songs, an indicator near the top of the Sync list shows you how much space you have remaining. If the indicator turns red and shows "Filled," you've gone over the limit. To remove a song from the Sync list, right-click its title and choose Remove from List. Do so until the indicator turns green again. Figure 24-32 shows an example where I've chosen many songs already, and have about 4.2 GB of space left on my portable player.

As always, you can arrange songs in the Sync list by dragging them up or down. Optionally, click Sync List, choose Sort, and choose a sort order. When you're happy with the songs you've selected and their order, click the Start Sync button at the bottom of the Sync list.

The contents pane of Media Player will show the synchronization progress as songs are copied to the device. When the Status column shows "Synchronized to Device" for every song, you're done. You can disconnect the device from the computer, plug in your headphones, and take your music with you.

FIGURE 24-32

Songs added to the Sync list.

Managing songs on a device

Portable media players are much more flexible than CDs. For example, you can delete individual songs from a portable device, and replace them with other songs. When your device is connected, it shows up as it own set of categories in the Navigation pane. When you click a category name under the device name, the contents pane to the right shows the contents of the device only, not the contents of your entire library.

Figure 24-33 shows an example. In the Navigation pane at left I've clicked the Music category name under E:, which is an RCA 8GB MP3 player. So the contents pane to the right is showing songs that are currently on the MP3 player. When viewing songs in that manner with your own device, you can right-click any song title and choose Delete to remove it from the device.

Manual syncing is easy (once you've played around with it a bit). Most people like to choose exactly what's on their portable player, so manual syncing is also the most commonly used method. To use auto syncing, you need to enable automatic syncing, and specify what syncs automatically. Let's look at that next.

Auto-syncing devices

Auto-sync is a method of keeping a portable player up-to-date with whatever content is currently available in your Media Player library. If your device doesn't have enough capacity to store your entire library, exactly what you end up with can be somewhat arbitrary. The first step is to connect the device to the computer, and make sure it's turned on.

FIGURE 24-33

Music on an MP3 player.

Next, click the Sync tab and then click the Sync Options button, point to your device name, and choose Set Up Sync. If you have not set up the device previously, you'll see the Device Setup dialog box, which asks if you want to sync temporarily (this session only) or permanently. If you choose the latter, you'll have additional options available for syncing, including the capability to specify which playlists are synced.

The Device Setup dialog box opens. The left column shows available playlists. The right column shows playlists that are currently used to sync songs to the device. To remove a playlist from the right column, click its name and choose Remove.

To add a playlist to the right column, click its name in the left column and click Add. To see Auto Playlists specifically designed for syncing, click the My Playlists button under Available Playlists and choose Sync Playlists.

If no playlist defines the kinds of songs you want to sync automatically, you can create your own. Click New Auto Playlist and give your playlist a name. For example, to make an Auto Playlist that copies new songs added to your library in the last week, create a criterion that specifies Date Added To Library Is After Last 7 Days.

Give the new playlist a name, perhaps New This Week, and save it. Then click the Add button to copy it from Available Playlists to Playlists to Sync. If that's the only playlist you put in the right column, then each time you connect your device, Media Player will copy only songs that you've added to your library within the last week.

Optionally, choose Shuffle What Syncs. If you do, each time you connect the device, files that are currently on the device will be removed automatically and replaced with songs that match the criteria of your selected Auto Playlists. So each time you connect the device, you automatically get however many songs your playlist provides added to the device.

Click Finish when you're done, and Media Player will sync based on your selections. Remove the device when the syncing is finished. Any time you want to change the contents of your player, just connect it to the PC and click the Finish button.

Choose between manual and auto sync

You can choose whether you want to use manual sync or auto sync at any time. Just connect your device, click the arrow under Sync, click the device name, and choose Set Up Sync. To use manual syncing, clear the checkmark next to Sync this Device Automatically. To enable auto syncing, select (check) that same check box. Then click Finish.

Setting player options

To see other options that your player supports, connect the player, right-click its name in the Navigation pane, and choose Advanced Options. A Properties dialog box for the device opens. The options available to you will depend on the capabilities of your player. If you're not sure what an option in the dialog box means, check the manual that came with your device or click the Help button in the dialog box for more information.

Note

Most portable players are USB mass storage devices. Once connected, these show up as a disk drive in your Computer folder. You can see the current contents of your device by opening its icon in your Computer folder. You can also erase any songs from the device using the same techniques you use to erase files from folders and drives. ■

Fun with Skins

Whenever you're using a program, the part that you see on the screen is just one snowflake on the tip of the proverbial iceberg. The real "guts" are in memory, and invisible. That part you see on the screen is called the *user interface*, abbreviated UI, and often referred to as simply the *interface* or *skin*. Some programs, including Windows Media Player, allow you to change the interface without changing the functionality of the program.

Windows Media Player comes with several skins for you to try out. These skins are for Now Playing mode, not for Library mode. To see them if Media Player is in Now Playing mode, press Alt to open the menu, and choose View ➪ Skin Chooser. If Media Player is in Library mode, right-click the area to the right of the breadcrumb, then choose View ➪ Skin Chooser.

Click each skin name in the left pane to get a preview of how Media Player will look if you apply the skin. To download additional free skins, click the More Skins button above the left column. When you find a skin you like, click the Apply Skin button.

Figure 24-34 shows an example where I'm using the Halo skin. Once you're in a skin, you'll need to point to various symbols and buttons on it to figure out what's up. You'll see the name of the control in a tooltip.

FIGURE 24-34

Media Player in the Halo skin.

When you're in the normal Full mode, you can click the Switch to Skin Mode button in the lower-left corner of Media Player's program window to switch to a skin. From the keyboard, press Ctrl+2 to switch to Skin mode. Press Ctrl+1 to switch back to Full mode. To get out of the Skin Chooser in Full mode, click the Back button.

Extending Media Player with Plug-ins

Plug-ins are optional add-on capabilities that you can purchase or, in some cases, download for free. A plug-in might be as simple as a new visualization or skin. Or it could be an audio or DVD driver or enhancer that extends the capabilities of Media Player. Some plug-ins add capabilities to Media Player. It all depends on what you download and install. To see your options, click Tools ➪ Download and choose Plug-Ins.

Some plug-ins are free, some aren't. Once you're at the site for downloading plug-ins, you'll need to review what's available and decide for yourself what's of value to you. If you don't see anything you like on the first page, click the link to get to the wmplugins.com site. Or, just browse to www.wmplugins.com with your Web browser. There you're more likely to find some freebies that you can try without paying for them.

To manage any plug-ins you acquire, click Tools ➪ Plug-ins and choose Options.

Converting File Types

Suppose you've ripped a bunch of CDs to WMA format, and then acquire a portable media device that only plays MP3s. Do you need to rip all those same CDs again? The answer is no. Media Player 12 can automatically convert files as it syncs them to your portable device. For example, it can convert WMA files to MP3 format. It can also convert video files.

To configure file conversion options, click Tools ➪ Options and click the Devices tab. Then, click the Advanced button to open the File Conversion Options dialog box (Figure 24-35).

FIGURE 24-35

File Conversion Options dialog box.

In the File Conversion Options dialog box, you can specify whether video or audio file conversion happens in the background. Syncing in the background can speed up syncing. By default, background conversion is on for video and off for audio.

You can also specify a better quality for video by choosing the Choose Quality Over Speed when Converting Video option. If you need more space for temporary files created during conversion, click the Change button and choose a different location. You can also specify the amount of disk space to allocate for the temporary files, and delete any temporary files currently in the temporary location.

For other types of conversion options, consider searching any download site for the type of conversion you need to perform. For example, you might go to `www.tucows.com` or `www.download.com`. Or, you could use a more generic search engine like Google. Type in the words that best define the type of conversion you need to perform, such as `Convert WMA MP4`. I'm also partial to Pocket DVD Studio, at `www.pqdvd.com`. It has versions to convert DVD for various devices including Zune, Pocket PC, iPod, and others.

Music, Metadata, and Searches

Tip

Whether or not you are in Windows Media Player, you can search for and group things based on metadata in any file. ■

Earlier in this chapter you discovered how you can store media information such as artist, album title, genre, and so forth with songs. That media information is a form of *metadata*. Metadata, in turn, is information *about* a file, and it doesn't apply only to music. Pictures, videos, Microsoft Office documents, and many other file types support metadata.

You don't have to be in Windows Media Player to take advantage of metadata. The Search features in Windows 7 allow you to search and group things based on metadata in any file. For example, if you click the Start button and type an artist's name into the Search box, songs by that artist show up in the Start menu.

Of course, there isn't a whole lot of room on the Start menu. So you could instead click Start, choose Search, and type jazz in the Search box, and you'll get all the files that have the word Jazz in their metadata or content. You could narrow that down to only files whose Genre property contains the word jazz by searching for genre:jazz.

You're also not limited to searching for one thing. You can specify multiple criteria separated by the words AND or OR (uppercase letters). For example, here's a search that finds all tracks in which the composer is either Beethoven or Mozart: composer:beethoven OR composer:mozart.

Tip

You might think that it should be composer:Beethoven AND composer:Mozart. But it doesn't work that way. A song can't have both Beethoven *and* Mozart as the composer. You're looking for tracks that have either Beethoven *or* Mozart as the composer. ■

If you want to locate all MP3 songs that have Clapton as an artist and a year greater than 2003, the following search would do the trick: type:mp3 AND artist:clapton AND year:>2003.

For experienced users, this is a far cry from the old days of searching for filenames. But it's not the kind of thing you master in a minute. Searches are only successful when you know how to construct them correctly. See Chapters 30 and 31 for the full story.

Wrap-Up

This chapter looked at the Windows Media Player main music capabilities, but all of its capabilities haven't been covered yet. In the next chapter you learn about using Media Player with DVDs and videos. If you have an edition of Windows 7 that includes Media Center, you can also use Media Center to play songs from your media library. See Chapter 26 for the goods on Media Center. The main points from this chapter include the following:

- Controlling sound volume on your computer is a necessary first step to playing music.
- The features taskbar along the top of Media Player's program window provides easy access to all of its main components.
- The Now Playing mode can show a visualization of music that's playing or the visual content of the playing video or DVD.
- The Navigation pane gives you access to all songs and other media you've downloaded or copied from CDs.
- You can rip (copy) songs from music CDs to your media library.
- You can burn your own custom music CDs.
- You can sync (copy) music to portable media devices.

DVD, Video, and More

There's more to Windows Media Player than ripping and burning CDs. Media Player can play digital media stored on DVD, Enhanced DVD, VCD, and SVCD disks. It can play video files you acquire online or create yourself in Movie Maker. You can even use it to manage photos and copy them to portable devices.

If you have Media Center with your version of Windows 7, you can use Media Center or Media Player to manage and watch recorded TV.

Watching DVD, VCD, and Such

If your computer has a DVD drive, you can use it to watch DVD movies — including movies you buy or rent at a movie store, as well as DVDs you create yourself using Windows DVD Maker. You can use the techniques described here to watch VCD and SVCD disks. You don't need a DVD drive for those kinds of disks; a CD drive will do.

Media Player 12 and Codecs

A *codec* is a compressor/decompressor that supports a specific type of video. Like previous versions, Media Player 12 will attempt to detect when a different codec is needed and try to provide a download location for the right codec. However, Media Player 12 adds support for H.264 video, AAC audio, Xvid video, and DivX video. With the addition of these codecs, Media Player 12 should be able to support the vast majority of video right out of the box.

Setting defaults for DVDs

You can choose a default program for playing DVDs. The default program is the one that opens automatically and plays a DVD when you put a DVD disk in your DVD drive. Here's how to set your default player:

1. Click the Start button and choose Control Panel.

2. Click Hardware and Sound.

3. Click AutoPlay.

4. Next to DVD Movie (Figure 25-1), choose Play DVD Movie Using Windows Media Player.

5. Click the Save button.

6. Close Control Panel.

FIGURE 25-1

Autoplay defaults for DVD movies.

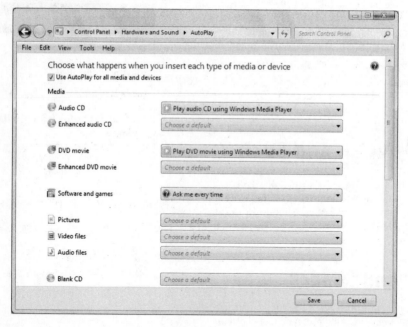

From that point on, whenever you put a DVD in your DVD drive, Windows Media Player should open and play the DVD automatically.

Playing a DVD or VCD

To play a DVD (or VCD), put the disk into the drive and wait a few seconds. Assuming that you chose Windows Media Player as the default player, the movie should start playing within a few seconds. If it plays full screen, and you want to view it in a window, right-click the screen and choose Exit Full Screen to get to the Windows Media Player program window. Or, click the Exit Full-Screen Mode button in the bottom-right corner of the display. If Media Player is in Library mode and you want to start playing a DVD, simply double-click the DVD in the Navigation pane.

When the movie is playing in Windows Media Player and the mouse is moving over the window, you'll see the controls shown in Figure 25-2. The controls disappear when you move the mouse out of the Media Player window or leave the mouse motionless for a little while. Likewise, in full-screen mode, the controls disappear after the mouse has been motionless for a little while.

FIGURE 25-2

Watching a DVD in Media Player.

The controls in the window are similar to controls on a DVD player, with a few extras. Here's how they work:

- **Stop:** Stops playback and rewinds to the beginning of the movie.
- **Previous/Rewind:** Click to go to the previous scene. Hold down the left mouse button to rewind.
- **Play/Pause:** Click to pause or resume playback.
- **Next/Fast Forward:** Click to skip to the next scene. Hold down the left mouse button to fast forward.
- **Mute:** Turn sound off. Click again to turn the sound back on.
- **Volume:** Adjust the sound volume.
- **View Full Screen:** Switch to full-screen mode. In full screen, right-click for playback controls or to exit full screen back to the Media Player program menu.

- **DVD Menu:** Click to access the DVD's menu options, as summarized here:

  - **Root Menu:** Takes you to the opening menu for the DVD. Typically offers options like Play Movie, Scene Selection, Language, and so forth. Click any item on the main menu to select it.

  - **Title Menu:** Takes you to a menu of titles, if available, on the current DVD. If the Root Menu option does nothing, try this one instead.

  - **Close Menu (Resume):** If you clicked Root Menu during playback, you can then click this button to resume playback where you left off.

  - **Back:** If the movie you're watching contains Internet links and you're navigating through Internet pages, it works like the Back button in a Web browser, taking you back to the previous page.

  - **Special Features:** Access the following options:

    - **Audio:** Choose the spoken language of the movie.

    - **Captions:** Show or hide closed captions.

    - **Camera Angles:** Lets you choose a camera angle on DVDs that offer multiple camera angles.

  - **Get DVD Information:** If the DVD you're viewing has media information on the Internet, choosing this option will download media information.

  - **Set Video Size:** Set the video playback size (see the following section).

  - **Full Screen:** Switch to full-screen mode.

Choosing the screen size

As your movie is playing or paused, right-click the movie. Or right-click an empty area to the left of the play controls and choose Video. Then choose options as summarized:

- **Fit Video to Player on Resize:** If selected, this option prevents Media Player from cropping the movie when the size of the video is larger than the program window. When you resize the program window to smaller than the dimensions of the video, the movie is resized as well.

- **Fit Player to Video:** If selected, Windows Media Player automatically resizes its own program window to avoid cropping out a portion of the movie when you first start playing a DVD movie or video.

The recommended setting for the preceding options is to leave both on (checked). Options lower on the menu size the visible video image as a percentage of the movie's actual dimensions:

- **50%:** Plays the movie at half its actual size (same as pressing Alt+1).

- **100%:** Plays the movie at actual size (same as pressing Alt+2).

- **200%:** Doubles the size of the movie (same as pressing Alt+3). You'd more likely use this option for small video clips than a DVD movie.

To quickly switch between full-screen mode and the player window, press Alt+Enter. In full-screen mode, you can right-click the screen for additional options.

Preventing screen savers during playback

If Windows is configured to play a screen saver after a period of inactivity, you probably don't want that kicking in while you're trying to watch a movie. To prevent your screen saver from disrupting your movie, follow these steps:

1. In Media Player Now Playing mode, right-click in the window and choose More Options. In Library mode, right-click beside the breadcrumb and choose Tools ➪ Options.

2. On the Player tab of the Options dialog box, clear the checkmark next to Allow screen Saver During Playback.

3. Click OK.

Setting parental controls and language defaults

You can set parental controls to prevent children from watching DVDs above a specific rating. You can also choose a default language for DVDs that support multiple languages. Here's how:

1. In Media Player, open the Options dialog box (choose Tools ➪ Options from the menu, or in Now Playing mode, right-click and choose More Options).

2. In the Options dialog box that opens, click the DVD tab.

3. Under DVD Playback Restrictions, click the Change button. Then use the button in the Change Rating Restriction box to choose a maximum rating (like G or PG-13) and click OK.

4. Optionally, to choose a default language for DVDs, click Defaults.

5. Choose a language for audio, caption, and DVD menu languages, and click OK.

6. Click OK to save your settings and close the dialog box.

Playing Video Files

A video file is a file on your hard disk that contains video and audio. These include videos you capture from video cameras, digital cameras, recorded TV shows, and videos you download from the Web. Video files come in many formats, and thanks to Media Player 12's support for additional formats, it can now play almost any type of video. The following sections will help you understand how to manage and play videos in Media Player.

Using your Videos Library

Tip

You can store video files in any folder you want. But to stay organized, you may want to put video files that are private to your user account in your Videos folder. Video files that you want to share with all users should go into the Public Videos folder. Both folders offer similar features. So before we get to playing videos, take a moment to look at your Videos folder. ■

To open your Videos folder, first click the Windows Explorer button on the taskbar to open the your Libraries. Then click Videos in the Navigation pane. Figure 25-3 shows an example where I already have some videos and other items in my Videos folder. Only the icons that look like thumbnails are actual videos. When you click one of those, it shows in the Preview pane (if the Preview pane is open).

FIGURE 25-3

Videos folder example.

Tip

To open and close optional panes, click the Organize button and choose Layout. See Chapter 28 for the full story on folders and panes. ∎

If you want to see filename extensions of video files, but they're not currently visible, click the Organize button and choose Folder and Search Options. Then click the View tab, clear the checkmark next to Hide Extensions For Known File Types, and click OK.

Recorded TV

Recorded TV shows are video files stored in the .dvr-ms (Digital Video Recording — Microsoft) format. You use Media Center (Chapter 26) to define times and channels to record, as on a VCR or DVD recorder. You can also decide where you want to store recorded TV shows in Media Center. And of course you can watch recorded TV shows in Media Center.

You can also watch recorded TV shows in Windows Media Player. To view your recorded TV shows in Media Player, click the Recorded TV branch in the Navigation pane.

If some of your recorded TV shows don't show up, Media Player may not be monitoring their folders. In Media Player toolbar, click Organize ➪ Manage Libraries ➪ Recorded TV. In the resulting Recorded TV Library Locations dialog box, click the Add button to add folders that contain recorded TV to the list of monitored folders.

Making Media Player the default video player

To watch a video file in Media Player, just open its icon (by clicking or double-clicking, depending on your click settings). If the video is stored in a format supported by Media Player, it should open in Media Player. If it opens in some other program, close that program. Then follow these steps to watch it in Media Player:

1. Right-click the video icon and choose Open With ➪ Choose Default Program.
2. Click Windows Media Player (or whatever program you want to set as the default).
3. To ensure that files of that type open in Media Player by default, choose Always Use The Selected Program To Open This Kind Of File.
4. Click OK.

Adding videos to your media library

You can store information about your video files in Media Player's library. Depending on how Media Player is configured, video files from your My Videos folder, and perhaps Public Videos folders, should already appear in Media Player. To find out, click Videos in the Navigation pane.

To add video files to your media library, monitor the folders in which they're stored. Here's how:

1. If you're not already in Windows Media Player, open that program.
2. Click Organize ➪ Manage Libraries ➪ Videos. My Videos and Public Videos appear in the Videos Library Locations dialog box by default.
3. Click the Add button and navigate to the drive and folder that contains other videos you want to include. Then click OK. Repeat this step for each folder you want to add.
4. Click OK in each open dialog box to save all of your changes.

Media files from the folders you specified are added to your library. As when working with music, you can use the View Options button to display icons in Tile, Icon, or Details view. You can also add your own media information to better organize your videos by genre, director, actor, or whatever. To add a genre to a video, choose the Details view, then click in the Genre column and type a tag, like SciFi, Sports, Nature, and so on.

By default, the Navigation pane doesn't show Genre as an option under the Videos branch. To add it, click Organize ➪ Customize Navigation Pane to open the Customize Navigation Pane dialog box. Under the Videos branch, place a check beside Genre and any other items you want to show, and click OK.

Figure 25-4 shows an example where I've already categorized video files by Genre. I clicked the Genre icon in the Navigation pane at the left to see video files stacked by categories.

Playing videos from your library

Playing videos in Media Player is no different from playing songs. In the library, just double-click the video's title or icon. Or right-click an icon, stack, or category name and choose Play.

FIGURE 25-4

Video files organized by Genre.

Managing Photos with Media Player

In Chapter 23 you discovered ways to acquire and manage photos with Windows Live Photo Gallery. There's no need to bring that information into Media Player, but you can if you want to. For example, if you have a portable media device that displays pictures, you might want to bring the photos into Media Player so you can sync music and video files.

To view photos in Media Player, the photos need to be in a folder that's monitored by Media Player. Or, you'll need to add that folder to your list of monitored folders. By default, the Pictures library appears in Media Player's Navigation pane, but without any options such as Tags or Date Taken. You can add those options by right-clicking the Navigation pane and choosing Customize Navigation Pane. Scroll down to find Pictures in the list and select the desired options.

To view photos in Media Player, click Pictures in the Navigation pane. Figure 25-5 shows an example where I'm viewing photos by Date Taken. Each stack represents a group of photos.

More on Playlists

In Media Player, you can include videos and photos in any music playlists you create. This is mostly useful for creating Auto Playlists for syncing to devices that support music, photos, and video. (When you play the playlist in Media Player, they play in sequence, not simultaneously. So you'll still see only a visualization or album art when music is playing.)

FIGURE 25-5

Viewing photos by Date Taken in Media Player.

Tip

If you want to create a movie that contains video, photos, and music, use Windows Live Movie Maker. If you want to copy Media Player content to a DVD as a data disk, use the Burn tab in Media Player. See Chapter 32 for details on burning files to DVD. ■

To create an Auto Playlist that includes music, photos, and/or videos, click the arrow beside the Create Playlist button in the toolbar and choose Create Auto Playlist. Or, right-click the name of an existing Auto Playlist and choose Edit. Name the playlist however you like. Under Music in My Library, add your criteria for music. Then, under And Also Include, set criteria for Pictures, TV, and Video as you see fit. Figure 25-6 shows an Auto Playlist named Todays Music Pix TV Vids that automatically displays all four types of files for media items added today.

You can use that Auto Playlist to keep your portable media player up-to-date with media content on your computer on a daily basis. To update manually, connect your device and click the Sync tab. Drag the playlist name from the Navigation pane into the List pane. Then click the Start Sync button.

To use the daily Auto Playlist for automatic syncing, first connect your device. Then right-click the device in the Navigation pane and choose Set Up Sync. Choose "Sync this device automatically." Then add the Auto Playlist to the Playlists to Sync column. Remove any other playlists that are in that Playlists to Sync column.

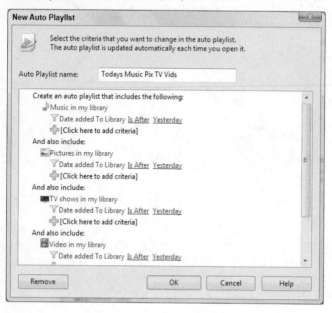

FIGURE 25-6

Auto Playlist for Music, Pictures, TV, and Video.

Tip

If you want to copy music (only) daily to your portable player, edit the playlist and remove the And Also Include criteria for photos, recorded TV, and video. Just click whichever criterion you want to remove, and then click the Remove button. ■

Limiting playlist size

If you discover that your Auto Playlists are too large, containing more content than you can fit on your portable player, you can limit the amount of content the playlist contains. Open the playlist for editing, and at the bottom of the Auto Playlist, click the + sign under And Apply The Following Restrictions To The Auto Playlist. You'll see the options shown in Figure 25-7. Your options are as follows:

- **Limit Number Of Items:** Choose this option to limit the number of items the playlist may contain. For example, if you choose 10, the Auto Playlist will list only the first 10 items that meet the criterion.

- **Limit Total Duration To:** Choose this option to set a maximum time limit to match the time duration of the disk to which you'll be copying items. For example, if you'll be copying playlist items to an Audio CD, the time limit is 80 minutes.

- **Limit Total Size To:** When syncing to portable devices, choose this option to limit the playlist items to the storage capacity of your device in megabytes (MB) or gigabytes (GB).

Click OK when you've finished setting criteria. To see which items the Auto Playlist includes, click its name under Playlists in the Navigation pane. Or click Playlists in the Navigation pane, and then double-click the playlist name in the Details pane. To use your new playlist for auto syncing, connect your portable device to the computer. Then right-click the device in the Navigation pane and click Set Up Sync. Choose the Sync This Device Automatically checkbox and remove any items listed in the Playlists To Sync column. Then add your new playlist to that same column.

FIGURE 25-7

Options for restricting an Auto Playlist.

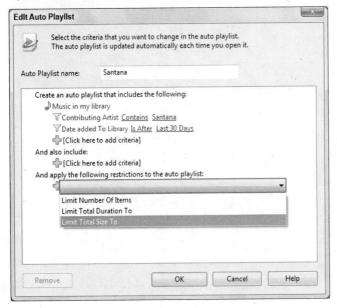

Limiting playlists to favorite items

When you manually create playlists by dragging items to the List pane, criteria you set in an Auto Playlist have no effect. But you can limit manual playlists to favorite items, providing you rate your items before dragging them over.

First, before you drag an album or category to the List pane, open the album or group and rate the songs. To rate a song, right-click its title in the contents pane and choose Rate. Or select several songs to which you want to apply the same rating, right-click any one selected song, and choose Rate. Give a four- or five-star rating to any songs you do want copied to playlists. Give a three-star or lower rating to songs you don't want copied.

To copy only favorites from the category to the playlist, right-click the album's icon or category name and choose "<playlist name> (Favorites Only)." Only the 4- and 5-star rated items appear in the List pane.

Skipping playlist items

When you're playing items in a playlist, you can skip over any item by clicking the Next button in the play controls. Media Player can remember which items you skipped, then skip them automatically the next time you play the list. It can also automatically omit skipped items when you save the playlist.

657

To choose how Media Player treats skipped items, click the List Options button above the list (shows an icon with a check mark on it) and choose Skipped Items, as in Figure 25-8. A checked option is active; an unchecked option is inactive. You can click the option to activate or deactivate it. The following section describes how those options work.

FIGURE 25-8

Options for skipping items.

Prompt Me To Remove Upon Save

Choosing (activating) the Prompt Me To Remove Upon Save option causes the message shown in Figure 25-9 to appear whenever you save a playlist that contains skipped items. You can choose whether you want to leave the skipped items in the saved playlist or omit them. If you choose to keep the items in the playlist, you can choose Skip During Playback to have the songs skipped over the next time you play the playlist.

If you choose the Don't Show This Message Again option, Media Player automatically saves the playlist, and skipped songs will be skipped on playback. Clear this option if you want to be prompted about these skipped items again.

FIGURE 25-9

Skipping options.

Wrap-Up

Windows Media Player 12 is the latest and greatest version of that program and comes free with Windows 7. Here's a quick summary of key points made in this chapter about using Media Player to watch DVD, videos, and photos:

- To watch a DVD movie in Media Player, insert the DVD disk into your drive and wait for Media Player to play.

- To download a non-streaming video from the Internet, right-click the link to the video file and choose Save Target As.

- To open your Videos folder, click the Start button, click your username, and open the Videos icon. (In the breadcrumb menu, click your username and choose Videos.)

- To view video files you've imported to Media Player, click Videos in the Navigation pane.

- For help, troubleshooting, and more information, click the Help button in the toolbar.

Fun with Media Center

W indows Media Center is an optional program that comes with the
Home Premium, Professional, and Ultimate Editions of Windows 7.
It brings all your media (pictures, music, video) together in one
easy-to-use center. If you connect your computer to a TV, you can use Media
Center to enjoy them on a TV screen. If the graphics card that lets you connect
to a TV screen came with a Windows Media Center remote control, you can
control Media Center with that. No need to use a mouse and keyboard.

A second advantage of Media Center is that it allows you to watch and record
live TV, but this requires special hardware in the form of a TV Tuner card or
PVR (Personal Video Recorder) card.

This chapter first looks at those aspects of Media Center that work with any
computer. That way, if you have Media Center, you can try out the things that
will work for you. Things that require special equipment are discussed later in
the chapter.

Starting Media Center

If you have an edition of Windows 7 that includes Media Center, use any of the
following methods to start it:

- Click the Start button and choose All Programs ➪ Windows Media
  Center.
- Press ▓ , type **med**, and click Windows Media Center.
- If you happen to have a Media Center remote control, click the button
  that shows the Windows Media Center logo.

If this is the first time you've used the program, it will take you through some
questions and show you some examples of its use. If you're not a technical
person, the trickiest part will be answering questions about your main monitor.
If you don't know the answer to a question and guess wrong, your screen will go
completely black. But don't panic, it will come back to life in 15 or 20 seconds.
Try again (but not with the same incorrect answer).

Tip

If you missed the initial setup options or need to make a change, choose Tasks on the home page and then click Settings ➪ General ➪ Windows Media Center Setup. ■

After you've completed all the steps, you'll be taken to Media Center's "home page." (I put that in quotation marks because it's not an Internet home page like on the Web. You don't have to be online to start and use Media Center on your PC.) Figure 26-1 shows what that home page looks like. Items in the corners only appear when you're using a mouse to control Media Center and only after you move the mouse. Note also that a few options might not show up in Media Center until you configure Media Center.

FIGURE 26-1

Windows Media Center home page.

The interface on Media Center is much different from the desktop. That's because it's designed to work on a TV screen and through a remote control. Even so, you don't have to hook up to a TV to use Media Center. You can use it on your computer with your mouse and keyboard.

Working Media Center with a mouse

Working Media Center with a mouse is relatively easy, although not intuitively obvious. Point above or below the names down the center of the screen or to the left or right of a horizontal row of names to see a white arrow. Then point to that to scroll through items. If your mouse has a wheel, you can use that to scroll up and down. Click any item to select it. Click the Back button in the upper-left corner to back out of a selected area. Click the round Media Center logo near the Back button to get to Media Center's home page.

As on your desktop, you can often find extra options by right-clicking the page. Often you'll find an option to change settings that apply to a page or to burn a CD/DVD from the content you're viewing.

Working Media Center with a keyboard

On a keyboard use the ↑, ↓, ←, and → keys to move around. If you use keys on the numeric keypad, make sure that the Num Lock key is turned off. When the item you want is highlighted, press Enter to select it. Press the Backspace key to back out of a selected area. Press Escape (Esc) to return to the home page.

Using a Media Center remote control

If you're using a Media Center remote control, use the arrow keys around the OK button to get around. Press the OK button to select the currently highlighted option. Use the Back button to back out of any area. Press the button that shows the Media Center logo to return to Media Center's home page.

The More button on a remote works like right-clicking. Often you'll find options to change settings, burn a CD or DVD from the current item, and more.

Plenty of other buttons on your remote control can be used for getting around in Media Center. Because there are different brands of remotes, I can't say exactly what's in yours. But you can usually tell what a button does just by looking at its label. Or, check the manual that came with your remote control for more information.

Moving and Sizing Media Center

Media Center usually opens full screen. But you don't need to leave it that way on a computer monitor. When you move the mouse, you'll see the standard Minimize, Restore, and Close buttons in the upper-right corner. Click the Restore button to shrink it down. Then drag any corner or edge to make it exactly the size you want. Figure 26-2 shows an example in which I have it down near the lower-right corner of the screen.

If you have multiple monitors, you can also drag the Media Center window, by its title bar, over to another monitor. After it's on the other monitor, you can maximize it there to fill that screen.

The next few sections talk about things you can do in Media Center on regular computers with regular monitors. The optional TV features are discussed later.

Media Center Playback Controls

Media Center can play picture slide shows, videos, music, movies, and TV shows. When you get something playing, you have two ways to control playback. If you're using a mouse, move the mouse a little to reveal the playback controls shown in Figure 26-3. Depending on what you're playing, some controls may be disabled (dimmed).

If you're using a remote control, those buttons won't appear on the screen. Use the corresponding buttons on the remote to control playback.

Things You Can Do without TV

You can do many things in Media Center that don't require a TV Tuner card or TV. You can do these things with Media Center showing full screen or in a smaller window on the desktop.

FIGURE 26-2

Media Center in the lower-right corner of the desktop.

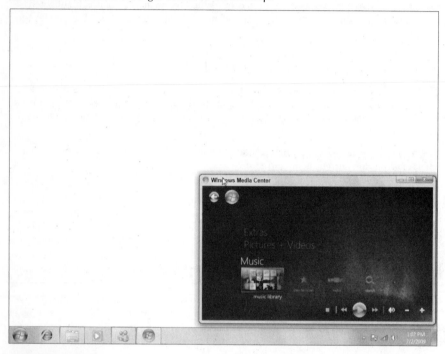

FIGURE 26-3

Playback controls for a mouse.

Playing music in Media Center

The Music portion of Media Center gets albums and songs from Windows Media Player. You can also listen to online radio stations from Media Center. Choose Music from the home page. Options that appear across the horizontal row are summarized here:

- **Music Library:** Lets you choose songs from Windows Media Player categories and playlists to play. You can create a queue of songs to play and more.

Note

If there is no music in your media library yet, you'll be prompted to add some. You can choose Yes if you have put songs in your media library. If you don't have a media library, you can learn to create one in Chapter 24. ■

- **Play Favorites:** Plays songs in your Media Player media library based on their ratings.
- **Radio:** Lets you locate and play music from radio stations if your PC includes an FM radio tuner.
- **Search:** Helps you find songs in your media library.

While music is playing, you'll see buttons as shown previously in Figure 26-3. Use them to view or change the queue (playlist), watch a music visualization, play a photo slide show with the music, and so forth. Use the playback controls to control volume, pause, stop, skip songs, and so forth. If you navigate away from the page shown in the figure, go to Media Center's home page and choose Now Playing to return.

Viewing pictures and videos in Media Center

You can use Media Center to view and play pictures and videos in your Windows Live Photo Gallery and Pictures folder. Click Pictures + Videos on the home page (see Figure 26-4) to see pictures and videos from your Windows Media Player library. Click Picture Library to view your still pictures, or Video Library to view your video library. Use Play Favorites to play picture slide shows and videos.

Movies and TV in Media Center

The Movies category on the home page lets you view movies on your PC. You can also use it to rent movies online and watch movies you've purchased. The TV category on the home page lets you view live TV (if your PC has a TV tuner) and also view recorded TV programs. Use the Guide item under each of the categories to browse online TV programs and movies. As always, your best bet is to simply explore your options.

Tip

When the movie is playing, use the playback controls as you would on a VCR to pause, resume, fast forward, rewind, and so forth. ■

Extras

The Extras option in the home page gives you access to the Extras Library, which contains games and other applications trusted by Media Center that you can access within Media Center. You can also access MSNBC news, Internet TV, online radio stations, and other online content.

FIGURE 26-4

Pictures + Videos in Media Center.

Sports

The Sports option lets you browse information about scores and statistics, players, and fantasy sports leagues. When tracking a specific player, you can view sport-specific statistics such as at bats, runs, hits, and so on (using baseball as an example). You need an online connection to the Internet for this feature.

Watching and Recording TV

If your computer has a TV tuner or Personal Video Recorder card, you can use Media Center to watch and record TV. If your computer doesn't already have one, you can purchase and install one or have one professionally installed. Ideally, you want a card that's specifically designed to work with Media Center. One that comes with a Media Center remote control is ideal if you think there's a chance you might want to connect your computer to a TV.

Tip

TV tuner devices for PCs come in two formats: as a card that installs in the computer or as a USB device. The USB format offers portability, enabling you to use the device on more than one computer. Portability isn't the only consideration, however, so choose a TV tuner that suits all your needs. ■

The TV Tuner device you purchase will provide a connection for cable TV or an antenna. You'll need to connect that to get TV reception. You don't need to connect to a TV screen, though. You can watch and record TV from any standard computer monitor.

Note

The TV Tuner device might also include other ports such as S-Video input or FM input. ■

To use the TV features, choose TV on Media Center's home page. You'll see three options: Recorded TV, Guide, and Live TV Setup. Before you start using Media Center for watching TV, you need to run through setup. Click Live TV Setup and follow the prompts to specify input type, scan for channels, and complete other setup and configuration tasks. If you see an item named Live TV rather than Live TV Setup, the configuration wizard has already been run. You can run it again if necessary from the Tasks option on the home page.

The Guide option takes you to your online program guide of upcoming TV shows shown in Figure 26-5.

FIGURE 26-5

Media Center Guide.

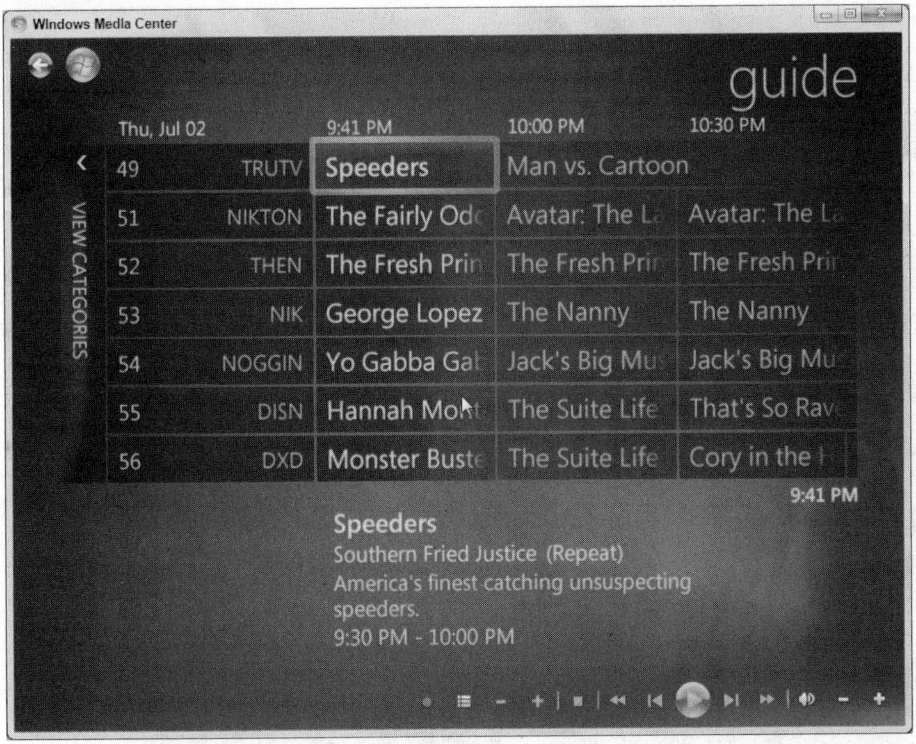

If you're using a remote control, you can scroll through times and channels using the navigation buttons. To watch or record a show that's currently airing, highlight its title and click the OK button. If you're using a mouse, move the mouse pointer onto the guide. You'll see some arrows just below the guide. Click those to scroll through times and channels. To watch or record a show that's currently airing, click its title.

Tip
Click View Categories at the left side of the guide to see shows organized into categories such as Most View, Movies, Sports, Kids, and so forth. ■

When a TV show is playing, you can use the playback controls for just about anything except fast forwarding "into the future." For example, you can pause playback and then resume later. Or you can rewind. But you can't fast forward live TV beyond what's been aired so far.

You don't want to pause live TV for too long, though. Pausing for a few minutes is fine. Pausing for hours won't work because there's a limit to how much live TV your hard drive will store during a pause. The exact limit depends on the storage capacity and free space on the drive. But it's always a matter of minutes, not hours.

Recording TV

You can record TV in two ways. One is to just hit the Record button in the playback controls while you're watching the show. Then Media Center will record from that point to the end of the show.

As an alternative to manual recording, choose shows to record on a regular basis. The easiest method is to open the guide and navigate to the show you want to record. Double-click it (with the mouse) or press the OK button on the remote control. You see options like those in Figure 26-6.

FIGURE 26-6

Options for recording an upcoming show.

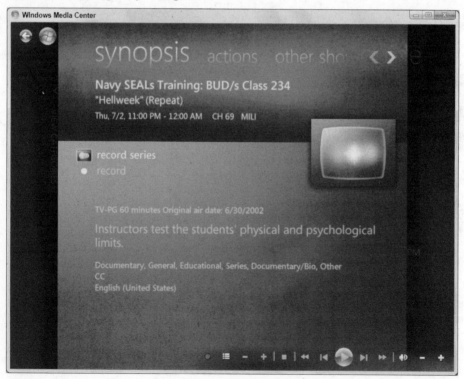

Click the Record button if you want to record only the selected show when it airs. Click Record Series to record all future airings.

To stop a recording in progress, right-click the red Record button in the play control of the Windows Notification area and choose Stop Current Recording. Or press the Stop button on your remote control.

It's important to keep in mind that recorded TV shows take up a lot of disk space. The higher the quality of settings chosen, the more disk space a recorded TV show requires. The numbers range from 5.6 GB per hour for 1080i high-definition down to about 1 GB per hour for fair resolution.

Tip

A very large hard disk can hold quite a bit of recorded TV. For example, a 2 TB hard disk can hold about 360 hours of 1080i high-definition TV. ■

To decide on a quality, you need to think in terms of available disk space and how long you intend to keep each show on the disk. Open your Computer folder to see available disk space on your hard drive. If the available space on a drive doesn't show in a meter, choose the Details view or right-click the drive's icon and choose Properties.

Tip

See Chapter 28 for information on drives, your Computer folder, and storage capacities. ■

You can configure default settings that apply to all recordings. I talk about how that works under "Personalizing Media Center" later in this chapter.

You don't really have to keep a TV show on your hard disk forever. If you have a DVD burner, and the show isn't copy-protected, you can burn the show to a DVD and then delete the original from your hard disk. I talk about CD and DVD burning from Media Center a little later in this chapter.

Watching recorded TV

To watch a recorded TV show, starting from Media Center's home page, choose TV, and then Recorded TV. Scroll through the shows and choose any one by clicking or by pressing OK on the remote control. You'll see options like those in Figure 26-7.

I assume the buttons are self-explanatory. They let you play or delete the show. Set a time limit on how long you'll keep it on your hard drive. You can also choose to record the series or view other times.

Recorded TV files

Each recorded TV show is stored as a file with a WTV filename extension. Unless you choose another location, they'll likely be placed in the Recorded TV subfolder in your Public folder. You can use the Folders list to navigate to that folder as in Figure 26-8.

Tip

Microsoft has replaced the DVR-MS file format used by Media Center in Windows Vista with the WTV format. The WTV format was actually introduced in the TVPack2008 OEM update for Windows Vista Media Center, so WTV files can be played on Windows Vista computers that have that update installed. ■

FIGURE 26-7

Options for a recorded TV show.

As with any file, you can right-click an icon to see different things you can do with it. For example, you can play a TV show in Windows Media Player rather than Media Center. You can also convert the file to DVR.MS format for compatibility with earlier versions of Windows Media Center.

Personalizing Media Center

Like most programs, Media Center has options that you can adjust to your own needs and preferences. To get to those settings, select Tasks on Media Center's home page and click Settings. You see buttons for changing General, TV, Pictures, Music, DVD, Start Menu and Extras, Extender, and Media Libraries as shown in Figure 26-9. I cover each in the sections to follow.

General Settings

Clicking General takes you to still more options for personalizing Media Center. Under Startup and Window Behavior, you'll find the following.

FIGURE 26-8

Icon for recorded TV show in the Recorded TV folder.

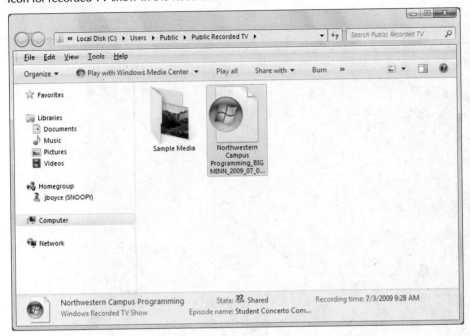

Startup and window behavior

The Startup and Window Behavior button takes you to general options for controlling how Media Center behaves, as follows:

- **Always Keep Windows Media Center On Top:** Choosing this option prevents other program windows on a computer monitor from covering Media Center's program window. It will also prevent you from switching to another program when Media Center is maximized to full-screen size!

- **Show a Warning Before Displaying Web Pages That Are Not Designed for Windows Media Center:** Some of the online services and other Web content you can get to in Media Center can't be operated through a remote control or the normal Media Center interface. Choosing this option ensures that you see a warning when you encounter such content, so you can cancel out if you want. That way, you won't get stuck on some page that you can't operate with a remote control.

- **Start Windows Media Center when Windows Starts:** Choosing this option makes Media Center open onto the desktop automatically each time you start Windows.

- **Show Taskbar Notifications:** Choose this option to ensure that you see Notification area messages telling you when Media Center is up to something, such as recording a scheduled TV show.

FIGURE 26-9

Media Center Settings page.

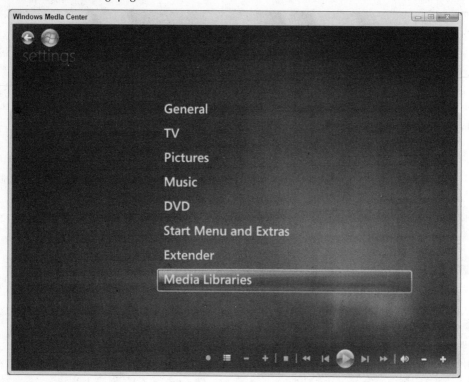

Visual and sound effects

The Visual and Sound Effects options let you enable, or disable, the transition animations between pictures in a slide show. Here you can also enable or disable the audio feedback you hear when navigating in Media Center, choose a color scheme for your Media Center display, and choose a background color for videos that don't fill the entire screen.

Windows Media Center setup

The Media Center Setup options allow you to set up your Internet connection, TV signal (if you have a TV Tuner), speakers, and TV/monitor. If you want to run through the initial setup process again, click Run Setup Again. That will take you through the entire process, step by step.

Parental controls

Media Center setup has parental controls that are separate from those in Windows 7. Think up a four-digit access code that you won't forget. (If you forget the code, you'll lock yourself out of blocked content.) Then click Parental Controls and enter that code as instructed on-screen.

After you've entered the code (twice), you're taken to a page where you can activate TV blocking and DVD blocking, change your access code, or turn off parental controls.

Automatic download options

The Automatic Download options allow you to enable or disable automatic downloading of media information and program guide data. If you disable downloading of media information, you'll see "Unknown" in place of many artist and album names, "Track" instead of song titles, and other generic information. Turn automatic downloading back on to replace the unknown and generic information with actual names and titles.

If you disable automatic program guide downloads, you'll need to update the program guide manually from time to time. To do that, go into the program guide, right-click a channel in the left column, and choose Get Latest Guide. If you're using a remote control, go into the guide, highlight a channel number, press the More button on the remote control, and choose Get Latest Guide.

Optimization

The Optimization option takes you to a page where you can schedule optimization tasks to run on a regular schedule. Be sure to choose a time when the computer will be on but you won't be needing Media Center, because you won't be able to use Media Center for the few minutes it takes to complete those tasks.

Privacy

Choose this option to view Microsoft's privacy policy statement, configure whether Media Center sends any usage data to Microsoft, and turn off the Most Viewed filter in the Guide.

TV settings

The TV option on the Settings page lets you configure TV recording and other aspects of using TV in Media Center. The Recorder option takes you to a page where you can view your recording history and set defaults for TV recording. The Recorder Storage button lets you choose where you want to store recorded TV. It has to be a hard drive, but not necessarily your C: drive.

You can't record TV straight to DVD in Media Center, but after you've recorded a show you can burn it to DVD. Verify that you can play the DVD in your TV's DVD player. Then you can delete the copy of the show that's still on your hard disk.

Use the Record on Drive option to choose where you want to store recorded TV (Figure 26-10). Choose the drive on which you want to store recorded TV shows. The maximum number of hours of recorded video that will fit on the selected drive is shown. The slider shows how much live TV can be buffered (stored) during a live TV pause.

The Media Libraries option allows you to specify folders that contain recorded TV, so Media Center can find them and add them to your library.

The Recording Defaults button takes you to still more options for controlling TV recording. Figure 26-11 shows the first few options. You have nine options in all. To scroll through hidden options, use the Up and Down buttons on a remote control. Or use the arrow buttons on your keyboard, or click the up and down arrows near the lower-right corner with your mouse.

Again, I think the options are self-explanatory. You can choose how long you want to keep recorded TV shows, a quality, a little extra leeway at the start and end of every show, and settings that apply only to recorded TV series. Other buttons on the TV page include the following:

- **Guide:** Use this button to configure the program guide, add missing channels, tell it what region you live in (in case the guide is incorrect), and manually update the guide.

FIGURE 26-10

Recorder Storage settings.

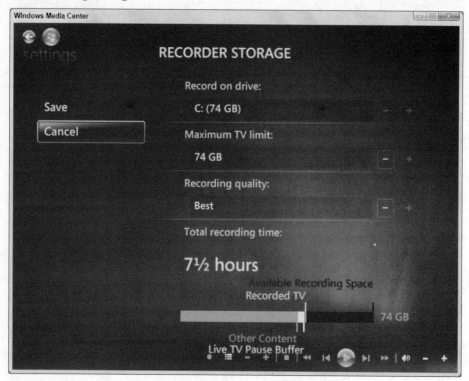

- **Set Up TV Signal:** Clicking this button takes you through a step-by-step wizard for configuring your incoming TV signal.

- **Configure Your TV or Monitor:** This is the same setting as the one under the General options. Use it to get the best picture quality on your TV or monitor.

- **Language:** Choose the preferred audio and caption languages.

- **Audio:** Choose Stereo, SAP, or any other audio option provided by your hardware.

- **Closed Captioning:** Turn closed captioning on or off and choose settings for text size, color, and related captioning properties.

Pictures settings

Clicking Pictures on the Settings tab shows you the options you can set for photos and slide shows. Again, I think they're self-explanatory. You can show pictures in random order (or not), show pictures from subfolders in your Pictures folder (or not), and show captions (the filename and date taken) with each picture (or not). You can also specify which types of photos to include in your slide show based on ratings and other criteria, enable a slide show screensaver, and specify whether you can use shortcut keys to set ratings on photos as you view them.

FIGURE 26-11

Recording defaults.

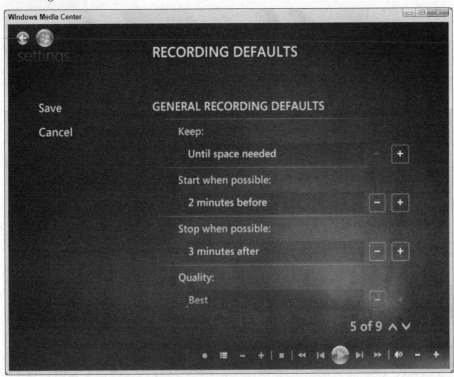

When you launch a slide show from the Music area to play along with the music, the song title usually appears briefly at the start of each song, and then again at the end. You can choose to have the song title shown the whole time that the song is playing, or not at all.

The Use Pan-and-Zoom option causes each picture in the slide show to pan and zoom into view. Clearing the Animated option makes each picture appear more abruptly without any special effects.

Music settings

The Music button provides options for controlling music playback in Media Center. You can specify which songs are included in your favorites, enable shortcut keys for adding ratings, and set options for the Now Playing window that determine when song information is displayed and the window's background. You can also specify which visualizations Media Center will use when playing music.

DVD settings

The DVD option lets you choose a default language for multi-language DVDs. Use the Audio option to set an audio mode for the Dolby decoder. You can also control closed captions for DVDs from the page. Use the Subtitle option to specify when subtitles are displayed. If you use a remote control to work Media Center, you can configure DVD navigation buttons according to your own preferences.

Start Menu and Extras

Use these options to control which items appear on the Media Center home page and in the Extras page. You can also set a handful of options for the Extras Library that control user experience and whether Media Center displays Internet security warnings.

Extender settings

Media Center extenders are devices and programs that extend Media Center's capabilities. For example, Microsoft Xbox 360 acts as an extender to share your Media Center library with other players in the house. You need to purchase an extender first. Then follow the instructions that came with that extender to hook it into Media Center on your PC.

Media libraries

Click Media Libraries to add folders to, or remove folders from, Media Center's watch list. Pictures, music, videos, recorded TV, and movies from all the folders you specify are added to Media Center automatically, so you can play them whenever you want.

The Tasks item on the home page provides more than just the Setting option. You'll find options for burning optical discs (CDs and DVDs), syncing with other devices, shutting down or restarting the computer, and adding extenders.

Burning CDs and DVDs from Media Center

Windows 7 offers many ways to burn CDs and DVDs. For example, Chapter 23 explores creating audio CDs with Windows Media Player. Chapter 32 explores the many other ways you can copy files to CDs and DVDs and create DVD video disks with Windows DVD Maker. The disks you end up with are the same whether you burn them using those techniques or Media Center.

Of course, with Media Center, it's easy to access all your media files (music, pictures, videos, recorded TV, and movies). You can do it all from a TV screen with a remote control, if that's the way you want to do it. Here's how it works, starting from within Media Center:

1. If you haven't already done so, put a recordable CD or DVD into the CD or DVD burner.

2. After a brief delay you should see Burn a CD or DVD. Click that (not the X that appears to the right of it).

Note
If the disc was already in the drive before you started Media Center, click Burn CD/DVD under Tasks in Media Center's home page. ∎

3. Choose which type of disc you want to create. The options available to you depend on the type of disc you inserted:

   - **Audio CD:** Create a music CD for playing in a stereo, CD player, or computer.

   - **Data CD:** Create a CD that contains files for playback on a computer only (and devices that can play audio files).

   - **Data DVD:** Create a DVD that contains files to be played on a computer.

- **Video DVD:** Create a DVD Video disc that contains video to be watched from a standard DVD player or on a computer.

- **DVD Slide Show:** Create a picture slide show on a DVD that can be played in a computer or watched on a TV with a DVD player.

4. Click or choose Next.

5. Follow the on-screen instructions.

Exactly what happens next depends on what you chose in step 3. But it's just a matter of reading and following the instructions that appear on the screen.

Note
You cannot burn protected content to Audio CDs or Video DVDs. However, in some cases you can copy them to data discs. ■

That's one way to burn CDs and DVDs from Media Center. Another is to navigate to the specific item you want to burn and start the process from there. In some cases you'll see a Burn CD or DVD button right on the screen. In other cases you might have to right-click the item to burn or press the More button on a remote control. For example, you can navigate to a recorded TV program where you can right-click a show to see Play, Delete, and other options for a TV show. Click Burn a CD/DVD to start the burn process.

Syncing, shutting down, and extenders

The Sync option in Tasks makes it easy to sync a compatible device with your Media Center content. Exactly how it works depends on the specific device you're using. If you can't get it to work by guessing, check the manual that came with the device for instructions on syncing with Windows 7 Media Center.

The Shut Down option in Tasks offers a way of closing Media Center from a mouse or remote control. You'll also have options to Log Off, Shut Down the computer, Restart the computer, or put the computer into Sleep mode.

Wrap-Up

Windows Media Center is a great tool for enjoying all forms of digital media. To keep up with what's happening, be sure to check out the Media Center Web site. The site is located at http://www.microsoft.com/windows/windows-media-center/default.aspx.

This chapter has covered the basics of Windows 7's Media Center to give you an overview of what it offers. Here's a summary of the basics:

- Windows Media Center comes with the Home Premium, Professional, and Ultimate Editions of Windows 7.

- You can use Media Center to enjoy all forms of digital media including photos, music, radio, video, movies, games, and TV.

- To start Windows Media Center, click the Start button and choose All Programs ⇨ Windows Media Center.

- Media Center gets photos from your Windows Live Photo Gallery and music from your Windows Media Player media library.

- If you have an appropriate graphics card, you can display Media Center on a TV screen and operate it with a remote control.

- If your computer has a TV Tuner or PVR (Personal Video Recorder) card, you can watch and record live TV in Media Center.

- Choosing Tasks ➪ Settings in Media Center takes you to many options for configuring and personalizing Media Center to your liking.

- Choosing Tasks in Media Center takes you to options for burning CDs and DVDs, syncing with compatible devices, adding extender devices, and shutting down your computer.

Troubleshooting Multimedia

Troubleshooting Pictures and Photos

Most problems I see in the "pictures and photos" category stem from people who don't know how to work their digital cameras. So, if you fall into that category, remember that the only place to learn about your specific camera is from the instructions that came with it. Here the focus is on common, everyday problems. At the end of the chapter I point out other resources for troubleshooting multimedia.

No Copy option when right-clicking a picture in a Web page

Not all Web browsers offer a copy option on the shortcut menu. Try browsing to the same page using Internet Explorer. Optionally, you can right-click a picture and choose Save Picture As to store the picture in your Pictures folder, or any other folder of your choosing. If you still can't copy or save a picture, the Web page could be disabling those features intentionally to prevent you from saving the picture. If that's the case, you might not be able to get a copy of the file. Note the URL of the file when you mouse over the image (if any), and try navigating directly to that URL to see if you can right-click and save the file from that URL.

Cannot copy thumbnail from my Pictures folder to open document

Thumbnails represent closed documents and cannot be copied and pasted into an open document. You'll either need to insert the picture into the open document using whatever commands that program supports, or open (double-click) the picture, right-click the open picture and choose Copy, and then paste the picture into an open document.

Troubleshooting Windows Media Player

Multimedia is a combination of computer hardware (your graphics card, CD or DVD drives, and the like) as well as software (Windows Media Player and the specific song or movie with which you're having a problem). It's not always easy to tease out exactly where a problem lies. The following sections cover solutions to some of the more common Windows Media Player maladies.

Error Message: "Invalid Function when trying to burn a CD"

Follow these steps to verify that your CD-R or CD-RW is able and ready to burn CDs:

1. Click the Start button and select Computer.
2. Right-click the icon that represents your CD or DVD drive and choose Properties.
3. Click the Recording tab.
4. Under Disc Burning, verify that you have selected the correct device under Select the Disc-burning Drive that Windows Will Use by Default. Also make sure that the correct drive (one with sufficient free space) is selected under Select a Hard Drive with Enough Free Space to Temporarily Store Files You're Burning to a Disc.
5. Click OK.

Some other program opens when you open an icon or insert a CD

If the problem arises when you double-click the icon for a song or video file, follow these steps:

1. Open the Default Programs applet by clicking Start ➪ Control Panel ➪ Programs ➪ Default Programs.
2. To change the default action that happens when you open an icon, click the Set Your Default Programs link.
3. Select the Windows Media Player from the Programs column and click the Choose Defaults for This Program link.
4. In the Set Associations for a Program window, check each file type you want associated with Windows Media Player and click the Save button.

If the problem arises when you insert a CD or DVD, follow these steps:

1. Open the Default Programs applet by clicking Start ➪ Control Panel ➪ Programs ➪ Default Programs.
2. Click the Change AutoPlay settings link.
3. In the Choose What Happens When You Insert Each Type of Media or Device window, choose the default application next to each type of media.
4. When you have finished making your selections, click the Save button.

Tip

Media Player can't play all types of media files. It can play only the file types listed on the Set Associations for a Program window under Set Program Associations. ∎

I'm unable to locate the menus within Media Player

If you're not able to find the menus within the new version of Windows Media Player, follow these steps:

1. Open Windows Media Player normally. Right-click in the empty space to the right of the Forward and Back navigation buttons as shown in Figure 27-1.

FIGURE 27-1

The menu that shows up after right-clicking in Windows Media Player.

2. Optionally, you can select Show Menu Bar from the menu shown in Figure 27-1 to permanently keep the menu available.

Cannot see captions when playing a CD or DVD

Verify that the CD or DVD you're playing offers captions or subtitles (not all do). In Windows Media Player, choose Play ⇨ Lyrics, Captions, and Subtitles ⇨ On if Available from Media Player's menu. Even if you've already done so, you may need to do so again after the computer goes into Stand By or Hibernate mode.

If the problem persists, choose Tools ⇨ Options from Media Player's menu. Then, click the Security tab, select (check) Show Local Captions When Present, and click OK.

Media Player can't find my MP3 player

Verify that the MP3 player is properly connected to the computer and turned on. If the player is brand new, wait a few minutes for Windows Media Player to detect the device. If nothing happens within several minutes, read the instructions that came with the device. You may need to install the original drivers and then update those drivers.

Once you've installed the drivers that came with the device, there may still be several minutes of delay while Media Player checks the Windows Update site for new drivers. Make sure that you go online, and stay online, for several minutes after connecting the device so that Media Player can check for updated drivers.

You might also want to check the player manufacturer's Web site for information on using the device with Windows Media Player. Not all devices are 100 percent compatible with Media Player.

Song titles don't appear after inserting a CD

Song titles only appear in the Rip window if 1) you're online when you insert the CD and 2) the CD media information is stored in the online CD database.

Error message appears with 0xC00 or other number

There are lots of these, more than I could even begin to fit into a single chapter. But the number you see in the message is ideal for online searching, because it's so unique. Microsoft's `search.microsoft.com` page is a good starting point, because it searches only Microsoft's site and includes a lot of technical information. If that fails, you can search the Web at large using Windows Live Search (`www.bing.com`), Google (`www.google.com`), or your search engine of choice.

All other Windows Media Player issues

Windows Media Player has its own Web page at `www.microsoft.com/windows/windowsmedia/player`. It also has its own troubleshooting page at the site. When you get to that page, click Help and Support in the left pane. You can also get to that page from within Windows Media Player. Right-click Media Player's title bar or press the Alt key and click Help ➪ Troubleshooting Online. Or, click the Help button in the toolbar.

Error Message: "Your system is currently set to 800 x 600 . . ."

This isn't an error message — more like a suggestion. Click OK to use Windows Media Player at the current resolution. Optionally, you can increase your screen resolution to 1024 x 768 or higher as described under "Choosing a screen resolution" in Chapter 10.

More Troubleshooting Resources

Multimedia is a complex topic and many things can go wrong. Troubleshooting multimedia requires some resourcefulness. If it's a problem with a camera or other media device, the manufacturer's Web site is a good first step. You can also check out the many forums at `www.microsoft.com/communities` for help with media and other problems.

Part VI

Managing Files and Folders

L ong gone are the days when people used floppy disks and small hard drives to manage a few dozen or a few hundred files. Today's enormous capacity hard drives let every user store thousands, even tens of thousands, of personal files in their personal computers. Microsoft was keenly aware that most people were struggling with managing enormous file collections when they designed Windows 7. And it really shows.

Chapter 28 starts off with the basics of what drives, folders, and files are all about. It's primarily intended for people who are new to all of this, or at least pretty fuzzy on what those terms are all about. Chapter 29 gets into the specifics of managing files and folders, including important skills for moving, copying, renaming, deleting, and recovering files.

Chapters 31and 32 get into the search index, perhaps the single most important and useful (and least understood) feature of Windows 7. As you'll discover in those chapters, the search index is basically a search engine for your own computer's content rather than the Internet's content. It's a real boon to those who have a lot of files stored on their hard drives.

Chapter 32 gets into the world of optical media, a.k.a. CDs and DVDs. Windows 7 has many features built right into it that make working with those discs easier than ever. Chapter 33 gets into features for protecting your files, including the Backup and Restore Center, previous versions of lost or damaged files, and BitLocker drive encryption for protecting data on portable computers. Chapter 34 covers common file management problems and their solutions.

Understanding Drives, Folders, and Files

B eginners and casual users are often thrown by terms like *drive, folder, file, icon, kilobyte, megabyte, gigabyte*, and so forth. Virtually every resource you turn to assumes that you already know what these things mean. Nobody ever bothers to explain them. That's because these terms and concepts have remained unchanged for the past 25 years or so.

Of course, just because those terms have been around for a long time doesn't mean they're common knowledge. In fact, for every person who does know what those terms are about, you can be sure many thousands don't. So in this chapter, I'm going to break from the tradition and explain what those terms mean.

Understanding Disks and Drives

Computers work with information. That information has to be stored on some type of *medium*. These days that medium is most likely to be in the form of a disk or a card. You can also store information on tape, but tape is used primarily for backup.

Your computer's hard disk

All the programs and information that's in your computer is actually stored on a disk. You never see that disk because it's inside a sealed case. That disk goes by many names including *hard disk, hard drive*, and *fixed disk*.

Essentially all of the data you work with, with the exception of information you browse to on the Internet, is stored on one or more hard disks in your computer. This includes Windows itself, your programs, and all of your documents, photos, videos, music, and other data.

Note
Don't confuse your hard disk with *memory* (also called RAM for *random access memory*). Your hard disk stores everything that's in your computer. Memory stores data temporarily while you are using it. ∎

IN THIS CHAPTER

Disk drives, disks, and memory cards

Navigating through folders with Windows Explorer

Clicking, viewing, and arranging icons your way

Stop losing saved files

You can also add extra hard drives to your system, either internally or externally. Each shows up as an icon in your Computer folder, as discussed later in this chapter.

Your main hard disk, drive C:, is called *a non-removable* disk because you can't just pop it out of the computer by pressing some button. Other types of disks are called *removable* media because you can pop them in and out of the computer quite easily. CDs and DVDs are examples of removable media.

Removable media

Removable media are disks and devices you can pop into and out of the computer at will. Most removable media require a specific disk drive, or *drive* for short. The drive is a device into which you can place the disk. The drive then spins the disk. A drive head can then read data from, or write data to, the disk as it is spinning. The sections to follow are about removable media.

Floppies and Zip disks

Floppy disks and Zip disks have been around a long time. They're both *magnetic media* (meaning they use magnetism to store data, like your hard disk). There was a time where virtually every PC came with a floppy disk drive built in for using floppy disks. But that's no longer the case. The extremely limited storage capacity of floppy disks has rendered them obsolete in today's storage-hungry world.

Zip disks are still in use, mainly because of their greater capacity than floppies, but are losing popularity to flash drives and external hard disks. A single Zip disk can store as much information as many floppy disks. How many depends on the capacity of the disk and the drive, but anywhere from 100 to 1,000 floppies per Zip disk is not unusual.

Few computers come with Zip drives built in. You can easily and inexpensively add either type of drive to your system. The most common reason to add a removable drive like a Zip drive is to provide a means of backing up files. However, you can also use writable CDs and DVDs for file backup, as well as flash drives and removable hard disks.

Note
Zip disks are not the same as Zip files, so don't confuse the two. In fact, the two aren't even related. A Zip disk is a type of storage media. A Zip file is a compressed file that can be stored on any type of disk. ■

Figure 28-1 shows examples of what a floppy disk looks like. A Zip disk looks very similar, it's just slightly larger. If you do have drives for these, make sure you put the disk in correctly. The sliding metal door faces the disk. The label should be facing upward. If there is no label on the disk, make sure the metal wheel in the center of the disk is facing down when you put the disk in the drive.

The write-protect tab in a floppy is used to prevent accidentally erasing or replacing important information on the floppy. When the write-protect tab is closed (you cannot see through the hole), you're free to do whatever you want with the disk. When the slider is open, you can only read the contents of the disk. You can't erase the disk or change its contents.

CDs and DVDs

CDs and DVDs are very popular storage media. The record companies use CDs to sell albums. The movie industry sells movies on DVDs. The computer industry uses both CDs and DVDs to distribute software. Figure 28-2 shows an example of a CD or DVD. The two look exactly alike, so the figure could be either.

FIGURE 28-1

Floppy disk.

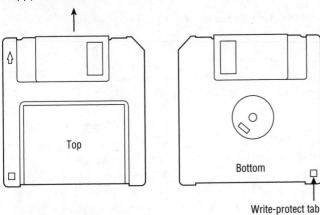

FIGURE 28-2

CD or DVD.

When putting a CD or DVD disk into its drive, push the eject button to open the drive, and make sure to insert the disk in the tray with the label facing up. Then push the eject button on the drive to close the drive.

To listen to music on a CD, you usually just stick the CD in your CD drive, wait a few seconds, and the CD starts playing in your default music program, usually in Windows Media Player. The same is true for most movie DVDs, but only if your computer has the appropriate hardware and software. Here's a quick rundown on where to look for more information on CDs and DVDs (besides this chapter):

- **Listen to, copy from, or create your own music CDs:** Chapter 24, "Making Music with Media Player."

- **Watch DVD movies:** Chapter 25, "DVD, Video, and More."

- **Copy computer files to and from CDs and DVDs:** Chapter 32, "Using CDs and DVDs."

Tip

You can use Windows Media Center (Chapter 26) to play CDs and watch movies, but only if you have a version of Windows 7 that includes Media Center. ∎

The most common mistake people make with CDs and DVDs is assuming they're the same. After all, they *look* the same. But they're not the same at all. Nor do you treat them like other kinds of disks. That's why I've dedicated a whole chapter (32) just to CDs and DVDs.

Portable devices

Technically, portable devices aren't disks or disk drives. But some can store files. For example, digital cameras store pictures. Portable MP3 players store songs. When you connect such a device to your computer, it looks like a disk drive to Windows 7, in the sense that it shows up in your Computer folder.

You can copy things to and from portable devices using many different techniques. For example, you can use Windows Live Photo Gallery (Chapter 23) to get pictures from a digital camera. Use Windows Media Player to copy songs to and from a portable MP3 player. You can also use more general techniques described in Chapter 29 to copy files to and from some portable devices.

Flash cards and memory sticks

Flash cards (also called *memory cards* and *memory sticks*) are a solid state medium, which just means there's no spinning disk or drive head involved in getting information to and from the card. Memory cards come in many shapes and sizes. Figure 28-3 shows some examples.

Most digital cameras and portable MP3 players use memory cards to store songs and pictures. When you connect the device to the computer, you get access to that memory card so you can copy files from it, or to it.

If your card has memory card slots, you also have the option of putting the card right into a slot. Each slot into which you can insert a card shows up as an icon in your Computer folder. When you insert a card into a slot, you can copy files from it (or to it) using techniques described in Chapter 29.

Flash drives

A flash drive (or *thumb drive*) isn't a disk at all. It's more like a little gizmo you hang from a keychain, though you can also hide them in pens and pocket knives. Furthermore, you don't need any special kind of drive for this storage medium because it *is* a drive. You just plug it into a USB port on your computer.

Tip

A flash drive is basically a memory card with a USB plug connected to it. ∎

Once the flash drive is plugged in, it looks and acts just like a disk drive to Windows. You can move or copy files to it and from it using any technique described in Chapter 29. Flash drives come in all shapes and sizes. To see examples, go to any online retailer that sells computer accessories (www.newegg.com, www.cdw.com, www.amazon.com, or wherever) and search for jump drive or flash drive.

FIGURE 28-3

Memory cards.

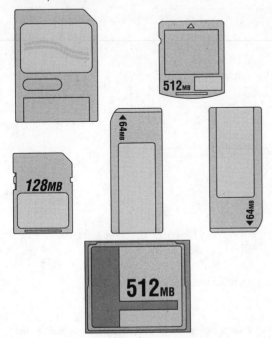

Viewing your computer's drives

Every disk drive in your computer is represented by an icon in your Computer folder. To open that folder, use whichever of the following techniques works for you:

- Click the Start button and choose Computer.
- Click the Start button, click your username, and open the Computer folder.
- Double-click the Computer icon on your desktop (if present).
- Tap 🪟, type comp, and click Computer.
- Press 🪟 +E (hold down 🪟, tap the E key, release 🪟).

Note

If you don't have a Computer option on the right side of your Start menu, but want one, right-click the Start button and choose Properties. Choose the Start Menu option and click the Customize button to its right. Choose Display as a Link under the Computer heading and click OK. ∎

Exactly what you see depends on what's available in your PC. Figure 28-4 shows an example of a PC with lots of different drives.

Don't expect your Computer folder to look like the one in Figure 28-4. All computers are different and have different drives, slots, and portable devices that can connect. But you should see at least two categories of drives.

FIGURE 28-4

Sample Computer folder.

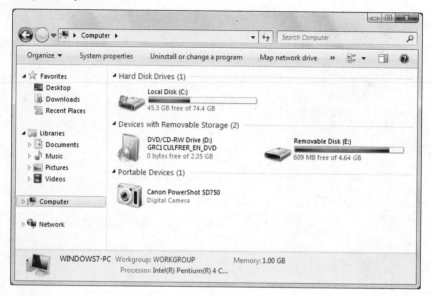

Note

Your Computer folder is unique in that it contains an icon for each disk drive in your computer, as well as for devices that can store files. Most other folders contain subfolders and files. ■

The first category is Hard Disk Drives. Your computer will have at least one of these named C:. That's that drive where everything in your computer is stored. One hard drive is sufficient for most users.

Under the Devices with Removable Storage, you'll see icons for other media. You might have a Floppy Disk drive (A:). You probably have a CD or DVD drive. Its letter could be D: or something else. In the figure, the DVD drive is D:. The computer in that picture also has a removable disk connected to it (E:).

The last category, Portable Devices, shows icons only for devices that are currently connected to your computer. If you don't have a camera or similar device connected when you open your Computer folder, you might not see a Portable Devices category. In the figure, I have a digital camera connected to the computer and turned on, so it shows up under Portable Devices.

You can leave your Computer folder open as you insert and remove disks. The names of icons that represent removable drives change to reflect the content of the disk that's currently in the drive. When you remove the disk, the name reverts to the generic name for the drive. That's a good thing to know if you're new to all of this and don't know what the icons in your own Computer represent on your system.

Sizes and capacities

Every disk is like a container in which you store things. There's a limit to how much data you can put on a disk. This is no different from any other container. For example, you can store water in a drinking glass, bucket, bathtub, or swimming pool. They're all containers for water. They just vary greatly in their *capacity* (how much water each can hold).

If we liken different computer media to water containers, a floppy disk is like a drinking glass. A CD is like a bucket, a DVD like a bathtub, your hard disk like a swimming pool. Memory cards, flash drives, and Zip disks vary in capacity, so it's tough to liken any one to a water container. But they're basically in the bucket-to-bathtub range.

With water we measure things in ounces, liters, gallons, and such. In the computer world the basic unit of measure is the *byte*. One byte equals roughly the amount of space required to store one character like the letter *a*. For example, the word *cat* requires three bytes.

Note

The smallest unit of measure is the *bit* (binary digit), which can contain either 0 or 1. A byte is eight bits. ■

Most disks can hold thousands, millions, or even billions of bytes. We tend to round their capacities to the nearest thousand, million, or billion bytes. That's because disk storage is cheap and plentiful and there's no point in fussing over a few thousand bytes here or there. Also, computer folks don't even use the words "thousand," "million," or "billion." We have shorter terms as follows:

- Kilo — thousand
- Mega — million
- Giga — billion
- Tera — trillion

That's all you really need to know about those terms. For those who like their numbers more exact, Table 28-1 shows the facts in detail.

TABLE 28-1

Buzzwords for Disk Capacities and File Sizes

Word	Abbreviation	Approximate (number)	Approximate (word)	Actual
Kilo	K or KB	1,000	Thousand	2^{10} or 1,024
Mega	M or MB	1,000,000	Million	2^{20} or 1,048,576
Giga	G or GB	1,000,000,000	Billion	2^{30} or 1,073,741,824
Tera	T or TB	1,000,000,000,000	Trillion	2^{40} or 1,099,511,627,776

Getting back to our analogy of water containers, here are approximate capacities of common disk types:

- **Floppy:** 1.44 MB
- **CD:** 650–700 MB
- **DVD:** 4.7 GB
- **Hard disk:** 40+ GB

The reason I have 40+ for hard disk is because hard disks are available in many different capacities from about 40 GB to 2 TB or more. Zip disks, memory cards, flash drives, and portable devices also vary greatly in capacity. The hard disk reigns supreme in its ability to store large amounts of information.

How much room is there?

Everything you store on a disk takes up some space. So once you start putting things on a disk, you have some used space and some free space. It's easy to see how much space you have on a disk.

When you open your Computer folder, each hard disk has a little meter beside it (in Tile view) that shows how much space is used (blue) and how much free space is still available for storing data (white). It also tells you how much under the bar. For example, back in Figure 28-4, Removable Disk E: has 609 MB left of free space. Its total capacity is 4.64 GB. In addition, the Details pane at the bottom of the Computer window shows capacity for the selected drive, as shown in Figure 28-4.

Tip

If your Computer folder doesn't show the meters, click Views in its toolbar and choose Tiles. If yours aren't grouped, point to the Type column heading, click the arrow that appears, and choose Group. If your hard drives aren't listed first, click the Type column heading. ■

To see how much space is left on a flash drive, floppy disk, or memory card, first insert the disk or card. Right-click the icon for that drive and choose Properties. You see a dialog box like the example shown in Figure 28-5. There you can see how much space is used, how much is still available, and the total capacity of the disk or card.

If you see 0 bytes capacity, that means you right-clicked the icon for a drive or slot that's empty. An empty drive has no capacity because there's no disk in it. The drive or slot doesn't have a capacity. The disk or card in it has a capacity. No disk or card in a drive means no capacity (0 bytes).

If you check the capacity of a CD or DVD that's already been burned, you might see 0 bytes free, even if the used space doesn't match the total capacity of that drive. That's because optical media (CDs and DVDs) don't work quite like other types. We'll get into all of that in Chapter 32.

FIGURE 28-5

Sample used space, free space, capacity.

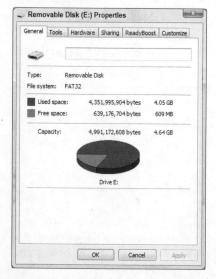

If you right-click the icon for a portable device, you might not see used space, free space, or capacity. Again, that's just because the Properties sheet for a portable device tends to show information about the device as a whole, not just its storage. It's no big deal though, because typically you copy files *from* portable devices, not to them. Also you tend to use programs like Photo Gallery and Windows Media Player to work with portable devices, not your Computer folder.

Viewing disk contents

Disks exist for one reason only — to store information. That information is stored in files, often organized into folders. To view the contents of a disk or memory card, insert it into its drive or slot and then open (double-click) its icon in your Computer folder. Make sure you insert the disk or card first, because it makes no sense to open the icon for an empty drive.

For example, if there is no floppy disk in your floppy drive, it makes no sense to open that icon. There has to be a disk in the drive whose contents you want to view. The same goes for CD/DVD drives and memory card slots.

Like your hard disk, external disks store data in folders and files. Each folder and file on the disk is represented by an icon. Double-click a folder's icon to view its contents. Double-click a file's icon to open the file and see its contents. Use the Back button to back out of a folder to wherever you were before.

Formatting disks

It seems just about everyone has heard of the concept of *formatting* a disk. But not many people really understand what that's about. So let's start with some basic rules of thumb:

- Not all disks need to be formatted. Only blank, unformatted disks and a few other types need to be formatted. But only once, not each time you use the disk.

- Never presume that you have to format a disk. If a disk needs to be formatted, you'll see a message telling you so and an option to format it right on the spot. If you don't see such a message, don't format the disk or even think about formatting the disk.

- Formatting a disk permanently erases the contents of that disk. Never format a disk unless you are 100 percent certain you will never need anything on that disk again for the rest of your life.

Don't even *think* about formatting your computer's primary hard disk. You won't be able to anyway. But formatting your hard disk would erase Windows 7, all of your installed programs, Contacts, saved e-mails, saved files — everything. You don't want to do that unless you really know what you're doing and are certain that you can easily get back everything you lost in the process.

About Folders

Information stored on a disk is organized into files. For example, a photograph is stored as a file. A song is stored as a file. The files may be organized into *folders*. Folders on a disk play exactly the same role as folders in a filing cabinet — to organize things so they're easier to find when you need them.

If you're confused as to why folders exist at all, look at it this way. Suppose you went to your filing cabinet (the real one with paper in it) and dumped the contents of every single folder onto your desk. You end up with a big messy pile of paper on your desk. Finding anything in that pile would not be easy. That's why we put things into folders in filing cabinets in the first place — to make it easy to find things when we need them.

Disks can store millions of files. If every time you opened a disk's icon you were faced with millions of filenames, you'd have the same basic problem as the mountain of papers on your desk. You'd spend all your time looking through icons and filenames rather than getting stuff done.

In short, folders on disks exist for exactly the same reason manila file folders in filing cabinets exist — to organize information. When you're looking at a disk's contents, it's fairly easy to tell which icons represent folders:

- The icon for a folder usually looks like a manila file folder.

- Folders are usually listed first.

Figure 28-6 shows some examples of icons that represent folders.

FIGURE 28-6

Icons that represent folders.

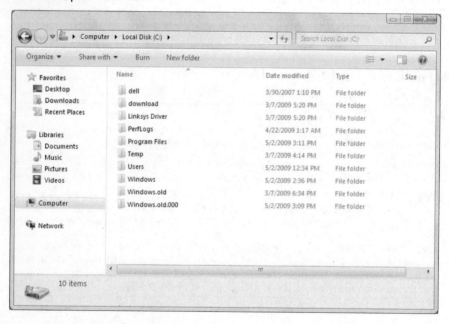

Viewing the contents of a folder

To open a folder and see what's inside, you just double-click the folder's icon. The name of the folder whose contents you're currently viewing always appears at the end of the breadcrumb trail near the top of the window. The contents of the folder appear in the main pane at the center of the window. Figure 28-7 shows an example where I'm viewing the contents of a library named Music.

It might seem odd that the folder named Music contains icons for still more folders. But that's the way it often works. Any folder can contain still more folders, files, or both. That's different from the way folders in a filing cabinet work. So let's take a look at that concept.

FIGURE 28-7

Viewing the contents of a folder.

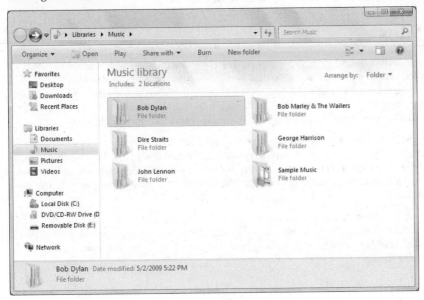

Folders in folders (subfolders)

In a filing cabinet, a folder usually contains documents, not other folders. But any computer folder can contain still more folders. We call the folders within a folder *subfolders* but they're still just folders. For example, Figure 28-7 is showing the contents of a folder named Music. All the folder icons that appear in the main pane are subfolders of that Music folder (but they're still just folders).

Subfolders allow you to organize information hierarchically so things are easier to find when you need them. For example, let's say you copy thousands of songs from your audio CDs into your Music folder with Windows Media Player. If you opened your Music folder and saw an icon for every single song, that could be a pain if you were looking for a specific song. You'd have to read through lots of file-names until you found the one you wanted.

To better organize things, Media Player organizes your songs by artist and album. So when you open your Music folder you see a folder icon for each artist. When you open an artist's folder, you see an icon for each album by that artist. And when you open the folder for an album, you see all the songs by that artist.

So once again, the important thing to remember about folders and subfolders is that they're really just a means of organizing files into groups — the same as folders in a filing cabinet. Of course, you need to know how to *navigate* through folders for any of this to be useful, because all of your files are stored in folders.

Parent folders

The folder in which a subfolder is contained is called the *parent* to that folder. For example, if you click the Start button and then click your username, you open the main document folder for your user account. That folder you opened is the parent to all the subfolders you see in the main pane.

Tip

When you're navigating through folders, it's easy to get to the current folder's parent. Just click its name in the Address bar. That name is the second-to-last one in the breadcrumb trail. ■

About Files

Every file has a filename and an icon. A file can be just about anything — a photograph, a song, a video clip, a typed report, a spreadsheet, a contact — whatever. In the preceding section, I likened a computer folder to a manila file folder in a filing cabinet. Using the same analogy here, a file is roughly equivalent to one thing you'd put inside a manila file folder. In fact, that's the whole idea. You organize your computer files into folders just as you organize your paper files into manila file folders.

In the preceding section, you also saw how the icon that represents a folder often looks like a manila file folder. Icons that represent files don't have a manila file folder in their icon, because that would just confuse things. Icons that represent files tend to look more like little dog-eared sheets of paper. On top of that sheet of paper you might see the logo of the program that opens or plays the file. More on that topic in a moment.

Figure 28-8 shows examples of some icons that represent files. But you have to bear in mind that there are thousands of different kinds of files, and thousands of different programs. So don't expect to find those exact examples anywhere on your system. The key thing is that the icons for files don't look like manila file folders.

FIGURE 28-8

Sample icons that represent files.

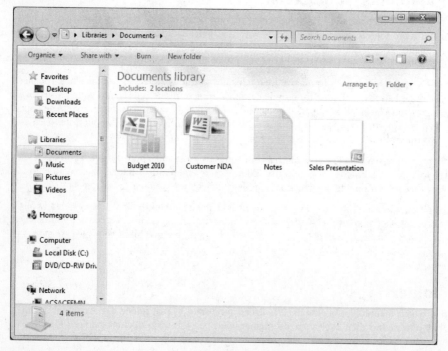

Pictures and videos are also files. But their icons don't always sport the dog-eared sheet of paper look. Instead, their icons usually look like the actual picture that's in the file, or a frame from the video in the file. Windows 7 shows them that way because it saves you from having to open the file to see what picture it contains. See Figure 28-9.

FIGURE 28-9

Sample icons for pictures.

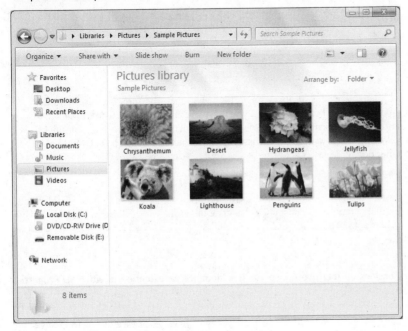

Opening and closing files

To see, change, or print what's in a file, you *open* that file. You do that in the same way you open a folder or the icon that represents a disk drive — by double-clicking the file's icon.

Tip
You might be able to open a drive, folder, or file by single-clicking its icon. It all depends on a setting in the Folder and Search Options dialog box described later in this chapter. ■

Document files never open by themselves. A file has to open within some program. There are thousands of different kinds of files, and thousands of different programs. So I can't tell you offhand what program that will be. But if you can open the file at all, it will open and appear within a program.

Note
Chapter 2 discusses the basics of using programs and program windows. ■

697

Showing/hiding filename extensions

Windows uses a file's *extension* to determine what program to use to open a file. The extension is a short abbreviation, preceded by a period, at the end of the filename as in the example shown in Figure 28-10.

FIGURE 28-10
_____

Filename and extension.

If you want to see the filename extension for a single file, right-click the file's icon and choose Properties. In the Properties dialog box that opens, you'll see the file's type (in words) followed by the extension in parentheses. For example, if you right-click the icon for a video file, you might see something like the following (the .wmv in parentheses is the filename extension that's hidden in Explorer's main contents pane):

Type of file: Windows Media Audio/Video file (.wmv)

To see filename extensions for all files in Explorer, click the Organize button and choose Folder and Search Options. In the dialog box that opens, click the View tab and clear the checkmark next to Hide extensions for known file types. Then click OK.

Note
Folders typically don't have extensions on their names, so you'll seldom see an extension in either its Properties sheet or Explorer. ■

If you opt to make filename extensions visible in Explorer, you have to be careful not to change the extension when renaming a file. Changing a file's extension doesn't change the file's type. It just assigns the wrong type to the file, which could make it impossible to open the file. You'll need to rename the file back to its original extension before you can open the file again.

Choosing a program to open a file

The program that opens automatically when you open a file icon is called the *default program* for that file type. But you're not stuck with that. If you have two or more programs capable of opening a file type, you can right-click the file's icon, choose Open With, and then click the name of the program you want to open the file with (see Figure 28-11). The file will open in the specified program this one time.

Changing the default program

If you want to permanently change the default program that opens when you open a particular type of file, right-click the file's icon and choose Open With as just described. But don't click a program name. Instead, click Choose Default Program. The Open With dialog box opens. Figure 28-12 shows an example. But the programs that appear in your dialog box depend on the type of file you right-clicked and the programs installed on your computer.

FIGURE 28-11

Choosing Open With.

You can click any program name to make it the default for opening files of the same type as the one you right-clicked. If the program you want to use doesn't show in the Open With dialog box, you can use the Browse button to choose the program's startup file. But you must know the name and location of that file in advance — the Browse button won't find it for you.

When choosing a program to open the file, make sure you choose a program that *can* open that file type. Otherwise you'll end up with an error message or gobbledygook when the file tries to open in that program.

To make the change permanent, select (check) the Always Use The Selected Program To Open This Kind Of File check box. Click OK after making your selections.

To test the change, double-click the icon for which you changed the default program. It should open in the program you specified. If you chose a program that cannot open that file type, you'll end up with an error message or a bunch of meaningless gobbledygook. If that happens, you need to get back to the Open With dialog box and choose a recommended program, or any program that you know for sure can handle that type of file.

FIGURE 28-12

The Open With dialog box.

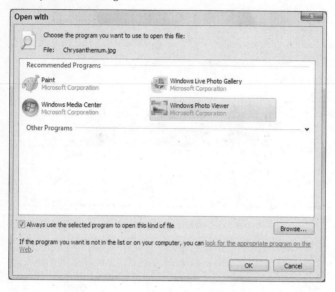

Windows cannot open this file

It's possible that Windows won't be able to open a file at all. For example, suppose someone sends you a Microsoft Excel spreadsheet attached to an e-mail message. If you don't have Microsoft Excel installed on your computer, Windows won't be able to open the file. Instead it will display an error message like the example in Figure 28-13.

If you're new to all of this, there's no easy way to guess what program might work to open the file. Like I said, there are thousands of file types and thousands of programs out there. Your best bet might be to ask the person who sent you the file what program you need to open the file. Or, ask them to send you the file in some other format that you can open.

FIGURE 28-13

When Windows can't open a file.

File paths

Every file on your system is in a specific location defined as the *path* to the file. The path starts with the drive letter (for example, C: for your primary hard disk), the folder in which the file is stored, and all the higher-level folders leading up to that folder. Each part of the path is separated by a backslash (\).

For example, let's say I'm in my user account (jboyce) and I save a file named `MyMovie.wmv` to my Videos folder. The path to that folder would be:

`C:\Users\jboyce\Videos\MyMovie.wmv`

Figure 28-14 shows why this is so. It starts with the fact that your hard disk has, at its highest level, at least three folders. One is named Program Files, and it contains subfolders and files for all of the programs that are installed on your system. A second folder named Users contains a subfolder for each user account. A third folder, named Windows, contains all the folders and files that make up the Windows 7 operating system.

FIGURE 28-14

C:\Users\jboyce\My Videos\MyMovie.wmv

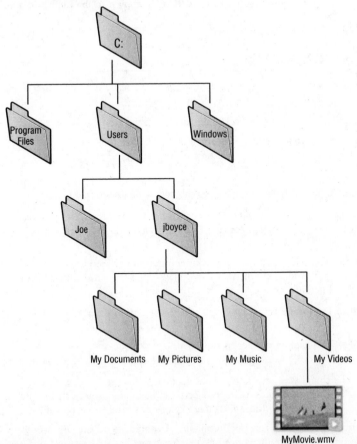

Caution

The Program Files and Windows folders contain files used by the system. Your best bet is to stay out of those folders. Never save your own files to those folders. Whatever you do, never delete, move, or rename a file in any of those folders. Doing so could render your computer useless until a professional can figure out how to fix your mistake! ■

Each user account folder in the Users folder contains the built-in folders people can use to store their documents. These include the Music, Pictures, and Videos folders among others.

The path C:\Users\jboyce\Videos\MyMovie.wmv tells Windows exactly how to get to the file. It has to start by going to the hard drive (C:), drilling down through the folders named Users and jboyce until it gets to the folder named Videos. There it will find the file named MyMovie.wmv. Figure 28-14 shows the basic idea, using a few sample folders from the folder hierarchy.

It isn't often that you need to know or type the path to a file. I only mention it because you'll see paths like that from time to time. The program you'll use to navigate through folders, Windows Explorer, makes it very easy to get around without worrying about paths.

Tip

If you ever do need to see the actual path to the folder you're currently viewing, there's an easy way to do it. Just click the folder icon at the left side of the Address bar. The breadcrumb trail in the Address bar changes to the actual path of the folder. The path is also selected so you can press Ctrl+C to copy it to the Clipboard and paste wherever appropriate. ■

Using Windows Explorer

Knowing about drives, folders, and files is certainly important. In fact, you really can't do much with a computer until you've mastered those concepts. To review:

- All computer information is stored on some medium, usually disks.

- All the stuff that's in your computer right now is stored on a hard disk that you never see or remove from the computer.

- Information is stored in files.

- Files are organized into folders just like files in a filing cabinet are organized into folders.

Once you understand the concepts, the next step is to learn how to use the tool that gives you access to drives, folders, and files. That tool is a program named *Windows Explorer* (or just *Explorer* for short).

Windows Explorer is the main program for getting around your computer to access all the disks, folders, and files available to you. Notice I didn't say Internet Explorer. Despite the name similarity, the two programs serve two entirely different purposes:

- **Windows Explorer** (or **Explorer**): Lets you explore and access stuff that's *inside* your computer.

- **Internet Explorer:** Lets you explore and access stuff that's *outside* your computer on the Internet.

That's a huge difference. For one thing, you have to be online (connected to the Internet) to use Internet Explorer, because the Internet exists outside of your personal computer. You don't have to be online to use Windows Explorer because all the stuff you're exploring is inside your computer.

There's also a big size difference. The Internet consists of millions of computers all over the world. A lifetime isn't nearly enough time to explore the entire Internet. Your own computer is just one computer. It doesn't take anywhere near a lifetime to explore your own computer! But you do have to invest some time in learning how to use Explorer if you want to be able to use everything your computer has to offer.

Opening Windows Explorer

You start most programs on your computer by going through the Start menu or All Programs menu. You *can* start Windows Explorer that way if you want to. Just click the Start button and choose All Programs ➪ Accessories ➪ Windows Explorer. But there's no reason to do that because Windows Explorer opens automatically whenever you open *any* folder. For example, if you click the Start button and then click your username, Documents, Pictures, Music, or Computer, Windows Explorer opens automatically to show you the contents of that folder.

Windows Explorer components

Windows Explorer has many optional panes and other gizmos. Figure 28-15 points out the names of the main ones. Some may not be visible when you first open a folder, but they're easy to show or hide, so don't worry about that.

FIGURE 28-15

Explorer panes and tools.

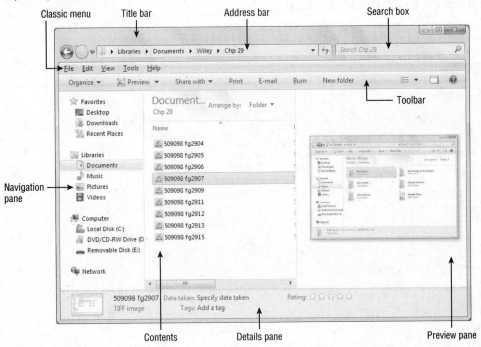

Here's a quick overview of the main components:

- **Title bar:** Use this to move the whole window as convenient. Use the Minimize, Maximize, and Close buttons to size the window as you would in any other program. (See "Sizing program windows" and "Moving a program window" in Chapter 2.)

- **Address bar:** Displays a breadcrumb trail (also called an eyebrow menu) of drives and folders leading up to the folder you're viewing. The name of the folder you're currently viewing appears at the end.

- **Search box:** Lets you search by name for an item within the current folder.

- **Search pane:** Lets you conduct a more thorough and exact search than the Search box. This topic is covered in Chapter 30.

- **Classic menus:** Similar to the menu bar in earlier versions of Windows. When this is hidden, you can tap the Alt key to make it visible.

- **Toolbar:** Buttons in the toolbar let you do things with files and folders in the contents pane. They change depending on the types of icons you select in the folder.

- **Navigation pane:** Makes it easy to get to any drive or folder in your computer.

- **Contents:** The contents of the folder you're currently viewing.

- **Preview pane:** When you select an icon, this pane provides a sneak peek into the file's contents, when possible. Otherwise it just shows an enlarged version of the icon.

- **Details pane:** Shows some detailed information about the icon(s) currently selected in the contents pane.

Show or hide optional panes

To show or hide optional components, click the Organize toolbar button and choose Layout as in Figure 28-16. Items that are currently showing have a light blue highlight. Items that aren't showing have no highlight. To show or hide an item, click its name on the menu.

FIGURE 28-16

Show or hide Explorer panes.

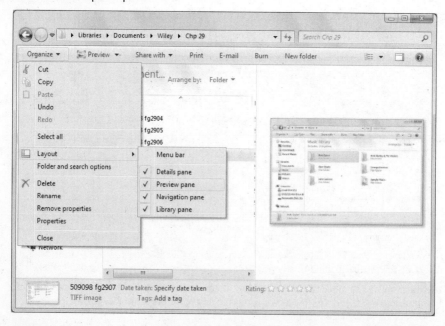

Navigating with the Address bar

No matter how you open Windows Explorer, it's easy to get just about anywhere from the Address bar. Don't assume that only the names in the Address bar matter. You can click the << or >> symbol (if any), or any triangle between names to see nearby places to which you can navigate just by clicking the item's name. Here's how it works:

- If you see the name of the folder you want to open, click that name.

- Otherwise, click the triangle to the right of any name to see its subfolders, as in Figure 28-17, and then click the folder you want to open.

FIGURE 28-17

Show or hide Explorer components.

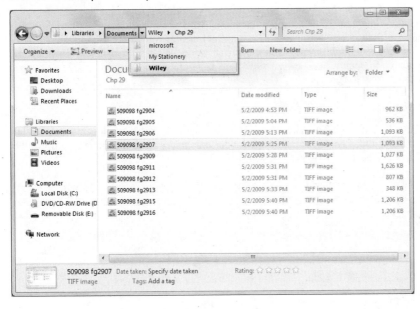

- Or click the << symbol at the left side of the trail to get to higher-level places.

- Or, click the Previous Locations button (the down-pointing triangle at the right side of the Address bar) or the Recent Pages button (the triangle to the right of the Forward button) to return to any recently visited folder.

Note
The button with the two curvy arrows is a Refresh button. That one doesn't take you to a different location. Rather, it just ensures that the contents of the folder you're currently viewing are up-to-date. ∎

You can also type the name of the folder to which you want to navigate right into the Address bar. But that only works with certain built-in folders. First, click the icon that appears at the left side of the Address bar. Then type the first few letters of the place you want to go. A drop-down menu will display matching locations as you type. When you see the name of the folder to which you want to navigate, click that name. Or type the entire name and press Enter.

Tip

You can type the URL (address) of an Internet location into the Address bar. When you press Enter, Internet Explorer will open to show the page at that URL. To return to Windows Explorer, close Internet Explorer or click the taskbar button on the folder you were in. ■

Of course, you can also use the Back and Forward buttons to the left of the Address bar to navigate. At first, both buttons may be disabled (dimmed) because there's no place to go back or forward to. But when you go from one folder to another, the Back button is enabled, so you can click that to return to the place you just left. After you click the Back button, the Forward button is enabled. Click that to return to the folder you just backed out of.

Navigating with the Navigation pane

You can get anywhere from the Address bar. But at times you may find it more convenient to use the Navigation pane. When open, the Navigation pane offers two ways to get around. The first way is the Favorites group at the top of the pane. That one shows links for commonly used folders, or any locations you want. Click any link to open it in the current window. Or right-click a link and choose Open in New Window to open it in a new window. This is handy when you want to move or copy files to the new location by dragging.

Tip

Choosing Open Folder Location opens a folder's parent folder. For example, right-clicking the Downloads folder in the Favorites box and choosing Open Folder Location opens your user folder (where Contacts, Favorites, My Documents, and other folders are located, along with Downloads). ■

FIGURE 28-18

Working the Navigation pane.

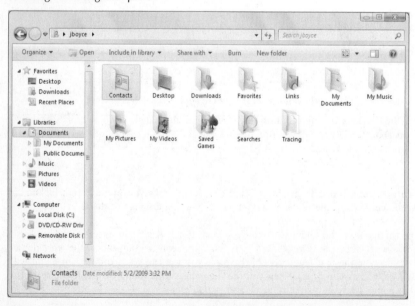

In the middle of the Navigation pane is the Libraries group, which gives you quick access to your user libraries. By default, these include Documents, Music, Pictures, and Video.

Below this group in the Navigation pane you'll find the Computer group, which includes items for your local and removable disks. You can expand each of these to access the folders they contain. Under the Computer group is the Network group, which gives you quick access to devices and shared resources on your local network.

To widen or narrow the Navigation pane, get the tip of the mouse pointer on its right border so the mouse pointer turns to a two-headed arrow. Then drag left or right.

You can expand and collapse libraries, drives, and folders in the Folders list to see more, or fewer, details. Click the white triangle next to any name to expand. Click the black triangle next to any name to collapse. Figure 28-18 shows where all these things are located.

When you click a folder name or drive in the Navigation pane, it opens in the current window. If you want to open the folder or drive in a separate window, right-click and choose Open in New Window.

Adding places to Favorites

The Favorites group can provide easy one-click access to any drive or folder on your system. Initially, you'll see a few shortcuts in it. But you can replace those with any you like. Just drag the icon for any item to which you want easy access into the Favorites group. Figure 28-19 shows an example where I'm in the process of dragging the Contacts icon from my user account folder into the Favorite Links pane. Release the mouse button to create the link.

FIGURE 28-19

Create your own favorite link.

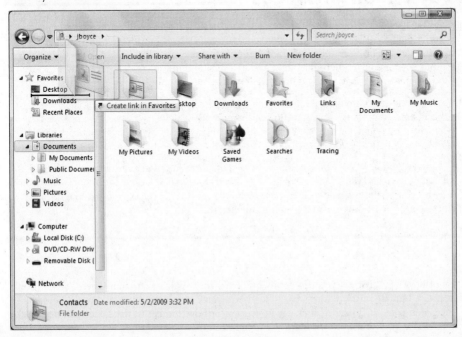

Managing Favorites

Managing favorites is easy too. Here are the basics of managing shortcuts in your Favorites:

- To rename a shortcut, right-click the shortcut, choose Rename, type the new name or edit the existing name, and press Enter.

- To alphabetize shortcuts, right-click Favorites and choose Sort by Name.

- To remove a shortcut you don't use, right-click it and choose Remove. Then choose Yes when asked for confirmation.

Note
Removing a favorite does not delete the associated folder. So don't worry about losing anything when you right-click and choose Remove. ■

Navigating from the contents pane

The main contents pane at the center of Explorer's program window shows you the contents of whatever folder you're viewing at the moment. If the folder you've opened contains subfolders, you can open a subfolder by double-clicking its icon, or by single-clicking, if you've configured Folder and Search Options for single clicking. After you've opened a subfolder, you can click the Back button to return to the parent folder.

If you want to open a subfolder in a separate window, right-click the folder's icon and choose Open in New Window. You can size and position the two open folder windows so you can see the contents of both. Then you can move files from one folder to the other just by dragging their icons.

What About E-mail Messages? ____

Computer files are like files in your filing cabinet. There's a basic assumption that you intend to keep them forever. E-mail messages aren't files, per se. They're *messages*, and they have roughly the same status as messages left on your telephone answering machine. There is a basic assumption that you don't intend to keep them. As such, messages are usually stored in folders that exist only in your e-mail client (the program you use to send and receive e-mail).

Attachments to e-mail messages are files. But they don't automatically go into the kinds of folders we're discussing in this chapter. An attachment stays in your e-mail client unless you specifically save the attachment to a regular folder like Pictures or Documents. Exactly how you save an attachment depends on your e-mail client, but typically you right-click the attachment's icon and choose Save or Save As.

If you happen to use Windows Live Mail as your e-mail client, your messages *are* actually stored in folders on your computer's hard disk. Each message in Windows Live Mail is stored as an .eml file in a hidden folder under your main user folder. If you use Windows Live Mail and want to explore it some more, see "Where and How Messages Are Stored" in Chapter 18.

Regardless of how you navigate, you can get to any folder on any drive on your system. Some people will want to use buttons in the Address bar. Others will want to use the more traditional Folders list in the Navigation pane. It doesn't matter which you use or how you get to the folder you need. All that matters is that you be able to get there when you need to.

Navigating to a disk drive

You can open any disk drive right from the Navigation pane. If you see a white triangle next to Computer in the Folders list, click the triangle to see all of your available drives. Click the name of the drive you want to open. Or right-click the drive and choose Open in New Window to open it in a new window. If the drive name shows a white triangle in the Folders list, you can click that triangle to see folders and files on the disk in the drive without opening the drive.

Tip

Here are a couple tricks you can use with USB drives in the Folders list. Right-click and choose Open As Portable Device to see how much space is available. Right-click and choose Eject to close the drive before pulling it from the USB slot. ■

Choosing an icon view

Once you've opened a folder, you can view its contents in several different ways. As usual, there's no right or wrong way, or good or bad way. There are just different ways, and you should use whichever one is most convenient at the moment. To choose how you want to view icons, click the Change Your View toolbar button to see the slider and options shown in Figure 28-20.

FIGURE 28-20

Choosing a view.

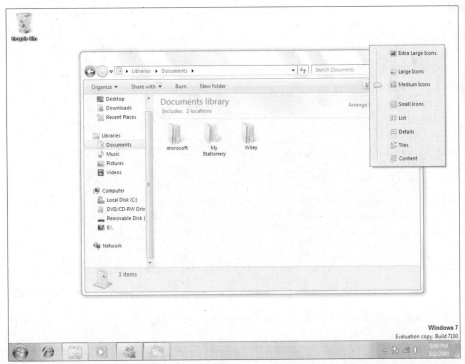

To choose how you want to view icons, click any option along the slider, or drag the box up and down the slider. If your mouse has a wheel, you don't even have to click the Views button. Just hold down the Ctrl key while you spin the mouse wheel as you would to size desktop icons.

Most of the options show each item as an icon and filename. The Tiles view shows the type and size of each file. For folders it just shows File Folder.

Using columns in the Details view

The Details view of a folder shows icons for folders and files in a tabular view like the example in Figure 28-19. You can use this view to show a lot of information about each folder and file. The column headings you see across the top of the display (Name, Date Modified, Type, and so forth) don't tell the whole story. You can choose columns to view as you see fit. Just right-click any column heading to reveal more column names as in Figure 28-21.

To add a column to the display, click its name on the menu. To remove a column, click its name on the menu to clear its checkmark. To see other columns to display, click More . . . at the bottom of the menu. Then select (check) the columns you want to see. Clear the checkmarks of columns you don't want to see. Then click OK.

If you choose more columns than can fit within the window, you'll see a horizontal scroll bar at the bottom of the contents pane. Use that to scroll left and right through the columns you've selected.

FIGURE 28-21

Right-click any column heading.

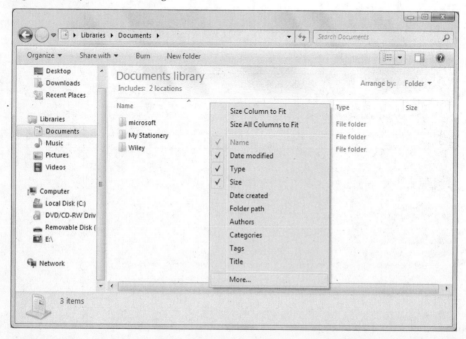

To size a column, put the tip of the mouse pointer on the right border of the column heading so the mouse pointer turns to a two-headed arrow. Then drag left or right. To move a column left or right, put the tip of the mouse pointer right on the column name, then drag left or right.

Tip

The techniques for moving and sizing columns aren't unique to the Details view. They work in just about any tabular view in any program. ■

Sorting icons

The View menu lets you choose different ways of viewing icons. The column headings under the tool-bar let you choose different ways of *arranging* the icon in a folder. Those column headings aren't only visible in the Details view. They're visible in all views. It might seem weird to have column headings showing when the icons aren't arranged into columns. But they're there for a good reason — you can click any one of them to sort and alphabetize icons on an as-needed basis.

To sort icons, you just click the column heading by which you want to sort. The first click usually puts them in ascending order (A to Z, smallest to largest, or oldest to newest). When icons are sorted into ascending order, the column heading shows an up-pointing triangle.

For example, when you click the Name column heading and see an up-pointing triangle in that column heading, you know the icons are in ascending alphanumeric order. Folders are always listed before files. So the folders will be listed first in alphanumeric order, followed by files in alphanumeric order. Figure 28-22 shows an example.

FIGURE 28-22

Icons in alphanumeric order.

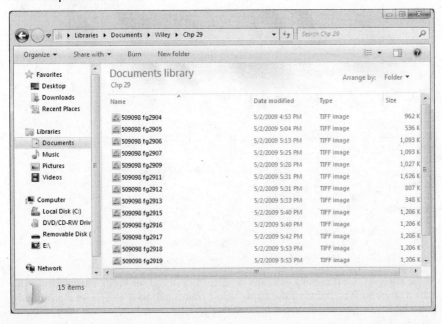

Tip

Alphanumeric order sorts by letters and numbers, not just letters (as with alphabetical order). ■

When you click the Date Modified column heading, you sort icons by the date they were last modified. The first click puts them in ascending order (newest to oldest). The second click puts them in descending order (oldest to newest).

You can sort icons by any column heading, in any view. When you see a >> symbol at the right side of the column headings, you can click it to sort by some other column. If the column on which you want to base the sort isn't available, you can add that column heading as described in the previous section.

Filtering a folder

When you point to a column heading in Details view, a triangle appears to the right of the column name. Clicking that triangle displays options for filtering icons in the folder. These options work best in folders or search results that contain lots of icons. The exact options you see vary from one column heading to the next, because different columns offer different ways of arranging things. As a general example, Figure 28-23 shows options that appear when you click the arrow next to Date Modified.

FIGURE 28-23

Click the arrow next to Date Modified.

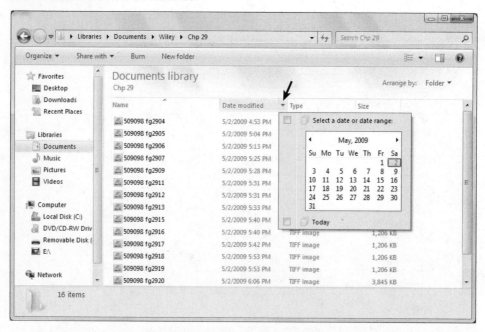

Depending on the selection you make in a column's header, you can end up with a filtered view of the folder's contents. For example, if you click the arrow beside Name and place a check in the A-H box, you will only see folders or files whose names begin with any letter from A through H. The column header then shows a checkmark at the right edge of the column to indicate that a filter is applied. Click the check and clear the check box for any selection to clear the filter view and show all items. The following section offers more detail.

Tip

To select only files of a certain type in a folder, group by the Type column. Then click the heading of the group whose icons you want to select. ■

Filtering is a means of temporarily hiding things when they're just in the way. For example, let's say you're viewing a folder that contains dozens, or even hundreds of icons. You want to focus on just the files and folders you modified today or yesterday. You don't want to delete the other icons. You just want to put them into hiding temporarily so you can focus on the more recently edited icons.

To view just the icons of files you modified today, you would select (check) the Today check box shown back in Figure 28-23. Then click outside the menu. Icons for files that were modified today remain visible while all other icons disappear. The Date Modified column heading shows a checkmark to serve as a visual reminder that you're not viewing all icons — only icons that meet certain Date Modified criteria, as in Figure 28-24.

FIGURE 28-24

The checkmark next to Date Modified tells you some icons are hidden.

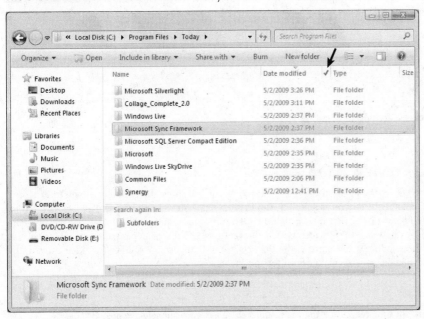

The Search box in the upper-right corner of a folder also plays a filtering role (Figure 28-25). As you type in the Search box, only files from the current folder and its subfolders that match those characters remain visible. Icons that don't match what you've typed are temporarily hidden from view. This makes it easy to quickly locate icons in a large folder based on their names. When you search from the Search box, the Address bar shows the words Search Results rather than the folder name. To undo the search and bring all icons from the folder back into view, click the X button beside the Search box.

Filter a view with the Search box.

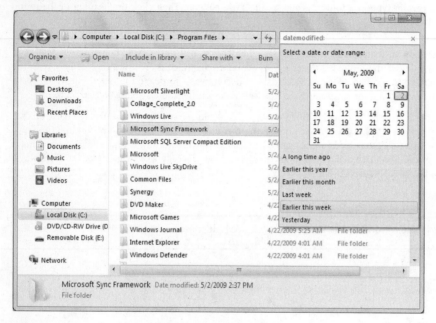

Note

Chapters 30 and 31 discuss searching in detail. ■

Using the Preview pane

The optional Preview pane at the right side of Explorer tries to show the contents of whatever icon is selected in Explorer. If no icon is selected, the Preview pane shows only the words "Select a file to preview." If the Preview pane isn't open, click the Organize button and choose Layout ➪ Preview Pane to open it. The window has to be wide enough to accommodate the contents pane and whatever else is showing. If the window is too narrow, the Preview pane disappears. You have to widen the window or close the Navigation pane to make room for the Preview pane.

Note

See "How to Select Icons" in Chapter 29 for the many different ways you can select icons. ■

What shows in the Preview pane depends on the type of icon you select, as follows:

- If you select a picture's icon, the pane shows that picture.
- If you select a music or video file, the pane shows options for playing that file.

- If you select an icon whose contents can be read directly by Windows 7, you see a portion of the file's contents in the pane.

- If you select a folder icon or any file that can't be previewed, the pane just shows No preview available.

As with any pane, you can widen and narrow the Preview pane by dragging its inner border. Just make sure you get the tip of the mouse pointer right on the bar, so you see the two-headed arrow before you hold down the left mouse button and start dragging. The wider you make the Preview pane, the larger the preview image.

Figure 28-26 shows an example where I've selected a video file icon in a folder. I've also pointed out the two-headed mouse pointer you need to see in order to widen or narrow the pane.

FIGURE 28-26

Preview pane, selected icon, and sizing mouse pointer.

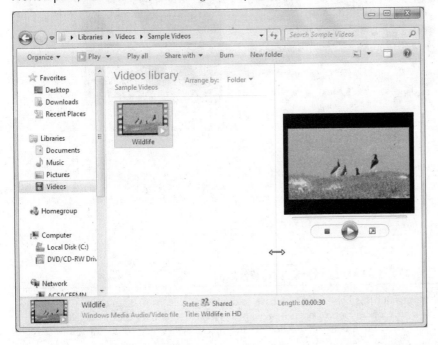

Using the Details pane

The optional Details pane at the bottom of Explorer's window also shows information about the currently selected icon or icons. To show or hide that pane, click the Organize button and choose Layout ⇨ Details Pane. How much information shows depends on the icon(s) you select and how tall you make the pane. Drag the upper border of the pane to make it shorter or taller.

Figure 28-27 shows an example where I've selected three icons that represent files containing pictures. Depending on the type of file(s) selected, you might be able to change the Authors, Tags, Comments, Categories, Status, Content Type, or Subject of the selected items right in the Details pane. That information becomes metadata used by the search index for quickly finding and arranging icons in a way that transcends their physical locations in folders. Chapter 31 describes metadata and searching in detail.

FIGURE 28-27

Details pane and three icons selected.

To Click or Double-Click?

As mentioned throughout this book, you may have to double-click icons to open them. Or you may only have to click once on an icon to open it. Whether you have to double-click or single-click is entirely up to you. The default is usually to double-click, because that method allows you to select icons by clicking, which is easier for people who haven't fully mastered the mouse.

You use the Folder and Search Options dialog box to choose between the double-click and single-click methods. Here's how:

1. Open any folder so you're in Windows Explorer.

2. Click the Organize button and choose Folder and Search Options. Or if you're using the Classic Menus, choose Tools ➪ Folder Options. Either way, the Folder Options dialog box opens as in Figure 28-28.

3. Under Click Items As Follows, choose how you want to handle icons:

   - **Single-click to open an item (point to select):** Choose this option if you want to be able to open icons by clicking once. If you choose this option, also choose one of the following:

- **Underline icon titles consistent with my browser:** Choosing this option will usually make all icon names look like hyperlinks (blue and underlined).

- **Underline icon titles only when I point at them:** Choosing this option leaves icon names alone so they look normal. The name only looks like a hyperlink when you touch it with your mouse pointer.

- **Double-click to open an item (single-click to select):** This is the more classical approach where you have to double-click icons to open them. If you're new to computers or have difficulty using a mouse, this might be your best bet.

4. Click OK.

FIGURE 28-28

The General tab of Folder Options.

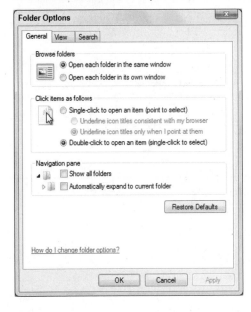

Tip

Here are a couple of other ways to get to Folder Options: Tap ![Windows logo], type fol, and click Folder Options under the Programs heading; or click the Start button and choose Control Panel ⇨ Appearance and Personalization ⇨ Folder Options. ∎

Personalizing folder behavior

The Folder Options dialog box offers many more options than double-click/single-click. On the General tab, you can choose from the following options:

- **Open each folder in the same window:** This is the default behavior where each time you open a folder, the current instance of Explorer shows the contents of that folder.

- **Open each folder in its own window:** Choosing this option causes each folder to open in a separate instance of Explorer. So you end up with an instance of Explorer for each open folder.

- **Show all folders:** This option in the Navigation pane group, when enabled, causes Windows Explorer to show additional icons in the Navigation pane, such as Control Panel and the Recycle Bin.

- **Automatically expand to current folder:** This option, if enabled, causes Windows Explorer to automatically expand the Navigation pane to show the currently opened folder.

When two or more folders are open, you can right-click the clock and choose the options Cascade Windows, Show Windows Stacked, or Show Windows Side by Side to arrange them in different ways on the desktop. Use taskbar buttons, Alt+Tab, or ⊞ +Tab to switch among them.

By default, the taskbar buttons for folder windows will collapse into a single taskbar Windows Explorer button. You can close them all in one fell swoop by right-clicking that taskbar button and choosing Close All Windows. You can also hover the mouse over the icon to see a preview of all windows in the group.

Options on the View tab

Clicking the View tab in the Folder and Search Options dialog box takes you to a whole bunch of options for controlling folder behavior (see Figure 28-29). Most of the options are self-explanatory. If you open a folder that shows icons for pictures and a Navigation pane, you'll be able to try out many on the fly. Just fill or clear a check box and click Apply to see how it affects that open folder.

FIGURE 28-29

The View tab of Folder and Search Options.

Caution

The settings you choose in Folder Options apply to all folders, not just the folder you have open at the moment. The one oddball exception is the first one on the tab. See "Personalizing your folder" later in this chapter for ways of customizing a single folder. ■

Some options aren't quite so obvious. In the interest of being complete, I'll run through them all in the sections that follow.

Always show icons, never thumbnails

If you choose this option, icons for pictures and videos will be generic icons rather than mini-pictures of the file's contents. It might help speed things along on an extremely slow computer. But to see the picture in a file, you'll need to open that picture. You won't be able to see the picture in Explorer.

This option has no effect on Windows Live Photo Gallery. That's because Windows Live Photo Gallery is a program, not a folder.

Always show menus

Choose this option if you want the classic menu bar to open automatically with Explorer. If you don't choose this option, the menu bar is hidden when you first open Explorer. To open it, tap the Alt key or click Organize ➪ Layout ➪ Menu Bar.

Display file icon on thumbnails

If you choose this option, thumbnails will show the logo of the default program for opening the file. If you clear the option, thumbnails show without the logo.

Display file size information in folder tips

This option is about the size of files and folders in terms of how much disk space they use, not the visual size of the icon on the screen. When you choose this option, you're telling Explorer to show a folder's size when you point to (rest the mouse pointer on) a folder's icon. That size is the sum of the sizes of all the files in the folder. For example, all the songs in the Music folder shown in Figure 28-30 are taking up 465 MB of disk space. You can see that in the tooltip that appears under the mouse pointer.

If you clear this option, the tooltip shows only the Date Created for the folder.

Display the full path in the title bar (Classic theme only)

This option applies only if you are using the Windows Classic desktop theme, which removes several of the Windows 7 features from the user interface, making it look like Windows XP and previous versions of Windows.

In Classic folders, the title bar normally displays only the name of the folder you're currently viewing, such as Music. If you choose this option, the title bar shows the complete path to the file, like C:\Users\YourUserAccountName\My Music.

FIGURE 28-30

Size of folder (465 MB) in folder's tooltip.

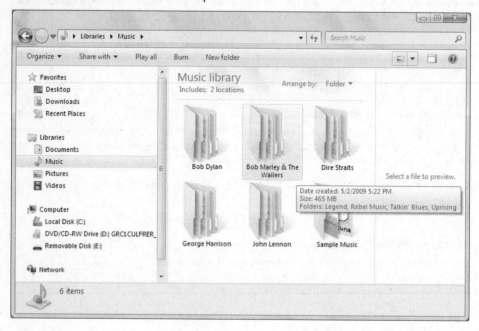

Show hidden files and folders

Hidden files are those that have the Hidden attribute checked on the Properties sheet. If you choose Don't Show Hidden Files, Folders, And Drives then files and folders that have the Hidden attribute checked won't appear at all in Explorer. If you choose Show Hidden Files, Folders, And Drives, you'll see those folders and files. But their icons are dimmed to distinguish them from items that aren't marked as hidden.

Tip

To get to the Properties sheet for a file or folder, right-click its icon and choose Properties. ■

Hide empty drives in the Computer folder

Choose this option to have Windows 7 hide drives that don't contain media. For example, if the CD drive is empty, that drive will not appear under the Computer branch of the Windows Explorer Navigation pane.

Hide extensions for known file types

As mentioned earlier in this chapter, most files have a filename extension that indicates the file type. That extension also determines which program will open when you open the file. A *known file* is one for which you already have a default program installed and defined.

FIGURE 28-31

Extensions hidden (left) and not hidden (right).

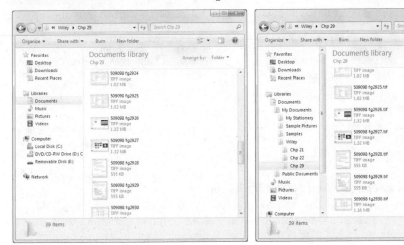

Choosing Hide Extensions For Known File Types hides filename extensions for known file types. So you see only the filename without the extension for those kinds of files as at the left side of Figure 28-31. Clearing that option displays filename extensions for all files, as at the right side of Figure 28-31.

As always, choosing one option or the other is strictly a matter of personal preference. Sometimes it's convenient to see filename extensions. Other times they might just seem to be adding unnecessary clutter. Of course, it only takes a few mouse clicks to turn them on or off. So you can easily change from one setting to the other as convenient.

There's a slight security risk to hiding filename extensions. Malware files delivered by e-mail sometimes have a dot in the filename, like MyDocument.txt.exe. If filename extensions are hidden, you only see MyDocument.txt because the extension is the part that comes after the last dot in the name. Text (.txt) files are harmless, so you might open the file. Executable (.exe) files can contain malware. Of course, millions of .exe files are perfectly safe, but one where someone is trying to hide the .exe extension is certainly suspicious, and probably not safe. Then again, opening e-mail attachments from people you don't know, in general, isn't safe either!

Hide protected operating system files (recommended)

Protected operating system files are files that Windows 7 needs to do its job. These files are for the computer's use. Choosing this option keeps those files hidden so you don't see their icons. This is the recommended choice based on the "out of sight, out of mind" theory. If you can't see files you shouldn't be concerned with, you don't have to wonder what they are. Nor can you do bad things, like delete or rename them, which could cause a lot of problems with your computer.

If you clear this option, those protected operating system files will be visible in Explorer. Do this at your own risk. If you mess with one of those files, you could render your computer inoperable.

Launch folder windows in a separate process

This oddly named option really has nothing to do with processes listed in Task Manager. Normally, Windows Explorer sets aside a little bit of memory to store the contents of the currently selected folder. As you go from one folder to the next, it overwrites that portion of memory with the current folder's contents.

If you choose this option, each folder's contents are stored in a separate area in memory. This won't change how things look on your screen. But if your computer crashes frequently while exploring folders, this setting might solve the problem.

Show drive letters

By default, whenever you open your Computer folder, each drive's icon displays both a friendly name and a drive letter (like C:). Choose this option if you want to hide the drive letters and see only the friendly name.

Show encrypted or compressed NTFS files in color

The NTFS file system used in Windows 7 lets you encrypt and/or compress folders. Choose this option if you want the names of those folders to appear in color, to distinguish them from regular unencrypted, uncompressed folders. Names of encrypted folders will be green. Names of compressed folders will be blue.

Note
To compress or encrypt a file, right-click its icon and choose Properties. Then, click the Advanced button in the Properties dialog box that opens. You can compress the folder (to reduce its size) or encrypt it to secure its contents. But you can't do both. ■

Show pop-up description for folder and desktop items

Selecting this option ensures that when you point to a file, folder, or desktop icon you see a tooltip like the example in Figure 28-32. If you clear this option, pointing to such an icon won't show the tooltip (or anything else).

Show preview handlers in Preview pane

When you select a file icon in Explorer, the Preview pane (if open) will attempt to show some content from that file. It doesn't work with all file types, so often you'll just see "No preview available."

If you clear this option, the Preview pane will never attempt to show the contents of any file icon you select. If it takes too long to show the contents of a file, and that's slowing you down, clearing this option will help speed things along. But you won't see the contents of any file you select.

Use check boxes to select items

Chapter 29 describes different ways you can select icons in a folder. If you find it difficult to use those techniques, choose this option to have each icon show a check box. Then you can select multiple icons by clicking their check boxes. You'll also see a check box next to the Name column heading. Select (check) that one if you want to select all icons in the folder.

Figure 28-33 shows an example. The files named Chrysanthemum, Desert, and Lighthouse are selected, as indicated by highlighting and their checkmarks. The figure also points out the location of the optional Select All check box.

FIGURE 28-32

Pointing to a folder icon shows a description in a tooltip.

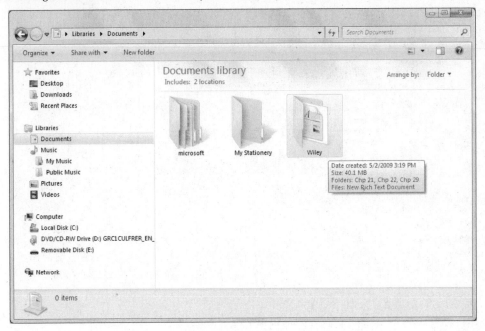

Use Sharing Wizard (recommended)

To share a folder or file with other users, you typically right-click the icon and choose Share, or select icons and click Share in Explorer's toolbar. When you choose this option, the Sharing Wizard opens to help you through the sharing process.

If you clear this option, the Sharing Wizard won't open when you click the Share button. Instead you're taken to the folder's Properties dialog box. There you share the folder by choosing specific options rather than using the simpler wizard.

When typing into list view

The options in this group determine what happens when you start typing in a list view. The default behavior is to select the item that matches what you are typing. You can instead choose to have the text you type appear in the Search Box instead.

Restore defaults

Click this button if you've experimented with settings and want to get things back the way they were originally set in Windows 7.

As always, be sure to click OK after changing options in the Folder and Search Options dialog box.

FIGURE 28-33

Use checkboxes to select icons.

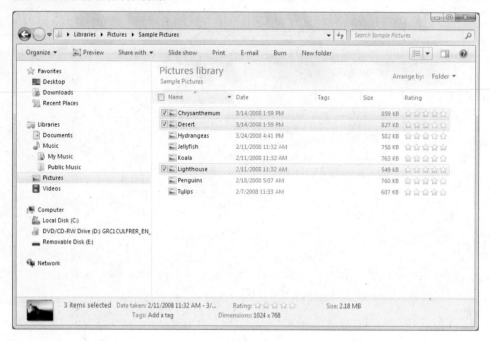

Saving Things in Folders

The most common complaint among casual computer users is the inability to find things they're certain they've saved. The reason this happens is because they don't choose *where* they want to save an item, or *what* they want to name it. They just click the Save button. This is roughly the same as handing an important paper document to a colleague and saying "stick this in the filing cabinet somewhere, but don't tell me where you put it." Finding that document later isn't going to be easy.

Another common mistake is to save things on external media like floppies, flash drives, CDs, and such. That's a bad idea. You only use external media to save *copies* of files that you've previously saved on your hard disk. The copy might be for backup, or to give to a friend. But either way it should be a copy of the file, not the one-and-only original file.

Tip

If the goal of storing a file on an external disk is to conserve hard disk space, ask yourself this: "How much hard disk space do I have available right now, and how much will I have after I save this file to my hard disk?" If the answer is "I don't know," you may be wasting your time, energy, and a ton of available hard disk space! ■

What folder should I use?

Windows 7 comes with several folders already created for you to store your files in. When you click the Start button and then your user account name, you see those folders. When you're saving a file, first ask yourself "What is this thing I'm saving?" Then based on your answer, use the folder whose name matches the type of thing you're saving:

- If it's a picture or photograph, save it in your Pictures folder.
- If it's a video, save it in your Videos folder.
- If it's a song or sound clip, save it in your Music folder.
- If it's any other kind of typed document or worksheet, save it in your Documents folder.

There's no rule that states you *must* save a file in a specific folder. Remember, folders exist mainly to help you organize files so they're easy to find later when you need them. Also, saving to a folder is no big commitment. You can easily move any file from any folder to another folder whenever you want.

How to save in folders

There are basically two times when you have to choose where to save a folder:

- After you've created a new document from scratch in some program and chosen File ⇨ Save from that program's menu, or closed the program and answered Yes when asked if you want to save it.
- When you've opted to download a file from the Internet and chosen Save.

In either case, a dialog box titled Save ... (perhaps Save As, Save Picture, or Save Webpage, or something like that) appears. It's in that dialog box where most people make their mistake. They click the Save button without first thinking about and specifying where to put the file and what to name it.

Tip

Why do the Save and Save As dialog boxes look the same for many different programs? The answer is: they *are* the same. Windows 7 includes a "stock" set of dialog boxes that any program can invoke when opening or saving files. Other programs provide their own custom dialog boxes to add capabilities, but most use the standard Windows dialog boxes. ∎

Saving in Windows 7-style dialog boxes

The Windows 7-style Save As dialog box is shown in Figure 28-34. The name at the end of the Address bar is the name of the folder where the file will be saved unless you specify otherwise. In the example shown, you can see that the file will be saved in the Documents folder for the user account named jboyce. At the very least, you should look at that name so you know where the file is going, and where you can find it in the future.

If you don't want to save the file to the folder that's suggested in the Address bar, navigate to the folder in which you want to save the file. A simple way to do this is to click the arrow to the right of your username so you can see the folders available to you. Then click the folder into which you want to save the document.

If you're an advanced user and want to save to a location that's not easily accessible from the Address bar, click Browse folders to expand the dialog box as shown in Figure 28-35. Then you can use the

Favorite Links or Folders list at the left side of the Save As dialog box to navigate to the location to which you want to save the file.

FIGURE 28-34

Sample Windows 7-style Save As dialog box.

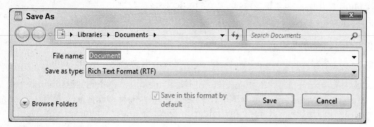

FIGURE 28-35

Save As dialog box with Browse folders open.

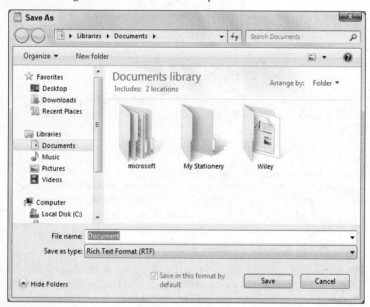

Caution

Another common mistake is to save the file in some inappropriate place like the Desktop, or a subfolder under C:\Program Files or C:\Windows. Those places are not for storing documents, so don't save things there. ■

Depending on the type of document you're saving, you may be given an option to enter *metadata* like an author, tags, or other information. Metadata is information *about* the file that is stored in the file's properties or Windows 7's search index. At first you might see only a couple of metadata options.

If you enlarge the Save As dialog box by dragging any corner or edge, you might see many more. Figure 28-36 shows an example from Microsoft Office Excel, which lets you include a thumbnail and add a tag.

FIGURE 28-36

Sample metadata options.

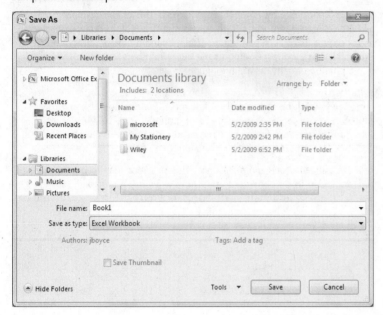

Fill in whatever metadata seems appropriate for your way of organizing and searching for things. If you're not up on Windows 7 style searching yet, don't worry about it. You can still add any information that seems reasonable. But the main thing to keep in mind when filling in the blanks is the question "If I lost this thing, what word(s) might I type into the Search box to find it?" Whatever words come to mind are the words you should put into metadata. Also keep in mind that Windows 7 can search within documents to find words or phrases in the document.

Tip

The Save Thumbnails . . . option lets you see the file's contents in the Preview pane. That's a handy feature because you can see at least some portion of the file's contents without opening the file. So if a file offers that option, you'd do well to select it. ∎

After you've chosen where you want to save the file (and filled in some metadata, if available), you can name the file. The next section offers advice on naming files.

Tips on Naming Things

Whenever you save a file or create a folder, you need to give it a name. Before you do, ask yourself "If I needed this thing a year from now, and forgot its name, what would I look for?" Whatever word pops into your head is probably the best name to give to the item. You're not limited to a single word, but you want to keep the name short. There's not always room to show the entire name of a file or folder. So put the most important word first so that if the name is cut off, you can at least see the most recognizable part of the name.

In some situations, it makes sense to name things by number. For example, this chapter (Chapter 28) was a file on my computer named 509098c28-doc (for inquiring minds, the first 6 digits come from the book's ISBN number). Each screenshot was its own, separate file. Those I named f2801, f2802, and so on, with the last two characters of each name corresponding to the figure number. So, when I view a list of the chapters, they are sorted alphanumerically, as are the figures.

When using numbers to name things, it's best to use the same amount of digits in each number. Otherwise, when you sort by name, they won't be in the order you expect. For example, I know there will never be more than 99 pictures in a chapter. So I use two-digit numbers for each figure. The 28 is the chapter number. The 01, 02, and 03 are the figure number. So the first figure is 2802 and the highest possible figure number is 2899. You can use hyphens in a name if you prefer, such as 28-04.

If you name things by date, consider using the *yyyymmdd* format. This provides for the best results when sorting by name. But again, you need to be consistent about it, always using four digits for the year, two for the month, and two for the day, for instance, 19990101 or 20071231. It's okay to use hyphens if you like.

Naming the file

After you've chosen *where* you want to save the file, the next step is to choose *what* to name it. Again, think to yourself "If I were to look for this thing six months from now, what name would I look for?" Then name the file accordingly. Keep the name short and specific. You can use spaces and some basic punctuation like apostrophes. The following characters are not allowed in a file name: \ / ? : * " > < | because those have special meanings and will be rejected.

Choosing a Save As type

It's usually best to leave alone the Save As Type drop-down at the bottom of a Save dialog box. The suggested type is the "normal" type for the type of file you're saving. If you have a good and specific reason for choosing a different type, then go ahead and choose it. But otherwise you might just create unnecessary headaches for yourself!

Click Save

The last step in the process of saving a file is to click the Save button in the dialog box. Before you do you might want to take a quick look at the last folder name in the Address bar again or the name in the Save In box so you know where you're about to save the file. Take another quick look at the name in the File Name box so you know its name. Then click Save. The file is saved to the folder you specified with the name you specified.

Opening the saved file

To open the file in the future, use Windows Explorer to navigate to the folder in which you placed the file, as described earlier in this chapter. Then double-click the file's icon.

Nothing Happens When I Save!

The *first* time you save a new document, the Save As dialog box opens so you can tell Windows where you want to put the file and what you want to name it. When you click Save, the document is saved.

Every time you save after that, the program saves only changes you made since your last save to that same file. It doesn't ask where to put the file or what to name it again. It just brings the currently saved copy up-to-date with what's on your screen. That's important, and not doing that often enough is yet another common beginner mistake.

It's important to save your work often because that's what keeps the permanent copy on your disk up-to-date with the copy you see on the screen. While creating or editing a document, you should save every two minutes or so. That way, if a power outage or other mishap wipes the document off your screen, the most you can lose is two minutes of work!

If the file you saved is a document, you may be able to re-open it by clicking the Start button, Recent Items, and then the filename. Or open the program you used to create the document, open its File menu, and click the filename at the bottom of the File menu. But keep in mind that those things only include recently used files. Your file won't stay in either list forever!

After you open the file, keep in mind that changes you make are not *saved* automatically by most programs. Changes you make to an open file are stored in RAM, not on the hard disk. If you want to save changes you've made, you must choose Save from the File menu while the document is open. Or remember to choose Yes when asked about saving your changes when you close the document.

Creating Your Own Folders

You can create your own folders at any time. For example, if you have many files in your Documents folder or some other folder, you might want to start organizing into subfolders within your Documents folder. You can create as many folders as you wish, and name them anything you wish. You can move or save any files you wish into any folder you create.

The main trick to creating your own folders is putting them where they make the most sense. Any folder you create will be a subfolder of some other folder. So the first thing you want to do is get to that *parent folder* — the folder in which your own custom folder will be stored. If you're new to all of this and are not sure what I'm talking about, here are some suggestions:

- If you're creating a subfolder to organize pictures, use your Pictures folder as the parent folder.
- If you're creating a subfolder to organize songs, use your Music folder as the parent folder.
- If you're creating a subfolder to organize videos, use your Videos folder as the parent folder.

- If you're creating a subfolder to organize some other type of files, use your Documents folder as the parent folder.

Like I said, you can create a folder anywhere you like. The preceding items are just suggestions. For example, you can create a folder on an external magnetic disk (floppy, Zip disk, flash drive, memory card, or external hard disk). In those cases, whatever disk is currently in the drive would be like the parent folder. Make sure you put a disk in the drive before you perform the following steps:

Caution

You can create folders on CDs and DVDs too, but not necessarily by following the steps here. See Chapter 32 for information on working with those kinds of disks. ■

1. In Windows Explorer, open the parent folder for the folder you're about to create. Or open your Computer folder and then open the icon for the disk drive on which you want to create a folder.

2. Do whichever of the following is easiest for you:

   - If you're using Classic menus, choose File ⇨ New ⇨ Folder.

   - Right-click some empty space below or to the right of icons in the current folder and choose New ⇨ Folder.

3. Type in a name of your own choosing and press Enter.

The new folder appears with the name you specified. When you double-click its icon to open it, you'll find it's empty. That's because it's brand new and you haven't put anything in it yet. (Click the Back button or press Backspace to leave the folder.)

Tip

If you're not happy with the name you gave to a folder, right-click its icon and choose Rename. Then type the new name or edit the existing name and press Enter. ■

You can move existing files into the folder using techniques described in Chapter 29. You can save new files to the folder just by opening the folder from the Save dialog box.

Creating folders on the fly while saving

There may be times when you're in the middle of saving a file and suddenly think "I should have created a new folder for this file and others like it." You don't have to cancel out of the current save operation to create a folder. Instead, navigate to the folder that will act as the parent to the new folder you want to create.

If you're using a Windows 7-style Save dialog box, right-click in the file list area of the dialog box as shown in Figure 28-37, and click New ⇨ Folder. If you're using an older-style Save dialog box, point to each toolbar button until you find the one that lets you create a new folder at the bottom of that same figure, and click it. A new empty folder appears in the main pane at the center of the dialog box. Type in a new name of your own choosing and press Enter.

Double-click the new folder's icon in the main pane of the Save As dialog box, so that name appears at the end of the Address bar or in the Save In box. Then click the Save button in the dialog box. Your file is saved in that new folder.

FIGURE 28-37

Create a folder on the fly while saving.

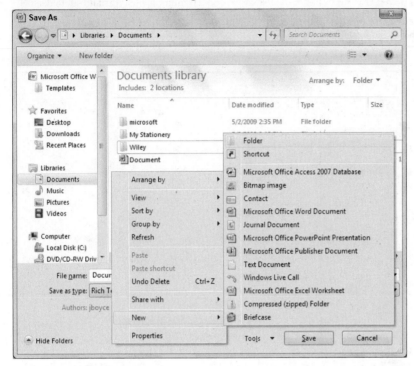

Personalizing your folder

You can customize a folder in several ways. Unlike the Folder Options described earlier, which apply to all folders, these settings apply to only one folder — the one whose icon you right-click, then specify your settings. To get started on customization, first right-click the icon you want to customize and choose Properties. In the Properties dialog box that opens, click the Customize tab to see the options shown in Figure 28-38.

Tip

You can't access the Customize tab when working from a Windows 7 library. For example, if you create a folder in your Documents folder and then open its properties, the Customize tab will be missing. However, you can open C:\Users\YourAccount\My Documents, where YourAccount is your Windows account name and then right-click the folder you want to customize and choose Properties. ■

Specify a folder type

All folders have a default view that defines what tools appear in the toolbar and how icons look when you first open the folder. To define a default view, click the button under "What kind of folder do you want?" and choose from the menu. There isn't any rule that says you must choose a specific kind.

But in general, you want to choose an option that reflects the type of items that the folder contains, or will contain:

- **General items:** Use this option if the folder will contain multiple file types and subfolders.
- **Documents:** Use this type if the folder will contain mostly non-media document files (text, spreadsheets, database data, and such).

FIGURE 28-38

Customize tab for a folder's properties.

- **Pictures:** Use this if the folder will contain pictures.
- **Music:** Use this if the folder will contain mostly albums or other subfolders that contain songs.
- **Video:** Use this if the folder will contain mostly video files.

If you want your selection to be applied to subfolders within the folder, choose Also Apply This Template to all subfolders.

Note

If you chose Remember Each Folder's View Settings in the Folder and Search Options dialog box, the view you were using when you left the folder will override the default view. ■

Folder pictures

Folder icons always look like partially opened manila file folders because like real-world manila file folders, computer folders are containers in which you store files (written documents, pictures, songs, videos, and such). Items in the folder icon represent one or more files that are actually in the folder. For example, folders that contain albums show the covers of albums that are in the folder, as in Figure 28-39.

FIGURE 28-39

Folder icons showing album covers.

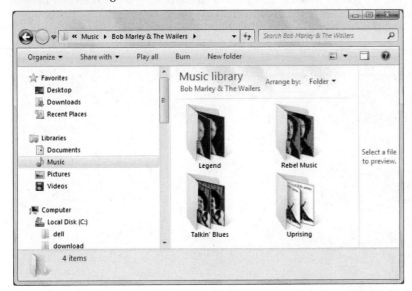

If you don't like the file that a folder icon shows, you can change it to a picture. Just click the Choose File button on the Customize tab and click the file you want the folder icon to show.

Tip

If you can't use a file because it's not the right type, you can take a screenshot of the open file you want to use. Save the screenshot as a JPEG file. Then use the JPEG as the folder's picture. ∎

If you ever change your mind and want to go back to the original, click the Restore Default button in the Properties sheet.

Changing a folder's icon

You can choose an entirely different icon for a folder. You'll likely lose the open folder effect you normally see in folder icons, so you might consider changing the folder's picture rather than its icon. But if you really want to change the folder's icon to something else, just click the Change Icon button. Click the icon you want to use, or use the Browse button to browse to any location that contains icon (.ico) files and choose an icon there.

If you change the icon and then change your mind, click the Change Icon button again and click Restore Default. Don't forget to click OK or Apply after changing any settings in any dialog boxes. Your changes won't take effect until you do.

If your changes don't take effect immediately, refresh the folder. (Right-click some empty space in the folder and choose Refresh, or press F5, or choose View ➪ Refresh from the menu bar in the folder.)

Read-Only, Hidden, and Advanced attributes

When you right-click a folder icon (or file icon) and choose Properties, the General tab of the Properties dialog box shows the options shown in Figure 28-40. The Read-Only and Hidden options often confuse folks, so let's take a moment to discuss what those are about.

FIGURE 28-40

General tab of a folder's Properties.

The Read-Only attribute can be empty, checked, or colored. Here's the difference:

- **Empty:** The contents of the folder can be read (viewed and opened) by everyone who has access to the folder.

- **Colored:** The contents can be read and written to (changed) by the owner of the folder (the person who created the folder). Other users with whom the folder is shared can view the contents of the folder, but not change its contents.

- **Checked:** Everyone can view the contents of the folder, but nobody (not even the owner) can change the folder's contents.

The Hidden attribute, if checked, makes the folder's icon invisible in the folder if the Do Not Show Hidden Files And Folders option in Folder and Search Options is selected. The folder's icon is dimmed if Show Hidden Files And Folders is selected in Folder and Search Options.

Clicking the Advanced button on the General tab reveals the options shown in Figure 28-41.

The Folder Is Ready For Archiving check box is handled automatically by Windows Backup. So it's unlikely you'd ever need to change that yourself. The check box is checked if you've never backed up the folder (or file), or if its contents have changed since the last backup. That tells Windows Backup to back it up again the next time you do a backup. The check box is empty if its contents haven't changed since the last backup. That tells Windows Backup that there's no need to back it up again.

FIGURE 28-41

Advanced folder or file attributes.

The Allow Files In This Folder To Have Contents Indexed In Addition To File Properties check box, if selected, allows Windows to index the contents of files in the folder, as well as the file properties. For example, if the folder contains Microsoft Office Word documents, Windows will index the contents of those documents, enabling you to search for and locate files based on words or phrases inside the documents.

The other two options in the dialog box deserve some special attention and are described next.

Compress contents to save disk space

Choosing this option tells Windows to automatically compress everything in the folder to reduce its disk space consumption. (This works only on hard disks that use the NTFS file system.) When you open a file from the folder, it's automatically decompressed for you. So the compression is transparent, in the sense that you don't have to constantly compress and decompress files yourself.

Caution

This option has nothing to do with Zip files (also called compressed folders). If your goal is to e-mail someone a Zip file, this option won't help at all. See "Zipping and Unzipping Files" in Chapter 14 for information on Zip files and compressed folders. ■

Folder and file compression is a good way to conserve disk space. But before you jump in and start compressing all your folders, there are some costs to consider. For one, there is a time cost. It takes a little time to automatically compress every file you save, and automatically decompress every file you open. Furthermore, many file types already have a degree of compression built into them. Putting such files into a compressed folder may have little or no effect on the amount of disk space they consume.

With today's computers, the amount of time it takes to compress and decompress a file on the fly is negligible. So, you can generally compress folders without worrying about a performance impact. However, you should generally not compress all of drive C:. Instead, just compress those folders where you store lots of documents that are taking up a lot of space. If you want to turn off compression for a folder, just clear the check box beside the Compress Contents To Save Disk Space option.

Encrypt contents to secure data

This check box lets you apply EFS (Encrypting File System) to the folder. EFS encrypts the contents of the folder (or a single file) to make it almost impossible to open without logging in to the computer using the account that encrypted it. EFS is not the most complete form of encryption available for PCs, but it is nevertheless a very effective tool for securing data.

Note

Companies that are concerned about data being compromised when computers are stolen often use *whole-disk encryption* to encrypt the computer's entire disk drive. This encryption is applied even below the operating system level, making it nearly impossible to decrypt the contents of the computer. EFS in Windows does not provide this type of whole-disk encryption, although you can encrypt an entire disk if you want to. In reality, whole disk encryption should really be called whole *system* encryption when the system is encrypted below the operating system. ■

First, understand that anyone who has access to your user account also has access to files in your encrypted folders. Therefore, there is no point in using EFS if your user account isn't password-protected.

If you forget the password to your user account, you will lose access to all files in the encrypted folders. To play it safe, you must make a backup copy of your encryption key, preferably on a CD-R or other disk where it can't be erased. You need to store that disk in a safe place, preferably in a fireproof safe.

Assuming you understand the risks and responsibilities, the act of encrypting a folder is easy. Just select (check) the Encrypt contents to secure data check box. Then follow the steps in the wizard that appears to make a backup copy of your encryption key (Figure 28-42). If you save that file to your hard disk, copy it to a CD-R or other medium, and delete the copy that's on your hard disk.

Note

An encryption key applies to all encrypted folders in your user account. So you'll only be prompted to back up your key the first time you encrypt a folder. ■

Once you've encrypted a folder, you really don't have to do anything else to secure its contents. When you save a file to that folder, or move a file into that folder, its contents are encrypted automatically. When you open a file, the contents are decrypted. So working with the files in the encrypted folder is like working with any other files in any other folder.

If someone tries to open a file in the encrypted folder from another user account, he will be denied access to the file. There is no way he can access anything in the folder unless he can get a copy of your encryption key.

FIGURE 28-42

Make a backup copy of your encryption key.

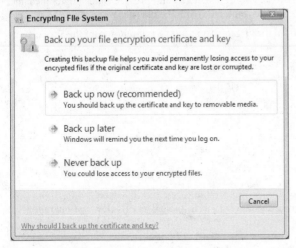

Note

For more information on encryption and backing up keys, search Windows Help for EFS and `certificate backup`. ■

After all this talk of creating folders, you may be wondering how to get some of your existing files into one. That's a topic for the next chapter. First, here's a quick recap of the important points from this chapter.

Wrap-Up

This chapter covered some basic facts about how computers store information. It also covered some basic (and some not-so-basic) skills for navigating through your system to find things. Here's a quick review:

- Everything that's in your computer is stored on your hard disk, typically drive C:.

- The Computer folder shows icons for all the disk drives in your system. To open that folder, click the Start button and choose Computer.

- A folder is a container in which files (and perhaps subfolders) are stored.

- Icons that represent folders usually look like little manila file folders. Double-click a folder's icon to open the folder and see what's inside.

- Windows Explorer (also called Explorer) is the program you use to navigate through and explore the contents of all the drives and folders in your system.

- You don't have to go through the All Programs menu to get to Windows Explorer. Any time you open a folder, Windows Explorer opens automatically.

- Explorer's Address bar, Navigation pane, and main contents window are all tools for navigating through drives and folders in your system.

- When saving a file, always navigate to an appropriate folder and provide a meaningful filename before you click Save. Otherwise, it may be difficult to find the file later when you need it.

- You can create your own folders from the Organize button in Explorer or from the Save dialog box.

- To customize a folder, right-click its icon and choose Customize.

Managing Files and Folders

Your computer's hard disk has enough space on it to store thousands of pictures, songs, and other files. Having lots of stuff in your computer can be a good thing, but only if you can find what you're looking for when you need it. Therefore, keeping things organized so they're easy to find is an important basic skill that every computer user needs to learn.

Chapter 28 discussed drives, folders, and files in terms of what they are and why you need them. There you also learned how to use Explorer to navigate your system and get to things you need. It also talked about how you can save things in such a way that prevents you from losing them.

This chapter picks up where that one left off. Here I assume you've read and understood most of that chapter. Now you're ready to start reorganizing what you already have. That requires knowing how to select, move, and copy files. Here you'll also discover other important techniques, like how to rename, delete, and un-delete files. These basic skills are important to acquire if you ever intend to use your computer for anything beyond basic e-mail and Web browsing.

How to Select Icons

There will be many times where you want to perform some operation on many files. For example, let's say you want to copy a couple dozen files to an external disk. You could do them one at a time, but that would take a lot of time and effort. Better and easier to *select* all the icons you want to copy, and copy them all in one fell swoop.

As you'll see, you have many ways to select icons. As always there is no right way or wrong way, no good way or bad way. It's usually a matter of choosing which method is easiest for you, or which method is best for whatever you're trying to accomplish.

Note
How you select icons depends largely on whether you're using the double-click or single-click method to open icons. If you don't know what that's about, see "To Click or Double-Click?" in Chapter 28. ∎

Thumbnails for pictures and videos are icons too. So all the techniques described in this chapter apply to thumbnails.

Select one icon

Selecting a single icon is easy. If you're using the double-click method to open documents or programs, you click (once) on the icon you want to select. If you're using the single-click method to open icons, you just point to the icon (rest the tip of the mouse pointer right on the icon you want to select). The selected icon will be highlighted to stand out from the others. The toolbar will likely change to reflect things you can do with that selected icon. If the Details pane is open, it will show information about the selected icon, as illustrated in Figure 29-1.

Tip

If you're new to selecting multiple icons, you might find it easiest in Windows 7 to use the check box feature to select icons. ■

FIGURE 29-1

Sample selected icon.

If you turned on the option to select icons using check boxes in Folder and Search Options, you have to point to the icon first, and then click its check box. The only thing that's unique about this method is that the selected icon's check box has a checkmark, as in Figure 29-2.

To turn on the option to use check boxes, click the Organize button and choose Folder and Search Options. Click the View tab in the dialog box that opens. Then scroll down to and check Use Check Boxes to select items. Click OK. The check box won't show on an icon until you point to or click the icon. See Chapter 28 for more information on folder options.

FIGURE 29-2

Selected icon shows a checkmark.

Tip

If you unintentionally keep opening files when you only intended to select their icons, consider using the double-click method to open icons. ■

Selecting all icons

If you want to select all the icons in a folder, use whichever of the following techniques is easiest for you:

- Click the Organize button and click Select All.
- Press Ctrl+A.
- If you're using Classic menus, choose Edit ➪ Select All.

All of the icons are selected.

Select a range of icons

You can easily select a range of icons using the mouse and keyboard. If there are many icons in the folder, you might consider using the View button (or the Ctrl key and your mouse wheel) to make the icons small enough so you can see all the ones you want to select. If the items you want to select have something in common, consider sorting the icons so the ones you want to select are adjacent to one another. To select multiple icons:

1. Select the first one by pointing or clicking.

2. Hold down the Shift key and click the last one.

Both icons and all the icons in between are selected. The toolbar changes to show things you can do with all of those icons. If the Details pane is open, it shows some information about the selected icons. The Size detail tells the combined size of all the selected icons. Figure 29-3 shows an example.

Range of icons selected.

Selecting and unselecting one at a time

To select a single icon without unselecting others, Ctrl+Click the icons you want to select (or unselect). Ctrl+Click means "hold down the Ctrl key as you click." For example, if you wanted to unselect only the Budget 2010 icon in Figure 29-3, you'd Ctrl+Click its icon. All the other icons would remain selected.

If you're using the single-click method to open icons, you can Ctrl+Click or Ctrl+point to select or unselect a single icon. It doesn't matter which, the result is the same.

Here's another way to look at it. When you select an icon by pointing or clicking, only that one icon is selected. Any other selected icons are instantly unselected. But if you hold down the Ctrl key as you go, other selected icons remain unchanged. So you can hold down the Ctrl key to select or unselect without disturbing other selected icons.

Of course you can use the Ctrl key to select multiple non-adjacent icons, as illustrated in Figure 29-4.

Selecting with the keyboard

You can select icons without using the mouse at all. First you have to make sure the keyboard focus is in Explorer's main contents pane. If you're not sure, press arrow keys on the keyboard until you notice the selection box moving from icon to icon within the main content pane. Then move the focus to the first icon you want to select using the navigation keys (←, →, ↑, ↓, Home, End, PgUp, PgDn).

FIGURE 29-4

Select multiple icons.

To select multiple adjacent icons, hold down the Shift key as you move through icons using the navigation keys. All icons through which you pass are selected. To select multiple non-adjacent icons, hold down the Ctrl key as you move from icon to icon with the navigation keys. When you get to an icon you want to select, tap the Spacebar (but don't let go of the Ctrl key). To unselect all selected icons with the keyboard, press any navigation key alone, without holding down Shift or Ctrl.

Select by filtering

Yet another way to select icons that have something in common is to filter out (hide) the icons you don't want to select. For example, let's say you want to select only files that were created or edited today. Click the arrow next to the Date Modified column heading and choose the Today option. Or, perhaps you want to select only Word and Excel files as in Figure 29-5. In that case, use the Type column to filter the view.

Tip

Don't forget that if you don't see a column heading you need, you can click the >> symbol at the end of the column headings to see other open columns. Or right-click any column heading to see other columns you can choose. Note that the >> symbol only appears when the window is not wide enough to show all columns. ■

You can also filter by using the Search box at the top of the folder. Just be aware that the search results might include files from subfolders. It all depends on your selection choice in Folder and Search Options, as discussed in Chapter 28. But for the sake of example, let's say you want to select all PNG and GIF images in a folder. You could type the following into the Search box for the folder:

```
type:gif OR type:png
```

or the following:

```
*.gif OR *.png
```

Just make sure you use an uppercase OR to separate the two types. The search results include only files with .gif and .png extensions.

FIGURE 29-5

Hide all except Word and Excel files.

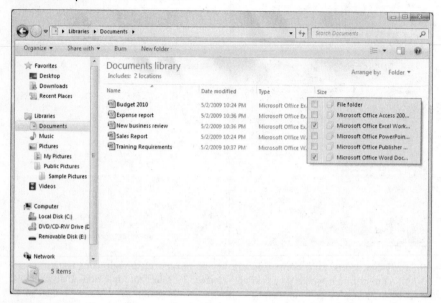

Caution

Using AND in the preceding examples wouldn't work because no file can have both a .gif extension AND a .png extension. Be sure to read Chapters 30 and 31 for a full understanding of how index searches work, because it's not always intuitively obvious. ■

When only the icons you want to select remain visible, select them all using any technique described earlier (for example, press Ctrl+A). None of the hidden icons will be selected. So you can move, copy, delete, or rename the selected icons without affecting anything else.

Selecting by lassoing

You can also select multiple icons by dragging the mouse pointer through them. But this is more difficult to do in Windows 7 than in older versions of Windows. The problem is that if you want to select by lassoing, you have to get the mouse pointer to some empty spot near the first icon you want to select, without selecting any icons. That's difficult in Windows 7 because there is little or no empty space between icons. What appears to be empty space isn't empty at all.

You can see this if you use the single-click method to open icons. Once you get the mouse pointer anywhere near an icon, you select the icon. Once you've selected an icon, if you start dragging, you only move the icon, you don't select multiple icons. The mouse pointer has to be in neutral territory (not on an icon) *before* you start dragging.

To see where the empty space is (if any) in the current view, press Ctrl+A to select icons. If there's any empty space at all it will be white. To select by dragging, you have to get the tip of the mouse pointer into a white area near the first icon you want to select. Then hold down the left mouse button and drag through all the icons you want to select.

Select most icons in a folder

The old "invert selection" technique from previous versions of Windows still works too. But the option is available only from the menu bar. As the name implies, invert selection unselects all selected icons and selects the ones that weren't selected. Say, for example, you want to select most, but not all, of the icons in a folder. You could start by selecting the few icons you *don't* want to select. Then press Alt to display the menu bar (if it's not already visible) and choose Edit ➪ Invert Selection.

Selecting from multiple folders

To select icons from multiple folders, perform a search that finds all the icons you want to select. In the search results, you can select all icons, or just specific icons using any of the preceding methods. For more information on performing searches, see Chapters 30 and 31.

Unselecting all icons

If you have one or more icons selected and want to unselect them all, click some neutral area to the right of, below, or between icons (if you can find such an area). Or click the Refresh button (the two arrows to the right of the Address bar).

Moving and Copying Files

Many reasons exist for moving and copying files. If you've been saving files in a willy-nilly manner, you may want to move them around into folders that make more sense so they're easier to find. Or, if you end up with hundreds or thousands of files in a folder and you get sick of looking through all their names, you might want to create some subfolders, and then move some of those files into subfolders.

If you have a bunch of files on external disks, you may want to copy them to your hard disk where they're easier to get to and work with. Or, if you need to send someone some files and they don't have e-mail, you might want to copy some files to an external disk to put in the mail. Then again, you may want to copy some files to an external disk as backups, just in case some mishap damages the copy on your hard disk.

Whatever your reason for moving or copying files, the techniques are the same. First, understand that there is a difference between moving and copying. The words mean the same things they do in English. When you move a file from one place to another, you still have only one instance of the file. It's just in the new location rather than the old location. When you copy a file, you end up with two instances: the original in the original location and an exact copy in the new location.

Moving and copying usually involves two locations. They may be two different folders in the same drive, or two entirely different drives. But that doesn't really matter because one location is always the *source*. The other location is the *target* or *destination*. Here's the difference:

- **Source:** The drive and/or folder that contains the files you want to move or copy (the "*from*" drive and/or folder).
- **Destination** or **target:** The drive and/or folder to which you want to move or copy files (the "*to*" drive and/or folder).

The source can be any folder on your hard disk, a floppy disk, a Zip disk, a thumb drive, a memory card, or a CD. The same is true for the destination in most cases, though copying files to CDs and DVDs requires methods that are different from those described in this chapter, as you discover in Chapter 32.

Moving files to a subfolder

One of the most common reasons to move files is when you create a new, empty subfolder within some existing folder. Then, you want to move some files into that new subfolder. That's easy to do:

- Drag any item onto the subfolder's icon, and release the mouse button.

- Or, select the items you want to move, and drag any one of the selected items to the subfolder's icon, and then release the mouse button.

The main trick is making sure that you get the mouse pointer right on the subfolder's icon. When the mouse pointer is right on the subfolder's icon, you'll see the words Move to foldername at the mouse pointer (where *foldername* is the name of the folder into which you're moving the file). For example, in Figure 29-6 I'm about to drop a selected icon into a subfolder named Sales. To drop the files into the folder, release the mouse button without moving the mouse pointer away from that folder.

FIGURE 29-6

About to drop selected icons onto a subfolder's icon.

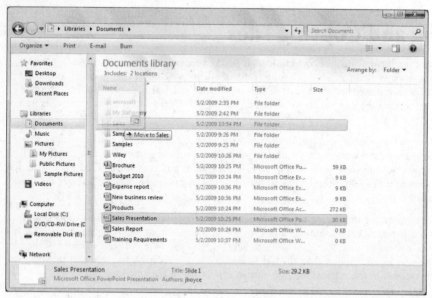

If you change your mind partway through the drag-and-drop operation, just tap the Esc key, and then release the mouse button. If it's too late for that because you've already dropped the items, press Ctrl+Z to undo the move.

If you want to copy, rather than move the files to a subfolder, drag with the right mouse button. After you drop, click Copy Here on the menu that appears. Optionally, you can drag with the left mouse button, but you have to press and hold down the Ctrl key before you release the mouse button.

Caution

Make sure you don't select the subfolder into which you want to move or copy the items. It won't work if you do it that way. Select only the items you want to move or copy into the subfolder. ■

Copying to/from external disks

You can copy things to external disks in many ways. But don't forget that size is limited on those. And the rules for copying to CDs and DVDs are different from those described here. You'll want to refer to Chapter 32 if you plan on copying files to a CD or DVD.

Anyway, you first have to know how much space you have on the external disk, which means you have to put it into its drive and open your Computer folder. When you view icons in the Computer folder as Tiles, each drive's available space shows with its icon. Or if you can see the drive's icon in the Folders list, right-click that and choose Properties. In the Properties sheet that opens, the Free Space number tells you how much room you have.

Then you need to know how much space the file(s) you're about to copy will require. For that, you can select the icons you intend to copy. If the Details pane is open, you'll see their combined size next to the Size: option. But that size isn't entirely accurate because it doesn't take into account the small amount of additional overhead involved in storing files on disk. For a more accurate size, right-click any selected icon and choose Properties. The Size on Disk number in the Properties sheet more accurately describes how much disk space you'll need to store all of the selected files. If there isn't enough space on the external disk, you'll need to select and copy fewer files.

Once you know the files will fit, you can use any of the techniques in the sections that follow to copy to the external disk, or for that matter, to copy files from an external disk or portable device (camera or music player) to your hard disk.

Moving and copying by dragging

You can move or copy any file (or selected files) to any location whose name you can see in the Navigation pane. You can also create a shortcut to the file. As usual, if you want to move or copy multiple items, first select their icons. Then just drag any one of them to the appropriate location in the Navigation pane as illustrated in Figure 29-7. That location can be any folder or any drive.

When dragging, make sure you get the tip of the mouse pointer right on the name of the drive or folder to which you want to copy. If you drag with the left mouse button, you'll see "move to ... " or "copy to ... " when the mouse pointer is in position. The rule is:

- If you drag to a different drive, Windows assumes you want to copy.
- If you drag to another folder on the same drive, Windows assumes you want to move.

This is because there's rarely any need to move a file to an external disk. External disks are mainly used for copies of files on your hard disk. Likewise, there's rarely any need to have two copies of the same file on your hard drive. But you're not stuck letting Windows 7 decide whether to move or copy. Just press and hold down Alt, Shift, or Ctrl before you release the mouse button to drop the files. That rule is:

- **Ctrl:** Files will be copied to the location.
- **Shift:** Files will be moved to the location.
- **Alt:** A shortcut to the file will be created

As an alternative to relying on the keys, you can drag with the right mouse button instead of the left. When you release the mouse button to drop, you'll see a menu like the one in Figure 29-8. Click

Move or Copy depending on what you want to do. Click Cancel if you change your mind and decide to do neither.

FIGURE 29-7

Drag icons to any drive/folder in the Navigation pane.

Move or copy using two open folders

It's not always easy getting the tip of the mouse pointer right on the destination drive or folder in the Navigation pane. You might find it easier to open both the source and destination locations at the same time. Then just drag from one open window to the other. They make much bigger targets.

The trick here is to open two instances of Explorer, one for the source and one for the destination. Then size and position so you can see at least some portion of both. For example, in Figure 29-9, the left window is a folder on the hard drive. The right window is a jump drive.

1. Open the source folder or drive (from which you want to move/copy files).

2. Click the Start button and open your Computer folder or user account folder, or right-click the Windows Explorer icon on the taskbar and choose Windows Explorer.

3. In the new folder window you just opened, navigate to the destination drive or folder.

4. Right-click the clock in the lower-right corner of the screen and choose Show Windows Side by Side, or simply size and position the windows to suit your needs as shown in Figure 29-9.

Tip

Windows Explorer is the program that displays folders. You can use all the techniques described in Chapter 2 to move and size its program window. ■

That gets you to the point where you can see both open folders. Now you just have to select the items you want to move or copy. Then drag them into the main center pane of the destination folder and drop them there. Or, right-drag the items so you can choose Move or Copy after you release the mouse button.

FIGURE 29-8

Menu when you right-drag and then drop.

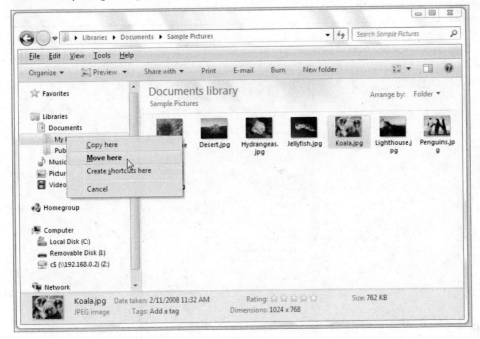

Caution

Don't drag to the Navigation pane in the destination window. Either close the Navigation pane in the destination location's window, or make sure you drag past it into the main center pane of that window. ■

Using cut-and-paste to move or copy files

You can also copy and paste files to copy them, or cut and paste to move files. The procedure goes like this:

1. Navigate to the drive or folder that contains the items you want to move or copy.

2. To move or copy multiple items, select their icons. Then:

   • To move the item(s), right-click its icon or any selected item and choose Cut or press Ctrl+X.

   • To copy the items(s), right-click its icon or any selected icon and choose Copy or press Ctrl+C.

3. Navigate to the destination drive or folder.

4. Paste using any of the following methods:

- Click the Organize button and choose Paste.

- Press Ctrl+V.

- Right-click some empty space in the main, center pane of the destination window and choose Paste.

FIGURE 29-9

Drag icons from one folder to the other.

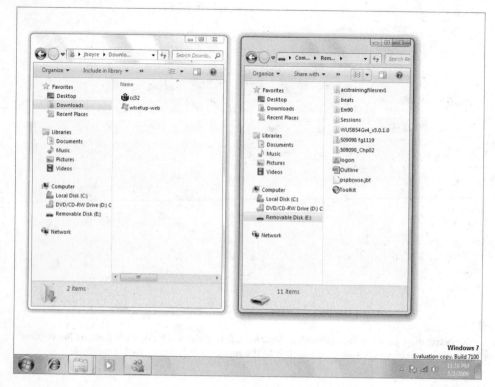

Making a copy in the same folder

There may be times when you want to make a copy of a file within the same folder. For example, maybe you have a large photo from your digital camera. You want to make a smaller version for e-mail or for use in documents. Of course, you don't want to shrink down your original because that's the best one to use for editing and printing. Here's the quick and easy way to make copies:

1. Select the icon (or icons) you want to copy.

2. Press Ctrl+C and then press Ctrl+V (to copy, then paste).

The copied files have the same name as the originals followed by – Copy as in Figure 29-10. You can rename the copies if you like, but it isn't necessary. You can make any changes you want to the copies. Those changes will have no effect on the originals.

FIGURE 29-10

Original files and copies.

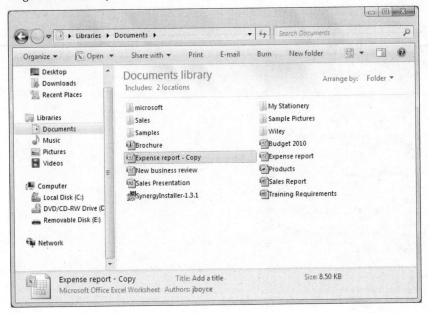

Tip

Click the Name column heading once or twice to get the files back into alphanumeric order, if needed. ∎

Undoing a move or copy

If you complete a move or copy operation and then change your mind, you can undo the action. But you have to do it soon because you can only undo your most recent action. For example, you can't move or copy, then do a bunch of other things, then come back and undo the move or copy. Use whichever technique is easiest for you to undo a move/copy:

- Press Ctrl+Z.
- Click the Organize button and choose Undo.
- Right-click some empty white space in the main pane of either folder and choose Undo Move or Undo Copy.

This location already contains. . .

A folder cannot contain two files that have the same name. If you move or copy a file into a folder (or onto a drive) and that destination already has a file with the same name as the one you're bringing in, you'll see a message like the one in Figure 29-11. Notice that the message simply explains what's going on and gives you some choices as to what you can do about it.

Before you make a decision, take a look at the source you're copying from and the destination to which you're copying. That appears just under each item's filename (E:\ and C:\Users\jboyce\My Documents in Figure 29-11). If that isn't where you intended to copy from and to, click Cancel to cancel the whole operation. Then rethink where you want to move/copy from and to, and start over. But this time make sure you get both locations right.

FIGURE 29-11

Destination already has file with that name.

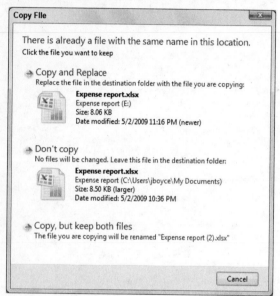

If the source and destination are correct, then think what you want to do about the copy that's already in the destination. Notice that the size and the date you last edited each file are listed next to each icon. Your options are clearly explained right in the message window:

- If you want to replace the file at the destination with the one you're moving or copying, click the first option, Copy and Replace (or Move and Replace).

- If you want to keep the file that's already at the destination and leave well enough alone, click Don't Copy, Don't Move, or Cancel. Either way, the move/copy operation will be cancelled and it will be just as though you never even tried to move or copy.

- If you want to keep the original but proceed with the move or copy, click the third option, Copy, but keep both files (or Move, but keep both files). If you choose this option, the file will be moved or copied. Its name will be the same as the original name followed by a number, like Expense report (2).

The bottom line here is that you can move or copy any file anywhere at any time. There are no restrictions. It's simply a matter of first knowing why you want to move or copy, because there is no point in doing such things purely for the heck of it. Then you need to know where the item is now and where you want to move or copy it to. Once all that is squared away, use either a dragging method or a copy-and-paste method described earlier to do the move or copy.

In addition to the techniques already described, you can get stuff into your computer using methods listed here:

- To get pictures from a digital camera into your computer, use Windows Live Photo Gallery (Chapter 23).

- To get music from a CD or portable music player into your computer, use Windows Media Player (Chapter 24).

- For information on copying *to* CD and DVD, see Chapter 32.

Renaming Files

Renaming a file or folder is simple. Just right-click the item you want to rename and choose Rename. The existing name will become highlighted in blue. You can type a new name, or edit the current name, and then press Enter.

If you've taken filename extensions out of hiding, that part of the name won't be highlighted. For example, the .docx extension on the Word document file shown in Figure 29-12 isn't highlighted. That's because you don't want to change the extension unless you *really* know what you're doing. Guessing is unlikely to work. At the very least, make sure you know the extension you're about to change. That way if you ruin the file, you can rename the file back to the original extension (in case you miss the opportunity to undo the rename).

Tip
Click once to select a file, pause briefly, then click the filename again to highlight the name and rename it. ∎

Undoing a rename

You can undo a rename like you can undo just about anything else. But as always, you have to do so fairly soon after the rename. Just press Ctrl+Z or click the Organize button and choose Undo. If it's too late for that, you have to rename the file again, back to its original name and extension.

So How Do I Change a File's Type?

You can't simply change a file's extension to change the file's type. If you can open the file, and it's not a music or video file, you may be able to just choose File ➪ Save As from the opening program's menu. Then set the Save As Type option to the file type you want, before you click the Save button.

If it's a music or video file, you'll likely need a conversion program. Search the Web or a download site like www.download.com or www.tucows.com for convert ext1 to ext2 (where *ext1* is the extension of the file type from which you want to copy, and *ext2* is the extension of the file type to which you want to copy) and see what programs you can find.

In some cases you simply need the right program or reader to open the file without converting it. Some common examples include .pdf files, which require Adobe Reader (www.adobe.com), QuickTime movies and iTunes (players are available from www.apple.com), and Office documents and snapshots. Viewers for many such files are available from download.microsoft.com.

FIGURE 29-12

Filename extension is not highlighted.

Renaming multiple files

To rename multiple files, select all of their icons using any methods described near the start of the chapter. Then right-click any one of them and choose Rename. Type the new name (again, don't change the extension if it shows up) and press Enter. The files will all be given the name you specified. All but the first will have numbers. For example, if you renamed to River, the files will be named River, River (2), River (3), River (4), and so forth.

Tip

If the lack of a number on the first renamed file bugs you, right-click its icon and choose Rename. Then add the (1) to the name yourself. ■

If you have a relatively large number of files and want to rename just a part of the filename for each one, you can turn to the Command Prompt to rename the files. For example, assume that you have a set of files named `img-old-01.jpg`, `img-old-02.jpg`, `img-old-03.jpg`, and so on in sequence. You want to replace the word "old" with the word "new." Here's how to do it:

1. Click Start ⇨ Accessories ⇨ Command Prompt to open a command console.

2. Type `CD \(path)` where `(path)` is the path to the folder where the files reside that you want to rename. For example, assuming the files are located in your Documents folder and your username is jboyce, type `CD \Users\jboyce\My Documents`.

3. Type the command `rename img-old-??.jpg img-new-??.jpg` and press Enter.

The question marks in the command essentially tell Windows to leave those characters alone. In this example, the sequential image numbers remain the same, and only the word in the middle of the filename is changed.

Before you try renaming multiple files using the command console in this way, I suggest you make a backup copy of the files in a different folder. That way, if you really mess up the filenames by typing an incorrect command, you can simply copy the files back to the original folder to restore the old filenames.

Deleting Files

In computers, the term *delete* is synonymous with "throw in the trash." That's important to know because you wouldn't want to throw in the trash any important paper documents from your filing cabinet. Likewise, you don't want to delete anything important that's in your computer.

It's easy to delete files and folders. Perhaps it is too easy, because it's a leading cause of headaches and disasters, especially among beginners and casual computer users who try to learn by guessing and figuring things out. Deleting and "moving to the Recycle Bin" are basically the same thing. So let's start with a couple of good rules of thumb. Before you delete an item or move it to the Recycle Bin, ask yourself two questions:

- Do I know exactly what this file (or folder) is?
- Am I 100 percent certain neither I nor my computer will need it in the future, ever?

If the answer to both questions is "Yes," go ahead and delete the file. If the answer to either question is "No," don't delete the file or move it to the Recycle Bin.

Caution

When you delete a folder, you delete all of the files and subfolders inside that folder! That means one small delete can lead to many lost files. Never delete a folder unless you're absolutely sure that the folder and its subfolders contain only files that you'll never need again. ■

Deleting is a simple process. If you want to delete a single file or folder, first select its icon. Optionally, if you want to delete multiple items in one fell swoop, select their icons. Then, do whichever of the following is most convenient for you:

- Right-click the icon (or any selected icon) and choose Delete.
- Press the Delete (Del) key.
- Choose File ➪ Delete from Explorer's menu bar.
- Drag the selected item(s) to the Recycle Bin.
- Click Organize ➪ Delete.

Because deleting is serious business, you'll be asked for confirmation before the item(s) are actually deleted. The confirmation appears as a question asking if you're sure, and gives you a choice on whether or not you want to proceed. Figure 29-13 shows examples of three such confirmation messages.

The idea is to read the message, then click Yes only if you're sure. If you're not so sure, you should click No. Clicking Yes deletes the files. Clicking No keeps the files right where they are.

Notice that the top and bottom messages ask if you're sure you want to send the items to the Recycle Bin, while the middle message asks if you're sure that you want to permanently delete the items. The difference is as follows.

When you send something to the Recycle Bin, you still get one last chance to change your mind. It's kind of like fishing something out of the wastepaper basket before you empty it for good. That doesn't mean you should put things you intend to keep in the Recycle Bin. You wouldn't put important papers in your trash can. Never put important files or folders in your Recycle Bin.

FIGURE 29-13

Asking for confirmation before deleting.

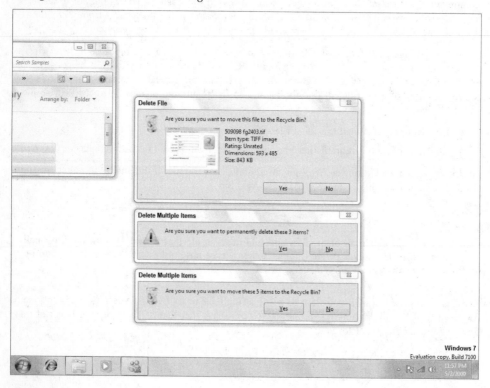

Caution

Despite its environmentally friendly name, the Recycle Bin *is* a trash can and should be treated as such. Neither the Recycle Bin nor your trash can are good places to put things you intend to keep! ∎

When you permanently delete a file or folder, there's no turning back. Whatever you permanently deleted is gone for good and there's no changing your mind and getting it back. Think of permanently deleting as being like putting something down the garbage disposal. Or dousing the thing with gasoline and burning it to ashes. There is no "undo" for such actions.

Tip

In some cases, it might be possible to use the Previous Versions feature described in Chapter 33 to recover a permanently deleted file. But to play it safe, you should treat all deletions as though they were permanent. There are also third-party programs that can recover deleted files, as well as data recovery services that can recover deleted data. However, the likelihood of recovering the deleted data decreases if any data is written to the disk before recovery is attempted. ∎

Using the Recycle Bin

The Recycle Bin stores copies of files you've deleted from your hard disk. To open your Recycle Bin, use whichever method is easiest for you:

- Open the Recycle Bin on the desktop.
- Click Recycle Bin in the Folder list in Explorer's Navigation pane.
- Click the leftmost arrow in Explorer's Address bar and choose Recycle Bin.
- Type `Recycle Bin` in Explorer's Address bar and press Enter.

When the Recycle Bin opens, it looks like any other folder. Figure 29-14 shows an example.

Each icon in the Recycle Bin represents an item that's in your computer trash can, so to speak. You have basically two ways to use the Recycle Bin:

- *Restore* files that you've accidentally deleted, so they go back to their original folders. (Same as fishing something out of your real trash can.)
- *Empty* the Recycle Bin, thereby permanently deleting the files within it to reclaim the disk space they were using. (Same as emptying your real trash can into a trash truck or incinerator.)

The sections that follow look at each option.

Recovering accidentally deleted files

If you accidentally deleted some files or folders from your hard disk, and if they were sent to the Recycle Bin, you can get them back, provided that you don't empty the Recycle Bin first. You have three ways to do that:

- To put all items back where they were, click Restore all items in the toolbar.
- To put a single item back where it was, right-click its icon and choose Restore.
- Optionally, you can select multiple icons, right-click any selected icon, and choose Restore to put all those selected items back where they were.

Each file and folder you restore will be returned to its original location.

Permanently deleting Recycle Bin files

When you feel confident that the Recycle Bin contains only folders and files that you'll never need again, click Empty the Recycle Bin in the toolbar. The icons in the Recycle Bin disappear. The files and folders that those icons represented are permanently deleted from your hard disk. The space they occupied is freed up for anything you might want to save in the future.

If you want to remove only one or a selection of files from the Recycle Bin, select those files, right-click, and choose Delete. Windows asks if you want to permanently delete the files, removing them from the Recycle Bin. Click Yes to delete them, or No to leave them in the Recycle Bin.

Tip

You can empty the Recycle Bin without opening it first. Right-click the Recycle Bin's icon, and choose Empty Recycle Bin. Just keep in mind that in doing so, you're presuming there's nothing in the Recycle Bin you intended to keep. ■

FIGURE 29-14

An open Recycle Bin.

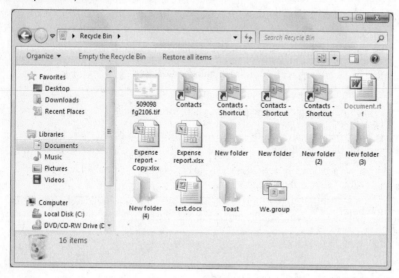

When you've finished with the Recycle Bin, you can close it as you would any other window — by clicking the Close (X) button in its upper-right corner.

For all intents and purposes, you should consider the files that were in the Recycle Bin as permanently gone. But if you messed up and emptied too early, you *might* be able to get some of the files that were in there back using the Previous Versions feature discussed in Chapter 33.

Creating and Deleting Shortcuts

Shortcuts provide an easy way to get to a file or folder without having to navigate through a bunch of folders. For example, let's say you have an external disk drive X. On that drive you have a folder named My Big Project inside another folder named Xternal Docs. To view the contents of your My Big Project folder, you have to open your Computer folder, open the icon for drive X:, open the Xternal Docs folder, and then open the My Big Project folder. Doing that repeatedly gets tiresome.

If you create a shortcut to My Big Project, you won't have to go through all those steps. You just have to open the My Big Project shortcut icon. That shortcut icon can be any place you like — on the desktop, in your Documents folder, in the Favorites pane, on the Start menu — or any combination thereof.

You can create a desktop shortcut to virtually any program, folder, or file just by right-clicking that item's icon and choosing Send To ➪ Desktop (create shortcut). You can also use any of the following methods to create a shortcut to a file or folder:

- Hold down the Alt key as you drag an icon to the folder in which you want to place the shortcut.

- Drag, using the right mouse button, the selected icon(s) to where you want to put the shortcuts. After you release the right mouse button, click Create Shortcuts Here.

- Copy the selected icon(s) to the Clipboard (press Ctrl+C or right-click and choose Copy). Then right-click some empty space at the location where you want to place the shortcuts and choose Paste Shortcut.

Once you have a shortcut, you can double-click (or click) its icon to open the item to which the shortcut refers.

It's important to understand that when you delete a shortcut to a resource, you delete only the shortcut. You don't delete the folder or file to which the shortcut refers. That means you can easily create a bunch of shortcuts to a folder you're working with right now.

Later, when you move on to another project in another folder, you can delete all those shortcuts and replace them with new shortcuts to whatever folder you're working in currently. But you have to make sure you delete the shortcuts only, not the real folder because when you delete the real folder, you also delete everything that's in that folder. You also render the shortcuts useless, because the location to which they refer no longer exists. When you try to open a shortcut that points to a non-existent file or folder, you see a message like the one in Figure 29-15.

FIGURE 29-15

Opening a shortcut that leads nowhere.

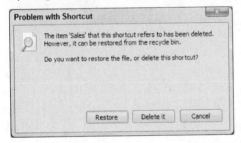

If you deleted the item recently and it's still in the Recycle Bin, click the Restore button. The original item will be taken out of the trash, put back where it belongs, and the shortcut will work. Otherwise, if there's no way to recover the item to which the shortcut refers, all you can do is delete the now-useless shortcut by clicking the Delete It button.

Note

If the shortcut refers to an item on external media (such as CD, flash drive, external USB drive), that disk has to be in its drive for the shortcut to work. ∎

If you're thinking about deleting an icon, but aren't sure if it's a shortcut or the real thing, there are ways to find out. For one thing, all icons on the Start menu, All Programs menu, and their submenus are shortcuts. Likewise, all links in the Favorites portion of Explorer's Navigation bar are shortcuts. Desktop icons you control from the Desktop Icon Settings dialog box are also shortcuts. I'm not suggesting you delete any of those unless you have a very good reason, but if you delete one, be aware that you're deleting only the shortcut and not the actual item.

Tip

Chapters 10 and 28 provide more detailed information about the items described in the preceding paragraph. ∎

Shortcut icons of your own making have many characteristics that make it easy to distinguish them from the items to which they refer. The most obvious is the curved arrow that appears right on the icon. The name of the icon usually has - shortcut at the end (if you don't rename the shortcut). The filename extension for a shortcut icon is always .lnk (for link). The size of a shortcut will always be tiny (1 KB or less). When you right-click the icon and choose Properties, the General tab shows the Type of File as Shortcut (.lnk). The Shortcut tab shows information about the icon and its target as in Figure 29-16.

Anatomy of a custom shortcut icon.

Like I said at the outset of this section, when you delete a shortcut you delete only the shortcut, not the item to which it refers. So you can create and delete shortcuts on the fly without losing any important files or folders. But the #1 rule of deleting still applies: Know exactly what you're deleting and why you're deleting it *before* you delete. It's as simple as that.

Managing Files with DOS Commands

This section is for people who were around in the DOS days and remember commands like CD (change directory), Copy (to copy files), and so forth. All those old DOS commands still work. Using DOS commands is useful in some instances, such as when you want to print a list of filenames or paste them into a file. So, we'll look at how all that works in this section.

Getting to a command prompt

The first step to using DOS commands is to get to the Command Prompt window (also called a *console window*). To do so, click the Start button and choose All Programs ⇨ Accessories ⇨ Command

Prompt. Or click the Start button, type com, and choose Command Prompt. A window reminiscent of ye olde DOS days opens, complete with the standard prompt that displays the folder (*directory* in DOS terms) that you're currently in. Figure 29-17 shows an example. Note that I've changed the colors for the console to be black text on a white background. The default is white text on a black background.

FIGURE 29-17

Command Prompt window.

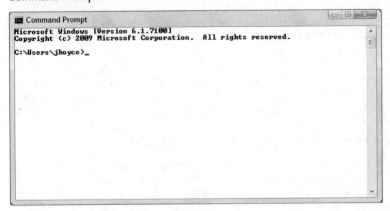

The Command Prompt window has a title bar and taskbar button. You can drag the window around by its title bar. To a limited extent, you can size the Command Prompt window by dragging any corner or edge, but the height is limited to the number of lines currently displayed within the window.

To get full control over the size of the Command Prompt window, you need to use its Properties dialog box. That Properties dialog box also lets you choose a cursor size, a Full Screen View, a font, text and background colors, and so forth.

You can get to the Command Prompt window's Properties dialog box in two ways. If you want to change properties for the current session only, right-click the Command Prompt title bar and choose Properties. If you want to change the defaults for future sessions as well, right-click the title bar and choose Defaults. The dialog box that opens is self-explanatory and is a normal Windows dialog box.

You can scroll up and down through the Command Prompt window using the vertical scroll bar at its right. The navigation keys don't work unless you right-click within the window and choose Scroll. You can't type normal characters in the scroll mode; you can just navigate up and down. To get out of scroll mode and back to normal typing, press Enter.

To exit a command prompt session, type exit and press Enter. Or close the Command Prompt program window by clicking its Close (X) button or by right-clicking its taskbar button and choosing Close.

Using the command prompt

The Command Prompt window works just like the screen did in DOS. You type a command and press Enter (assuming that you're not in the aforementioned "scroll mode," wherein typing normal characters just sounds a beep). After you press Enter, you see the results of the command and another command prompt appears. For example, if you enter Help (that is, type the word Help and press Enter), you see a list of all the supported DOS commands.

To get help with a command, type its name followed by a forward slash and question mark. For example, entering the command dir /? shows help for the Dir command. The Doskey feature is enabled automatically (again assuming that you're not in the bizarre scroll mode). So, you can use the ↑ and ↓ keys to retrieve previous commands from the current session. Press the ← and → keys to bring back and remove the previous command one character at a time.

Note
If the characters you type result only in a beep and nothing on the screen, right-click in the Command Prompt window and choose Scroll to get back to normal typing. ■

The mouse doesn't do much in the Command Prompt window. As mentioned, you can right-click the title bar (or its taskbar button) to get to the Properties sheet. You can right-click and choose Scroll to enter the (disturbing) scroll mode where navigation keys move through the window and normal characters do nothing but beep at you. (Though pressing Enter terminates the disturbing scroll mode.)

Copy and paste in the command prompt window

Right-clicking in the Command Prompt window provides some options that allow you to use copy and paste. It's a bit tricky, but handy when you want to copy a lengthy list of filenames into a Word, WordPad, or Notepad document. If you'll be using the keyboard to select only a portion of the text, you first want to use the scroll bar to get up to where you can see where you want to start selecting text. If you'll be using the mouse to select a portion of text, or will be selecting all the text in the window, it's not so important where you start.

To select the entire window, right-click within the window and choose Select All. To select only a portion of the window's contents, right-click within the Command Prompt window and choose Mark. You'll see a square cursor. To select with the keyboard, hold down the Shift key and use the ←, →, ↑, ↓, PgUp, and PgDn keys to extend the selection through the text you want to select. With the mouse, move the mouse pointer to the far-right edge of the window, hold down the left mouse button, and then drag diagonally through the text you want to select.

Once you've selected some text, press Enter to copy the selected text and also clear the selection. From there, you can paste the copied text into any document that accepts pasted text.

You can paste a command into the window, but it has to be a valid DOS command. Just right-click near the command prompt and choose Paste.

Navigating from the command prompt

Navigating to a particular drive at the command prompt is easy. Type the drive letter followed by a colon and press Enter. For example, entering d: takes you to drive D:. Entering c: takes you to drive C:.

Use the cd (Change Directory) command, just as you did in DOS, to go to a folder on the current drive. Two short cd commands you can use are

- cd\ takes you to the root folder of the current drive.
- cd.. takes you to the parent of the current folder.
- cd *folder* takes you to the subfolder specified by *folder*

Using wildcards

When specifying filenames in most DOS commands, you can use wildcard characters to represent characters in the filename. Use the ? character to represent a single character and the * character to represent multiple characters. For example, a?c.txt would match abc.txt, a2c.txt, aqc.txt, and so on. By comparison, a*c.txt would match abc.txt, a12345c.txt, anotherc.txt, and so on.

A common use for the wildcard is to find all files of the same type, such as *.jpg, which would match all JPG files. So, the following command would list all JPG files in the current folder:

```
dir *.jpg
```

The following section explains how to use the Dir command.

Printing a list of filenames

Perhaps the one thing that the DOS command has that Explorer doesn't is the ability to easily print a list of filenames from any folder, or even a parent folder and all its subfolders. Though you can print directly by following any command with >prn, I'm sure most people would prefer to get that list into a Word or WordPad document. From there you can edit and sort the filename list to your liking, and then print it.

You'll use the dir command to list the filenames. You may find some of the following optional switches useful for controlling how dir displays its output:

- /s — Include filenames from subfolders
- /b — Display filenames in bare format (no headings or summary)
- /w — Show in wide format
- /d — Same as wide, but sorted by columns
- /n — Use long list format with filenames to the far right
- /l — Use lowercase letters
- /o — Sort output by column as follows: N (by name), S (by size), E (by extension), D (by date), - (prefix for descending sort), G (group folder names first)

As an example of using the /o switch, the command dir /on lists filenames in ascending alphabetical order. The command dir /o-s lists filenames by size, in descending order.

Let's look at a practical example. Suppose that you've used Windows Media Player to copy lots of CDs to your Music folder. The songs are organized into folders by artist and album. But you want a list of all song filenames, from all the subfolders.

Step 1 is to get to the parent folder of all the files you want to list. The DOS command would be cd followed by the full path to that folder. For example, cd C:\Users\yourUserName\Music where *yourUserName* is the name of your user account.

Next, you need to enter a dir command with the /s switch to list the filenames from all the subfolders. You can use any other switches in combination with /s. For example, here's a dir command that lists all the filenames in bare format:

```
dir /b /s
```

Here's one that lists files in the columnar wide format with filenames listed alphabetically by name:

```
dir /d /on /s
```

You can try out various DOS commands to see which presents the most reasonable list of filenames. Then, when you get a decent list, enter that command again, but follow it with >filename.txt where *filename* is any name of your choosing. The file will be stored in whatever folder you're currently in. For this example, I'll use SongList.txt as the filename. So, you might enter a command like this at the command prompt:

```
dir /d /on /s >SongList.txt
```

You won't get any feedback on the screen after you redirect the output to a file. You can just exit the Command Prompt window. Then use Windows Explorer to navigate to the folder from which you ran the dir command. You'll find your SongList.txt file there. Right-click it and choose Open With ⇨ Microsoft Word (or whatever program you want to use to edit the file).

Tip

To quickly open a text from a DOS prompt, type the command notepad file.txt, where file.txt is the name of the text file you want to open. ∎

The list will look exactly like DOS output, which might not be ideal. But if you know how to use the program, it shouldn't be too tough to select and delete anything you don't want in the document. Then, save it, print it, and keep it for future reference.

Tip

If you're a Microsoft Office guru, you could create a macro to clean up the output from a DOS command, maybe even convert it to a list of comma-separated values. Then, you could save *that* file as a text file, and import it into an Access table or Excel spreadsheet. ∎

Whether or not this example of exporting filenames is of any value to you, I couldn't say. But it is just an example. If you know DOS, you may be able to come up with more useful applications of your own. You can do anything at the Command Prompt window that you could do in DOS, even copy and delete files. Remember, for a quick overview of all the DOS commands available in the Command Prompt window, just type help at the command prompt and press Enter.

Wrap-Up

Managing files and folders in Windows 7 is a lot like it was in earlier versions of Windows. You just have more ways of doing things. Here's a quick wrap-up of the main topics covered in this chapter:

- To select a single icon to work with, click it (if you're using double-click to open files) or point to it (if you're using single-click to open files).
- To select multiple icons, use Ctrl+Click, Shift+Click, or the drag-through method, whichever is appropriate to your goal and easiest for you to use.
- To move or copy selected files and folders, drag them to some new location, or use copy and paste, or use the Copy or Move options under File and Folder tasks in the Explorer bar.

- To rename a file or selected files, right-click and choose Rename.

- To delete a file or selected files, right-click and choose Delete.

- Small items you delete from your hard drive are just moved to the Recycle Bin.

- Large files, and files you delete from removable media, are not sent to the Recycle Bin.

- To recover a file from the Recycle Bin, right-click its icon and choose Restore.

- To permanently delete all the files in the Recycle Bin and reclaim the disk space they're using, empty the Recycle Bin.

- When you delete a shortcut to a resource, you delete only the shortcut — not the resource itself.

- If you're a DOS guru, you can still use DOS commands to manage files. Click Start and choose All Programs ⇨ Accessories ⇨ Command Prompt to get to the Command Prompt window.

Searching for Files and Messages on Your Computer

Hard disk storage in the twenty-first century is reliable, fast, and cheap. Just about every computer sold in the past few years has lots of it. The result is that people now store many thousands of files on their computers. To organize their folders, people use lots of folders and subfolders. Though it's certainly good to have lots of well-organized files on your hard disk, it has a couple of downsides. For one, drilling down through a ton of folders to get to a specific file gets tedious. For another, it's easy to forget where you put things and what you named them.

In earlier versions of Windows, you could use shortcuts and searches to help with these problems, but too many shortcuts just add that much more clutter to the screen. The old style of searching for things is slow and tedious. Searching for things in Windows 7 is a lot like searching for things on the Internet. You don't have to search for specific filenames. You can search for things by content and meaning. And in most cases the search results are instantaneous. You don't have to wait for the system to slog through the whole file system looking at every file.

Basics of Searching

Like filing cabinets, computers just store information. The information in your filing cabinet has no "meaning" to your filing cabinet. Likewise, the information in your computer has no meaning to the computer. Searching a computer is much like searching through a filing cabinet or the index at the back of a book.

In the next sections, I try to clear up some common misconceptions about searching. Along the way I offer some tips and techniques that should make it easier to find what you're looking for.

You're not asking it questions

The most basic thing you need to understand about searching is that you're not asking the computer a question. Computers don't understand human languages the way people do. As mentioned, searching a computer (or the Internet) is much like searching the index at the back of a book. You need to zero-in on a specific word or phrase. The more specific that word or phrase, the more specific the search results.

Let's use the Internet as an example. You certainly can search for something like:

What is the capital of Kansas?

You will likely get your answer from any Internet search engine. However, you'd probably get the same or similar results if you search for:

capital Kansas

The reason for this is because the "keywords" in the search are "capital" and "Kansas." The other words don't help to narrow the search much. That's because you're searching for words, not meaning. Virtually every page on the Internet contains the words "what," "is," "the," and "of," even if the page has nothing to do with Kansas or capital.

I'm not saying you *can't* conduct a search for "What is the capital of Kansas?" You certainly can if you want to, and you will get results. However, the results won't be much different than if you left out the *noise words*. A noise word is any word that appears in virtually all written documents and doesn't help describe what the page is about. Examples of noise words include the following:

a about an are but did how is it me my of should so than that the then there these they this to too want was we were what when where which who will with would you your

Some search programs will actually remove all the noise words before conducting the search. Others will include them. But sometimes that works against you because you find things in your search results that have nothing to do with what you were really searching for.

The bottom line is this: When you search for something, don't try to word it as a question. Instead, search for an exact word or phrase that has a specific meaning.

Be specific

The key to successful searches, whether on the Internet or on your computer, is to be specific. The more specific you are about what you're searching for, the better the results.

I'll use an Internet search as an example. Suppose I'm looking for quotes by Benjamin Franklin on health. If I search Google for *health*, I get links to about 1.2 billion pages. That doesn't help much because a lifetime isn't enough time to look through all those. If I search Google for *Benjamin Franklin*, I get links to 9.7 million Web pages. That's still too many.

If I search Google for *Benjamin Franklin health*, I get links to 1.5 million pages. If I search for *Benjamin Franklin quotation health*, I get links to 132,000 pages. Now, if I add the word *wise* to the search (because I know the quote contains that word), I get about 19,000 hits. Notice how the more specific words there are in the search, the smaller (and also better targeted) the search results. In fact, one of the first pages listed will probably contain exactly what I'm looking for. The moral of the story being: The more specific the search, the more specific the search results.

Tip

After you've clicked a link to a page, you can search that specific page for a word by choosing Edit ⇨ Find on this page (or pressing Ctrl+F) in Microsoft Internet Explorer. If you use some other Web browser, check its Edit menu or help for a similar feature. ■

Of course, searching the Internet and searching your own computer are two entirely different things, for the simple reason that the Internet exists *outside* your computer, and its searches don't include things that are inside your computer. But the general rule of specificity applies to all searches.

Spelling counts

When you write text for a human to read, you can get away with a ton of spelling errors. For example, the following sentence is loaded with spelling errors but you can probably still figure out what the sentence says:

Th kwik brwn dogg jmpt ovr teh lzy mune.

You can figure it out because you have a brain, and brains have many strategies for figuring things out based on context, the sounds the letters make when read aloud, and so forth. Computers don't have brains and can't figure things out.

Plenty of computer programs are available that can correct your spelling, suggest alternate spellings, and such, but those programs aren't as good as a human brain. I realize that spelling is one of those traits that some people are good at, and some people aren't. But knowing how to spell the words you're searching for is a good thing.

If you're not sure how to spell something, try typing it into a word processing system that has spell checking. Or, if that's not an option for you, try an online service like `www.spellcheck.net` or `www.dictionary.com`. If it's a tech term, try `www.webopedia.com`.

Where you start the search matters

You can search in many different places and for many different kinds of things. Where you start your search and what you search for matters a lot. For example, there's the World Wide Web, which consists of several billion pages of text that exist outside your computer. It makes no sense to search the Internet when you're looking for something that's in your own computer.

Inside your own computer are basically two types of searches to consider. One is a search for *help*. There you're typically looking for instructions on how to perform some task. Chapter 5 provides strategies for getting help with Windows 7. Chapter 14 offers suggestions for getting help with other programs. This chapter has nothing to do with searching for help.

This chapter is mostly about searching for programs, folders, files, and messages that are inside, or directly connected to, your computer; the kinds of things you can use even when you're offline (not connected to the Internet).

How Searching Works

Understanding how searches work in Windows 7 is critical to performing quick, successful searches. Most searches are performed on an *index*. The index is like the index at the back of this or any other book. It's basically a list of key words. Of course, Windows 7's index doesn't contain page numbers. In place of page numbers it contains filenames and locations. You never see the index with your own eyes. The index is built, maintained, and searched behind the scenes without any intervention on your part.

It's Not a Replacement for Search Companion

Readers who are familiar with XP's Search Companion need to realize that the search features in Windows 7 are a whole different ball game. You *can* use Windows 7's search features to find files, but that's just one tiny capability of the overall strategy. The search boxes are more like an Internet

continued

continued

search engine for your own computer. You don't have to look for filenames or wildcard characters. You can look for any word or phrase in any file, as well as file properties.

For instance, if you type `modified:this week` into the Search box at the bottom of the Start menu, you see items modified this week. Try typing the first name of someone in your Contacts folder to see what shows up for that person. If you type `word`, where *word* is a word from a file or Windows Live Mail message, you find all related items. It's all very different from searching for filenames and patterns. And in most cases the results are instantaneous. But you do have to invest a little time in learning how it works to take full advantage of its capabilities.

Some searches you perform will search the entire index. Others will search only for programs, or files, or e-mail messages, or contacts. Still others will ignore the index and search through every single folder on one or more drives. It all depends on where you start the search and how you perform the search. Let's start with common everyday searches that are fast and easy to do.

Tip

The Start menu Search box provides a quick and easy way to open programs, folders, files, and messages. ■

Quickie Start Menu Searches

The quick and easy way to find a program, favorite Web site, document file, contact, or e-mail or newsgroup message is to search right from the Start menu. Press ▨ or Ctrl+Esc, or click the Start button to open the Start menu. The Search box is at the bottom left of the Start menu (see Figure 30-1). It contains the words *Search programs and files*. The cursor is already in the Search box, so you can just start typing. You don't need to delete the words Search programs and files. They're removed the moment you type a character.

As soon as you type one character, the search results appear on the Start menu. Each character you type reduces the search results to include only items that contain those letters. You get instant feedback as you type. So you can just keep typing as many characters as necessary until you see the item you want. The search results are categorized as in the example shown in Figure 30-2.

Here's what each category represents:

- **Programs:** Programs that are currently installed on your computer and ready to use.
- **Control Panel:** Items that are in the Windows Control Panel.
- **Documents:** Documents in your user account files.
- **Music:** Music in your user account files.
- **Files:** Other types of files, including e-mail.

Unlike searches with previous Windows search technologies, Start menu searches don't look only at file and folder names. They look at the contents of files, tags, and properties as well. We talk about what those things are in Chapter 32. I mention it here in case you're wondering why some of the results in the Files group in Figure 32-2 don't show the word "money." It's because the word "live" appears within the message or contact's information.

FIGURE 30-1

Search box at the bottom left of the Start menu.

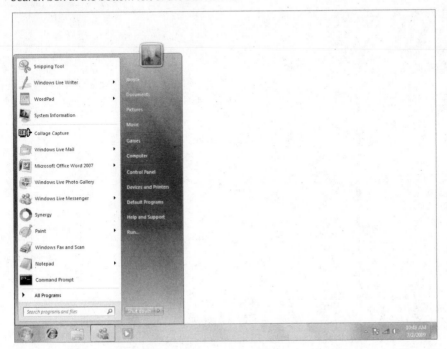

You can do many things with the search results, as follows:

- To open an item, click it.
- To see other things you can do with an item, right-click it.
- If an item you were expecting to find doesn't show up, or if you want to improve the search, click See more results.
- To discard the search results, press Esc or click the Start button again.

You can do wildcard searches from the Start menu, where * stands for any characters and ? stands for a single character. But do keep in mind that when you search from the Start menu, you're only searching the index, not the entire hard disk. So don't be too surprised if some files don't show up.

You can also do AND and OR searches from the Start menu. For example, a search for `*.jpg OR *.jpeg` finds files that have either a `.jpg` or `.jpeg` extension. I talk about these kinds of searches in more detail in this chapter and the next.

Customizing Start menu searches

You can customize the Start menu's search box to include or exclude certain information in search results. Right-click the Start button and choose Properties. On the Start Menu tab of the dialog box that opens, click the Customize button. Scroll down to the options shown in Figure 30-3.

FIGURE 30-2

Results of searching for "money".

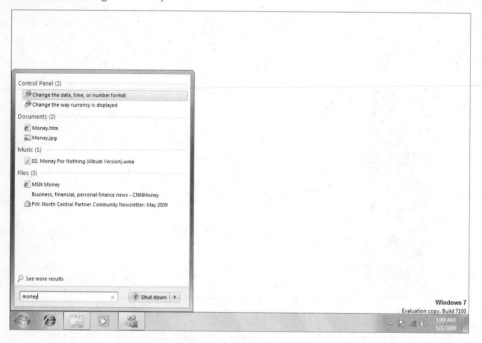

Here's what the two main options offer:

- **Search other files and libraries:** Searches files in the Documents, Music, Pictures, and other standard folders in your user account.

- **Search programs and Control Panel:** Searches through programs accessible from your Start menu and Control Panel.

Don't forget to click OK after making your selections.

Note

See, "Configuring Search Options," later in this chapter to learn how to configure other search settings for Windows 7. ■

Extending a Start menu search

If the thing you're looking for doesn't show up in your search, first check your spelling. Make sure the word you're searching for matches something on your computer. For example, if you're looking for photos of your dog named Spot, a search for Spot won't find them unless the photos have Spot in the filename, tags, or properties.

There isn't a whole lot of space to show things on the Start menu. Some things might not show up just because there isn't enough room. To see more items, click See more results at the bottom of the Start menu.

FIGURE 30-3

Start menu search options.

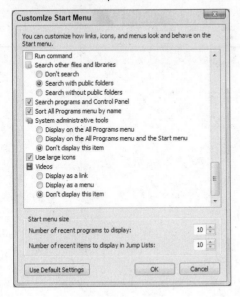

Start menu searches are ideal for finding the kinds of things most people use most often — programs, folders, Control Panel dialog boxes, favorite Web sites, messages, and documents (text, worksheets, pictures, music, and videos). If you're a quick typist, using the Search box can save you a lot of time you'd otherwise spend clicking and opening things through the traditional methods. But Start menu searches aren't the end of the story. Not by a long shot. There's much more, as you'll see.

Tip

The Search box in Windows Explorer's upper-right corner provides a quick and easy way to search the current folder and its subfolders. ■

Searching Folders and Views

By now you may have noticed Windows Explorer has a Search box in its upper-right corner. The Search box, by default, includes text that describes the search context, such as *Search Libraries* as in Figure 30-4.

Like the Search box on the Start menu, the one in Windows Explorer gives you instant keystroke-by-keystroke search results. But this one doesn't search for programs, messages, and such. Instead, this one searches only the current *view*. The view consists of all files and subfolders you see in the main content pane. The Search box in Explorer doesn't look strictly at file and folder names either. It looks at the contents of files that contain text, tags, and other metadata. So once again, you use it in much the same way you use an Internet search engine: Not just to search for a specific filename, but to search for keywords or phrases.

Search box in Explorer (all folders).

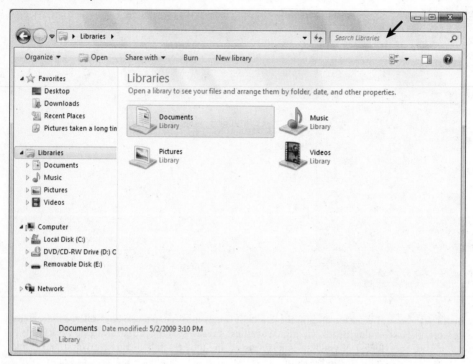

The Search box in Explorer works best when you have some idea where the item you're looking for is located. For example, let's say you have thousands of songs in your Music folder and its subfolders. You want to see all songs in the Jazz genre. Step 1 is to open your Music folder. Step 2 is to type the word Jazz into the Search box. Instantly, you see all songs in the Jazz genre.

You certainly aren't limited to searching a genre. You can type an artist's name to see all songs by that artist. You can type a few characters from a song title. Basically, you can type anything you want to find whatever it is you're looking for. Just keep in mind that you're searching only the current folder or view.

If you're looking for something that's in one of your user account folders, but don't know which one, start by opening your user account folder (click the Start button and click your username). That folder contains all the main subfolders for your user account, as in Figure 30-5. Then start typing whatever it is you're looking for into the Search box. Instantly, you see all files and folders from your user account that match or contain the text you've typed.

Note

Searching subfolders is optional. If you're not getting results from subfolders, you need to change a setting in the Folder and Search Options dialog box. ■

If you don't really want to search all the folders in Figure 30-5, no big deal. Just open (double-click) the folder you *do* want to search, and start your search from that folder's Search box.

FIGURE 30-5

Contents of a user account folder.

When you're first learning to use the Search box in Explorer, there will be times when you don't find a file you might have been expecting to find. This might happen for several reasons:

- The file isn't in the folder you're searching (or one of its subfolders).
- The way you spelled the search term in the Quick Search box doesn't match how it's spelled in the file(s).
- The file you were expecting to find isn't one of the common file types included in file searches launched from Explorer.

If you get more stuff than you were expecting, keep in mind the search isn't looking only at the filenames, or only at the columns you see in the results. It's searching properties that might not even be visible in the Details view and the contents of files that contain text.

Specifying search criteria

Anything you type into a Search box is a *search criterion*. Basically, the search criterion is telling Windows 7 "show me all items that have these characteristics." The *items* are things like files, folders, messages, contacts, and Internet Explorer favorites.

The search criterion can be as simple as a few characters of text. For example, you can click the Start button, type a person's name, and find whatever files and messages on your computer contain that person's name. You can specify search criteria in the Start menu search box, as well as in the Windows Explorer search boxes. You can also use multiple search criteria to locate items. First, let's take a look at how to perform a search using different types of search criteria.

Search by Date

You can narrow your search to specific kinds of dates by adding a date filter to your search. For example, you can search by Date Modified (the last time you opened, changed, and saved the file), Date Accessed (the last time you opened the file), or Date Created. If you are working in the Pictures folder, you can choose Date Taken from the Windows Explorer search box to find pictures taken (created) on a particular day or in a particular date range.

Here's an example. Click the Libraries button in the taskbar to open Windows Explorer. Click in the Search box and then click Date Modified from the drop-down menu that appears. You can then click a date from the date picker or click an option like Yesterday or Earlier this month. Windows 7 then searches in your libraries for the files that meet those criteria.

Although Date Modified is the only date option available when you search at the Libraries level, it isn't the only date criteria you can use to search. For example, you can search by date created, date modified, and last accessed. If you don't see the search option you need, you can type it.

Let's say today is March 31, 2010, and you've just created or downloaded a file. Only you clicked the Save button without choosing where to put the file, and you didn't notice the name of the file. So now you don't know where it is. So, open the parent folder where you downloaded the file, click in the Search box, and type `datecreated:today` to see all files created today. That might help you find the file.

To search for files within a range of dates, choose one of the date criteria (like Date Modified). In the calendar that drops down, click the start or end date. Then hold down the Shift key and click the other date. Or, simply click and drag across the date range with the mouse. Both dates, and all the dates in between, are highlighted (Figure 30-6). Windows 7 displays the files that fill the criteria within that date range.

FIGURE 30-6

Searching a date range.

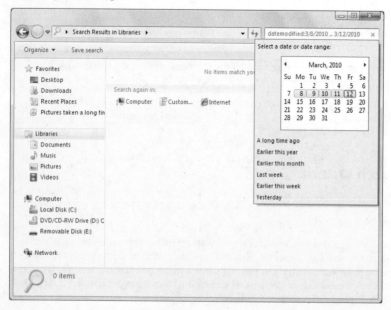

Search by Size

The Size option lets you search for files that are an exact size, or files that are larger or smaller than some size. For example, let's say you bought a second hard drive and want to move some large video files to it. You could search for Size and choose the Gigantic option, which finds files larger than 128 MB. Or, you can specify a particular size, such as 500 MB or 1 GB. To search by a specific size, click the Size option in the Search box and then type a size after the colon. Use the modifiers K for kilobyte, M for megabyte, and G for gigabyte.

Note

A megabyte (MB) is about 1,000 KB (exactly 1,024 KB). A gigabyte (GB) is about 1,000,000 KB (exactly 1,048,576 KB). ■

Search by Filename or Subject

In the Search box, you can type a specific filename or part of a filename. For example, a search for sunset finds all files that have the word "sunset" in the filename. You can use wildcard characters as in earlier versions of Windows (and DOS). Use ? to stand for a single character, and * to stand for any group of characters. For example, let's say you have files named Sunset (1), Sunset (2), Sunset (3), and so forth. A search for sunset* will find them all.

You can include filename extensions to narrow down the search. For example, a search for *.jpg finds all files that have a .jpg extension. A search for sunset*.jpg finds all files that start with sunset and end with a .jpg filename extension.

You can use the word OR (in uppercase letters, with a space before and after the word) to extend the search to multiple criteria. For example, consider the following typed into the Filename box:

*.jpg OR *.jpeg

When you click the Search button, you get all files that have either a .jpg extension or a .jpeg extension. Similarly, you could search for

sunset*.jpg OR sunset*.jpeg

to find all files that start with sunset and end with either .jpg or .jpeg.

You're not limited to just one OR. For example, placing the following in the Filename box

*.avi OR *.wmv OR *.mpg OR *.mpeg

finds all files that end with .avi, .wmv, .mpg, or .mpeg.

Caution

Make sure you use OR, not AND. It's a common misunderstanding that I discuss under "Power Searches" in Chapter 31. ■

If you are searching a folder that contains e-mail messages, you can search using e-mail-specific critiera. For example, you can search for e-mail messages that have a certain word or phrase in the Subject line. There's no need to use wildcards or filename extensions because the Subject line is just text, not a filename. To search by subject, click in the Search box and type subject:(subject text), where subject text is the text for which you are searching. You can also simply type the text in the Search box without the subject: modifier, but you will return results from matches other than in the subject of the e-mail messages. You can use other critiera like From and To when searching for e-mail messages, as well as enter text that appears in the body of the message.

Search by Kind

Windows 7 lets you search by the type of object you want to find. For example, you can search for contacts, documents, e-mail, feeds, folders, games, and more. If you don't see Kind: listed as a search criteria in the Search box, just type that keyword and a menu of object types drops down, enabling you to choose the kind(s) of objects for which to search (Figure 30-7).

FIGURE 30-7

Search by kind.

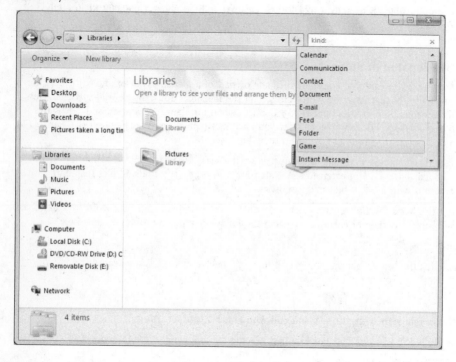

Tip

To search for multiple kinds of objects, use the OR logical operator with multiple kind: specifications. ∎

Search by Tags, Authors, Title, and others

Depending on what type of folder you are searching in, you'll see other boxes like Tags, Authors, or Title for specifying search criteria. These correspond to metadata stored in file properties. You can type in any word or phrase to search for files that have that word or phrase in the corresponding property. I talk more about those properties in Chapter 31.

Saving a search

Searches can be used in two ways. In some cases you might just be looking for a file you've lost track of. In that case, once you've found the file, there's probably no need to repeat the search in the future. You can just double-click the found file to open it. Then close the Search window.

There may be other times when you put some time into constructing a search to pull together files from multiple folders. For example, a search for `*.avi OR *.wmv OR *.mpg OR *.mpeg` shows all video files with those extensions. If you think you'll want to check up on your current video files often, it's not necessary to re-create the search from scratch each time. You can save the search. Any time you want to check up on your current video files, open the saved search. It will show you all *current* files that meet those criteria.

Saving a search is easy. After you've performed the search, you'll see a Save Search button in the toolbar. Just click that button and a Save As dialog box opens. The name of the search will reflect the search criteria you specified. But you don't need to keep that name. Type in any name that will be easy to recognize in the future. For example, in Figure 30-8 I've named a search I'm about to save Video Files. Windows 7 will suggest putting it in the Search folder for your user account. That's as good a place as any to keep it. So don't change that unless you have some good reason. You can also enter an Author name and Tags if you like. Then click the Save button.

FIGURE 30-8

Saving a search for video files.

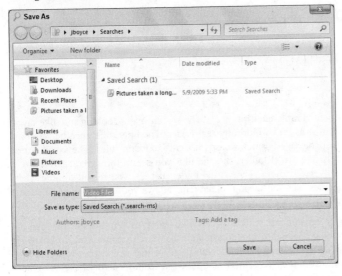

Using saved searches

Unless you specify otherwise, your saved searches are stored in the Searches folder for your user account and a link is automatically added to your Favorites. You can open that using any of the following techniques:

- Click the Start button, click your user account name, and open the Searches folder.

- If you're in a folder and the Navigation pane is open, click the search under Favorites (if available).

- Press ⊞, type `sear`, and click the saved search.

Unless you opened a specific search, the Searches folder opens. You'll see searches you've saved yourself. Figure 30-9 shows an example.

FIGURE 30-9

Saved searches.

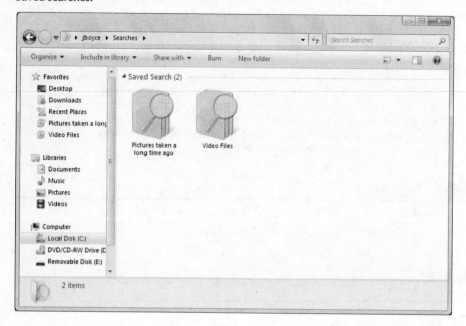

To perform a saved search, just open (double-click) its icon. The search opens looking just like any real folder. In fact, you can treat it just as you would any real folder. The only difference between a saved search and a real folder is that the saved search doesn't actually "contain" files. The saved search is a *virtual folder* that looks and acts like a real folder. But the files you see in the saved search are still in whatever folder you originally saved them. The virtual folder just lets you see all the files that match the search criteria *as though* they were all in one folder. This allows you to work with the files as a unit, regardless of their actual physical location in folders.

A search in Windows 7 is similar to an Internet search. When you search in Windows 7, or open a saved search, you're really just looking at links to files that match the search criteria. But do be aware that when you do something to a file in the search results, you perform that action on the actual file. For example, when you delete a file from a saved search, you delete it from its actual location. Likewise, if you restore that file from the Recycle Bin, you restore it back to its original location.

Wrap-Up

You have many ways to find things in Windows 7. The main points are that you can type a word in the Search box at the bottom of the Start menu to find items that contain that word, or search in Windows Explorer using a wide range of criteria.

For experienced users, the trick is to realize that the Search boxes are not at all like the Search Companion from Windows XP. Each box is more like a mini search engine for finding documents and messages based on content, properties, tags, or name. By default, only items in your user account are searched. If you want to include more items in those searches, see Chapter 31.

Here's a quick review of the main points covered in this chapter:

- Windows 7 has a built-in index of programs, files, folders, and messages in your user account. When you search the index, you get keystroke-by-keystroke results.

- To search from the Start menu, tap the ⊞ key, or press Ctrl+Esc, or click the Start button to open the Start menu. Then start typing your search text.

- To search for a file when you know its general location, open the folder or a parent folder of the item. Then use the Search box in Explorer's upper-right corner to search.

- You can specify multiple criteria in both the Start menu and in Windows Explorer by entering search keywords like datemodified, subject, size, and others, followed by a colon and the search parameter. You can combine multiple criteria in a single search.

- To save a search for future use, click Save Search in the Search window's toolbar.

- To reuse saved searches, click the Start button, click your username, and open the Searches folder. Or click Searches under Favorites (if available) in the Navigation pane of any folder.

If you frequently use files that are outside of your user account folders, see Chapter 31 for info on adding those folders to your search index.

Metadata and Power Searches

Chapter 30 was about different ways you can search your computer. When you search for files, you actually search an index of filenames and properties. The index isn't something you see on the screen. Nor do you have to do anything to create or update the index. Windows 7 takes care of all the details automatically and behind the scenes. The beauty of the index is that it allows Windows 7 to find things much more quickly than it could without the index.

The information about files that's in the index comes from each file's properties. Those properties are sometimes referred to as *metadata* because they're different from the file's content. The file's content is what you see on the screen when you open the file. The file's properties are stored in the file and visible from the file's Properties sheet.

Properties provide a way of organizing files that goes beyond their physical location in folders. This is a great help to people who have many files to manage, because sometimes a simple folder name and filename just aren't enough. Sometimes you want to see all files based on authorship, date created, tags, subject, or even comments you've jotted down about the file. In other words, you want to pull together and work with files in a way that transcends their physical locations in folders. Metadata in Windows 7's indexed searches allow you to do that quickly and easily.

Tip
You can view file metadata in Windows Explorer's Details pane. ■

Working with File Properties

Taking a wild guess, I'd say you can put several thousand different types of files on a PC. No one person needs them all or uses them all. Some are so esoteric you might never come across one. Some of those many different file types support the use of *properties*, some don't.

You can view and edit a file's properties in many ways. One way is to open the folder in which the file is contained, then select the file's icon. The Details pane, if open, display's the file's properties. If the Details pane isn't open, click the Organize button and choose Layout ⇨ Details pane. Or, click the Change Your View button in the toolbar and choose Details.

Initially, the Details pane might be too short to show all the file's properties, but you can drag its top border upward to see more properties. Figure 31-1 shows an example where I'm viewing the properties for a Microsoft Word 2007 document. Other file types will have other properties.

FIGURE 31-1

A file's properties in the Details pane.

Viewing properties sheets

Here's another way to view a file's properties: Right-click its icon and choose Properties. A dialog box opens. If that dialog box has a Details tab, that's where you're most likely to find the kinds of properties you can create and edit. You'll often hear the term *properties sheet* used to describe that set of properties, because it's kind of like a sheet of paper on which properties are written.

Figure 31-2 shows a couple of sample properties sheets. On the left is the properties sheet for the Word document shown in Figure 31-1. On the right is the properties sheet for a JPEG image. When there are more properties than fit in the box, use the scroll bar at the right side of the box to see others.

Every property has a name and a *value*. The value is some text, date, or number that's assigned to the property. In the properties sheets, the property names are listed down the left column. The value assigned to each property (if any) appears to the right of the property name.

Examples of properties sheets.

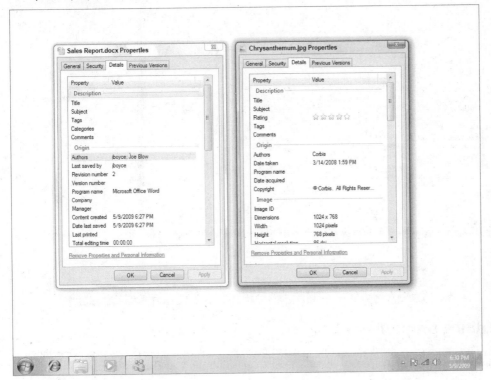

Viewing properties in columns

Yet a third way to view properties is through the Details view in Windows Explorer. In any folder (including the results of a search), click the Views button and choose Details. You'll see a few columns across the top of the contents pane. But what you see isn't necessarily all there is. The horizontal scroll bar across the bottom of the pane lets you scroll to other columns. You can also add columns to the view (or remove columns) by right-clicking any column heading, as in Figure 31-3. The menu that appears shows a few other columns from which you can choose. Click More ... at the bottom of that menu to see others.

Tip

See "Using columns in the Details view" in Chapter 28 for information on choosing, moving, and sizing columns in the Details view. ■

FIGURE 31-3

Choosing columns in Details view.

Editing properties

To change a file's properties, select its icon and make your changes in the Details pane. Or right-click the file's icon, choose Properties, click the Details tab, and make your changes there.

You can change properties for multiple files using the same basic method. You just have to select the icons for the files first. But there is a catch. You'll be limited to changing properties that all the selected files have in common. This can be a real pain when you're working with multiple file types. For example, many different types of files for storing pictures exist — JPEG, TIFF, PNG, BMP, and GIF to name a few. The newer file types, JPEG, TIFF, and PNG, offer many properties. The older file types, BMP and GIF, offer relatively few.

Figure 31-4 shows an example of what can happen when you select multiple file types. There I've selected all the icons in the folder, each of which is a picture. Then I right-clicked one of them, chose Properties, and clicked the Details tab. Hardly any properties are showing because all those different file types have few properties in common.

With old file types that support few properties, about the only thing you can do is convert them to newer file types. For example, I had a lot of GIF images on my system when I installed Windows 7. That file type doesn't offer any really usable properties. So I used the batch conversion feature of my graphics program (Paint Shop Pro) to convert them all to PNG files. I chose PNG because it supports transparency like GIF does.

FIGURE 31-4

Properties for multiple files of different types.

Note
PNG does not support animation, so you may not want to convert animated GIFs to PNG. ∎

If you have many files to which you want to assign new properties, you might consider creating a search that brings similar files together all under one roof, so to speak. Open the Libraries folder (or other folder that is a parent of the one you want to search) and click in the Search box to specify the types of files you want to work with. In Figure 31-5, I typed the following into the Filename box:

```
*.jpg OR *.jpeg OR *.tif OR *.tiff OR *.png NOT *.lnk
```

That brings together all the TIFF, JPEG, and PNG files in the search scope, and omits any shortcuts (.lnk files). (The .lnk files won't have many editable properties either.) Perform the search and then use column headings to sort items based on their current folder location. You can also add columns that allow you to see the properties you intend to work with. Of course, that's just an example. You can set up searches to find and organize things as you see fit.

Save the search when you're done so you can open and use it whenever you have time to work with properties. To change properties for any single file, click its name. To assign the same property value to multiple files, select their icons. Then use the Details pane or properties sheet to make your changes. It will take some time if you have many files to work with. But having all the files together in one place, and the properties of interest in plain view, can make the job less daunting.

FIGURE 31-5

Specify the types of files in the Search box.

Tip

Windows 7's Save As dialog box offers tools for entering metadata when you save a file. ∎

Setting Properties When You Save

Search indexes are nothing new. Database administrators have been using them for decades. Every time you do an Internet search, you're actually searching an index of Web sites somewhere. Windows XP and other operating systems allow for some limited indexed searching through add-on programs. But Windows Vista was the first Windows version to have indexed searching — its own built-in search engine — built in from the ground up. Windows 7 expands on and improves the search capabilities introduced in Vista. Other software developers understand the value of that. As the years roll by, new versions of old programs will include the ability to tag files and set properties at the moment you first save the program.

When you save a new file, be sure to look around for any options in the Save As dialog box that allow you to add tags or properties. Figure 31-6 shows an example where I'm in the Save As dialog box for a Microsoft Word 2007 document. As you can see, the dialog box allows me to add tags and authors right on the spot.

FIGURE 31-6

Save As dialog box for Word 2007.

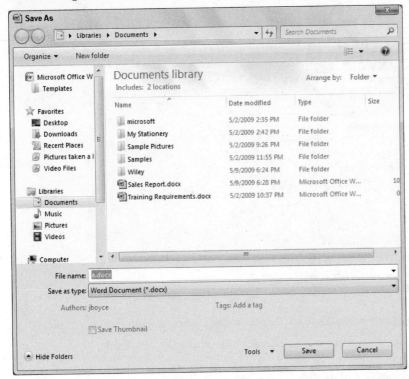

When you're faced with such options, think about words you might want to type into a Search box to find the file in the future. Ask yourself, "If I need this thing six months from now and forget its file name, what word might I use to search for it?" or "How should I categorize this file in relation to other similar kinds of documents?" As your collection of files grows, and your searching skills grow, the few moments you spend thinking up keywords for tags and properties will pay off in spades.

Tip

You have many options for personalizing and configuring Windows 7's Search tools. ■

Personalizing Searches

Getting the most from Windows 7's searches includes knowing how to tweak its settings to work in ways that support the kinds of things you do. You can tweak some aspects of indexed searches through the Folder and Search Options dialog box. To get to the search options, do any of the following:

- If you're in a folder, click the Organize button and click Folders and Search Options.
- Press ▉ or click the Start button, type fol, and then click Folder Options.

FIGURE 31-7

Search options.

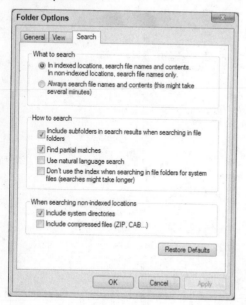

The Folder Options dialog box opens. Click the Search tab to see the options shown in Figure 31-7.

The first set of options under What to search dictates how searches are performed:

- **In indexed locations, search file names and contents. In non-indexed locations, search file names only:** This is the default setting and gives the best performance for searching documents, messages, and such.

Tip

If some files aren't showing up in your searches because they're not in your user account folders, these options really won't help. Better to extend the index to include those files. I talk about how you do that in the next section. ■

- **Always search file names and contents (this might take several minutes):** This option forces searches to look at the contents of non-indexed files, which can really slow things down. Better to index the non-indexed document files to get the speedier index searches.

The How to search options affect different aspects of Windows 7 searching. The Include subfolders in search results when searching in file folders causes Windows to search not only in the current folder, but also in any subfolders of the current folder when searching for files.

The Find partial matches option, when selected, lets you type a few characters into the Search box and still get a match. For example, let's say you have numerous files with the name Sarah in the filename, Artist name, or other property. When you type sar into the Search box, you see those items that contain Sarah. But if you clear the Find partial matches checkbox, it won't work that way. You wouldn't see items that contain Sarah until you typed all five characters, sarah.

The Use natural language search is an interesting option related to typing search criteria directly into the Search box. I talk about that under "Power Searches" later in this chapter. But here's the gist of it: If you don't choose that option, you have to type queries following strict syntax. For example, typing the following into the Search box on the Start menu displays all Windows Live Mail messages from George that contain the word "lunch":

```
from:george about:lunch
```

The following example would work, but only if Use natural language search is selected in the Search options:

```
from alan about lunch
```

The advantage is that the natural language option relaxes the rules, so that if you forget the colons the search still works. But sometimes that works against you because when you don't follow stricter syntax rules you can't always be sure exactly how Windows 7 is interpreting the query. How you see the query, and how Windows 7 sees it, might be two different ways. So the results from the search might not be what you were expecting.

The Don't use the index when searching in file folders for system files (searches might take longer) option applies when you search non-indexed locations. When you select that option, searches outside the index work like non-indexed searches from older Windows versions. The search looks at every file in every folder and doesn't even look at the search option. When you leave that option unselected, the search still uses the index for files in indexed locations. So that part of the search goes quickly. Then it falls back to the old non-indexed method, but only for files that aren't indexed.

The last two options apply only when you're searching non-indexed locations. Choose Include system directories if you want non-indexed searches to include Windows and other program files that are essential to proper functioning of your PC. These are not files you normally open or modify yourself. So it would only make sense to choose this option if you're a power user or administrator who needs frequent access to files in those locations. Otherwise you're just slowing down your searches for no good reason.

Choosing the Include compressed files (ZIP, CAB ...) option extends the search into compressed Zip folders and the like. Typically, people only use those for *archived* files that they don't use often, because the compression and decompression add some time overhead to opening and closing the files. Including their contents in searches can also slow down searches. But if you want to include those files' contents in your non-indexed searches, just select the check box.

As always, clicking Restore Defaults sets all options back to their original defaults. Those are the options that provide the best performance for indexed searches, and cover the things most people would typically want included in their searches.

Managing the Search Index

To get the best performance and value from the search index, you want to make sure it includes all of the files you regularly use in your work. But you don't want to go overboard and also include files you never, or rarely, use. If you do, you're forcing it to search through thousands of filenames and properties for no good reason. By default, Windows 7 maximizes the search index by including messages and documents from a limited number of folders.

Of course, many people use multiple hard disks to store their files. If you want to include files from other drives and folders, you'll need to add them to your search index. But do exercise some discretion. The larger the index, the more overhead involved in maintaining the index and the slower things go. Don't add a folder to the index if it contains a bunch of non-document files or files you don't open and use regularly.

Tip

Some indexing settings can be changed by regular users. Advanced settings can only be changed by a user with administrative rights. ■

What's with the Offline Files?

Offline files are files that primarily exist on some other computer. You use Sync Center, described in Chapter 48, to copy them to and from a portable notebook in a way the prevents the copies on your computer from becoming out of sync with copies on the main computer. The files are included in the search index, by default, because they're usually documents. And the search index is all about finding and opening documents quickly.

You can exclude offline files from the search index just by clearing the check box in the Indexed Locations dialog box. Any user can do that; administrative privileges aren't required. If you don't use offline files, there's no overhead to leaving that option selected. After all, if you don't use offline files, the folder is empty. It takes no time at all to index an empty folder.

Adding and removing indexed locations

Windows 7 indexes a certain set of folders by default. You can add or remove locations through the Indexing Options dialog box (Figure 31-8). Here are the steps:

1. Open the Indexing Options item from the Control Panel to open the Indexing Options dialog box.

2. Click Modify.

3. Expand drives and folders, as necessary, to get to the folder(s) you want to add. Use white triangles to expand, black triangles to collapse.

Caution

Items with checkmarks are already indexed. Don't clear any checkmarks unless you specifically want to remove that folder from your index. If you goof and lose track, click Cancel to leave the dialog box without saving any changes. ■

4. Select (check) the folder(s) you want to add. Choosing a folder automatically chooses all subfolders, so there's no need to select those individually. But you could clear the checkmark on one if you wanted to exclude it from the index. Those excluded folders will show up in the Excluded column in Indexing Options.

5. Click OK.

FIGURE 31-8

Indexing Options.

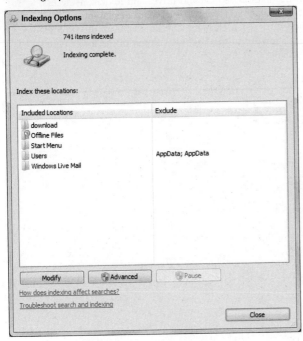

The folder is added to the index without any fanfare. About the only change you'll see is that the folder name appears in the Index These Locations list in Indexing Options. Use the scroll bar to the right of that list if the folder name isn't immediately visible. Also, if you look at the text near the top of Indexing Options, you'll see the number of items indexed.

If you're actively using the computer, you see a message indicating that indexing speed is reduced due to user activity. Not to worry, it just means that the index-building process is giving priority to things you want to do. The message is replaced by others when the index is being built at full speed, and when indexing is compete.

You can add as many folders as you wish, from as many drives as you wish, using those same methods. But again, prudence is a virtue. Remember, don't add folders just for the heck of it or because you don't know what's in a given folder. The more you can keep your index focused on files you want to find in searches and access through virtual folders, the better performance you'll get from the index.

Tip

With administrative rights, you can click Show All Locations in the Indexed Locations dialog box to show additional folders that are not shown by default. These include Offline Files folders for all users, rather than just the current user. You can also view user folders for users other than yourself when you click Show All Locations. ∎

Remove a location from the index

Removing a folder from the index is the opposite of adding one. Repeat the preceding steps to get to the Indexed Locations dialog box shown in Figure 31-9. Expand drives and folders, as necessary, so you can see the items you've selected (checked). If you want to exclude some subfolders from one of your indexed folders, expand that folder first. Then clear the checkmarks from the subfolders you don't want in the index. Those subfolders show up in the Exclude column in the lower pane of the dialog box. Click OK after making your changes.

FIGURE 31-9

The Indexed Locations dialog box.

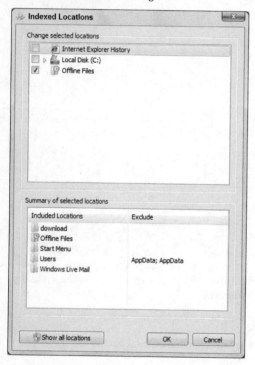

Choosing file types to index

The index intentionally excludes unknown file types, certain kinds of executable files, and libraries, because they're not normally the kinds of things you want to locate in a quick file search or virtual folder. You can add any file type you wish to your index, and you can remove any file type you don't want to see.

Filenames and properties of selected file types are always indexed. For files that contain text, like word processing documents and spreadsheets, you can choose whether or not to index file contents. The advantage of indexing file contents is that when you search for files, the file shows up even if the search term isn't in the filename or properties. The slight disadvantage is that it adds some size to the index. But in this case I think the advantage of including file contents probably outweighs the cost, unless you're using older, slower hardware and your searches are very slow.

To change options for file types, starting from the Indexing Options dialog box:

1. Click the Advanced button (enter an administrative password if prompted).

2. In the dialog box that opens, click the File Types tab. You see a list of all file extensions as in Figure 31-10:

    ● To include a file type, select its check box.

    ● To exclude a file type, clear its check box.

    ● If you opted to include a file type, choose whether you want to index properties only or properties and contents.

3. To add a file extension that isn't in the list, type the extension next to the Add button and click the Add button.

4. Click OK after making your changes.

FIGURE 31-10

Choosing file types to index.

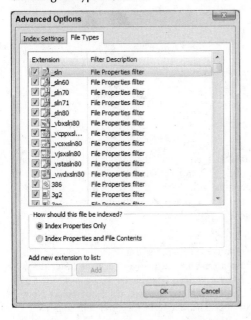

More advanced options

You can make some more advanced tweaks to the index to change how it operates. You'll see them when you first click the Advanced button in Indexing Options. Figure 31-11 shows those advanced options on the Index Settings tab.

Choosing Index encrypted files ensures that encrypted files are included in searches and virtual indexes. People encrypt files to keep prying eyes out. Keeping those same files out of the index adds another layer of security by making them invisible to basic file searches. But if that's not a problem for you and you want your encrypted files to show up in searches, just choose the option to index encrypted files.

FIGURE 31-11

Index Settings tab.

A *diacritic* (or diacritical mark) is an accent mark added to a letter to change a word's pronunciation. Some examples include the acute accent (á), circumflex (ˆ), and umlaut (ä). When used in file-names and properties, Windows 7 usually treats characters with diacritics as being identical to the character without the mark. Choosing Treat similar words with diacritics as different words changes the search behavior so that the diacritics are no longer lumped together as though they were a single character.

The Index location option lets you specify where you want to store the search index. The default is the c:\programdata\microsoft folder. If you have a separate hard drive that runs faster than your C: drive, you could relocate the index to that drive for better performance. Just make sure you choose a drive that's always attached to the computer, not a removable drive. Click the Select New button and use the Browse for Folder dialog box that appears to navigate the drive and folder in which you want to store the index.

Rebuilding the index

If you see error messages about a corrupt index, or the system is crashing when you try to perform a search, the problem might be a corrupted index. You can rebuild the index to see if that helps, but the process could take several hours. So if at all possible, you might consider doing this job as an overnighter. The process is simple: Just click the Rebuild button on the Index Settings tab of the Advanced Options dialog box shown in Figure 31-11.

You can continue to use the computer while the index is being rebuilt. Any searches you perform while the index is being rebuilt will likely be incomplete.

Power Searches

The ability to click the Start button (or press , type a few characters, and see all items that contain those characters is really a great thing. For most people it'll save a lot of time otherwise spent opening programs or navigating through folders to open a program, document, contact, or message. It's so useful you might not even need to bother with more complex searches.

When you do need a more complex search, you can just use the Search box in Windows Explorer to search for particular types of files, and limit the search by date, filename, size, or whatever. You can create complex searches and save them. When you want to do the same search again in the future, that's handy too. For folks who want still more, there's the query language.

You may have noticed that after you fill in the blanks in an Advanced Search and click the Search button, you see some text in the Search box. Take a look at Figure 31-12 for an example. There I set the date criterion to Date modified 5/9/2009. This puts the following into the Search box:

```
datemodified:5/9/2009
```

FIGURE 31-12

Sample search.

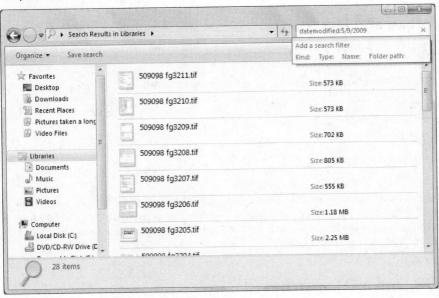

That little line of text, called a *query*, in the Search box is what's actually returning the search results. When you perform the search, Windows 7 actually looks through the whole index. But the query acts as a filter of sorts. Only items that meet the conditions set forth by the query show in the search results. In this example, only files whose Date Modified date is 5/9/2009 show in the search results. Items that don't match the criterion don't appear in the search results. Those items aren't deleted or changed in any way. They're simply "filtered out" so as not to show up in the search results.

You can type your own queries into the Search box to perform complex searches. But, it's not as simple as "asking a question" or typing a bunch of words at random. You have to follow some rules and write the query in such a way that it can be interpreted properly. Otherwise, the search returns the wrong items, or no items at all. The sections that follow look at some ways you can type your own complex queries.

Searching specific properties

When you type a word into the search box, the results show files that contain that word in their filename, contents, and properties. For example, a search for jazz finds songs in the Jazz music genre, any folder or file that has the word jazz in its filename or contents, and any file that has the word jazz in any property. In other words, you could end up with a whole lot of files in the search results.

You can always narrow a search down by specifying a property name followed by a colon and the text for which you're searching. For example, a search for genre:jazz finds only music files in the Jazz genre.

Similarly, a search for susan finds all files that have Susan somewhere in the file, name, or a property, whereas a search for from:susan finds only e-mail messages that have the name Susan in the From address (for a local e-mail client, not a Web e-mail client).

You can assign ratings to pictures and music files, and use ratings as a search word. For example, rating:5 stars finds files with 5-star ratings.

Greater than and less than

When you're searching a property that contains a date or number, you can use the following comparison operators:

- =: Equal to (this is assumed if you don't specify an operator below)
- >: Greater than
- >=: Greater than or equal to
- <: Less than
- <=: Less than or equal to
- <>: Does not equal

A search for rating:>=4 stars finds pictures and music with 4- or 5-star ratings. A search for width:<600 finds pictures with widths less than 600 pixels. The query modified:<2007 finds files last modified in 2006 or earlier. A search for kind:video size:<300KB finds video files less than 300 KB in size.

AND, OR, and NOT searches

You can use the keywords AND, OR, and NOT in searches. You must type the word in uppercase letters. Be sure to include a space before and after the word.

Not using any word is the same as using AND. For example, consider the following search:

Datemodified:5/9/2009 name:koala

That means the same thing as this:

Datemodified:5/9/2009 AND name:koala

Any time you create an AND query, you *narrow* the search results. Intuitively, you might think it would have the opposite effect. But that's not the way it works. The query is a filter. In order to show up in the search results, a file must meet *all* criteria posed by the filter. For example, files that don't have *koala* in the filename property won't show up at all, no matter what's in their Date Modified property. And files that were modified on dates other than 5/9/2009 won't show up either, even if they do have *koala* in the filename field.

Here's a common mistake that might help to better illustrate. Take a look at this:

```
filename:(*.jpg AND *.jpeg)
```

Intuitively, you might expect the result of this search to be files with .jpg and .jpeg extensions. But it's not. The result of this search is nothing! Why? Because the criterion is a filter, not a question. In order to get through the filter, a file would need to have a .jpg extension *and also* a .jpeg extension. But a file can't have two extensions. Every file has only one filename extension. Therefore, no single file could get past this filter.

When you want to *broaden*, not narrow, a search, you use OR. For example, take a look at this:

```
filename:(*.jpg OR *.jpeg)
```

To get past this filter a file needs to have either a .jpg *or* .jpeg extension. So the result of the search is all files that have either a .jpg or .jpeg filename extension.

Tip

If you don't see filename extensions in search results, click the Organize button and choose **Folder and Search Options**. Then click the **View** tab, clear the checkmark next to **Hide extensions for known file types**, and click **OK**. ■

By the way, you don't have to use the * and dot if you use extension:, ext:, or type: as the property name. For example, this search criterion also shows all files that have .jpg or .jpeg extensions:

```
ext:(jpg OR jpeg)
```

You're not limited to a single OR. Here's a search that shows all files that have .avi, .wmv, .mpg, and .mpeg extensions:

```
ext:(avi OR wmv OR mpg OR mpeg)
```

When you use type: you can use whatever appears in the Type column (in Details view) rather than the extension. For example, this search finds Microsoft Word documents:

```
type:word
```

This one finds Word documents that have the word John in the filename or inside the document text:

```
john AND type:word
```

Because the keyword AND is assumed if omitted, the following works the same as the preceding one:

```
john type:word
```

If you want to look only at the filename and not the contents, use the name: property. For example, here's a query that looks for Excel spreadsheets that have the word Festival in the filename:

```
name:festival type:excel
```

In addition to searching for extensions, you can use `kind:` to find certain kinds of files. For example, `kind:music` finds music files; `kind:picture` finds pictures; `kind:contact` finds contacts; `kind:e-mail` finds e-mail messages; and `kind:communication` finds messages and contacts.

The NOT keyword narrows a search by excluding items that match the criterion that follows. For example, when you use the `kind:` keyword you get both the file type as well as shortcuts that open the file type. To hide the shortcut files, use `NOT shortcut`. For example, here's a search criterion that shows all communications files excluding any shortcuts to those files:

```
kind:(communication NOT shortcut)
```

A search for `kind:video` shows all video files. This search shows all video files except the ones that have a `.mov` filename extension.

```
kind:video NOT extension:mov
```

It's not always necessary to specify the kind or type of file. For example, consider this query:

```
homecity:Cucamonga
```

That one finds all contacts whose Home City is Cucamonga. Because Contacts are the only type of file that have a Home City property, you'd probably only get contacts in the search results even without specifying `kind:contact`.

You can use `tag:` as a search property too. For example, the query `tag:(alec OR ashley)` finds files and that have either Alec or Ashley in the Tags property. The query `tag:(alec AND Ashley)` finds files that have both the names Alec and Ashley in the Tags property.

If you use the Comments and Categories properties in files, use `comment:` and `category:` to search just those properties. Similarly, you can use `title:` to search the Title property and `subject:` to search the Subject property.

Date and number searches

When searching for files based on a date, you can use the following property names for specific dates:

- **modified:** Date the file was last modified.
- **accessed:** Date the file was last opened.
- **created:** Date the file was created.
- **sent:** Date that a message was sent.
- **received:** Date that a message was received.
- **taken:** Date that a picture was taken.

To search a range of dates, use the keywords followed by a start date, two dots (..), and an end date. For example, to find all pictures taken between June 1, 2007, and September 1, 2007, use the criterion:

```
taken:6/1/2007..9/1/2007
```

You can also use comparison operators with date searches. For example, to see all files modified on or after January 1, 2007, use:

```
modified:>=1/1/2009
```

You can also use the following keywords with dates:

`today`

`tomorrow`

`yesterday`

`this week`

`last week`

`this month`

`last month`

`next month`

`this year`

`last year`

`next year`

For example, this search finds all files modified today:

`modified: today`

This search shows all files that were created this week:

`created:this week`

Here's a query that lists all picture files that were taken this month:

`taken:this month`

To see all files modified between some date (say 1/1/2009) and today, use this query:

`modified:>=1/1/2009 AND modified:<=today`

If you're interested in a certain month and year, use the month name and year like this:

`modified:july 2009`

For a day of the week, use the weekday name like this:

`modified:monday`

The comparison operators work with numbers too. When searching sizes, you can use KB, MB, and GB abbreviations. For example, here's a search criterion that finds all files that are 1 MB or greater in size:

`size:>=1MB`

Here is one that finds files larger than 2 GB in size:

`size:>2GB`

Here's one that finds files between 500 KB and 1,000 KB in size:

`size:>=500KB AND size:<=1000KB`

If you save music in various bit rates, here's a query that will find all files with bit rates greater than 300 kbps:

```
bitrate:>=300kbps
```

If you wanted only mp3 files with those large bit rates, use:

```
bitrate:>=300kbps AND type:mp3
```

Here's a query that finds all pictures whose height is 800 pixels or less:

```
kind:picture height:<=800
```

Searching for phrases

When searching for two or more words, you'll likely end up with documents that contain the words you specified, but not necessarily in the order you typed them. To prevent that problem, you can enclose the phrase is quotation marks. For example, typing this into a Search box displays all files that contain the words *dear* and *wanda* regardless of their relative positions to one another:

```
dear wanda
```

But typing the following into a Search box displays files where the words *dear* and *wanda* appear right next to each other in the document:

```
''dear wanda''
```

Message searching

For Windows Live Mail messages (both e-mail and newsgroup), key properties include to:, from:, about:, subject:, sent:, and received:. Both to: and from: can contain any word that appears in the To: and From: columns in the message. The about: keyword looks at the contents of the messages, not just the subject line. For example, here is a query that you could enter in the Search box on the Start menu that finds all messages from someone named Kay that contain the word *lunch*:

```
from:kay about:lunch
```

Here's a query that shows all messages addressed to Alan that arrived today:

```
to:alan received:today
```

Here's a search that shows all messages addressed to Susan, sent by Alan, that have *contract* in the Subject line:

```
to:susan from:alan subject:contract
```

Here's a query for e-mail messages sent this week from Alan to Wanda that contain the words chow mein:

```
to:wanda about:''chow mein'' from:alan sent:this week
```

Natural language queries

Earlier in this chapter you saw an option titled Use natural language search in the Folder and Search Options dialog box. If you choose that, you can omit the colons after property names, and use uppercase or lowercase letters in search queries. This really does make it easier to type most queries. For example, with natural language, the following query finds all messages from Susan that contain the word *dinner*:

```
from susan about dinner
```

This search finds all video files excluding ones with an `.avi` filename extension:

`kind video not avi`

Here's the natural language version of the query about chow mein e-mail messages:

`to wanda about chow mein from alan sent this week`

Here's a query that finds all files whose size is greater than 5 megabytes:

`size > 5MB`

Here's a natural language query that finds all songs by Led Zeppelin:

`music by zeppelin`

This natural language query finds all pictures that have the word *flower* in the filename:

`flower pictures`

Here's a natural language query that finds all files that contain the word *peas*, the word *carrots*, or both words:

`peas or carrots`

Here's a natural language search that finds files that contain the word *peas* and the word *carrots* (though not necessarily together):

`peas and carrots`

Here's one that finds files that contain all three words, *peas and carrots*, together:

`''peas and carrots''`

Looking for a file you just downloaded or saved today? Try this natural language search in the Search box on the Start menu:

`created today`

Here's a natural language search that lists all files modified yesterday:

`modified yesterday`

Here are some other natural language searches you can probably figure out without my telling you what they mean:

`e-mail received today`

`e-mail from alec received yesterday`

`contact message`

`pictures alec`

`genre rock`

`artists Santana`

`rating 5 stars`

Using natural language syntax doesn't mean you can ignore all of the other things described in this chapter. The folder from which you start the search still matters. And all of the other options in the Folder and Search Options and Indexing Options dialog boxes still apply. But in most cases you can type a useful search query with minimal fuss. If you can't get a search to work, try turning off natural language searches and use the stricter syntax with colons after property names.

Wrap-Up

Windows 7's searching and indexing features are a far cry from the Search Companion and other simple search tools of yesterday. Windows 7 searching isn't really about finding lost files, though you can certainly use it for that. But if you use it only for that, you're missing out on the big picture and some key features of Windows 7.

Windows 7 searches use an index of filenames, properties, and file contents to make searches quick and nimble. It also looks only at files in the search index, because that's a lot faster than slogging through the entire file system to look at every file in every folder. But it only works right if your index includes all the locations where you keep your frequently used document files.

One thing is for sure. If you've been managing thousands of files in hundred of folders, and are sick of opening programs and folders to get to things, you're sure to love the new search index. Maybe not at first, because you really have to understand what it is and how it works. And you may have to spend some time tweaking settings in a couple of dialog boxes. But once you're past that small bump in the road, you'll spend a lot less time *getting to* things, and a lot more time *doing* things!

Here's a summary of the main points covered in this chapter:

- The search index includes information about files stored in the file's properties sheets.
- When you select a file in a folder, the Details pane shows the properties currently assigned to the file.
- You can also view a file's properties by right-clicking its icon and choosing Properties. Most editable properties are on the Details tab.
- File properties are also visible in any folder's Details view. That includes virtual folders (saved searches).
- The search index generally covers all files in your user account, people in your Contacts folder, and Windows Live Mail messages.
- The Folder and Search Options dialog box provides some options for personalizing searches.
- The Indexing Options dialog box provides a means of customizing the index to better suit how you organize your files.

Using CDs and DVDs

CDs (compact disk) and DVDs (digital versatile disk) are media for storing information. In that regard, they're like any other type of storage media, such as hard disks. But unlike those other types of disks, CDs and DVDs are *optical* media, not magnetic media. That means they use a laser rather than a magnet to read and write data to and from the disk.

When you copy information to a CD or DVD, the laser essentially *burns* the data to the disk. That's why copying files to CDs is commonly referred to as *burning* to the disk.

This chapter focuses on the tools included in Windows 7 that you can use to use and create CDs and DVDs. First, let's take a quick look at the different types of optical media.

Understanding CDs and DVDs

Even though CDs and DVDs look exactly alike, there's a big difference in capacity. A CD holds about 650–700 MB of data. A DVD holds about 4.7 GB (or about 4,700 MB). In other words, one DVD can hold more information than six CDs. This is also why albums are sold on CDs and movies on DVDs — there isn't enough room on a CD to store a feature-length movie.

The newest media type, Blu-ray, has the same physical dimensions as CDs and standard DVDs, but uses a blue-violet laser that has a shorter wavelength than the red laser used on older formats. This shorter wavelength makes it possible for Blu-ray media to hold up to 50 GB (using dual-layer media). Because of its higher capacity, Blu-ray offers better image quality for movies than standard DVD. However, you must have a Blu-ray drive to play Blu-ray media.

To complicate matters, many different kinds of CDs and DVDs are available, including CD-ROM, CD-R, CD-RW, DVD-R, DVD-RW, DVD+R, DVD+RW, and DVD-RAM. So let's untangle that mess, starting with the most common types of disks — the CD-ROM and DVD-ROM.

Tip

CD and DVD drives have a top speed, indicated by an "x" number, such as 52x. This is the top burn speed, measured as a factor of the playback speed (which is 1x). Generally, the speed is irrelevant unless you are burning a lot of CDs or DVDs and need to reduce the amount of time it takes. If that's the case, buy a high-speed drive and blank media that has an equivalent or higher maximum burn rate. ∎

CD-ROM and DVD-ROM

The ROM in CD-ROM and DVD-ROM stands for *read-only memory*. The term "read only" means you can read (or play) the contents of the disk whenever you want. The disk is not *writable*. You can't add new files to the disk, remove files from the disk, or change files that are already on the disk.

CD-R, DVD-R, and DVD+R

The R in CD-R, DVD-R, and DVD+R stands for *recordable*. These are often referred to as *distribution media* because they're the blank disks that software companies, record companies, and the movie industry use to stamp out thousands of copies of the programs, albums, and movies they sell. In other words, they buy -R disks to create the -ROM disks that they sell you.

CD-RW, DVD-RW, DVD+RW

The RW in CD-RW, DVD-RW, and DVD+RW stands for *read/write*. The -RW disks are often called *backup media*. You can use a CD-RW, DVD-RW, or DVD+RW disk to back up important files. You can erase the disk and start over if you like, and you can delete individual files. In short, the -RW disks are much more like hard disks, just not as fast!

Data CD versus audio CD

CDs come in two capacities, commonly referred to as *data CDs* and *audio CDs*. A data CD has a capacity of about 650 MB, or enough space to store about 74 minutes worth of music. Those are best to use when your goal is to use the CD to store backup copies of files on your hard disk, or to distribute copies of files to other people.

An audio CD has a capacity of about 700 MB, or enough space to store about 80 minutes worth of music. Those are best to use when you want to create your own custom music CDs to play in your car stereo or in a CD player. You use Windows Media Player (Chapter 23) to create those custom music CDs.

DVD- versus DVD+

There are two DVD standards to consider, although the differences have little to do with DVDs as used in computers. They're more subtle differences having to do with how DVDs store data for watching movies on TV. So for the average computer user, choosing between a + and — DVD is largely a matter of knowing what works with your DVD player, DVD burner, and whatever other equipment you have.

Note

The only way to find out which types of disks your DVD equipment can handle is from the documentation for that specific equipment. As a rule, the DVD+ disks are compatible with more DVD players than the DVD-R disks. ∎

Disc, Disk, What's the Difference?

The only difference between a "disk" and a "disc" is the spelling. Computer people usually spell it "disk." The people who invented CDs and DVDs decided to spell it "disc." But no matter how you spell it, it's a medium on which you can store information. I'll use "disc" in places you're likely to see it spelled that way. Otherwise I'll stick with "disk" only because that's the way you'll see it spelled in other places throughout the book.

What Kind of Drive Do I Have?

If you just purchased a new computer, you might not be sure what type of drive you have. Getting information about your CD/DVD drive isn't difficult. You can get some information right from your Computer folder. First make sure there isn't a disk in the drive. Then open your Computer folder and take a look at the icon for the empty drive. The icon and description should provide some clues. To get more information, you can right-click that icon, choose Properties, and click the Hardware tab for more specific information. For example, in Figure 32-1, drive D: is a DVD/CD-RW drive.

FIGURE 32-1

Icon and Properties for a DVD drive.

There's also a System Information window you can use to get specs on your system. Click the Start button, type **sys**, and click System Information on the Start menu. In the window that opens, click the + sign (if any) next to Components and click CD-ROM. The pane to the right shows detailed information about the drive as in the example shown in Figure 32-2.

Unfortunately, knowing the make and model of the drive doesn't tell you all the different types of disks it can handle. For instance, the Hitachi drive shown previously can read and write virtually all CD and DVD disk types, but there's no indication of that in either figure. After you know the make and model of the drive, you can search the manufacturer's Web site for the model number for more detailed specs. Or you can use a general search engine like Google or Bing to search for both the make and model name (HL-DT-ST in my example).

FIGURE 32-2

System Information about a CD/DVD drive.

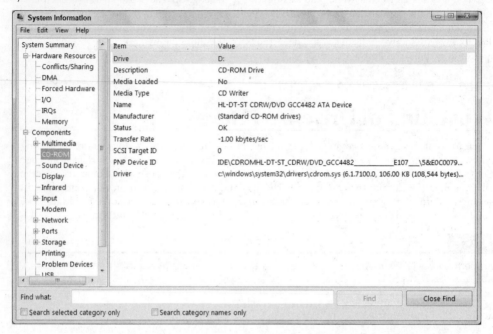

Of course, there's always the old-fashioned method of calling your computer manufacturer on the phone, or contacting them by e-mail, and asking about the drive. At the very least, you'll need to know the model of your computer. Then ask them what kinds of disks the drive can handle.

Using Disks that Already Contain Data

Using disks that already have information on them isn't too tough. Starting with the basics, if you have a DVD drive, you can read (use) both CD and DVD disks. If you have a CD drive, you can only use CD disks.

Playing the kind of CD that you buy in a music store is usually pretty easy. You stick the CD in your CD drive and, most likely, Windows Media Player will play it for you. To copy songs from that kind of CD, you *rip* the CD in Media Player. See Chapter 24 for the goods on how all that works.

To watch a DVD movie, you stick the DVD in your DVD drive and hope it plays. If you have a CD drive (not a DVD drive), it won't play at all. To copy files from DVDs, you typically have to use DVD ripping software.

Note
If you have Windows Media Center, that program might open rather than Media Player. See Chapter 26 for information on Media Center. ■

Exactly what happens when you insert a CD or DVD really depends on your AutoPlay options. Generally, Windows 7 does a pretty good job of figuring out what to do. For example, you might see an

AutoPlay dialog box asking what you want to do with the CD. The options in that dialog box depend on the contents of the disk and the programs installed on your computer. Figure 32-3 shows a general example. You just click whichever option describes what you want to do.

FIGURE 32-3

Sample AutoPlay dialog box.

Then again, nothing at all may happen after you insert a CD or DVD. It all depends on the type of drive you have, the type of disk you put in the drive, and how you've configured AutoPlay options. But no matter what happens, you can use your Computer folder to view the disk's contents.

What kind of disk is this?

As discussed in Chapter 28, every disk drive on your system is represented by an icon in your Computer folder. To open your Computer folder, click the Start button and choose Computer.

Tip

If you want your icons to look like the ones in the examples shown here, click the Views button in the toolbar and choose Tiles. ■

When your CD or DVD drive contains a disk, its icon changes to show some basic information about that disk. If the drive can handle that type of disk, the icon shows the disk type. If there's any empty space on the disk, you'll see just how much space there is. Figure 32-4 shows several examples using a single icon and how it looks with different types of disks in it. The figure shows three examples, but different icons are possible depending on the media type inserted in the drive.

FIGURE 32-4

Examples of a CD/DVD drive icon containing different disks.

Viewing a disk's contents

To see what's already on the CD or DVD in a drive, right-click its icon in your Computer folder and choose Open. You'll see its contents in Explorer. As with folders on your hard disk, any folders on the CD appear as manila file folders. Files are represented by document icons; if the disk is empty, no icons show.

Copying files from a CD or DVD

To copy files or folders from a CD, use any method described in Chapter 29. But first, if you skipped straight here without reading anything else, some quick reminders on when *not* to use the method described here:

- To copy songs from a commercial CD where songs are titled Track1, Track2, and so forth, and have .cda extensions, rip the CD using Windows Media Player (Chapter 24).
- To copy a movie from a video DVD that has a folder named Video_TS, use DVD ripping software to copy and convert to a more computer-compatible format such as .avi, .mpg, or .wmv.

Tip

Often you can copy the .vob files to a folder on your hard disk, then change the extension to .mpg. Typically the largest .vob file is the most important one. Smaller .vob files are often just background video scenes. ■

What's Video_TS and Audio_TS?

DVD Video disks (the kind of DVD disks you rent at video stores or create using Windows DVD Burner) store data in folders with names like Video_TS and Audio_TS. DVD players (the kind you connect to a TV) expect to find folders and files like that. The Audio_TS folder may be empty because it's commonly used for DVDs that contain music rather than video.

For other types of CDs that you or someone else created using a computer, the more traditional file-copying techniques from Chapter 29 will do. For example, you can select any icons and drag them to a folder name in the Navigation pane. Or open the destination folder in a separate Explorer instance and drag right into the folder as shown in Figure 32-5.

Note

You must drag to a specific drive or folder name in the Navigation pane. It won't work if you drag to empty space within that pane. ■

You can also use the copy-and-paste method from Chapter 29 to copy from a CD or DVD. If you specifically want to send the selected items to your Documents folder, right-click any selected icon and choose Send To ➪ Documents.

Tip

Windows 7's AutoPlay applet makes it easy to control CD and DVD behavior. ■

FIGURE 32-5

Copy from a CD or DVD by dragging.

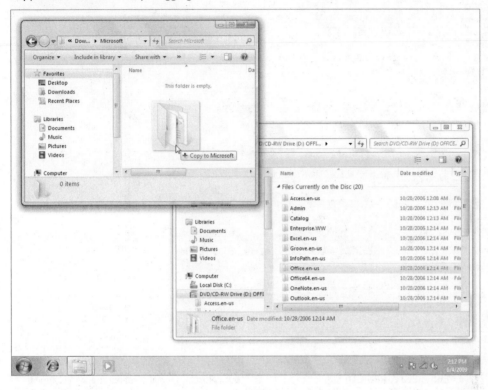

Changing what happens when you insert a CD or DVD

When you insert a CD or DVD into your CD or DVD drive, just about anything can happen. Exactly what happens depends on what kinds of files are on the disk and how Windows is configured to deal with those files. To configure how Windows responds to various types of CDs, use the AutoPlay program. To open AutoPlay, use whichever technique is easiest for you:

- Tap 🪟, type **auto**, and click AutoPlay on the Start menu.
- Click the Start button and choose Control Panel ➪ Programs ➪ Default Programs ➪ Change AutoPlay Settings.
- Right-click your CD or DVD drive's icon in your Computer folder and choose Open AutoPlay. Then click View More AutoPlay Options in Control Panel.

Regardless of which method you use, AutoPlay opens looking something like Figure 32-6. To ensure that your options play out, first make sure that the Use AutoPlay for All Media and Devices check box is checked. Then you can set options for responses to different types of CD content as summarized here.

- **Audio CD:** A commercial audio CD (the type you buy at a music store and can play in any stereo).

FIGURE 32-6

AutoPlay options (use scroll bar to see all options).

- **Enhanced Audio CD:** Similar to Audio CD, but contains special visual content that appears only when played in a computer.
- **DVD Movie:** A commercial DVD like you buy or rent in a video store.
- **Enhanced DVD Movie:** Similar to DVD Movie but with advanced features for computers and advanced playback equipment.
- **Software and Games:** A CD or DVD that contains a program or game you can play.
- **Pictures:** A CD or DVD that contains only picture files.
- **Video Files:** A CD or DVD that contains video files, such as the .wmv movies you create using Windows Movie Maker.
- **Audio Files:** A CD or DVD that contains compressed non-commercial music files stored in .wma, .mp3, or a similar format.
- **Blank CD:** An empty CD-R or CD-RW disk.
- **Blank DVD:** An empty DVD-R, DVD+R, DVD-RW, or DVD+RW disk.
- **Blank BD:** A blank Blu-ray disk.
- **Mixed Content:** A CD or DVD that contains two or more different kinds of files. For example, worksheets, word processing documents, pictures, and video clips.
- **HD DVD Movie:** A High-Definition DVD.

- **Blu-ray Disc Movie:** Similar to high-definition video but provides capacities up to 25 GB per disk.

- **DVD-Audio:** A DVD disk that contains music, no video.

- **Video CD:** Also known as a VCD, a CD that contains a movie.

- **Super Video CD:** Also known as SVCD, similar to Video CD with better quality and resolution.

The options available to you for each kind of disk depend on the programs installed on your computer. But some options apply to virtually all types of disks:

- **Ask Me Every Time:** When you insert a disk you'll see the AutoPlay dialog box with options relevant to the type of disk you inserted. That way you can decide what you want to do right on the spot.

- **Play <media type> using Windows Media Player:** Open Windows Media Player automatically and begin playing the media.

- **Open Folder to View Files using Windows Explorer:** When you insert a disk, Windows Explorer will open automatically to show you the contents of the disk.

- **Take No Action:** Absolutely nothing will happen on the screen after you insert the CD.

You're free to pick and choose whatever works for you. If ever you want to get things back to the way they were originally, click the Reset All Defaults button at the bottom of the AutoPlay window. Whatever options you choose, bear in mind that they won't be applied until you click the Save button at the bottom of the AutoPlay window.

Copying Files to Blank CDs and DVDs

When you put a blank CD or DVD in your drive, it'll take a few seconds for the disk to settle in. Then Windows will take whatever action you specified in AutoPlay. For example, if you chose Ask Me Every Time, you'll see a prompt like the example in Figure 32-7. Your choices are as follows:

FIGURE 32-7

Sample AutoPlay prompts for blank CDs and DVDs.

- **Burn . . . using Windows Media Player:** Choose this option if you want to copy music, pictures, or video from your Windows Media Player Media Library to the disk. You're taken straight into Windows Media Player. See "Burning DVD Data Disks with Media Player" later in this chapter for more information.

- **Burn a DVD Video Disc using Windows DVD Maker:** Choose this option to make a DVD you can watch on TV from video files, such as movies you created with Windows Movie Maker. You're taken straight to Windows DVD Maker.

- **Burn Files to Disc using Windows Explorer:** Choose this option if you want to copy any kind of files from any folder to the disk for use in this computer or another computer.

Assuming you opted to burn files using Windows, you see a dialog box like the one in Figure 32-8. The disk title need not be the date. You can replace that with a title of your own choosing, up to 16 characters in length.

Enter a brief title here.

Now you get to make some more decisions. Basically you get to choose between creating a Live File System disk (also called a UDF disk) or a Mastered disk (also called Mastered ISO). A Live File System disk is preferred if you want to treat the disk like a flash drive, where you can add and delete files at will. A Mastered disk is preferred only if you intend to use the disk in CD or DVD players, or computers that don't have Windows 7, Windows Vista, or Windows XP installed. You cannot delete individual files from a Mastered disk.

Here's how to proceed based on the kind of disk you want to create:

- If you want to create a Live File System (UDF) disk, and the disk being compatible with Windows XP or later isn't an issue for you, choose the Like a USB Flash Drive option and click Next.

- If you want to create a Mastered disk, choose With a CD/DVD Player.

If you didn't choose the Mastered (ISO) option, it will take a few seconds for Windows to format the disk. An Explorer window opens so you can start adding files to the CD. Because the disk is empty, you won't see any icons. You'll see Drag Items to this Folder to Add Them to the Disc where the disk's contents would otherwise appear.

Windows 7 by default will format an LFS disk using UDF 2.01, which is compatible with Windows XP or later. If you want to use a different format, you need to format the disk ahead of time using the Format command in My Computer. See "Formatting CDs and DVDs" later in this chapter for details on how to do that.

Tip

For a good discussion of different disk formats and compatibility, click the Which One Should I Choose link in the Burn a Disc dialog box. ■

When you have both the source folder and the disk's contents open in separate windows, size and position both the source and destination windows so you can see at least a portion of each, like in Figure 32-9. Then select and drag folders and files to the destination window (the window that shows the contents of the CD or DVD).

Drag items from any location (source) to the CD/DVD (destination).

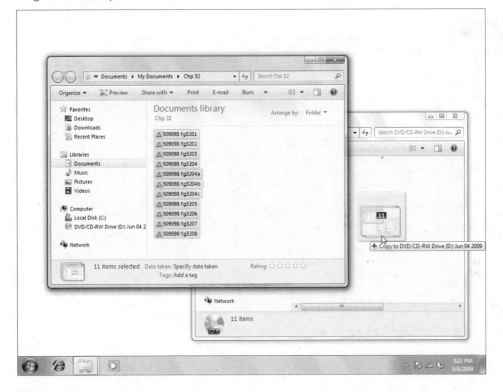

Tip

Right-click the current time in the lower-right corner of the screen and choose Cascade Windows to get the windows to a good size. Then drag the destination window down and to the right. See Chapter 2 for the basics on moving and sizing program windows. ■

You can navigate around through the source window and drag items from multiple locations into the destination window. You can keep doing that until the disk is full, or until you've copied all the files you want to copy, whichever comes first.

When you've finished copying files to the disk and want to remove it, push the eject button on the drive door. But don't expect the disk to pop out right away. It'll take about 15 to 30 seconds for

Windows 7 to close the session so the disk can be read in other computers. Just wait for the disk to pop out on its own. Don't try to force it. Don't worry, you'll still be able to add more files to the disk later, even after the session is closed.

Burning a Mastered (ISO) disk

If you chose the Mastered (ISO) format for the disk, icons for the files you drag into the disk's Explorer window are dimmed and show little arrows. That's because they're *temporary files* waiting to be burned to the CD. You'll also see reminder notifications, in the tray, telling you that there are files waiting to be written to the disk. You don't need to respond to that immediately. You can wait until all the files you intend to copy to the disk are in the window.

FIGURE 32-10

Files waiting to be burned to Mastered (ISO) disk.

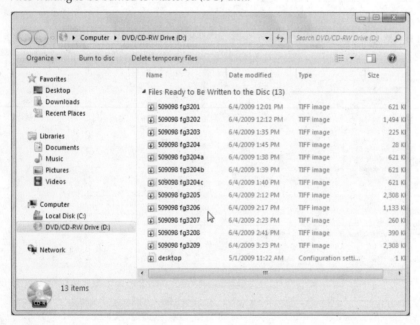

Tip

To remove a temporary file, right-click its icon and choose Delete. To remove them all, click the Delete Temporary Files button on the toolbar. Note that the original files will remain intact in their original locations. You're only removing the temporary file icons so the files aren't burned to the CD. ■

When you're certain you have temporary files for all the items you intend to copy to the disk, click the Burn to Disc toolbar button. You'll be prompted to add or change the disk title and choose a burn speed. Click Next, wait for the disk to be written, and then click Finish. Click the eject button on the drive to remove the disk.

Closing a Live File System (UDF)

When you copy files to a Live File System CD-R, DVD-R, or DVD+R disk and click the eject button, Windows closes the session so that the disk can be read by other computers. If, for whatever reason, the disk doesn't close and its contents don't show up in another computer, don't fret. You can bring the disk back to the computer in which you created it and close it there. Here's how:

1. Put the disk back into the CD or DVD drive on the Windows 7 computer (the same computer you used to create the disk).

2. If the AutoPlay dialog box opens, click the Close (X) button in its upper-right corner to take no action.

3. Open your Computer folder.

4. Right-click the drive's icon and choose Close Session.

The closing puts a little information about the disk contents onto the disk, which makes the disk readable to other computers. But it doesn't prevent you from adding more files to the disk later, so you're not making any big commitment when you close a session.

Adding more files later

You can add more files to your CD or DVD at any time in the future. Put the disk back in the drive. If the AutoPlay dialog box opens, click Open Folder to View Files. Or, right-click the drive's icon in your Computer folder and choose Open. Either way, the current disk contents will be visible in a standard Explorer window. Add more files by dragging them into that window, just as you did the first time.

Erasing Disks

Many writable CDs and DVDs can also be erased. But you have to erase the entire disk. You can't pick-and-choose individual files unless it's a Live File System (UDF) RW disk.

Before you erase a disk, be aware that the act is permanent. There is no Recycle Bin or other safety net. So if the disk contains the files that you value, and you have no other copies, copy the files to a folder on your hard drive *before* you erase the disk!

To erase a disk, first put it in the drive. If AutoPlay opens, choose Open Folder to View Files. If nothing happens, open your Computer folder to see the disk's icon. Then right-click and choose Open to view the disk's icon. The rest is easy:

- To erase the entire disk, click Erase this Disc in the toolbar (visible in Figure 32-11).

- To delete a single file, right-click its icon and choose Delete.

- To delete multiple files, select their icons and press Delete (Del), or right-click a selected icon and choose Delete.

Tip
Format CDs and DVDs so you can treat them like magnetic media. ∎

FIGURE 32-11

Erase entire disk from toolbar.

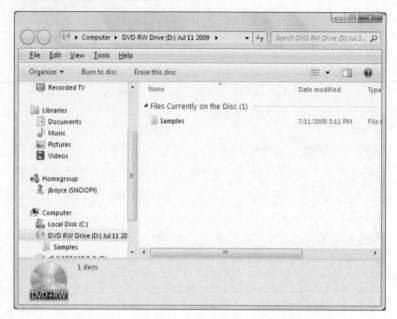

Formatting CDs and DVDs

You can format CDs and DVDs in two basic ways: Mastered (ISO) and Live File System (UDF). The Mastered (ISO) format is compatible with almost everything. When you create CDs to play in stereos or DVDs to watch on TV, Mastered (ISO) is usually selected for you because they're the only ones that play in such devices. The Mastered (ISO) format is also compatible with virtually all computers.

The Live File System (UDF) format is much more specialized. Its advantage is that you can copy files directly to the CD using drag-and-drop. There's no need to take the extra step of burning temporary files to the CD. The disadvantage to Live File System (UDF) is its incompatibility with CD players, stereos, DVD players, and even other computers. Exactly how compatible a UDF disk is with other computers depends on the UDF version you use as listed here:

- **UDF 1.50:** Compatible with Windows 2000, XP, and Server 2003. May be unreadable by Windows 98 and Apple computers.

- **UDF 2.00**: Compatible with Windows XP (and later) and Windows Server 2003 (and later). It might not be compatible with Windows 98 and Windows 2000.

- **UDF 2.01:** Compatible with Windows XP and Windows Server 2003. Earlier Windows versions and Apple computers might not be able to read these disks. This format is used if you don't specify another.

- **UDF 2.50:** Designed specifically for use in Windows Vista or Windows 7. Don't use this format if you intend to copy files from the disk to a computer that doesn't have Windows Vista or Windows 7 installed.

You can format a CD in a couple ways. When you first attempt to use a blank CD, you'll likely be presented with an option to title the CD. If you don't specify otherwise, the CD will be formatted in UDF 2.01 format.

You can also format a CD or DVD straight from the Computer folder. You might need administrative privileges when you take this approach. Right-click the disk's icon and choose Format. The dialog box shown in Figure 32-12 opens.

FIGURE 32-12

Format dialog box.

To choose a UDF version, choose a UDF option from the File System drop-down list. You can't, and don't need to, choose Mastered (ISO) here. That's because a Mastered (ISO) disk is really one that isn't formatted at all. If you want that kind of format, just click Close without formatting.

The Volume Label is the title of the CD. The Quick Format option is available only if the disk has already been formatted. The other options don't apply to CD or DVD disks and can't be changed. After choosing your options, click Start to format the disk.

Note
The 4.37 GB capacity you see for a DVD is normal, even when it says 4.7 GB on the disk. Capacities tend to be rough and vary depending on whether or not you format the disk. ∎

Tip
Copy files from folders to CD or DVD on-the-fly in Windows Explorer. ∎

Burn as You Go in Explorer

As discussed in Chapter 28, Windows Explorer is the program used to explore stuff *inside* your computer. When you're viewing the contents of a folder, you may notice a Burn toolbar button (see Figure 32-13). Clicking the Burn button adds the selected files to the disk.

FIGURE 32-13

Burn button in Explorer.

Anyway, the basic idea is to treat the disk as you would a flash drive. Leave the disk in the drive as you browse from folder to folder on your hard drive. When you come across a file you want to copy to the disk, select its icon. Or select multiple icons that you want to copy to the disk. Then click the Burn toolbar button. When you're ready to burn the files to disk, open the target drive in My Computer and click Burn to Disc in the toolbar, or right-click the drive in My Computer and choose Burn to Disc.

Tip

Create your own custom DVDs with Windows 7's built-in DVD Maker. ∎

Using Windows DVD Maker

Windows DVD Maker lets you create DVDs that play in any DVD player, so anyone who has a TV and DVD player can watch the disk you create. They don't need a computer. Some things to consider before you use DVD Maker:

- Your computer must have a DVD burner.
- The type of disk you use must be compatible with your DVD burner and DVD player. For general distribution to family and friends, DVD+R disks may be your best bet.
- If the video you want to put on a DVD is currently on video tape, use Windows Live Movie Maker to import the tape.
- You can add video, still pictures, or both to the DVD. Still pictures will play as a slide show.
- If your computer supports DVD+RW and DVD-RW disks, you can practice burning disks to those. That way if you're not happy with the results, you can erase the disk and start over. The RW disk may not work with your DVD player, but you should be able to watch it on your computer.

If you've ever rented a movie on DVD, you know that the movie typically opens to a main menu with options for viewing different content on the DVD. For example, you can click Scenes to choose specific scenes to watch. The DVDs you create with DVD Maker can also have an opening menu and scenes menu. You can design both menus in DVD Maker. The first step, of course, is to open the DVD Maker program.

Opening Windows DVD Maker

Before you open Windows DVD Maker, make sure you put a writable DVD into your computer's DVD burner. Then you can use any of the following methods to start DVD Maker:

- If an AutoPlay option appears, click Burn a DVD Video Disc using Windows DVD Maker.
- Click the Start button and choose All Programs ➪ Windows DVD Maker.
- Tap ⊞ , type **dvd**, and click Windows DVD Maker on the Start menu.

Adding photos and videos

After the Windows DVD Maker program starts, click Choose Photos and Videos. The main page for choosing photos and videos to put on a DVD is (appropriately) titled Add Pictures and Video to the DVD. Click the Add Items button to proceed. A typical Open dialog box titled Add Items to DVD opens.

In the Open dialog box, navigate to a folder that contains pictures or videos you want to add. These will likely be in your Pictures and Videos folders (unless you put them somewhere else). When you get to the folder that contains items you want to add to the disk, select their icons and click Add. Optionally, you can double-click a single icon to add it to DVD Maker. Figure 32-14 shows files added in Windows DVD Maker.

Files stored in incompatible file formats, like .mov videos, won't show up in the Open dialog box unless you choose All Files from the file type drop-down list. You'll need to convert those to a compatible format before burning to DVD. Use a third-party program like DeskShare's Digital Media Converter (www.deskshare.com) or AVS Video Tools (www.avsmedia.com) to convert the files.

FIGURE 32-14

Windows DVD Maker.

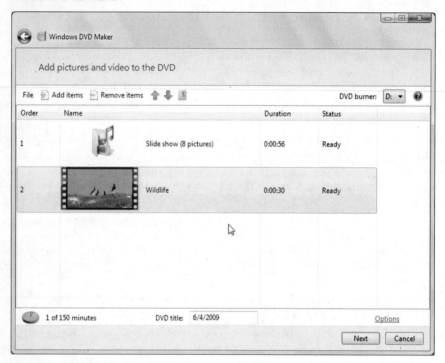

Note
Use any technique described under "How to Select Icons" in Chapter 29 to select icons in the Open dialog box. ■

You can click Add Items as many times as necessary to add all the items you want. Photos will be grouped together in a folder titled Slide Show. Each video will appear as its own icon.

Look to the indicator at the bottom-left side of the window to see how you're doing in terms of disk consumption. If you go over the limit, the indicator will show how far over you are. If you need to remove an item, right-click its name in the main pane and choose Remove, or click the item and click Remove Items in the toolbar. To change an item's position, click it and use the up and down arrows in the toolbar to move it up and down.

To make changes within a slide show, double-click the Slide Show folder and use the same tools to make your changes. Then click the Back to Videos button (to the right of the arrow buttons) to get back to the larger view.

Choosing DVD options

Near the lower-right corner of the window, you'll see an Options link. Click that to see the options shown in Figure 32-15 and described here:

- **Start with DVD Menu:** This is how most commercial DVDs work, by showing a menu of options before playing video.

FIGURE 32-15

DVD Video Options.

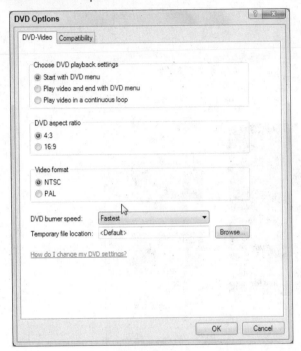

- **Play Video and End with DVD Menu:** The DVD starts playing as soon as it's in the DVD player without showing a menu. The menu doesn't appear until all items have played.

- **Play Video in a Continuous Loop:** The DVD never displays a menu. The video on the DVD plays continuously until removed from the DVD player.

- **4:3 Aspect Ratio:** Choose this option for playback on regular television screens.

- **16:9 Aspect Ratio:** Choose this option for playback on widescreen TVs.

- **NTSC:** Choose this option if the DVD will be played on DVD players in the United States and other countries that follow National Television Standards Committee standards.

- **PAL:** Choose this option if the DVD will be played in countries that follow PAL specifications.

- **DVD Burner Speed:** Choose a burn speed. Slower speeds are more reliable than faster speeds.

- **Temporary File Location:** Leave this empty unless you're certain your hard disk doesn't have enough free space to hold the temporary file created briefly during the burn process.

Make sure of your selections and click OK.

Optionally, fill in a title in the DVD Title text box near the bottom of the page. It's not necessary to fill the disk to capacity. When finished choosing videos and photos, click Next. You'll see a preview similar to that shown in Figure 32-16.

FIGURE 32-16

Ready to burn videos and pictures.

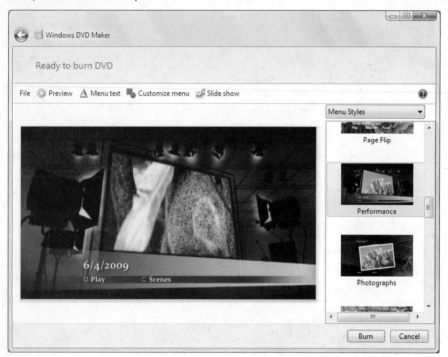

Designing the menus

Now you have the option to create a menu for your DVD. Of course this only makes sense if you didn't choose the option to show the DVD as a continuous loop in the Options dialog box. Scroll through all the styles in the right pane to find the one you want, and click that style. Click the Preview button to get a preview of how it will look when people play your DVD on their TV.

Tip

If you create your own custom styles, use the drop-down list at the top of the right pane to switch between Custom Styles and the built-in menu styles. ■

After you've chosen a basic menu style, feel free to style other aspects to your liking using the Menu Text, Customize, and Slide Show options described next.

Customize menu text

Clicking Menu Text takes you to a page where you can customize the text that shows on your DVD menu. Choose a font from the Font drop-down list. You can also choose to add boldface or italics, or change the font color.

Caution

Be sure to choose a font color that contrasts well with your selected background. Otherwise, the text will be difficult or impossible to see! ■

You can also change the wording of the DVD Title, Play Button, Scenes Button, and Notes Button. Use the Notes box to add your own personal text to the title as in the example shown in Figure 32-17. (The notes show on the screen when the person who is viewing the DVD clicks the Notes button on his or her screen.) To get a better look at how your text selections will look on the DVD, click the Preview button.

FIGURE 32-17

Menu Text options.

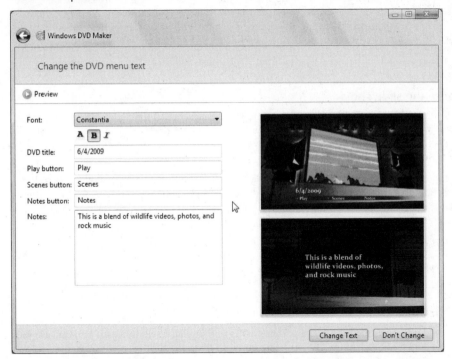

When you're happy with your changes, click the Change Text button.

Tip

The small preview screens to the right show how your changes affect the DVD's opening menu (top), and the screen that appears if the viewer clicks the Scenes button (bottom). If they're too small to see, you can enlarge the page to full screen by clicking the Maximize button near the upper-right corner. ■

Customize the menus

Click the Customize Menu button to style the DVD screen menu pages. The menu pages usually show some content from videos on the DVD, but you can use the Browse buttons to choose different videos or a still picture. As you browse through folders that contain pictures and video, only compatible files will show. If a file doesn't show, that means it's not an acceptable format for DVD Maker. Click the Browse button next to the Menu Audio option to choose a song or other sound file to play as background music while the menu is on the screen. You can use any unprotected wav, mp2, mp3, or wma song as the background music.

The Scenes Button Styles button lets you choose a style for buttons on the scenes menu bar. When you choose an option, the bottom preview pane shows how the buttons will look on the screen.

Click the Preview button in the upper-left corner to see how your choices will look on the DVD. At first you'll see the opening menu page. Click the Scenes button there to see the scene selection menu. After viewing the scene selection menu, click Menu near the bottom of the page to return to the DVD's menu. Click OK when you've finished previewing.

If you think you might want to use the same settings you've chosen here in future DVDs, click Save as New Style, give the style a name, and click OK. Styles you save appear down the right column of DVD Maker's program window when you choose Custom Styles from the button at the top of that pane.

If you don't want to reuse the same style in future DVDs, just click the Change Style button.

Customize the slide show

Any photos you added to the DVD are displayed as a slide show. Click the Slide Show button to customize how your slide show plays (Figure 32-18). You can choose background music for the slide show, and automatically adjust the duration of the slide show to match the duration of the music. Or, can set how long you want each picture to show.

You can choose from a variety of transitions to play between photos in the slide show. Choose Random to use multiple transitions between pictures. The Pan and Zoom check box ensures that still photos show some subtle motion during the slide show. Clear that check box to have each photo hold steady during the show.

Click the Preview button to see how your slide show will look with your current selections. When you're happy with your selections and slide show, click the Change Slide Show button. If you want to cancel your choices, click Don't Change.

Make the DVD

To create the DVD, click the Burn button. Then there's nothing left to do but wait. You can use the computer for other tasks while the DVD is being burned. When the disk is complete, remove it from the drive. When you exit DVD Maker, you'll be asked if you want to save your project. Choosing Yes saves all of your selections so you can make more copies of the DVD later, or make changes to it.

If you used a DVD disk that's compatible with your DVD player, put the DVD into the player and you should be able to watch it on TV. You can work its menus with your remote control as you would any other DVD movie.

If you copied to a DVD-RW for practice, you can still play the DVD on your computer using Windows Media Player or Media Center. On the computer screen, use the mouse to work the DVD menu. If you're not happy with the movie and want to try something else, you can erase the RW disk and reuse it to create a different DVD.

When all is said and done, close Windows DVD Maker by clicking its Close (X) button. You'll see a message asking if you want to save your project. The project consists of the items you chose to put on the DVD and all your customization selections. It's a good idea to save the project, because that will allow you to make more copies of the DVD. You can also change the project in case you decide to do something different with future DVDs. So click Yes and enter a name for your project. By default, the project will be saved to the Videos folder in your user account. That's as good a place as any to store the project. If you prefer a different location, just click the Browse Folders button and choose a different location. Then click Save.

FIGURE 32-18

Change slide show settings.

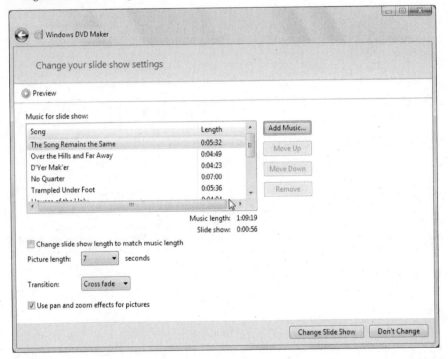

Tip

You need not burn the DVD before saving a project. You can close DVD Maker at any time and save your project, or click the File button in DVD Maker and choose Save Project. Also, understand that saving a project doesn't create a single project file with all of the photos and / or videos in that file. The project file only contains the definition of the project, not the content. ■

Opening a saved DVD project

When you want to burn another copy of a DVD, or resume work on a previously saved project, open the folder in which you stored your project. If that's the default Videos folder, click the Start button, click your user account name, and open your Videos folder. The icon for a saved DVD project looks like the example shown in Figure 32-19. Or, you can simply open DVD Maker and click File ➪ Open Project File, then select the existing project file and click Open.

FIGURE 32-19

Icon for a saved DVD project.

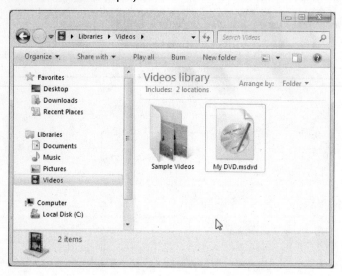

Double-click the icon of the project you want to open. DVD Maker opens with all of the videos and pictures you added. Any customization settings you chose before saving the project are still intact. If you just want to burn another copy of the DVD, click the Next button and then click Burn. If you want to change things before burning a DVD, use the same tools you used when creating the initial project:

- To change the disk title, use the DVD Title box near the bottom of the program window.
- To change how the video plays, use the Options link near the bottom of the program window.
- Click Add Items to add more items to the DVD.
- To remove a video from the DVD, click it and then click Remove Items.
- To reposition an item, click it and use the up and down arrows in the toolbar to move it up or down.
- To delete or rearrange pictures in a slide show, double-click the Slide Show folder and use the Remove Items and arrow buttons to make changes. Then click the Back to Videos button (just to the right of the arrow buttons).

To save your changes, click File in the toolbar and choose Save. You won't be prompted for a new filename. Your changes are saved to the current project. If you want to retain the original project and save the changed version as a new project, click the File button, choose Save As, and give this new project a different filename. To make a DVD from your new project, click Next and then click Burn.

DVD Maker help and troubleshooting

For more information on DVD Maker, and help with troubleshooting, click the Help button (blue button with question mark) in the DVD Maker program. Or click the Start button, choose Help and Support, and search for DVD Maker.

Wrap-Up

This chapter has been about the confusing world of CDs and DVDs. These disks use lasers, rather than magnets, to read and write data. Hopefully this chapter has given you the information and skills you need to use all the different kinds of CDs and DVDs. Here's a summary of the key facts:

- CDs and DVDs look the same, but there's a big difference in capacity. One DVD holds more information than six CDs.
- Virtually all DVD drives can handle CDs, but CD drives can't handle DVDs.
- The -R and +R disks are *recordable*. But once you burn a file to an -R disk you can't delete it or update it with a newer version of the file. These are mainly used to create music CDs for stereos and video DVDs for TVs.
- The -RW and +RW disks are reusable, in that you can erase information you've previously burned to the disk. These are preferred for making backup copies of important files.
- Use the AutoPlay Control Panel applet to choose what happens each time you insert a CD or DVD.
- To create CDs and DVDs that work like magnetic disks for storing computer files, use the Live File System (UDF) format.
- To create the kind of DVDs you can watch on a TV, use Windows DVD Maker.

Protecting Your Files

Some things on your hard drive are valuable. Music you purchase online costs money. Pictures and videos from digital cameras are irreplaceable. Documents you spent hours creating required an investment of your time. You wouldn't want to lose those things because of some technical problem or mistake you made, so it's a good idea to keep backups. That way, if you do lose the originals on your hard drive, you can just restore them from your backup copy.

In addition to the files you create and use yourself, many *system files* reside on your hard drive. These are files that Windows 7 needs to function properly. If those files get messed up, your computer may not work correctly. So you need some means of backing up those system files as well.

This chapter explains how to back up both your personal files and your system files. Of course, the backups won't do you any good if you can't use them when you need them. So, of course, I talk about how to use those backups should the need ever arise to get your system back in shape. I also talk about System Protection, which keeps copies of some files around temporarily, to help you fix minor mishaps on the spot, without having to fumble around with external disks.

Simple File Backups

A simple way to back up items from your user account is to copy them to an external disk. You can use any of the methods described in Chapter 29 for copying files to accomplish this sort of backup. You just need to make sure that the disk to which you're copying has enough space to store what you're copying.

To see how much stuff is in a folder in your user account, click the Start button and then click your username. Then point to the folder you're considering backing up, or right-click that folder and choose Properties. When you point, the size of the folder shows in a tooltip. When you right-click and choose Properties, the size of the folder shows up next to Size on Disk in the Properties dialog box (see Figure 33-1).

FIGURE 33-1

A folder's size in tooltip (left) and Properties (right).

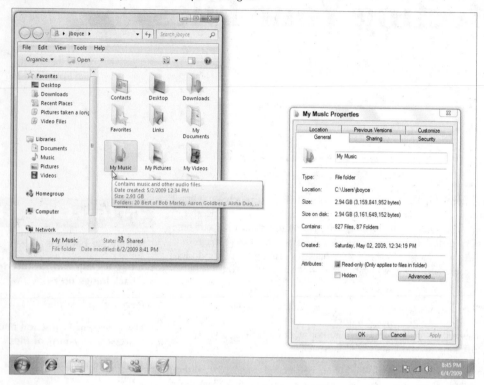

Note

Folder sizes show in tooltips only if you selected Show Pop-up Description for Folder and Desktop Items in the Folder Options dialog box. For more information on that and other terms and concepts used in this chapter, see Chapter 28. ■

To see how much space is available on a disk, insert that disk into the appropriate drive on your computer. Or if it's a flash drive, connect it to a USB port. Then open your Computer folder. With some kinds of drives you'll see the amount of available space right on the icon. For example, drive C: in Figure 33-2 has 32.4 GB free, the DVD in Drive D: has no free space left, and the remote network disk drive Z: has 3.01 GB free.

If there is no meter, choose View ⇨ Tiles from the toolbar. Or right-click the drive's icon and choose Properties to see the amount of free space in the Properties dialog box.

Tip

Remember, 1 KB is 1,024 bytes, 1 MB a little over a million $(1,024^2)$, and 1 GB about a billion $(1,024^3)$. ■

FIGURE 33-2

A disk's available space in the Computer folder.

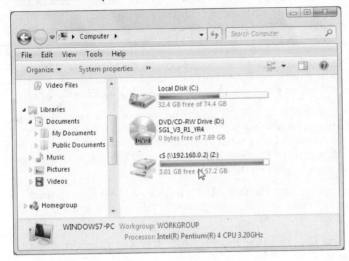

If there's enough space on the disk for the item you want to copy, just go ahead and copy it using any method described in Chapter 29. Should you ever lose or damage a file on your hard drive, you can get it back from the copy that's on the external disk.

It's difficult for me to tell you how to back up your e-mail messages because dozens, if not hundreds, of different e-mail services, and multiple e-mail clients exist. They don't all work the same. In fact, e-mail really has nothing to do with Windows 7 at all. It's a service provided by your ISP or mail service provider. Your only real resource for information on that is the tech support provided by your ISP or mail service (or someone who happens to use and know that same service).

If you use Windows Live Mail, you have some simple ways to back up important e-mail messages. One is to use the Backup and Restore Center described in the next section. Another is to simply copy your entire message store folder to another disk. You can find out where that is from the Maintenance button in the Options dialog box for Windows Live Mail (Chapter 18).

Optionally, you can save just your important messages as files. Create a folder, perhaps named Saved Messages, in your Documents folder. Then save copies of important messages to that folder. You can do so by clicking the message header and choosing Save As. Then specify that folder as the place to save the message. Or, just drag the message header out of Windows Live Mail and into that Saved Messages folder.

Each saved message will be a file with an .eml extension and an envelope icon. To back up your saved messages, just copy that Saved Messages folder to an external disk.

That's the quick-and-easy way to make backups of important files. More elaborate methods exist. The next two sections discuss ways of backing up all your files, and even your entire hard drive.

Tip
The Backup and Restore Center, introduced in Windows Vista and carried over to Windows 7, is a big improvement over the Backup programs from Windows XP and before. ■

Using Backup and Restore

Windows Backup is an alternative to the simple method for backing up files described earlier. It can back up individual folders, all files for all user accounts, or even your entire hard drive. Windows Backup works best if you have a second hard drive that you can use for backups. It can be an internal disk or an external hard drive connected through a USB port.

Very few computers sold come with multiple hard drives. So your system most likely has only one. If you want to back up to another hard drive, you'll either need to purchase and install one yourself, have it installed, or use an external hard drive that you can easily connect with a USB cable.

You can also back up to removable media like CDs and DVDs. It's not always easy to know in advance how many disks you'll need. It depends on how many files you back up, and whether or not you back up just your personal files or the entire hard drive. You might want to consider buying CDs or DVDs in spindles of 50 or 100. They're cheaper in those quantities. It won't take that many to make backups, but you'll probably find plenty of uses for the extras.

If you have a DVD burner, your best bet would be to use DVDs because one DVD holds as much information as about six CDs. Backup media (RW disks) are better than distribution media (R) disks for backup, because RW disks are reusable.

Finally, you can back up folders and files to a shared network folder. This option provides simplicity in that you don't have to change removable media. However, backups to tape or other removable media enable you to take your backups offsite to guard against a catastrophic incident such as a fire that destroys all of the computers on your network.

Starting Backup and Restore

Backup and Restore is a tool for backing up files in all user accounts, so you need administrative privileges to run it. If you're logged in to a standard account, log off. Then log back in to an administrative account. Use either of the following methods to open Backup and Restore:

- Press ![Start icon], type **back**, and click Backup and Restore.
- Click the Start button and choose Control Panel ⇨ System and Security ⇨ Backup and Restore Center.

Backup and Restore opens looking something like Figure 33-3.

Backing up files and settings

The Backup and Restore Center backs up all user files and personal settings in all user accounts by default. It does not back up Windows or any installed programs. Its main purpose is to make sure that you can recover documents like pictures, music, videos, and such in case you lose the originals on your hard drive.

The first file backup you perform might take several hours. It will run in the background so you can continue to use your computer during the backup. But the backup will consume some resources, slowing things down, so you may want to run the first backup overnight, starting it at a time when you can leave the computer on and running.

Before you start a backup, you should configure options for the backup. In Backup and Restore, click the Options button, and then click Change Backup Settings in the resulting dialog box. Windows 7 starts the Backup program and then displays a wizard similar to the one shown in Figure 33-4. In the first step, choose the device on which you will place the backup. Figure 33-4 shows three potential targets: a network drive, a local CD-RW drive, and a removable (flash) disk.

FIGURE 33-3

Backup and Restore with backup in progress.

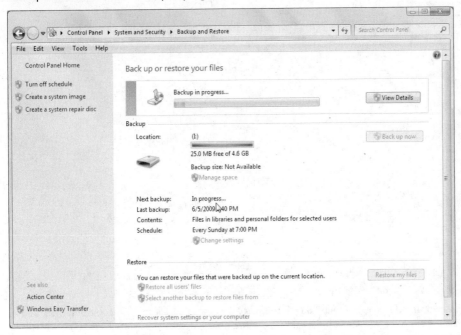

Choose the desired target for the backup and click Next. The wizard then presents you with two options. You can let Windows decide what to back up, or you can choose. If you allow Windows to choose, Windows backs up data files from your libraries, desktop, and default Windows folders, and also creates a system image that you can use to restore your computer should it crash. If you specify the option to let you choose what to back up, Backup and Restore displays the wizard page shown in Figure 33-5 when you click Next.

Use the Data Files branch to select which user libraries to include in the backup. Use the Computer branch to select other folders as desired. Optionally, select the check box Include a System Image of Drives to create an image that you can use to restore the computer if it crashes. Then, click Next.

Backup and Restore at this point displays a summary of what will be backed up and the target location. It also specifies the backup schedule. To change the schedule, click the Change Schedule link to open the wizard page shown in Figure 33-6. To perform a one-time backup, clear the Run Backup on a Schedule check box. Otherwise, choose the backup schedule from the drop-down lists on the page, and then click OK. When you're satisfied with the settings, click Save Settings and Run Backup.

If you specified a recurring schedule, Windows 7 will automatically back up files according to whatever schedule you specified. If you use an external hard drive for backups, you'll need to remember to connect that drive before the scheduled time arrives.

FIGURE 33-4

Choose a backup location.

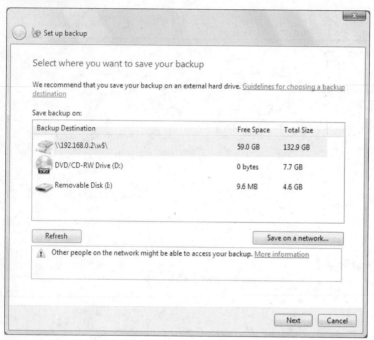

As mentioned, the first backup may take a while. But subsequent backups will copy only files that have changed since the last backup, so they'll go more quickly. Also, you won't have to answer all the same questions again. Subsequent backups will assume you want to keep the same settings.

If you back up to an external hard drive, the backup files will be in a folder that has the same name as the computer you backed up. If you delete the folder, you lose the backup. Exploring that folder won't reveal files in their original form. The backed up files are combined and compressed to minimize storage requirements. To restore from backups, use the method described in the next section.

I Lost/Messed Up My Backup Files

If you encounter a problem while trying to do subsequent backups, the reason might be because you inserted the wrong disk to back up to, or you deleted the folder or files that contain the previous backups. (Backups don't do you any good if you lose the backup disk or erase the backed up data.)

If you get in a jam where Windows encounters a problem on subsequent backups, use the Change Settings link in Backup and Restore Center to start a new backup from scratch. When you get toward the end of the wizard, watch for the option to do a complete backup and select (check) its check box. That will keep Windows from trying to limit the backup to files that have changed since the last backup and prevent the error message from returning.

FIGURE 33-5

Choose what to back up.

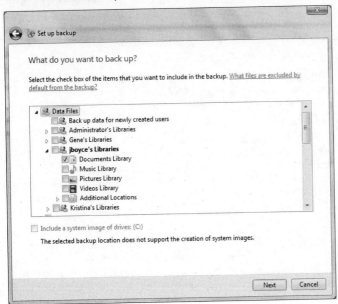

FIGURE 33-6

Set a backup schedule.

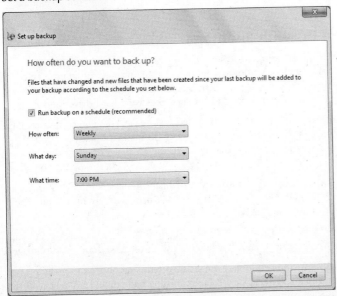

Restoring files from a backup

If there ever comes a time when you've lost or destroyed some important files, you can restore them from your backup. But understand that this method is only required if the files or folders are not in the Recycle Bin. Before you bother with the method described here, open the Recycle Bin and look for the missing file or folder. If you find what you're looking for, right-click it and choose Restore. The deleted item is right back where it was, and there's no need to proceed with the procedure described here.

Even if the folder or file isn't in the Recycle Bin, you might be able to use the quick-and-easy method described under "Returning to a previous version of a file or folder" later in this chapter. In fact, you might even be able to recover a file you didn't back up! Be sure to check out that section if you don't intend to restore a whole slew of backed-up files.

If neither of these methods helps you recover the lost items, you can restore from your backup. First, log in to the user account from which you lost the files. If you used a CD or DVD to make the backup, insert the disk into the drive. If you used an external hard drive, make sure that drive is connected and turned on. Then start Backup and Restore as described earlier in this chapter. Click the Restore My Files button. The Restore Wizard opens to take you step by step through the process of recovering files from the backup. It's just a matter of answering questions on each page and clicking Next.

When you get to the page shown in Figure 33-7, use the Browse for Files button to locate specific files to recover. Click Browse for Folders if you're trying to recover a folder. Click Search to locate a specific item to restore. When you find the file or folder you want to restore, click its icon and the Add button. You can repeat the process as necessary to add as many files and folders as needed to the list of files and folders to restore. When the list is complete, click Next to move on to the next steps.

On the last wizard page, you're given the option to restore items to their original location or a new location. Stick with the original location if you're recovering files you've accidentally deleted. If you still have the originals and want to use the restored files as extra copies, specify a different location for the restored files. Then click Restore.

Backing up the entire PC with an image

The Create a System Image link in the Backup and Restore Center backs up everything on your primary hard drive (drive C:). That includes Windows 7 and all of your installed programs. That backup takes considerably more time and storage space than a file backup, but it offers the advantage of being able to recover everything in the event of a disaster that makes your hard drive inoperable.

A complete PC backup is also different from a file backup in that it doesn't allow you to restore only specific lost files. It's an all-or-none thing. The most common use is to make a brand-new empty replacement hard drive contain exactly the same files that were on the old hard drive the last time you made a backup.

You don't need to back up your entire PC often, because the vast majority of files in your Windows and Program Files folders rarely, if ever, change. How often you back up is entirely up to you. The usual recommendation is every six months.

To back up your entire hard drive, click the Create a System Image link. A wizard opens to take you through the process step by step. You'll need to choose where you want to place your backup image.

If your primary hard drive is partitioned into multiple logical drives, you can choose to include or exclude those. Just make your selections and click Start Backup and the backup will begin. It will run in the background so you can continue to use your computer during the backup process.

FIGURE 33-7

Choose files and folders to restore.

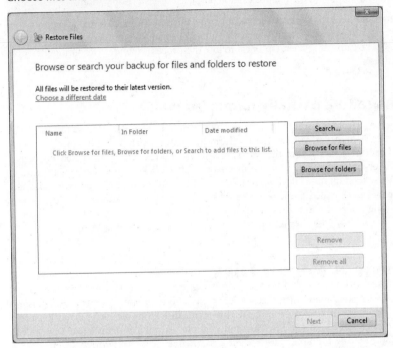

When the backup is complete, the drive to which you backed up has a new folder icon named WindowsImageBackup. The "image" part of the name stems from the fact that the backup is like a "snapshot" of the drive's contents. It's not the kind of image you can see with your own eyes, though. You can't open that folder and navigate through your original folders.

Restoring from an image to a new hard drive

If you lose your entire hard drive and need to replace it, use the following procedure to restore from your image backup. It's important to remember this is an all-or-none recovery. You cannot use this method to restore specific folders or files:

1. Leave the computer turned off (it won't start with a brand-new hard drive anyway).

2. If you backed up to DVD, insert the first DVD into your DVD drive. If you backed up to an external hard drive, connect that external hard drive to the computer.

3. Turn on the computer and hold down the F8 key while the computer is starting. If your keyboard has a Function Lock (or F Lock) key, make sure it's on or the F8 key might not work. The Advanced Boot Options page will appear.

Note

If you can't use the F8 key to get to the recovery options from the hard drive, put your Windows 7 Installation disk into a CD or DVD drive. Then start the computer and hold down the F8 key as the computer is starting. ■

4. When the Advanced Boot Options page appears, click Repair Your Computer.

5. In the System Recovery Options dialog box, click System Image Recovery, and follow the instructions on-screen to choose the image and complete the restore operation.

When you've completed all the steps, you should be able to start the computer normally without the backup disks. Everything will be exactly as it was at the time you made the backup. If you need to install other files you backed up using Back Up Files, follow the procedure under "Restoring files from a backup" to restore those.

Restore an image to a partially damaged disk

If your situation is such that you can still start the computer with Windows 7, but need to bring back previous programs, settings, and files, you can restore from the image file from Backup and Recovery. That will make your hard drive identical to the way it was when you created the image backup. Just open Backup and Recovery as described earlier in this chapter. Then click the Recover System Settings or Your Computer link at the bottom of Backup and Restore. Click Advanced Recovery Methods, and click Use a System Image You Created Earlier to Recover Your Computer. Backup and Restore gives you the option of backing up your current files or skipping that step. Follow the remaining steps in the wizard to optionally back up your files and then perform the restore.

Create a System Repair Disk

It's a good idea to create a system repair disk that will enable you to boot your computer and perform troubleshooting and repair steps if needed. You create this repair disk from the Backup and Restore Center. To create the disk, open Backup and Restore and click the Create a System Repair Disc link in the left pane. Backup and Restore prompts you to select a recordable CD or DVD drive. Insert a blank disk in the drive and click Create Disc.

To use the system repair disk, insert the disk in your computer's CD or DVD drive and restart the computer. When the computer prompts you to press a key to boot from CD, press a key. If you are not prompted to boot the system from CD, modify the computer's BIOS settings to include the CD or DVD drive as a bootable device.

After the system boots from the CD/DVD, you'll see a System Recovery Options dialog box. In this dialog box you can access several troubleshooting tools including Startup Repair, System Restore, System Image Recovery, Windows Memory Diagnostics, and a Command Prompt (which you can use to search for files, run troubleshooting commands, and so on). When you have finished troubleshooting, click either the Shutdown or Restart buttons, as desired.

Using System Protection

System Protection is yet another means of backing up important system files. Unlike either of the previous methods, it doesn't require or use any external disks. Nor does it back up any installed programs or all of Windows 7. Rather, it maintains copies of the most important system files needed for Windows 7 to operate properly, as well as hidden *shadow copies* of some of your own personal files.

The idea behind System Protection isn't to protect you from rare catastrophic hard drive disasters; it's to protect you from smaller and much more common mishaps. For example, you install some program or device that wasn't really designed for Windows 7, on the grounds that "It worked fine in XP so it should work fine here," only to discover that it doesn't work as well as you assumed it would (because it wasn't designed for Windows 7). Even after uninstalling the program, you find that some Windows 7 features don't work like they did before you got the notion to give the old program or device a try.

Another common mishap is when you make some changes to an important file, only they're not particularly good changes. But you save the changes anyway out of habit, thereby losing the original good copy of the file you started with. Sometimes System Protection can even help you recover a file that you deleted and removed from the Recycle Bin.

Turning System Protection on or off

System Protection is turned on by default for the drive on which Windows 7 is installed. That means it's protecting your Windows 7 operating system and also documents you keep in your user account folders like Documents, Pictures, Music, and so forth.

If you have documents on other hard drives, you can extend System Protection to protect documents on those drives, too. However, it would be best not to try to use System Protection to protect a hard drive that has another operating system installed on it, like Windows XP. Windows XP has its own System Restore feature.

System Protection is an optional feature. You can turn it on and off at will (providing you have administrative privileges, because it affects all user accounts). And you can choose for yourself which *volumes* it will monitor. (A volume is any hard drive or hard drive partition that looks like a hard drive in your Computer folder.) To get to the options for controlling System Protection, first open your System folder using any of the following techniques:

- Click the Start button, right-click Computer, and choose Properties.
- Click the Start button, type **sys**, and click System.
- Click the Start button and choose Control Panel ➪ System and Security ➪ System.

In the left pane of your System folder, click System Protection. The System Properties dialog box opens to the System Protection tab as in Figure 33-8.

To ensure that system protection for Windows 7 and user account files is turned on, first look in the Protection Settings box to verify that the Protection column shows "On" for your system disk (typically Drive C:). If the Protection column indicates that protection is off, click the Configure button to open the System Protection dialog box. Then, choose one of the first two settings in the Restore Settings group. You can also specify how much disk space to allocate to system protection with the Max Usage slider.

Caution

Note that if you turn off System Protection, all existing restore points are deleted. ■

If your computer contains other volumes, whether you apply System Protection to them depends on what is on the volumes and whether you find it worthwhile to enable system protection on them.

After you've made your selections, click OK. You're done. Nothing will happen immediately, but Windows 7 will create *restore points* every 24 hours. Each restore point contains copies of your important system files, and *shadow copies* of files on the volumes you specified.

System Protection needs a minimum of 300 MB of space on each protected volume for restore points. If necessary it will use from 3 to 5 percent of the total drive capacity. It won't grow indefinitely or consume a significant amount of disk space. Instead it will delete old restore points before creating new ones. Old restore points are of dubious value anyway.

FIGURE 33-8

System Protection tab in System Properties.

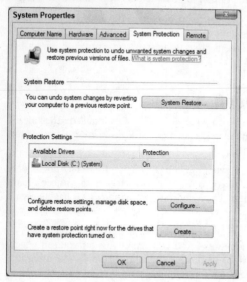

Creating a restore point

System Restore is the component of System Protection that protects your important system files — the ones Windows 7 needs to work correctly. System Restore automatically creates a restore point daily. It also creates a restore point when it detects that you're about to do something that changes system files. But you can also create your own restore points. This might be a good idea when you're about to install some older hardware or software that wasn't specifically designed for Windows 7. It's certainly not required, but it's a smart and safe thing to do.

To create a restore point, get to the System Protection tab shown back in Figure 33-8 and click the Create button. When prompted, you can type in a brief description as to why you manually created the restore point. Perhaps "Pre-Acme Widget install" if you're about to install an Acme widget. Then click Create and OK.

Next you install your Acme Widget or whatever. Take it for a spin, make sure it works. If it works fine and you don't notice any adverse effects, great. You can forget about the restore point and go on your merry way.

If it turns out that change you made wasn't such a great idea after all, first you have to uninstall it. That's true whether it's hardware or software.

After you've uninstalled the bad device or program, you can make sure no remnants of it lag behind by returning to the restore point you specifically set up for that program or device.

If you install other programs or devices after the bad one, don't skip over other restore points to the one you created for the new item. If you do, you'll also undo the good changes made by the good programs and devices, which will likely make those stop working! You have to be methodical about these things. Set the restore point, install the program or device, and test the program or device. If (and only if) you encounter problems, uninstall the device or program and return to the last restore point you set.

Returning to a previous restore point

Say you installed something that didn't work out, uninstalled it, and now you want to make sure your system files are exactly as they were before. You have two ways to get started on that:

- On the System Protection tab shown back in Figure 33-8, click System Restore.
- Press 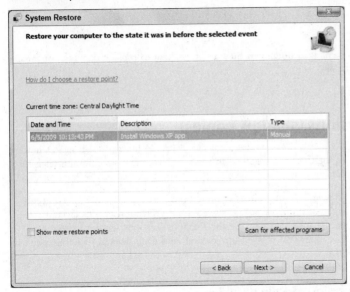, type **sys**, and click System Restore.

The System Restore Wizard starts. Just read what it says and follow its directions. When you get to the page shown in Figure 33-9, click the restore point you created just before the installation. If you forgot to create a restore point manually, click the most recent restore point in the list.

FIGURE 33-9

Choose the specific or most recent restore point.

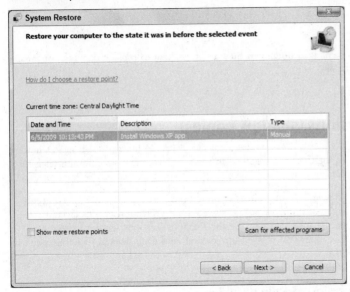

Click Next, then just continue on, reading and following the on-screen instructions. After you click Finish, your computer will restart and you'll see a confirmation about restoring your system files.

Note

For technical readers, I should mention that you can run System Restore from a command prompt. This is good to know if you can only start the computer in Safe Mode with the command prompt. Type **rstrui.exe** at the command prompt and press Enter. ■

Undoing a System Restore

If you use System Restore and restore points exactly as described in the preceding sections, things will go smoothly. If you try to use it in other ways, things probably will not go smoothly. In fact, returning your system to an earlier restore point might cause more problems than it solves. When that happens, you can undo that last restore. Here's how:

1. Open System Restore (click the Start button, type **sys**, and click System Restore).
2. Click Choose a Different Restore Point and click Next.
3. Choose the restore point labeled Undo and click Next.
4. Click Finish and follow the on-screen instructions.

Your computer will restart, and you'll see a confirmation message about undoing the restore point.

System Restore and the restore points you've just learned about have absolutely nothing to do with your document files. System Restore does not change, delete, undelete, or affect document files in any way, shape, or form. You should only use System Restore and restore points exactly as described. To take advantage of System Protection's ability to maintain shadow copies of documents, use the Previous Versions feature described next.

Tip

System Protection makes daily backups of changed document files too. Use them to replace damaged or missing files, even when you don't have a backup. ■

Using previous versions (shadow copies)

When System Protection makes copies of important system files every 24 hours, it also makes hidden *shadow copies* of every folder and file that was modified in the last 24 hours. The common term for that shadow copy is a *previous version* of the folder or file.

Previous versions of files are available only on volumes you checked on the System Protection tab shown back in Figure 33-8. They're also only available after System Protection creates at least one restore point. Once those criteria are met, you can use the Previous Versions feature to restore corrupted files, previous versions of files you messed up yourself, and even deleted files that aren't in the Recycle Bin.

Returning to a previous version of a file or folder

If you still have the icon for a corrupted or messed up file or folder, follow these steps to restore it to its previous version:

1. Right-click the file or folder's icon and choose Properties.
2. Click the Previous Versions tab. You'll see a list of available previous versions (if any), their source, and date. Figure 33-10 shows an example.
3. Click a previous version and then click Open to review it.
4. Close whatever program opened to show you the previous version.
5. If the version you just viewed is the one you want to recover, proceed to the next step. Otherwise repeat steps 3 and 4 until you find the version you want to restore.
6. Next, decide how you want to restore the file:
   - To replace the copy you have with the previous version, click Restore. Read the warning and follow the instructions.

FIGURE 33-10

Previous versions of a file.

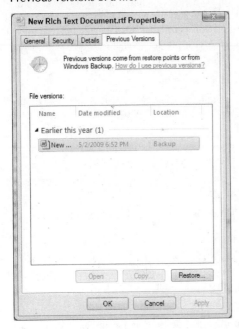

- To keep the copy you have and also recover the previous version, click Copy. Navigate to the folder in which you want to put the previous version and click Copy. When prompted about overwriting the existing file, choose Copy using a Different Name. The previous version of the file will have a (2) at the end of its filename to distinguish it from the copy that was already in the folder.

7. Click OK to close the Properties dialog box.

If the location in which the previous version was previously stored no longer exists, the Restore button will be disabled (dimmed). Try using the Copy button to save the file to a new location. Or click the Open button to open the file. Then save the open copy to an existing folder using the Save method of whatever program the file opened in. Pressing Ctrl+S or choosing File ➪ Save from the program's menu will usually do the trick.

Why no Previous Versions?

The Previous Versions tab of a file or folder might be empty for several reasons. System Protection might not be turned on for the drive in which the file is located. Or System Protection is turned on, but there is no restore point yet that contains the previous version. Automatic restore points are created every 24 hours. Also, restore points and shadow copies aren't kept around forever. Old ones are deleted to make room for new ones. If you accidentally deleted a file long ago, and also emptied the Recycle Bin, there may be no hope of recovering the file through Previous Versions unless you have a backup of the file on an external disk.

Restoring deleted files from previous versions

As you know, most files that you delete are held in the Recycle Bin, to give you a chance to change your mind. The file stays in the Recycle Bin until you empty the Recycle Bin. You should never empty the Recycle Bin unless you're sure there's nothing in it of value. But we all make mistakes, like emptying the Recycle Bin without first checking its contents. If you make that mistake and can't recover a deleted file from the Recycle Bin, you may be able to recover a previous version of the file instead. You need to know the original location from which you deleted the file. Then follow these steps:

1. Open the folder in which the accidentally deleted file was stored.

2. Get the mouse pointer onto a empty area within the folder. The easiest way is to get the mouse pointer about an inch below the last row of icons in the folder. You'll know the mouse pointer is touching an empty spot when no icon is selected (highlighted).

3. Right-click that empty space and choose Properties. Then click the Previous Versions tab in the dialog box. If previous versions of the folder are available, they'll be listed on that tab.

Note

If you see icons for a file rather than for the current folder, you right-clicked an icon rather than empty space within the folder. Click Cancel and try steps 2 and 3 again. ■

4. Double-click a previous version of the folder to see its contents. Try to choose a folder that's before, but close to, the date of accidental deletion. If the first folder you try doesn't contain the file you want, click its Close (X) button and try an earlier folder.

5. If you find the file you're looking for, right-click that file's icon and choose Copy.

6. Paste a copy of the file to a folder of your choosing or the desktop. For example, click the Start button, click Documents, and press Ctrl+V. A copy of the file is placed in your Documents folder.

7. Click OK to close the Properties dialog box.

That copy you pasted is a normal file that you can use in normal ways. You can move it from wherever you pasted it to whatever folder you like.

If you can't restore the accidentally deleted item from previous versions, but you have a backup on removable disks, use the method described under "Restoring files from a backup" earlier in this chapter to restore a copy.

Tip

BitLocker drive encryption ensures the confidentiality of data stored in portable computers. ■

Using BitLocker Drive Encryption

Backup and System Protection ensure the *availability* of your files, in that they allow you to restore lost or damaged files by restoring from a backup copy. BitLocker drive encryption isn't about availability. It's about *confidentiality*. If your notebook computer is lost or stolen, that's certainly a bad thing. But if it contains confidential personal, client, or patient information, that's even worse. BitLocker drive encryption ensures that lost or stolen data can't be read by prying eyes.

Tip
BitLocker differs from the Encrypting File System (EFS) in that EFS encrypts individual folders and files, whereas BitLocker encrypts the whole disk. ■

BitLocker drive encryption works by encrypting all the data on a hard drive. With BitLocker drive encryption active, you can still use the computer normally. All the necessary encryption and decryption takes place automatically behind the scenes. But a thief would be unable to access data, passwords, or confidential information on the drive.

BitLocker hardware requirements
BitLocker drive encryption uses an encryption key to encrypt and decrypt data. That key must be stored in a TMP Version 1.2 (Trusted Platform Module) microchip and compatible BIOS. Only newer computers come with the appropriate hardware preinstalled. You'll also need a USB flash drive to store a copy of the password.

Note
The first time you open the BitLocker task page, you'll see a message indicating whether you do, or don't, have a TPM Version 1.2 chip installed. If you're certain that you have such a chip, but Windows 7 fails to recognize it, check with your computer manufacturer for instructions on making it available to Windows 7. ■

Caution, Caution, and More Caution

BitLocker drive encryption is primarily designed for organizations that have sensitive data stored on notebooks and PCs. Theft of those data could have a negative impact on the organization, its customers, or its shareholders. While transparent to the user, the act of setting up BitLocker would normally be entrusted to IT professionals within the organization.

If you're not an IT professional, you need to be aware of the risks involved, especially if you plan to set up BitLocker on a hard drive that already contains files. First, always back up your data before re-partitioning a drive. Though many programs on the market allow you to repartition a disk without losing data, there's always a risk involved. A backup is your only real insurance. More importantly, understand that BitLocker is not for the technologically faint-of-heart. There is no way to undo any bad guesses or mistakes. If not handled with the utmost care, BitLocker can render your computer useless and your data unrecoverable. If you're not technologically inclined, but have a serious need for drive encryption, consider getting professional support in setting up BitLocker for your system.

In addition to a TPM chip, your hard drive must contain at least two volumes (also called partitions). One volume, called the *system volume*, must be at least 1.5 GB in size. That one contains some startup files and cannot be encrypted. The other volume, called the *operating system volume*, will contain Windows 7, your installed programs, and user account folders. Both volumes must be formatted with NTFS.

Encrypting the volume

When all the necessary hardware is in place, setting up BitLocker drive encryption is a relatively easy task:

1. Click the Start button, choose Control Panel, click System and Security, and then click BitLocker Drive Encryption.

2. If your hardware setup doesn't support BitLocker, you'll see messages to that effect. You cannot continue without appropriate hardware and disk partitions.

3. If all systems are go, click the option to turn on BitLocker.

4. If your TMP isn't initialized, a wizard takes you through the steps to initialize it. Follow the on-screen instructions to complete the initialization.

5. When prompted, choose your preferred password storage method, store the password, and click Next.

6. On the encryption page, select (check) the Run BitLocker system check and click Continue.

7. Insert the password recovery USB flash drive (or whatever medium you used for password recovery) and click Restart Now.

8. Follow the on-screen instructions.

The wizard will ensure that all systems are working and it's safe to encrypt the drive. Just follow the instructions to the end to complete the procedure.

Make sure you password-protect all user accounts to prevent unauthorized access to the system. Otherwise a thief can get at the encrypted data just by logging in to a user account that requires no password!

When the computer won't start

Once BitLocker is enabled, you should be able to start and log in to the computer normally. BitLocker will only prevent normal startup if it detects changes that could indicate tampering. For example, putting the drive in a different computer, or even making BIOS changes that look like tampering, will cause BitLocker to prevent bootup. To get past the block, you'll need to supply the appropriate password.

Turning off BitLocker

Should you ever change your mind about using BitLocker, repeat the steps under "Encrypting the volume" and choose the option to turn off BitLocker drive encryption.

More info on BitLocker

The setup wizard for BitLocker drive encryption is designed to simplify the process as much as possible for people using computers with TPM 1.2. Other scenarios are possible, but go beyond the scope of this book. For more information, search Windows Help for BitLocker. Or better yet, browse to www.TechNet.com and search for BitLocker.

Wrap-Up

Any way you slice it, having two or more copies of important files is better than having only one copy. The reason is simple and obvious: If you have two or more copies, you can afford to lose one copy. This chapter has been about different ways to make backup copies of important files. Here's a summary:

- To make simple backups of files on-the-fly, copy them to external disks as convenient.

- To back up all the document files in all user accounts, use the Back Up Files button in Windows Backup and Restore.

- To back up your entire hard drive, use the Back Up Computer button in Back Up and Restore.

- To recover deleted files or an entire hard drive image, use the Restore buttons in Backup and Restore.

- Use System Protection to make automatic daily backups of important system files and documents. These won't protect you from a hard drive disaster because they're on the same disk as the system files and documents. But they provide a relatively easy means of recovering from minor mishaps without messing with external disks.

- To use System Restore properly, create a restore point just before installing new hardware or software. If the new product creates a problem, uninstall it. Then return to your restore point to ensure all traces of the installation are wiped away.

- To restore a previous version of a file or folder, right-click the item's icon and choose Properties. Then click the Previous Versions tab to see what versions are available.

- To restore an accidentally deleted file, first try to restore it from the Recycle Bin.

- If you forget to restore the file before emptying the Recycle Bin, you can try the previous versions. Open the folder in which the file was stored. Right-click some empty space in that folder and choose Properties. Then click Previous Versions to view previous versions of the folder.

- If you can't restore a file using either of the preceding techniques, but you made a backup, use Restore Files in Backup and Restore Center to recover the file.

- For data confidentiality on portable computers, Windows 7 offers BitLocker drive encryption.

Troubleshooting Files and Folders

Troubleshooting Folders, Files, and Shortcuts

This section discusses some common problems and their solutions for working with files and folders in Windows Explorer. Remember, Windows Explorer is the program that opens whenever you open any folder. You don't need to specifically open Windows Explorer from the All Programs menu.

The Menu bar is missing from Explorer

Microsoft moved the most used functions to the different toolbars in Windows Explorer. Not all of the functionality appears on the toolbars, though. As mentioned in Chapter 28 under "Windows Explorer components," you can temporarily bring back the menu bar by tapping the Alt key.

If you want the menu to show up on a more permanent basis, do so by selecting Organize ➪ Layout ➪ Menu Bar.

Where is the Up button to navigate to the parent folder?

There is no Up button in Windows 7's Explorer. To go to the parent of the current folder, click its name in the address bar. Or click the arrow to the left of the current folder's name and choose a folder from there.

What happened to the Folders list?

The Folders list is in the Navigation pane. If the Navigation pane isn't visible, click Organize and choose Layout ➪ Navigation pane.

Slide Show is not available as an option in the Explorer toolbar

Based on the contents of the folder, Windows Explorer builds the items that appear on the toolbar on the fly. If Windows Explorer has determined that the folder you're looking at doesn't require the Slide Show option and you want that option, follow these steps to enable it:

1. Make sure no files are selected within the folder and choose Organize ⇨ Properties from the toolbar.

2. In the Properties window for the folder, click the Customize tab.

3. From the Optimize This Library For drop-down list, choose Pictures.

4. Check the box Also Apply This Template to All Subfolders if you want folders below this folder to also use the same format.

5. Click the OK button, and the Explorer interface should now contain the Slide Show button in the toolbar.

Tip

If you still don't see the Slide Show option in the toolbar, try viewing the folder outside of the Libraries view. Expand the Computer node in the Navigation pane and drill down to where the folder is located. Note that you can't set the properties for a folder when viewing it in the Libraries view. Instead, you need to drill down from the Computer node to get to it and set its properties there. ■

I don't see the file extensions on files

By default, the file extensions are not shown under Windows Explorer. Sometimes, it is necessary to alter the file extension of a file. To show the file extensions, follow these steps:

1. Select Organize ⇨ Folder and Search Options.

2. In the Folder Options window, select the View tab.

3. In the Advanced Settings section, scroll down to Hide Extensions for Known File Types, clear the checkmark from its checkbox, and click OK.

For more information on this topic, see the section titled "Options on the View tab," in Chapter 28.

When I try to select by dragging, the icons move, and nothing is selected

To *move* an item, you put the mouse pointer *on* the item you want to move, and then drag. To *select* items by dragging, start with the mouse pointer *near* the first item you want to select, but not at a point where it's actually touching an icon. It's tricky in Windows 7 because the mouse pointer selects when you get close to an icon. You can tell an icon is selected when the background color changes. The Tiles view is the easiest one to use when you want to select multiple icons by dragging.

Error message: "Application is using this file. You must close the file before proceeding"

Whenever you see this message, it means that the file you're trying to delete, rename, or move is currently open. Close the open document on the desktop (or from the taskbar, if it's minimized). Then, try again.

Error message: "If you change a file name extension, the file may become unusable"

You've attempted to rename both the filename and the extension. Changing a filename extension can be bad news because the extension will no longer accurately reflect the format of the data in the file. Choose No and then rename the file. This time, don't change the file extension.

Error message: "This location already contains a file with the same name"

No two files in a folder can have the same name. Here, you're trying to move or copy a file to a folder that already contains a file with the name of the one you're trying to move or copy. Your best bet would be to choose Keep This Original File. Next, rename the file or folder you're trying to move or copy and then move or copy the renamed file.

Optionally, if you choose Copy This File, the file that's already in the folder will be replaced by the one you're trying to move or copy, which means that the original file will be lost forever.

You're also given a third option of Copy Using Another Name that will copy the file to this folder and give the file you're copying a different name. Windows will give the new file the same name as the original but append a number enclosed with parentheses.

"Problem with Shortcut" dialog box opens

When a shortcut stops working, that means the folder, file, or Web page to which the shortcut refers no longer exists. In the case of a file or folder, you've deleted, moved, or renamed the original item since creating the shortcut. If the file or folder has been deleted and still remains in the Recycle Bin, Windows gives you the option of restoring the file or folder. If the file or folder has been deleted and removed from the Recycle Bin, Windows only gives you the options of deleting or keeping the shortcut. In the case of a Web page, either you're not online, or the Web page no longer exists at that location.

Deleting a shortcut from my desktop deletes it from all users' desktops

When you create a desktop shortcut in your own user account by right-clicking an icon and choosing Send To ➪ Desktop (create shortcut), that icon is unique to your desktop. So, when you delete the icon, it should disappear from your desktop only. That's because the icon is stored in the Desktop folder for your user account only. That folder's name is C:\Users\Username\Desktop, where *Username* is the name of your user account.

Sometimes, when you install a new program, that setup procedure automatically creates a new desktop shortcut icon on every user's desktop. That icon is stored in the Public Desktop folder at C:\Users\Public\Public Desktop. So, when you delete that icon from your desktop, you actually delete it from the folder and all other users' desktops.

If you just want to get the icon back, so that other users have it again, open the Recycle Bin and restore the icon from there.

Troubleshooting Documents

It's very frustrating trying to save a document that you've spent hours on only to have the system tell you that you can't save it. This section covers some of the common problems when trying to save your hard work.

You cannot save in the folder specified

The folder you've chosen in the drop-down list can't be used to store files. Click OK to close the message box. Choose a different folder, such as Documents, from the drop-down list. Then, click the Save button again.

Error message: "The file name is invalid"

The filename you entered contains an invalid character. Try a different filename; make sure that it doesn't contain any of the following characters:

\ : / * ? " > < |

Click the Save button to save the document with the new name.

My document isn't in the Open dialog box

Make sure that the location at the top of the Open dialog box is showing the name of the folder in which the document is contained. If it isn't, navigate to the appropriate folder. If the document still isn't visible in the main pane, change the file type option at the bottom-right corner of the dialog box to All Files or the type of file you're trying to open.

Troubleshooting CDs and DVDs

CDs and DVDs pose some unique problems because unlike most computer storage media, they use laser technology rather than magnetism. You can't read from and write to CDs and DVDs as you can other types of disks. And, CDs and DVDs are likely to generate some unique error messages, described and addressed in the sections that follow.

Error message: "Invalid function when attempting to write files to a CD"

You can write files only with CD-R and CD-RW drives, not a CD-ROM drive. Also, the recording capabilities of your CD-R or CD-ROM drive must be enabled as follows:

1. Click the Start button and choose Computer.
2. Right-click the icon for your CD drive and choose Properties.
3. In the Properties dialog box that opens, click the Recording tab.
4. Make sure that your drive shows up under Select the Disc-burning Drive that Windows Will Use by Default.
5. Click OK.

An invalid or outdated CD driver can also cause the problem. See Chapter 52 for the goods on finding an updated driver.

Finally, a conflict with third-party CD-burning software can generate this message. Try using that third-party program to copy files to a CD. For general information about Roxio CD-burning products, see www.roxio.com. See www.nero.com for general information on Nero Burn products.

I'm unable to read recorded CDs and DVDs on other computers

The most likely cause of this problem is that you did not properly close the session after you were finished copying information to the CD or DVD. To close the session:

1. Put the CD or DVD back into the drive.
2. Navigate to the contents of the disc if they don't come up automatically.
3. Right-click within the window and select Close session.

Even though you have closed the session, you can add more data to the disc later. Closing the session allows you to use the disc on other computers.

Troubleshooting Searches

Searches in Windows 7 are a whole new ballgame, nothing like Search Companion or similar tools from earlier versions of Windows. The kinds of searches that return keystroke-by-keystroke results don't search the entire file system. If they did, the searches wouldn't be nearly as fast. Searches that return keystroke-by-keystroke results are searching only the search index. By default, the search index includes only the kinds of things most users access all the time, such as documents, messages, programs, and dialog boxes.

Search didn't find my file

Where you start a search has a big effect. When you search using the Search box in the upper-right corner of a folder, you search only that folder and its subfolders. Limiting the search in that manner is what allows Windows 7 to return keystroke-by-keystroke results. For more traditional file system searches, you have to use the Search window, and extend the search beyond the search index.

Use techniques described in Chapters 30 and 31 to master Windows 7's instant searches.

More Troubleshooting Resources

For live help with troubleshooting files, consider the Microsoft.public.windows.7.file_ management newsgroup in Microsoft Communities. Whatever problem you're having, chances are you'll find someone who has had that same problem and solved it.

You can also search Windows 7's built-in Help and Support for the specific topic with which you're having a problem.

Part VII

Printing, Faxing, and Scanning

I've worked in the IT industry for 25 years, and have been hearing about the paperless office for almost all of that time. In reality, the truly paperless office doesn't exist. Sometimes, you just have to get a document onto paper, no two ways about it. Likewise, not everything can be downloaded or copied from disk. Sometimes, you can only get text or pictures from paper. Part VII covers both sides of the story.

Chapter 35 starts with the basics of installing and managing printers. If you already have a working printer, you can skip that one.

Chapter 36 moves onto the actual task of printing. Chapter 37 follows with a discussion of managing print jobs, which includes things like stopping a runaway printer before it wastes all your paper and ink!

When your only copy of a favorite photo is printed on paper, the only way to get it into the computer is by scanning it. Chapter 38 explains how to do that. It also covers faxing. Chapter 39 covers solutions to problems relating to printing, faxing, and scanning.

Installing and Managing Printers

I nstalling a printer is usually an easy job. There's one rule that applies to installing any hardware, and it certainly applies to printers. The rule is: *Read the instructions that came with the printer first.* Trying to save time by ignoring the instructions and winging it is likely to cost you more time in getting the thing to work.

In many cases, you'll have the option to connect the printer to a USB port or a printer port. If your computer is a member of a network, you might want to install a shared printer that's physically connected to some other computer. This chapter looks at different ways of installing printers, as well as techniques for managing installed printers.

IN THIS CHAPTER

Using your Devices and Printers folder

Choosing a default printer

Installing a new printer

Managing printer drivers

Setting default printer properties

Printer Properties versus Printing Properties

Two types of properties are covered in this chapter: *printer properties* and *printing properties.* The distinction isn't obvious from the terminology, so here's a general description to help you understand the difference:

- **Printer properties:** These properties apply to the printer itself, such as the way it is connected to the computer, whether and how it is shared on the network, the way the computer sends information to the printer, when the printer is available, and more.

- **Printing properties:** These properties apply to how the printer creates a printed document. These properties include things such as paper source, paper size, duplex printing, paper quality settings, print scaling, watermarks, and other document output properties.

In a way, you can think of printer properties as how the printer prints *all* documents and printing properties as how the printer prints *specific* documents. That's not 100% accurate, but it should begin to help you understand the distinction between the two.

If you are a typical Windows user, you will be more likely to spend time configuring printing properties than printer properties. If you are a power user or administrator, however, you'll no doubt spend some time configuring printer properties to control how the printer operates.

Before diving into printer and printing preferences, you need to get your printer installed. That's covered in the following section.

Opening the Devices and Printers Folder

New Feature

Windows 7 consolidates many types of devices as well as printers into a single folder to make it easier to manage devices connected to your computer. The Devices and Printers folder is the place to go to manage devices such as displays, keyboards, input devices, wireless network adapters, and printers.

Aside from actually printing documents, just about everything you do with printers will take place in the Devices and Printers folder. As with everything else in Windows 7, you can get to that folder in several ways. Use whichever works for you and is most convenient at the moment:

- Click the Start button and choose Devices and Printers from the right side of the Start menu.
- Tap ⊞, type **prin**, and click Devices and Printers under the Control Panel heading.
- Click the Start button and choose Control Panel ➪ View Devices and Printers under Hardware and Sound.

When you're in your Devices and Printers folder, you'll see an icon for each printer (or similar device) to which you can print. Figure 35-1 shows an example; your folder will, of course, look different.

Setting the default printer

If your Devices and Printers folder contains more than one printer icon, only one of them will be the *default* device for printing. By "default," I mean the printer that's used automatically if you don't specify something else. For example, many programs allow you to print a document to the default printer by pressing Ctrl+P. The program may not ask what printer you want to use. Instead, it just sends the document to the default printer.

In the Devices and Printers folder, the default printer is indicated by a checkmark. If you want to change the default printer, right-click the printer's icon and choose Set as Default Printer. The printer or device you specified will now sport the green checkmark, and will be used for printing when you don't specify some other printer or device.

Testing a printer

If you've just installed a printer and want to test it out, follow these steps (here, I'm assuming that you're already in the Devices and Printers folder):

1. Right-click the printer's icon and choose Printer Properties.
2. At the bottom of the Properties dialog box that opens, click the Print Test Page button.

FIGURE 35-1

Sample Devices and Printers folder.

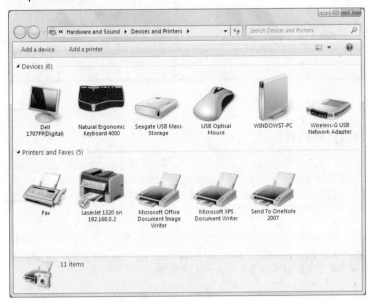

3. Wait a few seconds (few printers start immediately). The printer should print a sample page.

- If the page prints and doesn't look garbled, click OK in each open box.
- If nothing prints within 15 or 30 seconds, click Get Help with Printing for some tips on solving the problem.

If you had to click Get Help with Printing, follow the advice in the Help documentation first to resolve the problem. You can click the link Click to Open the Print Troubleshooter to launch the printing troubleshooter from the Control Panel. If you still can't get your printer to work, see Chapter 39 for more options. Also, keep in mind that hundreds of different makes and models of printers are available on the market, and no one rule that applies to all. So, don't overlook the documentation that came with your printer, or the printer manufacturer's Web site, which may provide troubleshooting advice.

Adding a Devices and Printers Option to Your Start Menu

You don't need to open your Devices and Printers folder to print things. When you want to print a document that's currently open on your screen, you can usually do so by pressing Ctrl+P, by clicking the Print button in that program's toolbar, or by choosing File ➪ Print from that program's menu bar.

continued

continued

Nonetheless, if you need to open your Devices and Printers folder often and don't have a Devices and Printers option on your Start menu, you can easily add that option. Right-click the Start button and choose Properties. Click the Customize button on the Start menu tab and scroll down through the list of Start menu options. Select (check) Devices and Printers and click OK. From then on, whenever you click the Start button, you'll see a Printers option on the right side of the Start menu.

Installing a New Printer

Before you can use a new printer, you need to connect it to the computer and install it. Many printers give you the choice of using the USB port to connect the printer, or a standard printer port. In most cases, USB will work just fine for printing. In fact, many of today's newer computers don't even have a parallel printer port, so USB might be your only option.

Tip

If your printer only offers a parallel port, and your computer does not have one, you can either buy an add-on adapter card to add the parallel port or buy a new printer that supports USB. ■

As mentioned at the beginning of this chapter, the main rule on installing a printer is to follow the instructions that came with it. Sometimes you need to install drivers first, sometimes you don't. There is no "one rule fits all" when it comes to installing printers, or any other hardware device for that matter. But in a pinch, where there are no instructions, the techniques in the following sections will be your best first guess.

Installing printers with parallel and serial port connections

If your printer is a typical plug-and-play printer that connects to the computer via an LPT port or COM port, the best approach is:

1. Save any unsaved work, close all open programs, shut down Windows, and turn off your computer.

2. Plug the printer into the wall, connect the printer to the computer's LPT or serial port, turn on the printer, and turn on the computer.

3. When Windows restarts, look for the *Found New Hardware* notification message to appear.

It's tough to say what will happen next. You might be prompted for a disk if Windows can't find the driver for the printer. If you see a notification message indicating that the printer is installed and ready to use, you're probably done.

Installing printers with USB and infrared connections

If your only option is to connect the printer through a USB port, or by infrared, the installation procedure should go like this:

1. Close all open programs on your Windows desktop, so that you're at the Windows desktop with nothing else showing.

2. Check the documentation that came with the printer, and if directed to install the drivers before connecting the printer to the computer, do so.

3. Plug the printer into the wall; connect the printer to the computer with its USB connection, or configure the infrared connection as instructed by the printer manufacturer.

4. Turn on the printer, and wait a few seconds.

You should see a message in the Notification area that tells you the device is connected and ready to use. You're done. The printer is installed and ready to go.

Regardless of which of these methods you use, you'll want to test the printer, and perhaps make it the default printer, as discussed later in this chapter.

Tip
If the printer documentation tells you to install the software before you attach the printer to the computer for the first time, don't skip that step. If you connect the printer before installing the drivers, Windows might have problems detecting the printer. ■

Installing a network, wireless, or Bluetooth printer

If your computer is a member of a home or small-business network, and you know of a shared printer on another computer in that network, you can use the technique described here to install that printer on your own computer. The same is true of many wireless and Bluetooth printers. But again, this procedure may not be necessary because Windows 7 often detects network printers and makes them available automatically. Be sure to check the manual that came with a wireless or Bluetooth printer for an alternative procedure before trying the method described here. Also, be sure to turn the printer on before you try to install it.

If you're trying to install a printer that's attached to another computer in your private network, make sure that both the printer and the computer to which the printer is physically connected are turned on. Make sure your network is set up and you've enabled discovery and sharing as discussed in Part X of this book. Then go to the computer that needs to access the network printer and perform the steps to follow on that computer. You install a network, wireless, or Bluetooth printer in much the same way you install a local printer. First open the Devices and Printers folder using any technique described at the start of this chapter.

If the printer's name appears in the Devices and Printers folder, you need not install it. If you want to make it the default printer, right-click its icon and choose Set as Default Printer. Then, close the Devices and Printers folder and Control Panel. You'll be able to use the printer as described in Chapter 36.

If there's no sign of the printer in your Devices and Printers folder, follow these steps to install it:

1. Click Add a Printer in the toolbar, or right-click some empty space in the folder and choose Add a Printer. The Add Printer Wizard opens.

2. Choose the second option, Add a Network, Wireless, or Bluetooth Printer, and click Next. The wizard searches the network for shared printers.

   - If the search finds the printer you're looking for, click its name and then click Next.

   - If the search doesn't find your printer, click The Printer that I Want Isn't Listed. If you know the UNC name or IP address of the printer to which you want to connect, fill in the appropriate information. Otherwise, click Browse, and navigate to the computer and printer to which you want to connect. Click the printer's name and click Select. Then click Next.

3. After the printer is successfully installed, click Next. On the next wizard page you can opt to print a test page and make the shared printer your default printer. Make your choices and click Finish.

An icon for the shared printer will show in your Devices and Printers folder. If you made it the default printer, it will also show a checkmark.

Managing Printer Drivers

Virtually all hardware devices, including printers, come with a special program called a *device driver*, or just *driver* for short. The driver provides the interface between the device and a specific operating system, such as Windows 7, Windows Vista, or Windows XP. You need to have the correct and current printer driver installed on your computer to get your printer to work correctly.

Tip

In most cases, the Vista version of a printer driver will work just fine for Windows 7. However, you should always use the Windows 7 version of a printer driver if one is available to ensure you have access to all of your printer's features. ■

Many printers come with the drivers on a CD. How you install a driver from the disk depends on the printer you're using, but an older printer may not even have a Windows 7 driver to offer. In that case, you'll need to look for a current driver online. Try Windows Update first by following these steps:

1. Click the Start button and choose All Programs ➪ Windows Update.
2. If Windows 7 doesn't start searching for updates immediately, click Check for Updates in the left column.
3. When the update search is complete, click the link for available updates (if any).
4. If the driver for your printer appears, go ahead and install it per the on-screen instructions.

If Windows Update doesn't find an updated driver, it might mean your printer manufacturer hasn't posted the driver on that site yet. Browse to the printer manufacturer's Web site and look around for a Drivers link or Support page with downloads. Or go to the Support page and send an e-mail asking if there's an updated driver for your printer model.

Setting Default Printing Properties

Remember the discussion early in this chapter about printing properties versus printer properties? This section explains how to configure the default printing properties that a printer will use to print documents.

Like objects on your screen, many devices have properties that you can customize. Most printers have such properties. You can make selections from those properties to define defaults for the printer. Those default settings for properties won't be set in stone. As you see in Chapter 36, you can override the defaults any time you print a document. The defaults are just a way of choosing a specific option every time you print a document.

As with other objects, a printer's properties are accessible from its icons. To view the properties for an installed printer, first open the Devices and Printers folder if you haven't already done so. Then, right-click the printer's icon and choose Printing Preferences. The options available to you depend on your printer. The options shown in Figure 35-2 are for an HP LaserJet 1320 printer.

FIGURE 35-2

Sample Printing Preferences.

The Printing Preferences dialog box varies from one printer to the next, and often offers multiple tabs, each with several options. The following sections cover some of the more common settings that you might want to set for your printer.

Making pages print in the right order

When you print a multiple-page document, you don't want to have to shuffle the pages around to get them in the correct order. You want the pages to come out of the printer in the right order. The Page Order property is the option that determines whether or not the pages are printed in the right order. The rules are as follows:

- If the pages come out of the printer face down, use Front to Back order.
- If the pages come out of the printer face up, use Back to Front order.

Said another way, if you have to reshuffle printed pages, choose whichever of those options currently *isn't* selected.

Portrait versus landscape printing

Unless your printing needs are very unusual, you'll probably want to print most of your documents in a portrait orientation. That's the orientation that normal letters and other documents use, so you'll almost always want to choose Portrait as your default orientation, as in Figure 35-2.

You can always override that default and print the occasional document in Landscape orientation (sideways, so the page is wider than it is tall). Chapter 36 talks about choosing Landscape orientation for a document on-the-fly.

Saving time and money

Printers, as a rule, are just plain slow. That's because they're clunky mechanical devices, and it takes time to move a page through a printer and get the ink or toner onto the paper. Faster printers are typically more expensive than slower ones. But, no matter what the cost or general speed of your printer, one general rule will apply: The higher the print quality of the document you're printing at the moment, the longer it will take to print.

Here's another fact about printers in general. Many printers are cheap, but ink cartridges typically are not. In some cases, it is actually cheaper to buy a new printer than to buy replacement cartridges for your printer.

The printer property that most determines how quickly your documents print and how much ink you use per document is called *print quality*. The higher the print quality, the longer it takes to print a document, and the more ink you use in the process. You can save time and money by doing all your day-to-day printing in Draft quality, perhaps even without color if you want to conserve color ink.

On my LaserJet printer, quality settings are on the Paper/Quality tab shown in Figure 35-3. The Econo Mode for the LaserJet 1320, for example, causes the printer to use less ink when it prints, but the quality of the finished document is naturally less. Your printer might have similar options.

As with other printer properties, setting the printer defaults to low-quality and black-and-white settings won't prevent you from printing the occasional color document. As you learn in Chapter 36, you can override those defaults any time you print a document. When you want to print a professional-looking report or a fine photo, just increase the print quality and activate color for the one print job.

Those three properties that I've just mentioned are the ones that most printers have. Beyond those, the properties vary greatly from one printer to the next. The only resource for learning all the details of your particular make and model of printer is the documentation that came with that printer, or the printer manufacturer's Web site.

Setting Printer Properties

If you are an average Windows user, you might never need to configure printer properties for a printer. In most cases, you'll be more concerned with printing properties that control how the printed documents look. If you are an advanced user or administrator, however, you'll likely need to understand how to configure printer properties.

FIGURE 35-3

Paper/Quality settings.

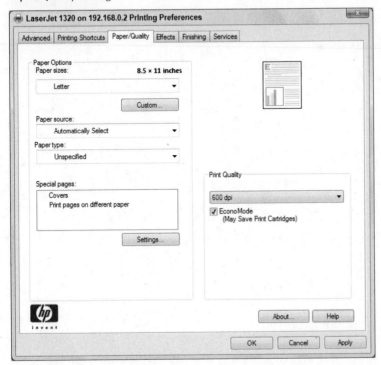

To configure properties for a printer, start by opening the Devices and Printers folder as described earlier in this chapter (you should find it on the Start menu.) Then, right-click the printer and choose Printing Properties to open a Properties dialog box similar to the one shown in Figure 35-4.

The tabs shown in the Properties dialog box for a printer can vary from one type of printer to another, but you will see some common settings between them. The following sections use the HP LaserJet 1320 as an example to illustrate common concepts such as port configuration, printer pooling, spooling options, and more.

Tip

Use the Print Test Page button on the General tab of a printer's Properties dialog box to test the printer. ■

Configuring printer ports

The Ports tab (Figure 35-5) lets you view and configure the printer's ports, which define the way the printer is connected to the computer. Typically, a printer will have only one port, but it is possible to have multiple ports.

The most common reasons to visit the Ports tab are to configure a printer for a different network port, or to switch from one LPT (parallel) port to another. You can also configure the printer to print by default to a file by selecting the File port.

FIGURE 35-4

Sample Properties dialog box.

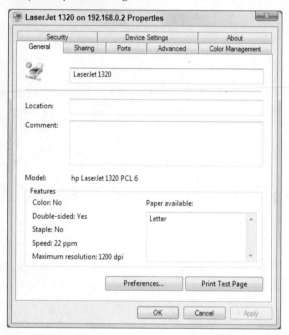

Some port types offer settings that you can configure. LPT ports, for example, enable you to specify the Transmission Retry setting, which determines how long the computer will wait for a response from the printer before timing out. For serial printers on a COM port, you can specify several settings that control the speed of the port and how data flows from the computer to the printer. To configure a port, select the port from the list and click Configure Port. Use the settings in the resulting dialog box to specify settings for the port.

If you need to add a new port for a printer, click the Add Port button. Windows displays the Printer Ports dialog box shown in Figure 35-6. Select the type of port you want to create and click New Port. If the selected port type supports creating new ports, Windows displays a dialog box or a wizard (depending on the port type) that you use to specify the settings for the new port.

Setting up printer pooling

A *printer pool* is a group of identical printers that Windows treats as a single printer instance. You can then print to the printer pool as if it were a single printer, and Windows handles sending the document to an appropriate printer in the pool. Before explaining pooling in more detail, take a look at how a *printer driver instance* differs from a *printer*.

A printer that you see listed in the Devices and Printers folder is really not a printer per se. Instead, it is an instance of a printer driver. The printer driver is the middleware between Windows and the printer hardware (the real *printer* in this discussion) that enables Windows to communicate with the printer. "Instance of a printer driver" means a named copy of the printer driver that has its own set of properties. You could have two instances of the same printer driver with different settings, both of which control the same printer. Or, you can have one instance of a printer driver that controls more than one printer, and that's a printer pool.

FIGURE 35-5

The Ports tab.

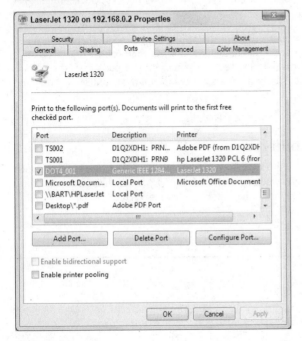

FIGURE 35-6

Printer Ports dialog box.

For example, assume your office has three identical network printers. You can create a printer pool using those three printers, assigning three ports to the single instance of the printer driver in your Devices and Printers folder. So, you might have one HP LaserJet 1320N network printer in your

Devices and Printers folder, for example, but that instance of the driver could actually print to any of the three printers.

Why would you want to do that? First, you only need to manage one instance of the printer driver in your computer, which can simplify printer and document management, particularly if you typically use the same settings for each one. Second, you don't have to worry about selecting a printer when you print. Instead, assuming you have assigned the printer driver instance for the pool as your default printer, you just click Print and send the document on its way. Windows decides which printer to send the document to.

To set up a printer pool, first install the printer driver for the printers in the pool. Then, open the properties for the printer from the Devices and Printers folder and select the Enable Printer Pooling option on the Ports tab. When that option is selected, you can select multiple ports from the ports list. Add ports as needed (such as additional TCP/IP ports for network printers), and select the ports for all of the printers in the pool. Then, click OK.

Configuring printer availability

You can specify when a printer is available. For example, you might want to restrict access to a printer to business hours to keep people for using it when no one is around. Whatever the reason, you configure printer availability from the Advanced tab of the printer properties (Figure 35-7).

FIGURE 35-7

The Advanced tab.

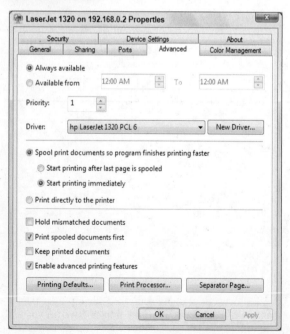

By default, a printer is configured to be always available. To limit its availability, click the Available From option, then use the spin controls to set the start and end times for the time range when the printer will be available. If you or a network user of a shared printer sends a document to a printer when it is not available, the document is held in the printer queue on the sending computer until the printer becomes available.

Setting other advanced options

As Figure 35-7 illustrates, Windows offers several other advanced options for configuring a printer. For example, the spooling options determine how the printer driver sends data to the printer. The option Spool Print Documents So Program Finishes Printing Faster causes documents to be spooled to an on-disk queue, where it waits until the printer driver can send it to the printer. To the printing application, printing is complete as soon as the last page of the document is sent to the queue and you can then continue using the program.

Alternatively, you can configure the printer driver to print directly to the printer, bypassing the on-disk document queue. The downside to this option is that you can't use the program until it finishes printing, which can potentially take much longer than sending the document to a queue if the document is complex or very large.

In most cases, today's computers are fast enough and have enough disk capacity that you will never need to print directly to the printer. If you are trying to print a huge document and have very little free space on your disk, however, sending the document directly to the printer could enable the document to print when it might not otherwise.

Following are some additional settings on the Advanced tab:

- **Hold Mismatched Documents:** The spooler checks the configuration of the printer against the document setup before sending the document to the printer. If the document setup doesn't match the printer, the document is held in the queue and not sent to the printer. You can then address the configuration mismatch, and restart the document from the queue to send it to the printer.

- **Print Spooled Documents First:** Documents that have completed spooling to the queue are printed before documents that are still spooling, even if they have a lower priority.

- **Keep Printed Documents:** Documents remain in the queue even after they are printed, enabling you to restart the document from the queue if needed to reprint them.

These are not the only properties available for a printer. I cover other properties, such as sharing properties, in other chapters.

Wrap-Up

That about wraps it up for installing and managing printers. In the next chapter, you learn how to print documents, how to choose color and quality settings on-the-fly, and so forth. The main points from this chapter are as follows:

- Many makes and models of printers exist. Your best resource for your specific printer is the documentation that came with that printer.

- Installed printers, and options for installing printers, are in your Devices and Printers folder. You can open that folder from the Start menu, Search box, or Control Panel.

- If you have access to multiple printers, right-click the icon for the printer you want to use on a day-to-day basis and choose Set as Default Printer.

- To test a printer, right-click its icon and choose Printer Properties. Then, click the Print Test Page button.

- The typical scenario for installing a printer that connects to a printer port is to shut down the computer, connect the printer and turn it on, and then restart the computer. In the case of USB printers, however, you often need to install the printer driver software before connecting the printer to the computer.

- To connect a printer by USB, don't shut down the computer. Instead, leave the computer on, connect the printer to the computer, and then turn the printer on. Check the printer documentation to see whether you need to install the drivers before connecting the printer.

- To ensure that your printer driver is appropriate for your operating system, check the Windows Update site and the printer manufacturer's Web site.

- To set default properties for day-to-day printing, right-click the printer's icon and choose Printing Preferences.

Printing Documents and Screenshots

Windows 7, in and of itself, doesn't print documents. The main reason is that Windows 7 can't even open documents. You use programs, not Windows, to print documents. Typically, you open the document first by clicking or double-clicking its icon. Then, you print the document from the program that opens.

This chapter looks at different ways to print documents. As everyone knows, printer ink, toner, and paper are expensive. For that reason, I'll be sure to present some techniques to help you get the most for your printing buck.

Printing a Document

If you have a printer, using it should be easy. First, you want to make sure that the printer is turned on, has paper, and is ready to go. Then if the document you want to print is open and on the screen, do whichever of the following is most convenient:

- Choose File ➪ Print from the program's menu bar.
- Click the Print button in the program's toolbar.
- Press Ctrl+P.

In many cases, you can print a document, or several documents, without first opening the document. To print a single document that way, right-click its icon and choose Print. To print multiple documents, select the icons first, using any technique from Chapter 29. Then click the Print button in the toolbar. Or, right-click any selected icon and choose Print, as shown in Figure 36-1.

Tip
If you select different types of files (such as Word and Excel documents), you can't print them from the context menu. You can print a group of files from the context menu only if they are of the same type. ■

What happens next depends on what program you're using, and which method you used. Often, right-clicking a closed document or pressing Ctrl+P starts the print job automatically. No further input is required.

FIGURE 36-1

Printing multiple closed documents.

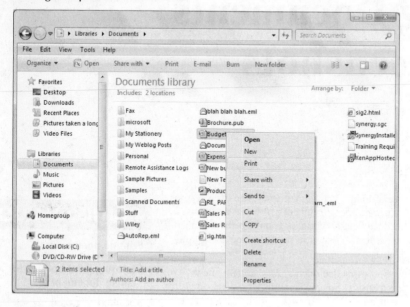

Tip

Don't expect the document to start printing immediately. There's always some prep work that needs to be done, and that will take a few seconds. ■

In most cases, printing a document will first take you to the Print dialog box. Exactly how the Print dialog box looks varies depending on the program and printer you're using. Figure 36-2 shows an example of a Print dialog box.

In the Print dialog box, click the Print or OK button to print to whatever printer is currently selected near the top of the dialog box. That's the simple approach, if you want to print the entire document immediately to the default printer. But as you can see in the sample Print dialog boxes, you may also have quite a few options to choose from before you click the Print or OK button.

Tip

See "Printing Pictures" in Chapter 23 for specifics on printing photos and other pictures. ■

Common printing options

Because different programs offer different Print dialog boxes, I can't really say exactly what you'll see when you print a document. However, the options shown in the sample dialog box are fairly common. Those common options include:

- **Select Printer:** If you have access to multiple printers (for example, when you're connected to a network), choose the printer you want to use.

FIGURE 36-2

Example of Print dialog box.

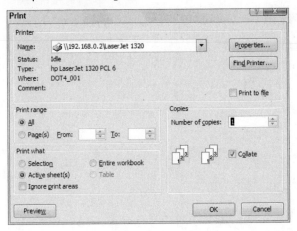

- **Page Range:** Choose which pages you want to print, ranging from *All* (the entire document), the *current page* (the page visible on your screen), *Selection* (only the text and pictures you selected in the document prior to choosing the Print command), or *Pages* (define a specific page, such as 1, or a range of pages, such as 2-5, to print only pages 2, 3, 4, and 5).

- **Manual Duplex:** Print pages back-to-back on printers that don't have the capability to do that automatically. (*Duplex* is the nerd word for *back to back*.) When you choose this option, odd-numbered pages will be printed first. You'll then be prompted to reinsert those pages, so the remaining pages can be printed on their backs.

- **Number of Copies:** Specify the number of copies to print.

- **Collate:** If this is selected, and you print multiple copies, pages are collated. If you print multiple copies, and clear the Collate option, you'll get multiple page 1s, followed by multiple page 2s, and so forth.

Choosing a print quality and other options

The general options that appear in the Print dialog box are almost universal. Depending on the make and model of your printer, you might have some other options to choose from. For example, you might be able to control the print quality of a document, opting for a quick draft or a time-consuming but better-quality job.

In most cases, you'll click the Properties button in the Print dialog box to get to those options. Figure 36-3 shows an example from an HP LaserJet 1320 printer. The figure shows options on both of the tabs in that dialog box.

Here's a description of some of the common options you'll find in a printer properties dialog box:

- **Orientation:** Portrait prints in the normal vertical orientation; Landscape prints horizontally across the page.

- **Page Order:** Front to Back prints pages from lowest page number to highest. It keeps printed pages in the correct order if those printed pages come out of the printer face down. Back to

FIGURE 36-3

Sample Printer Properties dialog box.

Front prints pages from last to first, which keeps them in order if the printed pages come out face up.

- **Pages per Sheet:** If you specify a number greater than one, multiple pages are reduced to fit on the page. For example, choosing 2 prints two document pages on each piece of paper, making each document half its actual size.

- **Paper Source:** If your printer has more than one paper feeder, use this option to choose which one you want to use. For example, if you can keep regular paper in one printer bin and envelopes in a second bin, choose the second bin whenever you want to print envelopes.

- **Media:** Lets you specify the type or quality of paper you're printing on, such as Plain Paper or Premium Photo Paper.

- **Quality Settings:** To conserve ink, consider choosing this option and using a low-quality setting, such as Draft, and perhaps Black and White or Grayscale printing, for day-to-day printing. Use higher-quality settings and color for more professional-looking documents and photos.

- **Color:** Lets you print a color document in black and white, to conserve color ink.

Tip

If you have to change print options often, consider setting the printer's default properties to the options you select often. See "Setting Default Printing Properties" in Chapter 35 for details. ■

After you've made your selections in the Printer Properties dialog box, click OK to return to the Print dialog box. There, you can choose additional options. Or, click the OK or Print button in the Print dialog box to start printing.

If you change your mind after starting the print job, there's no simple "undo" that can stop the print job. You'll have to open the printer's icon in the Printers folder, and then right-click the document job and choose Cancel.

Note
See Chapter 37 for information on canceling a print job. ∎

Still more print options

Depending on the program and printer you're using, you might also see an Options button in the Print dialog box. Clicking that button takes you to still more options like the ones shown in Figure 36-4. In that example, additional printing options for Microsoft Office Word 2007 are displayed.

FIGURE 36-4

Still more printing options.

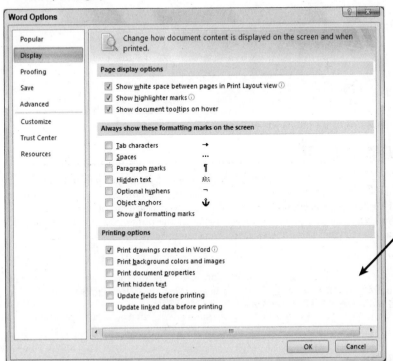

Most of the options in Figure 36-4 apply only to Word documents. For example, fields, forms, hidden text, and such are features of Microsoft Word documents.

FIGURE 36-5

Screenshot in a graphics program.

Printing the Screen

If you were around in the early days of computers with text screens, you might remember a time when you could print whatever was on the screen just by pressing the Print Screen key (perhaps abbreviated PrtScn, Prnt Scrn, or something like that). This was a so-called *screen dump*. It doesn't work that way in Windows. You can't print the screen directly to the printer. But you can *capture* the screen, paste it into a program, and print it from there. Here are the steps:

1.   Get the screen to look the way you want.

2.   To capture the entire screen, make sure no window is selected and then press the Print Screen key. To capture only the active window, dialog box, or message, select it to bring it to the foreground and then press Alt+Print Screen.

Note

If your keyboard has a Function Lock (or F Lock) key, it may need to be off for the PrtScn key to work. Some notebook computers require that you hold down an Fn or similar key while pressing PrtScn. ■

3.   Open your favorite graphics program.

4. Press Ctrl+V or choose Edit ➪ Paste from the graphics program's menu bar.

Tip

If you don't have a favorite graphics program, you can use the simple Paint program that comes with Windows. Click the Start button and choose All Programs ➪ Accessories ➪ Paint. ∎

A snapshot of the screen or program window opens in your graphics program. If your graphics program allows it, zoom out to get a more complete view. For example, Figure 36-5 shows a screenshot in Paint.

Tip

In some graphics programs, you can spin your mouse wheel to change the image's magnification. In others, you have to choose some option from the program's View menu, such as View ➪ Zoom. ∎

Once the screenshot is in a graphics program, print it as you would any other open document, using any technique described earlier in this chapter. If you plan to use the screenshot as a picture in a Web page, save it as a JPEG or Portable Network Graphics (PNG) file (if possible), using the Save As Type option in the Save As dialog box.

Tip

As an alternative to using the technique just described, you can use Windows 7's Snipping Tool to capture and annotate screenshots. See "Annotating Screenshots with Snipping Tool" in Chapter 14 for the whole story. ∎

Using Print Preview

Many programs offer a Print Preview feature that lets you see how a document will look on paper before you actually print it. That way, you'll know what to expect and avoid unpleasant surprises and wasted paper, such as expecting to print one page and ending up with twenty pages!

To use Print Preview, you'll need to open the document first, or browse to the Web page you want to print. Then, choose File ➪ Print Preview from the program's menu bar (assuming that the program you're using has a Print Preview feature). Or, right-click the page and choose Print Preview.

For example, suppose that you're considering printing a Web page that you're currently viewing. Before you start printing, you'd like to know how many pages will print and how things will look on paper. Click the arrow next to Print in the toolbar and choose Print Preview to see how the page(s) will look printed. Down at the bottom of the window you see a Page x of y indicator, where y tells you how many pages will print. Use the Show Multiple Pages drop-down list in the toolbar to display multiple pages, like in the example shown in Figure 36-6.

Use the arrows at the bottom of Print Preview to scroll through individual pages. Point to any button in the toolbar to see its name and purpose. To print straight from the Print Preview window, click the Print button at the left side of the toolbar. The Print dialog box will open. From there you should be able to choose specific pages to print. When you're finished with Print Preview, close it to return to the original program.

FIGURE 36-6

Internet Explorer's Print Preview window.

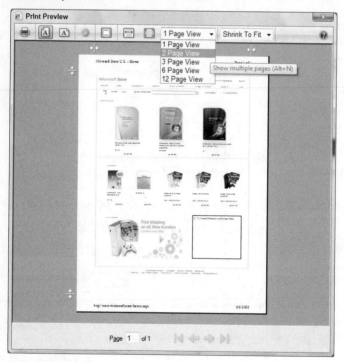

Wrap-Up

Printing should be a simple matter of choosing File ➪ Print from a program's menu bar, or right-clicking a document and choosing Print. Here's a quick recap of the main points of this chapter:

- To print the document you're currently viewing, choose File from that program's menu bar. Or, click the Print button in its toolbar or press Ctrl+P.

- To print a closed document from its icon, right-click that icon and choose Print.

- When the Print dialog box opens, you can choose a printer, a print quality, and other settings before you print.

- To print the screen, first capture the entire screen by pressing the Print Screen key. Or, press Alt+Print Screen to capture just the current window. Then, open any graphics program and press Ctrl+V. Finally, print the screenshot from that program.

- To see what an open document will look like before you print it, choose File ➪ Print Preview from the program's menu bar.

Managing Print Jobs

When you print a document, there's more going on than you might expect. The printer doesn't immediately start printing. Instead, the computer needs to convert your document to a set of instructions that tells the printer what to do. Then, those printer instructions have to be sent to the printer in small chunks, because the printer is a slow mechanical device compared to a computer, which is much faster.

Each document you print becomes a *print job* that has to wait its turn in line if other documents are already printing, or waiting to be printed. Most of this activity takes place in the background, meaning that you don't have to do anything to make it happen. In fact, you can just go about using your computer normally. There's no need to wait for the document to finish printing.

How Printing Works

When you print a document, quite a bit of work takes place invisibly in the background before the printer even "knows" there's a document to print. First, a program called a *print spooler* (or *spooler* for short) makes a special copy of the document that contains instructions that tell the printer exactly what to do. Those instructions don't look anything like the document you're printing. They're just codes that tell the printer what to do so that the document it spits out ends up looking like the document that you printed.

After the spooler creates the special printer file, it can't just hand the whole thing off to the printer as one giant set of instructions. Most printers are slow mechanical devices that can hold only a small amount of information at a time in a *buffer*. The buffer is a storage area within the printer that holds the data to be printed until it is printed. The amount of data that can reside in the buffer depends on the size of the buffer. In some cases, the buffer will hold a large number of pages. In others, it might only hold a single page, or in the case of a complex document such as a photo, and a relatively small buffer, only part of the page might fit in the buffer at one time.

Furthermore, when the spooler has finished creating the special printer file, there may be another document already printing. There may even be several documents waiting to be printed. So, the spooler has to put all the print jobs into a *queue* (line). All of this activity takes computer time (not *your* time, per se). And because each document has to be fed to the printer in small chunks, there's often time for you to do things like cancel documents you've told Windows to print but that haven't yet been fully printed.

To manage those print jobs, you use the *print queue*. If a document is already printing, or waiting to print, you'll see a tiny printer icon in the Notification area. When you point to that icon, the number of documents waiting to be printed appears in a tooltip, like the example shown in Figure 37-1. Double-click that small icon to open the print queue.

FIGURE 37-1

Printer icon in the Notification area.

As an alternative to using the Notification area, you can get to the print queue from the Devices and Printers folder. As mentioned in Chapter 35, you can use any of these techniques to open your Devices and Printers folder:

- Click the Start button and click Devices and Printers on the right side of the menu (if that option is available).

- Tap ⊞, type prin, and click Devices and Printers under the Control Panel heading.

- Click the Start button and choose Control Panel ➪ View Devices and Printers.

Once you're in the Printers folder, double-click the printer's icon to open its print queue.

Tip

To make a desktop shortcut to a specific printer, right-click the printer's icon in Devices and Printers and choose Create Shortcut. Any time you need to open the printer's queue, just double-click (or click) that shortcut icon on the desktop. ∎

Managing Print Jobs

The print queue for a printer contains all the documents that are currently printing or waiting to print. Figure 37-2 shows an example where I've already told Windows to print two documents. The first document I sent is currently printing. The other is waiting in line for its turn.

Sample documents in a print queue.

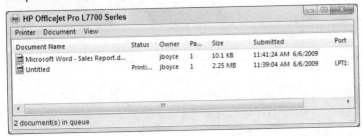

Managing a single document

To pause or cancel a specific print job, right-click its line in the print queue and choose one of the following options from the shortcut menu that appears:

- **Pause:** Stops printing the document until you restart it.
- **Restart:** Restarts the paused print job.
- **Cancel:** Cancels the print job so that it doesn't print and removes the job from the print queue.
- **Properties:** Provides detailed information about the print job. You can also set the document's priority. The higher the priority, the more likely the print job is to butt in line ahead of other documents waiting to be printed.

Managing several documents

To pause, restart, or cancel several documents in the queue, select their icons. For example, click the first job you want to change. Then, hold down the Shift key and select the last one. Optionally, you can select (or deselect) icons by holding down the Ctrl key as you click. Then, right-click any selected item, or choose Document from the menu bar, and choose an action. The action will be applied to all selected icons.

Managing all documents

You can use commands on the print queue's Printer menu, shown in Figure 37-3, to manage all the documents in the queue without selecting any items first. The options that apply to all documents are as follows:

- **Pause Printing:** Pause the current print job and all those waiting in line. See "Printing Offline" later in this chapter for an example of when this would be useful.

- **Cancel All Documents:** You guessed it — this cancels the current print job and all those waiting to be printed.

How Do I Stop This Thing?

Don't expect a paused or canceled print job to stop right away. Several more pages may print, even after you've canceled a print job. That's because the print queue sends chunks of a document to the printer's buffer. That buffer, in turn, holds information waiting to be printed. Canceling a print job prevents any more data from being sent to the buffer, but the printer won't stop printing until its buffer is empty (unless, of course, you just turn the printer off).

FIGURE 37-3

Printer menu in the print queue.

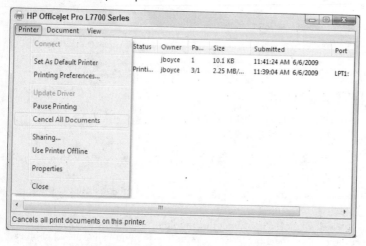

Changing print queue order

In the print queue, you can change the order in which documents in the queue will print. For example, if you need a printout right now, and there's a long line of documents waiting ahead of yours, you can give your document a higher priority so it prints sooner. In other words, your print job gets to butt in line ahead of others.

To change an item in the print queue's priority, right-click the item in the queue and choose Properties. On the General tab of the dialog box that opens, drag the Priority slider, shown in

Figure 37-4, to the right. The farther you drag, the higher your document's priority. Click OK. Your document won't stop the document that's currently printing, but it may well be the next one to print.

Priority slider in a print queue item's Properties dialog box.

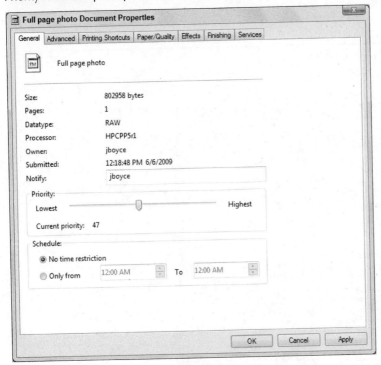

You can close the print queue as you would any other window — by clicking the Close button in its upper-right corner or by choosing Printer ⇨ Close from its menu bar. To get help with the print queue while it's open, choose Help from its menu bar.

Solving Common Printer Problems

If you experience a problem printing a document, the problem could well be something to do with the printer. Before you assume the worst and delve into any major troubleshooting, check for some of the more common problems that cause such errors, as listed next:

- Is the printer turned on and set online?
- Are both ends of the printer cable plugged in securely?
- Is there paper in the printer, and is it inserted properly?
- Is there a paper jam in the printer?
- Does the printer still have ink or toner?

More often than not, you'll find that the printer problem is something as simple as the printer being out of paper or ink.

If there seem to be no issues with the printer itself, you can do some troubleshooting in Windows. Open the Devices and Printers applet, right-click the printer, and choose Troubleshoot as shown in Figure 37-5. Windows 7 then runs through several troubleshooting steps to attempt to identify and fix the problem.

FIGURE 37-5

Troubleshoot a printer from Devices and Printers.

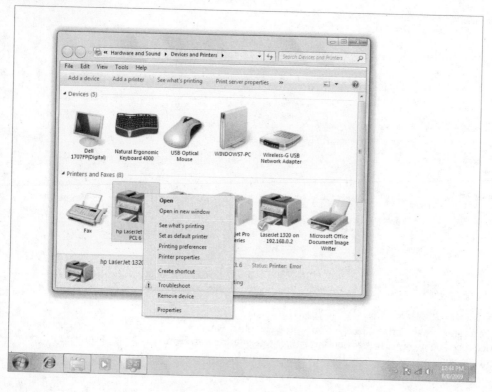

In some situations, Windows 7 will be able to identify the problem and fix it for you. In others, it will suggest a fix as shown in Figure 37-6.

Printing Offline

Printing offline is a means of going through the process of creating the spool file for the printer without actually printing the document. There are times when this is useful, such as when you're working on a notebook computer with no printer attached, but intend to print later when you can attach the computer to a printer or network.

FIGURE 37-6

Suggested troubleshooting action.

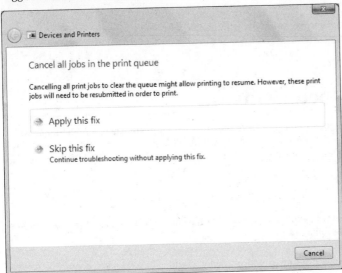

To make this work, open the printer's queue and choose Use Printer Offline from the Printer menu, as shown in Figure 37-7. The printer's icon will dim and show the word *offline*. You can disconnect the printer from the computer.

FIGURE 37-7

Use Printer Offline.

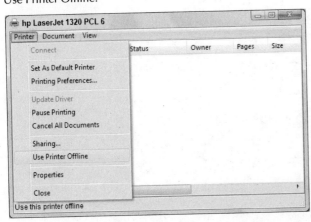

You can print any document while the printer is offline. Of course, the document won't actually print because the printer isn't connected to the computer. When you get back to the printer, connect the printer to the computer again. Open the Printers folder, right-click the printer's icon, and choose Use Printer Online. Any documents you "printed" while disconnected from the printer will start printing.

Caution

XPS documents are a great way to share electronic printouts with people who don't have the same program you used to create the document. ■

Creating XPS Documents

As an alternative to printing on paper, you can print to an XPS document. The XPS document will look exactly like the printed document will look, but it will be a file rather than a sheet of paper. You can then e-mail that XPS document to other people. Or, if you have a Web site, let people download it from your site.

Tip

You can also use this technique to print other people's Web pages to files on your own hard disk. You can view that file at any time; you don't need to be online. ■

To print to an XPS document, start printing as you normally would. For example, choose File ➪ Print from the program's menu bar. Or if you're in Internet Explorer, click the Print toolbar button. When the Print dialog box opens, choose Microsoft XPS Document Writer instead of your usual printer, as in Figure 37-8. Then click OK or Print.

FIGURE 37-8

Print an XPS document.

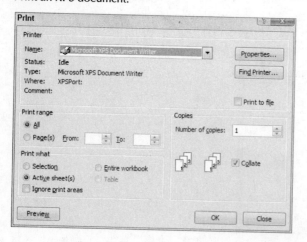

Because you're printing to a file, a Save As dialog box will open. There you can choose the folder in which you want to place the file, and give the file a name. Figure 37-9 shows an example where I'm about to print to a file named Budget 2010.xps in my Documents folder. Click Save.

FIGURE 37-9

Printing Budget 2010.xps in the Documents folder.

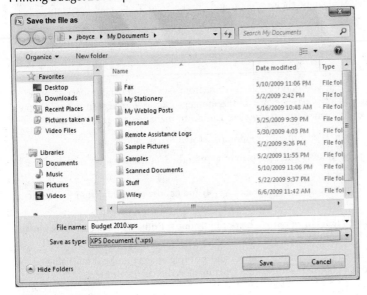

FIGURE 37-10

Icon for an XPS document.

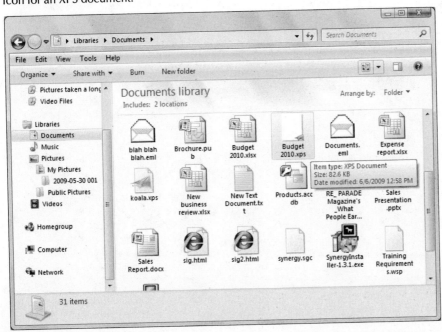

The Save As dialog box closes. To verify that the document was printed to a file, open the folder you printed to. The file is closed so it will look like an icon (see Figure 37-10), but you can treat it as any other document. For example, double-click the icon to open it. Or, if you want to e-mail it to someone using Windows Live Mail, right-click the icon and choose Send To ⇨ Mail Recipient.

Wrap-Up

The typical printing scenario is that you choose File ⇨ Print from a program's menu bar, or press Ctrl+P, to print whatever document you're viewing at the moment. But as you've seen in this chapter, there's more going on behind the scenes, and things you can do to manage your print jobs.

- Every document you print is a print job, temporarily stored in a print queue.

- To open the print queue, double-click the printer icon in the Notification area, or the printer's icon in the Printers folder.

- To manage print jobs in the queue, right-click any job and choose an option from the shortcut menu.

- To cancel all documents that are waiting to be printed, choose Printer ⇨ Cancel All Documents from the print queue's menu bar.

- To print to an XPS document rather than paper, start printing and get to the Print dialog box as you normally would but choose Microsoft XPS Document Writer as the printer.

Faxing and Scanning

F ax machines have been around for a long time, and it's a safe bet that you have at least a basic understanding of how faxing works, at least in the context of paper faxes. Essentially, you scan a document, the fax machine sends it to a recipient's fax machine, which then prints the fax.

There isn't as much reason to use faxes in today's world. If the item you want to send someone is a file, it's much easier to send an e-mail message to the recipient with a copy of the file attached. It doesn't matter what program you use for e-mail. They all allow you to attach files to messages.

On the other hand, if the person to whom you're sending a file doesn't have an e-mail account or can't accept attachments by e-mail, then fax might be your best alternative. You have the added benefit in Windows 7 of faxing right from your applications, with no need to print the document and scan it through a fax machine.

Tip
Though faxing and scanning are nothing new, Windows Fax and Scan provides new and easier ways to use fax equipment and scanners. ∎

What You Need for Fax

To use Fax, your computer must have either a fax modem that's connected to an analog phone line or access to a fax server on the same local network. A fax server is a program on a computer that has a fax modem installed and allows other computers in the network to send and receive faxes through that device. To use a fax server, you need to know the name of that server. If you didn't set up the fax server, ask the person who did for that name.

Note
If you have a multi-function printer that includes fax capabilities, you'll likely use the printer, not Windows or your computer, to send and receive faxes. See the manual that came with your printer for instructions. The information presented in this chapter may not apply. ∎

Opening Windows Fax and Scan

Windows Fax and Scan is the program that comes with Windows 7 for faxing and scanning. To open that program, use whichever of the following methods is most convenient for you:

- Click the Start button and choose All Programs ⇨ Windows Fax and Scan.
- Tap 🔳 , type fax, and click Windows Fax and Scan.

Figure 38-1 shows how the program looks when you first open it.

FIGURE 38-1

Windows Fax and Scan.

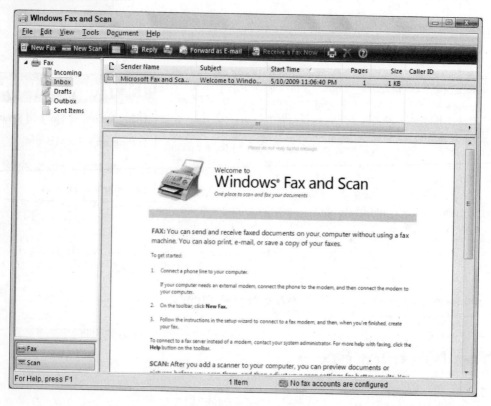

Creating a fax account

To send and receive faxes from your computer, you need a fax account. You need only set up the account once, not each time you want to use faxes. To create a fax account, open Windows Fax and Scan as described in the previous section. Make sure that you're viewing faxes rather than scans (click Fax in the left column if you're unsure). Then follow these steps:

1. In the menu bar, click Tools ⇨ Fax Accounts.
2. Click Add to create a new account.

3. On the first page to open, click the type of account you want to set up, either for a fax modem in your own computer or a fax server on your local network.

4. Follow the on-screen instructions depending on which type of account you're creating.

Note

If you're trying to connect to a fax server but don't know its name, ask your network administrator or the person who installed the fax server. Guessing won't work. ∎

When you're finished, the Fax Accounts dialog box shows the name of the fax account you created. Before you send or receive faxes, you'll want to configure the account to best suit your needs. See the next section if you're using a fax modem. See the section after next if you're using a fax server.

Configuring fax modem options

If you'll be using a fax modem in your own computer to send and receive faxes, you need to make some decisions about how you want to use it. The options available to you are in the Fax Settings dialog box. In Windows Fax and Scan, first make sure that you're in the Fax view (click Fax in the left column if you're not sure). Then follow these steps:

1. Choose Tools ⇨ Fax Settings from the menu.

2. If you want to send faxes from the fax modem, select (check) the first option, Allow the Device to Send Faxes.

3. If you want the fax modem to receive faxes, select Allow the Device to Receive Fax Calls on the General tab. Then choose one of the following options:

   - **Manually Answer:** Choose this option if you want to manually answer incoming calls by clicking the Answer Now button in Fax Monitor as described under "Receiving Faxes" later in this chapter.

   - **Automatically Answer after X Rings:** Choose this option if you want the fax modem to answer automatically. Then specify a ring delay (the number of times the phone must ring before the fax modem answers).

4. To configure fax alerts and how Fax Monitor operates, click the Tracking tab. You see the options in Figure 38-2.

5. Select or clear any options on the Tracking tab according to your personal preferences. If you don't have any preferences yet, select them all as in the figure.

6. Optionally, click the Advanced tab to configure options shown in Figure 38-3.

7. Finally, to grant faxing permissions to standard users, click the Security tab. Click the Everyone group and then use check boxes to allow permissions as you see fit.

8. Click OK.

Sharing Fax with a Voice Line

Faxing is easiest when you have a dedicated phone line for faxes. If the fax modem uses the same phone number as your voice phone, your best bet will be to choose Manually Answer. That way

continued

continued

if you hear the high-pitched tone of an incoming fax when you answer the phone, you can click the Receive Now button in Fax Monitor to accept the incoming fax.

Also, if you have an answering machine or service that automatically answers after X rings, you don't want Fax Monitor beating it to the punch every time. Otherwise nobody will be able to leave you a voice message!

FIGURE 38-2

Fax modem tracking options.

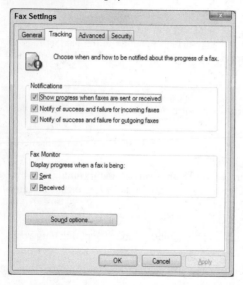

If you send and receive faxes through a fax server, there is no need to configure options for receiving faxes. Any faxes you receive will automatically be sent to your Inbox.

Defining Dialing Rules

If this will be the first time you're using your modem, you may need to take a moment to configure your dialing rules. For example, most locations in the United States require dialing a 1 before you dial a number outside your own area code. When dialing within your own area code, you might only need to dial seven digits. Or, if your area uses ten-digit dialing, you have to dial your area code plus the seven-digit phone number.

To configure dialing rules, open the Phone and Modem applet from the Control Panel (you can type phone and modem in the Start menu search box to find it). If this is the first time opening Phone and

Modem, Windows 7 displays the Location Information dialog box in which you enter your local area code and a couple of other self-explanatory options. Then, the Phone and Modem dialog box opens.

FIGURE 38-3

Advanced fax modem options.

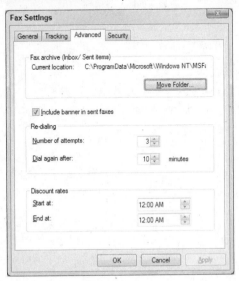

If you're using a modem with a desktop computer, you can set up one set of dialog rules for your location. If you use the modem in a portable computer and travel around, you can set up dialing rules for multiple locations.

The default location (the main location from which you dial) is referred to as My Location by default. Chances are you'll see that location in the Phone and Modem Locations as soon as the dialog box opens. If not, click the New button to create it. Use the New button to set up dialing rules for multiple locations, too.

To create or change dialing rules for any location listed in the Phone and Modem Options dialog box, click the location name and then click the Edit button. The first set of options, shown in Figure 38-4, are self-explanatory.

Keep in mind that all the options refer to where you're dialing *from*, not to, so you want to choose the country and specify the area code you're in when using the modem. If you need to dial a number carrier code for an outside line, choose the appropriate options, and specify the number you dial.

Call waiting can interfere with modems. So if there's a way to turn that off, choose the Disable Call Waiting option and specify the number you dial to disable that. Leave the Tone option selected unless you're in an area that still uses the old dial phones rather than buttons.

To create a rule for dialing area codes, click the Area Code Rules tab. Then click New to get to the options shown in Figure 38-5. The instructions on the tab explain how to define a rule. Remember that these rules apply to phone numbers you dial. For example, if you need to include the area code (but not a 1 prefix) when dialing within the 215 area code, enter that area code up top and select Include the Area Code near the bottom of the dialog box, as in the figure. Then click OK.

FIGURE 38-4

Edit Location dialog box.

If you need to define a rule for an area code and prefix combination (which is rare), you can specify the area code in the top box and then specify one or more prefixes under the Prefixes heading.

If you want all your phone charges to be put on a calling card, click the Calling Card tab. Choose the calling card company you use and click New. Then fill in the blanks to ensure that the calls are billed to your account. Click OK in all open dialog boxes after defining rules and accounts.

If you later discover that you're having a problem reaching a certain phone number, open the Phone and Modem Options dialog box again and choose the location from which you're dialing. Then click the Edit button to fix any rules or account information that might be causing incorrect dialing.

Setting Up Your Cover Sheets

It's generally a good idea to send cover sheets with faxes. You can define some general information to appear on cover sheets in advance, so you don't have to re-type that information every time you send a fax. If you've closed the Windows Fax and Scan program, re-open it using any of the methods described earlier in this chapter. Then choose Tools ➪ Sender Information from the menu bar. You'll see the dialog box shown in Figure 38-6.

FIGURE 38-5

Defining an area code rule.

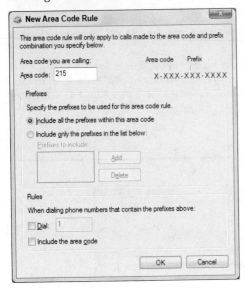

FIGURE 38-6

Defining sender information.

Fill in only as much information as you want to appear on each fax cover sheet. Then click OK.

Tip

Windows Fax and Scan offers a small selection of predefined cover pages, but you can also create your own. ■

Next, consider using the Fax Cover Page Editor to create a professional-looking fax cover sheet. To open the Fax Cover Page Editor, in Windows Scan and Fax, click Tools ➪ Cover Pages to open the Fax Cover Pages dialog box. Then, click New. Figure 38-7 shows the Fax Cover Page Editor program window with a few fields added to the cover page.

FIGURE 38-7

Fax Cover Page Editor.

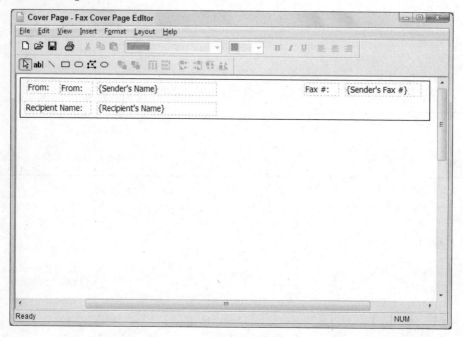

To insert fields into cover page, click Insert, then click Recipient, Sender, or Message, followed by the item you want to insert. The item then appears in the cover page and you can drag it into position and/or resize it as needed. Repeat the process to add to the cover page all of the fields you want. To align fields with one another, hold the Ctrl key and select the items you want to align, then click Layout and use the options in the Align Objects, Space Evenly, and Center On Page menus to lay out the fields on the page.

You can use the drawing tools in the Drawing toolbar to draw lines, squares, rounded boxes, polygons, circles, and ellipses, and also add text boxes to the page. The program is fairly simple to use, so I won't go into a lot of detail here. With several minutes of experimenting, you should be able to lay out a nice-looking cover page.

When you're ready to save the cover page so you can use it for your faxes, click File ⇨ Save. In the Save As dialog box, enter a name for the cover page and click Save.

Tip

Fax Cover Page Editor uses the folder My Documents\Fax\Personal CoverPages by default, but you can choose any folder you like. With your cover pages created, you're all set to start sending faxes. The next section explains how. ■

Sending Faxes

You can send faxes to people in two ways: right from the Windows Fax and Scan program, or from the program you used to create the document you want to scan. The end result is the same either way. Just use whichever method is easiest for you.

Faxing from Windows Fax and Scan

To create and send a fax from the Windows Fax and Scan program, open that program as described earlier in this chapter. Click Fax in the left column to ensure you're in the faxing mode. Then follow these steps:

1. Click the New Fax toolbar button and choose File ⇨ New ⇨ Fax from the menu.

2. If you want to include a cover sheet, click Cover Page and choose the style you want.

Tip

To create and manage your own fax cover sheets, choose Tools ⇨ Cover Pages from the Windows Fax and Scan menu bar. ■

3. To specify recipients, do any of the following:

    • Type the recipient's fax number directly into the box to the right of the To: button.

    • If the recipients are already in your Contacts, click To:, use the To ⇨ button to add each recipient's name to the Message Recipient's list, and then click OK.

    • To add recipients to your Contacts, click To:, click New Contact, and fill in the recipient's name and fax number (plus any other information you have). Click OK and then click To ⇨ to add the recipient to the Message Recipients list. Click OK.

Caution

If a recipient's name is red in the To: box, that means there is no fax number for that recipient. Edit the recipient's Contact information to include a fax number. ■

4. Fill in the Subject line with a brief description of the fax. If you send the fax to another computer, the Subject text will appear in the fax header, like the Subject line in an e-mail message.

5. Type the body of your fax in the main program window. You can use standard text selection techniques and options in the toolbar to format the text. (See "Basic text editing" in Chapter 14 for more information.)

6. Optionally, to insert a picture or file to send with your fax, click Insert on the menu bar to see the options shown in Figure 38-8. Then choose whichever option best describes what you want to insert as listed next.

FIGURE 38-8

Insert options.

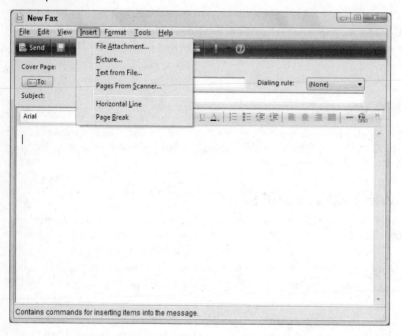

- **File Attachment:** Choose this option to attach any printable document to your fax. The file you choose will be converted to a TIF image and sent as part of the fax.

- **Picture:** Choose this option to insert a picture into the body of your fax message. When the picture is in the message, you can size it using the dragging handles. To wrap text around a small picture, right-click the picture and choose Properties, then set the Alignment property to Left or Right.

- **Text from File:** Choose this option to add text from any .txt, .htm, or .html file to your message. You can edit the inserted text using the same techniques used to edit text you typed yourself.

- **Pages from Scanner:** If you have one or more pages in your scanner to send, choose this option to scan the printed page(s) and add them immediately.

- **Horizontal Line:** Insert a horizontal separator line in the fax from margin to margin.

- **Page Break:** Start a new page in the fax.

7. Optionally, to preview how your fax will look to the recipient, choose View ⇨ Preview from the menu. Close the preview window when done.

8. Finally, to send the fax immediately, click Send. To schedule when the fax is sent, choose Tools ⇨ Options to see the options shown in Figure 38-9. Choose to send the fax when discount rates apply, or at a specific time of day. Then click OK.

The fax message will go to the Outbox until it is sent to the recipient. Once sent, a copy of the fax will be added to your Sent Items folder.

FIGURE 38-9

Sending options.

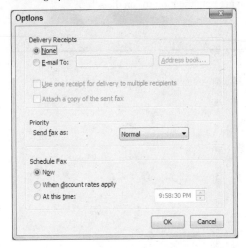

Sending faxes from programs

As an alternative to going through Fax and Scan, you can often fax a file using the same procedure you use to print. Open the document you want to fax using whatever program you typically use for that type of document. For example, open a document in Word, or a Web page in Internet Explorer.

Caution

When you fax a document, you send the recipient a non-editable image of the document. If you want to send an editable copy of the document, you should attach it to an e-mail message. ■

Next, choose File ➪ Print from the program's menu bar as though you were going to print the document yourself. When the Print dialog box opens, choose Fax from the list of available printers, as in Figure 38-10. Then click OK.

A copy of the document is converted to a TIFF picture and attached to a fax message in the New Fax window. Use the steps described in the previous section to choose a recipient, enter a Subject line, add a cover page, and set other options. When you're ready to send the fax, click Send.

If sent to a standard fax machine, the recipient sees the document printed on paper only. If the recipient is using software like Windows Fax and Scan, the document will be a TIFF image in their Inbox.

Receiving Faxes

If you've configured Windows Fax and Scan to receive faxes, you can receive incoming faxes in your Inbox. You might want to keep the Fax Monitor open at all times to make it easier to detect incoming faxes. This is especially important if you did not configure Fax and Scan to answer all calls automatically. To open Fax Monitor:

1. Open Windows Fax and Scan using any technique described near the start of this chapter.

2. Choose Tools ➪ Fax Status Monitor from the menu bar. The monitor opens as in Figure 38-11.

3. Optionally, close Windows Fax and Scan leaving only the monitor on the screen.

FIGURE 38-10

Choose Fax as the printer.

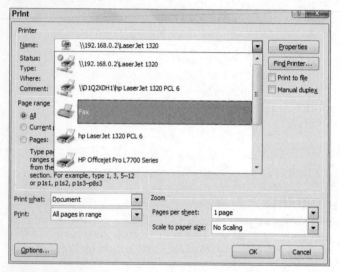

FIGURE 38-11

Fax monitor.

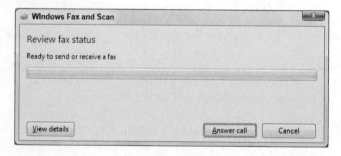

When the phone rings, you can pick up the handset on your phone to see who is calling. If you hear the high-pitched sound of an incoming fax, click Answer Call to accept the fax and add it to your Windows Fax and Scan Inbox.

Tip

Here's another way to get to your fax Inbox: Click the Start button and choose Documents. In the Navigation pane, expand Documents\My Documents and click Fax. ■

If you use a fax server rather than a fax modem in your own computer, you don't need to do anything to receive a fax. The fax server will add the fax to your Inbox automatically. Just check your Inbox occasionally to see what's available.

Working with Faxes

Windows Fax and Scan handles faxes in much the same way Windows Live Mail handles e-mail. New faxes you receive are placed in your Inbox. To see all the faxes in your Inbox:

1. Open Windows Fax and Scan using any method described near the start of this chapter.
2. In the left column, click Inbox under the Fax heading.

The top half of the main pane shows a header for each received fax. The header includes the sender's name, subject, time, pages, and other useful information. Click any header to see the contents of the fax message in the lower pane. Double-click any header to open the fax in a separate larger window. The rest is easy.

To reply to the fax, click the Reply toolbar button.

- To forward the fax to another fax recipient, click Forward as Fax in the toolbar.
- To forward the fax as an e-mail message, click Forward as E-mail.
- To close the fax, click the Close (X) button.

You can also work directly with fax headers in the top pane of your Inbox. For example:

- To print a fax, right-click its header and choose Print.
- To delete a fax, click its header and click the Delete (red X) toolbar button, or right-click the header and choose Delete.

For more information on faxing with Windows 7 and basic troubleshooting techniques, search Windows 7's help for fax.

Scanning Documents

A scanner is a device similar to a copy machine. You put a piece of paper in the scanner according to the instructions that came with your scanner. Then you scan the document. But unlike a copier, a scanner doesn't give a copy of the document on paper. Instead it stores a copy of the printed document as a file in your computer.

You use a scanner to get copies of things that exist only on paper into your computer. The scanned image is like a photocopy of the original. This means that even if the scanned document contains words, you won't be able to edit it in a program like WordPad, WordPerfect, or Microsoft Word.

If you want to edit a scanned document, you first need to use OCR (Optical Character Recognition) software to convert the scanned document to an editable form. Windows 7 doesn't come with OCR software built in. However, many programs that work with Windows do have built-in OCR capabilities. Chances are, when you bought your scanner, you got OCR software with it. To find out, check the documentation that came with your scanner.

If you have a scanner, you can use it to scan in three ways:

- You can use the scanning software that came with the scanner to scan any document. Use that method if neither of the following methods work with your scanner.

- If the item you want to scan is a picture or photograph, and Windows 7 recognizes your scanner, use Windows Live Photo Gallery described in Chapter 23 to scan.

- If the item you want to scan is not a picture or photo, and Windows 7 recognizes your scanner, you can use the techniques described in this section to scan the document.

Scanning with Windows Fax and Scan

To scan a document using Windows Fax and Scan, first open that program as described earlier in this chapter. At the bottom of the left pane, click Scan. Clicking Documents in the left pane lists all documents you've scanned with that program. If you haven't scanned yet, the list will be empty except for a sample scan, as in Figure 38-12.

To scan a document, load it into your scanner according to the scanner manufacturer's instructions. For example, if it's a flatbed scanner, place the document face down on the glass and close the cover. If it's the kind of scanner where you load pages into a document feeder, load them accordingly. Then follow these steps:

1. In Windows Fax and Scan, click New Scan in the toolbar or choose File ➪ New ➪ Scan from the menu bar.

2. In the New Scan dialog box (see Figure 38-13), you can choose a scan profile if you created one earlier.

3. Optionally, click the Preview button to see how the scanned image will look.

4. Optionally, use sizing handles in the preview area to crop out the portion of the document you want to scan.

FIGURE 38-12

Windows Fax and Scan in scan mode.

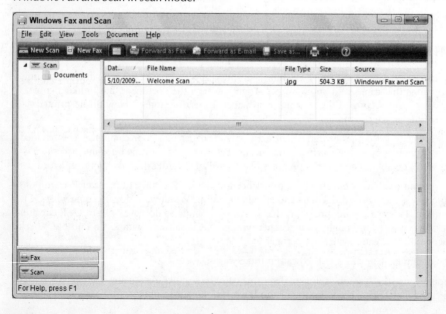

FIGURE 38-13

Choose a scan profile.

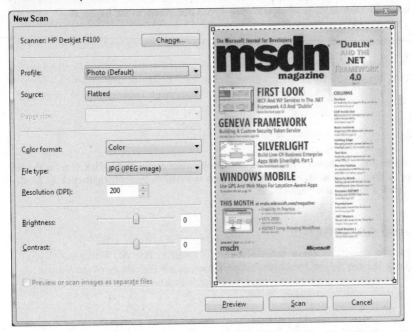

5. If there's anything you don't like about the preview image, use any combination of the following options to make adjustments:

   - **Source:** If your scanner offers multiple paper sources, choose the one that contains the document you're about to scan.
   - **Paper Size:** If you're using a non-standard paper size with an automatic document feeder, use this option to specify that size.
   - **Color Format:** Choose Color, Grayscale, or Black & White according to your preferences.

Tip

Use Black & White for text documents and forms that contain no shades of gray. Use Grayscale for photos and documents that do contain some shades of gray. ■

   - **File Type:** Choose your preferred file format. Bitmap Image is fine if you don't have a preference.
   - **Resolution:** Set this to 150 for clean standard printing. You can set it higher for more detailed scans. For example, if the preview of a scan looks like it's missing some text, try using a higher resolution.
   - **Exposure settings:** Use these options to adjust brightness and contrast if the preview image looks too dark or too flat.

6. If you changed any of these options, you can click Preview again to see how things will look. You can keep changing settings and clicking Preview until the scan looks the way you want.

Tip

If you want to save a profile with specific settings, choose Add Profile from the Profile drop-down list. Alternatively, adjust settings and preview the document until you get the results you want. Then you can click Save Profile to make it easy to reuse those same settings when scanning similar documents in the future. ■

7. Click Scan to scan the document. Wait for the scanner to scan the document.

By default, Windows Fax and Scan places newly scanned documents in the Scanned Documents folder, represented by the word Scan in the left pane. You'll see a header in that folder for every document you've scanned. To change the name of a scanned document, click its current name and type in a new name.

Tip

You can create additional folders under Scanned Documents to organize your scans. Right-click Scan in the left pane and choose New Folder to create a new folder. Then, to move a scanned document, right-click its header and choose Move to Folder, click a folder, and click OK. ■

Using scanned documents

Each document you scan is saved in the Scanned Documents folder in your My Documents folder. Clicking Documents at the left side of Windows Fax and Scan shows the names of those same documents. To print, e-mail, fax, delete, or do something else with a scanned document, right-click its header in the top main pane, as in Figure 38-14.

FIGURE 38-14

Right-click a scanned document header.

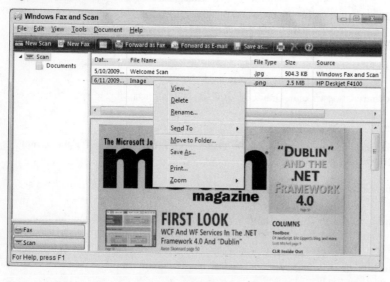

You'll find the same scanned documents in the Scanned Documents folder of you user account. Click the Start button and choose Documents ⇨ Scanned Documents.

Forwarding scanned documents automatically

If you use a scanner in a local network, you can automatically send a copy of all scanned documents to another computer on the network. Choose Tools ➪ Automatically Forward Scans from the Windows Fax and Scan menu (while you're in the scan mode).

To forward all scans to an e-mail address, choose the first option and specify the e-mail address. Or, choose the second option and specify the folder or UNC name of the folder to which you want to forward scanned documents.

Wrap-Up

Faxing and scanning are like two sides of the same coin. When you fax a document, you essentially send a photocopy of the document to a fax machine, or to a fax program on another computer. When you scan a document, you send a photocopy of the document to a file on your own computer's hard disk. You can use Windows Fax and Scan for both operations. Here's a quick wrap-up of the main points covered in this chapter:

- To open Windows Fax and Scan, click the Start button and choose All Programs ➪ Windows Fax and Scan.

- To work with faxes, click Faxes in the left column. To work with scans, click Scans in the left column.

- To create a new fax, click the New Fax toolbar button or choose File ➪ New Fax from the menu.

- To scan a document, load the document into the scanner and click the New Scan toolbar button. Or choose File ➪ New ➪ Scan from the menu bar.

- To work with a received fax or scanned document, right-click its header in the main pane in Windows Fax and Scan.

Troubleshooting Printing and Faxing

Troubleshooting Printing

Because no two printers are exactly alike, printing is more a matter of knowing your printer rather than knowing your computer or Windows. The best I can do here is to provide some general pointers that apply to most printers. But for specifics on your printer, the manual that came with the printer, or the main Web page for the product, will be your best bet.

First aid for printing problems

Before you start digging around the computer for solutions to a printing problem, check the most common physical problems:

- Make sure that the printer is plugged in and turned on.
- If the printer has an Online/Offline switch, make sure that it's online.
- Make sure that the printer cable is connected snugly at both the printer and computer ends.
- Make sure that the printer has paper.
- Make sure that the printer has ink or toner.
- Check for, and clear, a paper jam.

If none of the preceding help, take a look at the Help topics for printing, as described next.

Document appears to print, but nothing comes out of the printer

You may have selected a printer that produces files (like the Microsoft XPS Document Writer). After you choose File ⇨ Print to print a document, make

909

sure you choose an appropriate printer from the Print dialog box. To avoid making the mistake in the printer, make the printer you use most often the default printer, as discussed in Chapter 35.

Problem with a network printer

If your computer is a member of a network and your printing problems start right after installing or upgrading to Windows 7, the most likely problem is that the firewall has blocked communication with the printer. You'll need administrative privileges to unblock the firewall port. Follow these steps on each computer involved to enable them to share their printers:

1. Open the Windows Firewall applet from the Control Panel and click the link Allow a Program or Feature through Windows Firewall.

2. Click Change Settings, enter a password if prompted, and in the Allowed Programs and Features list, make sure that File and Printer Sharing is selected (checked) as shown in Figure 39-1.

3. Click OK and close Control Panel.

FIGURE 39-1

File and Printer Sharing enabled in Windows Firewall.

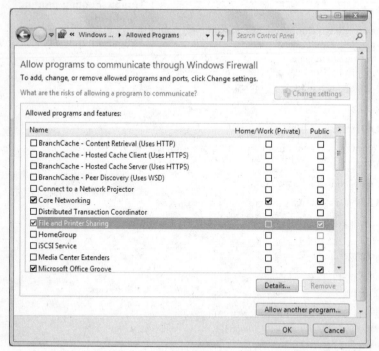

Printer prints garbage

If the printer used to print properly, turn off the printer. Then, close all open program windows and turn off the computer (click Start ⇨ Shut Down). Make sure that there is no paper jam in the printer, turn the printer back on, and wait a few seconds. Then, restart the computer normally.

If the trouble persists, delete all documents in the print queue and repeat the preceding procedure. If it still persists, consider updating the printer driver as discussed later in this chapter.

Advanced printing features are disabled

To use all the capabilities of a printer, you need to make sure that you have the most current printer drivers installed. Also, make sure that the printer's advanced features are enabled by following these steps:

1. Click Start ➪ Devices and Printers to open the Devices and Printers window.

2. Right-click the icon for the printer, and choose Printing Preferences.

3. Click the Advanced tab.

4. If you see Disabled next to Advanced Printing Features under Document Options, click that word and choose Enabled, as shown in Figure 39-2.

5. Click OK in all open dialog boxes.

FIGURE 39-2

Advanced Options dialog box for a sample printer.

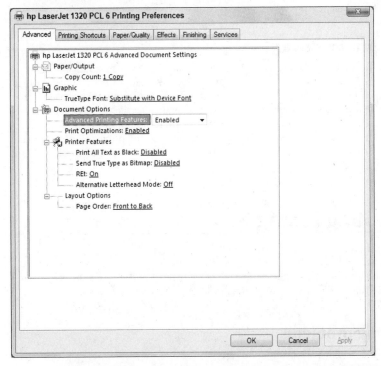

Printed colors don't match screen colors

On some Hewlett Packard and Canon BubbleJet printers, ICM (Image Color Management) may incorrectly color the printed page. To fix the problem, go to the Advanced Options and choose Disable ICM.

Error message "Problem communicating with printer"

This error occurs on some Lexmark printers that connect through a USB port. Getting the latest driver for the printer should resolve the problem. Optionally, you can turn off the USB hub's ability to turn off the device as follows:

1. Right-click the Computer link from the Start menu and choose Manage.

2. Click the Device Manager link on the left side of the window.

3. Click the arrow next to Universal Serial Bus controllers in the right pane.

4. Right-click USB Root Hub and choose Properties.

5. Click the Power Management tab.

6. Deselect the Allow the Computer to Turn Off This Device to Save Power check box.

7. Click OK in the Properties dialog box.

Note
If you have multiple USB root hubs, you'll need to repeat steps 4 through 7 for each one. ∎

8. Close Device Manager.

Updating your printer driver

A printer driver that's not specifically designed for Windows 7 can cause problems ranging from the printer not printing at all to garbled printer output. Most printer manufacturers submit updated drivers to Microsoft, so you may be able to update your printer driver right from Microsoft's Update Web site. You'll need to sign into a user account that has administrative privileges. Also, make sure your computer is online. Then open the Windows Update applet from the Control Panel and check for new updates. If there are no new updates for the printer, navigate to the printer manufacturer's Web site and search for a new driver. If you can't find a Windows 7 driver, you can probably use the Windows Vista version of the driver.

Troubleshooting Faxing

Like printing and scanning, faxing is more a matter of knowing your specific faxing hardware than it is about knowing your computer or Windows. Your best bet is to learn to use your fax hardware as described in the manual that came with the hardware device before you try to fax directly from Windows or a program. Again, the best I can do here is provide some general troubleshooting tips.

First aid for faxing problems

Windows 7 only provides access to your faxing hardware. To learn to use the fax that's part of an all-in-one printer, refer to the manual that came with the printer, or the manual that came with your fax modem or computer. If the fax device came with its own software, you may be better off using that software as opposed to Windows Fax and Scan.

Also, make sure that the fax phone port on your computer or printer is attached to a phone jack on the wall.

Tip

Remember, if you're trying to send a document that's already on your hard disk (as opposed to on paper only), you'll get better results by e-mailing the document as an attachment. ■

Printing and Faxing Troubleshooting Resources

Not all printers or fax modems are the same. Be sure to check the instruction manual that came with your printer or fax device for their troubleshooting suggestions.

You can also check Windows built-in help and support for troubleshooting tips. Click the Start button and choose Help and Support.

For additional help, post a question in the appropriate newsgroup at Windows Communities. See Chapter 18 for information on accessing the communities through Windows Live Mail.

Part VIII

Installing and Removing Programs

I n a sense, a computer is a simple machine that does only one thing — run programs. And that's the real beauty of it. It can be a stereo, TV, e-mail machine, Web browser, appointment book, a place to hang out online, a way to keep in touch with people, whatever you want it to be, because it is whatever program you have running at the moment.

The main reason why Windows is so popular and successful is because literally thousands of programs are available for it. Part VIII is all about finding and using programs that make your computer do what you want it to do.

Chapter 40 starts off covering installing programs from disks.

Chapter 41 covers getting older programs to run on Windows 7.

Chapter 42 covers important skills for repairing and removing programs. Chapter 43 covers different ways of configuring programs' default actions and processes. Chapter 44 gets into some of the more technical aspects of managing programs and processes. Chapter 45 wraps it all up with solutions to common software problems.

Installing and Upgrading Programs

Unlike documents, which you can freely copy to your hard disk and use on the spot, most new programs you acquire need to be installed before you can use them. The installation process configures the software to work with your particular hardware and software. The process also creates an icon or program group on your All Programs menu so that you can start the new program as you would any other.

You need to install a program only once, not each time you intend to use it. Once you've installed a program from a disk, you can put the disk away for safe keeping. You'll need the original installation disk to reinstall the program only if you accidentally delete it from your hard disk or if some sort of hard disk crash damages the program.

This chapter explores the common methods and issues you'll likely experience when installing programs for Windows 7. Keep in mind that the installation process, though similar across different programs, can still vary from one program to the next. So, the examples in this chapter are general, rather than specific.

Note
The rare exception to requiring installation is a self-contained program file that you simply copy to your computer and double-click to run. ■

Playing It Safe with Program Installations

Programs you buy in a store aren't likely to contain any malicious code such as viruses, worms, or spyware. Those things tend to be spread by e-mail attachments and free downloads from the Web. However, there's always an outside chance that the new program is incompatible with Windows 7 or a hardware device on your computer. So there may be times when you need to uninstall a program and then get all your system files back into shape to undo any changes made to your system by the new program.

Windows 7's System Protection greatly simplifies the task of getting things back in shape should a program installation or upgrade cause problems. But it only helps if it's turned on and you know how to use it. For details see "Using System Protection" in Chapter 33.

Updates versus Upgrades

Non-technical people often assume that updates and upgrades are the same thing. They aren't. An *update* is usually something you do online. There is nothing to buy at a store, no disk to insert in a disk drive. Updates are generally free, and often automatic (many programs scan for updates and offer them to you automatically). You don't have to make an effort to seek those out and install them.

Updates for some programs may not be quite so automatic. But you can often find out if any updates are available right from the program's Help menu. For example, in many Microsoft Office programs, you can choose Help ➪ Check for Updates from the program's menu bar to see what free updates are available for that program. In Office 2007 programs, click the Office button in the upper-left corner of the program window, click the Options button at the bottom of the menu (Word Options, Excel Options, etc.), click Resources in the left pane of the Options dialog box, and then click Check for Updates in the right pane.

Tip
You can also use Windows Update to check for Microsoft product updates. See Chapter 9 to learn about Windows Update. ■

Unlike updates, upgrades are usually not free. You have to purchase them and install them. For example, let's say you have Microsoft Office XP or 2003 installed on a computer. You want to get Office 2007 on that computer. In that case, you'd seek out an Office 2007 *Upgrade Edition* (which is cheaper than the regular edition). Then you'd install that upgrade edition right over your existing version. In other words, you wouldn't uninstall (remove) your existing version first.

Installing and Upgrading from a Disk

Before we get started here, know that you must have administrative privileges to install a program. In other words, you need to know the password for an administrative account on your computer. If you have a limited user account and don't know the administrative password, you'll need to get an administrator to install the program for you.

Most programs that you purchase will be delivered on a CD or DVD disk. You should always follow the installation instructions that come with such a program. But just so you know what to expect, here's how the process usually works, once you have the CD (or DVD) in hand:

1. Although not required, it's a good idea to run the installation with no other programs running to make sure you have plenty of memory available and any files that need to be updated by the installation will not be in use. Close all open program windows on your desktop by clicking their Close buttons or by right-clicking their taskbar buttons and choosing Close.

Note
You don't need to close programs whose icons are in the Notification area, unless specifically instructed to by the installation instructions for the program you're installing. ■

2. Insert the CD or DVD into your computer's CD or DVD drive and wait a few seconds.

3. Wait for the installation program to appear on your screen. If it doesn't appear within 30 seconds, see "Using the installed program" later in this chapter.

4. Follow the on-screen instructions to perform the installation.

That's really all there is to it. You will be presented with some questions and options along the way. Exactly what you see varies from one program to the next, but some common items include the End User License Agreement (EULA), and choosing a folder in which to store the program, which I discuss in a moment.

If nothing happens within half a minute or so after inserting a program's installation CD into your computer's CD drive, you may need to start the installation program manually. Here's how:

1. Open your Computer folder (click the Start button and choose Computer).

2. Open the icon that represents the drive into which you placed the disk.

3. If the installation program doesn't start automatically in a few seconds, open the icon named Setup or Setup.exe. (Click or double-click that icon.)

That should be enough to get the installation program started. From there you can follow the on-screen instructions to complete the installation.

The on-screen instructions and prompts you see during the installation will vary from one program to the next. The next section discusses some common things you're likely to come across when installing just about any program.

Note

You need not install a program every time you want to use it. You need install the program only once. From then on you can run it from the Start menu without the installation disk. ■

Common Installation Prompts

Even though every program is unique in some ways, you're likely to come across some common elements during a program installation. When you install a program, you probably won't see all the prompts described in the sections to follow, so don't be alarmed if your installation procedure is much simpler. (Be thankful instead.)

The initial CD or DVD prompt

Shortly after you insert the installation disk for a program, you may see a prompt like the one in Figure 40-1. Your choice there is easy — click the Run SETUP.EXE option (which might show an executable other than SETUP.EXE, as in Figure 40-1).

Enter an administrator password

Only people with administrative privileges can install programs in Windows 7. If you're signed into a limited account, you'll see a dialog box asking you to enter an administrative password. If you are already logged on with an administrative account, Windows 7 asks you if you want to allow the program to make changes to the computer. Click Yes to continue with Setup.

FIGURE 40-1

First prompt after inserting an installation CD.

The product key or serial number

Some programs (especially Microsoft's) require that you enter a product key or serial number to install the program. That number is usually on a sticker on the case or sleeve in which the program was delivered.

Tip

You may want to keep track of all your product keys in a WordPad document or other type of document in case you ever need to reinstall everything. Print a copy of the document and keep it safe in case your hard disk crashes. Belarc (www.belarc.com) offers a free program called Belarc Adviser that will list the product keys for all your installed programs, as well as a good deal more useful information about your systems. One of those free programs that's worth its proverbial weight in gold! Also check out Magical Jelly Bean Finder, at magicaljellybean.com/keyfinder. ■

If you do need to enter a product key or serial number, you'll see a prompt similar to the example shown in Figure 40-2. Type in the product key exactly as provided by the software developer, and click Continue (or whatever button the installation program offers to continue the installation process).

Compliance check

If you are installing the Upgrade Edition of a new program, and already have the older version installed on your computer, likely the installation program will detect the existing product and move through the upgrade. In other situations, particularly where you don't already have a previous edition of the program installed, you might be prompted to insert the CD for the old version and/or enter the product key for the old version. This depends entirely on the requirements of the application's upgrade program. Follow the prompts displayed by the upgrade program to provide the requested information.

Note

You might see a message asking what you want to do with the CD you just inserted. You do *not* want to install the program on the CD. The goal here is to simply prove you have the older version, not to install the older version. So if you do see a dialog box asking what you want to do with the CD, click the Close (X) button in the upper-right corner of that dialog box. ■

FIGURE 40-2

Enter a product key.

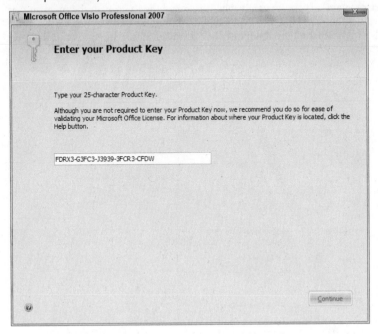

User information prompt

Some programs will offer prompts like the ones in Figure 40-3. These are optional, but useful. The username will automatically be entered as the Author name in any documents you create with the program. The initials will be used in settings where multiple people edit documents to identify changes you made to the document.

The End User License Agreement (EULA)

Just about every commercial program and most freeware and open source programs require that you accept the End User License Agreement (EULA) as part of the installation process. Figure 40-4 shows an example. The agreement is a legal document that defines your rights to the program, as well as the developer's retained rights.

The EULA differs from one program to the next. In most cases, the EULA gives you the right to install a program on one computer. However, that is not always the case. The EULA for Microsoft Office 2007 applications, for example, allows you to install the software on a licensed device (such as your desktop computer) and one portable device (such as your notebook PC). The intent of this clause is that you will only use the software on one computer at a time. What's more, you can access and use the software on the device remotely from any other device. For example, this means you can connect to your office PC from home and run the Office application remotely on your office PC (or vice versa).

Although many people never read the EULA when installing a program, you should take the time to do so. You'll discover interesting bits of information (such as being able to install Office on more than one computer), but also potentially discover possible problems. For example, I've seen EULAs for shareware and commercial programs that explain that the Setup program will install other, third-party applications along with the program, and that by accepting the EULA you are indicating your acceptance of those other programs. These programs might have nothing to do with the program you are installing, such as weather monitors, Internet Explorer add-ons and toolbars, and so on. Often the installation program will give you the option of not installing these additional programs, but that's not always the case. So, my best advice is to always read the EULA.

FIGURE 40-3

User information page.

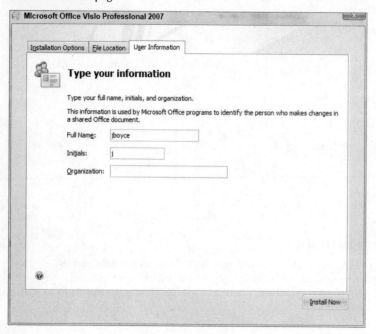

You can't install the program if you don't accept the terms of the agreement, so assuming you are happy (or at least resigned) to the terms of the EULA, select (check) the I Accept option and click Next, Continue, or whatever button continues the installation process.

Type of installation

Sometimes you'll be given some choices as to how and where you want to install the program. Figure 40-5 shows an example from Microsoft Office Visio Professional 2007. Unless your computer is low on disk space, it's generally a good idea to install the program with all features. Otherwise, months later you may go to use some advanced feature of the program only to get an error message saying it's not installed. A nice compromise in Microsoft Office Setup is to choose the Installed on First Use option for a feature, which causes Setup to run when you try to use a feature that is not yet installed. Then, you just pop in the CD or DVD, let Setup install the feature, and continue working.

FIGURE 40-4

Sample End User License Agreement.

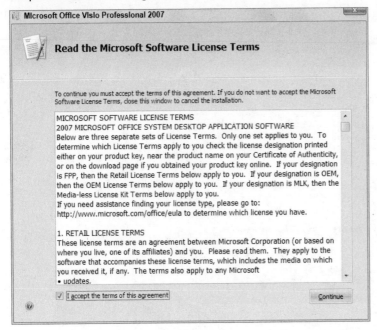

As to the "where" to install the program, there is rarely any reason to change the suggested location. That will typically be some folder in `C:\Program Files`. Don't change that unless you really have some good reason for doing it. Whatever you do, don't make the common newbie mistake of installing it in your Documents folder or someplace like that. You're not installing a document. You're installing a program. And it's best to keep all your programs in subfolders under `C:\Program Files`.

Installation summary

The installation procedure might give you a summary of the options you chose along the way. Typically you'll have a Back button or some other means to back up and make changes if needed.

Setup completed

The last page of the installation options might offer a couple of final options, like in the example shown in Figure 40-6. Whether or not you choose these options is relatively unimportant. You can check the Web for updates and additional downloads at any time, whether through the program itself or by visiting the software company's Web site (or the Microsoft Update site).

Some applications give you the option of keeping installation files on the computer rather than deleting them. Keeping the installation files can make it easier to change program settings or install missing components in the future. They usually don't take up any significant amount of disk space. Click Finish, remove the CD from the drive, and put it someplace safe in case you ever need to reinstall in the future.

FIGURE 40-5

Type of installation.

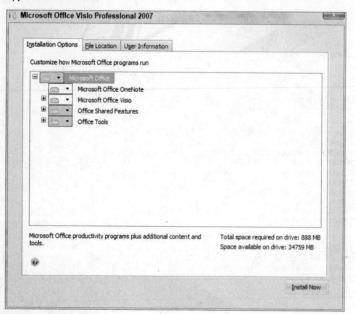

FIGURE 40-6

Setup complete.

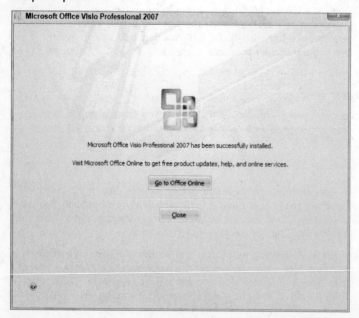

FIGURE 40-7

New program on the Start menu.

Note

Most insurance policies don't cover computer software. So if at all possible, consider keeping your original program CDs in a fireproof safe. ∎

Using the installed program

Once the program is installed, you can run it from the Start menu. In the preceding steps, I installed Microsoft Office Visio Professional 2007. So to run it, I'd click the Start button, then click the Visio item as shown in Figure 40-7. Or, I can choose All Programs ⇨ Microsoft Office, then click Microsoft Office Visio 2007.

Wrap-Up

Installing programs from CDs or DVDs is easy to do. It's basically a matter of putting the program installation disk into your CD or DVD drive and following the on-screen instructions. Here's a quick summary of the main points presented in this chapter:

- Consider creating a system restore point before installing any program. That way, if the new program creates problems, you can uninstall and return to the protection point to undo every change made during the program installation. Note that Windows 7 will create a restore point for you automatically in most situations.

- You need install a program only once, not each time you want to use it. Once installed, you run the program from the Start menu, without the program CD or DVD in the drive. In a few cases, the program requires the CD or DVD in the drive to validate that you have a licensed copy of the program (because possession of the CD or DVD implies that you haven't installed using someone else's media).

- If you're upgrading a program that's already installed, do not remove the existing version unless the installation instructions tell you to do so.

- The typical procedure for installing a new program is to insert the program's installation CD or DVD and follow the on-screen instructions.

- If nothing happens within a minute of inserting the installation disc, open your Computer folder, open the icon for the CD drive, and double-click the Setup or Setup.exe icon on the CD.

- When the installation is complete, store the installation disc in a safe place. In most cases you won't need it to run the program. But you may need it to reinstall the program should some mishap cause you to lose the program.

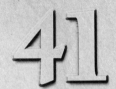

Getting Older Programs to Run

You can run almost any program that's installed on your computer just by clicking its startup icon on the All Programs menu. But, there are always exceptions to the rule. Chief among the list of exceptions are old programs that were originally written to work with earlier versions of Windows. Or, even worse, programs that were written to run on DOS.

That's not to say Windows *can't* run old programs. Most of the time, it can run an older program as-is, without any changes at all on your part. This is especially true if the program was written for Windows XP or later versions of Windows. So, before you assume that you have to do something to try to get an older program to run, try running the program normally. If it runs, you're done. If it won't run, then this is the chapter you need to (hopefully) get the program to run.

IN THIS CHAPTER

Old programs to avoid

Installing incompatible programs

Using the Program Compatibility Wizard

Quick and dirty compatibility

DOS commands and Windows 7

Understanding Program Types

A couple types of programs could be considered old in the context of this chapter:

- **DOS programs:** These programs were developed to run under various versions of the Disk Operating System (DOS) that was the precursor to Windows.

- **16-bit Windows programs:** These Windows applications were written for Windows 98 and earlier versions of Windows.

What does 16-bit mean? Three classes of Windows applications exist: 16-bit, 32-bit, and 64-bit. The number of bits indicates the maximum amount of addressable memory supported by the program. Table 41-1 indicates the differences.

Windows NT, Windows 2000, and Windows XP were all originally 32-bit operating systems. Windows XP was also offered in a 64-bit edition. Windows 98 and earlier were 16-bit operating systems. Windows Vista was offered in two versions, 32-bit and 64-bit. Likewise, Windows 7 is available in 32-bit and 64-bit versions. Suffice it to say, the higher the bits, the more capable the operating system. For the purposes of this chapter, the key point is that you can run a program on the OS it was designed for or (possibly) on a later version, but you can't go backwards. For example, you can run a 32-bit application on a 64-bit OS, but you can't run a 64-bit program on a 32-bit OS.

TABLE 41-1

Processor Technology and Directly Addressable Memory

Technology	Meaning	Memory Addresses
16-bit	2^{16}	65,536
32-bit	2^{32}	4,294,967,296
64-bit	2^{64}	18,446,744,073,709,600,000

DOS programs

Let's make a distinction between DOS programs and DOS commands that you can run in Windows 7. Consider "DOS programs" to refer to programs that were written specifically to run on a DOS operating system without (and prior to) Windows. It's so unlikely that you would want to run an old DOS program on Windows 7 that I don't even cover the topic in this chapter (although I do have a copy of Zork lying around somewhere that would be fun to play again ...). That doesn't mean you *can't* run that DOS program under Windows 7, because many of them will run without any major problems.

DOS commands that you run in a Windows 7 command console are actually DOS programs themselves. The difference is that they are developed by Microsoft and included as part of the Windows package, rather than being developed and marketed by third parties. I do cover DOS commands to some degree later in this chapter.

Old programs to avoid altogether

Windows 7 is a revision of the Windows Vista operating system, so almost all Vista programs should have no problems running on Windows 7. Likewise, many of your basic XP application programs will work. But you should validate compatibility for other kinds of programs before attempting to run under Windows 7. These include:

- **Old disk utility programs:** Older disk utility programs such as Norton Utilities and various disk compression and partitioning tools should never be run on Windows 7. Many older CD-burning programs are likely to cause problems too. If you have such a program, you should really upgrade to the Windows 7 version of that program, or find a similar product that's designed to work with Windows 7.

- **Old backup programs:** If you have an older backup program, using it in compatibility mode could prove disastrous. Even if you're able to perform the backup, there's an outside chance you won't be able to restore from the backup if and when you need to. Consider using Windows Backup, which came with your copy of Windows 7.

- **Old cleanup programs:** Older programs that purport to keep your computer running in tip-top shape, clean up your registry, and so forth should not be used at all in Windows 7. If you like the program, look into getting a version that's specifically written for or certified by the developer as compatible with Windows 7.

- **Old optimizing programs:** Programs designed to make your computer run at maximum performance won't necessarily make Windows 7 run that way. In fact, they may do a lot more harm than good. If you use such programs, check to see if there's a Windows 7 version available before you install the old version.

- **Old antivirus programs:** Virus detection and removal is dicey business, and needs to be handled with great care. Antivirus programs written for pre-Windows 7 versions of Windows should never be installed or run on a Windows 7 computer unless certified by the developer as compatible. The same goes for anti-spyware and other anti-malware programs. Better to seek out a Windows 7 version of the program than to presume the older version will work.

Installing Incompatible Programs

To install an older program, first try installing it normally. For example, if it's on a CD, insert the CD and wait for the installation program to appear automatically. If nothing starts automatically, open your Computer folder (click Start and choose Computer). Then open the icon for the drive that contains the installation disk and double-click the setup launcher program (typically setup.exe, setup, install.exe, or install). If Windows 7 determines that the program is older, you'll see the Program Compatibility Assistant shown in Figure 41-1.

FIGURE 41-1

Program Compatibility Assistant.

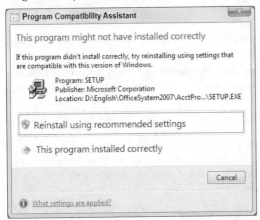

If you believe that the program installed normally, just click the second option. Otherwise, click the first option. Windows 7 will assign some compatibility mode attributes to the program and try the installation again. Hopefully, the second try will do the trick.

If you still have problems, here are some things to consider:

- If you're installing from a standard user account, log out and log in to an administrative account, then try to install from that account.

- If you have to create any file or folder names, use old 8.3 conventions (keep filenames to eight characters maximum with no blank spaces).

- If you get stuck in an installation program, use the Applications tab in Task Manager to end the stuck program. See Chapter 44 for details on Task Manager.

If all else fails, contact the program publisher (if they're still in business). They're the only ones who really know if the program will even run in Windows 7, and what's required to get it to run.

Using the Program Compatibility Wizard

Installing a program is one thing; getting it to run after it's installed is another. If an installed program won't start or isn't working right, try using the Program Compatibility Wizard on it.

The Program Compatibility Wizard provides a step-by-step means of configuring and testing an older program so that it will run in Windows 7. Before you bother to use it, try running the installed program without it. You could discover that the program runs just fine without any compatibility settings and save yourself quite a bit of trouble.

If you're sure an installed program isn't running, or is not running correctly, follow these steps to start the Program Compatibility Wizard:

Tip
You can right-click a program's icon and choose Troubleshoot Compatibility to launch the Program Compatibility Wizard. ■

1. Open the Control Panel and click the Programs category. Then click Run Programs Made for Previous Versions of Windows to launch the Program Compatibility Wizard.

2. Read the first wizard page and click Next.

3. On the second wizard page, choose the program for which you want to modify compatibility settings. Then, click Next.

4. If you want Windows 7 to try to determine the right settings on its own, click Try Recommended Settings. To specify your own settings, click Troubleshoot Program. The following steps assume you have selected the second option.

5. The wizard next prompts you to answer questions about the program (Figure 41-2). Selecting any of the first three causes the wizard to prompt you with related questions. For example, if you choose the option The Program Worked in Earlier Versions of Windows but Won't Install or Run Now, the wizard asks you to specify on which version of the OS it worked previously. Likewise, choosing the option The Program Opens but Doesn't Display Correctly results in a list of questions similar to that shown in Figure 41-3.

6. Complete the wizard by selecting options that relate to the problems you are having with the program.

The process is mostly trial-and-error. If the program runs when you finish the wizard, great. Otherwise you can run it again to try some different settings until you can get the program to work right.

Here are some general guidelines to help you get your programs running:

- If the program won't install or won't run, run the wizard, choose the option The Program Worked in Earlier Versions of Windows but Won't Install or Run Now and specify the operating system for which the program was written. For example, if it is a Windows 98 game, choose that OS from the OS list provided by the wizard.

- If you have problems with the program's display, choose the option The Program Opens but Doesn't Display Correctly and click Next. Choose the symptoms the program is exhibiting and click Next to let the wizard set display options as needed.

FIGURE 41-2

Program Compatibility questions.

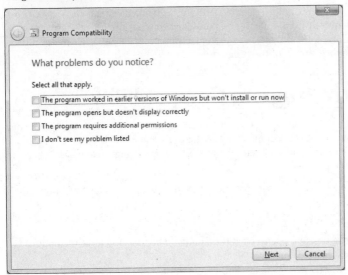

FIGURE 41-3

Display options for compatibility.

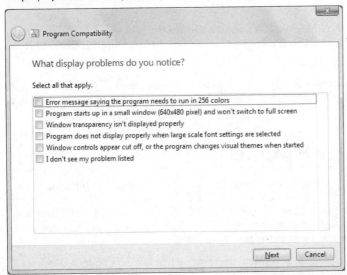

- If you think the program is having permissions issues, such as the program says it can't write a file, choose the option The Program Requires Additional Permissions. The wizard will configure the program to run as an administrator, which should resolve the issue.

There's no guarantee that the Program Compatibility Wizard will make the program run. Some programs are so old, and so far removed from modern computing capabilities, that there's just no way to force them to run. In those cases, the only hope is to contact the program publisher to see if they have any solutions or a compatible version of the program.

Quick-and-Dirty Program Compatibility

The Program Compatibility Wizard provides an easy way to choose and test settings for program compatibility. Those settings are stored on the Compatibility tab of the program file's Properties sheet. You can use the wizard to change compatibility settings, or you change settings manually right in the Properties sheet by following these steps:

1. Click the Start button, choose All Programs, and get to the startup icon that you'd normally click to run the program.

2. Right-click the program's startup icon and choose Properties.

3. In the Properties dialog box that opens, click the Compatibility tab. You'll see the options shown in Figure 41-4.

4. Choose Run This Program in Compatibility Mode For and then choose the operating system for which the program was written. If the program installs and runs, but exhibits other symptoms (such as display problems), leave this option unselected.

5. If you are having problems with the program's display, choose appropriate display settings in the Settings group.

6. If the program seems to have permission problems, select Run This Program as an Administrator.

7. If you want to apply the settings for everyone who uses the program, click the Change Settings for All Users button to open a similar Properties dialog box, and set properties there as needed.

8. Click OK.

The compatibility settings will stick to the program. So you can just start the program normally, from the All Programs menu, at any time. Just keep in mind there's no guarantee that you'll be able to force all programs to run in Windows 7.

Using Windows XP Mode

Microsoft recognizes that many small-to-midsize business users need to continue to run applications designed for previous versions of Windows on Windows 7, and that the compatibility features in previous versions of Windows were only a partial solution. To provide a better solution, Microsoft has developed a new compatibility platform that leverages new hardware virtualization technologies. This new platform is called Windows XP Mode and is part of the latest version of Windows Virtual PC.

Windows Virtual PC makes it possible to run virtual operating system instances under a Windows 7 host operating system. For example, given enough memory, you could run a Windows XP and a Linux virtual machine at the same time on one computer. In this example, Windows 7 is the host operating system and Windows XP and Linux are the guest operating systems. The guest OSs run in

FIGURE 41-4

Compatibility settings.

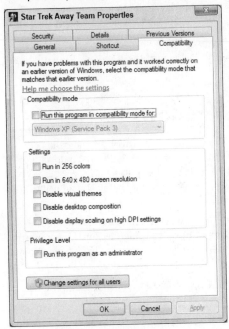

their own environments separate from one another and from the host OS. However, they can use the host's hardware, such as USB ports, printers, and so on.

Windows XP Mode runs the applications that you specify in a Windows XP virtual machine. The application running in Windows XP Mode appears to be installed like any other application on your desktop, but instead runs in the Windows XP virtual machine when launched.

To take advantage of Windows XP Mode in Windows 7, your computer's CPU must support either the Intel™ Virtualization Technology or AMD-V® feature, and that feature must be enabled in the computer's BIOS. To determine if your computer's CPU supports either of these features, first determine what type of CPU it has. Click Start, right-click Computer, and choose Properties. The resulting System applet shows the processor type. Look for either Intel or AMD to determine which type of CPU you have.

Next, visit http://www.microsoft.com/windows/virtual-pc/support/configure-bios.aspx and follow the appropriate link to download either the Intel or the AMD compatibility checker. These tools check your computer to determine whether the CPU supports the required virtualization technology.

If you computer meets the virtualization requirement, the next step is to download and install Windows Virtual PC from www.microsoft.com/windows/virtual-pc. Then, download and install Windows XP Mode from the same link. With both of those installed, you should see a Virtual Windows XP item under the Windows Virtual PC item in the Start menu. Clicking this launches the Windows XP virtual machine for the first time, and you are taken through a wizard that configures the XP environment where you specify whether to enable Windows updates, user account credentials to use in the virtual environment, and a few other items.

933

When the virtual environment finishes configuration and loads, you'll see a Windows XP desktop running in a window, complete with its own Start menu, taskbar, and other Windows XP elements. Next, in the Windows XP virtual machine, install the applications that you need to run in Windows XP Mode. After the installation is complete, you'll see a shortcut for the application in the Windows XP virtual machine's Start menu, and also in the host Windows 7 Start menu. You can launch the program from either shortcut.

To learn more about Windows Virtual PC and Windows XP Mode, visit the Windows Virtual PC site referenced previously.

Using DOS Commands in Windows 7

Readers who have used personal computers since the DOS days might still wish to enter the occasional DOS command. DOS commands will let you do things you can't really do in Windows. For example, in those rare instances where you can't delete a file in Windows, using a DOS erase or del command with the /F switch will often do the trick. You can use the DOS dir command to print filenames from a folder to paper or a text file.

There is one big catch to using commands in Windows 7. UAC may prevent you from doing things you'd otherwise take for granted. You can get around many of those by using the Run As Administrator option to open the command prompt. Here are two different ways to open the Command Prompt window:

- Click the Start button and choose All Programs ➪ Accessories ➪ Command Prompt. Or right-click Command Prompt and choose Run As Administrator.

- Press 🏁, type **cmd**, and choose cmd.exe or right-click cmd.exe and choose Run As Administrator.

The Command Prompt window that opens is much like DOS. By default you're taken to the home directory for your user account. But you can navigate around using the DOS cd command. For example, enter **cd..** to go to the parent directory, or **cd program files** to go to the Program Files folders.

To see a list of all supported commands, enter help at the command prompt. For the syntax of a command, type the command followed by /?. For example, entering dir /? displays the help for the dir command.

Note
You can change the height and width of the Command Prompt window. To do so, click its control menu in the upper-left corner and choose Properties. ■

You can copy-and-paste a lengthy pathname to a cd command to simplify opening that folder in a DOS window. In Windows, open the folder in Windows Explorer, highlight the path in the address bar as in Figure 41-5, and press Ctrl+C to copy it.

Tip
To see the name you need to type in order to launch any program, right-click the program's icon on the All Programs menu and choose Properties. The filename at the end of the Target path is the name you type in the Search or Run box. ■

FIGURE 41-5

Select a directory path.

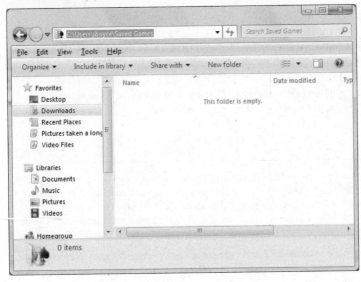

In the Command Prompt window, type **cd** and a space. Then right-click the Command Prompt window and choose Paste. Press Enter, and you'll be in that folder.

Use the `dir` command with various switches to view, or optionally print, all the filenames in a folder and also its subfolders if you like. For example, let's say you navigate to the Music folder for your account (`C:\Users\yourUserName\Music`). From that folder, entering

```
dir /s
```

lists all file and folder names for all artists, albums, and songs in your Music folder.

You can use the `/b`, `/n/`, and `/w` switches to choose how you want the information displayed. For example, entering

```
dir /s /w
```

shows filenames in the wide format.

To send `dir` output directly to the printer, try

```
dir /s /w > prn
```

You're probably better off sending the output to a text file rather than straight to the printer. That way you can open and edit the text file before you print. Or even import it into Excel or Access to make it more like tabular data. To send output to a file, end the command with a filename (or path and filename). For example, entering this command from the Music folder

```
dir /s /w >MyMusic.txt
```

puts the output listing in a file named MyMusic.txt in the Music folder. You can then open that file with any text editor or word processor to clean it up. If you have database management skills, you can import the data to Access or a similar program and treat it like any other tabular data.

Caution

This section is just a side topic for people who are already familiar with DOS. Don't experiment with DOS commands carelessly. You could lose a lot of files and have no means of getting them back! ■

To exit the Command Prompt window, enter the exit command or just close its window.

Wrap-Up

This chapter has focused on techniques for getting older programs to work in Windows 7. Windows 7 offers several tools to help with compatibility issues. Whether or not you have any luck with them depends on how old and how incompatible the program is. Most of your programs will run fine under Windows 7 with Compatibility Mode or Windows XP Mode. A few won't, until you upgrade to the Windows 7 version, but those should be few and far between. The main points are as follows:

- Most programs written for Windows XP and later are already compatible with Windows 7 and require no special handling.

- When you attempt to install an older program, the Program Compatibility Assistant kicks in automatically to help out.

- The Program Compatibility Wizard helps you with installed programs that won't start or run correctly.

- Compatibility settings are stored in the program file's Properties sheet, on the Compatibility tab.

- To use DOS commands in Windows 7 with minimal flack from UAC, choose Run As Administrator to open the Command Prompt window.

Repairing and Removing Programs

Most of the time, you will experience very few problems with your applications. Occasionally, however, you might need to repair a program that is having problems. Or, you might want to remove a program or a Windows feature that you are not using.

In this chapter, you learn techniques for managing installed programs. You learn how to change or repair programs, as well as to remove programs you no longer need or want. You'll do most of these tasks in Control Panel's Programs and Features applet.

Changing and Repairing Programs

Some large programs let you choose how you want to install the program. For example, you may be given options to do a Minimum Install, Typical Install, or Complete Install. You might do a Minimum or Typical installation to conserve disk space, but later discover you need a feature that only the Complete install would have provided.

Sometimes a program might become *corrupted* and not work properly anymore. That can happen when you inadvertently delete a file that the program needed. Or it might be caused by some minor glitch that compromised a file that the program uses.

The first step to changing or repairing a program is to get to the Programs and Features applet in Control Panel. Here's how:

1. Click the Start button and choose Control Panel.

2. In the category view, click Programs.

3. Click Programs and Features.

You can also get to Programs and Features from the keyboard. Press ![Windows key], type **fea**, and choose Programs and Features from the Start menu.

The page that opens lists all of your installed application programs. (It doesn't include programs that come with Windows 7.)

Not all programs offer change or repair options. To see what options an installed program offers, right-click the program name. Or, click the program name and take a look at the buttons above the list of program names. Things you can do with that program will be listed in a toolbar above the list. For example, in Figure 42-1, I clicked Microsoft Office Live Add-in, which offers options to Uninstall, Change, or Repair.

List of installed programs.

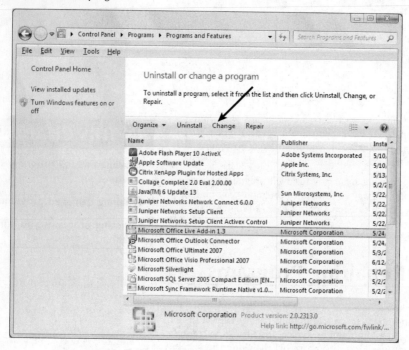

In most cases, you'll need the CD (or DVD) from which you originally installed the program to change or repair the program. If you have the CD handy, go ahead and put it in the CD drive. If AutoPlay asks what you want to do with the disk, choose Take No Action. If the installation program opens automatically, just cancel or close that program.

Note
Changes you make to a program affect all users. Therefore you must know the password for an Administrator account on your computer to change or repair programs. ■

Exactly how things play out from here will vary from one program to the next, so I can only provide some general guidelines and examples. But all you really have to do is make your selections and follow the instructions on the screen. For example, to repair a corrupted program, click the Repair button and do whatever the resulting instructions tell you to do.

The Change option for a program is generally for adding components you didn't install the first time around, though you can also remove any components you don't need. The exact process will vary from one program to the next, but a typical approach is to list all program features in a hierarchical tree, like the example in Figure 42-2.

FIGURE 42-2

Click an optional component.

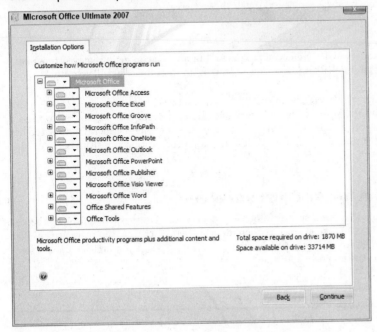

Note

Don't use Programs and Features to change settings within a program. Instead, use the program's Options or Preferences dialog box. Open the program as you normally would and look through its menus for a Tools or Preferences option. Or search that program's help for the word *preferences* or *options*. ■

In the tree, click a program feature to choose an action. For example, choose Run From My Computer to install a feature. To remove an optional feature, choose Not Available. That feature will be removed and its icon will display a red X. When you're finished making your selections, click OK or Next and follow the on-screen instructions.

Removing (Uninstalling) Programs

Unlike documents and other files, copying a program to your hard disk isn't enough to make it usable. You have to *install* programs before you can use them. Likewise, simply deleting the startup icon for a program isn't enough to remove the program from your system. You have to *uninstall* the program. All of this is because a program often consists of many files. For example, Microsoft Office comprises hundreds of files! Furthermore, installing a program makes other changes to the system. Uninstalling is necessary to undo those changes.

Note

You must be logged in to an administrative account, or know the administrator password for your PC, to remove a program. ■

Before you remove (uninstall) any program, make sure you know what you're removing and why. Just because you don't know what a program is or what purpose it serves, that doesn't mean you should remove it. Removing programs isn't likely to solve any computer programs, so you shouldn't remove a program as a means of solving some problem through sheer guesswork.

Caution

There is no Undo or Recycle Bin for reinstating removed programs. The only way to get a removed program back is to reinstall it from its original installation CD or download it again from the original Web site. ∎

With all those cautions out of the way, removing a program is quite simple. Assuming you're already on the Programs and Features applet, right-click the name of the program you want to remove and choose Uninstall. Or, select that program's icon or name and click the Uninstall button in the toolbar. If prompted, enter an administrative password. Follow any additional instructions that appear on the screen.

Uninstalling from the All Programs menu

If you don't find a program that you want to remove in Programs and Features, you might still be able to remove it right from the All Programs menu. Click the Start button, choose All Programs, and then look for an Uninstall or Remove option like the example in Figure 42-3. If you find such an option, you can click it to remove the program from your system.

FIGURE 42-3

Uninstall from the All Programs menu.

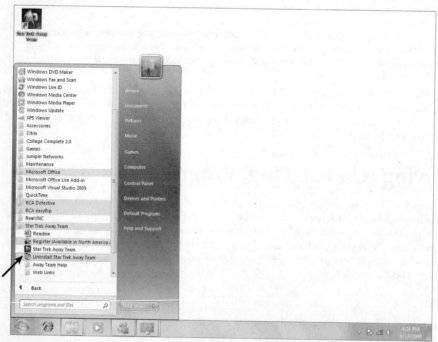

Dealing with stuck programs

Occasionally you might come across a situation where removing a program generates an error message before the program is completely removed. The first thing to do, of course, is to read the error message and see what options it offers. You may be able to finish the removal just by choosing options that the error message provides.

If you can't get rid of a program through the normal means or error message, your next best bet would be to install the program again. That might seem counterproductive, but the problem might be that the program only partially installed in the first place. A partially installed program may not have enough stuff installed to do a thorough removal. Once you've completed the initial installation, you should be able to remove the program without any problems.

Returning to a Previous Version

Tip
Returning to the previous version of a program is a quick and easy way to deal with program updates that cause more problems than they solve. ■

FIGURE 42-4

Restore the previous version of a program.

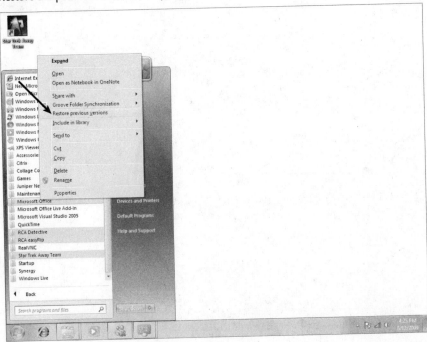

It seems computer programs are never done. Every program evolves through versions, each version a little bigger and better than its predecessor. But sometimes the latest and greatest version of a program won't quite work correctly on your computer. When that happens, you may be able to return to the previous version of the program with minimal fuss. Get to the program's startup icon on the All Programs menu and right-click it. If you see a Restore Previous Versions option like in Figure 42-4, click it. Then follow the on-screen instructions to return to the previous version.

Updates to programs are a little different than upgrades and can't always be removed using the Restore Previous Versions option. But should an update cause problems on your system, you can remove it. Click View Installed Updates in the left column of the Programs and Features window. The list of installed programs changes to a list of installed updates. As with programs, you can click an installed update to remove or change it.

Turning Windows Features On and Off

Tip

Unlike Add/Remove Windows Programs in Windows XP, Program Features in Windows Vista and Windows 7 allow you to turn features on and off without the hassles of installing and uninstalling. ■

FIGURE 42-5

Windows Features.

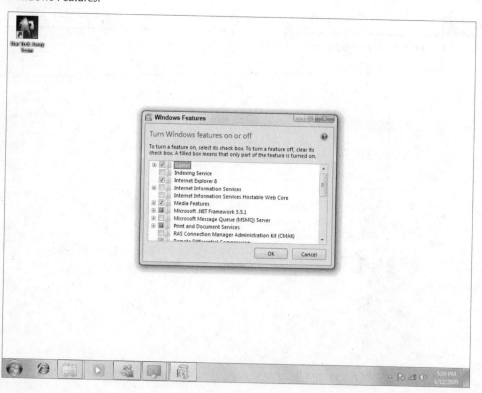

Windows 7 comes with many programs and features built right in. How many depends on which edition of Windows 7 you purchased. Regardless of the edition you bought, there may be some features you do want to use and some you don't.

To turn Windows Features on or off, get to the Programs and Features Control Panel applet discussed earlier in this chapter. (Press [⊞], type **fea**, and choose Programs and Features.) Then click Turn Windows Features On or Off in the left pane. A list of available Windows Features opens as in Figure 42-5. Items that are checked are currently installed and working. Unchecked features are not active. A filled check box represents a feature that's active, but also has additional subfeatures. Click the + sign next to a feature to see what subfeatures it offers.

Caution

Only turn off program features that you know and are certain you don't need. If you don't know what a feature is or does, better to err in favor of keeping it active than to find out, the hard way, that you shouldn't have disabled it! ∎

The rest is easy. To disable a feature or subfeature, deselect its check box. To enable a disabled feature, click its empty check box to select it. Click OK after making your changes.

Wrap-Up

Managing installed programs in Windows 7 is easy enough. It all takes place through the Programs and Features page. Here's a quick review of what's involved:

- You need administrative privileges to change, repair, or remove programs.
- Use Programs and Features to change, repair, or remove installed programs (click the Start button and choose Control Panel ➪ Programs ➪ Programs and Features).
- To see what options an installed program offers, click its name in Programs and Features and look at the buttons in the toolbar.
- Repairing a program generally involves reinstalling it from the original CD.
- Changing a program refers to installing features you didn't choose initially or removing features you don't use.
- Uninstalling a program removes it from your computer and from all user accounts.
- If a program upgrade creates problems on your system, use Restore Previous Versions on the startup icon's shortcut menu to revert to the previous working version.
- The Programs and Features window also provides an option to turn Windows features on and off.

Setting Default Programs

A s everyone knows, there are many different brands of toothpaste, shampoo, cars, and just about every other kind of product you can buy. The same is true of software. Everyone uses a Web browser to browse the Internet, and you have many different brands of Web browsers to choose from. There's Internet Explorer, which comes with Windows 7. There's also Safari, Firefox, and Google Chrome, to name a few.

For media players, Windows 7 comes with Media Player, Media Center, or both depending on which edition of Windows 7 you have. In addition to those, there's QuickTime, Musicmatch, and many others. When you have two or more programs capable of handling the same type of document, you might want to make one the *default program* that opens automatically when you open a document. Setting such defaults is what this chapter is all about.

Setting Default Programs for Files

Typed text, pictures, music files, and video clips are all examples of documents and other types of files that you can create or download to your computer. There are thousands of different file types. Each type is indicated by its filename extension. For example, a picture might be a JPEG (.jpeg or .jpg), bitmap (.bmp), GIF (.gif), TIFF (.tif or .TIFF), Portable Network Graphics (.PNG), or any of a couple dozen other formats.

When you click (or double-click) a file icon, the file opens in whatever is the *default program* for its type. If you have more than one program that can open the file type, you can override the default and open the file with some other program. Right-click the file's icon and choose Open With as in Figure 43-1. The Open With option will be available only if you have two or more programs installed that can open that type of file.

If you want to keep the current default program for this type of file, and override that just this time, click the name of the program you want to use to open the file.

FIGURE 43-1

Sample Open With options for a JPEG picture.

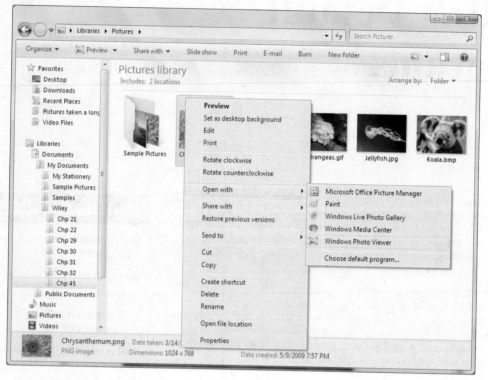

If you want to change the default program that Windows always uses to open that type of file, click Choose Default Program at the bottom of the Open With menu. The Open With dialog box shown in Figure 43-2 opens.

I Don't See Any Filename Extensions

If Windows is configured to hide filename extensions, you won't see them in your Pictures folder or other folders. But you can point to a file icon and see the filename extension in the tooltip that appears at the mouse pointer. Optionally, you can make filename extensions visible by clearing the checkmark next to Hide Extensions for Known File Types in Folder Options. You can open the Folder Options dialog box from the Organize button in any folder (click Folder and Search Options). Or open Control Panel, choose Appearance and Personalization, and then choose Folder Options. In the Folder Options dialog box, click the View tab and scroll down to the Hide Extensions option.

Click whatever program you want to use for opening that type of document. Also, make sure the Always Use the Selected Program to Open This Kind of File option is selected (checked). Otherwise your new choice won't be saved.

FIGURE 43-2

The Open With dialog box.

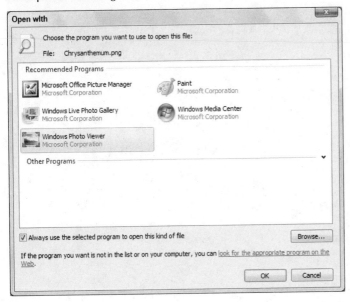

If you can't find the program you want to use as the default, you can click the Browse button to look for it. Just make sure that the program you want to use is capable of opening that type of document.

Setting default programs using the Open With dialog box is just one way to do it. Many programs have options within them that let you choose which file types you want to associate with the program. The settings within the program might even override the settings you specify in Windows. So sometimes you have to go into the program that's acting as the default for a file type, and make a change there.

Unfortunately, there's no one-rule-fits-all for the hundreds of programs that allow you to change associations within a program. Typically you start by opening the program and choosing Tools ➪ Options or Edit ➪ Preferences or something like that, to get to the program's main options. To illustrate, I'll use QuickTime (Version 7) as an example, because many people have that program.

In QuickTime, you first open the QuickTime player from the All Programs menu. Then choose Edit ➪ Preferences ➪ QuickTime Preferences from its menu bar. Click the Browser tab, click File Types, and you're taken to a dialog box where you can specify file types that should open automatically in QuickTime. Select (check) the file types you do want to open in QuickTime automatically. Clear the checkmarks for those file types for which QuickTime should not act as the default program. Figure 43-3 shows an example.

Of course, there's no right or wrong program to associate with a given file type. The choice is up to you. You just have to make sure to always specify a program that *can* open files of a given type. For example, it wouldn't make sense to associate video or audio files with Microsoft Word or Excel, because those programs don't play multimedia files.

FIGURE 43-3

File Types preferences for QuickTime 7.

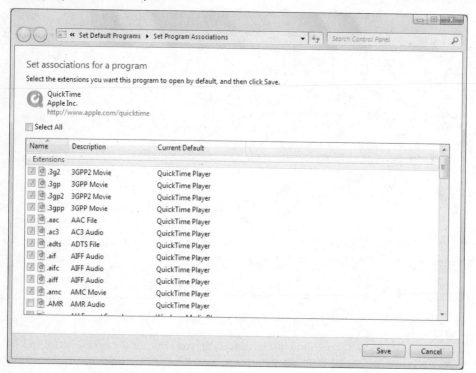

Using the Default Programs Page

Right-clicking a document's icon and choosing Open With is the quick-and-easy way to set a default program on the fly. But it's not the only method. And you're not limited to setting defaults based on file types either. You can also set defaults for *protocols*. A protocol is a standardized way of doing things. Different Internet services use different protocols. For example, the Web uses HTTP, which stands for Hypertext Transfer Protocol.

You can also set default actions for CDs, DVDs, and devices you connect to your computer. Use the Default Programs page in Control Panel to set all of these different kinds of defaults. To get there, use whichever method is easiest for you:

- Click the Start button and choose Control Panel ➪ Programs ➪ Default Programs.
- Press ⊞ , type **def**, and choose Default Programs.

You'll see the options shown in Figure 43-4 and summarized here.

- **Set Your Default Programs:** Use this option to choose default programs for your user account only.
- **Associate a File Type or Protocol with a Program:** Like the preceding item, except you start by choosing a file type or protocol rather than a program.

FIGURE 43-4

Default Programs page.

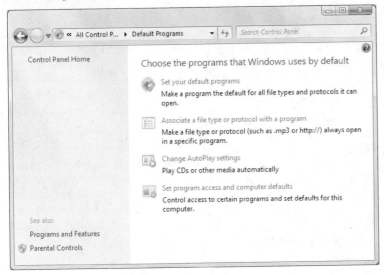

- **Change AutoPlay Settings:** Use this option to change what happens when you insert a CD or DVD or connect a camera to your computer.

- **Set Program Access and Computer Defaults:** This one is strictly for administrators. It sets defaults for Internet access and media players for all user accounts.

The sections that follow describe each option.

Set your default programs

The first item in Default Programs lets you pick and choose which file types and protocols you want to associate with programs. When you click that option, you're taken to a page like the one in Figure 43-5.

Click a program name in the left column to see a description of that program in the right column. Then you can choose one of the following options below that description:

- **Set This Program as Default:** Choose this option to make the selected program the default for all file types and protocols it can handle.

- **Choose Defaults for This Program:** Limit the program to act as the default for only certain file types and protocols.

Choosing the second option takes you to a list of all the file types and protocols that program supports, as in Figure 43-6. You can scroll through the list and select (check) the file types and protocols for which the program should act as default. Clear the checkbox of any file type or protocol for which you want some other program to act as the default. Then click Save to return to the previous page.

When you've finished choosing defaults for programs, click OK to return to the main Default Programs page.

FIGURE 43-5

Choose a program in the left column.

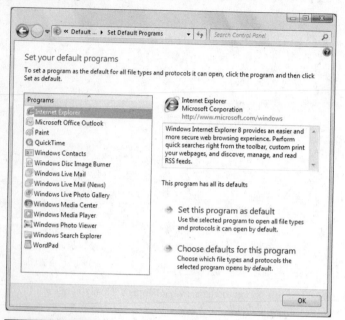

FIGURE 43-6

Choose file types and protocols for a program.

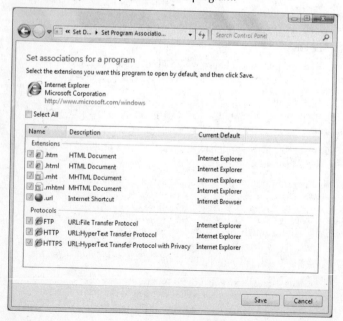

Associate a file type or protocol with a specific program

The second option in Default Programs is similar to the first. But rather than starting with a program, you start with a file type or protocol. When you click Associate a File Type or Protocol with a Specific Program you see options similar to those in Figure 43-7.

File types and protocols.

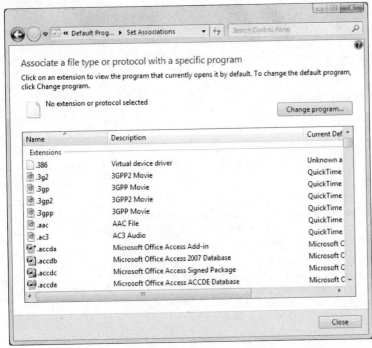

File types are listed first, in alphabetical order. Protocols are separate at the bottom of the list. Use the scroll bar to scroll through the list. To assign a default program to a file type or protocol, first click the item you want to change and click the Change Program button. Then use the Open With dialog box that opens to choose a program.

Note

Don't worry about items marked as Unknown Application. Most of those aren't documents anyway and don't need to have a default program. You don't have to assign a default program to every item in the list! ■

Change AutoPlay settings

AutoPlay is a Windows 7 feature that lets you choose what program you want to use to play content on CDs, DVDs, and devices. Chances are you've already seen the AutoPlay dialog box at least once, after you inserted a CD or DVD, or connected a camera or disk drive. Figure 43-8 shows an example.

FIGURE 43-8

AutoPlay dialog box for a removable disk.

The AutoPlay dialog box lets you choose the action you want to take with the selected media. For a removable device that always has pictures on it, you might choose one of the Import Pictures and Videos options. Until you set a default AutoPlay option, however, Windows will continue to ask you what you want to do when you attach the device.

When you click View More AutoPlay Options in Control Panel, you get to see all of your current AutoPlay default settings, as in Figure 43-9. You can also get there by clicking Change AutoPlay Settings in the Default Programs item in the Control Panel. Scroll to the bottom of the list to find icons for devices you connect to your computer, such as digital cameras.

Note

Chapter 32 describes all the different types of CDs and DVDs and provides some suggestions for choosing AutoPlay defaults. ∎

The Shift Key Doesn't Work Like It Used To

In previous versions of Windows, you could hold down the Shift key while inserting a disk or connecting a device to override the default action for the device. You can still do that in Windows 7. But the AutoPlay dialog box still opens. (The default program doesn't open.) To prevent the AutoPlay dialog box from opening when using the Shift key, you need to deselect the Use AutoPlay for All Media and Devices check box at the top of the AutoPlay page shown in Figure 43-9.

To change the default action for any item, click the current action and choose the action you want from the menu that drops down. Click Save after making your changes to return to Program Defaults.

FIGURE 43-9

Change AutoPlay settings.

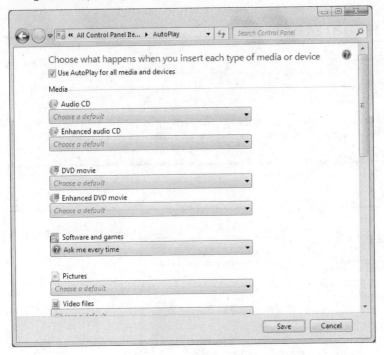

Set program access and computer defaults

Anybody who has a user account can choose defaults using any of the methods described in this chapter. The Set Program Access and Computer Defaults option is strictly for computer administrators. It sets defaults that apply to all user accounts, and can even be used to limit programs that they can use. This is most often used in corporate settings when administrators want very tight control over how staff members use their computers. But anyone with an administrative user account on a home computer can use it to control family members' program use as well.

Because the Set Program Access and Computer Defaults option can so severely limit what all users can do, you need administrative privileges just to start it. If you're in a standard user account, you'll need to log out. Then log in to an administrative account to open that option. When you first open it, you'll see three options:

- **Microsoft Windows:** Choose this option if you want to set the Internet programs that came with Windows 7 as the default programs.

- **Non-Microsoft:** Choose this option if you don't want to use any Microsoft Internet programs.

- **Custom:** Choose this option if you want to use a combination of Microsoft and non-Microsoft Internet programs.

After you choose one of these options, you'll see more options under that category. The exact options vary depending on what you choose. But they work in a similar manner. I'll use the Custom category, shown in Figure 43-10, as an example, because it offers the most options.

What's a Java Virtual Machine?

Java is a programming language often used with Internet programs and applets (small programs embedded in Web pages). The virtual machine (also called a runtime environment) allows those programs to run on your computer. It's not a mandatory item, unless you use programs that require it or visit Web sites that require it.

Typically, if you needed the Java virtual machine, you'd be prompted to download it automatically when it's required. You can also download and install it at any time from www.java.com/download.

FIGURE 43-10

Program Access and Computer Defaults.

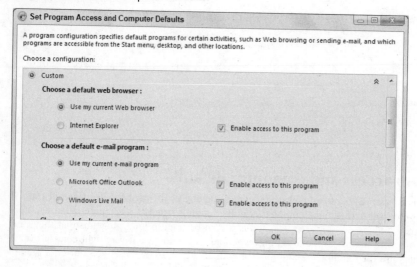

As you can see in Figure 43-10, the first options let you choose the default Web browser, e-mail client, and media player for online music and video. Scrolling down lets you choose a default instant messaging program and Java virtual machine. The options available to you depend on what programs you have installed on your computer at the moment. For each program, you have the following options:

- **Use My Current:** Choose this option to keep whatever program you're currently using as the default program. This will be the only option when you don't have multiple programs to choose from.

- *<program name>*: To specify a program as the default, click the option button to the left of its name.

- **Enable Access to This Program:** Choosing this option allows users to run the program. Clearing the check box hides the program's icon on the Start menu and elsewhere, preventing users from running the program.

There will be times when you can't choose exactly the option you want. Or when you choose an option, the selected program doesn't comply. That's because the programmers who create these programs aren't required to make them work with the Program Defaults selections. If that's a problem, your only recourse is to contact the program publisher. They may have a newer version that's compatible with setting program defaults in Windows 7.

Click OK when you've finished making your selections. You might see a message stating that your choices might not work because of current file associations. If you click Yes, Windows 7 will try to change the File Associations to go with the new default program automatically. If it doesn't work, you can change file associations manually.

Wrap-Up

Default programs are programs that start automatically when you open a document or use an Internet protocol like e-mail or the Web. When you have two or more programs that can open a document or use an Internet protocol, you can choose which one acts as the default. Choosing a default doesn't preclude you from using other programs. The default just determines which program is used when you don't specify otherwise. Windows 7 offers several methods of choosing default programs:

- To set the default for a file type on the fly, right-click a file's icon and choose Open With ⇨ Choose Default Program.

- To use some program other than the default for a document, right-click the icon, choose Open With and the name of the program you want to use.

- The Program Defaults page in Control Panel provides ways of setting multiple default programs from a single page.

- The Set Your Default Programs option lets you choose a program and specify the documents and protocols for which it should act as the default.

- The Associate a File Type or Protocol with a Program option lets you first choose a filename extension or protocol, and then choose the program that will be the default.

- Change AutoPlay Settings lets you choose what happens when you insert a disc or connect a device.

- Set Program Access and Computer Defaults allows an administrator to control defaults and programs for all user accounts.

Managing Programs and Processes

You are no doubt familiar with the terms *application* and *program*. These two terms describe program code that, whether one component or several components, serve a specific function. For example, a word processor is an application. Some applications, however, comprise multiple *processes* running at the same time. In addition, a process can comprise multiple threads of execution, each performing a specific task. Though you typically concern yourself with programs, you sometimes need to think about the processes that make up a program, particularly if one of those processes fails. That's where Task Manager comes into play.

Task Manager is a program included with Windows 7 for viewing and managing running programs and processes. You can use it to seek out performance bottlenecks, close hung programs and processes without restarting the system, and more.

Getting to Know Task Manager

Task Manager is a program that lets you view and manage running programs and processes, as well as view performance data for your computer and network. You can start Task Manager in several ways:

- Press Ctrl+Alt+Del and click Start Task Manager.
- Right-click the clock or an empty spot on the taskbar and choose Start Task Manager.
- Click Start and enter `taskmgr`.

Tip

If a program is hung (frozen), right-clicking the taskbar might not work. But pressing Ctrl+Alt+Del might still work. If Ctrl+Alt+Del doesn't work to bring up the Task Manager and the computer is unresponsive, cycling power on the computer is generally the only way to get it going again. ■

Figure 44-1 shows the Task Manager. It behaves much like any program window. It has a button on the Windows taskbar when open. You can drag the program window around by its title bar. Size it by dragging any corner or edge. You can also configure it so it stays on the top of the stack of open windows so you can always see it. You can change that by choosing Options ➪ Always On Top from its menu.

FIGURE 44-1

Task Manager in its normal view.

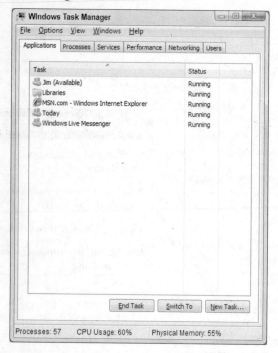

FIGURE 44-2

Task Manager mini-mode.

Tip

Regardless of how you start Task Manager, when it opens Task Manager displays whichever tab was open when it was last run. ■

Task Manager also has a mini-mode where the title bar, menu bar, and tabs are hidden, as in Figure 44-2. When you're in that mode, double-click the empty space inside the window border (such as to the left of the End Task button) to go to the normal mode. Double-click that same area, or to the right of the tabs, in the normal mode to go to mini-mode.

Tip

If you don't want Task Manager to show up on the Windows taskbar, click Options ⇨ Hide When Minimized. ■

Choosing Task Manager Views

You can view and use Task Manager in several ways. On the Options menu in the menu bar, you have the following options:

- **Always On Top:** Choosing this option ensures that Task Manager is always on the top of the stack when it's open, so no other program windows can cover it.

- **Minimize On Use:** If selected, this option just minimizes Task Manager whenever you choose the Switch To option to switch to another running program.

- **Hide When Minimized:** Normally when you minimize Task Manager, only its taskbar button remains visible. Choosing this option also hides the taskbar button when you minimize Task Manager.

Whenever Task Manager is open, you'll see a small green square in the Notification area unless Task Manager is configured to show notifications only. Pointing to that icon displays the current CPU (processor) usage, as shown in Figure 44-3. When Task Manager is minimized, you can double-click that little square to bring Task Manager back onto the desktop.

If you prefer to have Task Manager show only notifications and remove it from the tray, click the Show Hidden Icons button on the tray and choose Customize. In the Notification Area Icons applet, find Windows Task Manager in the Icons list, choose Only Show Notifications from the drop-down list, and click OK.

On the View menu in Task Manager, you have the following choices:

- **Refresh Now:** Causes Task Manager to refresh all of its data immediately, regardless of the Update Speed setting.

- **Update Speed:** Task Manager needs to use some computer resources to keep itself up to date with what's happening in the system at the moment. The Update Speed option lets you choose how often Task Manager updates itself as follows:

  - **High:** Updates Task Manager twice per second.

  - **Normal:** Updates Task Manager every two seconds.

  - **Low:** Updates Task Manager every four seconds.

  - **Paused:** Updates Task Manager only when you choose View ⇨ Refresh Now.

FIGURE 44-3

Task Manager notification icon.

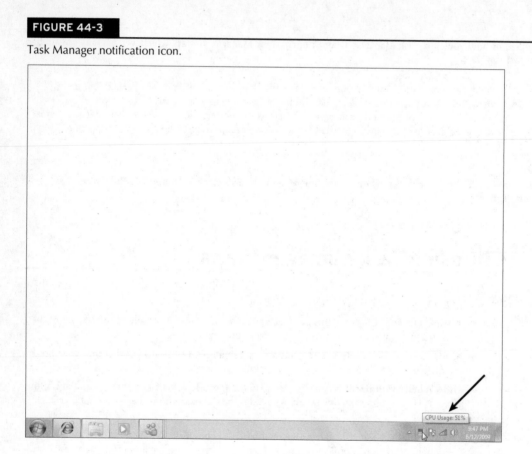

Not Responding? Task Manager to the Rescue

One of Task Manager's most useful roles is that of dealing with problems that cause programs, or your whole computer, to *hang* (to "freeze up," so that the mouse and keyboard don't work normally). Even when you can't get the mouse or keyboard to work, pressing Ctrl+Alt+Del and choosing Start Task Manager may get Task Manager open for you.

Closing frozen programs

Once Task Manager is open, click the Applications tab. If a particular program is hung, its Status column will usually read Not Responding rather than Running. To close the hung program, click its name in the Task column, and then click the End Task button. Task Manager will try to close the program normally, so that if you were working on a document at the time, you may be able to save any changes. (So, don't expect the program to close immediately.)

If the program won't close, you'll see a warning that moving ahead will close the program leaving unsaved work behind. To forge ahead, click End Now. The program may try to restart itself, depending on how it is designed.

Most likely, a process of reporting the problem and finding a solution will start after you end a program in this way. If you choose to allow Windows to send information about the program error, Windows sends information to a database of problems and searches that database for known problems and their solutions. You won't always get a solution to the problem, but many times I've received information about an incompatible device driver or other issue by allowing Windows to report the problem.

If you don't have time to wait through that whole reporting process, you can cancel out of each dialog box by clicking its Cancel button.

Switching and starting tasks

If the system is hung in such a way that you can't use the Start menu or taskbar normally, and you want to work with open program windows individually, Task Manager provides some ways to accomplish that.

To bring a running program to the top of the stack of windows on the screen, and make it the active window, click its name in the list of running tasks, and then click the Switch To button. If you were working on a document in that program, you can save your work, and then exit the program normally (assuming that program is running normally).

If you need to bring up a diagnostic program or debugger, or simply need to start some other program, and you know the startup command for that program, click the New Task button. The Create New Task dialog box, shown in Figure 44-4, opens. Type the startup command for the program (or the complete path to the program, if necessary), and click OK.

FIGURE 44-4

Create New Task dialog box.

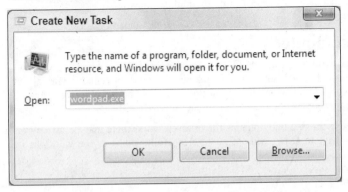

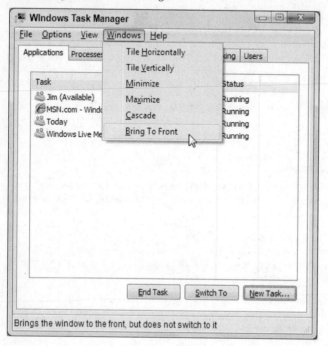

FIGURE 44-5

Window options in Task Manager.

The Windows menu shown in Figure 44-5 offers many of the same window-arranging options you see when you right-click the clock. You can click any program name in the Tasks column (on the Applications tab) and choose Bring to Front to bring a buried program window to the top of the stack. This is handy when a hung program is hogging up the entire screen, and you need to see something, perhaps to save some work in progress, behind that hung program window.

Restarting a hung computer

If your computer is so locked up that you can't get to Task Manager, or stop the offending program, you can try other things. If pressing Ctrl+Alt+Del works, taking you to the options in Figure 44-6, you can try any of the options shown. Logging off or restarting will likely be your best bet. If at all possible, Windows will attempt to give you a chance to save any unsaved work.

If the program that's hung is also the one that contains the unsaved work, there may be no way to save that work. You might just have to restart without saving. Hopefully you save your work often so you don't lose too much work.

Tip

You can configure some programs to save automatically, such as every few minutes. Check the program's options to see if this capability is available in the programs you use most often. ■

FIGURE 44-6

Options when you first press Ctrl+Alt+Del.

Peeking at Resource Usage

In addition to helping you deal with hung programs, Task Manager lets you see which processes in your system are using computer resources. These resources include the computer's memory and its Central Processing Unit (CPU). The CPU is where the program execution actually takes place, and the memory is where the application code and your data reside.

Exactly how fast your computer runs at any given moment depends on the resources available to it at that moment. For example, if you have half a dozen programs running, all doing intensive tasks, they are eating up CPU resources. If you start another program, that program may run slower than usual, because the other running programs are consuming CPU resources.

Likewise, everything you open stores something in RAM. If RAM is nearly full, and you start another program that needs more memory than what's currently left in RAM, Windows has to start sloughing some of what's currently in RAM off to the hard disk (called *virtual memory*) to make room. It takes time to do that, so everything slows down.

The status bar along the bottom of Task Manager's program window gives you a bird's-eye view of what is going on in your system, and how much of your available resources are being used by all of the running processes. Going from left to right along the status bar at the bottom of the Task Manager window you see these columns by default:

- **Processes:** Shows the total number of processes currently running on the system.
- **CPU Usage:** Shows what percentage of CPU capability is currently being used by the processes.
- **Physical Memory:** Shows the amount of physical memory in use.

Physical Memory versus Virtual Memory

The term *physical memory* refers to the actual amount of RAM, on computer chips, installed in your computer. When you right-click Computer and choose Properties, the number to the right of the words "Installed Memory (RAM)" indicates the amount of physical memory installed on the motherboard inside your computer.

When things are busy in RAM, Windows moves some lesser-used items out to a special section of the hard disk called a *paging file*. The paging file looks and acts like RAM (to the CPU), even though it's actually space on your hard disk. Although Windows can be configured to not use a paging file, Windows by default sets aside some hard disk space for this paging file. (More on that topic in Chapter 49.)

A *page fault* is when the CPU "expects" to find something in RAM, but has to fetch it from virtual memory instead. The term *fault* is a bit harsh here, because a certain amount of memory paging is normal and to be expected. Other terms used in this context include *Nonpaged memory* for physical memory and *Paged memory* for virtual memory.

Managing Processes with Task Manager

Whereas applications usually run in windows and are listed on the Applications tab in Task Manager, processes have no program window. We say that processes run in the background, because they don't show anything in particular on the screen.

Your running applications are actually one or more processes. You can see which process correlates with a given program by right-clicking that program's name on the Applications tab and choosing Go To Process. To see all currently running processes, click the Processes tab in Task Manager. Each process is referred to by *its image name* (in most cases, the name of the program's main executable file), as in the example shown in Figure 44-7.

The Processes tab shows its information in columns. You can size columns in the usual manner (by dragging the bar at the right side of the column heading). You can sort items by clicking any column heading. For example, you can click the Memory (Private Working Set) column to sort processes by the amount of memory each one takes up, in ascending order (smallest to largest) or descending order (largest to smallest). Seeing those in largest-to-smallest order lets you know which processes are using up the most memory.

FIGURE 44-7

Processes tab in Task Manager.

Here's what each column shows:

- **Image Name:** The name of the process. In most cases, this matches the name of the file in which the process is stored when not open.

- **User Name:** The user account in which the process is running. The System, Local, and Network Service built-in accounts are used by Windows to run a variety of core operating system processes.

- **CPU:** The percent of CPU resources that the process is currently using.

- **Memory (Private Working Set):** The amount of memory the process is currently using.

- **Description:** A description of the process.

Memory usage is probably the main cause of slow-running computers. The more stuff you cram into RAM, the more Windows has to use the paging file, and hence the slower everything goes. You can see which processes are hogging up the most RAM just by clicking the Memory (Private Working Set) column heading until the largest numbers are at the top of the list.

Hidden processes

Normally, the Processes tab only shows processes running in the user account into which you're currently logged. Clicking Show Processes from All Users shows the true number of running processes (but requires administrative privileges).

Multiple users not logging out of their accounts is one of the most common reasons for computer sluggishness. If users are using Switch User to leave their accounts, you'll see why when you view processes for all users. There's just a lot of unnecessary stuff going on when people don't log out of their user accounts when they've finished using the computer.

Task Manager might not show old 16-bit processes. To show or hide those processes, choose Options ⇨ Show 16-bit Tasks from Task Manager's menu bar. That menu option is available only when you're viewing the Processes tab.

Common processes

You can end any running process by right-clicking its name and choosing End Process (or by clicking its name and clicking the End Process button). But doing so isn't a good idea unless you know exactly what service you're terminating. If a process represents a running program with unsaved work, ending the process will close the program without saving the work.

Some processes are required for normal operation of the computer. For example, dwm.exe (Windows Desktop Manager) and explorer.exe are important parts of Windows 7. So you definitely don't want to mess with those.

Note
Just because a process is near the top of the list when you sort things in largest-to-smallest order doesn't mean the biggest items are hogs or outrageously large. Even seemingly large numbers like 50,000 K and 60,000 K are trivial when you consider how much RAM most systems have, and how cheap it is to add more. ∎

If you're unsure about a process, you can search for it by name on Google, Bing, or any other search engine. Just be sure to check out multiple sources, and read carefully. Virtually every resource you find will tell you that perfectly legitimate and necessary processes like dwm.exe and explorer.exe could be Trojan, spyware, or other malicious item. But *could* is not synonymous with *is*. So read carefully and don't assume the worst.

Choosing columns in processes

The four column names that appear in Task Manager by default don't tell the whole story. When you're viewing the Processes tab in Task Manager, you can choose View ⇨ Select Columns to choose other columns to view. Each column shows some detail of the process, mostly related to resource consumption. A programmer might use this information to fine-tune a program she's writing. Beyond that, it's hard to think of anything terribly practical to be gained from this information. But here's a quick summary of what the other, optional columns show:

- **Base Priority:** The priority assigned to the process. When the CPU is busy, low-priority processes have to wait for normal and high-priority processes to be completed. To change a process's priority, right-click its name and choose Set Priority.
- **Command Line:** The command, with parameters, that was used to initiate the process.
- **CPU Time:** Total number of seconds of CPU time this process has used since starting. The number will be doubled for dual-processor systems, quadrupled for systems with four processors.
- **CPU Usage:** The amount of processor time, as a percent of the whole, this process has used since first started (the CPU column).
- **Data Execution Prevention:** Specifies whether DEP is enabled or disabled for the specified process. DEP is a set of hardware and software technologies that help prevent malicious code from running by marking some areas of memory as non-executable.
- **Description:** A description of the process.
- **GDI Objects:** The number of Graphics Device Interface objects used by this process, since starting, to display content on the screen.

- **Handles:** The number of objects to which the process currently has handles.
- **I/O Other:** Non-disk input/output calls made by the object since it started. Excludes file, network, and device operations.
- **I/O Other Bytes:** The number of bytes transferred to devices since the process started. Excludes file, network, and device operations.
- **I/O Reads:** The number of file, network, and device Read input/output operations since the process started.
- **I/O Read Bytes:** The number of bytes transferred by Read file, network, and device input/output operations.
- **I/O Writes:** The number of file, network, and device Write input/output operations since the process started.
- **I/O Write Bytes:** The number of bytes transferred by Write file, network, and device input/output operations.
- **Image Path Name:** The path to the executable specified in the Image Name column.
- **Memory - Working Set:** The amount of memory used by the process (also called the process's *working set*) since starting.
- **Memory - Peak Working Set:** The largest amount of physical memory used by the process since it started.
- **Memory - Working Set Delta:** The change in memory usage since the last Task Manager update.
- **Memory - Private Working Set:** Amount of memory allocated to the process's private data.
- **Memory - Commit Size:** The amount of virtual memory currently committed to the process.
- **Memory - Paged Pool:** The amount of system-allocated virtual memory that's been committed to the process by the operating system.
- **Memory - Non-paged Pool:** The amount of physical RAM used by the process since starting.
- **Page Faults:** The number of times the process has read data from virtual memory since starting.
- **Page Fault Delta:** The change in the number of page faults since the last Task Manager update.
- **PID (Process Identifier):** A number assigned to the process at startup. The operating system accesses all processes by their numbers, not their names.
- **Session ID:** The Terminal Session ID that owns the process. Always zero unless Terminal Services are in use on the network.
- **Threads:** The number of threads running in a process.

Tip

A thread is a tiny sequence of instructions that the CPU must carry out to perform some task. Some programs divide tasks into separate threads that can be executed in parallel (simultaneously), to speed execution. This is called *multi-threaded execution.* ■

- **User Account Control Virtualization:** Specifies whether UAC is virtualized for the specified process. When enabled, data is written to a user area rather than to a system area.
- **User Name:** The user, user account, or service that started the process.
- **User Objects:** The number of objects from Window Manager used by the object, including program windows, cursors, icons, and other objects.

Much of the information available from the extra columns on the Processes tab is summarized on the Performance tab.

Monitoring Performance with Task Manager

The Performance tab in Task Manager, shown in Figure 44-8, provides both graphical and numeric summaries of CPU and memory resource usage. To watch resource usage, leave Task Manager open and "always on top" as you run programs and use your computer in the usual ways. If you have multiple processors, or a multi-core processor, each may be represented in a separate pane in the CPU history as at the top of the figure. Choose View ➪ CPU History to decide whether you want to see a single pane or multiple panes.

FIGURE 44-8

Performance tab in Task Manager.

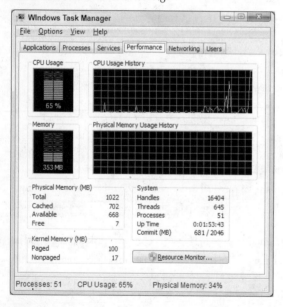

Tip

Double-click any chart or a blank area inside the window to show an expanded chart or to restore it to its previous size. ■

Here's what all the things you see on the Performance tab represent:

- **CPU Usage:** Indicates how much of the CPU's capacity you're using at the moment.

- **CPU Usage History:** Shows CPU usage over time. Choosing View ➪ Show Kernel Times adds a second red line to the chart, which shows the amount of CPU resources used by kernel operations (core operating system processes).

- **System:** The number of handles, threads, and processes running at the time, how long the system has been up, and amount of memory committed of total available.

- **Physical Memory (MB):** The total amount of physical memory in the system, the amount that's currently available, and the amount used by the System Cache, which maps to data stored in files. Each measurement is expressed in megabytes.

- **Kernel Memory (MB):** The total paged and nonpaged memory used by the operating system kernel and device drivers.

The Performance charts are useful for identifying major *performance bottlenecks*. For example, if the CPU Usage and History charts run high, your CPU is working very hard. An errant application can consume inordinate amounts of CPU capacity. Also, reducing the number of running programs will reduce CPU load.

A common performance bottleneck is limited physical memory. Running lots of programs with limited memory forces the system to use lots of virtual memory, which in turn slows down performance because of the added overhead of swapping pages in and out. Increasing the amount of virtual memory (as discussed in Chapter 49) can help, but the best solution is to add more RAM (physical memory) to the system.

Tip

Microsoft's published minimum requirement is 1 GB of RAM for 32-bit Windows 7 and 2 GB for the 64-bit edition, although Windows 7 will run with less. Naturally, having more than the specified minimums will provide better performance. With the relatively low cost of memory today, it's not unreasonable to have from 2 GB to 4 GB of physical memory. ■

Networking and Users Tabs

The Networking and Users tabs in Task Manager display information about your network and user accounts. The Networking tab, shown in Figure 44-9, shows network traffic, or the amount of network bandwidth used. If you have multiple network interface cards installed on the computer, each is displayed in its own chart.

FIGURE 44-9

Networking tab in Task Manager.

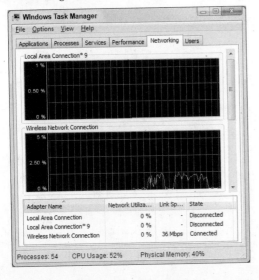

The Users tab shows the names of people currently logged in to the computer. Most users will see only themselves, even if other users are logged in. If you're an administrator and select Show Processors from All Users on the Processes tab, the Users tab will show all current users. Users who are logged in but have used Switch User to exit their accounts will show as Disconnected.

If people not logging out of their accounts is causing your system to run slowly, you can send a message to those users asking them to log off when done using the computer. Click a username and then click Send Message. Then write a reminder to log out when done. The users will see the message next time they go into their account.

If you select a user and click Logoff, that user will be logged off and any unsaved data will be lost. In general, this is a bad idea, so try to get the user to log off normally before taking this action.

Wrap-Up

Task Manager is a handy tool for terminating hung programs (programs that are not responding), and for monitoring computer resource usage. Task Manager also provides detailed information that's of interest only to programmers and network administrators. The main things to know about Task Manager are as follows:

- To open Task Manager, press Ctrl+Alt+Del and click Start Task Manager or right-click the time and choose Start Task Manager.
- The Applications tab shows the names of all running applications. To end a program that's not responding, right-click its name and choose End Task.
- To see which process an application relates to, right-click the application name and choose Go To Process.
- The Processes tab shows all running processes, including application programs, background programs like antivirus software, and operating system processes.
- The Performance tab presents a bird's-eye view of overall CPU and memory usage.
- The Networking tab shows network bandwidth usage.
- The Users tab shows which users are currently logged in.

Troubleshooting Software Problems

Troubleshooting Installation

Essentially, all programs designed for Windows Vista will work with Windows 7. However, not all programs that were designed for Windows XP (or earlier versions of Windows) will work with Windows 7. In fact, you should avoid installing utility and security programs unless they are specifically written for Windows 7 altogether. (Most basic application programs will run fine.)

If you can't get an older program to install, or it doesn't work after you install it, check the program manufacturer's Web site to see if they have a Windows 7 version available. Or, use the methods discussed in Chapter 41 to configure settings that might enable the older program to run on Windows 7. Or, consider installing and using Windows XP Mode with Windows Virtual PC to run the application. If these steps fail, you can take some general troubleshooting steps to hopefully get the program working properly.

Troubleshooting Programs

Because so many programs are available for Windows, no troubleshooting magic bullets exist that will solve all problems. Every program is unique and every problem is unique.

One of the most common mistakes people make is to not learn to use a program. They guess and hack their way through it, and when things don't work the way they guessed, they think there's something wrong with the program, when in fact, the problem is that the person using the program has no clue how to use it correctly. Troubleshooting can't fix ignorance; only learning can fix that.

You must eventually understand that every program has its own built-in Help for a reason — it's because every program is unique. The only way to get information about a specific program is from the Help that came with that program, or from the support Web site for that program. The Help menu, which is always the last item on the menu bar, provides all the help options available to you.

The whole concept of troubleshooting only applies when you *do* know how to do something, but things don't work the way the documentation from which you learned said they should work.

Anyway, the big trick is to not just try one resource and then give up. There is no book, Web page, person, place, or thing that has all the answers to all questions, nor the solutions to all problems. Sometimes you really have to dig around for a solution. Start with the narrowest, most simple solution and work your way out from there, as follows.

Try the Help that's available from the program's menu bar.

Then try the program manufacturer's Web site. With Microsoft products, you may want to try searching www.bing.com, http://support.microsoft.com, or http://office.microsoft.com for Office products. At the program manufacturer's Web site, look around for other support options such as FAQs (Frequently Asked Questions), Troubleshooting, and Discussion Groups or Newsgroups.

For Microsoft products, you'll also want to go to http://support.microsoft.com and click the Select a Product link for links to support for specific products. The Microsoft Public Newsgroups link on that same page will take you to areas for specific products where you can post questions and get answers.

Don't forget, too, that you can search the entire planet using a search engine like Google or Bing. Though, when you're searching the entire planet, you want to use as many exact, descriptive words as possible in your search. Otherwise, you'll get links to more pages than you could visit in a lifetime. Include the product name, version number, and specific words that describe what you're looking for.

Tip

To find out what version of a program you're using, choose Help ⇨ About ... from that program's menu bar. Or, you can also check the version in Control Panel. Open Control Panel, click Programs, and click Programs and Features. The Version column shows the program version. ∎

When searching the Web, use specific keywords and skip the noise words like "how." For example, if you're looking for help with Windows Live Mail backups, get all of the appropriate words into your search as in Backup Windows Live Mail. To find specific phrases, enclose the phrase in quotes. Be as specific as you can possibly be. The more specific you are when typing your search words, the better your results will be.

Note

I confess that I would be lost without Google. When my team experiences a problem with a server for which we don't have a ready fix, invariably the first place we turn is Google. We're not alone in that. The check engine light recently came on in my car, and the service manager told me they searched Google to find the probable cause for the error code that made the light come on. ∎

Researching Application Errors

Many software errors will provide hexadecimal memory locations in their error messages. Sometimes, searching for the number won't do any good. The title bar may provide some clues as to exactly what caused the problem. Look through the error messages for some unique keywords that you can enter into different support search engines.

Searching for a combination of the program name and keywords from the error message text can sometimes provide clues. You may want to start with a narrow search, such as `http://support.microsoft.com` to avoid getting too many hits. If that doesn't work, you can broaden the search to all of Microsoft.com (`www.bing.com`). If all else fails, you can search all five billion (or so) pages in Google's index at `www.google.com`.

But the key thing, in all searches, is to get the most unique words from the message into your search string. For example, if searching for the hexadecimal memory addresses from the error message doesn't return useful results, you could try a combination of other words. If you keep getting results that are clearly not germane, such as pages about UNIX system problems when you're searching for a Windows issue, preface with a minus sign the keyword you want exclude. For example, searching Google using `Windows 7 backup restore -UNIX -Linux` will return hits for pages that contain the words `Windows`, `7`, `backup`, and `restore`, but not pages that also include the words `UNIX` or `Linux`.

Ideally, you'll want to try to dig up as much information about the error as you can via the Web. Search the company's Web site; because they are the ones who created that application, they may be able to provide additional information.

Editing the Registry

After researching a software problem, you might find that the solution involves a "registry hack," also known as *editing the registry*. This is serious business with little margin for error. Never attempt to fix a problem by guessing at a registry hack. When you do get specific instructions on making a registry change, make sure you make *exactly* the change indicated in the message. Even the slightest typographical error can cause a world of problems. If you're not a technical person and don't want to risk creating a really big mess you can't rectify, consider hiring a professional to resolve the problem.

Before you launch into registry hacking, you need to understand what you're doing. First, be aware that the registry is a database where Windows and other programs store data that they need to operate properly on your computer. The average computer user typically doesn't need to know that the registry exists. In fact, I'm sure most do not. There is absolutely nothing that's "user friendly" about the registry. In fact, it's probably just about as "user hostile" as you can get. Microsoft provides the Registry Editor described in this chapter because programmers and other IT professionals occasionally need to view or modify registry entries.

Caution
The registry is not a safe place to mess around. Pay attention to all cautions in this chapter! ■

How registry data is organized

The Windows registry comprises several *hives*, each of which holds specific types of data. Within each hive, the registry uses *keys* and *subkeys* to organize data. Just as a folder can contain subfolders, a key can contain subkeys.

The registry doesn't store files or documents, however. Rather, it stores *values*. Some of these values make sense to the average user, but some do not. For example, if you have Microsoft Office installed, there is a value in the registry that stores the path to the Office installation folder, and the value is typically `C:\Program Files\Microsoft Office\Office 12\`. That's easy to understand. However, you'll also find a lot of values in the registry that look something like {89820200-ECBD-11cf-8B85-00AA005B4383}!8,0,7100,0, and it's highly unlikely that this value will mean anything to you. But whether or not the value of a given registry entry makes sense to you, they make sense to the application that is using the value, and that value must be entered exactly as required.

Hives, keys, and subkeys

I get into the specifics of editing the registry in a moment. But first, Figure 45-1 shows an example of the Registry Editor as it might look when you first open it. The names listed down the left column are *hives*. As defined by Microsoft, a hive is a logical group of keys, subkeys, and values in the registry that has a set of supporting files containing backups of its data. So, each hive contains keys, subkeys, and data. Each hive stores a particular type of information, as summarized in Table 45-1. Note that most keys have a standard abbreviation, such as HKCU for HKEY_CURRENT_USER.

Tip

To open Registry Editor, click Start, type regedit, and press Enter. ■

Standard hives at left in the Registry Editor.

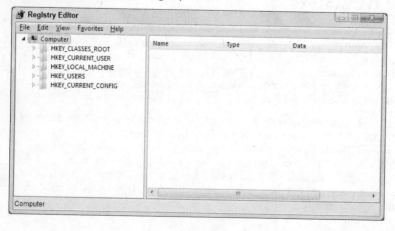

When you click the white triangle next to a hive, it expands to display its key. Most of the keys have subkeys, and those subkeys might also have subkeys of their own. In that case, the subkey itself will have a white triangle too, which you can click to see another level of subkeys. For example, in Figure 45-2, I've expanded the HKEY_CLASSES_ROOT key to reveal its subkeys. Each subkey represents a particular file type in that case. I've also expanded a few subkeys in that example.

You'll often see a reference to a specific subkey expressed as a path, in much the way that you might see a file's location and name expressed as a path. For example, the path to a file might be expressed as C:\Users\jboyce\Pictures\Summit01.jpg. The path tells Windows exactly where to find the file Summit01.jpg in my Pictures folder.

A registry path is the same idea, and even uses backslashes to separate the key and subkey names. For example, the highlighted subkey in Figure 45-2 is at Computer\HKEY_CLASSES_ROOT\.3g2\ OpenWithProgIds.

TABLE 45-1

Standard Root Keys

Name	Abbreviation	Description
HKEY_CLASSES_ROOT	HKCR	Stores information about document types and extensions, registered programs that can open each file type, the default program for each file type, and options that appear when you right-click an icon.
HKEY_CURRENT_USER	HKCU	Stores information about the person who is currently using the computer, based on which user account that person is logged in to, and settings that particular user chose within his or her account.
HKEY_LOCAL_MACHINE	HKLM	Stores information about all the hardware that's available to the computer, including devices that might not be plugged in at the moment.
HKEY_USERS	HKU	Stores information about all users, based on user accounts you've defined via Control Panel.
HKEY_CURRENT_CONFIG	*<none>*	Similar to HKEY_LOCAL_MACHINE, this key stores information about hardware available to the computer. However, this key limits its storage to hardware that's connected and functioning currently.

Sometimes you'll see instructions telling you the path to a key or subkey, like HKEY_CURRENT_USER\Control Panel\Appearance\Schemes. You have to manually expand each folder down the path to get to the subkey. Figure 45-3 shows the result of following that sample path. The values in the Data column for that key are mostly binary numbers; a good example of just how user *un*friendly the registry can be!

Key values

The data stored in a subkey is called a *value*. The value is a specific piece of information that can be stored as a string (text) or a number. However, the terms "string" and "number" don't tell the whole story, because those types can be further broken down into the specific *data types* listed in Table 45-2.

In the vast majority of situations, you'll be working with strings, DWORDs, or QWORDs when you create or modify registry entries. Entering a string in the registry is just like entering a string in a text box. When you enter DWORD and QWORD values, however, you enter those either as a decimal or a hexadecimal value. I won't go into detail about the differences here, and if you want a clearer understanding of hexadecimal numbering, a quick search on the Web will turn up lots of explanations and examples. Just keep in mind that when you edit a DWORD or QWORD value, you need to choose the option that matches the value you are entering. Figure 45-4 shows an example of a value entered as a decimal number.

FIGURE 45-2

The HKEY_CLASSES_ROOT and some subkeys expanded.

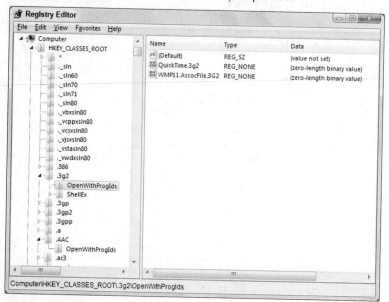

FIGURE 45-3

The HKEY_CURRENT_USER\Control Panel\Appearance\Schemes subkey selected.

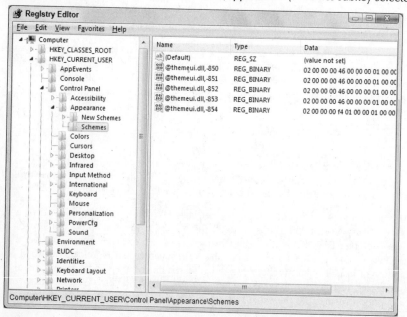

TABLE 45-2

Registry Value Data Types

Name	Data type	Description
Binary Value	REG_BINARY	Raw binary data used mostly by hardware components. Often displayed in hexadecimal format.
DWORD Value	REG_DWORD	An integer often used to store parameters for device drivers and services. Subtypes include related types such as DWORD_LITTLE_ENDIAN and REG_DWORD_BIG_ENDIAN with the least significant bit at the lowest/highest address, respectively.
Expandable String Value	REG_EXPAND_SZ	A variable-length string often used to store data for application programs and services.
Multi-String Value	REG_MULTI_SZ	A string that actually consists of multiple substrings separated by spaces, commas, or other special characters.
String Value	REG_SZ	A simple fixed-length text string.
Binary Value	REG_RESOURCE_LIST	A series of nested arrays (lists) often used by hardware and device drivers. Usually displayed in hexadecimal.
Binary Value	REG_RESOURCE_REQUIREMENTS_LIST	A series of nested arrays (lists) containing a device driver's hardware resources, displayed in hexadecimal.
Binary Value	REG_FULL_RESOURCE_DESCRIPTOR	A series of nested lists of actual hardware device capabilities, usually displayed in hexadecimal.
None	REG_NONE	Data with no particular type that's displayed as a Binary Value in hexadecimal.
Link	REG_LINK	A string naming a symbolic link.
QWORD Value	REG_QWORD	A 64-bit number displayed as a binary value.

FIGURE 45-4

The Edit DWORD (32-bit) Value dialog box.

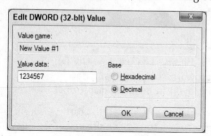

If the troubleshooting steps that you are using direct you to enter a decimal value, click the Decimal option and then type the value specified. If you need to enter a hexadecimal value, click the Hexadecimal option before you type the value.

Backing up the registry

Every time you start your computer, Windows automatically creates the registry based on the hardware and software available to it. Then, it makes a backup copy of that registry. When you plan to manually change the registry, you should also make a backup copy of the registry just before you make your change. Because when it comes to editing the registry, there is no margin for error and even a tiny typographical error can have far-reaching, unpleasant consequences.

Tip

The System Restore feature described in Chapter 33 also makes periodic backup copies of the registry. ∎

You need administrative privileges to edit the registry. The program you use is named regedit. You can start it using either of these methods:

- Tap 🪟 , type regedit, and click regedit.exe on the Start menu.
- Click the Start button, choose Run, type regedit, and press Enter.

Note

If you don't have a Run option on your Start menu, you can add it. Right-click the Start button and choose Properties. Then click Customize, check Run Command in the list of programs, and click OK in each open dialog box. ∎

The Registry Editor opens. You *always* want to make a backup of the registry before you change anything. It's easy to do:

1. Choose File ➪ Export from the menu bar in the Registry Editor.
2. Choose a folder and enter a filename of your own choosing.
3. To export the entire registry, choose All under the Export Range heading.
4. Click the Save button.

That's it. In the event of a disaster, you can choose File ➪ Import from the Registry Editor's menu bar to restore all the entries you copied in the preceding steps.

Making the registry change

You can change any value in the registry. First you need to get to the appropriate subkey. For example, let's say that you've found the solution to some problem via Microsoft's Web site. Part of that solution involves changing a value in the following subkey:

```
HKEY_LOCAL_MACHINE\SOFTWARE\Microsoft\Windows\CurrentVersion\Run
```

The first step is to get to the subkey by expanding the HKEY_LOCAL_MACHINE, SOFTWARE, Microsoft, Windows, and CurrentVersion node. Then click Run. The pane to the right shows values in the subkey. The status bar shows the complete path name as in Figure 45-5.

FIGURE 45-5

HKEY_LOCAL_MACHINE\SOFTWARE\Microsoft\Windows\CurrentVersion\Run selected.

To change a subkey's value, double-click that value. A dialog box will open allowing you to make a change. The appearance of the dialog box depends on the type of value you're editing. Figure 45-6 shows a general example.

Caution

Make sure you get to the correct key, and make *exactly* the change your instructions tell you to. Even the slightest mistake here could cause big problems down the road. ■

The Value Data box contains the value you can edit. Make your change there and click OK. Then close the Registry Editor. You have finished making your registry change.

FIGURE 45-6

Dialog box to edit a DWORD value.

Whether or not you see any change on the screen depends on the value you changed. Many registry hacks will have no effect until you close the Registry Editor, close all open program windows, and restart the computer.

If it turns out you created more problems than you solved, you can restore your registry from the backup you make. Open the Registry Editor and choose File ➪ Import to import the backed-up file. Otherwise, if all seems well, you can delete the backed-up registry file.

Troubleshooting Tips

I've been troubleshooting computer problems of one kind or another for a quarter of a century (yes that makes me feel old). In that time, I've learned one important fact that will help ensure success over failure: You *must* be methodical.

Don't start changing program settings, Windows settings, registry settings, deleting files, and taking other action without an understanding of what you're doing. Just as important, don't make lots of changes at once. Instead, make a single change, see if it fixes the problem, and then try the next if needed.

Here are some key pieces of advice:

- When searching the Web for answers, be as precise as possible. Include as many keywords as possible that are related to the issue. If you are receiving an error message, enclose the exact error message in quotes in your search.

- Ask yourself what has changed. Did you add something new? Did you change a setting? Knowing when the problem started occurring and what changes happened right before it could give you a great head start on finding the solution.

- Make one change at a time, testing the problem after each change to see if it is resolved.

- Keep notes. As you make a change or test something, make a note of it so you'll know what you changed and when.

- Don't be surprised to find that what appears to be a single problem could actually be multiple problems.

- Use restore points to restore your system to the state it was in just prior to when the problem started occurring.
- Make backups of your critical data before you make any drastic changes.
- Make backup copies of the registry key in which you are about to make changes before you make those changes.

Help with Troubleshooting Software

For more help with troubleshooting programs, search Windows Help and Support or post a question in the appropriate newsgroup at Microsoft Communities.

Part IX

Hardware and Performance Tuning

Computer hardware is the physical components you can touch or hold in your hand. This includes the many gadgets you can connect to your computer, such as cameras and disk drives. Part IX is all about the hardware and gadgets.

Chapter 46 starts off with the general tools and techniques for installing hardware, getting it to work, and removing hardware that you no longer use.

Chapter 47 focuses on working with Bluetooth devices, which are devices that use the Bluetooth wireless technology to interact with your computer.

Chapter 48 covers the Sync Center, a single point of entry for syncing your computer with many different kinds of devices.

Chapter 49 looks at hardware from the standpoint of performance — getting the most from the hardware you already have.

As always, we end the part with a discussion of common hardware and performance problems and solutions to make those problems go away.

Installing and Removing Hardware

A typical computer consists of hardware, firmware, and software. These three components work together to make the computer both usable and useful. This chapter will help you understand each of these with a focus on installing and removing hardware in Windows 7.

Before jumping into hardware-related tasks, take a quick look at just what hardware, firmware, and software really are.

Hardware, Firmware, and Software Demystified

Hardware is any physical device used by the computer, whether internal to the computer (such as the CPU on the computer's motherboard), or attached externally to the computer. A discrete hardware component that performs a given function is generally referred to as a hardware device or just *device* for short. You can use numerous types of hardware devices with a computer. Printers, scanners, mice, keyboards, monitors, disk drives, digital cameras, MP3 players, modems, and routers are all examples of hardware devices.

Before I describe firmware, it helps to get a better understanding of *software*. Software is program code that is written to perform a given function. For example, all of the program code that makes up WordPad is software. Likewise, all of the program code that constitutes Windows 7 is software.

Device drivers are also software. A device driver is a program that serves as an intermediary between a piece of hardware and an application or the operating system. For example, a display driver enables Windows 7 to communicate with and control your computer's display. Likewise, a printer driver enables Windows 7 to communicate with and control a printer.

Firmware is also software, in the context that it is program code. The difference is in how the program code is stored. Firmware is program code stored in a hardware device, typically in read-only memory. For example, the program code that makes your Apple iPod or your digital camera work is firmware.

Generally, as a typical Windows 7 user you will deal with firmware only when updating firmware on your removable devices, such as MP3 players. You will be adding device drivers and working with Windows updates much more so than you will with firmware.

A Few Words about Device Drivers

As indicated in the previous section, device drivers enable the Windows operating system to communicate with and control devices. Although Windows 7 comes with a very large number of device drivers for a wide range of devices, most device drivers are written by and distributed by the manufacturers of a given device. For example, your video adapter's device driver was written by the company that designed and manufactured the adapter.

Device drivers are very much device-specific. That is, a device driver written for one device won't work for a different type of device. For that reason, make sure you have the necessary device driver(s) for a device before you install it. If you have just purchased a new device that requires a device driver not included with Windows, that driver will be included with the new device, typically on a CD. Because the version of the device driver was developed specifically for the device, you don't have to obtain an updated driver before installing the new device. However, you can certainly visit the manufacturer's Web site to see if an updated driver is available that adds features or fixes issues with the version you have. I recommend installing the device with the driver you have, then checking later for an updated driver as needed.

Using Hot-Pluggable Devices

Many modern hardware devices are *hot-pluggable*, which means you just connect them to your computer and start using them. There's no need to shut down the computer before connecting the device. Nor is there any need to go through a formal installation process after you connect the device. However, you should always read the instructions that came with a device before you connect it for the first time because sometimes you need to install some software before you connect the device. When that's the case, as stated earlier the software is usually on a CD that comes with the device.

Tip

Because Windows 7 includes a large library of device drivers, you can just connect a device and begin using it without going through the process of installing a device driver yourself. For example, you can connect any USB flash drive and begin using it right away. Because most digital cameras look and act to Windows 7 as flash drives, you can do the same with cameras. ■

Hot-pluggable devices generally connect to the computer through one of three main ports: USB, IEEE 1392, or PC Card (different versions called PCMCIA, Cardbus, and ExpressCard). We look at those in the sections that follow.

Connecting USB devices

USB (Universal Serial Bus) is the most common type of hot-pluggable device. USB is used by flash drives, digital cameras, some types of microphones, external disk drives, and many other types of devices. Like most technologies, USB has evolved over the years, and three versions of USB are currently on the market.

The main differences among USB standard versions have to do with speed. USB 1.0 and 1.1 have two speeds: Low Speed (1.5 Mbps) used by mice and keyboards, and Full Speed (12 Mbps), more often used by digital cameras and disk drives. USB 2.0 added a third, High Speed, data rate, which can transfer data at the much faster rate of 480 Mbps.

USB 2.0 is downwardly compatible with USB 1.1 and 1.0, which means that you can use a USB 2.0 device in a computer with USB 1.x ports. However, the device will transfer at the 12 Mbps speed rather than the 480 Mbps speed available only in USB 2.0. So you don't really need to know exactly which type of USB your computer has. If you plug a USB 2.0 device into a USB 1.0 or 1.1 port, Windows will display a message telling you that you'd get better performance from a USB 2.0 port. The device will still work; it'll just be a lot slower than if you'd plugged it into a USB 2.0 port.

Tip

If you want to learn more about a technology mentioned in this chapter, such as USB, IEEE 1394, IDE, SATA, or whatever, browse to www.wikipedia.org or www.webopedia.com and search for the acronym of interest. ■

There are three different USB plug shapes, named Type A, Type B, and Mini-USB or On-the-Go (OTG). The computer has female Type A ports, into which you plug the male Type A plug on the cable. The device might have Type A, B, or a mini-port. Figure 46-1 shows the symbol for USB and the general shape of USB ports on the computer. Examples of Type A, B, and mini-ports are shown to the right of those. The plugs are all keyed so that they only fit one way. Try pushing the plug gently into the port, and it if won't fit, flip the plug over and try again.

FIGURE 46-1

USB symbol, ports, and plug types.

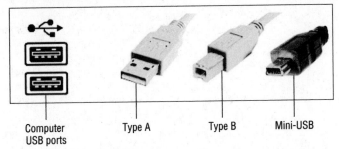

Computer USB ports   Type A   Type B   Mini-USB

Connecting a USB device should be easy, providing you've done any preliminary installations required by your specific device. The steps are as follows:

1. If the device has an on/off switch, turn it off.

2. Connect the device to the computer using the appropriate USB cable.

3. If the device has an on/off switch, turn it on.

The very first time you connect a device, you might get some feedback on the screen indicating that Windows is loading drivers for the device. That message will be followed by one indicating that the device is ready for use.

In many cases, you'll get an AutoPlay dialog box after you've connected the device. Figure 46-2 shows an example. From the AutoPlay dialog box, click whichever option best describes what you want to do with the device. In the case of a hard drive, that would most likely be the Open Folder to View Files option, unless you were using that hard drive to store one specific type of file.

What's "Speed up my system" and ReadyBoost?

Some USB devices can be used to speed up your system with ReadyBoost. When you plug a flash drive into a USB port, AutoPlay options might include an option to speed up your system using ReadyBoost. ReadyBoost is a Windows 7 feature designed to speed up some operations by using flash memory as intermediary storage between the processor and the hard drive. It only works with USB devices that actually can play that role. Flash memory has fast random I/O capabilities, and therefore isn't supported by all USB devices. See Chapter 49 for more information on ReadyBoost.

FIGURE 46-2

Sample AutoPlay dialog box for an external hard drive.

Connecting IEEE 1394 devices

IEEE 1394 (often called 1394 for short) is a high-speed (800 Mbps) standard typically used to connect digital video cameras and high-speed disk drives to computers. The symbol and plug shape for an IEEE 1394 port are shown in Figure 46-3. IEEE 1394 also goes by the names FireWire and iLink.

Tip

1394a supports speeds up to 400 Mbps, and 1394b supports speeds up to 800 Mbps. ∎

Connecting a 1394 device is much the same as connecting a USB device:

1. Leave the computer running, and turn the device off (if it has an on/off switch).
2. Connect one end of the 1394 cable to the computer and the other end to the device.
3. Turn on the device and wait.

As always, what happens next depends on the device.

FIGURE 46-3

FireWire symbol and plug shape.

PC Cards

PC Cards, Cardbus, and ExpressCard cards are commonly used on notebook computers. The device is usually a little larger and thicker than a credit card. Figure 46-4 shows an example of a PC Card wireless network adapter.

FIGURE 46-4

PC Card.

Connecting a PC Card to a notebook computer is simple. Just slide the card into the slot, right side up, and push until it's firmly seated. As with USB and FireWire devices, you should get some feedback on the screen indicating when the device is connected and ready for use. How you use the device depends on the type of device you inserted.

Using memory cards

Memory cards are hot-pluggable storage devices. Figure 46-5 shows examples of some memory cards. Most memory cards are used in digital cameras and jump drives. You just connect the camera or jump drive to a USB port to access the content on the memory card. However, if your computer has slots for memory cards, you can also insert the card directly into the appropriate slot.

After you insert a memory card into a slot, you should get some feedback on the screen indicating that the card is ready for use. That may be in the form of an AutoPlay dialog box, or an Explorer window may open to show you the contents of the card. Either way, the card will be treated as a USB mass storage device, as discussed next.

FIGURE 46-5

Examples of memory cards.

Memory cards and USB mass storage

Memory cards and USB devices that store data act like disk drives when you connect them to a computer. As such, each will have an icon in your Computer folder when it's connected. Figure 46-6 shows an example where I have connected an external hard drive (Drive I:), a flash drive (Drive F:), and a memory card (Drive H:) through USB ports. Drive Z: is a mapped network drive.

Using such a device is no different from using any other disk drive. To see the contents of the device, open its icon. Use the standard techniques to navigate through folders, to delete files and folders, and to move and copy files and folders. See Chapters 28 and 29 for the necessary buzzwords and basic skills.

Disconnecting hot-pluggable devices

Before you disconnect a hot-pluggable device from a computer, you might want to make sure it's not in the middle of a file transfer, or holding a file that you have open in some program. To do that, look in the Notification area and see if there's one that looks like the one pointed to in Figure 46-7. (That icon shows only when you have a storage device attached.) Note that the icon doesn't display a tooltip, but if you view its settings in the Notification Area Icons applet in Control Panel, you'll see that its name is Safely Remove Hardware and Eject Media.

To safely remove a device, click the Safely Remove Hardware and Eject Media icon. The menu shown in Figure 46-8 opens listing each connected mass storage device. Click the action you want to take from the menu.

FIGURE 46-6

External devices in Computer folder.

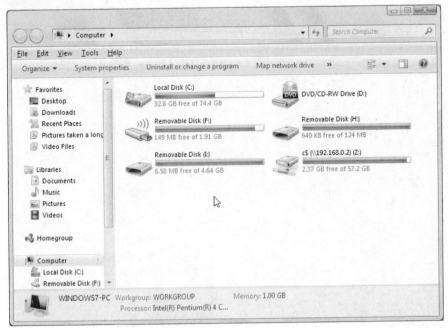

Tip

If it's difficult to reach around to the back of the computer to connect a USB or FireWire device, just leave that end of the cable plugged into the computer. Disconnect the cable from the device, and leave that end of the cable within easy reach for future connections. Or, get an external USB or FireWire hub, connect the hub to the back of the computer by its cable, and leave the hub on your desk within easy reach. ■

Simply click the Eject command for the drive you want to disconnect. The media will not physically eject from the computer, but Windows will close it and display a message that the device can safely be disconnected from the computer. You can then safely remove it from the computer.

Not all devices are hot-pluggable. Some require a more elaborate connection and installation procedures. Those kinds of devices are discussed in the next section.

Not-So-Hot-Pluggable Devices

Hardware devices that aren't hot-pluggable require a bit more effort than hot-pluggable devices. Most require that you turn off the computer, connect the device, turn the device on, and then turn the computer back on. You might also need to install some software to get the device to work. It all depends on the device you're connecting. As always, you have to read the instructions that came with the device for specifics. I can only provide general guidelines and examples here that give you an idea of what to expect.

Safely remove hardware icon.

Most computers have the ports pointed out in Figure 46-9. Your computer may have more or fewer such ports, and your ports probably won't be arranged exactly like that. On a notebook computer, some of the ports will likely be on the side of the computer, perhaps hidden under a sliding or hinged door. But the basic shape of each port will be as shown in the figure.

You can install some devices inside the computer case. These connect to sockets inside the computer case on the *motherboard* (also called the *mainboard*). The motherboard is a circuit board that provides the wiring between all the hardware devices that make up the system, including the CPU, memory (RAM), internal disk drives, and everything else. The sockets that accept these devices are called *expansion slots*, and the devices that go in them are typically called *adapter cards*.

Figure 46-10 provides a general idea of what different types of internal slots and ports look like.

Installing expansion cards

Many internal hardware devices are PCI Cards, which slide into a PCI slot. The slots are positioned so that one end of the card lines up perfectly with the back of the computer, exposing one or more external connectors. Figure 46-11 shows a general example of what such a card looks like.

Newer motherboards may have PCI Express (PCIe) and PCI Express 16. These provide faster communication between the motherboard, which in turn allows for more powerful expansion cards. The PCI Express 16 slot is ideal for high-powered graphics cards designed to work with advanced graphics and large High Definition TV screens. The AGP (Accelerated Graphics Port) port is designed specifically for a graphics card.

FIGURE 46-8

Safely Remove Hardware menu.

Before you buy an expansion card, you need to know what slots are available on your motherboard. Before you install a card, you need to read the instructions that came with the card. There is no one-rule-fits-all fact that applies to all of the thousands of hardware devices you can add to a PC. You should install the device exactly as instructed in the instructions provided by the manufacturer of the device. Winging it is likely to lead to many hours of hair-pulling frustration. It's also very important that you turn off the computer before opening the case to install a card. Remove the power cord too. Ideally, you should wear an antistatic wrist strap so that you don't generate any static electricity that could damage any of the components in the computer, potentially rendering it unusable and voiding your warranty.

Tip
You can buy an antistatic wrist strap at computer hardware stores, including online stores such as TigerDirect (www.tigerdirect.com), CompUSA (www.compusa.com), CDW (www.cdw.com), and Cyberguys (www.cyberguys.com). ∎

Many AGP and PCIe 16 slots have a locking mechanism to hold the card steady in the slot. You have to make sure that it's in the unlocked position before you try to insert the card into the slot. When installing the card, push firmly on the card to make sure you really get it in there. Don't force it and break it, but push it in well enough to ensure that it's firmly and evenly seated within its slot. If the slot has a locking mechanism, push it into the locked position. Put the case cover back together again, plug in the power cord, and then turn on the PC.

FIGURE 46-9

Ports on the back of a computer.

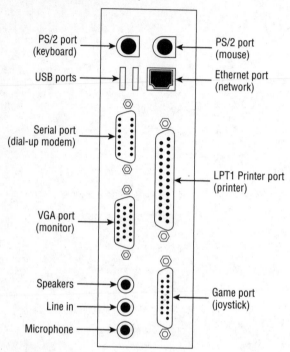

PS/2 port
(keyboard)

PS/2 port
(mouse)

USB ports

Ethernet port
(network)

Serial port
(dial-up modem)

LPT1 Printer port
(printer)

VGA port
(monitor)

Speakers

Line in

Game port
(joystick)

Microphone

Caution

When removing a card that has a locking device, don't forget to slide it into the unlocked position. Trying to force the card out of the locked slot would likely cause a lot of damage! ∎

If the device is plug-and-play (as many modern devices are), the rest should be easy. The computer should boot up normally, but you won't necessarily get to the desktop right away. Instead, Windows should detect the new device, and go through an installation procedure to get the device working. You'll get some feedback on the screen as that's happening, in the form of Notification area messages. When the notification messages stop and the desktop looks normal, the device should be ready to use.

Installing more memory (RAM)

Installing more RAM isn't exactly like installing other devices, because you're not likely to get any feedback at all on the Windows desktop when you're done. RAM is such an integral part of the computer that it doesn't really get "installed." The processor just detects it as soon as you turn on the power. One of the few places you'd even see that you have more RAM is on the General tab of the System Properties dialog box.

The key consideration to adding more RAM is finding the right type of memory. You need to match the type and speed of your existing RAM chip, and you need an available DIMM slot on the motherboard. Also, every motherboard has a limit as to the maximum speed and type of memory it can handle. When you build a PC, you know exactly what's involved. But when you buy a prebuilt PC, it's not always easy to find out what you need to know.

FIGURE 46-10

Slots on a computer motherboard.

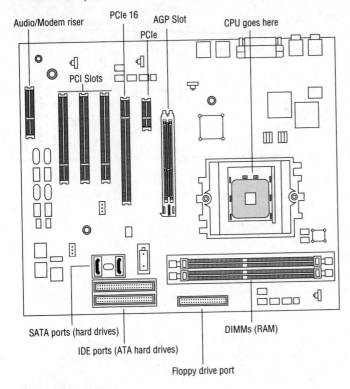

FIGURE 46-11

A sample expansion card.

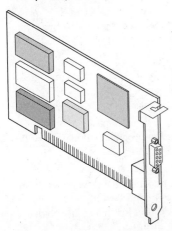

Upgrading the CPU

Every motherboard has a certain maximum CPU speed it can handle. You won't know what that is unless you can get the specs on your exact motherboard. Rather than try to upgrade just the CPU, you'd probably be better off upgrading the motherboard, CPU, and RAM while you're at it. That way you can speed up everything, but still use your existing hard drive, CD/DVD drive, mouse, keyboard, monitor, and everything else. Or, for a little extra, you can probably purchase a new PC almost as inexpensively as upgrading your old one.

A barebones kit might be the best way to go. With a barebones kit you can get a motherboard, CPU, RAM, and power supply already assembled in a new case. You then transfer your existing hard drive, CD drive, mouse, keyboard, monitor, and everything else to that new case. You get the benefits of a newer, faster computer without the expense of buying an entirely new PC.

Your best bet is to go to the computer manufacturer's Web site and find the main Web page for your exact model of computer. You can often find out exactly what type and speed of RAM chip is currently installed using that method. PNY (a company that sells RAM chips) has a Memory Configurator link on its home page (www.pny.com). When you click that link, it asks some basic questions about your system and then tells you which RAM chips will work with that system.

Tip

The PNY site also has installation guides, which might help you get the feel for what you'll be doing when you purchase more RAM. Remember, you have to look inside the computer and see if you even have an available slot for adding more RAM first. ∎

Even so, installing more RAM isn't really something for the technologically timid to undertake. Even the slightest mistake could prevent the computer from starting at all. If the speed of the new chip doesn't exactly match the speed of the existing chip, the computer will start but you're likely to end up with endless error messages when you try to do just about anything.

Installing a second hard drive

If you need more hard disk space, installing a second hard drive is a good option. Hard disk space is cheap, and it's a lot easier to just add another drive than it is to try to pinch a few more megabytes out of a single drive by compressing files and moving things out to removable disks.

Most internal drives are relatively easy to install. What's more, with today's computers, the computer will automatically detect the drive type on boot. If you don't feel up to the task of installing a new internal drive, however, consider an external drive.

Tip

If the computer doesn't recognize the new disk, enter the computer's BIOS Setup program and make sure the BIOS is configured to auto-detect drives on the new drive's interface. ∎

External hard drives are relatively simple to install. Basically you just connect the drive to a USB or FireWire port. If you already bought an internal hard drive but haven't connected it yet, you can convert it to an external drive just by putting it in an external drive enclosure. Just make sure you get an enclosure that has the right internal connectors (IDE or SATA) for your drive.

Tip

To see examples of hard drive enclosures, search an online retailer such as www.newegg.com, www.tigerdirect.com, or even froogle.google.com for external drive enclosure. Drives that connect via USB 2.0 can move data at 480 Mbps, which is plenty fast for a hard drive and won't be a performance bottleneck. ■

Hard drives for most non-server PCs fall into two main categories, SATA (Serial ATA) and PATA (Parallel ATA), more commonly referred to as IDE (Integrated Drive Electronics) drives. (The ATA stands for Advanced Technology Attachment.) SATA is the newer, faster, and easier technology.

Note

Servers and some workstations use SCSI (Small Computer System Interface) drives. However, SATA drives provide faster data rates than SCSI drives. ■

The original SATA drives moved data at a good 150 Mbps (150 million bits per second). The newer SATA II drives move data at 300 Mbps, and third-generation SATA drives support 600 Mbps. Before adding a second SATA drive, you'll need to make sure your motherboard has SATA connectors, and whether they are the appropriate connectors for the type of SATA device you want to install.

IDE drives come in multiple speeds too, ranging from 33 Mbps to 133 Mbps. The maximum speed your PC can use depends on the speed of the IDE connectors on the motherboard.

IDE drives have an unusual configuration where you can connect two drives to a single IDE port. One drive is called the master drive, the other the slave drive. You have to physically set a jumper on the drive to make the drive either master or slave. Then you have to connect the drive to the right place on the cable. The master goes at the end of the cable. The slave goes on the plug in the center of the cable, as illustrated in Figure 46-12.

FIGURE 46-12

Older style internal IDE drives.

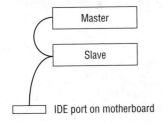

Again, your best bet before installing any hardware device is to follow the instructions that came with the device — to a tee — before you even turn the computer back on and use Windows to configure the device. If in doubt, have a pro install the hardware for you. But, assuming you've installed the drive, either internally or externally, you can then use Windows 7 to partition and format the drive.

Primary and extended partitions

You can divide a basic disk into multiple *partitions*. Each partition looks like a separate item in your Computer folder. The drive can be divided into a maximum of four *primary* partitions, or three primary partitions and one *extended* partition. The difference is that a primary partition can be used as a *system partition*, meaning you can install an operating system on it and boot the computer from it.

An extended partition can't be a boot disk and can't contain an operating system. However, you can divide an extended partition into multiple logical drives, where each logical drive has its own drive letter and icon in the Computer folder, and looks like a separate drive.

In Windows XP and previous versions of Windows, you could explicitly create extended partitions using the Disk Management console. Microsoft changed that in Windows Vista, and that change carries over to Windows 7. Now rather than the option to create either a primary or extended partition, Disk Management gives you the option of creating a new simple volume. The type of volume created when you use this command depends on the number of partitions already on the disk. The first three partitions you create are created as primary partitions. The fourth is created as an extended partition.

Tip

If you do need an extended partition, you can use the DiskPart command in a command console to create it. To learn more about DiskPart, open a command console and enter diskpart. At the DiskPart command prompt, enter Help to see a listing of commands. ■

Another concept to understand is that you can use three types of disks in Windows 7:

- **Basic:** This is the type of disk supported by DOS and all previous versions of Windows.
- **Dynamic:** This type of disk was introduced in Windows 2000. Dynamic disks support the following types of volumes:
  - **Simple:** These volumes comprise space for a single dynamic disk, and can use a single region on the disk or multiple regions on the disk.
  - **Spanned:** These volumes comprise space on more than one physical disk (they span multiple physical drives, hence the name).
  - **Striped:** These volumes stripe the data for a single logical volume across multiple physical disks, providing improved performance by distributing the read/write load across multiple disks.
- **GPT:** This stands for Globally Unique Identifier Partition Table. GPT supports theoretical volume sizes up to 18 EB. The primary advantages to using GPT are the very large volume size and the large number of partitions you can create on a GPT disk. Disk structure is also optimized for performance and reliability.

Tip

EB stands for exabyte, which is equal to about a million terabytes. ■

Which disk type you choose really depends on the type of disk and your needs. If you are installing a very high-capacity disk in a Windows 7 computer, I recommend using GPT. If you need to create a spanned or striped volume, use a dynamic disk. For general-purpose disks, a basic disk is fine.

Partitioning and formatting the disk

Caution

Repartitioning and/or reformatting a disk that already contains files will result in the *permanent* loss of all files on that disk. You should not attempt to repartition or reformat an existing disk unless you fully understand the consequences, and are fully prepared to recover any lost files. Again, if you don't have any formal training and experience in technical matters, it's best to leave this sort of thing to the pros. An in-depth treatment of these more technical hardware matters is beyond the scope of this book. ■

After you have a new hard drive installed, you can restart Windows 7 and use the Disk Management tool to partition and format the drive. Log in to an account with administrative privileges for this task.

If the Computer Management tool doesn't start automatically after you've logged in, you can get to it by following these steps:

1. Click the Start button, right-click Computer, and choose Manage.

2. Click Disk Management in the left column.

Tip

Optionally, press ⊞ **, type** comp **, and click Computer Management. Then choose Disk Management in the Computer Management tool that opens.** ■

The new drive appears at the bottom of the display, most likely as Disk 1 (assuming the system has one other disk drive, which will show as Disk 0). The drive's space is indicated by a striped bar showing Unallocated in the lower-left corner.

To partition the drive as a basic disk with a simple volume:

1. Right-click within the unallocated space of the new drive and choose New Simple Volume.

2. On the first page of the New Simple Volume Wizard that opens, click Next.

3. The next wizard page asks what size you want to make the partition, and suggests the full capacity of the disk. You can choose a smaller size if you intend to divide the disk into multiple partitions. After you make your selection, click Next.

4. The next wizard page asks you to assign a drive letter to the drive. It suggests the next available drive letter, which is a good choice. Click Next.

5. The next wizard page asks how you want to format and label the disk. Your options are as follows:

   - **Do Not Format this Volume:** If you choose this option, you'll have to format the partition later. I suggest that you not choose this option.

   - **File System:** Your choices here depend on the disk type. For volumes on basic and dynamic disks, you can choose between exFAT and NTFS. On a GPT disk, you can only choose NTFS.

   - **Allocation Unit Size:** This defines the cluster size. The Default option automatically chooses the best allocation unit size given the type and capacity of the disk, so that would be your best choice.

   - **Volume Label:** This is the name that appears with the drive's icon in My Computer. You can enter any name you want up to 12 characters in length (including spaces). You can also change that name at any time in the future.

   - **Perform a Quick Format:** If you choose this option, formatting will go quickly, but the drive won't be checked for errors. Better to leave this option unselected.

   - **Enable File and Folder Compression:** Only available if you chose NTFS as the file system, this option automatically compresses all files and folders on the drive. This conserves disk space, but there is a minimal performance overhead for the compression/decompression as the drive is used. You can still compress individual files and folders if you leave this option unselected.

6. Click Next after making your selections.

7. The last wizard page summarizes your selections. Click Finish.

Now you get to wait for the disk to be formatted. This could take some time, depending on the size of the volume. You can continue to use your computer while the drive is being formatted, or leave it until it finishes.

If you set up the drive as one large partition, you're done when the Formatting indicator reaches 100%. You can close the Computer Management tool and Control Panel.

If you are partitioning the disk into smaller units, you can repeat the steps outlined previously for each partition. Just make sure that you right-click an unpartitioned portion of the disk in step 1. If you create an extended partition with the DiskPart command, you will need to add one or more physical volumes to the disk through the Disk Management console. Just right-click the extended partition and choose New Simple Volume, then follow the steps described previously to create the new volume. Repeat the process for any other volumes you want to create in the extended partition.

Figure 46-13 shows an example with a secondary drive (Disk 1) containing two partitions, drives E: and F:. Their volumes' labels are Music and Docs, respectively.

FIGURE 46-13

Two physical hard drives in the Disk Management tool.

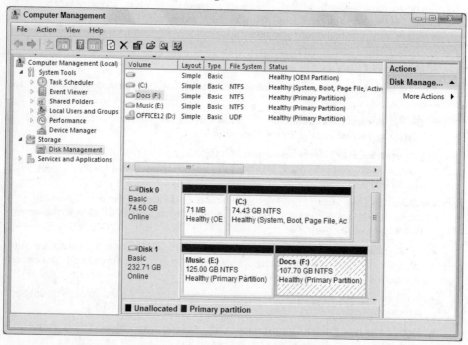

When all the partitioning and formatting is complete, exit the Computer Management tool. Access the drive as you would any other — through the Computer folder. Figure 46-14 shows an example. Notice how each Hard Disk Drive icon represents a drive (or partition) defined in the Disk Management tool.

FIGURE 46-14

Drives and partitions as viewed through the Computer folder.

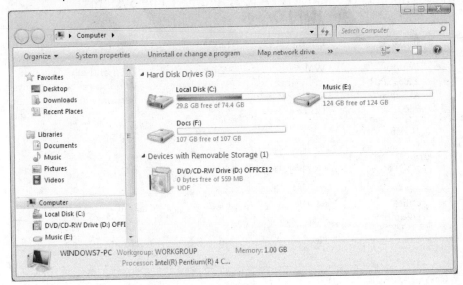

Other hard drive operations

This section covers some general issues concerning hard disks. All of these operations pose some risk of data loss, and should be attempted only by people who understand the risks and are confident they have backups of all important data.

Converting a FAT disk to NTFS

Windows 7 offers four different file systems for formatting a hard drive. The earliest file system, FAT (File Allocation Table), was used in DOS, and the earliest versions of Windows. FAT32 was introduced with Windows 95. NTFS (New Technology File System) was introduced in Windows NT 4.0, largely to support user access control required in domain networking. Extended FAT (exFAT) is a new file system that removes several limitations of the older FAT file systems while providing compatibility with other operating systems and devices.

When you divide a hard drive into multiple volumes, you can format each independently of the other. (A volume is any partition or logical drive that has its own drive letter and icon in My Computer.) NTFS is the preferred file system for Windows 7 because of its better performance and stronger security. There's no reason to use one of the FAT file systems unless you have multiple operating systems installed and can choose one or the other at startup. For example, if you can boot to Windows 7 and Linux, the Linux operating system will not be able to access files on a local NTFS volume.

Each file system imposes minimum and maximum volume sizes, and a maximum file size. Keep in mind that these file systems apply only to the hard drives, not to media like CDs or DVDs. Table 46-1 summarizes the differences among the file systems.

Tip

See the section, "The exFAT File System," later in this chapter to learn more about the exFAT file system. ∎

TABLE 46-1

Differences among NTFS, exFAT, FAT32, and FAT File Systems for Hard Drives

	NTFS	exFAT	FAT32	FAT
Locally accessible to	Windows 7, 2008, 2003, XP, and 2000	Windows XP, Vista, and 7; Linux	Windows 95 and later	DOS and all Windows versions
Minimum volume size	10 MB		512 MB	1 MB
Maximum volume size	> 2 TB*	64 ZB**	32 GB	4 GB
Maximum file size	Entire volume	64 ZB	4 GB	2 GB
Access Control Lists (ACLs)	Yes	No	No	No

*Terabyte, a trillion bytes or 1,024 GB.
**Zettabyte, a sextillion bytes or 1 billion terabytes

Caution

Changing the file system on a drive poses some risk of data loss, and should be attempted only by people who understand the risks and are prepared to recover from any loss of data. ■

You can convert a FAT or FAT32 file system to NTFS, but it's not possible to go in the other direction. That is, you can always upgrade to NTFS, but you cannot downgrade. Be sure to close all open documents and program windows prior to starting the conversion. To convert a FAT or FAT32 volume to NTFS, use the following syntax with the command console `convert` command:

```
convert drive: /fs:ntfs
```

where *drive* is the letter of the hard drive you want to convert. Advanced users can enter `convert /?` at the command prompt, or search Windows Help and Support for more advanced options. To enter the command:

1. Close all open documents and program windows.
2. Click the Start button and choose All Programs ⇨ Accessories ⇨ Command Prompt.
3. Type the command using the syntax shown. For example, to convert hard disk drive D: from FAT or FAT32 to NTFS, type `convert d: /fs:ntfs`.
4. Press Enter, and follow the instructions on the screen.

If you're converting your system drive (C:), you'll need to restart the computer to start the conversion. Don't use the computer during the conversion process.

Shrinking and extending partitions

Tip

You can shrink and extend partitions without reformatting, either from the Disk Management tool or by using the DISKPART command. ■

You can shrink existing partitions to free up unallocated space. And if you have any unallocated space, you can extend existing partitions into that space. As always, there is some risk in doing this. Therefore, you should back up everything before even attempting to shrink or extend a partition.

Caution

The techniques described in this section will *not* increase the amount of hard disk space you have. The techniques described in this section are best left to professionals and highly knowledgeable computer users. The slightest error could cost you everything on your hard drive! Not recommended for casual computer users. ■

You can shrink a basic volume that's either raw (unformatted) or formatted with NTFS quite easily right in the Disk Management tool. You can shrink to the current used space size or to the first unmovable files (such as a paging file) on the volume. To shrink a volume, just right-click it at the bottom of the Disk Management screen and choose Shrink Volume. A dialog box opens to show how far you can shrink the selected volume. Just make your selection and click OK.

Likewise, if you have some unallocated space on the drive, you can extend an existing partition into that space. A wizard opens to take you step-by-step through the process.

For more information on extending and shrinking volumes, including spanned volumes, search the Help in the Disk Management tool.

Changing a volume label

A *volume label* is the name of a volume as it appears in your Computer folder. By default, each volume is labeled Local Disk. To change a drive's Volume Label, right-click its icon in your Computer folder and choose Properties. On the General tab of the Properties sheet, type the new name into the first text box, where you see External HD in Figure 46-15.

Changing a drive letter

Drive letters A, B, and C are reserved for floppy disk drives and your hard drive, and cannot be changed. Beyond those first three letters, you can assign drive letters as you see fit. Just be aware that when you do, Windows will *not* update your settings and programs to the change. All settings you've made concerning locations of files in all programs will be invalid. Virtual folders and items in Media Player and Live Photo Gallery will need to be updated to reflect the new drive locations. If you're not sure how to deal with these things, better not to change any drive letters.

Caution

Changing drive letters is an operation that's best left to experienced users who understand the consequences and can solve, on their own, the problems that are likely to follow. ■

No two drives can have the same drive letter. If you need to swap two drive letters (for example, change drive E: to drive F: and change drive F: to drive E:), you'll need to temporarily leave one of the drives without a letter or assign it an unused drive letter. The Disk Management tool, which you need to make this change, will allow you to do that. Here's how it works:

1. Get back to the Disk Management tool described at the start of this section.

2. Right-click the graphical representation of the drive whose letter you want to change. Or, to change a removable drive, right-click its drive letter as in Figure 46-16. Choose Change Drive Letter and Paths.

3. If the new letter to which you want to assign the drive is available, click Change, choose the new drive letter, and click OK. Otherwise, if you want to assign the current drive's letter to a different drive, click Remove and click Yes.

4. Repeat steps 2 and 3 until all drives have the letters you want them to have. Then close the Disk Management tool.

The new drive letters will show up the next time you open your Computer folder.

FIGURE 46-15

Changing a volume label.

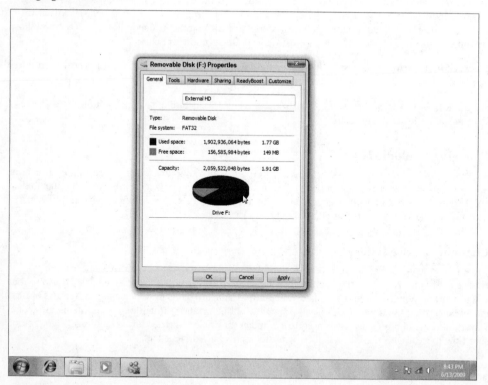

The exFAT file system

Microsoft has developed a new file system called exFAT, for Extended FAT. exFAT is also sometimes referred to as FAT 64 (for 64-bit).

FIGURE 46-16

Changing a drive letter.

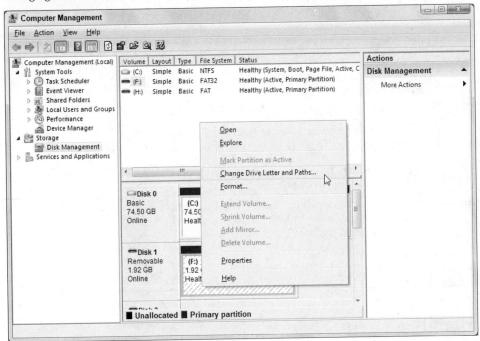

exFAT is not intended as a replacement for NTFS. Rather, exFAT is geared primarily toward mobile personal storage, such as used in MP3 players and other mobile devices. exFAT offers several advantages:

- Theoretical volume size of 64 ZB (recommended size 512 TB).
- Theoretical maximum file size of 64 ZB (recommended size 512 TB).
- Supports more than 1,000 files per directory.
- Provides cluster bitmap for fast storage allocation.
- Better contiguous on-disk layout, useful for recording movies.
- Is extensible.

exFAT is supported natively by Windows 7 and Windows Vista, and is supported under Windows XP through the application of hotfix 955704. Windows Vista does not support the use of exFAT with ReadyBoost, but Windows 7 does support it. exFAT is also supported under Linux through kernel update.

If you want to optimize performance for removable media such as flash drives, consider formatting the drive with exFAT. However, keep in mind that the device will only be usable in a computer that supports exFAT.

Removing Hardware

Hot-pluggable devices don't follow the type of removal discussed in this section. To remove a USB or FireWire device, or a PC card or memory card, see the section titled "Disconnecting hot-pluggable devices" earlier in this chapter. This section is about removing more complex devices like internal components. Before you follow the procedures described in this section, make sure you understand what you're removing and why you're removing it. Do not attempt to fix some problem by removing devices through sheer guesswork.

You'll need administrative privileges to perform the tasks described here. It might be best to sign into a user account before you get started so you don't have to rely on privilege escalation along the way.

Before you physically remove a device from the system, first uninstall it through Device Manager by following these steps:

1. Click the Start button, right-click Computer, and choose Manage, then click Device Manager in the left pane to open Device Manager.

2. Expand the category in which the device is listed. Then right-click the name of the device you intend to remove and choose Uninstall, as in Figure 46-17.

3. Click OK.

FIGURE 46-17

Uninstall a hardware device.

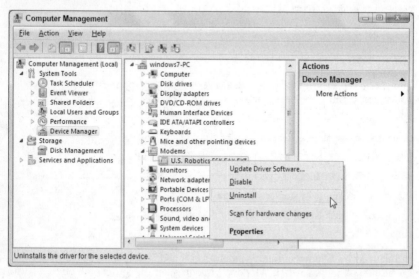

Now you need to shut down the computer, unplug the power cord, and physically remove the device from the system. Then plug the machine back in, start it up, and everything should be back to the way it was before you ever installed the device. If you set a protection point just before installing the hardware, you can return to that protection point just to make sure.

Updating Drivers

At the start of this chapter I discussed the importance of using Windows 7 drivers with your hardware. The quickest and easiest way to get an updated driver for a device is usually to search for it online by following these steps:

1. Open Device Manager (tap ⊞, type dev, and choose Device Manager).

2. Right-click the device that needs an updated driver and choose Update Driver Software as in Figure 46-18.

3. Click Search Automatically for Updated Driver Software and follow the on-screen instructions.

FIGURE 46-18

Update a device driver.

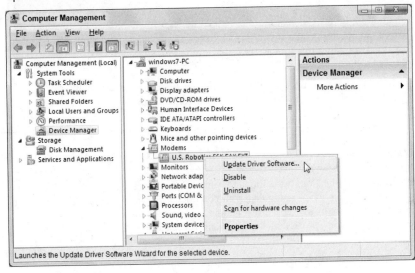

Often, that's all it takes. You might need to restart the computer after the driver installation is complete.

If that method doesn't work, you may have to go to the product manufacturer's Web site and search for a Windows 7 driver there. If you find the driver, make sure to follow the manufacturer's instructions carefully to download and install the updated driver. If you can't find a driver specifically for Windows 7, but you do find one for Windows Vista, that driver should work.

Dealing with Devices that Prevent Windows 7 from Starting

There may be times when a newly installed hardware device prevents Windows 7 from starting properly. In most cases, such devices will be disabled automatically so that Windows 7 can start. If it works that way, you can typically follow the steps described in the preceding section to try and get the updated driver online.

If Windows 7 cannot disable or work with the new device, you may be able to start in Safe Mode and either get updated drivers there, or disable the device manually. Here are the steps:

1. Close all open programs and documents and save any work in progress.

2. Restart the computer (click the arrow next to the Power button and choose Restart).

3. As the computer is restarting, press the F8 key a few times right after completion of the POST (Power On Self Test).

Caution

If your keyboard has a Function Lock (F Lock) key, keep an eye on it during the reboot process. If it turns off at any time, be sure to turn it back on before pressing F8. ■

4. When the Advanced Boot Options appear, choose Safe Mode with Networking.

5. Log in to the Administrator account.

When you're at the desktop, follow the procedure described under "Updating Drivers" to search for updated drivers. If you cannot find updated drivers, your best bet might be to disable the device by right-clicking its name and choosing Disable from the shortcut menu. Close Device Manager and restart the computer again normally.

If you had to disable the device, it won't work when you restart the computer normally. But at least you can get Windows 7 started and try to find an updated driver through the product manufacturer's Web site.

Wrap-Up

This chapter has been about connecting, installing, and removing hardware. Some of this material is intended for more advanced users who are familiar with computer hardware. If some of the content was beyond your technical capabilities or comfort level and you need to install or remove some hardware, consider having the job done professionally. The main points of this chapter are summarized here:

- Most modern devices are hot-pluggable, which means you just connect them to the computer as needed.

- Always read and follow the instructions that came with a device before connecting it to your computer. Winging it will likely result in frustration.

- Hot-pluggable devices that act as storage devices have icons in your Computer folder while connected. You can transfer files to and from such a device using basic techniques described in Chapter 29.

- More advanced hardware devices generally require shutting down the computer, connecting the device, turning the device on, and then starting the computer again.

- Use the Disk Management tool to partition and format a new drive.

- To remove a hot-pluggable storage device, click the Safely Remove Hardware icon in the Notification area and stop the device before physically removing it.

- To remove other devices, first uninstall them in Device Manager. Then shut down the computer and physically remove the device from the system.

Using Wireless Bluetooth Devices

I n a nutshell, Bluetooth is a wireless technology that provides wireless communications among computers, printers, mobile phones, PDAs, digital cameras, and other electronic devices. You can connect as many as eight devices together with Bluetooth, with one device acting as the master device and up to seven slave devices (this is called a piconet; you can have up to two piconets). For example, you could have a desktop PC, a notebook, PDA, digital camera, MP3 player, digital video camera, headphones, and mobile phone all linked together wirelessly. They could all share a high-speed Internet connection, share data, and use a single printer.

The World of Bluetooth

As of late 2009, the current Bluetooth version is 3.0. Bluetooth transfers data at up to 3 Mbps, which is slower than 802.11b (11 Mbps) and 802.11g (54 Mbps). So, if you're thinking of setting up a permanent wireless network between computers, you may want to stick with the 802.11 standards described in Chapter 51 of this book. But when it comes to connecting noncomputer Bluetooth devices, wirelessly connecting a printer, or occasionally transferring files between computers, Bluetooth can't be beat.

There are three types of Bluetooth devices, classified by the range across which devices can communicate:

- **Class 1:** Transmit and receive data up to 330 feet (100m).
- **Class 2:** Transmit and receive data up to 32 feet (10m).
- **Class 3:** Transmit and receive data up to 3 feet (1m).

Some Bluetooth buzzwords and concepts that you'll encounter in this section as well as in the instructions that come with Bluetooth devices are as follows:

- **Discovery:** A Bluetooth device finds other Bluetooth devices to which it can connect through a process called discovery. To prevent Bluetooth devices from connecting at random, discovery is usually turned off by default on a Bluetooth device. You manually turn on discovery when you are ready for that device to be discovered. After a device has been discovered, you can turn discovery off.

- **Discoverable:** A discoverable (or *visible*) Bluetooth device is one that has discovery turned on, so other Bluetooth devices within range can "see" and connect to the device.

- **Pairing:** Once two or more Bluetooth devices have discovered one another and have been paired (connected), you can turn off their discovery features. The devices will forever be able to connect to one another, and unauthorized foreign devices will not be able to discover and hack into the paired devices.

- **Encryption:** A process by which transferred data is encoded to make it unreadable to any unauthorized device that picks up a signal from the device. Bluetooth offers powerful 128-bit data encryption to secure the content of all transferred data.

- **Passkey:** Similar to a password, only devices that share a passkey can communicate with one another. This is yet another means of preventing unauthorized access to data transmitted across Bluetooth radio waves.

- **Bluejacking:** A process by which one user sends a picture or message to an unsuspecting person's Bluetooth device.

A noncomputer gadget such as a phone or PDA that supports Bluetooth is called a *Bluetooth device*. A standard desktop PC or laptop computer usually isn't a Bluetooth device. However, many newer laptops do include Bluetooth capabilities. But as a rule, it's easy to turn your PC or laptop into a Bluetooth device. You just plug a Bluetooth USB adapter — a tiny device about the size of your thumb — into any available USB port, and presto, your computer is a Bluetooth device. Making your computer into a Bluetooth device doesn't limit it in any way. It just extends the capabilities of your computer so that you can do things such as:

- Connect a Bluetooth mouse, keyboard, or other pointing device

- Use the Add Printer Wizard to use a Bluetooth printer wirelessly

- Use a Bluetooth-enabled phone or dial-up device as a modem

- Transfer files between Bluetooth-ready computers or devices by using Bluetooth

- Join an ad hoc personal area network (PAN) of Bluetooth-connected devices (an ad hoc network is an "informal" network, where devices connect and disconnect on an as-needed basis, without the need for a central hub or base station)

Bluetooth devices use radio signals to communicate wirelessly. When you install a Bluetooth adapter on your PC or laptop, you also install *radio drivers*. Windows 7 comes with many radio drivers preinstalled.

Note
If a built-in radio driver doesn't work with your device, install the drivers that came with the device per the device manufacturer's instructions. ∎

Configuring Your Bluetooth Adapter

If you plan to share a single Internet account among several computers or Bluetooth devices, you should install your first Bluetooth USB adapter in the computer that connects directly to the modem or router. That will give other Bluetooth devices that you add later easy access to the Internet through that computer's Internet connection.

After you've installed a Bluetooth adapter, you'll find a new icon named Bluetooth Devices in Control Panel. To get to it, click the Start button, choose Control Panel, and click Network and Internet. The Bluetooth icon looks like a letter B as shown in the Device Functions area of the Device Properties dialog box that is shown Figure 47-1. You might also notice a Bluetooth icon in the Notification area.

FIGURE 47-1

New icon on a PC that's configured as a Bluetooth device.

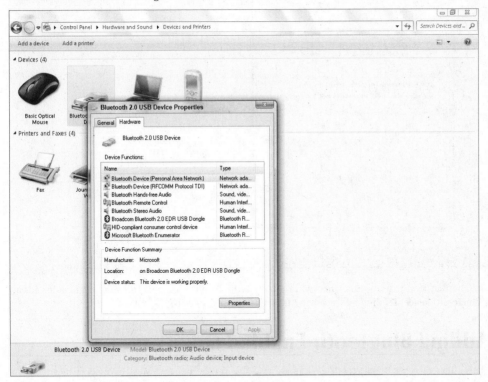

Tip

To return to the Category view in Control Panel, click Control Panel in the Control Panel window address bar. You also can click the Back button until you get there. ■

The Bluetooth Settings dialog box will be your central point for installing Bluetooth. To open that dialog box, double-click the Bluetooth Devices Notification area icon, or open the Devices and Printers icon in Control Panel. Initially, the Devices tab in the dialog box will be empty. But as you install devices and join devices to a Bluetooth PAN, you'll see the names of those devices listed on that tab.

The Options tab in the Bluetooth Settings dialog box, shown in Figure 47-2, provides general options for controlling discovery and the ability to install Bluetooth devices. If you don't see a Bluetooth Devices icon in your Notification area, make sure to select the Show the Bluetooth Icon in the Notification Area check box.

FIGURE 47-2

Options tab of the Bluetooth Settings dialog box and Notification area shortcut menu.

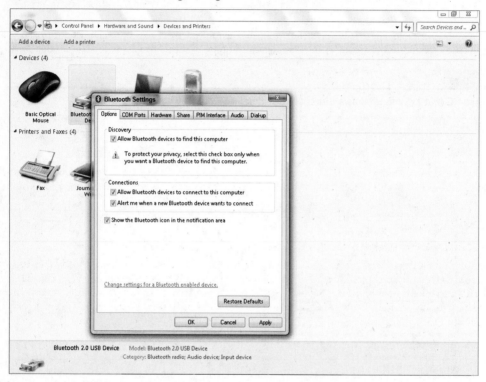

The shortcut icon that appears when you right-click the Notification area, provides options for adding a Bluetooth device, sending and receiving files, and joining a PAN.

Adding Bluetooth-Enabled Devices

Many different types of Bluetooth devices are available on the market. Most have some means of making the device discoverable (visible) to other devices. Whether or not you have to make your PC discoverable to install a device depends on the type of installation you're about to perform. As always, you need to read the documentation that came with your device for specifics. But if you do need to make your computer discoverable, it's simply a matter of choosing the Allow Bluetooth Devices To Connect To This Computer option, visible in Figure 47-2.

On the shortcut menu for the Bluetooth Devices notification icon, the Add a Bluetooth Device option opens the Add Bluetooth Device Wizard, which takes you step by step through the process of adding a device. The sections that follow discuss general techniques for adding Bluetooth devices, many of which will involve the Add Bluetooth Device Wizard.

Installing a Bluetooth printer

To install a Bluetooth printer, follow the printer manufacturer's instructions for turning on the printer and enabling its ability to connect to a computer. Then, on your PC:

1. Click the Start button and choose Devices and Printers. Or, click Start and choose Control Panel. If Control Panel opens in Category view, click Hardware and Sound. Select the Devices and Printers link to continue.

2. Click Add a Printer.

3. On the first wizard page, select the Add a Network, Wireless or Bluetooth Printer option.

4. Windows will start searching for your Bluetooth-compatible printer. If Windows is unable to locate the printer, it probably means that either the printer is not powered up or there is a problem with the Bluetooth device connected to your computer. Try clicking the link The Printer That I Want Isn't Listed and then select Add a Bluetooth Printer.

5. After your printer has been found, follow the remaining wizard instructions until you can click the Finish button to complete the job.

When it is installed, you should be able to print from any Bluetooth device according to the instructions that came with that device. To print a document from your computer, follow the usual procedure (choose File ➪ Print from the program's menu bar), and choose the Bluetooth printer from the Printer Name options in the Print dialog box.

Install a Bluetooth keyboard or mouse

To install a Bluetooth keyboard or mouse, you may need to first connect the device by cable, or use a cable-connected mouse or keyboard to provide the initial connectivity. Some newer Bluetooth keyboards and mice do not require this initial connection. Also, you must know how to make your mouse or keyboard discoverable (visible). If you're not sure how to get started, refer to the instructions that came with the mouse or keyboard.

If you're installing a keyboard, check its documentation to see if the keyboard supports the use of a passkey. And if so, find out if it already has a pre-assigned passkey, or if you can use a passkey of your own choosing. Then, to perform the installation, follow these steps:

1. Open the Devices and Printers window.

2. Click Add a Device. Windows searches for Bluetooth devices, namely the Bluetooth keyboard or mouse you intend to install. When Windows locates the device, a listing appears in the Select a Device to Add to This Computer window.

3. Click the discovered device's name, and then click Next.

4. If you're adding a keyboard, do one of the following as appropriate for your device:

   • To have Windows create a safe, random passkey, click Choose a Passkey for Me.

   • If your device has a predefined passkey, choose Use the Passkey Found in the Documentation, and then type the passkey.

   • If you want to create your own custom passkey, click Let Me Choose My Own Passkey, and then type a passkey.

   • If the device doesn't support the use of passkeys, choose Don't Use a Passkey.

5. Click Next and follow the remaining instructions presented by the wizard.

Install a Bluetooth mobile phone

Some Bluetooth mobile phones can connect to a computer to synchronize phone books and transfer files. Some (but not all) mobile phones can also act as modems to connect to the Internet. Make sure that you read the documentation that came with the phone so that you understand how to make the phone discoverable, how to name the phone (if necessary), basic information on setting up a passkey, and whether or not you can use the phone as a modem.

If your mobile phone can act as a modem, you'll need a dial-up Internet account to connect to the Internet. Most likely this will be a mobile service provider. This service may also be in addition to your regular mobile service. You'll need to know your user name, password, carrier code or phone number, and other basic account information prior to setting up your Internet account. Only your Internet service provider (or mobile service provider) can give you that information.

The exact procedure for installing a Bluetooth phone will vary from one phone to the next. But to get started, make sure that discovery and the ability to add new devices is enabled on your PC. Then, follow these steps:

1. Open the Devices and Printers window.

2. Click Add a Device. Windows searches for Bluetooth devices, namely the mobile phone device you intend to install. When Windows locates the device, a listing appears in the Select a Device to Add to This Computer window.

3. Click the discovered device's name, and then click Next.

4. Follow the instructions presented by the wizard, and as specified by the mobile phone manufacturer.

If the phone you installed in the preceding steps can act as a modem, you can then proceed with the following steps to set up a Bluetooth connection to the Internet:

1. Open the Network and Sharing Center folder by clicking the Start button and choose Control Panel. If Control Panel opens in Category view, click Network and Internet. Open the Network and Sharing Center icon.

2. Click Set Up a New Connection or Network from the Change your network settings a Connection list.

3. Click Next.

4. Select the option Set Up a Dial-up Connection and then click Next.

5. If your computer sees the mobile phone connected via Bluetooth, it will prompt you for setup information. When the information is filled out, click the Connect button to continue.

6. When you have successfully dialed your ISP, either click the Browse the Internet Now link or click the Close button.

When your connection is configured, you should be able to get online by opening Network and Sharing Center from the Control Panel. Click the Connect to a Network link on the left side of the window. The Connect to a Network dialog box will list all of the available connections that have been set up on your system. Select the connection and click the Connect button. The mobile phone should dial based on the information you included. When you're finished using the Internet connection, click the Disconnect link within Network and Sharing Center next to the mobile connection.

Connect a Bluetooth BlackBerry

To connect a Bluetooth BlackBerry device to your computer, make sure that you first make the BlackBerry discoverable (visible) and (if necessary) give the BlackBerry a name. Complete the following steps:

1. Make sure that the BlackBerry option for Discoverable is set to Yes under the Bluetooth settings.

2. From within Windows 7, open the Devices and Printers window.

3. Click Add a Device. Windows searches for the Bluetooth mobile phone device. When Windows locates the device, a listing appears in the Select a Device to Add to This Computer window.

4. Click the discovered device's name, and then click Next.

5. From within Windows 7, select the box My Device Is Set Up and Ready To Be Bound and then click the Next button.

6. Follow the remaining steps in the wizard including setting the passkey so that your computer and BlackBerry can communicate.

After the wizard completes, Windows may prompt for additional software to be installed. You can tell Windows to look locally and on the Internet or to load the software for the device from a CD provided by the vendor.

Connect a Bluetooth Windows Mobile device

To connect a Bluetooth Windows Mobile device to your computer, make sure that you know the handheld PC well enough to make it discoverable (visible), and (if necessary) to give the handheld a name. Complete the necessary steps, and then follow these steps on your PC:

1. Open the Devices and Printers window.

2. Click Add a Device. Windows searches for the Bluetooth Windows Mobile device. When Windows locates the device, a listing appears in the Select a Device to Add to This Computer window (see Figure 47-3).

3. Follow the instructions in the Add a Device Wizard to install your Pocket PC. Enter the passphrase when prompted, and then click Close when the wizard completes.

After you've completed the wizard, the Windows Mobile Device Center application should start.

From this point on, the Windows Mobile device is paired with your computer. You should be able to follow the instructions that came with your Windows Mobile device to synchronize that device with your PC.

Install a Bluetooth Palm PC

To connect a Bluetooth Palm PC to your computer, make sure that you know the handheld PC well enough to make it discoverable (visible) and (if necessary) to give the handheld a name. Complete the necessary steps, and then follow these steps on your PC:

1. Open the Devices and Printers window.

2. Click Add a Device. Windows searches for the Bluetooth device, namely the Palm PC you intend to install. When Windows locates the device, a listing appears in the Select a Device to Add to This Computer window.

3. Follow the instructions presented by the Add a Device Wizard.

Now you can install on your PC any other software that came with your Palm PC (unless, of course, you've already installed that software). To use your synchronization software, follow the instructions that came with your Palm PC.

FIGURE 47-3

The Add a Device window showing a Bluetooth device to add to Windows.

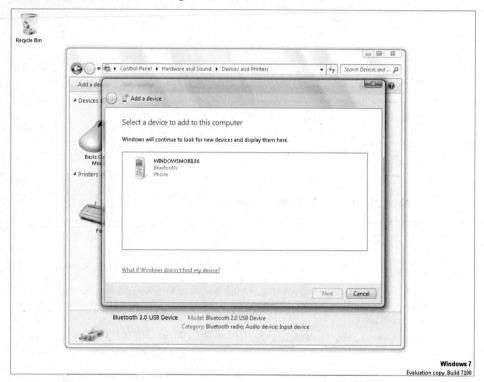

Joining a Bluetooth personal area network

A Bluetooth personal area network (PAN) is a short-range wireless network used to connect devices together wirelessly. It's commonly used to connect a laptop to a desktop PC, though it can be used to connect other types of Bluetooth devices. As a rule, there's not much to joining Bluetooth devices to a Bluetooth network. Most of the action takes place automatically behind the scenes.

To understand the basic procedure, let's assume you already have a desktop computer with a functional Internet connection. You've already installed a Bluetooth USB adapter on that computer, so it's now a Bluetooth device. On that desktop computer, right-click the Bluetooth adapter in the Devices and Printers window and click Bluetooth Settings. Click the Options tab, and make sure that the Allow Bluetooth Devices to Connect to This Computer option is selected.

On a laptop computer, plug in a second Bluetooth USB adapter. You want to connect the laptop to the desktop in a personal area network. To do so, starting from the laptop computer, follow these steps:

1. Right-click the Bluetooth Devices Notification area icon and choose Join a Personal Area Network. A list of Bluetooth devices should appear. If at least one device does not appear, click the Add a Device button and follow the steps to locate a Bluetooth-enabled computer. When the search completes, you should see a list of all of the available devices.

2. Click the name of the computer to which you want to connect, and click the Connect or Next button.

3. Choose a passkey method from the next wizard screen (the Choose a Passkey for Me option is sufficient), and then click Next.

4. You'll be given a passkey. On the other computer, you'll be asked to type in that same passkey. Type in the passkey exactly as shown in the first computer and click Next.

5. Follow any remaining instructions in the wizards on both computers until you get to the final page and then click the Close button in each wizard.

Once the connection is established, you should have Internet access on both computers. You can share printers and folders, and move and copy files between computers using the techniques described in Chapters 29 and 35.

Note, however, that if you made the Bluetooth connection to only one computer in an existing LAN, you'll have access only to the shared resources on the Bluetooth-enabled computer, not all the computers in the LAN.

Troubleshooting a Bluetooth network connection

If you can't get any connectivity at all using Bluetooth, try the following remedy:

1. Go to the computer that's having trouble connecting to the PAN.

2. Open the Network and Sharing Center by clicking the Start button and choose Control Panel ⇨ Network and Internet ⇨ Network and Sharing Center.

3. Scroll down to the Bluetooth Network Connection group. If you're unable to locate the Bluetooth Network Connection group, you'll need to follow the steps outlined earlier including entering a passkey from the other system in the PAN.

By the time you complete the wizards on both screens, you should have a connection. The Network and Sharing Center folders on each PC should have similar Bluetooth network entries.

Sharing an Internet connection

If you're unable to get Internet connectivity from the laptop computer, go to the computer that's connected to the modem or router. Open Network and Sharing Center and choose Manage Networks (or Manage Wireless Networks) from the left side of the screen. Right-click that Internet connection icon and choose Properties.

In the Properties dialog box for the Internet connection, click the Sharing tab and choose Allow Other Network Users to Connect through This Computer's Internet Connection.

Also, check the settings for the Windows Firewall:

1. Press ▦ , type **fire**, and click Windows Firewall with Advanced Security. Or click the Start button and choose Control Panel ⇨ System and Security ⇨ Windows Firewall.

2. Click the Inbound Rules item in the Console Tree (this is on the left hand side of the Windows Firewall with Advanced Security window), as shown in the example in Figure 47-4.

3. In the Inbound Rules area, select a networking option, such as the Core Networking rules, and click Properties on the Actions area (right-hand side of the window).

4. On the General tab, click Enabled. Repeat this for all the Core Networking rules.

With these settings you should now be able to connect to the Internet from the other computers in the PAN.

FIGURE 47-4

The Windows Firewall with Advanced Security window.

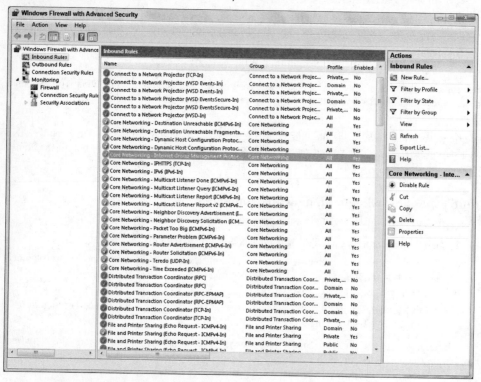

Transferring files between Bluetooth devices

When you connect two computers in a Bluetooth network, you can move and copy multiple files between computers using the techniques described under "Transferring Files between Computers" in Chapter 53.

You can also use the Send a File and Receive a File options on the Bluetooth Devices shortcut menu as an alternative. However, you can't move files that way, and you can only copy one file at a time. So, this method usually is best for transferring files to a non-computer Bluetooth device. But still, if you want to transfer one file between computers using this method, here are the steps:

1. On the computer to which you plan to send a file, right-click the Bluetooth Devices icon in the Notification area and choose Send a File, as shown in the example in Figure 47-5. The Bluetooth File Transfer Wizard opens and waits for you to send a file from the other computer.

2. In the Bluetooth File Transfer Wizard that opens, choose the Bluetooth device to which you want to send the file (see Figure 47-6).

3. Click the Next button.

4. Click the Browse button, choose the file you want to send, and then click Open.

5. Click Next.

6. On the receiving computer, the wizard asks if you want to receive the file from the other device.

7. Click Yes.

8. When the transfer is complete, click the Finish button in the last wizard page on both computers, as shown in the example in Figure 47-7.

FIGURE 47-5

Use the Notifications area icon to choose whether to send a file or receive a file between Bluetooth devices.

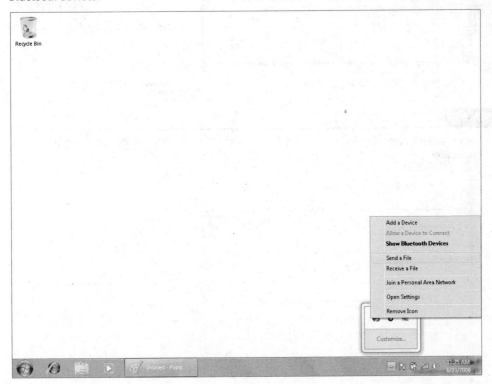

Remember, many different Bluetooth devices are available on the market. If none of the techniques described here help you make the connection between two computers in a personal area network, be sure to refer to the instructions that came with your Bluetooth device.

FIGURE 47-6

Select a Bluetooth device to send a file to.

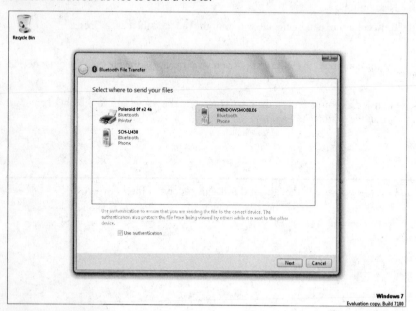

FIGURE 47-7

Showing a successfully transferred file between a laptop and Windows Mobile device using a Bluetooth connection.

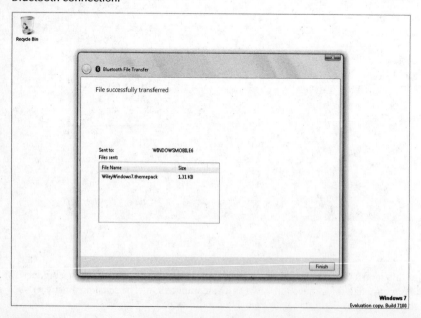

Wrap-Up

This chapter has been about installing and configuring Bluetooth devices and Bluetooth networks. Bluetooth devices provide an excellent alternative to many commonly wired devices. Also, they usually are fast and easy to set up and can provide a great way to communicate between computers without having to rely on more complex networking. Here's a recap of the technologies covered in this chapter:

- Bluetooth is currently at version 3.0 and allows you to connect cell phones, PDAs, mice, keyboards, and other Bluetooth devices.

- To turn a computer into a Bluetooth device, simply connect a Bluetooth USB adapter to a USB port on the computer.

- To connect a Bluetooth device to a computer, activate discovery on the device, bring it within range of the computer, right-click the Bluetooth Devices icon in the Notification area, and choose Add a Device.

- To create a personal area network between two or more computers, add a Bluetooth USB adapter to each computer. Then, right-click the Bluetooth Devices Notification area icon and choose Join a Personal Area Network.

- Regardless of what type of device you intend to connect to your computer, always read the instructions that came with the device first.

Syncing Devices

I f you've ever had files on a remote device that you wish you could easily take with you and keep in sync, Windows Sync Center and Offline Files provide the solutions that fit your need. The two solutions work together to remove the time-consuming chore of always copying data between a remote system and your local computer. This chapter discusses the many options for scheduling and conflict resolution that Sync Center provides.

Sync Center works with many devices, including PDAs, flash drives, and portable music players. I briefly discuss these topics, but the majority of functionality regarding synchronizing these devices is included with the software that comes with the device.

Syncing with Network Files

One of the most common uses for Windows synchronization is for offline files. This is most frequently used for laptop computers but can also be used with desktop systems. To do this, you'll need to have a network location set up on your local computer that connects to a server (see Chapter 52). You are able to set up offline files to synchronize the data on the server down to your local system. This makes the content available when you are away from that server.

You can edit the data while disconnected from the network, and Sync Center will make sure that the changes you have made while disconnected will be sent back to the server when you're connected back to the network. In the event someone has edited or changed the files on the server, Sync Center will ask for your assistance. Setting up offline files requires several steps, the first of which is making the files and folders available offline.

Using Sync Center for offline files

The first step to setting up offline files is to add a network location to your system if you don't already have one. This is covered in more detail in Chapter 53. When you have a network location configured, clicking your Computer link should look similar to Figure 48-1.

IN THIS CHAPTER

Synchronizing with content on the network

Setting schedules and events for synchronizations

Dealing with conflicts that occur in synchronizations

Dealing with other types of devices

FIGURE 48-1

A list of Network Locations on my computer.

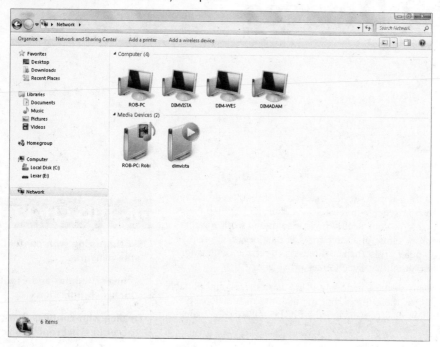

When you have at least one network location configured, you need to right-click the location and select Always Available Offline. A dialog box will appear showing the progress of the synchronization. At this point, the content has synchronized to your local system, and you can disconnect from the network and still use the files that once existed only on the server. You're able to right-click the Network Location again and this time select Sync. This will make sure that the two locations, the server and your local computer, are synchronized. This process could be a little tedious if you always needed to remember to sync your files before disconnecting. To automate this process, you can schedule the task of synchronizing the files and folders.

Note
Synchronizing with network locations works only on Network Locations local to your network. You are not able to use File Transfer Protocol (FTP) network locations to synchronize content. The Always Available Offline option is not available for network locations not connected to the local network. ∎

Using Sync Center

To configure offline files to run on a scheduled basis, you'll need to configure Sync Center using the following steps:

1. Click the Start button and choose All Programs ⇨ Accessories ⇨ Sync Center. Or press ⊞ , type `sync`, and click Sync Center.

2. When Sync Center is open, click the link View Sync Partnerships under the on the left side of the window as shown in Figure 48-2.

FIGURE 48-2

Sync Center with the default appearance for offline files.

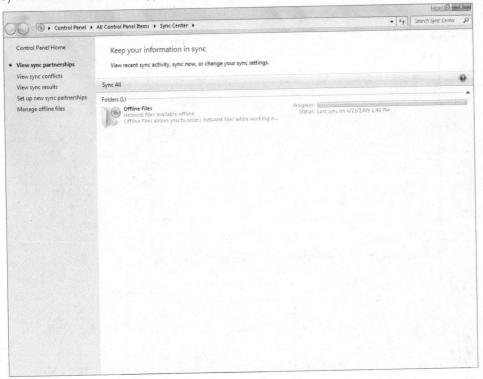

3. Right-click the Offline Files entry and choose Schedule for Offline Files, which will start the Offline Files Sync Schedule dialog box.

4. Select the network location that you want to synchronize and click the Next button.

5. You're now able to determine what starts the file synchronization. As shown in Figure 48-3, you can choose a recurring date and time or have the synchronization start as a result of an event that takes place on your computer.

6. Based on the selection, you'll initially see two different screens. If you choose the first option, At a Scheduled Time, you'll see the screen shown in Figure 48-4, which allows you to set when the schedule should start and how often it should occur. The drop-down box allows you to select a range of units from minutes up to months. This means you could schedule the synchronization to happen every minute.

7. If you choose the second option, When an Event Occurs, you'll see the screen shown in Figure 48-5, which allows you to choose an action that will cause synchronization. You can trigger the synchronization based on when you log on, when you lock Windows, when you unlock Windows, or when the system is idle for a given amount of time.

FIGURE 48-3

Offline Folders gives you the option for setting the schedule for synchronization.

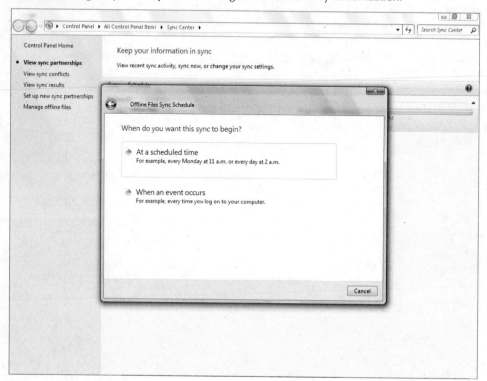

8. Regardless of what option you choose to trigger the file synchronization, there is a More Options button in both of the windows shown in Figures 48-4 and 48-5. Clicking this button provides you the opportunity to tell Windows when to start and stop synchronization. After you've made any changes to the More Scheduling Options dialog box shown in Figure 48-6, click the OK button.

9. Next, you'll need to name your synchronization schedule. Enter a descriptive name in the Name text box and click the Save Schedule button.

When your schedule is configured, it will run either based on the time schedule you set or based on the events on the computer. You're able to view, edit, or delete your schedule by opening Sync Center, right-clicking the Offline Folder entry, and choosing Schedule for Offline Folders as before in previous steps. This time, you're prompted with a dialog box that allows you to create a new schedule, view or edit an existing schedule, or delete an existing sync schedule. Clicking the View or Edit Existing Schedule option runs you through the steps similar to the ones you used to create the original schedule. You're also able to click the Schedule button in the toolbar to bring up the scheduling functions for offline files.

You still have some additional settings to configure offline files, including disk usage and encryption settings, which are covered next.

FIGURE 48-4

Set a schedule based on time for file synchronization.

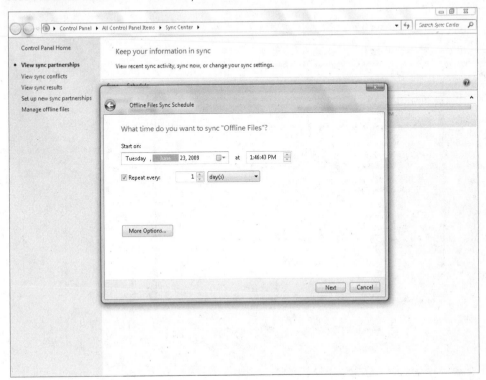

Settings for offline files

Beyond setting the network locations to synchronize and deciding when to synchronize the files and folders, Windows also allows you to set some additional options for offline files. To get to these settings, you'll need to use the Manage Offline Files features located in the Sync Center. Click Start and type **sync**. Choose Sync Center and click the Manage Offline Files link on the left side of the Sync Center window. The Offline Files dialog box, shown in Figure 48-7, opens with the General tab selected.

- **Disable Offline Files:** This button disables all of the file synchronizations you have set up. If you currently have file synchronization disabled, the button will read Enable Offline Files. If you disable Offline Files, you'll need to restart your system for the changes to take effect.

- **Open Sync Center:** This button opens Sync Center.

- **View Your Offline Files:** Clicking this button brings up a window that shows all of your synchronizations. To see your offline files, open an Explorer window, click Computer, then Network, and finally click the Network Location on which the sync files are stored. An example of the path used during this writing is shown in the navigation bar in Figure 48-8. Network folders that have been synced include green wave circles in the bottom-left corner of the icons.

FIGURE 48-5

Setting the options to trigger the synchronization based on an event.

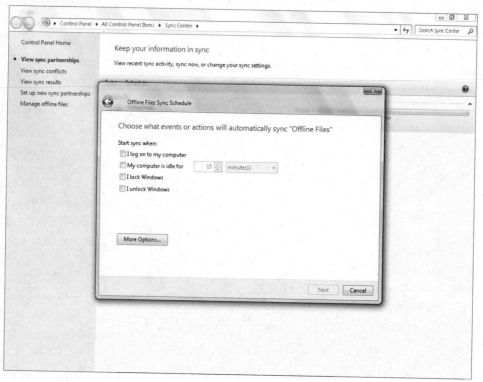

It's necessary to keep track of the amount of space your offline files are using and put limits on the amount of disk space used. To do this, you'll need to click the Disk Usage tab in the Offline Files dialog box. To make adjustments to the default values, click the Change Limits button, which will bring up the dialog box shown in Figure 48-9.

Make changes to the values using the slide bars; after you've set your limits, click the OK button to continue.

It is fairly common today that you hear of some institution that has had a laptop stolen with confidential information. Knowing this, Microsoft has included an option to encrypt any data with offline files synchronized with your local computer. Microsoft has also made it very easy to set up security. By clicking the Encryption tab within the Offline File dialog box, you're able to click the Encrypt button to encrypt the data that resides on your local system. When you do encrypt the data, only the data that resides on your local system is encrypted, not the data that resides on the server with which you are synchronizing. There is also no need for you to attempt to decrypt the files before using them. The decryption takes place when you attempt to use the synchronized file.

The final tab within the Offline Files dialog box is for working with a slow network connection. Clicking the Network tab allows you to determine how your system works after it determines you have a slow network connection. If you open up the network location that is currently being synchronized with your local system and double-click a file, Windows will use a cached version if it determines the network connection is too slow. With the settings on the Network tab, you're able to determine whether you would rather wait for the real version of the file. If the On Slow Connections, Automatically Work Offline option is checked, Windows will use the local version of the file. Additionally, Windows will check to see whether you still have a slow connection every five minutes by default. You're able to change this setting by setting the Check for a Slow Connection Every option.

FIGURE 48-6

Additional options for scheduling your synchronization.

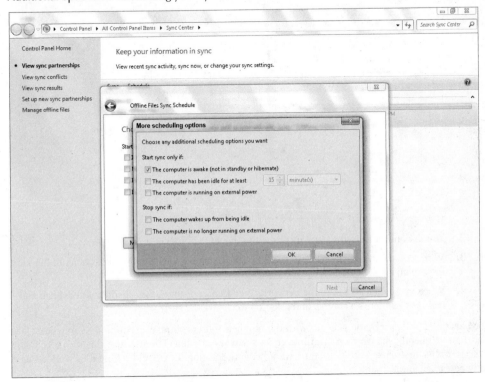

With all of the settings for Offline Folders and Sync Center, you're well on your way to using offline files. If you've set up the schedule, you'll have the latest versions of the files on your system based on your schedule. You've also determined how much disk space to dedicate to offline files and set up encryption if the data you are storing is sensitive. On occasion, you may hit a conflict in your synchronizations. This happens when the file on the remote computer changes and you also make changes to the file using your local offline version.

Dealing with conflict

Sync Center really comes in handy when you have a conflict with synchronization. The most common scenario is outlined in the following steps:

1. You have set up synchronization using offline files to a folder named Important Documents located on a remote server.

FIGURE 48-7

The General tab for the Offline Files dialog box.

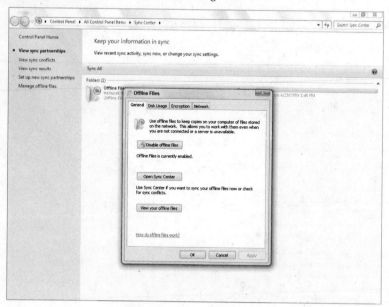

2. You disconnect from the network and edit some of the files within the folder.

3. While you are away and disconnected from the network, a coworker makes copies to the same files up on the server.

4. When you connect back to the network, Sync Center resumes the schedule you defined and realizes that there's a conflict and asks you to resolve the issue.

The likelihood of this scenario goes up with the number of users you have sharing the same data. Files that don't frequently change won't run into this scenario very often. To introduce this scenario, follow these steps but first make sure that you have a network location set up and offline files working as outlined earlier in the chapter:

1. Verify that your synchronization schedule is working by opening Sync Center within the Control Panel. Make sure that you verify that the status of your synchronization is fairly recent by clicking View Sync Partnerships as shown in Figure 48-10.

2. Disconnect from the network either by disconnecting your network cable or using the Disable This Network Device button shown in Figure 48-11. You can get to this window by selecting Networking and Sharing Center in the Control Panel. Click Change Adapter Settings on the left side of the Control Panel. Click Disable This Network Device or right-click the network adapter and choose Disable.

3. With your network connection disabled, navigate to the Offline Files. To do this, open your Computer folder; the files will be located under the Network group. Select a file you can edit. This can be any type of file including a text document, an image, or any other file you can afford to make changes to. When you are done making changes, save the file. The contents of the file will be stored locally on your system, and your system will attempt to synchronize the next time you connect to the network.

FIGURE 48-8

A listing of the synchronized files.

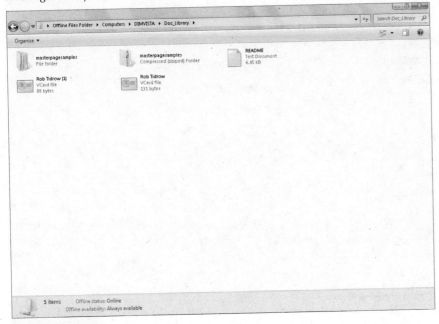

FIGURE 48-9

The dialog box used to set limits on the amount of space used by offline files.

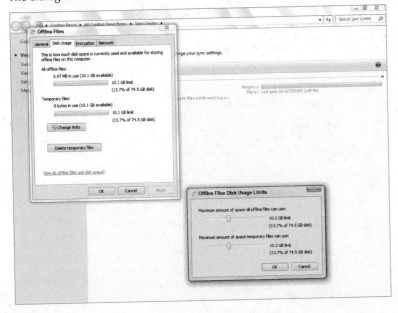

FIGURE 48-10

The status of the synchronization is fairly recent.

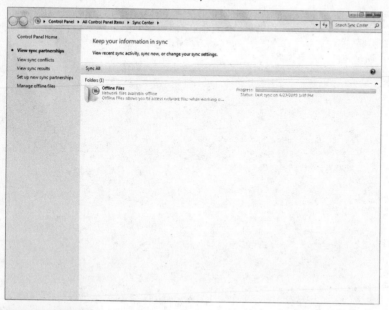

FIGURE 48-11

Disconnect from your network connection.

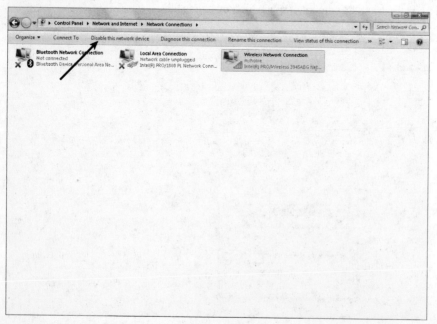

4. From another system on the network, connect to the original location of the file (this is the location of the file with which you were originally syncing). Open the file and make some changes to the same file that you made changes to in the previous step. Save your changes to the network location.

5. Go back to the computer that was recently disconnected from the network and reconnect. To reconnect to the network, open the Network and Sharing Center again and click Change Adapter Settings. Select your original network connection and click the Enable This Network Device button.

6. When connected to the network, open Sync Center if you've closed it. The status will change from Disconnected (see Figure 48-12) as Sync Center tries to resync your files. This time, however, the system notifies you that there was a conflict with the synchronization.

FIGURE 48-12

Sync Center indicates that Sync Center is disconnected.

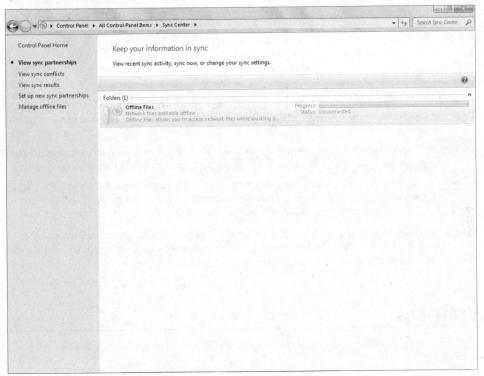

7. Clicking the Conflict link lists all of the files that had a synchronization conflict. The Details column indicates that "A file was changed on this computer and the server while this computer was offline." Right-clicking the entry provides three options:

- **View Options to Resolve Conflict:** This option enables you to keep the local version on your system and overwrite the changes on the server. You have the option to use the version on the server and overwrite your local copy. Finally, you have the option to keep both of them.

- **Ignore:** Selecting Ignore removes the conflict from the list. Both of the files remain in their original states — the one on your local system and the one on the remote system. However, the next time synchronization occurs, the same synchronization conflict will occur.

- **Properties:** The Properties dialog box shows the details regarding the type of partnership along with the date and details regarding the synchronization conflict.

Microsoft has provided quite a few options for dealing with the synchronization conflicts that arise with offline folders. In addition to the conflicts showing up in Sync Center, there is also a notification from the Notification area on the taskbar, which will notify you when a conflict has occurred. In the previous examples, the Offline Files entry within Sync Center is referred to as a sync partnership.

Synchronizing with Other Devices

Synchronizing with devices other than files and folders within a network location provides you with the ability to keep devices other than just your computer synchronized. One of the biggest differences is that most devices that provide synchronization capability do so using the software that comes with the device. The software will usually set up a partnership within Sync Center, but the majority of the configuration and maintenance is done within the software applications that come with the device. Because each device that provides syncing options is different, I've included some general guidelines for working with different devices:

- The first step is to follow the instructions provided by the manufacturer. They will provide details specific to the product and the steps necessary for installing the software and configuring the device.

- It is necessary to connect the device in some way to the computer. This may include connecting the device via USB, or you may be required to connect the device via a Bluetooth connection.

- Not all devices are designed to work with Sync Center. If you open Sync Center and your device does not show up as an available partner after clicking Set Up New Sync Partnerships, your device manufacturer may address synchronization in its own software.

The most important guideline is to follow the documentation provided by the manufacturer of the device. Also, if the device appears to have problems communicating with your computer, you should update to the latest available drivers found online at the product's Web site.

Wrap-Up

This chapter has gone into the details of Sync Center and also how to synchronize offline folders. Specifically, it covered:

- The basics of setting up synchronization for a network location.

- Using Sync Center to view partnerships. Specifically, using Sync Center to view the Offline Files partnership.

- Setting schedules and different events for starting synchronizations.

- Configuring the details regarding Offline Files for Disk Usage, Encryption, and what to do when synchronizing over a slow network connection.

- How to deal with conflicts that occur when synchronization determines a file has changed in two locations while your system has been disconnected from the network. The details for available options were also discussed to resolve the synchronization failure.

- The available options for connecting and synchronizing other types of devices to keep content on the devices in sync with your computer.

Performance Tuning Your System

Compared to most machines, a computer requires virtually no maintenance. That's because it has fewer moving parts compared to other machines. However, you can do to some things to keep your computer running at its optimum.

For example, the more the hard drive is used to store data, the more fragmented the data on the drive becomes. That doesn't pose any problems for reading the data, but it does slow down the process. To speed it up again, you can defragment the drive. This topic, and others that will help you optimize your computer's performance, are covered in this chapter.

Getting to Know Your System

A computer system is made up of many different components. The two main components that make up the actual "computer" are the CPU and RAM. The overall speed of your system is largely determined by the speed of your CPU and the amount of RAM in your system. The speed of a CPU is measured in gigahertz (GHz), billions of instructions per second, or for older (and slower) systems in megahertz (MHz), millions of instructions per second.

The amount of RAM determines how much data the CPU can work with at any one time without accessing the much slower hard drive. RAM chips do come in various speeds. But the amount of RAM you have, more so than its speed, really determines the overall speed of your system. RAM is measured in megabytes (MB) or gigabytes (GB). A megabyte is roughly a million bytes. (A byte is the amount of memory required to store a single character, such as the letter "A"). A gigabyte (GB) is 1,024 megabytes. In short, the faster your CPU and the more RAM the computer has, the better its performance.

Knowing your CPU and RAM

To see the brand name and speed of your processor and the amount of RAM you have, right-click your Computer icon from the Start menu and choose Properties. Or, tap ![Windows key], type sys, and click System. The System Control Panel applet that opens shows that basic computer information as well as information about the version of Windows you're using, as in the example shown in Figure 49-1.

The System applet.

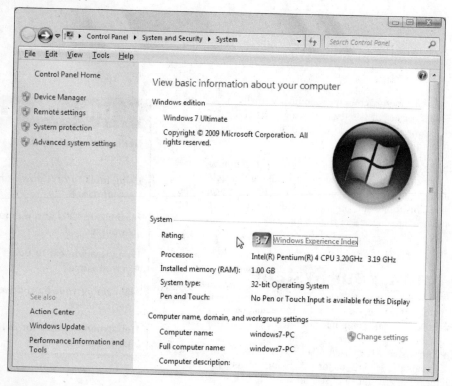

Note

The Windows Experience Index provides a quick snapshot of the major components that determine how you experience Windows 7 on your computer. ∎

Windows Experience Index

The first thing most people will notice is the Windows Experience Index. It is not a measure of your computer's overall speed or ability. Rather, it's an indicator of the weakest component in the system, the one that's most likely to give you a less than optimal experience. So don't interpret the value as being a general measure of your computer's overall performance. For a better understanding of what the number means, click the Windows Experience Index link next to the number to open Performance Information and Tools, shown in Figure 49-2.

FIGURE 49-2

The Performance Information and Tools applet.

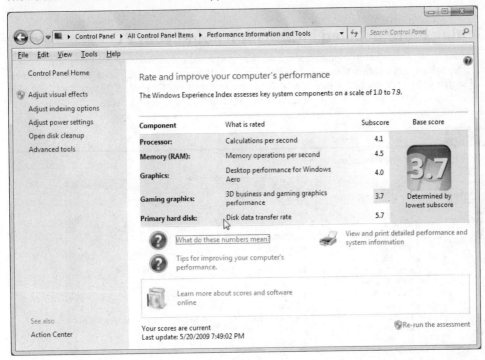

The second page shows that the 3.7 rating on that computer comes from the Gaming Graphics category. Notice that the index isn't an average. It's strictly the lowest score. Even with a relatively low score, your Windows 7 computer could perform quite well. For example, if you don't use any 3D business applications or 3D games, a low score for that item would likely not affect your experience with Windows. The items that have the most impact on overall computer speed are the processor, memory, and primary hard drive. If those scores are high, performance in general will be good.

Note

None of the numbers in the index relate to Internet speed. The primary factor that determines how long it takes you to download files or other data from the Internet is the bandwidth (speed) of your Internet connection. The faster your Internet connection, the less time it takes to download data. However, the other performance indicators can impact your Internet experience. Browsing on a slow computer will not be as fast as on a fast computer. ■

The Performance and Information Tools page shown in Figure 49-2 provides links to more information about the meanings of the numbers, ways to improve your computer's performance. The Re-Run the Assessment link performs all the tests needed to calculate those numbers. If you changed some hardware in your system, but still got the same performance rating, you could use that link to re-run the tests against your new hardware.

The View and Print Detailed Performance and System Information link shows all the information from the page, and additional details, and includes a button to print the page. The other blue links provide general information.

Getting more detailed information about your PC

You can get more detailed information about all the components that make up your computer system from the System Information program. To open System Information, click the Start button and choose All Programs ⇨ Accessories ⇨ System Tools ⇨ System Information. Or press 🏁 , type sys, and click System Information. The System Information window shown in Figure 49-3 opens.

FIGURE 49-3

The System Information program window.

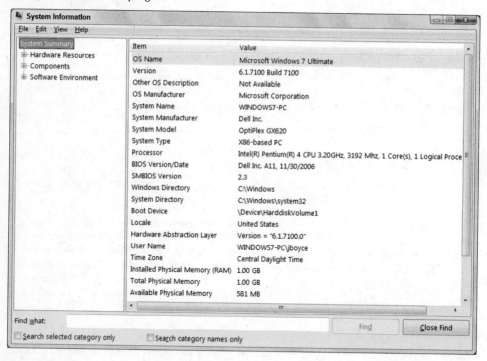

The left column of System Information organizes your system information into expandable and collapsible categories. For example, clicking the + sign next to the Components category expands that category to display subcategories and the names of specific device types. When you click a specific type, such as Drives under the Storage category, the pane on the right shows information about the components installed in your computer system.

You don't actually do any work in the System Information program. Its job is to just present the facts about your particular computer's installed hardware and software. However, you can export a copy of the System Information data to a text file, which in turn you can open, format, or print using any word processing program or text editor. To export a copy of your system information to a file, just choose File ⇨ Export from System Information's menu bar.

You can also print your system information, either in whole or in part. To print all of your system information, first click System Summary at the top of the left column. To print just a category, first click a category name, such as Components. Then, choose File ⇨ Print from System Information's menu bar. In the Print dialog box that opens, choose All if you want to print everything, choose Selection to print just the text you may have selected, or choose Current Page to print the page you are viewing. To close System Information, click its Close (X) button or choose File ⇨ Exit.

Maximizing CPU and Memory Resources

Your operating system (Windows 7) takes care of managing the CPU and memory for you. Even so, you can do some things to improve performance as it relates to your system's memory and CPU. The following sections offer some tips.

Conserving memory

One of the best things you can do to improve your computer's performance is ensure that it has plenty of memory. Initially, that means making sure the computer has a sufficient amount of physical memory installed. You should consider 1 GB a minimum, although Windows can run with less. If you use lots or programs at once, or use applications that require a lot of memory, consider having at least 2 GB of RAM in the computer, if not 4 GB.

Having a lot of memory is part of the solution, but managing the memory you do have is equally important. You can optimize your computer's RAM in these ways:

- **Reduce the number of programs you run concurrently:** If you aren't using a program, close it to reclaim the memory it is using. You can always open it again later if you need it.

- **Minimize the number of programs you install on your computer:** Do you really need a program on the tray that tells you what the weather is like outside? Do you really need a gadget on the desktop that shows a tiny slide show? All of the little add-on programs you install and run on your computer, even if they are running in the background, consume resources. The fewer, the better.

Reducing the number of programs running at one time not only improves performance from a memory perspective, but it also reduces the load on the CPU, making processing cycles available to those programs that do need to be running.

Managing virtual memory

In the very early days of DOS, a computer could run only one program at a time. Programs had to be written to fit in the available (and minimal) memory in the computer. In today's Windows OS, you can run almost as many programs as you want at one time. The capability to run multiple programs is due to the design of today's CPUs and of the OS itself. The capability to manage memory effectively for all of those programs is due in part to the use of *virtual memory*.

Modern computers can use two types of memory. The first type is *physical memory* (RAM), which consists of physical memory chips on memory modules (small circuit boards) that plug into the computer's motherboard.

Tip

The amount of RAM shown on the General tab of the System Properties dialog box (see Figure 49-1) is the amount of physical RAM in your system. ■

The second type of memory is *virtual memory*, and Windows 7 uses the computer's hard drive for that, using a file on the drive as a place to store data as an alternative to physical memory. The area on the hard drive that's used as virtual memory is called a *paging file*, because data is swapped back and forth between physical and virtual memory in small chunks called pages. When you fill up both your physical memory and virtual memory, the computer doesn't just stop and display an error. Rather, it displays a message in advance, warning that the computer is running low on virtual memory and suggesting that you make room for more.

Because the virtual memory is just a paging file on the hard drive, you can easily add more just by increasing the size of the paging file. You don't have to buy or install anything. This is unlike physical memory, in that the only way to increase physical memory is to buy and install more RAM.

To manage virtual memory in Windows 7, open the System applet from the Control Panel and click the Change Settings link. In the resulting System Properties dialog box, click the Advanced tab and click the Settings button in the Performance group. Then, click the Advanced tab in the resulting Performance Options dialog box (Figure 49-4). The Virtual Memory area on this dialog box shows the total paging file size for all drives. To adjust the settings, click the Change button to open the Virtual Memory dialog box shown in Figure 49-5.

FIGURE 49-4

The Advanced tab of the Performance Options dialog box.

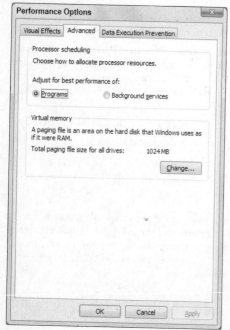

FIGURE 49-5

The Virtual Memory dialog box.

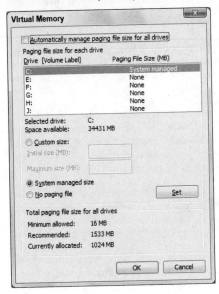

In most cases, it makes sense to select the top check box Automatically Manage Paging File Size for All Drives to allow Windows to adjust the page file.

If you don't want Windows to manage the page file for you, your main options in the Paging File Size for Each Drive area of the Virtual Memory dialog box are as follows:

- **Custom Size:** You choose where you want to put your paging file(s), their initial size, and maximum size.

- **System Managed Size:** Tells Windows to create and size the paging file automatically for you.

- **No Paging File:** Eliminates the paging file from a drive. Not recommended unless you're moving the paging file from one drive to another.

If you have multiple hard drives, you can get the best performance by using the least busy drive for virtual memory. For example, if you have a D: drive on which you store documents, it may be better to use that, rather than the C: drive, because the C: drive is pretty busy with Windows and your installed programs.

If you have multiple *physical drives*, you can get a little performance boost by splitting the paging file across the two drives. A single drive that's partitioned into two or more partitions, to look like multiple drives, doesn't count. You don't want to divide the paging file across multiple partitions on a single drive, because that will have the reverse effect of slowing things down.

If you do opt for a custom size, you can work with any one hard drive at a time. The drives are listed by letter and label at the top of the dialog box. In the example shown, all of the partitions actually reside on a single drive.

Tip

The Disk Management tool discussed in Chapter 46 lists hard drives by number. If you have a single physical hard drive, it will be Disk 0. If you have two physical hard drives, they'll be listed as Drive 0 and Drive 1, and so forth. ■

If you don't select the check box at the top of the Virtual Memory dialog box, you'll need to set the paging file sizes individually. For example, to move the paging from drive C: to D:, first click Drive C: at the top of the dialog box, choose No Paging File, and then click the Set button. Then, click Drive D:, choose Custom Size, set your sizes, and click Set.

The Total Paging File Size for All Drives section at the bottom of the dialog box shows the minimum allowable size, a recommended size, and the currently allocated size (the last measurement being the sum of all the Initial Size settings). The recommended size is usually about 1.5 times the amount of physical memory. The idea is to prevent you from loading up *way* more stuff than you have physical RAM to handle, which would definitely make your computer run more slowly.

If your computer keeps showing messages about running out of virtual memory, you'll definitely want to increase the initial and maximum size of the paging file. A gigabyte (1,024 MB) is a nice round number. But if the computer runs slowly after you increase the amount of virtual memory, the best solution would be to add more physical RAM.

If you do change the Virtual Memory settings and click OK, you'll be asked if you want to restart your computer. If you have programs or documents open, you can choose No and close everything first. But because the paging file is only created when you first start your computer, you'll eventually need to restart the computer to take advantage of your new settings.

Priorities, foreground, and background

Your computer's CPU and RAM are very busy places, with potentially thousands of tasks occurring at one time. To try to optimize performance, Windows prioritizes those tasks. Your application programs typically run in the *foreground*, which means that when you click an item with your mouse or do something at the keyboard, fulfilling that request gets top priority in terms of being sent to the CPU for execution.

Most processes, by comparison, run in the *background*. This means that they get a lower priority and have to momentarily step aside when you tell Windows or an application to do something. For example, printing a document is treated as a low-priority background process, and for a good reason. All printers are basically slow, mechanical devices anyway. So, by making printing a low-priority process, you can continue to use your computer at near normal speeds while the printer is slowly churning out its printed pages.

Controlling CPU priorities

By default, programs that you're using are given a higher priority than background processes. It's possible to reverse that by giving processes a higher priority than applications. If you have an intensive background task running and want to give it higher priority, you can reverse the order. Or, if you want to make sure that your applications are getting top priority, as they should be, follow these steps:

1. Right-click your Computer icon from the Start menu, and choose Properties to open the System window for your system.

Tip

The System icon in Control Panel also opens the System window. If Control Panel opens in Category view, click System and Security and click the System link. ■

2. Click the Advanced System Settings link on the left side of the screen to bring up the System Properties dialog box. Click the Advanced tab in the System Properties dialog box.

3. Under the Performance heading, click the Settings button. The Performance Options dialog box opens.

4. In the Performance Options dialog box, click the Advanced tab shown previously in Figure 49-4.

The Processor Scheduling options determine whether your actions, or processes, get top priority when vying for CPU resources to do their jobs. If you choose Background Services, your computer may not be as responsive as you'd like, but background tasks will get higher priority. So for example, if you are running a scan of your system in the background and want it to finish faster, select Background Services in the Performance Options dialog box and click OK.

Note

Choosing Background Services won't make your printer print any faster. There's really nothing you can do to speed printing, other than use the printer's Draft mode (if it has one). But even so, printers are just inherently slow mechanical devices. ■

Monitoring and Adjusting Performance

Windows 7 includes a great selection of tools to help you monitor and tune your system's performance. You've already seen a couple of them, notably the Performance Information and Tools applet described earlier in this chapter. The following sections explore this tool in more detail, along with several others that will help you keep your system running at its best.

Performance Monitor

Performance Monitor, included in Windows 7, has also been available under previous versions of Windows. It provides an interface for viewing performance counters on your system. To run Performance Monitor, first open the Action Center (click the Action Center button on the tray and click open Action Center). Then, in the left pane of the Action Center, click View Performance Information. Finally, in Performance Information and Tools, click Advanced Tools in the left pane and click the Open Performance Monitor link. Figure 49-6 shows the Performance Monitor.

Tip

To save several steps opening Performance Monitor, click the Start button and enter perfmon. ■

Note

Performance Monitor is a very complex application and could easily cover several chapters of detail. For this reason, I'm covering only some of the basic functions of the application. To get more information, search for Performance Monitor under Windows Help and Support. ■

FIGURE 49-6

Performance Monitor.

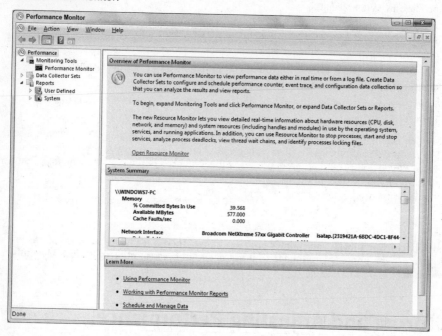

When Performance Monitor opens, the Performance branch in the left pane is selected and the Performance Monitor window displays general information about the program, a system summary, and some links to learn more using Performance Monitor. Though the System Summary area shows current performance data, you'll probably prefer to see a visual representation. To do so, click Performance Monitor under the Monitoring Tools branch in the left pane. Figure 49-7 shows an example.

The line crossing the screen as you watch the Performance Monitor plots your system's CPU activity. The graph has a timeline along the bottom and a percentage on the side. Only tracking the CPU doesn't provide much more information than what Task Manager provides. By adding counters to the grid, you can track your system's performance. To add more counters to the graph, follow these steps:

1. Start by clicking the plus (+) sign in the toolbar located just above the graph.

2. The Add Counters dialog box, shown in Figure 49-8, shows all of the available performance objects for your system. In the left column, click the arrow to the right of the performance objects to expand and display the available counters for that object. I've selected Network Interface in Figure 49-8.

3. Depending on the counter you select, you may also have the option of selecting an instance of that counter. In the case of the Network Interface object, there are multiple network interfaces on my computer, as shown in the Instances of Selected Object list box. I selected the Bytes Total/Sec as the counter and then chose the wireless adapter on my system for the instance.

4. Optionally, you can select the Show Description check box so you can view additional information about the counter.

FIGURE 49-7

Performance graphs in Performance Monitor.

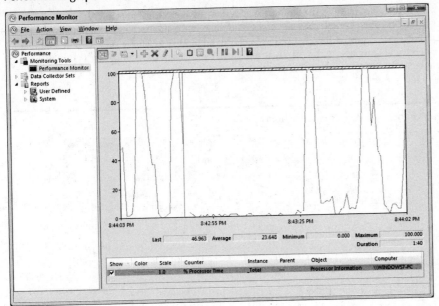

FIGURE 49-8

The Add Counters dialog box.

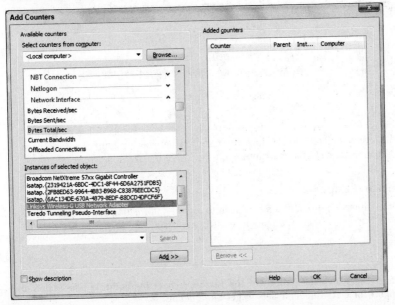

5. Click the Add button to move the selection over to the Added Counters section of the window.

6. When you've selected all of the counters you want to monitor, click the OK button to return to the graph.

7. As shown in Figure 49-9, the counter is added to the bottom of the window. If you select the counter in the list and click the highlighter icon in the toolbar, it will highlight that specific counter. In this case, it has changed the color to a bold black. This is very helpful when you have several counters on the screen at the same time. When the highlighter is turned on, clicking any counter in the list causes that counter to be highlighted.

FIGURE 49-9

Network Interface object added to Performance Monitor.

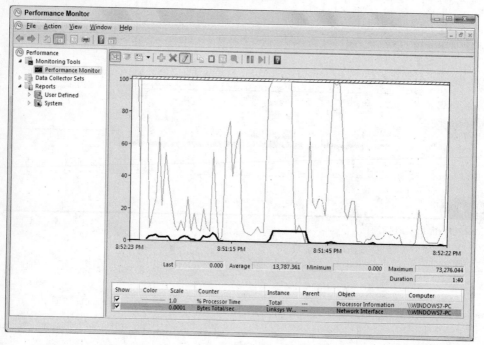

The scale of the graph is set automatically. In the case of the previous example, if the network utilization went off the screen, you're able to adjust the scale for that specific counter so you have more meaningful information instead of a line running off the top of the graph.

Data Collector Sets and Reports

The Performance Monitor interface provides a mechanism to log the information and events that occur on your system. Besides just logging the information, it also provides a way for you to use reports to look at the information.

Note

Data Collector Sets and Reports are very involved topics. For this reason, I cover the basics in this section and suggest searching Help and Support for Data Collector Sets to get more details. ∎

In the previous section you learned about performance counters in Performance Monitor using two examples, % Processor Time and Bytes Total/Sec. A data collector set, as its name implies, is a set of objects that collect data about your computer. So, you might create a data collector set that gathers data about specific items. For example, you could create a data collector set to gather information about network performance using a variety of network counters. Or, you might create one to analyze drive performance by using multiple drive counters.

Within the Performance Monitor interface, you're able to create User-Defined Data Collector Sets, but let's start with the predefined Data Collector Sets. To get started, follow these steps:

1. Click the arrow to the left of Data Collector Sets to expand the tree beneath it. Then expand the System icon beneath Data Collector Sets and click System Performance.

2. Right-click System Performance and choose Start, or click the Start button in the toolbar. The system will start collecting data for the different components of the collector.

3. Let the system run for a while, and when you're ready, right-click System Performance again and choose Stop this time, or click the Stop button in the toolbar. Stopping the collector may take a few seconds.

4. Next, navigate to the Reports section within Performance Monitor and expand the System branch as shown in Figure 49-10. In this figure, two performance reports are listed.

FIGURE 49-10

System Performance reports.

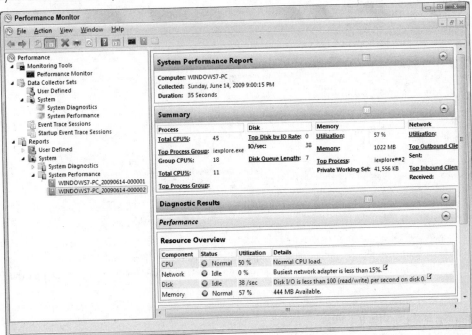

5. Expand or collapse different areas by clicking the arrows next to each group. Use the vertical scroll bar to see all of the different report categories.

Generating system performance reports in Performance Monitor can help you understand where bottlenecks might exist in your system. For example, you can quickly identify an overtaxed CPU, problems with network saturation, or other issues.

In addition to creating performance reports with Performance Monitor, you can also create diagnostic reports. In the left pane, under Data Collector Sets, expand System and click System Diagnostics. Then, click Start in the toolbar. Wait as Performance Monitor creates the report. While the report data is being gathered, the icon next to the System Diagnostics branch shows a small green arrow. This is replaced by an hourglass while Performance Monitor generates the report. When the icon returns to normal, the report is finished. You'll find a new report under the Reports\System\System Diagnostics branch in the left pane. Click the report to view its contents. Figure 49-11 shows an example of a diagnostic report.

FIGURE 49-11

A diagnostic report.

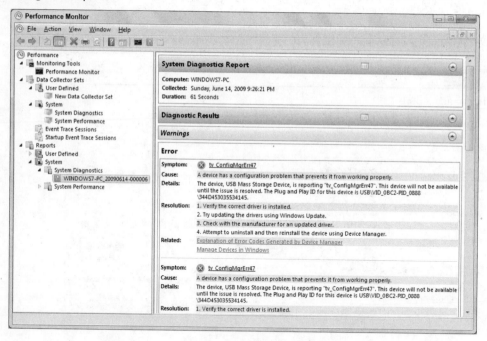

As with a performance report, expand and collapse different categories in the report to view the information in the report. The information in the report can help you pinpoint hardware errors and other problems.

Creating Data Collector Sets

You're able to create your own User-Defined Data Collector Sets, which involves adding data from one of the four categories. From the properties window of the collector, you're able to set a variety of properties for each type, such as the sample interval maximum number of samples, registry keys to monitor, and many more.

You can add the following four types of data collectors to your custom Data Collector Sets:

- **Event Trace data:** This data is gathered when different system events occur on your system.
- **Configuration data:** This data is gathered from changes that occur to the registry of your system.
- **Performance Counter data:** This information is the same information that you're able to gather from Performance Monitor, discussed earlier in the chapter.
- **Performance Counter Alert:** This data is gathered when a performance counter you specify reaches a point either above or below a value that you define.

As I explained previously, creating data collection sets assumes a certain level of technical capability and knowledge about how the computer and its components functions. Those topics are far outside the scope of this book. So instead, I'll focus on the mechanics of creating the data collector set:

1. Open Performance Monitor and expand the Data Collector Sets branch.
2. Right-click User Defined and choose New ➪ Data Collector Set to start the Create New Data Collector Set wizard (Figure 49-12)

FIGURE 49-12

Create New Data Collector Set wizard.

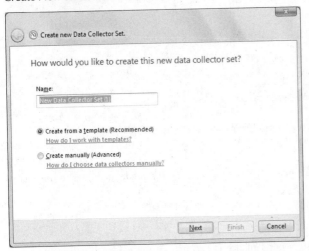

3. Enter a descriptive name in the Name text box.
4. Decide whether to create the data collector set from a template or from scratch (manually). If you choose the Create from a Template option, you can add data collectors to the ones already in the template. Click Next.
5. If you opted to start from a template, the wizard next prompts you to choose a template. Select one and click Next. Otherwise, the wizard prompts you to choose a type of data collector to add. In this example, let's assume you choose to start from a template, so choose Basic from the offered templates and then click Next.
6. Specify the directory where you want the data to be saved and click Next.
7. In the final page of the wizard, click Finish.

The new data collector set should now appear under the User Defined branch in the left pane. Let's assume that you now want to add some additional data collectors to the set. Right-click in the right pane (or on the new data collector set's name in the left pane) and choose New ➪ Data Collector.

Performance Monitor opens the Create New Data Collector Wizard (Figure 49-13). Specify a name for the collector and choose one of the four collector types, described previously in this section. For example, to add a performance counter, choose Performance Counter Data Collector. Then, click Next.

FIGURE 49-13

Create New Data Collector wizard.

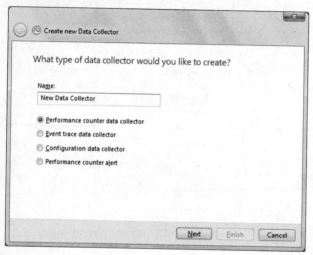

Depending on the type of collector you choose, the wizard prompts for information about the collector. Specify the information needed to configure the collector to obtain the data you're looking for, and then click Finish.

After you create the data collector set, you can use it just as you can the predefined ones in the System branch.

Resource Monitor

Another handy tool for monitoring system performance is Resource Monitor, which collects and displays real-time information about the CPU, disk, network, and memory. To open Resource Monitor, first open Performance Information and Tools from the Control Panel. Click Advanced Tools in the left pane, and then click Open Resource Monitor. Figure 49-14 shows Resource Monitor.

The Overview tab, shown in Figure 49-14, offers summary information about each of the four categories. To view activity for a specific process, select the check box next to the process' image name in the CPU list. Then, click the category header for a category to view the data filtered by the selected process. For example, Figure 49-15 shows network activity filtered for Internet Explorer.

Each of the other tabs in Resource Monitor provides data specific to the specified category. For example, to see detailed information about memory utilization, click the Memory tab. The top area of each tab shows the running processes. You can filter by one or more processes by selecting them from the list. Deselect the Image check box to clear the filter.

FIGURE 49-14

Resource Monitor.

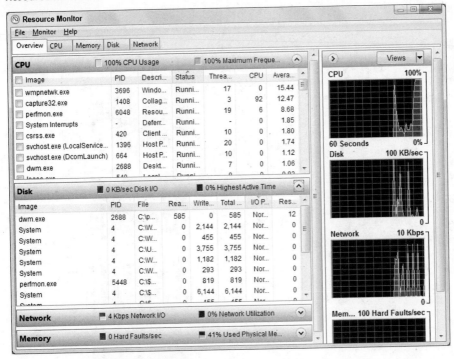

Reliability Monitor

Reliability Monitor provides information regarding your system's overall stability. It tracks data and generates a report similar to the one shown in Figure 49-16, which indicates a relative reliability index from 1 to 10. Reliability Monitor uses five groups of information to determine the index, including application failures, Windows failures, miscellaneous failures, warnings, and informational events. To open Reliability Monitor, open Action Center, expand the Maintenance group, and click View Reliability History.

Tip

Reliability Monitor starts monitoring your system right after the operating system is installed, and will keep one year's worth of data for analysis. Reliability Monitor requires 28 days of information before it will accurately determine a stability index. The line in the graph will also be dashed until Reliability Monitor has 28 days of information. ■

The icons on the chart in Reliability Monitor indicate the type of event that occurred on the specified date. The letter i inside a blue circle is an informational event, such as an update being applied successfully to the system. A yellow triangle with an exclamation mark inside indicates a warning. An example would be a warning that a driver did not install successfully. Failures are indicated by a white X inside a red circle. Examples include an application hanging or Windows shutting down unexpectedly.

FIGURE 49-15

Network activity filtered for Internet Explorer.

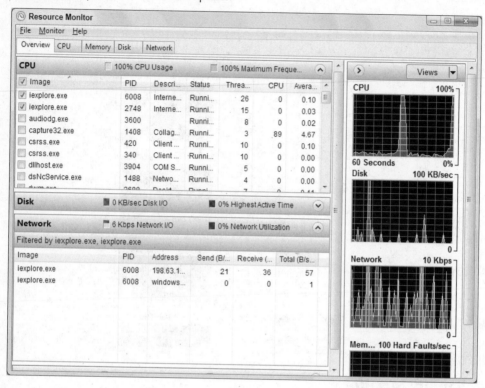

You can view the events for a particular day by clicking that day in the chart. Details for that day appear in the bottom Details pane. When viewing the graph in Weeks view, clicking a week in the graph shows all items for that week in the Details pane. Whichever view you use, double-clicking an item in the Details pane displays full information about the event. For example, Figure 49-17 shows the results of double-clicking an event related to Microsoft Office Live Add-in Sign-in.

Reliability Monitor is a great tool for keeping track of the events that have occurred with your computer over a long period of time. It can be particularly useful in identifying repetitive problems or problems with specific items.

Tip

Windows ReadyBoost uses flash memory, rather than your hard drive, for the paging file. This allows programs to get drive data more quickly, providing a faster, more fluid computing experience. ∎

Using Windows ReadyBoost

Historically, PCs had two ways to store data: memory and the hard drive. Memory (RAM) is very fast. But it's volatile, meaning everything in it gets erased the moment you shut down the computer. The hard drive isn't nearly as fast. But it has *persistence*, meaning that it retains information even when the computer is turned off.

Reliability Monitor report of overall system stability.

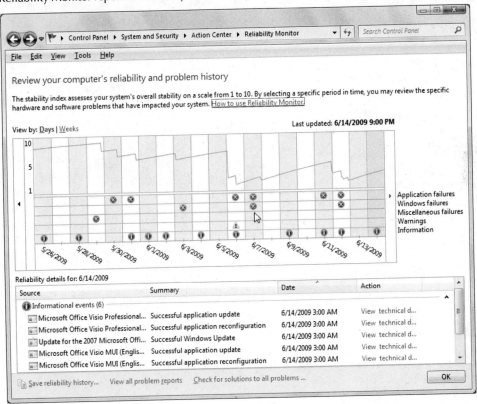

RAM is also more expensive, and therefore scarcer than hard drive storage. For example, a typical desktop computer might have 1 or 2 gigabytes of RAM. The hard drive, on the other hand, will likely hold tens or even hundreds of gigabytes of data.

Windows 7 automatically uses the paging file (discussed earlier in this chapter) to store the data and conserve RAM.

The downside to using the paging file is that the processor cannot move data to and from it as quickly as it can with RAM. The paging file becomes a little performance bottleneck. Prior to Windows Vista, there was no real solution to the problem. Windows Vista introduced a solution called ReadyBoost that lets Windows 7 use flash memory for the paging file. For paging file operations, flash memory is about 10 times faster than a hard drive, which means ReadyBoost can get rid of many little short delays and offer a faster, smoother overall computing experience. Windows 7 also supports ReadyBoost.

FIGURE 49-17

Details for an event in Reliability Monitor.

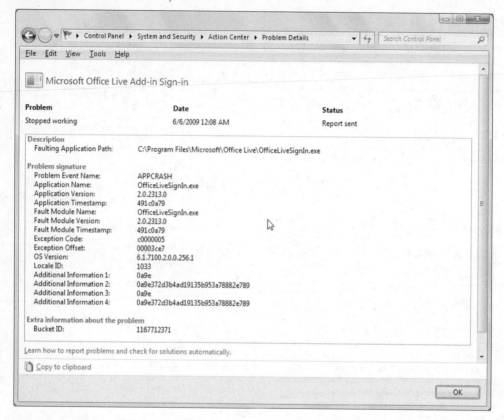

Note

Contrary to some popular belief, ReadyBoost doesn't add more RAM to your computer. It improves performance by using flash memory, rather than the hard drive, to store and access frequently used disk data.

Windows 7 takes care of all the potential problems that using flash memory for disk data might impose. For example, it keeps the actual paging file on the drive in sync with the copy on the flash drive. So if the flash memory suddenly disappears (as when you pull a flash drive out of its USB slot), there's no loss of data. Windows 7 even compresses and encrypts the data on the flash drive using high-strength AES encryption. If someone steals a ReadyBoost flash drive from your computer, they will not be able to read data from it to steal sensitive information. ■

There are basically three ways to get ReadyBoost capabilities in your system. One is to use a *hybrid* hard drive, which puts the flash memory right on the drive. Another is to have ReadyBoost capability on the computer's motherboard. If you have neither of those, the third approach is to use a USB flash drive for ReadyBoost. This is a small device, usually small enough to fit on a keychain, which you just plug into a USB 2.0 port on your computer.

Not all flash drives are ReadyBoost capable. They vary greatly in their capacity and speed. Windows 7 will only use a flash drive for ReadyBoost if it makes sense to do so. A 4 GB flash drive with fast random I/O capability is a good choice for ReadyBoost.

If you already have a USB flash drive, and want to see if it's ReadyBoost capable, just plug the drive into a USB slot. After Windows 7 recognizes and analyzes the drive, you'll get some feedback on the screen like the example shown in Figure 49-18.

FIGURE 49-18

Windows recognizes a new USB device and allows me to speed up my system using it.

Note
ReadyBoost requires that you use a USB 2.0-compliant flash drive. Anything preceding USB 2.0 is too slow to work as a ReadyBoost device. ■

If you want to use the device as virtual memory, select the Speed Up My System option. After you've selected that option, the properties for the removable disk will pop up. You can also bring up that dialog box by opening your Computer folder, right-clicking the drive's icon, and choosing Properties.

Select the Use This Device option and then you are able to set the amount of space for ReadyBoost. By default, Windows sets the value to the recommended amount and also lets you know that the space you allocate won't be available for general use. When you've set your value, click the OK button.

ReadyBoost works by copying as much of the information as possible from virtual memory to the USB thumb drive. There is still a copy of all of the information within virtual memory; the system now knows to look at the ReadyBoost device first. If the system can't find the information there, it will look to the real virtual memory located on your hard drive. By keeping the original copy on your hard drive, you're able to remove your USB thumb drive without disrupting the computer.

Don't expect to see everything suddenly run faster with ReadyBoost. Its benefits might not be immediate. Remember, the main purpose of ReadyBoost is to eliminate the short delays you might experience when loading certain programs, switching among open programs, and other activities that usually involve a paging file. With time, you should experience quicker response times in those areas. You might even find your computer starts more quickly because it takes less time to load programs at startup.

Trading pretty for performance

All the visual effects you see on your screen while using Windows comes with a price. It takes CPU resources to show drop-shadows beneath 3D objects, make objects fade into and out of view, and so forth. On an old system that has minimal CPU capabilities and memory, those little visual extras can bog down the system.

To change settings that control visual effects, open Performance Information and Tools from the Control Panel. In the left pane, click Adjust Visual Effects to open the Performance Options dialog box shown in Figure 49-19.

FIGURE 49-19

The Visual Effects tab of the Performance Options dialog box.

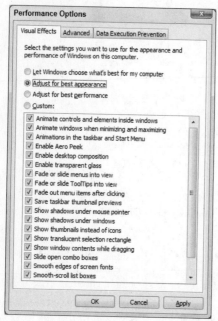

The Visual Effects tab of the Performance Options dialog box lets you choose how much performance you're willing to part with for a "pretty" interface. As shown in Figure 49-20, the Visual Effects tab gives you four main options:

- **Let Windows Choose What's Best for My Computer:** Choosing this option automatically chooses visual effects based on the capabilities of your computer.

- **Adjust for Best Appearance:** If selected, all visual effects are used, even at the cost of slowing down performance.

FIGURE 49-20

The Disk Cleanup dialog box.

- **Adjust for Best Performance:** Choosing this option minimizes visual effects to preserve overall speed and responsiveness.

- **Custom:** If you choose this option, you can then pick and choose any or all of the visual effects listed beneath the Custom option.

How you choose options is entirely up to you. If you have a powerful system, the visual effects won't impact performance much, if at all. So, there's no need to turn off the visual effects. But if your computer isn't immediately responsive to operations that involve opening and closing menus, dragging, and other things you do on the screen, eliminating some visual effects should help make your computer more responsive.

Maintaining Your Hard Drive

While the CPU and RAM are the most important factors for system performance, your hard drive plays an important role in determining the overall speed of your computer. That's because the hard drive comes into play when you're opening programs or documents, when you're saving documents, or when you're moving and copying files. It also comes into play when you are running low on RAM by moving less-used applications to your hard drive from RAM. So, keeping the hard drive running as near peak performance as possible will have a positive impact on system performance.

Recovering wasted hard drive space

At any given time, some of the space on your hard drive is being eaten up by *temporary files*. As the name implies, temporary files are not like the programs you install or documents you save. Programs and documents are "forever," in the sense that Windows never deletes them at random. The only time a program is deleted is when you use Programs in Control Panel to remove the program. Likewise, documents aren't deleted unless you intentionally delete them and also empty the Recycle Bin.

The files in your *Internet cache*, also called your *Temporary Internet Files* folder, are good examples of temporary files. Every time you visit a Web page, all the text and pictures that make up that page are stored in your Internet cache. When you use the Back or Forward button to revisit a page you've viewed recently, your browser just pulls a copy of the page out of the Internet cache. That saves a lot of time when compared to how long it would take to re-download a page each time you clicked the Back or Forward button to revisit a recently viewed page.

Caution

Before you click the Disk Cleanup tool, be forewarned that the process could take several minutes, maybe longer. It's never *necessary* to use Disk Cleanup to get rid of temporary files. ■

To recover some wasted disk space, click the Disk Cleanup button on the Properties sheet for the hard drive. Open the Computer folder, right-click a drive, and choose Properties. In the Properties dialog box, click the Disk Cleanup button. Disk Cleanup then analyzes the drive for expendable files. Eventually, you'll get to the Disk Cleanup dialog box shown in Figure 49-20. The Files to Delete list shows categories of temporary files. When you click a category name, the Description below the names explains the types of files in that category. All the categories represent temporary files that you can definitely safely delete. There won't ever be any important programs or documents you saved on your own in the list of temporary files.

The number to the right of each category name indicates how much drive space the files in that category are using, and how much space you'll gain if you delete them. Choose which categories of files you want to delete by selecting (checking) their check boxes. If you don't want to delete a category of files, clear the checkmark for that category. The amount of drive space you'll recover by deleting all the selected categories appears under the list. After you've selected the categories of files you want to delete, click OK. The files are deleted and the dialog box closes.

Deleting System Restore files and unwanted features

If you click the Clean Up System Files button in Disk Cleanup, a More Options tab appears on the Disk Cleanup dialog box. Clicking that tab provides two more options for freeing up drive space:

- **Programs and Features:** Takes you to the Programs and Features window, where you can uninstall programs and Windows Features you don't use.

- **System Restore and Shadow Copies:** Deletes all restore points except the most recent one. This can be significant because system protection files are allowed to consume up to 15 percent of your available drive space.

For more information on removing programs, see Chapter 42. For more information on restore points, see "Using System Protection" in Chapter 33.

Defragmenting your hard drive

When a drive is newly formatted, most of the free space on the drive is available in a contiguous chunk. This means the disk *clusters* (the smallest amount of storage space that can be allocated) are side-by-side in contiguous fashion. As Windows writes a file, it can do so in contiguous clusters, writing the entire file in one pass. When it reads the file back, it can also do so in one pass, making drive performance as good as possible.

However, the more a drive is used, the more fragmented the data becomes. Instead of writing data contiguously, Windows writes it here and there on the drive, splitting up the file into fragments (thus the term fragmentation).

Tip

Defragmentation is not necessary for solid state drives. ∎

When that happens, the drive head has to move around a lot to read and write files. You might even be able to hear the drive chattering when things get really fragmented across the drive. This puts some extra stress on the mechanics of the drive and also slows things down a bit.

To really get things back together and running smoothly, you can *defragment* (or *defrag* for short) the drive. When you do, Windows takes most of the files that are split up into little chunks and brings them all together to make them contiguous again. It also moves most files to the beginning of the drive, where they're easiest to get to. The result is a drive that's no longer fragmented, doesn't chatter as much, and runs faster.

Defragmenting is one of those things you don't really have to do too often. Four or five times a year is probably sufficient. The process could take a few minutes or up to several hours. So, it's another one of those tasks you'll probably want to run overnight. However, note that Windows 7, by default, defragments the drive. You can view the current schedule, if any, in the Disk Defragmenter program.

Tip

You don't have to stop using the computer while Windows defragments the drive. You can continue to use it as you normally would. Doing so, however, continues to generate read/write operations on the drive, which ultimately slows down the defragmentation process. For that reason, it's best to run the defragmentation operation while you are not using the computer. ∎

To defragment a hard drive, starting at the desktop:

1. Open your Computer folder by clicking the Start button.
2. Right-click the icon for your hard drive (C:), and choose Properties.
3. In the Properties dialog box that opens, click the Tools tab.
4. Click the Defragment Now button. The Disk Defragmenter program opens, as shown in Figure 49-21.

Tip

When it says you don't *need to* defragment, that doesn't mean that you can't or shouldn't. It just means the drive's not badly fragmented. But you can still defragment it. ∎

5. In the Disk Defragmenter dialog box, you're able to set up a schedule to run the defragmenter or click the Defragment Now button. The program will start analyzing your drive and may take as long as a few minutes or up to a few hours.
6. When the defragmentation is complete, the icon on the left side of the screen should turn to a green circle with a checkmark.

FIGURE 49-21

The Disk Defragmenter default settings.

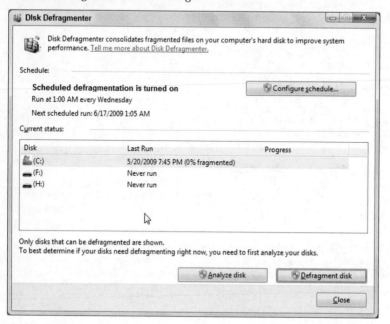

Disk Defragmenter defragments all the fragmented files and moves some frequently used files to the beginning of the drive, where they can be accessed in the least time with the least effort. Some files won't be moved. That's normal. If Windows decides to leave them where they are, it's for good reason. You may hear a lot of drive chatter as Disk Defragmenter is working. That's because the drive head is moving things around to get everything into a better position.

When Disk Defragmenter is finished, you can just close any open dialog boxes and the Disk Defragmenter program window.

The Power Settings

The power settings under Power Options in the Control Panel provide features that enable you to adjust the performance of your system while conserving energy. To get to the power options for your system, click the Start button and select Control Panel. If the Control Panel opens in Category view, click the System and Security link. Then click the Power Options icon. The Power Options applet will open, shown in Figure 49-22. Click the down arrow beside Show Additional Plans to show the High Performance plan.

The Power Options applet provides the basic configuration for the power options on your system. The three plans listed, Balanced, Power Saver, and High Performance, are the default power plans for the system. You're able to alter the settings for the three default plans by either clicking the Change Plan Settings link beside the plan or, for the selected plan, clicking either Choose When to Turn Off the Display or Change When the Computer Sleeps from the left column. Clicking any of these links brings up the Edit Plan Settings dialog box shown in Figure 49-23.

FIGURE 49-22

The different options for power settings.

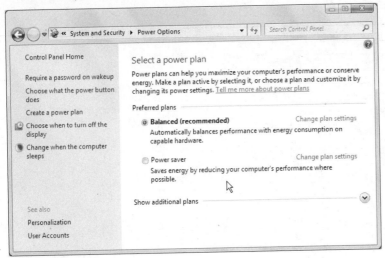

FIGURE 49-23

The basic options for setting the power conservation features of Windows 7.

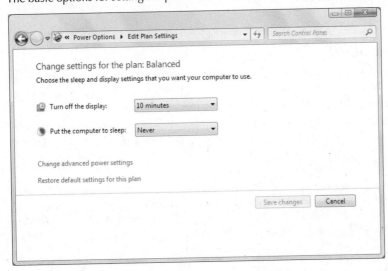

Adjusting either of these options will alter the default plan you have selected. Clicking the Change Advanced Power Settings link brings up the Power Options dialog box, which includes the Advanced Settings tab shown in Figure 49-24.

With these options, you're able to drill down on individual options at a more granular level. If you change something that you think you shouldn't have, you can click the Restore Plan Defaults button to get back to where you were. Note that notebook computers have additional power options not typically available on desktops.

The Advanced power settings.

Create a power plan

If none of the default options meet your needs and you'd like to build your own power plan, click the third link on the left side of the Power Options applet, Create a Power Plan. Clicking this link brings up the window shown in Figure 49-25.

To make it easier, Windows lets you create your power plan from one of the three defaults. You're also able to name the plan on this page. After you've set the name of your plan, click Next. The next window allows you to set when you want to turn off the display and when you want to put the computer to sleep.

After you've configured these last two options, click the Create button. When you are back at the Power Options applet, your plan should be first on the list and selected. If you want to change some of the advanced options in your plans, click the Change Plan Settings link and then click Change Advanced Power Settings as mentioned earlier in the chapter.

System settings

Clicking the first two links on the left side of the Power Options applet, either Require a Password on Wakeup or Choose What the Power Button Does, takes you to the System Settings page shown in Figure 49-26.

FIGURE 49-25

The first step to creating your own power plan.

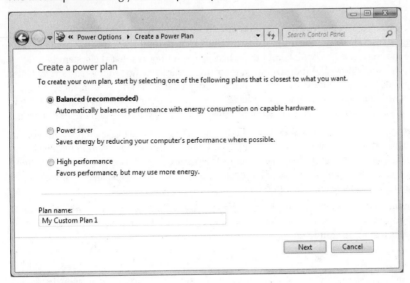

FIGURE 49-26

Options for power buttons and password protection.

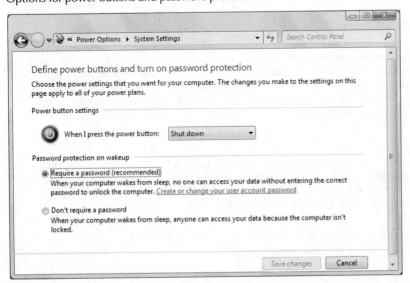

With older computers, when you pressed the power button, the system would power off. With current computers, the power buttons take on a different role. Under the first heading in this window, Power Button Settings, you determine what happens when the power button is pushed. You're given three options, discussed here:

- **Sleep:** If you select this option, the data you are working on will be stored in memory and to the hard drive. The system will run using very little power until you press the keyboard or move the mouse. On a notebook computer, when Windows notices that the system is running low on battery power, Windows will start writing the information to the hard drive. Upon restarting, the system will move all of the information from the hard drive to memory, just as the system was left originally. Usually, it takes 2 to 3 seconds to bring the computer back from Sleep. Sleep mode is not limited to notebooks. Most newer desktop computers also support it.

- **Hibernate:** Using this option will take all of the information you have in memory and write it to the hard drive, then shut down the computer. Upon resuming, your system understands that there is a file on the hard drive that contains the picture of what was in memory, and the system copies the information from the hard drive to memory. This is a snapshot of what you had running when the system went into hibernation.

- **Shut Down:** This selection will shut down the computer without saving any of the data you have in memory. Windows will prompt you to save your work before you shut down. This method does a graceful shutdown of Windows.

After you've determined which option you want, click the Save Changes button.

On the System Settings window, you're also able to set the password option for what happens when the computer wakes up. As indicated by the text next to each of the options, when your system wakes from Sleep, the user may be prompted for a password. Obviously, the more secure option is to use a password. However, if this is your home system and you are the only one with physical access to the system, it's sufficient to pick the second option.

Tip

Windows 7 includes a technology called ReadyDrive, which combines hard drives with flash memory to help with performance and power consumption. When the hard drive spins down to conserve battery life, some of the information can still be accessed from the flash memory on the hard drive. The flash memory consumes a fraction of the power compared to that of a typical hard drive. The advantage of ReadyDrive for notebook PC users is that Windows 7 can read data that is cached in the drive's flash memory without spinning up the drive, conserving battery life and extending drive life. ■

Note

The settings described in this section are the most common settings based on the hardware. For instance, if you're using a laptop, you may have two additional or different options on the left side of the Power Options window: Choose What Closing the Lid Does and Choose What Power Buttons Do. These options are specific to the system and offer additional options for power management. ■

With all of the power options available in Windows 7, you should be able to conserve resources on your system while still making your system very responsive. The power options will probably benefit a portable user more so than a desktop user.

Wrap-Up

The components of your computer system that most affect performance are its CPU and memory, but hard drive performance also affects overall system performance. (Internet access speed is determined primarily by the bandwidth of your Internet connection, but can also be affected by slow system performance.) As an alternative to buying a faster computer, you can do some things to make your current computer run faster, and keep it running at top speed. The main points in this chapter are as follows:

- The System Information program provides detailed information about all the components that make up your computer system.

- To ensure that your computer is responsive to your every mouse click and keyboard tap, Windows automatically prioritizes programs as foreground (high-priority) and background (low-priority) tasks.

- When your system runs out of physical memory (RAM), Windows automatically uses a portion of the hard drive as virtual memory to handle the overflow.

- ReadyBoost uses flash memory to store frequently accessed disk files to provide a faster, more fluid computing experience.

- If your computer is usually sluggish and unresponsive, consider turning off some of Windows 7's visual effects.

- The speed of your hard drive determines how long it takes to open and save files.

- To keep your hard drive running at top speed, consider deleting temporary files, scanning for and fixing bad sectors, and defragmenting the drive a couple of times a year.

- Power settings play a role in your system's overall performance and can also be adjusted to conserver power, especially when using a laptop.

Troubleshooting Hardware and Performance

This chapter discusses some common problems and their solutions for hardware on your system including the normal components of a computer. Additionally, information for troubleshooting Bluetooth connectivity is included. Finally, some information for troubleshooting general performance issues is addressed.

First Aid for Troubleshooting Hardware

Whenever you have a hardware problem that's causing a device to misbehave or just not work at all, finding an updated driver will usually be your best bet. But even before you do that, you might want to try Windows built-in Troubleshooting tools to see if they can resolve the problem.

New Feature

Windows 7 integrates troubleshooting components into a single applet in the Control Panel, replacing the Help and Support troubleshooting tools in previous versions.

To get help on programs, hardware, and drivers, open the Troubleshooting applet from the Control Panel (Figure 50-1). Each of the items in this Control Panel applet provides a troubleshooting wizard that can automatically search for, detect, and potentially fix problems. The applet offers the following groups:

- **Programs:** Launch the Program Compatibility Wizard, which enables you to apply settings to programs to make them run as if they were running in an earlier version of Windows. For example, you can potentially run a Windows 98 program under Windows 7 by configuring its compatibility settings for Windows 98. This group also includes items for troubleshooting printers, Media Player, and Internet Explorer.

FIGURE 50-1

The Troubleshooting applet provides options for troubleshooting hardware and driver issues.

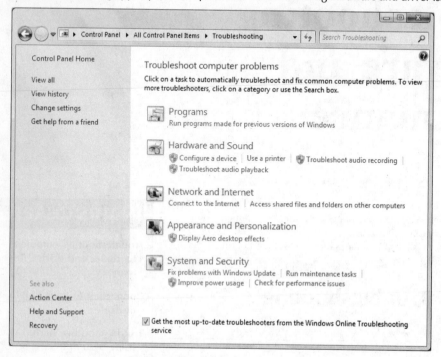

- **Hardware and Sound:** Use the Hardware and Sound item to scan for hardware changes and troubleshoot problems with general devices, printers, network adapters, and audio devices.

- **Network and Internet:** Troubleshoot problems connecting to the Internet or accessing shared files and folders on a local area network. Also troubleshoot Homegroup, incoming network connections, and DirectAccess.

- **Appearance and Personalization:** Troubleshoot problems with the Windows Aero desktop visual effects (such as transparent windows).

- **System and Security:** Troubleshoot problems with Windows Update, modify power settings, check for computer performance issues, and run maintenance tasks including cleaning up unused files and shortcuts. Also check search and indexing problems, and adjust performance settings.

The Troubleshooting applet lists only some of the items for each category. Click the group name (such as Hardware and Sound or Network and Internet) to see all of the troubleshooting tools for that category. Figure 50-2, for example, shows the System and Security category.

Tip

Make sure to leave enabled the option at the bottom of the Troubleshooting window, Get the Most Up-to-Date Troubleshooters from the Windows Online Troubleshooting Service, to allow Windows to update the troubleshooters as new or modified ones become available. ■

FIGURE 50-2

The System and Security category.

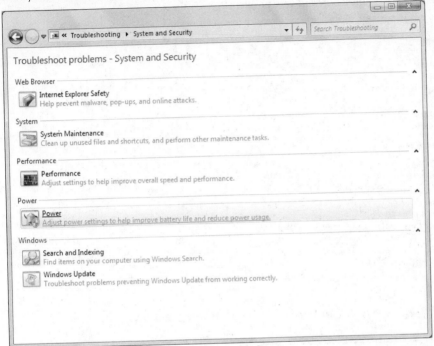

A second alternative is to troubleshoot from the hardware device's Properties dialog box in Device Manager. To open Device Manager, tap ⊞, type `dev`, and click Device Manager. Or click the Start button, right-click Computer, and choose Properties. Then click the Device Manager link on the left side of the screen. In Device Manager:

1. Right-click the name of the device that's causing problems and choose Properties.

2. If the device shows an error in the Device Manager (Figure 50-3), use that information to begin troubleshooting. For example, if Device Manager indicates that there is no driver installed, try installing or reinstalling the device's driver.

3. If needed, use the options on the Driver tab to reinstall the drivers for the device. You can also disable the device from this tab and eliminate potential conflicts with other devices.

4. On the Resources tab (Figure 50-4), check for a conflict message under Conflicting Device List and resolve problems by reassigning resources to the conflicting devices, or by disabling one of them. Note that not all hardware devices will have a Resources tab.

Tip

If you've made a hardware change but Windows hasn't noticed the change, open Device Manager and choose Action ⇨ Scan for Hardware Changes to have Windows rescan the system. For example, if you have an external modem that was turned off when you turned on the computer, rescanning should cause Windows to redetect the modem after you have turned it on. ■

FIGURE 50-3

Use Device Manager to help troubleshoot hardware problems.

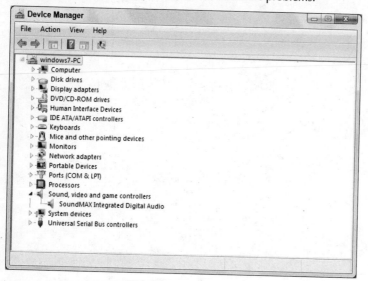

FIGURE 50-4

The Resources tab.

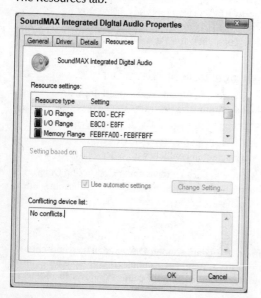

Dealing with Error Messages

Error messages come in all forms, from simple warnings to the *stop errors* and "the blue screen of death," which causes the computer to stop dead in its tracks. The more serious errors are often accompanied by one or more of the following pieces of information:

- **An error number:** An error number will often be a hexadecimal number in the format 0x00000*xxx* where the italicized numbers could be any numbers in the message.

- **Symbolic error name:** Symbolic error names are usually shown in all uppercase with underlines between words, such as PAGE_FAULT_IN_NONPAGED_AREA.

- **Driver details:** If a device driver caused the problem, you might see a filename with a `.sys` extension in the error message.

- **Troubleshooting info:** Some errors will have their own built-in troubleshooting advice, or a Help button. Use that information to learn more about what went wrong.

Whenever you get an error message that you can't solve just by reading the advice presented on the screen, go to `http://support.microsoft.com` and search for the error number, or the symbolic error name, the driver name, or some combination of words in the text or troubleshooting of the error message.

If searching Microsoft's support site doesn't do the trick, consider searching the entire Internet using Google or Bing. You never know, someone out there may have had the same problem and posted the solution somewhere on the Internet. When using a search engine, provide as much detail as possible to get the best results for your problem.

Tip

Odd as it might seem, a Google search will often turn up pages on Microsoft's own support site that can be difficult to find when searching at the Microsoft site. You can include "site:support.microsoft.com" in the search criteria in Google to help narrow down your search results to the Microsoft site. ∎

Performing a Clean Boot

The biggest problem with hardware errors is that even a tiny error can have seemingly catastrophic results, like suddenly shutting down the system and making it difficult to get the system started again. Clean booting can also help with software problems that prevent the computer from starting normally or cause frequent errors.

Not for the technologically challenged, this procedure is best left to more experienced users who can use it to diagnose the source of a problem that's preventing the computer from starting normally. The procedure for performing a clean boot is as follows:

Note

A clean boot is not the same as a clean install. During a clean boot, you may temporarily lose some normal functionality. But once you perform a normal startup, you should regain access to all your programs and documents, and full functionality. ∎

1. Close all open programs and save any work in progress.
2. At the Windows desktop, click Start and enter `msconfig`.

3. The System Configuration Utility opens.

4. On the General tab, choose Selective Startup and make sure the Load Startup Items check box is cleared.

5. Click the Services tab.

6. Select Hide All Microsoft Services and click the Disable All button.

7. Click OK and click Restart to reboot.

To return to normal startup after diagnosis, open the System Configuration Utility. On the Services tab, click Enable All. On the General tab, choose Normal Startup and click the OK button.

Using the System Recovery Options

For more severe problems that require repairing an existing Windows 7 installation, troubleshooting startup issues, system and complete PC restoration, using Windows Memory Diagnostic Tool, or getting to a command prompt, you'll need to use the System Recovery Options. This method should only be used by experienced users who can perform such tasks from a command prompt.

To boot from the Windows disc, first make sure that the drive is enabled as a boot device in the BIOS with a higher priority than any hard drives. Insert the Windows disc into the drive. Restart the computer and follow these steps:

1. During the POST, watch for the Press Any Key to Boot from CD or DVD prompt, and tap a key.

2. After all files load from the disc, click the Next button on the page that is prompting for language, currency, and keyboard type.

3. On the next page, click the Repair Your Computer link near the bottom of the page.

4. Windows will bring up the System Recovery Options dialog box, which looks for an existing installation of Windows 7. If your system requires special hard drive controller drivers, you can click the Load Drivers button so your installation of Windows 7 can be located. If you see your version of Windows 7 in the list box, select it and click the Next button.

5. The next window shows all of your options for recovery.

The System Recovery Options window provides different troubleshooting tools based on your set of circumstances:

- **Startup Repair:** Use this option if your system won't start up. This could be for any number of reasons including a bad or misconfigured driver, an application that attempts to start at startup but causes the system to hang, or a faulty piece of hardware.

- **System Restore:** System Restore restores back to a designated restore point. By default, Windows is making restore points of your computer that store the state of your system. You'll be able to choose a restore point for your system from a previous day when you knew your system was performing correctly. The System Restore option will not alter any of your personal data or documents.

- **System Image Recovery:** For this feature to work, you would need to have done a backup in the past. Windows will search hard drives and DVDs for valid backups to restore from. See Chapter 33 for information on backing up your system.

- **Windows Memory Diagnostic:** Some of the issues you may be experiencing may be the result of memory problems. Windows Memory Diagnostic Tool will perform tests against the RAM in your system to see if there are any problems. For this tool to run, click the link, which will prompt you to restart your computer now and check for problems or to check for problems the next time you restart.

- **Command Prompt:** The Command Prompt option is for experienced users who need to access the file system and run commands specific to Windows 7. Only choose this option if you're sure you need it, and be careful when using the Command Prompt.

When you're finished using the System Recovery Options, you can click either Shut Down or Restart to exit. For additional information on System Recovery Options, use Help and Support and search on System Recovery Options.

Troubleshooting Performance Problems

This section covers basic troubleshooting in terms of using Task Manager and Control Panel tools to monitor and troubleshoot performance. Keep in mind that hardware and software go hand in hand, so performance problems can be caused by either one. For example, if a device is malfunctioning or improperly configured, it can lead to performance problems. Likewise, having too many programs running at one time can eat up valuable memory and processor time, also foiling performance. So, don't assume that performance problems are always caused by hardware or software — the problem could well be one, the other, or both.

FIGURE 50-5

Task Manager sorting the processes based on CPU percentage.

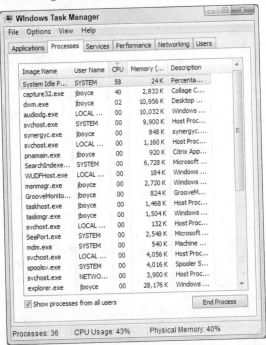

If your CPU Usage chart consistently runs at a high percentage in Task Manager, you may be running two or more firewalls. Most likely, you'll need to disable and remove any third-party firewalls, or disable the built-in Windows Firewall.

Also, scan your system for viruses, adware, and other malware, and remove all that you can find to eliminate their resource consumption.

If neither of the previous suggestions fixes your problem, you may need to see if an individual process is keeping your system overly busy. To do this, use one of these methods to start the Task Manager:

- With Windows running and while logged on to the computer, press Ctrl+Alt+Del and click Start Task Manager.
- Click Start and type taskmgr to locate and start Task Manager.
- Right-click the taskbar and click Start Task Manager.

Once you're in Task Manager, click the Processes tab and then click Show Processes from All Users. This will list all of the processes running on the system. Next, sort the information in the grid based on CPU, as shown in Figure 50-5. Just click the CPU column to sort by CPU utilization.

Tip

If a task is spiking CPU utilization but not staying at a consistently high rate, first identify the processes by sorting by CPU, then when you've determined which processes are using the most CPU time, sort by process name to watch how those processes are using the CPU. ∎

You should be able to identify the process that is using the majority of your CPU. You have a couple of options at this point:

- Use the name of the process under the Image Name column to search the Internet to see if the process is a valid file or a potential virus. If it is a virus of some form, you'll need to update your virus definitions and rerun your virus scan. If it does not appear to be a virus, you'll need to contact the vendor who provided the software to see if they can help troubleshoot the problem.
- Short term, you can right-click the process and choose End Process. Sometimes applications run into problems or situations the developer never imagined and the process gets stuck in a loop, which taxes the CPU. Restarting the application will reset the process, hopefully avoiding the circumstances that put the application in a loop. In addition to using Task Manager, Windows 7 includes several other utilities located in the Performance Information and Tools Control Panel applet (see Chapter 51).

Wrap-Up

Many thousands of hardware devices are available that you can use with Windows, and no one rule that applies to troubleshooting all of them. So you'll likely have to consider all of your resources. Be sure to check the manual that came with the hardware device first. If that doesn't work, the device manufacturer's Web site will likely be your next best bet.

When you need to ask a question, post a question in the appropriate newsgroup in Microsoft Communities.

Part X

Networking and Sharing

Networking is all about getting two or more computers to talk to each other. Not over the Internet, but within a private network in your home or office. Networked computers can share resources, like an Internet account, printer, and files. Networking and sharing is what Part X is all about.

Chapter 51 starts off with a discussion of network hardware, the physical components you need to get computers connected. It covers both traditional wired networks and the newer Wireless Wi-Fi variety.

Chapter 52 covers the ways in which you share resources on a network. After you've shared a resource, other computers on the network can access it through the network. Chapter 53 describes how that works.

Chapter 54 covers the kinds of problems many people encounter when trying to set up their own networks and offers solutions to overcome those problems.

Creating a Home Network

I f you have two or more computers, you may already be using what's known as a *sneaker network*. For example, to get files from one computer to another, you copy files to a flash drive or CD. Then, you walk over to the other computer and copy the files from the disk to that computer. Wouldn't it be nice if you could just drag icons from one computer to the other without having to use a floppy or CD?

What if you have several computers, but only one printer, one Internet connection, or one DVD burner? Wouldn't it be nice if all the computers could use that one printer, that one Internet connection, and that one burner? All of these things are possible if you connect the computers to one another in a *local area network* (LAN).

After you've purchased and installed networking hardware, you're ready to set up your network. Windows 7 includes features that remove the complexities commonly associated with network configurations.

This chapter describes how to configure Windows for different types of hardware setups. Remember, you should always follow the instructions that came with your networking hardware first. After all, those instructions are written for the exact products you've purchased.

What Is a LAN?

A *local area network* (sometimes referred to as a *LAN*, a *workgroup*, a *private network*, or just a *network*) is a small group of computers within a single building or household that can communicate with one another and share *resources*. A resource is anything useful to the computer. For example:

- All computers in the LAN can use a single printer.
- All computers in the LAN can connect to the Internet through a single modem and Internet account.
- All computers in the LAN can access shared files and folders on any other computer in the LAN.

In addition, you can move and copy files and folders among computers using exactly the same techniques you use to move and copy files among folders on a single computer. However, it's not entirely necessary to move or copy a document that you want to work on, because if a document is in a shared folder, you can open and edit it from any computer in the network. This is good, because you only have one copy of the document, and you don't have to worry about having multiple, slightly different copies of the same document all over the place to confuse matters.

Planning a LAN

To create a LAN, you need a plan and special hardware to make that plan work. For one thing, each computer will need a device known as a *network interface card* (NIC) or *Ethernet card*. Those you can purchase and install yourself. However, many PCs come with an Ethernet card already installed for connecting to a wired network. In that case, you'll have an RJ-45 port on the back of the computer. It looks a lot like the plug for a telephone, just a little bigger. You just plug one side of an Ethernet cable into that port, and plug the other side of the cable into a network hub or wall jack. You can also connect computers without any cables at all by using wireless networking hardware. Exactly what you need, in terms of hardware, depends on what you want to do. The rest of this chapter describes your options.

Creating a Wired LAN

If you have two or more computers to connect, and they're all in the same room and close to one another, you can use a traditional Ethernet hub and Ethernet cables to connect the computers with cables. You'll need exactly one NIC and one traditional Ethernet cable for each computer in the LAN. Figure 51-1 shows an example of four computers connected in a traditional LAN. Notice how each computer connects to the hub only — no cables run directly from one computer to another computer.

By the way, even though the printer in Figure 51-1 is connected to the same computer as the modem, that's just an example. The printer can be connected to any computer. In fact, you could have several printers connected to several computers. All computers will be able to use all printers, no matter which computer that printer is (or those printers are) connected to. In addition, a printer with a network interface need not be connected to a computer at all, but rather can be connected directly to the network.

Traditional Ethernet speeds

When it comes time to purchase network interface cards, cables, and a hub, you'll need to decide on the speed you want. As with everything else in the computer industry, network speed costs money. However, in the case of networks, the cost differences are minor, whereas the speed differences are huge. The three possible speeds for Ethernet LANs are listed in Table 51-1.

If it's difficult to relate the numbers to actual transfer rates, consider a dial-up modem, which tops out at 50 Kbps. That's 50,000 bits per second. A 100Base-T network moves 100,000,000 bits per second. That's 2,000 times faster or, in other words, you only have to wait 1/2,000 as long for the same file to transfer across a 100Base-T connection. So, a file that takes 33 minutes (2,000 seconds) to transfer over a dial-up modem takes 1 second to transfer over a 100Base-T network.

FIGURE 51-1

Example of four computers connected in a traditional Ethernet LAN.

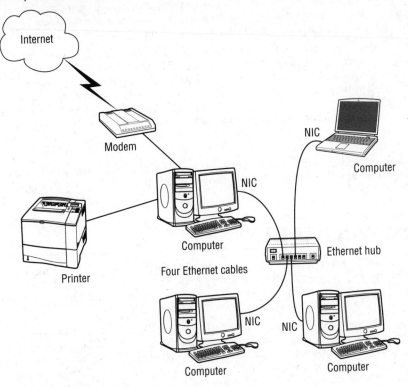

TABLE 51-1

Common Ethernet Network Component Speeds

Name	Transfer Rate (speed)	Bits per Second	Cable
10Base-T	10 Mbps	10 million	Category 3 or better
100Base-T	100 Mbps	100 million	Category 5 or better
Gigabit Ethernet	1 Gbps	1,000 million (billion)	Category 6 or better

The slowest component rules

When purchasing hardware, it's important to understand that the slowest component always rules. For example, if you get Gigabit Ethernet cards, but connect them to a 100Base-T hub, the LAN will run at 100Mbps. The faster Gigabit NICs can't force the slower hub to move any faster.

It makes sense if you envision the electrons going through the wire as cars on a freeway. Let's say lots of cars are zooming down a 10-lane freeway, but there's some road construction where the freeway narrows to one lane. Cars are going to pile up behind that point, because the one-lane portion is slowing things down. Where the one lane reopens back to 10 lanes, cars will still be trickling out of the *bottleneck* — the single lane — one at a time. The 10 lanes at the other side of the bottleneck can't "suck the cars through" the bottleneck any faster than one car at a time.

Likewise, if your computers are connected together with a Gigabit LAN, but all share a single broadband connection to the Internet, your Internet connection is still 512 Kbps. Your fast LAN can't force the data from your ISP to get to your computer any faster than 512 Kbps. Furthermore, if two people are using the 512-Kbps broadband connection at the same time, they have to share the available bandwidth, meaning that each user gets only 256 Kbps. But, if only one person is online, she gets the full 512 Kbps because she's not sharing any bandwidth when nobody else is online.

Note

If you have only two computers to connect, and each has an Ethernet card, you don't really need a hub. Instead you can connect the two computers directly using an Ethernet *crossover cable.* ■

Creating a Wireless LAN

Wireless networking reigns supreme when it comes to convenience and ease of use. As the name implies, with wireless networks you don't have to run any cables. Plus, no computer is tied down to any one cable. For example, you can use your notebook computer in any room in the house, or even out on the patio, and still have Internet access without being tied to a cable.

To set up a wireless LAN, you need a wireless NIC for each computer. To set up an *ad-hoc* wireless network, that's all you need. The computers can communicate with each other, so long as they're within range of one another. If you want Internet connectivity for all of the computers in a wireless LAN, you'll need some kind of access point that acts as a central location for all the computers and also provides an Internet connection. Typically, that device would be a Wireless Broadband Router, as illustrated in Figure 51-2.

Wireless Broadband Router

The big advantage of wireless networking is, of course, the lack of cables. This is especially handy on a notebook computer, because the computer isn't tethered to one location by a cable. Granted, you can't stray too far from the wireless access point (100 to 150 feet or so), but that will probably be sufficient in most cases.

Also, many universities and other locations offer public Internet access from any computer that has an 802.11b, 802.11g, or 802.11n wireless network interface. So, if you create your home wireless network using either of those standards, you'll also be able to use public Wi-Fi Internet access where it's available.

Tip

The only disadvantages to wireless networking, as compared to wired networks, are speed and reliability. 802.11n wireless networks run at about 300 Mbps. It's not as fast as the 100 Mbps or 1 Gbps speeds of traditional Ethernet cables, but still more than fast enough for typical networking tasks. Reliability isn't a problem with the technology, per se. Rather, it has to do with the rare "blind spot" here and there where the computer just won't connect to the network. ■

FIGURE 51-2

Example of four computers connected in a wireless LAN.

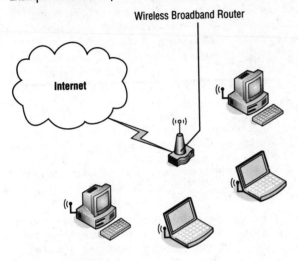

Wireless Broadband Router

Internet

TABLE 51-2

Wireless Networking Standards and Speeds

Standard	Speed	Range	Public Access
802.11b	11 Mbps	100–150 feet	Yes
802.11a	54 Mbps	25–75 feet	No
802.11g	54 Mbps	100–150 feet	Yes
802.11n	600 Mbps	150–300 feet	Yes

Wireless networks are built around four different standards. 802.11n is the newest, although as of this writing it is still in draft and not technically a standard. Table 51-2 summarizes the main differences between the four standards. The Public Access column refers to Internet Wi-Fi hotspots such as those found at some airports, hotels, and other places.

In most cases, when setting up your network you're really setting up two networks. The first network involves the computer-to-computer communication. This includes the wireless setup or a wired setup talked about earlier in the chapter. The second network is the Internet. Connecting to the Internet involves some form of an ISP. Today, two of the most popular methods are either a standard dial-up modem connection or a broadband connection. If you're sharing an Internet connection, one device in your network will have physical access to the Internet and the other computers will share the connection. The one device that actually sees the Internet can either be a computer or you can purchase an inexpensive device that connects to the Internet called a Broadband Router.

The 802.11n Standard

The 802.11n Standard, which offers theoretical speeds up to 600 Mbps, is expected to be approved by IEEE in late 2009 or early 2010. Several manufacturers offer 802.11n products, but until the standard is approved, there is no guarantee of interoperability between manufacturers. However, after the standard is approved, expect manufacturers to provide firmware updates for their products to make them fully compatible.

Other useful wireless goodies

If you already have a wired network with Internet connectivity, and just want to add some wireless computers to that network, you don't need a Wireless Broadband Router. Instead, you need a *Wireless Access Point* (WAP). First you'll need to configure the hub, as per the manufacturer's instructions, by connecting it directly to one of the computers in your wired network. Then you can disconnect the WAP from the computer and connect it directly to the hub for your wireless network. The wireless computer can use the same shared Internet connection that the wired network uses.

Getting a wireless network to cover a whole house can be a challenge, especially if you have two or more floors. If you want to extend Wi-Fi to the entire house, you may need to use one or more *wireless range expanders* to extend the reach of the network. Putting one near the staircase is a good idea when you need to reach upstairs or downstairs. You can also use multiple access points to achieve the same results.

A Wi-Fi finder can also be helpful. It's a device that's small enough to fit on a keychain and it measures the strength of a wireless network signal at wherever you're standing. It can help you determine where the edge of a signal is, which is a good place to put a range expander to get more coverage.

Acquiring and Installing Network Hardware

Now that you know what you need to network two or more computers, you need to purchase and install networking hardware. There's little I can do to help you with that, except give you a couple quick pointers:

- If you're not too keen on opening the computer case and installing things inside the computer, consider getting hardware that connects to the computer via USB ports. Typically, you just plug the devices in, and you're done.

- If you'll be adding a notebook to the network, you'll probably want a PC Card NIC (not to be confused with a PCI card, which goes in a motherboard slot inside the computer).

If you're new to all of this and just want to see what some of this stuff looks like, here are some Web sites you can visit. They're all network hardware manufacturers, not retailers:

- D-Link: www.d-link.com
- Gigafast: www.gigafast.com
- LinkSys: www.linksysbycisco.com
- Netgear: www.netgear.com
- SMC Networks: www.smc.com
- TrendNET: www.trendnet.com
- U.S. Robotics: www.usr.com

In terms of actually purchasing the products, you can find these products at any store that sells computer supplies, including many of the large office supply chains such as Staples and OfficeMax. Of course, you can buy the devices online at any Web site that sells computer stuff. Shopping jaunts include Web sites such as www.amazon.com, www.cdw.com, www.cyberguys.com, www.officemax.com, www.staples.com, www.tigerdirect.com, and www.walmart.com, just to name a few.

After you've acquired the hardware, you need to install it. I can't help you much there either. You'll have to follow the manufacturer's instructions on that one, because there is no one-rule-fits-all when it comes to installing hardware. As a general rule of thumb, you'll probably want to:

- Get the hub or router (if any) set up first.
- Install the network interface cards second.
- Connect all the cables last.

Once all the hardware is connected and installed, you're ready to set up the network. That part isn't so complicated because Windows does a great job of searching out networks. You work through that next.

After the Hardware Setup

A couple of steps are involved in actually setting up the networking hardware. First, make sure that the hardware you purchased is installed based on the manufacturer's instructions. This may include plugging in the device, then connecting the device to the Internet, and finally plugging in the other computers to the device. When this is complete, you can run the Set Up a Network Wizard to let Windows finish the process.

Caution

Read and follow the network hardware manufacturer's instructions carefully before you configure your network. If there's any conflict between what they say and what's stated in this chapter, do as the manufacturer's instructions say. Failure to do so will lead to many hours of hair-pulling frustration! ■

Close any open programs and documents before you start configuring your network. The type of network hardware you have set up will determine what configuration you'll need to use. Here's where to look, depending on your network configuration:

- If you have an Ethernet network, and your modem is inside of, or connected to, one computer in the network, you'll use Internet Connection Sharing (ICS) to share a single Internet account. See the section titled "Setting Up a Wired Network with an ICS Host."

- If you have a router or residential gateway that all computers in your network connect to, you will *not* use Internet Connection Sharing. Each computer will have its own direct access to your Internet account via the router. See the section titled "Setting Up a Wired Network with a Router."

- If you have a wireless network, see the section titled "Setting Up a Wireless Network" later in this chapter.

- If you want to set up a Bluetooth personal area network, see Chapter 47, "Using Wireless Bluetooth Devices."

Be sure to turn off all computers before you install the networking hardware. Then install all of the networking hardware and turn on all of the computers. Chances are, Windows 7 will detect the hardware and start setting things up automatically. If you see any prompts asking what type of network you're installing, make sure you specify that it's a *private* network (not a public network). When asked about file sharing, make sure you make choices that allow for file and printer sharing among computers in the private network.

With those buzzwords and tips in mind, let's move on to the specifics of things to do after you get all the network hardware in place and all the computers turned on.

Setting Up a Wired Network with an ICS Host

The method for setting up a network described here applies only for a network that's connected by cables (not a wireless network). If you're using a router, see the section titled "Setting Up a Wired Network with a Router." If you're setting up a wireless network, see the sections on setting up a wireless network.

The scenario where these instructions do apply is illustrated in Figure 51-3. Only one computer in the network is connected to the Internet. That computer might have an internal modem that connects directly to a phone or cable jack on the wall. Or, it might have an external modem that connects to that one computer and a wall jack. That same computer uses a separate cable to connect to the network hub.

In such a network, the computer that connects to the wall jack (or modem and wall jack) is the only computer that can access the Internet on its own. We call that computer the *Internet Connection Sharing Host*, or ICS host for short. You must know, beforehand, which computer has that Internet connection. If you don't, and try to guess your way through it, your network won't work. To play it safe, you should sit down at the computer, and make sure you can get online. Leave that computer online as you configure the ICS host.

Setting up the ICS host

With all your hardware in place, and your ICS host online, you're ready to start setting up the ICS host. Go to the computer to which the modem is directly connected and log in to a user account that has administrative privileges. Then open the Network and Sharing Center using either of the following methods:

- Click the Start button and choose Control Panel ➡ Network and Internet ➡ Network and Sharing Center.
- Tap 🪟 , type net, and click Network and Sharing Center.

From the Network and Sharing Center follow these steps:

1. In the left column, choose the Change Adapter Settings link to view all of the available network connections on your computer.

2. Right-click the icon that represents the Internet connection and choose Properties.

3. In the Properties window for that connection, click the Sharing tab as shown in Figure 51-4.

4. Select Allow Other Network Users to Connect through This Computer's Internet Connection and click OK.

That's it for the computer that's connected directly to the Internet. You'll need to configure the network connection for every computer in your network, as discussed next.

FIGURE 51-3

Example of networks with an ICS host.

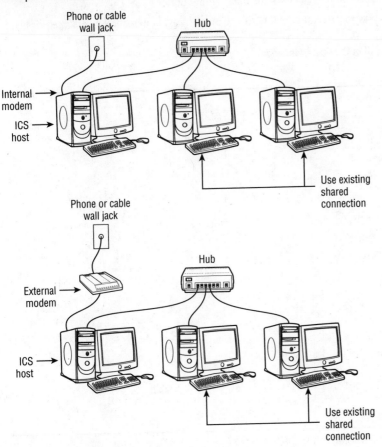

Setting up other computers

You need to configure the rest of the computers on your network to use the ICS host connection to the Internet. But first, make sure that you are still online, or can get online, from the ICS host. You want a live Internet connection as you set up other computers in the network. To connect the next system to the Internet, follow these steps:

1. Open the Control Panel and click View Network Status and Tasks to open Network and Sharing Center.

2. Click Change Adapter Settings in the left pane.

3. Right-click the network connection and choose Properties.

4. On the Networking tab, double-click Internet Protocol Version 4.

5. Choose Obtain an IP Address Automatically and click OK, then click OK to close the network connection's property sheet.

6. Click Start ⇨ Internet Explorer.

7. Click Tools ⇨ Internet Options to bring up the Internet Options window.

8. Click the Connections tab and click the LAN Settings button.

9. Clear check boxes as shown in Figure 51-5 (you can leave Automatically detect settings checked).

10. Click OK on all of the open windows.

FIGURE 51-4

The Sharing Properties sheet for the ICS host connection.

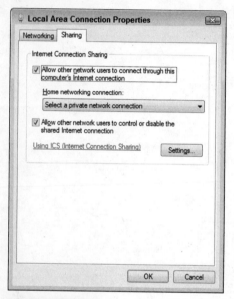

FIGURE 51-5

The LAN settings within Internet Explorer.

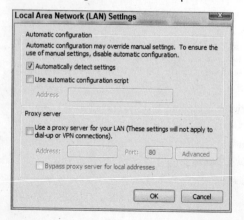

Remember, you need to follow the preceding steps for every computer you want connected to the Internet. When you've finished, you should be able to get online from every computer in the network. You should now be able to go straight to Chapter 53 to view shared resources on your network.

Setting Up a Wired Network with a Router

If your computer connects to the Internet through a residential gateway or router, there won't be an Internet Connection Sharing host. With a residential gateway, you'll likely have an Ethernet hub to which all computers, and the gateway, attach. The gateway, in turn, connects to a cable or DSL modem, which in turn connects to a phone jack or cable jack on the wall, as shown in Figure 51-6.

FIGURE 51-6

Sample residential gateway network.

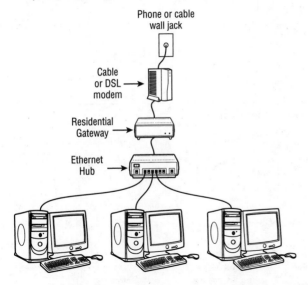

A router behaves in much the same way as a residential gateway, but everything is combined in a single unit. In fact, the router will look like a modem. But the big difference is that you can connect several computers — not just one computer — to the router. Figure 51-7 shows an example.

With a router or residential gateway, your first step will usually be to get online from one computer. You'll need to refer to instructions that came with your router, as well as your ISP's instructions, to do that. Windows will attempt to find the network for you. To see where you stand, follow these steps:

1. Click the Start button and choose Control Panel.

2. If Control Panel opens in Category view, click the Network and Internet icon.

3. Open the View Network Status and Tasks link below Network and Sharing Center.

4. As shown in Figure 51-8, the system is connected to a local network, but the local network does not have a connection to the Internet.

5. After reconfiguring the wiring connecting the network hardware and opening Network and Sharing Center, the network now looks like Figure 51-9.

FIGURE 51-7

Sample router connection to the Internet.

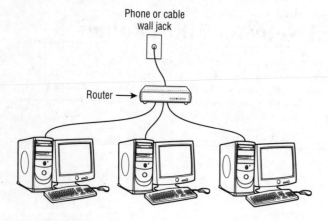

FIGURE 51-8

A computer connected to the network but no Internet connection.

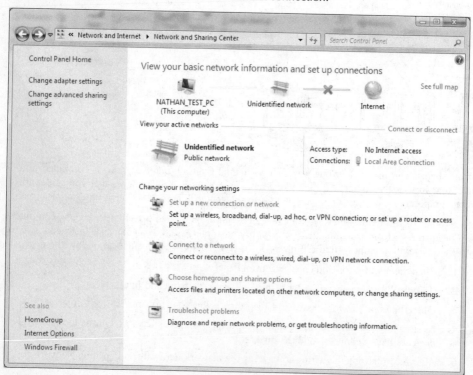

In Figure 51-9, Windows sees the local network and also sees the Internet connection from the local network. If your networking hardware is configured correctly, Windows sees the network and will set it up for you appropriately.

If your network is configured correctly for the first computer, try configuring your next system on the network using the steps outlined earlier.

If you have wireless devices that you want to connect to the network, follow the instructions in the next section.

FIGURE 51-9

A computer connected to the network and also connected to the Internet.

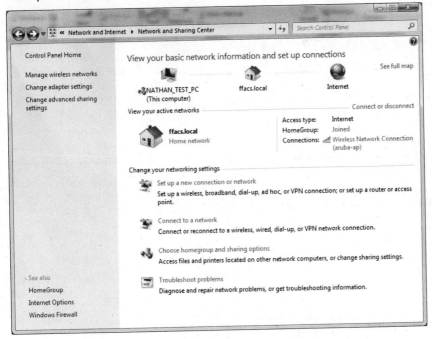

Setting Up a Wireless Network

There's something about the term "wireless" that makes it seem as though it must be easier than "wired." In truth, wireless networking is quite a bit more complicated terminology-wise. There are lots of buzzwords and acronyms everyone assumes that you already know. So, before we get into this topic, let's get all of that out of the way.

The 802.11 standard

The Institute of Electrical and Electronics Engineers, Inc., abbreviated IEEE and pronounced *EYE-triple-E*, is an organization of some 360,000 electrical engineers who develop many of the standards that PC products use to interact with one another. The IEEE isn't big on giving fancy names to things. They prefer numbers (which somehow seems fitting). Names often get tacked on later. For example, what is now called Ethernet is actually IEEE 802.3. What Apple calls FireWire and Sony calls iLink is actually IEEE 1394.

Note

The home page for IEEE is at www.ieee.net. ∎

IEEE created the 802.11 standard for most wireless networking today. Several revisions to the original specification have been proposed, with 802.11a, 802.11b, 802.11g, and 802.11n being the four that actually have made it to market as I write this chapter. Most likely, you'll be using 802.11g or 802.11n, because they are the standard to which most of the recently released wireless networking products adhere.

Access point, SSID, WEP, and WPA

Wireless networking requires some kind of *wireless access point*, also called a *base station*. The base station is the central unit with which all computers in the network communicate. It's the same idea as a hub in Ethernet networking. It's just that there are no wires connecting computers to the access point. Instead, each computer has a wireless network interface card (NIC), as illustrated in Figure 51-10.

FIGURE 51-10

Wireless communications all go through an access point or base station.

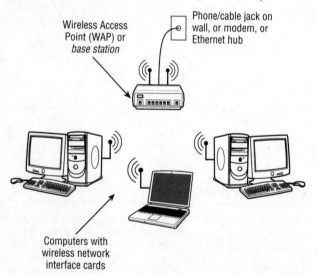

The access point in a wireless network plays the same role as the hub in a wired network, in that all traffic goes to the access point first, and is passed on to the appropriate destination from there. The problem is, with wireless networks, you have radio waves, which aren't confined to the inside of a wire. Radio waves go all over the place, just like when you throw a rock in the water and make waves that spread out in a circle.

The radio waves can be a problem when you have multiple wireless networks that are close to each other. For example, let's say that a company has several departments, and each department has its own, separate wireless network. If the departments are fairly close to each other in the same building, it's possible that network messages from one department might get picked up by another department's wireless access point, which in turn might send the message off to a computer in its own network rather than to the correct recipient.

To avoid that problem, you need some means of discriminating among multiple wireless access points. For example, you need some means of setting rules like "these six computers in the marketing department communicate only with each other through access point X, while these 12 computers in Accounting communicate with each other, only, through access point Z." The way you do that in today's wireless networking is through things such as network names, SSID, WEP, and WPA.

About SSIDs

Every wireless network has a unique name called a *service set identifier* (SSID) or just a *wireless network name* for simplicity. The access point in the network holds the SSID, and broadcasts it out at regular intervals. When you start a wireless network computer, it scans the airwaves for SSID. When you set up a wireless network access point (by reading the manufacturer's instructions, of course), you assign an SSID to your access point.

The name you assign doesn't have to be anything fancy, but it should be unique enough to avoid conflict with any close neighbors who also have wireless networks. The SSID doesn't provide any real network security. After all, the access point broadcasts the SSID out some distance from the access point. So if some hackers happened to be driving by with a notebook computer, they might be able to pick up the name of your wireless LAN from the car. Then they could join your network and receive data being sent by computers in your network. WEP and WPA are encryption tools designed to avoid such intrusions.

About WEP and WPA

Open System Wired Equivalent Protocol (WEP) is a wireless security protocol that protects wireless network data from falling into the wrong hands. Before any information leaves your computer, it's encrypted using a WEP key. The key is a simple string of characters that you can generate automatically, or have Windows generate for you.

Wi-Fi Protected Access (WPA) is a newer and stronger encryption system that supports modern EAP security devices such as smart cards, certificates, token cards, one-time passwords, and biometric devices. Eventually, IEEE will release a new 802.11i standard, which will offer the type of security currently found only in WPA. If your wireless networking hardware supports both WEP and WPA, you should go with WPA because that's the wave of the future.

Installing the wireless networking hardware

The most critical step in setting up a wireless network is installing the hardware devices. It's imperative that you follow the instructions that came with the device to a tee, because guessing almost never works. In particular, it's important to note that even devices that plug into a hot-pluggable port like USB devices or a PC Card need you to install drives *before* you install the hardware device. That's unusual for hot-pluggable devices, and most people just assume that they can plug in the device and go. But it just doesn't work that way with wireless networking devices.

Connecting to available networks

The main trick to wireless networking is setting up the base station (access point). Typically, you do this by choosing one computer to operate the access point, and you configure the access point from that computer. There you give the network its name (SSID) and choose your encryption method. The access point then begins transmitting that name at regular intervals.

On any computer that's to join the LAN, you install a wireless network adapter. On a notebook computer, it's likely that a card resides internal to the system. On a desktop computer, you can install an internal wireless network adapter, connect one to a USB port, or even slide one into a Compact Flash slot.

Once you've installed the network adapter, you can check and configure one of the available networks by following these steps. If you have enabled security on your access point, move on to the next set of steps. To connect to an unsecured access point, follow these steps:

1. Click the Start button and choose Control Panel.
2. If Control Panel opens in Category view, click the Network and Internet icon.
3. Open the View Network Status and Tasks link below Network and Sharing Center.
4. As shown in Figure 51-11, the system is not connected to a network, but this window indicates that wireless networks are available.

FIGURE 51-11

Windows sees that networks are available.

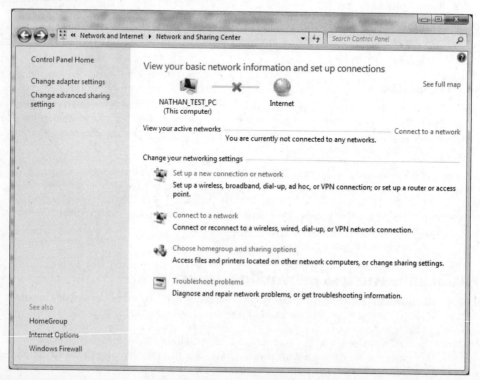

5. After clicking the Connect to a Network link, you will see what networks Windows says are available in screens similar to Figure 51-12.

FIGURE 51-12

Windows sees two networks.

6. If you choose an unsecured network and click the Connect button, Windows may prompt you with a window confirming that you want to connect to an unsecured network. Click to connect to the unsecured network.

7. After Windows has successfully connected to the network, a dialog box may pop up asking what type of network you just connected to. To learn more about the different types of network categories, search for Network Categories under Windows Help and select "What are network categories?"

If you have enabled either WEP or WPA encryption at your access point, you can follow these steps to get connected to your wireless network:

1. Click the Start button and choose Control Panel.

2. If Control Panel opens in Category view, click the Network and Internet icon.

3. Open the View Network Status and Tasks link below Network and Sharing Center.

4. As shown in Figure 51-11, the system is not connected to a network, but this window indicates that wireless networks are available.

5. After clicking the Connect to a Network link, you will see what networks Windows says are available in a screen similar to Figure 51-12.

6. Click the desired wireless network and then click Connect.

7. Windows prompts for the network security key (Figure 51-13). Type the key and click OK. Windows will connect to the wireless network.

FIGURE 51-13

Windows prompts for the network security key.

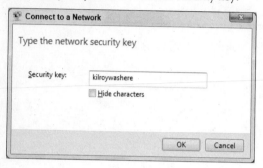

If you need to retype the network security key or change other wireless properties, follow these steps:

1. Open the Control Panel and click View Network Status and Tasks.

2. Click Manage Wireless Networks in the left pane.

3. In the Manage Wireless Networks window, right-click the wireless connection and choose Properties. Figure 51-14 shows the Connection tab of this dialog box.

FIGURE 51-14

Wireless Network Properties allow you to connect to this network automatically.

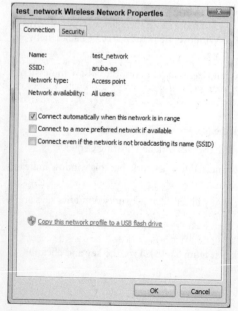

4. Click the Security tab shown in Figure 51-15.

Security tab for a wireless network connection.

5. Select the security type, encryption type, and enter a network security key based on the configuration of your access point. Then, click the OK button.

6. Click the wireless network icon in the tray to view the available networks, click the network you want to connect, and click Connect. After a few seconds your system should be connected to your local network and also the Internet if you have configured your router. To test this, use Internet Explorer and try browsing to a Web site.

The notification icon

Windows 7 can include your network connectivity information within the Notification area. The icon for a wired connection is a computer with a network cable beside it. The icon for a wireless connection is a set of signal strength bars. If you don't see an icon, check to make sure that it's not just hidden by clicking the < button at the left side of the Notification area. If you still don't see the icon, right-click an empty space on the taskbar and select Customize Notification Icons. Beside the Network item, click the drop-down list under the Behaviors column and choose Show Icon and Notifications. Then, click the OK button.

When you've finished, you're ready to move on to Chapter 52 where you learn to share resources and use those shared resources from any computer in the network.

Wrap-Up

A local area network (LAN) consists of two or more computers that can communicate with one another through networking hardware. Multiple computers in a network can share a single Internet account, share printers, and share files and folders. Moving and copying files between networked computers is a simple matter of dragging and dropping. No fumbling around with floppies, CDs, or other removable disks is required. The main points to remember when it comes to buying network hardware are as follows:

- The first step to creating a LAN is to purchase the computer networking hardware.
- Each computer in the network needs a network interface card (NIC) installed.
- Ethernet LANs provide the fastest speeds, but require running special Ethernet cables.
- Wireless networking provides complete freedom from cables and wires.
- USB networking devices are easy to install and don't require opening the computer case.
- On a notebook computer, you can use a PC Card NIC (not to be confused with PCI card) to connect to the network or an integrated wireless network card.
- After you acquire your network hardware, you have to set it all up per the manufacturer's instructions. When you've finished that step, you can use the Network and Sharing Center to help configure the hardware.

Sharing Resources on a Network

A local area network (LAN) consists of two or more computers connected through some sort of networking hardware. In a local area network, you can use *shared resources* from other computers in much the same way as you use local resources on your own computer. In fact, the way you do things in a LAN is almost identical to the way you do things on a single computer.

For example, everything you learned about printing documents on your own computer earlier in this book works just as well for printing on a network printer. Opening a document on some other computer in a network is no different from opening a document on your own computer.

Before you can access shared resources, however, you need to share them. You have more than one method for sharing resources, and this chapter covers those methods. Before getting into the particulars of resource sharing, the following section takes a quick look at some terminology.

Some Networking Buzzwords

Networking has its own set of buzzwords. All the buzzwords you learned in earlier chapters still apply, but you have some new words to learn, as defined here:

- **Resource:** Items you use on the network, including a folder, shared media, a printer, or other device.

- **Shared resource:** A resource accessible to other users within a network. A shared folder is often referred to as a *share* or *network share*.

- **Local computer:** The computer at which you're currently sitting.

- **Local resource:** A folder, printer, or other useful thing on the local computer or directly connected to the local computer by a cable. For example, if there's a printer connected to your computer by a cable, it's a local resource (or more specifically, a *local printer*).

- **Remote computer:** Any computer in the network other than the one at which you're currently sitting.

- **Remote resource:** A folder, printer, or other useful thing on some computer other than the local computer. For example, a printer connected to someone else's computer on the network is a remote resource (or more specifically, a *remote printer*).

Figure 52-1 shows an example of how the terms *local* and *remote* are always used in reference to the computer at which you're currently sitting.

FIGURE 52-1

Examples of local and remote resources, from your perspective.

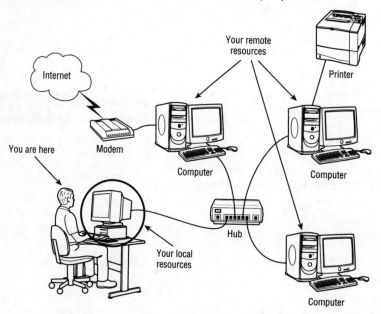

Methods for Sharing in Windows 7

Windows 7 includes three methods for sharing resources, each of which has its own advantages. The following sections explain these different methods.

Tip

See Chapter 24 to learn about sharing media with Media Player. ■

Homegroups

Homegroups are a new feature in Windows 7 designed to simplify resource sharing and access for home networks. The first Windows 7 computer added to a network creates the homegroup, and then other Windows 7 computers on that same network can join the homegroup. Once your computer is part of the homegroup, you have access to the resources shared by the other computers in the homegroup.

Note
See "Windows 7 Homegroups" later in this chapter to learn how to create and join a homegroup. ■

When you use a homegroup for sharing, you specify which folders you want to share. You can share those folders with either read or read/write permissions with the rest of the homegroup. You can also set permissions on a per-user basis to allow one person to access a folder or file but not others.

Only Windows 7 computers can participate in a homegroup. A computer running any edition of Windows 7 can join a homegroup, but computers running Windows 7 Home Basic and Windows 7 Starter can only join a homegroup, not create one.

Note
Computers in a homegroup do not have to belong to the same workgroup. ■

Workgroup

Although homegroups are a great new way to share resources in a network, only the Windows 7 computers on the network can participate. Computers running other versions of Windows cannot participate in the homegroup. In these situations, you can use workgroups to share resources on the network.

A Windows PC, regardless of the version of Windows it is running, must be a member of either a workgroup or a domain (covered in the next section). A workgroup isn't a boundary that controls security. Rather, workgroups provide a means for organizing and discovering resources on the network.

The default workgroup name in Windows is, not surprisingly, Workgroup. Computers that share the same workgroup name and which reside on the same network segment appear grouped together when you browse the network. Figure 52-2 shows a workgroup.

To access shared resources in a workgroup, you must have an account on the computer that is sharing the resource. Assuming a small home network of three computers and the desire to access resources on each one, this means you either need to have your own account on each computer or you create a common account on each computer that everyone uses for sharing resources.

Domain

In a domain environment, one or more domain controllers running Windows Server host all user accounts in a centralized directory called Active Directory (AD). Typically, rather than belong to a workgroup, your computer would be joined to the domain. When you log on, you log on with a domain account (stored in AD) rather than a local account (stored on your local computer).

In a domain, AD handles authentication services. So, if you share a folder on your computer, you can specify which other domain users or groups can access that shared resources, and what permissions they have in it. The advantage of this type of resource sharing is that every user needs only a single user account in AD, and that account can be used to access resources anywhere on the network.

How to choose?

If you are setting up a home network and all of your computers are running Windows 7, a homegroup probably makes the most sense. If your home network includes Windows Vista or Windows XP computers, using a common workgroup to share resources is a good option. Or, you can use a hybrid model where your Windows 7 computers share their resources through a homegroup and other computers use the workgroup.

FIGURE 52-2

Browsing a workgroup for shared resources.

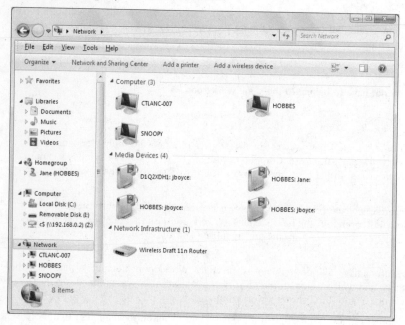

In a business network, the number of computers generally dictates whether you choose a workgroup or a domain model for sharing. You can set up a Windows workstation as a file server, create an account for each person on the network on that computer, and use it to share resources. Whether you choose that route or use a domain and Windows Server for sharing really depends on how you will be using the network. In most cases, when you get about 5–10 computers, a domain and server make the most sense.

Tip

Windows client computers running Windows Vista and earlier are limited to a maximum of 10 concurrent connections, making them useful for centralized sharing in small networks but not in larger ones. Windows 7 supports up to 20 concurrent connections. ∎

Note

Using a domain for sharing implies that you have one or more centralized file and print servers on the network, so sharing from your client computer is unlikely (although possible). For that reason, I don't cover domain sharing in detail in this chapter. ∎

Turn on Sharing and Discovery

Before you start sharing resources on your network, you need to make sure you configure Windows 7 to enable it to share and access shared resources. By default, Windows does not make network resources available to everyone. Instead, Windows 7 requires users to explicitly share resources before others can access them.

A first step on each computer is to make sure sharing and discovery is enabled, and all computers belong to the same workgroup. You need administrative privileges to makes these kinds of changes, so log in to an account that has those privileges before you get started. Then get to the Network and Sharing Center using either of these methods:

- Click the Start button and choose Control Panel ➪ Network and Internet ➪ Network and Sharing Center.
- Press ⊞, type **net**, and click Network and Sharing Center.

The center opens as in Figure 52-3.

FIGURE 52-3

Network and Sharing Center.

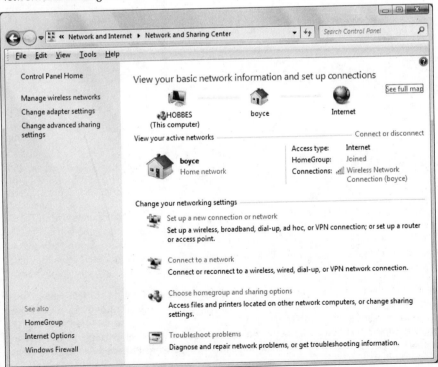

Tip

If you see any messages about connecting to your network for the first time and questions about the network type, choose Home Network. Your local network is a private network. The Internet is a public network. ■

If you see Unidentified Network or Public Network where the figure shows a Home Network, click the link under View Your Active Networks. Change the setting to Home Network as in Figure 52-4.

FIGURE 52-4

Select the network location type.

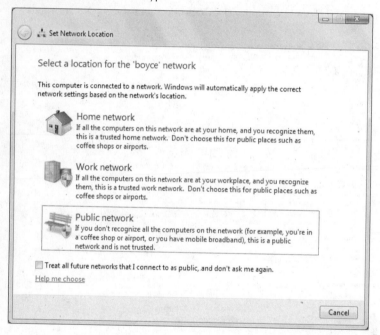

Designating the network as a home network makes it discoverable to other computers within the same private network. However, it's important that all computers belong to the same workgroup, particularly if you are going to use workgroup sharing rather than a homegroup. So on each computer you also want to make sure Network Discovery is turned on and all computers have the same workgroup name.

In the Network and Sharing Center, click Change Advanced Sharing Settings in the left pane to open the Advanced Sharing Settings dialog box (Figure 52-5). In the dialog box, turn on Network Discovery and File And Printer Sharing under the Home or Work profile. If you want to use the Public folders, also choose the option to turn on Public Folder Sharing. If you want to enable people to access shared resources without a user account, choose the option Turn Off Password Protected Sharing. Otherwise, turn on this option. Finally, if you are using a homegroup, you can specify that Windows manages the homegroup connections automatically, or choose to use user accounts and passwords in the homegroup. Leave this option at the default of Allow Windows to Manage Homegroup Connections.

If yours is a small network and you won't be using a domain for sharing, make sure all computers are in the same workgroup. On a Windows 7 or Windows Vista computer, click the Start menu, right-click Computer, and choose Properties. In the resulting System dialog box, click Advanced System Settings in the left pane, then click the Computer Name tab (Figure 52-6). On a Windows XP computer, click the Start menu, right-click My Computer, and choose Properties to open the System Properties dialog box.

FIGURE 52-5

Advanced Sharing Settings dialog box.

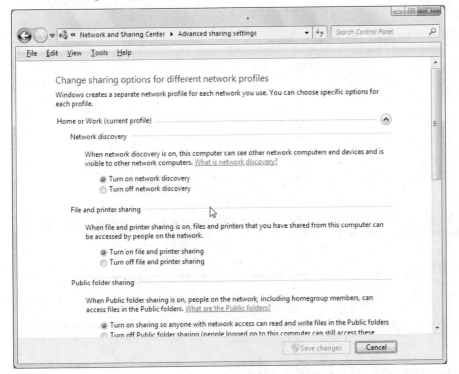

The Computer Name tab shows the current computer name, description, and workgroup name. If the workgroup isn't what you need it to be, click the Change button. In the resulting Computer Name/Domain Changes dialog box, click the Workgroup option and type the required workgroup name in the Workgroup text box. Then, click OK. Click OK again to close the System Properties dialog box.

When you've turned on all the Sharing and Discovery options and set the workgroup name, you're ready to move to the next computer in the network and repeat the process. Once all of the computers have sharing and discovery enabled and belong to the same workgroup, they'll be able to find each others' shared resources. But it's still up to each user to decide what they want to share. The sections that follow look at techniques for sharing resources.

FIGURE 52-6

The Computer Name tab of the System Properties dialog box.

Note

You can share media files from Windows Media Library, rather than from the folders in which those files are contained. See Chapter 24 for details. ■

New Feature

H omegroups simplify setting up a home network and sharing resources on the network.

Windows 7 Homegroups

Homegroups are a new feature in Windows 7 that simplify setting up a home network and sharing resources on the network. When you set up a Windows 7 computer, Windows creates a homegroup automatically if one doesn't already exist, and generates a network password for the homegroup. With that network password, other Windows 7 computers on the network can join the homegroup, and users on those computers can access resources that are shared by other computers in the homegroup.

Tip

Computers must be running Windows 7 to participate in a homegroup, and support for homegroups is included in all editions of Windows 7. However, Windows 7 Starter and Windows 7 Home Basic can participate in a homegroup but cannot create one. ■

Finding or changing the homegroup password

If Windows 7 doesn't find an existing homegroup, it creates one. From that point on, you can add other Windows 7 computers to that existing homegroup. All you need is the homegroup password, which Windows 7 creates automatically when it creates the homegroup.

If you don't already know the homegroup password, open the Control Panel and under Network and Internet, click Choose Homegroup and Sharing Options. In the Homegroup applet, click View or Print the Homegroup Password. A dialog box opens (Figure 52-7) and displays the password. Click Print This Page if you need a printed copy.

FIGURE 52-7

View or print your homegroup password.

As mentioned previously, Windows 7 sets the homegroup password when it sets up the homegroup. If needed, you can change the password. To do so, first make sure all of the computers in the homegroup are turned on. Then, open the Homegroup applet as explained previously and click Change the Password. In the resulting dialog box, click Change the Password. Windows generates a new password that you can use, or you can type your own password. In either case, click Next when you're satisfied with the new password.

Next, go to each of the other computers on the homegroup and open the Homegroup applet from the Control Panel. Windows 7 detects that the password has changed and gives you the opportunity to change it (Figure 52-8). Click the Type New Password button, type the new password, and click Next. After the password has been changed, click Finish. Repeat the process on all of the other Windows 7 computers on your homegroup.

Set a new homegroup password.

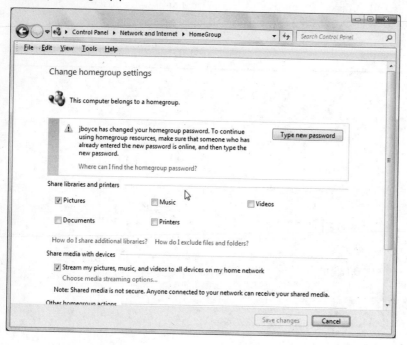

Joining a homegroup

When you add a new Windows 7 computer to your network, you can add it to your homegroup (although you don't have to unless you want the computer to participate in the homegroup). To add a computer to the homegroup, boot the computer and make sure the computer is on the network. See Chapter 51 if you need help with that.

Next, open the Control Panel and then open the Homegroup applet. Click the Join Now button, then in the resulting Join a Homegroup dialog box (Figure 52-9), choose which items you want to share. Then, click Next. Type the homegroup password, click Next, and click Finish.

Sharing items with the homegroup

If you change your mind about what you want to share with the homegroup, you can change sharing options accordingly. To do so, open the Homegroup applet from the Control Panel (Figure 52-10). If you just want to choose which items to share, place a check beside those you want to share and deselect the check box by those you don't want shared.

FIGURE 52-9

Choose the items to share with the homegroup.

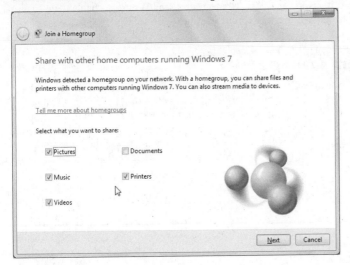

FIGURE 52-10

Sharing items with the homegroup.

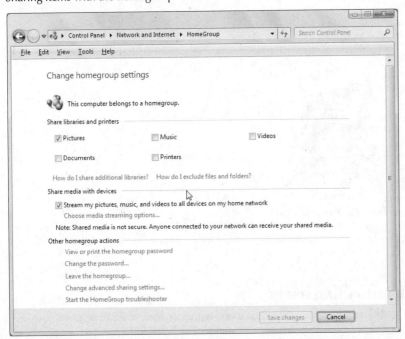

You can easily share other items with your homegroup. To do so, open the folder containing the item you want to share. For example, if you want to share a folder in the My Documents folder, open My Documents, click the folder, and in the toolbar click Share With, then choose Homegroup (Read) to give others the capability to read items in the folder, Homegroup (Read/Write) to enable them to also write to the folder, or Nobody to remove the folder from sharing.

Excluding items from sharing

In some situations, you might want to share a folder or library, but exclude access to certain folders or even individual files. Excluding a folder or file is simply a matter of setting its sharing to Nobody. Open the folder containing the folder you want to exclude, or in the case of an individual file, open the folder containing the file. Click the item you want to exclude, click Share With in the toolbar, and choose Nobody. That library, folder, or file will not show up when others browse the homegroup. On the system where the item resides, it will have a lock icon beside it to indicate that it is not shared (Figure 52-11).

FIGURE 52-11

Excluded items show a lock icon.

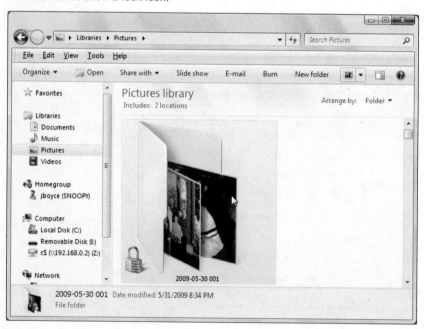

Sharing with individual users

You can also share folders and files with individual users, but those users must have an account on your computer and access the files from that same computer. For example, if you have a single home computer you share with your spouse and children, you might want to share a folder with only your spouse and not the children. To share the folder or file, open the folder containing the item to be shared, click it, and click Share With in the toolbar. Choose Specific People to open the File Sharing dialog box, choose an account from the drop-down list, and click Add. Then, click Share to close the dialog box.

To access a folder or file that has been shared in this way, open the Network folder, expand the local computer, then the Users folder, and finally the user who is sharing the folder or file.

Using Public Folders

Windows 7 (and Windows Vista) includes a Public folder from which files are shared automatically. This feature is similar to the Shared Documents folder in Windows XP. You can simply move any files that you intend to share across all user accounts or computers in a private network to that folder. To get to that folder:

1. Open any folder (for example, click the Start button and choose Computer or your user name).

2. Expand a library in the left pane until you see the library's Public folder, as in Figure 52-12.

FIGURE 52-12

Public folders in various libraries.

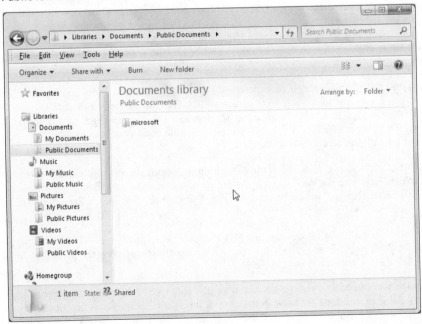

The Public folders you see in the Navigation pane are actually all contained in a single folder named Public in the Users folder. (The default path is C:\Users\Public.) The Public folder is organized much like your Documents folders. It contains subfolders for storing Documents, Downloads, Music, Pictures, and Videos. If you have the Premium or Ultimate Edition of Windows 7, it also contains a Recorded TV folder, in which Media Center–recorded TV files are stored.

Tip
Clicking the leftmost button in the address bar of any folder also provides a quick link to the Public folder. ■

Perhaps the easiest way to move files into a Public folder would be to open one of its subfolders, like Public Documents or Public Pictures. Then open the folder that contains the files you want to share. Size and position the two windows so you can see both. Then drag files from one folder to the other. See Chapter 29 for more information on moving and copying files.

The Public folder is shared in a way where every user on the computer (and in the network) has free reign over its contents. In other words, every user has equal rights to the Public folder. If you have files you want to share more selectively, such as only with certain people or only with certain permissions, use the method described previously in the section, "Sharing with individual users."

Advanced Sharing

Advanced Sharing allows a user with administrative privileges to set custom permissions for multiple users, control the number of simultaneous connections and caching for offline files, and set other advanced properties. Some of these topics require training in or knowledge of network administration. The Public folder and selective sharing methods described in the preceding sections should be adequate for a home network, and much easier to work with.

For people who understand the concepts (and potential problems) involved, I'll just quickly run through the process. Locate the folder you want to share, right-click that folder's icon, and choose Properties. Click the Sharing tab and click Advanced Sharing. Elevate your privileges (if prompted) and choose Share This Folder. Then click the Apply button. Set the number of simultaneous users up to a maximum of 20 and (optionally) add a comment.

To configure sharing permissions, click the Permissions button to open the Permissions dialog box for the shared folder. Here you can view existing sharing permissions and also add and remove users and groups. You'll notice that you are limited to specifying Full Control, Change, or Read permission sharing levels.

If the disk where the shared folder resides is on an NTFS volume, you can also set NTFS permissions, which are more flexible than sharing permissions. To set NTFS permissions, open the properties for the folder and click the Security tab (Figure 52-13).

On the Security tab you can add or remove users and groups and specify the permission levels for each one. The available permissions are more granular than the sharing permissions described previously, giving you finer control over what each user or group can do in the folder. As you assign permissions, keep in mind that the most restrictive permissions apply. For example, if you share a folder and apply Full Control for all users, but then set NTFS permissions so that all users have only Read access, then the more restrictive NTFS permissions will apply and users will only be able to read items in the folder, not modify them.

FIGURE 52-13

Security tab for NTFS permissions.

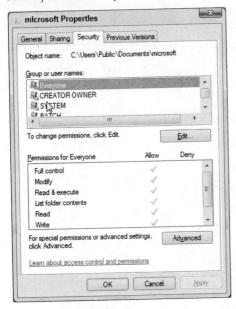

Identifying Shared Folders

In Windows 7 you have a few methods for identifying which folders are shared. First, in Windows Explorer, click a folder. If the folder is shared, you'll see the words "State: Shared" in the status bar at the bottom of the window.

You can also use the Shared Folders snap-in with the Computer Management console to see which folders are shared. To open Shared Folders, click Start, right-click Computer, and choose Manage. When the Computer Management console opens, expand the Shared Folders branch and click Shares. The folders that are shared, whether visible or hidden, appear in the right pane.

You can also use the NET command in a command console to see what is shared. Open a command console and type the command **NET SHARE** to see a listing of shared resources.

Sharing a Printer

Printers in a local area network will usually be connected to one of the computers in that network. To ensure that the printer is shared, so everybody in the network can use it, follow these steps:

Tip

With the right hardware, you can connect a printer directly to a LAN without going through a computer. With that type of arrangement, you need only to make sure that the printer is turned on and connected to the network, and configured with network settings appropriate for your network. ■

FIGURE 52-14

Sharing a printer.

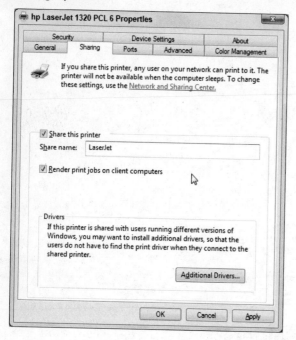

1. Go to the computer to which the printer is connected by cable. If either is turned off, turn on the printer first and the computer second.
2. Click Start ⇨ Devices and Printers.
3. Double-click the icon of the printer that you want to share.
4. Double-click Customize Your Printer to open the Properties dialog box for the printer.
5. Click the Sharing tab, then select Share This Printer, type a name in the Share Name text box, and choose to render print jobs on the client as in Figure 52-14.

Note

The Render Print Jobs on Client Computers option lets each user control print jobs from his or her own computer. In earlier versions of Windows, most print jobs had to be managed from the printer to which the computer was physically attached. ■

6. Click OK.

When you click the printer's icon in Devices and Printers, the status bar will indicate that the printer is shared. The printer should show up automatically in all network computers' Print dialog boxes. If it doesn't show up on a particular computer, see Chapter 35 for information on installing a shared network printer.

What about Sharing Programs?

Though you can share folders and documents freely on a LAN, there's no way to share programs. You can only run programs currently installed on your computer and accessible from your All Programs menu. If you try to open a document on another computer, but don't have the appropriate program for that document type, you can't open the document.

Don't bother trying to copy an installed program from one computer to another — except in rare cases it won't work. Only programs that you specifically install on your own computer will run on your computer.

The only solution will be to install the necessary program on your own computer. If the program you need is free, like Adobe Acrobat Reader, you can download and install the program in the usual manner. (For Acrobat Reader, go to www.adobe.com and click Get Adobe Reader.)

Wrap-Up

People create computer networks to share resources among computers. Resources include things such as an Internet connection, media files, folders, and printers. Windows 7's sharing and discovery makes it relatively easy to share resources and discover them. This chapter has focused on the "sharing" part. In summary:

- To turn on sharing and discovery, open the Network and Sharing Center. Make sure you are connected to your private network and that all computers in the network share a common workgroup name.

- For maximum ease-of-use, turn on all the options under Sharing and Discovery.

- Use a homegroup to easily share resources among Windows 7 computers on a small network.

- To share your media library, open Windows Media Player, click the button under Library, and choose Media Sharing.

- To share a printer, use the Sharing tab of its Properties dialog box.

- One way to share files is to move them to the Public folder or one of its subfolders.

- Use the Computer Management console or the NET SHARE command to see which folders are shared.

Using Shared Resources

Chapters 51 and 52 covered all the basics of setting up and sharing resources on a private home or small business network. This chapter assumes that you've already done all of that. Nothing in this chapter will work until the network is set up, you've turned on network sharing and discovery on each Windows 7 computer, and shared some things on the network.

This chapter looks at how you find and use shared resources from computers within the network. It looks at opening documents from remote resources, moving and copying files between networked computers, using remote printers, and ways of using shared media.

UNC Paths

Before diving too deep into methods for accessing network resources, let's take some time to delve into a topic that will help you navigate network resources more easily — UNC paths.

UNC stands for Universal Naming Convention. A UNC path is expressed in the form:

```
\\MachineName\PathName
```

where `MachineName` is the name of the computer and `PathName` is a folder path on that computer. For example, assume that your network includes a computer named SNOOPY that you use as a file server. On that computer is a folder that you have shared as SharedDocs. Within that SharedDocs folder is a subfolder named Contracts. The UNC path to the Contracts folder would be \\SNOOPY\SharedDocs\Contracts. Note that the UNC path is not case-sensitive.

A UNC path makes it easy to navigate the network, particularly when you know the path name already. Using a UNC path is often quicker than navigating to the Network folder, then to a remote computer, and drilling down through its shared folders. Instead, you can open the Computer folder, click in the address bar, and simply type the UNC path to the remote share that you want to use.

Another point to understand is that you can specify the IP address of the remote computer in place of the computer name in the UNC path. So, assuming that our trusty computer named SNOOPY has the IP address 192.168.0.5, the UNC path to the Contracts folder would be \\192.168.0.5\SharedDocs\Contracts.

Now that you're up to speed on UNC paths, let's take a look at how to access network resources.

Accessing Remote Resources

Every Windows 7 computer on which you've enabled network sharing and discovery should show up in every computer's Network folder. The same is true of any Windows Vista and XP computers in the network that have at least one shared resource (such as the built-in Shared Documents folder). To open the Network folder on a Windows 7 computer, use whichever technique is most convenient:

- Click the Start button and choose Network.
- Press ![Windows logo], type **net**, click Network and Sharing Center, and then click the icon for the network in the network map.
- If you're already in a Windows Explorer folder, click Network in the Folders list.

Tip

The Network icon does not appear on the Start menu by default. Right-click the taskbar and choose Properties, then click the Start Menu tab, click Customize, select Network, and click OK. ■

The first time you open the Network folder on a computer, it might take a few seconds for it to discover other computers in the network. But within a few seconds you should see an icon for each computer in the network as in the example shown in Figure 53-1. Notice how each computer is also accessible from the Folders list after expanding the Network category in that list.

Each computer's icon is like a folder in that when you open it, you see shared resources from that computer. That includes a folder icon for each shared folder and printer icons for any shared printers connected to that computer.

If you use the Network folder often, you'll want to make sure it's easy to find its icon. To put a Network icon on your desktop, right-click the desktop and choose Personalize. In the left column, click Change Desktop Icons. Select the Network check box (and the check boxes of any other icons you want) and click OK.

If you don't have a Network option on the right side of your Start menu, you can add one using methods for customizing the Start menu discussed in Chapter 10.

To add Network to your Favorite Links in Windows Explorer, open a folder and make sure you can see the Navigation pane. Open the Folders list, and then drag the Network icon in the Folders list into the Favorites Bar.

Tip

Any time you're in Windows Explorer, clicking the leftmost arrow in the address bar usually provides a quick link to the Network folder. ■

FIGURE 53-1

Sample Network folder.

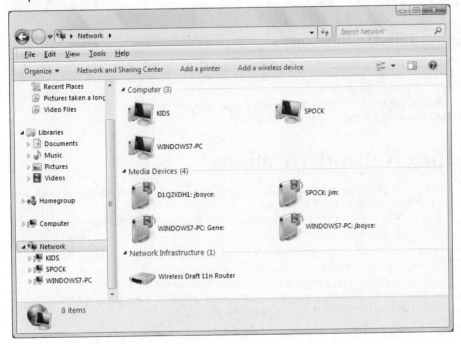

Opening Remote Documents

One of the advantages to having a network is that you can put documents in shared folders and open them from any computer in the network. For example, you might put all your important work documents in a shared folder on your main work computer. If you also have a portable computer you can use outside on sunny days (or from the sofa on lazy days), you can work directly with those documents from the remote computer.

The process is really no different from opening a document on a local computer. You could, for instance, just navigate to the folder, via the Network folder, in which the document is stored. Or, open the Computer folder, type the UNC path to the shared folder in the address bar, and press Enter. Then, double-click (or click) the document you want to edit, and the document will open from the remote computer (providing that the local computer has the appropriate program installed for working with that type of document).

Optionally, you can go through the program's Open dialog box to get to the document. Here's how:

1. Open the program you want to use and choose File ➪ Open from its menu bar.

2. In the Open dialog box, click Network (if available) at the left side of the dialog box.

3. First select the computer on the network where the document resides. Then navigate to the folder for (or a parent folder to) the document. If you have to open a parent folder, just navigate down through the subfolders until you get to the document's icon.

4. Click or double-click the document's icon.

Once the document is open, you can edit it or print it however you like. When you save the document, your changes will be saved at the original location. If you want to save a local copy of the document to work with, choose File ➪ Save As from the program's menu bar, navigate to a local folder such as your Documents folder, and save your copy there.

Opening a Read-Only copy

If you try to open a document that someone already has open on another computer, you might see a message telling you what your options are. Those options will vary from one program to the next. For example, you might be offered the option to open a read-only copy of the document, or open a copy of the document. If you choose to open a read-only copy, you can then choose File ➪ Save As in the program and save a local copy that you can modify.

Creating Network Locations

If you have your own Web site, or permission to upload to an FTP site, SharePoint site, or really anything on the Internet to which you can upload files, you can add an icon for that location to your Computer folder. Doing so will allow you to upload files to that location using the same techniques you use to save a file to your own computer.

You'll need to know the URL (address) to which you can download. Chances are you'll need a username and password as well. The people who own the site to which you'll be uploading will provide that information when you set up your account. They might also provide upload instructions. But as long as you know the URL and your username and password, you should be able to use the technique described here in addition to whatever method they provide.

To create a link to the Internet location, follow these steps:

1. Open your Computer folder.
2. Right-click any unused space in the window and choose Add a Network Location.
3. Click Next on the first wizard page.
4. Click Choose a Custom Network Location and click Next.
5. Type the complete URL of the remote site. For example, if it's a Web site you own, include the http://. For instance, in Figure 53-2 I'm about to create a shortcut to the www.boyce.us site. If the shortcut is to an FTP site for which you have upload permissions, use the ftp:// prefix on the URL. Click Next. To see a list of examples, click the View Examples link in the middle of the window.
6. If the remote resource requires a username and password, you'll be prompted to enter your credentials. Enter the credentials and click OK.
7. The next wizard page will suggest the URL (without the http:// or ftp:// prefix) as the name of the shortcut icon. You can replace that with any name you like, because it's used only as the label for the shortcut. Type the desired name and click Next.
8. On the last wizard page, you can select (check) the check box Open This Network Location When I Click Finish if you want to see the remote folder immediately. Or clear the check box if you don't want to see that right now. Then click Finish.

When you double-click the icon for the remote site, it will open in Windows Explorer, looking much the same as any local folder on your own hard disk. You may not have quite as many options to choose from in the Explorer bar. Figure 53-3 shows an example where I've opened a SharePoint site.

FIGURE 53-2

Providing the URL of an Internet resource.

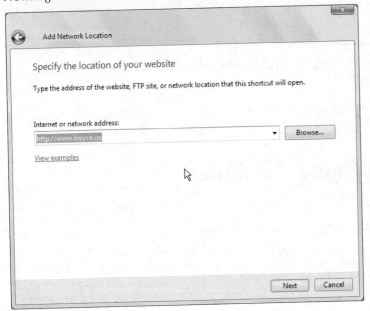

FIGURE 53-3

SharePoint site as a folder in Windows Explorer.

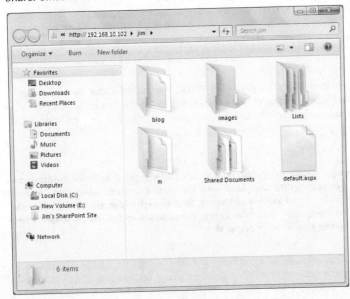

You can treat the folder as you would any other. For example, you can create a new folder, or rename or delete existing files and folders by right-clicking, just as you would in any folder on your C: drive. You can also move and copy files to/from the site. Things will be slower than on your own computer, because the remote resource could be thousands of miles away, but the techniques should all be the same.

Tip

You can rename any icon, at any time, under Network Locations just as you would any other icon. Just right-click the icon and choose Rename. ■

If things don't work as described here, your best resource for getting answers would be the people who provided the site. They're the only ones who know the details of that site.

Saving to a Remote Computer

Any time you save a new document — whether it's one you've created yourself, or something you're downloading — a Save As dialog box (or something similar) will open, enabling you to save the file. The dialog box will have a Folders list so that you can choose where you want to save the document.

As with the Open dialog box, you can choose the Network folder from the Folders list to get to all of the locations in your Network folder, and then navigate to wherever you want to save the file from there. Or, click in the text box where you would normally enter the filename and instead enter a UNC path to the folder where you want to store the file. After the folder opens in the dialog box, enter the filename.

Downloading Programs to a Network Share

If you regularly download programs to install on multiple computers, consider using the folder named Public Downloads within your Public folder. After you save a downloaded program file to that folder, you'll be able to install it on all the computers in the network. You still have to install it on each computer individually, but there is no need to download it on every computer, especially if you're sharing a not-so-speedy Internet connection.

Start by creating the Public Downloads folder in your own Public Documents folder, or on another shared folder on your network. Then, initiate the download as you normally would. When the File Download dialog box appears, click Save. In the Save As dialog box, navigate to the shared Public Downloads folder and save the file there.

Tip

You can download the file from the computer where the Public Downloads folder resides, or from another computer on the network. The advantage of performing the download from the same computer where the file will be stored is that you minimize network traffic. If you are instead saving to a shared folder across the network, the file comes through the network to your computer, then goes across the network to the shared folder, effectively doubling the network traffic and slowing down the process. ■

After the file has been downloaded, you can access it from any other computer on the network to install the program. Just browse the network from the computer where you want to install the program, open the shared Public Downloads folder, and double-click the file to begin the installation.

Note

Some programs need to be installed from a local copy of the file, rather than across the network. If you have problems installing across the network, copy the file across the network to the local computer and install from that local copy. ■

Transferring Files between Computers

Moving and copying files on a LAN is virtually identical to doing so on a single computer. You can use any of the techniques described in Chapter 29 to select, move, or copy files from any folder on your own computer to any shared folder or from any shared folder to any folder on your own computer. You can also use those same techniques to move and copy files between shared folders on any two remote computers on the network.

For example, let's say you're sitting at a computer named Hobbes, and you have a bunch of files in a subfolder named Shared Docs\Common Downloads on a computer named Spock. So, the UNC path would be \\Spock\SharedDocs\Common Downloads. You want to copy one or more files to the Downloads folder of your own user account on Hobbes. Just open the Network folder. Then open the Spock, SharedDocs, and Common Downloads folders. Then, click the Start button and open the Documents folder for your user account. It might be easiest if you size and position the windows so you can see the contents of both as in Figure 53-4.

FIGURE 53-4

Remote shared folder (top) and local folder (bottom).

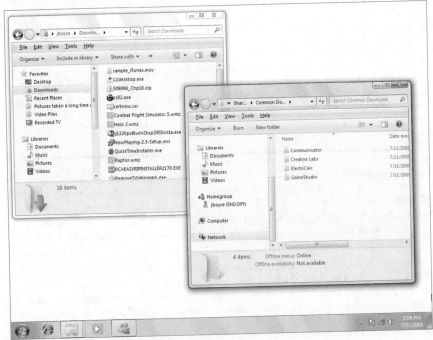

With both folders open, as in the figure, you can select the files you want to copy in the remote folder using any technique you like, as discussed in Chapter 29. To copy (rather than move) the items to the remote folder, right-drag any selected icon to the remote folder, and then choose Copy Here after you release the mouse button. (If you drag using the left mouse button, the files will be moved, rather than copied.) That's all there is to it. As I said, it's no different from moving and copying files between folders and drives on your own computer, except that you have to use the Network folder or a UNC path to open the remote folder.

Mapping Drive Letters to Shared Folders

Some programs require that you assign a drive letter to remote resources. You can assign any unused drive letter to a resource. For example, if you already have drives A: through F: in use, you can assign drive letters G: through Z: to any shared resource. To map a drive letter to a shared folder:

1. Go to the computer on which you need to assign a drive letter to a remote share.

2. Open any folder (such as the Computer folder), press the Alt key to view the Classic menu, and choose Tools ⇨ Map Network Drive from Explorer's menu bar. The Map Network Drive dialog box opens.

3. Click the Browse button if the Folder entry is not filled in already to open the Browse for Folder dialog box.

4. In the Browse for Folder dialog box, click the name of the shared resource to which you want to map a drive letter, so its name is selected (highlighted). For example, in Figure 53-5 I'm about to map the drive letter Y: to the shared Download folder on a computer named Spock.

5. Click OK.

6. If you want the drive to be mapped automatically each time you log on, select the Reconnect at Logon check box.

7. Click Finish.

The remote resource will open. You can close that folder, and also close the Network folder. Because you've mapped a drive letter to the remote resource, it will appear in your Computer folder. Figure 53-6 shows an example where I've mapped two resources, where Y: is mapped to the Download folder on the computer named Spock, and Z: is mapped to the hidden root share of drive C: on the computer with an IP address of 192.168.0.2.

Hidden Shares

Windows creates a hidden administrative share for each drive connected to the computer. These shares, which share the root of the drive, take the name of the drive letter followed by a $ sign. For example, the administrative share for drive C: is C$, for drive E: would be E$, and so on. If you have an administrative account on the remote computer, you can map to its hidden share using the UNC path. For example, to connect to drive C: on a computer named Spock, you would use the UNC path \\Spock\C$.

These shares are called hidden shares because they do not appear when you browse the network for resources. For example, you won't see these shares in the Network folder. In addition, you can create your own hidden shares. When you share the resource, just add a $ sign at the end of the share name. See Chapter 52 to learn more about sharing resources on the network.

FIGURE 53-5

Map Network Drive dialog box.

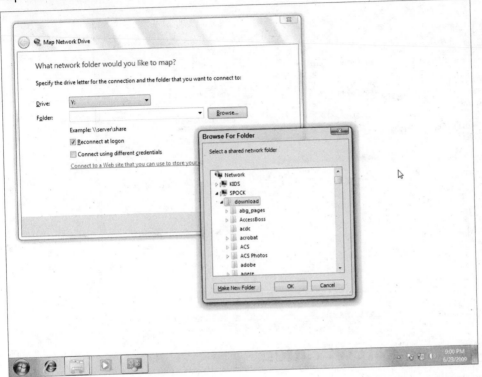

From that point on, you can access the folder either by going through the Network folder as usual, or you can just open your Computer folder and open the resource's icon under Network Location.

Tip

If the folders in your Computer folder aren't arranged like the example in Figure 53-4, use the menu bar in your Computer folder by pressing the Alt key to choose View and then choose either Sort By or Group By to alter the order and grouping of the folders. You can also access these options by right-clicking an empty area in your Computer folder. ■

Note

Even though a mapped network drive shows up as a disk drive in the Computer folder, a shared network resource need not be a disk drive at all. It can be a folder. The term "network drive" just refers to the fact that the shared resource "looks like" a drive, by virtue of the fact that it has a drive letter and icon in your Computer folder. ■

Disconnecting from a network drive

In your Computer folder, you can disconnect from any network drive by right-clicking the drive's icon and choosing Disconnect. If you chose the option Reconnect at Logon when you previously mapped the drive, the shared resource will no longer be mapped the next time you log on to the computer.

FIGURE 53-6

Drives Y: and Z: are actually shared resources on other computers.

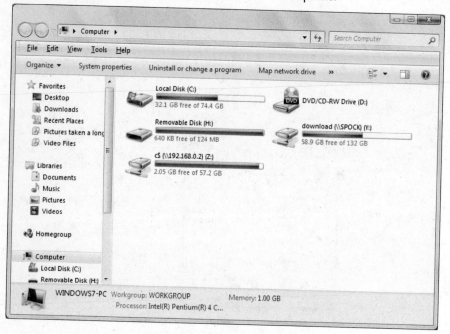

Using a Shared Printer

You use a shared printer from a remote computer exactly as you use a local printer. Choose File ▷ Print from the program's menu bar. When the Print dialog box opens, look for the shared printer, click it, and click the Print button.

If the shared printer doesn't show up in the Print dialog box, you can either add it right from the Print dialog box or you can install it from the Devices and Printers applet. To install it from the Printers dialog box, click Find Printer to open the Network folder. Expand the computer where the printer is shared, right-click the printer, and choose Connect. Windows will connect to the printer and prompt you to let it install the drivers for the printer.

You can also install the printer using the method described under "Installing a network, wireless, or Bluetooth printer" in Chapter 35. If that's the printer you'll use most often, make it the default printer as described in Chapter 35.

Whichever method you use to add the printer, after the printer is installed, choose File ▷, select the newly installed printer, and click Print.

Caution

You can play shared media from a Windows 7 computer on any other Windows 7 computer in the network, and on compatible networked digital media players. ■

Using Shared Media

Shared media are different from shared files because they're *streamed* to the local computer when played. This allows you to play the media files on non-computer network devices such as the Xbox 360 or a networked digital media player. Exactly how you work such a device depends on the device. You'll need to refer to the instructions that came with the device for specifics.

You can access the shared media by opening Windows Media Player normally. In the left pane, you should see each of the devices on the network that are sharing their media. Click the arrow next to a device to access its shared music, as shown in Figure 53-7.

You can also browse for media devices (and computers that are sharing their music libraries) from the Network folder. When you open the Network folder, you'll see a section named Media Devices that shows all of the streaming media devices on the network (Figure 53-8). Just double-click a device to open its library in Media Player.

For more information on using Windows Media Player, see Chapter 24.

FIGURE 53-7

jim (spock) is a remote shared library.

FIGURE 53-8

Shared media in the Network folder.

Wrap-Up

This chapter looked at ways to access shared network resources from computers in the same private network.

- To get to shared folders on other computers in the network, first open the Network folder on the computer at which you're sitting.

- To open a remote document from within a program, choose File ➪ Open from the program's menu bar, as usual. Then, choose the Network folder from the Folders drop-down list in the Open dialog box.

- To save a document to a remote computer, choose File ➪ Save (or File ➪ Save As), and choose your Network folder from the Folders drop-down list.

- To create a Network Location link to an Internet site, right-click within your Computer folder and choose Add a Network Location.

- To move or copy files between computers in a network, use your Network folder to open the source and/or destination folders. Then, use the standard techniques described in Chapter 29 to select, move, or copy the files.

- To use a shared printer, print normally but select the shared printer's name in the Print dialog box.
- If you don't see a shared printer in the Print dialog box, install the printer on the local computer using techniques described in Chapter 35.
- To play shared media using Windows Media Player, open the Network folder and double-click the shared media's icon.

Troubleshooting Networks

Networking has considerably improved with each new version of Windows, so you should experience fewer networking problems with Windows 7. However, Windows is just a part of the equation. Problems can occur with networking hardware, whether on your computer or elsewhere on the network. When that happens, you can use several troubleshooting techniques to identify and fix the problem. This chapter explores these techniques.

Letting Windows Troubleshoot the Network

Whenever you have a problem with a network, whether wired or wireless, you should always check your network hardware first. Even experts have been known to spend much time trying to troubleshoot a network problem from mouse and keyboard, when the problem turned out to be a loose cable.

If on a wired network, make sure the computer is firmly connected to the hub using an appropriate cable. For example, if you're using gigabit Ethernet, use Cat 6 straight through cables (not crossover cables) to connect all computers to the hub. Make sure each cable is firmly plugged in. If the hub and cards have indicator lights, they should be green when the computer is properly connected. The amber light only flashes when there's data crossing the cable.

Tip

How can you tell a straight cable from a crossover cable? Hold the two ends of the cable side-by-side, with the retaining clip facing away from you. The colors will be in the same order left-to-right on both connectors on a straight cable. ∎

For a wireless network, make sure the wireless access point is turned on and its connection to the wired segment (such as the switch, or DSL or cable modem) is connected.

1131

Always refer to the installation and troubleshooting documentation that came with your networking hardware. Remember, not all products are exactly alike. You have to understand and properly install whatever network hardware you've purchased. Windows 7 can only use that hardware for networking if that hardware is properly installed and working correctly.

If you're confident that the hardware is working properly, then you can use several techniques to help with troubleshooting. For example, Windows can perform some automated troubleshooting. Here's how to start the process:

1. Click Start ➪ Control Panel. If the Control Panel is in Category view, select View Network Status and Tasks under Network and Internet. If the Control Panel is in Classic view, click Network and Sharing Center.

2. Click Troubleshoot Problems at the bottom of the window (Figure 54-1).

FIGURE 54-1

Network and Sharing Center.

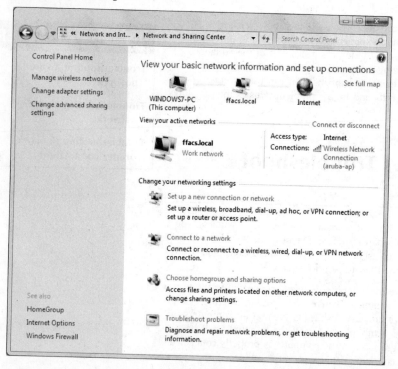

3. After selecting Troubleshoot Problems, Windows searches for troubleshooting packs, which enable it to troubleshoot specific types of problems. Figure 54-2 shows the list of troubleshooters.

4. Locate and click the troubleshooter that you believe is related to the problem your computer is experiencing. Windows 7 opens a troubleshooting wizard. Click Next to allow the wizard to attempt to resolve the problem.

Hopefully, the diagnostics will solve the problem for you. If not, you can take some general steps to troubleshoot the problem yourself.

FIGURE 54-2

Windows offers several network troubleshooters.

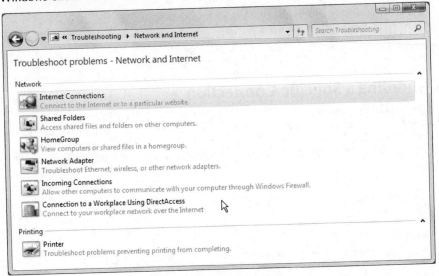

Manual Troubleshooting

If you are troubleshooting a wired network connection, make sure you have verified that all cables are securely connected and that you see link lights on both ends of the connection (at the computer and at the hub). Also, make sure the hub is powered on, and for an Internet connection, that the WAN connection for the Internet connection is plugged into the hub.

The two most common problems with wireless networking are:

- The computer from which you're working is too far away from the router or access point.
- The hardware isn't properly configured, as per the manufacturer's instructions.

A Common Network Problem

A common problem connecting to another system on your network is the Windows Firewall. By default, Windows does not allow sharing between two computers. This is something that you need to enable within the Windows Firewall.

To enable file sharing, click Start ⇨ Control Panel to bring up the Control Panel. If the Control Panel is in Category view, you'll need to click System and Security and then click Windows Firewall. If the Control Panel is in Classic view, you'll need to double-click Windows Firewall. Leave the firewall On and click the Allow a Program or Feature Through Windows Firewall link. Click Change Settings to enable the controls on the Allowed Programs dialog box. Then, select (check) File and Printer Sharing and place a check beside the network where you want to enable sharing (Private, Public, or both). Then, click OK.

Always check the troubleshooting material in the hardware manufacturer's documentation first. When you're confident that the computer is in range and the hardware is set up properly, use the network troubleshooters as described earlier in this chapter to troubleshoot the problem.

If Windows is unable to identify and fix the problem with your network, you can use a selection of tools and techniques to manually test the network. The following sections explore these techniques and tools.

Troubleshooting a Specific Connection

To troubleshoot a specific connection, open the Control Panel and click View Network Status and Tasks under the Network and Internet heading. In the resulting Network and Sharing Center, click Change Adapter Settings in the left pane. Windows 7 then displays the computer's network connections (Figure 54-3). To troubleshoot and repair a connection, right-click the connection and choose Diagnose.

FIGURE 54-3

Network Connections.

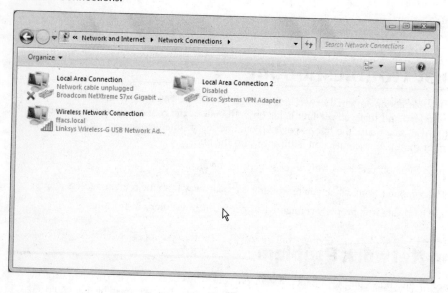

If the connection is still not working as you expect it, you can perform a few tests from a command console to isolate the problem.

Testing from a Command Console

A handful of command-line tools are available that you can use to troubleshoot a network issue. The first is the ping command.

ping

Ping sends test packets to an IP address that you specify, and if the connection is working, returns a reply. By default, ping sends four test packets to the specified address, but you can specify the number of requests to send or have ping continue sending until you stop it.

To troubleshoot using the ping command, first ping your local computer using the `ping localhost` command.

You should receive four replies. If not, there is an issue with the configuration of your network adapter, and you need to troubleshoot and/or repair that connection before testing further.

If you do get four replies when pinging localhost, try pinging past your own computer. For example, if you are troubleshooting an Internet connection, ping the IP address of your gateway. If you are using a wireless connection, ping the IP address of your wireless access point. On a wired network, ping the router. Work your way out from your computer, pinging successively further until you identify where the packets are dying. For example, if you can ping your gateway but no further, the problem likely lies with your Internet provider.

Note
Bear in mind that ping failures do not necessarily mean a problem at the device you're pinging. For example, if your gateway device is configured to drop ping packets, you won't receive a response. ∎

tracert

Another command you can use to troubleshoot a network connection is tracert. This command traces the route to a specified address, and is useful for identifying a point of failure in your connection. For example, if you perform a tracert to a public Internet server, but the tracert fails at your gateway, you probably have a problem with the gateway device. If the tracert fails at a location on the Internet (or on your ISP's network), the issue is not with your network.

To use tracert, open a command prompt and execute the `tracert (address)` command. `(address)` is the address or host name of the device to which you want to trace. As with ping, a failure at a certain point doesn't necessarily indicate a problem at that point, because the device could simply be dropping that traffic. However, if you can successfully return packets from beyond your own network, you have validated that your network is functioning properly.

Tip
The tracert command can be useful in identifying a point in the path with high latency (a point where response is slow). ∎

The following is a sample output from the `tracert` command:

```
C:\Users\jboyce>tracert www.irs.gov
Tracing route to a321.g.akamai.net [65.183.241.214]
over a maximum of 30 hops:

  1    4 ms    1 ms    1 ms  192.168.10.1
  2    1 ms    1 ms    1 ms  66-228-235-245.prtel.com
                              [66.228.235.245]
  3    2 ms    2 ms    1 ms  64-118-7-18.fergus.prtel.com
                              [64.118.7.18]
```

```
4      2 ms    2 ms    5 ms    undrootzer0.prtel.com [64.118.7.1]
5      2 ms    2 ms    2 ms    borderZer0.prtel.com [66.228.226.225]
6      9 ms    8 ms    9 ms    mrnet-ParkRegion-DS3.ply.mr.net
                               [137.192.200.17]

7     10 ms   13 ms    8 ms    ge-6-16.car1.Minneapolis1.Level3.net
                               [4.79.160.9]
8     10 ms    9 ms   12 ms    ae-11-11.car2.Minneapolis1.Level3.net
                               [4.69.136.102]
9     26 ms   31 ms   36 ms    ae-5-5.ebr2.Denver1.Level3.net
                               [4.69.136.110]
10    27 ms   25 ms   28 ms    ae-22-52.car2.Denver1.Level3.net
                               [4.68.107.39]
11    52 ms   38 ms   30 ms    360-NETWORK.car2.Denver1.Level3.net
                               [4.53.2.26]

12    35 ms   37 ms   39 ms    66.62.160.66
13    29 ms   32 ms   30 ms    a65-183-241-214.deploy.
                               akamaitechnologies.com
                               [65.183.241.214]

Trace complete.
```

Ipconfig

The ipconfig command displays network configuration and is particularly useful for viewing your TCP/IP settings, such as IP address, DNS server addresses, and gateway. To view the configuration for all interfaces, use the ipconfig /all command.

Windows displays the configuration for all network adapters, similar to the following listing:

```
C:\Users\jboyce>ipconfig /all


Windows IP Configuration

    Host Name . . . . . . . . . . . . : windows7-PC
    Primary Dns Suffix  . . . . . . . :
    Node Type . . . . . . . . . . . . : Hybrid
    IP Routing Enabled. . . . . . . . : No
    WINS Proxy Enabled. . . . . . . . : No
    DNS Suffix Search List. . . . . . : ffacs.local

Wireless LAN adapter Wireless Network Connection:

    Connection-specific DNS Suffix  . : ffacs.local
    Description . . . . . . . . . . . : Linksys Wireless-G USB Net-
work Adapter
    Physical Address. . . . . . . . . : 00-14-BF-7F-D7-2A
    DHCP Enabled. . . . . . . . . . . : Yes
    Autoconfiguration Enabled . . . . : Yes
```

```
Link-local IPv6 Address . . . . .: fe80::5814:d848:db25:731b%12
                                   (Preferred)
IPv4 Address. . . . . . . . . . .: 192.168.10.22(Preferred)
Subnet Mask . . . . . . . . . . .: 255.255.255.0
Lease Obtained. . . . . . . . . .: Friday, June 19, 2009
                                   12:23:41 PM
Lease Expires . . . . . . . . . .: Friday, June 26, 2009
                                   12:37:47 PM
Default Gateway . . . . . . . . .: 192.168.10.1
DHCP Server . . . . . . . . . . .: 192.168.10.20
DHCPv6 IAID . . . . . . . . . . .: 301995199
DHCPv6 Client DUID. . . . . . . .: 00-01-00-01-11-8C-F3-7F-00-
                                   14-22-50-C3-34

DNS Servers . . . . . . . . . . .: 192.168.10.20
                                   66.228.226.10
                                   66.228.232.5
NetBIOS over Tcpip. . . . . . . .: Enabled

Ethernet adapter Local Area Connection:

Media State . . . . . . . . . . .: Media disconnected
Connection-specific DNS Suffix  .:
Description . . . . . . . . . . .: Broadcom NetXtreme 57xx
Gigabit Controller
Physical Address. . . . . . . . .: 00-14-22-50-C3-34
DHCP Enabled. . . . . . . . . . .: Yes
Autoconfiguration Enabled . . . .: Yes

Tunnel adapter isatap.{4C3F69DA-1468-489A-9EDF-040EFC5816C6}:

Media State . . . . . . . . . . .: Media disconnected
Connection-specific DNS Suffix  .:
Description . . . . . . . . . . .: Microsoft ISATAP Adapter
Physical Address. . . . . . . . .: 00-00-00-00-00-00-00-E0
DHCP Enabled. . . . . . . . . . .: No
Autoconfiguration Enabled . . . .: Yes

Tunnel adapter isatap.ffacs.local:

Media State . . . . . . . . . . .: Media disconnected
Connection-specific DNS Suffix  .: ffacs.local
Description . . . . . . . . . . .: Microsoft ISATAP Adapter #2
Physical Address. . . . . . . . .: 00-00-00-00-00-00-00-E0
DHCP Enabled. . . . . . . . . . .: No
Autoconfiguration Enabled . . . .: Yes

Tunnel adapter Teredo Tunneling Pseudo-Interface:

Media State . . . . . . . . . . .: Media disconnected
Connection-specific DNS Suffix  .:
```

```
        Description . . . . . . . . . .: Microsoft Teredo
Tunneling Adapter
        Physical Address. . . . . . . .: 00-00-00-00-00-00-00-E0
        DHCP Enabled. . . . . . . . . .: No
        Autoconfiguration Enabled . . .: Yes
```

In addition to showing you the configuration of your computer's network interfaces, ipconfig can also renew a DHCP address lease. If your connection failed to obtain an IP address, force another attempt with the ipconfig /renew command.

You can also use ipconfig to flush the DNS resolver cache. Each time you try to access a network resource by its host name, such as www.wiley.com, the DNS resolver on your computer attempts to resolve the host name to its IP address. The resolver first looks in the local cache for the host, and if it finds the entry there, returns the results without attempting an external DNS query. However, if the entry is not in the cache, the DNS resolver queries your DNS server(s) for the results.

In addition to caching positive results, Windows 7 also caches negative results. So, if you attempted to connect to a resource and the query failed to return results, the resolver won't attempt to query DNS again until the previous query becomes stale. You can clear out the cache to remove all results, which causes the DNS resolver to query the DNS servers again for the results. Use the ipconfig /flushdns command to flush the resolver cache.

Troubleshooting Network Printer Connections

If you're unable to locate a printer on your network, you should first make sure that the printer is shared correctly off of the remote system. First verify that you can print when you are sitting at the computer connected directly to the printer. When you're able to print from the computer connected to the printer, you need to verify that print sharing is enabled. To do this, follow these steps:

1. Click Start ⇨ Control Panel. If the Control Panel is in Category view, click View Network Status and Tasks under Network and Internet. If the Control Panel is in Classic view, choose Network and Sharing Center.

2. When the Network and Sharing Center window opens, click Change Advanced Sharing Settings in the left pane to show Advanced Sharing Settings, as shown in Figure 54-4.

3. Choose the option Turn on File and Printer Sharing, and click Save Changes.

4. Open Devices and Printers from the Start menu and double-click the printer you want to share.

5. In the printer's dialog box that opens, double-click Customize Your Printer to open the properties for the printer.

6. Click the Sharing tab and verify that the Share This Printer check box is checked, and click OK.

After you have verified that the printer has been shared correctly, move to the computer from which you are trying to connect. Open Network and Internet from the Control Panel, and click View Network Computers and Devices. Double-click the remote computer and then the printer to which you are trying to connect. You can double-click the printer to install it on your system.

FIGURE 54-4

Configuration for sharing a printer.

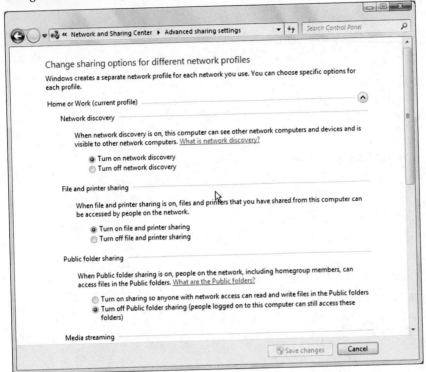

Use All Available Resources

As mentioned, you always want to check the most obvious things first (network cables, or making sure you're within range on a wireless network). Links in the left pane of the Network and Sharing Center, as well as the troubleshooting link at the bottom, can provide First Aid help after you've eliminated the more obvious suspects as the source of the problem.

Finally, don't forget Windows Communities. Chances are, someone in Communities has already experienced and resolved the very problem you're experiencing. The Microsoft.public.windows.networking_sharing community is the perfect location to ask questions about Windows 7 networking. You can get to the newsgroups from the Windows Communities link in Help and Support. Or set up Windows Live Mail as a newsgroup reader for Communities. See Chapter 20 for more information on that topic.

Part XI

Appendixes

If you purchased a new computer recently, Windows 7 was probably already installed on it. If your computer is running Windows Vista, however, you'll need to install Windows 7. You have two options for installing Windows 7: upgrade or perform a new installation. Appendix A explains how to upgrade Windows Vista to Windows 7. Appendix B explains how to perform a new installation of Windows 7.

Appendix C rounds out this part, providing a lengthy list of shortcut keys you can use in Windows 7 and in some of the applications that come with Windows 7 as an alternative to using the mouse.

IN THIS PART

Appendix A
Upgrading to Windows 7

Appendix B
Installing Windows 7 on a New System

Appendix C
Universal Shortcut Keys

Upgrading to Windows 7

I f you purchased your PC with Windows 7 already installed and have no interest in dual-booting, you need to hang a U-turn. There's nothing in this appendix for you. Go straight to the Introduction, or Chapter 1, at the beginning of this book, and forget all about this appendix.

If you purchased an upgrade version of Windows 7 to replace your current version of Windows and you haven't yet installed that upgrade, this is the place to be. To tell you the truth, you really don't have to read this entire appendix to install your upgrade. You really just have to do this:

1. Insert the disc that came with your Windows 7 upgrade into your computer's disc drive and wait a few seconds.

2. Follow the instructions that appear on the screen to install Windows 7 by upgrading your current version of Windows.

When the installation is complete, remove the new disc from your disc drive, put it someplace safe, and ignore the rest of this appendix. If these two steps don't quite get the job done, please read on.

There is one point that I need to stress. It's important that you know that Windows 7 can upgrade only from Windows Vista and no versions of Windows before it. I have run the beta version of the Windows 7 Upgrade Advisor and, although the systems tested on were able to support Windows 7, I was required to perform a custom installation on Windows XP machines, which creates a new OS instance rather than an upgrade.

IN THIS APPENDIX

Windows 7 system requirements

Pre-installation housekeeping

Installing Windows 7

Windows 7 System Requirements

Windows 7 has the same hardware requirements as Windows Vista, but requires a bit more hardware horsepower than versions of Windows prior to Vista. The more hardware capability you have, the better Windows 7 will run. The recommended minimum hardware requirements are as follows:

*   1 GB of RAM for 32-bit (x86) versions; 2 GB of RAM for 64-bit (x64) versions

- A 1.0 Gigahertz (GHz) 32-bit (x86) or 64-bit (x64) processor
- At least 16 GB free space available for 32-bit (x86) versions; 20 GB for 64-bit (x64) versions
- DirectX 9 capable GPU with WDDM 1.0 driver or higher (128 MBs of VRAM is required for the Aero theme)

Before upgrading your installation of Windows Vista, it would be a good idea to run the Windows Upgrade Advisor available at `www.microsoft.com/windows/windows-7/upgrade-advisor.aspx` as a free download. The tool generates a report that will indicate any shortcomings of your system and what you need to do to upgrade your computer if necessary.

Pre-installation Housekeeping

If you've been using your PC for a while with an earlier version of Windows, you'll want to do some things before you begin your upgrade:

- If your computer has any time-out features, such as the power-down features found on some portable PCs, disable those features now.
- If you have an antivirus program handy, run it now to check for, and delete, dormant viruses that may still be lurking on your hard drive.
- Disable your antivirus software after you've run the check. Leave it disabled until after you've completed the upgrade.
- Make sure that any external devices (printers, modems, external disk drives, and so on) are connected and turned on so that Windows 7 can detect them during installation.
- If at all possible, back up the entire hard drive at this point. At the very least, jot down all the information you need to connect to your Internet account. Back up all your documents, e-mail messages, names and addresses, and anything else you'll need after you complete the upgrade.

I realize that few people outside the corporate world have a means of backing up their entire hard drive. But you should be able to at least back up documents, e-mail messages, names and addresses, and so forth. Windows 7 includes Windows Easy Transfer that fills that need. See Chapter 12, "Transferring Files from Another Computer," for information on Easy Transfer.

Note
See Chapter 33 for some general pointers on backing up documents. ∎

Installing Windows 7

To upgrade an existing version of Windows Vista, start your computer normally. You'd do well to restart the computer and get to a clean desktop with no open program windows or dialog boxes. Then put the Windows 7 disc in your disc drive and wait for the Welcome screen to open. If nothing appears on the screen within a minute or so, follow these steps:

1. Open My Computer.
2. Open the icon for your disc drive. If the Welcome screen opens, skip the next step.
3. Click (or double-click) the setup (or `setup.exe`) file on the disc.

By now, you should definitely see on your screen some options for installing Windows 7. To get things rolling:

1. Choose the Install Now option.

2. When the Get Important Updates for Installation window appears, you're able to go online to get the latest updates for your installation of Windows 7. If you choose this option, your system needs to stay connected throughout the installation.

Note
Before clicking Install, you can use the Windows Easy Transfer, an application included with Windows 7, for copying your files and settings to a different computer. See Chapter 12 for more information on Easy Transfer. ■

The installation procedure will begin. You might notice that the screen goes blank once in a while during the installation. Don't be alarmed; that's normal. If the screen goes blank for a long time, try moving the mouse around a bit to bring it back. From here on out, you can just follow the instructions on the screen.

Installation options

The exact procedure from this point on will vary a bit, depending on what version of Windows 7 you're installing. Also, the specific hardware that's connected to your computer will affect the information that the setup procedure requests. Each request is largely self-explanatory, but here's a summary of the items you're likely to encounter along the way.

- **Regional, Currency, and Language Options:** Choose your preferred location, currency, and keyboard layout.

- **Product Key:** Type the product key. You should be able to find it on the sleeve in which the Windows 7 disc was delivered.

- **License Terms:** If you agree with the terms and conditions of the license, select the I Accept the License Terms check box.

- **Upgrade or Custom Installation:** If you decide that you want to do a fresh installation, choose the Custom option. This will not keep your personal files and programs. The Upgrade option will.

- **Compatibility Report:** The installation application will look at your existing configuration and indicate whether it finds devices that are incompatible with Windows 7.

- **Security Settings:** These settings let you determine how you want to protect your system.

- **Date and Time Settings:** Set the date and current time, choose your time zone, and decide whether you want Windows to automatically adjust the time for daylight savings changes.

Reenabling old startup programs

You may discover that some of the programs that used to start automatically on your computer don't do so after you've installed Windows 7. You can follow these steps to get those programs to start automatically again in the future:

1. Click Start, type **msconfig**, and then press Enter. This runs the System Configuration tool, which does not have an icon in the Windows menu.

2. Click the Startup tab.

3. To enable all previous auto-start programs, click the Enable All button. Optionally, select only those programs you want to auto-start.

4. Click OK.

5. Click the Start button, click the arrow to the right of the Power button, and select Restart.

Windows 7 should restart with the programs from your previous version of Windows open and running.

Installing Windows 7 on a New System

If you've just built a new computer from scratch, or if you've replaced your old drive C: with a new hard drive, you will have to do a *clean install* of Windows 7. From a purely technological standpoint, this is really your best option. You don't have to bring any of the old "baggage" with you, but therein lies an issue.

You can opt to do a clean install even if you already have a version of Windows installed on the hard drive; however, you must realize that doing so is *very* serious business. When you do a clean install, you wipe out everything on your hard drive. And I do mean *everything* — all programs, documents, settings, Internet account information — everything. There's no getting *any* of that stuff back, either. Just to make sure nobody misses this important fact, let me say it with a big caution icon:

Caution

The procedures described in this chapter are for advanced users only. You should know your hardware, your system's BIOS setup, all your Internet account information, how to export, back up, and restore messages, contacts, Favorites, and the like, and how to find technical information about your hardware components on your own before attempting any of the techniques described in this chapter. Don't confuse a "clean install" with a "clean boot." ■

Gearing Up for a Clean Install

Most experts prefer to do a clean install when they upgrade to a new version of Windows, largely because it gets everything off to a clean start. Besides, it's a great excuse for upgrading to a bigger and faster hard drive. You can use your

IN THIS APPENDIX

Gearing up for a clean installation

Doing the clean installation

Completing the installation

original hard drive as a second hard drive and easily transfer documents from that drive to the new drive after you've installed Windows 7 on the new drive. However, you'll still need to reinstall all your programs and redo all your settings after you complete the installation.

Back up all your data

If you intend to keep your existing C: as the C: drive after the clean install, it's important that you understand that you will permanently lose everything on that drive during the clean install. Therefore, you should:

- Write down all of your Internet connection data so that you can reestablish your account after the clean install.

- Back up or export all your e-mail messages, names and addresses, Favorites, and anything else you'll want after the clean install so that you can recover them. Remember, whatever you don't save will be lost forever. However, this does not apply for Web-based e-mail accounts that do not store messages on your computer.

- Back up all your documents, because each and every one of them will be wiped out along with Windows and all your programs.

Caution

A clean install permanently erases everything on your hard drive, which is basically everything that's "in your computer." Users who do not fully understand the ramifications of this should not attempt to do a clean install of Windows 7 or any other operating system. It's extremely difficult to recover data from an erased drive, but if you need that kind of help, you can turn to a data recovery service such as Driver Savers (www.drivesaversdatarecovery.com). ∎

If Windows is currently installed on the C: drive you intend to reuse, you can use the Windows Easy Transfer to back up all your documents and settings, as covered in Chapter 12. Ideally, you want to back up the data to another computer in the network. Windows Easy Transfer allows you to transfer files and folders, e-mail settings, and many other personal items from your existing computer to the new computer or hard drive. You can do this by using a USB Easy Transfer cable, the network, DVDs or CDs, or other external USB devices.

Given that hard drives are so inexpensive these days, it almost seems a shame *not* to start the clean install from a new hard drive. You don't have to worry about losing any data from the old drive if you do a clean install of Windows 7 to a new drive.

Make sure that you can boot from your CD or DVD

By far, the easiest way to do a clean install on a new drive is to boot from the Windows 7 disc. You'll want to make sure that you *can* do this before you do anything inside the computer. Most discs aren't bootable, so you need to insert the Windows disc into the drive and restart the computer. Watch for the Press any key to boot from CD or DVD countdown message, and tap the spacebar before the countdown runs out. (In case you're curious, it's five seconds.)

If you see the Windows is loading files message, you know you can boot from a disc. Press Ctrl+Alt+Del to reboot before setup actually starts, and remove the disc from the drive while the system is rebooting. Then, shut down the PC altogether.

If you can't boot the system from the Windows disc, you need to adjust your BIOS settings. Again, this isn't something I can tell you how to do specifically, because it depends on your system's BIOS.

But the usual scenario is to press F2 or Del as the computer is starting up to get to your BIOS setup. After you get into the BIOS settings, make sure that booting from the disc drive is enabled and that the disc drive has a higher priority than the hard drive.

If you'd rather not adjust your BIOS settings, many computers have the option of allowing you to select the boot device. Pressing a key during the startup process tells the BIOS that you want to select your boot device this one time. It can be the F10, F11, or F12 key, but you'll want to check your computer's documentation to find out which key it actually is.

If you do opt to change the BIOS settings, put the Windows disc back into the disc drive, save your BIOS settings, and exit so that the computer reboots again. If you got it right, you should see the Windows is loading files message again on restart, indicating that you've successfully booted from the disc. Cancel that startup as well, by pressing Ctrl+Alt+Del, and remove the disc from the drive before the computer gets another chance to boot from the disc.

Installing a new C: drive

If you're upgrading your C: drive along with your version of Windows, Step 1 is to hide existing hard drives from the system altogether so that to the BIOS, the new drive appears to be the only hard drive in the system. Simply disconnecting the power and interface plugs from the backs of the drives will do the trick.

Caution

Never do anything inside your system case while the computer is turned on or even plugged into a power outlet. Wear an antistatic wrist strap to prevent static discharge from wiping out components and the warranties that go with them! ∎

The next step involves getting the new drive installed to the point at which it's at least recognized by the BIOS. I can't tell you how to do that because the procedure varies from one drive manufacturer to the next. You must follow the instructions that came with the drive, or the instructions on the drive manufacturer's Web site, to get to the point at which the system recognizes that drive at startup.

Chances are, the drive manufacturer's instructions will include steps to partition and format the drive. You should probably do so even if you intend to repartition and reformat the drive during the Windows 7 clean installation. You still won't be able to boot from the drive, but at least the drive will be recognized as C during the Windows installation.

It's also important to note which connection architecture your system uses, which determines how the drive plugs into the motherboard. The vast majority of new systems today use Serial ATA (or SATA) interface. Systems from a couple of years ago used both SATA and the older Parallel ATA (or PATA). SATA cables are thin and have plastic connector tips, somewhat like USB. PATA cables are wide and flat and the connector blocks have two rows of holes.

The other part of the installation requires knowing how the drive will be powered. If you have a laptop, you need a 1.8-inch or 2.5-inch drive, and it will be bus powered. For desktop drives, you will either have the older Molex (white-tipped) power adapters or the newer, more common black- or red-tipped SATA power tips. Most systems have both Molex and SATA power adapters inside, but you need to pay close attention to the power that the drive needs. Some sATA drives come with Molex power ports, and you can find Molex-to-SATA type adapters online or in certain PC stores.

If you intend to handle the hard drive installation on your own, you need to become familiar with these interfaces and make sure that you get the correct drive to support it.

Doing the Clean Install

When you feel confident that you'll be able to get back everything you want from your hard drive, you're ready to start the clean install. Put the Windows disc in the disc drive and shut down the computer. Then, restart the computer and boot from the disc. Your system's screen will go blank with a progress bar across the bottom of the screen while it copies some setup files. After the copy, the screen will change to a blue and green background, and you'll be given a mouse pointer. Follow these steps to continue the installation:

1. At the Install Windows dialog box, select the Language, Time, and Currency format and the type of keyboard; then click the Next button.

2. Click the Install now link, and you'll be prompted for the product key. After entering the product key, click the Next button.

3. If you accept the license terms, select the I Accept the License Terms box and click the Next button.

4. Select the Custom option to continue.

5. The next dialog box lists all the drives and partitions that the installation application sees on your system. Select the partition on which you want to install Windows 7. If you don't see your drive, the controller your hard drive is connected to might require a special driver that the installation application doesn't know about. You can click the Load Driver link to load the driver provided by the controller's manufacturer. Clicking the Drive Options link enables the option to format the drive before installing Windows 7.

6. Select the partition on which Windows 7 will be installed and click the Format link. The installation application will prompt that the data on the drive will be erased and permanently deleted. Click the OK button as long as you are sure that your database has been saved elsewhere.

7. After the drive is formatted, the Total Size and Free Space columns will be almost identical. Don't worry about any discrepancies. They are a result of how file systems and the formatting process works. Click the Next button to continue. At this point, the installation application will start copying files.

The Rest of the Installation

Copying the files and installing them to your system takes some time. When the installation continues, follow these steps:

1. You are prompted to create a username and password and optionally to choose a picture for your account.

2. Next, you need to create a name for your computer or use the name that the installation application has chosen for you. You can also choose a background image for your desktop.

3. In the Help Protect Windows Automatically dialog box, choosing Use Recommended Settings is usually best.

4. Choose your time zone and set the date and time in the Review Your Time and Date Settings dialog box; then click the Next button.

5. Finally, click the Start button, and the Windows 7 installation is complete.

The installation checks your system's performance for a short time and then asks you to log in. At this point, Windows 7 has been installed, and you're ready to start using it.

Universal
Shortcut Keys

H ere is a quick reference to shortcut keys that are used throughout Windows 7. Many application programs use the same shortcut keys. That's why I've titled this appendix *Universal Shortcut Keys*. Of course, any program can have additional shortcuts to its own unique features. Those are visible in drop-down menus, as in the example shown in the Home group on the Microsoft Word 2007 ribbon shown in Figure C-1. The *key+key* combination to the right of each menu command is the shortcut key for using that command from the keyboard without the menu.

Many programs show shortcut keys in the tooltip that appears when you point to a button or icon (see Figure C-2). I'm pointing to the B (Boldface) button in Microsoft Excel 2007. Below the mouse pointer, you can see that Ctrl+B is the shortcut key for boldfacing text.

Virtually every program also comes with its own help. Typically, you get to that by pressing Help (F1) while the program is in the active window. Or choose Help from that program's menu bar. Use the Help feature of that program to search for the term *shortcut* or *shortcut keys* to see whether you can find a summary of that program's shortcut keys.

Of course, Windows 7 has its own Help, too, which you can learn about in Chapter 5 of this book. For help with shortcut keys, click the Start button and choose Help and Support. Type **shortcuts keys** as your search text and press Enter. The search results will include shortcut keys for Windows 7 and many programs that are built into 7.

FIGURE C-1

Shortcut keys on items in the Word 2007 ribbon.

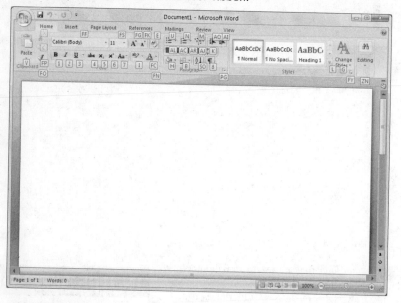

FIGURE C-2

Microsoft Office 2007 shortcut key hints.

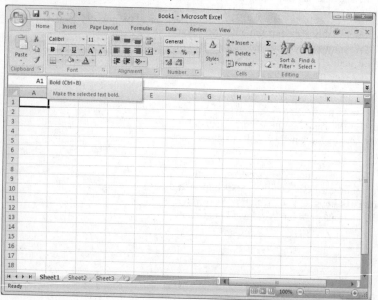

General Shortcut Keys

To do this	Press this key
Copy selected icon(s)	CTRL+C
Cut selected icons(s)	CTRL+X
Paste cut or copied text or item(s) to current folder	CTRL+V
Undo your most recent action	CTRL+Z
Delete selected icon(s) to Recycle Bin	DELETE or DEL
Delete selected icons(s) without moving to Recycle Bin	SHIFT+DELETE
Rename selected icon(s)	F2
Extend selection through additional icons	SHIFT+*any arrow key*
Select all items in a document or window	CTRL+A
Search for a file or folder	F3
Display properties for selected icon	ALT+ENTER
Close program in the active window	ALT+F4
Open the shortcut menu for the active window	ALT+SPACEBAR
Close the active document in multiple document program	CTRL+F4
Show Flip 3D	⊞ +TAB
Switch between open programs	ALT+TAB
Cycle through open programs in the order they were opened	ALT+ESC
Cycle through screen elements on the desktop or in a window	F6
Display the shortcut menu for the selected item	SHIFT+F10
Open/close the Start menu	CTRL+ESC or ⊞
Open menu or perform menu command	ALT+underlined letter
View menu bar in active program	F10 or Alt
Move left or right in menu bar	← and →
Move up or down in menu	↑ and ↓
Select highlighted menu command	ENTER
Refresh the active window	F5
View the folder one level up in Windows Explorer	BACKSPACE
Cancel the current task	ESC
Open Task Manager	CTRL+SHIFT+ESC
Copy dragged item to destination	CTRL+*drag*
Move dragged item to destination	CTRL+SHIFT+*drag*

Dialog Box Keyboard Shortcuts

Description	Key
Choose option with underlined *letter*	ALT+*letter*
Select a button if the active option is a group of option buttons	Arrow keys
Open a folder one level up if a folder is selected in the Save As or Open dialog box	BACKSPACE
Go to previous tab	CTRL+SHIFT+TAB
Go to next tab	CTRL+TAB
Same as clicking OK	ENTER
Same as clicking Cancel	ESC
Help	F1 key
Display the items in the active list	F4 key
Move to previous option	SHIFT+TAB
Select or deselect the check box	SPACEBAR
Move to next option	TAB

Windows Explorer Keyboard Shortcuts

Description	Key
Collapse the selected folder	− on numeric keypad
Display all the subfolders under selected folder	* on numeric keypad
Select or collapse parent folder	←
Expand current folder or move to next subfolder	↓
Display the contents of the selected folder	+ on numeric keypad
Display the bottom of the active window	END
Display the top of the active window	HOME
Open selected folder in new instance	SHIFT+Double-Click

Ease of Access Keyboard Shortcuts

Description	Key
Open Ease of Access Center	⊞ +U
Switch the MouseKeys either on or off	LEFT ALT+LEFT SHIFT+NUM LOCK
Switch High Contrast either on or off	LEFT ALT+LEFT SHIFT+PRINT SCREEN
Switch the ToggleKeys either on or off	NUM LOCK for five seconds
Switch FilterKeys either on or off	RIGHT SHIFT for eight seconds
Switch the StickyKeys either on or off	SHIFT five times

Windows Help Shortcut Keys

To do this	Press this key
Open Windows Help and Support	F1 or ⊞ +F1
Display the Table of Contents	ALT+C
Display the Connection Settings menu	ALT+N
Display the Options menu	F10
Move back to the previously viewed topic	ALT+←
Move forward to the next (previously viewed) topic	ALT+↓
Display the customer support page	ALT+A
Display the Help home page	ALT+HOME
Move to the beginning of a topic	HOME
Move to the end of a topic	END
Search the current topic	CTRL+F
Print a topic	CTRL+P
Move to the Search box	F3

Microsoft Natural Keyboard Shortcuts

Description	Key
Display or hide the Start menu	⊞
Lock the computer	⊞+L
Display the System Properties dialog box	⊞+BREAK
Show the desktop	⊞+D
Open Computer folder	⊞+E
Search for file or folder	⊞+F
Search for computers	CTRL+⊞+F
Display Windows Help	⊞+F1
Minimize all the windows	⊞+M
Restore all minimized windows	⊞+SHIFT+M
Open the Run dialog box	⊞+R
Show Flip 3D	⊞+TAB
Open Ease of Access Center	⊞+U
Open Windows Mobility Center	⊞+X

Text Navigation and Editing Shortcuts

Description	Key
Move cursor down one line	↓
Move cursor left one character	←
Move cursor right one character	→
Move cursor up one line	↑
Delete character to left of cursor	BACKSPACE
Move cursor to start of next paragraph	CTRL+↓
Move cursor to start of previous paragraph	CTRL+↑
Move cursor to start of previous word	CTRL+←
Move cursor to start of next word	CTRL+→
Select all	CTRL+A
Copy to Clipboard	CTRL+C
Copy the selected text to destination	CTRL+*drag*
Select to end of paragraph	CTRL+SHIFT+→

Description	Key
Select to end of word	CTRL+SHIFT+→
Select to beginning of word	CTRL+SHIFT+←
Select to beginning of paragraph	CTRL+SHIFT+↑
Select to end of document	CTRL+SHIFT+END
Select to top of document	CTRL+SHIFT+HOME
Paste Clipboard contents to cursor position	CTRL+V
Cut to Clipboard	CTRL+X
Undo last action	CTRL+Z
Delete selected text or character at cursor	DEL
Cancel the current task	ESC
Select to character in line above	SHIFT+↑
Select to character in line below	SHIFT+↓
Select character to left	SHIFT+←
Select character to right	SHIFT+→
Select from cursor to here	SHIFT+Click
Select to end of line	SHIFT+END
Select to beginning of line	SHIFT+HOME
Select text down one screen	SHIFT+PAGE DOWN
Select text up one screen	SHIFT+PAGE UP

Windows Character Map Shortcut Keys

Description	Key
Move up one row	↑
Move down one row	↓
Move to the left or to the end of the previous line	←
Move to the right or to the beginning of the next line	→
Move to the last character	CTRL+END
Move to the first character	CTRL+HOME
Move to the end of the line	END
Move to the beginning of the line	HOME
Move down one screen at a time	PAGE DOWN
Move up one screen at a time	PAGE UP
Switch between Enlarged and Normal modes	SPACEBAR

Microsoft Internet Explorer Shortcuts

To do this	Press this Key
Add "www." to the beginning and ".com" to the end of text in address bar	CTRL+ENTER
Add the current page to favorites	CTRL+D
Click the Information bar	SPACEBAR
Close current tab (or the current window if tabbed browsing is disabled)	CTRL+W
Close other tabs	CTRL+ALT+F4
Close Print Preview	ALT+C
Close the current window (if you have only one tab open)	CTRL+W
Copy selection to Clipboard	CTRL+C
Display a list of addresses you've typed	F4
Display a shortcut menu for a link	SHIFT+F10
Display first page to be printed	ALT+HOME
Display last page to be printed	ALT+END
Display next page to be printed	ALT+↓
Display previous page to be printed	ALT+←
Display zoom percentages	ALT+Z
Find on this page	CTRL+F
Go to home page	ALT+HOME
Go to selected link	ENTER
Go to the next page	ALT+↓
Go to the previous page	ALT+← or BACKSPACE
Go to the Toolbar Search box	CTRL+E
Help	F1
Move back through the items on a Web page, the address bar, or the links bar	SHIFT+TAB
Move back through the list of AutoComplete matches	→
Move backward between frames (if tabbed browsing is disabled)	CTRL+SHIFT+TAB
Move focus to the Information bar	ALT+N
Move forward through frames and browser elements (if tabbed browsing is disabled)	CTRL+TAB or F6

To do this	Press this Key
Move forward through the items on a Web page, the address bar, or the links bar	TAB
Move forward through the list of AutoComplete matches	↓
Move selected item down in the Favorites list in the Organize Favorites dialog box	ALT+↓
Move selected item up in the Favorites list in the Organize Favorites dialog box	ALT+↑
Move the cursor left to the next punctuation in the address bar	CTRL+←
Move the cursor right to the next punctuation in the address bar	CTRL+→
Move to the beginning of the page	HOME
Move to the end of the page	END
Open a new tab in the foreground	CTRL+T
Open a new tab in the foreground from the address bar	ALT+ENTER
Open a new Web site or page	CTRL+O
Open a new window	CTRL+N
Open Favorites	CTRL+I
Open Feeds	CTRL+J
Open History	CTRL+H
Open links in a new background tab	CTRL+Click
Open links in a new foreground tab	CTRL+SHIFT+Click
Open search query in a new tab	ALT+ENTER
Open the Organize Favorites	CTRL+B
Page Setup	ALT+U
Paste Clipboard contents	CTRL+V
Print the current page or active frame	CTRL+P
Refresh the current Web page	F5
Refresh the current Web page regardless of timestamp	CTRL+F5
Save the current page	CTRL+S
Scroll down a line	↓
Scroll down a page	PAGE DOWN
Scroll up a line	↑

To do this	Press this Key
Scroll up a page	PAGE UP
Select all items on the current Web page	CTRL+A
Select frames to print in framed Web site	ALT+F
Select the text in the address bar	ALT+D
Set printing options and print the page	ALT+P
Stop downloading a page	ESC
Switch between tabs	CTRL+TAB or CTRL+SHIFT+TAB
Switch to a specific tab number	CTRL+n (where n is a number between 1 and 8)
Switch to the last tab	CTRL+9
Toggle between full-screen and regular views	F11
Toggle Quick Tabs on or off	CTRL+Q
Type the number of the page you want displayed	ALT+A
Zoom in	ALT+PLUS SIGN
Zoom in 10 percent	CTRL+PLUS SIGN
Zoom out	ALT+MINUS SIGN
Zoom out 10 percent	CTRL+MINUS SIGN
Zoom to 100 percent	CTRL+0

Index

Index

Index

Index

Index

Index

Index

Index

Index

Index

Index

Index

Index

Index

Index

The books you
read to succeed.

**Get the most out of the latest software and leading-edge technologies
with a Wiley Bible—your one-stop reference.**

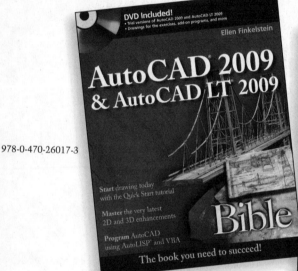

978-0-470-26017-3

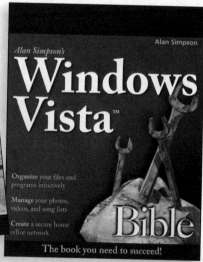

978-0-470-04030-0

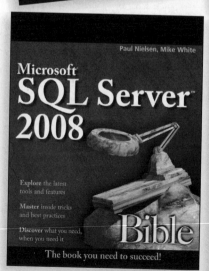

978-0-470-25704-3

978-0-470-37918-9